CONSUMER BEHAVIOR

FIFTH EDITION

CONSUMER BEHAVIOR

John C. Mowen
Oklahoma State University

Michael Minor
University of Texas—Pan American

Prentice-Hall

Upper Saddle River, New Jersey 07458

Acquisitions Editor: Whitney Blake
Associate Editor: John Larkin
Editorial Assistant: Rachel Falk
Vice President/Editorial Director: James Boyd
Marketing Manager: John Chillingworth
Associate Managing Editor: Linda DeLorenzo
Managing Editor: Dee Josephson
Manufacturing Buyer: Kenneth J. Clinton
Manufacturing Supervisor: Arnold Vila
Manufacturing Manager: Vincent Scelta
Design Manager: Patricia Smythe
Interior Design: Ox & Company
Cover Design: Marsha Cohen
Cover Image: © J.M. Gilmore/Stockworks, Six Heads

Copyright © 1998, 1995 by Prentice-Hall, Inc.
A Simon & Schuster Company
Upper Saddle River, New Jersey 07458

Library of Congress Cataloging-in-Publication Data

Mowen, John C.
    Consumer behavior / John C. Mowen, Michael Minor.—5th ed.
        p.   cm.
    Includes bibliographical references and indexes.
    ISBN 0-13-737115-2 (hardcover)
    1. Consumer behavior. 2. Consumers—United States. I. Minor,
Michael, II. Title.
HF5415.32.M68 1997
658.8'342—dc21   97-3101
                                                     CIP

Prentice-Hall International (UK) Limited, London
Prentice-Hall of Australia Pty. Limited, Sydney
Prentice-Hall Canada, Inc., Toronto
Prentice-Hall Hispanoamericana, S.A., Mexico
Prentice-Hall of India Private Limited, New Delhi
Prentice-Hall of Japan, Inc., Tokyo
Simon & Schuster Asia Pte. Ltd., Singapore
Editora Prentice-Hall do Brasil, Ltda., Rio de Janeiro

Printed in the United States of America

10 9 8 7 6 5 4 3 2 1

CONTENTS

CHAPTER 2

PART TWO

INDIVIDUAL CONSUMER PROCESSES

CHAPTER 3

CHAPTER 4

CHAPTER 5

Behavioral Learning   129

CHAPTER 6

Consumer Motivation and Affect   159

PART THREE

THE CONSUMER ENVIRONMENT

CHAPTER 14

THE CONSUMER ENVIRONMENT AND THE IMPACT
OF SITUATIONAL INFLUENCES   451

CHAPTER 15

CHAPTER 18

CULTURAL PROCESSES II: THE SUBCULTURAL ENVIRONMENT AND DEMOGRAPHICS

589

PREFACE

Our work on the fifth edition of *Consumer Behavior* has three goals. First, we want to continue to achieve the goal of producing a book that provides a current, balanced, comprehensive, and treatment of the field. Readers will discover within the chapters the latest research in the field of consumer behavior, whether it pertains to the dramaturgical analysis of white-water rafting and sky-diving, to the investigation of customer relationships, or to the latest research on consumer decision making. As in previous editions, our goal in writing *Consumer Behavior* is to create a book that is current and comprehensive as well as interesting and fun to read.

The second goal of the fifth edition is to make full use of modern electronic technology. A "Home Page" on the World Wide Web has been created by the first author, John Mowen. The "Home Page" contains four items of benefit to students and instructors. First, it contains detailed cases that can be downloaded for use in class. (The teacher's manual contains the case solutions.) Second, it contains the overheads of lecture slides that are provided to instructors in hard copy and on a compact disk that accompanies the text. Thus, students can download from the World Wide Web the lecture outlines used by instructors. Third, the "Home Page" contains copies of advertisements that can be downloaded and employed as teaching tools to illustrate the use of consumer behavior concepts. Fourth, the "Home Page" contains hot links to other home pages that have consumer behavior content. For example, one hot link is to the home page of the VALS II home page. Here students can take the psychographic profile and find out which of the VALS II categories in which they fall.

The third goal of *Consumer Behavior* is to provide students with a means of identifying the managerial relevance of the consumer behavior concepts. For the fifth edition each chapter begins with a short case. The material contained in the chapter is related to the case, and at the end of the chapter, a "managerial applications analysis" of the case is performed. In addition, at the end of each chapter a new case is presented. (The solution to these short cases are found in the Teacher's Manual.)

In sum, the fifth edition of *Consumer Behavior* provides:

- High Knowledge Content
- High Experiential Content
- High Managerial Content
- High Technology Content.

Another major addition to the fifth edition of *Consumer Behavior* is a second author. Michael Minor (Associate Professor of Marketing at University of Texas, Pan American) has joined John Mowen on the textbook. On the last edition, Michael revised two chapters and did a terrific job. He is an expert on international issues in consumer behavior and on topics related to culture, subculture, and public policy. He is a great addition to the team.

In addition to completely updating the textbook, adding the cases, and providing cyberspace materials in support of *Consumer Behavior*, the total supplement package to the text continues to be outstanding. A one-hour video tape has been produced specifically for *Consumer Behavior* and is available to adopters of the text. The videotape features John Mowen as the narrator and uses advertisements and other video materials to create four, high-impact, fast-paced video lecturettes. Fully discussed in the Teacher's Manual, these lecturettes can be incorporated into classes. Fifty+ four-color transparencies of key advertisements and figures have been produced to enhance the teaching of the class. In addition, the teacher's manual and test item file has been thoroughly expanded and updated. Finally, the Prentice-Hall Presents CD-ROM contains numerous additional advertisements and consumer behavior related materials from the Prentice-Hall library.

We believe that instructors and students will find the fifth edition of *Consumer Behavior* to be exciting to read, balanced, and managerially relevant. With *Consumer Behavior*, instructors do not have to sacrifice content in order to obtain a technologically sophisticated, fascinating, and managerially relevant text that is at the "cutting-edge" of the field.

Of course, without the support of numerous individuals the fifth edition would not have been possible. Many individuals at Prentice-Hall, Inc. deserve recognition. We would like to thank our editor, Whitney Blake, for her able guidance and attention to the details of the process. We also commend Rachel Falk for always being there to help us. Finally, Linda DeLorenzo is thanked for doing a superb job in producing an eye-catching book.

We also express our appreciation to the following colleagues for their reviews of various portions of the fifth edition of the text:

Beverlee B. Anderson	*California State University—San Marcos*
James Cagley	*University of Tulsa*
Rajendar Garg	*Indiana University of Pennsylvania*
Ronald Goldsmith	*Florida State University*
Douglas Hausknecht	*The University of Akron*
James H. Leigh	*Texas A&M University*
Kay Palan	*Iowa State University*
Edward A. Riordan	*Wayne State University*
Leslie Staggers	*Frostburg State University*
Stuart Van Auken	*California State University—Chico*

We would also like to thank James Lee, a doctoral student at Oklahoma State University for his outstanding efforts in updating the Teacher's Manual, obtaining permissions, and developing material for the World Wide Web and the compact disk that accompanies the text.

Finally, our deep gratitude goes to our families (John's family: Maryanne, Katie, and Cara; and Michael's family: Karen and Amy for their support, confidence, and good humor. They are truly special people!

JCM and MM

I

Introduction

1

AN INTRODUCTION TO CONSUMER BEHAVIOR

INTRODUCTORY CASE

The Many Faces of Consumer Behavior

What do you see when you look at the painting on the cover of this textbook? When we showed the cover to our students, they absolutely loved it. They reacted with exclamations, such as "cool," "in-style," and "hip." Several said, "It's a lot better than your last edition's cover." In contrast, when our faculty member colleagues looked at the cover, they grimaced, and did things like shield their eyes and say, "ugh, eye catching isn't it."

The different reactions of students and faculty illustrate one of the key points of consumer behavior. That is, different consumer segments can react with completely different emotions and feelings to exactly the same stimulus. Indeed, one of our great fears in selecting this cover was that because faculty select the textbook, its colorful cover could turn them off.

The painting on the cover is a metaphor for the many faces of consumer behavior. The abstract representation of the six people staring out at you could represent the emotions that consumers experience—from sadness, to anger, to caution, to happiness. On the other hand, the cover could represent different consumer segments—from Asians, to Hispanics, to Blacks, to women. Certainly, the divergent re-

actions of our students and faculty colleagues illustrate the concept that consumer behavior is about people and their perceptions.

Indeed, the many faces of consumer behavior is no better illustrated than by the curious world of plastic surgery in which physicians seek to recreate faces—and bodies.

Perhaps inspired by the physical transformations of celebrities like Cher, Michael Jackson, and Pamela Anderson, consumer interest in cosmetic surgery is exploding. It is estimated that more than 50,000 aesthetic surgeries were performed in the United States in 1997, and the approval rating for having such surgery has risen over 50 percent in the last decade. Some argue that Americans are reaching the point where they regard their bodies as "meat cages" to be molded as desired.[1]

A major difficulty with cosmetic surgery, however, is overblown expectations. As one expert noted, "The problem is [people think] that surgery is going to fix a relationship or help with work or make life happier."[2] But why shouldn't they when advertisements for certain procedures promise a personal metamorphosis?

Cosmetic surgery illustrates the thin line between "normal" and "deviant" consumer behavior.[3] Consider the thoughts of a plastic surgeon who was cutting into a 20-year-old woman's chest. Although everyone in the surgical unit agreed that her natural breasts were perfectly shaped, she desired breasts that were "much larger." The surgeon described his field like a marketer: "A lot has to do with regional preferences. In the South and West, big breasts are the thing, whereas in the East, the enlargements are more modest, and in the Midwest, there's nothing."[4] Indicating that he would make her breasts as large as he could within the "parameters of normal," the surgeon vowed, "I'm not going to do anything weird."

Unfortunately, plastic surgery can turn out "weird." Patients can erroneously assume that doctors know what is good for them and when to stop. For example, one woman seeking facial perfection had a series of face lifts until, after her fifth operation, her sideburns were behind her ears.[5] One surgeon defended his practice this way: "I'm not the one telling the person she has flat cheekbones—that's her decision. I know how to fix them." But what are the ethical implications of such an attitude?[6]

INTRODUCTION

Why do women and men risk pain and possible physical deformity to enhance their appearance? What motivates consumers to purchase a particular brand of athletic shoes or eat in a specific restaurant? Why do teenagers enjoy being scared half to death at horror movies? Why are automobile companies hooked on giving rebates to consumers to sell their cars? Why do students and faculty members prefer different text book covers? How can consumers be persuaded to wear seat belts? These are the kinds of questions that consumer researchers address.

Consumer behavior is an exciting field of study. In fact, a wonderful aspect of taking a course in this field is the wealth of examples you will encounter. Because you are all consumers, you can draw on your own daily experiences in the marketplace to understand consumer behavior concepts and theories. This book will provide you with copious illustrations of how consumer behavior concepts are used by corporations, public policy makers, and nonprofit organizations.

The chapter-opening case reveals how closely connected consumer behavior is to our everyday lives. The decision to undergo cosmetic surgery is a consumer behavior just as purchasing jewelry, cosmetics, cologne, or a nice suit is. While relatively few of us have (yet) had cosmetic surgery, we all know people who sport a pierced earring, nose ring, or tattoo—all of which involve a form of surgery. One goal of the surgery is to make the person more physically attractive. And certainly all of us have made a purchase of clothing, jewelry, or cosmetics for the same purpose.

Furthermore, just as fashion crazes come and go, so do fads in cosmetic surgery. One recent rage is the "metal scalp implant." After anesthetizing the patient, the surgeon makes a 1-inch incision on the top of the head and inserts a metal bar containing four threaded posts between skin and bone. Spikes, which can be up to 4 inches long, are then screwed into the posts so that they stick up into the air above the skin.[7]

The study of consumer behavior is critical for managerial decision making. As the introductory case suggested, cosmetic surgery is a lucrative business. In order to be successful in this business, plastic surgeons—and the hospitals to which they are connected—must market their product. The marketing process requires them to understand consumer needs and wants so that they can offer the types of plastic surgery products—from liposuction to breast augmentation to hair implants—desired by potential consumers and develop promotional messages this audience will find appealing. Thus when targeting middle-aged men, for example, they will emphasize the need to compete against younger rivals. They may also use the findings of consumer research to more effectively segment their market. For instance, research has shown that the market for plastic surgery is better on the coasts than in the midsection of the United States. Figure 1-1 contains an advertisement for one cosmetic surgery clinic.

The field of consumer behavior also has relevance to international marketing. The study of cross-cultural processes and of how people in different countries react to marketing efforts is central to international marketing. Plastic surgery's siren call is being heard around the world. For instance, President Carlos Menem's penchant for fixing his

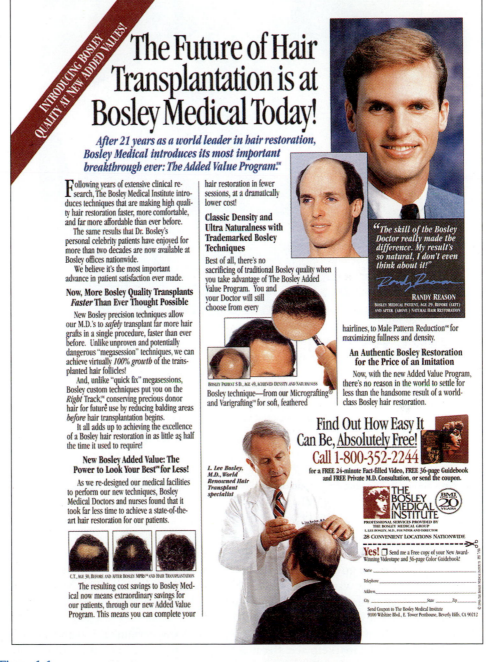

Figure 1-1

This ad for The Bosley Medical Institute touts one type of cosmetic surgery—hair transplantation.

THE NEW LIFT BRA

©1996 SARA LEE INTIMATES. WONDERBRA IS A REGISTERED TRADEMARK OF CANADELLE, INC.

GRAVITY SCHMAVITY.

THE ONE AND ONLY
wonderbra

INTRODUCING THE NEW LIFT BRA,
AN EVERY DAY WONDERBRA DESIGNED TO PUT MOTHER NATURE BACK IN HER PLACE.
ROBINSON MAY, FAMOUS BARR, L.S. AYERS, MEYER & FRANK, FOLEY'S, HECHT'S, FILENE'S, KAUFMANN'S, LORD & TAYLOR

Figure 1-2
Women have flocked to purchase the Wonderbra as a non-surgical means of enhancing the bustline.

receding hairline and his ex-wife's many face lifts seem to have induced almost the entire country of Argentina to go "under the knife." Argentina's best-selling book in 1996 was about plastic surgery (it was titled *Las Mascaras de la Argentina*, or "The Masks of Argentina"). One Argentinian psychiatrist explained the phenomenon this way: "This surgery, this frivolity, is the consequence of our terrible history."[8]

Finally, the study of consumer behavior brings into focus certain ethical and social responsibility issues in the marketplace. Because the patient-physician relationship involves such high levels of trust, it is essential that both parties behave ethically. Massive lawsuits charging that silicone breast implants have caused very serious health problems have led many women to avoid breast augmentation surgery in favor of less risky approaches to create the desired illusion. Figure 1-2 presents an ad for a product designed to enhance a woman's bustline without surgery—the Wonderbra.

WHAT IS CONSUMER BEHAVIOR?

Consumer behavior is a young discipline: the first textbooks for the field were written only in the 1960s. Its intellectual forebears, however, are much older. For example, the American sociologist/economist Thorstein Veblen discussed "conspicuous consumption" in 1899, and in the early 1900s writers began to suggest how psychological principles could help advertisers.[9] In the 1950s ideas from Freudian psychology were popularized by motivation researchers and used by advertisers. The marketing concept was also enunciated in the 1950s, which highlighted the importance of the study of consumer behavior.

As stated by Theodore Levitt, the **marketing concept** embodies "the view that an industry is a customer-satisfying process, not a goods-producing process. An industry begins with the customer and his needs, not with a patent, a raw material, or a selling skill."[10] Once it was understood that an organization can exist only as long as it fulfills its exchange partners' (i.e., customers') needs and wants, the study of the consumer became an essential part of doing business.[11]

Consumer behavior is defined as the study of the buying units and the exchange processes involved in acquiring, consuming, and disposing of goods, services, experiences, and ideas. This simple definition contains a number of important concepts. First, note the inclusion in the definition of the word "exchange." A consumer is inevitably at one end of an **exchange process** in which resources are transferred between two parties. For example, an exchange takes place between a doctor and a patient: the physician trades medical services for money. Other resources—such as feelings, information, and status—may also be exchanged between the parties.

This textbook views the exchange process as a fundamental element of consumer behavior. Exchanges occur between consumers and firms. They also occur between firms, as in industrial buying situations. Finally, exchanges take place between consumers themselves, as when a neighbor borrows a cup of sugar or a lawn mower.

Consider again our definition of consumer behavior. Notice that we use the term **buying units** rather than *consumers*. This is because purchases may be made by groups as well as by individuals. In fact, an important study area for consumer researchers is organizational buying behavior. Particularly in business-to-business marketing, the purchase decision may be made by a group of people in a buying center rather than by an individual. Fortunately, the same basic principles that apply to consumer behavior apply as well to organizational buying behavior.

Our definition of consumer behavior also suggests that the exchange process involves a series of steps, beginning with the acquisition phase, moving on to the consumption phase, and ending with the disposition of the product or service. In investigating the

acquisition phase, researchers analyze the factors that influence consumers' product and service choices. Indeed, most of the research in consumer behavior has focused on the acquisition phase. One factor associated with the search for and selection of goods and services is product symbolism—that is, people often acquire a product to express to others certain ideas and meanings they have about themselves. For example, some men and women undergo cosmetic surgery and wear body rings or tattoos to make a symbolic statement to others about the kind of person they are.

The consumption and disposition phases of the exchange process have received much less attention from consumer researchers. In investigating the **consumption phase,** researchers analyze how consumers actually use a product or service and the experiences they obtain from such use. The consumption experience is particularly important for service industries. In some industries, such as restaurants, amusement parks, and rock concert promotions, the consumption experience is the reason for the purchase.

The **disposition phase** refers to what consumers do with a product once they have finished using it. In addition, it addresses consumer satisfaction levels after purchasing a good or service. Our introductory case, for example, dealt with patients' level of satisfaction with the results of their cosmetic surgery. When consumers have unrealistic expectations of a product, they are unlikely to realize anticipated outcomes, and they will probably be highly dissatisfied. From the surgeon's perspective, customer dissatisfaction increases the likelihood of a lawsuit. From the patient's point of view, unfulfilled expectations may bring a loss of self-esteem and possibly even more cosmetic surgery to set things right. Thus the woman described in the opening case, who after five face lifts found her sideburns behind her ears, was still searching for a plastic surgeon to rectify the travesty.

The student of consumer behavior will be struck by the diversity of the field. It incorporates theories and concepts from all the behavioral sciences, so that when studying the acquisition, consumption, and disposition of products, services, and ideas, you will also explore the discipline of marketing, psychology, social psychology, sociology, anthropology, demography, and economics.

WHY STUDY CONSUMER BEHAVIOR?

Understanding consumers and the consumption process brings a number of benefits, among them the ability to assist managers in their decision making, provide marketing researchers with a knowledge base from which to analyze consumers, help legislators and regulators create laws and regulations concerning the purchase and sale of goods and services, and assist the average consumer in making better purchase decisions. Moreover, studying consumer behavior will enhance your understanding of the psychological, sociological, and economic factors that influence all human behavior.

Consumer Analysis as a Foundation of Marketing Management

The importance of understanding the consumer is found in the definition of **marketing** as a "human activity directed at satisfying needs and wants through human exchange processes."[12] From this definition emerge two key marketing activities. First, marketers attempt to satisfy the needs and wants of their target market. Second, marketing involves the study of the exchange process in which two parties transfer resources between each other. In the exchange process firms receive monetary and other resources from consumers, who, in return, receive products, services, and other resources of value. For marketers to create a successful exchange, they must understand the factors that influence consumers' needs and wants.*

Indeed, **consumer primacy** is the principle on which the entire field of marketing rests.[13] This principle insists that the consumer should be at the center of the marketing effort. As Peter Drucker, the well-known management scholar, has stated, "Marketing is the whole business seen from the point of view of its final result, that is, from the customer's point of view."[14] Similarly, in his critique of General Motors Corporation, Ross Perot proclaimed that for the company to turn around, its managers must perceive that "the consumer is king!"[15]

Public Policy and Consumer Behavior

A knowledge of consumer behavior can also assist in the development of public policy. **Public policy,** as it pertains to consumer behavior, is the development of laws and regulations that impact consumers in the marketplace. In its legislative, regulatory, and judicial roles, the federal government often deals with consumer issues. Periodically, for example, proposals surface to limit, or even eliminate, the ability of cigarette manufacturers to advertise their product. Recently, consumer research on the impact the advertising character Joe Camel has had on children figured prominently in the formulation of new federal regulation of the tobacco companies.

Also falling into the public policy domain of consumer behavior is the study of consumer *mis*behavior, sometimes called "the dark side of consumer behavior." Consumers can act unethically, misuse products, and engage in behaviors that risk life and limb. Recall from the chapter-opening case the desire of the young woman to enlarge her breasts to unnatural proportions. This could be considered an example of consumer misbehavior—albeit in this instance the surgeon refused to go along entirely with the consumer's wishes.

Consumer Behavior and Altruistic Marketing

The ideas and concepts of marketing are also applicable to nontraditional business areas. Various nonprofit groups—such as political parties, religious organizations, and charitable groups (e.g., United Way of America)—engage in consumer research. However, rather than marketing tangible products, these organizations are purveying intangible ideas. The United Way, for instance, seeks to convince the public that if thousands of individuals volunteer to help others through nonprofit organizations, such as Big Brothers/Big Sisters and the Red Cross, Americans can make the United States a better place to live.

Indeed, consumer researchers have recently argued that many of the most important problems our society faces today involve choices that consumers make. Examples are decisions to eat high-fat foods, smoke, drink and drive, take illicit drugs, and purchase the services of a prostitute. Research by consumer behavior scholars can suggest ways to influence people to act more responsibly in their consumption of such dangerous goods and services. Thus consumer researchers contribute to the new field of **altruistic marketing,**

---

*In 1985 the American Marketing Association developed the following definition of marketing: "Marketing is the process of planning and executing the conception, pricing, promotion, and distribution of ideas, goods, and services to create exchanges that satisfy individual and organizational objectives." Although this definition emphasizes the importance of the exchange concept, it neglects the concept that marketing functions to fulfill the needs and wants of *consumers*. In our view, the definition's downplaying of the consumer focus is a setback for marketing. The field of consumer behavior can assist the marketer to correct this underemphasis.

a field of study that (1) researches the causes of negligent consumer behavior and (2) applies the findings to develop treatment and/or preventive methods to reduce the maladaptive actions of consumers.[16]

The Personal Value of Consumer Behavior

A general knowledge of consumer behavior also has considerable **personal value.** For one thing, it helps people become better consumers by revealing to them how they and others go about their consumption activities. For another, it aids consumers in the buying process by informing them about the strategies companies use to market their products. In addition, knowledge of the factors that influence consumption has intrinsic value for many people: they enjoy learning why product rumors start, why subliminal advertising messages are unlikely to influence buying, and why some product endorsers (e.g., the basketball player Michael Jordan) are so much more effective than others (e.g., the basketball player Patrick Ewing). Finally, understanding one's own personal consumption motivations as well as those of others is part of a well-rounded person's education in contemporary America.

We can make the overall statement that the study of consumer behavior provides three types of information: (1) an orientation, (2) facts, and (3) theories. Studying the consumer orients managers and public policy makers to consider the impact of their actions on ordinary people. The field also provides useful facts, such as the size of various demographic groups. In addition, the study of consumer behavior helps us to formulate valuable social theories. *Theory* is a misunderstood term that tends to be ridiculed—as in such statements as: "That's only theory; it has nothing to do with what really happens." Actually, nothing is more practical than a theory. Detectives develop theories of why a certain crime was committed—and doing so often helps them solve the case. Medical doctors develop theories of why a person gets sick—and those theories can point the way to a cure. And business managers develop theories of why a product fails to sell—and use them to reposition the product or make a better one.

A **theory** is a set of interrelated statements defining the causal relationships among a group of ideas. Theories may be large or small, but every valid theory has research support. A major

Reasons for Studying Consumer Behavior

1. Consumer analysis should be the foundation of marketing management. It assists managers to:
   a. Design the marketing mix.
   b. Segment the marketplace.
   c. Position and differentiate products.
   d. Perform an environmental analysis.
   e. Develop market research studies.
2. Consumer behavior should play an important role in the development of public policy.
3. The study of consumer behavior will enable one to be a more effective consumer.
4. Consumer analysis provides knowledge of overall human behavior.
5. The study of consumer behavior provides three types of information:
   a. A consumer orientation.
   b. Facts about human behavior.
   c. Theories to guide the thinking process.

TABLE 1-1

practical reason for studying consumer behavior is that the field offers a variety of theories that do have research support and that can be used to understand and solve managerial and public policy problems. Table 1-1 summarizes the reasons for studying consumer behavior.

THREE RESEARCH PERSPECTIVES ON CONSUMER BEHAVIOR

A key feature of the field is its research base. As a social science, consumer behavior employs research methods and procedures from psychology, sociology, economics, and anthropology. To generalize, research in consumer behavior is organized according to three research perspectives that act as guides in thinking about and identifying the factors that influence consumer acquisition behavior. These three perspectives are: (1) the decision-making perspective, (2) the experiential perspective, and (3) the behavioral influence perspective.[17]

The Decision-Making Perspective

Throughout the 1970s and into the early 1980s, researchers viewed the consumer as a decision maker. From this perspective, buying results from consumers perceiving that they have a problem and then moving through a rational process to solve that problem. The **decision-making perspective** portrays consumers as taking a series of steps when making a purchase. These steps include problem recognition, search, alternative evaluation, choice, and postacquisition evaluation. The roots of this approach are in cognitive and experimental psychology and certain areas of economics.

If you think back to our cosmetic surgery example, you will see that the decision-making perspective in this situation focuses on the steps consumers take when deciding which physician to hire to do their cosmetic surgery. In analyzing this choice process, researchers would attempt to identify the characteristics consumers seek in their cosmetic surgeon, such as medical qualifications, bedside manner, ability to explain risks, and price charged.

The Experiential Perspective

The **experiential perspective** on consumer buying proposes that in some instances consumers do not make purchases according to a strictly rational decision-making process. Instead, they buy certain products and services in order to have fun, create fantasies, or feel desired emotions.[18] Classified within the experiential perspective would be purchases made on impulse and purchases made to seek variety. Variety seeking occurs when consumers switch brands simply because they are bored with their old brand and feel stimulated by the prospect of a new one.[19] Many consumer services and products bought for leisure purposes have a strong experiential component—for example, rock concerts, symphonies, amusement parks, and movies. The fundamental goal of these leisure products is to create feelings among consumers.

Advertisers frequently use emotional appeals to influence consumers. Figure 1-3 shows an advertisement that creates positive feelings in many people. Note that this ad also points up the increasing importance of the international dimensions of consumer behavior.

A researcher analyzing the introductory case from the experiential perspective would focus on identifying the feelings, emotions, and symbols that accompany the purchase of cosmetic surgery. The roots of the experiential perspective are in motivational psychology and in certain areas of sociology and anthropology. Researchers who take an experiential perspective frequently use **interpretive research methods.** Interpretivists believe that researchers inevitably influence the data-collection effort, concentrate on

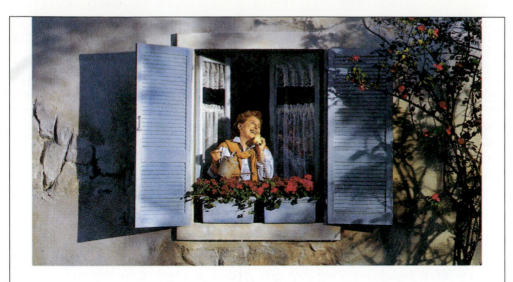

Figure 1-3

For many consumers, this AT&T ad strongly influences feelings and emotions

understanding rather than predicting behavior, and think that reality is socially constructed. They frequently employ naturalistic research methods—that is, methods in which the investigator directly observes and records the activities of interest or even deliberately participates in those activities.[20] Interpretivists can even be found recording the folklore and traditions of a society to obtain an understanding of that society's consumption processes.[21]

The Behavioral Influence Perspective

The **behavioral influence perspective** assumes that strong environmental forces propel consumers to make purchases without necessarily first developing strong feelings or beliefs about the product. According to this perspective, the consumer neither goes through a rational decision-making process nor relies on feelings to purchase a product or service. Instead, the consumer's purchase action directly results from environmental forces, such as sales promotion devices (e.g., contests), cultural norms, the physical environment, and economic pressures.[22]

Researchers analyzing our opening case from the behavioral influence perspective would look to determine if exceedingly strong group or social pressures were propeling people to have their noses pierced or their breasts enlarged. A person acting under strong environmental pressures may actually have a strong distaste for a procedure, but seek to have it performed anyway. The roots of the behavioral influence perspective are found in behavioral learning theory, which we discuss in Chapter 5.

We should note here that most buying behavior involves some elements of all three perspectives. For example, purchasing the services of a plastic surgeon involves some decision making, such as when the consumer searches for information, evaluates alternatives, and makes a rational choice. However, it is also likely that an experiential process is operating—that is, strong emotional elements are driving the consumer to engage in an action that has a high level of symbolic meaning (such as undergoing a face lift to achieve a youthful image). Finally, strong social pressures may well be pushing the consumer to this cosmetic "improvement." In sum, it is useful to examine consumer behavior from each perspective to fully appreciate the impact of logical decision making, of feelings and emotions, and of environmental influencers on consumer behavior.

EXCHANGE PROCESSES AND CONSUMER BEHAVIOR

Central to the study of consumer behavior are exchange processes. Whenever a good, service, idea, or experience is transferred from one entity to another, an exchange takes place. Formally, **exchange** may be defined as a process that involves the "transfer of something tangible or intangible, actual or symbolic, between two or more social actors."[23]

The idea that exchange is fundamental to marketing has been accepted for over 40 years. In 1957 Wroe Alderson, one of the early founders of the field, wrote, "Marketing is the exchange which takes place between consuming groups and supplying groups."[24] Similarly, Philip Kotler defined marketing as "a social process by which individuals and groups obtain what they need and want through creating and exchanging products and value with others."[25] In 1975 Richard Bagozzi proposed that exchange is the most basic element of the marketing function.[26] Finally, in 1985 the American Marketing Association defined marketing as "the process of planning and executing the conception, pricing, promotion, and distribution of ideas, goods, and services to create exchanges that satisfy individual and organizational objectives."[27] Note how in each of these definitions the concept of exchange is central to defining the field of marketing.

Prerequisites for Exchange

For an exchange to take place, five conditions must be met:

1. Two or more parties must be present.
2. Each party must have something that is of value to the other party.
3. Each party must be capable of communication and delivery.
4. Each party must be free to reject or accept the other's offer.
5. Each party must believe that it is appropriate or desirable to deal with the other.[28]

An important issue when investigating exchange is explaining why one person is willing to give up one thing to receive something else in return. If one person has one collection or assortment of goods and another person has a second collection or assortment of goods, what will make them enter into an exchange? The basic reason for exchanging one good for another is that different people possess divergent tastes and preferences. As described by economists, consumers act to increase the total utility of the assortment of goods they possess by making exchanges. Therefore the fundamental principle driving exchange is that people have different utility functions. Thus if I have something that has lower value to me than it has to you, and if you have something that has lower value to you than it has to me, we have a basis for exchange.[29] In such instances both parties profit from the exchange because each receives something that he values more than what he gave up.

What Are the Elements of Exchange?

Researchers have worked hard to identify what is exchanged between two people or between two social units (e.g., a family and a firm).[30] Some have proposed that six types of resources are exchanged: goods, services, money, status, information, and feelings.[31] Others have suggested that there are only four fundamental resources: material resources (e.g., goods and money), social resources (e.g., other people), physical resources (e.g., one's physical assets, such as seeing and hearing), and information resources (e.g., one's knowledge and skills).[32] Table 1-2 gives examples of each of the six categories of resources. Figure 1-4 presents an ad for Perrier bottled water in which a variety of resources are offered for exchange.

The exchange process itself is diagrammed in Figure 1-5. The figure shows that each party to the exchange possesses certain resources. The resources input by one party represent his or her costs, and become the outcomes received by the other party. Outcomes are derived, not only from the resources exchanged, but also from the experiences had by engaging in the exchange act. Thus each party may derive rewards or costs from the exchange process itself in addition to those obtained from the goods, services, or money transferred.

Examples of the Six Categories of Resources

1. *Feelings*. Expressions of affectionate regard, warmth, or comfort.
2. *Status*. Evaluative judgment conveying high or low prestige, regard, or esteem.
3. *Information*. Any advice, opinion, or instruction.
4. *Money*. Any coin or token that has some standard of exchange value.
5. *Goods*. Any product or object that has exchange value.
6. *Services*. Any performance of labor done for someone else.

Source: Based in part on Gregory Donnenworth and Uriel Foa, "Effects of Resource Class on Retaliation to Injustice in Interpersonal Exchange," *Journal of Personality and Social Psychology*, Vol. 29 (1974), pp. 785–793.

TABLE 1-2

©1992 Great Waters of France, Inc.

Along the dusty road to Santa Fe, you'll find

some great Navajo blankets,

more than a few hot chili peppers and maybe

even a legend or two.

Perrier. Part of the local color.

Figure 1-4
What are the resources offered for exchange in this ad for Perrier bottled water?

Dimensions of Exchange Relations

Four types of consumer exchange relations have been identified: (1) restricted versus complex, (2) internal versus external, (3) formal versus informal, and (4) relational versus discrete (see Table 1-3). We briefly discuss the dimensions of each in this section.

Restricted versus Complex Exchanges A **restricted exchange,** which is the simplest type of exchange, involves two parties interacting in a reciprocal relationship.[33] Examples are a consumer and her stockbroker and a patient and his physician. At the most complicated level of exchanges, one finds **complex exchanges,** which involve a set of three or more actors enmeshed in a set of mutual relations. An example is a channel of distribution in which an automobile goes from manufacturer (e.g., Ford Motor Company) to a dealer, which then sells it to a customer. In a complex exchange each party depends upon the other to supply resources—even though car buyers and manufacturers are separated by a dealer, the consumer depends upon the manufacturer to

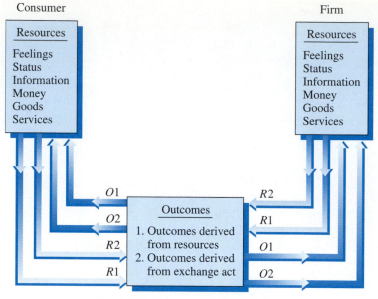

R1 and R2 = Resources input to exchange
O1 and O2 = Outcomes received from exchange

Figure 1-5
Diagram of the exchange process.

build a quality product. Similarly, the manufacturer depends upon consumers purchasing its autos.

Internal versus External Exchanges The second dimension of exchange relations concerns whether they occur within a group (an internal exchange) or between parties that are in separate groups (an external exchange).[34] An example of an **internal exchange** is the complex sets of relations that occur within a family. Internal exchanges involve a situation in which the members of the organization or group avoid going into the market to obtain a particular good or service, but instead satisfy that need within the organization. An ex-

Types of Exchange Relations

1. Restricted vs. Complex
   A. *Restricted exchange*. Concerns a two-party relation.
   B. *Complex exchange*. Involves a set of three or more actors.
2. Internal vs. External
   A. *Internal exchange*. Occurs within a group.
   B. *External exchange*. Occurs between groups.
3. Formal vs. Informal
   A. *Formal exchange*. Involves explicit written or verbal contracts.
   B. *Informal exchange*. Involves unwritten, unspoken, social contracts.
4. Relational vs. Discrete
   A. *Relational exchange*. Creates long-term relations.
   B. *Discrete exchange*. Constitutes one-time exchange in which no relations are formed.

TABLE 1-3

ample of an **external exchange** is the transactions that occur between a manufacturing firm and retailers. Here members of the group (retailers) are importing goods or services from an outside source (the manufacturer) to fulfill a need.

Although consumer researchers have generally focused on understanding external exchanges, internal exchanges are also important. For example, should an automobile company produce its own car motors (e.g., as General Motors does for most of its cars), or should it purchase the engines from an outside supplier (e.g., Ford buys motors from Yamaha for its Taurus SHO car).

Formal versus Informal Exchanges Exchanges can occur either formally or informally. A **formal exchange** involves an explicit, written, or verbal contract. Formal exchange is characteristic of external exchanges. In an **informal exchange** unwritten, social contracts are created between parties. This type of exchange is more frequent in internal exchanges, where social norms and peer pressure replace formal contracts.

One arena in which informal exchanges are common is dating. From an unromantic point of view, people possess a set of resources that are exchanged when they date—for example, physical beauty, intelligence, money, a high-status occupation, a good personality. These characteristics are the resources exchanged when individuals become involved in romantic exchanges. Thus the dating process arguably consists of men and women exchanging various personal resources.

One researcher investigated personal dating advertisements placed in *The Washingtonian* magazine and *New York* magazine.[35] In both magazines men and women publish short descriptions of themselves and of the type of person they would like to meet. Here is an example:

> Very attractive, college-educated, professional female (in science), 28, 5'8", dark hair, exercise fanatic, active and outgoing, seeks male counterpart: Tall, handsome, (blond?), muscular, secure, professional man (Law, MD) under 36, for sports, fun dates, and possibly great relationship. Note and photo appreciated.

After performing a content analysis of the personal advertisements in these two magazines, the researcher found that the resources offered and sought in such ads fell into ten categories: love, physical attractiveness/beauty, money, occupational status, educational status, intellectual status, entertainment services, information-personality, information-ethnic, and information-demographic. Table 1-4 depicts both the set of resources that men

---

Resource Exchanges Between Men and Women in the Dating Setting

I. Resources hypothesized to be advertised by men and women

    A. Women advertise physical attractiveness, love, entertainment services, and information.

    B. Men advertise money, educational status, intellectual status, and occupational status.

II. Actual resources found in study to be advertised and sought

    A. Women offered physical attractiveness.
        Women sought monetary resources and love.

    B. Men offered monetary resources and occupational status.
        Men sought physical attractiveness and love.

Source: Elizabeth C. Hirschman, "People as Products: Analysis of a Complex Marketing Exchange," *Journal of Marketing*, Vol. 51 (January 1987), pp. 98–108, published by the American Marketing Association.

TABLE 1-4

and women were hypothesized to offer and seek and the set of resources they actually did offer and seek. It was hypothesized that women would offer (and men would seek) physical attractiveness, love, entertainment services, and information. In contrast, it was proposed that men would offer (and women would seek) money, educational status, intellectual status, and occupational status.

The study results bore out these hypotheses: women more often than men did indeed offer physical attractiveness and seek monetary resources, while men tended to offer monetary resources and seek physical attractiveness. Somewhat sadly, both men and women sought love much more frequently than they offered it.

Relational versus Discrete Exchanges Exchanges are also categorized according to whether they are discrete or relational. A **discrete exchange** is a one-time interaction in which money is paid for an easily measured commodity. Discrete exchanges are quick purchases that do not involve the creation of a relationship. In contrast, a **relational exchange** is a transaction that involves a long-term commitment in which trust and social relations play an important role.[36]

Relational exchanges have been equated to a marriage between the buyer and the seller. As one author stated, "The sale merely consummates the courtship. Then the marriage begins. How good the marriage is depends on how well the relationship is managed by the seller."[37] Thus when viewed from a relational exchange perspective, transactions are analyzed in terms of their history and anticipated future. Relational transactions emphasize the social relations between the exchange parties as well as the benefits derived from the characteristics of the product or service obtained. Consumers in such an exchange make a long-term commitment with the marketer to reduce overall transaction costs (e.g., by minimizing search costs), lower risk, and gain the positive feelings derived from interacting with someone who is liked. Table 1-5 depicts some of the characteristics of relational exchanges.

Examples of relational exchanges are found in both the industrial and consumer sectors. For instance, a company producing a complex product—such as a jet aircraft, a submarine, or a large building—must contract with other corporations to supply specific components and services. One survey of banking, high-tech, and manufacturing customers found that respondents viewed "the personal touch" as the most important element of good service. The personal touch was defined as "how committed a company representative is to a client and whether he or she remembers a customer's name." The personal touch factor was found to be more important than convenience, speed of delivery, and how well the

---

Some Characteristics of Relational Exchanges

1. *Timing*. Long term, reflects an ongoing process.
2. *Obligations*. Obligations are customized and detailed. Promises are made, and laws and regulations may apply.
3. *Relationship expectations*. Conflicts are anticipated, but they are countered by trust and efforts to create unity.
4. *Rewards*. Rewards are derived from economic and noneconomic means.
5. *Communications*. Communications are extensive through formal and informal means.
6. *Cooperation*. A great deal of cooperation is needed to maintain exchange.
7. *Power*. Increased interdependence increases the importance of judicious application of power in the exchange.
8. *Planning*. There is a significant focus on the process of exchange. Detailed planning is required for future exchanges.

TABLE 1-5

Figure 1-6
PaineWebber emphasizes relationship quality in this print ad.

product worked.[38] Actually, "personal touch" is simply a term for what happens in relational exchanges. Figure 1-6 presents an ad from PaineWebber that emphasizes the importance of building relationships between broker and client.

Social relations are particularly important in facilitating exchanges at home buying parties. Indeed, the term **market embeddedness** has been used to describe a situation in which the social ties between buyer and seller supplement product value and thereby increase the perceived value of the exchange.[39] The importance of social relations has been recognized by companies, such as Tupperware and Mary Kay Cosmetics, that frequently employ home parties to sell their merchandise. At these parties are found a hostess, a demonstrator, and several invitees, and usually there are close relationships within the group of invitees as well as between the invitees and the hostess.

Table 1-6 summarizes the most significant research findings concerning relationship exchanges.

ETHICAL ISSUES IN CONSUMER EXCHANGE RELATIONS

Within exchanges, trust between buyer and seller is an extremely important element. One factor influencing trust is the ethical conduct of both parties. **Ethics** is the study of normative judgments about what is morally right and wrong, good and bad.[40] Ethical judgments are based on standards that:

1. Deal with serious human injuries and benefits.
2. May or may not be laid down by authoritative bodies.
3. Override self-interest.
4. Are based on impartial considerations.

Ethical judgments frequently involve a conflict between one's self-interest and a moral standard of conduct. Thus plastic surgeons are obligated to put their clients' interests first, rather than their own. When making a decision that has ethical implications, it is necessary to use impartial considerations. The decision should be based on moral guidelines rather than on who is helped or hurt by the outcome of the action.[41]

The problems faced by cosmetic surgeons in their relationship with patients illustrate an ethical dilemma. An **ethical dilemma** is defined as: "A decision that involves the trade-off between lowering one's personal values in exchange for increased organizational or personal profits."[42] In sum, whenever consumers engage in exchange relationships, ethical principles are likely to come into play.

Generally, an **ethical exchange** has the following components:

1. Both parties know the full nature of the agreement they are entering into.
2. Neither party to the exchange intentionally misrepresents or omits to give relevant information to the other.
3. Neither party to the exchange unduly influences the other.[43]

Figure 1-7 presents an exchange matrix that examines how marketing resources flow in exchange situations. The source of the resource is the information sender (which may be either the business firm or the consumer) and the recipient of the resource is the information receiver (which, again, may be either the business firm or the consumer). When one business extends resources to another business, it is engaging in **industrial marketing.** When a business sends resources to consumers, it is engaging in **consumer marketing.** In both cases ethical issues should inform the firm's actions. The firm should fulfill all commitments it has made concerning its inputs to the exchange. In particular, service, product, and informational inputs should be performed as promised or implied.

Most discussions of ethics deal with industrial or consumer marketing. Typically, they focus on the firm's actions in such areas as misleading advertising, selling products that do not live up to the claims made for them, producing unsafe products, exerting undue influence (e.g., bribery), and failing to disclose important relevant information (e.g., not telling a customer that a product was used previously). But consumers also have a responsibility to act ethically in their exchanges with firms and other consumers. If an acquaintance wants to buy your old car, you have an ethical duty to warn the person of any safety problems you've noted in driving the car, to avoid coercing the person to make the purchase, and to avoid misleading the person in terms of how the car will perform.

Consumers are also obliged to act ethically in their dealings with business firms. So when a consumer returns a product to a firm, she has an ethical duty to return it in satisfactory condition. She also should refrain from misleading the firm about her reasons for returning the product. For example, it is not ethical to purchase a dress, wear it on a single special occasion, and then return it to the store, claiming that it doesn't fit properly. Similarly, consumers should refrain from **free riding,** an unethical act in which a person obtains a resource from a firm, such as information, and then fails to pay back resources in return. For example, you may go to a full-service camera store to get product information and to identify satisfactory alternatives. If you obtain product information from sales personnel and then use that information to make a shrewd purchase from a low-cost discount store that does not offer personal service, you are guilty of free riding. Your action was unethical because you never had any intention of making a purchase at the full-service store. You have done that retailer real harm in deliberately extracting informational and service resources for nothing.

The relationship between consumers and businesses is a reciprocal one. When sufficient numbers of consumers act unethically, businesses feel compelled to respond in order

	Information Receiver	
Information Sender	Business	Consumer
Business	Industrial marketing	Consumer marketing
Consumer	Consumer-induced contact	Personal marketing

Figure 1-7

Consumer exchange matrix. (*Note:* Ethical principles should govern the exchange process in each cell of the matrix.)

to survive. For instance, if sufficient numbers of consumers engage in free riding at the full-service camera store, the store will eventually either close down or become a discount store. In either case consumers will lose an important source of marketplace information. Similarly, if too many consumers abuse return privileges, companies will be forced to install "no-return" policies. As you can see, ethics is a two-way street. Consumers have a right to expect businesses to act ethically, but firms also have a right to expect consumers to behave ethically.

It is critical for firms to develop an internal culture that emphasizes core ethical values.[44] Researchers have identified four rules that managers should follow to ensure that their decisions are ethical.[45] Although originally designed for managers, the rules have been slightly rewritten to make them applicable to consumers as well.

1. *The golden rule.* Act in a way that you would expect others to act toward you.
2. *The professional ethic.* Take only actions that would be viewed as proper by an objective panel of colleagues.
3. *Kant's categorical imperative.* Act in a way such that the action you take in particular circumstances could be a universal law of behavior for everyone facing those same circumstances.
4. *The TV test.* Always ask, "Would I feel comfortable explaining this action on TV to the general public?"

AN ORGANIZING MODEL OF CONSUMER BEHAVIOR

To give you an overview of the broad field of consumer behavior, we have developed the organizing model shown in Figure 1-8. This consumer behavior model has five primary components that form the core areas of study in the field: the buying unit, the exchange process, the marketer's strategy, the individual influencers, and the environmental influencers.

Buying units are the customers for products, services, experiences, and ideas offered by marketers. They are connected to the marketer via an exchange relationship. Buying units may consist of either an individual, a family, or a group that makes a purchase decision. In addition, buying units may be consumers (i.e., individuals and households) or profit/nonprofit organizations making purchases. In summation, the principles of consumer behavior apply to business-to-business marketing as well as business-to-consumer marketing.

The term *marketer* is used extremely broadly in the model; a marketer could be a firm selling a good or service, a nonprofit organization, a government agency, a political candidate, or another consumer who wishes to sell or trade something. The marketer seeks

---

Consumer Behavior Factoid

Question: In which university major do students admit to the most cheating?

Answer: A survey of 15,000 college students from "prestigious" universities revealed that 76 percent of business majors reported that they cheated—a higher percentage than in any of the other six majors surveyed. (Education majors cheated the least.) In addition, more business students than any others were found to be "regulars"—that is, they cheated more than four times while in school.

Source: Rick Tetzeli, "Business Students Cheat Most," *Fortune*, July 1, 1991, pp. 14–15.

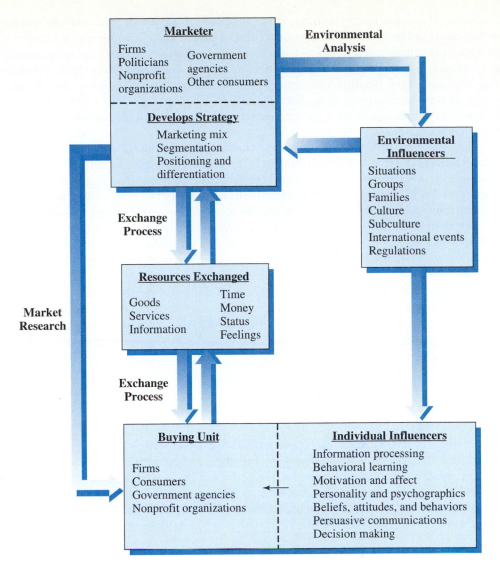

Figure 1-8
An organizing model of consumer behavior.

to create an exchange with consumers by implementing a marketing strategy designed to reach long-term customer and profit goals. A major focus of this text is on how an understanding of the exchange process, the individual influencers, and the environmental influencers can be used to develop marketing strategy.

A **marketing strategy** is implemented by creating segmentation and positioning objectives for a product that an organization or individual wishes to exchange with a consumer. **Segmentation** refers to the division of the marketplace into relatively homogeneous subsets of consumers with similar needs and wants. **Positioning** refers to influencing how consumers perceive a brand's characteristics relative to those of competitive offerings. In order to further the exchange and reach their segmentation and positioning objectives, marketers develop a marketing mix. The **marketing mix** consists not only of the product itself, but also of how it is priced, promoted, and distributed.

To develop a marketing strategy, managers perform environmental analysis studies to anticipate the likely effects of environmental influencers, and then use market research to obtain information on individual consumers. On the basis of this analysis and research, they create positioning and segmentation strategies and implement them through the marketing mix. Because consumer behavior findings and ideas have critical relevance to the development of marketing strategy, Chapter 2 discusses how consumer behavior concepts can be used by managers to market their goods, services, ideas, and experiences.

Notice that the model of consumer behavior connects the buying unit to both individual influencers and environmental influencers. **Individual influence factors** are those psychological processes that affect individuals engaged in acquiring, consuming, and disposing of goods, services, and experiences. **Environmental influence factors** are those factors outside the individual that affect individual consumers, decision-making units, and marketers.

The individual influencers and the environmental influencers lie on a continuum that moves from a highly micro to a broad macro focus. Market analysis begins at the individual end of the continuum, with the most basic psychological processes involving perception and learning. The analysis moves along the continuum to the study of personality, attitudes, persuasion, and, finally, consumer decision making. At this point on the continuum, the emphasis changes from the study of the individual to the investigation of the impact of situations and groups on consumer behavior. At the most macro end of the continuum, consumer researchers examine how people in different nations and cultures acquire, consume, and dispose of goods, services, experiences, and ideas.

The Organization of the Text

The major sections of this textbook correspond to the consumer behavior model shown in Figure 1-8. Part I provides an overview of the field and comprises two chapters. In this chapter we defined consumer behavior and presented the consumer behavior model we will use throughout the book. In Chapter 2 we identify how knowledge of consumer behavior can be used to create a marketing strategy. There we discuss how consumer behavior concepts are employed by managers of organizations to develop the marketing mix, segment the marketplace, position and differentiate products, perform environmental analysis, and conduct market research.

Part II consists of a set of chapters on the factors that influence individual consumers. As shown in Figure 1-8, the major individual influencers are: information processing; behavioral learning; motivation and affect; personality and psychographics; beliefs, attitudes, and behaviors; persuasive communications; and decision making.

Part III considers the environmental influencers that affect buyers and sellers. These include consumer situations, group and exchange processes, the family, culture, demographics and subcultures, international and cross-cultural consumer behavior, and the "dark side" of consumer behavior.

Summary

Consumer behavior is a broad field of study that investigates the exchange process through which individuals and groups acquire, consume, and dispose of goods, services, ideas, and experiences. The principles of consumer behavior are useful to business managers, government regulators, and nonprofit organizations, as well as to ordinary people. For marketing managers, knowledge of consumer behavior has important implications for environmental analysis, product positioning, the segmentation of the marketplace, the design of market research, and the development of the marketing mix.

That consumer behavior has a strong impact on marketing management is not surprising. Modern marketing managers have embraced the "marketing concept"—the idea that understanding consumer needs and wants will facilitate the exchange processes and achieve profits for the company. They therefore see satisfying consumers as the focal point of the marketing effort.

Consumer behavior is an applied discipline. Though it borrows theories and knowledge from other fields, such as anthropology, sociology, demographics, economics, and psychology, it is a discipline in its own right. Consumer researchers are developing their own body of knowledge to supplement knowledge they've obtained from other fields.

Central to the field of consumer behavior is the study of exchange processes. Exchange is the process through which something tangible or intangible, actual or symbolic, is transferred between two or more social actors. It is the most basic element of the marketing function. For an exchange to take place, a number of elements must be present. First, each party must have the freedom to accept or reject the other's offer. Second, when exchanges take place, resources are transferred between the parties. These resources include goods, services, money, status, information, and feelings. Finally, exchanges may be restricted or complex, internal or external, formal or informal, and relational or discrete. Increasingly, marketers are focusing on creating relational exchanges. The term market embeddedness is used to describe the situation in which the social ties between a buyer and seller supplement product value and therefore increase the perceived value of an exchange.

An emerging area of study in consumer behavior is ethics—normative judgments concerning what is morally right and wrong, good and bad. Ethical judgments are grounded in standards that pertain to serious human injuries and benefits, that may or may not be laid down by an authority, that override self-interest, and that are based on impartial considerations. In the field of consumer behavior ethical issues pertain to actions engaged in by both businesses and consumers. Thus consumers, like businesses, can, and do, act unethically.

Three research perspectives on consumer acquisition behavior were identified: the decision-making perspective, the experiential perspective, and the behavioral influence perspective.

The organizing model of consumer behavior presented in this chapter is composed of five primary elements: the individual influencers, the consumer environment, the exchange process, the buying unit, and the marketer. The entire textbook is organized around this model.

K E Y   T E R M S

acquisition phase
altruistic marketing
behavioral influence
    perspective
buying unit
complex exchanges
consumer behavior
consumer marketing
consumer primacy
consumption phase
decision-making perspective

discrete exchange
disposition phase
environmental influence
    factors
ethical dilemma
ethical exchange
ethics
exchange
exchange process
experiential perspective
external exchange

formal exchange
free riding
individual influence factors
industrial marketing
informal exchange
internal exchange
interpretive research
    methods
market embeddedness
marketing
marketing concept

marketing mix
marketing strategy
personal value
positioning
public policy
relational exchange
restricted exchange
segmentation
theory

R E V I E W   Q U E S T I O N S

1. Define the term *consumer behavior*. Why is consumption viewed as a process?

2. Identify the reasons for claiming that an understanding of consumer behavior is the foundation for developing marketing strategy and planning.

3. How can the study of consumer behavior assist managers in doing an environmental analysis?

4. How can the study of consumer behavior assist managers in positioning and differentiating products and services?

5. How can the study of consumer behavior help managers to segment the marketplace?

6. Through what means does consumer behavior assist the market research function?

7. In what ways can the study of consumer behavior provide consumers, managers, and public policy makers with theories, facts, and an orientation?

8. What are the behavioral science fields from which consumer behavior draws some of its theories and concepts?

9. Draw a diagram of the consumer behavior model presented in the text.

10. Describe the three research perspectives marketers can use to analyze the consumer purchase process.

11. Why is the concept of exchange fundamental to the understanding of marketing and consumer behavior?

12. Identify the basic prerequisites for exchange.

13. Identify the six categories of resources that are exchanged.

14. Define ethics in the context of consumer behavior.

15. What standards should be used to judge whether an action is ethical?

16. Briefly describe the two broad levels of analysis from which consumer behavior may be analyzed—that is, the individual influencers and the environmental influencers.

D I S C U S S I O N   Q U E S T I O N S

1. Consider the soft-drink industry. Through what means do such companies as Coca-Cola, PepsiCo, and Dr Pepper attempt to differentiate their products from those of other soft-drink companies? (Think in terms of product characteristics and images.)

2. Define the concept of environmental analysis. What environmental factors may surface in the next ten years to influence soft-drink consumption? (*Hint*: Think in terms of changes in the global marketplace and of demographic trends.)

3. Define the concept of market segmentation. Using your knowledge of the automobile industry, try to identify different segments of customers that auto manufacturers attempt to reach.

4. Define the concept of consumer primacy. Next, identify several ways in which marketers can demonstrate to customers that they subscribe to the principle of consumer primacy. Finally, describe two or three instances in your own buying experience in which marketers or retailers failed to follow this principle.

5. Consumer researchers are highly interested in demographic trends. Identify three major demographic trends that may influence corporate market planning for makers of golf clubs or microwave ovens.

6. Identify three types of purchases you have made that were based mostly on a careful, rational thought process. Briefly explain the nature of the thought process behind each purchase.

7. Identify three purchases you have made that were based mostly on a desire to obtain feelings and experiences. What feelings and experiences were you hoping to obtain from each purchase?

8. Identify three purchases you have made principally because of environmental pressures. What was the nature of the pressure that encouraged each purchase?

9. Identify a relational exchange that you have had with a retailer or service provider. What characteristics of the exchange made you consider it relational?

10. Students are in an exchange relationship with a university. Discuss the resources you have exchanged with your university. To what extent are the costs and benefits received by your university and its students equitable? (For a discussion of equity theory, see Chapter 13.)

11. Identify an ethical dilemma students commonly face. What factors should they consider in attempting to resolve the dilemma?

ENDNOTES

1. Charles Siebert, "The Cuts That Go Deeper," *The New York Times Magazine*, July 7, 1996, p. 34.

2. Kathy Healy, "Plastic Surgery Addicts," *Allure*, April 1993, pp. 80–82.

3. Healy, "Plastic Surgery Addicts."

4. Charles Siebert, "The Cuts That Go Deeper," *The New York Times Magazine*, July 7, 1996, pp. 20–25, 34, 40–44.

5. Healy, "Plastic Surgery Addicts."

6. Healy, "Plastic Surgery Addicts," p. 81.

7. Joe Aylward, "Don't Try This at Home," *Newsweek*, August 12, 1996, p. 5.

8. Jonathan Friedland, "Argentina Is a Land of Many Faces, Fixed by Plastic Surgeons," *The Wall Street Journal*, February 2, 1996, pp. A1, A5.

9. Scott Ward and Thomas Robertson, "Consumer Behavior Research: Promise and Prospects," in *Consumer Behavior: Theoretical Sources*, Scott Ward and Thomas Robertson, eds. (Upper Saddle River, NJ: Prentice Hall, 1973), pp. 3–42.

10. Theodore Levitt, "Marketing Myopia," in *Modern Marketing Strategy*, Edward Bursk and John Chapman, eds. (Cambridge, MA: Harvard University Press, 1964).

11. Philip Kotler, *Marketing Management Analysis, Planning, and Control*, 4th ed. (Upper Saddle River, NJ: Prentice Hall, 1980), p. 21.

12. Brent Stidsen, "Directions in the Study of Marketing," in *Conceptual and Theoretical Developments in Marketing*, Neil Beckwith et al., eds. (Chicago: American Marketing Association, 1979), pp. 383–398.

13. As cited in Kotler, *Marketing Management*, p. 3.

14. Frank Houston, "The Marketing Concept, What It Is and What It Is Not," *Journal of Marketing*, April 1986, pp. 81–87.

15. Ross Perot, "How I Would Turn Around GM," *Fortune*, February 15, 1988, p. 45.

16. Richard E. Petty and John T. Cacioppo, "Addressing Disturbing and Disturbed Consumer Behavior: Is It Necessary to Change the Way We Conduct Behavioral Science?" *Journal of Marketing Research*, Vol. 33 (February 1996), pp. 1–8.

17. John C. Mowen, "Beyond Consumer Decision Making," *Journal of Consumer Marketing*, Vol. 5 (Winter 1988), pp. 15–25.

18. Morris Holbrook and Elizabeth C. Hirschman, "The Experiential Aspects of Consumption: Consumer Fantasies, Feelings, and Fun," *Journal of Consumer Research*, September 9, 1982, pp. 132–140.

19. For a review of variety seeking, see Leigh McAlister and Edgar E. Pessemier, "Variety Seeking Behavior: An Interdisciplinary Review," *Journal of Consumer Research*, December 9, 1982, pp. 311–322. Also see Werner Kroeber-Riel, "Emotional Product Differentiation by Classical Conditioning," *Advances in Consumer Research*, Vol. 11, Thomas Kinnear, ed. (Ann Arbor, MI: Association for Consumer Research, 1984), pp. 538–543.

20. Russell Belk, John Sherry, and Melanie Wallendorf, "A Naturalistic Inquiry into Buyer and Seller Behavior at a Swap Meet," *Journal of Consumer Research*, March 14, 1988, pp. 449–469.

21. John Sherry, "Some Implications of Consumer Oral Tradition for Reactive Marketing," in *Advances in Consumer Research*, Vol. 11, Thomas Kinnear, ed. (Ann Arbor, MI: Association for Consumer Research, 1984), pp. 741–747.

22. Michael L. Rothschild and William Gaidis, "Behavioral Learning Theory: Its Relevance to Marketing and Promotions," *Journal of Marketing*, Vol. 45 (Spring 1981), pp. 70–78. Also see Peter H. Reingen and Jerome B. Kernan, "More

Evidence on Interpersonal Yielding," *Journal of Marketing Research*, Vol. 16 (November 1979), pp. 588–593.

23. Richard Bagozzi, "Marketing as Exchange," *Journal of Marketing*, Vol. 39 (October 1975), pp. 32–39.

24. Wroe Alderson, *Marketing Behavior and Executive Actions* (Homewood, IL: Richard D. Irwin, 1957).

25. Philip Kotler, *Marketing Essentials* (Upper Saddle River, NJ: Prentice Hall, 1984).

26. Bagozzi, "Marketing as Exchange."

27. "AMA Board Approves New Marketing Definition," *Marketing News*, March 1, 1985, p. 1.

28. Philip Kotler, *Marketing Management*, 4th ed. (Upper Saddle River, NJ: Prentice Hall, 1980).

29. These ideas are based on the law of exchange articulated by Wroe Alderson, *Dynamic Marketing Behavior* (Homewood, IL: Richard D. Irwin, 1965).

30. Franklin Houston and Jule Gassenheimer, "Marketing and Exchange," *Journal of Marketing*, Vol. 51 (October 1987), pp. 3–18. This excellent article was the basis for a number of the ideas expressed in the section on exchange processes.

31. Uriel Foa and Edna Foa, *Societal Structures of the Mind* (Springfield, IL: Charles C. Thomas, 1974). Please note that Foa and Foa employed *love* as the sixth resource rather than *feelings*. We made this change in our text because we believe that *love* is an inappropriate term for the types of feelings engendered in a consumer exchange. Furthermore, in some contexts negative, rather than positive, feelings are communicated.

32. Dennis Bristow and John C. Mowen, "The Resource Exchange Model of Motivation," Faculty Working Paper, College of Business Administration, Oklahoma State University, Stillwater, OK 74078.

33. Richard P. Bagozzi, "Toward a Formal Theory of Marketing Exchanges," in *Conceptual and Theoretical Developments in Marketing*, O. C. Ferrell, Stephen W. Brown, and Charles W. Lamb, Jr., eds. (Chicago: American Marketing Association, 1979), pp. 32–39.

34. Robert F. Lusch, Stephen W. Brown, and Gary J. Brunswick, "A General Framework for Explaining Internal vs. External Exchange," *Journal of the Academy of Marketing Science*, Vol. 20 (1992), pp. 119–134.

35. Elizabeth C. Hirschman, "People as Products: Analysis of a Complex Marketing Exchange," *Journal of Marketing*, Vol. 51 (January 1987), pp. 98–108.

36. F. Robert Dwyer, Paul Schurr, and Sejo Oh, "Developing Buyer-Seller Relationships," *Journal of Marketing*, Vol. 51 (April 1987), pp. 11–27.

37. Theodore Levitt, *The Marketing Imagination* (New York: The Free Press, 1983), p. 111.

38. "What Customers Really Want," *Fortune*, June 4, 1990, pp. 58–68.

39. Jonathan K. Frenzen and Harry L. Davis, "Purchasing Behavior in Embedded Markets," *Journal of Consumer Research*, Vol. 17, June 1990, pp. 1–12.

40. Morris B. Holbrook, Ethics in Consumer Research: "An Overview and Prospectus," *Advances in Consumer Research*, Vol. 21, Chris T. Allen and Deborah Roedder John, eds. (Provo, UT: Association for Consumer Research, 1994), pp. 566–571.

41. For a recent discussion of ethics and marketing, see Craig J. Thompson, "A Contextualist Proposal for the Conceptualization and Study of Marketing Ethics," *Journal of Public Policy and Marketing*, Vol. 14, (Fall 1995), pp. 177–191.

42. Gene R. Laczniak and Patrick E. Murphy, "Fostering Ethical Marketing Decisions," *Journal of Business Ethics*, Vol. 10 (1991), pp. 259–271.

43. Manuel Velasquez, *Business Ethics: Concepts and Cases* (Upper Saddle River, NJ: Prentice Hall, 1982).

44. Anusorn Singhapakdi, Kenneth L. Kraft, Scott J. Vitell, and Kumar C. Rallapalli, "The Perceived Importance of Ethics and Social Responsibility on Organizational Effectiveness: A Survey of Marketers," *Journal of the Academy of Marketing Science*, Vol. 23, (Winter 1995), pp. 49–56.

45. Laczniak and Murphy, "Fostering Ethical Marketing Decisions."

2

CONSUMER BEHAVIOR AND THE MARKETING MANAGER

The "New Coke" Debacle

In April 1985 the Coca-Cola Company announced with much fanfare that it had developed a new and better-tasting formula for its flagship beverage. The company took the radical step of reformulating Coke because of the success of the Pepsi Challenge, in which person after person selected Pepsi over Coke in blind taste tests. To make matters worse, for the first time Pepsi's supermarket sales were surpassing Coke's. Market research on over 100,000 consumers confirmed that most people thought the new formulation tasted better than Pepsi, so Coke's management thought it had a winner in its "New Coke."

Within days of the announcement, however, a massive consumer revolt was underway. Over 40,000 letters poured into corporate headquarters in Atlanta. One writer fumed, "I don't think I would be more upset if you were to burn the flag in the front yard."[1] Lawsuits were filed against the company. In May a Seattle promoter established a 900-number whose goal was to force Coca-Cola to bring back the original formulation. In June sales of Pepsi-Cola surged by 14 percent. Even after Coca-Cola hired Bill Cosby to endorse "New Coke," a poll found that of the 45 per-

cent of Americans who had tasted the new drink, 59 percent preferred the old drink.[2] In an attempt to explain the public's reaction, one executive stated, "It didn't matter how New Coke tasted: what these people resented was the audacity of Coca-Cola in changing the old taste."[3]

On July 19, 1985, the company folded under the pressure and announced that it was bringing back the old formula—now to be called "Coca-Cola Classic"—but would also retain "New Coke." On the day of the announcement the company's consumer affairs department received 18,000 calls of gratitude. Surveys indicated that the company's action improved its image with the public. In fact, by the end of 1985, Coca-Cola's image ratings had moved from a position lower than Pepsi's to one substantially higher than Pepsi's.[4]

The cola wars continued, however. In 1987 both Pepsi and Coca-Cola launched advertisements in which Pepsi challenged Coke Classic and New Coke challenged Pepsi. Getting in on the fray, *The Wall Street Journal* commissioned a taste test of Coke Classic, Pepsi, and New Coke, which revealed that 70 percent of the 100 tasters confused the three colas. When confronted with this result, some tasters accused the testers of shaking the bottles to throw them off. Others attributed their confusion to the testers' use of plastic cups rather than glass.[5] Interviews with the tasters revealed a strong emotional component to their brand preferences. When asked why he wouldn't drink Pepsi, one person replied, "It's too preppy. Too yup. The New Generation—it sounds like Nazi breeding. Coke is more laid back." In contrast, one Pepsi drinker said, "I relate Coke to the status quo. I think Pepsi is a little more rebellious, and I have a little rebellion in me."[6]

Even after bringing back the "Old Coke," the company continued to market the new drink. Nine months after the new brand's introduction, it was being outsold by "Classic" by nine to one in Minneapolis and by eight to one in Dallas. However, in Detroit "New Coke" outsold "Classic."[7] Three years after its introduction, "New Coke" had claimed only 2.3 percent of the market, although the company was spending twice as much to advertise it as it was spending on ads for "Classic."[8]

For all its problems with "New Coke," the company's worldwide share of the soft-drink market moved from 38 to 42 percent between 1985 and 1997.[9] (Each share point is worth $500 million in sales.) This story of Coca-Cola's initial marketing disaster and subsequent triumphant turnaround furnishes a textbook case of how managers can use consumer behavior principles to develop a successful marketing strategy.

INTRODUCTION

This chapter will use the "New Coke" debacle and the Coca-Cola Company's subsequent turnaround to demonstrate why an understanding of consumer behavior principles is critical for developing managerial strategy. To develop a successful managerial strategy, decision makers must understand five managerial application areas: (1) environmental analysis, (2) market research, (3) segmentation, (4) product positioning, and (5) marketing mix development. (Table 2-1 briefly defines each of these areas.) All five application areas require an in-depth knowledge of consumer behavior concepts.

The crucial importance of consumer behavior principles to managerial strategy is illustrated by the different reactions of consumers to "New Coke" in various U.S. cities. While

Five Managerial Application Areas of Consumer Behavior Concepts

Managerial Application Area	Definition
1. Environmental analysis	The assessment of the external forces that act upon the firm and its customers, and that create threats and opportunities.
2. Market research	Applied consumer research designed to provide management with information on factors that impact consumers' acquisition, consumption, and disposition of goods, services, and ideas.
3. Segmentation	The division of the marketplace into distinct subsets of customers with similar needs and wants, each subset to be reached with a different marketing mix.
4. Product positioning	The attempt to influence product demand by developing and promoting a product with specific characteristics that differentiate it from competitors.
5. Marketing-mix strategy	The coordination of marketing activities involving product development, and the promotion, pricing, and distribution of the product.

TABLE 2-1

the beverage did poorly in Minneapolis and Dallas, it did extremely well in Detroit. This variation in response suggests that Coca-Cola needed to segment its market by geography. The segmentation of a market into homogeneous groups of consumers with similar needs and wants is an important application area of consumer behavior concepts. In addition to doing **geographic segmentation,** companies are targeting women as a market segment. Figure 2-1 shows an ad from Chevrolet that targets female automobile buyers.

When we found there was a race our cars couldn't possibly win, we decided to sponsor it.

Chevrolet is proud to sponsor America³- the first all-women's team in America's Cup history.

Winning is a tradition at Chevrolet. From Daytona to Baja, we've had more first place finishes than you could shake a checkered flag at. But it doesn't come easy. It takes technology, talent and teamwork. And then some. The same dedication goes into winning the America's Cup. That's why we're proud to sponsor America³ — with the first all-women's team to compete in the 144-year history of the race. Because like us, they won't settle for second best. So on behalf of Chevrolet, good luck America³. We're behind you all the way as you set sail to make America's Cup history.

GENUINE CHEVROLET™

For more information about Chevrolet and America³, please call 1-800-950-CUBE.
Chevrolet and the Chevrolet Emblem are registered trademarks of the GM Corp. ©1995 GM Corp. All Rights Reserved. Buckle up, America!

Figure 2-1
Women have become an important market segment targeted by automakers such as Chevrolet.

Coca-Cola in the 1990s

In the 1990s Coca-Cola continued to struggle to develop a marketing strategy for its "New Coke." By 1991 the brand was no longer one of the top-10 soft drinks, and the company began experimenting with a new name for the drink. In a market test in Spokane, Washington, the brand was called "Coke II." After a large promotional push, Coke II's market share jumped to four percent, but then fell back quickly after the test ended.[10] By 1997 Coke II had less than 1 percent share of the national soft-drink market, and the company had demoted the brand to a backup role. However, there was still the possibility that if Pepsi resumed its promotional taste tests, Coke could counter with its own evidence showing that most people prefer Coke II to Pepsi.

If Coke II has performed so poorly in the marketplace over the last dozen years, what accounts for Coca-Cola's increasing share of the soft-drink market? The answer is that the Atlanta-based company learned from its mistake. It moved away from a megabrand strategy of focusing on its two major cola beverages—Coke Classic and Diet Coke—and began reinvigorating its "old" noncola beverages, such as Sprite, Minute Maid, Nestea, and Hi-C. In addition, it launched new brands—PowerAde, Fruitopia, and Barq's Root Beer—that consumers could differentiate from one another and that were designed to appeal to new market segments. By 1996 the company had hired 21 different advertising agencies to promote its brands around the world.[11] As will be discussed later in the chapter, Coca-Cola's new strategy is based on sound consumer behavior principles.

Organization of the Chapter

First, we discuss the five areas of managerial strategy to which consumer behavior principles apply. Then we present a three-step process for using consumer behavior concepts to analyze and solve marketing problems. We end the chapter with a demonstration of how this three-step approach can be used to analyze the introductory case.

THE MANAGERIAL APPLICATION AREAS OF CONSUMER BEHAVIOR CONCEPTS

As we stated in the chapter introduction, consumer behavior concepts can be used to develop marketing strategy in five fundamental areas: environmental analysis, market research, segmentation, positioning and differentiation, and the development of the marketing mix. In this section of the chapter we analyze each of these areas, beginning with environmental analysis.

Environmental Analysis

Environmental analysis consists of the assessment of the external forces that act upon the firm and its customers, and that create threats and opportunities. In large organizations the environmental analysis may be performed by either the market research department or the strategic planning group. In smaller organizations the CEO and key staff members generally perform this task. Every firm, large or small, should monitor a number of components of its external environment.[12] These include the demographic, economic, natural, technological, political, and cultural environments. Table 2-2 lists the consumer behavior areas that are applicable to an understanding of these six environments.

The consumer researcher's goal should be to predict changes in these environments and how the changes will influence consumers. For example, the publisher of this textbook, Prentice Hall, must be able to predict demographic changes in the textbook mar-

Market Environments and Their Applications to Consumer Behavior Areas

Environment	Consumer Behavior Area
Demographic	Population changes and cultural values of various demographic groups based on such factors as age, sex, income, education, ethnicity, and geography.
Economic	Factors influencing consumer economic sentiment and patterns of savings and spending.
Natural	Consumers' reactions to changing weather patterns and to natural disasters such as earthquakes.
Technological	The diffusion of technological innovations and consumers' reactions to the innovations; the user-friendly characteristics of machines and computers.
Political	The impact of laws, rules, and regulations on consumers.
Cultural	Rituals, values, mores, customs, and norms of a culture and how they influence consumption behavior within that culture.

TABLE 2-2

ket. An analysis of population trends suggests that between 1996 and 2000 the number of high school students will increase dramatically, while the number of children entering grade school will decline considerably. These demographic trends have major implications for the publisher's corporate strategy: they indicate that resources should be shifted from one area (elementary school textbooks) to another (high school textbooks).

The field of consumer behavior focuses on how the cultural, demographic, group, and situational environments can lead to marketing opportunities or liabilities. All these areas are discussed in detail in Part III of this text. Since the field places less emphasis on how the economic, natural, and technological environments affect consumer behavior and marketing strategy, we will discuss these areas more briefly here.

The Economic Environment and Consumer Behavior The economic environment consists of the set of factors—involving monetary, natural, and human resources—that influence the behavior of individuals and groups. At the local, national, and international levels, the economic environment influences the consumption patterns of millions of people. Over the long term it can dramatically affect the lifestyle and well-being of entire nations. For example, in the nineteenth century Britain was the wealthiest country in the world. One hundred years later British consumers' standard of living lagged far behind that of consumers in the United States, Germany, Japan, and Scandinavia.

One area of economics has particular relevance to consumer behavior. Called **behavioral economics,** it is the study of the economic decisions made by individual consumers and the behavioral determinants of those economic decisions.[13] Although economic theories like the law of demand can be applied to individuals, traditional economists are most comfortable talking about aggregates of people. (The law of demand states that there is an inverse relationship between the price of a product and the quantity demanded of that product.) Behavioral economists, however, analyze consumers individually. This radical new approach, developed by George Katona, proposes that the attitudes, motives, and expectancies of individual consumers can be drawn upon to make predictions concerning the economy as a whole.[14]

Behavioral economists have made three major contributions to the understanding of consumer spending patterns. First, they originated and documented the idea that the consumer sector of the economy strongly influences the course of the aggregate economy.

Actually, the recognition that the U.S. economy had become consumer driven provided much of the impetus for the development of behavioral economics. Fully two-thirds of our gross national product comes from consumer spending. Second, behavioral economists investigated what factors influence the decisions of families to buy or save. Traditional economists, in contrast, tend to confine their study to how such decisions affect the economy.

The third contribution made by behavioral economists was the development of a new methodology for predicting aggregate economic activities on the basis of consumer surveys. Survey research methodology was a major break from the traditional econometric studies of the economy. In the survey approach representative samples of consumers are interviewed to obtain information on their attitudes and expectations about their future buying behavior. Surveys of consumer sentiment, begun in 1946, are done at the University of Michigan Survey Research Center. Other groups, such as the Conference Board, have developed their own indices of consumer sentiment. Such indices are important today in helping private and governmental forecasters anticipate the future course of the economy. Table 2-3 sets out the questions found in the Index of Consumer Sentiment.

The Natural Environment and Consumer Behavior Features of the natural environment important to the marketer include the types of raw materials available, pollution, consumer fear of contracting deadly diseases, the expansion of desert regions around the globe, and various weather phenomena, such as hurricanes and droughts. Each of these factors can influence consumption behavior.

Shortages of raw materials, such as oil, can dramatically influence product prices and spur consumers to change their buying patterns. Pollution can wipe out or degrade important waterways and ruin industries. For example, the oyster industry in the Chesapeake Bay in Virginia has been severely harmed by pollution. The effects of disease on consumer behavior are illustrated by the fear of AIDS in recent years. The threat of contracting this deadly disease has induced most sexually active people to change their behavior. Even alterations in weather patterns have been linked to short-term changes in consumer behavior. Obviously, cold snaps and rainy spells directly influence consumers' purchase of clothing.

Index of Consumer Sentiment

1. We are interested in how people are getting along financially these days. Would you say that you (and your family living there) are better off or worse off financially than you were a year ago? Why do you say so?

2. Now looking ahead—do you think that a year from now you (and your family living there) will be better off financially, or worse off, or just about the same as now?

3. Now turning to business conditions in the country as a whole—do you think that during the next 12 months we'll have good times financially, or bad times, or what?

4. Looking ahead, which would you say is more likely—that in the country as a whole we'll have continuous good times during the next five years or so, or that we will have periods of widespread unemployment, or depression, or what?

5. About the big things people buy for their homes—such as furniture, a refrigerator, a stove, television, and things like that—generally speaking, do you think now is a good or a bad time for people to buy major household items? Why do you say so?

Note: The survey asks respondents about their plans to purchase automobiles over the next year.

Source: Richard T. Curtin, "Indicators of Consumer Behavior: The University of Michigan Surveys of Consumers," *Public Opinion Quarterly*, Vol. 46 (1982), pp. 340–353.

TABLE 2-3

Interestingly, however, evidence is emerging that the weather may also affect people's moods and thus, indirectly, their buying behavior.

The Technological Environment and Consumer Behavior

Technological changes are not only an important source of new-product ideas, they can dramatically affect the lifestyle of consumers as well. The birth control pill, television, radio, the computer, the automobile, and the airplane have all transformed our lifestyles. (Consumer lifestyle, or the way people live, is discussed in Chapter 7 of the text.) The consumer researcher needs to anticipate changes in the technological environment and how these will influence the lifestyle and consumption patterns of consumers.

An often overlooked area of research relating technology to consumer behavior is that of investigating the man-machine interface—or how to produce machines and products that can be used without too many problems. The issue is usually put as making machines "user-friendly." (This issue will be discussed in some detail in Chapter 3.)

The Reciprocity of Consumers and the Environment

An important concept in consumer behavior is that consumers influence the environment, just as the environment influences them. For example, changes in consumer spending and saving patterns can strongly affect the economy. By the same token, changes in the behavior of millions of people can influence the natural environment. For instance, among the primary causes of the expansion of the deserts in Africa are the actions of people who overgraze their cattle and cut down trees for firewood.

Market Research

Market research is applied consumer research designed to provide management with information on factors that affect consumers' acquisition, consumption, and disposition of goods, services, and ideas. Unless market researchers have a firm grasp of these factors, they will have no way of determining what to measure or what pitfalls may endanger their research.

The problems Coca-Cola encountered in responding to the Pepsi Challenge illustrate why it is necessary to have a solid grounding in consumer behavior principles when doing market research. Coca-Cola's managers went to great lengths to keep the development of the new soft drink a secret. Market researchers were not allowed to tell consumers who tasted the test beverages what they were drinking. Had they had a better understanding of consumer behavior and taste perception, these managers would have recognized that their approach was doomed to failure. Taste, after all, is highly subjective—it is influenced by expectations aroused by knowledge of what one is consuming. And consumer behavior is powerfully affected by the human need for behavioral freedom. When "Old Coke" was suddenly yanked from the marketplace, millions of loyal customers felt that their freedom to purchase a beverage they had loved from childhood had been violated. The psychological reaction to a loss of behavioral freedom is anger and the strong desire for retaliation. Thus Coca-Cola faced a consumer boycott and a massive defection to competitors.

Consumer researchers also provide market researchers with many of the scales and instruments they need to measure myriad issues—from attention to advertisements, memory for promotions, attitudes, and decision processes to customer satisfaction and personality and psychographic characteristics. Table 2-4 summarizes the categories of scales and instruments developed by consumer researchers and used by corporate marketing research groups.

In some cases consumer research can make the difference between receiving regulatory approval to market a product and not. For example, in 1996 Procter & Gamble (P & G)

Categories of Consumer Behavior Scales and Instruments Used by Market Researchers

Consumer Behavior Category	Market Research Use
Information processing	Assess exposure, attention, comprehension, and memory for messages, brand names, etc.
	Assess level of consumer product involvement.
	Assess sensory perceptions, such as taste, smell, sound.
	Identify associations between brands and other entities.
Behavioral learning	Identify factors that reinforce and punish consumers.
	Identify factors that elicit emotional reactions.
	Identify the characteristics of models that spur consumer action.
Motivation	Develop measures of affective reactions to advertisements.
	Develop measures of basic consumer needs.
	Develop measures of perceived risk of brands.
	Assess perceptions of cause for poor product performance.
Personality and psychographics	Develop measures of personality characteristics for segmentation and message design.
	Develop lifestyle measures for segmentation and message design.
Beliefs, attitudes, and behaviors	Measure beliefs, attitudes, and behaviors to pinpoint segments, identify positioning strategies, and develop marketing mix.
Decision making	Identify how consumers make buying decisions in order to develop an overall marketing strategy.
Customer satisfaction	Develop measures of satisfaction and product quality.
Consumer situations	Develop measures of the physical environment to predict consumer attitudinal, emotional, and behavioral responses.
Group processes	Develop measures of word-of-mouth communications.
	Develop measures of decision-making dominance.
Culture and subcultures	Measure changes in the demographics of cultures and subcultures.
	Measure changes in cultural and subcultural values.
	Identify trends of popular culture and rituals of behavior.
Dark side of consumer behavior	Measure trends in unethical consumer behavior.
	Measure differences in consumers' tendencies to engage in compulsive consumption.

TABLE 2-4

began marketing a man-made fat substitute named Olestra that can be used for cooking potato chips, french fries, and the like. Olestra has a huge market potential among the diet-conscious because it cannot be absorbed by the body and therefore saves the consumer calories. The downside of this product is that it may cause "abdominal cramping and loose stools." Before it permitted the marketing of Olestra, the Federal Drug Administration (FDA) forced P&G to do consumer research to assess the product's effects on the human gastrointestinal system. Although some problems were found, the FDA regarded them as minor and approved the product.

Even after receiving the FDA's approval, P&G continued to do consumer research on Olestra. When a potato chip product made by Frito-Lay that was fried in Olestra was initially test-marketed in several midsized cities, P&G researchers carefully monitored consumer response. The company discovered only one alleged adverse health effect for every 3,000 bags of chips sold—a rate significantly lower than that found in the tests it had done for the FDA. This consumer analysis helped to combat charges made by one consumer group that Olestra is unsafe and should be banned.[15] (See the accompanying Consumer Behavior Factoid on another consumer research issue associated with the use of Olestra.)

The Segmentation of the Marketplace

Market segmentation is defined as the division of a market into distinct subsets of customers having similar needs and wants, each of which can be reached with a different marketing mix.[16] For segments to be useful, they should possess the characteristics of *measurability*, *accessibility*, and *substantiality*. In order to measure a segment, a manager must be able to assess its characteristics, needs, and wants via various demographic, psychographic, attitude, and/or personality measures. For a market segment to be accessible, customers must be reachable via the marketing mix. A market segment that cannot be reached by promotional messages and the product itself is not a viable target. Finally, for a segment to be managerially useful, it must be substantial enough in size and income to generate sufficient sales.

The advantage of segmentation is that it allows a company to tailor a marketing mix to the needs and wants of homogeneous subsets of customers. Dividing a market into subsets of consumers who have particular needs and wants not shared by the general consumer lets a company expand the total market potential for a general class of product. For example, the overall market potential for watches was increased when watchmakers identified specialized needs and wants of consumers for fashion watches, diving watches, running watches, pocket watches, dress watches, and so forth. If only one type of all-purpose watch were offered, sales of watches would be much lower than they currently are. By developing watches for particular segments, watchmakers increased the total number of watches sold.

Bases for Segmenting Consumer Markets Segments are identified by finding groupings of consumers with similar needs and wants. For consumer goods, a market segment may be composed of millions of people. For industrial goods, a segment is normally composed of hundreds or thousands of companies. The problem for the manager is in identifying

---

Consumer Behavior Factoid

Question: Over a three-month period what proportion of consumers will experience gastrointestinal problems?

Answer: Medical researchers have found that over a three-month period 70 percent of men and women will have at least one bout of gastrointestinal illness. For Procter & Gamble, this is a decidedly nontrivial statistic because it presents a serious problem in the marketing of Olestra. A substantial percentage of people who call P&G with complaints about Olestra are misat-tributing the cause of their gastrointestinal problems. As will be discussed in Chapter 6, people are strongly motivated to attempt to determine the cause of their problems. Therefore, companies must take appropriate steps to handle situations in which their products are being erroneously blamed for a problem.

Source: Raju Narisetti, "P&G Says Fake-Fat Olestra Gets Fewer Complaints Than Expected," *The Wall Street Journal*, July 25, 1996, p. B3.

the *bases for segmentation*—in other words, on what variables can distinct grouping of people or companies be identified? Because the bases of segmenting consumer and industrial markets are somewhat different, we will discuss these two markets separately.

There are four classifications of segmentation variables for consumer markets: (1) the characteristics of the person, (2) the nature of the situation in which the product or service is purchased, (3) geography, and (4) the culture and subculture adopted by the consumer. Table 2-5 summarizes these variables, which we will now explain briefly.

Bases for Segmenting the Consumer Market

I. **Characteristics of the Person**
   A. *Demographics*

1. Age	6. Education
2. Sex	7. Family size
3. Income	8. Occupation
4. Religion	9. Ethnicity
5. Marital status	10. Nationality

   B. *Consumption behavior*
   1. Benefits sought
   2. Demand elasticity
   3. Brand loyalty
   4. Usage rate
   5. Other—purchase occasion, media usage, etc.

   C. *Psychographic profile*
   D. *Personality characteristics*
   1. Need for cognition
   2. Tolerance for ambiguity
   3. Risk-taking propensity
   4. Connectedness vs. separateness

II. **Situation**
   A. *Task definition*
   B. *Antecedent states*
   C. *Time*
   D. *Physical surroundings*
   E. *Social surroundings*

III. **Geography**
   A. *National boundaries*
   B. *Regions*
   C. *State boundaries*
   D. *Urban/rural*
   E. *Zip code/census block*

IV. **Culture**
   A. *Cultural mores, customs, values, and norms*
   B. *Subcultural mores, customs, values, and norms*

TABLE 2-5

Characteristics of the Person. Every individual has a unique set of needs, wants, and aspirations. Fortunately for marketers, however, certain needs and wants are shared by large enough numbers of people so that a particular product or service can be developed to cater to them. The sum of individual consumers who share these needs and wants constitutes a market segment. Characteristics of the person useful for market segmentation may be divided into four categories: demographics, consumption behavior, psychographic profile, and personality characteristics.

DEMOGRAPHIC CHARACTERISTICS In Chapter 18 on subcultures we will discuss a number of **demographic characteristics,** including age, sex, income, religion, marital status, education, family size, occupation, ethnicity, and nationality. Such demographic measures of consumers have two important uses in the segmentation process. First, they can be employed, either singly or in combination, to describe various subcultures whose members share certain values, needs, rituals, and behaviors. For example, a combination of education, occupation, and income can be used to develop a measure of consumers' social class. Similarly, a combination of age, marital status, and number of children can be utilized to ascertain the stage of consumers' family life cycle. Thus demographic variables help to identify cultures and subcultures the marketing manager can target with a particular marketing mix.

Second, demographic variables can be used to describe consumers who are classified into segments via other means. Suppose that the product manager of Coca-Cola Classic wants to segment his brand's consumers into heavy, medium, and light users so that he can target different promotions to each group. The manager may initiate a telephone survey that contacts 3,000 people and asks them how frequently they consume soft drinks in general and Coca-Cola Classic in particular. Let's say that of the 3,000 people contacted, 1,000 fall into the medium-usage category and the product manager decides to target these people for promotional messages and sales promotions (e.g., contests, coupons) to get them to increase their consumption. How does the manager reach this segment? By including in the consumer survey a series of questions that elicit demographic information such as respondents' age, ethnicity, geographic location, sex, education, and income, the manager will learn how to reach this group in a cost-effective way.

Demographic information is the most important type of information for segmentation purposes, primarily because demographic data are the most readily available data on individual consumers. The federal government collects a wealth of demographic information through its census. Magazines, newspapers, and television and radio stations gather demographic data on their audiences, while private research companies collect and sell demographic information on various groups of people. With this wealth of available demographic data, a manager shouldn't have much trouble identifying the demographic characteristics of a target market and using this information to make rational choices concerning the type of media to use to reach it as well as to make pricing and distribution decisions.

In the chapter-opening case we saw that one important early task for Coca-Cola's marketing researchers was to develop a profile of the consumers of "New Coke." By knowing the age, ethnicity, income level, and geographic location of these consumers, the company could more precisely target the people who were heavy users of the brand.

CONSUMPTION BEHAVIOR A complementary approach to using demographic variables to segment the market is to divide consumers into homogeneous groups based on various aspects of their buying behavior. The most important bases for **behavioral segmentation** are price elasticity, benefits sought, and usage rate.

Segmentation by **price elasticity** is based on the economic concept that different groups of consumers react divergently to changes in the price of a product or service. Demand-elastic customers will modify their buying habits a great deal in response to price changes, while demand-inelastic customers will not.

Breakfast is supposed to be the most important meal of the day. Not the most expensive.

So we've lowered the price of all our cereals.

In fact, we reduced the everyday price on every cereal we make. As much as a dollar a box. We didn't make the boxes smaller. Or put any less in them. After all, we're not in the business to cut corners or make our cereals as cheaply as possible. You see, we are a company of people not unlike you. We shop in the same supermarkets. We know the value of a dollar. We believe we are doing the right thing.

Post

Breakfast made right.™

Figure 2-2

Post lowered the price of its cereals. As a result, it gained market share when consumers with elastic demand curves shifted their buying preferences.

Post, the cereal company, segmented its market according to demand elasticity. As the advertisement reproduced in Figure 2-2 shows, the company lowered the price of its cereals so that they cost significantly less than competing products made by Kellogg's. This strategy allowed Post to target price-conscious consumers with elastic demand curves.

Airlines also use demand elasticity to price their product. Business-class and first-class sections have been created for people willing to pay more for greater seating space and higher levels of service. The airlines also charge more for tickets sold to travelers who reserve seats close to departure time. These price-inelastic customers are generally wealthier people, business travelers, and people traveling because of an emergency. In contrast, price-elastic consumers are typically vacationers who plan far enough in advance to make their reservations early, as well as people willing to use another mode of travel (e.g., the automobile) if the price of an airline ticket is too high.

Another example of segmentation via **demand elasticity** involves coupon distribution. Coupon users are a distinct consumer segment (Table 7-4 in Chapter 7 on personality provides a "coupon-proneness scale" to help identify them). People who don't use coupons are relatively demand inelastic because they are willing to pay a higher price for a product than people who clip coupons. The demand-elastic coupon clippers are willing to invest the time and effort to collect coupons in order to lower the price of their purchases.

Managers find that developing strategies to target different demand-elasticity segments has a number of advantages. Foremost, this practice allows a company to increase its total sales and, possibly, the overall efficiency of its operations. For the airlines, seats that would not have been filled without a demand-elasticity strategy will have occupants. Because the marginal cost of filling empty seats in a plane is minimal, almost the entire fare from such passengers go directly to the bottom line. Correctly done, demand-elasticity segmenting will not downgrade the image of the product. In other words, customers will not think less of the quality of the product simply because it is lower priced.

Another basis for segmenting by demand elasticity is according to benefits sought by consumers. The idea behind **benefit segmentation** is to develop products and services with the specific qualities desired by homogeneous groups of consumers. For example, many consumers are very calorie-conscious. Figure 2-3 presents an ad for Juicy Fruit chewing gum that promotes the product's benefit as "saving calories."

The third important basis for market segmentation is **usage behavior.** A company using this approach attempts, through market research, to identify the light, moderate,

Figure 2-3

Juicy Fruit chewing gum repositions itself as a snack food that substitutes for nasty, calorie-laden cookies.

and heavy users of its products or services. Next, it seeks to determine the demographic and psychographic characteristics of these three groups of users so management can create strategies to target one or more of them by manipulating the marketing mix. Perhaps the usage behavior segment most coveted by marketers is the collector. See the nearby Consumer Behavior Factoid for information on collectors.

In addition to segmenting by usage rate, a marketing manager can segment by user status. From marketing research the manager may be able to obtain profiles of consumers who are nonusers, ex-users, potential users, first-time users, and regular users. Or the manager may decide to segment by brand loyalty. Consumers who are brand loyal to the product or service may be separated from other user groups for special promotional messages. Alternatively, the manager may decide to try to reach users who tend to switch between brands through sales-promotion devices such as coupons or contests.

PSYCHOGRAPHIC AND PERSONALITY CHARACTERISTICS As we will describe in Chapter 7, markets may be segmented by the psychographic and personality characteristics of consumers. *Psychographics* refers to the analysis of consumers' lifestyles, interests, activities, and opinions. *Personality* refers to the distinctive patterns of behavior, including thoughts and emotions, that characterize a person's response to various situations in life.

In most instances psychographic or personality segmentation is combined with behavioral segmentation. That is, the marketer first divides consumers into heavy, moderate, and light users of a brand and then analyzes one or more of these segments via psychographic inventories and/or personality inventories. Finally, the marketer designs promotional messages and distribution and pricing strategies that will be most effective for this segment's personality or psychographic characteristics. For example, when Merrill Lynch wanted to identify the psychographic characteristics of heavy users of brokerage services, it employed a psychographic inventory called VALS, which stands for "values and lifestyles." The brokerage firm found that the upwardly mobile, independent-thinking psychographic segment labeled "achievers" described the heavy users of brokerage services quite well. Since the VALS inventory showed that achievers are not followers, but leaders who make their decisions independently, Merrill Lynch changed its advertising theme from herds of bulls thundering across the plains to a single bull making intelligent directional choices.[17]

The Nature of the Situation. In Chapter 14 we discuss why the situation within which a product or service is purchased is an important influence on consumption behavior. Here we will note that consumer situations consist of those temporary environmental factors that form the context within which a consumer activity occurs at a particular time and place. For many types of products, segmentation by situation is the rule. Clothing and footwear, for example, have to be designed specifically for climate (i.e., warm or cold weather, sunshine or rain) as well as for tasks (e.g., party, work, casual). Research has shown that the situation strongly affects people's choice of snack food, meat products, and fast-food chains.[18] For example, consumers will purchase very different snack foods for a cocktail party than for a picnic.

Consumer Behavior Factoid

Question: How much does a good toy scalper make per year?

Answer: Toy scalpers buy popular toys that are in short supply and resell them to collectors. Perhaps the most collected toy is the Barbie Doll. Estimates are that between 200,000 and 3 million people collect Barbies. A good toy scalper is estimated to make $50,000 per year.

Source: Joseph Pereira, "If You Can't Locate That Special Plaything, Call, or Blame, a Scalper," *The Wall Street Journal,* June 24, 1996, pp. A1, A12.

Geography. For many products and services, an important basis for segmentation is geography. Managers can employ geography to segment the market by region or by the size of cities, counties, or even census blocks. Other means of geographic segmentation include density of population and climate. As illustrated by the "New Coke" case, a brand's sales can vary dramatically across geographic regions.

Over the past decade researchers have combined the fields of geography and demography (the study of demographics) to create the new discipline of *geodemographics*. Geodemographic analyses allow the marketer to analyze the demographic characteristics of groups of people who live in particular census blocks or zip codes. Companies are increasingly turning to this new discipline for help in segmenting the marketplace. Geodemographics is particularly useful for deciding where to locate a new business, such as a grocery store, fast-food restaurant, or golf course. We will have much more to say about geodemographics in Chapter 18.

Culture and Subculture. *Culture* may be defined as the way of life of the people of a society. *Subculture* is defined as a division of a national culture. A subculture is based on some unifying characteristic, such as social status or nationality; its members share a set of behaviors that are somehow distinct from the national culture in which they live. For example, the United States, Japan, and Germany have distinctive national cultures, yet within each of these cultures myriad subcultures coexist. We explore cultural, subcultural, and cross-cultural issues in Chapters 17, 18, and 19.

Culture is most clearly used as a segmentation variable when companies are engaged in international marketing. Within a national culture, marketers frequently target subcultures. Usually these subcultures are described by demographic variables. Thus particular religious groups, such as Mormons, Born-Again Christians, and Jews, may be identified as targets for a marketing offering. Similarly, a product may be developed and promoted to carefully selected ethnic groups. For example, an insurance company may target Asians or Hispanics for a particular type of insurance product.

Segmenting Industrial Markets Like consumer markets, industrial markets may be divided into segments, although there are a number of differences in how this is done. Perhaps the major difference concerns the types of information available on industrial firms compared to data on consumers. For example, the federal government has developed a system for categorizing all businesses into homogeneous groups. Called the **Standard Industrial Classification System (SIC),** this database classifies and identifies groups of business firms that produce the same type of product. The SIC system helps industrial marketers to identify potential new customers, estimate the market potential for their products, and delineate groups of companies that are likely to have similar product or service needs.

One suggestion for segmenting industrial markets involves macrobases and microbases.[19] **Macrosegmentation** consists of identifying groups of companies having similar buying organizations and facing similar buying situations. Table 2-6 identifies a number of macrobases for segmentation. Examples of segmentation categories based on the characteristics of the organization are the size of the company, its geographical location, its usage rate, and whether it is centralized or decentralized. An example of a segmentation category based on characteristics of the purchasing situation is whether the purchase is a new task, a modified rebuy, or a straight rebuy.

Microsegmentation consists of identifying the characteristics of the decision-making units within each of the various macrosegments. Obviously, this requires an in-depth knowledge of buying organizations. One basis for microsegmentation is the key decision criteria used by the buying organization. Analogous to benefit segmentation in consumer marketing, this approach involves identifying the product and producer attributes sought by buyers, such as product quality, delivery reliability and speed, and supplier reputation.

Some Macrobases of Segmentation	
Segmentation Basis	**Example**
1. Characteristics of buying organization	
a. Size	Small, medium, large; can be based on overall sales
b. Geographic location	New England vs. Southwest
c. Usage rate	Light, moderate, heavy user
d. Buying structure	Centralized vs. decentralized
2. Product application	
a. SIC code	Varies by product
b. End market served	Varies by product
3. Characteristics of purchasing situation	
a. Type of buying situation	New task, modified rebuy, straight rebuy
b. Stage in decision process	Early vs. late stage

Source: Based on Michael D. Hutt and Thomas Speh, *Industrial Marketing Management* (New York: The Dryden Press, 1981), p. 112.

TABLE 2-6

Product Positioning and Product Differentiation

Through **product positioning** an organization influences how consumers perceive a brand's characteristics relative to those of competitive offerings. The goal of product positioning is to influence demand by creating a product with specific characteristics (i.e., brand attributes) and a clear image that differentiates it from competitors. **Product differentiation** is the process of manipulating the marketing mix to position a brand so that consumers perceive meaningful differences between it and its competitors.

Product positioning and segmentation go hand-in-hand. First a segment of customers may be identified, and then a product may be developed and positioned to fill the needs of that segment. For example, when Starbucks announced in 1996 that it would open coffee shops in Japan, the news sent shivers down the spines of Japanese coffee bar owners. Starbucks had recognized that the Japanese are the world's third largest coffee consumers, and yet the country was a relatively untouched market. Starbucks is positioned as an upscale, hip place to drink espresso, caffé latté, caffé mocha, and Seattle coffee. Because its image is so differentiated from that of the native mom-and-pop coffee bars in Japan, its earnings potential in that country is extremely high. One Japanese advertising executive described the current coffee merchants in his country as "like a dry lake bed—void of new ideas." He said, "That's why the whole industry is stirred up about Starbucks."[20]

Two types of positioning strategies may be followed. In **specific positioning,** the company seeks to create in consumers' minds strong linkages among the product, certain key attributes, and benefits. Market leaders particularly seek to establish attribute-need linkages in order to create a strong product image. In this approach the goal is to differentiate the brand's qualities from the competition's without mentioning other brands specifically. Crest toothpaste did this effectively by creating the image of a strong tooth-decay fighter.

The second positioning strategy is frequently employed by brands that are not market leaders. In this approach, called **competitive positioning,** the "secondary" brand attempts to position itself in relation to the market leader. The goal is to emphasize the "secondary" brand's attributes in relation to the leading brand's. Companies employing this approach often use some type of comparative advertising.[21]

Pepsi has developed an interesting positioning strategy vis-à-vis Coke in which it promotes Pepsi-Cola as a "hip" product targeted to the more unconventional consumer. Coca-Cola, interestingly, does not appear to have a clear positioning strategy. Instead, as the sales leader, it attempts to stand above the competition and let the other soft-drink companies react to its moves.

A key problem for marketers has always been assessing a brand's position. Perhaps the most frequently used approach involves the creation of a **perceptual map** that shows how consumers position various brands relative to each other on a graph whose axes are formed by product attributes.

Figure 2-4 presents one such map designed to assess consumers' perceptions of various types of meat products by asking them to rate the products on a series of attributes.[22] A computer program developed at Bell Laboratories, called Multidimensional Preference Scaling, was used to create this perceptual map. A number of attributes are clustered together in the upper right-hand quadrant of the figure—"very healthy," "low fat," "low calorie," and "very tender." The products positioned closest to these attributes are fish, chicken, and tuna fish. In contrast, "great taste" and "good aroma" are associated with beef roast, pork roast, pork chop, and ham.

The perceptual map shown in Figure 2-4 helps to explain why beef consumption has fallen quite dramatically in the United States over the past 10 years. Consumers have become pressed for time and highly concerned about their health over the past decade, and beef and pork roasts are both positioned a good distance from the attributes of "quick to prepare" and "healthy." Note that the foods that have been coming on strong in recent years—fish, chicken, and turkey—are all much closer to these attributes.

One benefit of creating a perceptual map is that it tells the marketer whether consumers differentiate one product from another. As Figure 2-4 shows, consumers cluster beef roast,

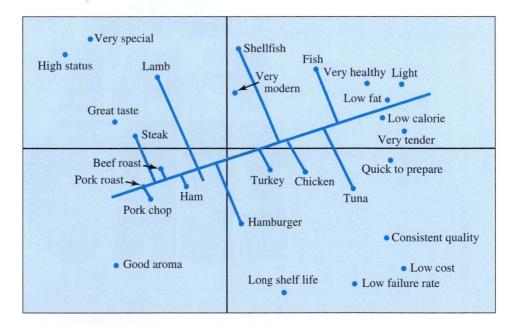

Figure 2-4 **A perceptual map of meats.**
(SOURCE: Adapted from a discussion in John Kinski, "Consumer Perceptions of Meat Products," Master's Thesis, Oklahoma State University, 1985.)

pork roast, pork chops, and ham together. In other words, they do not differentiate well among these products.

Companies gain a number of benefits when consumers can differentiate their brand from others. Some marketing researchers have argued that product differentiation adds perceived value to the product, and that this increase in perceived value boosts the "leverage" of the various components of the marketing mix.[23] In the pricing area, for example, brand differentiation can allow a company to command premium prices for its product. In the promotion area, product differentiation helps creative personnel develop messages that promote only the brand advertised and not competitors as well. An example of a clearly differentiated brand that has been able to use a claim effectively is Mercedes with its unique selling proposition "Engineered like no other car in the world." Mercedes cars *do* stand out for their engineering vis-à-vis other brands in the United States, so Mercedes can price its cars significantly higher in the United States than in Germany.

In addition to positioning a new brand, companies sometimes need to reposition an existing brand. **Repositioning** is defined as changing how consumers perceive a brand's characteristics relative to those of competitive offerings. Figure 2-5 presents an ad for Louis Rich ham that seeks to reposition the brand as a low-fat product. The company's goal is to differentiate its product from other pork products (and beef) as a good-tasting, but fat-free, product.

One quite successful repositioning strategy was employed by Snickers, the top-selling candy bar, in the 1980s. When Mars, the maker of the product, recognized that consumer

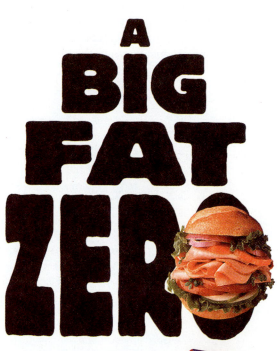

Finally—a no-fat ham that's big on taste, with zero fat.* New LOUIS RICH® FREE™ fat-free ham. Nothing but great taste.

SWITCH TO RICH...Louis Rich®

©1994 Louis Rich Company   *zero grams per serving

Figure 2-5

Louis Rich seeks to reposition ham as a low-fat product.

preferences were shifting toward wholesome, nutritious foods, it seized the opportunity to reposition Snickers from a candy to a snack food. This move made sense because the snack-food market is more than twice the size of the candy market ($22+ billion versus about $10 billion). Using the 1984 Olympic games as the springboard for its effort, Mars solicited former Olympic athletes to extoll Snickers as a snack. A key line in the 30-second ad spots was: "Packed with peanuts, Snickers really satisfies."[24] The advertising campaign, which continued into the 1990s, substantially increased overall sales for the brand.

Marketing-Mix Development

The creation of a **marketing mix** involves the initiation and coordination of activities concerning the development of the product, its promotion, its pricing, and its distribution. The facts, theories, and concepts of consumer behavior that directly affect marketing-mix development are discussed in the following subsections.

Product Development We use the term *product* here very broadly to include physical objects, services, places, and organizations.[25] Principles of consumer behavior can be applied to four areas of the new-product development process: idea generation, concept testing, product development, and market testing.

Consumer behavior concepts probably have the greatest impact on the **idea generation** phase of new-product development. Five major areas of consumer behavior analysis are useful to managers when they are thinking up ideas for new products: consumer attitudes, lifestyle changes, situational factors, other cultures, and subcultures. For example, consumer attitudes about existing products can be studied to identify consumers' desires for particular product attributes. If consumers do not think that existing products possess the attributes they want, a new-product opportunity may exist. When Colgate-Palmolive found that people wanted a toothpaste that dispensed more easily, it developed a pump that was economical and easy to use. As a result, Colgate rapidly increased its share of the toothpaste market until it threatened to usurp Crest's number-one position.

Concept testing involves the pretesting of the product idea. A *product concept* is the particular "consumer meaning that the company tries to build into a product idea."[26] Let's say the product concept for a new personal computer is to build a computer that consumers perceive to be user-friendly, portable, IBM-compatible, powerful, and low-priced. To determine whether there is a market for such a product concept, the firm would do product-positioning analysis as well as surveys to identify consumers' attitudes toward such a concept.

If the company finds that consumers perceive the product concept as management intends, it will begin the **product-development** process, which consists of developing, testing, naming, and packaging prototypes. A variety of consumer behavior concepts are important in this phase. For example, researchers should try to find out how consumers process information about the product. Is the product user-friendly (i.e., not too complex for the average person)? Is its packaging attention-getting? Can consumers remember the product's name?

Researchers must also pay attention to the attitude-formation process when testing both product and packaging. Do consumers like the prototype product? Do they believe the claims made for it? Do they like its packaging?

Once the product-development phase is satisfactorily concluded, the product may be market tested. **Market testing** involves placing the product into limited distribution to consumers in order to identify potential problems and test the entire marketing mix. In this phase additional attitudinal measures are taken to determine if consumers are forming the expected beliefs, affective reactions, and buying intentions. In addition, managers examine postpurchase satisfaction. Are consumers happy with the product after purchase? Are they rebuying it? Are they showing signs of developing brand loyalty? Managers will also want to know if consumers are using the product in the expected situations. Since the general goal of the market test is to determine if the marketing strategy is working, all the consumer behavior areas previously mentioned apply in this phase of new-product development.

Throughout the entire new-product–development process, managers must be concerned with the products and actions of competitors, for consumers will not perceive the brand in isolation. Assessment of how the product compares to competitive offerings is therefore crucial. A decision to move into full-scale production would be a gross mistake if based on the finding that consumers rate your product as "good" on various attributes, while they rate competitors as "excellent" on the same attributes. Furthermore, managers cannot assume that the competitive environment will remain constant during the product-development process. This process is exceptionally risky because changes occurring in the cultural, economic, and natural environments mean that managers are constantly trying to hit a moving target.

Figure 2-6 presents an ad for TasteTations, a hard candy Hershey introduced in 1996. Before it spent millions to launch the new brand, the company engaged in a careful product-development process.

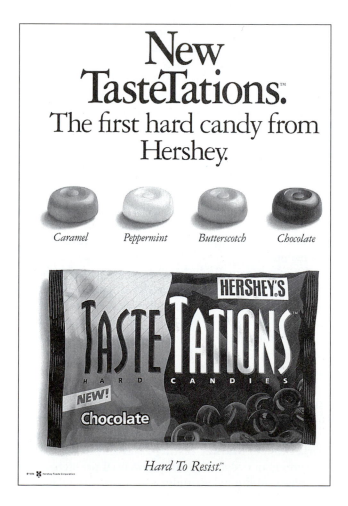

Figure 2-6

Hershey went through a product-development process prior to launching TasteTations in 1996.

Promotional Strategy For the manager developing a marketing mix, consumer behavior concepts and principles have their greatest application in the promotional strategy area, which covers everything from advertising to personal selling to sales promotion to public relations. The strategic and practical implications of consumer behavior for the promotional activities of the firm are discussed in the following subsections.

At least 10 of the major concepts discussed in this text are applicable to advertising. Table 2-7 identifies these concepts and gives a brief idea of how each may be applied.

Advertising and Personal Selling. In developing advertising materials, it is useful for managers to sketch out the kinds of ideas, images, and feelings they want the creative people to attempt to evoke in consumers. One approach to developing the advertising theme is to analyze the motivations and psychographic characteristics of the target market. Developing a theme and image for the product is particularly crucial for products such as beer, perfume, and cigarettes.

Budweiser's beer-drinking frog ads exemplify an advertising campaign based on knowledge of the demographic and psychographic characteristics of a target market. Targeted to Generation X consumers (people born after 1964), the ads show ugly, but cute, green frogs going to great lengths to "get a Bud." In one ad a frog shoots out its tongue to latch onto a speeding Budweiser truck. In another a gang of frogs hijacks an alligator to invade a party and make off with a case of Bud. While these scenarios sound ridiculous, the ads are absurd in an irrerevant way that appeals to Generation X.

Consumer attitude is another important area for advertisers. Many advertisements aim to instill certain beliefs in consumers about the attributes of a product. Market researchers

Advertising Applications of Consumer Behavior	
Consumer Behavior Concept	**Application**
Cultural/subcultural values	Development of advertising themes.
Opinion leader analysis	How to reach and influence opinion leaders.
Analysis of decision maker	How to reach and influence decision makers.
Personal influence	Effects of endorsers and identification of influence techniques.
Motivation	Development of advertising themes, how to reduce risk and reactance, how to encourage consumers to make appropriate attributions.
Information processing	Gaining attention, increasing recall and recognition, how consumers organize perceptions, factors influencing the reception of information.
Learning	Creating affective responses through classical conditioning, encouraging modeling behavior, analyzing the contingencies of the environment.
Attitudes	How to create beliefs, identifying important attributes to emphasize, how to change attitudes, effects of various types of messages on consumers.
Psychographics/personality	Develop profiles of target audience in order to reach and appeal to them more effectively.
Decision process	How to engage problem-solving activities, how to assist search behavior, providing information for evaluation activities, providing information to influence postpurchase evaluations.

TABLE 2-7

cannot know which beliefs they should instill unless they first identify the product attributes that the target market views as most important. The advertiser also needs to know what type of message will influence beliefs. Should fear appeals be used, or would a celebrity endorser be more effective? Should comparative advertising be employed? A knowledge of attitude formation and change can assist the manager in answering these types of questions.

Many areas of consumer behavior that are important to advertisers are also important to salespeople. An understanding of attitude formation and change processes helps marketers to develop specific messages for their sales force. Similarly, an analysis of cultural/subcultural differences between the sales force and customers will enable the company to forestall inappropriate statements or actions by salespeople. For example, managers will want to ensure that a sales force that deals with Japanese businesspeople does not come on so quickly or act so informally that they offend the more reserved and polite Japanese.

An especially important consumer behavior area for selling is personal influence. Particularly when engaging in personal selling as opposed to industrial selling, managers need to be knowledgeable about various influence techniques. For example, research on self-perception processes suggests that salespeople should do all they can to entice consumers to touch a product, use it, and explore it thoroughly. The more consumers explore a product behaviorally, the more likely they are to picture themselves owning that product—and therefore the more willing they will be to buy it.

Sales Promotion. Sales promotion has been defined as embracing all the supplementary promotional activities done in addition to advertising and personal selling.[27] It includes such tactics as supplying product literature through direct mail, providing dealer incentives, using point-of-purchase (POP) materials, and offering consumer incentives.

Consumer behavior principles can help managers plan in all of these areas, but for direct mail, POPs, and consumer incentives, the applications are especially strong. Direct-mail marketers' goal is to identify highly specific segments of consumers to whom they can send advertising materials or catalogs. The need here is to pinpoint a segment of consumers who are good prospects for the product and then influence that group directly through the mail. Sophisticated direct-mail marketers develop precise demographic and psychographic profiles of a targeted segment. By using the demographic data obtained from ZIP codes and the census in combination with information gleaned from lists of magazine and catalog readers, marketers can identify segments quite precisely.

Point-of-purchase (POP) displays in retail stores, like packaging, seek to intrigue consumers and make them pay attention to the product. Knowledge of consumers' perceptual processes is a very valuable aid in designing POP materials.

The third area of sales promotion where consumer behavior principles have a strong application is sales incentives, such as price-off deals, sampling, contests, rebates, premiums, coupons, and trading stamps. Notice that many of these incentives change the price the consumer pays for the product. Consumer behavior concepts relevant to understanding the impact of sales-promotion devices include behavioral learning (Chapter 5), consumer motivation (Chapter 6) and consumer decision making (Chapters 11–13).

Public Relations. Public relations is a broad area that focuses on the interface between the corporation and consumers. Principal concerns here are managing publicity about the firm and handling consumer questions and complaints. The areas of consumer behavior that apply most directly to public relations are attitude formation and change. Public relations managers must be especially concerned with the effects of negative publicity on the firm and its products. As we noted earlier in the text, negative information has a disproportionate impact on consumer attitudes, so the public relations staff must monitor the news media and consumers constantly to identify quickly any negative information about the company that is seeping into the marketplace. Examples of negative information PR managers have to deal with are rumors, product recalls, product disasters (e.g., an airplane crash), corporate financial problems, illegal activities of senior corporate officials, and complaints by consumer groups about advertising.

In planning public relations activities the manager must be concerned with how the public will perceive both the source of the information and the specific message. Corporate officials often act as spokespersons for the company, so companies that have a high public profile should provide training to these individuals on how to present themselves in public.

Pricing and Distribution One major application of consumer behavior principles in the area of pricing is in predicting the likely impact of price changes on consumers. That is, how will consumers react when companies raise or lower the price of a product? Perception plays a central role here. As we will explain in Chapter 3, unless the price change is greater than some threshold level, consumers may not even notice it. So if the price is being lowered, it should be lowered enough so that consumers will perceive a significant change. In contrast, if the price is being raised, in most instances it should not be raised by so much that consumers perceive a difference. Pricing issues will be discussed in Chapters 11 and 12 on consumer decision making and in Chapter 8 in the section focusing on the price-quality relationship.

Consumer behavior principles also apply to the distribution component of the marketing mix. In particular, understanding how consumers make their purchase decisions (Chapters 11–13) will have an impact on product distribution. That is, the extent to which consumers engage in search behavior should influence the intensity of a company's distribution efforts. If the product is one bought under low-involvement conditions, consumers will probably not engage in much search behavior before making their purchase. Therefore companies selling low-involvement products should place their brands in as many retail outlets as possible so they will be readily available whenever consumers need them. Coca-Cola furnishes a classic example of this distribution strategy. In most urban areas a consumer can find a vending machine or retailer selling Coke within several hundred feet of wherever the consumer is standing.

Another consumer behavior area that has application to physical distribution is geodemographics (see Chapter 18). Companies must plan where to place new retail outlets and distribution centers. Careful analysis of population shifts among the various regions of the country can reap high dividends in terms of containing costs and matching product distribution to growth areas. Similarly, decisions on where to place shopping centers and retail stores in cities and towns should take into account population patterns and geodemographics.

CONSUMER BEHAVIOR AND SOLVING MANAGERIAL PROBLEMS

To develop managerial solutions to marketing problems, the analyst needs to understand consumer behavior concepts, the managerial strategy elements, and how to combine these two types of information into viable managerial plans. We advocate a four-step **managerial applications analysis:**

Step 1: Gather information and identify the problem/opportunity.

Step 2: Identify the relevant consumer behavior concepts and determine how they apply to the problem.

Step 3: Develop a managerial strategy by identifying the managerial implications of each applicable consumer behavior concept.

Step 4: Summarize the managerial recommendations that emerge from the managerial implications.

In Step 1 the analyst gathers as much information as possible about the problem (or opportunity) and carefully sifts through this information to identify the fundamental question(s) that needs to be answered. This step is crucial because the rest of the analysis will be useless if the information gathered at this point is inadequate or if the problem is not accurately identified.

In Step 2 the analyst systematically examines the problem(s) by identifying the consumer concepts that are relevant to it. Each topic area at both the individual level of analysis (Part II of this text) and the environmental level of analysis (Part III) is evaluated for potential application to the problem. The key consumer behavior concepts used in this analysis are found in bold letters in each chapter and are listed in the Key Terms section at the end of each chapter.

In Step 3 the analyst identifies the managerial implications of the consumer behavior concepts. These implications will involve one or more of the five managerial strategy areas we discussed earlier: the marketing mix, segmentation, positioning/differentiation, environmental analysis, and market research. The analyst examines how the various consumer concepts affect each relevant managerial area and develops suitable managerial strategies from the concepts. On the basis of this analysis, a solution to the problem is identified.

In practice, Steps 2 and 3 are usually combined. That is, the analyst identifies a consumer concept applicable to the case, and then develops its managerial implications. Next the analyst identifies a second applicable consumer concept and develops its managerial implications, and so forth. The information gathered in Steps 2 and 3 is entered into a table in which the applicable consumer behavior concepts are placed on the left and their managerial implications on the right. Table 2-8 provides this managerial applications analysis for the "New Coke" case.

Finally, in Step 4 the analyst summarizes the marketing actions that should be taken as a result of the analysis of consumer behavior concepts and their managerial implications.

A MANAGERIAL APPLICATIONS ANALYSIS OF THE "NEW COKE" CASE

We will use the "New Coke" case that began this chapter to illustrate the four steps of the managerial applications analysis and to demonstrate the importance to marketing managers of understanding the field of consumer behavior. It is highly probable that had Coca-Cola's executives carefully considered certain consumer behavior concepts, principles, and theories, the ego-bruising and costly affair described at the outset of this chapter could have been avoided.

Step 1: Problem Identification

The problem identified in the launch of "New Coke" is: What factors caused Coca-Cola's marketing strategy to go awry? In order to answer this question, extensive information about the problem must be gathered. Here, the details presented earlier in the chapter will suffice for our demonstration. In an actual managerial applications analysis, however, managers could only fully understand the parameters of the problem by obtaining a good deal more information.

The Managerial Applications Analysis of the "New Coke" Case

Consumer Concepts	Managerial Implications
Brand Loyalty/ Relational Exchange	**Marketing Research.** Perform appropriate research to determine the impact of eliminating the brand on consumers with high levels of brand loyalty.
	Product Strategy. Carefully analyze whether eliminating "Old Coke" would break bonds of trust with customers.
	Promotional Strategy. Develop promotional strategies that would minimize the negative effects on brand loyalty.
Consumer Expectations	**Market Research.** Perform studies to examine the effects on consumers of providing the brand name of the beverages when performing the taste tests in order to account for the impact of expectations.
Consumer Motivation	**Market Research.** Perform studies to determine if strong psychological reactance would result from the decision to eliminate "old Coke."
	Marketing Mix. If reactance could be a problem, decide whether a new brand should be developed rather than eliminating "old Coke."
Self-Concept	**Market Research.** Identify the images consumers obtain from Coke and competing brands and how these images are linked to consumers' self-concepts.
	Segmentation. Identify segments of consumers of sufficient size and buying power whose self-concept matches that of Coke's image.
	Positioning. Develop a positioning strategy that links the image of Coke to the self-concept of the target market identified.
	Promotion. Develop advertising and sales promotion campaigns that implement the positioning strategy.
Demographics/ Subculture	**Market Research.** Determine how various demographic and subcultural groups perceive new and old Coke and whether these groups respond divergently to different promotional themes.
	Segmentation. As appropriate, segment the market based upon the demographic and subcultural differences.
	Promotional Strategy. Develop divergent promotional strategies and sales promotions to the segments identified.
	Environmental Analysis. Identify potential long term changes in the size of the demographic and subcultural groups identified.

TABLE 2-8

Steps 2 and 3: The Consumer Behavior Analysis and Its Managerial Implications

The second and third steps occur in tandem, as we noted earlier. In the "New Coke" case five consumer behavior concepts are relevant: brand loyalty and relational exchange, consumer expectations, consumer motivation (psychological reactance), self-concept, and demographics and regional subcultures. Each concept and its managerial implication are briefly discussed in this section. In addition, Table 2-8 summarizes the analysis performed in Steps 2 and 3 of the managerial applications analysis.

Brand Loyalty and Relational Exchange Managers must carefully analyze their customers' brand loyalty and the nature of the exchange relationship between their organization and its customers. This analysis should be based on the perceptions of the customer. Many

Coke drinkers had a fierce loyalty to the beverage and felt as though they had a long-standing relational exchange with the company. They had been Coke drinkers all their lives, and when the firm changed the taste of its flagship brand, they perceived that the company was showing contempt for them. In effect, the company was breaking a bond of trust by changing the taste of a product that many customers had happily consumed for years.

Recall that in Step 3 of the managerial applications analysis the analyst identifies the managerial implications of the consumer concept identified. We can see that in the "New Coke" case the concept of relational exchange influenced two managerial areas: the marketing mix and market research. The basic decision of whether to eliminate the current brand and launch a totally new one involved the "product element" of the marketing mix. Coca-Cola executives should have done careful marketing research to determine whether eliminating the original beverage would break the bonds of trust the company had established with its customers over half a century. If after examining the research findings the company decided to go ahead with the product change, managers should have used relational exchange ideas to develop a promotional strategy—another marketing mix element. That is, using ideas from relational exchange, Coca-Cola's executives should have created a strategy for presenting the new product to consumers in a way that would lower their perception of an exchange inequity.

Consumer Expectations The concept of consumer expectations helps managers see how people's expectations influence their perceptions and interpretations of information, such as that received through the taste sense. Coca-Cola's executives and researchers failed to consider the effects of consumer expectations in their market research. Because they used blind tests, they were unable to ascertain the effects of consumer expectations on taste and therefore to obtain a realistic estimate of potential consumer reactions to the new formula. Clearly, Coca-Cola should have had its researchers do some tests in which consumers knew the brand names of the colas they were tasting.

Consumer Motivation To keep their strategy secret from competitors, Coca-Cola's managers decided not to inform the research participants that they were considering a change in Coke's formula. As a result, they were staggered by the vehemence of the negative response to the introduction of "New Coke." This emphatic rejection of the new brand was an effect of the emotional state called *psychological reactance*, which we discuss in Chapter 6 on motivation and affective processes. Psychological reactance occurs when people perceive that their freedom of choice has been violated.[28] People in this state are aroused to take steps to restore their behavioral freedom, and Coke drinkers did so with a vengeance.

The concept of reactance applies to both the market research and the marketing mix in this case. In the realm of market research, the implication is that a group of test consumers should have been sworn to secrecy and then asked how they would react to the withdrawal of regular Coke from the marketplace. The implication for the marketing mix is that the company should not have tampered with "Old Coke" but instead introduced and promoted an entirely new brand to compete against Pepsi.

Self-Concept Self-concept (see Chapter 7) is another consumer behavior concept that applies to the Coke case. As *The Wall Street Journal*'s taste test demonstrated, Coke and Pepsi drinkers have very different images of themselves. We know that consumers frequently buy a specific brand because its image connects with their **self-concept.**

Self-concept has application to four managerial areas in this case. First, market research should have been designed to discover what images consumers connect with Coke and competing brands. Second, this information should have been used to pinpoint segments of consumers who wish to identify themselves with a particular cola's image. Third, the company should have developed a positioning strategy for portraying Coke's image. Finally, Coca-Cola should have created a promotional strategy to implement that positioning strategy.

Demographics and Regional Subcultures The "New Coke" debacle also illustrates the need for marketers to consider demographics and regional subcultures (see Chapter 18). People in different regions of the United States often have markedly different tastes and preferences. Coca-Cola should have conducted market research to identify these differences, and if they were found to be significant, the company should have segmented its market by region and developed different promotional strategies for each region. Finally, corporate managers should have done an environmental analysis to gauge how long-term changes in regional population distributions would impact their marketing strategy. If, for example, urban centers were expected to shrink, that could indicate trouble for "New Coke."

Step 4: Managerial Recommendations

Five recommendations emerge from our managerial applications analysis of the "New Coke" case.

Recommendation 1 Before deciding to launch the new product, management should have done sophisticated marketing research that considered consumer expectations, brand loyalty, and the brand image of Coke and Pepsi. Had this been done, the problem of reactance would have been identified prior to the launch of the product and the company would have found itself with three alternatives: abandon the launch of the new product; launch it, but employ a different marketing mix strategy; or bring the new beverage out under a different brand name.

Recommendation 2 If the decision was made to launch "New Coke" and eliminate "Old Coke," managers should have employed a different promotional strategy, one that used an advertising campaign to minimize reactance and reduce the negative feelings of loyal Coke drinkers.

Recommendation 3 If managers decided instead to bring out the new beverage under a new brand name, they should have performed market research so that they could carefully segment the market. The researchers would have clearly identified the characteristics of consumers currently loyal to Coke as well as the characteristics of the new segment they would be targeting for the new brand. All the segmentation variables identified earlier in the chapter would be used in this effort. The likely outcome would have been to target the new beverage to Pepsi drinkers who are young, urban, and hip.

Recommendation 4 If managers went with Recommendation 3, after identifying the characteristics of the target market for the new brand, they would develop a positioning and differentiation strategy for it. There would be two essential elements to this strategy: clearly distinguish the new brand from Coke, and position it to appeal to Pepsi drinkers. The positioning strategy, of course, would be executed through the marketing mix—particularly the promotional strategy element of that mix.

Recommendation 5 If the decision was to bring out a second brand, it would be critical to perform an environmental analysis to identify trends in demographics and popular culture so that effective promotional messages could be designed to reach the new target market.

As you may have noted, Coca-Cola appears to be following many of these recommendations in its current strategy. Recall from the case that the company has replaced its megabrand strategy with one that calls for bringing out numerous new products designed to appeal to a cross-section of consumer segments. Management now uses 21 advertising agencies to maximize its ability to position and differentiate the company's brands from one another. All of this is being done, however, while maintaining a strong focus on the company's major brands—Coke and Diet Coke. At the 1996 Olympic Games, for example, Coca-Cola spent over $60 million advertising and promoting these brands.[29]

SUMMARY

Consumer behavior principles and research assist managerial decision making in five different areas: environmental analysis, market research, segmentation, product positioning, and marketing-mix development. All of these elements are interdependent.

Environmental analysis involves assessing the external forces that act on the firm and its customers and that create threats and opportunities. When doing an environmental analysis, the researcher investigates the demographic, cultural, situational, group, economic, natural, and technological environments.

Market research is applied consumer research designed to provide management with information on factors that affect consumers' acquisition, consumption, and disposition of goods, services, and ideas. Unless market researchers have a firm grasp of these factors, they have no way of determining what to measure or what pitfalls to avoid doing research.

Market segmentation is defined as the division of a market into distinct subsets of customers with similar needs and wants, each of which can be reached with a different marketing mix." Useful segments possess the characteristics of *measurability*, *accessibility*, and *substantiality*. The advantage of segmentation is that it allows the company to tailor the marketing mix to meet the needs and wants of homogeneous subsets of customers. Since these subsets have particular needs and wants not shared by larger groupings of consumers, segmentation expands the total market potential for a general class of product. A number of factors on which people and companies can be grouped have been identified. For consumer markets, there are four classifications of segmentation variables: (1) the characteristics of the person, (2) the nature of the situation in which the product or service is purchased, (3) geography, and (4) the consumer's culture and subculture. Segmentation of industrial markets is often based on the Standard Industrial Classification System developed by the federal government.

Product positioning and product differentiation are other key managerial application areas for consumer behavior concepts. Through product positioning, an organization influences how consumers perceive a brand's characteristics relative to those of competitive offerings. The goal is to influence demand by creating a product with specific characteristics (i.e., brand attributes) and a clear image that differentiate it from competitors. Product differentiation is the process of manipulating the marketing mix so as to position a brand in a manner that allows consumers to perceive meaningful differences between it and its competitors. Positioning a product and segmenting customers go hand-in-hand. First, a segment of customers is identified, and then a product is developed and positioned so that it fulfills the needs of that segment.

Marketing-mix development, the final application area of consumer behavior concepts, involves the coordination of activities concerned with product development, as well as the promotion, pricing, and distribution of the product. The facts, theories, and concepts of consumer behavior directly affect the development of the marketing mix. In this textbook the term *product* is used very broadly to include physical objects, services, places, organizations, and so forth. Principles of consumer behavior can be applied to four separate areas of the new-product–development process: idea generation, concept testing, product development, and market testing.

We detailed a four-step process for solving marketing problems. First, gather information and identify the problem/opportunity. Second, identify the relevant consumer behavior concepts and determine how they apply to the problem. Third, develop a managerial strategy by identifying the managerial implications of each applicable consumer behavior concept. Finally, summarize the managerial recommendations that emerge from the managerial implications.

behavioral economics
behavioral segmentation
benefit segmentation
competitive positioning
concept testing
demand elasticity
demographic characteristics
environmental analysis

geographic segmentation
idea generation
macrosegmentation
managerial applications
  analysis
market research
market segmentation
market testing

marketing mix
microsegmentation
perceptual maps
price elasticity
product development
product differentiation
product positioning
repositioning

self-concept
specific positioning
Standard Industrial Classification System (SIC)
usage behavior

REVIEW QUESTIONS

1. Identify the five key managerial strategy areas in which consumer behavior concepts can assist managers.

2. Identify five of the six environmental areas in which consumer behavior information may be of assistance to managers. Give two specific examples of the consumer behavior information that would be useful in each area.

3. What is meant by the idea of a reciprocity between consumers and the environment?

4. Identify and give examples of two different types of positioning.

5. What is a perceptual map? How can perceptual maps be used to help position products?

6. How have managers attempted to reposition Snickers?

7. What are the three factors necessary to have a managerially useful segment?

8. Identify the bases for segmenting the consumer market.

9. What is the single most important type of information that marketers should gather for purposes of segmentation? Why?

10. What is meant by behavioral segmentation? What are three types of behavioral segmentation?

11. What are two bases for segmenting industrial markets?

12. What are the four areas of product development in which consumer behavior principles may assist managers?

13. List eight of the 10 consumer behavior concepts that are useful for promotional strategy. Give an example of an application for each of the concepts.

14. Identify one example of how a consumer behavior principle can assist the manager in each of the following areas: sales promotion, public relations, pricing, and distribution.

15. What is the difference between product positioning and product differentiation?

DISCUSSION QUESTIONS

1. You are a member of the planning department at General Motors' corporate headquarters. You have just been assigned the task of identifying the likely environmental factors that will influence consumer tastes and preferences for automobiles over the next 10 years. Outline the various factors you would consider in making such an analysis.

2. Consider the use of Freon in air conditioners. Identify as many uses as you can for air conditioners. Discuss the relationship between air conditioner use and the reciprocity of the consumer with the natural environment.

3. Identify two current examples of specific and competitive positioning of products or services. How effective do you consider each of these marketing strategies to be?

4. Perceptual maps can be used to identify a brand's position relative to competitors. Using your personal knowledge and understanding of universities that high school students in your region consider, develop a perceptual map that the "typical" student might have of these universities.

5. Consider the automobile industry or some other major industry you know something about, such as cosmetics. Among the brands of autos or cosmetics with which you are familiar, which are highly differentiated from other brands? Which are poorly differentiated? How could the poorly differentiated brands be better distinguished from their competitors?

6. Again, consider the automobile industry or some other major industry you know something about, such as cos-

metics. Identify as many variables as you can on which that industry appears to segment its marketplace. Then identify specific brands that target the various segments. Are there segments of the marketplace that have not been adequately reached?

7. Suppose that universities and colleges decided to engage in benefit segmentation and specifically mention the benefits they provide in their promotional activities. First, identify the various benefits that colleges and universities offer students. Then sketch out a print advertisement for your college or university that promotes the benefits it offers.

8. Imagine that you work in the marketing department of a company that has developed a prototype of a new processed beef product. The product tastes and looks just like a high-quality piece of steak. However, it is made of beef chuck and costs about half as much as sirloin steak. Furthermore, it contains about half the calories and cholesterol of sirloin steak. Outline the consumer behavior considerations you would keep in mind in developing the marketing mix for the product.

ENDNOTES

1. Thomas Oliver, *The Real Coke, The Real Story* (New York: Random House, 1986).

2. Leah Rikard, "Remembering New Coke," *Advertising Age*, April 17, 1995, p. 6.

3. Ibid.

4. Ibid.

5. Betsy Morris, "In This Taste Test, the Loser Is the Taste Test," *The Wall Street Journal*, June 3, 1987, p. 31.

6. Betsy Morris, "Coke vs. Pepsi: Cola War Marches On," *The Wall Street Journal*, June 3, 1987, p. 31.

7. Ibid.

8. "Coke 'Family' Sales Fly as the New Coke Stumbles," *Advertising Age*, January 27, 1986, pp. 1, 91.

9. Andrew Wallenstein, "Coca-Cola's Sweet Return to Glory Days," *Advertising Age*, April 17, 1995, p. 4.

10. Laura Bird, "Coke II: The Sequel," *Adweek's Marketing Week*, Vol. 31 (July 30, 1990), pp. 4–5.

11. Wallenstein, "Coca-Cola's Sweet Return," p. 4.

12. Philip Kotler, *Marketing Management: Analysis, Planning, and Control*, 4th ed. (Upple Saddle River, NJ: Prentice Hall, 1980), pp. 23–24.

13. W. Fred van Raaij, "Economic Psychology," *Journal of Economic Psychology*, *Vol. 1*, (1981), pp. 1–24.

14. George Katona, "Consumer Savings Patterns," *Journal of Consumer Research*, 1, June, 1974, 1–12.

15. Raju Narisetti, "P&G Says Fake-Fat Olestra Gets Fewer Complaints Than Expected," *The Wall Street Journal*, July 25, 1996, p. B3.

16. Kotler, *Marketing Management*, p. 195.

17. Joseph Plummer, "Emotions Important for Successful Advertising," *Marketing News*, April 12, 1985, p. 18.

18. Russell W. Belk, "Situational Variables and Consumer Behavior," *Journal of Consumer Research*, Vol. 2 (December 1975), pp. 157–164.

19. Michael D. Hutt and Thomas Speh, *Industrial Marketing Management* (New York: The Dryden Press, 1981).

20. Norihiko Shirouzu, "Japan's Staid Coffee Bars Wake Up and Smell Starbucks," *The Wall Street Journal*, July 25, 1996, p. B1.

21. Kotler, *Marketing Management*.

22. John Kinski, "Consumer Perceptions of Meat Products," Master's Thesis, Oklahoma State University, 1985.

23. Thomas Robertson, Joan Zielinski, and Scott Ward, *Consumer Behavior* (Glenview, IL: Scott, Foresman, 1984).

24. Bess Gallanis, "Positioning Old Products in New Niches," *Advertising Age*, May 3, 1984, p. M50.

25. Kotler, *Marketing Management*.

26. Ibid., p. 231.

27. Edmund Faison, *Advertising: A Behavioral Approach for Managers* (New York: John Wiley & Sons, 1980).

28. Mona Clee and Robert Wicklund, "Consumer Behavior and Psychological Reactance," *Journal of Consumer Research*, Vol. 6 (March 1980), pp. 389–405.

29. Jeff Jensen and Chuck Ross, "Centennial Olympics Open as $5 Bil Event of Century," *Advertising Age*, July 15, 1996, pp. 1, 27.

II

Individual Consumer Processes

3

INFORMATION PROCESSING I: INVOLVEMENT AND PERCEPTION

INTRODUCTORY CASE

Ford Fails to Learn from the Past

In the 1995 model year over 500,000 Ford Tauruses were sold, making the Taurus the best-selling automobile in the world. In the next model year Ford Motor Company introduced a new, redesigned Taurus. Developed after extensive marketing research to determine consumer needs, wants, and styling preferences, the radically revamped Taurus had styling cues derived from the ellipse.

Because the Taurus, and its twin the Mercury Sable, are Ford's bread-and-butter vehicles, their success in the marketplace is critical to the firm's profitability. When initial sales in the 1996 model year fell off by more than 20 percent, the price of Ford's stock went down in what was a bull market.

Arguing that the sales decline was only temporary and that consumers would gradually warm up to the new design, the company's general manager claimed, "It is such a revolutionary change that people have to get used to it."[1] *Automotive News* suggested that one reason for the new Taurus's slow sales was Ford's ads had failed to prep consumers that the car's radical new design was meant to signal the approach of the twenty-first century.[2] A research analyst concurred that the

company's advertising campaign had not prepared the public for the dramatic styling innovations—for example, the unique oval instrument panel that echoed the car's elliptical shape. The company had actually had 48 employees working months to create that futuristic dashboard.[3]

Ford's failure to prepare consumers for the new vehicle is quite surprising considering that the company had had experience with consumer resistance to startlingly new designs. When it created the original Taurus in 1986, Ford was introducing a revolutionary car with a highly aerodynamic body. In the mid-1980s the teardrop-shaped vehicle was unique, and the marketing department worried that the design was too radical for the mass market. To reduce expected consumer resistance, Ford deliberately violated established auto marketing principles by publicizing its innovative design instead of keeping it a secret. Six months before the model's launch, the company released photos of the Taurus to the press.

As the automotive press learned more about what Ford was trying to do, it rallied to support the company. *Car and Driver* said,

"The Ford Motor Company wants the masses to see its provocative new cars now, so that the shock will have worn off by the time they go on sale in the fall." Noting the dramatic design of the vehicles, the magazine added, "No wonder Ford is sweating bullets."[4]

The marketing strategy worked, and the Taurus was a massive success. By 1992 it was the top-selling car in the world. The launch of the redesigned Taurus in 1996 threatened this success, however, because Ford's managers had forgotten the lessons learned 10 years earlier.

INTRODUCTION

One of the most vexing problems marketers encounter is how to ensure that consumers receive, comprehend, and remember information about their product or service. The problem is particularly worrisome for advertisers, who can spend millions of dollars developing and executing a national campaign, only to find that consumers fail to be exposed to the information, fail to attend to it, fail to comprehend it, or fail to remember it. The topic of information processing is rooted in these concerns. **Consumer information processing** is the process through which consumers are exposed to information, attend to it, comprehend it, place it in memory, and retrieve it for later use.

The introductory case illustrates three concepts related to consumer information processing: the orientation reflex, adaptation, and perception. When people are first exposed to a stimulus, such as a photo of a new automobile, they have some initial reaction to it. If the stimulus is highly novel, they will reflexively orient to it in a type of "flight or fight" reaction called an *orientation reflex*. A major goal of advertisers and product designers is to capture consumers' attention by creating a stimulus that will excite an orientation reflex. The revolutionary design of the Taurus certainly accomplished this goal.

One pitfall marketers try to avoid is creating a stimulus so novel that its very newness produces a negative reaction. The initial negative reaction to the unexpected can be reduced, however, if the consumer is exposed to the stimulus a number of times. Then the feelings generated will tend to become more positive. This process is called *adaptation*.[5]

In 1986 Ford's strategy of flouting marketing tradition by publicizing the car prior to its introduction helped consumers adapt to the novel shape of the Taurus. This element of the company's promotional strategy was one of the reasons for the Taurus's phenomenal success. However, in 1996 Ford ignored the lessons it had learned a decade earlier and introduced a radical new look for the Taurus without preparing its customers for the new shape. Partly because of the radical new design and partly because of its higher price, initial consumer response to the new Taurus was tepid. However, after consumers adapted to the design, buying interest increased, and the Taurus again became the world's leading selling car. Figure 3-1 shows an ad for the 1996 Taurus.

The introductory case also illustrates the role of perception in consumer behavior. *Perception* refers to what happens when consumers are exposed to, attend to, and comprehend stimuli in the consumer environment. Within this process people use all of their senses— sight, hearing, smell, taste, and touch. In the development of the 1996 Taurus instrument panel, Ford's engineers sought to deliver a design that was not only visually appealing, but also highly user-friendly. They created ridges and valleys of controls that were easy to feel as well as to see, so that consumers could use their sense of touch to find the proper control. Thus the engineers employed principles of perception to help consumers adapt to the complex instrument panel.

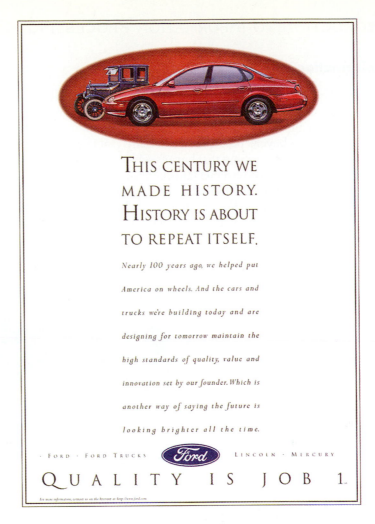

Figure 3-1
Consumers were somewhat slow to adapt to the radical styling of the 1996 Ford Taurus.

An Introduction to Information Processing

What Is Information?

Information may be defined as the content of what is exchanged with the outer world as we adjust to it and make our adjustment felt upon it.[6] By reacting appropriately to information, or by generating information ourselves, we adapt to and influence the world around us. For example, a buyer's purchase of a socially visible product, such as clothing or a watch, provides information about that buyer's self-concept to others. Similarly, companies communicate meaning to consumers through the information transmitted in their advertisements. Thus the symbols employed in print advertisements are information units employed to influence consumers. For example, the ad for Kodak Royal Gold 200 film found in Figure 3-2 uses symbols of special occasions to stress the importance of purchasing the best photographic film available.

Figure 3-2
Kodak employs symbols of special occasions to tell consumers why they should purchase Royal Gold 200 film.

Consumer information is obtained through the senses of vision, hearing, taste, smell, and touch. There is an important distinction between raw stimuli and the perception of those stimuli. Raw stimuli are composed of sound waves, light waves/particles, bits of chemicals, textures, and levels of temperature. Perception—the interpretation of and the meanings derived from the stimuli—results from information processing. Different people often assign divergent meanings to exactly the same stimulus because their perception of that stimulus is influenced by their expectations as well as by their particular background. Marketers, therefore, cannot assume that because two people receive exactly the same stimulus from an ad they will perceive it and react to it in a similar manner. If you ask two avid fans of opposing basketball teams how well a game was refereed, for example, you will likely get two very different opinions because of the differences in the way they perceived the game.

What Is Information Processing?

As we noted earlier in the chapter, consumer information processing is the process through which consumers are exposed to information, become involved with it, attend to it, comprehend it, place it into memory, and retrieve it for later use. Figure 3-3 is a simplified diagram of consumer information processing. Notice that three important factors influence information processing: perception, the level of consumer involvement, and memory.

The first factor—**perception**—is the process through which individuals are exposed to information, attend to that information, and comprehend it. In the initial **exposure stage** consumers receive information through their senses. Then, in the **attention stage,** they allocate processing capacity to a stimulus. Finally, in the **comprehension stage,** they organize and interpret the information in order to obtain meaning from it. **Comprehension** is the process of making sense of stimuli so they may be understood. One goal of this chapter is to impress upon you the importance of perceptual processes in consumer behavior.

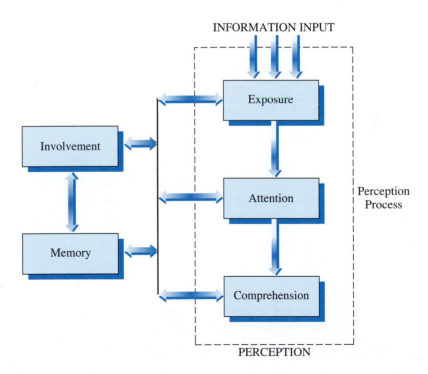

Figure 3-3
Consumer information-processing model.

The second factor that influences information processing is the degree of involvement of the consumer in the task. Involvement level influences whether the consumer will move from the exposure to the attention and, ultimately, to the comprehension stage of perception. In addition, involvement influences memory functions. Because an understanding of involvement is central to the understanding of information processing and perception, we will discuss this important construct in the next section.

The final component of the information-processing model is the memory function. As you can see in Figure 3-4, memory plays a role in each of the stages of perception. It guides the exposure and attention processes by allowing consumers to anticipate stimuli they may encounter. It also assists consumers' comprehension process by storing knowledge about the environment. This knowledge can then be retrieved and used to help consumers understand the meaning of a stimulus. Because of the large role memory plays in information processing, we devote Chapter 4 to memory and cognitive learning.

CONSUMER INVOLVEMENT

Consumer involvement is the perceived personal importance and/or interest consumers attach to the acquisition, consumption, and disposition of a good, a service, or an idea.[7] As their involvement increases, consumers have a greater motivation to attend to, comprehend, and elaborate on information pertaining to the purchase.

The most important factors influencing a consumer's involvement level are: (1) the type of product under consideration, (2) the characteristics of the communication the consumer receives, (3) the characteristics of the situation within which the consumer is operating, and (4) the consumer's personality. For example, consumer involvement generally increases when the product or service under consideration is more expensive, socially visible, and risky to purchase. Communications can also raise involvement by arousing the consumer's emotions. The situation—or context within which a purchase is made—also influences involvement. Thus if the purchase goal is a gift for an important person, such as a fiancée, the consumer's involvement is likely to increase. Furthermore, the consumer's personality governs involvement to some extent, which is why different consumers can react so divergently to the same products, situations, and communications. Figure 3-4 diagrams the interrelationships among personality, product, communication, and situation.[8]

Types of Consumer Involvement

Researchers have identified several different types of involvement. An important distinction is that between situational and enduring involvement.[9] **Situational involvement** occurs over a short time period and is associated with a specific situation, such as the need to replace a product that has broken down (e.g., an automobile). In contrast, **enduring involvement** occurs when consumers show a consistent high level of interest in a product and frequently spend time thinking about the product. It is the combination of situational and enduring involvement that determines the consumer's **involvement responses**—that is, the complexity of information processing and the extent of decision making by the consumer.[10]

What happens when someone who has a high enduring involvement with a product suddenly needs to purchase that product? Research indicates that in such circumstances the effects of enduring and situational involvement combine—that is, the consumer experiences a high number of involvement responses because the total level of involvement is equal to the enduring plus the situational involvement levels.[11] (Table 3-1 presents a scale designed to measure consumers' enduring involvement with products.)

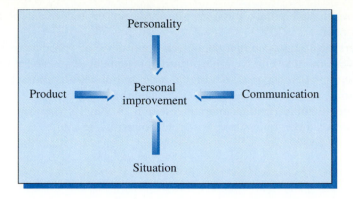

Figure 3-4

The factors that influence consumer purchase involvement. (*Source:* Based in part on John H. Antil, "Conceptualization and Operationalization of Involvement," in *Advances in Consumer Research,* Vol. 11, Thomas C. Kinnear, ed. [Ann Arbor, MI: Association for Consumer Research, 1984], pp. 203–209.)

Research has also revealed that involvement has multiple dimensions. Each of the following factors acts to increase a consumer's level of involvement with a purchase:

1. *Self-expressive importance:* products that help people express their self-concept to others.
2. *Hedonic importance:* products that are pleasurable, interesting, fun, fascinating, and exciting.
3. *Practical relevance:* products that are essential or beneficial for utilitarian reasons.
4. *Purchase risk:* products that create uncertainty because a poor choice would be extremely annoying to the buyer.[12]

The importance of each of these dimensions varies according to the type of good or service being purchased as well as the characteristics of the consumer. The purchase of expensive jewelry, for example, entails a high degree of self-expressive importance, hedonic importance, and purchase risk for most consumers, but has little practical relevance. In contrast, the purchase of a refrigerator generally has high practical relevance

Scale for Measuring Consumers' Enduring Involvement with Products

1. I would be interested in reading about this product.
2. I would read a *Consumer Reports* article about this product.
3. I have compared product characteristics among brands.
4. I usually pay attention to ads for this product.
5. I usually talk about this product with other people.
6. I usually seek advice from other people prior to purchasing this product.
7. I usually take many factors into account before purchasing this product.
8. I usually spend a lot of time choosing what kind to buy.

Source: This scale was developed by Edward F. McQuarrie and J. Michael Munson, "A Revised Product Involvement Inventory: Improved Usability and Validity," *Diversity in Consumer Behavior: Advances in Consumer Research,* Vol. 19 (Provo, UT: Association for Consumer Research, 1992), pp. 108–115.

TABLE 3-1

and entails considerable purchase risk, but has little self-expressive and hedonic importance to most people.

Researchers have suggested that the overall importance of a product in a person's life also affects involvement level.[13] Examples of survey statements employed to measure overall importance are: "Choosing a—is a big decision in one's life"; "I attach great importance to selecting a—"; and "Decisions about selecting a—are serious, important decisions." Managers should conduct market research to identify the extent and type of involvement targeted consumers have with the product being sold.

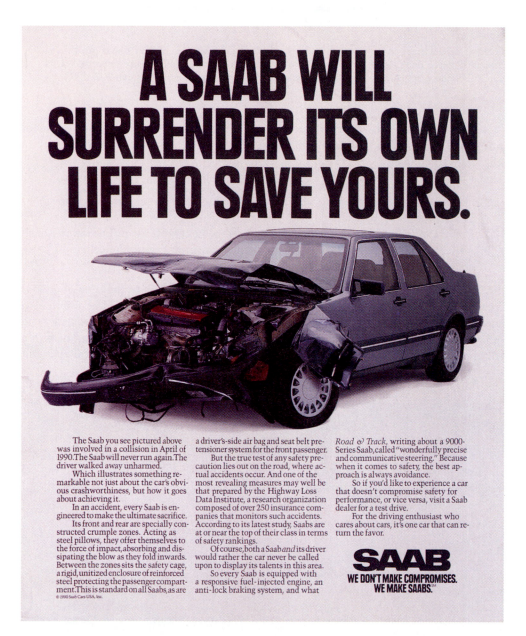

Figure 3-5

Saab uses a detailed message to target buyers involved in extended decision making.

Consumer Involvement: Some Important Points

1. *Definition:* Involvement is the level of perceived personal importance and/or interest evoked by a stimulus.
2. The level of involvement is influenced by the characteristics of the product, the situation, the communication, and the consumer's personality.
3. Two types of involvement have been identified: *situational involvement*, which occurs over a short period of time and is associated with a specific situation, and *enduring involvement*, which represents a longer commitment and concern with a product class.
4. Four dimensions of involvement have been identified: *self-expressive, hedonic importance, practical relevance*, and *purchase risk*.
5. The effects of high involvement include greater depth of information processing, increased arousal, and more extended decision making.

TABLE 3-2

The Effects of High Involvement

What happens when a consumer's involvement increases? The available evidence suggests that as the level of involvement goes up, consumers process information in more depth. Accompanying this increased information processing is a general increase in arousal levels. Consumers are more likely to think hard about a decision when it is made under high-involvement circumstances.[14] They are also more likely to engage in an extended decision process and move through each of the decision stages in a more deliberate manner. Some authors have suggested that the decision process differs so much between high- and low-involvement circumstances that it is justifiable to speak of two categories of decision making: limited decision making in low-involvement circumstances and extended decision making in high-involvement circumstances.[15]

Since consumers tend to give more diligent consideration to the information they receive as their involvement in the prospective purchase increases, advertisers should develop more complex messages for high-involvement purchases. The Saab advertisement shown in Figure 3-5 illustrates this concept. Indeed, the ad's headline—"A Saab Will Surrender Its Own Life to Save Yours"—immediately indicates to the reader that the message is relatively complex. Saab can afford to use a complex approach in its advertising because its target market consists of people who are highly involved in the buying process.

In summary, the involvement concept is critical to understanding not only information processing but also a variety of other consumer topics. For example, a consumer's involvement level has important implications for memory processes, the decision-making process, attitude formation and change, and word-of-mouth communication.[16]

Table 3-2 summarizes the important ideas about consumer involvement, a topic we discuss intermittently throughout this textbook.[17]

THE EXPOSURE STAGE

As shown in the model presented in Figure 3-3, exposure to a stimulus is the first step in information processing. Information exposure activates a consumer's sensory organs so that the entire mechanism of information processing can begin. To influence consumers, marketers must expose them to information via marketing communications. An example of what happens when marketers fail to expose consumers to their product through marketing communications is the fate of Planter's Peanuts in the early 1990s.

Between 1991 and 1994 Nabisco slashed advertising spending on this brand by 70 percent. As one sales representative for the product line said, "Mr. Peanut disappeared." Because of the drastic cut in ad spending, consumers were not exposed to Planter's Peanuts and sales of the product fell from $60 million in 1993 to about $15 million in 1996.[18]

One salient characteristic of consumer information processing in the exposure stage is its selectivity. Through a process known as **selective exposure,** consumers actively choose whether or not to expose themselves to information. It is noteworthy that as they become more involved with a particular type of product consumers are more likely to selectively expose themselves to information about that product.

The concept of selective exposure is of great importance to advertisers because consumers' tendency to selectively screen information can dramatically lower the effectiveness of advertising dollars. For example, when the Super Bowl is televised, sanitation supervisors at water departments have found that water consumption fluctuates dramatically. For periods lasting about two or three minutes, water-holding tanks are drained and the system is strained to capacity. This sudden increase in water usage—called the "flush factor"—occurs during commercial breaks, when people leave their televisions to rush to their bathrooms. Thus advertisers are spending huge amounts to reach consumers who are avoiding exposing themselves to their commercials.[19]

Television viewers' ability to engage in selective exposure to commercials has risen with the spread of cable television and the popularization of remote-control devices that allow people to rapidly and easily switch channels. This practice is called **zapping,** or channel surfing, in the industry, and it is estimated that at any one time about six to 19 percent of consumers are zapping commercials by remotely switching channels. One study found that 64 percent of homes that have cable regularly zap advertisements.[20]

At an advertisers' symposium on the zapping problem and the related issue of audience loss during commercial messages, the consensus was that the erosion rate for television commercials was 59 percent. In effect, only about four out of every 10 people watching a television program actually observe a commercial. The professionals realized that reducing the audience erosion problem required making more appealing commercials. As one executive commented, advertisements need to be made so interesting that people will *want* to view them.[21] Table 3-3 lists some other suggestions for dealing with the audience erosion problem.

The Study of Sensation

Exposure to a stimulus activates a consumer's sensory organs. The study of **sensation** is the investigation of the ways in which people react to the raw sensory information they receive through their sense organs. Its goal is to analyze people's raw responses to a stimulus *before* they attend to it, comprehend it, and give it meaning. For example, someone studying sensation might ask, "How loud does a sound have to be before it is detected?" or "How much difference must there be in the level of the hem of a skirt before a consumer can detect the difference?" The topic of sensation has a number of important applications to product development and promotion.

Once a consumer is exposed to information, whether or not that consumer goes on to actively attend to the stimulus is determined by a number of factors. One is the intensity of the stimulus. The lowest level at which a stimulus can be detected 50 percent of the time is called its **absolute threshold.** As the intensity of a stimulus (e.g., the loudness of an advertisement) increases, the likelihood that it will be sensed also increases. Advertisers therefore have an incentive to make their commercials as loud as they can—without offending the consumer. Indeed, a common complaint by consumers is that television advertisements are louder than the programs they accompany. Although the *maximum* in-

Methods to Reduce Problems of Audience Erosion

1. Format change	Place less important material in the interior of programs. Zapping occurs most at the beginning and end of programs.
2. Spread commercials	Since consumers often switch from network shows to cable programming, place more ads on cable channels.
3. Strategic timing	Zapping frequently occurs 5 to 10 seconds into the commercial. Place important material early in commercials. Also, try to obtain first position in a series of commercials.
4. Budget more for print and other media	With audience erosion in television growing, why not place more emphasis on other media? *Reader's Digest* has run ads in trade magazines pointing out the erosion problem on TV.
5. Persuade networks to show fewer ads	Audiences may be reacting to commercial clutter and advertising overload by zapping commercials.

Source: Extracted from Bernie Whalen, "$6 Billion Down the Drain!" *Marketing News*, September 14, 1984, pp. 1, 37, 38.

TABLE 3-3

tensity of sound in a commercial is no greater than that in a program, advertisers do take steps to create the sensation that the loudness is greater—for example, by recording the entire commercial near the peak allowable sound level.

Subliminal Perception

Closely related to the physiological concept of absolute threshold is the psychological concept of subliminal perception. In 1957 audiences at a movie theater in New Jersey were exposed to messages that said "Drink Coca-Cola" and "Eat popcorn." The messages were superimposed on the movie and presented so quickly that the audience did not consciously realize they had appeared. The marketing firm that created the messages claimed—albeit without presenting any evidence—that sales of Coke and popcorn increased dramatically at the theater.

Some people were shocked and angry when they learned what had been done. A writer at *The New Yorker* compared the stunt to "breaking and entering" people's minds. Others, however, saw great potential in subliminal messages, and soon a radio station was broadcasting the subaudible message that "TV's a bore."[22]

The term *subliminal* means "below threshold"—that is, below the absolute threshold and therefore unreportable. **Subliminal perception** refers to the idea that stimuli presented below the level of conscious awareness may nonetheless influence behavior and feelings. Three different types of subliminal stimulation in advertising have been identified: briefly presented visual stimuli, accelerated speech in low-volume auditory messages, and embedded or hidden sexual imagery or words in print advertisements.[23] In fact, one author has written two books claiming that advertisers intentionally embed erotic and death symbols in print advertisements.[24]

Does subliminal advertising work? According to one psychologist, "No, what you see is what you get."[25] He argues that subliminal stimuli are extremely weak and most certainly overridden by a host of other, more powerful messages. In addition, because people are generally in control of their overt responses to stimuli, they screen out attempts to persuade them to do something they don't want to do.

Recently, however, evidence has been accumulating that the effects of subliminal advertising are strong enough to cause concern. One study investigated the effects of "subliminal embeds" on the ratings of ads by college students, who were simulating consumers. Two actual print ads were used—one for a popular cigarette and the other for a well-known brand of scotch whiskey. After the stimuli were pointed out by the experimenters, students reported that they could identify the nude body of a woman in the liquor ad and the representation of male genitals in the cigarette ad. A second version of each ad was created by having a professional photographer airbrush out the embedded material. Four other groups of students then evaluated the four ads. The results revealed differences in the ratings for the control (airbrushed ads) and the embedded ads for the liquor advertisement, but not for the cigarette ad. A second study was run, in which measures of autonomic arousal were taken. In this study the students showed evidence of differences in arousal for both advertisements containing the embedded material.[26]

Other research supports the argument that subliminal advertising has an effect on consumers. For example, researchers found that presenting the word "Coke" at levels below the absolute threshold increased the thirst ratings of subjects.[27] Similarly, another group of researchers presented slides of a well-known brand of soap for washing wool at a rate of one-sixtieth of a second—a speed of presentation much too quick for conscious recognition—during a film on how to wash woolens. Those who had been exposed to the slides rated the brand significantly higher than subjects who had not received this subliminal information.[28]

Assuming they are real, how do we account for the effects of subliminal advertising? Two theories have been proposed.[29] The first, **incremental effects theory,** states that, over many presentations of a stimulus, a stimulus representation is gradually built into the consumer's nervous system. At some point this representation reaches a behavioral threshold and causes changes in the consumer's actions—without the consumer's ever recognizing the cause of these changes. The incremental effects theory assumes that numerous repetitions of the stimulus are needed. Indeed, both the Coke study and the woolen study used multiple repetitions.

The second theory, the **psychodynamic theory of arousal,** assumes that unconscious wishes to engage in some behavior can be activated by unconsciously presented stimuli. In the study using the liquor advertisement, for example, the students harbored an unconscious wish for sexual activity that was activated by the image of a nude female body embedded in the advertisement. Thus the activation of an unconscious wish presumably influences the actual perception of an advertisement.

To sum up, current research on subliminal perception indicates that this is not an idea that should be dismissed. Clearly, additional research needs to be done, not least because of the public's intense interest in the topic. Consumers spend an estimated $50 million a year on audiotapes with subliminal messages designed to help them quit smoking or lose weight, raise their self-esteem, and improve their sexual functioning. As one author noted, however, researchers will have to take great care to eliminate alternative explanations of the effects.[30]

The Just Noticeable Difference Threshold (JND)

Besides the *absolute* threshold, there is a *difference for stimuli* threshold. The **just noticeable difference (JND)** is the minimum amount of difference in the intensity of a stimulus that can be detected 50 percent of the time.

The study of just noticeable difference thresholds has important implications for marketing research. For instance, food and beverage companies are interested in producing products that give the optimum taste at the lowest cost.[31] In formulating a recipe for a product, they frequently have to choose between two ingredients that differ in price. The relevant question is: Will a change in ingredient create a just noticeable difference in the taste of the product?[32]

Weber's Law and the JND

One important point about the just noticeable difference is that it varies with the level of the stimulus. The relationship between the size of the JND and stimulus intensity is known as Weber's Law, after its discoverer, the German scientist E. H. Weber. **Weber's Law** states that as the intensity of the stimulus increases, the ability to detect a difference between the two levels of the stimulus decreases. Weber identified a formula to express these relationships:

$$JND = I \times K$$

where *I* is the intensity level of the stimulus and *K* is a constant that gives the proportionate amount of change in stimulus level required for its detection.

One marketing application of Weber's Law is to pricing. A retailers' rule is that mark-downs must be at least 20 percent before consumers recognize them.[33] This 20 percent figure is equivalent to *K*, the constant in Weber's Law. For example, if a diamond ring is priced at $1,200, it would have to be marked down by $240 for the price change to be meaningful (i.e., $1,200 × .20 = $240). And, if the diamond were priced at $8,000, the markdown would have to be $1,600 to be effective. As you can see, the JND increases in size proportionate to *K* as the dollar value of a purchase increases. This application is controversial because, strictly speaking, a small difference between two prices (say $1,000 and $1,001) is clearly *noticeable*; it just has little *meaning* to the consumer. More will be said about this issue later in the chapter.

Information on absolute and difference thresholds may influence packaging strategy as well. Why does Campbell's Soup package its pork and beans in a 20 3/4-ounce can while its major competitor uses a 21-ounce can? The reason is probably because consumers do not notice the difference. When Bohemia Beer lowered the quantity of beer in each bottle from 12 to 11 ounces, the company used the cost savings to increase the beer's ad budget and develop a fancier container for it. As a result, sales nearly doubled.[34] The JND principle applies to increases in the size of portions as well as to decreases. A 12-month test convinced M&M/Mars that increasing the size of its candy bars would raise sales by 20 to 30 percent. As a result, the company changed nearly its entire product line.

Table 3-4 identifies a number of marketing uses of the JND concept.

Although marketers seldom overtly acknowledge that they are using Weber's Law, much evidence shows that they fully understand its implications. For example, Procter & Gamble made no fewer than 19 changes in the wrapper of Ivory Soap between 1898 and 1965,[35] but the difference between any two of these changes was extremely subtle. However, when

Some Marketing Examples of the JND	
Area of Application	**Example of Use**
Pricing	When raising the price, try to move less than a JND.
	When lowering the price for a sale, move more than a JND.
Sales promotion	Make coupons larger than the JND.
Product	Make decreases in size of food product less than JND (e.g., in shrinking candy bars).
	When the word *new* is used, make sure the product change is greater than the JND.
Packaging	To update package styling and logo, keep within the JND.
	To change image, make styling changes greater than the JND.

TABLE 3-4

the 1898 and 1998 wrappers are compared, the differences are astounding. P&G altered the wrapper gradually enough to stay within most consumers' JND with each change.

As we said above, gradual increases in size are just as likely to go undetected by consumers as decreases. For example, in 1954 Burger King's "small" soda contained 8 ounces. In 1996 it held 16 ounces. Generally, food packages have increased in size over the years, but because the changes have been slight, few Americans realize that they are "automatically" consuming more calories than they did 20 years ago.[36]

There is a potential problem marketers should be aware of when applying psychological concepts like Weber's Law to consumer behavior problems. Sometimes the *idea* applies quite well, but the exact *process* through which it operates does not match the consumer behavior context. Weber's Law describes quite accurately the *sensory* impact of changes in the intensity of a stimulus. The question is: Does a change in sales price influence consumers at the sensory level, or rather at a *cognitive* level where the information is being interpreted? If the change in sales price influences people at the comprehension stage rather than at the sensory level, Weber's Law is, strictly speaking, being misapplied. Indeed, we strongly suspect that in most consumer behavior situations the term *just noticeable difference* is inappropriate and that a more appropriate term would be *just meaningful difference*.

Practically speaking, however, it makes little difference to the marketing manager whether Weber's Law is being misapplied from a psychological perspective. The important point is that this psychological concept helps managers understand the relationship between the level of the stimulus and the amount of change that must take place in the stimulus to be noticeable.

Consumer Adaptation

Closely related to the concepts of the absolute threshold and the JND is that of **adaptation.** Everyone has direct experience of the process of adaptation. When you first immerse yourself in a hot bath, you may find the steaming water nearly unbearable. After a few minutes, however, you will experience the water as quite pleasant. This change in sensation does not happen because the water got colder. Rather, it happens because your nerve cells have adapted to the water's temperature and are no longer firing signals to your brain telling it that the bath water is too hot. Adaptation, then, occurs when an individual has repeated experience with a stimulus. The **adaptation level** is the amount or level of the stimulus to which the consumer has become accustomed. It is the reference point to which changes in the level of the stimulus are compared.

The concept of adaptation has implications for both product and advertising strategies. Since consumers become adapted to a certain look, style, or message over some period of time, to keep product or service communications fresh, marketers should vary them periodically. You have probably noticed that the EverReady® Energizer Bunny ads have for many years used the same theme of the drum-banging rabbit "going and going and going" to drive home the idea that these batteries last a long time. Yet the message has not become boring because of the highly creative use of dozens of humorous variations on the theme. The result is a long-running advertising campaign that has propelled the brand to market leadership.

The Butterfly Curve

In the early 1990s U.S. airlines began losing market share to foreign carriers on transatlantic flights. In seeking to explain why American, TWA, and other airlines were rated lower than competitors, one airline executive suggested that the reason was not poorer service. He maintained that the service on foreign airlines isn't actually better, but "different. It seems better because it's not what [customers] normally get."[37] Is there any merit in this executive's conclusion?

The idea that something slightly different may be perceived more positively is supported by an effect called the **butterfly curve,** which is illustrated in Figure 3-6. The vertical axis denotes the degree of liking for a stimulus, while the horizontal axis denotes the level of the stimulus and the position of the adaptation level. (If you want to know the origin of the name of this concept, look hard and you'll see that the humps in the figure resemble the wings of a butterfly.) The butterfly curve shows that preference for a stimulus is greatest at points just higher and just lower than the adaptation level. At the adaptation level itself, preference declines slightly because the person has become habituated to the stimulus. Preference steadily decreases as the stimulus moves farther and farther from the adaptation level.[38]

The butterfly curve neatly explains why fashion trends change so often. Consumers quickly become adapted to a certain look, and their pleasure in it palls. Designers then modify the current look in some relatively small way, and it appears fresh and interesting because the stimulus has diverged from the adaptation level. The up-and-down movement of skirt hems over the years well illustrates the principle. The width of men's ties and lapels shows the same tendency.

The butterfly curve also suggests that radical fashions are adopted slowly because when introduced they are too far away from the adaptation level. For example, when Madonna first wore a bustier, the public was horrified. However, after several years consumers adapted, and bustiers became familiar sights on urban dance floors and even in that Middle American fashion kingdom—the mall.

Another consumer behavior phenomenon that can be accounted for by the butterfly curve is **spontaneous brand switching.** Consumers frequently switch brands, even when they are not unhappy with the brand they previously used. The phenomenon seems to occur most frequently with low-involvement products in which there is little difference between brands. Consumers may switch brands because they have thoroughly adapted to the one they are used to buying and are susceptible to a new stimulus. In changing brands, the consumer moves off the adaptation level, and therefore experiences some increment in the pleasure received from the product class. That companies implicitly recognize this phenomenon is borne out by the frequent appearances of "new and improved" versions of products.

Another way in which companies apply the concept of the butterfly curve is to periodically change their logos and other corporate symbols to give their products a "fresh look." In 1996 General Mills, Inc., again updated the look of its 75-year-old famous (but fictitious) endorser of its cake mixes and other products, Betty Crocker. Figure 3-7 shows

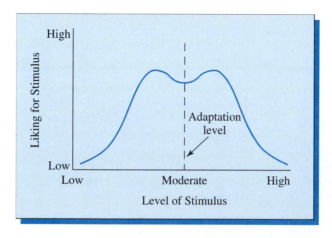

Figure 3-6
Butterfly curve.

Figure 3-7

The changing images of Betty Crocker over the years illustrate the concept of the butterfly curve.

photos of all seven "Betty Crockers" used by the company. The Consumer Behavior Factoid answers the question, "How was the new image of Betty Crocker chosen?"

THE ATTENTION STAGE

Marketers are vitally concerned with attracting consumers' attention. In order for consumers to comprehend information and place it into long-term memory, they must first attend to it. **Attention** is the allocation of cognitive capacity to an object or task so that information is consciously processed. Thus when someone attends to an advertisement, a public relations piece, or a personal-selling communication, that person is allocating mental capacity to the task. The more demanding the task, or the more involved the person is in it, the greater the amount of attention the person will focus on it.[39]

Types of Attention

Researchers have distinguished a number of different types of attention. A primary differentiation is between preattention and attention. As we noted above, when someone attends to a stimulus, such as an advertisement, that person is consciously aware of receiving information. In contrast, during preattention a person is unconsciously and automatically scanning the environment. Thus **preattention** can be defined as an unconscious process in which consumers automatically scan the features of the environment. It is an intermediate stage between exposure and conscious attention to a stimulus. During preattention the person initially evaluates information obtained to determine whether it is important enough to be processed further. If it is, the person allocates additional cognitive resources to the stimulus and moves into the attention stage of information processing.[40]

Preattention processes can influence consumer feelings. In one study a pictorial ad was placed either to the left or the right of an accompanying editorial.[41] The consumer researcher found that when the ad was to the left of the editorial, respondents liked it more than they did when it was to the right. The researcher explained this difference by theorizing that when the ad was at the left of the editorial, the information it contained was transferred to the right hemisphere of the brain, which is responsible for holistic perceptions that directly affect feelings and emotions. As a result, the respondents had preconsciously processed the ad favorably when it was in the left position, without realizing that its placement relative to the editorial had affected their conscious evaluations of it. We will have more to say about consumers' unconscious formation of feelings and affect in Chapter 8 on attitude formation.

A consumer's attention can be activated either voluntarily or involuntarily. When consumers actively search out information that has personal relevance for them, their attention is said to be voluntary. **Voluntary attention** is selective. As their involvement with a particular product increases, through a process called **selective attention,** consumers focus on information that is relevant to them. Thus a man who is interested in buying an expensive camera will actively seek information about the product. When reading newspapers, he will be on the lookout for ads and articles about the product sought. Conversely, he will tend not to focus attention on marketing communications he does not perceive as relevant to his quest. Consumers' tendency to selectively attend to communications is a major problem for advertisers on television and radio. Exposing consumers to a message doesn't do any good if they decide to ignore it because of their low involvement level.

Attention can also be involuntary. **Involuntary attention** occurs when consumers are exposed to something surprising, novel, threatening, or unexpected and they respond autonomically by turning toward and allocating attention to the stimulus. This response, which the consumer cannot consciously control, is called an **orientation reflex.**[42] Because most advertisements are unrelated to the immediate goals of their targets, marketers go to some trouble to elicit the orientation reflex. Figure 3-8 portrays an ad from ITT Automotive that features a huge stop sign. Because we are conditioned to respond to stop signs, the ad elicits an orientation reaction.

Both voluntary and involuntary attention are followed by an allocation of cognitive capacity to the stimulus. Whenever people attend to information, they experience physiological arousal. This arousal may be manipulated by an increase in blood pressure, a change in brain wave patterns, a quickening of breathing, a slight sweating of the hands,

ITT AUTOMOTIVE
CREATED SOMETHING THAT MAKES DRIVING
SAFER THAN EVER BEFORE.

(WE'LL GIVE YOU A HINT.)

ITT Automotive is not only a pioneer in hydraulic drum and disk brake technology, it has become the world's leading innovator and manufacturer of four-wheel passenger car anti-lock brake and traction control systems. Eighteen of the most highly regarded auto makers here and abroad depend on them.

ITT Automotive, part of ITT's Manufactured Products group, is also a global supplier of a variety of other products: ITT Koni shock absorbers. ITT SWF windshield wiper systems, switches and rear lighting modules. Fluid handling systems. Plus a wide range of body hardware and structural components.

In addition, we've given the green light to reinvest $2.7 billion in ITT Automotive for engineering, R&D and capital expansion over the next five years. At ITT, our mission is to make your car a safer place. Stop, and think about it. **ITT** We're adding more than just our name.

Figure 3-8

The stop sign triggers an orientation reflex that increases the likelihood that consumers will pay attention to this ad for ITT Automotive.

dilation of the pupils, even a rise in eardrum temperature. So one way of assessing the impact of advertisements is to measure such physiological signals in consumers who are viewing the ad. An example is by measuring heart rates or pupil sizes.

Capturing Consumers' Attention

Marketers attempt to capture consumers' attention by varying the nature of the stimulus they receive. The goal is to activate the orientation reflex by adroitly creating stimuli that surprise, threaten, or violate expectations. The clever use of surprise is illustrated by the "big eye" in the United Airlines ad reproduced in Figure 3-9. Similarly, the "Budweiser Frogs" in the TV ads are effective partly because of the use of surprise.

Figure 3-9
The computer-enhanced image of the woman's eye creates surprise and draws attention to this United Airlines ad.

A variety of strategies can be employed to activate the orientation reflex. For example, movement attracts attention. Thus on highways and in cities retailers use neon signs that simulate motion. Unusual sounds can also activate the orientation response, which is why television advertisers have taken to using distinctive nonverbal sounds. For example, ads for the financial corporation Shearson Lehman Brothers had a buzzing sound that grew louder as the commercial progressed. The ad agency created the noise to mimic the sound of thinking, which was called "Minds Over Money" in the ad campaign. Shearson's executives found that ad awareness increased by 50 percent with the use of the funny sound. General Electric reported a similar positive response to its "beep ads," in which a symphony of peculiar beeps was played by digital kitchen appliances.[43]

Another stimulus factor that influences attention is the size or magnitude of the stimulus. All else being equal, large-print advertisements are more attention-grabbing than small-print ones, and a loud television commercial is more likely to be processed than a soft one.

Color also draws attention, particularly when it contrasts with a sea of black-and-white print materials and consumers are in a low involvement state.[44] Thus graphic artists who employ the Gestalt principle of contrast increase the likelihood that consumers will attend to an advertisement. This principle refers to the substantial divergence of a stimulus from surrounding background stimuli. A loud noise in a quiet room and a print ad with very little copy in a sea of verbose ads illustrate the Gestalt concept of contrast.

Finally, marketers can command attention by placing ads in circumstances in which consumers have little choice but to attend to the information presented to them. An outstanding example of this tactic is the commercials that are shown in movie theaters before the film begins. Theater operators, however, are extremely cautious about what kinds of ads to show for fear of annoying customers. In fact, theater chains regularly screen ads to ensure that they are appropriate and avoid a hard sell. Thus the commercials you see in movie theaters tend to be highly lavish productions. Although the cost per thousand viewers is higher than that for television advertising, it is claimed that theater advertising is recalled three times better. Still, many national advertisers are reluctant to use movie advertising for fear of associating their products with violent or sex-laden movies. In addition, Walt Disney Productions forbids theater owners from showing advertisements with any of its movies.[45]

Table 3-5 summarizes the stimulus factors marketers use to attract consumers' attention.[46]

THE COMPREHENSION STAGE

As we noted earlier in the chapter, in the comprehension stage of information processing consumers perceptually organize and interpret information in order to derive meaning from it. **Perceptual organization** refers to the processes through which people perceive the shapes, forms, figures, and lines in their visual world. In the **interpretation process** people draw upon experience, memory, and expectations to attach meaning to a stimulus.

Comprehension is a particularly important concept for advertisers. Researchers have found that when people fail to correctly comprehend an advertisement, they are generally less persuaded by it.[47] In one study a random sample of 1,347 adults was asked to read a short communication and immediately afterward given a six-item quiz on its contents. Somewhat surprisingly, the respondents answered only 63 percent of the questions correctly. Considering that these respondents were in a high-involvement state and answered the questions immediately after reading the communication, this research indicates that consumer miscomprehension is a major problem for marketers.[48] (Table 3-6 presents the communication and the quiz used in the study.)

Perceptual Organization

What do you see when you look at Figure 3-10? The ad's goal is to have you perceive the light and dark images as various types of lightbulbs. Philips Lighting Company made excellent use of the principle of closure to create this ad. This principle of perceptual organization says that our perceptual system automatically fills in incomplete lines to form a coherent image. Through the process of closure, then, people comprehend a "whole" figure, even if there are gaps in it.

Much of the work on perceptual organization was done by German psychologists active in the early part of this century. Called **Gestalt psychologists,** these researchers attempted to identify the rules that govern how we take disjointed stimuli and make sense

---

Advertisement and Quiz for Comprehension Study

INCREASE YOUR CAR'S CARGO CAPACITY
By Slaton L. White

When you replace your large car with a smaller, more fuel-efficient one, expect to forfeit a lot of storage space. Many of the newer cars have sacrificed trunk space for less weight—all in the name of fuel economy. Short of jettisoning one of the kids, leaving your luggage behind, or buying a mini pickup instead of a car, what options does the owner of a downsize automobile have when he wants to head out on vacation or carry large, bulky cargo?

Basically, there are two options: tow the gear in a trailer or tote it on the roof. Both choices involve trade-offs, most noticeably a measurable decrease in fuel economy as well as a marked change in the car's handling characteristics. However, many manufacturers offer a broad range of products designed to minimize the trade-offs.

Sample Quiz

The instructions for the quiz were as follows:

Based upon the passage you just read, which of the following statements is True and which is False?

Remember: Base your answers *only* upon what you think the passage said or implied.

1. To increase space for a downsize automobile, there are three main options. (False/Fact)
2. When a trailer is added, a subcompact has all the advantages of a larger car. (False/Inference)
3. Toting gear on a roof will decrease fuel economy. (True/Fact)
4. In general, you should *not* buy a subcompact if you have a family unless you have to. (False/Inference)
5. Manufacturers offer products that are designed to minimize problems with towing. (True/Fact)
6. You should *not* give in to a lack of space if you own a subcompact car. (True/Inference)

TABLE 3-6

Figure 3-10

Principles of closure and figure-ground are illustrated in this ad for Philips lightbulbs. (Courtesy of Philips Lighting Company.)

out of the shapes and forms to which we are exposed. *Gestalt* is the German word for "pattern" or "configuration," which suggests these psychologists' quest to understand how people perceive patterns in the world.

Figure 3-11 illustrates a number of Gestalt rules of perceptual organization. Many of these rules deal with how people decide what things go together. For example, the "rule of common fate" states that elements that move in the same direction are assumed to belong to each other. Other rules applicable to the problem of deciding "what-goes-with-what" are similarity, proximity, and closure.

Another question of interest to the Gestalt psychologists was how people distinguish figure from ground in their visual world. Example 4 in Figure 3-11 illustrates the figure-ground principle. At one moment the reversible figure resembles two faces looking at each other. The next moment it looks like a vase. The image switches back and forth because our brain cannot decipher whether the black or the white portion of the drawing is the figure. The figure-ground principle is useful to advertisers, who want their product to be the figure moving against the background of an ad because it is the figure that attracts attention.

In marketing, perceptual organization is generally applied to visual communications, such as print and television advertising and package design. For example, when drawing an ad, the artist may consciously or unconsciously use Gestalt principles to create the desired effect, paying particular attention to the figure-ground concept because a product will not be noticed unless it stands out from the background of a print ad. If, however, the advertiser's goal is to associate the product with something else desirable—such as a celebrity endorser—the principles of proximity, closure, and common fate could be more useful.

Researchers have recently confirmed that consumers' feelings about a product can be influenced by Gestalt processes such as closure. One study involved severely cropping vi-

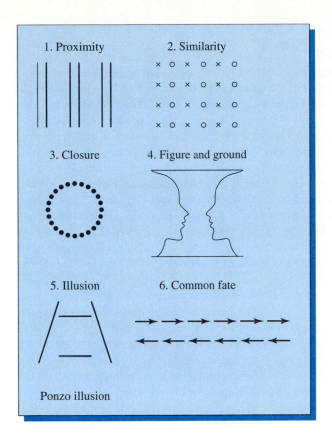

Figure 3-11
Some principles of perceptual
organization.

sual material in ads for beer and jeans and showing the ads to subjects who had been divided into high- and low-involvement groups (the high-involvement subjects were offered the chance to win a pair of jeans).[49] If the respondents were highly involved in the task and if an object in the ad was severely cropped (e.g., a truck in the beer ad was cropped off), evaluations of the product were higher than when the object was not cropped. The study's authors concluded that when an object in an ad is cropped, the viewer's perceptual system attempts to "close" the image and make sense of it. This forces the viewer into a more extensive analysis of the ad, which, in turn, raises the viewer's evaluation of the product. These and similar study results suggest that the employment of Gestalt principles such as closure can favorably affect consumer evaluations of advertisements and products.

Interpretation

Through the interpretation process, consumers arrive at an understanding of what a stimulus is. The process begins during the attention phase and continues after it, as consumers attempt to gain an understanding of what the stimulus is and how they should react to it. In this interpretation phase of information processing, people retrieve from long-term memory information pertinent to the stimulus, as well as expectancies regarding what the stimulus "should be like." Personal inclinations and biases also influence consumers' interpretation of the stimulus.

As we pointed out earlier, a major headache for marketers is that consumers often interpret the same stimulus differently. In fact, cross-cultural marketing affords some classic examples of differential interpretation. Colors, for instance, have different meanings in different countries. Yellow flowers, which are a sign of death in Mexico, denote infidelity in France.[50]

The Role of Expectations   Consumer expectations strongly affect their comprehension and interpretation of marketing stimuli. **Expectations** are a person's prior beliefs about what should happen in a given situation. The fact that expectations influence the interpretation of information created a big problem for Adolph Coors, in 1988, when the company decided to change the label on its flagship brand from "Banquet Beer" to "Original Draft." The change was made in response to Miller Brewing Company's successful new market entry "Genuine Draft." Unfortunately, many Coors drinkers in the Southwest believed that the taste of the beer had been altered—for the worse—along with the label. As one Coors executive explained, "We tried to convince them it was the same product, and they'd say, 'Oh, no it isn't.' " But for many Coors drinkers, label change translated into beverage change. As a result of this expectation, they perceived a change in taste where there was none. When the company reverted to the old label, a Coors distributor described customers as being elated and saying, "You brought it back just for me?" His response to each was, "You bet I did, old buddy."[51]

The moral is that market researchers should assess the impact of consumers' expectations on their evaluations of marketing stimuli. One research study vividly demonstrates how taste perception can be affected by visual cues that influence taste expectations. In this study vanilla pudding was colored either dark brown, medium brown, or light brown by adding a tasteless and odorless food coloring. Respondents were then asked to rate the puddings on a variety of scales. About 62 percent said the dark-colored pudding had the best chocolate flavor and was the thickest. The lighter-colored puddings were rated as more creamy than the dark pudding. In the words of the researchers, "It's the consumer's subjective perception of the product that counts, not the product's objective reality."[52] Other researchers have found that food colored in unexpected hues (e.g., potatoes dyed blue) can actually make people physically ill.[53]

Expectations also influence how people perceive the gas gauge in their car, as the accompanying Consumer Behavior Factoid describes.

The Price-Quality Relationship   Consumer expectations can also have an important impact on pricing strategies. In general, the greater the price, the less likely a consumer is to buy a particular product. (Basic microeconomic theory makes this prediction through the idea

---

Consumer Behavior Factoid

Question: When Cadillac improved the accuracy of the gas gauge in one of its models, how did consumers react?

Answer: Consumers were very unhappy. They perceived that their new car was getting very poor gas mileage even though, in reality, its engine was more fuel efficient than the engines in previous models. Cadillac engineers identified two reasons for the misperception. First, consumers expect their gas gauge to stay on "full" for a long period of time. Second, they expect to drive many miles before the gas gauge reaches the "halfway" point. For many years car manufacturers had been rigging gas gauges to "lie" to drivers: they would stick on "full" too long, use up well over half the tank before the gauge moved to the "halfway" point, and read "empty" long before the tank ran out of gas. By the way, Cadillac soon changed the calibration of the gas gauge on this model to meet customer expectations, and Cadillac drivers were extremely happy about the great gas mileage of their new cars.

Source: Mac Demere, "Little White Lies from Your Dashboard," *Motor Trend,* September 1996, p. 79.

of the downward sloping demand curve.) However, in some circumstances consumers develop expectations concerning the **price-quality relationship.** That is, within a certain price range for a product, they expect that higher prices indicate greater quality.[54] The price-quality relationship is probably ingrained in people from childhood through hearing such aphorisms as "You get what you pay for." One summary of the evidence on the price-quality relationship noted that price may be used to indicate the quality of a product in the following circumstances:

1. The consumer has some confidence that in this situation price predicts quality.
2. There are real or perceived quality variations among brands.
3. Actual quality is difficult to judge by objective means or by brand name or store image.
4. Larger differences in price have a greater impact on perceived quality differences than do smaller price differences.
5. Consumers use price as an indicator of quality more frequently for familiar brands than for unfamiliar brands.[55]

Recent research indicates that a product's characteristics and its price combine to impact consumers' perceptions of its quality. Significantly, the more information consumers receive about a product's characteristics, the less likely they are to use price as a quality indicator. Researchers have also found that perceived quality and perceived price combine to influence the perceived value of a brand. In this case, interestingly, the higher the price of the product, the lower its perceived value. **Perceived value,** then, can be defined as the trade-off consumers make between perceived quality and perceived price when evaluating a brand.[56]

To conclude, there is a price-quality relationship, but it is not a simple one. In certain circumstances consumers will infer *quality* from a high price. However, a higher price will also lower the perceived *value* of a brand. The implication for managers is that they need to exercise extreme care in raising prices as a means of increasing sales.

SEMIOTICS

Consider the problem faced by video movie distributors: How do you get consumers to even notice, let alone rent, a video of a movie they have never heard of that is lost in a sea of video boxes at the local Blockbuster? Answer: Make a dynamite video box. The strategy was put succinctly by one executive: "A box has to look mainstream, sell the cast, tell the story, and jump off the shelf."[57] So: How do you make a dynamite video box that "jumps off the shelf"? Answer: Use great symbolism.

When the NC-17 video for *Showgirls* was released in 1996, the video box, as described in *The New York Times*, showed a "curve of flesh running from a woman's head to her toes. On the box of an R-rated alternative . . . the skin extends only through the cleavage."[58] The length of the "curve" symbolized the extent of the nudity in the two versions of the film. While *Showgirls* was a flop in theaters, the video sold extremely well, partly because of the symbols used on the video box.

The investigation of symbols and their meanings is called **semiotics.** This field of study originated in the desire to analyze how people obtain meaning from **signs,** or the words, gestures, pictures, products, and logos used to communicate information from one person to another. Even nonverbal sounds can communicate meaning. For example, Harley-Davidson attempted in 1995 to trademark the distinctive sound made by its motorcycles. The guttural growl of Harley bikes has been compared to a growling animal saying "potato-potato-potato." According to a spokesperson for the company, "A lot of owners tell us they buy a Harley just for the sound." That sound, of course, symbolizes much more than the motorcycle itself. It also stands for the Harley-Davidson image of macho, nonconformist, independent men and women. Competitors are fighting Harley's petition in court because the ability to trademark a product's sounds threatens to open up a Pandora's box of problems. As one critic pointed out, "How about Rice Krispies? Do you think you can trademark the snap, crackle, pop?"[59]

The discipline of semiotics has been studied in one form or another since before the time of Socrates.[60] Indeed, some have argued that what sets the human species apart from other animals is our ability to adroitly use and manipulate symbols.[61] Semiotics is highly relevant to the entire area of promotional strategy in marketing because it is through the use of various symbols or signs that marketers communicate information about a product or service to consumers.

Semiotics is also highly useful for gaining an experiential perspective on consumer behavior. In order to understand how people emotionally react to symbols in the environment, one must know the shared meanings of various signs. Figure 3-12 shows the logo of Eskimo Joe's, a restaurant/bar in Stillwater, Oklahoma. (Stillwater is the home of Oklahoma State University, where one of the authors of this textbook teaches.) What does this logo with grinning Eskimo and drooling dog symbolize to you? When the logo was developed for the restaurant, it was meant to represent a place to have a

Figure 3-12

Eskimo Joe's logo symbolizes cold beer and a good time. (Courtesy of Stan Clark Worldwide.)

good time, one where you could buy the coldest beer in town. The logo proved so successful that Eskimo Joe's owner, Stan Clark, started putting it on T-shirts. By 1992 the Eskimo Joe's T-shirts were the second-largest-selling promotional T-shirts in the world—exceeded only by those of New York's Hard Rock Cafe. In fact, the success of the T-shirt spawned a new enterprise that is far more profitable to Stan Clark than the restaurant business—selling clothing all over the world. He is now a wealthy entrepreneur, largely owing to the appealing symbolism of a grinning Eskimo named Joe and his dog Buffy.

Semiotics has relevance to a number of consumer behavior areas—consider the Freudian symbolism in advertising, symbols used to express one's self-concept, and signs employed in cross-cultural communications. Researchers working in this field emphasize that meaning is partly determined by cultural context. Thus a sign may have entirely different meanings in two different cultures. For instance, animals are frequently paired with products in the United States because Americans admire and cherish many animals. In some Asian cultures, however, animals are viewed negatively. Advertisements by an optical company showing cute little animals wearing eyeglasses failed miserably in Thailand because animals symbolize a lower form of life to the Thais.

Symbols and signs are used to communicate meaning to others. A theoretical framework has been proposed for explaining how signs function as communications. This paradigm, called *semiosis analysis*, is shown in Figure 3-13. Semiosis analysis involves identifying an object, a sign, and an interpretant. The object is the thing whose meaning is to be communicated (e.g., a product, a person, an idea); the sign is the symbol or set of symbols used to communicate the meaning of the object; and the interpretant is a person's reaction to and meaning derived from the sign.[62]

In Figure 3-13 the object whose meaning is to be communicated is a shirt. The sign is the logo on the shirt—this could be a pony (Ralph Lauren), a boot (L. L. Bean), or a "swoosh" (Nike). Logos are developed to impart meaning to the object. Thus the interpretants for the pony logo may be expensive, high quality, sophisticated, snooty, and stylish, while those for the boot logo may be practical, high quality, and outdoor-oriented. Interpretants derived from the swoosh logo could be sports-oriented, high quality, and (maybe) sexy.

The decoding of symbols occurs in the comprehension stage of information processing. Marketing and advertising managers must be alert to the use of symbols and how their target market will interpret them. Indeed, advertising has been described as "the modern substitute for myth and ritual and, directly or indirectly, it uses semiotics (the science of signs) to invest products with meaning for a culture whose dominant focus is consumption."[63]

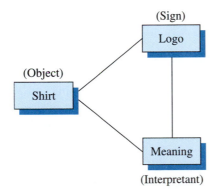

Figure 3-13
Semiosis analysis.

We learn the meaning of signs in our culture fairly early in life through acculturation. It seems that preschoolers have only a minimal ability to recognize the social implications of consumption choices. By the second grade, however, children are capable of making inferences about what it means to purchase a Camaro versus a Caprice or a new, modern house versus an older, traditional one. By the sixth grade, these skills are almost fully developed in most youngsters. Interestingly, some research shows that college students evidence the most consumption stereotyping of any age group, and that this stereotyping tendency weakens with age.[64]

Semiotics is particularly applicable to brand positioning. For example, colleges and universities are currently working hard to refine—in some cases, to change—their logos and mascots. According to the university trade publication *The Chronicle of Higher Education*, universities are attempting to "Create a catchy symbol that paints a thousand words about the college and entices people to buy shirts and notebooks bearing the emblem." In the words of one college official, a distinctive logo "sets an institution apart in the eyes of alumni, donors, and students." In addition to helping to position a university, logos can bring a university millions of dollars, either directly through the sale of T-shirts, hats, and other memorabilia, or indirectly through the licensing of the logo to vendors, typically for about $1.00 per use. (Thus $1.00 of the price of a T-shirt goes to the university for the use of its logo.) When Villanova University updated its logo to a more aggressive-looking wildcat, profits from license fees jumped nearly 600 percent.[65]

Semiotics and the study of symbols are fascinating areas of study for marketers. Ideas from this field will appear throughout the text.

A MANAGERIAL APPLICATIONS ANALYSIS OF THE FORD TAURUS/SABLE CASE

The managerial implications of knowing how consumers process information are broad-ranging. The introductory case on the Ford Taurus and Sable illustrates how an understanding of consumer perceptions can influence managerial strategy. Our analysis in this section examines the case from the perspective of 1994–1995, when marketers at Ford Motor Company were deciding how to introduce the new Taurus and Sable.

Problem Identification

The basic marketing problems suggested by the case are these: How will consumers perceive the radical new designs of the revamped Taurus and Sable models? What, if anything, should Ford do to minimize negative reactions?

The Consumer Behavior Analysis and Its Managerial Implications

Several concepts derived from the study of perception would be useful in developing managerial strategies for answering these questions: consumer involvement, the just noticeable difference, the butterfly curve, and perceptual organization. Table 3-7 presents the managerial implications of these consumer concepts for the Taurus/Sable case.

Consumer Involvement For most consumers, purchasing a car is a high-involvement decision. Obviously, consumers with a high situational involvement due to an immediate need to purchase an auto are very likely to attend to promotional materials about car lines. Less

Managerial Implications of Consumer Behavior Concepts in Ford Taurus/Sable Case

Consumer Behavior Concept	Managerial Implications
Involvement	*Market research*. Identify market segments having enduring and/or situational involvement. *Segmentation*. Create different marketing strategies for reaching consumers with enduring vs. situational involvement. *Promotional strategy*. Develop divergent messages and use different media to reach different targeted segments.
Just noticeable difference	*Product design*. Ensure that the Taurus/Sable is noticeably different from competitors. *Promotional strategy*. Enhance perception that the Taurus/Sable is a unique vehicle. *Environmental analysis*. Analyze competition in order to develop a unique vehicle.
Butterfly curve	*Promotional strategy*. Release photos of cars early to hasten the adaptation process.
Perceptual organization	*Promotional strategy*. Focus advertising on the unique design of the vehicles rather than "trick up" the ads with extraneous visual material (e.g., beautiful models) to create a brand image.

TABLE 3-7

obviously perhaps, consumers with a high level of enduring involvement also tend to expose themselves to and attend to such messages even if they are not currently in the market for an auto.

Consumer involvement has implications for several managerial areas, especially marketing research, segmentation analysis, and promotional strategy. Ford should have conducted market research studies to identify market segments with different levels of product involvement and targeted these segments with different messages or reached them through different media. (As noted earlier, scales have been developed to assist marketers in assessing variations in enduring involvement.) For example, it would have made sense for Ford to specifically target as a market segment consumers with high enduring involvement with autos, for such people are opinion leaders. By identifying the characteristics of this group, the magazines they read, and so forth, management could have designed advertisements that would reach and influence them.

The Just Noticeable Difference The "just noticeable difference" applies in this case to product design, promotional strategy, and environmental analysis. The radical redesign of the Taurus and Sable should have suggested to management that consumers would readily perceive a just noticeable difference between these models and other cars in the market. Readily identifiable differences have strong implications for positioning. Figure 3-14 presents a perceptual map of how consumers would likely perceive the Taurus and Sable in relation to competing models in the same product category. Note that the two Ford models are positioned as being moderately priced and highly expressive. The competitor closest to this position is the Dodge Intrepid, but this car is significantly less expensive. The figure suggests that Ford could have built a strong brand image for its Taurus and Sable models as moderately priced, highly expressive, and technologically advanced.

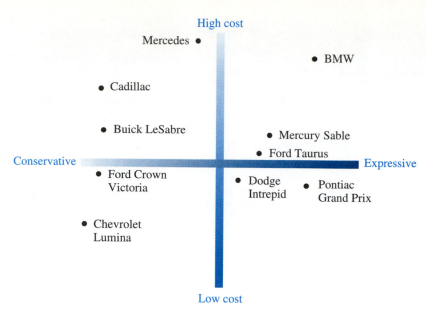

Figure 3-14
Positioning of Taurus/Sable autos.

Butterfly Curve The butterfly curve has implications for promotional strategy. Because of the radical redesign of the new models, Ford should have guessed that consumers' initial reactions would be negative. As we pointed out in the introductory case, the company could have mimicked its 1986 strategy of publicizing the cars' design a full six months prior to their launch date to prepare consumers for the startling look of the cars. Management's failure to do this was certainly a factor in the initial resistance to the brand.

The obverse side of the coin was that with such a distinctive product, Ford was in the enviable position of not having to worry about capturing consumers' attention, though the radical reshaping of the models could cause an orientation reaction when customers first encountered the company's promotional materials. Ford should have capitalized on the elliptical design of the cars by advertising them early on as heralds of a new age—the twenty-first century.

Perceptual Organization The principles of perceptual organization have particular application to promotional strategy. The distinctive design of the Taurus/Sable models made these cars stand out. Indeed, the obvious advertising strategy would be to simply show photographs of the car in various settings emphasizing use—or in settings with symbolic value. Because of their unique design, there was little danger that the Taurus/Sable could be swallowed up by the background in such advertisements.

Managerial Recommendations

Four managerial recommendations emerge from our consumer behavior analysis of this case.

Recommendation 1 Employ marketing research to profile consumers who have high and low involvement in the automobile purchase process. Then segment the market into high-

and low-involvement consumers and develop different promotional strategies to reach and influence these segments.

Recommendation 2 Take advantage of the fact that consumers perceive a wide difference between the Taurus/Sable and their competitors to clearly differentiate the models in advertisements and sales messages.

Recommendation 3 The concept of the butterfly curve suggests that when companies produce a highly novel design like the new Taurus, they must adapt consumers to it gradually by releasing photos and information about the brand well before launching the product.

Recommendation 4 Principles of perceptual organization suggest that the models' radical shape will clearly stand out against the background of ads. Instruct graphic artists to take advantage of this by positioning the cars in ads in ways that enhance consumers' perception of them as figures moving against the background.

SUMMARY

Information processing is the process through which consumers are exposed to information, attend to it, comprehend it, place it in memory, and retrieve it for later use. Several areas are closely related to the study of information processing, including the study of consumer involvement and the processes of exposure, attention, comprehension, and memory. The field of semiotics also has strong relevance for the study of comprehension processes.

Consumer involvement refers to the level of perceived personal importance and/or interest a stimulus evokes. Situational involvement is short-term; it changes as the person, product, situation, or communication changes. In contrast, enduring involvement refers to a longer-term commitment and concern with a product class. A number of dimensions of involvement have been identified, including self-expressive importance, hedonic importance, practical relevance, and purchase risk.

Exposure refers to the process in which consumers initially receive information through their senses. Consumers selectively expose themselves to information. Advertisers try to prevent consumers from selectively exposing themselves to television commercials through remote-control channel changing, or "zapping." Marketers need to understand sensation—the immediate impression left by the firing of nerve fibers in response to the physical stimulation of the senses—since it is an important aspect of the exposure process. Aspects of sensation especially important for marketing are absolute and differential thresholds, the adaptation level, the butterfly curve, and subliminal perception.

Attention is another important area of information processing. Preattention is the process through which people unconsciously analyze information for its relevance and importance to them. Voluntary attention refers to consumers' active search for information in order to achieve some type of goal. Through selective attention consumers focus on stimuli that match their goals. Involuntary attention refers to consumers' exposure to a surprising, novel, or unexpected stimulus. Through the orientation reflex, people focus attention on such a stimulus in order to comprehend its nature.

Comprehension, another important area in information processing, refers to how consumers organize and interpret information. Marketers need to recognize that different people can perceive the same stimulus in quite divergent ways because of variations in expectancies and in the ways in which they organize information.

Semiotics is the study of symbols and the meanings that people obtain from signs, or the words, gestures, pictures, products, and logos used to communicate information from one person to another. Semiosis analysis identifies how signs function to communicate information and involves identifying an object, a sign, and an interpretant (a person's reaction to and the meaning derived from a sign).

absolute threshold
adaptation
adaptation level
attention
attention stage
butterfly curve
comprehension
comprehension stage
consumer information processing
consumer involvement

enduring involvement
expectations
exposure stage
Gestalt psychologists
incremental effects theory
information
interpretation process
involuntary attention
involvement responses
just noticeable difference (JND)

orientation reflex
perceived value
perception
perceptual organization
preattention
price-quality relationship
psychodynamic theory of arousal
selective attention
selective exposure
semiotics

sensation
signs
situational involvement
spontaneous brand switching
subliminal perception
voluntary attention
Weber's Law
zapping

REVIEW QUESTIONS

1. Define the concept of information.

2. Define the concept of information processing.

3. Distinguish the concepts of exposure, attention, and comprehension.

4. What is meant by the term *consumer involvement?*

5. What are the types of consumer involvement? What happens when consumers are in a high-involvement state?

6. Briefly discuss what happens during the exposure stage of information processing.

7. What does the study of sensation involve?

8. Can subliminal perception have an impact on consumers? Why or why not?

9. What are absolute and difference thresholds?

10. Discuss the concepts of selective exposure and attention.

11. Define and give a marketing example of Weber's Law. Why is it better to use the term *just meaningful difference* rather than *just noticeable difference* in marketing?

12. What is meant by adaptation level? How does adaptation level relate to the butterfly curve?

13. Discuss what is meant by attention. What are two types of attention?

14. What happens during the comprehension stage of information processing?

15. What is the relationship between expectations and interpretation?

16. Identify five of the six principles of perceptual organization discussed in this chapter.

17. Briefly discuss the relationship that consumers frequently perceive between price and quality.

18. What is meant by the term *semiotics?* What happens during semiosis analysis?

DISCUSSION QUESTIONS

1. Consumer involvement is influenced by the product, the situation, the communication received, and the personality of the individual consumer. Give two examples each of high- and low-involvement products, high- and low-involvement situations, and high- and low-involvement communications. Describe a case in which you were highly involved with a product and an acquaintance was not, noting how this involvement difference affected information processing for the two of you.

2. Select three products with different prices, ranging from less than a dollar to thousands of dollars, and for each product indicate what you would consider to be

the JND for a sale price. To what extent do your JNDs exemplify Weber's Law?

3. How much use do you think clothing designers make of the concept of the adaptation level? If they understood the concept of the butterfly curve, would that make a difference in their behavior?

4. Select three print advertisements. Identify in each all the instances you can of stimulus factors being used to gain your attention.

5. Using the same three advertisements, identify as many examples as you can of perceptual organization.

6. Look through magazines that contain cigarette and liquor advertisements. Find three possible examples of subliminal messages in the ads. Do you think these embedded symbols were placed there deliberately?

7. Interview five of your friends to discover cases in which they used price as an indicator of quality. To what extent do these cases match the occasions discussed in the chapter when price is most frequently used as an indicator of quality?

8. Watch a popular television show, such as *Friends*. Discuss how consumer products/services were used as symbols to help develop the plot of the show.

9. Go through one or more popular magazines, carefully examining the print advertisements. Identify three examples of symbols used in the ads. Then conduct a semiosis analysis for each ad showing how the signs communicate meaning about the product or service.

ENDNOTES

1. Keith Naughton and Kathleen Kerwin, "Backfiring at Ford," *Business Week*, December 25, 1995, pp. 36–37.

2. Lindsay Chappell, "Taurus Takes Industry Slings and Arrows—Again," *Automotive News*, February 19, 1996, pp. 1, 77.

3. John Pierson, "Ford Labors Over Tin Buttons and Dials in Quest for a Driver-Friendly Dashboard," *The Wall Street Journal*, May 20, 1996, pp. B1, B7.

4. Rich Ceppos, "The 1986 Mercury Sable," *Car and Driver*, March 1985, pp. 43–46.

5. Charles Osgood, *Method and Theory in Experimental Psychology* (New York: Oxford University Press, 1964).

6. Norbert Wiener, "Cybernetics in History," in *Modern Systems Research for the Behavioral Scientist*, Walter Buckley, ed. (Chicago: Aldine, 1968), pp. 31–36.

7. Richard L. Celsi and Jerry C. Olson, "The Role of Involvement in Attention and Comprehension Processes," *Journal of Consumer Research*, Vol. 15 (September 1988), pp. 210–224. See also Anthony Greenwald and Clark Leavitt, "Audience Involvement in Advertising: Four Levels," *Journal of Consumer Research*, Vol. 11 (June 1984), pp. 581–592. For a general review of the strength of involvement effects, see Carolyn Costley, "Meta Analysis of Involvement Research," in *Advances in Con-*sumer Research*, Vol. 15, Michael Houston, ed. (Provo, UT: Association for Consumer Research, 1988), pp. 554–562.

8. See John H. Antil, "Conceptualization and Operationalization of Involvement," in *Advances in Consumer Research*, Vol. 11, Thomas C. Kinnear, ed. (Ann Arbor, MI: Association for Consumer Research, 1984), pp. 203–209.

9. Marsha Richins and Peter H. Bloch, "After the New Wears Off: The Temporal Context of Product Involvement," *Journal of Consumer Research*, Vol. 13 (September 1986), pp. 280–285.

10. Marsha Richins, Peter H. Bloch, and Edward F. McQuarrie, "How Enduring and Situational Involvement Combine to Create Involvement Responses," *Journal of Consumer Psychology*, Vol. 1 (1992), pp. 143–153.

11. Richins, Bloch, and McQuarrie, "How Enduring and Situational Involvement Combine."

12. These four dimensions were obtained from a synthesis of several research articles: Kapil Jain and Narasimhan Srinivasan, "An Empirical Assessment of Multiple Operationalizations of Involvement," *Advances in Consumer Research*, Vol. 17 (Provo, UT: Association for Consumer Research, 1990), pp. 594–602; Thomas Jensen, Les Carlson, and Carolyn Tripp, "The Di-mensionality of Involvement: An Empirical Test," *Advances in Consumer Research*, Vol. 16 (Provo, UT: Association for Consumer Research, 1989), pp. 680–689; Robin Higie and Lawrence Feick, "Enduring Involvement: Conceptual and Measurement Issues," *Advances in Consumer Research*, Vol. 16 (Provo, UT: Association for Consumer Research, 1989), pp. 690–696.

13. Kenneth Schneider and William Rodgers, "An 'Importance' Subscale for the Consumer Involvement Profile," *Advances in Consumer Research*, Vol. 23, Kim Corfman and John Lynch, eds. (Provo, UT: Association for Consumer Research, 1996), pp. 249–254.

14. Richard E. Petty, John T. Cacioppo, and David Schumann, "Central and Peripheral Routes to Advertising Effectiveness: The Moderating Role of Involvement," *Journal of Consumer Research*, Vol. 10 (September 1983), pp. 135–146.

15. Herbert Krugman, "The Impact of Television in Advertising: Learning Without Involvement," *Public Opinion Quarterly*, Vol. 30, pp. 583–596.

16. Jong-Won Park and Manoj Hastak, "Memory-Based Product Judgments: Effects of Involvement at Encoding and Retrieval," *Journal of Consumer Re-*

search, Vol. 21 (December 1994), pp. 534–547.

17. For a discussion of how increased involvement and physiological arousal impact the processing of information, see: David M. Sanbonmatsu and Frank R. Kardes, "The Effects of Physiological Arousal on Information Processing and Persuasion," *Journal of Consumer Research*, Vol.15 (December 1988), pp. 379–385.

18. Alex Markels and Matt Murray, "Call It Dumbsizing: Why Some Companies Regret Cost-Cutting," *The Wall Street Journal*, May 14, 1996, pp. A1, A6.

19. Bernie Whalen, "$6 Billion Down the Drain!" *Marketing News*, September 14, 1984, pp. 1, 37.

20. "Background on Zapping," *Marketing News*, September 14, 1984, p. 36.

21. Whalen, "$6 Billion Down the Drain!"

22. Timothy E. Moore, "Subliminal Advertising: What You See Is What You Get," *Journal of Marketing*, Vol. 46 (Spring 1982), pp. 38–47.

23. Ibid.

24. W. Key, *Subliminal Seduction* (Englewood Cliffs, NJ: Prentice Hall, 1973).

25. Moore, "Subliminal Advertising."

26. William Kilbourne, Scott Painton, and D. Ridley, "The Effect of Sexual Embedding on Responses to Magazine Advertisements," *Journal of Advertising*, Vol. 14 (1985), pp. 48–56.

27. Del Hawkins, "The Effects of Subliminal Stimulation on Drive Level and Brand Preference," *Journal of Marketing Research*, Vol. 7 (1970), pp. 322–326.

28. R. Cuperfain and T. K. Clarke, "A New Perspective on Subliminal Perception," *Journal of Advertising*, Vol. 14 (1985), pp. 36–41.

29. Joel Saegert, "Why Marketing Should Quit Giving Subliminal Advertising the Benefit of the Doubt," *Psychology and Marketing*, Summer 1987, pp. 107–120.

30. Philip M. Merikle and Jim Cheesman, "Current Status of Research on Subliminal Perception," in *Advances in Consumer Research*, Vol. 14, Melanie Wallendorf and Paul Anderson, eds. (Provo, UT: Association for Consumer Research, 1987), pp. 298–302.

31. David Stipp, "A Flavor Analyst Should Never Ask, 'What's for Lunch?' " *The Wall Street Journal*, August 3, 1988, pp. 1, 10.

32. Bruce Buchanan, Moshe Givon, and Arieh Goldman, "Measurement of Discrimination Ability in Taste Tests: An Empirical Investigation," *Journal of Marketing Research*, Vol. 24 (May 1987), pp. 154–163.

33. Richard Lee Miller, "Dr. Weber and the Consumer," *Journal of Marketing*, January 1962, pp. 57–61.

34. John Koten, "Why Do Hot Dogs Come in Packs of 10 and Buns in 8s or 12s?" *The Wall Street Journal*, September 21, 1984, pp. 1, 26.

35. See Leon G. Schiffman and Leslie L. Kanuk, Figure 6–1, in "Sequential Changes in Packaging That Fall Below the J.N.D.," *Consumer Behavior* (Upper Saddle River, NJ: Prentice Hall, 1983), p. 140.

36. "Cup Runneth Over," *UC Berkeley Wellness Letter*, May 1996, p. 8.

37. Jonathan Dahl, "Tracking Travel," *The Wall Street Journal*, May 15, 1990, p. B1.

38. Flemming Hansen, *Consumer Choice Behavior* (New York: Collier Macmillan, 1972).

39. Daniel Kahneman, *Attention and Effort* (Upper Saddle River, NJ: Prentice Hall, 1973). This section relies heavily on ideas from this classic book.

40. Chris Janiszewski, "Preattentive Mere Exposure Effects," *Journal of Consumer Research*, Vol. 20 (December 1993), pp. 376–392.

41. Ibid.

42. Ibid.

43. Sana Siwolop, "You Can't (Hum) Ignore (Hum) That Ad," *Business Week*, September 21, 1987, p. 56.

44. Pamela S. Schindler, "Color and Contrast in Magazine Advertising," *Psychology and Marketing*, Vol. 3 (1986), pp. 69–78. Also see Joan Meyers-Levy and Laura A. Peracchio, "Understanding the Effects of Color: How the Correspondence Between Available and Required Resources Affects Attitudes," *Journal of Consumer Research*, Vol. 22 (September 1995), pp. 121–138.

45. Ronald Alsop, "Coming Attractions: TV Ads At Movie Houses Everywhere," *The Wall Street Journal*, July 3, 1986, p. 17.

46. The factors that influence attention are closely related to the effects of salience on memory. These issues are discussed in the next chapter. Also see John Lynch and Thomas Srull, "Memory and Attentional Factors in Consumer Choice: Concepts and Research Methods," *Journal of Consumer Research*, Vol. 9 (June 1982), pp. 18–37.

47. David W. Stewart, "The Moderating Role of Recall, Comprehension, and Brand Differentiation on the Persuasiveness of Television Advertising," *Journal of Advertising Research*, Vol. 25 (March-April 1986), pp. 43–47.

48. Jacob Jacoby and Wayne D. Hoyer, "The Comprehension/Miscomprehension of Print Communication: Selected Findings," *Journal of Consumer Research*, Vol. 15 (March 1989), pp. 434–443.

49. Laura A. Peracchio and Joan Meyers-Levy, "How Ambiguous Cropped Objects in Ad Photos Can Affect Product Evaluations," *Journal of Consumer Research*, Vol. 21 (June 1994), pp. 190–204.

50. E. T. Hall, *The Hidden Dimension* (New York: Doubleday, 1966).

51. Marj Charlier, "Beer Drinkers in Texas, California Don't Swallow Change in Coors Label," *The Wall Street Journal*, December 29, 1988, p. B4.

52. Gail Tom, Teresa Barnett, William Lew, and Jodean Selmants, "Cueing the Consumer: The Role of Salient Cues in Consumer Perception," *Journal of Consumer Marketing*, Vol. 4 (Spring 1987), pp. 23–27.

53. M. Tysoe, "What's Wrong with Blue Potatoes?" *Psychology Today*, Vol. 19 (December 1985), pp. 6, 8.

54. Kent B. Monroe, "The Influence of Price Differences and Brand Familiarity on Brand Preferences," *Journal of Consumer Research*, Vol. 3 (June 1976), pp. 42–49. Also see Valarie Zeithaml and Merrie Brucks, "Price as an Indicator of Quality Dimensions," paper presented at the 1987 Association for Consumer Research Annual Conference, October 9–11, Cambridge, MA. Chr. Hjorth-Anderson, "The Concept of Quality and the Efficiency of Markets for Consumer Products," *Journal of Consumer Research*, Vol. 11 (September 1984), pp. 708–718.

55. Kent B. Monroe and Akshay R. Rao, "Testing the Relationship Between Price, Perceived Quality and Perceived Value," paper presented at the 1987 Association for Consumer Research Annual Conference, October 9–11, Cambridge, MA.

56. Tung-Zong Chang and Albert R. Wildt, "Price, Product Information and Purchase Intention: An Empirical Study, *Journal of the Academy of Marketing Science*, Vol. 22 (Winter 1994), pp. 16–27.

57. Peter M. Nichols, "Dressed Up and Vying to Catch Your Eye," *The New York Times*, January 26, 1996, pp. H9, H20.

58. Ibid.

59. Anna D. Wilde, "Harley Hopes to Add Hog's Roar to Its Menagerie of Trademarks," *The Wall Street Journal*, June 23, 1995, p. B1.

60. David Mick, "Consumer Research and Semiotics: Exploring the Morphology of Signs, Symbols, and Significance," *Journal of Consumer Research*, Vol. 13 (September 1986), pp. 196–213.

61. Kenneth Boulding, *The Image* (Ann Arbor: University of Michigan Press, 1956), p. 44.

62. Charles Sanders Peirce, *Collected Papers*, Charles Hartshorne, Paul Weiss, and Arthur W. Burks, eds. (Cambridge, MA.: Harvard University Press, 1931–1958). David Mick, in "Consumer Research and Semiotics," noted that scholars have had great difficulty determining precisely what Peirce meant by the "interpretant."

63. Richard Zakia and Mihai Nadin, "Semiotics, Advertising, and Marketing," *Journal of Consumer Marketing*, Vol. 4 (Spring 1987), p. 6.

64. Russell Belk, Kenneth Bahn, and Robert Mayer, "Developmental Recognition of Consumption Symbolism, *Journal of Consumer Research*, Vol. 9 (June 1982), pp. 4–17.

65. Julie L. Nicklin, "Marketing by Design," *The Chronicle of Higher Education*, March 22, 1996, pp. A33, A34.

THE COMPACT DISC LONGBOX:

A PACKAGING DILEMMA

In the early 1980s consumers were introduced to a new audio medium that has since revolutionized the music industry—the compact disc (CD). When compact disks began to replace long-playing records (LPs), marketers had to decide how to package them. The first solution was to put the jewel box (i.e., the hard, clear plastic disc casing) inside a cardboard box measuring 6 by 12 inches, commonly called the *longbox*. This packaging allowed the retailer to replace one LP with two CDS, because of their smaller size. It was a clever and efficient way of changing packaging without replacing shelves. Moreover, the size deterred thieves.

The use of longboxes, however, quickly came under criticism. The jewel box measures only 5 by 5 by 1.5 inches, which means the longbox represented a wasted use of resources that increased shipping, storing, and manufacturing costs and added anywhere from $.75 to $1.50 to the cost of a CD.[1] Furthermore, in 1989 longboxes accounted for some 20 million pounds of garbage.[2]

Some people advocated eliminating longboxes on the grounds that this would decrease the price of CDs by lowering shipping, storage, and manufacturing costs and save natural resources. In rebuttal, retailers claimed that getting rid of the longbox would have negative effects on the consumer. For one thing, changing packaging would require new retail display fixtures and mandate new theft deterrence measures, which would increase the cost of CDs. For another, two-thirds of CDs are impulse purchases in which the buying decision is made within 8 seconds.[3] Reducing the size of the CD package would discourage consumers from paying attention to new artists and albums because graphics are a key element of attracting attention for impulse sales. As an executive of a major music retail chain said, "we deliver feelings, nothing we sell, people need . . . but it is an integral part of their lives."[4]

Those who want to ban the longbox claim that shrinking the size of the package would not reduce actual stimulus size because most CD titles now use the top 5 square inches of the longbox merely to reproduce the cover of the booklet.[5] Furthermore, in countries that sell discs only in jewel boxes, CD sales have been quite successful.[6]

Actually, some companies have found that eliminating the longbox increases CD sales. One alternative that is supposed to help solve the security problem while enhancing the product image is to put the jewel boxes into a special locked cabinet or glass casing. However, Roger Whiteman, vice president of inventory and distribution for a major music store chain, rejects this idea: "Psychologically, there's an attraction to browsing, and it allows people to touch the product. The CD in just the jewel box looks more expensive than in a dirty, grubby, old longbox." Still, he believes that longbox displays are a "mishmash to the eye" and prefers a uniform jewel box because "When you have a wall of just jewel boxes in a uniform, colorful display, it can only attract customers."[7] Further, a uniform package could decrease the possibility of information overload and might therefore lead to better buying decisions by consumers.

By 1997 the CD packaging industry had settled on the jewel box. However, the problem of the security of the CDs continued. Many retailers moved to a system in which the CD is placed in a plastic security box with a magnetic strip that activates an alarm if it is not removed by store personnel. The problem is that the boxes cost $.21 each. For a major retailer with 30,000 CDs, the cost is high for the complete system, which includes security boxes, alarm system, and labor.

Case developed by Cody Roberts and Jeri Jones.

Questions

1. What are the major problems facing the music industry concerning the use of longboxes?

2. Which concepts from perception apply to the longbox case, and how do they apply to the problems faced by the music industry?

3. Develop a managerial applications analysis. Using applicable information-processing concepts as a foundation for your answer, describe the managerial strategies the music industry should follow in attempting to deal with CD packaging.

References

1. Robert Simonds, "A Modest Proposal on CD Packaging," *Billboard Magazine*, Vol. 101 (October 7, 1989), p. 2.
2. Gerry Wood, "Save Mother Earth: Bag the CD Longbox," *Billboard Magazine*, Vol. 102 (June 9, 1990), p. 6.
3. Geoff Mayfield, "Dealers Defend Longbox: CD Packaging Argued at NARM Meet," *Billboard Magazine*, Vol. 101 (October 7, 1989), p. 1.
4. Ed Christman and Nigel Hunter, "NARM '90: National Association of Recording Merchandisers Conference," *Billboard Magazine*, Vol. 102 (March 17, 1990), p. N3.
5. Simonds, "A Modest Proposal on CD Packaging," p. 3.
6. "Quid Pro Quo Indicated on 6-by-12 Box," *Billboard Magazine*, October 21, 1989, p. 11.
7. Trudi Miller, "Pandora's Longbox Opened in Canada: Retailers Scramble for CD Pack Options," *Billboard Magazine*, Vol. 102 (June 9, 1990), pp. 6, 45, 50.

CHAPTER FOUR

INFORMATION PROCESSING II: MEMORY AND COGNITIVE LEARNING

INTRODUCTORY CASE

The Xerox Copier Failure

It was 1980, and industrial buyers were shunning Xerox Corporation's new 8200 office copier. Xerox's management was stunned because it was the first time that consumers had balked at one of its products. Meanwhile, the market share of Japanese competitors was jumping. Why were Xerox's customers rejecting the 8200? A technological masterpiece, the copier boasted the three most advanced features demanded by businesses—collating, enlarging, and reducing capabilities. In the lab the copier worked perfectly. It was reliable, contained an onboard computer, and produced excellent copies.

Xerox instituted a crash program to find out why the 8200 was a market failure. The project manager brought in cognitive scientists, anthropologists, and the repair personnel who were the closest to the product's users. The problem quickly became apparent: ordinary people could not use the copier. As the project manager said, "No one paid attention to the human interface—to the user. People had to wade through buttons and visual noise and manuals for all features, including the most frequently used one, copying a page or two."

Consumers who had used the 8200 copier outright hated it.

As a result of this analysis, the 8200 was totally redesigned. Clear, graphic displays and touch-screen menus were created that quickly and easily guided users through the machine's operations. By paying attention to the customer, Xerox was able to redesign and relaunch its copier—and this time it succeeded in the marketplace.

INTRODUCTION

In the nearly 20 years since the failure of the Xerox 8200 office copier, product designers have continued to overlook the consumer when developing new products. Indeed, many products have become so complicated that even engineers with Ph.D.s cannot figure them out. An analyst for *Business Week* warned, "Manufacturers of consumer products are not only losing the interest of their customers but they're also alienating them." Users do not want

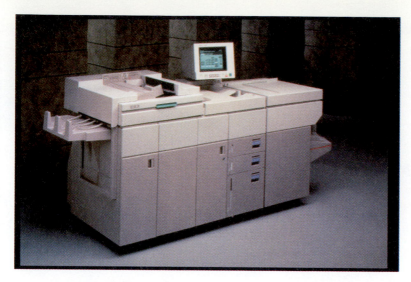

Figure 4-1

In order to make the processing of information easier for consumers, Xerox designs copiers, such as the model 5775, that are highly user-friendly. (Courtesy of Xerox Corporation.)

overly complex and temperamental machines. Certainly the ability to make personal computing simpler was the key factor in the early success of Apple's Macintosh. As one Apple executive explained, "On the desktop today, 80% of computing power is going toward ease of use, such as menus, windows, and popups. Only 20% is actually going toward doing the job, such as calculating your spreadsheet."[1]

Xerox Corporation did learn from its mistake with the original 8200: the company redesigned the copier and regained its market-leading position. Figure 4-1 presents a photo of a recent Xerox copier that won an award for its user-friendliness.

The problem of prohibitively complex consumer products illustrates the role of memory and knowledge in consumer information processing, the subject of this chapter. We begin by presenting a simplified model of memory. Then we discuss the role of consumer knowledge in the purchase process. Next, we explain how forgetting occurs as well as how affective processes influence memory. We conclude the chapter with a discussion of the implications of these topics for understanding the Xerox 8200 failure.

A SIMPLIFIED MEMORY MODEL

In the last chapter on consumer information processing, we focused on perception—that is, the exposure, attention, and comprehension stages of the process. We also presented a diagram of information processing (Figure 3-3) that showed memory affecting each of these stages. Memory, a major topic of this chapter, is the faculty that allows consumers to anticipate the stimuli they might encounter and therefore to selectively expose themselves to desired stimuli. Similarly, memory influences attention processes by guiding consumers' sensory systems so they can focus selectively on particular stimuli. Finally, the expectations and associations elicited in memory by the stimuli encountered affect consumers' comprehension.

Figure 4-2 presents a simplified model of memory. This **multiple-store model of memory** identifies three types of memory storage systems: sensory memory, short-term memory, and long-term memory.[2] As you can see from the figure, information is first reg-

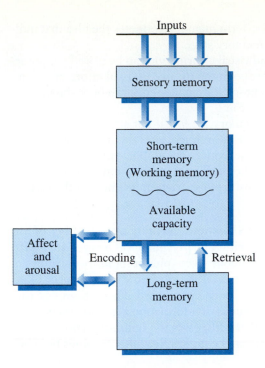

Inputs

Sensory memory

Short-term memory (Working memory)

Available capacity

Affect and arousal

Encoding

Retrieval

Long-term memory

Figure 4-2
A simplified memory model.

istered in sensory memory. This is where the preattention stage occurs, as the person briefly analyzes the stimulus unconsciously to determine if additional processing capacity should be allocated to it. If at this stage the stimulus is perceived to be related to the person's goals, the additional capacity will be allocated to it and the information will shift to short-term, or working, memory, where it will be actively processed. Short-term memory is connected to long-term memory through encoding and retrieval processes. **Encoding** refers to transference of information from short- to long-term memory for permanent storage, while **retrieval** refers to the accessing of that stored information so that it can be utilized in short-term memory. Note that the figure conceptualizes affective and arousal states as influencing both short-term and long-term memory.

Sensory Memory

A sight, sound, touch, or taste is perceived when a stimulus activates nerve fibers in the person's sensory organs. This perception becomes a part of the person's sensory memory. Lasting only a fraction of a second, the **sensory memory** of a stimulus consists of the immediate impression caused by the firing of the nerve cells. Because the nerve fibers fire for only very short lengths of time in response to outside stimulation (in most cases for less than a second), the stimulus information will be quickly lost unless it is further processed.[3] The firing of the nerve cells is monitored in the preattention stage. If the information is relevant to the person or activates an orienting response, it will be actively monitored in short-term memory.

Short-Term Memory

Short-term memory is the site where information is temporarily stored while being processed. For example, when a consumer thinks about a television commercial or actively attempts to solve a problem, the cognitive processing is occurring in short-term memory.

Working memory, a common term for short-term memory, connotes the idea that individuals actively process information in this memory stage.

Evidence indicates that both auditory and visual information can be stored temporarily in short-term memory. It is, however, more common to encode visual information into words or sounds for further processing.[4] Auditory stimuli, it seems, can be maintained in short-term memory longer than visual stimuli can.[5]

Just as the images contained in sensory memory are lost if not attended to, so is the information contained in short-term memory. Research indicates that if the information is not rehearsed, it will be lost within about 30 seconds because short-term memory has a limited storage capacity.[6] **Rehearsal** is the silent repetition of information to encode it into long-term memory. One way information is lost from short-term memory is through its replacement by other information.[7]

The Limited Capacity of Short-Term Memory Short-term memory has a number of important characteristics. First, it has limited capacity. The psychologist George Miller proposed that the average person can process only about seven (plus or minus two) chunks of information at a time.[8] A *chunk* may be conceptualized as a single meaningful piece of information; this could be a single letter, a syllable, or an entire word. This recognition that people can handle seven (plus or minus two) chunks of information at a time has been labeled **Miller's law.** Some researchers think that Miller was too optimistic about the capacity of short-term memory. Indeed, in consumer contexts five (plus or minus two) bits may be a better estimate.

Because of its limited capacity, short-term memory acts like a bottleneck. If the consumer receives more information than can be handled, some of this information will be lost. This limited capacity of working memory is one reason customers were highly uncomfortable with the Xerox 8200 copier discussed in the introductory case. The machine required users to process large amounts of data quickly. Because of the limitations of "working memory," only small amounts of information can be processed at a time. If too much information is received at once, the problem-solving process breaks down. This is what happened to people attempting to use the 8200 copier, and as a result, customers stopped buying the machine.

The term **information overload** is used to describe the situation in which more information is received than can be processed in short-term memory. In addition to being unable to process all the information, consumers may react to overload by becoming aroused and by narrowly focusing their attention on only certain aspects of the incoming stimuli.[9] They may simply make a random choice, not buy anything, or focus on the wrong product qualities when confronted with a buying decision.

Two questions about information overload are of importance to marketers. First, *can* consumers become overloaded with information? Research has yielded an unequivocal "yes" to this question.[10] In the consumer societies of the United States, Western Europe, and many parts of the Far East, so many product choices abound, with so many options and characteristics, that consumers have far more information available to them than they can possibly process.

Research on the second question—*do* consumers become overloaded?—is somewhat controversial.[11] On one side of the argument is the evidence that people actively manage the information they receive to avoid becoming overloaded. According to this view, they "stop far short of being overloaded."[12] On the other side is the conviction that highly motivated consumers often collect so much information that they cannot possibly handle all of it, and this information overload actually decreases the quality of their purchase decisions.

We believe that information overload does commonly occur in consumers. Take a situation in which a salesperson is explaining the characteristics of a complex product such as a computer to an uninformed buyer. The person can quite easily be overwhelmed by all these facts. The consumer is therefore likely to become aroused and nervous and to focus on narrow aspects of the product, which may not be important for his purposes. Such overarousal can lead to a poor purchase decision, which is just the opposite of what the well-intentioned salesperson had in mind. The introductory case on the Xerox 8200 copier illustrated the difficulties companies get into when their products are so complicated that they produce information overload in consumers. Information overload is also common when consumers are making a purchase in a culture whose language is foreign to them.[13] In these circumstances, most people become highly aroused and uncomfortable.

Involvement and Short-Term Memory Capacity The amount of arousal a person feels influences the capacity of short-term memory.[14] In high-involvement situations consumers are usually more aroused and more attentive, which expands their short-term memory capacity to its maximal extent. In low-involvement conditions, however, the arousal level is apt to be low, so consumers focus relatively little memory capacity on the stimulus. Advertisers generally maintain that the number of copy points that can be transmitted in a televised commercial is about three or four. If "copy points" are viewed as analogous to "chunks of information," this indicates that the cognitive capacity of consumers vis-à-vis television advertising is quite low. This makes perfect sense considering that most television advertising is done in low-involvement situations in which viewers' arousal levels are low, and they are allocating little cognitive capacity to the task of processing the information in the ad. For companies that advertise on television (or radio), then, the lesson is: Keep your messages simple.

Transfer of Information from Short-Term to Long-Term Memory One of the functions of short-term memory is to assist in the transfer of information to **long-term memory,** where it is permanently stored. As a person allocates more capacity to a stimulus, the likelihood of its being transferred to long-term memory increases. One means of allocating increased capacity to a stimulus is through the process of rehearsal. This process can involve either the silent verbal repetition of information or the application of more energy to the task. A common example of rehearsal is your silent repetition of a telephone number between the time you looked it up and the time when you completed dialing it.

One researcher investigated the impact of rehearsal on the recall of advertised products by young children. The children, aged four to nine, either rehearsed or did not rehearse, product names by saying them aloud. The results revealed that when the children rehearsed the names of the products, they were better able to recall information about the brands. The implication for advertisers is that commercials that induce repetition of material (e.g., jingles and slogans) may improve the transfer of information from consumers' short-term to long-term memory.

How long does it take to transfer a chunk of information into long-term memory? According to researchers, that depends on just how the information is to be recalled from long-term memory. If the goal is simply to recognize that a stimulus has been seen, it may take only two to five seconds for transfer if the information is processed. In contrast, if the goal is to recall the information without assistance at a later time, the transfer time is longer—from five to 10 seconds for a single chunk.

These differences in transfer times have important implications for marketers. When developing messages for consumers, the marketer should consider whether the objective is to present the consumer with a recognition task or a recall task. For a **recognition task,** information is put in front of a consumer, who then simply judges whether that information has been previously seen. For a **recall task,** the information must be retrieved by the consumer from long-term memory. In recognition tasks, then, memory recall is aided, while in recall tasks it is unaided.

Grocery shopping usually involves consumers in a recognition task. If the product sought is of a low-involvement nature, such as laundry detergent, the shopper may merely scan the shelves for ideas on what to buy. The shopper is engaging in a recognition task. Because of the lower information processing demands of the recognition task in comparison to a recall task, fewer repetitions of an advertisement are required. Thus, marketers should carefully consider whether the buying task involves recognition or recall. If recall is required, more repetitions of the ad (along with a higher budget) will be required.

Figure 4-3 reproduces a print ad for Goodyear tires that shows two people water-skiing behind a car. It is likely to activate consumers' recognition memory for a popular television commercial that had a man and woman water-skiing behind a car driving through

Figure 4-3

This print ad for the Aquatred tire should activate recognition memory for television ads that featured skiers being pulled by a car driving over a thin layer of water.

shallow water. In addition, by eliciting recognition memory, the print ad has surplus meaning that goes beyond its written and pictorial content.

In other instances the direct recall of a product name from memory may be required. Suppose that a group of friends decides to go out to lunch on the spur of the moment. Each person will name a restaurant choice, and from this list of options the group will pick a restaurant. The set of restaurants recalled from memory is called the **consideration set.** Any restaurant whose name is not recalled from memory will simply not become part of the consideration set. Obviously it is crucial that a company's product be included in the consideration set for it to have a chance to be chosen in such circumstances. Whenever unaided recall is the consumer task for a product, firms have to go to greater lengths to expose consumers to messages about their brand.

Because short-term memory has a limited capacity, information temporarily stored there will be replaced when new information is input, and the earlier material may not be transferred to long-term memory. When consumers watch television or read a magazine, they are bombarded by dozens of advertisements competing for their attention. **Clutter** is the name marketing people give to this problem of too many ads. Consider the Super Bowl, an annual extravaganza that lasts over three hours. During that time viewers see 65+ commercials. After one Super Bowl game a few years ago, a market research firm analyzed consumer recall for ads placed by the game's leading sponsor—PepsiCo. It turned out that fewer than half the respondents could remember *any* ads for PepsiCo's products. So PepsiCo spent $6.8 million on commercials broadcast amid so much clutter that, in the words of one researcher, "it was hard for any company to break through."[16]

Studies of how information is transferred from short-term to long-term memory suggest that clutter is a major problem for advertisers. It impedes the ability of consumers to move information from temporary storage in short-term memory to permanent storage in long-term memory, particularly when unaided recall is required.[17] Table 4-1 summarizes some important points concerning short-term memory.

Long-Term Memory

In contrast to short-term memory, long-term memory has an essentially unlimited capacity to store information permanently.[18] The information stored in long-term memory tends to be either visual or semantic. *Semantic concepts* are the verbal meanings we attach to words, events, objects, and symbols. Thus long-term memory stores the meanings of words, symbols, and so forth, along with the associations among these various semantic concepts that we acquire. Long-term memory can also store information in terms of its sequence of occurrence (episodic memory), its modality (e.g., visual, smell, touch senses), and its affective, or emotional, content.[19]

Summary of Short-Term Memory (STM) Processes
1. STM has a limited capacity of 7, plus or minus 2, chunks of information.
2. STM is the site where information is processed and temporarily stored.
3. Information overload can occur if more information is received than can be processed in STM.
4. As involvement levels increase, consumers may allocate more capacity to a stimulus.
5. Information is transferred from STM to long-term memory by allocating more capacity to it. One method for allocating more capacity is rehearsal of the material to be learned.

TABLE 4-1

The permanent nature of long-term memory is illustrated by the enduringness of brand names. In 1987 General Motors brought back the name Nova for a new car model after not using it since 1980 because of translation problems. (In Spanish *Nova* can be interpreted to mean "no go.") Despite the seven-year lapse, GM knew that consumers retained an image of the brand as reliable and low in cost, so the company decided the name would be appropriate for a new car it was building jointly with Toyota. Herbert Krugman, an important scholar-practitioner in marketing, noted, "Bringing back well-known brand names could be a clever idea because so much of the marketing work is done. People's memory of old advertising campaigns and packaging is remarkably persistent."[20]

Relative Superiority of Picture versus Word Memory An important finding from psychology and consumer behavior is that pictures are generally more memorable than their verbal counterparts, particularly under low-involvement circumstances.[21] In one study consumers received one set of information about a brand from the written copy of a print ad and a different set of information from the ad's pictorial content. The visual material pertained to one characteristic of the brand (its durability) and the verbal material to another (its value for the money). The results of the study revealed that consumers recalled and recognized significantly more pictorial information than verbally presented information.[22] Thus the aphorism "A picture is worth a thousand words" has some scientific support.[23]

Another study found that if the words in a message have high-imagery content, then the use of pictures is not so important. (A high-imagery word would be *table*; a low-imagery one would be *future*.) In this study high- and low-imagery versions of advertisements were created. Some of the messages were accompanied by a photograph; others were not. It was found that the photograph did not significantly enhance recall of the message when high-imagery words were used, but did when low-imagery words were used. Two managerial implications can be drawn from this research: first, advertisers should use high-imagery words whenever possible; and second, the use of photographs in an ad significantly increases recall if the verbal message has a relatively low-imagery content.[24]

Researchers have also found that visual material is particularly easily recognized if the objects to be remembered are perceived as interacting in some way. So when using a famous endorser to plug a product, the advertiser should show that endorser actually using the product in everyday scenes.[25]

The following generalizations can be made about the effects of the verbal and pictorial content of ads on memory:

1. Pictorial content is usually recognized and recalled more readily than verbal content, particularly if the verbal material has low-imagery content.
2. Verbal material is best recalled when it is processed under high-involvement circumstances.
3. If consumers are engaged in high-involvement information processing, advertisers generally get better overall recall results if they present different information about the product via verbal and pictorial means.
4. Words and pictures can be used to complement each other in ads.[26]

Memory-Control Processes

Understanding how people get information into and out of memory is just as important for the consumer researcher as understanding how memory is structured. Called **memory-control processes,** these methods of handling information can operate unconsciously as well as consciously to influence the encoding, placement, and retrieval of data.[27]

Encoding As we saw, rehearsal influences whether or not information will be transferred from short-term to long-term memory. How that information is coded will have a great impact on the speed of transfer as well as on the placement of the information in memory. With a topic new to them, consumers may simply repeat a stimulus over and over during rehearsal or attempt to link it to other information already present in their long-term memory. As the topic becomes more familiar, consumers grow more adept at coding information on it by drawing associations between it and the information they already have in memory, and the storage process speeds up proportionally.[28]

Research has shown that when given new information on a topic, experts on that topic can recall the information much better than novices can because they have already developed elaborate memory networks and knowledge structures into which the new information can be placed. For this reason they can encode the information more efficiently and retrieve it more speedily. They are also better able than the novice to discriminate between important and unimportant data.[29] The ability to distinguish between important and unimportant information helps the expert to make better decisions. (Decision-making processes are discussed in Chapters 11, 12, and 13.)

Marketers should be governed by an understanding of the encoding process when they are developing brand names. The closer a product name fits with consumers' associations about the product class, the better consumers will be able to recall the name. One researcher has argued that highly concrete names that are easily visualized are remembered better than less concrete names because they are coded both visually and verbally and also because they fit better into consumers' existing knowledge structures. In the study carried out by this researcher subjects were presented with either high-imagery or low-imagery brand names. Examples of high-imagery names were *ocean*, *orchestra*, *frog*, and *blossom*. (An instance of a product with a high-imagery name is Head & Shoulders shampoo.) Examples of low-imagery names were *history*, *capacity*, *truth*, *moment*. The subjects recalled more of the high-imagery names.[30]

Retrieval and Response Generation The act of remembering consists of two processes: retrieval and response generation. As described earlier, the retrieval process involves a search through long-term memory to identify within it the information the individual wants to recall. In **response generation** the individual develops a response by actively reconstructing the stimulus.[31] So the consumer does not access stored replicas of the encoded stimulus information, but instead activates and reconstructs traces of stimuli into a recollection of the stimulus. People use logic, intuition, expectations, and whatever else is available to help them reconstruct a memory.

A major goal of advertisers is to improve consumers' ability to retrieve information from memory. One time-tested means of doing this is to provide retrieval cues on the packaging of a product to assist consumers' memories during decision making. Such **retrieval cues** may be created by placing the verbal or visual information originally contained in an ad on the packaging (or on the product itself).[32] This technique is frequently employed by marketers of children's cereals—many feature animals both in their ads and on the cereal boxes.

Another common means of assisting consumers' retrieval and response generation is to employ music in advertisements. There is good evidence that people recall sung messages better than spoken ones. In fact, many jingles stay in consumers' heads for years. The maker of Mounds/Almond Joy brought back the "Sometimes you feel like a nut" jingle because even though the company had not played it for years, customers still remembered it. By bringing it back, the firm could reach them *and* capture an entire new generation of consumers with its jaunty message.

Summary of Long-Term Memory (LTM) Processes
1. LTM has unlimited capacity.
2. Information is stored semantically and visually, by its sequence of occurrence, by its modality, and in terms of its emotional content.
3. LTM is essentially permanent.
4. Generally, picture memory is superior to word memory.
5. The memory-control processes of encoding and response generation influence what is stored in and retrieved from memory.

TABLE 4-2

A recent study empirically tested the impact of attaching a message to music by having a message either sung or read to consumers. The result: Respondents could recall significantly more words when the three verses of the message were sung. The study's author convincingly argued that music is a very powerful retrieval cue that substantially improves recall.[33]

Table 4-2 summarizes key points on the impact of long-term memory on consumer information processing.

CONSUMER KNOWLEDGE

A person's knowledge about the consumption environment is stored in long-term memory. **Consumer knowledge** has been defined as the amount of experience with and information about particular products or services a person has.[34] As an individual's consumer knowledge increases, it becomes possible for that individual to think about a product across a greater number of dimensions and make finer distinctions among brands. For example, someone with a good deal of knowledge about wine can think in terms of several dimensions, such as a wine's color, bouquet, "nose," acidity, and provenance. A novice, by contrast, might think in terms of only one dimension—say, how much he or she likes a wine's taste.

Three types of consumer knowledge have been identified. The first is objective knowledge, or the correct information about a product class that the consumer has stored in long-term memory. The second type is subjective knowledge, or the consumer's perception of what or how much he or she knows about a product class. Interestingly, there are wide differences between how much people *think* they know and how much they *really* know, so objective and subjective knowledge are not highly correlated.[35] The third type of knowledge is information about the knowledge of others. In the Xerox case we presented at the beginning of this chapter, the product managers failed to consider—or perhaps obtain—this third type of knowledge—that is, they had little understanding of how much consumers knew about running a complicated copying machine. Lacking this knowledge, they designed the 8200 copier for themselves rather than for their customers.

What are the major implications of consumer knowledge for marketing managers? First, as consumer knowledge increases, consumers become better organized, grow more efficient and accurate in their information processing, and display better recall of information. Managers therefore need to consider the state of consumer knowledge when they are developing a product. Xerox Corporation obviously failed to consider the consumer knowledge of its targeted customers when developing the 8200 copier. Different people have different amounts of experience with and knowledge of products. The engineers who designed the copier had extensive knowledge of complex machinery, so for them the 8200 was quite simple to use. Customers, however, had much less knowledge in this area, so for them the new copier proved intractable. They were extremely dissatisfied with the product—and with Xerox Corporation for foisting it upon them. Products must be designed for their eventual users, not for the engineers who dream them up.

The second implication for marketing managers is that information on the extent of consumer knowledge should influence promotional strategy. Specifically, a message targeted to a knowledgeable prospect can be much more complex than one addressed to a novice.

Product managers have a large stake in influencing what consumers learn about their products. A firm's promotional activities can educate consumers, and the beliefs formed through such education may directly influence consumers' attitudes and actions regarding the product. What consumers learn through such education often affects how they interpret their experience with the product. If a firm promises splendid performance for a product in its advertisements and the product fails to live up to the expectations aroused by the promise, consumers' psychological interpretation of their experience with the product is likely to be negative—even if the product, in fact, performs quite decently.

How Do Consumers Gain Knowledge?

Knowledge is obtained through the process of cognitive learning. **Cognitive learning** is defined as the processes through which people form associations among concepts, learn sequences of concepts (e.g., memorize a list), solve problems, and gain insights. Such learning involves an intuitive hypothesis-generating process in which people adapt their beliefs to make sense of new data.[36] Thus cognitive learning is an *active* process in which people seek to control the information they obtain.

An important issue for marketers is how people learn in the consumer environment. One influential article on this question proposed that consumers learn both through education and through experience.[37] **Learning through education** involves obtaining information from companies through advertising, sales personnel, and the consumer's own directed efforts to seek data. **Learning through experience** is gaining knowledge through actual contact with products. Learning through experience is generally a more effective means to gain consumer knowledge. It promotes better retrieval and recall because the consumer is involved in the learning experience, and the information obtained is more vivid, concrete, and salient.

The Gestalt Theory of Cognitive Knowledge Gestalt psychologists believe that biological and psychological events do not happen or influence behavior in isolation of each other. Rather, people perceive inputs from the environment as part of a total context.

The Gestalt psychologists were early cognitive theorists whose work was a marked departure from that of other learning theorists in the first half of the twentieth century. Whereas other psychologists viewed man as a static organism who responded automatically to inputs from the environment, the Gestalt psychologists focused on the active, creative nature of human learning and action.[38] As one noted consumer researcher stated:

> When we look at an automobile, we do not see glass and steel and plastic and bolts and paint. We see instead an organized whole, an automobile. And perhaps not even just an automobile but also comfortable transportation, prestige, status, and a symbolic sense of achievement. This is the familiar Gestalt dictum; the whole is different from, if not greater than, the sum of the isolated parts.[39]

The work of the Gestalt psychologists has important implications for marketers. Market researchers tend to perceive a product in terms of its individual characteristics—price, color, features, reliability, and so forth. But consumers tend to perceive a product as an integrated whole. In isolation, a particular color or style may be judged unacceptable. However, when seen in the overall context of a product, the characteristic could be quite satisfactory. Thus, considered in isolation, plaid car seats might seem silly; when placed in a sports car, however, bold multicolor seats might look quite good.

Another contribution of the Gestalt school is the idea that consumers engage in problem solving and have sudden bursts of insight. Although consumer researchers have emphasized low-involvement learning processes in recent years, many products or situations actually activate consumers to begin problem-solving activities. For example, people can become highly involved in purchasing an automobile, selecting mutual funds for their retirement savings, or choosing a college to attend.

The Associationist Theory of Cognitive Knowledge Another approach to cognitive learning is to analyze the associations consumers form between marketing stimuli. Early experimental work within the associationist school was done by Hermann Ebbinghaus in the late nineteenth century. It was Ebbinghaus who discovered what was later called *serial learning*.

The study of **serial learning** is concerned with how people place into memory and recall information received in a sequential manner. Consider the typical commercial break in a television show, when viewers are exposed to six or more advertisements. An important question for marketers is whether an ad's position in the series influences how well it is remembered. We say that there is a **serial-position effect** when the order of presentation of information in a list influences recall of the information in the list. As you can see from the curve in Figure 4-4, researchers have found that items at the beginning of the list and those at the end are the most readily learned. Items in the middle of the list are learned much less rapidly.

A serial-learning effect has been discovered by consumer researchers. In one study respondents watched a series of three commercials and were then asked to recall information about each of the ads. Significantly less information was remembered about the middle of the three advertisements.[40]

One explanation for the serial-learning effect is that the beginning and end of a list become anchors for learning. Because of the limitations of short-term memory, people pick reference points for when to start and end the learning process. Since only limited amounts of information can be stored in short-term memory at a time, it is those items right around the beginning and end of the list—the reference points—that are recalled most readily.

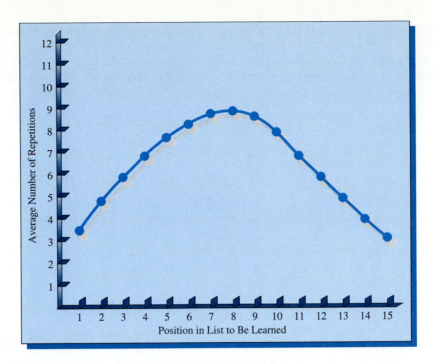

Figure 4-4

Serial-position effect: a hypothetical example. More repetitions are required to learn the material in the middle of the list. (*Source*: The hypothetical curve shown here is based in part on serial-position curves found in Charles E. Osgood, *Method and Theory in Experimental Psychology* [New York: Oxford University Press, 1964].)

Many more repetitions of the material may be required before items in the middle can be recalled.

The serial-learning effect has some important implications for marketers. One is that key information in an advertisement should be placed at the beginning or end of the message, for if important information is embedded in the middle, it may take many more repetitions of the advertisement for consumers to learn it. By the same token, advertisers should strive to get their commercials placed either at the beginning or the end of a series of television ads.[41]

Marketers should also know that in some instances the first information received in a list tends to be recalled better than the last, according to research on the "pioneering advantage." The **pioneering advantage** occurs in marketing when the first brand to enter a product category achieves a long-term edge over competitors. Studies have shown that information on the pioneer is perceived as more interesting and novel than information on later entrants. The benefits of being the first to enter the marketplace have the most observable effects among consumers who follow a product category and monitor the entry of brands into it.[42]

Besides studying how consumers learn lists of information, the associationists investigated how consumers remember words that are paired with each other. In a task called **paired-associate learning,** people are asked to associate a series of response words with stimulus words. For example, three stimulus-and-response pairs might be Maytag—quality, Toyota—"Oh-what-a-feeling," and peas—Jolly Green Giant. *Maytag*, *Toyota*, and *peas* are the stimulus words, and subjects are asked to recall from memory the response words of *quality*, "*Oh what a feeling*" and *Jolly Green Giant*, respectively. An important finding in paired-associate studies is that learning is speeded up if the stimulus-and-response items can be readily associated with each other and are already familiar to the subject.[43] Learning is especially rapid if mental images are developed of the linkage of the stimulus and response words.

Research on paired-associate learning suggests that associations are learned most rapidly when the following conditions are met:

1. The stimulus and response words are easily pronounceable.
2. The person is familiar with both the stimulus and the response words.
3. The stimulus and response words are meaningful.
4. The stimulus and response words are easily associated.
5. Visual images are created to link the stimulus and response words together.

You may have noted that these recommendations are totally consistent with the work cited earlier in the chapter on the effects of visual processing and the encoding of information.

Marketers appear to instinctively use ideas from paired-associate learning to create cooperative advertising campaigns. In such campaigns two distinct products are promoted together. For example, Alka-Seltzer and H&R Block developed a joint campaign in which the product and the service were touted as helping "tax-time upsets." As one Alka-Seltzer manager said, "Alka-Seltzer has a heritage of being caring, empathetic, like Mother Teresa. This touches an underlying emotion at tax time."[44]

When an ad is positioned beside another annoying ad or a disturbing news story, the impact of the promotion is often reduced and may even become negative. Some of the earliest work in cognitive learning was performed by researchers who developed the concept of the **law of contiguity,** which states that things that are experienced together become associated.[45] Marketing managers have a strong intuitive awareness of this law, which is why most companies check to ensure that their television advertisements will not be shown in conjunction with programs that could be offensive to their target market.

Semantic Memory Networks

One aspect of consumer knowledge is **semantic memory,** which refers to how people store the meanings of verbal material in long-term memory. Researchers have found that semantic memory is organized into networks.[46] Figure 4-5 depicts a memory network for automobiles. It shows a series of memory nodes that represent stored semantic concepts; the lines connecting the nodes indicate the existing associations among them. According to one popular theory of semantic memory, information is recalled from a semantic network via spreading activation.[47] That is to say, when a stimulus activates one node, the impulse spreads throughout the network, activating its other nodes. Each node that is activated represents a memory that is recalled.

Researchers have proposed that five types of consumer information can be stored in the memory nodes of a semantic network:

1. The brand name.
2. The brand's characteristic advertisement.
3. Other advertisements about the brand.
4. The product category.
5. Evaluative reactions to the brand and the ads.[48]

Suppose that the Corvette node in Figure 4-5 is activated in someone's semantic memory network by an advertisement for the car. The activation of that node would set off a chain of activation whereby a number of additional nodes in the person's semantic net-

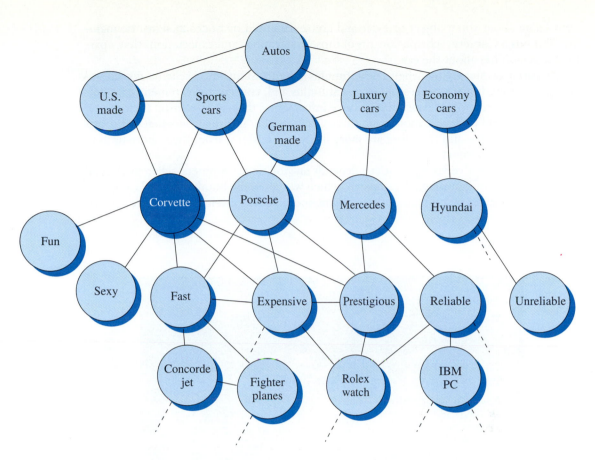

Figure 4-5
A semantic memory network for *Corvette*.

work would be activated. All these nodes, of course, are the associations the person has with the semantic concept *Corvette*—for example, *sports car*, *fast*, *expensive*, and *prestigious*. In addition, other, similar brands of cars might be activated in the person's memory (e.g., Porsche), along with various evaluative reactions stored there. (Since individual consumers have unique memory structures, the activation of any semantic concept may result in quite divergent sets of associations.)

Our example of a memory network for *Corvette* demonstrates how consumers form a set of semantic associations with a brand name. A consumer's **brand knowledge** consists of a "brand node in memory to which a variety of associations have been linked."[49] Thus in Figure 4-5 the brand name *Corvette* forms a node with which a variety of concepts are associated, such as the model's characteristics (e.g., fast and expensive), brand connections (Porsche), and evaluative reactions (e.g., fun, sexy).

Schemas

The total package of associations brought to mind when a node is activated is called a *schema*. Specifically, a **schema** is an organized set of expectations a person holds about an object. Schemas (the plural is sometimes written *schemata*) are "stored frameworks of knowledge about some object or topic and are represented by nodes in semantic memory."[50] Thus a Corvette schema consists of those associations and expectations that a particular person has about the car.

Research has shown that when a new stimulus is inconsistent with a schema, consumers engage in more diligent processing of that stimulus and, consequently, remember it better. In other words, when consumers receive information that deviates from their expectations, they tend to devote more cognitive capacity to that information—that is, process it in greater depth—and therefore are more likely to transfer it from their short-term to their long-term memory.[51]

A good deal of advertising creativity depends on violating consumers' schemas. A good example is the "milk mustache" campaign, which was rated the number-one ad campaign in the United States by one group. In highly memorable ads physically attractive celebri-

Figure 4-6

The award-winning "milk mustache" advertising campaign is so memorable because the ads violate consumers' schemas of what sophisticated athletes, actresses, and other celebrities should look like.

ties are photographed with a semicircle of milk over their upper lip (see Figure 4-6 for one of these ads). The ads attract so much attention and are remembered so vividly because in their startling childlikeness they violate our schemas of what celebrities drink and how they should look.

One study tested the effects of a stimulus that deviates from consumers' expectations in a personal-selling situation.[52] Customers in a clothing store were confronted by a salesperson who interacted with them in an unexpected manner. Surprised by the sales approach, the customers paid more attention to the information conveyed by the salesperson and recalled it better later. The study concluded that when subjects were approached by salespeople who conformed to their expectations, their product evaluations were not affected by the quality of the sales presentation. However, when the seller violated the "salesperson schema," subjects recalled more about the product from the presentation and had a more positive attitude toward the product.

FORGETTING

If long-term memory is permanent, why do we forget things placed in it? The answer is that information placed in long-term memory is sometimes extremely difficult to retrieve. In one study over 10,000 people were polled on advertisements they could remember. It turned out that 53 percent of the respondents were unable to remember *any* specific ad they had seen, heard, or read in the last 30 days.[53] The result was devastating to advertising managers because the recall of ads is an important measure of advertising effectiveness.

Researchers have investigated the phenomenon of forgetting for many decades. Our discussion in this section relates some of their findings.

Interference Processes

Two kinds of interference cause problems in encoding, retrieval, and response generation: proactive interference and retroactive interference. In the **retroactive interference** process, new material presented after old material has been learned interferes with the recall of the old material. That is, the learning of new material blocks the retrieval or response generation of the old material from memory. With **proactive interference** the process works the other way around: material learned prior to the new material interferes with the learning of the new material.[54]

Forgetting that results from retroactive and proactive interference can create serious problems for marketers. There is an enormous potential for interference in the recall of advertisements because of the great number of promotional messages Americans are exposed to every day. In a recent series of studies investigating interference processes in an advertising context,[55] respondents were given a series of print ads to read and then questioned on them. The studies' conclusion was that advertising for competing brands, as well as for other products offered by the same manufacturer, could inhibit consumers' ability to remember brand information. The interference effects were particularly pronounced when the competing material was similar to the target information.

Indeed, it is a classic research finding that interference between sets of material to be learned increases as the similarity of their content increases.[56] Relying upon these findings in experimental psychology, one would predict that if consumers are exposed to a series of commercials for products in which similar types of claims are made, they will become confused and their learning will be impeded. Traditional work on retroactive and proactive interference suggests that confusion grows proportionally to the degree that the competing commercials involve similar types of products, or that different products use similar adjectives to describe their performance (such as *high-quality*, *low-cost*, *low-maintenance*).

Recently, however, researchers have found that interference effects occur only for *unfamiliar* brands.[57] The results showed that recall for familiar brands was not affected by information from either familiar or unfamiliar competing brands. This phenomenon provides important advantages in the marketplace for brands that are familiar to consumers. If, indeed, the advertising of familiar brands interferes with the advertising of unfamiliar brands, while the converse does not occur, the pioneering advantage discussed earlier in the chapter becomes an even more important factor in the marketplace.

The von Restorff Effect Another finding from studies of recall that is intriguing to advertisers has become known as the **von Restorff effect.**[58] Experiments have shown that a unique item in a series of relatively homogeneous items is recalled much more easily, because the effects of proactive and retroactive interference are minimized. The von Restorff effect is illustrated by the ad campaign for Infiniti automobiles. In 1990 Nissan Motor Corporation U.S.A. introduced its new flagship line of cars with an unusual series of ads in which "rocks and trees" were shown rather than the cars themselves. While controversial at the time, the ads scored very high on recall tests. Figure 4-7 presents one of these ads. (*Note*: The case study at the end of this chapter discusses this Infiniti ad campaign.)

The von Restorff effect illustrates the importance of **information salience,** or the level of activation of a stimulus (e.g., a brand name) in memory.[59] Generally, the more salient something is, the more likely it will be encoded into memory and later recalled. For obvious reasons, salience for a product is increased right after a consumer purchases it. Marketers can also raise the salience of a product by making it unique, by advertising it continually, or by using cues such as point-of-purchase displays to remind consumers of it.[60] One of the advertiser's primary goals should be to make an advertisement highly salient to consumers through such stimulus devices as novelty, contrast, color, surprise, movement, and size.

If one brand is highly salient to consumers, research has found that the recall of competing brands is generally lower.[61] Thus if a brand manager can develop a marketing mix that makes her brand highly salient to consumers, their recall of competing brands may be inhibited through retroactive interference. When the presence of the salient brand in memory inhibits the recall of competitor brands, those brands may slip out of the consumer's consideration set.

The Zeigarnik Effect Another factor that influences whether something will be forgotten is the Zeigarnik effect, named after the German Gestalt scientist who discovered it. The **Zeigarnik effect** occurs when an individual is involved in a task that is interrupted or not completed.[62] Comparisons of recall for information from a task that has been interrupted

Figure 4-7

An early ad for Infiniti cars illustrating the von Restorff effect. The prose in the ad read, "In our mind, the balance of three things is essential to making a luxury car luxurious: performance, comfort, styling." The ad continued at a later point, ". . . balance . . . it's why walls that were built 200 years ago haven't fallen down, and why designs that are classic in 1990 will still stand up in 2010." Over 80 percent of consumers in Infiniti's target market could remember the ads.

versus from one that has been completed consistently show that material from the interrupted task is recalled better.[63]

This effect partly explains the effectiveness of "soap opera" ads, such as those created for Taster's Choice coffee that feature an ongoing romance between a man and a woman. Naturally, the trials and tribulations of this couple revolve around drinking coffee. Each ad is a miniepisode in a soap opera that ends with the couple caught in an unresolved conflict. Such endings pique the interest of consumers, so that they "hold in mind" the ad until the conflict is resolved in the next commercial episode.

Time and Forgetting

Through the operations of proactive and retroactive interference, recall of verbal information decreases over time. Classic work by Ebbinghaus tracked this loss of recall[64], and the results of one of his experiments are shown in Figure 4-8. After people learned a list of nonsense words (e.g., *xlp, mqv*), the percentage of words they could remember decreased dramatically at first, and then leveled off.

The rapid forgetting that took place immediately after learning in this experiment occurs in advertising as well. In a classic experiment Zielske had an advertisement for a product run for a group of housewives once a week for 13 weeks.[65] At the end of the 13-week period, 63 percent of his respondents could recall having seen the ad. The ad was not shown to them after the 13-week run, and forgetting displayed the same pattern as that found by Ebbinghaus 70 years earlier: it occurred very rapidly at first, and then leveled off. After 20 weeks, those who could recall the ad had dropped to under 30 percent; by the time nine months had passed, fewer than 10 percent of respondents could remember the ad.

In addition to showing one group of housewives one ad a week for 13 weeks, Zielske ran 13 ads, spaced 4 weeks apart, for another group of housewives. In this group the ability to recall the ads increased slowly, so that by the end of the year some 48 percent of respondents could remember the ads.

This difference in results has important implications for advertisers. If an advertiser's goal is rapid awareness of a product, then a high frequency of ads over a short period of time will be most effective. The downside of this strategy is that consumers will rapidly

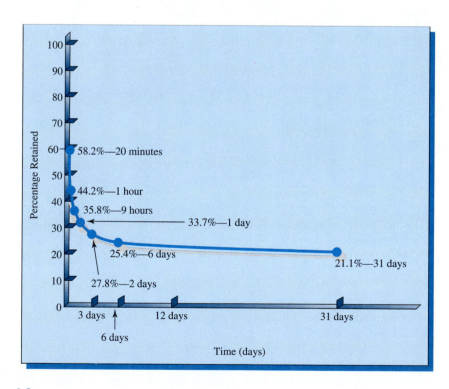

Figure 4-8

Relationship between time and forgetting. (*Source:* Data from H. Ebbinghaus, *Memory*, H. A. Ruger and C. E. Bussenius, trans. [New York: New York Teachers College, 1913].)

Consumer Behavior Factoid

Question: How many commercial messages do consumers receive a day, and of these, how many are they aware of and how many do they actively process?

Answer: The average consumer receives between 200 and 500 commercial messages a day, is aware of 15 percent of these messages and actively processes only 4–5 percent of them.

Source: Scott A. Hawkins and Stephen J. Hoch, "Low-Involvement Learning: Memory without Evaluation", *Journal of Consumer Research, 19* September 1992, 212–225.

forget the commercial message after the burst of advertisements ends. If the advertiser's goal is to build long-term awareness of the ad, the commercials should be pulsed so that the ads are seen by consumers regularly over a long period of time. Some advertisers prefer to combine these approaches by using a high-intensity ad campaign to bring out a product, and then pulsing regularly after the introduction to maintain consumers' awareness of the product.

Think back to the Xerox case detailed at the beginning of the chapter. What effects would the passage of time have on the recall of information about how to run the copier? Unless employees used it frequently, they would probably have difficulty remembering the 8200's complicated controls. Thus they would experience frustration each time they attempted to use the copier.

AFFECT AND MEMORY

One of the major themes of this text is that marketers must be alert to consumers' experiential/affective processes. The term **affect** refers to feelings, emotions, and moods. Researchers in recent years have developed theories describing how feelings influence memory and judgment that are useful to marketers.[66] Consumer behavior research in this area has concentrated on the relationship between consumers' mood states and their memory processes. As noted by one prominent researcher, "Mood is important and its effects need to be accounted for. Mood states pose an important and difficult challenge because information-processing theorists have seldom dealt with the affective system."[67]

A **mood** is a transient feeling state that occurs in a specific situation or time. It is not a personality variable, because moods are temporary in nature, whereas personality is long-lasting. Neither is it an emotion, which is more intense and attention-claiming.[68] But even though short in duration and mild in intensity, moods influence the recall of information. It has been found that people are better able to remember information that has the same affective quality as their mood state. Thus when people are sad, they are more likely to recall information that is sad; and conversely, when they are happy, they are more likely to recall happy information. Indeed, there is evidence that mood states influence the encoding of and retrieval of information, as well as how information is organized in memory.[69]

In one study consumers were asked to think about happy, sad, or neutral past experiences in order to induce positive, negative, or neutral moods. They were then shown a single print advertisement for a Mazda RX7 sports car and requested to form an impression of the car while reading the ad. The researchers found that the subjects' induced mood affected their rating of the car 48 hours later. It was hypothesized that when the subjects read the ad, their mood state influenced how they encoded the information. Subjects in a sad mood encoded a lower evaluation of the Mazda than subjects in a neutral mood state. The highest ratings of the car came from subjects who encoded the ad information when in a positive mood state.[70]

In another study subjects saw either a sad television show (e.g., *60 Minutes*) or a happy one *(Real People)* and then were asked to evaluate a commercial that ran during the show. The subjects recalled more information about the ad when it was embedded in the television show that induced a happier mood. One possible explanation of this finding is that a positive mood influences consumers to elicit from memory a broader and more integrated set of knowledge categories, and the result is a more effective encoding of information.[71]

The research on the relationship between affect and memory suggests that marketers should generally attempt to put consumers in a positive mood when they are presenting them with information on a product or service. A number of devices can be used to create such a mood, among them using humor in an advertisement and purchasing a nice meal for a client in a personal-selling situation. Another implication of the research is that, to the extent that using a product causes negative moods, it may inhibit the learning of information and therefore slow the learning process. The latter effects seem to have occurred in consumers attempting to learn to use the Xerox 8200 copier.

Summary of Major Implications of Memory Processes for Promotional Strategy

Memory Area	Implications
Short-term memory	Develop messages that match the capacity level of consumers' STM.
Long-term memory	Enhance message presentation by using vivid visual information as well as verbal information.
Consumer knowledge	1. Construct messages that match target's knowledge.
	2. Construct messages inconsistent with consumer schemas.
	3. Attempt to understand target market's schemas and semantic memory networks that include your product/service, and create messages that fit into these schemas.
Forgetting	1. Create promotional material with distinctive characteristics in order to minimize interference in target market's memory caused by competing material.
	2. Create interruptions in advertisements that enhance their recall.
	3. To maintain memory for ads, use a pulsing strategy of showing ads periodically, rather than spending an entire budget in a short time period.
Cognitive learning	1. Recognize that consumers are insightful information processors who perceive products as integrated wholes.
	2. Make use of the law of contiguity by pairing product/service with positive associations.
	3. Do not bury key product information in the middle of a commercial.
	4. Avoid allowing your advertisements to be buried in the middle of a series of commercials.
Affect and memory	In general, attempt to cause people to be in positive mood states when evaluating your product/service.

TABLE 4-3

Table 4-3 summarizes the major implications of memory processes for promotional strategy.

A MANAGERIAL APPLICATIONS ANALYSIS OF THE XEROX 8200 CASE

Problem Identification

Xerox Corporation needed to identify and correct the factors responsible for the failure of its 8200 copier in the marketplace.

The Consumer Behavior Analysis and Its Managerial Implications

Four consumer behavior concepts from the chapter have implications for managers in this case. Table 4-4 summarizes these concepts and gives their managerial applications.

Miller's Law Miller's law suggests that because of the limited capacity of short-term memory, consumers cannot be overloaded with too much information. Xerox's problem was that the complexity of its copier pushed consumers to process well over 10 bits of information at a time, which overloaded them. Miller's law also applies to product design. Managers must ensure that products are designed from the start so that they do not overtax consumers with information. In sum, products must be user-friendly—and the Xerox 8200 failed that test.

Managerial Implications of Consumer Behavior Concepts in Xerox 8200 Case	
Consumer Behavior Concept	**Managerial Implications**
1. Short-term memory	*Product design*. Design products so that they are user-friendly and do not overload consumers with information.
	Promotional strategy. Design instructions so that they are simple and easy to follow.
2. Consumer knowledge	*Market research*. Do appropriate studies to develop an understanding of the amount of expertise various consumer groups have.
	Segmentation. Select appropriate consumer groups as market segments to target.
	Product design. Develop product so that the degree of difficulty of its use matches the knowledge of the target market.
	Promotional strategy. Develop promotions with a level of sophistication that matches target market's.
3. Forgetting	*Product design*. Design product so that it has sufficient cues to assist users' recognition memory. Recognize when developing product that memory decays rapidly.
4. Consumer mood states	*Product development*. Design products with minimal potential to create frustration in consumers.
	Promotional strategy. Work up instructions that humor consumers and put them a positive mood state.

TABLE 4-4

Consumer Knowledge The employees who used the 8200 copier had little expertise running complicated copiers, and as a result, they became frustrated when they found they had to process a lot of information merely to perform a simple task. The consumer knowledge concept applies to market research, segmentation, product design, and promotional strategy. Xerox should have done market research to determine consumers' level of expertise, and then identified segments based on these levels of expertise. It then could have designed a product that matched the level of knowledge of the target market it selected for the 8200. Finally, the company should have developed a promotional strategy that used messages describing the product's benefits in terms that matched its targeted market's knowledge of the product category.

Forgetting If consumers use a complex product only infrequently, they are not likely to remember how to operate it because of the rapid forgetting that occurs for new information. If Xerox's managers had understood the consumer behavior concept of forgetting, they would have used a different product-development and promotional strategy. The 8200 copier would have been designed to minimize the effects of rapid consumer forgetting. In addition, managers would have kept in mind the findings on consumer forgetting in developing instructions for the use of the product. Simple icons placed on the 8200 that activated recognition memory and facilitated the retrieval of product information would have been very helpful. (*Note*: The development of product-use instructions is part of the general category of promotions.)

Mood Finally, Xerox should have considered the effects of mood on information processing and memory. We know that negative mood states can inhibit the processing and learning of information. The frustrations users of the 8200 encountered no doubt caused a negative affective state, which lowered their ability to learn how to operate the machine. Had Xerox managers developed and issued clear instructions on the use of the copier, the company could have minimized frustration and negative moods in consumers.

Managerial Recommendations

Recommendation 1 To avoid information overload, follow Miller's law by designing products so that consumers do not have to process more than seven new bits of information at any point in time.

Recommendation 2 Perform marketing research to identify the knowledge level of consumers, and then design product and promotions based on this information.

Recommendation 3 To minimize consumer forgetting, develop product-use instructions that employ written material and icons that facilitate recognition memory and enhance retrieval.

Recommendation 4 Develop instructions that enhance consumer mood states, which will facilitate information processing and the successful use of products.

SUMMARY

According to the model of memory presented in this chapter, information is input into sensory memory, and if it relates to the consumer's goals, it will be shifted into short-term memory for further processing. The more elaborate the processing done in short-term memory, the greater the likelihood that the information will be permanently stored in long-term memory.

Short-term memory is characterized by a limited processing capacity: seven (plus or minus two) chunks of information (Miller's law). If more information is received than can be processed, the person enters a state of information overload. The capacity of short-term memory is influenced by the consumer's involvement level. As involvement increases, capacity also generally increases.

Encoding refers to the movement of information from short-term memory into long-term memory. Retrieval is the process of recalling information from long-term memory back into short-term memory. The probability that information will be coded into long-term memory increases as the person puts more cognitive effort into the task by rehearsing the information or by connecting it with other knowledge already stored in memory. Encoding also benefits when associations can be drawn between the new information and other knowledge held in memory.

The retrieval of information from long-term memory is enhanced if the consumer has cues available to assist the recall. Stored in long-term memory are verbal, visual, and other information that originated in the senses. In addition, people can encode sequences of events, or episodes, in memory. Picture memory seems to be superior to verbal memory, so using a visual image that depicts verbal information in some manner enhances memory of that information.

Consumer knowledge—also encoded in long-term memory—refers to a person's familiarity with and expertise concerning a product or service. It has a number of characteristics, one of which is the number of dimensions in which a person can think about something. Knowledge is also organized into the semantic memory, which refers to how people store the meanings of verbal material in their long-term memory. In semantic memory concepts are represented by nodes that are connected together. The activation of one node by a stimulus may result in a spreading activation, so that information related to connected nodes is also recalled.

The study of forgetting is particularly important for advertising managers. One impediment to the recall and recognition of information is information interference. Proactive interference makes it more difficult to encode information, and retroactive interference impedes the retrieval of information from memory.

Memory can be enhanced by making use of the von Restorff and Zeigarnik effects. The von Restorff effect occurs when a unique item in a series of relatively homogeneous items is recalled more easily because it is more salient and that counteracts some of the effects of interference. The Zeigarnik effect occurs when a task or story is interrupted, causing people to engage in deeper processing and form a stronger memory trace.

People tend to forget information with time because of interference processes. Advertisers should therefore consider pulsing messages—using them on and off over a long period of time—rather than repeating the same message over and over again in a brief time period. They should also avoid putting important information in the middle of a message, where it is susceptible to the serial-position effect. That is, interference makes it harder for people to encode and retrieve information in the middle of a message because they tend to use the beginning and end of the message as reference points for the learning process.

Cognitive learning theorists have tackled the question of how we develop knowledge. One group, called Gestalt psychologists, depicted consumers as active problem solvers who perceive products and services in terms of their environmental context. Another group, the associationists, proposed that people acquire knowledge by the law of contiguity, which states that things that are experienced together tend to become associated. Consumer researchers should therefore analyze the kinds of entities with which a product or service is associated, because if a product is paired with something negative, consumers may well make an unfortunate association.

Marketers need to recognize the role of affect in memory processes. A consumer's mood state often influences brand evaluations. Marketers should therefore try to create positive mood states in consumers when giving them information to increase the chances that they will evaluate the product or service positively.

affect
brand knowledge
clutter
cognitive learning
consideration set
consumer knowledge
encoding
information overload
information salience
law of contiguity

learning through experience
learning through education
long-term memory
memory-control processes
Miller's law
mood
multiple-store model of
    memory
paired-associate learning
pioneering advantage

proactive interference
recall task
recognition task
rehearsal
response generation
retrieval
retrieval cues
retroactive interference
schema
semantic memory

sensory memory
serial learning
serial-position effect
short-term memory
von Restorff effect
working memory
Zeigarnik effect

REVIEW QUESTIONS

1. What are the three types of memory that have been proposed? How do they differ?

2. What happens when information overload occurs?

3. What is the difference between a recognition and a recall task?

4. Compare the effectiveness of picture memory and word memory under high- and low-involvement conditions.

5. What is a memory network?

6. Define and give examples of memory-control processes.

7. Discuss what happens in short-term memory. What is the relationship between involvement and short-term memory?

8. How is information transferred from short-term to long-term memory?

9. Summarize the major findings concerning long-term memory and knowledge processes.

10. Why does forgetting occur?

11. What is the relationship between time and forgetting?

12. What is the serial-position effect?

13. What is the law of contiguity?

14. What is the relationship between affect and memory?

15. What is the difference between learning through education and learning through experience?

DISCUSSION QUESTIONS

1. Attend carefully to three television advertisements. Identify the number of "copy points" (i.e., chunks of information) in each ad. To what extent do you think consumers will remember these points? What factors might influence the placement into memory of these copy points?

2. Go through a magazine and locate three print advertisements. Identify the number of copy points in the ads. Compare the number of copy points you found in the print ads to the number you observed in the television ads. What factors might account for any differences you discovered?

3. Describe two instances of consumer recognition tasks and two instances of consumer recall tasks. Do you find any differences in the advertising associated with the products identified in each instance?

4. It has been said that "one picture is worth a thousand words." Relate this adage to the capabilities of picture versus word memory. What are the implications for advertisers?

5. Draw a diagram of your memory network for fast-food restaurants.

6. Suppose that you had to develop a name for a new product—a soybean-curd (tofu)–based dessert that uses real fruit, has no cholesterol, and does not bother people who have digestive difficulties with milk-based products (a sizable portion of the population). Create several names for the product and identify how each utilizes the various memory-control processes.

7. Go to a grocery store and find as many examples as you can of point-of-purchase (POP) advertising that effectively help consumers associate national advertising with the brand on the grocery shelves. What are the memory factors that make the POP displays more or less effective?

8. Outline a fictitious ad for any product that makes use of the Zeigarnik effect.

9. Outline a fictitious ad for any product that makes use of the von Restorff effect.

ENDNOTES

1. This quote and the introductory case are based on Bruce Nussbaum and Robert Neff, "I Can't Work This Thing!" *Business Week*, April 29, 1991, pp. 58–66.

2. James R. Bettman, "Memory Factors in Consumer Choice: A Review," *Journal of Marketing*, Vol. 43 (Spring 1979), pp. 37–53. Actually, the evidence is mixed as to whether there are three types of memory, and if so, whether memories are stored in three separate locations in the brain. Other approaches to memory have been proposed; one suggests that short- and long-term memories are distinguished only by the depth of processing. Researchers have also identified another type of memory, called *implicit memory*. For a discussion of this concept, see Abhijit Sanyal, "Priming and Implicit Memory: A Review and Synthesis Relevant for Consumer Behavior," in *Diversity in Consumer Behavior*: *Advances in Consumer Research*, Vol. 19, John F. Sherry, Jr., and Brian Sternthal, eds. (Provo, UT: Association for Consumer Research, 1992), pp. 795–805. For even newer views of memory processes, see Alan J. Malter, "An Introduction to Embodied Cognition: Implications for Consumer Research", *Advances in Consumer Research*, Vol. 23, Kim Corfman and John Lynch, eds. (Provo, UT: Association for Consumer Research, 1996), pp. 272–276. Still, the multiple-store approach has a strong intuitive appeal and its predictions are generally consistent with other approaches to memory, so this is the model we have chosen to discuss.

3. George Sperling, "The Information Available in Brief Visual Presentations," *Psychological Monographs*, Vol. 74 (1960), p. 498.

4. D. F. Fisher and R. Karsh, "Modality Effects and Storage in Sequential Short-Term Memory," *Journal of Experimental Psychology*, Vol. 87 (1971), pp. 410–414.

5. S. W. Keele, *Attention and Human Performance* (Santa Monica, CA: Goodyear Press, 1973).

6. Herbert Simon, *The Sciences of the Artificial* (Cambridge, MA: MIT Press, 1969).

7. Richard M. Shiffrin and R. C. Atkinson, "Storage and Retrieval Processes in Long-Term Memory," *Psychological Review*, Vol. 76 (1969), pp. 179–193.

8. George A. Miller, "The Magical Number Seven, Plus or Minus Two: Some Limits on Our Capacity to Process Information," *Psychological Review*, Vol. 63 (1956), pp. 81–97. Other researchers have disputed Miller's law, some arguing that short-term memory is limited to processing as few as 3 chunks of information simultaneously, others claiming it can deal with as many as 20 chunks.

9. Daniel Kahneman, *Attention and Effort* (Upper Saddle River, NJ: Prentice Hall, 1973).

10. Jacob Jacoby, "Perspectives on Information Overload," *Journal of Consumer Research*, Vol. 10 (March 1984), pp. 432–435.

11. Robert S. Owen, "Clarifying the Simple Assumption of the Information Load Paradigm," in *Diversity in Consumer Behavior*: *Advances in Consumer Research*, Vol. 19, John F. Sherry, Jr., and Brian Sternthal, eds. (Provo, UT: Association for Consumer Research, 1992), pp. 770–776. Also see Naresh Malhotra, "Reflections on the Information Overload Paradigm in Consumer Decision Making," *Journal of Consumer Research*, Vol. 10 (March 1984), pp. 436–440.

12. Ibid., p. 435.

13. Claudia Dolinsky and Richard Feinberg, "Linguistic Barriers to Consumer Information Processing: Information Overload in the Hispanic Population," *Psychology and Marketing*, Vol. 3 (1986), pp. 261–271.

14. Kahneman, *Attention and Effort*.

15. M. Carole Macklin, "Rehearsal Processes in Children's Recall of Advertised Products," in *Proceedings of the Division of Consumer Psychology*, Wayne Hoyer, ed. (Washington, DC: American Psychological Association, 1986), pp. 21–25.

16. Kevin Goldman, "Barrage of Ads in Super Bowl Blurs Messages," *The Wall Street Journal*, February 3, 1993, p. B6.

17. Tom J. Brown and Michael L. Rothschild, "Reassessing the Impact of Television Advertising Clutter," *Journal of Consumer Research*, Vol. 20 (June 1993), pp. 138–146. This important article found little evidence of the negative effects of clutter on the recognition of advertisements embedded in television programming. Additional research, however, is required before we can conclude that clutter presents few, if any, problems for advertisers.

18. For a more detailed description of memory and memory-control processes, see Bettman, "Memory Factors in Consumer Choice."

19. Benton Underwood, "Attributes of Memory," *Psychological Review*, Vol. 76 (November 1969), pp. 559–573.

20. Ronald Alsop, "Old Chewing-Gum Favorites Find There's Life After Death," *The Wall Street Journal*, September 11, 1986, p. 37.

21. Terry Childers and Michael Houston, "Conditions for a Picture-Superiority Effect on Consumer Memory," *Journal of Consumer Research*, Vol. 11 (September 1984), pp. 643–654.

22. Terry Childers, Susan Heckler, and Michael Houston, "Memory for the Visual and Verbal Components of Print Advertisements," *Psychology and Marketing*, Vol. 3 (Fall 1986), pp. 147–150.

23. Recent research has found, however, that this superiority of visual over verbal recall may not be true in preschool children. See M. Carole Macklin, "The Impact of Audio-visual Information on Children's Product-Related Recall," *Journal of Consumer Research*, Vol. 21 (June 1994), pp. 154–164. For additional information on the persuasive effects of visual and verbal information, see Charles S. Areni and K. Chris Cox, "The Persuasive Effects of Evaluation, Expectancy and Relevancy Dimensions of Incongruent Visual and Verbal Information", *Advances in Consumer Research*, Vol. 21, Chris Allen and Deborah Roedder John, eds. (Provo, UT: Association for Consumer Research, 1994), pp. 337–342.

24. H. Rao Unnava and Robert E. Burnkrant, "An Imagery-Processing View of the Role of Pictures in Print Advertising," *Journal of Marketing Research*, Vol. 28 (May 1991), pp. 226–231.

25. For a review of this literature, see Kathy Lutz and Richard Lutz, "Effects of Interactive Imagery on Learning: Applications to Advertising," *Journal of Applied Psychology*, Vol. 62 (August 1977), pp. 493–498.

26. Michael Houston, Terry Childers, and Susan Heckler, "Picture-Word Consistency and the Elaborative Processing of Attributes," *Journal of Marketing Research*, Vol. 24 (November 1987), pp. 359–369. Closely related is the field of mental imagery. For a review of this area, see Laurie A. Babin, Alvin Burns, and Abhijit Biswas, "A Framework Providing Direction for Research on Communications Effects of Mental Imagery-Evoking Advertising Strategies," in *Diversity in Consumer Behavior: Advances in Consumer Research*, Vol. 19, John F. Sherry, Jr., and Brian Sternthal, eds. (Provo, UT: Association for Consumer Research, 1992), pp. 621–628.

27. Bettman, "Memory Factors in Consumer Choice."

28. R. N. Kanungo, "Effects of Fittingness, Meaningfulness, and Product Utility," *Journal of Applied Psychology*, Vol. 52 (August 1968), pp. 290–295.

29. Elizabeth J. Cowley, "Recovering Forgotten Information: A Study of Consumer Expertise," *Advances in Consumer Research*, Vol. 21, Chris Allen and Deborah Roedder John, eds. (Provo, UT: Association for Consumer Research, 1994), pp. 58–63.

30. Kim Robertson, "Recall and Recognition Effects of Brand Name Imagery," *Psychology and Marketing*, Vol. 4 (Spring 1987), pp. 3–15.

31. Bettman, "Memory Factors in Consumer Choice."

32. Kevin L. Keller, "Memory Factors in Advertising: The Effect of Advertising Retrieval Cues on Brand Evaluations," *Journal of Consumer Research*, Vol. 14 (December 1987), pp. 316–333.

33. Wanda T. Wallace, "Jingles in Advertising: Can They Improve Recall?" in *Advances in Consumer Research*, Vol. 17, Marvin Goldberg and Gerald Gorn, eds. (Provo, UT: Association for Consumer Research, 1990), pp. 239–242.

34. Joseph Alba and J. Wesley Hutchinson, "Dimensions of Consumer Expertise," *Journal of Consumer Research*, Vol. 13 (March 1987), pp. 411–454.

35. C. Whan Park, David L. Mothersbaugh, and Lawrence Feick, "Consumer Knowledge Assessment," *Journal of Consumer Research*, Vol. 21 (June 1994), pp. 71–82.

36. Stephen J. Hoch and John Deighton, "Managing What Consumers Learn from Experience," *Journal of Marketing*, Vol. 53 (April, 1989), pp. 1–20.

37. Ibid.

38. David Horton and Thomas Turnage, *Human Learning* (Upper Saddle River, NJ: Prentice Hall, 1976).

39. Harold H. Kassarjian, "Field Theory in Consumer Behavior," in *Consumer Behavior: Theoretical Sources*, Scott Ward and Thomas Robertson, eds. (Upper Saddle River, NJ: Prentice Hall, 1973), p. 120.

40. Marvin Goldberg and Gerald Gorn, "Happy and Sad TV Programs: How They Affect Reactions to Commercials," *Journal of Consumer Research*, Vol. 14 (December 1987), pp. 387–403.

41. Frank R. Kardes and Paul M. Herr, "Order Effects in Consumer Judgment, Choice, and Memory: The Role of Initial Processing Goals," in *Advances in Consumer Research*, Vol. 17, Marvin Goldberg and Gerald Gorn, eds. (Provo, UT: Association for Consumer Research, 1990), pp. 541–546.

42. Frank R. Kardes and Gurumurthy Kalyanaram, "Order-of-Entry Effects on Consumer Memory Judgment: An Information Integration Perspective," *Journal of Marketing Research*, Vol. 29 (August 1992), pp. 343–347.

43. Horton and Turnage, *Human Learning*.

44. Sandra Atchison, "Block, Block, Fizz, Fizz," *Business Week*, March 30, 1987, p. 36.

45. Horton and Turnage, *Human Learning*.

46. John Lynch and Thomas Srull, "Memory and Attentional Factors in Consumer Choice: Concepts and Research Methods," *Journal of Consumer Research*, Vol. 9 (June 1982), pp. 18–37.

47. Alan Collins and Elizabeth Loftus, "A Spreading Activation Theory of Semantic Processing," *Psychological Review*, Vol. 56 (1975), pp. 54–59.

48. J. Wesley Hutchinson and Daniel Moore, "Issues Surrounding the Examination of Delay Effects of Advertising," in *Advances in Consumer Research*, Vol. 11, Thomas Kinnear, ed. (Provo, UT: Association for Consumer Research, 1984), pp. 650–655.

49. Kevin Lane Keller, "Conceptualizing, Measuring, and Managing Customer-Based Brand Equity," *Journal of Marketing*, Vol. 57 (January 1993), pp. 1–22.

50. Tom J. Brown, "Schemata in Consumer Research: A Connectionist Approach," in *Diversity in Consumer Behavior: Advances in Consumer Research*, Vol. 19, John F. Sherry, Jr., and Brian Sternthal, eds. (Provo, UT: Association for Consumer Research, 1992), pp. 787–794.

51. Houston et al, "Picture-Word Consistency."

52. Mita Sujan, James Bettman, and Harish Sujan, "Effects of Consumer Expectations on Information Processing in Selling Encounters," *Journal of Marketing Research*, Vol. 23 (November 1986), pp. 346–353.

53. Julie Franz, "$95 Billion for What: Ads Remembered as Forgettable in 1985," *Advertising Age*, Vol. 57 (March 3, 1986), p. 4.

54. Ernest Hilgard, Richard Atkinson, and Rita Atkinson, *Introduction to Psychology* (New York: Harcourt Brace Jovanovich, 1975).

55. Raymond Burke and Thomas Srull, "Competitive Interference and Consumer Memory for Advertising," *Journal of Consumer Research*, Vol. 15 (June 1988), pp. 55–68.

56. Charles E. Osgood, *Method and Theory in Experimental Psychology* (New York: Oxford University Press, 1964).

57. Robert Kent and Chris T. Allen, "Competitive Interference Effects in Consumer Memory for Advertising: The Role of Brand Familiarity," *Journal of Marketing*, Vol. 58 (July 1994), pp. 97–105.

58. Ibid.

59. Joseph Alba and Amitava Chattopadhyay, "Salience Effects in Brand Recall," *Journal of Marketing Research*, Vol. 23 (November 1986), pp. 363–369.

60. John Lynch and Thomas Srull, "Memory and Attentional Factors in Consumer Choice: Concepts and Research Methods," *Journal of Consumer Research*, Vol. 9 (June 1982), pp. 18–37.

61. Ibid.

62. Osgood, *Method and Theory in Experimental Psychology*.

63. An interesting question concerns which is recalled better—the interrupted story or the inserted material causing the interruption. Research indicates that the inserted material may actually be more salient. See Richard Harris, Ruth Sturm, Michael Klassen, and John Bechtold, "Language in Advertising: A Psycholinguistic Approach," *Current Issues and Research in Advertising*, Vol. 9 (1986), pp. 1–26.

64. H. Ebbinghaus, *Memory*, H. A. Ruger and C. E. Bussenius, trans. (New York: Teachers College, 1913).

65. Hubert A. Zielske, "The Remembering and Forgetting of Advertising," *Journal of Marketing*, Vol. 23 (January 1959), pp. 231–243.

66. G. H. Bower, "Mood and Memory," *American Psychologist*, Vol. 36 (1981), pp. 129–148.

67. Thomas Srull, "Memory, Mood, and Consumer Judgment," in *Advances in Consumer Research*, Vol. 14, Melanie Wallendorf and Paul Anderson, eds. (Provo, UT: Association for Consumer Research, 1986), pp. 404–407.

68. Meryl Gardner, "Mood States and Consumer Behavior: A Critical Review," *Journal of Consumer Research*, Vol. 12 (December 1985), pp. 281–300.

69. Patricia A. Knowles, Stephen J. Grove, and W. Jeffrey Burroughs, "An Experimental Examination of Mood Effects on Retrieval and Evaluation of Advertisement and Brand Information," *Journal of Academy of Marketing Science*, Vol. 21 (Spring 1993), pp. 135–142. Also see Meryl Gardner, "Effects of Mood States on Consumer Information Processing," *Research in Consumer Behavior*, Vol. 2 (1987), pp. 113–135.

70. Srull, "Memory, Mood, and Consumer Judgment."

71. Goldberg and Gorn, "Happy and Sad TV Programs."

ROCKS, TREES, AND INFINITI

In September 1989 Nissan Motor Corporation U.S.A. started a revolutionary automobile advertising campaign. The ads featured "rocks and trees" and philosophical musings rather than information about the vehicle's characteristics, such as its handling, performance, and safety features. For example, in various ads viewers were shown a rock wall, haystacks, a flowing stream, the sky, leaves blowing, and waves pounding a beach. The television ads used minimal dialogue. An announcer talked about the car in terms of nature, not in terms of its characteristics.

One two-page print advertisement was called "Beauty in Balance." On one page the reader saw a closeup photo of the intricate detail of a stone wall layered by a master mason. The second page contained sparse dialogue: "In our minds, the balance of three things is essential to making a luxury car luxurious: performance, comfort, styling. No one idea is more important than the other. Each idea contributes in its way to a personal definition of luxury." After a few more brief comments, the ad continued: "Balance. It's why walls that were built 200 years ago haven't fallen down and why designs that are classic in 1990 will still stand up in 2010."

The goal of the Infiniti campaign was to create customer awareness, and it worked beautifully. The car did not officially become available for sale until November 8, 1989, but three weeks earlier people began asking for it in showrooms across the country.[1] Research revealed that the ads were highly effective in two areas. First, they brought consumers into showrooms: an overwhelming 80 percent of customers who walked into showrooms said they had seen the commercials. As one Chicago area sales manager noted, "The advertising clearly worked. The number of people coming in here has been tremendous. It's been like an auto show."[2] Information compiled by the company showed that 80 percent of Infiniti's target market—households with an annual income of $60,000 or more—could identify the brand marque in aided awareness tests. Customers commented that the Infiniti advertising was unusual, that they had never seen anything like it.

The second benefit of the advertising campaign was that it created high brand awareness. A Gallup survey conducted in November 1989 concluded that Infiniti ads were rated highest in "top-of-the-mind" awareness. And despite the fact that no performance information was furnished in the advertisements, consumers were well versed on the car. As a dealer in Van Nuys, California, noted, "They seemed to have read every article ever written about Infiniti. In fact they knew more about the cars than the salesman."[3]

Infiniti sold 1,723 cars in its launch period, the seven weeks ending December 31, 1989—which works out to an annual rate of 12,800 cars. Unfortunately, these figures were far below what company executives had expected: they had projected sales of 30,000 cars by year-end 1990. In contrast, the sales of Toyota's upscale competitor, the Lexus, were extremely strong in that same period. Introduced two months prior to the Infiniti ads, the Lexus ads were more conventional. They displayed the car and emphasized its benefits. While Nissan sold 1,723 Infinitis in seven weeks in the late fall of 1989, Toyota sold over 4,500 Lexus cars in that same period.[4]

A postcampaign analysis of the Infiniti launch concluded that although awareness of Infiniti advertising was high, the response to it was mixed. Some dealers were furious when sales of the luxury sedans faltered, and their immediate reaction was to blame the problem on the peculiar advertising. Comedian Jay Leno captured many consumers' feelings about the high-toned ads when he joked, "The new Japanese car, Infiniti, isn't selling well. I guess the advertising isn't working, although I understand the sale of rocks and trees is up 300 percent."

Although Nissan had planned on showing the "rocks and trees" ads for a full year after the Infiniti was launched, the poor sales caused the company to revise its plans. In April 1990 new ads were created that focused on the cars. As one Nissan manager described them, "The new ads are more traditional in terms of beginning to tell a story, the voice-overs now will reinforce the visual elements of the commercials."[5] With the new advertising campaign, Infiniti's sales picked up. Interestingly, during the recession of 1990–1991, Infiniti's sales increased 45 percent, the highest increase shown by any luxury car.[6]

Questions

1. Define the advertising problem faced by Infiniti's managers when the company was about to launch the vehicle two months after Toyota had introduced the Lexus.

2. What consumer concepts from the chapter apply to this case?

3. Discuss the managerial applications of the consumer behavior concepts to the case.

References

1. Cleveland Horton, "Infiniti Ads Pull Traffic," *Advertising Age*, November 27, 1989, pp. 2, 112.

2. Scott Hume, "Infiniti Shoots to Top of Best Recalled Ads," *Advertising Age*, January 8, 1990, p. 10.

3. Ibid.

4. Cleveland Horton, "Infiniti Ads Trigger Auto Debate," *Advertising Age*, January 22, 1990, p. 49.

5. Cleveland Horton, "Infiniti Revises Ads: Snubs Nature Theme," *Advertising Age*, April 9, 1990, p. 2.

6. Mark Landler, "Mercedes Finds Out How Much Is Too Much," *Business Week*, January 20, 1992, pp. 92–96.

5

BEHAVIORAL LEARNING

Helping People to Help Each Other

Providing social services to the poor on a shoe-string budget is a critical problem for many nonprofit organizations. Most depend on volunteers, but as a spokesperson for an agency in Miami phrased the problem: "How [can] you get people to volunteer to perform various services for others, such as doing household chores for a person in the hospital, driving an elderly man to see a doctor, or making repairs on a house for an invalid?"

A solution was suggested by a professor at the District of Columbia School of Law. Why not treat the hours that someone gives to volunteer work as though they were currency? Volunteers would receive credits that would be banked, to be refunded at a later date when they themselves needed help. The idea, the professor said, is for "the economy to give a reward and incentive for decency that is as automatic as the market's reward for selfishness."

The professor's plan was implemented in Miami and quickly caught on at other locations in the United States. In Miami a work force of 700 regular volunteers was established, and social services dramatically increased. For example, the number of meals delivered to the housebound elderly increased from 200 per day to 1,600. Moreover, the dropout rate among volunteers was low—under 10 percent. Indeed, the major problem with the program seems to be that volunteers are reluctant to cash in on their credits. After roughly a year of operation only 1.1 percent of the credits had been redeemed.

The beauty of the program is illustrated by the experience of Elsa Martinez. For several months she had helped others by driving them on errands and by doing some of their shopping and cleaning. Then this unmarried 64-year-old garment worker learned that she had a brain tumor. In her time of need, the people she had befriended sent flowers and visited her in the hospital. Ms. Martinez whispered gratefully from her bed, "When you're sick, they come."[1]

INTRODUCTION

Researchers typically distinguish two types of consumer learning: cognitive learning and behavioral learning. As we saw in the last chapter, cognitive-learning theorists focus on relatively complex topics, such as how people retain verbal material (e.g., advertising messages), how they have insights, and how they plan. Most cognitively oriented theorists view learning as occuring via information processing.

This chapter explores another view of learning: behavioral learning. According to the behavioral influence perspective, behavior is a response to environmental stimuli. The thrust of this approach is to apply scientific methods to solving practical problems rather than to develop theories using explanations of internal processes within the person.[2]

Behavioral learning is a process in which experience with the environment leads to a relatively permanent change in behavior or to the potential for such a change. Like all learning, it results from experience—not from changes in physiology caused by growth, injury, or disease. Thus temporary states, like those induced by drugs, are not classified as learning.

An instance of behavioral learning is described in the introductory case to this chapter. Facing the practical problem of how to influence people to act prosocially, the managers of a social services program in Miami devised a system in which reinforcements were provided for helping others. As a result, volunteer work increased dramatically in that city.

Researchers have identified three major approaches to behavioral learning: classical conditioning, operant conditioning, and vicarious learning. In *classical conditioning*, behavior is influenced by a stimulus that occurs prior to the behavior and elicits it in a manner that has the appearance of being a reflex. In *operant conditioning*, behavior is influenced by the consequences of the behavior. Finally, in *vicarious learning* (also called *observational* or *social learning*), people observe the actions of others and model or imitate those actions.

Although consumers engage in all three types of behavioral learning, advertisers are particularly interested in classical conditioning because it tells them how to identify stimuli (e.g., messages, sights, or sounds) that elicit positive reactions from consumers. Their goal is to condition their good or service to the positive stimulus so that the product will elicit positive reactions whenever consumers think about or encounter it.

Operant conditioning was the primary means by which the Miami program increased prosocial behavior. The principles of operant conditioning are used in many marketing activities. Sales promotions, such as coupons, contests, and "giveaways," are based on the operant-conditioning principle of providing consumers with reinforcers to influence their later behavior.

Vicarious, or observational, learning underlies the common advertising strategy of showing appealing models using a product and experiencing positive outcomes from its use. The hope here is that consumers will imitate the model and purchase the product. Figure 5-1 shows a Nike ad that effectively employs observational-learning ideas.

Our goal in this chapter is to give you an understanding of each approach to behavioral learning and suggest how managers can use all these approaches to develop and execute marketing strategy. We begin with a discussion of classical conditioning.

CLASSICAL CONDITIONING

In **classical conditioning,** a neutral stimulus is paired with a stimulus that elicits a response. Through the repetition of this pairing, the neutral stimulus eventually becomes able to elicit the response all by itself. The Russian physiologist Ivan Pavlov discovered this phenomenon when he was working with dogs. The dogs had the messy propensity of beginning to salivate profusely (the response) every time meat powder (the stimulus) was presented to them. The **unconditioned stimulus (UCS)** of the meat powder reflexively elicited the **unconditioned response (UCR)** of salivation. At one point in his work Pavlov noticed that the dogs housed in his lab also salivated profusely when they heard the ringing of the bell that signaled the arrival of their food.

Figure 5-1

Nike used principles of observational learning in this effective ad for its cross-training shoes.

Humans also have a variety of such stimulus-response linkages. For example, puffing air into someone's eye elicits the response of blinking. Playing soothing music may elicit the response of relaxation. The soothing music is an unconditioned stimulus, and the reflexive response it elicits is an unconditioned response.

In classical conditioning, a previously neutral stimulus, called the **conditioned stimulus (CS),** is repeatedly paired with the eliciting stimulus, called the unconditioned stimulus (UCS). Note that in this pairing the CS needs to occur prior to the UCS, so that it predicts the UCS. After a number of such pairings, the ability to elicit a response is transferred to the CS. The response elicited by the CS is called the **conditioned response (CR).**

Current research on classical conditioning emphasizes that mere contiguity (or closeness in time) of the pairing of the CS with the UCS is not enough to achieve classical conditioning.[3] Rather, conditioning results from the informational relationship of the CS and the UCS. For the CS to provide information about the UCS, it must predict the occurrence of the UCS. For optimal conditioning, the CS should slightly precede the UCS in time.[4]

Consumer Behavior Factoid

Question: What is the relative proportion of spending on sales promotions versus advertising by companies in the United States?

Answer: Because they feel it is imperative to directly influence consumer behavior, companies spend approximately twice as much on sales promotions as they do on advertising.

Source: Purushottam Papatla and Lakshman Krishnamurthi, "Measuring the Dynamic Effects of Promotions on Brand Choice, *Journal of Marketing Research*, Vol. 33 (February 1996), pp. 20–35.

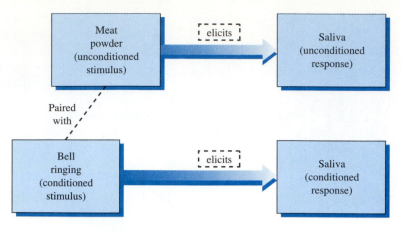

Figure 5-2

The classical-conditioning framework.

Figure 5-2 depicts the framework of classical conditioning established in Pavlov's experiments with dogs. The presence of the meat powder (the UCS) was preceded in time by the ringing of a bell (the CS). After a number of such pairings, the mere ringing of the bell elicited the conditioned response of salivation (the CR) in the dogs. You may have observed the same kind of phenomenon in your cat or dog at "feeding time."

Studies of Classical Conditioning in Consumers

Researchers have found that a variety of stimuli can classically condition consumers—music, for example. In one experiment the tempo of music played in a grocery store was varied over a nine-week period, so that at various times customers heard no music, slow-tempo music, or fast-tempo music. There were significant differences in the way customers moved when fast- as opposed to slow-tempo music was played. When the pace at which they moved between two points was measured, it was found that those exposed to fast-tempo music moved significantly faster than did those hearing slow-tempo music.

Interestingly, daily gross sales at the store were significantly higher in the slow-tempo condition—actually 38 percent higher than in the fast-tempo condition.[5] Without making wild generalizations based on one study performed in one grocery store over a period of only nine weeks, we may speculate on how music influences consumer behavior. The shoppers may have been classically conditioned throughout their lives to respond to music in certain predictable ways. Thus, hearing fast-paced music played in a grocery store, they moved faster, and that fast pace impeded buying. Perhaps, to speculate on another context, slow-paced, pleasant music relaxes patients in a dentist's waiting room enough to raise their threshold for pain when they get into the dentist's chair.

Researchers have identified other phenomena that act like classical conditioning. For example, the author of the grocery store study has replicated his findings in a carefully designed study set in a restaurant. Fast-tempo and slow-tempo music were alternated over several weeks. When slow-tempo music was played, customers stayed longer and ordered more drinks at the bar. The estimated gross margin of the restaurant was significantly higher because of the increased bar sales.[6]

In another study researchers conducted four experiments to test for classical-conditioning effects in an advertising–consumer behavior setting.[7] After carefully applying the procedural controls necessary to distinguish classical conditioning from other processes, the authors found evidence of classical-conditioning effects. The unconditioned stimuli in this study were pictures of beautiful landscape scenes, and the conditioned stimulus was a fictitious brand of toothpaste. The conditioned response was evaluated by various measures of attitude toward the brand. When the toothpaste ad was paired with the landscape scenes, people's attitude toward the ad was significantly more positive than in the control conditions. Results across the four experiments strongly supported this classical-conditioning interpretation.

Additional research has provided tantalizing evidence of classical-conditioning processes at work among consumers.[8] The author of these studies discovered that stimuli associated with spending money (specifically, credit card insignias) may actually elicit a spending response in consumers. In this carefully controlled series of studies, one group of subjects was placed in a spending situation where a MasterCard sign was in view, while another group of subjects was placed in the same situation, but without the presence of the sign. The MasterCard sign caused respondents to:

1. Make buying decisions more quickly,
2. Indicate they would spend more on a clothing purchase and other consumer goods,
3. Estimate that they would give more to a charity, and
4. Actually give more to a charity.

In explaining his results the author proposed that credit cards have become paired with the buying act in our society. Here is how the pairing works. For many people, the buying act has the properties of an unconditioned stimulus that elicits the unconditioned response of positive feelings. Through many pairings of the credit card with the buying act, the credit card becomes a conditioned stimulus that elicits a conditioned response of positive feelings. The positive feelings elicited by the credit card, in turn, make it more likely that someone will spend money when it—or a sign symbolizing it—is present.

Figure 5-3 is a photograph of the credit card placards that are frequently placed in highly salient locations in stores to attract consumers' attention.

In yet another set of studies researchers analyzed the extent to which positive attitudes could be conditioned to various unknown and known brands of colas. The unconditioned stimuli were photos of beautiful water scenes, and the conditioned stimuli were the various brands of colas. The results provided evidence of classical conditioning: that is, people's attitudes were changed in the experimental conditions. But the researchers noted two important additional findings: first, it was attitudes toward the unknown colas that changed the most, and second, the conditioning occurred only when the subjects had some awareness of a relationship between the conditioned stimulus and the unconditioned stimulus.[9]

The broad conclusion of recent studies, then, is that consumers respond to a variety of stimuli in a manner consistent with a classical-conditioning interpretation. Because the early research in this field involved conditioning animals to salivate to bells or to demonstrate other "rudimentary" behaviors, for a long time there was a tendency to view classical conditioning as a simple process in which organisms "stupidly" react to stimuli. Today researchers take a much more sophisticated view of the phenomenon. One internationally recognized researcher in the field encapsulated this new perspective when he argued that the organism "is better viewed as an information seeker using logical and perceptual relations among events, along with its own preconceptions, to form a sophisticated representation of the world."[10]

Table 5-1 summarizes the key concepts found in classical conditioning that apply to consumer behavior.

Other Classical-Conditioning Concepts That Apply to Consumer Behavior

Two additional concepts from classical conditioning are relevant to consumer research: sign tracking and higher-order conditioning. We discuss them in this section, along with the problem of determining the conditions necessary to induce effective classical conditioning.

Figure 5-3

Retailers often prominently display credit card insignia. Research has indicated that such displays may act as conditioned stimuli that elicit buying behavior.

Sign Tracking Consumer researchers have strong evidence that, through advertising, products may become conditioned stimuli and elicit a positive emotional response in consumers. In addition, the classical-conditioning process may cause consumers to pay more attention to a product. This attention-drawing faculty of conditioned stimuli is rooted in a phenomenon called **sign tracking**.[11] Organisms have the tendency to attend to, to orient themselves toward, and to approach a conditioned or unconditioned stimulus. Substantial evidence indicates that the ability of the unconditioned stimulus to draw attention to itself can be transferred to the conditioned stimulus. Thus if a product is paired with an unconditioned stimulus so that it eventually becomes a conditioned stimulus, it may also acquire the ability to draw attention itself. With all the commercial clutter today, a product that can induce people to engage in sign tracking is a major advantage in getting the marketer's message attended to and stored for later use. For example, in a grocery store the process of sign tracking may cause consumers to notice first the brands that act as conditioned stimuli.

Figure 5-4 is a photograph that well illustrates the phenomenon of sign tracking. It shows a college student and his dog avidly reading the second edition of *Consumer Behav-*

ior by John Mowen. While we believe that the book is interesting to people, how in the world could it so absorb a dog? The answer is that a clever photographer had the student hold a dog biscuit against the book. A strong reinforcer, the biscuit caused the dog to engage in sign tracking and stare at the food treat.

Higher-Order Conditioning Of particular importance to marketers is the concept of **higher-order conditioning,** which says that a conditioned stimulus can, in and of itself, act to classically condition another previously neutral stimulus. Indeed, most of the stimuli marketers use to create conditioned stimuli are probably themselves conditioned stimuli. For example, the pairing of a particular sports announcer, such as John Madden, with exciting sports events has made his voice a conditioned stimulus for many people. Thus just hearing John Madden produces a certain degree of excitement in many Americans. His voice can therefore be used as a stimulus to classically condition a brand, such as ACE Hardware stores. Note that the voice of John Madden is *itself* a conditioned stimulus.

One approach companies frequently use is to associate their products—or even their company—with the flag or with patriotic themes. The flag can be conceptualized as a conditioned stimulus that, in turn, conditions other previously neutral stimuli through a higher-order conditioning process.

Requirements for Effective Conditioning

To classically condition a response most effectively, a number of requirements need to be met.[12] First, when seeking to condition a neutral stimulus, marketers should ensure that the stimulus precedes in time the appearance of the unconditioned stimulus. The concept is that the conditioned stimulus needs to *predict* the occurrence of the unconditioned stimulus. In commercials, therefore, the product should be shown before the unconditioned stimulus appears. By preceding the UCS, the CS provides information to the organism on its occurrence.

A second requirement for effective classical conditioning in marketing is that the product must be paired *consistently* with the unconditioned stimulus. If the product is seen very frequently and the unconditioned stimulus only rarely, conditioning is much less likely to occur. This finding suggests that television advertising should be supported by a strong sales-promotion effort. For example, if a celebrity endorser is used as the unconditioned

Figure 5-4
This photo illustrates how a dog biscuit held against a textbook can cause a dog to engage in sign tracking and appear to be interested in the book.

stimulus in television advertising, his or her picture should be prominently paired with the product in point-of-purchase displays.

A third requirement is that both the conditioned stimulus and the unconditioned stimulus be highly salient to the consumer. Particularly in television commercials, the product and the unconditioned stimulus should stand out from the background of the advertisement as well as from the clutter of competing ads.

How many pairings of conditioned stimulus and unconditioned stimulus are necessary to obtain classical conditioning? Recent research indicates that learning can be surprisingly rapid, depending on the organism and the kind of conditioning. In a number of cases, in fact, only one pairing of conditioned stimulus and unconditioned stimulus is necessary for conditioning to occur.[13]

Managerial Applications of Classical Conditioning

Perhaps the most important application of classical-conditioning concepts in marketing involves conditioning positive emotional responses to brands via promotional activities. How can managers identify strong unconditioned stimuli with which their product or service can be paired? Experience has shown that a variety of unconditioned stimuli elicit positive emotional responses in consumers: sexy actors and actresses, patriotic music, exciting sporting events, and beautiful scenery, for example. These positive emotional reactions are the unconditioned responses. By pairing on numerous occasions a product (the conditioned stimulus) with the unconditioned stimulus (e.g., a sexy actor), the marketer tries to elicit a positive emotional response in the consumer to the product itself.

Figure 5-5
Could this ad for Levi's 531 jeans be using principles of classical conditioning?

Excellent examples of this process at work are the television advertisements for various brands of beer and colas shown in the mid-1990s. For example, in commercials for Coors Light beer, pictures of the beverage were followed by views of the scantily clad bodies of highly attractive men and women. Hard-driving background music enhanced the overall emotional impact of the advertisements.

Figure 5-5 is an ad for Levi's 531 jeans titled "Everything Basic Evolves." It is targeted to men who desire a looser fit in their jeans. The photo of the young man soaring through the air evokes highly positive feelings in consumers seeking freedom and independence. An interesting question is whether the ad is using a classical-conditioning approach. Probably—because positive emotional reactions will be triggered in men who resonate to the look depicted in the photo.

Classical-conditioning processes also influence shopping behavior as well as attitudes toward products, and therefore have application to distribution issues. As we noted earlier, music influences the speed with which consumers move in a grocery store and dine in a restaurant, and, through a similar process, the appearance of credit card signs encourages spending. These findings imply that the physical design of stores, restaurants, banks, and other buildings catering to consumers should be considered in terms of its emotional impact on people.

But Is It Classical Conditioning?

We cannot leave this subject without a warning about interpreting the results of consumer studies of classical conditioning. The idea that advertisers can classically condition consumers to respond positively to their products is a highly controversial one. Actually, some critics claim that a completely different mechanism explains the results found in consumer behavior studies.[14] They say that the presence of the unconditioned stimulus, such as pleasant music, puts people in a better mood, and this change in mood state causes the stimulated consumers to retrieve positive thoughts from their memories. It is these positive thoughts that account for consumers' preference for the classically conditioned brands. (Notice that this proposal of how mood affects information processing is consistent with our discussion of mood in the last chapter.)

For the marketing manager or public policy person, this is an interesting argument but one that doesn't alter the main point—which is that by following the proper conditioning procedures, marketers can influence consumer behavior. Managers have little interest in knowing whether the influence results from classical conditioning or mood effects.

OPERANT CONDITIONING

From the cognitive perspective, learning results from some change within the learner's brain. Although not observable, this change is assumed to involve the existence of a memory trace, as postulated by the Gestalt psychologists, or the creation of new protein chains, as recently proposed by physiological psychologists. In contrast, the operant-conditioning perspective resolutely avoids reference to any mental processes. Indeed, the dominant theoretician of the scientific movement known as behaviorism, B. F. Skinner, refused to allow his students to use such words as *mind*, *thoughts*, *wants*, *needs*, *motivations*, or *personality* as anything other than behaviors.

Skinner and his followers never denied the *existence* of thoughts and feelings. Rather, they insisted that these were simply covert or hidden behaviors that resulted from conditioning by their consequences. In the behavioristic view feelings and thoughts do not *cause* actions, but *are* actions.[15] Skinner even disliked using the word *learning*, because for many people it connotes some kind of internal mental operation that itself causes behavior.[16]

Just what are operants and operant conditioning? **Operants** are the naturally occurring actions of an organism in the environment. Dogs walk, bark, and sniff. Pigeons peck at objects. Human babies crawl, babble incessantly, and love to put disgusting things into their mouths. Examples of consumer operant behaviors are purchasing a product or service, telling friends or acquaintances about a product's performance, writing or calling the manufacturer about product problems, and searching for the best product or the best price for a product.

Operants are not elicited reflexively by some stimulus; rather, their initial cause is the natural tendency of organisms to explore their environment.[17] In fact, another name for operants is **instrumental responses**—which stresses that operants serve as the organism's instruments for obtaining reinforcements from the environment.

Early in this chapter we defined operant conditioning as behavior influenced by the consequences of the behavior. Formally, **operant conditioning** may be defined as a process in which the frequency of occurrence of a behavior is modified by the consequences of that behavior.[18] Thus when a consumer buys a product (a behavior), the consequences of that purchase, or behavior, will affect the probability of its occurring again. If the behavior is positively reinforced—say, the product performs well or friends compliment the buyer on the purchase—the likelihood of the purchase being repeated increases. But if the behavior is punished—say, because the product fails or friends ridicule the purchase—the likelihood that the consumer will make the same purchase again decreases.

In the operant-conditioning perspective, then, a behavior is selected according to the environmental consequences of the action. Plainly this theory is consistent with an evolutionary explanation of behavior. Just as the entire human species evolved in response to environmental pressures, individual people adapt and evolve their actions in response to the contingencies of the environment, which selectively reinforces or punishes actions. Some theorists have even argued that culture evolves in the same manner: the customs and mores of a people are selected by the consequences of that people's collective actions.[19]

Operant-conditioning concepts have wide application to consumer behavior and marketing management. Especially important to marketing managers is the study of all the reinforcers and punishers that accompany the purchase of a product—that is, the analysis of the **contingencies of reinforcement** consumers receive when they purchase and use a good or service. The relationship, or *contingency*, between the consumer's behavior and when the reinforcers and punishers occur influences the likelihood of that behavior occurring again. Take a consumer who goes into a fast-food restaurant to buy lunch. A variety of stimuli will act to reinforce or punish her—such as the cleanliness of the restaurant, the speed of the service, the courtesy of the employees, and the quality and price of the food. Managers must carefully analyze these contingencies of reinforcement to determine their impact on customers.

Table 5-2 defines eight key concepts of operant conditioning. A number of these are discussed in the paragraphs that follow.

Reinforcement and Influencing Behavior

We said earlier that a **reinforcer** is anything that occurs after a behavior and changes the likelihood that the behavior will be repeated.[20] There are three different types of reinforcers. A **positive reinforcer** is an appropriate reward that is given immediately after a behavior occurs to increase the likelihood that the behavior will be repeated. Giving consumers $25 if they agree to test-drive a car is an example of a positive reinforcer. During the recession of 1980–1982 Chrysler found that the $25 payment did increase the likelihood that consumers would test-drive its cars.

A **negative reinforcer** is the removal of an aversive stimulus. Here a behavior that results in the elimination of something negative is reinforced, and is thus more likely to occur again in the future. Negative reinforcers are somewhat hard to find in marketing because their use would involve ethical problems. One humorous example comes from a nonprofit organization that operated a shelter for teenagers. The shelter ran a fund drive it called "The Great Gerbil Giveaway." Targets received a letter saying that their name had been

Some Basic Operant-Conditioning Principles

Reinforcer. A stimulus that increases the probability of repetition of the behavior that it follows.

Positive reinforcer. A stimulus whose *presence* as a consequence of a behavior increases the probability of the behavior recurring.

Negative reinforcer. A stimulus whose *disappearance* as a consequence of a behavior increases the probability that the behavior will recur.

Secondary reinforcer. A previously neutral stimulus that acquires reinforcing properties through its association with a primary reinforcer.

Punisher. A stimulus whose presence after a response decreases the likelihood of the behavior recurring.

Shaping. A process through which a new operant behavior is created by reinforcing successive approximations of the desired behavior.

Extinction. A gradual reduction in the frequency of occurrence of an operant behavior resulting from a lack of reinforcement of the response.

Schedule of reinforcement. The frequency and timing of reinforcers form a schedule of reinforcement that can dramatically influence the pattern of operant responses.

Source: These definitions are based on material found in G. S. Reynolds, *A Primer of Operant Conditioning* (Glenview, IL: Scott, Foresman, 1968).

TABLE 5-2

placed in a drawing to receive two gerbils—but they could buy insurance against the possibility of winning the gerbils for a $5 or $10 contribution to the shelter. The letter noted that without the insurance, "you just might WIN Gus and Gwendolyn who, we have it on an unimpeachable authority, 'Go for the Gusto,' and have multiplying personalities."[21] In other words, recipients had to engage in the behavior of making a cash contribution to avoid receiving a negative reinforcer in the form of two gerbils. Of course, the premise was that most people would willingly cough up $5 to avoid the nuisance of receiving such a prize.

The third type of reinforcer, called a **secondary reinforcer,** is a previously neutral stimulus that acquires reinforcing properties through its association with a primary reinforcer. Early in life all reinforcers are primary. *Primary reinforcers* are stimuli that are necessary for life and basic happiness, such as food, water, salt, and soft touching. Over time, previously neutral stimuli can become secondary reinforcers if they are paired over and over with primary stimuli. As a result of this pairing, a neutral stimulus will take on reinforcing properties similar to those of the primary stimulus. Thus if a mother coos softly just before softly touching her baby, after a while the cooing itself will become reinforcing to the baby. A mother might in this manner inadvertently condition a baby to cry to be picked up. If she coos each time she picks up the child, the cooing becomes a secondary reinforcer, leading the baby to emit behaviors simply to obtain the cooing.

In the marketing environment most reinforcers are secondary. A product performing well, a reduction in price, a friendly "hello" by a salesperson—all are examples of secondary reinforcers. But even though they are secondary reinforcers, they have a major impact on behavior.

Another operant-conditioning concept of importance to marketers is that of a punisher. A **punisher** is any stimulus whose presence after a behavior decreases the likelihood that that behavior will recur. A key goal of marketers is to avoid punishing consumers for using their product or service. If you think about it, there are a great number of punishers in the environment that discourage people from making product purchases—for example, poor product performance, ridicule of the product by friends, irritating actions or remarks by a salesperson, and stock outages of the product.

The makers of J&B Scotch furnished an interesting—and rare—example of a deliberate use by a marketer of a punisher.[22] The company offered buyers of a $15 bottle of Scotch a free watch, radio, or movie videocassette with their purchase. Amazingly, the gift was actually worth more than the bottle of Scotch. How could the company afford to do this? The answer is that in order to get the gift, customers had to take the trouble to soak the label off the whiskey bottle. This task was so hard that few consumers bothered to go through with it. J&B management had correctly anticipated that the mere *offer* of an expensive premium (i.e., the watch, radio, or videocassette) would be sufficiently reinforcing to stimulate purchases of the product—and that there would be so much "slippage" that the offer would not cost them much. **Slippage** refers to the percentage of customers who purchase a product but fail to redeem a premium offer. Since J&B had extensive knowledge of the target market, management's gamble that few customers would go to the trouble of redeeming the premium was a rational one. Thus, in this case, a punisher kept most consumers from cashing in on the offer.

Extinction and Eliminating Behaviors   Once an operant response is conditioned, it will persist as long as it is periodically reinforced. If, however, the operant response is not reinforced for an extended number of occasions, it will tend to disappear. This disappearance of a response due to lack of reinforcement is called **extinction.** Interestingly, *immediately* after reinforcement ceases, the vigor of the response may actually increase. To see why, suppose that a salesman over the years has reinforced a customer for buying his product by taking her out to lunch each time she purchases the product. Suddenly the salesman decides that this is too expensive and quits providing free lunches. The customer's initial reaction is to purchase the product sooner than necessary to see if she can get the salesman to provide the accustomed lunch again. If he doesn't and she becomes angry or annoyed about the withdrawal of the reinforcer, the eventual outcome of his action could be the extinction of the buying response.

Schedules of Reinforcement   How reinforcers are applied can have an enormous impact on consumers' behavior. A reinforcer does not have to be applied each time a particular behavior is emitted in order to reinforce it. In intermittent **schedules of reinforcement** the behavior is reinforced after a certain number of repetitions or after a certain length of time has passed. One advantage to marketers of using schedules of reinforcement is that the operant responses are more resistant to extinction: the reinforcer can be omitted for quite a while, yet the behavior will persist.

Automobile rebates are a good example of an intermittent schedule of reinforcement. Auto rebates employ what is called a *variable interval schedule*—that is, the timing of rebates varies. In some years one rebate follows hard upon another, but in other years a considerable length of time passes between rebate programs. This intermittent schedule conditions consumers to wait for rebates; such behavior resists extinction. To take another common example, casino slot machines employ a variable ratio schedule so that there is a winner only after the one-armed bandits are fed coins an indeterminate number of times. Casinos are adept at using principles of operant conditioning to entice consumers to gamble. The nearby consumer behavior factoid discusses the use of "comps" as reinforcers.

Discriminative Stimuli

Discriminative stimuli are stimuli that only occur in the presence of a reinforcer. They are, in effect, signals that indicate the reinforcer will be given if the desired behavior is emitted. Because the discriminative stimulus is invariably paired with the reinforcer, the likelihood of the operant response occurring increases. The organism learns to emit the operant response when the discriminative stimulus is present, and not to emit it when the stimulus is absent. There is nothing special about a discriminative stimulus. For example, the word *sit* has no particular impact on a dog—until it is followed by a dog biscuit (if the animal does sit on the floor). If the word is consistently followed by a reward after the behavior has appeared, it will gradually come to elicit the instrumental response of sitting.

From an operant-conditioning perspective, the messages and information that consumers receive about products and services are discriminative stimuli[23]—that is, they signal the reinforcements that result from a purchase. Discriminative stimuli are found in advertisements, on product packaging, and in the brand names, product logos, and other symbols used by marketers. The strategy of using branded products illustrates the managerial use of discriminative stimuli. Companies with broad product lines usually prominently identify each product as a member of the same brand family. Thus Campbell's Soup Company clearly displays its name on every one of its soup products to cue consumers that each is produced by the same company. Campbell's distinctive cans have become discriminative stimuli indicating to consumers that their contents will be reinforcing. The use of corporate logos has a similar function. Figure 5-6 diagrams the relationship among the discriminative stimulus, the behavior, and the reinforcer.

Stimulus Discrimination and Generalization An important goal of marketers is to use appropriate tactics to cause consumers to differentiate their brands from those of competitors. Product differentiation operates much like stimulus discrimination in operant conditioning. **Stimulus discrimination** occurs when an organism behaves differently toward two similar stimuli. Thus Procter & Gamble would like for consumers to discriminate between P&G's Crest toothpaste and its competitor, Colgate toothpaste, by buying Crest when confronted with the two brands on a drugstore shelf. When a consumer is reinforced for responding to a particular stimulus, the probability of the response recurring in the presence of other, similar stimuli increases.

Figure 5-6
The relationship among the discriminative stimulus, the behavior, and the reinforcer.

Stimulus generalization occurs when an organism reacts similarly to two or more distinct stimuli. Suppose that a consumer is reinforced for buying a new type of coffee by really enjoying its taste. The next time that person is in the grocery store he sees that brand amid other new brands and decides to try one of the other brands. In this case the buying response is said to have generalized from one brand to another. In general, the greater the similarity between stimuli, the greater the likelihood that stimulus generalization will occur.

Since stimulus discrimination and generalization are essentially opposite sides of the same coin, whenever stimulus generalization occurs, one can say that stimulus discrimination has not occurred. The extent of stimulus generalization depends on the nature of the discriminative stimulus that signals the presence or absence of the reinforcer or punisher that is contingent on a behavior. A major goal of marketers when attempting to differentiate products, then, is to identify the discriminative stimulus that consumers use to decide whether they will respond to a product or service favorably or unfavorably. This may be a product's price, its packaging, its advertising, or how it is distributed. Basically, in controlling the elements of the marketing mix, the manager is attempting to make use of discriminative stimuli to differentiate and position a product or service.

A good example of stimulus discrimination and generalization is found in battles companies have fought over the color of pain relief tablets. American Home Products Corporation actually went to court to prevent generic competitors from emulating the "terra cotta" color of its Advil (ibuprofen) pain relief tablets. The company had spent over $100 million advertising the distinctive color of its tablets. It argued that the distinctive color was part of the brand's image, and that if competitors could usurp the color, consumers might be misled into thinking a generic ibuprofen tablet was Advil. In defense, the generic companies claimed they were not trying to mislead consumers, but contended that it is impossible to convince the public that two brands contain the same chemicals if they are different colors. As the attorney for the generic company stated, "The issue is psychological." Recognizing the psychological significance of the tablet color and accepting the generic companies' argument that their brands differed enough from Advil to prevent consumer confusion, the judge ruled that some generic ibuprofen tablets could be colored "Advil brown."[24]

The Advil case illustrates marketers' use of the behavioral concepts of stimulus generalization and stimulus discrimination. American Home Products used a discriminative stimulus—a terra cotta–colored tablet—to help sell Advil. Its competitors made generic tablets of the same color—employing the principles of stimulus generalization to sell their products. The other companies had found that for generic ibuprofen tablets to be successful on the market, consumers must perceive them as having the same ingredients as the original—Advil.

Shaping Consumer Responses

Have you ever wondered how animal trainers are able to get animals like dogs, killer whales, and elephants to do bizarre tricks? Certainly, jumping through a hoop of fire is not an instinctive behavior for the average killer whale. The process by which animals are taught such amazing tricks is **shaping.** Through shaping, trainers create totally new operant behaviors in animals by selectively reinforcing behaviors that successfully approximate the desired instrumental response.

A brief example should clarify the shaping process. A number of years ago the first author of this text used the shaping process to teach his dog, Troon, how to catch a Frisbee. First, Troon was introduced to the Frisbee by using it to play tug-of-war with him on the lawn. Troon loved tug-of-war, and this became the reinforcer that was used to control his behavior. After getting him accustomed to tugging on the Frisbee, I began to hold it out to get him to jump for it. Troon quickly mastered this behavior and would run and jump for the Frisbee with abandon. Each time that he successfully grasped the Frisbee from my hand without tearing my arm off, I reinforced him by playing tug-of-war with the Frisbee. After Troon learned to jump for the Frisbee, I began to drop it just before he took it from my hand. Every time he successfully caught it in the air, I reinforced him. If he failed to catch it, I did not reinforce him. Over a period of days Troon became progressively better at adjusting his jump to catch the Frisbee—as I gradually tossed it farther and farther away. After about a month of training, I could throw the Frisbee as far as I wanted and he would speed after it and catch it in midair. Importantly, he would always bring it back to be reinforced with the tug-of-war game.

Companies follow a similar shaping procedure when they arrange contingencies to shape new operant behaviors in consumers. For instance, a car dealership might use shaping to encourage consumers to buy cars by, first, providing free coffee and doughnuts to anyone who comes into the dealership. Next the dealership might offer $5 to any licensed driver who agrees to test-drive a car. Third, the dealer would offer a $500 rebate to anyone who buys a car. Finally, the dealership would provide outstanding service to any customer who brings in the car for maintenance. The ultimate desired consumer behavior is repeat buying from the dealership. To obtain that behavior, actions by the consumer that lead to that desired ultimate behavior are selectively reinforced.[25]

Similarly, the desired ultimate behavior of buying a low-involvement product in a grocery store can be shaped by giving consumers a free sample of the product. The consumer who takes the sample is reinforced by its good performance. Next the consumer is given a coupon to shape the behavior of buying the product in the store. Once that behavior is reinforced by the product's good performance, it can be maintained by giving the consumer additional coupons of a lesser value. Over a period of time the product's performance may be the only reinforcer required to keep the consumer buying it.[26]

Similarities Between Operant and Classical Conditioning

A number of the characteristics of operant conditioning are similar to those found in classical conditioning. Like classical conditioning, operant conditioning is more likely to occur as the number of pairings between conditional and unconditional stimuli increases. Extinction, discrimination, and stimulus generalization also take place in much the same ways in both types of conditioning.

Sometimes operant-conditioning and classical-conditioning processes overlap. In discussing the credit card study earlier in the chapter, we noted that both operant and classical conditioning seemed to be going on. The "MasterCard" stimulus may be conceptualized as a type of discriminative stimulus—that is, it was paired with the act of buying (i.e., anyone who has a credit card needs only to pull it out to buy something). Buying something is an instrumental response that is frequently followed by a reinforcer, such as other people's approval of the buyer's purchase. However, the credit card also acts as a conditioned stimulus that precedes the unconditioned stimulus of the possession of a product—which elicits the unconditioned response of good feelings. Hence the presence of the credit card itself may elicit a conditioned response of good feelings.

Operant Conditioning and Marketing

Operant-conditioning principles are applicable to most areas of marketing strategy. For example, operant-conditioning concepts are very useful in the personal-selling and sales-promotion areas of the promotional mix. Salespeople are in close enough contact with their clients to successfully reinforce desired behaviors. With the skillful use of social reinforcers (i.e., compliments, pats on the back, and smiles), they can create a situation in which they themselves become secondary reinforcers. Then clients may buy from them largely for the reward of having them around. Skilled salespeople can also employ monetary reinforcers (e.g., free lunches, Christmas gifts, rebates, and pricing discounts) to shape the buying response. However, managers should be aware of the potential for ethical or even legal problems if such reinforcements turn into real or imagined bribes.

Operant-conditioning principles are also useful in the sales-promotion area—provided managers recognize that behavioral learning can sometimes work against their efforts. For example, when General Motors offered 2.9 percent financing on its cars some years ago, buyers rushed to GM showrooms. After a few months the promotion was discontinued, and customers disappeared. Just as pigeons learn to respond to changes in a reinforcement schedule of feeding, so had consumers learned to respond to GM's changes in sales promotions. The owner of a Buick dealership noted that his customers are buying cars the way they buy shirts: "They wait for a sale: and if they miss it, they aren't worried."[27] Recently, an empirical study of consumers' purchases of liquid detergents confirmed the anecdotal evidence that not only do sales promotions erode brand loyalty, they also increase consumers' price sensitivity.[28]

Despite these well-known problems, sales promotions remain a critical component of the marketing mix—so crucial that firms spend more on them than they do on advertising. It is estimated that over 50 percent of the sales volume of many products depends on sales promotions.[29] Clearly, promotions have a positive influence on sales in the short term, and these effects are explained well by operant conditioning. Figure 5-7 shows an ad General Motors used to entice consumers into adopting its credit card. The reinforcer here is a potentially large cash discount on the purchase or lease of a new GM car or truck.

Perhaps the most important implication of operant-conditioning principles in marketing is in the area of product performance. How a product performs has strong reinforcing qualities. If it performs well, the chances that the consumer will repurchase it go up. Conversely, if it performs poorly, the buyer is punished and is much less likely to repurchase the product.

Managers can use operant-conditioning concepts when segmenting their market. If they determine that some groups of people are "deal-prone"—that is, respond particularly well to sales-promotion devices—they can direct promotional messages specifically to these segments.

As noted earlier in this section, operant-conditioning principles help position and differentiate a product. Particularly pertinent in this area are the concepts of stimulus discrimination and stimulus generalization. A marketing manager's goals here are to (1) use discriminative stimuli that help to position the product (through stimulus generalization) and (2) differentiate the product through stimulus discrimination.

Applied Behavior Analysis

There is a technology available to guide managers when they are applying operant-conditioning techniques. It is called *applied behavior analysis*, and has been shown in numerous cases to be an effective means of altering people's behavior. **Applied behavior analysis** has been defined as a process in which environmental variables are manipulated to alter behavior.[30] Manufacturers and marketers can use it to vary the contingencies of the environment by structuring reinforcements, discriminative stimuli, and punishers in a manner that modifies the behavior of consumers. Indeed, consumers can also use it to modify their own behavior.

Table 5-3 lists the steps managers need to take to develop a consumer behavior-modification program. The process begins with the identification of the behavior that is to be modified. For example, management might want to pull people into a store in a mall.

Figure 5-7

General Motors Corporation uses operant-conditioning principles in a highly effective sales-promotion campaign to entice consumers to sign up for its new credit card—up to $1,000 off each year on a new GM car.

Next, in a straightforward series of steps, managers develop measures to determine how often the behavior currently occurs, identify reinforcers that may influence the behavior, and create a behavior-modification strategy.

To return to our example of the store that wants to draw in more customers, an applied behavior analysis might determine that currently only one in 20 people at the mall enter the store. Management then considers what reinforcers might be used to attract customers into the store. One possibility is to give a small gift to some proportion of customers who come into the store. This kind of intermittent schedule of reinforcement has been found to have only a moderate initial impact, but it does remain effective over a long time period.

Remember, however, that relying too heavily on reinforcers can cause problems. If a product or service has few intrinsic reinforcing properties and is purchased largely because of external reinforcers (i.e., sales promotion devices), people will not buy it when the reinforcers are withdrawn. Thus marketers who offer frequent price discounts to reinforce consumers for buying their brand may find that buying behavior is controlled by the discount rather than by any positive features of the brand. Then, of course, if the price discounts are discontinued, consumers may well shift to other brands.[31]

Steps in Using Applied Behavior Analysis
1. Identify the specific behavior you want to change.
2. Determine how to measure how frequently the behavior occurs.
3. Identify the environmental reinforcers and punishers that shape the behavior.
4. Develop a procedure to use these reinforcers/punishers to shape the behavior.
5. Test the behavior-modification strategy.
6. Evaluate the costs and benefits of the strategy.

Source: Based on William Gaidis and James Cross, "Behavior Modification as a Framework for Sales Promotion Management," *Journal of Consumer Marketing*, Vol. 4 (Spring 1987), pp. 65–74.

TABLE 5-3

OBSERVATIONAL LEARNING

The third major approach to learning links aspects of cognitive learning to operant conditioning. **Observational learning,** which is also called **vicarious** or **social learning,** refers to the phenomenon whereby people develop "patterns of behavior" by observing the actions of others.[32] Such patterns of behavior can vary from purchasing a product, to learning a skill (e.g., riding a bicycle), to avoiding illegal drugs.

Three important ideas have emerged from observational-learning theory.[33] First, observational-learning theorists view people as symbolic beings who foresee the probable consequences of their behavior and vary their behavior accordingly. Second, people learn by watching the actions of others and noticing the consequences of those actions (i.e., by vicarious learning). Social-learning theorists stress the importance of models in transmitting information. A **model** is someone whose behavior others observe and attempt to emulate. Third, people have the ability to regulate their own behavior, and through this self-regulatory process, they supply their own internal rewards and punishments by feeling either self-critical or self-satisfied.

Notice how social-learning theory reconciles certain cognitive-learning and operant-conditioning principles. The idea that human beings are symbolic and can foresee consequences is fully compatible with principles of cognitive learning. The belief that reinforcers control behavior is derived from operant conditioning. To these principles observational-learning theory adds the concept that people can learn by observing how the behaviors of others are reinforced and punished. Note that the social-learning perspective differs from operant-conditioning theory in the contention that the reinforcers and punishers do not always have to occur to the person being influenced in order for learning to take place. People can also learn from observing the actions of others.

A further difference is that social-learning theorists argue that people can control their own behavior by creating their own reinforcement structure. As symbolic beings with expectations, we reward ourselves for doing something well or properly. Consumers, for instance, often reward themselves for finishing a grinding job by making a purchase that pleases them. Similarly, we can punish ourselves for doing something we disapprove of. For example, one of the authors of this book knew a man who enjoyed playing golf. One day, this man borrowed a five-wood from a golf pro to try it out with the intention of purchasing it if he liked it. During the round, he hit the club well and was ready to make the purchase. However, on the seventeenth hole—in a fit of anger—he accidentally broke his driver after hitting a poor shot. Ashamed of himself, the man decided not to purchase the five-wood as a means of punishing himself for doing something so foolish.[34]

Factors Influencing a Model's Effectiveness

The characteristics of the model, the observer, and the modeled consequences all influence the effectiveness of social learning. Interestingly, the characteristics of the model that enhance vicarious learning are highly similar to those that increase the effectiveness of information sources. (We discuss source effects in greater detail in Chapter 10, which deals with communications processes.)

The effectiveness of a model is increased in the following instances:

1. The model is physically attractive.
2. The model is credible.
3. The model is successful.
4. The model is similar to the observer.
5. The model is shown overcoming difficulties and then succeeding.[35]

Figure 5-8 shows an ad for Omega watches featuring Michael Schumacher, the world famous Formula 1 race car driver. Note that he exhibits many of the characteristics of an effective model.

Different kinds of people react divergently to the consequences of the behavior of models. Those who are dependent and lack self-esteem seem to be particularly prone to model the behavior of successful people, but any person who highly values the consequences of a modeled behavior tends to imitate that behavior.[36]

According to observational-learning theorists, it is the consequences of a model's behavior that determine whether the action will be emulated. Vicarious learning occurs most readily when the consequences of a behavior are very clear and salient to the observer. In addition, the more positively the observer evaluates those consequences, the greater the tendency to imitate the model's behavior.

In a consumer setting, it makes a great deal of sense for people to learn from the outcomes—negative (i.e., mistakes) as well as positive—that others have experienced. Word-of-mouth communication may have a modeling component. For instance, if your neighbor describes in detail the positive consequences of purchasing a certain product, you may react to the information by emulating her and buying the product yourself. Albert Bandura, the psychologist who has done much of the work on vicarious learning, has argued that new-product adoption is based partly on vicarious learning from "pioneers," who are more adventurous about trying out the new than the average person is. From a social-learning perspective, it is the observation of the actions of these models and their consequences that determines whether other people will buy new products or services. According to Bandura, "Models not only exemplify and legitimate innovations, they also serve as advocates for products by encouraging others to adopt them."[37]

Marketing Uses of Social-Learning Theory

Vicarious-learning principles can be employed by marketing managers for three major purposes. First, a model's actions can be used to create entirely new types of behaviors. Second, a model can be used to decrease the likelihood that an undesired behavior will occur. Third, the model can be used to facilitate the recurrence of a previously learned behavior.[38]

Just as positive reinforcers can induce consumers to undertake new actions, such as visiting a retail store they have never been to before, so may observing the actions of others cause them to engage in the model's behavior. Advertisers lean heavily on social-learning theory when they feature attractive endorsers whom they hope consumers will emulate. In this type of ad the model's behavior—using the product—is often positively reinforced by having other people congratulate the model on his or her purchase. The advertiser's

Figure 5-8
This ad for the Omega Speedmaster watch uses principles of vicarious learning to influence the behavior of consumers.

hope is that consumers will obtain vicarious reinforcement from the ad so that the probability of their buying the product will increase.

Convincing consumers to engage in new behaviors is an urgent concern of companies that are marketing innovative products. IBM, for instance, in trying to broaden the appeal of its personal computers, made ads that incorporated principles of observational learning. One series of commercials had regular people, such as a "good-old-boy" farmer, going into a computer store, purchasing an IBM, and then using it effectively. The farmer was shown being reinforced by the positive consequence of amazing his neighbors with his expertise at his new IBM personal computer.

Modeling can also be used to inhibit undesirable behaviors. In these instances the model is shown being punished for engaging in a behavior. To combat the drug problem among young Americans, people who have been harmed by drugs have appeared in ads urging others to "say no." In one campaign ex-football star Mercury Morris described how drug use had ended his football career and nearly destroyed his life. The goal of these messages is to show the bad consequences of drug use and thereby discourage the young from taking the path the "ruined" celebrity did.

The third way advertisers employ vicarious-learning principles is to enhance the likelihood that consumers will repeat an already learned behavior. Here the behavior of the model acts as a kind of discriminative stimulus to tell consumers when that behavior is appropriate. Examples of this type of vicarious learning are marketers' attempts to reposition a product or service. For instance, the Florida Citrus Growers have for years striven to persuade consumers to drink orange juice at times other than breakfast. Their advertisements feature attractive people downing orange juice after swimming or playing hard at sports. The behavior of drinking orange juice at breakfast is already in most Americans' repertoire. By using the models' actions as discriminative stimuli, the ads attempt to persuade consumers to drink orange juice on other occasions. The goal of the strategy, of course, is to raise the total sales of orange juice.

Table 5-4 summarizes the managerial implications of classical conditioning, operant conditioning, and observational learning.

A Final Word of Warning

Although classical-conditioning, operant-conditioning, and observational-learning principles are highly useful to managers and public policy makers, a word of warning is in order. As we noted earlier in the chapter, some authorities have criticized the consumer research that supports the applicability of classical conditioning to marketing. Similarly, in many of the consumer behavior examples of operant conditioning, it seems questionable that people can be conditioned with so few pairings of behavior with reinforcer. Other behavioral theories—such as associative learning—may explain the findings in both classical- and operant-conditioning studies. Nonetheless, for the manager, the key issue is whether one can influence consumer behavior by implementing classical-conditioning, operant-conditioning, and observational-learning procedures. The answer is a definite "yes." For the manager interested only in obtaining results, exactly what processes account for the behavioral change is of little importance.

A MANAGERIAL APPLICATIONS ANALYSIS OF THE MIAMI VOLUNTEER PROGRAM

Problem Identification

A Miami social service agency confronted the problem of how to furnish badly needed services to the community without spending large amounts of taxpayer dollars.

The Consumer Behavior Analysis and Its Managerial Implications

The Miami volunteer program was implemented to save money by attracting volunteers to perform social services. It succeeded in drawing people into volunteer work partly because it employed a variety of behavioral-learning concepts—in particular, ideas from

Managerial Applications of Behavioral-Learning Principles

I. Classical Conditioning

   A. Marketing Mix

      1. Recognize that ads may be used to create positive emotional responses.

      2. Pay close attention to the in-store environment and how various stimuli, such as lighting and music, influence consumers.

      3. Recognize that the consumer's attention may be attracted through the sign-tracking process by using unconditioned stimuli.

   B. Segmentation

      1. Use market research to identify segments that may respond positively to unconditioned stimuli.

   C. Environmental Analysis

      1. Identify environmental stimuli that may create positive or negative emotional responses.

   D. Market Research

      1. Perform studies to identify positive and negative unconditioned stimuli and their impact on consumers.

II. Operant Conditioning

   A. Marketing Mix

      1. Develop sales promotions based on operant-conditioning principles.

      2. Have sales personnel use operant conditioning to shape customers.

      3. Recognize that the product or service acts as a reinforcer or punisher.

      4. Assess distribution to ensure there are no punishers that will decrease the likelihood of buying behavior.

   B. Segmentation

      1. Analyze different segments to determine if they respond differentially to reinforcers or punishers.

   C. Environmental Analysis

      1. Perform an in-depth analysis to identify the reinforcers and punishers that influence the purchase of a product or service.

   D. Market Research

      1. Use market research to analyze the differential reinforcing or punishing properties of various stimuli on the target market.

III. Observational Learning

   A. Marketing Mix

      1. Use models in advertising to:

         a. Facilitate the occurrence of previously learned behavior.

         b. Decrease the likelihood of undesired behaviors.

         c. Create entirely new behaviors.

   B. Segmentation

      1. Conduct research to determine if specific target groups are prone to engage in observational learning.

   C. Market Research

      1. Conduct studies to identify characteristics of the model that are most appealing to the target group.

TABLE 5-4

operant conditioning and observational learning. The credits people received for volunteering acted as secondary reinforcers that modified their behavior. By influencing individuals to join the program, the credits brought people together. The result was that participants in the program obtained another positive reinforcer in the form of gratitude from those they helped. In summary, the contingencies of reinforcement provided by the program made the behaviors of participants resistant to extinction. As a result, few volunteers dropped out.

Observational-learning concepts also helped to ensure the success of the Miami program. Program participants acted as models for new volunteers and potential recruits. By seeing volunteers receive personal benefits from participation, others came to emulate those volunteers' behavior.

Table 5-5 summarizes the consumer behavior concepts pertinent to this case and their managerial implications. In the table three behavioral-learning concepts are identified as having particular relevance: secondary reinforcers, contingencies of the environment, and modeling.

The work credits, which served as the secondary positive reinforcer in the program, were an important part of the program's strategy. (In this case the program itself is the product being sold.) Because the credits were the principal inducement used to attract volunteers, the program's success depended on developing promotional materials that clearly informed potential participants about them. The use of the credits also acted to position the program as helping people to help themselves, rather than as giving handouts. From an operant-conditioning perspective, providing a reward to someone who does nothing to earn it merely reinforces that individual for doing nothing.

Contingencies of the environment are relevant to environmental analysis and product development. Before implementing the Miami program, the administrators carefully analyzed the contingencies of the environment to ensure that participants would be positively reinforced for desired behaviors and punished for undesired actions by the withdrawal of rewards.

Managerial Implications of Consumer Behavior Concepts in the Miami Volunteer Program	
Consumer Behavior Concept	**Managerial Implications**
Secondary reinforcers	*Promotional strategy*. Effectively communicate the rewards that will be obtained for joining program.
	Product. The credits are the primary product of the program.
	Positioning. Use credits to position the program as helping people help themselves.
Contingencies of the environment	*Environmental analysis*. Analyze reinforcers and punishers in the environment that impact volunteer behavior.
	Product development. Create service that maximizes the number of positive reinforcers and minimizes the number of punishers received.
Modeling (observational learning)	*Promotional strategy*. Have volunteers serve as models for the behavior of new recruits.

TABLE 5-5

Observational learning is particularly relevant to the development of promotional strategy. In promoting the program, the designers thought it important to have credible and successful volunteers visit various clubs and organizations to describe what they were doing. These people served as models because, listening to them, others decided to emulate their behavior and join the ranks of volunteers.

Managerial Recommendations

Recommendation 1 Use secondary reinforcers, such as credits, as a means of influencing behavior.

Recommendation 2 Employ environmental analysis to identify the reinforcers and punishers that impact behavior.

Recommendation 3 Develop services that maximize the number of positive reinforcers experienced by consumers.

Recommendation 4 Because volunteers act as models for the behavior of new recruits, encourage interaction among the current volunteers with the new recruits.

SUMMARY

Behavioral learning is a process in which experience with the environment leads to a relatively permanent change in behavior or the potential for such a change. Marketers study behavioral learning because it is the foundation for investigating the behavioral influence perspective on consumer buying. Three different types of behavioral learning were identified: classical conditioning, operant conditioning, and observational learning.

In classical conditioning, a stimulus of some type elicits behavior or an unconditioned response. The behaviors of most interest in consumer behavior contexts are the positive and negative emotional responses that may be elicited by various stimuli. When a previously neutral stimulus (the conditioned stimulus) is paired with the eliciting stimulus (the unconditioned stimulus), the neutral stimulus gradually comes to elicit the response.

Classical conditioning can help advertisers create positive feelings in consumers as they think of a particular product. As shown by several studies, an unconditioned stimulus, such as music, may elicit an unconditioned response of positive feelings. If a product is paired appropriately with the unconditioned stimulus, the product may become a conditioned stimulus. It then will have the ability to elicit the conditioned response of positive feelings.

Two classical-conditioning concepts useful to marketers are sign tracking and higher-order conditioning. Sign tracking refers to the tendency of organisms to attend to, orient themselves toward, and approach an unconditioned stimulus. In higher-order conditioning, a conditioned stimulus acts to classically condition another previously neutral stimulus. In most instances the stimuli used to influence consumers take on their influential properties as a result of higher-order conditioning.

Operant conditioning changes an organism's behavior as a consequence of something happening after the behavior. Operants are the naturally occurring actions of an organism in the environment. In a consumer behavior setting, operants include such activities as purchasing a product or service, engaging in word-of-mouth communication, and complaining about a product to a service manager. From an operant-conditioning perspective, behavior is influenced by the reinforcers and punishers received after engaging in an action.

Reinforcers are stimuli that increase the likelihood that a behavior occurring prior to the reinforcer will be repeated. Punishers are stimuli that decrease the likelihood of a behavior recurring. Marketers must be particularly concerned about the rewards and punishments that consumers receive while using their products or services. Important reinforcers/punishers that may influence consumer behavior include the performance of the product purchased, favorable and unfavorable information and reactions the consumer receives from other people about products and services purchased, and the consumer's interactions with sales personnel.

For consumer researchers, another important operant-conditioning concept is that of the discriminative stimulus. Discriminative stimuli are those that occur in the presence of a reinforcer and do not occur in its absence. These stimuli signal to the consumer that a reinforcer is likely to result when the consumer acts in a certain way. Marketers use such discriminative stimuli as advertisements, brand names, packaging, and other symbols to indicate to consumers that they will be positively reinforced if they purchase a product.

Marketers often try to arrange reinforcers and punishers to shape consumers so that they will act in totally new ways. In a consumer setting, a salesperson may attempt to shape a person's behavior by using various sales-promotion devices and social reinforcers (e.g., pats on the back). Of course, the ultimate behavior that the salesperson wants to shape is a buying response. The technology of applied behavior analysis was developed to help marketers use operant-conditioning techniques to influence behavior.

The third behavioral-learning theory we discussed is observational learning, also called vicarious or social learning. This theory proposes that people develop patterns of behavior by modeling their behavior on the actions of others. Observational-learning theorists view people as symbolic beings who learn by observing others and the outcomes of their actions. Further, these researchers believe that people can act to control their own behavior by providing their own rewards and punishments contingent on their behavior. Advertisers frequently use models to (1) teach consumers entirely new behaviors, (2) encourage them to learn to avoid engaging in undesirable actions, and (3) facilitate the repetition of previously learned behavior.

Marketing managers and public policy officials should recognize that much behavioral-learning research has been performed on animals. It is therefore arguable whether the principles derived from this research can be directly applied to human learning. Still, evidence is accumulating that these principles can be used to influence consumer behavior.

applied behavior analysis
behavioral learning
classical conditioning
conditioned response (CR)
conditioned stimulus (CS)
contingencies of reinforce-
    ment
discriminative stimuli

extinction
higher-order conditioning
instrumental responses
model
negative reinforcer
observational learning
operant conditioning
operants

positive reinforcer
punisher
reinforcer
schedules of reinforcement
secondary reinforcer
shaping
sign tracking
slippage

social learning
stimulus discrimination
stimulus generalization
unconditioned response
    (UCR)
unconditioned stimulus
    (UCS)
vicarious learning

REVIEW QUESTIONS

1. Define the concept of behavioral learning. What are the three major theoretical perspectives on learning in a consumer setting?

2. What is meant by observational learning? Identify and describe three important ideas that result from its study.

3. Define operant conditioning and describe its process.

4. Discuss the different effects of positive and negative reinforcers.

5. What is meant by extinction?

6. What is meant by a schedule of reinforcement?

7. How do marketers use discriminative stimuli to influence consumer behavior?

8. Give an example of how a marketer might shape a consumer response.

9. What are the primary differences between classical and operant conditioning?

10. What are the relationships among conditioned stimuli, unconditioned stimuli, conditioned responses, and unconditioned responses in classical conditioning?

11. Identify two managerial uses for each of the theories of learning discussed in the chapter.

DISCUSSION QUESTIONS

1. Observational learning is an important means of socialization for children, teenagers, and adults. Consider the content of popular prime-time television shows. What are the patterns of behavior that people may learn as a result of watching prime-time television? What, if any, are the public policy implications of your analysis?

2. Identify the five major consumer reinforcers. How can a salesperson use these reinforcers to influence the behavior of prospective clients?

3. Try to remember the worst experiences you ever had in a restaurant. What were the various ways in which you were punished for eating there?

4. One problem many college instructors face is getting students to participate in classroom discussions. De-

velop a systematic plan in which reinforcers are applied to shape students to participate frequently in classroom discussions.

5. Develop the outline of an advertising campaign for a new line of bath towels that includes television commercials and point-of-purchase displays that make use of classical-conditioning ideas. Be sure to identify the conditioned stimulus, the unconditioned stimulus, the conditioned response, and the unconditioned response.

6. Visit a supermarket or mall in your area. Take along a notebook and record specific examples of how retail stores use behavioral-learning principles to influence consumers. Which of the three types of behavioral learning provided most of your examples?

ENDNOTES

1. Steven Waldman, "Credit for Good Deeds," *Newsweek*, January 15, 1990, p. 61.

2. J. Paul Peter and Walter Nord, "A Clarification and Extension of Operant Conditioning Principles in Marketing," *Journal of Market-ing*, Vol. 46 (Summer 1982), pp. 102–107.

3. Robert Rescorla, "Pavlovian Conditioning: It's Not What You Think It Is," *American Psychologist*,

Vol. 43 (March 1988), pp. 151–160. Note that a "cognitive revolution" has taken place in the understanding of classical conditioning. The idea that actions follow stimuli in a reflexive manner is no longer held by most theorists. See Terence A. Shimp, "The Role of Subject Awareness in Classical Conditioning: A Case of Opposing Ontologies and Conflicting Evidence," in *Advances in Consumer Research*, Vol. 18, Rebecca Holman and Michael Solomon, eds. (Provo, UT: Association for Consumer Research, 1991), pp. 158–163.

4. An excellent review of the applications of classical conditioning and operant conditioning to marketing may be found in Walter R. Nord and J. Paul Peter, "A Behavior Modification Perspective on Marketing," *Journal of Marketing*, Vol. 410 (Spring 1980), pp. 36–47.

5. Ronald E. Milliman, "Using Background Music to Affect the Behavior of Supermarket Shoppers," *Journal of Marketing*, Vol. 42 (Summer 1982), pp. 86–91.

6. Ronald E. Milliman, "The Influence of Background Music on the Behavior of Restaurant Patrons," *Journal of Consumer Research*, Vol. 13 (September 1986), pp. 286–289.

7. Elnora W. Stuart, Terence A. Shimp, and Randall W. Engle, "Classical Conditioning of Consumer Attitudes: Four Experiments in an Advertising Context," *Journal of Consumer Research*, Vol. 14 (December 1987), pp. 334–349.

8. Richard A. Feinberg, "Credit Cards as Spending Facilitating Stimuli: A Conditioning Perspective," *Journal of Consumer Research*, Vol. 13 (December 1986), pp. 348–356.

9. Terence A. Shimp, Elnora W. Stuart, and Randall W. Engle, "A Program of Classical Conditioning Experiments Testing Variations in the Conditioned Stimulus and the Context," *Journal of Consumer Research*, Vol. 18 (June 1991), pp. 1–12.

10. Rescorla, "Pavlovian Conditioning," p. 154.

11. Francis K. McSweeney and Calvin Bierley, "Recent Developments in Classical Conditioning," *Journal of Consumer Research*, Vol. 11 (September 1984), pp. 619–631.

12. Ibid.

13. Rescorla, "Pavlovian Conditioning."

14. Chris Allen and Thomas Madden, "A Closer Look at Classical Conditioning," *Journal for Consumer Research*, Vol. 12 (December 1985), pp. 301–315.

15. Gordon Foxall, "Radical Behaviorism and Consumer Research: Theoretical Promise and Empirical Problems," *International Journal of Research in Marketing*, Vol. 4 (1987), pp. 111–129.

16. B. F. Skinner, *Contingencies of Reinforcement: A Theoretical Analysis* (New York: Appleton-Century-Crofts, 1969).

17. G. S. Reynolds, *A Primer of Operant Conditioning* (Glenview, IL: Scott, Foresman, 1968).

18. This section on operant conditioning relies heavily on Reynolds, *A Primer of Operant Conditioning*.

19. Gordon R. Foxall, "Consumer Choice as an Evolutionary Process: An Operant Interpretation of Adopter Behavior," *Advances in Consumer Research*, Vol. 21, Chris T. Allen and Deborah Roedder John, eds. (Provo, UT: Association for Consumer Research, 1994), pp. 312–317.

20. William Gaidis and James Cross, "Behavior Modification as a Framework for Sales Promotion Management," *Journal of Consumer Marketing*, Vol. 4 (Spring 1987), pp. 65–74. Gordon Foxall has developed another view of the types of reinforcers in which he distinguishes hedonic from informational reinforcers. See Foxall, "The Behavioral Perspective Model of Purchase and Consumption: From Consumer Theory to Marketing Practice," *Journal of the Academy of Marketing Sciences*, Vol. 20 (Spring 1992), pp. 189–198.

21. Dolores Curran, "Putting the 'Fun' Back in Fundraisers," *Eastern Oklahoma Catholic*, April 21, 1991, p. 21.

22. Richard Edel, "No End in Sight to Promotions' Upward Spiral," *Advertising Age*, March 3, 1987, pp. S1–S8.

23. Foxall, "Radical Behaviorism."

24. Ronald Alsop, "Advil Loses Claim to the Color Brown." *The Wall Street Journal*, April 9, 1987, p. 27.

25. This example can be found in Peter and Nord, "A Clarification and Extension of Operant Conditioning Principles in Marketing."

26. A version of this example can be found in M. L. Rothchild and W. C. Gaidis, "Behavior Learning Theory: Its Relevance to Marketing and Promotions," *Journal of Marketing*, Vol. 45 (Spring 1981), pp. 70–78.

27. Melinda Guiles, "Latest Incentives on Cars Prove Confusing and Fail to Stir Much Showroom Traffic," *The Wall Street Journal*, January 30, 1987, p. 17.

28. Purushottam Papatla and Lakshman Krishnamurthi, "Measuring the Dynamic Effects of Promotions on Brand Choice," *Journal of Marketing Research*, Vol. 33 (February 1996), pp. 20–35.

29. Robert C. Blattberg and Scott A. Neslin, *Sales Promotions: Concepts, Methods, and Strategies* (Upper Saddle River, NJ: Prentice Hall, 1990).

30. Gaidis and Cross, "Behavior Modification as a Framework."

31. Carol A. Scott, "The Effects of Trial and Incentives on Repeat Purchase Behavior," *Journal of Marketing Research*, Vol. 14 (August 1976), pp. 263–269.

32. Albert Bandura, *Social Learning Theory* (Upper Saddle River, NJ: Prentice Hall, 1977).

33. Ernest Hilgard, Richard Atkinson, and Rita Atkinson, *Introduction to Psychology* (New York: Harcourt Brace Jovanovich, 1975).

34. John C. Mowen, "Today's Round of Golf and My Expensive Mistake," *Personal Diary*, May 15, 1988, p. 69.

35. Charles C. Manz and Henry P. Sims, "Vicarious Learning: The Influence of Modeling on Organizational Behavior," *Academy of Management Journal*, Vol. 6 (January 1981), pp. 105–113.

36. Bandura, *Social Learning Theory*.

37. Ibid., p. 51.

38. Nord and Peter, "A Behavior Modification Perspective."

THAT GREAT NEW PEPSI CAN

The sleek Lamborghini pulls up to the Halfway Café somewhere out in nowhere. Its gull-wing door opens, and the beautiful form of supermodel Cindy Crawford emerges from the cockpit. Writing in *Advertising Age*, columnist Bob Garfield described the scene this way: "Simultaneously smoldering and insouciant, she emerges from the gull-wing door of her Lamborghini Diablo like Venus on the half-shell. We are way out in the country, at the crossroads of astonishing loveliness and transcendent sexuality. Watch her as she ambles sleekly across the dusty parking lot. This is no mere stroll; it is a ballet for the glands—her supple, sinuous, slow-motion feline languor on the surface concealing the coiled, smoldering, feral cat beneath. In other words: what a dish."[1]

Crawford glides to the soda machine, inserts some coins, and a Pepsi emerges. She throws back her head, closes her eyes, and gulps the cold beverage.

But Crawford is not alone. Two young boys, perhaps 10 years old, happen upon the scene. Drawn by curiosity at the sight of the car, they move closer to the vision and hide behind a fence. They are enchanted, their mouths agape.

The scene shifts rapidly between Crawford and the peeping boys. Finally, after having been refreshed, she turns to leave. At that instant one of the awestruck boys manages to utter a short sentence. He says in astonishment, "Is that a great new Pepsi can, or what?" The camera then cuts back to Crawford, and a voiceover narrator says, "Introducing a whole new look at Pepsi and Diet Pepsi." The camera again moves to the boys, and the second boy declares, "It's beautiful."

In analyzing the ad Bob Garfield raised the question of whether it objectifies women. His answer: "yes and no." He said that the ad does objectify Crawford in a "wry and self-conscious way, toying with men's libidos at least partly to make light of them." He continued, "It's not the Old Milwaukee 'Swedish Bikini Team,' which uses a coarse parody of men's adolescent preoccupations as a transparent pretext to trot out a paratroop squad of busty blondes wiggling their pulchritude at the camera." Instead, Garfield suggested that the Pepsi ad explores the meaning of beauty, whether in the form of the female or of the logo on a can of soda. He said, "Cindy Crawford in slow motion is a goddess, with aesthetic appeal exceeding erotic, sure to transfix women as well as men."[2]

But the critical issue is, "Will the ad have a positive effect on consumers?" This question is answered affirmatively by the last two sentences in Garfield's column: "Not incidentally, every time you see this new logo you will conjure up Cindy Crawford. And that, I believe, is advertising."[3]

Questions

1. What was the managerial problem that Pepsi executives were attacking in developing the Cindy Crawford commercial?
2. What consumer concepts from behavioral learning apply to the Pepsi commercial? Explain.
3. Develop a managerial applications analysis that describes the effects of the commercial. Specifically, discuss/show how the consumer behavior concepts identified relate to managerial strategy.
4. Discuss the ad in terms of the objectification of women. Do you think that women's groups should be upset by the advertisement?

References

1. Bob Garfield, "Sultry Cindy Saunters into Pepsi's Portfolio," *Advertising Age*, January 13, 1992, p. 46.
2. Ibid.
3. Ibid.

6

CONSUMER MOTIVATION AND AFFECT

INTRODUCTORY CASE

"Frequent Flier Junkies"

A major religious charity raised the average contribution from its direct-mail campaign from $46 to $126 in one year. How was this amazing feat accomplished? By offering one American Airlines frequent flier mile for every dollar donated, the charity increased not only the amount given but also the percentage of those donating (from 10 to 35 percent).[1]

The idea of giving out frequent flier miles originated in 1981 at American Airlines. Initiated to build brand loyalty among veteran airline travelers, frequent flier programs gradually expanded beyond providing free miles for airline travel. In the mid-1980s airlines began selling miles to "travel partners," such as car rental agencies, credit card purveyors, and hotels. In the early 1990s the list of firms giving away frequent flier miles expanded exponentially. By mid-decade, miles could be obtained from restaurants, mortgage firms, investment houses, and even roofing companies.

For some people, accumulating frequent flier miles has become an obsession. One consumer described collecting frequent flier miles as "a compulsion. I live, eat, and breathe the United Airlines Mileage Plus Program."[2] In the late 1980s the problem of mileage maniacs grew to epidemic proportions for the airlines. One lawyer and her husband had six credit cards, each of which netted a free mile for every dollar spent. When they applied for another card, they were rejected, but still they collected 2,500 free miles. Her husband described the lawyer as addicted: "It's like drugs; you first start small and it gets bigger."[3]

Before 1995 some frequent flier junkies cheated by enlisting people to ride airlines under their names. How to deal with such rule flouters who ultimately drove up costs for everyone was a major problem for the airlines.[4] The problem was resolved for them in 1995, when the fear of terrorist attacks on airlines caused the Federal Aviation Administration to require airlines to examine the IDs of all travelers. By checking IDs, of course, airlines could determine whether the person with the ticket was the person who had bought it.

Even absent the cheating, the airlines suffered huge revenue losses as a result of all the free miles passengers were racking up. In the early 1990s the estimated total cost of frequent flier programs approached $940 million.[5] By the mid-1990s, however, the unfunded liability problem had largely vanished because the airlines had placed deadlines on when the miles had to be used. (But they played fair. Miles earned before the change was instituted could be kept indefinitely.) Moreover, the airlines learned how to sell "free miles" to other companies for use in their promotions. By 1995, nearly half the miles were being sold to other companies at a rate of $.02 per mile. American Airlines earned roughly $300 million this way. Because frequent fliers fill seats that would otherwise be empty, this revenue is virtually pure profit. For example, at $.02 per mile, a 25,000-mile round trip domestic ticket earns the airline $500. The extra cost for that additional passenger ranges from about $43 to $93, depending upon the airline. So selling frequent flier miles has become a profit center for the airline industry.

What makes consumers act as though frequent flier miles are worth far more than their actual value? One explanation offered by *The Wall Street Journal* is that the miles have "become a jar of mad money for families, a vacation-enabling fund untouchable for paying bills, saving for college or providing for retirement." Indeed, when United Airlines offered consumers a choice of free miles or a cash rebate in a promotional campaign, most consumers chose the miles. One consultant said, "Cash is not what consumers want anymore. The whole lure of something for nothing is very powerful. Miles are almost a second national currency."[6]

INTRODUCTION

The investigation of motivation is central to understanding the acquisition, consumption, and disposition of goods, services, and ideas. As the introductory case suggests, airline companies improved their finances in the mid-1990s when they learned how to cash in on the motivation of consumers to obtain frequent flier miles. Understanding consumer needs and desires has such practical importance that corporations spend billions of dollars researching ways to motivate people to purchase their automobiles, clothing, perfume, medical services, and jeans. On the dark side of consumer behavior, public policy makers seek to determine what motivates people to buy such deviant goods as cocaine, heroin, and other addictive substances.

Motivation studies also help to explain the popularity of such risk-taking sports as skydiving, mountain climbing, and hang gliding. Researchers have found that people enjoy the physical sensations these sports deliver, as well as the emotional arousal and the sense of achievement and camaraderie they bring. According to actuarial studies, the death rate among skydivers is 1 per 700 participants per year. The riskiest sport of all, though, seems to be hang gliding: 1 in 250 participants dies each year.[7] By testing themselves at their limits of skill and courage, enthusiasts of extreme sports experience emotional highs. Indeed, many of our leisure pursuits are designed to create hedonic experiences. One newly offered extreme hedonic experience is described in the nearby consumer behavior factoid.

These ideas underline the importance of the study of motivation for marketing managers. Prior to discussing the various theories of motivation on which managers can form marketing strategy, however, we must precisely define the concept of motivation.

WHAT IS MOTIVATION?

Motivation refers to an activated state within a person that leads to goal-directed behavior.[8] It consists of the "drives, urges, wishes, or desires that initiate the sequence of events leading to a behavior."[9] Figure 6-1 presents a simple model of the flow of events that occurs when consumers experience a motivational state. The model identifies five key concepts of motivation studies: need recognition, drive state, goal-directed behavior, incentive objects, and affect. These concepts are discussed in the paragraphs that follow.

Motivation begins with the presence of a stimulus that spurs the recognition of a need. This stimulus may come from inside the consumer: feeling hungry and longing for a change of scene are examples of internal stimuli that can result in the recognition of a need (to eat, to travel). The stimulus can also come from outside the consumer: for example, from an advertisement or a friend's comment about a product. If the stimulus causes a divergence between the person's desired state of being and her actual state of being, a need results. In other words, **need recognition** occurs when the person perceives that there is a discrepancy between an actual and a desired state of being. For example, you could feel a need for a compact disc player because you dislike the sound quality of your tape player (i.e., the actual state) and/or because you realize that a CD player would provide a much clearer, cleaner sound (the desired state).

Researchers differentiate between expressive and utilitarian needs.[10] **Expressive needs** are desires to fulfill social and/or aesthetic requirements. They are closely related to the maintenance of the person's self-concept. For example, you may feel an expressive need when your outdated clothing fails to match your self-concept of fashion plate. **Utilitarian needs** are desires to solve basic problems, such as filling a car's gas tank or buying necessities, such as food and clothing.

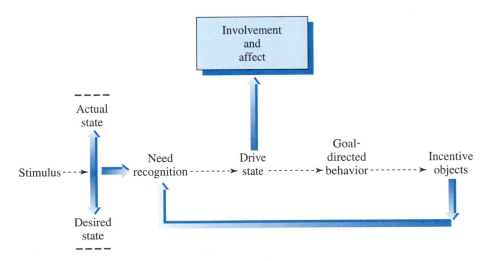

Figure 6-1
A simple model of motivation.

We can make two generalizations about the operation of needs. First, needs can be either innate or learned. Consumers are genetically programmed to have various physiological needs—for food, air, water, and perhaps human contact. But they also learn many of their needs through secondary conditioning processes and consumer socialization (see Chapters 5 and 16). Second, a person's needs can never be fully satisfied, for if one need is fulfilled, another will spring up to take its place. Marketers, of course, create products and services precisely to incite and fulfill this endless succession of needs.

Once a need is aroused, it produces a drive state. A **drive** is an affective state in which the person experiences emotions and physiological arousal. The arousal can be measured in different ways: by paper-and-pencil surveys, for example, or by monitoring physiological processes, such as changes in heart rate, blood pressure, and pupil size. The level of a drive state influences the person's level of involvement and affective state. As drive increases, feelings and emotions intensify, resulting in higher levels of involvement and information processing.

When people experience a drive state, they engage in goal-directed behavior. **Goal-directed behavior** consists of the actions taken to relieve the person's need state—in the consumer context, examples are searching for information, talking to other consumers about a product, shopping for the best bargain, and purchasing products and services.

You may have noticed the similarity between *needs* and *problem recognition* and between *goal-directed behavior* and the *search for information*. We fully discuss consumer decision making in Chapters 11, 12, and 13. Here we will just note that consumer decision making is activated when the consumer recognizes that a problem exists, and problem recognition occurs when the consumer's actual state of being differs from a desired state of being. So problem recognition and need activation are essentially synonymous concepts, and goal-directed behavior and the search for information are closely related. In each instance the consumer engages in a series of behaviors to fulfill a need or solve a problem. In sum, concepts from motivation studies are extremely helpful for understanding consumer decision making.

Consumer incentives are the products, services, information, and even other people consumers perceive will satisfy a need. If you look back to Figure 6-1, you will see that the incentive objects are connected back to the need recognition stage, where they act to narrow the gap between the actual and the desired state. Incentive objects are similar to reinforcers, and consumers will direct their behavior to obtain them to fulfill needs. In the introductory case frequent flier miles are an excellent example of a consumer incentive object.

As we've indicated throughout this section, when consumers become motivated, they experience feelings. This important topic is the subject of the next section.

THE CONCEPT OF AFFECT

As noted earlier in the chapter, a felt need produces a drive state that creates affective reactions in consumers. **Affect,** or feelings, can be defined as a "class of mental phenomena uniquely characterized by a consciously experienced, subjective feeling state, commonly accompanying emotions and moods."[11] Thus affect is a broad term that encompasses both emotions and moods. Emotions are distinguished from moods by their greater intensity and their greater psychological urgency.[12] Examples of emotions are anger, distress, fear, interest, joy, and surprise.[13] Researchers have found that when their goals are satisfied, people experience positive feelings. In contrast, when events thwart the achievement of their goals, people experience negative feelings.[14]

Areas of Application of Affective Processes to Consumer Research

Areas of Application of Affective Processes to Consumer Research

1. *Experiential perspective.* The experiential perspective asks researchers, managers, and individuals to consider the role of affect in motivating consumer behavior. Areas of particular interest are: investigating leisure pursuits, the affective impact of advertising, and the role of affect in the purchase of high-involvement products.

2. *Attitude formation.* Affect is one component of an attitude regarding a product, advertisement, or other object. (See Chapter 8.)

3. *Information processing.* Affective states may influence memory, cognitive capacity, and attention. (See Chapters 3 and 4.)

4. *Choice behavior.* A choice may be based on the rule of selecting the option that makes one feel the best. This is called the *affect referral heuristic.* (See Chapter 11.)

5. *Postpurchase processes.* Affect is closely linked to postpurchase satisfaction, brand loyalty, and complaining behavior. (See Chapter 13.)

6. *Communication processes.* Messages can be created that focus on eliciting emotions. (See Chapter 10.)

7. *Situational influences.* Mood states result in part from the consumer situation and represent a mild affective state. (See Chapter 14.)

TABLE 6-1

Table 6-1 summarizes the seven areas of consumer research for which the study of affect has implications. When analyzing a managerial or public policy problem, marketers need to consider the causes and impact of consumers' affective states.

The Structure of Emotions

Table 6-2 presents one attempt to identify the fundamental emotions that people experience in life.[15] This taxonomy of affective experience by Carroll Izard has been used extensively by consumer researchers. For example, in one study the researchers asked people about their feelings regarding the new cars they had just purchased. Measures were taken of the 10 emotions listed in Table 6-2: interest, joy, surprise, anger, distress, disgust, contempt, fear, shame, and guilt. As might be expected, satisfied customers reported being pleasantly surprised and interested, while dissatisfied owners revealed a general pattern of anger, disgust, contempt, guilt, and distress—which made them generally hostile customers.[16]

Izard's Taxonomy of Affective Experience

1. Interest	5. Distress	8. Fear
2. Joy	6. Disgust	9. Shame
3. Surprise	7. Contempt	10. Guilt
4. Anger		

Source: Carroll Izard, *Human Emotion* (New York: Plenum Press, 1977).

TABLE 6-2

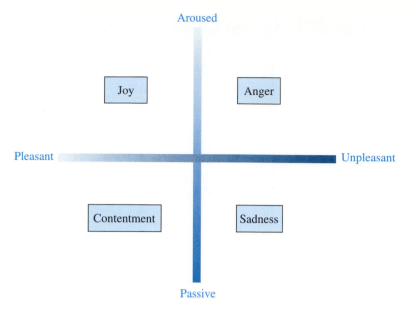

Figure 6-2

The two-dimensional structure of emotions. The boxed words represent the emotions that emerge from the combination of the two dimensions of "pleasant-unpleasant" and "passive-aroused."

Researchers have found that emotions like those identified in Table 6-2 are derived from two basic bipolar dimensions of affective responses: (1) pleasant-unpleasant and (2) aroused-passive.[17] Figure 6-2 portrays this two-dimensional structure of emotions. Within the squares formed by the two dimensions, one can place specific emotions, such as joy, anger, contentment, and sadness. If, for example, you feel very unpleasant and aroused, you are experiencing the emotion of anger. In contrast, if you feel very pleasant and quite passive, you are probably experiencing the emotion of contentment. Recent research has confirmed that these dimensions are experienced by consumers of television advertisements.[18]

Three questions concerning affect are pertinent to consumer research. First, do people in a consumer setting experience emotions with sufficient strength for them to have an impact on behavior? Second, if people do feel strong emotions in such a setting, do they experience the full range of feelings identified in Table 6-2? Finally, do individual consumers differ in the intensity with which they experience emotions?

Do Consumers Experience Strong Emotions? To test whether consumers feel strong emotions, all one has to do is to go to the complaint department of a major corporation. In a few hours' observation, one will witness the full gamut of negative emotions, from anger to rage to depression. Similarly, if one is at a busy airport in the midst of bad weather, one will see plenty of consumers in a highly charged affective state.

Consumers also experience strong positive feelings. For example, the movie *Phenomenon*, starring John Travolta, brought tears to the eyes of most people who saw it in the summer of 1996. At the extreme end of positive affective responses, perhaps, are the emotions experienced by those who engage in high-risk sports (e.g., hang gliding).

Of interest to marketers, however, is whether consumers really feel anger, fear, sexual desire, surprise, and so forth when viewing a television commercial or print ad. Certainly, if they do, these emotions must be experienced at a relatively low intensity. And if a feeling is that low-key, does it affect behavior? The evidence suggests that even weak feelings have an impact on cognition and behavior.[19] For example, a well-executed advertisement that depicts fear may cause consumers to have a lower-intensity, but nonetheless detectable, fear response.[20]

Figure 6-3 shows an ad that uses such a fear appeal to promote condom usage. Wouldn't the ad create some anxiety, particularly in those leading an active sex life with numerous partners who are not now using condoms? It makes a highly emotional point with the simple words "An ounce of prevention . . . because there is no cure."

Message strategies are based in part on the kind of emotion the advertiser wants to elicit in the target audience. In fact, messages are often labeled in terms of the emotions they elicit. Thus communications researchers speak of fear appeals, guilt appeals, sexual appeals, and of commercials that appeal to people's desire to have fun. Message development will be discussed in detail in Chapter 10.

Do Consumers Experience the Full Range of Emotions? The second question about affect that is pertinent to consumer research is whether people in a consumer setting experience the full range of emotions and feelings identified in Table 6-2. One consistent finding by consumer researchers is that the response to advertisements has two emotional dimensions.[21] One consists of positive affective states, the other of negative affective states. The implication of this finding is that a single message or event can simultaneously create both good and bad feelings in consumers.

Such combinations occur quite often. For example, a frequent advertising theme involves the achievement of a goal through a great deal of effort. The military services often

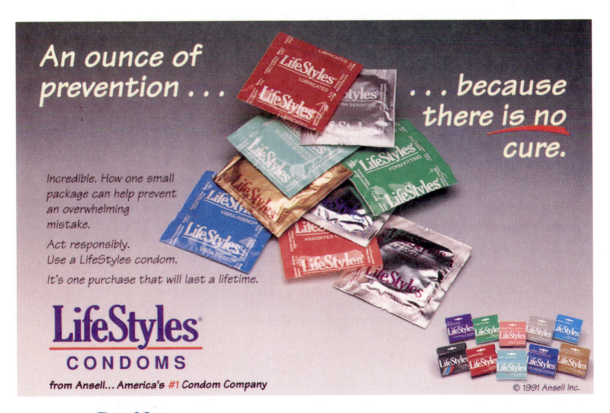

Figure 6-3
An illustration of a fear approach designed to create emotions.

use this approach in their advertising. Thus in one memorable commercial a group of young men are shown jumping out the back of a hovering helicopter and rappeling to the ground. The voiceover narrator says, "Rangers never do things the easy way." The advertisement simultaneously creates in viewers negative feelings of fear and anxiety and positive feelings of pride, excitement, and camaraderie.

When the analysis moves from advertising to consumer responses to products and services, the range of affective responses increases dramatically. For example, consumers who purchase an automobile that turns out to be a lemon experience anger, disgust, and contempt. People who illegally purchase the services of prostitutes experience a range of emotions, including sexual desire, fear, and power.

Thus the anecdotal evidence suggests that consumers do experience the two dimensions of emotional experience described earlier. That is, their emotions may be positive or negative and active or passive.

Do Consumers Differ in Intensity of Emotions?   Our third question concerning affect was whether there are individual differences in the strength with which consumers experience emotions. Researchers have found that different people react with divergent affect intensity to the same emotional stimulus. Thus **affect intensity** refers to the stable tendency of some people to react more strongly than others to an emotion-producing situation.[22] Recent studies confirm that people who score high on affect intensity respond more strongly to advertisements than those who score lower on this measure.[23] In particular, high-affect-intensity individuals react with greater empathy and feelings of pain and discomfort to fear appeals than do low-affect-intensity people. Moreover, high-affect-intensity people tend to show a more positive attitude toward the object of the advertisement. These findings imply that people with high affect intensity may be an important segment for marketers whose products lend themselves to strong emotional appeals.[24]

SOME GENERAL THEORIES OF MOTIVATION

Most textbook discussions of motivation focus on certain well-known broad theories, such as Maslow's hierarchy of needs and Murray's list of human needs. (See Figure 6-4 for a brief review of both sets of needs.) Indeed, by the time students take a consumer behavior course, they have usually encountered the Maslow hierarchy in several other classes. It may therefore surprise you to learn that research findings on these theories have been quite inconsistent. In particular, Maslow's hierarchy has been criticized for not being hierarchical because young adults have been found to focus more on self-actualization needs than "mature" adults do.[25] This finding is obviously inconsistent with Maslow's concept of self-actualization as the last human need to be realized.

One recent study, however, did yield results that were interpreted as consistent with Maslow's hierarchy of needs.[26] The researchers described products as meeting various needs identified in the hierarchy—from more basic needs (e.g., basic function and safety needs) to higher-order needs (e.g., beauty and self-expressive needs). They found that consumers were willing to pay as much as 30 percent more for a brand that would satisfy their expressive as well as their basic needs. While these results do not necessarily support the concept that needs form a hierarchy, they do suggest that "higher-order" needs strongly influence consumer behavior.

While Maslow's hierarchy has received mixed reviews, one broad theory of motivation has gained substantial research support—and that is McClelland's theory of learned needs.

A.   Maslow's Hierarchy of Needs

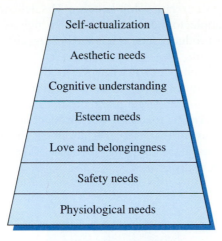

Self-actualization

Aesthetic needs

Cognitive understanding

Esteem needs

Love and belongingness

Safety needs

Physiological needs

B.   Murray's List of Human Needs

Abasement	Harm avoidance
Achievement	Infavoidance
Affiliation	Nurturance
Aggression	Order
Autonomy	Play
Counteraction	Rejection
Defendance	Sentience
Deference	Sex
Dominance	Succorance
Exhibition	Understanding

Figure 6-4

Needs identified by Maslow and Murray. (*Source:* A. H. Maslow, *Motivation and Personality,* 2nd ed. [New York: Harper & Row, 1970]; and H. A. Murray, *Exploration in Personality* [New York: Oxford, 1938].)

McClelland's Theory of Learned Needs

David McClelland developed an important stream of research around the idea that three basic learned needs motivate people: the needs for achievement, affiliation, and power. Those with a high **achievement motivation** seek to get ahead, strive for success, and take responsibility for solving problems. In one study McClelland found that 83 percent of students with a high need for achievement entered occupations that demanded an ability to take risks and to make decisions and that offered the potential for great success, such as business management.[27]

McClelland seemed to view his **need for affiliation** as similar to Maslow's belongingness need. The need for affiliation is what motivates people to make friends, to join groups, and to associate with others. Those with a high need for affiliation rank the desire to be with others ahead of the need to succeed. For example, in one study subjects were given the opportunity to choose a partner to assist them on a task. Those with a high need for achievement chose a partner with demonstrated competence, while those with a high need for affiliation were more likely to choose a friend. Apparently, people with a high need for affiliation based their decision more on the desire to enjoy the experience than to succeed at the task.[28]

The **need for power** refers to the desire to obtain and exercise control over others. The goal is to influence, direct, and possibly dominate other people. The need for power can have either of two directions, according to McClelland. It can be positive, resulting in persuasive and inspirational power; or it can be negative, resulting in the desire to dominate and obtain submission from others.

There has been some research investigating the relationship between McClelland's ideas and consumer behavior. One study, for example, found that people with a high need for achievement tend to buy more outdoor leisure products, such as skis and boating equipment, than do those with a low need for achievement.[29]

A clear prediction from McClelland's work is that products can be advertised with motivational themes derived from the three basic consumer motivations he identified. The marketer would need to analyze the characteristics of the target market to determine its dominant motivational need, and then design advertising that placed the product in such a context. Figure 6-5 is an example of an advertisement that uses an achievement theme. In the ad for Champion, which makes athletic clothing, the copy talks about the effort one must exert in practice in order to succeed when it really counts.

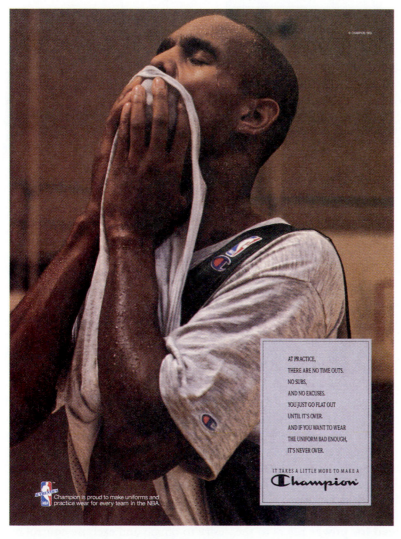

Figure 6-5
Champion uses an achievement motivation theme in this ad.

The trend in consumer research over the past 20 years, however, has been moving away from developing broad theories of motivation, such as McClelland's social needs, toward creating more restricted midrange theories that explain narrower facets of human behavior. Each of the midrange theories of motivation discussed in this chapter is supported by research, so we are fairly confident of its validity.

MIDRANGE THEORIES OF MOTIVATION

Figure 6-6 lists the midrange theories of motivation we describe in this section. Notice that the order of description is from the more physiologically based theories (e.g., opponent-process theory) to the more cognitively oriented (e.g., attribution theory). Thus at one end of the continuum opponent-process theory seeks to explain such phenomena as why people feel exhilarated after doing something frightening, such as parachute jumping, or bad after doing something exhilarating, such as taking a drug. At the other end of the continuum, attribution theory seeks to explain how people go about determining the causes of their actions and the actions of others.

Opponent-Process Theory

A researcher once made an interesting observation about the emotional reactions of parachutists. During their first free fall, before the parachute opens, they usually experience terror. They yell, their eyes bulge, their bodies go stiff, and they breathe irregularly. Upon landing safely, they at first walk around stunned with stony-faced expressions. Then they begin smiling, talking, gesticulating, and showing every indication of being elated. Why would someone who was in terror only minutes before suddenly become elated? The answer seems to lie in a theory of motivation called the *opponent-process theory of acquired motivation.*[30]

According to **opponent-process theory,** when someone receives a stimulus that elicits an immediate positive or negative emotional reaction, two things occur. First, the person has the immediate positive or negative emotional reaction. Then the person experiences a second emotional reaction that has a feeling opposite to that initially experienced. The overall feeling experienced is a combination of these two emotional reactions. Because the second emotional reaction is delayed, the overall episode consists of the consumer first experiencing the initial positive or negative feeling, and then, after some time

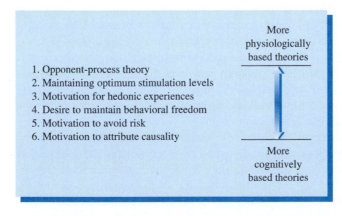

More
physiologically
based theories

1. Opponent-process theory
2. Maintaining optimum stimulation levels
3. Motivation for hedonic experiences
4. Desire to maintain behavioral freedom
5. Motivation to avoid risk
6. Motivation to attribute causality

More
cognitively
based theories

Figure 6-6
Some midrange theories of motivation.

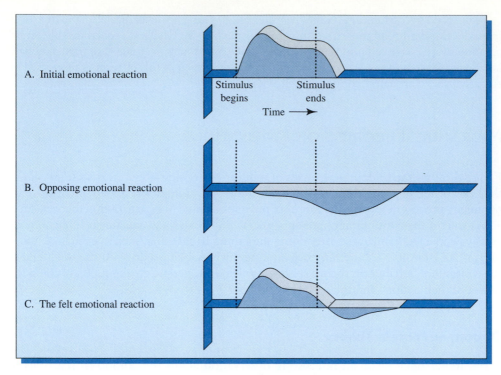

A. Initial emotional reaction

Stimulus
begins

Stimulus
ends

Time ——➤

B. Opposing emotional reaction

C. The felt emotional reaction

Figure 6-7

A diagram of opponent-processes for an initially positive stimulus, e.g, taking an addictive drug.

period, experiencing the gradual decline of this feeling and its replacement by the opposite feeling. So the parachutists first felt extreme fear, but after landing, their fear turned into the opposite emotion—elation. Figure 6-7 diagrams these relationships.

The idea that pleasure and pain often go together has been noted for many centuries. Consider these words of Plato found in the work *Phaedo*:

> How strange would appear to be this thing that men call pleasure! And how curiously it is related to what is thought to be its opposite, pain! The two will never be found together in a man, and yet if you seek the one and obtain it, you are almost bound always to get the other as well, just as though they were both attached to one the same head. Wherever the one is found, the other follows up behind.

Although opponent-process theory is quite simple, it has broad explanatory power. It can be used to account for a variety of consumer behaviors, such as drug addiction, cigarette smoking, jogging and marathoning, sauna bathing, and video game playing. Why do seemingly sane people put themselves through the pain of running a marathon? The answer may be that through the operation of opponent processes the pain that accompanies the endurance run is followed by great physiological pleasure. When combined with the reinforcement the runner receives from friends and acquaintances, the overall experience of marathoning may be felt as an extremely positive one.

Opponent-process theory also explains certain dysfunctional buying behavior—for example, sinking into debt through overusing credit cards. In order to make themselves feel better, people with this tendency buy something they really can't afford and charge it. After the purchase, however, they begin to feel bad because of the negative rebound (as predicted by the theory). The arrival of the credit card bill exacerbates their negative feelings. To combat these negative feelings, they go out to the local mall or call a favorite mail-order firm to make another purchase. Their behavior results in a vicious circle of financial problems.

Priming Another concept to emerge from opponent-process theory is priming. **Priming** is a phenomenon in which a small amount of exposure to a stimulus (e.g., food, playing a video game, watching television) leads to an increased drive to be in the presence of that stimulus. An example most people can relate to is taste cravings. After eating one potato chip, it is extremely hard to stop. The taste of the first potato chip activates the taste buds so that the drive to consume additional chips is greater than the drive to eat the first one. Priming influences many consumers in their ingestion of drugs (e.g., cocaine and alcohol) and food (e.g., nachos and rich desserts).

Priming is understood as follows from the perspective of opponent-process theory. When the person begins to consume the reinforcing stimulus, the opposite motivation has not yet had a chance to start building up. Without any counteracting motivation, the experience is intensely pleasurable, resulting in a strong drive to continue consuming. Eating that first potato chip creates a strong sensation. Because the opposite feeling (e.g., a sickening satiation) has not yet been activated, the tendency to continue consuming the salty snack is extremely strong.

Marketers intuitively use principles of priming on a regular basis. Providing samples in a supermarket is a classic example of priming. One study found that giving out free samples of donuts in a grocery store made shoppers spend more than they had intended.[31]

Maintaining Optimum Stimulation Levels

A growing body of research evidence indicates that people have a strong motivation to maintain an optimum level of stimulation.[32] An **optimum stimulation level** is a person's preferred amount of physiological activation or arousal, which may vary from very low (e.g., sleep) to very high (e.g., severe panic). People are so motivated to maintain their optimum level of stimulation that they will generally take action to correct the level whenever it becomes too high or too low.

A person's level of stimulation at any given point in time is influenced by internal and external factors. Internal factors include age, learning history, and personality characteristics. For example, people who crave higher levels of stimulation score high on a scale that measures sensation seeking.[33] To maintain the high levels of stimulation they require, sensation seekers are apt to engage in such risky activities as parachute jumping, mountain climbing, and gambling. External factors that influence the stimulation level are those that affect the uncertainty and risk of the environment. For example, sensation seekers frequently pursue entrepreneurial careers because they enjoy the risk.

In summary, people attempt to manage their actions and the environment to maintain their optimum stimulation level. When the level of arousal is too high, for them, they take steps to lower it, and when it is too low to suit them, they alter their behavior to raise the stimulation level.

The motivation to maintain an optimum stimulation level has obvious implications for marketers because so many products and services arouse or depress consumers' activation levels. For example, various types of drugs lower arousal levels (e.g., sleep aids) or raise arousal levels (e.g., stimulants such as caffeine and amphetamines). Many popular leisure activities strongly affect arousal levels, such as parachute jumping, white-water rafting, and hunting. Indeed, even the desire to attend sporting events is influenced in part by the need for excitement. Similarly, some rides at amusement parks are designed chiefly to scare those who dare them. If you want to test your own arousal-seeking tendencies, complete the scale found in Table 6-3.

The desire to maintain an optimum level of stimulation may account for some spontaneous brand switching and variety seeking among consumers.[34] Many consumers periodically change brands for no apparent reason. For example, they buy a particular brand of toothpaste consistently for a long period of time, and then suddenly switch to another brand. When asked why they switched, they will often say that they just wanted a change. The likely reason for much spontaneous brand switching is that the consumer was bored and wanted to vary her everyday life to temporarily change her activation level.

One study found that people who need higher activation levels tend to engage in greater amounts of brand switching, to reveal greater innovativeness in product purchases, and to be greater risk takers.[35] More recently, other researchers found that those with higher optimum stimulation levels:

Engage in greater amounts of information seeking.
Feel more boredom with repetitive ads.
Reveal higher levels of variety seeking when choosing fast food.
Exhibit greater tendencies to gamble and seek risk.[36]

A Scale to Measure Arousal-Seeking Tendencies

Directions: Answer each of the questions with a "yes" or "no." The greater the number of "yes" answers you have, the more you tend to seek to be aroused.

1. I frequently change the pictures on my walls.
2. I enjoy seeing people in strange clothing.
3. I continually seek new ideas and experiences.
4. I get bored when I am always around the same people and places.
5. I enjoy doing foolhardy things just for the fun of it.
6. People view me as an unpredictable person.
7. I like surprises.
8. I enjoy having lots of activity going on around me.
9. I like a job that offers change, variety, and travel even if it involves some danger.
10. I enjoy dangerous sports like mountain climbing, airplane flying, and skydiving.
11. I feel restive when I am safe and secure.
12. I would like to try the group-therapy techniques involving strange body sensations.

Source: Adapted from a scale developed by Albert Mehrabian and James Russell, *An Approach to Environmental Psychology* (Cambridge, MA: MIT Press, 1974).

TABLE 6-3

The chapter-opening case illustrates the application of optimum-stimulation-level theory to consumer behavior, for one factor motivating people to accumulate frequent flier miles is the need to engage in leisure activities—specifically, traveling—that will move them to the desired arousal levels.

The Motivation for Hedonic Experiences

The desire for hedonic experiences is closely related to the need to maintain an optimum stimulation level. In consumer research **hedonic consumption** refers to the needs of consumers to use products and services to create fantasies, to feel new sensations, and to obtain emotional arousal.[37]

Though the systematic study of hedonic consumption dates only to the late 1970s, it has roots in other areas of study, such as the motivation research that began in the 1950s. Early motivation researchers usually adopted a Freudian perspective in interpreting consumer behavior. They focused on the emotional reasons for people's consumption patterns and emphasized how products could be used to arouse and fulfill fantasies. (Freudian ideas are discussed in greater detail in Chapter 7 on personality and psychographics.) In addition, the hedonic consumption approach borrows concepts from sociologists on the symbolic nature of products—that is, products not simply as objective entities but also as tokens of emotional and social significance. Thus diamonds are not simply pretty carbon crystals but also symbols of love, permanence, and status.

Desires to Experience Emotion The term **hedonism** generally refers to gaining pleasure through the senses. In the consumer behavior context, however, it is a more complex term, for the feelings that consumers seek may not be uniformly pleasurable. People seek to experience a variety of emotions, including love, hate, fear, grief, anger, and disgust. At first thought it might seem odd that people would seek out negative experiences. However, remember that roller coasters are built to create fear. Even their names—such as "Screamer" and "The Beast"—are designed to instill fright. Horror movies are intended to frighten and disgust people. And Steven King has made millions of dollars selling narratives of fear. In sum, people go to movies and read books to experience both positive and negative secondhand emotions, such as love, excitement, and fear.

One point made by hedonic consumption theorists is that emotional desires sometimes dominate utilitarian motives when consumers are choosing products.[38] From a utilitarian perspective, why would a sane man send a woman a dozen roses? Today the gesture will cost him fifty dollars or so—for a gift that will perish within a couple of days. A gift of roses only makes sense in terms of the flowers' symbolic value and the emotions created in the recipient by such symbolism.

The types of products and services that hedonic consumption researchers investigate are found within the "experiential research perspective"—and are quite different from those traditionally analyzed. Most consumer research has focused on packaged goods (e.g., toothpaste, beer, cigarettes, laundry detergent). In contrast, hedonic research concentrates on such products as movies, rock concerts, theater, dance, pornography, and sporting events, which are intrinsically more emotionally involving than toothpaste or toilet paper. Hedonic relevance comes from a product's symbolic value and the emotion it is anticipated to elicit in the consumer.

Figure 6-8 presents an ad with a clear hedonic appeal.

Desires for Leisure Activities Another type of hedonic consumption rests on the desire to engage in leisure activities—that is, those activities pursued in "free time" or "nonwork time." Actually, "leisure" is a personal experience. What one person defines as leisure, another may consider work.[39] Leisure is multidimensional, and a number of different needs

Figure 6-8

Guess what hedonically based feelings the advertiser is attempting to elicit in this perfume ad.

propel people to seek it. For example, people use leisure activities to express themselves to others. They also use them to obtain pleasure and to maintain their optimal stimulation level. Among the other principal reasons people engage in nonwork activities are the following:

1. Desire for intrinsic satisfaction. Here the activity is viewed by the consumer as rewarding in and of itself—for example, reading a good book. Performing the activity does not have to lead to any extrinsic rewards—monetary or otherwise. Some theorists have even argued that **intrinsic satisfaction** is the key defining element of leisure and that all other concepts merely explain how that intrinsic satisfaction is obtained.[40]

2. Involvement in the activity. Here the activity is so totally absorbing that the person forgets all about everyday life while engaged in it—for example, in playing a pickup game of basketball, a young man becomes so absorbed that no thought intervenes between him and this intensely pleasurable activity.

3. Perceived freedom. Here the activity is utterly without coercion. The person has the **perceived freedom** to engage or not to engage in it—for example, taking a long, luxurious hot bath. In this line of thought all experience is conceptualized as either obligatory or discretionary. Activities that one is obligated to perform are categorized as nonleisure, while those that one is free to perform or not are categorized as leisure.[41]

4. Mastery of the environment or of oneself. Here the person attempts to learn something well or to overcome some obstacle. The idea is to test oneself or to conquer the environment—an example of an activity that provides both kinds of mastery is mountain climbing. Sports and intellectual games such as chess are especially conducive to feelings of mastery.

5. Arousal. The need for arousal is a major motivator of leisure activities. Leisure pursuits that are novel, complex, and risky can temporarily raise the arousal levels of consumers, which produces pleasurable feelings.[42] An example is bungee jumping.

To refer back to the introductory case, the motivation to obtain hedonic experiences is another factor that motivates consumers to pursue frequent flier miles. The miles represent a ticket to exciting leisure activities, and as such are an incentive object that consumers desire.

The Desire to Maintain Behavioral Freedom

One of the motivators of leisure activities mentioned in the last section was the desire to engage in activities without externally imposed restrictions. This desire to maintain behavioral freedom has broad implications for marketers. When their freedom to select a product or service is impeded, consumers respond by reacting against the threat. The consequent motivational state has been labeled *psychological reactance*.[43]

The term **reactance** describes the motivational state of someone whose behavioral freedom has been threatened. The reaction among loyal users of Crayola crayons to an action taken by the product's producer, Binney & Smith, in 1990 illustrates the effects of consumer reactance. That year Binney & Smith managers decided to retire eight colors from the popular 64-crayon flip-top box and replace them with more contemporary hues. Thus "boring" colors like raw umber, maize, and lemon yellow were eliminated in favor of sexy new hues like wild strawberry, fuchsia, teal blue, and cerulean. Some consumers reacted to the change by forming a boycott. In one protest march people even carried a coffin, for, as a marcher said, "They call it a retirement. I call it a burial." A first-grader named Ebony Faison said plaintively, "Whenever I draw me, I use raw umber. What color should I color now?"[44] In the year following the change the company received more than 300 calls and letters a month protesting the action. A Binney & Smith spokesperson admitted, "We were aware of the loyalty and nostalgia surrounding Crayola crayons, but we didn't know we hit such a nerve."[45]

Marketers intentionally use reactance principles to influence consumers. They know that sharp restrictions of supply can make demand for a product soar because its perceived value increases as a result of reactance. For example, researchers have found that one-day-only sales intensify consumers' desires to make purchases much more than three-day sales. Auto companies like Ferrari and Porsche make use of reactance by turning out exceedingly expensive limited-production models. For example, in 1990 the sticker price on a 475-horsepower Ferrari F40 was a mere $350,000. However, since only 1,000 were built, demand increased and the asking price quickly rose to over $1 million. As one dealer explained, "If you say to a rich man, 'You can't have it,' he'll want it more. That's part of the appeal."[46] In sum, restricting people's ability to obtain a product or to buy during a sale increases their desire to engage in the action.[47]

Two types of threats can lead to reactance. **Social threats** involve external pressure from other people to induce a consumer to do something. Examples are pressing the consumer to buy a certain product, go to a certain play, or vote for a particular political candidate. If the pressure is too great, the consumer may react against it—resulting in a "boomerang effect." In such instances the consumer moves in the opposite direction intended by the person exerting the pressure. In personal selling, the potential for the boomerang effect is great because salespeople must take definite steps to persuade customers to buy their products. However, if they push too hard, they risk alienating the prospect and losing the sale. A time-tested strategy is to give customers the right information so they can persuade themselves that the product is the right one to buy.

A second threat to behavioral freedom that leads to reactance comes from impersonal sources. Generally, **impersonal threats** are barriers that restrict the consumer's ability to buy a particular product or service. For instance, there may be a shortage of the product, someone else may buy it, making it unavailable to the consumer, or the price of the product may rise, making it unaffordable to the consumer. In each case something comes between the consumer and the purchase of the product. The consumer's likely reaction to the barrier is to reevaluate the product and want it even more. Even the decision to buy one product instead of another can result in the person's reevaluating the unchosen alternative more positively.[48]

For consumers to experience reactance, three requirements must be met. First, the consumer must believe that he or she has the freedom to make an unhindered choice in a given situation. Lacking the ability to make a free choice—perhaps because alternative products are unavailable—the consumer will not experience reactance. Second, the consumer must feel his or her personal freedom is threatened. Third, the buying decision must be one that is of some importance to the consumer.[49]

Interestingly, companies sometimes find it profitable to create reactance via their advertising messages. For example, Avia Athletic Footwear placed the following stern message in its ads: "For athletic use only. If you're after frilly, faddish shoes, open someone else's catalog." This may seem a foolish approach since 80 percent of all athletic shoes sold in the United States are for street use. However, as Avia's vice president for marketing explained, the company is banking on human nature: "People will yearn to buy shoes just because you tell them not to. It's the perfect strategy for our core customer (serious athletes); and, if executed correctly, it will be very effective with the non-core as well."[50]

Reactance theory also applies to our chapter-opening case. Because of the financial liabilities they were incurring, the airlines considered simply dropping their frequent flier programs. Had they done that, however, consumers would have lost the behavioral freedom to use the free miles they had accumulated—and that would have created a huge backlash, to say nothing of legal problems. The ingenious solution was to phase in new programs with time limits and honor the old commitments. In this way the airlines avoided the effects of reactance, and simultaneously greatly reduced their financial liability. (The nearby consumer behavior factoid discusses reactance and speeding in the state of Montana.)

The Motivation to Avoid Risk

Perceived risk is defined as a consumer's perception of the overall negativity of a course of action based upon an assessment of the possible negative outcomes and of the likelihood that those outcomes will occur.[51] Note that perceived risk embraces two major concepts: the negative outcomes of a decision and the probability that these outcomes will occur.

Consumers constantly face decisions that involve uncertainty and the possibility of negative outcomes. Examples are buying new products or untried services, determining where to go on a vacation, selecting a retailer to purchase a product from, and choosing whether to take up a dangerous sport. Actually, almost any decision a consumer can make involves uncertainty. A general rule derived from consumer research over the past 25 years is that people usually seek to avoid risks they perceive as being too great. So, in general, con-

Question: When did Montana change its laws to eliminate speed limits on its highways and give consumers the behavioral freedom to go as fast as they want?

Answer: Actually, the state never eliminated speed limits. However, in 1995 Montana did eliminate all specific speed restrictions in favor of one "basic rule," which states that vehicles should be driven so that others are not unreasonably endangered. Thus when an out-of-state driver was clocked going 94 mph on a two-lane winding road, he was fined because he was driving too fast for those conditions.

The difficulty with the "basic rule" is that, while it gives people the behavioral freedom to drive at an appropriate speed, it places personal responsibility on them to use common sense. Ironically, since the "basic rule" became the only law in this area, some drivers become incensed when stopped for speeding because their behavioral freedom to drive as fast as they want is being limited.

Source: Tom Vines, "Freedom on the Montanabahn," *The Wall Street Journal,* July 3, 1996, p. A10.

sumers are risk averse, but there are exceptions to this rule. As we noted earlier in the chapter, some consumers actively seek risk in order to optimize their activation levels.[52]

Types of Consumer Risks The first discussion of the concept of perceived risk appeared in marketing literature in 1960.[53] Since then, consumer researchers have expended a good deal of effort trying to identify the various types of risk that impact consumers. Table 6-4 lists the seven major types of risk to which consumers respond.[54] These are financial, performance, physical, psychological, social, time, and opportunity loss risks.

Marketers often gear their promotional work toward lowering consumers' perceived risk. Advertisements frequently point out how the product or service being touted lowers risk. A good example is insurance ads stressing the reduction of financial risk. But automobile manufacturers like Volvo mention the reduction of physical risk when bragging about the safety of their cars, and many advertisements for personal-use products have a reduction-of-social-risk theme. Thus there are products to help you ward off "ring around the collar," bad breath, and dandruff. Deodorant ads often trade on social embarrassment.

Types of Perceived Risk

1. *Financial.* Risk that the outcome will harm the consumer financially (e.g., will buying a car cause financial hardship?).

2. *Performance.* Risk that the product will not perform as expected (e.g., will the car really accelerate faster than a Porsche 928?).

3. *Physical.* Risk that the product will physically harm the buyer (e.g., will the car collapse in a crash?).

4. *Psychological.* Risk that the product will lower the consumer's self-image (e.g., a swinging single wonders, will I look like a typical housewife if I buy this car?).

5. *Social.* Risk that friends or acquaintances will deride the purchase (e.g., will my best friend think that I am trying to show him up by buying a Porsche?).

6. *Time.* Risk that a decision will cost too much time (e.g., will buying a sports car cost me time because I have to tune it so frequently?).

7. *Opportunity loss.* Risk that by taking one action the consumer will miss out on doing something else he or she would really prefer to do (e.g., by buying a Porsche 928, will I miss out on buying several expensive oil paintings?).

TABLE 6-4

Figure 6-9
Gillette cleverly uses a social-risk theme to promote a deodorant.

Figure 6-9 presents an ad for Dry Idea that promises you will "never let them see you sweat."

Factors Influencing the Perception of Risk Consumer behavior researchers have found a number of factors that influence the amount of risk consumers perceive in a given situation. The prime influencer is personality. The following personal characteristics have been associated with a greater willingness to accept risk: higher self-confidence, higher self-esteem, lower anxiety, and lower familiarity with the problem or decision. People who tend to make choices from a wider range of alternatives also tend to see lower risk in a particular selection.[55]

Situational factors also influence risk perception. One situational variable is the nature of the task. For example, voluntary risks are more acceptable to people than involuntary risks.[56] When consumers choose to drive a car on a trip or opt for a ski vacation, they are taking a voluntary risk. When they live in a house near where a nuclear power plant is being built or undergo surgery for a life-threatening condition, they are taking an involuntary risk. For voluntary activities, consumers systematically perceive less risk than actually exists, while for involuntary activities, they tend to overrate the risk. Another situational variable that influences risk perception concerns how the purchase is to be made. Most consumers perceive that there is a greater risk in shopping through the mail than in buying in a retail store.[57]

The characteristics of the product or service itself also affect consumers' perception of risk. In general, products or services whose use may result in highly negative outcomes are seen as riskier. Factors associated with such negative outcomes are cost, social visibility, and potential physical danger.

Risk perception is also influenced by the saliency of the potential negative outcomes of a purchase or activity. When these are highly salient, they are generally easier to remember, and that may make consumers perceive the product or service as riskier than it really is.[58] When a ValuJet passenger plane crashed into the Everglades swamp in Florida in 1996, this startup airline was grounded for many months until questions over its safety and maintenance practices could be resolved. The publicity about the crash, and about the safety of new airlines in general, scared consumers so that their perception of the risk of flying on any new airline increased. The result was that passengers avoided newer carriers like Kiwi International Air Lines and Frontier Airlines. As one airline president said, media coverage of the ValuJet crash left the impression that "If you're not a major airline, you're not safe."[59]

In summary, the amount of perceived risk in a purchase is likely to increase if:

1. The product is expensive in terms of time or money for the target market.
2. Others will evaluate the purchaser on the basis of his or her choice of brand.
3. Consumers get ego satisfaction from owning the product.
4. Consumers perceive that they could be harmed physically, psychologically, or socially by purchasing the product.
5. Consumers have to give up purchasing other products or services to buy the product.
6. The activity is of an involuntary nature, and the outcome is out of the consumer's control.

When managers discover through market research that consumers perceive a significant risk in purchasing their brand, they should take immediate steps to lower that perception. Table 6-5 lists a number of strategies developed to lower consumer perceptions of risk.

It is also possible to capitalize on the risk averseness of the average consumer by developing an advertising campaign that focuses on how a particular product or service reduces risk. General Motors has successfully used such a strategy. In a campaign focusing on the physical risk of driving an automobile, GM has forcefully pointed out the good safety record of many of its cars. Figure 6-10 presents one of these ads.

How Do Consumers Reduce Perceived Risk? Since some degree of perceived risk is inherent in nearly all consumer decisions, people must have methods that help them make buying decisions with some confidence. One important theory is that consumers compare

Managerial Strategies to Lower Consumer Perceptions of Risk

1. Price the product higher than average.
2. Give good warranties and guarantees.
3. Distribute the product through retailers that have a high-quality image.
4. Use a high-quality sales force composed of people who can give consumers convincing reassurance.
5. Provide prompt service to lower the time risk.
6. Obtain seals of approval (e.g., Underwriters Laboratories Approved).
7. Develop an extensive image-building campaign for the product *and* the company.
8. Provide hot-line numbers consumers can call to get information.
9. Give free trials, test drives, etc. (e.g., "test drive an Apple").
10. Provide lots of information about the product through brochures, packaging, instructions, writeups in magazines, and a trained sales force.
11. Possibly have trusted endorsers promote the product.
12. Focus on developing good word-of-mouth communications about the product.

TABLE 6-5

their perception of the amount of risk present in a buying decision to their personal criterion of how much risk is acceptable.[60] If the perceived risk is greater than the acceptable risk, the consumer is motivated to reduce the risk in some way or forgo the purchase.

What actions do consumers take to reduce the amount of risk they perceive in a buying decision? In general, risk-reduction strategies involve taking steps to lower the perceived likelihood of negative outcomes. There are six popular risk-reduction strategies:

1. Be brand-loyal—consistently purchase the same brand that has proved satisfactory in the past.
2. Buy through brand image—purchase a quality national brand.
3. Buy through a store image—shop at a retailer you trust.
4. Seek out information so you can make a well-informed decision.
5. Buy the most expensive brand, which is likely to be of high quality.
6. Buy the least expensive brand in order to reduce financial risk.

Why Do Consumers Sometimes Seek Risk? As we saw earlier in the chapter, people sometimes seek risk rather than attempt to avoid it. The pursuit of risk generally pertains to experiential-hedonic activities, such as participating in dramatic sports (e.g., parachuting) or amusement park rides and taking addictive and/or illegal drugs to get "high." Behavioral learning approaches such as optimum-stimulation-level theory and opponent-process theory partially explain why people willingly risk their lives at highly dangerous activities, but they are insufficient. Physiological processes are needed to complete the explanatory picture.

One group of researchers has suggested that there are three fundamental reasons for engaging in high-risk sporting activities: normative, hedonic, and personal efficacy motives. The attraction to parachuting, hang gliding, and bungee jumping seems to revolve around the normative need to comply with the desires and expectations of others. This motive is especially dominant at the early stages of participating in the sport: the neophyte takes up the dangerous activity to become part of an elite group. Hedonic motives predominate when people seek arousal, pleasure, fun, and incorporation into "the flow." One experiences "the flow" when one is totally absorbed in the experience. People describe such a state as feeling as though "nothing else in the world exists but the moment itself."[61]

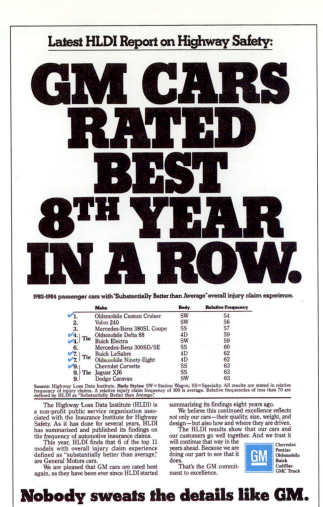

Figure 6-10
General Motors points out that its cars may reduce physical risk for drivers and passengers.

The third motive for engaging in high-risk sports is personal efficacy. After they overcome their worries about safety and equipment, participants begin to focus on the pleasures of developing their skills. As they become more proficient at the sport, participants gain a feeling of achievement and increased self-confidence that leads to the construction of a new identity based on the sport and its subculture. The new identity is equivalent to a kind of transcendence.

To sum up the findings about consumer risk, when purchasing basic goods and services (e.g., clothing, household goods, medical services, and food), people actively seek to minimize their risk. However, when engaged in hedonic consumption, consumers actively seek risk. Finally, when making financial investments, consumers may take on extra risk because of the potential monetary rewards such risk makes possible. In this area consumers are making risk-reward trade-offs.

The Motivation to Attribute Causality

In everyday life events happen to consumers for which they seek an explanation. A good or service may perform well below expectations, a product endorser may strongly tout a brand of soft drink, a salesperson may flatter a customer's ego, or a plane may crash—in each case consumers will seek to understand the cause for the action. They will want to know why the product brought dissatisfaction, why the endorser advocated the soft drink, why the salesperson was so ingratiating, and why the plane crashed.[62]

The explanation of the processes through which people determine the causes of actions has been labeled attribution theory.[63] According to **attribution theory,** we attempt to determine whether the cause for an action was something internal or external to the person or object in question. Thus in the case of the endorser, a consumer may ask whether this person recommended the product because he or she actually liked it (an **internal attribution**) or because he or she was paid to endorse it (an **external attribution**). Similarly, when asked why you bought a particular brand, you will try to determine whether the cause for your action was something internal to the product (e.g., the product's good qualities) or external to it (e.g., pressure from a salesperson or a temporary reduction in price).

People are motivated to make attributions concerning the cause of an action so that they can determine how to act in the future. So if a consumer decides that an endorser is advocating a product merely because he or she got paid a great deal of money to do so, the consumer will discount the message. That is, the consumer will attribute the cause of the message to an external factor (i.e., the money) rather than to an internal factor (i.e., the endorser's liking for the product), and the advertising message will not affect the consumer's attitude toward the product. (The Shaquille O'Neal factoid illustrates the difficulties companies can have with highly paid endorsers.) Because consumers tend to make external attributions concerning the endorsements of highly paid celebrities, companies seek "virgin" endorsers—celebrities who have not previously endorsed products. In 1997 an example of a "virgin" endorser was Barbra Streisand.

On the other side of the coin are circumstances that cause attributions that can benefit a brand. Suppose you purchase a high-priced brand. If asked why you bought such an expensive product, you will probably point to its high quality. It is as though you said to yourself, "The product *must* be good, or why would I have paid such a high price for it?" You made an internal attribution simply because the product cost a lot and you bought it.

Attribution theory is actually composed of a family of theories, each of which explains how people determine causality in various situations. We do not have the space to discuss all of these component theories. We will examine only the two we consider most important to marketing: the augmentation-discounting model of Harold Kelley and the fundamental attribution error.

The Augmentation-Discounting Model Harold Kelley was one of the first social psychologists to articulate basic ideas about how people make attributions of causality. He was interested in determining how people decide whether an action represents the actor's true beliefs—or has been caused by external forces (so that it says little about what the actor really believes). Kelley's work led him to propose two important concepts: the augmenting principle and the discounting principle.[64]

The augmenting-discounting model is based on the idea that people examine the environmental pressures impeding or propelling a particular action to determine the underlying cause for the action. Discounting occurs when the person making the attribution decides that external pressures are provoking someone to act in a particular way—in other words, his actions are to be expected given the circumstances. In these cases the one making the attribution believes that the actions of the observed person were caused by the environment rather than by that person's actual beliefs, feelings, and desires. In other words, the observer *discounts* the action as representing the other's real beliefs. In summary, the **discounting principle** may be stated as follows: The ostensible cause of a given outcome is discounted if other, more plausible causes are also present. An example is making the judgment that an endorser is praising a particular product because she is being paid to do so.

What happens if a person moves *against* environmental pressures to do something? In this instance the action is unexpected given the circumstances, so the observer will tend to believe that the person must have been highly internally motivated. In summary, the **augmenting principle** states that when a person moves against the forces of the environment to do something unexpected, observers are more likely than otherwise to judge that the action represents the actor's actual opinions, feelings, and desires. Suppose a computer salesperson tells a prospective customer that a computer made by her competitor is superior to one she sells. Since the salesperson is moving against her own best interests, the consumer will be more inclined to judge that she really believes the statement she is making. Incidentally, the augmentation principle also implies that this unexpected statement by the salesperson will increase the consumer's trust in her.

The augmenting-discounting model applies to many consumer behavior problems. Certainly one of marketers' major difficulties is how to induce consumers *not* to discount their messages. Consumers are well aware of the pressures that exist to sell products and to make a profit, so whenever they watch television advertisements or open promotional mail, they are primed to discount the message by making an external attribution. In fact, it may be taken as a general rule that most consumers do not believe promotional messages accurately describe the characteristics of products. For instance, one study found that over 59 percent of respondents found "statistical" claims in advertisements to be unbelievable.[65]

Since consumers are prone to discount messages, marketers frequently strive to create the impression that a message is going against the pressures of the environment. Take the ad reproduced in Figure 6-11, where R. J. Reynolds Tobacco Company is telling young people "You don't have to smoke to express yourself." Coming from a tobacco company, the message is certainly unexpected and seemingly against the company's interests.

Figure 6-11

By implicitly arguing against young people smoking, R. J. Reynolds is using the augmenting principle to encourage consumers to view the company as trustworthy.

The likely result is an augmentation of consumers' belief in the trustworthiness of the company.

Another way to counteract consumer discounting of advertising messages is to use person-on-the-street interviews. By employing seemingly randomly selected people to advocate the product, the advertiser hopes to give viewers the impression that there was no external pressure for the advocacy. Pepsi-Cola ran an effective campaign against Coca-Cola with its "Pepsi Challenge" series, in which people were asked to taste the two colas and give their preferences. More people in the taste test favored Pepsi, and the ads dramatically improved the brand's market share. In response, Coke had its endorser, Bill Cosby, suggest that the people taking the Pepsi Challenge deliberately chose Pepsi in order to get on television. Coke's goal, obviously, was to give the audience a reason to discount the Pepsi message.

A powerful means of counteracting discounting is to have your product appear in a movie. It is well known that a movie appearance can hugely boost a product's sales: the classic case was the use of Reese's Pieces in the megahit *E.T.: The Extra Terrestrial*. Since then, companies have been willing to pay handsome fees to get their brand featured in a movie,[66] though the practice has come under fire by consumer activist groups, which charge that it is unethical to disguise advertising as art this way. But despite the pressure of these critics, you can expect to see the practice of paying movie makers to feature branded products in their films to continue. Brand managers know that most consumers discount the testimonials of product endorsers, so they are determined to expose people to their brands in "nonselling" circumstances that enhance the authenticity of the product.

The Fundamental Attribution Error People are biased to make internal attributions.[67] That is, when an individual engages in an action, observers tend to believe that action was caused by the person's true beliefs and preferences—even when the actor really had no choice in the matter. This bias to make internal attributions is called the **fundamental attribution error.**

Evidence of the fundamental attribution error was found in a study in which respondents received persuasive messages from an automobile salesperson. Some of the participants were told that the salesperson had received special incentives to sell the car—called the "Austin"—while others were not told this. Those in the special incentive condition learned that the salesperson would get a bonus for selling the Austin and that the sales manager was pushing him to sell the car. Somewhat amazingly under the circumstances, the respondents inferred that the salesperson's attitudes were consistent with the sales message. The researcher reported that "Even when the salesperson clearly had no choice in the views that he or she expressed, subjects inferred that the product was more valuable when the salesperson spoke favorably compared to unfavorably."[68]

Besides being useful for investigating how consumers react to advertising and personal-selling messages, attribution theory can be applied to several other problem areas in consumer behavior. For example, the attributions consumers make concerning a product's failure can have strong implications for a corporation. If consumers attribute the cause of the failure to the company, that could have severely negative long-term effects on the firm's business. But if they attribute a product problem to bad luck and chance, the negative repercussions for the company are generally minimal.[69] Johnson & Johnson's ability to rapidly rebuild Tylenol's market share after some Tylenol pills were poisoned by a demented character in the early 1980s illustrates this point. Consumers were favorably impressed by the company's valient efforts to recall all the outstanding product from the market and repackage the brand to make the pills tamper-proof. Therefore they attributed the cause of the poisonings to bad luck rather than to the corporation.

Attribution theory also has managerial implications for sales promotion. When companies make heavy use of sales-promotion devices, they should be concerned about the attributions consumers make concerning why they bought the product. If consumers attribute the cause of their purchase to the sales-promotion device (e.g., a rebate or prize), the company may find it extremely difficult to build repeat purchase behavior and brand

Managerial Applications of Attribution Theory

A. *Develop believable advertisements*. Use strategies that enhance message augmentation by influencing consumers to perceive that the endorsement was made for internally caused, rather than externally caused, reasons.

Develop messages that give both sides of arguments. Particularly include messages that would be unexpected from the organization.

B. *Resolve product problems*. Respond quickly and proactively to product problems to enhance consumer beliefs that the cause of the problem should be attributed to bad luck rather than to the intentions or negligence of the firm.

C. *Assess sales promotions*. Use sales promotions cautiously to avoid having consumers attribute the cause of their purchase to the incentive rather than to the product's qualities.

TABLE 6-6

loyalty.[70] Managers, then, should do all they can to encourage consumers to attribute their purchase of a product or service to the brand rather than to some situational variable like a rebate.

Table 6-6 summarizes the managerial applications of attribution theory.

A MANAGERIAL APPLICATIONS ANALYSIS OF THE FREQUENT FLIER CASE

Problem Identification

The chapter introductory case detailed the incredible behavioral impact that frequent flier miles have had on consumers. The problem can be framed in the following manner: What are the consumer behavior concepts that help us understand the strong behavioral impact of frequent flier programs?

The Consumer Behavior Analysis and Its Managerial Implications

Five concepts from motivation studies help us to understand the strong appeal of frequent flyer miles to consumers: (1) the general motivation model, (2) consumer affect, (3) optimum-stimulation-level theory, (4) motivation for hedonic experiences, and (5) reactance. Table 6-7 presents the managerial implications of these concepts for the frequent flier case. Note that the frequent flier program is a sales-promotion technique, so each of the consumer concepts applies to promotional strategy within the marketing mix.

The general model of motivation has application to promotional strategy. Frequent flyer miles are a consumer incentive: they are instrumental to fulfilling consumers' goals to experience interesting leisure activities and obtain hedonic experiences. Therefore they are a highly effective sales-promotion device—so effective that nonairline companies have been buying the miles from airlines so they can give them away to consumers as part of their own sales promotions.

Consumer affect is another important component of any promotional strategy. The analyst should ask what kinds of feelings may be elicited by this promotional device. Frequent fliers—especially frequent flier junkies—experience a range of feelings, including interest, surprise, joy, and even fear. One factor contributing to the positive affect stimulated by this program is the "illusion" that the miles are free. Because consumers do not

Managerial Implications of Consumer Behavior Concepts in the Frequent Flier Case

Consumer Behavior Concept	Managerial Implications
1. General motivation model	*Promotional strategy*. Frequent flier miles can be used as a sales-promotion device to encourage consumers to act.
2. Consumer affect	*Market research*. Identify how consumers with different levels of affect intensity respond to alternative ads in which people are shown having fun.
	Segmentation. Segment the market on affect intensity.
	Promotional strategy. In ads show people having fun because they are using their frequent flier miles.
3. Optimum stimulation	*Market research*. Perform studies to determine if consumers who seek frequent flier miles differ in desired optimum stimulation from the general public.
	Segmentation. If frequent fliers differ in desired optimum stimulation level, employ a segmentation strategy.
	Promotional strategy. Develop ads with themes that appeal to individuals in the segment identified.
4. Hedonic experiences	*Market research*. Identify the divergent needs for leisure that motivate people to seek frequent flier miles.
	Segmentation. Develop segmentation strategies based on the analysis of the different travel needs being satisfied.
	Promotional strategy. Develop and target ads to consumers with specific leisure/travel needs.
5. Reactance	*Promotional strategy*. Use as an advertising theme the idea that frequent flier miles give consumers the freedom to go and do what they want.
	Product development. When changes in the structure of the frequent flier program are made, carefully consider customers' desire for behavioral freedom. Be aware that significant restrictions on the use of miles already earned will lead to consumer dissatisfaction.

TABLE 6-7

directly pay for the miles, they are convinced they are getting something for nothing—always a highly pleasurable experience.

Consumer affect has application to promotional strategy, market research, and segmentation. First, in developing advertising campaigns, airlines and other companies employing frequent flier miles as a sales-promotion device should show people having fun using their miles. Second, market research is required to determine how consumers with divergent levels of affect intensity respond to such advertising. Third, if differences in affect intensity are found to relate to preferences for advertising, managers should use this variable for segmentation purposes. For example, people who are low in affect intensity will probably respond better to informational ads than to emotional ads.

An interesting aspect of the motivation to obtain frequent flier miles is that consumers may participate in such programs to optimize their stimulation levels. The excitement and energy of traveling make the miles highly desirable—particularly to those who are chronically underaroused. Optimum-stimulation-level theory has application to promotional strategy, market research, and segmentation. As with affect intensity, market research can be used to determine if individuals with differing chronic needs for stimulation respond divergently to advertising messages. If so, managers would be wise to segment the marketplace and target appropriate promotional messages to the various segments.

Closely related to the concept of optimum stimulation level is the motivation to obtain hedonic experiences. The hedonic desire for leisure activities clearly plays a role in motivating consumers to obtain frequent flier miles, for the miles are the instruments that allow them to experience intrinsic satisfaction, gain perceived freedom, and manage their arousal levels to their satisfaction. Motivation for hedonic experiences has application to market research, positioning, and segmentation. First, research should be done to analyze the divergent leisure needs that consumers expect frequent flier miles to fulfill. Managers can use this analysis to identify divergent segments of consumers. It should then be possible for nonairline companies to consider whether it is possible to position their good or service by linking it to frequent flier miles.

Finally, the consumer behavior concept of reactance also applies to this case. One of the central attributes of frequent flier miles is that they give consumers the freedom to go wherever they want. Ironically, even though the miles can only be used for travel purposes, these programs offer consumers more freedom than monetary rebates would because consumers might feel obligated to use a money rebate for necessities rather than for leisure pursuits.

The concept of reactance applies to the approach the airlines took to reduce their future liability for frequent flier miles. By phasing in the new program and permitting customers to use their accumulated miles as originally promised, the companies refrained from limiting consumers' behavioral freedom.

Reactance theory also pertains to promotional strategy and product development. Nonairline companies can use behavioral freedom as an advertising theme: By buying our product and getting frequent flier miles, you can go where you want to go and do what you want to do. In the area of product development, airlines should carefully consider the impact of changes in the structure of frequent flier programs on consumer desires for behavioral freedom because significant restrictions in the use of the miles will certainly lead to unhappiness.

Managerial Recommendations

A number of managerial recommendations emerge from the frequent flier case. These include:

Recommendation 1 Frequent flier miles act as a consumer incentive, and can be used as a potent sales promotion device.

Recommendation 2 In advertisements show consumers experiencing fun and excitement through their use of frequent flier miles.

Recommendation 3 Segment consumer markets on their divergent need for arousal, and target different promotional themes to the groups.

Recommendation 4 Promote using frequent flier miles as a means of gaining personal freedom.

SUMMARY

Motivation refers to an activated state within a person that leads to goal-directed behavior. According to our model of motivation, a stimulus creates a gap between a desired state and an actual one. When such a gap exists, the individual recognizes a need state that leads to a drive state and goal-directed behavior. The individual's goal-directed behavior is focused on obtaining incentive objects that are perceived to move the actual state closer to the desired state. In a consumer behavior context, marketers hope to create products that fulfill the needs initiating the goal-directed behavior.

Accompanying a motivated state are various feelings and emotions. These affective states are characterized by consciously experienced internal sensations, which include feelings of anger, distress, fear, interest, joy, and surprise. In consumer settings, these various feelings have a positive dimension and a negative dimension, so the same situation can cause both positive and negative feelings to occur simultaneously.

There are a number of general theories of motivation, but overall McClelland's theory of learned needs has received the most research support. McClelland's theory suggests that different people have divergent needs for achievement, affiliation, and power.

Six midrange theories of motivation were discussed in this chapter: opponent-process theory, optimum-stimulation-level theory, motivation for hedonic experiences, the desire to maintain behavioral freedom, the motivation to avoid risk, and the motivation to attribute causality. The core concept of opponent-process theory is that whenever a person receives a positive or negative stimulus, two processes are activated sequentially. First, the process with the same affective content as the stimulus is elicited; thus if the stimulus is positive, initial feelings are positive. Shortly after the initiation of the primary response, a second, opposing response begins to occur. The sum of these two processes is the overall feeling the subject experiences. Opponent-process theory can explain a wide variety of seemingly reckless consumer actions, ranging from participation in daredevil sports to taking drugs.

People take action to raise or lower their input of stimulation to maintain their optimum level of stimulation. Thus consumers may go to an amusement park to raise their level of activation or consume alcohol to lower their activation.

Some researchers argue that consumers have a need to experience fantasies, feelings, and emotional arousal. The study of these needs is at the core of the experiential perspective on consumption. The need for hedonic experiences may well be an extension of the need to maintain an optimum stimulation level. Consumers will in certain instances allow hedonic or emotional desires to dominate utilitarian motives in choosing products. Researchers who emphasize the experiential side of consumer behavior tend to focus on different types of products and services. Rather than investigating the buying of consumer durables and package goods, they study the consumption of such services as rock concerts, dancing, sporting events and the purchase of symbolic goods such as automobiles and jewelry.

The fourth midrange theory of interest to consumer researchers is reactance theory, which holds that consumers have a need to maintain their behavioral freedom. When they feel this freedom threatened, they react in ways intended to restore it. Companies can threaten a consumer's behavioral freedom in a variety of ways, such as by having their salespeople push customers too hard or by suddenly withdrawing a product from the marketplace, as we saw in Chapter 1 in the case of Coca-Cola. When consumers feel their freedom is threatened, they take opposing action, such as refusing to buy from a pushy salesperson or filing a lawsuit to get a product placed back on the market.

Although consumers sometimes engage in high-risk activities, they generally seek to avoid risk. Researchers have identified a number of consumer risks, including financial, performance, and social risks. The two components of risk are the negative outcomes that are possible from a course of action and the probability that those outcomes will occur. Overall risk is assessed by combining these two. Among the factors that influence consumers' perception of risk, the most important are the situation, the characteristics of the individual, and the nature of the product.

The last midrange theory we discussed, attribution theory, proposes that people attempt to identify why various events occur in order to gain an understanding of their environment and their own actions as well as the actions of others. The fundamental attribution error refers to people's tendency to attribute the cause of someone's actions to that person's personality and disposition rather than external causes. Marketers and consumer researchers should try to determine the attributions that consumers make—particularly concerning the actions of product endorsers and sales personnel. If consumers believe that these corporate representatives are merely hyping the product rather than trying to assist consumers, they will place little trust in their statements.

REVIEW QUESTIONS

1. Define the concept of motivation. Draw the model of motivation presented in Figure 6-1 and indicate how needs, drives, and goal-directed action interrelate.

2. What are the seven needs identified by Maslow?

3. What are the three needs identified by McClelland?

4. Discuss how the opponent-process theory of acquired motivation can explain why someone becomes elated after making a parachute jump.

5. Define the concept of priming. How can it be used by retailers to increase sales?

6. Define the concept of optimum stimulation level. How can the desire to maintain optimum stimulation levels lead consumers to purchase products or engage in specific types of leisure activities?

7. What is meant by the term *hedonic consumption?* What types of products and services tend to fall into the hedonic consumption category?

8. Name four reasons people engage in nonwork leisure other than the desire to maintain optimum stimulation levels.

9. Define the concept of reactance. What factors can lead consumers to engage in reactance?

10. Define the concept of perceived risk. Identify five of the seven types of risk to which consumers may respond.

11. Identify five of the six ways discussed in the text through which consumers may act to reduce risk.

12. What occurs when a consumer makes an attribution? Why are people motivated to make attributions?

13. Discuss what is meant by the augmenting and discounting principles.

14. A number of managerial strategies that can potentially lower consumer perceptions of risk were mentioned in the chapter. Identify six of these possible strategies.

15. Define the concept of affect. Does advertising influence consumers' affective states?

DISCUSSION QUESTIONS

1. Following are a number of slogans that have been used by corporations and the military. Indicate which of the needs identified by motivational theorists each slogan best represents.
   a. "Be all that you can be." (U.S. Army)
   b. "Join the Pepsi generation." (Pepsi-Cola)
   c. "For all you do, this Bud's for you." (Budweiser)
   d. "Get a piece of the rock." (Prudential)
   e. "All my men wear English Leather, every one of them." (English Leather)
   f. "We have one and only one ambition. To be the best. What else is there?" (Lee Iacocca for Chrysler)

2. You are on an advertising team assembled to develop a campaign for a new running shoe. Develop three slogans that could be used in the campaign. Each slogan should illustrate one of the needs identified by McClelland.

3. Priming may be a potent method of encouraging consumers to purchase large amounts of a product. How could the following types of companies make use of priming: a sausage manufacturer, a movie distribution company, an auto dealership?

4. Consider your own leisure activities. Which of these activities do you engage in to increase your level of activation?

5. You are marketing director for a company that makes camping equipment. Develop the copy for a print advertisement for a backpack. The advertisement should utilize three of the five reasons identified in this chapter for engaging in nonwork activities.

6. Reactance often causes problems for companies in their personal-selling efforts. However, under some circumstances reactance can be beneficial to companies. Try to identify one or more of these instances.

7. A major problem mail-order companies face is that consumers perceive a greater risk in purchasing from them than from retail stores. List some of the steps that mail-order companies can take to reduce this perceived risk.

8. What are some actions advertisers can take to convince consumers to attribute internal rather than external motivations to endorsers of products?

9. Make a list of your own leisure activities, along with your reasons for engaging in each. Compare your reasons to those given in the text for engaging in nonwork activities.

10. Identify in specific terms two ads that have caused you to experience positive affect and negative affect.

ENDNOTES

1. Scott McCartney, "Free Airline Miles Become a Potent Tool for Selling Everything," *The Wall Street Journal*, April 15, 1996, pp. A1, A6.

2. Robert Rose, "Frequent-Flier Plans Become Obsessions," *The Wall Street Journal*, September 9, 1988, p. 29.

3. Michael Manges, "Frequent-Flier Awards Tougher to Sell as Airlines Tighten Rules, Press Brokers," *The Wall Street Journal*, September 9, 1988, p. 29.

4. Robert Rose, "There's Still Time to Triple Miles," *The Wall Street Journal*, September 9, 1988, p. 29.

5. Peter Nulty, "Why Do We Travel So*!?*! Much?" *Fortune*, March 28, 1988, pp. 83–88.

6. Scott McCartney, "Free Airline Miles," p. A6.

7. Richard L. Celsi, Randall L. Rose, and Thomas W. Leigh, "An Exploration of High-Risk Leisure Consumption Through Skydiving," *Journal of Consumer Research*, Vol. 20 (June 1993), pp. 1–23.

8. Ernest Hilgard, Richard Atkinson, and Rita Atkinson, *Introduction to Psychology*, 6th ed. (New York: Harcourt Brace Jovanovich, 1975).

9. James A. Bayton, "Motivation, Cognition, Learning—Basic Factors in Consumer Behavior," *Journal of Marketing*, Vol. 22 (January 1958), pp. 282–289.

10. Robert A. Westbrook, "Product/Consumption-Based Affective Responses and Postpurchase Processes," *Journal of Marketing Research*, Vol. 24 (August 1987), pp. 258–270.

11. Meryl Gardner, "Effects of Mood States on Consumer Information Processing," *Research in Consumer Behavior*, Vol. 2 (1987), pp. 113–135.

12. Deborah J. MacInnis and Bernard J. Jaworski, "Information Processing from Advertisements: Toward an Integrative Framework," *Journal of Marketing*, Vol. 53 (October 1989), pp. 1–23.

13. Carroll E. Izard, *Human Emotion* (New York: Plenum Press, 1977).

14. John P. Murray, Jr., and Peter A. Dacin, "Cognitive Moderators of Negative-Emotion Effects: Implications for Understanding Media Context," *Journal of Consumer Research*, Vol. 22 (March 1996), pp. 439–447.

15. Ibid.

16. Robert A. Westbrook and Richard L. Oliver, "The Dimensionality of Consumption Emotion Patterns and Consumer Satisfaction," *Journal of Consumer Research*, Vol. 18 (June 1991), pp. 84–91.

17. James A. Russell, "A Circumplex Model of Affects," *Journal of Personality and Social Psychology*, Vol. 36 (1980), pp. 1152–1168.

18. Haim Mano, "Assessing Emotional Reactions to TV Ads: A Replication and Extension with a Brief Adjective Checklist," *Advances in Consumer Research*, Vol. 23, Kim Corfman and John Lynch, eds. (Provo, UT: Association for Consumer Research, 1996), pp. 63–69.

19. Chris Allen, Karen Machleit, and Susan Marine, "On Assessing the Emotionality of Advertising via Izard's Differential Emotions Scale," in *Advances in Consumer Research*, Vol. 15, Michael Houston, ed. (Provo, UT: Association for Consumer Research, 1988), pp. 226–231.

20. For an empirical study of the impact of advertisements on affect and decision making, see Haim Mano, "Emotional States and Decision Making," in *Advances in Consumer Research*, Vol. 17, Marvin Goldberg et al., eds. (Provo, UT: Association for Consumer Research, 1990), pp. 577–584.

21. See Julie Edell and Marian Burke, "The Power of Feelings in Understanding Advertising

Effects," *Journal of Consumer Research*, Vol. 14 (December 1987), pp. 421–433. Also see Westbrook, "Product/Consumption-Based Affective Responses."

22. Randy Larsen and Ed Diener, "Affect Intensity as an Individual Difference Characteristic: A Review," *Journal of Research in Personality*, Vol. 21, pp. 1–39.

23. David J. Moore, William D. Harris, and Hong C. Chen, "Exploring the Role of Individual Differences in Affect Intensity on the Consumer's Response to Advertising Appeals," *Advances in Consumer Research*, Vol. 21, Chris Allen and Deborah Roedder John, eds. (Provo, UT: Association for Consumer Research, 1994), pp. 181–187.

24. David J. Moore, William D. Harris, and Hong C. Chen, "Affect Intensity: An Individual Difference Response to Advertising Appeals," *Journal of Consumer Research*, Vol. 22 (September 1995), pp. 154–164.

25. Lynn Kahle, David Bousch, and Pamela Homer, "Broken Rungs in Abraham's Ladder: Is Maslow's Hierarchy Hierarchical?" *Proceedings of the Society for Consumer Psychology*, 1988.

26. Richard Yalch and Frederic Brunel, "Need Hierarchies in Consumer Judgments of Product Designs: Is It Time to Reconsider Maslow's Hierarchy?" *Advances in Consumer Research*, Kim Corfman and John Lynch, eds. (Provo, UT: Association for Consumer Research, 1996), pp. 405–410.

27. David McClelland, "Achievement and Entrepreneurship: A Longitudinal Study," *Journal of Personality and Social Psychology*, April 1965, pp. 1, 389–392.

28. E. H. French, "Effects of the Interaction of Motivation and Feedback on Test Performance," in *Motives in Fantasy, Action, and Society*, J. W. Atkinson, ed. (New York: Litton Educational Publishing, 1958).

29. David H. Gardner, "An Exploratory Investigation of Achievement Motivation Effects on Consumer Behavior," Association for Consumer Research, 1972 Proceedings of Third Annual Conference, pp. 20–23.

30. Richard L. Solomon, "The Opponent-Process Theory of Acquired Motivation," *American Psychologist*, Vol. 35 (August 1980), pp. 691–712.

31. Sandon A. Steinberg and Richard F. Yalch, "When Eating Begets Buying: The Effects of Food Samples on Obese and Nonobese Shoppers," *Journal of Consumer Research*, Vol. 4 (March 1978), pp. 243–246.

32. Jan-Benedict E. M. Steenkamp and Hans Baumgartner, "The Role of Optimum Stimulation Level in Exploratory Consumer Behavior," *The Journal of Consumer Research*, Vol. 19 (December 1992), pp. 434–448. Also see Michael Driver and Siegfried Streufert, "The General Incongruity Adaption Level (GIAL) Hypothesis," Paper No. 114, Institute for Research in the Behavioral, Economic, and Managerial Sciences, Krannert Graduate School of Management, Purdue University, West Lafayette, IN.

33. Marvin Zuckerman, *Sensation Seeking: Beyond the Optimum Level of Arousal* (Hillsdale, NJ: Lawrence Erlbaum, 1979).

34. Satya Menon and Barbara E. Kahn, "The Impact of Context on Variety Seeking in Product Choice," *Journal of Consumer Research*, Vol. 22 (December 1995), pp. 285–295.

35. P. S. Raju, "Optimum Stimulation Level: Its Relationship to Personality, Demographics, and Exploratory Behavior," *Journal of Consumer Research*, Vol. 7 (December 1980), pp. 272–282.

36. Steenkamp and Baumgartner, "The Role of Optimum Stimulation Level in Exploratory Consumer Behavior."

37. Morris Holbrook and Elizabeth Hirschman, "The Experiential Aspects of Consumption: Consumer Fantasies, Feelings, and Fun," *Journal of Consumer Research*, Vol. 9 (September 1982), pp. 132–140.

38. Elizabeth Hirschman and Morris Holbrook, "Hedonic Consumption: Emerging Concepts, Methods, and Propositions," *Journal of Marketing*, Vol. 46 (Summer 1982), pp. 92–101.

39. Suzana de M. Fontenella and George M. Zinkhan, "Gender Differences in the Perception of Leisure: A Conceptual Model," in *Advances in Consumer Research*, Vol. 20, Leigh McAlister and Michael L. Rothschild, eds. (Provo, UT: Association for Consumer Research, 1992), pp. 534–540. Also see Lynette S. Unger and Jerome B. Kernan, "On the Meaning of Leisure: An Investigation of Some Determinants of the Subjective Experience," *Journal of Consumer Research*, Vol. 9 (March 1983), pp. 381–392.

40. Seppo Iso-Ahola, *The Social Psychology of Leisure and Recreation* (Dubuque, IA: William C. Brown, 1980).

41. Douglass K. Howes, "Time Budgets and Consumer Leisure-Time Behavior," in *Advances in Consumer Research*, Vol. IV, William Perreault, ed. (Ann Arbor, MI: Association for Consumer Research, 1977), pp. 221–229.

42. Philip Hendrix, Thomas Kinnear, and James Taylor, "The Allocation of Time by Consumers," in *Advances in Consumer Research*, Vol. V, William Wilkie,

ed. (Ann Arbor, MI: Association for Consumer Research, 1979), pp. 38–44.

43. Jack W. Brehm, *A Theory of Psychological Reactance* (New York: Academic Press, 1966). For a review of consumer research on reactance, see Greg Lessne and M. Venkatesan, "Reactance Theory in Consumer Research: The Past, Present, and Future," in *Advances in Consumer Research*, Vol. 16, Thomas K. Srull, ed. (Provo, UT: Association for Consumer Research, 1989), pp. 76–78.

44. Virginia Daut, "Roses Were Reds, Violets Blues, Till They Redid Crayola's Hues," *The Wall Street Journal*, September 11, 1990, p. B1.

45. Suein L. Hwang, "Hue and Cry over Crayola May Revive Old Colors," *The Wall Street Journal*, June 14, 1991, p. B1.

46. Carrie Dolan, "Well, Would You Expect 475 Horses to Sell for Peanuts?" *The Wall Street Journal*, February 15, 1990, p. 1.

47. Greg J. Lessne, "The Impact of Advertised Sale Duration on Consumer Perceptions," in *Development of Marketing Science*, Vol. 10, J. M. Hawes, ed. (Atlanta: Academy of Marketing Science, 1987), pp. 115–117.

48. Darwyn Linder and Katherine Crane, "Reactance Theory Analysis of Predecisional Cognitive Processes," *Journal of Personality and Social Psychology*, Vol. 15 (July 1970), pp. 258–264.

49. Mona Clee and Robert Wicklund, "Consumer Behavior and Psychological Reactance," *Journal of Consumer Research*, Vol. 6 (March 1980), pp. 389–405.

50. Marcy Magiera, "Avia Ads Say Shoo to Non-Athletes," *Advertising Age*, August 22, 1988, p. 4.

51. G. R. Dowling, "Perceived Risk: The Concept and Its Measurement," *Psychology and Marketing*, Vol. 3 (Fall 1986), pp. 193–210. For another discussion of problems in defining the concept, see James Bettman, "Information Integration in Consumer Risk Perception: A Comparison of Two Models of Component Conceptualization," *Journal of Applied Psychology*, Vol. 60 (1975), pp. 381–385.

52. For a recent discussion and model of perceived risk, see Grahame R. Dowling and Richard Staelin, "A Model of Perceived Risk and Intended Risk-Handling Activity," *Journal of Consumer Research*, Vol. 21 (June 1994), pp. 119–134.

53. Raymond A. Bauer, "Consumer Behavior as Risk Taking," in *Dynamic Marketing for a Changing World*, Robert S. Hancock, ed. (Chicago: American Marketing Association, 1960), p. 87.

54. Five of the risks listed in Table 6-4 were identified by Jacob Jacoby and Leon Kaplan, "The Components of Perceived Risk," in *Advances in Consumer Research*, Vol. 3, M. Venkatesan, ed. (Chicago: Association for Consumer Research, 1972), pp. 382–383. "Social risk" was identified by J. Paul Peter and Michael Ryan, "An Investigation of Perceived Risk at the Brand Level," *Journal of Marketing Research*, Vol. 13 (May 1976), pp. 184–188. "Opportunity Cost" was identified by William Zikmund and Jerome Scott, "A Factor Analysis of the Multidimensional Nature of Perceived Risk," *Proceedings of the Southern Marketing Association* (Houston, TX, 1973), p. 1036.

55. Thomas Pettigrew, "The Measurement and Correlates of Category Width as a Cognitive Variable," *Journal of Personality*, Vol. 26 (December 1968), p. 532.

56. Baruch Fischhoff, Paul Slovic, and Sarah Lichtenstein, "Which Risks Are Acceptable?" *Environment*, Vol. 21 (January 1979), pp. 17–38.

57. Homer Spence, James Engel, and Roger Blackwell, "Perceived Risk in Mail-Order and Retail Store Buying," *Journal of Marketing Research*, Vol. 7 (August 1970), pp. 364–369.

58. Valerie S. Folkes, "The Availability Heuristic and Perceived Risk," *Journal of Consumer Research*, Vol. 15 (June 1988), pp. 13–23.

59. Susan Carey and Martha Brannigan, "Fearful Fliers Avoid Discount Carriers," *The Wall Street Journal*, August 30, 1996, p. B1.

60. Donald Popielarz, "An Exploration of Perceived Risk and Willingness to Try New Products," *Journal of Marketing Research*, Vol. 4 (November 1967), pp. 368–372.

61. Celsi, Rose, and Leigh, "An Exploration of High-Risk Leisure Consumption Through Skydiving."

62. Brian K. Jorgensen, "Consumer Reaction to Company-Related Disasters: The Effect of Multiple versus Single Explanations," *Advances in Consumer Research*, Vol. 21, Chris Allen and Deborah Roedder John, eds. (Provo, UT: Association for Consumer Research, 1994), pp. 348–353.

63. For a general review of the attribution process in consumer behavior, see Valerie Folkes, "Recent Attribution Research in Consumer Behavior: A Review and New Directions," *Journal of Consumer Research*, Vol. 14 (March 1988), pp. 548–565.

64. Harold H. Kelley, "The Process of Causal Attribution," *American Psychologist*, Vol. 28 (February 1973), pp. 107–128.

65. Nancy Millman, "Product Claims Not Believable," *Advertising Age*, March 15, 1984, pp. 1, 32.

66. Laura Bird, "A Star Is Brewed as Beer Scores in Hit Film," *The Wall Street Journal*, July 8, 1993, p. B8.

67. Lee Ross, "The Intuitive Psychologist and His Shortcomings: Distortion in the Attribution Process," in *Advances in Experimental Social Psychology*, Vol. 10 (New York: Academic Press, 1977).

68. Robert Baer, "Overestimating Salesperson Truthfulness: The Fundamental Attribution Error," in *Advances in Consumer Research*, Vol. 17, Marvin Goldberg et al., eds. (Provo, UT: Association for Consumer Research, 1990), pp. 501–507.

69. John R. O'Malley, Jr., "Consumer Attributions of Product Failures to Channel Members," *Advances in Consumer Research*, Vol. 23, Kim Corfman and John Lynch, eds. (Provo, UT: Association for Consumer Research, 1996), pp. 342–345.

70. Carol Scott, "The Effects of Trial Incentives on Repeat Purchase Behavior," *Journal of Marketing Research*, Vol. 4 (August 1976), pp. 263–269.

"In-Your-Face Advertising"

Furious, the clothing saleswoman stated, "It's an invasion of our privacy. It's dangerous. It's annoying. I have made a concentrated effort to boycott any products advertised here." Another woman said, "It's so unnecessary. Anyone who would advertise in doctors' waiting rooms is an immediate turnoff. I resent it."[1]

What raised the anger of these working women? The answer: captive advertising. Found in movie theaters, doctors' offices, airports, health clubs, and a growing number of other locations, captive advertising barrages consumers with advertising messages while they are engaged in another activity, such as waiting or exercising. One marketing professor warned, "People are going to become more and more violent in their reactions and in terms of trying to avoid such gimmicks."[2]

The use of what is disparagingly called "in-your-face advertising" is growing rapidly. A company called Health Television Network supplies programming for health clubs that is 70 percent exercising and health shows and 30 percent advertising. Turner Broadcasting has launched the "Airport Channel" to capture people waiting for planes, and another company has a "checkout channel" barraging people standing on line in supermarkets.

Members of the Vertical Club, a health club for the well-to-do, launched a petition against captive advertising that was sent to all the companies that advertised on the Health Television Network. Criticizing the advertising as the equivalent of a "commercial police state," the petitioners also attacked the network through press releases. A spokesperson for Dannon Company, which advertises on the network, remarked ruefully, "Obviously, we aren't reaching someone if they're annoyed by the message."[3] A manager at Playtex, Inc., called a leader of the petitioners to assure him that the company would pull its ads.

Some companies have long had a policy of not associating themselves with any type of captive advertising. Walt Disney Productions, for example, has a general policy of refusing to allow movie theaters to show advertisements for products or services prior to projecting a Disney movie.

Executives at Health Club Television decided to defy the petitioners. One manager called them a bunch of rich malcontents who represented only a minority of club members. According to this spokesperson, marketing research indicates that over 80 percent of people *like* Health Club Television.

Questions

1. Define the problem of "in-your-face advertising" from the perspectives of Health Club Television, the health club itself, and the advertising company.

2. What consumer behavior concepts concerning consumer motivation and affect apply to this case?

3. What are the managerial implications of these consumer behavior concepts for each of the entities involved?

4. What are the ethical implications, if any, of "in-your-face advertising"?

References

1. Joanne Lipman, "Consumers Rebel Against Becoming a Captive Audience," *The Wall Street Journal*, September 13, 1991, pp. B1, B8.

2. Ibid.
3. Ibid.

7

PERSONALITY
AND PSYCHOGRAPHICS

The U.S. Army Targets Its Customers

In 1980 the survival of the all-volunteer U.S. Army was threatened. For three consecutive years recruiting had fallen below the 100,000 annual goal. Moreover, there was a problem with quality. Fully 45 percent of new recruits were high school dropouts, and 75 percent measured below average on intelligence tests.

One cause of the Army's dismal recruiting effort was unfocused advertising. Campaigns changed at the whim of military brass and congressional leaders. Believing that the Army wasn't for sissies, these influential people demanded "blood and guts" ads. For example, in a campaign called "This is the Army," soldiers were seen trudging through a swamp, when suddenly one man was sucked under the slime. A recruiter noted that potential enlistees sometimes walked out after being shown the film. As he commented, "Being shot and killed in some foreign country never appealed to recruits."[1]

A consultant recommended that the Army first change its product and then its advertising message. A new marketing program was developed that promised recruits $15,200 toward their college education in return for enlisting. In addition, the "Be All You Can Be" ad

campaign was launched. The writer of the slogan explained, "I wanted a line that could be used in the Army, not just in the ads." In one of these ads a young man and woman are shown leaving a college class. The man mentions that the woman seemed to know a lot about computers. She responds that she learned about them in the Army. Amazed, he asks, "You were in the Army, too? What branch?" She replies, as she effortlessly hops over a fence, "Airborne." Totally incredulous, he looks up into the sky and responds, "You mean you jumped out of airplanes?"

The Army also employed patriotic themes in its ads. For example, in one ad a young man is shown returning home and asking his brother whether his father is still angry with him for joining the Army. When the young man walks hesitatingly into the living room in his dress green uniform, his father takes a long look at him and then hugs him. Another ad, called "Dear Dad," was developed to communicate the idea that Army service is an exciting and rewarding adventure that develops character. It ends with a group of soldiers firing a canon—a closing shot designed to emphasize the importance of military teamwork.

Interestingly, when consumer researchers showed this ad to focus groups, the target market failed to perceive the teamwork message. Rather, they wondered how learning to fire a canon would translate to civilian life.[2]

In the mid-1990s, under congressional mandate, the Army "downsized" by 25 percent—which took some of the pressure off Army recruiters. Still, it was crucial to continue to recruit promising young men and women to avoid having a military top heavy with old soldiers. The Army knew what kind of recruits it needed for the new streamlined force it contemplated: flexible people who could think on their feet and who exhibited intelligence, tact, and discretion. To attract such recruits, ads for ROTC students emphasized how the Army builds business leaders. For example, one print ad read, "In college, he decided to take Army ROTC. Today, he's deciding the future of a company."[3]

The changes in product and promotional strategy instituted in the early 1980s succeeded. The proportion of recruits in the bottom 25th percentile of intelligence fell from 56 percent in 1980 to 19 percent in 1982, while the proportion of recruits who had a high school diploma went up from 54 percent in 1980 to 91 percent in 1984. Most importantly, recruitment quotas were being met. The marketing strategy of communicating that the U.S. Army pays for college, while building leadership skills recruits will find useful in the civilian world, continues today.[4]

INTRODUCTION

In this chapter we introduce the concepts of personality, the self-concept, and psychographics. Each is a factor that causes individual differences in consumer behavior. **Individual-difference variables** describe how one individual differs from another in distinctive patterns of behavior. These variables have three important managerial uses. First, if sufficient numbers of people share certain personality, self-concept, or psychographic characteristics, they may constitute a segment that can be targeted by a firm. Second, by understanding a target market's personality, self-concept, and/or psychographic characteristics, managers can craft promotional messages that will optimally tap into the group's needs and wants. Third, it may be possible to position a brand based on a dominant individual-difference characteristic of a target market.

These ideas are illustrated in the U.S. Army case that began the chapter. The target market of the Army's marketing campaign was (and is) young men and women who share the personality trait and self-concept of being adventurous and seeking personal growth. These characteristics partly define the market segment the Army sought to reach with its advertisements. The Army promoted itself to its target market by employing themes in its advertising—such as "Be All That You Can Be"—that are consistent with adventure and personal growth. Indeed, the ads sought to position the U.S. Army as an organization that helps young people achieve these goals.

The use of personality measures in consumer research is our first topic in this chapter. The word *personality* comes from the Latin *persona*, which means "actor's face mask." Like a mask, a personality is worn as a person moves from situation to situation during a lifetime. *Personality* is defined as "the distinctive patterns of behavior, including thoughts and emotions, that characterize each individual's adaptation to the situations of his or her life."[5] For consumer researchers, the goal is to identify personality variables that distinguish large groups of people from one another.

Next we analyze the self-concept, which is an important component of personality. The *self-concept* is defined as the "totality of the individual's thoughts and feelings having reference to himself as an object."[6] People have a strong need to act consistently in accor-

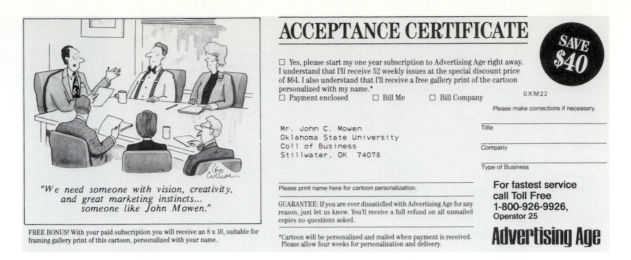

Figure 7-1

This direct-mail sales promotion seeks to bolster John Mowen's self-concept.

dance with who and what they think they are.[7] In addition, they purchase products and services to build their self-image and to express themselves to others.

Building customers' self-esteem is an important marketing tactic. Figure 7-1 shows a direct-mail advertisement that the first author of this text received from *Advertising Age*. With the certificate, he could save $40 on a subscription to the trade publication. To bolster his ego—and those of thousands of other recipients of the same sales promotion—a cartoon was printed on the certificate. In the cartoon a manager says, "We need someone with vision, creativity, and great marketing instincts . . . someone like John Mowen." Of course, he saw through this blatant attempt to flatter his ego: he knew that each recipient of the ad had his or her name printed in the cartoon. (It should be added, however, that he continues to subscribe to this terrific trade publication.)

Third, we investigate *psychographic analysis*—a market research tool for measuring consumers' lifestyles. In the early 1990s, with cigarette smoking declining among the well-to-do and the better-educated, RJR Nabisco decided to target a distinct group of women—called *virile females*—for its new cigarette. The company employed psychographic analysis to identify the characteristics of this target market. The virile female was described as follows:

> She is a "white 18–24-year-old female. She has only a high school degree and work is a job, not a career. Her free time is spent with her boyfriend, doing whatever he is doing. That includes going to tough-man competitions, tractor pulls, hot rod shows, and cruising. She watches lots of television, entertainment she can afford, in particular—Roseanne. One of her chief aspirations is to have an ongoing relationship with a man."[8]

RJR Nabisco's promotional strategy for Dakota cigarettes was based on this psychographic profile, but it backfired when critics discovered the company's plan. As one anti-smoking lobbyist stated, Dakota advertising "represents an effort through false image-based advertising to lure young, healthy women to smoke."[9]

We conclude the chapter with an assessment of how concepts derived from research on personality, the self-concept, and psychographics apply to the U.S. Army recruiting case and discuss the managerial implications of these consumer concepts.

PERSONALITY AND CONSUMER BEHAVIOR

The concept of **personality** has four essential aspects (summarized in Table 7-1). First, to be called a personality, a person's behavior should show consistency across time. Second, the behaviors should distinguish the person from others: a personality characteristic cannot be shared by all consumers.

The third aspect is that personality characteristics are not rigidly connected to specific types of behavior. Thus researchers cannot accurately predict an individual's actions on one specific occasion from a single measure of personality.[10] In specific terms, how many cans of peas a person will buy or the type of furniture that person will purchase cannot be predicted by looking at his or her specific personality characteristics, for such choices depend on the interaction of personality, situation, and product. The complex interactions of forces within and between these factors make simple stimulus-response connections between personality and purchase unlikely. In short, the consumer must be viewed as a dynamic whole.

One reason there are such low correlations between personality measures and behavior is that single measures of behavior are highly unreliable.[11] One study investigating the correlation between a scale assessing cat owners' and dog owners' emotional attachment to their pets and their tendency to feed them human food. The researchers found that the correlation increased when the number of days assessed was increased.

Aspects of Personality
1. Behavior shows consistency.
2. Behaviors distinguish one person from another.
3. Behaviors interact with the situation.
4. Single measures of personality cannot predict specific behaviors, such as which brand of car a consumer will purchase.

TABLE 7-1

The moral is that behavior must be measured on multiple occasions to assess personality-behavior relationships accurately.

The fourth aspect of personality is that it moderates the effects of advertising messages and marketing situations on consumer behavior. A **moderating variable** is an individual-difference variable that interacts with the consumer situation and/or the type of message being communicated. Consumer situations are those temporary environmental factors that form the context within which a consumer activity occurs. (Consumer situations will be discussed further in Chapter 14.) One type of situation is the social context in which purchases take place. Researchers have found that consumers act differently when other people are observing their purchase behavior than when they believe they are unobserved. This situational variable may interact with a personality characteristic that distinguishes individuals on their tendency to conform to social pressures when making purchases. The **ATSCI** (attention to social comparison information) scale (see Table 7-2) has been developed to measure this disposition to conform.[12]

Figure 7-2 shows how the situational context may interact with a person's tendency to conform to others to influence purchase behavior. Most of the time people go shopping with plans to make certain purchases. Does the social situation impact the extent that a

A Scale Developed to Measure the Attention to Social Comparison Information (ATSCI)

1. It is my feeling that if everyone else in a group is behaving in a certain manner, this must be the proper way to behave.
2. I actively avoid wearing clothes that are not in style.
3. At parties I usually try to behave in a manner that makes me fit in.
4. When I am uncertain how to act in a social situation, I look to the behavior of others for cues.
5. I try to pay attention to the reactions of others to my behavior in order to avoid being out of place.
6. I find that I tend to pick up slang expressions from others and use them as part of my own vocabulary.
7. I tend to pay attention to what others are wearing.
8. The slightest look of disapproval in the eyes of a person with whom I am interacting is enough to make me change my approach.
9. It's important to me to fit into the group I'm with.
10. My behavior often depends on how I feel others wish me to behave.
11. If I am the least bit uncertain as to how to act in a social situation, I look to the behavior of others for cues.
12. I usually keep up with clothing style changes by watching what others wear.
13. When in a social situation, I tend not to follow the crowd, but instead behave in a manner that suits my particular mood at the time.

Note that each item is scored 0 (always false) to 5 (always true) and that item 13 requires reverse scoring.

Source: Scale developed by William O. Bearden and Randall L. Rose, "Attention to Social Comparison Information: An Individual Difference Factor Affecting Consumer Conformity," *Journal of Consumer Research*, Vol. 16 (March 1990), pp. 461–471.

TABLE 7-2

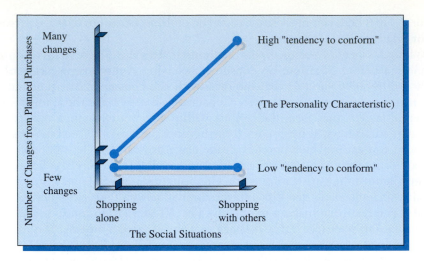

Figure 7-2

A personality (attention to social comparison information) by situation (whether or not shopping with others) interaction. (*Note*: The "tendency to conform" is a personality characteristic based on the Attention to Social Comparison Scale. See William O. Bearden and Randall L. Rose, "Attention to Social Comparison Information: An Individual Difference Factor Affecting Conformity," *Journal of Consumer Research*, Vol. 16 [March 1990], pp. 461–471.)

consumer *fails* to make her intended purchases? As shown in Figure 7-2, a person who has a *low tendency to conform* will tend to make her desired purchases whether she is shopping alone or with a group. In contrast, someone with a *high tendency to conform* will make many more changes in purchase plans when shopping with a group than when shopping alone. Thus the personality variable ATSCI moderates the impact of the situation on consumer behavior.

Two distinct approaches to personality can be identified: psychoanalytic theory and trait theory. The application of these theories to consumer research is discussed in the next two sections.

Psychoanalytic Theory

Sigmund Freud's **psychoanalytic theory of personality** has had a major impact on our understanding of human behavior. Freud argued that the human personality results from a dynamic struggle between inner physiological drives (such as hunger, sex, and aggression) and social pressures to follow laws, rules, and moral codes. He proposed that human beings have a conscious, preconscious, and unconscious mind, and that the forces that drive our behavior are largely unconscious, and hence not available for scrutiny. This idea that individuals are aware of only a small fraction of the forces that propel their actions revolutionized the understanding of the human personality.[13]

The Structure of the Personality According to Freud, the personality is the product of the clash of three forces—the id, ego, and superego. Present at birth, the **id** encompasses the physiological drives that propel a person to action. These drives are completely unconscious and form a chaotic cauldron of seething excitations.[14] The id requires instant gratification of its instincts. That is, it operates on the **pleasure principle,** moving the person to obtain positive feelings and emotions.

As the child grows, the ego begins to develop. The function of the **ego** is to curb the id's appetites so the person can function effectively in the world. Freud stated that the ego stands for "reason and good sense while the id stands for untamed passions."[15] He viewed the ego as the conscious part of the mind that operated on the **reality principle,** moving the person to be practical and to function efficiently in the world.

The **superego** can be understood as the conscience or "voice within" a person that echoes the morals and values of parents and society. As with the id, only a small portion of the superego is available to the conscious mind. According to Freud, it is formed during middle childhood, through the process of identification. The superego actively opposes the id, and one role of the ego is to resolve these conflicts. It is this focus on the clash between id and superego that classifies the psychoanalytic view of personality as a conflict theory.

Psychoanalytic Theory and Promotional Strategy After being embraced by **motivation researchers** in the 1950s, psychoanalytic thought, with its emphasis on plumbing dreams, fantasies, and symbols to identify the unconscious motives behind people's actions, had a

Figure 7-3
This ad for Italian Cappuccino coffee employs fantasy images to create feelings and emotions in consumers.

major impact on marketing. Advertising firms hired psychoanalysts to help them develop promotional themes and packaging that would appeal to consumers' unconscious minds. Some marketing researchers still use Freudian theory to identify the symbols and fantasies that unconsciously propel people to buy.

Advertisers also frequently try to move consumers to fantasize about the consequences of using their product. Figure 7-3 is a nice illustration of the type of ad that seeks to evoke dreamy fantasies. Here General Mills attempts to link drinking its "New Italian Cappuccino" brand of coffee with romance by showing dreamlike figures rising from a steamy cup. The ad's copy (i.e., "more than just a cup of coffee") reinforces the pictorial romance.

Psychoanalytic theory has posited a number of **symbols** that are of use to marketers—for example, phallic (male) and ovarian (female) symbols. Figures that are long and cylindrical are phallic symbols, whereas those that are round and receptive are ovarian symbols. Indeed, some writers have sold large numbers of books by sensationalizing the charge that advertising agencies employ these sexual symbols in ads to arouse sexual energy, or **libido,** and thereby generate sales.[16] Clearly some companies do use such symbols in their ads quite deliberately. The concave shape of Jovan perfume and the convex shape of Jovan aftershave, for instance, are obviously sexual symbols. Figure 7-4 shows a less obvious example of the art. In this ad for MerCruiser boat engines the erect figure of the skier, as interpreted from a Freudian perspective, is a phallic symbol.

Besides the libido—or life-seeking sexual drive—psychoanalytic theory posits a death wish that drives people to destructive acts. The ancient symbol of this drive is the death mask—a facial cover portraying the contorted face of someone in mortal pain. One author has argued that liquor companies insert death masks into the ice cubes in their liquor ads to activate the death wish of heavy drinkers and thereby get them to consume more of their product.[17]

Do advertising agencies really engage in such activities? The answer is a qualified no. More than a dozen years ago a college professor conducted a survey asking advertising people if they ever deliberately embedded a subliminal message—such as a word, a symbol, or a sexual organ—into advertising artwork for a client. Of those surveyed, 96 percent said they did not. When asked if they knew of anyone doing it, 91 percent said they did not.[18] These are very low percentages. Granted, not everyone would admit to such practices, but there is reason to think that the critics' diatribes about subliminal trickery in ads are exaggerated. After all, in a society where the popular media feast on highly explicit portrayals of sex and violence, subliminal messages of sex and death will have little or no impact on consumers. One must distinguish, however, between subliminal messages and symbolism. Symbolism, such as the egg-shaped packaging of L'eggs hose, can have a strong impact on consumers through the meaning conveyed.

Psychoanalytic Theory and Consumer Research The psychoanalytic approach to personality has had its greatest impact on marketing in the area of consumer research. Consumer behavior research is highly indebted to psychoanalytic projective techniques developed to identify the unconscious motives that spur people to action. Among these techniques are word association tasks, sentence completion tasks, and thematic apperception tests (TATs). (TATs are ambiguous drawings about which people are asked to write stories.)

Freud's major therapeutic technique was to have his patients lie on a couch and relax both physically and psychologically. The idea was that in this relaxed state they would lower their defenses and begin to understand their unconscious motivations. Later psychologists began to bring people together for group therapy. These two approaches have been translated by marketers into the tools of depth interviews and focus groups. **Depth interviews** are long, probing "one-on-one" interviews undertaken to identify consumers' hidden rea-

THIS IS THE ENGINE MORE OF THE BEST SKIERS ARE LEANING TOWARD.

A world class skier can tell more about an inboard from 43 feet than most people can right under their nose. Then again, when engine performance is the difference between planting a turn and planting your face, you become a quick study.

That's why our engineers worked directly with competition skiers to design the new MerCruiser 350 Magnum Tournament Ski.™ What resulted may be the most uncompromising inboard in skiing history.

We started with a 350 cubic inch block. Thanks to an aggressive new camshaft design, it delivers 265 propshaft HP and smoother torque across a broader speed range than

any engine in its class. A precisely calibrated carb provides rock-steady acceleration without surging. And to get you off to a fast start, we added the same Thunderbolt IV® ignition (virtually maintenance free), high rise manifold and PlusPower™ Exhaust proven on our revolutionary Magnum stern drives.

Over the last two years, MerCruisers have been certified in more AWSA tournament tow boats than anyone. But until you see your dealer, you won't know the difference

an engine this good can make. The new 350 Magnum Tournament Ski. If you're leaning toward performance, you may just fall in love.

THE NEW 350 MAGNUM TOURNAMENT SKI

The Only Logical Choice

Products of **BRUNSWICK**MARINE   ©1991 Brunswick Corporation.

MerCruiser STERN DRIVES & INBOARDS

Figure 7-4

From a psychoanalytic perspective, the erect figure of the skier is a phallic symbol.

sons for purchasing products and services. In **focus groups** five to ten consumers are encouraged to talk freely in long sessions about their feelings and thoughts concerning a product or service.

To illustrate how the depth interview works, we will use an example from the McCann-Erickson ad agency. The agency's researchers were charged with finding out why low-income women in the South were not responding positively to a new roach killer in a tray, which the manufacturer believed was more effective and less messy than traditional antiroach products. When psychologists performing depth interviews asked Southern female respondents to draw roaches, the women portrayed the roaches as male scavengers. One woman wrote, "A man likes a free meal you cook for him; as long as there is food he will stay." Paula Drillman, the director of strategic planning at McCann-Erickson, concluded that the women preferred traditional roach killers to the new product because "Killing the roaches with a bug spray and watching them squirm and die allowed [them] to express their hostility toward men and have greater control over the roaches."[19]

Trait Theory

The trait theory approach to personality classifies people according to their dominant characteristics or traits. A **trait** is "any characteristic in which one person differs from another in a relatively permanent and consistent way."[20] Trait theories describe people in terms of their predispositions on a series of adjectives. In this approach, a person's personality results from a particular combination of traits. Table 7-3 lists 16 trait pairs developed by one trait psychologist for this purpose. Notice that several of the characteristics sought by Army recruiters in the introductory case appear in the table. As you will recall, the Army seeks to attract recruits who are: bright rather than dull, aggressive rather than docile, conscientious rather than expedient, and controlled rather than undisciplined.

The early research on consumer personality done in the 1960s employed trait theories borrowed from psychologists. One study, for example, profiled the traits of Ford owners versus Chevrolet owners.[21] Other studies analyzed the traits of owners of convertibles versus owners of compacts versus owners of standard models,[22] and of smokers of filtered cigarettes versus smokers of nonfilter brands.[23] The results of these studies were generally weak and inconclusive—and, ultimately, severely criticized.[24]

Borrowing scales directly from psychology produced such disappointing results because the measured personality characteristics did not have direct relevance to the specific buying behavior being investigated. If a consumer researcher wants to measure the tendency of a target group to use coupons, for instance, the trait of "coupon proneness" should be measured rather than a more general personality characteristic identified by psychologists. Only in this way can trait theory be useful to marketers.

A trait scale must also be reliable and valid. **Reliability** is evidenced when the scale is internally consistent (i.e., each question measures the same general construct) and gives similar results when an individual is retested after a period of time. **Validity** is evidenced when the scale is shown to measure the trait that it is designed to assess. Over the past 15 years consumer researchers have developed a number of valid and reliable scales to measure personality traits that have relevance to marketing managers. Used properly, these scales can assist managers in segmenting the market, positioning a product, and/or developing effective promotional appeals. We briefly describe a number of these scales in this section.

---

16 Personality Traits Identified by Cattel

1. Reserved vs. outgoing
2. Dull vs. bright
3. Unstable vs. stable
4. Docile vs. aggressive
5. Serious vs. happy-go-lucky
6. Expedient vs. conscientious
7. Shy vs. uninhibited
8. Tough-minded vs. tender-minded
9. Trusting vs. suspicious
10. Practical vs. imaginative
11. Unpretentious vs. polished
12. Self-assured vs. self-reproaching
13. Conservative vs. experimenting
14. Group-dependent vs. self-sufficient
15. Undisciplined vs. controlled
16. Relaxed vs. tense

Source: Adapted from R. Cattel, H. Eber, and M. Tatsuoka, *Handbook for the Sixteen Personality Factor Questionnaire* (Champaign, IL: Institute for Personality Ability Testing, 1970).

TABLE 7-3

Coupon Proneness and Value Consciousness Recent consumer research has found that consumers' tendency to redeem coupons is based partly on their view of coupons and partly on their value consciousness.[25] *Value consciousness* denotes the amount of concern a consumer has for the need-satisfying properties of a product in relation to its price. In contrast, *coupon proneness* denotes the tendency to buy a product because the purchase offer includes a coupon, which the consumer views almost as an end in itself. Table 7-4 presents the scales developed to measure coupon proneness versus value consciousness.

In one study 350 adults were asked how frequently they had redeemed coupons in the past month, and then requested to complete the two scales in Table 7-4. The survey results revealed that the coupon-proneness trait was strongly related to coupon-redemption behavior. Interestingly, the trait of value consciousness also predicted the use of coupons even after the impact of the coupon-proneness trait had been accounted for. It seems that the traits of coupon proneness and value consciousness are distinct, and that both influence consumer buying behavior.

Items Composing Coupon-Proneness and Value-Consciousness Scales

All items are 7-point scales ranging from *strongly agree* to *strongly disagree*. All scale items were coded/recoded so that higher scores reflect higher levels of the construct.

Coupon Proneness

1. Redeeming coupons makes me feel good.
2. I enjoy clipping coupons out of the newspapers.
3. When I use coupons, I feel that I am getting a good deal.
4. I enjoy using coupons, regardless of the amount I save by doing so.
5. I have favorite brands, but most of the time I buy the brand I have a coupon for.
6. I am more likely to buy brands for which I have a coupon.
7. Coupons have caused me to buy products I normally would not buy.
8. Beyond the money I save, redeeming coupons gives me a sense of joy.

Value Consciousness

1. I am very concerned about low prices, but I am equally concerned about product quality.
2. When grocery shopping, I compare the prices of different brands to be sure I get the best value for the money.
3. When purchasing a product, I always try to maximize the quality I get for the money I spend.
4. When I buy products, I like to be sure that I am getting my money's worth.
5. I generally shop around for lower prices on products, but they still must meet certain quality requirements before I will buy them.
6. When I shop, I usually compare the "price per ounce" information for brands I normally buy.
7. I always check prices at the grocery store to be sure I get the best value for the money I spend.

Source: Scales developed by Donald R. Lichtenstein, Richard G. Netemeyer, and Scot Burton, "Distinguishing Coupon Proneness from Value Consciousness: An Acquisition-Transaction Utility Theory Perspective," *Journal of Marketing*, Vol. 54 (July 1990), pp. 54–67.

TABLE 7-4

Attention to Social Comparison Information We said earlier in the chapter that a second trait of importance to marketers is the tendency of consumers to pay attention to social comparison information. The ATSCI scale, you will recall, assesses the extent to which consumers conform to social pressures to make purchases.[26] Those who score high on the scale are very aware of how others react to their behavior and are prone to change their behavior and attitudes to conform to group standards. More will be said about the ATSCI scale in Chapter 9, on attitudes, beliefs, and behavior changes.

Tolerance for Ambiguity **Tolerance for ambiguity** is a trait that predicts how a person will react to situations that have varying degrees of ambiguity or inconsistency.[27] People who are tolerant of ambiguity react positively to situational inconsistency, while those who are intolerant of ambiguity view situational inconsistency as threatening and undesirable. To revert to the introductory case, tolerance for ambiguity is a trait that Army recruiters look for—especially in officer candidates.

Three different types of situations have been identified by psychologists as ambiguous[28]: (1) the completely new situation about which a person has little information; (2) the highly complex situation that overwhelms a person; and (3) the situation that contains contradictory information. These situations may be characterized as (1) novel, (2) complex, and (3) insoluble.

Tolerance for ambiguity is a trait that influences people in a number of consumer tasks. For example, one study found that individuals categorized as tolerant of ambiguity reacted more positively to products perceived as new than those intolerant of ambiguity. When introducing a new product, then, managers should attempt to identify a segment that is tolerant of ambiguity and tailor their appeals to this group. Unless such a segment can be identified, it will probably be very difficult to launch the new product successfully.

The tolerance-for-ambiguity scale has relevance to the search for information consumers undertake when making a product choice. One study investigating the factors that influence the extent of this search found that consumers who are tolerant of ambiguity are more likely to do an extensive search for information when the product choice is complex or the product is novel.[29] Individuals with a higher tolerance for ambiguity apparently enjoy gleaning information about products. So if the firm's target market consists largely of people who are tolerant of ambiguity, managers should probably produce informative pamphlets and brochures to accompany the product. If, on the other hand, the target market is intolerant of ambiguity, the best strategy may be to give out relatively little information about the product and rely on more emotional appeals.

The Need for Cognition The **need for cognition** measures the extent to which consumers have an intrinsic motivation to engage in problem-solving activities.[30] Consumers who consistently do so are said to have a high need for cognition. People with this trait become highly involved in their purchases—they think before they buy.[31] They are influenced most by the quality of the arguments in an advertising message because they examine it more carefully, and they tend to have greater recall of the information in the ad than people with a low need for cognition do. Researchers have also found that consumers with a low need for cognition are influenced more by the characteristics of the source—especially physical attractiveness and likability—than by the quality of the arguments in an ad.[32]

Information on a target market's need for cognition is valuable to advertisers[33] because more complex messages may be developed for consumers with a high need for cognition than for those with a low need. When targeting "thinkers," then, marketers should consider using print advertising and create messages that are quite detailed and provide strong arguments for purchasing the brand. Television is a better medium when targeting consumers with a low need for cognition. For this group, messages should be simple and delivered by attractive and likable people. The need-for-cognition personality variable is discussed further in Chapter 10 on persuasive communications.

Separateness-Connectedness **Separateness-connectedness** is a variable that measures the extent to which people perceive their self-concept as autonomous (separated from other people) versus interdependent (united with other people).[34] Connected people consider significant others as part of themselves or as an extension of themselves, while separated people distinguish themselves from others and set a clear boundary between "me" and "not me." Researchers have found that separateness-connectedness (SC) differs across a number of demographic variables. For example, females have been found to have a more "connected" self-concept than males, and people from Asian cultures evidence a more "connected" self-concept than people from the United States, Canada, and Europe.

A recent study has shown that the SC trait moderates consumer responses to advertisements.[35] Respondents first completed the SC scale, and two weeks later were asked to evaluate advertisements for the Discover credit card that had either a separated or a connected theme:

Separated Theme: "Our marriage brings me and Chris together, but it doesn't make me lose my self identity. I have a world of my own and I am keeping individuality and unique life style. . . . Be what you want, but always be you. Your credit card shouldn't be like someone else's."

Connected Theme: "Our marriage brings us together and it makes each "me" become part of the "us." Our family becomes our life. . . . We contribute to our relationship by our communal activities and joint decisions."

The researchers found that individual differences in this variable moderated respondents' attitude toward the ads. Those who scored high on separateness rated the "individualistic" ad highly and the "communal" ad lower. The results for respondents who scored high on connectedness were just the opposite: they gave the "communal" ad a high rating and the "individualistic" ad a lower one.

One clear managerial implication of these findings is that advertisers should match the theme of their messages to the self-concept of their target market. Another is that marketers can base segmentation and brand positioning on the SC construct. For instance, a brand could be positioned as made for "individualists" and targeted to men, or positioned as made for "those who are connected" and targeted to women.[36]

Figure 7-5 shows a SAAB ad that nicely illustrates the use of a "separated" theme in its tag line: "Find your own road." Saabs have long been known for their quirky design (e.g., the ignition switch is on the console rather than on the steering column or dashboard), and their buyers tend to be individualists.

Additional Personality Trait Scales

Consumer researchers have assessed a number of other traits that have relevance to marketing managers, among them vanity,[37] "deal proneness,"[38] cognitive complexity,[39] verbal versus visual information processing,[40] gender schema theory,[41] anxiety,[42] ethnocentrism,[43] extroversion/neuroticism,[44] need for emotion,[45] compliance, aggression, and detachment.[46] They have even developed a scale to measure people's tendency to engage in compulsive consumption.[47] Some of the questions on this instrument that successfully identified compulsive buyers are: "Bought things even though I couldn't afford them"; "Felt others would be horrified if they knew of my spending habits"; "Felt anxious or nervous on days

Figure 7-5
This ad for the Saab 9000 Aero is likely to appeal to consumers with a "separated" self-concept who prize autonomy and independence.

I didn't go shopping"; "Bought something in order to make myself feel better." Those who answer "yes" to a large number of such questions may have a compulsive consumption personality and may need the assistance of a professional clinician.

On the Managerial Use of Scales Measuring Personality Traits

The key issue for marketing managers and market researchers, of course, is how to make practical use of personality scales. We have indicated the specific uses of the various trait measures as we have discussed them. Here we will state a general rule: To employ personality measures, the manager must first segment the market by either the purchase behavior or the demographic characteristics of targeted consumers. Suppose, for example, the goal is to get moderate users of a soft-drink brand such as Pepsi-Cola to buy the brand more often. Managers would first obtain samples of consumers classified as low, moderate, and high users of the brand. They would then pay these people to complete an inventory of personality scales and compare the personality traits of the three groups. The next step would be to create advertisements that employed themes consistent with the traits that differentiated moderate users from low users. In addition, the demographic characteristics of the moderate users would be identified.

Identifying the demographic characteristics of a target market is extremely important—in fact, companies often begin with this step. For example, the demographic characteristics of the target market for Chrysler's Eagle Vision automobile are: 25–40 years of age, college educated, two children, high income. Once this description is obtained, market researchers can pay a sample of individuals with these characteristics to complete a series of personality inventories (e.g., tolerance for ambiguity, attention to social comparison information, need for cognition, and separateness-connectedness). Using the responses to these questions, the marketing manager can develop promotional messages that are most likely to appeal to this group. The manager might also consider positioning the car on the basis of the target market's dominant personality characteristic. For example, if the target market is "high need for cognition" people, the Eagle Vision could be promoted as the "thinking person's car." In contrast, if the target is "connected people," the car could be positioned as "designed for those committed to others."

In conclusion, personality information is usually gathered after the market researcher segments the market either demographically or behaviorally. Census information provides market researchers with a great deal of data on the demographic characteristics of the populations of the United States, Canada, and Western Europe. However, no government systematically collects information on the personality characteristics of its population, and it is much too expensive for a firm to gather such data on its own. Therefore, managers have no choice but to first profile their target market based on product-usage characteristics and/or readily available demographic information. Only after the target market is demographically described can they seek to profile its personality characteristics.

THE SELF-CONCEPT IN CONSUMER RESEARCH

The **self-concept** represents the "totality of the individual's thoughts and feelings having reference to himself as an object."[48] It is as though the individual "turns around" and evaluates in an objective fashion just who and what he or she is.[49] Because people have a need to behave consistently with their self-concept, this perception of themselves forms part of the basis for their personality. By acting in a manner consistent with their self-concept, consumers maintain their self-esteem and gain predictability in interactions with others.

Russell Belk, a well-known consumer researcher, has suggested that possessions play a major role in establishing a person's identity. Our possessions actually become part of ourselves, and as such form an **extended self.** His argument may be summarized in his statement that "we are what we have [which] may be the most basic and powerful fact of consumer behavior."[50]

People have more than one self-concept. Table 7-5 identifies eight dimensions of the self-concept. The *actual self* refers to how a person actually perceives himself or herself, while the *ideal self* describes how a person would like to perceive himself or herself.[51] The *social self* concerns how a person believes that others perceive him or her, in contrast to the *ideal social self*, which is how a person would like others to view him or her. The *expected self* describes how a person would like to act, and the *situational self* portrays how a person would like to act in various contexts. For example, at a sporting event a person might want to be carefree, but when conducting a business deal, the same person would want to be serious. The *extended self* denotes the impact of possessions on self-image. Researchers have also identified a self-perception called *possible selves*, which refers to what a person perceives that he or she would like to become, could become, or is afraid of becoming. The "possible selves" perspective has a more future orientation than the other self-concept types.[52] Finally, we believe there is a ninth self, based on the extent to which people define themselves in terms of others or groups with whom they are affiliated—in other words, a self based on the separateness-connectedness trait variable we described earlier in the chapter.

Various Types of Self-Concept

1. *Actual self.* How a person *actually* perceives himself or herself.
2. *Ideal self.* How a person *would like* to perceive himself or herself.
3. *Social self.* How a person thinks *others* perceive him or her.
4. *Ideal social self.* How a person *would like others* to perceive him or her.
5. *Expected self.* An image of self somewhere in between the actual and ideal selves.
6. *Situational self.* A person's self-image in a specific situation.
7. *Extended self.* A person's self-concept that includes the impact of personal possessions on self-image.
8. *Possible selves.* What a person would like to become, could become, or is afraid of becoming.

TABLE 7-5

Symbolic Interactionism and the Self

The **symbolic interactionism** perspective views consumers as living in a symbolic environment and constantly interpreting the symbols around them.[53] In every society members develop shared meanings as to what symbols represent. Further, by linking themselves to certain of these symbols, people can depict to others their own self-concept.

The metaphor of the "looking-glass self" is crucial to the symbolic interactionist perspective.[54] A looking glass, of course, is a mirror, and the idea is that people obtain signals about who they are by observing the reactions of others to themselves. It is as though we see ourselves reflected in the faces of other people as we interact with them and define ourselves partly according to how we perceive those reflections. People's self-concept, then, is influenced by whom they believe is observing them at any particular time. Thus a woman may be shy and retiring in the office because that is how she believes her bosses and co-workers view her, but among her friends on weekends she may be a party animal. Looking into the mirror of her friends' faces, she views herself quite differently from the person she sees reflected back to her in her colleagues' faces in the office.

The Self-Concept and Product Symbolism Symbols, you will recall from Chapter 3, are things that stand for or express something else. According to the symbolic interactionists, people often buy products not for their functional benefits, but rather for their symbolic value.[55] Products, then, are symbols, and consumers' personalities can be defined by the products they use.

Many consumer researchers believe that people view their possessions as an extension of themselves. In fact, various studies have found a definite relationship between a person's self-image and certain products that the person buys. Products noted for this self-image/product-image congruence are: automobiles; health, cleaning, grooming, and leisure products; clothing, food, and cigarettes; home appliances and home furnishings; and magazines.[56] Retail store patronage can also be a function of self-image.

Just what makes it likely that a product will be viewed as a symbol by consumers? Of prime importance is the product's ability to communicate the consumer's self to others. Communicative products have three characteristics.[57] First, they are visible—that is, their purchase, consumption, and disposition are readily apparent to others. Second, they show variability—that is, some consumers have the resources to own them, whereas others do not. If everyone owned the product and it was identical for everyone, it could not be a symbol. Third, symbolic products have personality. *Personalizability* refers to the extent to which a product denotes a stereotypical image of the average user. One can easily see how such symbolic products as automobiles and jewelry possess the characteristics of visibility, variability, and personalizability.

The ties made by Nichole Miller are good examples of symbolic products. The company prints six new ties a month—all targeted to upscale consumers purchasing gifts for someone special.[58] One of the authors of this textbook analyzed the types of Nicole Miller ties that were on sale in 1996. This content analysis, which identified seven categories of ties, is presented in Table 7-6. Notice that most of the ties fit into one of three categories: sports (e.g., football, basketball, baseball, and golf), food/drink (wine, restaurants), and professions (e.g., law, teacher, dentist). The other categories were holidays/special events (e.g., Christmas ties), hobby/leisure pursuits (e.g., painting, music), shopping and buying (e.g., shopping bags, Barbie Dolls), and miscellaneous (stop signs, political parties, cacti, and a Texas tie). When a man wears a $60 Nichole Miller tie, he is publicly associating the idea symbolized in the tie with his own self-concept. So when I wear my Nichole Miller tie with books printed on it, I am stating that teaching is an important part of my self-concept. The success of Nichole Miller, Inc., suggests that many consumers value these high-status ties as symbolic communications of their self-concept to others.

Figure 7-6 is an ad for another symbolic product—Mont Blanc pens. It explicitly links the possession of this expensive writing instrument to an expression of personality. A Mont Blanc pen possesses all three characteristics of products that communicate the self-concept: it has visibility in use because of its distinctive shape and color; it has variability because few people can afford to pay hundreds of dollars for a fountain pen; and it has personalizability because it makes a statement about the type of person who would invest in such a costly writing instrument.

The importance of recognizing the symbolic nature of products is depicted in Figure 7-7. In this figure are three boxes, representing (1) a person's self-concept, (2) an audience or reference group, and (3) a product that acts as a symbol. In Step 1 the consumer buys a product that communicates his or her self-concept to the audience. In Step

What Elements of the Self-Concept Do Nichole Miller Ties Project to Others?*

Content Analysis Category	Number of Ties†	Examples of Category
1. Sports	37	Baseball, football, basketball, golf, lacrosse
2. Professional occupation	37	Lawyer, teacher, stock broker, physician, dentist, home builder
3. Food and drink	30	Wine, gin, chopstick, munchies, Italian food, chili peppers, coffee
4. Hobbies and leisure	15	Painting, music, crossword puzzles, gambling, photography
5. Holidays and special events	10	Christmas, Halloween, birthdays
6. Shopping and buying	8	Cuff links, shopping bags, cruises, Barbie Dolls
7. Miscellaneous	8	Cacti, Texas, New York, political parties, stop signs, safe sex

*This table is based on a content analysis done by John C. Mowen of Nichole Miller ties in the company's Denver, Colorado, Cherry Creek store in August 1996.

†Number of ties represents the number of different types of ties in each category. Thus in the "sports" category, there were 37 different tie designs employing a sports theme.

TABLE 7-6

Figure 7-6

This ad suggests that ownership of a Mont Blanc pen is a means of expressing one's self-concept to others.

2 the consumer hopes that his or her audience will have the desired perception of the symbolic nature of the product. Finally, in Step 3 the consumer hopes that the audience will perceive him or her as having some of the same symbolic qualities as the product.[59] Thus consumers may be conceptualized as purchasing products to communicate symbolically various aspects of their self-concepts to others. The theory that consumers se-

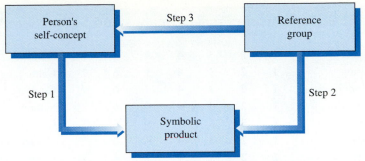

Step 1: Person buys product that is symbolic of self.
Step 2: Reference group associates product with person.
Step 3: Reference group attributes to person the symbolic qualities of the product.

Figure 7-7
The communication of self to others via symbolic products.

lect products and stores that correspond to their self-concept is known as the **image congruence hypothesis.**[60]

A Scale to Measure the Self-Concept and Product Image

Market researchers sometimes have a problem determining how to assess the self-concept of consumers in a market segment, as well as the image that these consumers have of a brand. For an optimal match of segment and product, one scale should be used to assess both product image and self-image. A scale designed for this purpose is shown in Table 7-7.[61] The 15 items on the scale are presented in a semantic differential format to consumers. (A semantic differential scale uses bipolar adjectives, such as light-heavy, on which a person rates something.) Consumer researchers ask members of the target market to rate themselves and various products on the scale. Brands that receive ratings that are similar to consumers' self-ratings are predicted to have an image that corresponds to these consumers' self-concept. This scale is a promising approach for assessing congruities between product image and consumer self-image, although more work needs to be done to test the scale's reliability and validity.

The advertisement for the Toyota Camry shown in Figure 7-8 illustrates how manufacturers can directly link the personality of the automobile to that of targeted consumers. The ad copy boldly states, "If you could describe a car by a personality trait, this one would be the strong and silent type." Durability and a quiet ride are two positive attributes in an automobile, just as strength and a quiet personality can be highly positive traits in a person. For consumers who like to think of themselves as the strong and silent type—or who appreciate those qualities in others—the ad is highly appealing.

One's Body and the Self-Concept

In the introductory case to Chapter 1 we discussed cosmetic surgery as a consumer behavior phenomenon related to the self-concept. This relationship of plastic surgery to consumers' self-concept was investigated in a study reported in 1991. The researcher conducted depth interviews with nine people who had undergone various types of plastic surgery, such as breast augmentation or reduction, wrinkle removal, and nose or chin reshaping.[62] Most of these patients had sought cosmetic surgery during role transitions, such as after a divorce or upon changing jobs.

The researcher found that, in general, the respondents' self-esteem improved greatly after the surgery. They felt much more confident in social and intimate situations, which substantially improved their view of their social self. The author suggested that plastic

A Scale to Measure Product Images and Self-Images*

1. Rugged	1	2	3	4	5	6	7	Delicate
2. Exciting	1	2	3	4	5	6	7	Calm
3. Uncomfortable	1	2	3	4	5	6	7	Comfortable
4. Dominating	1	2	3	4	5	6	7	Submissive
5. Thrifty	1	2	3	4	5	6	7	Indulgent
6. Pleasant	1	2	3	4	5	6	7	Unpleasant
7. Contemporary	1	2	3	4	5	6	7	Uncontemporary
8. Organized	1	2	3	4	5	6	7	Unorganized
9. Rational	1	2	3	4	5	6	7	Emotional
10. Youthful	1	2	3	4	5	6	7	Mature
11. Formal	1	2	3	4	5	6	7	Informal
12. Orthodox	1	2	3	4	5	6	7	Liberal
13. Complex	1	2	3	4	5	6	7	Simple
14. Colorless	1	2	3	4	5	6	7	Colorful
15. Modest	1	2	3	4	5	6	7	Vain

*Consumers are asked to rate either their actual, ideal, or social self-concept on the scale. They are then asked to rate one or more brands on the same scale. Brands whose pattern of responses most closely match a consumer's self-concept are expected to be preferred by a consumer.

Source: Adapted from Naresh K. Malhotra, "A Scale to Measure Self-Concepts, Person Concepts, and Product Concepts," *Journal of Marketing Research*, Vol. 18 (November 1981), pp. 456–464.

TABLE 7-7

surgery enables a person to take control of his body and its appearance. Just as the car he drives and the clothing he wears say something about who and what a person is, so too does the state of his body. In discussing the reasoning of one male respondent named Chuck, the author commented, "Just like any other stock or commodity in his portfolio, Chuck could manage his body to increase his overall return from it."[63]

The Self-Concept and Promotional Strategy When engaging in advertising or personal selling, companies should seek to enhance the self-image of consumers. American Express Corporation successfully used such a strategy in its "Do You Know Me?" campaign. In 1980 slightly over 100 million credit cards were owned by U.S. consumers; by 1995 consumers had almost 350 million credit cards in their hands. How can such an increase be explained?[64] Owning a credit card—especially a prestigious one like American Express—enhances a person's self-esteem. As one psychologist said, "The great modern nightmare is discovering that you're unrecognized, a nobody. With that card you can be surrounded by strangers, but you walk up and say, 'Look what I've got in my hand.' "[65] American Express Corporation used this need to propel itself into leadership in the credit card industry in the 1980s.

Materialism: You Are What You Own

An important component of one's self-concept is one's connections to the material world. It has been argued that "What we possess is, in a very real way, part of ourselves."[66] Indeed, the pioneer American psychologist William James stated in 1890 that we are the sum total of all our possessions.[67]

How else can you describe the all-new Toyota Camry? Try well-built, good-looking and, yes, even intelligent.

Take, for example, our two new engines with more well-appreciated power than ever before. There's an enhanced 185 hp V6 engine. Also available is an energetic 135 hp 4-cylinder engine. Whichever you prefer, both are attached to a more rigid body thanks to the increased use of high-strength tensile steel.

Now turn the key and what you'll discover is that noise, vibration and harshness have all surprisingly been hushed. That's because our engineers have, once again, done the unexpected.

They employed new anti-vibration subframes. They utilized new hydraulic engine mounts. They even smoothed body surfaces to cheat the wind.

All of which you'll find as either a luxury or, quite possibly, a necessity.

Depending on your personality, of course.

IF YOU COULD DESCRIBE A CAR BY A PERSONALITY TRAIT, THIS ONE WOULD BE THE STRONG AND SILENT TYPE.

THE ALL-NEW 1992 CAMRY.
WE JUST COULDN'T LEAVE WELL ENOUGH ALONE.

"I love what you do for me."
TOYOTA

Call 1-800-GO-TOYOTA for a brochure and location of your nearest dealer. Get More From Life... Buckle Up! © 1991 Toyota Motor Sales, U.S.A., Inc.

Figure 7-8
Toyota explicitly links the Camry to a particular type of consumer self-image.

Four types of possessions help to make up our personal sense of self: (1) body and body parts, (2) objects, (3) places and time periods, and (4) persons and pets. Body parts vary in importance to people. Eyes, hair, heart, legs, and genitals have been identified as most essential to the sense of self, while the throat, liver, kidneys, chin, knees, and nose are perceived as less central to the self. The implication is that if you lose a body part central to your identity, you will feel a loss to your very identity. Most evidence suggests that women more than men perceive their bodies as central to their identities.

That different body parts have different levels of importance to consumers' self-concept has an important practical consequence. A major medical problem in our time is finding donors for organ transplants. From a psychological perspective, transplanting important body organs is extremely traumatic for both the donor and the recipient. We know that decisions by next of kin to donate organs of a deceased person are at least partly based on how sacrosanct they perceive the organs to be. Thus organs important to the self-concept—such as the eyes and heart—are most frequently vetoed for donation.[68]

After body parts, objects are people's most important possessions. Highly important material possessions are dwellings, cars (particularly for men), and favorite clothing. (Clothing is a type of second skin that embellishes the self that we present to others.) Collections of objects are extremely important to some people's sense of self.[69] Because they represent the person's judgment and taste, collections serve as extensions of the self. Besides rendering information about a person's past experiences, collections are used to express a person's fantasies. Thus the middle-aged man who collects baseball cards by the thousands may be keeping alive his boyhood desire to be a major league ball player.

Recently, researchers have been investigating individual differences with regard to how highly consumers value their possessions. The tendency to seek happiness through ownership of objects has been called *materialism*. Formally, **materialism** may be defined as the importance a consumer attaches to worldly possessions. At the highest levels of materialism, such possessions assume a central place in a person's life and are the greatest sources of satisfaction and dissatisfaction.[70]

People with the following characteristics are rated as having high levels of materialism:

1. They are less willing than others to donate body organs for transplants.
2. They are more approving of spending large amounts of money on cars and houses.
3. They are less likely to want to eat at expensive restaurants.
4. They are more likely to view Christmas as a time for shopping.
5. They are less likely to believe that other people will appreciate their help.

Much work remains to be done in exploring the impact of individual differences in materialism on consumption behavior, but from what we do know, materialism seems to relate to several important consumer behavior areas, such as consumption **innovativeness** and brand loyalty. Efforts are under way to develop scales to measure individual differences in materialism. Table 7-8 is one such scale. Here three dimensions of materialism are identified, namely, the extent that purchasing and possessing material goods (1) are used by the person to define success, (2) are central to the person's lifestyle, and (3) are important to the person's happiness.[71] Because materialism is also a cultural value, it will be discussed further in Chapter 17 on cultural processes.

Compulsive Buying as a Personality Trait

A major societal problem in the United States is overspending that results in personal bankruptcy. While falling deeply into debt can be the inevitable consequence of factors beyond a person's control—such as unexpectedly losing a job—it can also result from compulsive buying. Compulsive buying has been described as "chronic, repetitive purchasing that becomes a primary response to negative events or feelings."[72] It is a highly negative component of consumer behavior, for compulsive buyers have lower self-esteem, fantasize more frequently than "normal," and suffer higher-than-average levels of depression and anxiety.

A Scale to Measure Materialism

Success Subscale

I admire people who own expensive homes, cars, and clothes.

Some of the most important achievements in life include acquiring material possessions.

I don't place much emphasis on the amount of material objects that people own as a sign of success.

The things I own say a lot about how well I'm doing in life.

I like to own things that impress people.

I don't pay much attention to the material objects other people own.

Centrality Subscale

I usually buy only the things I need.

I try to keep my life simple as far as possessions are concerned.

The things I own aren't all that important to me.

I enjoy spending money on things that aren't practical.

Buying things gives me a lot of pleasure.

I like a lot of luxury in my life.

I put less emphasis on material things than most people do.

Happiness Subscale

I have all the things I really need to enjoy life.

My life would be better if I owned certain things I don't have.

I wouldn't be any happier if I owned nicer things.

I'd be happier if I could afford to buy more things.

It sometimes bothers me quite a bit that I can't afford to buy all the things I'd like.

TABLE 7-8

Consumer researchers have developed an instrument to measure people's tendency to engage in compulsive buying.[73] It has been used quite successfully to identify consumers who are at risk of becoming compulsive buyers and thereby getting into a financial hole. Some of the yes-or-no statements on this measure are:

- Bought things even though I couldn't afford them.
- Felt others would be horrified if they knew of my spending habits.
- Felt anxious or nervous on days I didn't go shopping.
- Bought something in order to make myself feel better.

Answering "yes" to one or two of the questions on the scale does not necessarily mean someone has a problem. However, a consistent pattern of "yes" answers indicates that the person is a serious overspender who should seek professional assistance. Incidentally, this instrument is a nice example of how consumer behavior research can be used to enhance society and its individual members.

LIFESTYLE AND PSYCHOGRAPHIC ANALYSIS

A third approach to identifying individual differences among consumers is to measure their lifestyles through psychographic analysis. **Psychographic analysis** is a type of consumer research that describes segments of consumers in terms of how they live, work, and play. It is much used by marketing professionals today.

Consumer Lifestyles

"Lifestyle" has been defined simply as "how one lives."[74] It has also been used to describe three different levels of aggregation of people: the individual, a small group of interacting people, and larger groups of people (e.g., a market segment).[75]

The consumer concept of lifestyle is quite distinct from that of personality. **Lifestyle** denotes how people live, how they spend their money, and how they allocate their time. It is, therefore, concerned with consumers' overt actions and behaviors, in contrast to personality, which describes the consumer from a more internal perspective[76]—that is, the consumer's "characteristic pattern of thinking, feeling, and perceiving."[77]

Lifestyle and personality are closely related, of course. A consumer whose personality is categorized as low risk is unlikely to have a lifestyle that includes speculating in the futures market or pursuing such leisure activities as mountain climbing, hang gliding, and jungle exploration.

While related to each other, however, lifestyle and personality need to be distinguished for two important reasons. First, they are conceptually distinct. *Personality* refers to the internal characteristics of a person, while *lifestyle* refers to the external manifestations of those characteristics—or how a person lives. Although both concepts describe the individual, they describe different aspects of that individual.

Second, lifestyle and personality have different managerial implications. Some authors have recommended that marketing managers sequentially segment the market by first identifying lifestyle segments and then analyzing these segments for personality differences.[78] By first identifying people who show consistent patterns of behavior in buying products, using their time, and engaging in various activities, marketers are able to define a large number of individuals with similar lifestyles. After that segment has been identified, they can use appropriate personality inventories to broaden their understanding of the internal factors underlying the lifestyle patterns.

Just how are lifestyles measured by marketers? The answer is by psychographic analysis, which we discuss next.

Psychographic Analysis

Psychographics means different things to different researchers. The term connotes the idea of describing (*graph*) the psychological (*psycho*) makeup of consumers. In practice, however, psychographics is employed to assess consumers' lifestyles by analyzing their activities, interests, and opinions (AIOs). The goals of psychographic research are usually of an applied nature. That is, psychographic studies are used by market researchers to describe a consumer segment in ways that help an organization better reach and understand its customers. Psychographic studies usually include questions designed to assess a target market's lifestyle, its personality characteristics, and its demographic characteristics. In summary, **psychographics** is the quantitative investigation of consumers' lifestyles, personalities, and demographic characteristics.

Companies make extensive use of psychographic analysis. As described earlier in the chapter, Chrysler Corporation's consumer researchers developed a demographic profile of the target market for its Eagle Vision car: a young, highly educated, high-income couple with two children under 10 years of age. In addition, the company determined a number of psychographic characteristics of the target market: the couple dislikes television but enjoys jazz music, works out twice a week, collects Art Deco objects, and takes three vacations a year.[79]

Psychographics and AIO Statements To get a sense of consumers' lifestyles, psychographic researchers use questions called **AIO statements** that seek to reveal consumers' activities, interests, and opinions. *Activity questions* ask consumers to indicate what they do, what they buy, and how they spend their time. *Interest questions* focus on consumers' preferences and priorities. And *opinion questions* inquire about consumers' views and feelings concerning world, local, moral, economic, and social affairs. Table 7-9 is a representative sample of AIO items.

There are no hard-and-fast rules for developing AIO items. In fact, one dimension on which these items frequently differ is level of specificity. Highly specific AIO questions ask respondents to provide information on their attitudes and preferences regarding a specific product or service. A researcher for General Mills, for example, might be interested in consumer perceptions of Post Grape-Nuts and ask respondents to agree or disagree with the following highly specific questions:

I find Grape-Nuts to be too hard to chew.
Grape-Nuts remind me of the outdoors.
When I eat Grape-Nuts, it makes me feel healthful.

AIO questions can, however, be much more general. Some highly general questions researchers might ask consumers to agree or disagree with are:

I consider myself an outdoor person.
I believe in world peace.
I think cities are where the action is.

Researchers have different purposes for asking the two types of questions. The highly specific questions give them information on what consumers think about a product and

---

Some Typical Questions Found in AIO Inventories

1. *Activity Questions*
   a. What outdoor sports do you participate in at least twice a month?
   b. How many books do you read a year?
   c. How often do you visit shopping malls?
   d. Have you gone outside of the United States for a vacation?
   e. To how many clubs do you belong?
2. *Interest Questions*
   a. In which of the following are you most interested—sports, church, or work?
   b. How important to you is it to try new foods?
   c. How important is it to you to get ahead in life?
   d. Would you rather spend 2 hours on a Saturday afternoon with your wife or in a boat fishing alone?
3. *Opinion Questions (Ask the respondent to agree or disagree.)*
   a. The Russian people are just like us.
   b. Women should have free choice regarding abortion.
   c. Educators are paid too much money.
   d. CBS Inc.™ is run by East Coast liberals.
   e. We must be prepared for nuclear war.

TABLE 7-9

how that product relates to themselves. Out of such data products may be developed or changed and specific messages created. Indeed, unique selling propositions may be formulated on the basis of this information. A **unique selling proposition** is a quick, hard-hitting phrase that captures a major feature of a product or service. For example, the makers of Wheaties have for many years used the unique selling proposition "The Breakfast of Champions."

General AIO questions are more useful for developing profiles of consumer markets, which help managers understand the general lifestyle of a targeted segment. Using this profile, advertisers can develop ideas for ad themes and settings. In the "Project Virile Female" we described earlier in the chapter, RJR Nabisco found that one important aspiration of its target market was to have an ongoing relationship with a man. Such knowledge suggests the company should employ an advertising theme in which an attractive male is highly visible.

The psychographic inventory currently most popular with corporations is VALS (Values And Lifestyles). More recently, though, consumer researchers have become intrigued by another approach, called LOV (List Of Values). We explore these two inventories and how they can aid marketing managers in the next two sections.

The VALS Psychographic Inventories

Probably the best-developed psychographic inventory of consumers is the **VALS lifestyle classification scheme** developed by the Stanford Research Institute (SRI). For years VALS has been widely used by U.S. corporations to segment their markets and to guide them in developing advertising and product strategies.[80]

SRI has, in fact, developed two psychographic inventories that are currently used by firms. The first, called **VALS** or **VALS 1,** is based on motivational and developmental psychological theories—particularly Maslow's hierarchy-of-needs theory. The second approach, called **VALS 2,** is designed specifically to measure consumer buying patterns.

The Original VALS Inventory The originators of VALS viewed consumers as moving through a series of stages they called a *double hierarchy*. Shown in Figure 7-9, the double hierarchy consists of four general categories of people:[81] (1) the **need-driven person,** (2) the **outer-directed person,** (3) the **inner-directed person,** and (4) the **integrated person.** Table 7-10 summarizes the characteristics of all these VALS groups.

Because the VALS inventory is so popular with marketers, it has inspired numerous studies describing the consumption and activity differences among the various VALS groups. One example is work performed for the Beef Industry Council. The beef industry faced major problems in the 1980s and 1990s because of declining per capita consumption of beef in the United States.[82] Seeking to understand this ominous trend, the

---

Consumer Behavior Factoid

Question: What is the "Tank Tops 'n Tennis Shoe" market segment?

Answer: This psychographic segment comprises 17 percent of golfers in the United States. They are young males with lower incomes who play golf at public courses in casual attire. Other segments of golfers are: Dilettante Duffers, Pull-Carts, Public Pundits, Junior Leaguers, and Country Club Traditionals. Today 24 million Americans are golfers.

Source: Deborah Bosanko, *American Demographics,* July 1995, pp. 16–18.

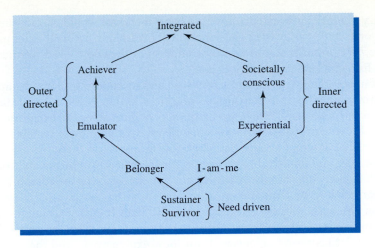

Figure 7-9

The VALS double hierarchy. (*Source*: Arnold Mitchell, *The Nine American Lifestyles* [New York: Macmillan, 1983].)

The VALS Market Segments

1. *The Need-Driven Group*
   a. *Survivors*. Marked by poverty, old age, poor health, and poor education.
   b. *Sustainers*. Also marked by poverty, but feel left out of things. Have not given up hope. Younger than survivors, frequently a minority, sustainers are more self-confident, do more planning, and expect more of the future than do survivors.

2. *The Outer-Directed Group*. Focus on what other people think of them and gear their lives to the visible, tangible, and materialistic.
   a. *Belongers*. Middle-class America. Most are white, have middle incomes, and are middle-aged or older. They cherish the institutions of family, church, and country.
   b. *Emulators*. Intensely striving to get ahead by imitating achievers. Highly ambitious, but spend rather than save.
   c. *Achievers*. Wealthy, high-income, self-employed professionals. Conservative and Republican in political persuasion.

3. *The Inner-Directed Group*. Inner-focused, they seek intense involvement tasks.
   a. *I-am-me group*. Young, unmarried, and marked by major shifts in emotions, feelings, and viewpoints. Enthusiastic, daring, and seeking new ideas and possessions.
   b. *Experientials*. Highly involved in activities, such as causes, hedonism, or sports. Independent, self-reliance, and innovative. Moderate incomes and in late 20s.
   c. *Societally conscious*. Small, successful, mature, liberal group concerned with societal issues. The inner-directed equivalent of the achievers.

4. *The Integrated Group*. Composing 2% of the population, they approximate the self-actualized person. Mature, balanced people who have managed to "put together" the best of the characteristics of the inner- and outer-directed personalities. Although the integrated have the highest incomes of any of the VALS groups, their small numbers make them difficult to target successfully.

TABLE 7-10

Beef Industry Council authorized a survey of consumers that would classify them into the VALS categories and analyze their consumption of beef, lamb, fish, and other main-course foods. Table 7-11 provides an index of consumption by the eight VALS segments of beef, lamb, fresh fish, chicken, and turkey breast.

As you can see plainly in the table, survivors and sustainers do not consume much of *any* meat, presumably because they are too poor to afford it. Achievers and the societally conscious, on the other hand, are heavy consumers of meat across all categories, as well as of fresh fish. Income probably plays a major role in explaining these results—the achievers and societally conscious groups have high incomes and can therefore afford to eat all types of meat, fish, and poultry. However, lifestyles also clearly influence the consumption patterns of VALS groups, for the experiential segment eats very little lamb, whereas the I-am-me's eat much more than average.

Partly on the basis of this VALS analysis, the Beef Industry Council's advertising agency recommended that the council target its promotions of beef to active contemporary adults—in VALS terms, achievers, I-am-me's, experientials, and the societally conscious. These groups were considered good segments to target because they are all growing in numbers, because the achievers and the societally conscious are opinion leaders, and because the I-am-me's and the experientials had somewhat negative attitudes toward beef that perhaps could be changed. An interesting question is whether ignoring the belongers, who were by far the largest market for beef, was a proper course of action for the advertising agency to recommend to the council.

Figure 7-10 is an advertisement for the Pontiac Firebird. This ad employs a theme meant to appeal to the "experiential" psychographic group.

The VALS 2 Inventory Criticisms of VALS 1 spurred SRI to bring out a second psychographic inventory, called VALS 2. The goal of VALS 2 is to identify specific relationships between consumer attitudes and purchase behavior. As summarized in Table 7-12, this inventory divides the American population into eight segments based on their self-identity and their resources.

For the first dimension—self-identity—the VALS 2 researchers identified three different consumer orientations. People oriented toward "principle" make consumer choices based upon

A VALS Analysis of Meat and Fish Consumption*

	Beef	Lamb	Fresh Fish	Fresh Chicken	Turkey Breast
Survivors	64	21	62	69	41
Sustainers	77	54	111	93	62
Belongers	98	96	90	97	75
Emulators	102	62	111	107	63
Achievers	115	125	108	107	155
I-am-me	90	174	119	90	110
Experiential	95	36	79	100	85
Societally conscious	109	160	121	108	154

*Based on an index in which 100 is average. The respondents were asked to indicate if they had eaten the product in the last 7 days.

Source: T. C. Thomas and S. Crocker, *Values and Lifestyles—New Psychographics* (Menlo Park, CA: SRI, 1981).

TABLE 7-11

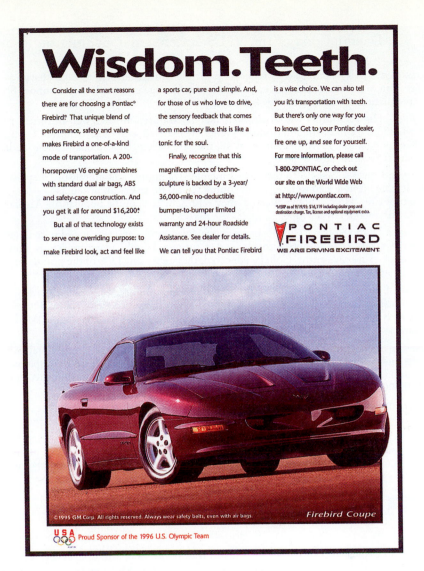

Figure 7-10
This ad for the Firebird is targeted to experiencers in the VALS 2 framework. Experiencers are young, enthusiastic individuals who like sports and risk taking.

their beliefs rather than upon their feelings, events that happen to them, or a desire for the approval of others. People oriented toward "status" make consumer choices based on their perception of whether others will approve of their purchases. Finally, people oriented toward "action" make purchase decisions based on their desires for activity, variety, and risk taking.

For the second dimension of the VALS 2 classification scheme—resources—the researchers included not only consumers' financial-material resources but their psychological and physical resources as well. Figure 7-11 shows the VALS 2 network. People with abundant resources are at one end of the spectrum, and those with minimal resources occupy the other end.

VALS 2 was used by Transport Canada (the equivalent of the U.S. Department of Transportation) to survey travelers at Canadian airports. Survey results revealed that most travelers were actualizers (37 percent). Actualizers have high incomes, and they buy

1. *Actualizers.* High resources with focus on principle and action. Active, take-charge expression of taste, independence, and character. College educated, they compose 8% of the population. Median age is 43. Income is $58,000.

2. *Fulfilleds.* High resources with focus on principle. Mature, satisfied, well-informed people for whom image has little importance. Generally married with older children. Composing 11% of population, their median age is 48, they are college educated, and their median income is $38,000.

3. *Believers.* Low resources with focus on principle. Traditional and moralistic, they live predictable lifestyle tied to family and church. Loyal to American products— noninnovative. High school educated, they represent 16% of the population. Median age is 58, with income of $21,000.

4. *Achievers.* High resources with focus on status. Successful, career-oriented individuals. Low risk takers, they respect authority and status quo. Highly image conscious, they buy expensive, expressive autos. College educated, they represent 13% of the population. Average age is 36 and average income is $50,000.

5. *Strivers.* Low resources with focus on status. Impulsive and trend conscious, these individuals seek social approval for actions. Money defines success for them. They frequently have some college education and represent 13% of the population. Median income is $25,000 and median age is 34.

6. *Experiencers.* High resources with focus on action. Young, enthusiastic individuals who like sports and risk taking. Single and impulsive purchasers, they have not yet completed their education. Representing 12% of the population, their average age is 26 and their income is $19,000.

7. *Makers.* Low resources with focus on practical action. Conservative and practical, they focus on family, working with their hands. They represent 13% of the population. Median age is 30 and income is $30,000. High school educated.

8. *Strugglers.* Poor, with little education, they have few resources and must focus on living for the moment. Cautious but loyal shoppers, they represent 14% of the population. Median age is 61 and income is $9,000. High school educated.

TABLE 7-12

products as an expression of their good taste, independence, and character. These characteristics suggested to the researchers that stores like The Sharper Image or the Nature Company would do well in airports. As the researcher explained, "Actualizers are a good market for quality arts and crafts."[83] Table 7-13 identifies the activity patterns and buying patterns of the eight VALS 2 categories.

Before we leave the subject of the VALS inventories, we should note that a problem with assessing the utility of both VALS 1 and VALS 2 is that they are proprietary instruments (i.e., not in the public domain). The Stanford Research Institute highly restricts access to these instruments by outside consumer researchers, so their reliability and validity are difficult to assess.[84] However, the survey itself is available on the World Wide Web.

The List of Values (LOV) Scale

An analytic instrument that shows promise of correcting some of the problems noted with VALS is the **List of Values (LOV) scale.** The goal of the LOV scale is to assess people's dominant values.[85] Although not strictly a psychographic inventory (i.e., it does not use AIO statements), LOV has been applied to the same types of problems as VALS has. Further, because it is available for public scrutiny, its validity and reliability can be assessed. The nine values assessed by LOV are:

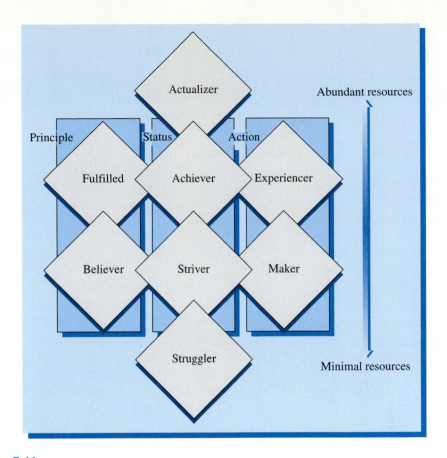

Figure 7-11

The VALS 2 framework. Principle, status, and action are the three dimensions of self-orientation proposed by SRI. (*Source:* SRI International.)

1. Self-fulfillment
2. Excitement
3. Sense of accomplishment
4. Self-respect
5. Sense of belonging
6. Being well-respected
7. Security
8. Fun and enjoyment
9. Warm relationships with others

When LOV is used for market research, questions assessing respondents' demographic profiles are added to the questions designed to identify the nine values. The LOV scale has three dimensions. Questions regarding the first four items (i.e., self-fulfillment, excitement, sense of accomplishment, and self-respect) represent individual values that are internal in nature. The next three questions (i.e., regarding sense of belonging, being well-respected, and security) represent values that focus on the external world. Thus a person who worries a lot about crime and unemployment would probably have a need for security. The last two questions (i.e., regarding fun and enjoyment and warm relationships with others) measure respondents' interpersonal orientation.[86]

After extensive testing, it was determined that the LOV differentiates consumers along these three dimensions of internal, interpersonal, and external focus quite well. One

Buying and Activity Patterns of VALS 2 Segments

Activity Patterns

Item	Segment							
	Actualizer	Fulfilled	Believer	Achiever	Striver	Experiencer	Maker	Struggler
Buy hand tools	148	65	105	63	59	137	170	57
Barbecue outdoors	125	93	82	118	111	109	123	50
Do gardening	155	129	118	109	68	54	104	80
Do gourmet cooking	217	117	96	103	53	133	86	47
Drink coffee daily	120	119	126	88	87	55	91	116
Drink domestic beer	141	88	73	101	87	157	123	50
Drink herbal tea	171	125	89	117	71	115	81	68
Drink imported beer	238	93	41	130	58	216	88	12
Do activities with kids	155	129	57	141	112	89	116	32
Play team sports	114	73	69	104	110	172	135	34
Do cultural activities	293	63	67	96	45	154	63	14
Exercise	145	114	69	123	94	143	102	39
Do home repairs	161	113	85	82	53	88	171	58
Camp or hike	131	88	68	95	84	156	158	33
Do risky sports	190	48	36	52	59	283	171	7
Socialize weekly	109	64	73	90	96	231	94	62

Buying Patterns

Item	Segment							
	Actualizer	Fulfilled	Believer	Achiever	Striver	Experiencer	Maker	Struggler
Own SLR camera	163	124	80	138	83	88	115	29
Own bicycle > $150	154	116	90	33	83	120	88	43
Own compact disc player	133	108	119	97	96	94	94	69
Own fishing equipment	87	91	114	87	84	113	142	67
Own backpacking equipment	196	112	64	100	56	129	148	29
Own home computer	229	150	59	136	63	82	109	20
Own < $13K import car	172	128	80	143	68	109	89	44
Own > $13K import car	268	105	70	164	79	119	43	32
Own medium/small car	133	117	89	101	112	92	112	54
Own pickup truck	72	96	115	104	103	91	147	52
Own sports car	330	116	43	88	102	112	90	5

Note: Figures under each segment are the index for each segment (100 = base rate usage).

Source: SRI International.

TABLE 7-13

recent study, for example, revealed that people with an emphasis on internal values seek to control their lives. This desire for control extended to such consumer decisions as where to eat and where to shop, and was expressed as a need to obtain good nutrition and to avoid food additives by purchasing "natural" foods. In contrast, those with an external orientation tended to avoid natural foods, perhaps out of a desire to conform to the preferences of the larger society.[87]

A Consumption Lifestyle Inventory

A new lifestyle inventory identifies nine "consumption communities."[88] The developers of this inventory employed a behavioral segmentation approach in which people's actual expenditure patterns were used to cluster them into groups of consumers with similar spending patterns. Table 7-14 describes the nine consumption lifestyles that make up this inventory.

A Warning

Psychographic research has become extremely popular over the past 20 years, with consumer researchers and corporations investing large amounts of time and money in these studies. Nevertheless, there is a risk that pigeonholing consumers this way will grossly oversimplify the buying process and therefore mislead marketing managers. Consumer buying results from the interaction of the person, the product-service offering, and the buying situation. The amount of behavior that can be explained by a single-minded focus on personality or psychographics is apt to be quite small.

The danger of oversimplification arises because psychographic analysis tends to provide neat and tidy descriptions of consumers that do not do justice to them. For example, the description of the "virile female" given earlier in the chapter is a fairly stereotypical picture of these women that does not portray them fully or very accurately.

A MANAGERIAL APPLICATIONS ANALYSIS OF THE U.S. ARMY CASE

Problem Identification

The problem faced by the U.S. Army was how to develop a marketing strategy that would appeal to high-quality young men and women. What are the consumer behavior concepts from this chapter that apply to the problem?

Nine Consumption Lifestyles

1. *Functionalists*. Spend money on essentials. Average education, average income, largely blue-collar. Tend to be less than 55 years old and married with children.

2. *Nurturers*. Young. Lower income. Focused on child-rearing, initial household startup, and family values. Above-average education.

3. *Aspirers*. Focused on enjoying the "high life" by spending above-average amounts on status goods—particularly housing. Highest total expenditures of the nine groups, but only fourth highest in income level. Possess classic "Yuppie" characteristics. Highly educated, white-collar, and married without children.

4. *Experientials*. Spend above-average amounts on entertainment, hobbies, and convenience goods. Average in education but above-average incomes because they hold white-collar jobs.

5. *Succeeders*. Established households. Middle-aged. Highly educated. Highest incomes of the nine groups. Spend a great deal on education and self-advancement. Spend above average on work-related expenses.

6. *Moral Majority*. High expenditures on educational organizations, political causes, and church. In empty-nest stage. Second-highest incomes. Single wage earner.

7. *The Golden Years*. Frequently retired, but with third-highest incomes. Engaged in buying second homes or remodeling. High expenditures on laborsaving products and entertainment.

8. *Sustainers*. Mature, oldest group. Frequently retired. High level of income spent on necessities and alcohol. Lowest education levels, second-lowest incomes.

9. *Subsisters*. Low socioeconomic status. Above-average percentage live on welfare. Many are single-earner families and single parents. Above-average number of minority groups.

Source: Based on Susan Fournier, David Antes, and Glenn Beaumier, "Nine Consumption Lifestyles," in John F. Sherry, Jr., and Brian Sternthal, eds., *Advances in Consumer Research*, Vol. 19 (Provo, UT: Association for Consumer Research, 1992), pp. 329–337.

TABLE 7-14

The Consumer Behavior Analysis and Its Managerial Implications

A number of insights result from analyzing the U.S. Army's recruitment strategy using concepts from personality, the self-concept, and psychographics. From the psychoanalytic perspective, one can identify appeals to the id, ego, and superego in the strategy. Appealing to the rational ego, the Army focused on convincing recruits that military service would let them achieve the goals of a college education and a good civilian job. Appealing to the primitive id, the Army emphasized adventure. Finally, appeals to the superego were made in such ads as the one showing a young man coming home to a proud father.

Trait theory also has relevance to the Army's marketing campaign. In working up a segmentation strategy, managers could have developed a profile of traits that described the target market. Some of the traits considered desirable in new recruits would be: bright (not dull), serious (not happy-go-lucky), conscientious (not expedient), tough-minded (not tender-minded), aggressive (not docile), and controlled (not undisciplined). These traits could be assessed in the battery of tests given to potential recruits and used as themes in promotional material and in sales presentations by recruiters.

Research on tolerance for ambiguity suggests that Army recruits should be assessed on the scale. The targeted market of qualified young men and women would possess moderate to high levels of tolerance for ambiguity. Ads depicting soldiers exhibiting flexibility and adaptive behavior would attract recruits capable of acting creatively and independently.

One interesting problem is whether the Army should use ads with a teamwork theme. As described in the introductory case, the commercial showing soldiers working as a team to fire a cannon was not received well by the target market. The separated-connected self-concept of recruits has application to this problem. Because young men tend to have a separated self-concept, advertisements glorifying teamwork will probably not be effective with them. Rather, teamwork is something that has to be taught to young males in basic training.

Other ideas based on the self-concept are relevant to the Army's recruitment strategy. Images in advertisements should focus on potential recruits' ideal self-image. Thus market research should be performed to identify the goals and ambitions of the target market. If these include college, achievement, and self-actualization, then promotional materials should portray individuals using the Army to achieve these ends. The use of well-chosen models who depict the ideal self-concept would be an excellent strategy.

Of course, psychographics also has important implications for developing the full description and profile of the target market. Because psychographic analysis is managerially oriented, this application borrows many relevant approaches for use. The psychographic analysis might include materials from trait theory, self-concept scales, and AIO inventories. It should describe the target market on relevant demographic variables. Possibly, VALS 1 or 2 psychographic inventories could be used to delineate the target market. In particular, the researcher would want to develop promotional materials that would appeal to belongers, who make up the largest segment of the population. The LOV scale could also be used in psychographic analysis to determine the values of particular importance to the target market.

The changes in product and promotional strategy the Army made in the 1980s illustrate a number of consumer behavior areas besides personality and psychographics. For example, the college tuition incentive is a sales-promotion device whose effectiveness could be explained by behavioral learning principles. Similarly, "Be All You Can Be" is a strong appeal to self-actualization and achievement motivations.

Table 7-15 is a succinct presentation of the managerial applications analysis for the U.S. Army ad campaign. A consistent pattern emerges in the table. In each case the consumer concept applies to three managerial areas—market research, segmentation, and promotional strategy. This outcome should be expected. Personality, the self-concept, and psychographics are used principally to segment the marketplace and identify positioning strategies for products. Then market research is done to identify the segments based upon the personality, self-concept, and psychographic variables. Finally, individuals in the segments are reached via the marketing mix. In particular, promotional campaigns are built around the knowledge gained about the personality and psychographic characteristics of the target market.

The U.S. Army advertising campaign case well illustrates these ideas. In the advertisements one finds appeals to the id, the ego, and the superego. To develop these ads, market research was required to determine that such appeals would be effective with the targeted group. The ads themselves had to be created and then tested to ensure that they would have the desired impact. In a similar manner, concepts from trait theory and from tolerance for ambiguity could have been used to describe the target market and to develop promotional strategy.

The self-concept is a particularly important idea that managers should consider when doing market research, segmenting the marketplace, and developing promotional campaigns. Market research should be conducted to determine the ideal self-image of potential target groups. In addition, it can be employed to identify whether the target market has a "connected" or "separated" self-concept. Promotional campaigns can then be developed to show how purchasing the product (in this case joining the U.S. Army) will enhance the target's actual self-image or be consistent with the connectedness or separateness of the self-concept. The Army ad showing the young man and woman leaving a college class together nicely appealed to the ideal self-image of some young women. The ad struck a responsive chord in those women whose ideal self-image consists of

Managerial Implications of Consumer Behavior Concepts in the U.S. Army Case

Consumer Behavior Concept	Managerial Implications
1. Psychoanalytic theory	*Market research*. Perform studies to identify psychoanalytic characteristics of target market.
	Segmentation. Employ characteristics as segmentation variables.
	Promotional strategy. Develop ads that appeal to the segments based upon the groups' response to id, ego, or superego themes.
2. Trait personality theory	*Market research*. Perform studies to identify the traits that are characteristic of the target market. Such traits include tolerance for ambiguity and separateness-connectedness.
	Segmentation. Employ traits as segmentation variables and develop a marketing mix that appeals to recruits' personality.
	Promotional strategy. Develop ad themes that are consistent with the traits identified in the target market.
3. Self-concept	*Market research*. Perform studies to identify the ideal self-concept that characterizes the target market.
	Promotional strategy. Develop advertising themes that appeal to the ideal self-concept identified.
	Product design. Identify the self-concept aspirations of the target market, and develop programs that help recruits to achieve these aspirations.
4. Psychographics	*Market research*. Perform studies to identify the lifestyle characteristics of the target market of U.S. Army recruiters.
	Segmentation. Use the psychographic profiles that are developed to segment potential recruits into categories.
	Promotional strategy. Develop advertising themes and/or sales promotions that are consistent with the lifestyle aspirations of the target market.
	Product design. Develop programs and training consistent with the mission of the Army and the lifestyles that recruits seek.

TABLE 7-15

being adventurous and confident. By placing the ad within the context of going to college, the Army appealed to an important long-term goal of young recruits of both sexes.

Information gleaned from the psychographic analysis should also be used to make decisions regarding segmentation, market research, and promotional strategy. In addition, psychographics can be used to identify appropriate positioning objectives. Then, based upon knowledge of the psychographic characteristics of the target market, advertisements could be developed that position the U.S. Army in a manner consistent with the desired lifestyle sought by the group. Such lifestyle depiction in advertisements can be highly effective. For example, the U.S. Army positioned itself as exciting, modern, and achievement oriented in ads, as well as ready to assist recruits to get a college degree and find a job in the civilian work force. When the military moved away from its original "blood and guts" appeals to this more sophisticated positioning strategy, its recruitment success improved dramatically.

A final point needs to be made concerning ethics. The Army has been criticized for conveying a false impression of what military life is like. (As a Ranger-qualified member of the U.S. Army many years ago, one of us can vouch that it is not all high technology and adventure.) The decision to enlist in the military is far more important than deciding between Gleem and Crest toothpaste. It is a decision that will affect a recruit's entire life. Therefore puffery in military promotional materials must be carefully monitored.

Managerial Recommendations

Three managerial recommendations for the U.S. Army emerge from the analysis of the case.

Recommendation 1 Employ market research to identify the personality, self-concept, and psychographic characteristics of potential target markets.

Recommendation 2 Employ the personality, self-concept, and psychographic characteristics that differentiate groups of consumers as segmentation variables.

Recommendation 3 Develop promotional themes that appeal to the unique needs of consumer segments based upon the personality, self-concept, and psychographic characteristics of the segments.

SUMMARY

Concepts derived from research on personality and the self-concept and from psychographics analysis are very useful for segmenting markets, developing market research, creating promotional strategy, and positioning products. Personality was defined as the "distinctive patterns of behavior, including thoughts and emotions, that characterize each individual's adaptation to the situations of his or her life." Although marketers cannot expect to predict from a personality profile the specific brands a consumer will purchase, they can use such profiles to increase their understanding of the factors that motivate and guide a consumer's purchases. Two different approaches to the study of personality were identified in the chapter: the psychoanalytic and the trait approach.

Psychoanalytic theory views the personality as the product of conflicts among the id, the ego, and the superego. It has had a major influence on marketers through motivation research. In the trait approach consumers are classified according to their dominant characteristics. Over the past 10 to 15 years, the trait approach has been used extensively by consumer researchers. Some of the trait theories employed by consumer researchers are coupon proneness, value consciousness, tolerance for ambiguity, need for cognition, and separateness-connectedness.

The study of the self-concept is also relevant to marketing managers. The self-concept is the totality of a person's thoughts and feelings with reference to himself or herself as the object. Many products are bought partly to reflect the consumer's self-concept. These products are symbols representing the buyer's self to others.

Marketers have in recent years moved away from the study of personality to a greater focus on identifying consumers' psychographic characteristics. Psychographic analysis is the quantitative investigation of consumers' lifestyles, cognitive styles, and demographics in ways that are useful for marketing decision making. The goal of psychographics is to describe individual consumers in a manner that helps managers segment the marketplace, position products, and develop a marketing-mix strategy. Marketing researchers borrow questions for psychographic inventories from every feasible source.

Psychographic inventories contain questions that assess three different aspects of consumers: their lifestyles, personalities, and demographic characteristics. *Lifestyle* refers to how people live, how they spend their money, and how they allocate their time. It is assessed by asking consumers questions about their activities, interests, and opinions.

Whereas *personality* refers to consumers' characteristic patterns of thinking, feeling, and perceiving, lifestyle is concerned with their overt actions and purchases. Psychographic inventories include demographic questions to further define the characteristics of individual consumers.

One of the most frequently used psychographic inventories is the VALS (Values And Lifestyle) classification scheme. In the original approach, called VALS 1, consumers are divided into four broad groups: need-driven, inner-directed, outer-directed, and integrated. In VALS 2, a revision of the scheme, eight different consumer segments were identified based on their self-identity and the amount of resources possessed. Numerous companies and organizations have used VALS to segment their markets and to help them develop a marketing mix. Another analytic tool marketing managers use is the List of Values (LOV) scale, which is designed to assess the dominant values of a person. Still another approach to psychographic analysis is the Consumption Lifestyle Inventory, which identifies groups of people in terms of their expenditure patterns.

AIO statements
ATSCI
depth interviews
ego
extended self
focus groups
id
image congruence
hypothesis
individual-difference
variables

inner-directed person
innovativeness
integrated person
libido
lifestyle
List of Values (LOV) scale
materialism
moderating variable
motivation researcher
need-driven person
need for cognition

outer-directed person
personality
pleasure principle
psychoanalytic theory of
personality
psychographic analysis
psychographics
reality principle
reliability
self-concept
separateness-connectedness

superego
symbolic interactionism
symbols
tolerance for ambiguity
trait
unique selling proposition
validity
VALS 1 and 2
VALS lifestyle classification
scheme

REVIEW QUESTIONS

1. Compare and contrast the concepts of personality and psychographics.

2. Discuss the structure of personality developed by Freud.

3. In what areas has psychoanalytic theory had an impact on marketing?

4. Describe what is meant by trait theory. What has been the major problem with the use of trait theory by marketers?

5. To what types of consumer tasks might the concept of tolerance of ambiguity be relevant? What types of consumer situations have been identified as ambiguous?

6. Define what is meant by self-concept. Identify five of the six different types of self-concepts.

7. Explain how consumers communicate themselves to others via symbolic products.

8. A scale has been developed to measure product images and self-images. Give some examples of the questions that would be on this scale. What procedure would respondents have to go through in order for researchers to assess the relationship between product image and self-image?

9. Define the terms *consumer lifestyle* and *psychographics*.

10. Provide three examples of questions that would be classified as designed to obtain psychographic information on activities, interests, opinions.

11. Outline the basics of the VALS I and VALS II psychographic inventories.

12. Compare and contrast the LOV scale to VALS.

13. What are the major managerial uses of personality, the self-concept, and psychographics?

DISCUSSION QUESTIONS

1. Consider your own preferences for food and automobiles. How do your preferences differ from those of your friends? Review the trait theories identified in the text. Speculate on what traits might explain these differences.

2. Go through a magazine looking carefully at the print advertisements. Identify two ads that seem to be using Freudian symbolism. To what extent do you think people are influenced by these symbols?

3. One function of the superego, according to Freudian theory, is to create guilt. To what extent do advertisers use guilt as a mechanism to promote their products? Cite some specific examples.

4. Fantasy is a technique frequently used by marketers of perfumes, autos, and other products with heavy symbolism. Do a draft version of a print advertisement for a new perfume called Temptation. Develop the ad so that fantasy is its major theme.

5. In working up a trait profile of personality, it is important to utilize adjectives that are closely associated with the product or service. Develop a 10-item trait scale designed to identify the trait characteristics of heavy consumers of diet foods.

6. Rate yourself on the scale provided in Table 7-7. Next, rate two of your material possessions that are particularly important to you on the scale. How closely did you rate the material possessions to how you rated yourself?

7. Go through a popular magazine, such as *Newsweek* or *Time*, and identify advertisements that use products as symbols of the self. Why are these products used to express the self-concept to others?

8. Go to the World Wide Web and complete the VALS survey provided on the Web. Its location is: http://future.sri.com/vals/ovalshome/htm.

ENDNOTES

1. Janet Meyers, "Learning to Deploy a Strategic Weapon," *Advertising Age*, November 9, 1988, pp. 94, 96.

2. Major Gary Lee Keck and Barbara Mueller, "Observations: Intended Vs. Unintended Messages," *Journal of Advertising Research*, March/April 1994, pp. 70–78.

3. Dyan Machan, "We're Not Authoritarian Goons," *Forbes*, October 24, 1994, pp. 246–248.

4. Major General Kenneth W. Simpson, "Recruiting Quality Soldiers for America's Army," *Army*, October 1994, pp. 159–163.

5. Walter Mischel, "On the Future of Personality Measurement," *American Psychologist*, Vol. 32 (April 1977), p. 2. For a general review of personality in consumer behavior, see Harold H. Kassarjian and Mary Jane Sheffet, "Personality and Consumer Behavior: An Update," in *Perspectives in Consumer Behavior*, 4th ed., Harold H. Kassarjian and Thomas S. Robertson, eds. (Upper Saddle River, NJ: Prentice Hall, 1991), pp. 81–303.

6. Morris Rosenberg, *Conceiving the Self* (New York: Basic Books, 1979).

7. Darrell Bem, "Self-Perception Theory," in *Advances in Experiential Social Psychology*, Vol. 6, L. Berkowitz, ed. (New York: Springer Press, 1965).

8. Alix M. Freedman and Michael McCarthy, "New Smoke from RJR Under Fire," *The Wall Street Journal*, February 20, 1990, pp. B1, B4.

9. Judann Dagnoli, "RJR's Dakota Test Faces Counterattack," *Advertising Age*, March 12, 1990, p. 6.

10. Harold H. Kassarjian and Mary Jane Sheffet, "Personality and Consumer Behavior: One More Time," American Marketing Association 1975 Combined Proceedings, Series No. 37, 1975, pp. 197–201.

11. John Lastovicka and Erich Joachimsthaler, "Improving the Detection of Personality-Behavior Relationships in Consumer Research," *Journal of Consumer Research*, Vol. 14 (March 1988), pp. 583–587.

12. William O. Bearden and Randall L. Rose, "Attention to Social Comparison Information: An Individual Difference Factor Affecting Consumer Conformity," *Journal of Consumer Research*, Vol. 16 (March 1990), pp. 461–471.

13. For an interesting overview of psychoanalytic theory, see Spencer Rathus, *Psychology* (New York: Holt, Rinehart and Winston, 1981).

14. Sigmund Freud, "New Introductory Lectures," in *The Standard Edition of the Complete Works of Freud*, Vol. 22, James Strachey, ed. (London: Hogarth Press, 1964).

15. Ibid.

16. Wilson Bryan Key, *Subliminal Seduction: Ad Media's Manipulation of a Not So Innocent America* (Upper Saddle River, NJ: Prentice Hall, 1973).

17. Ibid.

18. Jack Haberstroh, "Can't Ignore Subliminal Ad Charges," *Advertising Age*, September 17, 1984, pp. 42, 44. Also see John Caccavale, Thomas Wanty, and Julie Edell, "Subliminal Implants in Advertisements: An Experiment," in *Advances in Consumer Research*, Vol. 9, Andrew Mitchell, ed. (Ann Arbor, MI: Association for Consumer Research, 1981), pp. 418–423.

19. Ronald Alsop, "Advertisers Put Consumers on the Couch," *The Wall Street Journal*, May 13, 1988, p. 17.

20. Ernest Hilgard, Richard Atkinson, and Rita Atkinson, *Introduction to Psychology*, 6th ed. (New York: Harcourt Brace Jovanovich, 1975).

21. F. B. Evans, "Psychological and Objective Factors in the Prediction of Brand Choice," *Journal of Business*, Vol. 32 (October 1959), pp. 340–369.

22. R. Westfall, "Psychological Factors in Predicting Consumer Choice," *Journal of Marketing*, Vol. 26 (April 1962), pp. 34–40.

23. A. Kaponin, "Personality Characteristics of Purchasers," *Journal of Advertising Research*, Vol. 1 (January 1960), pp. 6–12.

24. Harold Kassarjian, "Personality and Consumer Behavior: A Review," *Journal of Marketing Research*, Vol. 8 (1971), pp. 409–418.

25. Donald R. Lichtenstein, Richard G. Netemeyer, and Scot Burton, "Distinguishing Coupon Proneness from Value Consciousness: An Acquisition-Transaction Utility Theory Perspective," *Journal of Marketing*, Vol. 54 (July 1990), pp. 54–67.

26. William O. Bearden and Randall L. Rose, "Attention to Social Comparison Information: An Individual Difference Factor Affecting Consumer Conformity," *Journal of Consumer Research*, Vol. 16 (March 1990), pp. 461–471. The study presented here was but one of four studies discussed by these authors. In this study the differences between low- and high-ATSCI subjects were not large. The trend over the four studies, however, is strong.

27. Stanley Budner, "Intolerance for Ambiguity as a Personality Variable," *Journal of Personality*, Vol. 30 (1962), pp. 29–50.

28. Ibid.

29. Charles Schaninger and Donald Sciglimpaglia, "The Influence

of Cognitive Personality Traits and Demographics on Consumer Information Acquisition," *Journal of Consumer Research*, Vol. 8 (September 1981), pp. 208–215.

30. James W. Peltier and John A. Schibrowsky, "Need for Cognition, Advertisement Viewing Time, and Memory for Advertising Stimuli," *Advances in Consumer Research*, Vol. 21, Chris T. Allen and Deborah Roedder John, eds. (Provo, UT: Association for Consumer Research, 1994), pp. 244–250.

31. Curtis P. Haugtvedt, Richard E. Petty, and John T. Cacioppo, "Need for Cognition and Advertising: Understanding the Role of Personality Variables in Consumer Behavior," *Journal of Consumer Psychology*, Vol. 1, no. 3, pp. 239–260.

32. Curt Haugtvedt, Richard Petty, John Cacioppo, and Theresa Steidley, "Personality and Ad Effectiveness: Exploring the Utility of Need for Cognition," in *Advances in Consumer Research*, Vol. 15, Michael Houston, ed. (Provo, UT: Association for Consumer Research, 1988), pp. 209–212.

33. Curtis P. Haugtvedt, Richard E. Petty, and John T. Cacioppo, "Need for Cognition and Advertising: Understanding the Role of Personality Variables in Consumer Research," *Journal of Consumer Psychology*, Vol. 1, no. 3, pp. 239–260.

34. Cheng Lu Wang and John C. Mowen, "The Separateness-Connectedness Self Schema: Scale Development and Application to Message Construction," *Psychology and Marketing*, in press.

35. Wang and Mowen, "The Separateness-Connectedness Self Schema."

36. For additional work on "affiliation versus autonomy seeking," see Susan Schultz Kleine, Robert E. Kleine III, and Chris T. Allen,

"How Is a Possession 'Me' or 'Not me'? Characterizing Types and an Antecedent of Material Possession Attachment," *Journal of Consumer Research*," Vol. 22 (December 1995), pp. 327–343.

37. Richard G. Netemeyer, Scot Burton, and Donald R. Lichtenstein, "Trait Aspects of Vanity: Measurement and Relevance to Consumer Behavior," *Journal of Consumer Research*, Vol. 21 (March 1995), pp. 612–626.

38. Donald R. Lichtenstein, Richard G. Netemeyer, and Scot Burton, "Assessing the Domain Specificity of Deal Proneness: A Field Study," *Journal of Consumer Research*, Vol. 22 (December 1995), pp. 314–326.

39. George Zinkhan and Abhijit Biswas, "Using the Repertory Grid to Assess the Complexity of Consumers' Cognitive Structures," in *Advances in Consumer Research*, Vol. 15, Michael Houston, ed. (Provo, UT: Association for Consumer Research, 1988), pp. 493–497.

40. Evelyn Gutman, "The Role of Individual Differences and Multiple Senses in Consumer Imagery Processing: Theoretical Perspectives," in *Advances in Consumer Research*, Vol. 15, Michael Houston, ed. (Provo, UT: Association for Consumer Research, 1988), pp. 191–196. Also see Deborah MacInnis, "Constructs and Measures of Individual Differences in Imagery Processing: A Review," in *Advances in Consumer Research*, Vol. 14, Melanie Wallendorf and Paul Anderson, eds. (Provo, UT: Association for Consumer Research, 1987), pp. 88–92.

41. See Bernd H. Schmitt, France LeClerc, and Laurette Dube-Rioux, "Sex Typing and Consumer Behavior: A Test of Gender Schema Theory," *Journal of Consumer Research*, Vol. 15 (June 1988), pp. 122–128.

42. See Ronald Hill, "The Impact of Interpersonal Anxiety on Consumer Information Processing," *Psychology and Marketing*, Vol. 4 (Summer 1987), pp. 93–105.

43. Terence Shimp and Subhash Sharma, "Consumer Ethnocentrism Construction and Validation of CETSCALE," *Journal of Marketing Research*, Vol. 24 (August 1987), pp. 280–289.

44. Todd A. Mooradian, "Personality and Ad-Evoked Feelings: The Case for Extroversion and Neuroticism," *Journal of the Academy of Marketing Science*, Vol. 24 (Spring 1996), pp. 99–109.

45. Niranjan V. Raman, Prithviraj Chattopadhyay, and Wayne D. Hoyer, "Do Consumers Seek Emotional Situations: The Need for Emotion Scale," *Advances in Consumer Research*, Vol. 22, Frank R. Kardes and Mita Sujan, eds. (Provo, UT: Association for Consumer Research, 1995), pp. 537–542.

46. Terence Shimp and Subhash Sharma, "Consumer Ethnocentrism: Construction and Validation of the CETSCALE," *Journal of Marketing Research*, Vol. 24 (August 1987), pp. 280–289. For information on the CAD scale, see J. Noerager, "An Assessment of CAD," *Journal of Marketing Research*, Vol. 16 (February 1979), pp. 53–59.

47. Ronald J. Faber and Thomas C. O'Guinn, "A Clinical Screener for Compulsive Buying," *Journal of Consumer Research*, Vol. 19 (December 1992), pp. 459–469.

48. Morris Rosenberg, *Conceiving the Self* (New York: Basic Books, 1979).

49. Mehta and Belk, however, note that concepts of self differ cross-culturally. Thus Hindus are less susceptible to the Western view of self as both subject and object. See Raj Mehta and Russell Belk, "Artifacts, Identity, and Transition: Favorite Possessions of

Indians and Indian Immigrants to the United States," *Journal of Consumer Research*, Vol. 17 (March 1991), pp. 398–411.

50. Russell W. Belk, "Possessions and the Extended Self," *Journal of Consumer Research*, Vol. 15 (September 1988), pp. 139–168. The quote is found on p. 160.

51. For an excellent review of the self-concept in consumer behavior, see M. Joseph Sirgy, "Self-Concept in Consumer Behavior: A Critical Review," *Journal of Consumer Research*, Vol. 9 (December 1982), pp. 287–300. Also see Newell D. Wright, C. B. Claiborne, and M. Joseph Sirgy, "The Effects of Product Symbolism on Consumer Self-Concept," in *Diversity in Consumer Behavior, Advances in Consumer Research*, Vol. 19, John F. Sherry, Jr., and Brian Sternthal, eds. (Provo, UT: Association for Consumer Research, 1992), pp. 311–318.

52. Amy J. Morgan, "The Evolving Self in Consumer Behavior: Exploring Possible Selves," *Advances in Consumer Research*, Vol. 20, Leigh McAlister and Michael L. Rothschild, eds. (Provo, UT: Association for Consumer Research, 1993), pp. 429–432.

53. George H. Mead, *Mind, Self and Society* (Chicago: University of Chicago Press, 1934).

54. Charles H. Cooley, *Human Nature and the Social Order* (New York: Scribner's, 1902).

55. Sidney J. Levy, "Symbols for Sale," *Harvard Business Review*, Vol. 37 (1959), pp. 117–124.

56. Russell W. Belk, Kenneth D. Bahn, Robert N. Mayer, "Developmental Recognition of Consumption Symbolism," *Journal of Consumer Research*, Vol. 9 (June 1982), pp. 4–17.

57. Rebecca H. Holman, "Product as Communication: A Fresh Appraisal of a Venerable Topic," in *Review of Marketing*, Ben M. Enis and Kenneth J. Roering, eds. (Chicago: American Marketing Association, 1981), pp. 106–119.

58. Susan Wildes, Public Relations Coordinator, Nichole Miller, Inc., telephone conversation, August 13, 1996.

59. Edward L. Grubb and Harrison Grathwohl, "Consumer Self-Concept, Symbolism, and Market Behavior: A Theoretical Approach," *Journal of Marketing*, Vol. 31 (October 1967), pp. 22–27. However, the author conceived of these relations from the work of Fritz Heider on balance theory. See Fritz Heider, *The Psychology of Interpersonal Relations* (New York: John Wiley, 1958).

60. Sak Onkvisit and John Shaw, "Self-Concept and Image Congruence: Some Research and Managerial Issues," *Journal of Consumer Marketing*, Vol. 4 (Winter 1987), pp. 13–23.

61. Naresh K. Malhotra, "A Scale to Measure Self-Concepts, Person Concepts, and Product Concepts," *Journal of Marketing Research*, Vol. 18 (November 1981), pp. 456–464.

62. John Schouten, "Selves in Transition: Symbolic Consumption in Personal Rites of Passage and Identity Reconstruction," *Journal of Consumer Research*, Vol. 17 (March 1991), pp. 412–425.

63. Ibid., p. 419.

64. Charles McCoy and Steve Swartz, "Big Credit-Card War May Be Breaking Out, to Detriment of Banks," *The Wall Street Journal*, March 19, 1987, pp. 1, 24.

65. Ibid., p. 24.

66. Russell Belk, "My Possessions Myself," *Psychology Today*, July/August 1988, pp. 50–52.

67. William James, *The Principles of Psychology*, Vol. 1 (New York: Henry Holt, 1890).

68. Russell Belk, "Materialism: Trait Aspects of Living in the Material World," *Journal of Consumer Research*, Vol. 12 (December 1985), pp. 265–280.

69. Russell Belk, Melanie Wallendorf, John Sherry, Morris Holbrook, and Scott Roberts, "Collectors and Collecting," in *Advances in Consumer Research*, Vol. 15, Michael Houston, ed. (Provo, UT: Association for Consumer Research, 1987), pp. 548–553.

70. Belk, "Materialism."

71. Marsha L. Richins and Scott Dawson, "A Consumer Values Orientation for Materialism and Its Measurement: Scale Development and Validation," *Journal of Consumer Research*, Vol. 19 (December 1992), pp. 303–316. For another materialism scale, see Russell Belk, "Materialism: Trait Aspects of Living in the Material World," *Journal of Consumer Research*, Vol. 12 (December 1985), pp. 265–280.

72. Ronald J. Faber and Thomas C. O'Guinn, "A Clinical Screener for Compulsive Buying," *Journal of Consumer Research*, Vol. 19 (December 1992), pp. 459–469.

73. Ibid.

74. Del Hawkins, Roger Best, and Kenneth Coney, *Consumer Behavior: Implications for Marketing Strategy* (Plano, TX: Business Publications, 1983).

75. W. Thomas Anderson and Linda Golden, "Lifestyle and Psychographics: A Critical Review and Recommendation," in *Advances in Consumer Research*, Vol. 11, Thomas Kinnear, ed. (Ann Arbor, MI: Association for Consumer Research, 1984), pp. 405–411.

76. Lifestyle has been distinguished from "cognitive style" by Anderson and Golden, "Lifestyle and Psychographics."

77. Ron J. Markin, *Consumer Behavior: A Cognitive Orientation* (New York: Macmillan, 1974).

78. Sunil Mehotra and William D. Wells, "Psychographics and Buyer Behavior: Theory and Recent Empirical Findings," in *Consumer and Industrial Buying Behavior*, Arch Woodside, Jagdish N. Sheth, and Peter D. Bennett, eds. (New York: North-Holland, 1979).

79. Doron P. Levin, "Chrysler's New L/H, as in Last Hope," *The New York Times*, July 12, 1992, Section 3, p. 1.

80. For an in-depth discussion of VALS, see Arnold Mitchell, *The Nine American Lifestyles* (New York: Macmillan, 1983), p. 57.

81. Ibid., p. 6.

82. 1985 Meat Board Consumer Marketing Plan, National Live Stock and Meat Board, 1985.

83. Rebecca Piirto, "VALS the Second Time," *American Demographics*, July 1991, p. 6.

84. A number of researchers have noted that there are problems with the original VALS inventory. See John L. Lastovicka, John P. Murray, Jr., and Eric Joachimsthaler, "Evaluating the Measurement Validity of ATSCI Typologies with Qualitative Measures and Multiplicative Factoring," *Journal of Marketing Research*, February 1991, pp. 11–23. Also see Lynn R. Kahle, Sharon Beatty, and Pamela Homer, "Alternative Measurement Approaches to Consumer Values: The List Values (LOV) and Values and Life Style (VALS)," *Journal of Consumer Research*, Vol. 13 (December 1986), pp. 405–409; Sharon E. Beatty, Pamela Homer, and Lynn Kahle, "Problems with VALS in International Marketing Research: An Example from an Application of the Empirical Mirror Technique," in *Advances in Consumer Research*, Vol. 15, Michael Houston, ed. (Provo, UT: Association for Consumer Research, 1988), pp. 375–380.

85. Kahle et al., "Alternative Measurement Approaches to Consumer Values."

86. Pamela Homer and Lynn Kahle, "A Structural Equation Test of the Value-Attitude- Behavior Hierarchy," *Journal of Personality and Social Psychology*, Vol. 54 (April 1988), pp. 638–646.

87. Kahle et al., "Alternative Measurement Approaches to Consumer Values." Also see Thomas P. Novak and Bruce MacEvoy, "On Comparing Alternative Segmentation Schemes: The List of Values (LOV) and Values and Life Styles (VALS), *Journal of Consumer Research*, Vol. 17 (June 1990), pp. 105–109. For a recent article that further explores the LOV scale, see Wagner A. Kamakura and Thomas P. Novak, "Value-System Segmentation: Exploring the Meaning of LOV," *Journal of Consumer Research*, Vol. 19 (June 1992), pp. 119–132.

88. Susan Fournier, David Antes, and Glenn Beaumier, "Nine Consumption Lifestyles," *Advances in Consumer Research*, Vol. 19, John F. Sherry, Jr., and Brian Sternthal, eds. (Provo, UT: Association for Consumer Research, 1992), pp. 329–337.

MATERIALISM WANES AND IZOD'S SALES PLUMMET

When the United States went into a full-scale recession in 1991 and 1992, companies selling luxury goods had to scramble. It was so sad. Sales of Dom Pérignon champagne were flat, and Cartier couldn't move its $10,000 watches. Ferraris selling for $300,000 in 1989 languished at $150,000 in 1991. Poor babies!

Carolyne Roehm, the wealthy fashion designer, commented on the new restraint in spending. She said, "It's almost looked down upon." The son of billionaire Marvin Davis said that people have stopped talking about "how much money they've just made, what boat they're going to buy or what fancy vacation they've just taken." The chairman of The Sharper Image said that in this environment "People want to live well for less." As a result, during the 1991 Christmas season the company carried so many $25 items "that people will be surprised it's The Sharper Image."[1]

One suffering wine merchant came up with an interesting marketing strategy. He invited his best clients to a polo match and served free French Burgundy and Bordeaux wines costing as much as $100 a bottle. His goal was to convince his customers that spending $100 on a bottle of wine for your friends is not the same thing as conspicuous consumption.

Meanwhile Crystal Brands, Inc., was attempting to create a marketing strategy for its troubled Izod Lacoste polo shirts. Its managers decided to bring out a new version of its shirt with a crest to be priced at $30 to $35—a full 20 percent lower than the shirt with the alligator on the front. (Actually, the crest is a crocodile.) In the early 1980s the company sold $450 million worth of the Izod shirts. At one time Saks Fifth Avenue devoted an entire wall to the 24 shades the shirts came in, but by the late 1980s, most retailers had phased out the brand. Price discounting by retailers and a plethora of cheap "knock-offs" had seriously tarnished Izod.

In dissecting Izod's problems, one analyst argued that a consumer rebellion was underway against visible logos on everything from shirts to jeans to cars. He said, "People today are embarrassed to say that they identify with a logo. They want to say, 'I'm a more interesting and individualistic person.' "[2]

Izod's strategy was to market its lower-priced crested shirts under the Izod brand to retailers selling moderately priced merchandise and sell the "alligator" shirts under the Chemise Lacoste label to upscale retailers. Since the Izod name had become so closely associated with the Chemise Lacoste label, the big question was whether the cheaper crest shirt would harm sales of the more expensive alligator shirt. The next question was whether, in poor economic times with people avoiding symbols of excess, consumers would go for the " 'gator."

Unfortunately, the answer was "yes" to the first question and a resounding "no" to the second. In 1994 Izod Lacoste filed for bankruptcy. The next year, the company sold all its assets to Phillips Van Heussen Corporation, which is still trying to resurrect the struggling brand.[3]

Questions

1. Identify the problems faced by Izod Lacoste.
2. Discuss which consumer behavior concepts from this chapter apply to the case.
3. Discuss the managerial implications of the consumer behavior concepts relevant to the problems faced by Izod Lacoste.

References

1. Francine Schwadel and Judith Valente, "With Money Tight and Ostentation Passé, Luxury Goods Suffer," *The Wall Street Journal*, September 3, 1991, pp. 1, 4.

2. Teri Agins, "Izod Lacoste Gets Restyled and Repriced," *The Wall Street Journal*, July 22, 1991, pp. B1, B4.

3. "Crystal Brands to Sell Almost All Its Assets," *The Wall Street Journal*, January 26, 1995, p. B2.

8

CONSUMER BELIEFS, ATTITUDES, AND BEHAVIORS

INTRODUCTORY CASE

"Americans Are Truckin' "

"[It] helps you pick up girls. I've even had girls follow me home."

What miraculous possession caused Bradley Bonner to boast so much? It was his Chevy Z71, 4X4 pickup with 38-inch wheels and a body jacked up 6 feet into the air. Bonner is not alone in his infatuation with a truck. Consumer demand for trucks, sport utility vehicles, and vans soared in the mid-1990s. In fact, the two leading brands of vehicles sold in the United States (including cars) during this period were the Ford F-Series and the Chevy C/K pickup trucks.[1]

The explosive growth in demand for trucks and sport utility vehicles is driven by attitude changes in the huge baby-boom generation. Chrysler Corporation's director of market research has said that baby boomers do not want to be like their parents, adding that Chrysler's mistake in the 1980s was to assume that this generation would want the same boxy cars their parents owned.[2] Auto manufacturers responded quickly in the 1990s to this change in consumer attitudes regarding sport utility vehicles and trucks. Between 1996 and 1998 Acura, Toyota, Lexus, Infiniti, Mercedes-Benz, Lincoln, and BMW all brought to mar-

ket new versions of these vehicles. By 1996 trucks, sport utility vehicles, and vans accounted for over 40 percent of all light vehicles sold in the United States.

As the image of sport utility vehicles and pickup trucks became more upscale, dealers altered their marketing strategy to keep pace. For example, some Land Rover dealers created 25-yard off-road courses for test-driving. After navigating one steeply sloping terrain, a customer described the experience as "amazing—my kids thought they were on a roller coaster." In addition, Land Rover dealers redecorated their buildings so they would look like exclusive clothing stores, such as Ralph Lauren's or Burberry's. The manager of one Land Rover dealership said, "If you want a really good mountain bike, you don't go to Wal-Mart. You go to a specialty store. We're creating an environment that reflects a lifestyle." The president of Land Rover of North America commented on the importance of creating a highly positive experience for people who come into a dealership. Car buying, he said, "is literally the most horrible retail experience any customer can imagine. Why not make it easy, and why not make it fun?"[3]

Fun is one reason baby boomers purchase trucks and sport utility vehicles. When he pulled up to a charity ball in his jacked-up Chevy short-body pickup, a wealthy financier exulted, "The reaction I get from virtually everybody who sees it . . . is: 'Boy, I bet that's a lot of fun to drive.' And it is!" A woman who bought a Ford Explorer described her new driving attitude: "I turn on the country-and-western station and think: 'Thelma and Louise have nothing on me.' "[4]

Why are these vehicles so much fun to own? For one thing, they look different from the ordinary car. Most consumers cannot tell one oval family car from another, but it is impossible to miss a jacked-up Chevy short-bed. Another thing that makes sport utility vehicles and pickup trucks desirable today is that they have become gentrified lifestyle vehicles. As one dealer said, they are "simultaneously up-town and down-town."[5] Moreover, consumers view these vehicles as practical, flexible, nonconformist, and environmentally sound (the last perception is erroneous: in fact, trucks, vans, and sport utility vehicles get worse gas mileage and cause more pollution than cars). Another reason for their popularity is they have the potential for going "off-road." Finally, their low price is an advantage. Since there are fewer government regulations on these vehicles, manufacturers have to spend fewer dollars on safety features and emissions-control equipment and can therefore sell them more cheaply.

INTRODUCTION

The concepts of beliefs, attitudes, and behavior are closely linked. As a result, the generic phrase *consumer attitude formation* is often used to describe the study of the relationships among beliefs, attitudes, and behaviors. More has been written on consumer attitudes than on any other single topic in the field.[6] Our goal in this chapter is to describe the interrelationships of beliefs, attitudes, and behavior and to explain how knowledge of these interrelations can assist marketing managers and public policy makers in their work.

Closely associated with beliefs, attitudes, and behaviors is the term *product attribute*. An attribute is a feature of a product about which consumers form beliefs. For example, two key attributes of sport utility vehicles are their off-road capabilities and their spaciousness. Figure 8-1 presents a print ad for the RAV4, which emphasizes both these attributes. How product attributes and other factors influence the formation and change of beliefs, attitudes, and behavior is perhaps the most important set of consumer behavior ideas for the marketing manager or public policy maker to know. The next section defines these crucial ideas.

THE CONCEPTS OF BELIEFS, ATTITUDES, AND BEHAVIORS

The starting point for understanding the relationships among beliefs, attitudes, and behaviors is in the study of consumer belief formation.

Consumer Beliefs About Product Attributes

Consumer beliefs are all the knowledge a consumer has and all the inferences a consumer makes about objects, their attributes, and their benefits. **Objects** are the products, people, companies, and things about which people hold beliefs and attitudes. **Attributes** are the characteristics or features that an object may or may not have. Two broad classes of attributes have been identified. *Intrinsic attributes* are those that pertain to the actual quality of a product, while *extrinsic attributes* are those that apply to external aspects of the product, such as its brand name, packaging, and labeling.[7] Finally, **benefits** are the positive outcomes that attributes provide to the consumer.

It is critical for managers to identify the salient attributes that consumers employ to evaluate a brand. For example: What are the characteristics of the perfect pet dog? Steven M. Brown asked this question. His answer: The perfect dog is healthy, has a coat that does not shed, and is gentle. The problem was that when he looked for such a dog, he found it did not exist. Most pedigreed dogs are plagued by genetic diseases, many are aggressive, and others tend to shed excessively. Mr. Brown's solution was to create his own dog—a "watwheat." Over the next decade he carefully bred Portuguese water dogs with soft-coated

Figure 8-1

In this ad for the RAV4, Toyota emphasizes the attributes of off-road capability, people space, and cargo space.

wheaten terriers. The result was such a success that by the 1990s customers were clamoring for his $800 puppies.[8]

Managers must recognize that beliefs about objects, attributes, and benefits represent consumer perceptions, and therefore, beliefs generally differ from one consumer to another. They must also remember that their own beliefs about a particular brand may be very different from those of the target market. Beliefs, which as we said represent the associations that consumers form among objects, attributes, and benefits, are based in cognitive learning. People form three types of beliefs (see Figure 8-2):

1. Object-attribute beliefs
2. Attribute-benefit beliefs
3. Object-benefit beliefs.

Object-Attribute Beliefs The knowledge that an object possesses a particular attribute is called an *object-attribute belief*. Object-attribute beliefs link an attribute to an object, such as a person, good, or service.[9] Thus the belief that a sport utility vehicle rides high off the road is an object-attribute belief. Through object-attribute beliefs consumers define what they know about something in terms of its various attributes.

Attribute-Benefit Beliefs People seek products and services that will solve their problems and fulfill their needs—in other words, that have attributes that will provide recognizable benefits. This link between attributes and benefits represents the second type of belief, called an *attribute-benefit belief*. An attribute-benefit belief is the consumer's perception of the extent to which a particular attribute will result in, or provide, a particular benefit. The perception that a vehicle that rides high off the ground provides a better view of the road is an attribute-benefit belief. Table 8-1 gives examples of some attributes and their potential benefits in a hypothetical "perfect" sports car.

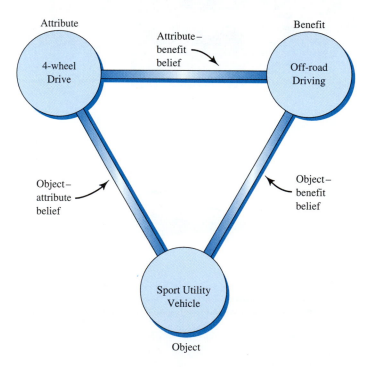

Figure 8-2
Forming beliefs among objects, attributes, and benefits.

Examples of Attributes and Their Benefits for the "Perfect" Sports Car	
Attribute	**Benefit**
Large engine	Quick acceleration
	Allows driver to pass more safely.
	Allows driver to navigate winding roads more quickly.
	Creates feelings of excitement and fun.
Superior suspension	Allows driver to navigate winding roads more quickly.
	Heightens arousal when going fast around corners.
	Creates feelings of excitement and fun.
Small size	Helps improve acceleration.
	Improves gas mileage.
Good gas mileage	Lowers expenses.
Low sticker price	Lowers expenses.
Good repair frequency	Saves money and time.
Futuristic styling	Makes owner feel good.
	Turns people's heads.

TABLE 8-1

Object-Benefit Beliefs The third type of belief is formed by linking an object with a benefit. An *object-benefit belief* is a consumer's perception of the extent to which a particular product, person, or service will lead to a particular benefit. In the case of a sport utility vehicle, an object-benefit belief would be that by buying a Ford Explorer or Jeep Cherokee I will have a very good view of the road.

Consumer Beliefs and Their Managerial Implications

The beliefs that consumers hold about brands, corporations, and other objects in the consumer environment have several important managerial implications. First of all, managers need to recognize that consumers' product-attribute beliefs may not match reality. Halo effects are one source of consumer misperceptions. A **halo effect** occurs when consumers assume that because a product is good or bad on one product characteristic, it is also good or bad on another product characteristic. Thus a consumer who believes that the Explorer sport utility vehicle has good traction may believe that it provides good handling as well.

Managers also should recognize that positioning, differentiation, and segmentation strategies can be based on a brand's attributes. For example, Jeep sport utility vehicles are positioned and differentiated from other brands on the basis of their ruggedness and ability to navigate in snow and mud. The study of attributes and their benefits applies to segmentation strategy as well. Within the marketplace are many groups of consumers seeking specific product benefits. Any of these groups may become an important segment for a company to target via benefit segmentation. **Benefit segmentation** involves the division of the market into relatively homogeneous groups of consumers based on a similarity of benefits sought.

Companies can usually identify groups of people who seek products that satisfy specific needs. Thus some consumers have a shared need for the benefit of being able to drive in deep snow, and these individuals form an important market segment for four-wheel-drive sport utility vehicles. Procter & Gamble has built huge market shares for many of its brands through its strategy of focusing on how a product provides a benefit that fulfills one particular consumer need. For example, Crest toothpaste's dominant market share was built around one primary benefit—prevention of tooth decay. Similarly, Charmin toilet tissue built its market share by providing the benefit of softness.

The analysis of attributes and benefits can also affect promotional strategy. Different segments of consumers have varying amounts of knowledge about the attributes and benefits of products. Researchers have found that consumers with a great deal of knowledge (i.e., experts) process information differently from novices. In one research study information on computers was expressed in the form of attributes (e.g., large RAM memory capacity expandable to 100 megabytes) or benefits (e.g., large memory capacity adequate to handle heavy-duty word processing better than the existing word processors).[10] The results revealed that experts had a more positive evaluation of the product when they received the attribute information, while novices had a more positive evaluation when they received the benefit information. These results suggest that managers should carefully determine the expertise of their target market before they decide whether to advertise a brand by presenting attribute information, benefit information, or a combination of the two.

Attribute Importance Attributes differ widely in importance to consumers. **Attribute importance** is defined as a person's general assessment of the significance of an attribute for products or services of a certain type.[11] Figure 8-3 is a diagram depicting the factors that influence attribute importance. This approach takes an information-processing perspective, arguing that attribute importance is directly influenced by the amount of attention consumers pay to a specific attribute. Thus the greater the attention directed to an attribute, the more important that attribute becomes.

Four elements determine the amount of attention consumers direct to an attribute: (1) characteristics of the message recipient; (2) characteristics of the message; (3) factors that influence the response opportunity of the recipient; and (4) the characteristics of the product. An example of a message recipient characteristic that influences attention is the consumer's needs and values. Another is the consumer's self-concept. Thus if a consumer has a self-concept that includes "ruggedness," the attribute of toughness in a truck should attract his or her attention.

The second element, advertising, can direct consumers' attention to an attribute and cause them to allocate cognitive capacity to that attribute (i.e., make them think about it). The result may be an increase in the perceived importance of the attribute. Thus making the ad copy that pertains to one product attribute highly concrete and vivid may direct consumers' attention to that attribute and enhance its perceived importance. Figure 8-4 presents an ad that AT&T employed in its massive campaign for "The I plan." This surrealistic message focuses the viewer's attention on the bald man's ears in order to get consumers to think more about sound quality of telephone calls as a product attribute.

Figure 8-3
Factors influencing attribute importance. (*Source:* Based on Scott Mackenzie,"The Role of Attention in Measuring the Effect of Advertising on Attribute Importance," *Journal of Consumer Research*, Vol. 13. September 1986, pp. 174–195.)

Soon, people who have AT&T will be closer

than people who don't.

The long distance service you thought couldn't get any better is about to—with a breakthrough from AT&T Bell Labs. And in the coming months, it's going to make AT&T's sound quality dramatically superior to any other long distance company. You'll hear it virtually everywhere you use AT&T. It sounds so much clearer, closer, more natural, even 8 out of 10 people who don't have AT&T prefer it. AT&T TrueVoice,™ coming free. Just another part of The *i* Plan." *i* is for innovation. Call 1 800 932-2000 for a demonstration.

©1995 AT&T Based on customer preference study of domestic long distance calling. Deployment from 9/93 through 12/94.

Figure 8-4
AT&T seeks to increase the importance of sound quality to consumers in this surrealistic ad.

The characteristics of the message can also influence attribute importance when the advertiser is trying to "demarket" the use of a product. **Demarketing** refers to attempts by regulatory agencies and nonprofit organizations to reduce the frequency of consumer behaviors that have a negative impact on the consumer or society. Efforts to reduce illegal drug use, cigarette smoking, and alcohol drinking are all demarketing attempts. One method of demarketing the consumption of alcoholic beverages and cigarettes is to place warning labels on bottles and packages. The goal of these warning labels is to influence consumer attitudes by identifying an attribute that results in a negative outcome (i.e., harm to one's health). The problem with such warnings is that it is hard to make the negative attribute sufficiently salient to consumers to influence their behavior.

In investigating the effects of warning labels for alcoholic beverages, researchers varied the size of the warning labels that were placed in magazine ads for alcoholic beverages. In a second study they developed warnings for commercials that were embedded in a sports-oriented television show. The results revealed that increasing the size of the warning label did affect consumers' recall of the message. The researchers found, in fact, that inconspicuous labels were no better than having no label at all. For the television ad, the impact of the warning label was greater when it was both shown onscreen and stated verbally. The researchers' conclusion was that increasing the saliency of the warning labels enhanced their impact.[12]

The third element influencing the attention consumers direct to a product attribute is response opportunity factors. These are factors that determine the extent to which a person must process information about an attribute. Response opportunity is increased when information about the attribute is repeated and when consumers are not distracted from processing information about the attribute.

From a manager's perspective, it is crucial to know the relative importance that a target market assigns to the attributes of a product. If a brand possesses the attributes consumers prize in that product, managers can design promotions that encourage consumers to form the brand-attribute linkage. In addition, they should consider positioning the brand on this attribute. If, on the other hand, a brand possesses an attribute that consumers do not perceive to be important, managers should create messages that change consumers' perception of the attribute's importance.

The final element that affects the attention consumers pay to an attribute is the characteristics of the product. One such characteristic is perceived quality. In one study researchers investigated the impact of adding a new feature, or attribute, to either an inferior, lower-quality brand or to a higher-quality one. The results revealed that the new attribute increased perceived value to a greater extent for the low-quality brand than for the higher-quality one. The researchers therefore concluded that a new attribute has greater importance to consumers when added to a lower-quality brand.[13]

Another study found that even irrelevant attributes can raise consumers' evaluation of a brand if the attribute is unique to that brand. Respondents evaluated "down jackets" after the researchers had created an irrelevant attribute by describing the fill as either "Alpine class" or "regular" class. The explanation of the fill's warmth, however, was exactly the same for each class. The study found that when a higher price was charged for the jacket, respondents rated the jacket more positively if the irrelevant attribute (i.e., Alpine class) was used to describe the fill—and they did so even if they were told that the attribute was irrelevant! The higher price seemed to justify the presence of the "new," but irrelevant, attribute in consumers' eyes.[14]

Price as an Attribute Price is one of the most important attributes evaluated by consumers, and managers need to be acutely aware of its role in the formation of consumer attitudes. In some instances consumers are highly price sensitive (i.e., demand elastic), so that a high price relative to competitors may eliminate the product from consideration. In other cases, however, price can be used as a surrogate indicator of product quality, with the result that a higher price is viewed positively by certain segments of the market. (Chapter 3 has more on the price-quality relationship.) Product price, then, can be either a positive or a negative influence on consumers. This is an important concept for managers to remember.

Researchers have identified seven dimensions of the price attribute, five negative and two positive.[15] In its *negative role* a concern for price has been found to influence people to be:

1. *Value conscious*—the extent to which consumers are concerned with the ratio of product quality to price.
2. *Price conscious*—the extent to which consumers focus exclusively on paying low prices.
3. *Coupon prone*—the extent to which consumers respond to a purchase offer that includes a coupon.

4. *Sale prone*—the extent to which consumers respond to a purchase offer that includes a temporary reduction in price.
5. *Price mavens*—the extent to which consumers become sources of information to others about prices in the marketplace.

In its *positive role* price has been found to influence consumers in two types of circumstances:

1. *Price-quality relationship*—the extent to which consumers use price as an indicator of quality.
2. *Prestige sensitivity*—the extent to which consumers form favorable perceptions of the price attribute based on their sensitivity to other people's perceptions of the status signaled by higher prices.

Those researching the negative-positive dimensions of price found individual differences in the extent to which people respond to each of these seven dimensions of price sensitivity and concluded that these individual differences strongly affect shopping behavior. For example, consumers who were value conscious tended to read *Consumer Reports* magazine more frequently, while those who were price conscious looked more frequently at advertisements for grocery store sales. It almost goes without saying that consumers who were coupon prone redeemed coupons more frequently.

We can sum up the price attribute by saying that price is a multifaceted concept that takes on quite different meanings for consumers depending upon the characteristics of the consumer, the situation, and the product.

Consumer Attitudes

The word *attitude* comes from the Latin *aptus*, which means "fitness" or "adaptedness." In the eighteenth century *attitude* generally referred to physical posture, and to this day the word can denote a general physical orientation with respect to something else. In the nineteenth century Charles Darwin used the word in a biological sense to mean a physical expression of an emotion. Indeed, well into the twentieth century researchers linked attitudes with physiological tendencies to approach or avoid something.[16]

Over the past 30 years the term *attitude* has been defined in numerous ways. The definition that best captures the ideas developed in this text was put forth by L. L. Thurstone, who was one of the originators of modern attitude measurement theory. Thurstone defined an **attitude** as "the amount of affect or feeling for or against a stimulus."[17] Note how he links the word to *feelings* rather than *beliefs*. The use of *attitudes* to refer to affect or a general evaluative reaction is common among consumer behavior researchers today. Here are some of the current definitions:

- Attitudes are "the categorization of an object on an evaluative continuum."[18]
- The "major characteristics that distinguish attitude from other concepts are its evaluative or affective nature."[19]
- Attitudes are the core of our likes and dislikes for certain people, groups, situations, objects, and intangible ideas."[20]

Whereas beliefs are our cognitive knowledge about an object, attitudes are the feelings or affective responses that we have about objects.

The Functions of Attitudes If a market researcher asks consumers how much they like something or how they feel about something, their answers will reveal their attitudes toward the object. Once an attitude is formed, it is stored in long-term memory—to be retrieved on appropriate occasions to help the person deal with an issue or problem. In this way people use attitudes to help them interact more effectively with their environment. So when we speak of the functions of attitudes, the goal is to identify the use to which the attitude is put.[21]

Of all the functional theories of attitudes that have been developed, the one that appeals most to marketers was proposed by Daniel Katz. Katz identified four functions of attitudes: utilitarian, ego-defensive, knowledge, and value-expressive.[22]

The Utilitarian Function. The utilitarian function of attitudes refers to the idea that people express feelings to maximize the rewards and minimize the punishments they receive from others. In the utilitarian sense, attitudes guide behavior to gain positive reinforcers and avoid punishers—the expression of an attitude is like an operantly conditioned response. Indeed, Katz specifically identified an attitude as an operantly conditioned behavior. For example, a salesperson might learn that making positive comments to a client (i.e., expressing favorable attitudes) is more likely to result in a sale (i.e., a positive reinforcer). Similarly, a consumer might express a positive attitude toward a particular singer like Gloria Estefan to gain the affection of someone known to love the popular recording artist.

The Ego-Defensive Function. The function of attitudes as ego defenders is to protect people from basic truths about themselves or from the harsh realities of the external world. The ego-defensive function, also called the *self-esteem maintenance function*, relies on psychoanalytic theory (discussed in Chapter 7). Thus an attitude, like prejudice against minorities, functions as a defense mechanism in bigots who don't want to acknowledge their own basic insecurities.

An example in a consumer setting would be smokers who hold a positive attitude toward their habit in order to defend themselves against the reality of what they are doing to their bodies. Similarly, consumers may purchase and express positive attitudes toward beauty aids and diet products to defend themselves against underlying feelings of physical inadequacy.

The Knowledge Function. Attitudes may also serve as standards that help people to understand their universe. In this role attitudes assist people to give meaning to the unorganized and chaotic world. For example, consumers may develop certain attitudes toward salespeople in "loud" jackets or toward retail stores with soft music and plush interiors. Whenever they come into contact with such a salesperson or store, they interpret the encounter according to their established attitudes. This procedure simplifies the world for them. Thus consumers who take a negative view of salespeople who wear loud jackets will probably automatically resist selling efforts from such people without having to stop and think about it. The attitude simplifies the encounter for them, allowing them to focus on matters they regard as more important.

Through the knowledge function, people's attitudes form a frame of reference by which they interpret the world. Consumers' attitudes, therefore, heavily influence how they selectively expose themselves and attend to marketing communications. The knowledge function also helps to explain some of the effects of brand loyalty. By maintaining a positive attitude toward a product, consumers can simplify their lives. Brand loyalty certainly reduces the amount of search time required to find a product to fulfill a need. Thus if you have a positive attitude toward Crest, you will probably purchase it every time you run out of toothpaste instead of putting yourself through an extensive search process for other alternatives.

Value-Expressive Function. The value-expressive function of attitudes refers to how people express their central values to others—which is why it is also called the *social identity function*. The expression of attitudes may even help an individual define his or her self-concept to others. In consumer settings the value-expressive function can be seen in instances in which people express positive views about various products, brands, and services in order to make a statement about themselves.[23] In the ad for Rolex watches displayed

Right: Tibetan antelopes.

George Schaller on the Tibetan plateau at 12,000 feet.

Chang Tang—the name means northern plain in Tibetan—is high, austere, and largely unexplored. Rolling away to the horizon, its immensity is broken only by snowcapped ranges. Vegetation is scant, with neither shrubs nor trees to break the expanse. Just a few nomadic herdsmen inhabit the fringes.

Wolves still prowl the plains and snow leopards stalk their prey among the crags; wild yaks forage on the hillsides and herds of Tibetan antelopes migrate over unknown paths. This is a landscape untouched by civilization, virtually the same today as it was over a hundred years ago.

George Schaller, science director

Site of the Chang Tang Reserve in the Tibet Autonomous Region.

of Wildlife Conservation International, has spent four decades in wild and rugged places, studying wildlife, and fighting

"We have the chance to save one of the last unspoiled ecosystems on our planet."
George Schaller

for its survival. And now Schaller and his Chinese and Tibetan colleagues have helped establish a huge reserve in the Chang Tang.

Although the reserve is already the size of Arizona, they hope to expand it to conform to the migrations of antelopes and yaks.

There, Tibet's last great herds can roam free, and the nomads can maintain their traditional culture.

Schaller explains, "If we don't protect the Chang Tang now, the magnificent species found here could soon vanish forever."

Under such harsh and remote conditions, the right equipment is not only important, it's imperative. Which is why George Schaller wears a rugged Rolex Oyster Perpetual timepiece.

ROLEX

Rolex Oyster Perpetual Explorer in stainless steel with matching Oyster bracelet.
Write for brochure. Rolex Watch U.S.A., Inc., Dept. RLX, Rolex Building, 665 Fifth Avenue, New York, N.Y. 10022-5383.
Rolex, ♛, Oyster Perpetual, Explorer and Oyster are trademarks.

Figure 8-5

In this ad for Rolex watches George Schaller voices an attitude that illustrates the value-expressive function of attitudes.

in Figure 8-5, the naturalist George Schaller says, "If we don't protect the Chang Tang now, the magnificent species found here could soon vanish forever." This attitudinal statement expresses a set of values held by Mr. Schaller, with which Rolex hopes that its target market will identify.

Behaviors and Intentions to Behave

As we have stressed in this text, the primary goal of the marketer is to understand, predict, and influence the behavior of consumers. **Consumer behaviors** consist of all the actions consumers take to acquire, use, and dispose of products and services. Some consumer behaviors are: buying a product or service, providing word-of-mouth information about a product or service to another person, disposing of a product, and collecting information for a purchase.

Before they take action, people often develop behavioral intentions regarding the likelihood of their taking that action. **Behavioral intentions** may be defined as the intentions of consumers to behave in a particular way with regard to the acquisition, disposition, and use of products and services. Thus a consumer may form the intention to search for information, to tell someone else about an experience with a product, to buy a particular product or service, or to dispose of a product in a certain way. As discussed in more detail later in this chapter, the formation of behavioral intentions tends to occur in high-involvement circumstances.

HOW BELIEFS, ATTITUDES, AND BEHAVIORS ARE FORMED

Beliefs, attitudes, and behaviors are formed in two distinct ways. In direct formation a belief, attitude, or behavior is created without either of the other states occurring first. Thus, as the behavioral influence perspective suggests, a behavior can be induced without the consumer first forming strong attitudes or beliefs about the object toward which the behavior is directed. Similarly, as the experiential perspective suggests, an attitude (i.e., a feeling) may be created without the consumer first developing specific beliefs about the attitudinal object.

After a belief, attitude, or behavior is formed directly there is a tendency for the three states to build upon one another to create a hierarchy. In this way the consumer may first form beliefs about a product, then develop attitudes toward it, and finally purchase it. Or the consumer may first engage in the behavior of buying a product and then form beliefs and attitudes toward that product. When the formation of one state (e.g., a belief) results in the creation of another state (e.g., an attitude), the indirect formation of an attitude has occurred. In the next two sections we explore how beliefs, attitudes, and behaviors may be formed either directly or indirectly.

The Direct Formation of Beliefs, Attitudes, and Behaviors

Disparate processes cause the direct formation of beliefs, attitudes, and behaviors, and these processes are directly linked to the three research perspectives on consumer behavior we described earlier in the text. Belief formation corresponds to the decision-making perspective. Thus beliefs are viewed as being formed primarily through cognitive-learning principles. In contrast, the direct formation of attitudes is linked to the experiential perspective, so attitudes are viewed as resulting from sources that directly elicit emotional responses (e.g., mere exposure and classical conditioning). In addition, the affective responses that are associated with attitudes may result from behavioral influence processes such as classical conditioning. Finally, the direct creation of behavior corresponds to the behavioral influence perspective—specifically operant conditioning—so that behavior is viewed as resulting from environmental or situational factors.

Creating Beliefs Directly The direct formation of beliefs takes place through the information-processing activities of the consumer. Information about the attributes and benefits of a product is received, encoded into memory, and later retrieved from memory for use. Figure 8-6 shows an advertisement for Dr. Scholl's callus removers that attempts to create the following specific beliefs about the product: fast, safe, eliminates pain, eliminates corns, and eliminates calluses. The goal of the ad is to influence the reader's beliefs via information processing and cognitive learning.

Forming Attitudes Directly Earlier in the chapter, we defined attitude as the amount of affect or feeling for or against a stimulus object, such as a person, a product, a company, or an idea. Three mechanisms explain how attitudes are formed directly: behavioral-learning processes, a process called the *mere-exposure phenomenon*, and mood states.

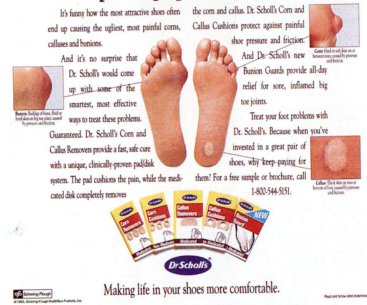

Keeping up with fashion shouldn't mean putting up with pain.

It's funny how the most attractive shoes often end up causing the ugliest, most painful corns, calluses and bunions.

And it's no surprise that Dr. Scholl's would come up with some of the smartest, most effective ways to treat these problems.

Guaranteed. Dr. Scholl's Corn and Callus Removers provide a fast, safe cure with a unique, clinically-proven pad/disk system. The pad cushions the pain, while the medicated disk completely removes

the corn and callus. Dr. Scholl's Corn and Callus Cushions protect against painful shoe pressure and friction. And Dr. Scholl's new Bunion Guards provide all-day relief for sore, inflamed big toe joints.

Treat your foot problems with Dr. Scholl's. Because when you've invested in a great pair of shoes, why keep paying for them? For a free sample or brochure, call 1-800-544-5151.

Dr. Scholl's

Making life in your shoes more comfortable.

Figure 8-6

The goal of this ad is to influence consumers' beliefs about attributes and benefits.

Behavioral Learning and Attitude Formation. Attitudes may be created directly through the behavioral-learning processes of classical conditioning, operant conditioning, and observational learning. (For a detailed description of these processes, see Chapter 5.) From a classical-conditioning perspective, an attitude is a conditioned emotional response that can be elicited by a conditioned stimulus. Researchers have found evidence of the classical conditioning of attitudes in a consumer behavior setting.[24] One set of four studies showed quite convincingly that attitudes toward a brand could be influenced by using the unconditioned stimuli of pleasing pictures, such as a mountain waterfall. The "hot," "sexy" ads for Calvin Klein's products are an ubiquitous illustration of one company's attempt to classically condition consumers so that its brand elicits certain feelings and emotions.

Attitudes may also result from operant-conditioning processes. For instance, during the course of a conversation with friends about various cars, you may make certain statements about alternative models. The positive and negative responses of your friends may act to reinforce or punish your evaluations. Evaluations that are positively reinforced are likely to recur, while those that are punished are likely to be suppressed. Thus social reinforcement is a major factor influencing attitude formation.

The operant conditioning of attitudes is closely related to the utilitarian function we referred to earlier in the chapter. As conceived by Katz, attitude expression is a learned response resulting from reinforcement and punishment.[25] From this perspective, the affect that makes up the feeling base of the attitude is the outcome of operant conditioning.

Vicarious learning may also lead to the direct formation of attitudes. The observation of important others expressing their feelings and evaluations of products may cause the target audience to model these actions. In such a process consumers form their attitudes by taking on the attitudes of opinion leaders. Very popular celebrity endorsers, such as Andre Agassi or Whoopi Goldberg, may have such an effect on their admirers.

Mere Exposure and Attitude Formation. Another method for creating positive feelings in consumers is to repeatedly expose them to a stimulus. All else being equal, through the **mere-exposure phenomenon,** people's liking for something may increase simply because they see it over and over again.[26] The all-else-equal caveat is important, for if consumers perceive the stimulus negatively, repeated exposures will probably lead to an intense dislike of the stimulus.[27]

An interesting aspect of the mere exposure phenomenon is that it does not seem to be cognitively based. Rather, the positive feelings created by repeated exposures often occur without the consumers consciously knowing or perceiving that the object is familiar.[28] Figure 8-7 is a mundane picture of a Wal-Mart parking lot. The retailer is having a back-to-school sale. But notice the Coca-Cola logo on the tent. In the consumer environment images of Coke are ubiquitous. At least some of Coke's long-standing appeal comes from the mere-exposure effect.

Figure 8-7
The Coca-Cola logo, which can be found just about everywhere, is a good illustration of the mere-exposure effect.

The mere-exposure effect has important implications for marketers. If a corporation can manage to put its product, name, or symbol in front of consumers often enough, it may be able to subtly influence the feelings of large numbers of people. The omnipresence of the Coca-Cola name is an example. We see it repeatedly flashed on television, at baseball parks, in theaters, in restaurants, on buses, and just about everywhere else. It is no accident that Coke is the largest-selling soft drink.

Moods and Attitude Formation. Mood also has a direct impact on consumers' attitude formation. It has been found that when consumers are initially exposed to an object, their mood state at the time affects the attitude they form toward the object. So when consumers first learn about a new product, such as a digital audio recorder, their mood at that time will influence their evaluation: a good mood increases the chances of a positive evaluation and a bad mood increases the chances of a negative evaluation. The managerial implications of this phenomenon are obvious: when introducing them to new products, retailers should do everything possible to put consumers in a positive affective state.[29] Recall the comment by the president of Land Rover of North America in the introductory case. When he said that the car-buying experience should be fun, he was recognizing the importance of creating positive moods among potential buyers.

Creating Behavior Directly Consumer researchers have traditionally viewed the behavior of buying a product or service as occurring *after* the formation of beliefs and attitudes. However, in certain circumstances purchase behavior may be influenced directly without consumers first developing strong beliefs or attitudes about the product. As we said in Chapter 5, behavior is directly influenced when strong situational or environmental forces propel the consumer to engage in an action. The design of the physical environment is an excellent example of how behaviors can be directly induced.[30] The appropriate arrangement of aisles in a supermarket can move customers toward high-margin food and nonfood items. Similarly, the seating arrangement in a restaurant can either enhance or detract from customers' ability to interact during their meals, thereby influencing the rate of turnover during prime eating hours. Sales-promotion tactics are likewise designed to directly influence behavior.

Operant conditioning is also used to influence behavior directly. The advantage, according to its proponents, is that people are often unaware they are being conditioned. Shaping is a good example of the direct influence of behavior through operant conditioning.

Auto dealerships are skillful shapers of behaviors. They know how to apply reinforcers to create new behaviors. For instance, Buick attempted to improve sales of its slow-selling Regal by coordinating sales-promotion efforts with the Buick Open golf tournament. The division ran a large contest, called the Longest Drive Sweepstakes, that gave every person who entered a Buick showroom a chance of winning $126,000. Anyone who test-drove a Regal received a sleeve of golf balls. Finally, the customer was given large discounts on the purchase of a Regal.

The direct influence of behavior has not received much attention from researchers, so the frequency of its occurrence among consumers is unknown. Our guess is that future research will show that a great many consumer activities are directly induced.

Hierarchies of Beliefs, Attitudes, and Behaviors

Behaviors, attitudes, and beliefs can be formed indirectly as well. In these instances they link up to form hierarchies of effects. The term **hierarchies of effects** was coined to delineate the order in which beliefs, attitudes, and behavior occur. It is the type of purchase process that controls which hierarchy a consumer will form. Table 8-2 identifies the four

Purchase Processes and Their Possible Hierarchies of Effects

Purchase Process	Hierarchy of Effects
1. High involvement	Standard learning hierarchy: Beliefs—affect—behavior
2. Low involvement	Low-involvement hierarchy: Beliefs—behavior—affect
3. Experiential/impulse	Experiential hierarchy: Affect—behavior—beliefs
4. Behavioral influence	Behavioral influence hierarchy: Behavior—beliefs—affect

TABLE 8-2

possible purchase processes and the hierarchy of effects associated with each process. The four hierarchies are the high-involvement hierarchy, the low-involvement hierarchy, the experiential hierarchy, and the behaviorial influence hierarchy.

Decision-Making Hierarchies The early proponents of hierarchies of effects proposed that consumers first form a belief about an object, then develop affect (feelings) toward that object, and finally engage in some behavior relative to the object (e.g., purchasing a product). This pattern—beliefs leading to affect, which, in turn, leads to behavior—is called the **standard learning hierarchy**[31] or the **high-involvement hierarchy.** Earlier in the text we defined involvement as a state of motivation resulting from the level of importance the consumer attaches to a purchase. As involvement in the buying decision increases, the consumer tends to engage in a more extensive search for information about alternative products and, consequently, to form a large number of beliefs about those alternatives. The consumer is also likely to take the time to evaluate and compare alternatives. Through such problem-solving activities, the consumer forms certain attitudes. With the formation of these beliefs and attitudes, the consumer's behavioral intentions are likely to result in the behavior of purchasing the product or service. In short, when consumers are highly involved in a particular purchase decision, they engage in extended problem-solving activities and move through the standard learning hierarchy—belief formation, then attitude formation, and then behavior.

In the mid-1960s consumer researchers began to recognize that many, if not most, consumer purchases do not fit the pattern of the high-involvement hierarchy.[32] Many times consumers purchase products without developing any feelings or affect beforehand. In these cases it was proposed that consumers first form beliefs about a product, which are followed directly by the product's purchase. Only after the purchase do they form an attitude toward the product.[33]

Attitudes follow purchase behavior when the consumer's involvement with both product and purchase situation is low.[34] The flow of events is quite different in a low-involvement decision. In these cases consumers are not motivated to do extensive problem solving. Instead, they move through a limited decision process in which they consider just a few product alternatives in a superficial manner and therefore form only a limited number of beliefs about those alternatives. Because they do not evaluate the alternatives closely, they may not form any attitudes concerning them. In low-involvement situations, then, attitudes tend to occur only after the good or service is bought and experienced, when consumers reflect on how they feel about it. So when consumers have low involvement in a purchase, they tend to engage in limited problem solving and move through what is called a **low-involvement hierarchy**—belief formation, then behavior, and finally attitude formation.[35]

Experiential Hierarchy From the experiential perspective, consumers engage in a behavior because they strongly desire to obtain certain feelings or excitement. In this conceptualization the hierarchy of effects is initiated by feelings or attitudes. For example, a friend may ask you to go to a rock concert. Your decision will probably be based on the feelings that you have toward the group performing and the concert setting. If questioned about your reasons for going, you will be able to voice a series of beliefs, but these beliefs are probably far less influential in your decision than your feelings. In fact, you may state these beliefs merely to justify your decision.[36]

The **experiential hierarchy** begins with a strong affective response, is followed by behavior based on these strong feelings, and ends with beliefs developed to justify the behavior. Impulse purchases exemplify the experiential hierarchy. In an **impulse purchase** a strong positive feeling is followed by the buying act.[37]

The hypothesis that affect can occur prior to the formation of strong beliefs is intuitively appealing, but it is controversial. Very little research has been conducted that directly tests for the existence of the experiential hierarchy. The major reason for identifying such a hierarchy is to emphasize the point that for some purchases affective processes appear to dominate and precede rational decision making. Indeed, some researchers have noted that emotions may predominate even in some highly involving situations. For example, when purchasing a house or a car, the stakes may be so high that information processing stops for some people and feelings and emotions take over.

Affective reactions can also have a strong impact on behaviors that provoke fear in some people, such as giving blood. In one study investigating the role of emotion in blood donations, the authors found that for those less experienced at giving blood, emotional responses of sadness, contempt, and joy played a major role in predicting donations. Interestingly, for those most experienced at giving blood, the emotion of fear was negatively associated with donations. That is, the least fearful donors had the greatest likelihood of donating blood.[38]

Figure 8-8 portrays a print ad for United Airlines that incorporates many of the ideas that underlie the experiential hierarchy. In particular, note the focus on creating affective responses.

Behavioral Influence Hierarchy The **behavioral influence hierarchy** predicts that strong situational or environmental forces can propel consumers to buy a product without having formed either feelings or affect about that product. Recall the study described in Chapter 5 that found that when grocery stores played slow-paced music, buying increased because the music caused consumers to walk more slowly through the store. This is an instance of buying behavior being directly influenced without beliefs or attitudes intervening.

Whenever behavior is induced directly through the operation of environmental or situational factors, the hierarchy of effects begins with the behavior. Whether feelings or beliefs follow the behavior cannot be definitely answered at this time, though one researcher has argued that the hierarchy moves from behavior to feelings to beliefs.[39] This has been called the "Do-Feel-Learn" hierarchy. Common experience seems to support such a view—people do at times feel very good or very bad after a purchase. (Postpurchase processes are discussed in greater detail in Chapter 13.)

The study of beliefs and attitudes and their relationship to purchase behavior has major implications for promotional strategy. How companies promote a brand depends upon the type of buying process that the brand's target market engages in when purchasing products in the brand's category. Table 8-3 summarizes some promotional strategies that companies may use depending upon the buying process involved.

CONNOISSEUR CLASS

Comfort comes to a head.

Your ears will tell you. Your eyes will show you. Your mouth confirms the assessment. In Connoisseur Class,™ contentment reaches a crescendo.

Your seat, deep and wide, surrounds you. The CD audio sings. Godiva® chocolate tempts you. You're flying into the state of total relaxation.

Connoisseur Class is international business travel elevated to its highest form of civility.

Come fly the airline that's uniting the world. Come fly the friendly skies.

UNITED AIRLINES

Figure 8-8
United Airlines seeks to create positive affective reactions through this ad.

Additional Comments on Hierarchies of Effects Twenty-five years ago consumer behavior researchers had a simplistic one-dimensional view of the relationship of beliefs, feelings, and behavior. Today the view is highly complex, with various authors proposing that different hierarchies of effects operate under various buying circumstances. Indeed, the current view may well be overly complex. For example, does it make sense to say that when a consumer is engaged in a routine decision process *absolutely* no affect exists prior to purchasing a product? Or is it likely that in impulse purchases the consumer has formed *no* beliefs about the product? Such reasoning leads to the realization that the various hierarchies of effects are idealized representations of consumer buying behavior. Regardless of the decision process involved, it is likely that consumers have some rudimentary beliefs and some vague attitudinal feelings about a product or service before they buy it. What the various hierarchies of effects give managers is a feel for the relative emphases of beliefs, attitudes, and behavior within the various purchase processes.

Some Promotional Strategies Based on the Type of Consumer Purchase Process	
Buying Process	**Possible Promotional Strategies**
High involvement	Emphasize developing product-attribute and product-benefit beliefs through cognitive-learning procedures. Can stress print advertising and personal selling. Help create affect through product demonstrations and advertising using classical-conditioning procedures.
Low involvement	Emphasize developing product-attribute beliefs through repetition of simple messages. Tie point-of-purchase displays to advertising. Place product and displays in high-traffic area.
Experiental/impulse	Emphasize the fun and feelings that can be obtained by experiencing the product or service. Emphasize creating affect through the classical conditioning of positive feelings toward the product.
Behavioral influence	Use sales-promotion techniques, such as sweepstakes, rebates, samples, or coupons.

TABLE 8-3

PREDICTING CONSUMER ATTITUDES THROUGH MULTIATTRIBUTE MODELS

As noted earlier in the chapter, the formation of consumer attitudes in high-involvement situations may be best described by **multiattribute models.** These models identify how consumers combine their beliefs about product attributes to form attitudes about various brand alternatives, corporations, or other objects. Multiattribute models assume that consumers are using the standard hierarchy-of-effects approach in which beliefs lead to attitude formation, which, in turn, leads to purchase behaviors.

Numerous multiattribute models have been developed.[40] We present two of them in this section. The first focuses on predicting the attitude that a consumer forms toward a specific attitude object, such as a product, service, person, or idea. The second model focuses on predicting the behavioral intentions of consumers to perform some type of action, such as buying a product or service. The behavioral intentions model appeared after the attitude-toward-the-object model, and in fact builds upon the earlier approach.

Attitude-Toward-the-Object Model

Of all the different multiattribute models that have been developed to predict a consumer's attitude toward an object, the one that has received the most attention from consumer and marketing researchers is the **attitude-toward-the-object model,** or the Fishbein model.[41] This model identifies three major factors that predict attitudes. First are the salient beliefs that a person has about an object. **Salient beliefs** are those attribute-object beliefs activated when a person evaluates an attitudinal object. From an information-processing perspective, these are the beliefs that are activated in memory when attention is focused upon an object. Salient beliefs usually concern the attributes that are important to the consumer.

The second component of the Fishbein attitude-toward-the-object model is the strength of the belief that an object has the attribute in question. The strength of the object-attribute linkage is usually assessed by asking a consumer, "How likely is it that object x possesses attribute y?" For example, suppose that a researcher wished to determine the strength of consumers' belief that a Land Rover has high ruggedness and excellent handling. She would ask them to answer the following questions:

1. How likely is it that Land Rovers are extremely rugged?
   Extremely unlikely 1 2 3 4 5 6 7 8 9 10 Extremely likely
2. How likely is it that Land Rovers have excellent handling?
   Extremely unlikely 1 2 3 4 5 6 7 8 9 10 Extremely likely

The third component of the Fishbein model is the evaluation of each of the salient attributes. These evaluation ratings provide an assessment of the goodness/badness of the salient attributes. For example, in the Land Rover example some consumers may evaluate "ruggedness" positively and others evaluate it negatively. (That is, while "ruggedness" allows the vehicle to go off the road, it also makes the vehicle look awkward and slow.) Researchers obtain evaluation ratings of an attribute by asking consumers how good or bad the attribute is. In the Land Rover example the researcher would ask consumers to answer the following two questions:

1. How bad/good is it for a vehicle to be extremely rugged?
   Very bad −3 −2 −1 0 +1 +2 +3 Very good
2. How bad/good is it for a vehicle to have great handling?
   Very bad −3 −2 −1 0 +1 +2 +3 Very good

There are probably wide variations in consumers' evaluations of the goodness/badness of the attribute of ruggedness in a Land Rover. Some consumers may prize a vehicle that allows drivers to go off-road, while others may be indifferent to that attribute but greatly desire a vehicle that has more sports car characteristics. So on this attribute consumer ratings may range widely from −3 to +3. In contrast, for most people, the attribute "great handling" is a positive characteristic. Few would want a vehicle to have poor handling. On the other hand, many consumers simply desire a car that handles safely and adequately. The trade-offs for great handling are high costs and a harsh ride, which many consumers seek to avoid. So on this attribute evaluations would probably range only from 0 to +3.

To predict a consumer's attitude, managers can combine information on the evaluation and strength of the salient beliefs via the following algebraic formula:

$$A_o = \sum_{i=1}^{N} b_i \, e_i$$

where A_o = the overall attitude toward object o

b_i = the strength of the belief concerning whether object o has some particular attribute i

e_i = the evaluation of the goodness or badness of attribute i

n = the number of beliefs

Table 8-4 presents a hypothetical example of the attitudes held by two market segments—Macho Mikes and Racy Ritas—regarding three vehicles: a Land Rover, a Toyota RAV4, and a Toyota Celica. Macho Mikes are young males who are risk takers, like to participate in sports, and love to drink beer. Racy Ritas are young professional women who live in urban areas and work out at health clubs. We are assuming that members of each market segment evaluated the three vehicles on five salient attributes: sporty styling, great handling, high cost, ruggedness, and off-road capability.

An inspection of Table 8-4 shows that the Macho Mikes prefer the RAV4, followed by the Land Rover and the Celica. In contrast, Racy Ritas like the Celica the best, followed

Predicting the Attitudes of Two Consumer Segments

Segment A: Macho Mikes

Attribute	e_i	Land Rover b_i	Land Rover $b_i \times e_i$	RAV 4 b_i	RAV 4 $b_i \times e_i$	Celica b_i	Celica $b_i \times e_i$
Sporty styling	−1	5	−5	7	−7	7	−7
Great handling	+1	5	5	6	6	8	8
High cost	−3	8	−24	2	−6	7	−21
Ruggedness	+3	7	21	9	27	4	12
Off-road Ability	+3	7	21	9	27	1	3
Attitude score =			18		47		−5

Segment B: Racy Ritas

Attribute	e_i	Land Rover b_i	Land Rover $b_i \times e_i$	RAV 4 b_i	RAV 4 $b_i \times e_i$	Celica b_i	Celica $b_i \times e_i$
Sporty styling	+2	4	8	6	12	8	16
Great handling	+3	5	15	3	9	9	27
High cost	−1	8	−8	2	−2	7	−7
Ruggedness	+1	7	7	7	7	5	5
Off-road Ability	−3	9	−27	9	−27	2	−6
Attitude score =			−5		−1		35

Note: b_i = strength of attitude (1 = extremely unlikely, 10 = extremely likely).
$\quad e_i$ = evaluation of goodness/badness (−3 = very bad, +3 = very good).
$\quad A_0$ = Attitude toward object 0.

TABLE 8-4

by the Land Rover and the RAV4. Looking at the table, one finds that the belief ratings of these two very different market segments were similar for the three autos. Each group viewed the Land Rover as costly, rugged, and possessing off-road capability. The RAV4 was thought to cost less than the Land Rover and the Celica, while the Celica was perceived as having sporty styling and good handling, but as lacking in ruggedness and off-road capability. (An ad for the Celica is found in Figure 8-9.) What caused the extreme differences in the preferences of the two market segments was the wide variation in their evaluations of the attributes. Macho Mikes strongly desired ruggedness and off-road capability, and Racy Ritas craved sporty styling and great handling.

In sum, the attitude-toward-the-object model suggests that three factors influence attitude formation: (1) consumers' salient attributes for an object; (2) the extent to which consumers believe that the object possesses these attributes; and (3) the degree of positivity/negativity with which these attributes are evaluated. Marketing managers must therefore know the salient attributes that consumers expect in a product and how positively or negatively they rate these attributes in order to develop an attractive product and promote it successfully. Remember, one important role of promotional messages is to influence consumers' beliefs concerning the extent to which an object possesses an attribute.

How does Fishbein's attitude-toward-the-object model deal with differences in attribute importance? Interestingly, the model makes no direct attempt to measure the

IT HAS BEEN SAID THAT BEAUTY IS IN THE
EYE OF THE BEHOLDER. BEHOLD.

People are not just attracted to beauty. They are drawn to it.

For twenty-five years that has been the abiding principle in designing the Toyota

Celica. Restyled for 1996, Celica's sleekly sculptured aerodynamics take this

principle to a new level. And with Toyota's legendary reputation for reliability,

you don't have to look hard to see that Celica's beauty is more than just skin

deep. All of which makes Celica as beautiful to drive as it is to look at.

But, then, what else would you expect from a company that approaches manufacturing

as an art?   TOYOTA CELICA
                                                   I love what you do for me

Call 1-800-GO-TOYOTA or visit our Web Site at: http://www.toyota.com for a brochure and location of your nearest dealer.
©1996 Toyota Motor Sales, U.S.A., Inc. Buckle Up! Do it for those who love you.

Figure 8-9
The Toyota Celica is known for its beautiful lines, precision handling, and reliability.

differential importance of attributes, but this omission has little or no effect on its ability to predict attitudes because consumers assess the importance of an attribute when they give evaluation ratings. Indeed, researchers have found that as the importance of an attribute increases, the evaluation ratings become more extreme.[42] Thus if an attribute is not important, its evaluation rating will be close to zero on the "goodness-badness" dimension—which is equivalent to rating the attribute as having low importance.

Global Attitudes versus Attitudes-Toward-the-Object The measure of attitude obtained from a multiattribute model is an indirect measure of attitude. In other words, when using this model, the researcher estimates the level of consumers' attitudes toward an object by measuring the strengths of their beliefs about the attributes possessed by the object and their evaluations of these attributes. But it is also possible to directly measure consumers' global attitudes. A **global attitude measure** is a direct measurement of the overall affect and feelings held by a consumer regarding an object.

To measure global attitudes several questions are asked on semantic differential scales—which request respondents to rate an object on various scales anchored by opposite-meaning adjectives. For example, global attitudes regarding the Land Rover might be assessed in the following manner:

Please describe your feelings about Land Rovers by circling the appropriate number on the scales.
Good 1 2 3 4 5 Bad
Positive 1 2 3 4 5 Negative
Like 1 2 3 4 5 Dislike

Whenever possible, market researchers collect data on global attitudes as well as sufficient information to predict consumer attitudes through an attitude-toward-the-object model. The results of the two estimates can then be compared. If global attitudes and predicted attitudes match closely, researchers can be confident they have a good understanding of the factors influencing consumer attitude formation. But, if the predicted and the global attitudes do not correlate, they know additional research is required.

When Do Attitudes Predict Behavior?

One of the most vexing problems for a consumer researcher involves explaining why a carefully gathered body of knowledge about consumer attitudes toward a product can fail to predict purchase behavior. In fact, many consumer researchers have become rather pessimistic about the ability of attitudes to predict overt behavior.[43] The present view of the issue is that one must learn to recognize the factors that influence the extent to which attitudes predict behaviors.[44] The following six factors are thought to be decisive:

1. *Involvement of the consumer.* Attitudes are likely to predict purchase behavior only under conditions of high involvement, when the standard learning hierarchy operates.

2. *Attitude measurement.* The attitude measurement has to be both reliable and valid—and be at the same level of abstraction as the measure of behavior. For example, if the behavior involves contributing to a specific charity, such as the American Cancer Society, the attitude questions cannot deal with less specific (i.e., more abstract) questions about consumers' attitudes toward charities in general. A similar point concerns the variable of time. If the behavior involves buying a new Porsche within the next six months, the measure should include a time parameter. The longer the time between attitude measurement and the time of the behavior, the weaker the relationship is.

3. *Effects of other people.* The desires of other people toward the purchase and the consumer's motivation to comply with these desires influence the extent to which attitudes predict behavior.

4. *Situational factors.* Situational factors, such as holidays, time pressures, and sickness, may intervene so that measured attitudes fail to predict behavior well.

5. *Effects of other brands.* Even though a consumer's attitude toward a brand is quite favorable, if that consumer's attitude toward another brand is even more favorable, the other brand is probably the one that will be purchased. One of the reasons the attitude-toward-the-object model has problems predicting behavior is that it fails to measure attitudes toward other objects.

6. *Attitude strength.* For an attitude to influence behavior, it must be held with sufficient strength and conviction to be activated in memory.[45] The degree of association between an attitude and an object varies across a continuum. At one end of the continuum is the nonattitude: the consumer essentially has neither positive nor negative feelings about a particular brand. At the other end of the continuum is the extreme attitude: the consumer feels very strongly about the brand. Numerous studies have demonstrated that the stronger the attitude, the more likely it is to be retrieved from memory and to subsequently influence behavior.

One way of measuring the strength of an attitude is through a procedure called *response latency*. The researcher asks respondents to press either a "like" or "dislike" key on a computer when a series of products are displayed, with the computer measuring how long it takes respondents to press a button. It is assumed that the longer the response latency, the weaker the attitude held by the consumer. This assumption was borne out by one study in which this procedure was followed for 100 products, such as various candy bars, salty snack foods, chewing gums, and canned foods. After completing the rating task, the respondents were given an opportunity to choose from ten of the products the five they most preferred. The results revealed that the more accessible in memory the attitude (i.e., the more quickly the "like" computer key was pushed for a brand), the more likely the person was to select the brand.[46]

These findings are consistent with the idea that the expression of an attitude is a constructive process. When asked to state an attitude toward an object, people search through their memories to retrieve information concerning their feelings. Because memory is a constructive process in which any information available is used to assist the recall process, what attitude is recalled depends in part on what is current, salient, and available in memory. As a result, situational circumstances and moods may well influence the attitude people express. Indeed, some researchers have found that merely asking someone to think about his or her attitude toward something can itself change the attitude. That is, people seek to justify their statements by giving reasons for their feelings, and this process of giving reasons can make new attributes salient and thereby change their views. The lesson is that market researchers should take indirect measures whenever possible to forestall the process of thinking that can influence the attitude expressed.[47]

For all our sophisticated measures, the task of predicting consumer actions is still extremely difficult. Just consider the nightmare of trying to predict whether or not consumers will purchase a new music album in a market known for its fickle and bewildering taste. Can you guess what percentage of new albums succeed in the marketplace? The nearby consumer behavior factoid answers this question.

The six factors that limit the ability of attitude-toward-the-object models to predict behavior were recognized by Martin Fishbein and his colleagues. They realized that a person may have a positive *attitude* toward buying a brand, such as a Land Rover, but never engage in the *behavior* of buying it. To improve marketers' prediction prowess, they developed another model. Rather than concentrating on consumers' *attitude* toward the object, this model focuses on predicting *intentions* to behave in a specific manner, such as purchasing a product.

The Behavioral Intentions Model

The behavioral intentions model, also called the **theory of reasoned action,** was developed by Martin Fishbein and his colleagues expressly to improve the ability of the attitude-toward-the-object model to predict consumer behavior. It extends that basic model in several ways.[48] First, it proposes that behavior results from the formation of specific intentions to behave. Thus the behavioral intentions model does not attempt to predict behavior per se, but rather intentions to act.

Second, the model contains a new construct called the *subjective norm*. The **subjective norm** (SN) assesses what consumers believe other people think that they should do. In other words, SN introduces into the formulation the powerful effects of reference groups on behavior.

The third change in the model involves the object to which attitudes are directed. Instead of assessing the consumer's attitude toward the brand itself, the model assesses the consumer's attitude toward the overt behavior of purchasing the product. The key difference here is that the focus is on the consumer's perception of what the consequences of the purchase will be. Assessing the consequences of the purchase rather than whether or not the product possesses certain attributes helps the researcher take into consideration factors that may act to impede consumers' intentions to behave. For the purchase of a sport utility vehicle, some consequences of the purchase might be: (1) buying the car would cause the person to forgo a vacation; (2) buying the car would cause the person to have to deal with obnoxious salespeople; and (3) buying the car would involve the person in getting a loan at very high interest rates. Attitude models that assess only the attitude toward the object cannot measure such factors.

Algebraically, the behavioral intentions model is expressed as

$$B \approx BI = w_1(A_B) + w_2(SN)$$

where:

$$B = \text{behavior}$$
$$BI = \text{behavior intention}$$
$$A_B = \text{attitude toward performing the behavior}$$
$$SN = \text{the subjective norm}$$
$$w_1 \text{ and } w_2 = \text{empirically determined weights}$$

The weights (w_1 and w_2) are determined empirically through regression analysis, and A_B and SN are obtained directly from consumers via questionnaires. In fact, A_B and SN are themselves indexes that are obtained through other measures. Specifically, the attitude toward the behavior is obtained from the following equation:

$$A_B = \sum_{i=1}^{n} b_i \, e_i$$

where:

$$A_B = \text{attitude toward performing the behavior}$$
$$b_i = \text{the person's belief that performing the behavior will result in consequence } i$$
$$e_i = \text{the person's evaluation of consequence } i$$
$$n = \text{the number of beliefs}$$

Note that this equation is very similar to the one used in other multiattribute models. The major difference is in the belief variable. Rather than assessing the person's belief that an object has an attribute, the behavioral intentions model assesses the person's belief that performing a particular behavior will result in a particular consequence.

The equation for obtaining the subjective norm is

$$SN = \sum_{j=1}^{n} NB_j \, MC_j$$

where:

$$SN = \text{subjective norm}$$
$$NB_j = \text{the normative belief that a reference group or person } j \text{ thinks that the consumer should or should not perform the behavior}$$
$$MC_j = \text{the motivation to comply with the influence of referent } j$$
$$n = \text{number of relevant reference groups of individuals}$$

The subjective norm is calculated much as a belief is. The normative belief is equivalent to a belief statement, and the motivation to comply is like an importance rating. Thus for each person or reference group, these ratings are multiplied, and the result is added across all people or reference groups considered.

Researchers have found that a person's beliefs about normative pressures to engage in a behavior can play a dominant role in determining whether that person behaves in a particular way. For example, a study investigating the use of condoms by adults revealed that perceived normative pressure was by far the best predictor of condom usage. Pressure from socially important people was more important than other variables, such as AIDS knowledge, perceived susceptibility to the disease, and condom use outcome expectancies.[49]

A number of researchers have tested the behavioral intentions model against the standard multiattribute models. In general, the results reveal that the behavioral intentions model is superior.[50] However, various authors have suggested that the model as specified may not be completely accurate. They especially question the role of the subjective norm variable, for the evidence suggests that purchase behavior is influenced much more by the attitudinal component than by the subjective norm component of the model.[51]

The Mere-Measurement Effect An intriguing question for consumer researchers is whether merely asking consumers about their purchase intentions influences their subsequent purchases. In order to test this **mere-measurement effect,** researchers asked nearly 5,000 consumers whether they intended to purchase a new car or computer. In this study they employed a six-point scale ranging from "yes, within six months" to "never." Next they determined whether the respondents actually made such a purchase during the next six months and compared the results to those for a control group of 5,000 similar consumers who had not been asked the purchase intent question. The finding was that consumers who had been asked the purchase intent question were significantly more likely to make the purchase, regardless of whether they answered "yes" or "no" to the question. While the overall increase in tendency was slightly less than 1 percent, this is a meaningful change, for in consumer goods industries such as autos and soft drinks, a 1 percent change in sales translates into tens of millions of dollars in profits.[52]

Additional research on the mere measurement effect found that when current users of a brand were asked about their intentions to repurchase the brand, their likelihood of making the purchase increased. Interestingly, when the question was asked of consumers who were *not* current users of the brand, they more frequently purchased brands having the largest market share. These results provide an urgent new reason for doing marketing research: the very act of asking behavioral intentions questions could very well increase the likelihood that consumers will purchase a product.[53]

Table 8-5 summarizes some of the managerial applications of the concepts concerning consumer beliefs, attitudes, and behaviors discussed in this chapter.

A Managerial Applications Analysis of the "Americans Are Truckin'" Case

Problem Identification

The introductory case concerned the rising popularity of trucks and sport utility vehicles. A key issue for product managers of both types of products is to determine what factors are responsible for the recent surge in consumer interest in these vehicles and to create strategies for sustaining present high sales levels.

The Consumer Behavior Analysis and Its Managerial Implications

The concepts discussed in this chapter that explain the popularity of trucks and sport utility vehicles are: attribute importance, the value expressive function of attitudes, multiattribute models, and the behavioral intentions model. The implications of these concepts

Examples of Managerial Applications of Key Chapter Concepts

I. Beliefs

   A. *Market Research*

      1. Conduct studies to determine the belief structure and needs and wants of consumers concerning your brands and competitive brands.

   B. *Marketing Mix*

      1. Develop products possessing attributes that provide the benefits sought by consumers.

      2. Use promotional strategy to form consumer beliefs and attributes of benefits.

   C. *Segmentation*

      1. Segment market based on the similar benefits sought by large numbers of consumers.

   D. *Positioning and Differentiation*

      1. Position and differentiate products based on the attributes they possess.

   E. *Environmental Analysis*

      1. Conduct studies to determine the belief structure and needs and wants of consumers for competitive brands.

II. Attitudes

   A. *Market Research*

      1. Conduct studies to determine the global attitudes of consumers regarding your brands, sales personnel, retail stores, and corporations, and those of your competitors.

   B. *Marketing Mix*

      1. Use advertising to form positive attitudes by associating the product with positively evaluated spokesperons, music, and images.

      2. Train sales force, retail clerks, and other personnel to create positive feelings among customers.

      3. Carefully analyze the distribution system to ensure the minimization of factors, such as stockouts and dirty facilities, that create negative feelings.

III. Multiattribute Models

   A. *Market Research*

      1. Conduct studies to predict attitudes toward the object and intentions to behave, and compare the outcomes of these analyses to measures of global attitudes and to actual behavior.

   B. *Marketing Mix*

      1. Use results of multiattribute attitude studies as the basis for making appropriate changes in the product, pricing, promotion, and distribution strategy to create more positive attitudes and to influence behavioral intentions.

IV. Hierarchies of Effects

   A. *Market Research*

      1. Conduct market research studies to determine the operative hierarchy of effect.

   B. *Marketing Mix*

      1. Develop strategy based on the type of hierarchy of effect the target market uses. For example, if it is a high-involvement hierarchy, focus on using promotional strategy to create beliefs. If it is an experiential hierarchy, focus on creating appropriate affective states. For the behavioral influence hierarchy, use sales-promotion devices to influence behavior.

TABLE 8-5

for this case are summed up in Table 8-6. By skillfully developing a managerial strategy for understanding these factors, managers can increase the chances of sustaining the booming sales of vans, trucks, and sport utility vehicles.

Attribute Importance The key features that differentiate sport utility vehicles and trucks from automobiles are their ruggedness and their off-road capabilities. If dealers can make these attributes more salient and important to consumers, sales of these vehicles will increase. In addition, to attract women and urban dwellers, managers should work on making the attribute of luxury more salient. (Range Rover and Lexus already do this.)

Attribute importance has a number of managerial implications. First, market research should be performed to identify those attributes that have the most importance to consumers—such as ruggedness, off-road capabilities, and luxury. (This can be done either by having consumers rank-order the attributes or by using conjoint analysis—a sophisticated methodology used with good results by some companies.) Second, attributes found to be extremely important should be used to develop a benefit segmentation strategy. Third, brands should be positioned and differentiated on the basis of the salient attributes. Finally, an environmental analysis should be done to monitor changes in the regulatory and consumer environments.

Managerial Implications of Consumer Behavior Concepts in the "Americans Are Truckin' " Case

Consumer Behavior Concept	Managerial Implications
1. Attribute importance	*Market research*. Perform research studies to identify the consumer characteristics to target in the benefit segmentation strategy.
	Promotion. In ads emphasize off-road capability of vehicles and ability to navigate in mud and snow. In demonstrations have consumer drive vehicle over off-road course.
	Positioning and differentiation. Use the salient attributes of ruggedness and off-road capability to position and differentiate these vehicles from automobiles.
	Segmentation. Use benefit segmentation strategy to identify consumers who seek ruggedness and off-road capability.
	Environmental analysis. Carefully monitor changes in consumer environment, such as increased focus on protecting the environment, that may cause consumers to move away from these gas-hungry, pollution-causing vehicles.
2. Value expressive function	*Promotional strategy*. Depict consumers as showing off their vehicles to express their personal values of ruggedness and practicality.
3. Multiattribute models	*Market research*. Perform studies to determine degree of goodness/badness and the belief ratings for key attributes, such as ruggedness, price, comfort, and repair frequency.
4. Behavioral intentions model	*Market research*. Perform studies that identify factors that will influence consumer perceptions of the attitude toward the act, such as building off-road courses. Also take steps to maximize the positive benefits of normative influence, such as involving children in purchase who could influence their parents.
	Promotional strategy. In the personal selling of the product take appropriate steps to maximize the pleasure of purchasing a vehicle at the dealership.

TABLE 8-6

There is at present, for example, a movement to require trucks and sport utility vehicles to add costly pollution-control equipment. There is also the danger that consumers may once again gravitate to vehicles that get good gas mileage and are environmentally-friendly.

Value-Expressive Function of Attitudes The promotional strategy for these vehicles should include ads portraying consumers showing off their rugged trucks and sport utility vehicles in a way that makes it plain they are using these products to express their personal values to others.

Multiattribute models Managers should conduct market research studies to identify goodness/badness and belief ratings of key attributes of these vehicles, such as their ruggedness, off-road capability, price, comfort, and repair frequency. Then, of course, they can build their positioning and differentiation strategies around the attributes on which their vehicle rates highly.

Behavioral Intentions Model Managers should also do research to determine which factors influence consumer perceptions of the attitude toward the act. A good example is the off-road course that some Range Rover dealers built. Moreover, they should take steps to maximize the positive benefits of normative influence. One such step would be to draw consumers' children into the purchase process by encouraging parents to take their youngsters along when test-driving the off-road course. The hope, of course, is that the kids will be so delighted with the ride that they will urge their parents to buy the vehicle. In the promotional-strategy arena it would be a good idea to show customers enjoying the buying experience in television and print ads. Another way to maximize the positive aspects of the purchase process is to ensure that all dealerships use low-pressure sales tactics.

Managerial Recommendations

Four specific recommendations emerge from the managerial applications analysis:

Recommendation 1 Use benefit segmentation strategy within the product class of pickup trucks and sport utility vehicles in order to differentiate and position a brand. For example, Lexus positions its sport utility vehicles as luxurious and comfortable.

Recommendation 2 Continuously monitor the consumer environment to identify any changes in the goodness/badness ratings of vehicle ruggedness and environmental friendliness. Changes in the importance of these attributes would dramatically influence consumers' attitudes toward sport utility vehicles and pickup trucks.

Recommendation 3 Keep taking steps to influence consumer attitudes toward the act of buying the vehicles. Strategies that make the purchase experience pleasurable and that favorably affect the attitudes of important others (e.g., kids) will positively influence sales.

Recommendation 4 Help consumers to express their values through the brand by providing ancillary products that bear the brand's emblems and logos. Harley-Davidson dealers sell jackets, scarves, and jewelry with the brand emblem prominently displayed. Dealerships can do the same for pickup trucks and sport utility vehicles.

SUMMARY

Discerning the interrelationships among beliefs, attitudes, and behaviors is highly important to the marketing manager, the marketing researcher, and the public policy maker. Beliefs describe the knowledge a person has about objects, attributes, and benefits. An object, such as a particular brand, possesses various attributes and provides various benefits. Consumers' beliefs about the extent to which a brand has specific attributes and benefits may be formed through exposure to ads and the processing of information contained in them, from friends, or through direct experience of the product. Product attributes are the characteristics that a product may or may not have. Product benefits are the positive and negative outcomes provided by the product's attributes.

Certain attributes are often extremely important to consumers, so managers should do research to identify those attributes that are crucial to their target market. They can then use these attributes in the benefit segmentation strategy to position and differentiate the product, as well as in the initial product design and the promotional strategy. One attribute that is often extremely important to consumers is price. In some cases a high price plays a negative role—that is, it decreases the likelihood of purchase. In other instances, however, a high price positively influences buying via the price-quality relationship and prestige sensitivity.

Consumer attitudes represent the amount of affect or feeling that a person holds for or against a stimulus object, such as a brand, a person, a company, or an idea. In high-involvement situations consumers form attitudes because they hold a number of beliefs about an object that are positive or negative. Attitudes may also be formed through principles of classical and operant conditioning. The mere-exposure phenomenon suggests that positive feelings can be induced by repeated exposures to a previously neutral stimulus.

Consumption behaviors were discussed in two different ways: intentions to behave and actual consumer behavior. Intentions to behave refer to the statements consumers make when questioned on the likelihood that they will engage in some behavior, such as buying a product, supporting a political candidate, or visiting a retail store. Actual behavior refers to an overt consumer act, such as purchasing a product or service, visiting a retail store, or voting for a particular political candidate.

Attitudes serve four different functions for consumers. First is the utilitarian function: consumers express an attitude to maximize rewards and minimize punishments from others. Second is the value-expressive function: consumers express an attitude to make a statement to others about what they believe to be important and valuable. Third is the ego-defensive function: consumers seek to maintain their self-concept by holding attitudes that protect them from unpleasant truths about themselves or the external world. Fourth is the knowledge function: consumers use attitudes to help them comprehend a complex universe.

Consumption behavior can result from a number of different processes that are governed partly by the type of buying process in which the consumer is engaged. When the consumer is in a high-involvement situation, the standard learning hierarchy operates: behavior occurs after beliefs are formed and attitudes are created. In the low-involvement hierarchy behavior appears to occur after a limited number of beliefs are formed: attitudes play only a minor role in influencing behavior and are formed only after the consumer purchases and uses the product. In the experiential hierarchy affect occurs first, followed by behavior. Impulse purchases exemplify an experiential purchase. The behavioral influence hierarchy is usually followed in situations where strong situational or environmental forces propel the consumer to engage in the behavior.

Multiattribute models were developed to predict consumer attitudes in high-involvement circumstances. The attitude-toward-the-object model combines information on the likelihood that an object possesses an attribute with consumer evaluations of the goodness/badness of that attribute to predict an attitude. The behavioral intentions model predicts consumers' intentions to behave in a certain way by obtaining information on their attitude toward performing the behavior and on their subjective norm, (what they believe other people think they should do). Recently, researchers have discovered that the mere attempt to measure behavioral intentions can influence the likelihood that a consumer will purchase a brand.

attitude
attitude-toward-the-object
    model
attribute importance
attributes
behavioral influence
    hierarchy

behavioral intentions
benefit segmentation
benefits
consumer behaviors
consumer beliefs
demarketing
experiential hierarchy

global attitude measure
halo effect
hierarchies of effects
high-involvement hierarchy
impulse purchase
low-involvement hierarchy
mere-exposure phenomenon

mere-measurement effect
multiattribute model
objects
salient beliefs
standard learning hierarchy
subjective norm
theory of reasoned action

REVIEW QUESTIONS

1. Define the concepts of belief, attitude, and behavior.

2. Distinguish among attribute-object, attribute-benefit, and object-benefit beliefs.

3. Why should researchers attempt to identify the importance of product attributes to consumers? What are the factors that tend to influence attribute importance?

4. What is meant by the idea that beliefs, attitudes, and behaviors may form into hierarchies of effects?

5. What processes account for how beliefs are directly formed?

6. What processes account for the direct formation of attitudes?

7. Identify three ways in which behaviors may be induced without the consumer first forming strong attitudes or beliefs.

8. How do the hierarchies of effects differ in high- and low-involvement circumstances?

9. How do the hierarchies of effects differ in experiential versus behavioral influence processes?

10. What conditions limit the ability of attitudes to predict behavior accurately?

11. What is meant by a multiattribute attitude model?

12. Differentiate the attitude-toward-the-object model from the behavioral intentions model.

13. What are the four functions of attitudes identified by Katz?

14. Why would a market researcher want to assess consumer global attitudes?

15. What is the mere-measurement effect?

DISCUSSION QUESTIONS

1. List as many attributes as you can that consumers may seek in an automobile. You should be able to identify at least ten attributes. Select five of them and determine what benefits consumers receive if these characteristics are present in an automobile.

2. Consider the sport utility segment versus the family car segment of the car market. Rank in order the five attributes that you think are most important for each of these segments.

3. One industry that has had a notoriously hard time identifying the benefits of its product to consumers is the home computer industry. Identify the important attributes of home computers. What are the tangible benefits consumers can receive from these attributes? How can these benefits be communicated to consumers?

4. Rough out a print advertisement that seeks to influence consumer beliefs about two attributes of a new soft drink. (You must create the new drink and identify its benefits.)

5. Describe the most recent commercial you have seen for a soft-drink maker or a beer company. Which of the hi-

erarchies of effects does the company seem to be assuming that consumers are using? Why?

6. Go through magazines to find a print advertisement that seems to view consumers as in a high-involvement state and for which a multiattribute model might describe attitude formation. Discuss how the advertisement attempts to influence consumers' attitude formation by giving information on multiple attributes.

7. Consider your own attitudes. Identify examples of attitudes you hold that represent each of the four functions of attitudes postulated by Katz.

8. Using the attitude-toward-the-object model, interview five of your friends and assess their attitudes regarding a local fast-food restaurant. What are the managerial implications of this exercise for the restaurant?

9. Go through the multiattribute model computed for Macho Mikes and Racy Ritas. Why would these two market segments differ in both their belief ratings and their evaluations of many attributes? Write a description of these two market segments based on the information given in Table 8-4.

1. James B. Treece, Stephanie Anderson, Gregory Sandler, and Kate Murphy, "Why We Love Trucks," *Business Week*, December 5, 1994, pp. 70–80.

2. Michael M. Phillips, "Selling by Evoking What Defines a Generation," *The Wall Street Journal*, August 13, 1996, p. B1.

3. Keith Naughton, "The Ralph Lauren of Car Dealers," *Business Week*, November 20, 1995, pp. 153–155.

4. James B. Treece et al., "Why We Love Trucks."

5. Ibid.

6. James Helgeson, Alan Kluge, John Mager, and Cheri Taylor, "Trends in Consumer Behavior Literature: A Content Analysis," *Journal of Consumer Research*, Vol. 10 (March 1984), pp. 449–454.

7. For a recent discussion of intrinsic and extrinsic attributes, see Paul S. Richardson, Alan S. Dick, and Arun K. Jain, "Extrinsic and Intrinsic Cue Effects on Perceptions of Store Brand Quality," *Journal of Marketing*, Vol. 58 (October 1994), pp. 28–35.

8. Otis Port, "When It Comes to Cuddles, This Dog Is Best in Breed," *Newsweek*, April 1, 1991, p. 82.

9. M. Fishbein and I. Ajzen, *Belief, Attitude, Intention, and Behavior: An Introduction to Theory and Research* (Reading, MA: Addison-Wesley, 1975).

10. Durairaj Maheswaran and Brian Sternthal, "The Effects of Knowledge, Motivation, and Type of Message on Ad Processing and Product Judgments," *Journal of Consumer Research*, Vol. 17 (June 1990), pp. 66–73.

11. Scott Mackenzie, "The Role of Attention in Mediating the Effect of Advertising on Attribute Importance," *Journal of Consumer Research*, Vol. 13 (September 1986), pp. 174–195.

12. Todd Barlow and Michael S. Wogalter, "Alcoholic Beverage Warnings in Magazine and Television Advertisements," *Journal of Consumer Research*, Vol. 20 (June 1993), pp. 147–156.

13. Stephen M. Nowlis and Itamar Simonson, "The Effect of New Product Features on Brand Choice," *Journal of Marketing Research*, Vol. 32 (February 1996), pp. 36–46.

14. Gregory S. Carpenter, Rashi Glazer, and Kent Nakamoto, "Meaningful Brands from Meaningless Differentiation: The Dependence on Irrelevant Attributes," *Journal of Marketing Research*, Vol. 31 (August 1994), pp. 339–350.

15. Donald R. Lichtenstein, Nancy M. Ridgway, and Richard G. Netemeyer, "Price Perceptions and Consumer Shopping Behavior: A Field Study," *Journal of Marketing Research*, Vol. 30 (May 1993), pp. 234–245.

16. This brief history of attitudes was adapted from Richard Petty, Thomas Ostrom, and Timothy Brock, *Cognitive Responses in Persuasion* (Hillsdale, NJ: Lawrence Erlbaum, 1981).

17. The definition was found in Petty et al., *Cognitive Responses in Persuasion*, p. 31.

18. Chris T. Allen, Karen A. Machleit, and Susan Schultz Kleine, "A Comparison of Attitudes and Emotions as Predictors of Behavior at Diverse Levels of Behavioral Experience," *Journal of Consumer Research*, Vol. 18 (March 1992), pp. 493–504. For a similar definition, see Darrel J. Bem, *Beliefs, Attitudes, and Human Affairs* (Belmont, CA: Brooks/Cole, 1970).

19. Fishbein and Ajzen, *Beliefs, Attitude, Intentions, and Behaviors*.

20. Phillip Zimbardo, E. Ebbesen, and C. Maslach, *Influencing Attitudes and Changing Behavior* (Reading, MA: Addison-Wesley, 1977). It should be noted that some researchers have defined attitudes in terms of three separate components: cognitions (beliefs), affect (feelings), and conation (behavioral intentions). However, such a conceptualization fails to distinguish these concepts such that each has its own set of determinants. Indeed, some evidence indicates that beliefs and feelings reside in completely different physiological systems. Thus beliefs may reside in a cognitive system influenced by cognitive-learning principles, while feelings and affect may reside in the autonomic nervous system, which is affected more by classical-conditioning principles. This is why we have chosen to separate the definitions of beliefs and attitudes in this text. For more information on this issue, see W. A. Scott, "Attitude Measurement," in *The Handbook of Social Psychology*, 2nd ed., Vol. 2, G. Lindzey and E. Aronson, eds. (Reading, MA: Addison-Wesley, 1968); T. M. Ostrom, "The Relationship Between the Affective, Behavioral, and Cognitive Components of Attitudes," *Journal of Experimental Social Psychology*, Vol. 5 (1969), pp. 12–30; and Robert A. Zajonc and Hazel Markus, "Affective and Cognitive Factors in Preferences," *Journal of Consumer Research*, Vol. 9 (September 1982), pp. 123–131.

21. Our discussion of the functions of attitudes is based on Charles Kiesler, Barry Collins, and Norman Miller, *Attitude Change: A Critical Analysis of Theoretical Approaches* (New York: John Wiley, 1969).

22. Daniel Katz, "The Functional Approach to Attitudes," *Public Opinion Quarterly*, Vol. 24 (1960), pp. 163–204. Also see

Sharon Shavitt, "Products, Personalities and Situations in Attitude Functions: Implications for Consumer Behavior," in *Advances in Consumer Research*, Vol. 16, Thomas Srull, ed. (Provo, UT: Association for Consumer Research, 1989), pp. 300–305.

23. For an excellent discussion of the functions of attitudes and the role of attitudes in consumer behavior, see Richard J. Lutz, "The Role of Attitude Theory in Marketing," in *Perspectives in Consumer Behavior*, Harold Kassarjian and Thomas Robertson, eds. (Englewood Cliffs, NJ: Prentice Hall, 1991), pp. 317–339.

24. Elnora Stuart, Terence Shimp, and Randall Engle, "Classical Conditioning of Consumer Attitudes: Four Experiments in an Advertising Context," *Journal of Consumer Research*, Vol. 14 (December 1987), pp. 334–349.

25. Kiesler et al., *Attitude Change*.

26. Robert Zajonc, "The Attitudinal Effects of Mere Exposure," *Journal of Personality and Social Psychology* monograph, Vol. 9 (1968), p. 2, pt 2.

27. Mackenzie, "The Role of Attention in Mediating the Effect of Advertising on Attribute Importance."

28. William Wilson, "Feeling More Than We Know: Exposure Effects Without Learning," *Journal of Personality and Social Psychology*, Vol. 37 (June 1979), pp. 811–821.

29. John Hadjimzrcou, John W. Barnes, and Richard S. Jacobs, "The Effects of Context-Induced Mood States on Initial and Repeat Product Evaluations: A Preliminary Investigation," *Advances in Consumer Research*, Vol. 23, Kim P. Corfman and John G. Lynch, Jr., eds. (Provo, UT: Association for Consumer Research, 1996), pp. 337–341.

30. Walter Nord and J. Paul Peter, "A Behavior Modification Perspective on Marketing," *Journal of Marketing*, Vol. 44 (Spring 1980), pp. 36–47.

31. Michael Ray, "Marketing Communications and the Hierarchy-of-Effects," in *New Models for Mass Communications*, P. Clarke, ed. (Beverly Hills, CA: Sage Publications, 1973), pp. 147–176.

32. Robert Lavidge and Gary Steiner, "A Model for Predictive Measurements of Advertising Effectiveness," *Journal of Marketing*, Vol. 25 (October 1961), pp. 59–62.

33. Richard W. Olshavsky and Donald H. Granbois, "Consumer Decision Making—Fact or Fiction?" *Journal of Consumer Research*, Vol. 6 (September 1979), pp. 93–100.

34. Herbert Krugman, "The Impact of Television Advertising: Learning Without Involvement," *Public Opinion Quarterly*, Vol. 29 (October 1961), pp. 59–62. A variety of definitions of involvement have been proposed. For a good review, see John H. Antil, "Conceptualization and Operationalization of Involvement," in *Advances in Consumer Research*, Vol. 11, Thomas C. Kinnear, ed. (Provo, UT: Association for Consumer Research, 1984), pp. 203–209.

35. For an excellent discussion of low-involvement decision making, see F. Stewart De Bruicker, "An Appraisal of Low-Involvement Consumer Information Processing," in *Attitude Research Plays for High Stakes*, John Maloney and Bernard Silverman, eds. (American Marketing Association, 1979), pp. 112–130.

36. Such justifications would work through a self-perception process. See Bem, *Beliefs, Attitudes, and Human Affairs*.

37. Dennis W. Rook and Stephen J. Hoch, "Consuming Impulses," in *Advances in Consumer Behavior*, Vol. 12 (Provo, UT: Association for Consumer Research, 1985), pp. 23–27.

38. Chris T. Allen, Karen A. Machleit, and Susan Schultz Kleine, "A Comparison of Attitudes and Emotions as Predictors of Behavior at Diverse Levels of Behavioral Experience," *Journal of Consumer Research*, Vol. 18 (March 1992), pp. 493–504.

39. These ideas were expressed to me by Professor Russell Belk.

40. There have been numerous approaches to the study of attitudes. For a discussion of several of them, see Richard J. Lutz, "The Role of Attitude Theory in Marketing," in *Perspectives in Consumer Behavior*, 4th ed., Harold H. Kassarjian and Thomas S. Robertson, eds. (Upper Saddle River, NJ: Prentice Hall, 1991), pp. 317–339.

41. For a full discussion of the Fishbein model, see Fishbein and Ajzen, *Belief, Attitude, Intention and Behavior*.

42. For a recent discussion of this issue, see Mackenzie, "The Role of Attention in Mediating the Effect of Advertising on Attribute Importance."

43. Allan Wicker, "Attitudes versus Actions: The Relationship of Verbal and Overt Behavioral Responses to Attitude Objects," *Journal of Social Issues*, Vol. 25 (Autumn 1969), p. 65.

44. Robert Cialdini, Richard Petty, and John Cacioppo, "Attitude and Attitude Change," *Annual Review of Psychology*, Vol. 32 (1981), p. 366.

45. Linda F. Alwitt and Ida E. Berger, "Understanding the Link Between Environmental Attitudes and Consumer Product Usage: Measuring the Moderating Role of Attitude Strength," in *Advances in Consumer Research*, Vol. 20, Leigh McAlister and Michael Rothschild, eds. (Provo, UT:

Association for Consumer Research, 1992), pp. 189–194.

46. Russell H. Fazio, Martha C. Powell, and Carol J. Williams, "The Role of Attitude Accessibility in the Attitude-to-Behavior Process," *Journal of Consumer Research*, Vol. 16 (December 1989), pp. 280–288.

47. Timothy D. Wilson, Douglas J. Lisle, and Dolores Kraft, "Effects of Self-Reflection on Attitudes and Consumer Behavior," in *Advances in Consumer Research*, Vol. 17, Marvin Goldberg, Gerald Gorn, and Richard Pollay, eds. (Provo, UT: Association for Consumer Research, 1990), pp. 79–85.

48. Icek Ajzen and Martin Fishbein, "Attitude-Behavior Relations: A Theoretical Analysis and Review of Empirical Research," *Psychological Bulletin*, September, 1977, pp. 888–918. Note that the behavioral intentions model is now called the "theory of reasoned action." We have retained the older name to emphasize its focus on predicting behavioral intentions.

49. Martin Fishbein, Susan E. Middlestadt, and David Trafimow, "Social Norms for Condom Use: Implications for HIV Prevention Interventions of a KABP Survey with Heterosexuals in the Eastern Caribbean," in *Advances in Consumer Research*, Vol. 20, Leigh McAlister and Michael Rothschild, eds. (Provo, UT: Association for Consumer Research, 1992), pp. 292–296.

50. One example of an article finding the behavioral intentions model to be superior to attitude-toward-the-object model is Michael J. Ryan and E. H. Bonfield, "Fishbein's Intentions Model: A Test of External and Pragmatic Validity," *Journal of Marketing*, Vol. 44 (Spring 1980), pp. 82–95. Note that research is continuing on behavioral intentions models. For a recent comparison of three models of behavioral intentions, see Richard Netemeyer, J. Craig Andrews, and Scrinvas Durvasula, "A Comparison of Three Behavioral Intentions Models: The Case of Valentine's Day Gift-Giving," in *Advances in Consumer Research*, Vol. 20, Leigh McAlister and Michael Rothschild, eds. (Provo, UT: Association for Consumer Research, 1992), pp. 135–141.

51. R. J. Pomazal and J. J. Jaccard, "An Informational Approach to Altruistic Behavior," *Journal of Personality and Social Psychology*, Vol. 33 (1976), pp. 317–326. Also see M. J. Ryan and E. H. Bonfield, "The Fishbein Extended Model and Consumer Behavior," *Journal of Consumer Research*, Vol. 2 (September 1975), pp. 118–136. Another problem with the Fishbein attitude models is that placing the evaluation of the consequences on unidimensional scales anchored by "good" and "bad" is inappropriate, according to researchers. As we discussed in Chapter 6 on motivation and af-fect, people tend to evaluate the goodness and badness of an object on separate dimensions. The same phenomenon appears to apply to attitudes as well. Thus two scales should be used to evaluate the goodness/badness of each attribute. For example, if consumers were evaluating attitudes toward the attribute of "strength of cleaning power" of a dishwashing detergent, they would be asked to rate the attribute on two evaluative scales: "neutral" to "good" and "neutral" to "bad." In a study investigating coupon usage, the researchers found that the positive consequences of coupon usage (e.g., monetary savings and approval from a spouse) are relatively independent of the negative consequences (e.g., time spent collecting coupons and shopping at nonpreferred stores). See Terence Shimp and Alican Kavas, "The Theory of Reasoned Action Applied to Coupon Usage," *Journal of Consumer Research*, Vol. 11 (December 1984), pp. 795–809.

52. Vicki G. Morwitz, Eric Johnson, and David Schmittlein, "Does Measuring Intent Change Behavior?" *Journal of Consumer Research*, Vol. 20 (June 1993), pp. 46–61.

53. Gavan J. Fitzsimons and Vicki G. Morwitz, "The Effect of Measuring Intent on Brand-Level Purchase Behavior," *Journal of Consumer Research*, Vol. 23, (June 1996), pp. 1–11.

A FOUL TASTE AT PERRIER

Perrier Group of America, Inc., the U.S. unit of France's Source Perrier S.A., announced a highly embarrassing product recall on February 9, 1990, after North Carolina regulators released a report stating that this high-priced bottled water was contaminated with benzene, a poisonous liquid shown to cause cancer in laboratory animals. Even though the U.S. Food and Drug Administration (FDA) said that the benzene levels did not pose "a significant short-term health risk," Perrier management decided to request the removal of the brand from supermarkets and restaurants in the United States and Canada.[1]

A Source Perrier official stated at the time that the company believed the contamination could be traced to an employee's mistaken use of fluid containing benzene to clean the machinery on the bottling line that fills Perrier bottles for North America. Initially, the recall affected only the United States and Canada—an inventory of some 70 million bottles. Soon it was made worldwide, however, because Dutch and Danish officials also found benzene in some Perrier bottles.

The incident turned into a public relations disaster as the company's explanation for the recall kept changing. After traces of benzene were found in Perrier bottles in other parts of the world, company officials altered their original explanation. Benzene, they now said, is naturally present in carbon dioxide (the gas that makes Perrier bubbly) and is normally filtered out before the water is bottled—except that workers had inexplicably failed to change the filters. Perrier still insisted that its famous spring in Vergeze, France, was unpolluted.[2] These inconsistent statements further raised consumers' suspicions.

The big question was what long-term effects the contamination incident would have on Perrier, which had positioned itself as a naturally pure water. The strong underpinning for the success of bottled waters is their perceived safety compared with ordinary tap water. Tom Pirko, a beverage consultant, described the revelations of contamination as "the worst possible thing that could happen to a bottled water company. Purity is the franchise. The last possible thing that Perrier can afford to have happen is for the American public to

think there is benzene in their spring, whether it gets filtered out or not."[3]

Complicating the company's problem was the fact that the product disappeared from the marketplace for three to five months—a hiatus that severely tested consumers' loyalty. As one marketing expert commented, "When a brand is consumed daily, out of sight is out of mind." The prospect of a Perrier-free market seemed to pose only minor difficulties for supermarkets and restaurants. "Typically, bars and restaurants carry just one sparkling brand," an analyst noted. "Until now that has been Perrier. Now other sparkling waters will have a chance to get into Perrier's stronghold." Tom Kaplan, general manager of a restaurant in Los Angeles, noted, "Now consumers have decided that other brands are better or at least as good, so Perrier no longer holds the monopoly on water."[4]

The recall came at a tough time for Perrier. In 1989 Perrier was the leading imported water, holding about 6 percent of the U.S. bottled water segment. But success brought intense competition from other bottled water brands in the 1990s. While the total category was growing at about 10 percent annually, Perrier's growth slowed to about 5 percent a year. In an effort to regain market share lost during the months-long recall, Perrier Group spent $25 million in a U.S. advertising campaign whose message was: "Perrier. Worth waiting for." (In 1989 Perrier Group had spent just $6 million on U.S. advertising.) In the opinion of marketing experts, the mere increase in advertising was a good start, but the ads themselves did little to ease the problem. Many found them lacking in sincerity and credibility.[5] Perhaps more dangerous to Perrier was that while it was off the market some consumers made the discovery that any bottled water would do. Exacerbating the problem was the FDA's decision to make Perrier drop the words "Naturally sparkling" from its label since its investigators had discovered that Perrier artificially carbonates its water after taking it out of the ground.

By 1995 Perrier sales had fallen to one-half their 1989 peak. Even so, the brand was still number two in the marketplace—a distant second to Evian. Some experts think that because the brand endured through the crisis, it has a chance of coming back. One recommended strategy is to focus on building relationships with bars and clubs in order to broaden distribution.[6]

One comeback strategy management did employ was to bring out new brands that do not have the Perrier name attached to them. By 1996 the company owned seven of the top ten brands of bottled water—and the future of bottled water looks good. Sales of this product already represent 10 percent of the total beverage market, and they are growing. Overall sales of bottled water have increased by 25 percent since 1990, and consumers are more and more worried about the quality of municipal water.[7]

Questions

1. Define the problems Perrier faced.
2. Identify the consumer concepts related to beliefs, attitudes, and behaviors most relevant to this case. What does each concept say about the case?
3. Develop the managerial applications analysis for the Perrier case based on the applicable consumer concepts. What managerial actions should Perrier have taken to minimize the crisis? What actions should it take in the future?

References

1. E. S. Browning, Alix M. Freedman, and Thomas R. King "Perrier Expands North American Recall to Rest of Globe," *The Wall Street Journal*, February 15, 1990, pp. B1, B4.
2. Alix M. Freedman and Thomas R. King "Perrier's Strategy in the Wake of Recall: Will It Leave the Brand in Rough Waters?" *The Wall Street Journal*, February 12, 1990, pp. B1, B4.
3. "Perrier Finds Mystique Hard to Restore," *The Wall Street Journal*, December 12, 1990, pp. B1, B3.
4. G. Prince, "Best Sellers—Ranking the Top Soft Drink, Beer and Bottled Water Brands and Companies," *Beverage World*, March 1991, pp. 24–33.
5. "Perrier's Back—Whimsical Campaign to Support Its Return," *Advertising Age*, April 23, 1990, pp. 1, 84.
6. Ylonda Gault, "Flat Perrier Pours Bubbly Ads," *Crains New York Business*, May 22, 1995, p. 22.
7. Dan Shope, "Upper Macungie Perrier Plan Rides Wave of Demand for Bottled Water," *Allentown Morning Call*, April 7, 1996, p. D1.

CHAPTER NINE

ATTITUDE, BELIEF, AND BEHAVIOR CHANGE

Changing Attitudes About Drugs: A Marketing Challenge

In the 1980s it was cocaine. Now, in the last half of the 1990s, heroin is becoming the drug of choice for many. The combination of low price, high purity, and publicity about its use by glamorous celebrities has led to a dramatic increase in heroin addiction in the United States. A 1995 study found that 50 percent of high school seniors "did not perceive great risk in trying heroin once or twice."[1]

An urgent public policy question is whether advertising can change people's beliefs, attitudes, and behaviors regarding drug use. A real-world test took place in the late 1980s, when a partnership between the media and advertising agencies resulted in a major campaign called "Drug-Free America." This campaign treated the threat to America's youth as a marketing problem. As Executive Director Tom Hedrick stated, the campaign "is competing with drug pushers for market share of nonusers." Hedrick went on to say, "Everything we've been doing goes back to the belief in advertising's power to communicate messages strong enough to change attitudes and affect behavior over time."[2] Between March 1987 and November 1988 media support for the campaign totaled $150 million. In 1988 alone TV networks aired 2,000 free spots.

The campaign was based on solid market research foundations. The first study involved conducting over 7,000 interviews in malls across the United States to obtain information on the attitudinal basis of drug use. Four target groups were identified for separate analysis: 9- to 12-year-olds, 13- to 17-year-olds, college students, and adults. As the study's director stated, it "was designed to reveal the matrix of attitudes that form the basis of drug abuse—rather than focus on the phenomenon of drug abuse itself—and to track attitudinal change over time."

Information gleaned from the research formed the basis for the advertising campaign. One finding was that, among 9- to 12-year-olds, contact with older siblings had the greatest influence on attitudes and behavior regarding drugs. Furthermore, older siblings who used drugs feared they would negatively influence their younger brothers and sisters. Among the 13- to 17-year-olds, an important factor was whether friends were involved with drugs.

A year after the first study was completed, a second study was undertaken to assess changes in attitudes. These results indicated that across the United States attitudes toward drug use were becoming more negative. Furthermore, in the geographic areas the antidrug campaign had chosen for high media exposure, attitude change was greater on most variables than in low-exposure areas. Several of the ads seemed to have had a particularly strong impact. For example, one ad (called "Fried Brains") achieved a 95 percent recognition rate among college students—and 75 percent gave it positive ratings.

Nevertheless, data released in late 1996 indicated that between 1992 and 1995 drug use among U.S. teenagers more than doubled.[3] Moreover, interest in heroin had dramatically increased. As one expert pointed out, "You got a million needles tattooing kids. You got a million needles piercing their ears, piercing their noses, piercing their lips. You get a million needles shooting drugs into their veins. And to them it's all the same thing. I don't think the kids can differentiate the behaviors."[4]

The 1996 Partnership group (a nonprofit coalition of professional advertisers) began planning a new campaign to change attitudes, beliefs, and behaviors toward heroin. The question was: What factors should be considered in designing the campaign to change attitudes, beliefs, and behaviors about drugs?

INTRODUCTION

In discussing beliefs, attitudes, and behavior in the last chapter, we focused on how they are formed and how they may be predicted. Many times in marketing, however, the goal is to implement a persuasion process that changes people's preexisting attitudes and beliefs in order to influence their behavior. **Persuasion** is defined as the explicit attempt to influence beliefs, attitudes, and/or behaviors.

It can be argued that consumers rarely enter a situation with absolutely no preexisting attitudes and beliefs about an object. Whenever a new product or service is introduced by a firm, consumers may already have an initial positive or negative feeling toward it because of their previous experience with the firm's products. So even when introducing new products, communicators are seeking to persuade consumers.

This chapter's introductory case illustrates key points about attitude, belief, and behavior change. For example, one factor that influences consumer attitudes is the consumer's attitude toward the advertisement. Those running the "Drug-Free America" campaign recognized how crucial it was that the target markets react positively to their ads. Market research revealed that the targets—particularly college students—had a positive reaction to the "Fried Brains" ad, and it was believed this positive attitude would influence their attitude toward taking drugs. Figure 9-1 presents the ad; as you can see, its message is clear and powerful.

Figure 9-2 presents a model of belief, attitude, and behavior change. Note that the change process begins with a persuasive communication. Next information processing of the message occurs. At this point the change process can take three different paths: the decision-making path, the experiential path, or the behavioral influence path.

From the decision-making perspective, the persuasion process begins with a change in beliefs. Once beliefs are changed, the route to persuasion is based upon whether the consumer is engaged in high- or low-involvement information processing. In the first major section of this chapter we explain the decision-making view of persuasion and present an important approach, called the elaboration likelihood model.[5] Then we go on to show how the multiattribute models of attitude formation can be used to understand attitude, belief, and behavior change. The nearby consumer behavior factoid describes what can go wrong when advertisers take the wrong route to persuasion.

Figure 9-1

This ad received positive ratings on attitude-toward-the-ad measurements.

In the second major section of the chapter we discuss the experiential path to persuasion. As Figure 9-2 shows, the experiential path involves changing attitudes directly, without necessarily influencing beliefs first. We present three theoretical approaches to the experiential path to persuasion: balance theory, the impact of reactance and dissonance on attitudes, and the consumer's attitude toward the advertisement.

In the third major section of the chapter we consider several strategies for behavioral change that follow the behavioral influence path. These strategies involve using techniques that induce consumers to comply with requests, without their necessarily forming beliefs or attitudes about the object of the behavior. In Figure 9-2 the decision-making path is shown as moving directly from information processing to behavior change.

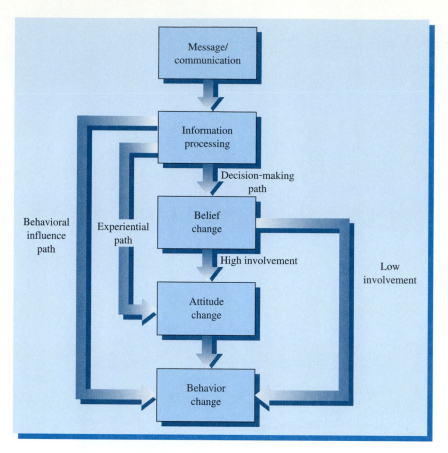

Figure 9-2

Paths to belief, attitude, and behavior change.

We conclude the chapter with an analysis of how the concepts discussed here apply to the important task of changing consumers' beliefs, attitudes, and behaviors regarding drug use.

THE DECISION-MAKING PATH TO PERSUASION

The Elaboration Likelihood Model

One approach to understanding the persuasion process, called the **elaboration likelihood model** (ELM), illustrates the decision-making path to belief, attitude, and behavior change. In the ELM (depicted in Figure 9-3) the persuasion process begins when the consumer receives a communication. The term **communication** is defined broadly here to cover all aspects of the message, including its source, type, and channel (e.g., television, radio, or print media). Upon receiving the message, the consumer begins to process it. Depending on such factors as the message content, the nature of the consumer, and the consumer's situation, the communication is processed with higher or lower amounts of involvement.

As we stated in Chapter 3, involvement refers to the perceived personal relevance of the information. Depending upon the amount of involvement, belief and attitude change may take one of two routes.[6] When high-involvement information processing occurs, the person is said to take the **central route to persuasion.** In low-involvement circumstances, the consumer is said to take the **peripheral route to persuasion.**

The Central Route to Persuasion When attitude and belief change take place via the central route, consumers attend more carefully to the message being received. They more diligently consider the communication and compare it to their own attitudinal position. If they are able to process the information, they will likely generate a number of cognitive responses to the communication.[7] (Cognitive responses are the favorable and/or unfavorable thoughts consumers generate as a result of a communication.) Depending partly upon the extent to which these cognitive responses are supportive or nonsupportive of the message, consumers may undergo a belief change. If beliefs are changed, they may next experience an attitude change. When belief and attitude changes occur through the central route to persuasion, the effects are relatively enduring and predictive of behavior.[8]

When persuasion takes place through the central route, consumers are said to employ central cues when evaluating the message. **Central cues** are those ideas and supporting data that bear directly on the quality of the arguments developed in the message.[9]

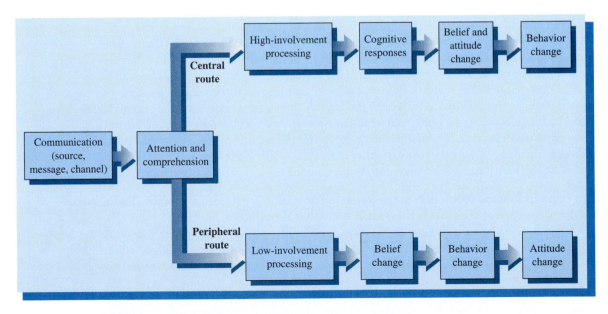

Figure 9-3
The elaboration likelihood mode of persuasion.

The Peripheral Route to Persuasion When consumers engage in low-involvement information processing, they move through the peripheral route to persuasion. In these instances cognitive responses are much less likely to occur because people are not carefully considering the pros and cons of the issue. Instead, they use peripheral cues to determine whether to accept or reject the message. **Peripheral persuasion cues** include such factors as the attractiveness and expertise of the source, the mere number of arguments presented, and the positive or negative stimuli that form the context within which the message was presented (e.g., pleasant music). Under low-involvement circumstances, consumers' beliefs may change, but it is unlikely that their attitudes and feelings are also influenced. Any attitudes that are formed will probably be temporary and unpredictive of behavior.[10] In short, under low-involvement conditions, the buying task is not important enough to cause people to develop feelings regarding the product.

Central and peripheral cues have differential effects on consumers depending on which persuasion route is operative. Under low-involvement circumstances, peripheral cues have a greater impact on belief and behavior change than central cues do. So such factors as the likability and physical attractiveness of an endorser will have a greater effect on consumers than the quality of the arguments under low-involvement conditions. In contrast, under high-involvement circumstances, central cues have the greater impact on beliefs, attitudes, and behaviors.

The elaboration likelihood model is directly related to the decision-making perspective on consumer behavior. That is, the route to persuasion depends on the involvement of the consumer. With the central route to persuasion, greater amounts of information processing occur and the high-involvement hierarchy of effects operates. In contrast, with the peripheral route to persuasion, less information processing takes place and the low-involvement hierarchy of effects operates.

The Truth Effect You have probably heard the old aphorism: "If you say something often enough, people will come to believe you." This proverb has direct bearing on a marketing phenomenon known as the *truth effect*. According to the **truth effect,** if something is repeated often enough, people who are in a low-involvement processing mode will believe it. This occurs regardless of the actual truth value of the statement. Thus the truth effect illustrates one type of peripheral cue that may act to persuade consumers in low-involvement conditions—the repetition of information.[11]

Is the truth effect important to marketers? The answer is a definite "yes." Consumers are exposed to hundreds of communications a day from advertisers and other communicators. In most instances they pay insufficient attention to consider their truthfulness. The net result is a situation that enhances the possibility that frequently repeated messages will be perceived as true. If you think back to the introductory case, you will see that the truth effect has important public policy implications. When consumers constantly receive messages from music, movies, and books that using heroin is cool, the perceived "truth" of the idea that the drug is *not* dangerous is enhanced. That is why hard-hitting, skillfully produced messages that provide accurate information on the ravages of heroin use are required.

Are There Individual Differences in the Route to Persuasion? The elaboration likelihood model proposes that individuals chronically use either a central or a peripheral route. Researchers have found that consumers do consistently differ in how diligently they process information. To measure the extent to which consumers chronically exhibit high- versus low-involvement processing of information, they have developed a construct called the **need for cognition.**[12]

Individuals' need for cognition varies on a continuum from very low to very high. Consumers who have a propensity to engage in effortful cognitive activities are said to have a high need for cognition. These people tend to habitually evaluate the quality of arguments and require a central route to persuasion. Other consumers have a low need for cognition and require a peripheral route to persuasion. Plainly, information on a target market's need for cognition is useful to advertisers so they can create more complex messages for consumers with a high need for cognition and simpler messages for consumers with a low need for cognition. Table 9-1 presents a portion of the need-for-cognition scale.

The need for cognition influences how consumers will respond to central and peripheral cues contained in advertisements. When researchers investigated how advertisements influenced high- versus low-need-for-cognition consumers, they manipulated a "central cue" by creating ads that had either high- or low-quality arguments for why consumers should buy a particular brand of typewriter.[13] The results of the study, depicted in

The Need-for-Cognition Scale

1. I really enjoy a task that involves coming up with new solutions to problems.
4. I would prefer a task that is intellectual, difficult, and important to one that is somewhat important but does not require much thought.
10. Learning new ways to think doesn't excite me very much.*
12. I usually end up deliberating about issues even when they do not affect me personally.
13. I prefer just to let things happen rather than try to understand why they turned out that way.*
15. The idea of relying on thought to make my way to the top does not appeal to me.*
16. The notion of thinking abstractly is not appealing to me.*
18. I find it especially satisfying to complete an important task that required a lot of thinking and mental effort.
19. I only think as hard as I have to.*
21. I like tasks that require little thought once I've learned them.*
22. I prefer to think about small, daily projects than long-term ones.*
23. I would rather do something that requires little thought than something that is sure to challenge my thinking abilities.*
24. I find little satisfaction in deliberating hard and for long hours.*
29. I don't like to have the responsibilities of handling a situation that requires a lot of thinking.*
31. I feel relief rather than satisfaction after completing a task that required a lot of mental effort.*
32. Thinking is not my idea of fun.*
33. I try to anticipate and avoid situations where there is a likely chance that I will have to think in depth about something.*
37. I think best when those around me are very intelligent.
39. I prefer my life to be filled with puzzles that I must solve.
40. I would prefer complex to simple problems.
41. Simply knowing the answer rather than understanding the reasons for the answer to a problem is fine with me.*
43. It's enough for me that something gets the job done, I don't care how or why it works.*

Note: Only the 22 items found to be most highly related to the construct are shown. Items marked with an asterisk are reverse scored.

Source: John T. Cacioppo and Richard E. Petty, "The Need for Cognition," *Journal of Personality and Social Psychology*, Vol. 42 (1982), pp. 116–131.

TABLE 9-1

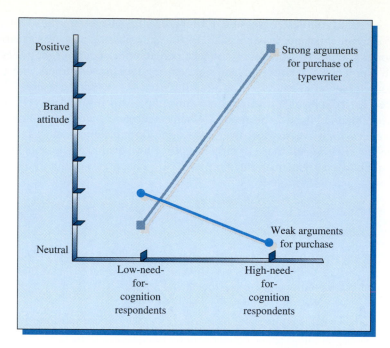

Figure 9-4

The need for cognition moderates the impact of argument quality on brand attitudes. (*Source*: Curtis P. Haugtvedt, Richard E. Petty, and John T. Cacioppo, "Need for Cognition and Advertising: Understanding the Role of Personality Variables in Consumer Behavior," *Journal of Consumer Psychology*, Vol. 1 [1992], p. 250.)

Figure 9-4, demonstrate that the quality of the arguments had virtually no effect on the low-need-for-cognition respondents. Indeed, these respondents produced slightly higher ratings of brand attitude in the weak-argument condition. The results were just the opposite among the high-need-for-cognition respondents: they rated the typewriter much more positively in the strong-argument condition.

These results point out the importance of doing research to identify a target market's need for cognition. Target markets that have a high need for cognition will focus on central cues, such as argument quality, while those that have a low need for cognition will emphasize peripheral cues, such as pictorial images, the physical attractiveness of endorsers, and the number (rather than the quality) of arguments.

Comprehension and the ELM Historically, consumer researchers have argued that the comprehension of a message was a prerequisite for persuasion. That is, potential buyers must understand what the message is saying to be influenced by it. Today researchers believe that the relationship between comprehension and persuasion is more complex.

One series of studies presented respondents with messages that were easy or hard to comprehend about a new invention—a replacement eraser for ordinary lead pencils. In addition, the expertise of the inventor was varied. Some respondents learned that the inventor was an expert—an engineer at Stanford University with numerous patents. Others learned that the inventor was a novice in this area—a realtor who held no other patents. It turned out that when the message was difficult to comprehend, the subjects relied on the expertise of the source to evaluate the product. However, when the message was easily comprehended, the expertise of the inventor had no impact on people's attitudes.[14]

The results of these studies are consistent with the ELM. When the message is easily comprehended, high levels of processing can occur. Consequently, respondents attend to the factual material in the message, and source expertise has little or no impact on their attitudes. In contrast, when messages are difficult to comprehend, consumers have a hard time processing them and resort to peripheral cues, such as source expertise, to form brand attitudes.

Consumers' level of involvement also affects whether they will miscomprehend advertising messages. Thus people who use a peripheral route to persuasion are more likely to draw inaccurate conclusions from advertisements that employ inconspicuous qualifications. Everyone has seen ads in which a claim is made in large type within the body of the ad, and then is qualified in small print at the bottom of the ad. The small-print statement is an *inconspicuous qualification*. For example, a manufacturer might boldly proclaim that its CD player is the easiest-loading compact disc player in the body of an ad, and then, at the bottom of the ad, state in small type that it is "easier to load compared to brands with magazine changers."[15] Are companies that employ inconspicuous qualifications guilty of deceptive advertising?

The managerial implications of the research on comprehension and persuasion are direct. Because consumers often differ widely in knowledge about a product category, advertisers must take care when creating messages that are complex and potentially difficult to comprehend. If less knowledgeable consumers receive such a complex message, they will probably form attitudes toward the brand based on the perceived expertise of the source of information. With this in mind, firms should use experts in advertisements that are difficult for many consumers to comprehend.

When a consumer issue becomes a public policy issue, arguments can become highly charged. Anyone seeking to persuade people in this kind of situation should combine elements of the central and the peripheral routes to persuasion. In other words, messages should couple effective arguments with emotionally charged peripheral cues. The nearby consumer behavior factoid addresses this issue.

Multiattribute Models and the Decision-Making Path to Persuasion

The concepts that underlie multiattribute models of attitude formation can be applied by marketers to change the beliefs, attitudes, and behaviors of a target audience.

Persuasion and the Attitude-Toward-the-Object Model In the last chapter we presented the attitude-toward-the-object model, which proposes that an attitude results from three factors: (1) the salient attributes on which a person evaluates an object; (2) a rating of the person's evaluation of the "goodness" or "badness" of the various attributes of an object;

Consumer Behavior Factoid

Surfer Questions

Question 1: Who is the "man in the gray suit"?

Answer: A man-eating shark.

Question 2: What is chumming?

Answer: The practice of throwing out massive quantities of blood and dead animals to attract sharks. When a charter boat captain began chumming near a beach in California, all the surfers became alarmed. They employed a central route to persuasion by developing an impressive series of arguments for why the practice harmed sharks, polluted the beaches, and endangered the ecosystem. In addition, they used peripheral cues, such as surfboards with 2-foot bites taken out of them, to stir emotions. Macabre jokes were also circulated. Example: "How do you escape a shark? Answer: Swim faster than your buddy."

Source: Carey Goldberg, *The New York Times*, March 10, 1996, p. Y9.

and (3) a rating of the person's beliefs about the extent to which the object possesses each of the attributes.

This model implies that communicators have three basic options for changing an existing attitude. First, they can attempt to change consumers' perceived evaluation of an attribute of a product. As noted earlier in the chapter, this was one goal of the "Drug-Free America" campaign—to show just how negative the outcomes of using drugs can be.

In the second strategy, rather than attempt to change consumers' evaluation of an existing attribute, a new attribute is introduced. An example is found in an ad for Rembrandt Mouth rinse that informs consumers that the brand is alcohol free (see Figure 9-5). Because the most popular mouthwash (Listerine) is 52 proof, Rembrandt has effectively added a reason for buying its brand.

The third strategy for influencing attitudes through a multiattribute model approach is to change consumers' beliefs about a product attribute by changing the attribute itself. This is probably the easiest approach of the three because a company can use a variety of methods to implement it. For instance, commercials could use demonstrations or trustworthy endorsers to show and explain the change.

Figure 9-5
Rembrandt mouth rinse seeks to persuade by adding the attribute that it has no alcohol.

Persuasion and the Behavioral Intentions Model The behavioral intentions model suggests still other approaches to attitude change. One strategy is to influence consumer perceptions of the consequences of a behavior. The "Drug-Free America" campaign identified at least one new consequence of taking drugs: passing one's addiction on to one's offspring. Many women may not have realized that taking a drug such as cocaine can addict a child before birth or one who is nursing. By making this negative outcome of using cocaine salient, the campaign directed a strong appeal to pregnant women and nursing mothers not to use drugs.

A second implication of the behavioral intentions model for attitude change involves the subjective norm component. The model explicitly considers the impact of other people on a consumers' intentions to act. The Drug-Free America campaign recognized the crucial role of peer groups in teenagers' lives—which was confirmed by the market research study—and developed advertisements that showed one peer helping another avoid drugs.

Researchers have found that different people react divergently to what others may think of them. The scale known as Attention to Social Comparison Information (discussed in Chapter 7) is used to assess this tendency. One study investigated whether consumers' attention to social comparison information influenced their color choice for a sweatshirt after they received a persuasive message from their peers. The results revealed that color choice was more likely to be influenced by peers among those students who were sensitive to social comparison information. The implication is that managers should give consumers with a high need to conform information about the preferences of members of their peer group.[16]

Table 9-2 summarizes the implications of multiattribute models for attitude change and behavior.

THE EXPERIENTIAL PATH TO ATTITUDE CHANGE

The persuasion process can also take an experiential path. When consumers follow the experiential path, attitudes are influenced directly, and beliefs about the object or behavior do not necessarily change beforehand. Four theoretical approaches can be used to understand the experiential path to persuasion: balance theory, social judgment theory, the impact of reactance and dissonance on attitudes, and attitudes toward the advertisement.

Balance Theory

Researchers have found that attitudes may be changed by creating cognitive imbalance in the target audience. The objective is to make use of people's tendency to maintain cognitive consistency among the various ideas and concepts they hold. **Cognitive consistency** is the name applied to the human desire to maintain a logical and consistent set of interconnected attitudes. Thus by deliberately creating cognitive inconsistency, the skillful communicator can induce consumers to change their attitudes in order to bring their cognitive system back into balance. To discuss the mechanisms behind the operation of cognitive consistency, we must first explain balance theory.

Balance theory was originated by one of the founders of social psychology, Fritz Heider.[17] As originally conceived, the theory dealt with the cognitive relationships that an observer (*o*) perceives among himself/herself, another person (*p*), and an impersonal object (*x*). In a consumer behavior setting, the observer is the consumer, the other person might be a product endorser, and the impersonal object is a brand. The observer, person, and object are called *cognitive elements*. Balance theory states that cognitive elements may form

Five Methods of Changing Attitudes: A Multiattribute Perspective

Method 1

Change the perceived evaluation of the attributes.

Advantage: Can increase the attitude rating of a product or service without changing the product or service in any way.

Disadvantage: Very difficult to do because evaluation ratings are often tied to the consumer's self-concept.

Method 2

Change the product-attribute beliefs.

Advantage: Easier to do because the company can use demonstrations or trustworthy sources to present the message. Beliefs about the extent to which products contain attributes are not usually connected to the consumer's self-concept.

Disadvantage: May involve changing the product.

Method 3

Add a new attribute for consideration.

Advantage: Beliefs and attitudes are easier to change when they are weakly held.

Disadvantage: May involve changing the product or service. Requires extensive promotional efforts to get new information to target market.

Method 4

Influence perceptions of consequences of behavior.

Advantage: Can identify consequences not previously recognized.

Disadvantage: Target may not evaluate consequences as desired or may not perceive them to be likely.

Method 5

Influence perceptions of reference group's reactions to behavior.

Advantage: Reference groups have a large impact on intentions to behave.

Disadvantage: Motivation to comply may be very low.

TABLE 9-2

a system in which each is linked to the other in a manner similar to the linkage of nodes in a semantic memory network (see Chapter 4).

Figure 9-6 shows a triad of elements that form a cognitive system. Notice that two types of connections join the cognitive elements: sentiment connections and unit relations. A sentiment connection is identical in definition to the term *attitude* as used in this text. Thus **sentiment connections** are the observer's evaluations of another person and an attitudinal object. They are the positive or negative feelings that the observer has toward that other person and object. Sentiment connections are given a positive or negative algebraic sign depending upon whether the feeling toward p or x is positive or negative.

The second type of connection, **unit relation,** occurs when the observer perceives that the person and object are connected to each other. The factors that govern whether a person will perceive a connection are the same principles of perceptual organization that we discussed in Chapter 3. Thus p and x would be perceived as having a unit relation through such principles as proximity, similarity, continuation, and common fate. As with sentiment connections, the relationship between p and x may be either positive or negative. A positive unit relation indicates that p and x are perceived as related and as forming a unit; a negative sign indicates that the two elements are in opposition to each other. A "0" sign indicates that no relation is perceived between p and x. In the last case the observer would

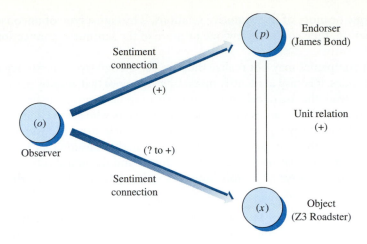

Figure 9-6
An example of cognitive elements in a balance-theory framework.

not view the three elements as forming a unit, and no cognitive consistency forces would operate.

The basic premise of balance theory is that people prefer to maintain a balanced state among the cognitive elements of p, o, and x if they perceive these elements as forming a system. A balanced state was defined by Heider as one in which the cognitive elements fit together harmoniously with no stress for change. Such "harmony" occurs when the multiplication of the signs of the connections between the elements results in a positive value. As shown in Figure 9-7, a balanced state results from three positive signs or from two negative signs and one positive sign. An imbalanced state occurs when two signs are positive and one is negative, or when all three signs are negative.

Heider's key point is that balanced states are preferred to imbalanced states. Further, he said that when people experience an imbalanced state, they are motivated to change

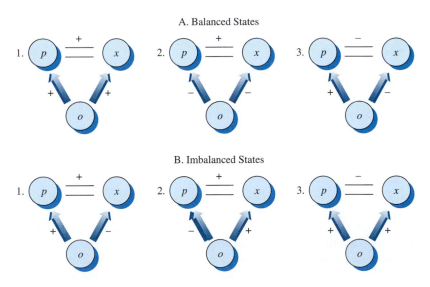

Figure 9-7
Examples of balanced and imbalanced states.

the signs of one or more of the cognitive relations. Through a type of unconscious mental rationalization, they come to view one or more of the sentiment connections and unit relations differently.

Although companies may not realize they are using cognitive consistency procedures to change attitudes, it is easy to identify marketing strategies that employ principles of balance theory. Indeed, the use of celebrity endorsers to sponsor products fits balance model principles quite well. Companies strive to select endorsers who are viewed very positively by consumers. From the perspective of balance theory, these firms are attempting to maximize the strength of the sentiment connection between the consumer (*o*) and the endorser (*p*) and to create a unit relation between the endorser and the brand (*x*).

There are various ways of establishing this unit relation. Three of the most common are:

1. *Hiring endorsers who are known experts at using the product.* For example, a tennis star, like Steffi Graf, would endorse a company's tennis racket or tennis shoe.
2. *Signing the endorser to a long-term exclusive contract, so that the celebrity is associated only with the company's brand and no others.* Manufacturers of perfumes and cosmetics have long used this strategy. For example, Elizabeth Taylor was signed to endorse White Diamonds perfume exclusively.
3. *Having the endorser consistently wear or use the product in public, so that he or she is strongly associated with the brand.*

Consumers, however, do not always oblige marketing managers by changing their attitudes according to plan. In general, consumers change the sign of the weakest connection in an imbalanced cognitive system.[18] Thus if they perceive that a celebrity is endorsing a brand simply for the money, they will not develop a unit connection between the celebrity and the product—and therefore will not undergo an attitude change. It is very possible that celebrities like Michael Jordan who endorse many products gradually lose their effectiveness because consumers fail to form unit connections between them and all the products they extol.

At this location the authors intended to place an ad for the BMW Z3 Roadster that illustrates principles of balance theory. A sentiment connection links the consumer to James Bond—an exciting and likable character—and a unit connection links Bond to the Z3. In order to have a balanced set of cognitions, consumers will adopt a favorable attitude toward the Z3. Unfortunately, we could not obtain permission to use the ad.

Social Judgment Theory

The second theoretical approach that is relevant to the experiential path is **social judgment theory.** According to this theory, the same factors that influence psychophysical judgments influence attitude expression. From a social judgment perspective, when individuals have an attitude toward an object, they compare any incoming message about that object to their initial attitude. The initial attitude, which was formed through prior experience with and feelings and beliefs about the object, acts as a frame of reference for their judgment. It is an anchor to which their perception of the new message is compared on a judgment scale ranging from very negative to very positive.[19]

Consider the drug case that began this chapter. Suppose a university student receives a communication that insists that taking drugs is extremely dangerous. The student already has an attitude about the danger of drugs, which acts as her frame of reference to which new communications about drugs are compared. The question addressed by social judgment theory is: How does the student perceive the new communication and how does it influence her attitude toward taking drugs?

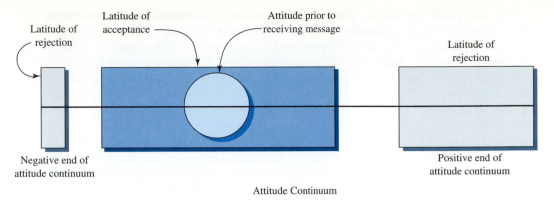

Latitude of rejection

Latitude of acceptance

Attitude prior to receiving message

Latitude of rejection

Negative end of attitude continuum

Positive end of attitude continuum

Attitude Continuum

Figure 9-8
Latitudes of acceptance and rejection.

Latitudes of Acceptance and Rejection One of the findings of social judgment theory is that people form **latitudes of acceptance** and **latitudes of rejection** around their attitudinal frames of reference. (Figure 9-8 diagrams the latitudes of acceptance and rejection.) Immediately surrounding their initial attitude is an area of acceptance, and communications falling within this range on the judgmental scale will tend to be assimilated. According to a concept known as the **assimilation effect,** such a communication—or attitude statement—will be viewed as more congruent with the receiver's initial attitude toward an object than it really is because it falls within the latitude of acceptance. Receivers are likely to indicate that they agree with the attitude statement because, in effect, their own initial attitude is pulling them toward the message. When this happens, persuasion has occurred. Thus social judgment theory suggests that in order to change an attitude, the message should fall just within the target market's latitude of acceptance.

What happens when the message (attitude statement) falls into the latitude of rejection—an area on the scale of judgment that is well outside the latitude of acceptance? When people perceive an attitudinal statement as falling into their latitude of rejection, they will reject it. They may even view it as more opposed to their own initial attitude than it really is, and thus reject it vehemently. The net result is that attitude change occurs in the direction opposite to that intended by the communicator—a phenomenon known as the **contrast effect.**

These findings suggest that it is extremely difficult to change the attitudes of someone who holds extreme views on a topic. Reverting to our introductory case, the implication is that antidrug messages should be designed to change the opinions of people who hold only "somewhat favorable" attitudes toward drugs, for those who express extremely positive attitudes are unlikely to be influenced by antidrug messages.

The Effects of Commitment to a Position and Involvement People vary in their ability to accept or tolerate positions different from their own, but generally a strong commitment to a position widens the latitude of rejection and narrows the region of acceptance.[20] The level of commitment is associated with the extremity of a position—that is, when receivers' initial position is either very positive or very negative, they tend to be more committed to that position.

A second factor associated with the size of the latitudes of acceptance and rejection is the receiver's level of involvement. When receivers are highly involved in the issue and hold an extreme position on it, their latitudes of acceptance and noncommitment are smaller and their latitude of rejection larger.

The managerial implication of these findings is that persuasion becomes more diffi-cult as consumers' levels of commitment and involvement rise. People who are highly in-volved in a purchase usually exert more energy in searching for information and in exam-ining the information they obtain. Consequently, they are better prepared to reject communications containing information that does not match their initial attitudes. This conclusion meshes well with the elaboration likelihood model. According to that model, you will recall, consumers who are highly involved tend to generate more counterargu-ments to advertising messages. The result is that they may reject communications that do not fit their frame of reference, without giving much thought to the ideas contained in the messages. True believers in causes exhibit this tendency. Thus an ardent antibusiness cru-sader may reject any positive statements about American corporations because the com-munication is positive—that is, it falls into her latitude of rejection.

Latitudes of Price Acceptance   Researchers have found that consumers form latitudes of price acceptance. A latitude of price acceptance surrounds a reference price, which con-sumers form through experience with a product category. The region of price insensitiv-ity around a reference price is larger for consumers who (1) have a higher reference price, (2) are more brand loyal, and (3) go a longer interval between purchases. If a target mar-ket has a wide latitude of price acceptance, managers can increase prices in larger incre-ments without dampening product demand.[21]

The Impact of Reactance and Dissonance on Attitudes

When consumers have to make a brand choice, they may feel anxious about the purchase—especially if it is an expensive or important one. Immediately before making the choice, they often feel conflicted about which brand to buy or whether they should make the pur-chase at all. Similarly, shortly after making an important purchase, consumers often ex-perience severe anxiety and doubt about whether they have made the correct choice. These negative feelings before or after a purchase are caused by the psychological processes of reactance and dissonance. Since these processes usually operate in high-involvement circumstances where salespeople are involved, it is important that companies and their sales personnel have a good understanding of them.

Predecisional Reactance   In comparing brands, consumers may have a negative affective reaction if they perceive that their behavioral freedom is being threatened in some way. (You will recall from our discussion in Chapter 6 that such threats to behavioral freedom often do result in reactance.) Why would the prospect of making a choice cause people to believe that their behavioral freedom is being threatened?

The explanation is a bit complicated but psychologically sound. When a consumer must make a choice between two or more brands, at least one of the choices must be given up.

Question: What happened when a re-tailer put $1,000 king-size beds on its floor?

Answer: Sales of less expensive beds in-creased. As explained by the retailer's managers, the costly beds made the regular-priced mattresses seem much less expensive. Another way of putting it is

that the high-priced beds expanded con-sumers' reference price so that the regular-priced beds were now within their latitude of acceptance.

Source: Karen Blumenthal, "Sleeping Giants: Beds Get Bigger, Beefier," *The Wall Street Journal*, March 20, 1996, p. B1.

Consumer Behavior Factoid

Particularly if the choice is important and involves a high degree of financial and social risk, the threat of giving up one of the choices can create a reactance state. That is, because both options have positive features, a choice inevitably means giving up the benefits of the brand not chosen. This leads to a loss of freedom to have those benefits. Because people desire to restore their behavioral freedom, the feelings regarding the rejected option become more positive. Thus, prior to the choice, the expected loss of behavioral freedom causes the consumer's evaluations of the alternatives to converge. Ironically, the very act of giving up a desired alternative can cause attitudes toward that alternative to become more favorable.

If feelings about two important alternatives tend to converge before the consumer makes the purchase decision, what happens to these feelings immediately after the decision is made? The evidence suggests that shortly after making an important decision people experience reactance in the form of buyer's regret. One study investigated the postdecisional feelings of Army recruits who had just chosen their occupational specialties—an extremely important decision with potential life-and-death consequences.[22] These recruits were asked to rate their feelings about their decision at various times after the choice. Shortly after the decision, their ratings of their choice went down—the recruits had had the proverbial second thoughts. Although no research has been done on the predecisional and postdecisional effects of reactance in the consumer area, it is likely that a similar effect operates, so that after an important purchase consumers reevaluate the unchosen alternative as superior to the chosen one.

Postpurchase Cognitive Dissonance A number of years ago, one of the authors of this text bought a new home. The decision was extremely difficult because he had to decide between two homes that both had very positive features. The reactance from this tough choice was so severe the next day that he felt almost ill—a not uncommon experience when reactance causes the unchosen alternative to be viewed more favorably than the alternative selected. Psychologists call this state of discomfort *cognitive dissonance*. Real estate agents call it *buyer's regret*.

Cognitive dissonance is an unpleasant emotional state that is felt when there is a logical inconsistency among cognitive elements. In the author's case, the knowledge that he had purchased a house that he liked less than the alternative made him feel extremely uncomfortable. Leon Festinger, the originator of dissonance theory, stated that "two elements are in a dissonant relation if, considering these two alone, the obverse of one element would follow from the other."[23] The cognitive elements were the knowledge that he bought a house that he didn't like and that he is a careful, prudent decision maker. These two ideas were in conflict and created a dissonant state. According to Festinger, the experience of dissonance is an aversive state, and people act to reduce it. After purchasing a product, consumers use three different means to reduce dissonance:

1. They break the link between their self-concept and the product by returning it or complaining about it.[24]
2. They acquire new information by reading material relevant to their purchase.
3. They reevaluate the desirability of the chosen alternative in a positive direction and the desirability of the unchosen alternative in a negative direction.

The first means has quite negative implications for the brand, for if the consumer seeks to lower dissonance by returning the product or by engaging in negative word-of-mouth communications about it, the company loses one or more sales of the product. The second means—resolving the cognitive dissonance by obtaining greater amounts of information—can be positive or negative for the brand, depending on the kind of material the consumer reads. The third approach to handling dissonance—reevaluating the desirability of the chosen alternative—is positive for the brand. As the consumer gradually changes his perception of the brand purchased and the brand(s) not purchased in order to lower the dissonance, his feelings toward the brand he chose become more favorable and his feelings toward the brands he did not chose become less favorable.

In one study investigating the predictions of dissonance theory, consumers were asked to choose among a number of different record albums.[25] In the high-dissonance condition the albums were all rated favorably, while in the low-dissonance condition one of the albums was clearly preferred by most of the participants. The researchers found that in the high-dissonance condition preference for the chosen album increased after the purchase, while preference for the albums not chosen decreased. In the low-dissonance situation preferences remained essentially unchanged after the purchase. This finding supports the third means of dissonance reduction: reevaluation of the chosen alternative in a favorable direction is commonly used by consumers to reduce dissonance.

Table 9-3 presents six factors that influence the degree of dissonance consumers experience after a purchase.[26] The first two factors are interrelated. To experience dissonance, the consumer must have favorable feelings toward two or more of the alternatives, for if one of the brands is clearly superior to the others, no dissonance will be felt. Then the second factor comes into play: the brands that are perceived to be similar must be rated differently on different attributes. In other words, if the brands are perceived to be similar in every way, it would not make any difference which was chosen. A great deal of conflict will only be felt when one brand is good in some areas and not so good in others, and the other brand is rated good in the areas in which the first is lacking.

The remaining factors listed in the table are quite logical. The consumer must be able to choose freely among the alternatives. When someone is forced to choose one brand—say, because of price or availability—dissonance will not be experienced. Further, the consumer must be committed to the decision. If it is possible to back out of it at any time, dissonance will not be felt. The purchase must be a highly involving one that entails substantial perceived risk.[27] (The risk could be financial, social, time, performance, etc.) In such instances it is important to make the best choice, and people are therefore more likely to feel conflicted about their decision. Finally, there is the personal tendency to experience dissonance—some consumers generally feel more conflicted and doubtful about their purchases than others do.

Figure 9-9 diagrams the potential effects of reactance and dissonance on purchases in high-involvement, free-choice circumstances. Note that prior to the purchase predecision reactance may cause a convergence of preferences for the alternatives. Immediately after purchase, though, a phase of buyer's regret may occur in which the unchosen alternative is preferred. Over a period of time, however, the effects of dissonance may act to influence preferences so that the buyer's liking for the purchased product increases and that for the forgone product decreases.

Factors Associated with the Creation of Cognitive Dissonance

1. Two or more alternatives are rated similarly in overall favorability.
2. Two or more alternatives, although rated similarly, are perceived to differ on specific attributes.
3. The person has free choice.
4. The person is committed to the decision.
5. The person is highly involved in the purchase.
6. The tendency of the person is to experience dissonance.

TABLE 9-3

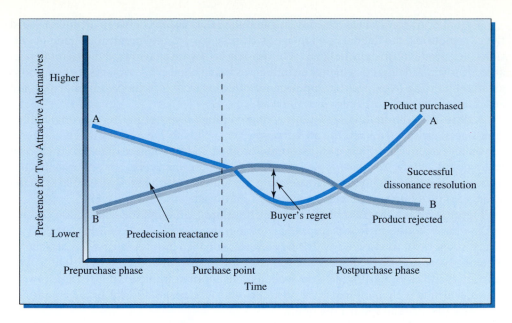

Figure 9-9

The effects of reactance and dissonance before and after purchase. In the example product A was purchased. Dissonance was reduced enough for the buyer to still prefer product A some time after making the purchase. (In the predecision reactance phase, attitudes toward alternatives A and B tend to converge. In the buyer's regret phase, the effects of reactance are fully felt and the buyer may like the unchosen alternative, option B, more than the chosen alternative, option A. In the dissonance resolution phase, the discomfort of liking the unchosen alternative more than the chosen alternative is reduced through a psychological reevaluation process.)

Managers need to recognize the effects of dissonance and reactance and have a strategy for counteracting them. Whenever consumers find it hard to choose between brands, they are likely to experience a severe case of buyer's regret. Sales personnel who are aware of this can take steps to minimize the negative impact of reactance and dissonance. For example, the real estate agent who sold the house to one of us allayed buyer's regret by effusively pointing out the terrific features of the house and the low price paid for it. One means, then, of lowering dissonance is to provide consumers with information that supports their purchase decision.[28]

Attitudes Toward the Advertisement

The final theoretical approach that is relevant to the experiential path to attitude change is changing consumers' brand attitudes without necessarily changing their beliefs. This approach involves influencing consumer attitudes toward the advertisement. Researchers have found that consumers develop attitudes toward advertisements just as they do toward brands,[29] and these attitudes toward ads influence their attitudes toward the brand. **Attitude toward the ad** refers to a consumer's general liking or disliking for a particular advertising stimulus during a particular advertising exposure.[30] (Recall that college students particularly liked the "Fried Brains" ad referred to in the introductory case.) Attitudes toward advertisements depend on a number of factors, including the ad's content and imagery vividness, the consumer's mood, the emotions the advertisement elicits in the consumer, and the consumer's liking for the TV program in which the ad is embedded.[31] These factors influence attitude toward the ad under both high- and low-involvement conditions, and whether or not the consumer is familiar with the brand.[32]

A number of researchers have investigated the relationships between attitude toward the ad, emotions, the degree of ad imagery, attitude toward the brand, and brand cognitions (i.e., product-attribute beliefs).[33] One finding is that attitude toward the ad influences attitude toward the brand, which then influences brand choice.[34] Another is that emotions elicited by the ad (e.g., positive and negative affect as well as feelings of dominance and arousal) influence the attitude toward the ad.[35]

A third research finding is that ads containing high levels of imagery strongly affect consumers' attitudes toward the ad.[36] *Imagery* here refers to the extent that an ad causes consumers to envision their own use of the product and to connect the ad to their own feelings and beliefs. Ads that employ concrete words, use vivid verbal or pictorial images, instruct consumers on how to imagine using the brand, and are highly plausible have the strongest impact on consumers' attitudes toward the ad.

Figure 9-10 is a diagram of all these relationships. Although the connections shown in the figure require further research and testing, they are plausible and have some empirical support. In the figure advertising content is divided into verbal and pictorial components. Note that each component influences the formation of brand cognitions as well as feelings and emotions. In turn, the feelings and emotions influence the attitude toward the ad, which may then influence the attitude toward the brand. Finally, brand cognitions influence the attitude toward the brand.[37]

While attitude toward the ad clearly has important effects on brand cognitions, such effects may be only temporary.[38] That is, because ad attitudes are composed of feelings and emotions, their persuasive impact may be short-lived.

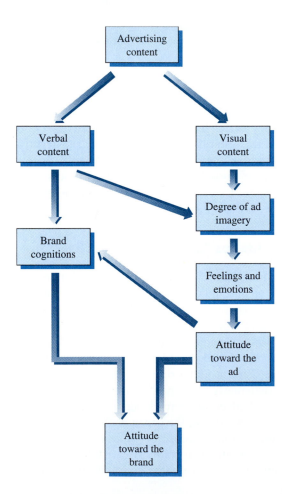

Figure 9-10

Attitude toward the ad and the persuasion process.

Another beneficial impact of creating strongly positive attitudes toward ads in consumers is that it increases the time they will spend watching the commercial. Consumers have two direct means of controlling the time they spend watching an ad: they can "zap" the ad by switching to a new channel, or they can "zip" the ad by fast-forwarding through programs already recorded. Researchers have found that both zipping and zapping are reduced as the pleasure and arousal caused by an ad increases.[39] In order to reduce zipping and zapping, then, firms should create ads with positive emotional and informational qualities.

Do professional copywriters use the theories developed by "academic" researchers in creating advertisements? According to one study, no.[40] It seems that copywriters do employ theories, but the theories are their own rather than researchers'. For instance, copywriters do not appear to employ the concept of attitude toward the ad in developing the pictorial and verbal components of ads. Also, they act as though all receivers of advertising communications are in a high-involvement state. Who is right—the pros or the academics? Further studies are needed before we can answer that question.

THE BEHAVIORAL INFLUENCE ROUTE TO BEHAVIOR CHANGE

So far, we have discussed the processes through which beliefs and attitudes are changed. As we noted in Chapter 8, through behavioral influence techniques people's actions can be affected without necessarily influencing either their beliefs or their attitudes about the behavior. For example, the ecological design of buildings and spaces can strongly affect people's actions without their being aware of the influence. Similarly, strong reinforcers or punishers in the environment can induce people to take actions that they would prefer to avoid. An extreme illustration of the effects of behavioral influence techniques is the armed robber who says, "Your money or your life." Most of us would unhesitatingly give up the first in preference to the second—even though we would rather not have to make the choice.

Sticking a gun in someone's ribs gets results because it drastically changes the reward-cost matrix for outcomes. There are, of course, much more subtle means of influencing the cost-benefit ratio for actions. Four of these means are discussed in this section: the ingratiation technique, the foot-in-the-door technique, the door-in-the-face technique, and the even-a-penny-will-help technique. These four techniques of personal influence are directly relevant to personal selling component of the promotional mix, and it is the function of marketing research to evaluate their success.

Ingratiation Tactics

The term **ingratiation** refers to self-serving tactics engaged in by one person to make himself or herself more attractive to another.[41] We use "attractiveness" here to denote the overall positivity or negativity with which one person views another. Ingratiators build on the knowledge that as one increases one's attractiveness, the likelihood that another will comply with one's wishes also increases. Ingratiation is a subtle way of obtaining power over another. Of course, we all try to make ourselves more attractive to favored others, but with ingratiators, the efforts are manipulative and calculating.

Several ingratiation techniques are available to marketers. Note that the common denominator among them is that the ingratiator subtly rewards the target.

- *Appearing to be similar to the target.* One of the strongest research findings in the social sciences is that people like others who are similar to them. Thus a skillful ingratiator attempts to assess his target and rapidly identify that person's attitudes, opinions, and interests. The ingratiator then modifies his own statements to match the perceived beliefs of the other. If successful, the target perceives the ingratiator as similar and consequently likes him more.

- *Conforming to the target's wishes.* One way of building up another person's ego is to agree with her and conform to her wishes. In this manner the target is made to feel important. By rewarding the target this way, the ingratiator increases his own importance to the target.
- *Offering compliments and gifts.* The ingratiator can build power by directly rewarding the target through compliments (e.g., "You solved that problem brilliantly") or through gifts (e.g., picking up a lunch tab).[42]
- *Expressing liking.* People tend to like others who like them. If the ingratiator can persuade the other that she is viewed with genuine affection, the target is likely to return the liking.
- *Asking advice.* By asking for advice, the ingratiator makes the other feel as though she is respected. This is actually an indirect method of telling the other that she is liked.
- *Remembering someone's name.* By remembering someone's name, the ingratiator gives a compliment to the other and makes it more likely that the person will comply with a request.[43]

Ingratiation tactics are very effective for achieving power in a short-term relationship, such as a personal-selling situation. Indeed, one of the primary tactics of the skilled salesperson is to create a "close relationship" with the client. There is one major drawback to this technique, however. If the target recognizes that she is being deliberately manipulated, the influence attempt is likely to boomerang—resulting in a loss rather than a gain of power. Hence the *ingratiator's dilemma*: The ingratiator cannot be too obvious in his attempts to reward the target for fear of being caught out and alienating the target. On the other hand, for the approach to be successful, the target must be rewarded and know it.[44]

The likelihood of the ingratiator being caught is quite high in a sales situation. There is a natural power difference between the prospect and the salesperson. The prospect knows that the salesperson wants to make a sale, and is wary of his influence attempts. The salesperson's goal is to come across as sincere and nonmanipulative.

The Foot-in-the-Door Technique

There is an old saying that if a good salesman can merely get his foot in the door, he can make the sale. That adage has scientific support—hence the popularity of the foot-in-the-door technique. Here is how it works: A requester increases the likelihood that a prospect will say yes to a moderate request if the person is first persuaded to say yes to a smaller request. By getting a prospect to let him in the door, the skilled salesman has persuaded the prospect to capitulate to a small request. The task of selling the prospect the product then becomes that much easier.

The **foot-in-the-door technique** operates through a self-perception mechanism. By complying with the first, small request, the prospect forms an impression that he is the type of person who does such a thing. Later, when the second request is made, the prospect is likely to agree to the request simply out of the need to be consistent with that self-perception.[45]

The foot-in-the-door technique has been shown to influence people in a wide variety of settings. For example, in comparison to control groups, subjects who were first asked to do something very small more frequently agreed to a larger request when asked—this was true for such requests as giving blood, counting traffic for a fictitious safety committee, and completing market research surveys. Similarly, one study found that people who were first contacted over the phone and asked a few short questions were later more likely to complete a long written questionnaire than were people who had not been contacted first on the phone.[46]

The foot-in-the-door technique is applicable to a number of areas in marketing, but has been used most frequently to increase the response rate to market research surveys. A more important area of use, however, is in personal selling. Selling a product consists of a series of steps. For example, if a stockbroker can persuade a potential client to visit her office, the task of selling that person stock becomes substantially easier because a stock purchase is consistent with the prospect's previous behavior of going to visit the broker.

The Door-in-the-Face Technique

The **door-in-the-face technique** also involves making two requests. However, instead of being very small, the initial request is extremely large. In fact, it is so large that no one is expected to comply with it. After the respondent says "No!" to the first request, the requester makes a second, smaller request—which seems eminently reasonable by comparison. Studies show that, in comparison to control groups that did not receive the initial request, those subjected to the two-step approach demonstrated a greater degree of compliance to the second request. Some areas in which the door-in-the-face technique has been found to work are: asking people to complete marketing surveys, to take juvenile delinquents to the zoo, and to count automobiles for a traffic safety committee.

Logic suggests that the self-perception mechanism that accounts for the effectiveness of the foot-in-the-door technique should doom the door-in-the-face technique. After all, if a person says no to a first request, the self-perception norm indicates that he or she should be more than able to say no to a second request. But a completely different mechanism is operating in the door-in-the-face strategy—the norm of reciprocity.[47] The **norm of reciprocity** states that if a person does something for you, you should do something in return for that person. This norm greases the wheels of society by ensuring that our efforts to help someone else will not go unreciprocated. The door-in-the-face strategy invokes this norm illicitly—because the requester never really expects the person to agree to the initial large request, only the second, more modest request. However, the requester makes it appear that *he* has given up something by retreating to a smaller request, so the target feels that she must return the favor. The only possible way of reciprocating the imaginary favor is to say yes to the second request.

The door-in-the-face technique is more limited in application than the foot-in-the-door strategy. Because it is based on the norm of reciprocity, the second request must be a smaller portion of the first request. Thus if the large request is to complete a long survey, the second request should involve completing a shorter version of the survey. A second limitation of the door-in-the-face approach is that the *same person* must make both requests because it is essential that the target be made to feel that the requester is actually giving up something when making the second request. If a different requester makes the second request, the target will not perceive that anything has been given up. A final limitation is that the second request must immediately follow the first. The two requests can be made even a week or two apart with the foot-in-the-door approach, but to create the impression that a concession is being made, the two requests must be close in time (certainly within an hour or so) with the door-in-the-face strategy.

The Even-a-Penny-Will-Help Technique

The foot-in-the-door and the door-in-the-face techniques are based on the norms of consistent self-perception and reciprocity, respectively. The **even-a-penny-will-help technique** is based on the universal tendency for people to want to make themselves "look good." Most often used in charity contexts, in this approach a solicitor asks the target to give money. Then, he adds on the phrase "even a penny will help" to the end of the appeal. The goal is to make people feel foolish if they say no to the request. The problem for the target, of course, is that it is impossible to give simply a penny, because that would also look ridiculous. Thus the target tends to give whatever is normatively appropriate for the situation and the charity.

Researchers have found that the total of donations to a charity increases when this technique is used. Although the targets give, on average, slightly less money than donors who do not receive the "penny" request, many more of them comply—and this more than compensates for the slightly smaller individual contributions.[48]

This compliance tactic can be implemented in other ways besides saying "even a penny will help." For instance, a market researcher could ask respondents to complete a survey and add the phrase "even answering a question or two would help." A salesperson making a "cold call" could state "even two minutes of your time would be appreciated." The adaptations of the technique are endless.[49]

Managerial and Ethical Implications of the Techniques of Personal Influence

The four behavioral influence techniques we discussed are implemented by firms and by charities, by honest salespersons and by everyday people. Unfortunately, they can also be used by the unscrupulous for illicit ends. Each technique has a Machiavellian edge in that the influencer is attempting to manipulate another person by engaging in subtle subterfuge. In the case of the door-in-the-face technique, for example, the influencer lies to the respondent, because the first request is a sham. This tactic is patently in conflict with the critical principle that marketers and researchers should never lie to consumers. Fortunately, the ability to abuse the compliance techniques is self-limiting—that is, if overused, these tactics will be seen through by consumers, who will then turn against the firms or people who use them.

A MANAGERIAL APPLICATIONS ANALYSIS OF THE "DRUG-FREE AMERICA" CASE

Problem Identification

The problem faced by public policy makers in this case can be phrased as follows: How do you change consumers' beliefs, attitudes, and behaviors concerning the use of illegal drugs?

The Consumer Behavior Analysis and Its Managerial Implications

Several of the concepts described in this chapter are applicable to this problem: multiattribute models, social judgment theory, attitude toward the ad, balance theory, and the truth effect. Table 9-4 summarizes the managerial implications of each of these consumer behavior concepts.

Multiattribute Models   The behavioral intentions model suggests two approaches marketers can take to influence intentions and behavior. First, communications can be developed to influence the target audience's attitude toward the behavior—specifically, ads that point

Managerial Implications of Consumer Behavior Concepts in the "Drug-Free America" Case

Consumer Behavior Concept	Managerial Implications
1. Multiattribute models	*Market research.* Identify the factors that will most influence beliefs about the consequences of drug use and about peer perceptions of drug use.
	Promotional strategy. Based on the market research, develop and test messages that have maximal persuasive impact on the target audience, using persuasive tactics derived from the multiattribute models (e.g., adding beliefs and influencing attitudes toward the act and perceptions of normative influence).
2. Social judgment theory	*Market research.* Identify characteristics of individuals with "nonextreme" attitudes toward drugs.
	Promotional strategy. Develop ads with messages that fall within these individuals' latitude of acceptance.
3. Attitude toward the ad	*Promotional strategy.* Develop commercials with messages and imagery likely to create positive attitudes toward the ad.
	Market research. Prior to rolling out the full campaign, conduct studies to test audience's attitude toward the ads that have been shown.
4. Balance theory	*Promotional strategy.* Create ads that develop a unit connection between the negative results of using heroin and the act of taking the drug.
5. Truth effect	*Promotional strategy.* Develop an ad campaign in which the target audience frequently receives messages in order to capitalize on the truth effect.

TABLE 9-4

out the dire consequences of consuming illicit drugs. For example, one ad in the campaign showed a woman with a gun stuck up her nose and the word "COCAINE" written in bold letters at the bottom of the page. Second, messages can be created to influence the target audience's perceptions of how key reference persons—such as older siblings or friends in a peer group—view the behavior. Some of the ads in the "Drug-Free America" campaign have suggested that teenagers should help their friends avoid drugs. By influencing teenagers to believe that important others view drug use negatively, the ads may change behavioral intentions.

Clear implications for marketing research and promotional strategy emerge from these ideas. First, market research should be performed to identify what consequences the target market perceives as particularly negative. Second, studies should be done to determine the best way to influence teenagers' perceptions of how their peers perceive drug use. Using the results of this research, the directors of the campaign could develop advertising messages with a maximum likelihood of persuading the target group to shun drugs.

Social Judgment Theory According to social judgment theory, extreme attitudes are difficult to change because the latitude of acceptance for a message is very small in people who are highly committed to a position. One of the first steps the strategists of the "Drug-Free America" campaign took was to authorize a large-scale market research study. Managers cannot expect to develop effective persuasive messages without first obtaining information about the target market and the initial attitudes of its members. The study conducted for the antidrug campaign identified the extent of attitude commitment among members of the target market. Its conclusion was that messages should be targeted to consumers with midrange attitudes toward drugs, because these young people were more susceptible to persuasion than drug enthusiasts.

These ideas have direct application to market research, segmentation, and advertising strategies. Market research should be done to identify the demographic characteristics of individuals with midlevel attitudes on drug use. These individuals with nonextreme attitudes would then become a segment that is targeted for the advertising communications. By knowing the demographic characteristics of the target market, managers could select appropriate media (e.g., magazines, television shows) to use.

Attitude Toward the Ad Another consumer concept that applies to the case is the consumer's attitude toward the advertisement. Marketing researchers involved in the "Drug-Free America" campaign ran studies to determine if consumers were reacting positively to their ads. The research showed that targeted consumers—particularly college students—were receiving the ads positively. A positive attitude toward the ads should impact these individuals' attitude toward taking drugs. Consumers' attitudes toward ads should always be assessed, and the results should be employed to develop promotional messages.

Balance Theory Balance theory suggests that there is a triad in which the *consumer* evaluates a message from a *person*, who is connected to the *object* of the message (e.g., heroin). In developing a strategy for the campaign against heroin use, the marketing director decided to stress the need to stop people at risk from starting a habit. The goal was to deglamorize heroin usage by showing the horrors of addiction and the nightmare of withdrawal. One ad, for example, showed a photo of a beautiful young woman prior to her addiction. A second photo showed her displaying the ravages of addiction, which included the loss of all her teeth. Of course, these ideas were directly tied to the promotional materials, so that the campaign was all of a piece. The goal was to cause the targeted group to perceive a negative sentiment relation with addiction—to create a positive connection between addiction and heroin that would, in turn, cause a negative sentiment relation (i.e., attitude) toward heroin.

Truth Effect The truth effect suggests that if people hear a message over and over again, they will come to believe it, particularly if it concerns what is a low-involvement issue for them. Through the romanticization of heroin in songs and movies, the false idea that this is not a truly dangerous drug is being communicated to young people again and again. One objective of the advertising campaign was to counter this truth effect by communicating the message "Heroin kills" frequently and across diverse media, (print, television, and radio). These ideas apply to the managerial area of promotional strategy.

Managerial Recommendations

Five managerial recommendations emerge from our consumer analysis.

Recommendation 1 Employ market research to identify the demographic characteristics of the target market, as well as to develop and test ad themes.

Recommendation 2 Target ads to consumers who do not hold extremely positive or extremely negative views of illegal drugs.

Recommendation 3 Develop messages that influence targeted consumers to develop a positive attitude toward the ad.

Recommendation 4 Deglamorize heroin use by linking the drug to negative images of withdrawal (consequences of the act) and social isolation from friends (normative influence).

Recommendation 5 Employ the truth effect by developing a campaign in which the message "Heroin kills" is communicated over and over again to the target market.

SUMMARY

This chapter explained how attitude, belief, and behavior change can take any one of three different paths: the decision-making path, the experiential path, or the behavioral influence path. The study of attitude, belief, and behavior change is closely related to the study of persuasion, which is the explicit attempt to influence people's beliefs and attitudes.

The elaboration likelihood model (ELM) explains the persuasion process from within the decision-making perspective. The ELM suggests that the mode through which persuasion takes place varies according to whether the consumer is in a high- or low-involvement state. Under high-involvement conditions, the consumer moves through the central route to persuasion, focusing on the nature of the arguments presented in a message. Under low-involvement conditions, the consumer moves through the peripheral route to persuasion, focusing on a different set of cues—such as the attractiveness of the source of information and the context within which the information is presented. When the peripheral route to persuasion is operative, consumers may come to believe a message that is repeated over and over again—a result known as the truth effect.

From the perspective of the elaboration likelihood model, under high-involvement conditions, multiattribute models are predictive of attitude change. The attitude-toward-the-object model suggests that there are three ways to change attitudes: (1) change the belief that the object possesses an attribute; (2) change the evaluation of the positivity of an attribute; or (3) add a new attribute. The behavioral intentions model suggests other ways to change the intentions of consumers: (1) by influencing their perceptions of the consequences of a behavior; (2) by influencing their perceptions of reference groups' reactions to a behavior. The second method can be very powerful if consumers have a high need to conform to the preferences of their reference (peer) group.

The experiential approach proposes that people's attitudes can be changed directly without first influencing their beliefs. From a balance theory perspective, attitudes are changed directly by creating cognitive imbalance. Cognitive imbalance is present if multiplying the signs of the cognitive elements (the observer, o, another person, p, and the impersonal object, x) results in a negative value. Because consumers have a need to maintain cognitive consistency, they tend to change one of the signs (usually the weakest in intensity) to restore balance. According to balance theory, there are two types of connections between the cognitive elements: sentiment connections, which resemble attitudes and involve the person's feelings about an object; and unit relations, which are established when the person perceives that two objects are connected to each other.

Social judgment theory, the second theory that applies to the experiential approach to attitude change, assumes that attitudes may be placed on a scale anchored by highly positive or negative feelings. Around the consumer's original attitude is a latitude of acceptance. If information falls within the latitude of acceptance, it tends to be accepted by consumers. In such instances an assimilation effect occurs, as the original attitude is moved toward the position of the new information on the scale. If information is perceived by a consumer as being so far from the original attitude that it falls within the latitude of rejection, it is likely to be rejected. In such instances a contrast effect may occur—that is, the consumer's original attitude moves in a direction opposite to what the communicator intended.

The third theoretical approach that can help us understand the experiential path is the impact of reactance and dissonance. Reactance refers to the consumer's need to give up one desirable brand in order to purchase another. Feelings of reactance can lead the consumer to come to like the unchosen alternative more than the chosen one. The recognition of this postpurchase preference creates feelings of cognitive dissonance, because one cognition does not logically follow from another. (That is, I chose the brand that I like less.) The result is psychological discomfort. To help people reevaluate their chosen alternative more favorably, some companies communicate with buyers after the purchase to positively reinforce them for their choice.

The final theoretical approach to understanding the experiential path to attitude change is derived from work on attitudes toward the advertisement. Consumers' attitude toward an ad may influence their attitude toward the brand—regardless of their beliefs about the product's attributes. The research in this area indicates that managers should test consumer attitudes toward prototype ads extremely carefully before they launch an ad campaign.

In the behavioral influence path to persuasion, consumers' behavior is influenced directly, without their forming strong beliefs or attitudes prior to taking action. A number of behavioral influence techniques were discussed in the chapter. Ingratiation is the use of self-serving tactics to make oneself more attractive to another. Some of these tactics are: appearing to be similar to the target, flattering the target, and giving the target gifts. In the foot-in-the-door approach, another behavioral influence technique, the influencer first asks the target to do something very small, and then follows with a moderate-sized request. The door-in-the-face technique takes the opposite route: first the influencer asks the target to do something very large—without really expecting to get a positive response—and then makes a much more modest request. Both approaches increase compliance. The foot-in-the-door technique works through a self-perception mechanism, while the door-in-the-face technique works through the norm of reciprocity. Finally, the even-a-penny-will-help technique involves adding a phrase to the end of a request suggesting that even a very small amount of money or time from the donor would be valuable. This technique raises the percentage of people complying with the request without greatly reducing the size of donations.

assimilation effect
attitude toward the ad
balance theory
central cues
central route to persuasion
cognitive consistency
cognitive dissonance

communication
contrast effect
door-in-the-face technique
elaboration likelihood model
even-a-penny-will-help
   technique
foot-in-the-door technique

ingratiation
latitude of acceptance
latitude of rejection
need for cognition
norm of reciprocity
peripheral persuasion
   cues

peripheral route to
   persuasion
persuasion
sentiment connections
social judgment theory
truth effect
unit relation

REVIEW QUESTIONS

1. According to the elaboration likelihood model, there are the two routes to persuasion. What are they? What factors cause a consumer to move through one route rather than the other?

2. Which route of persuasion tends to result in more long-lasting attitude change? Why?

3. According to the attitude-toward-the-object model, there are three ways in which attitudes may be changed. What are they?

4. According to the behavioral intentions model, what are the means through which intentions may be changed?

5. Define *sentiment connections* and *unit relations* as used in balance theory.

6. What are the three ways of forming a unit relation between an endorser and a product?

7. What is meant by the terms *latitude of acceptance* and *latitude of rejection*?

8. What factors influence the width of a person's latitude of rejection?

9. From a social judgment perspective, how should one go about attempting to change an attitude?

10. How does reactance influence consumer attitudes?

11. What causes postpurchase dissonance to occur?

12. What are the means through which consumers can resolve dissonance?

13. What is a contrast effect?

14. What factors may influence the formation of an attitude toward an ad?

15. How may the attitude toward the ad influence attitudes toward the brand?

16. What is meant by ingratiation? What are the means of ingratiation?

17. How does the foot-in-the-door compliance technique work?

18. How does the door-in-the-face compliance technique work?

19. How does the even-a-penny-will-help technique work?

DISCUSSION QUESTIONS

1. Survey current advertisements for the following companies: Pepsi-Cola, Volvo, McDonald's, and IBM. Which of these ad campaigns would you say involve central routes to persuasion and which ones involve peripheral routes to persuasion? State your reasons in each case.

2. Over the past 15 years American auto manufacturers have been losing market share in the United States because consumers perceive U.S. autos to be of poorer quality than Japanese cars. Assuming that U.S. manufacturers have overcome their quality problems by now, how might they persuade consumers of this fact?

   a. Sketch out an advertising campaign for the Dodge Neon designed to change consumers' perceptions of its quality using the attitude-toward-the-object model.

   b. Sketch out a campaign for the Neon using balance theory principles.

   c. What are the implications of social judgment theory for the two advertising campaigns?

3. Multiattribute models have a great deal to say about changing attitudes. Develop three concrete ideas for using multiattribute models to persuade teenagers not to smoke.

4. Identify two advertisements that you have a positive attitude toward and two ads that you regard negatively. Do your attitudes toward the ads influence your perceptions of the products? Discuss the ads and their impact in relation to the model presented in Figure 9-10.

5. Some analysts have argued that Wendy's fast-food restaurants are having problems in the marketplace because of a lack of cleanliness around the restaurants. Discuss what your recommendations to management would be for changing consumer attitudes toward

Wendy's. In doing so, make sure you refer to the consumer concepts discussed in this chapter.

6. Think back upon one or two major decisions that you have made in the past, such as buying a car or selecting a college or university. Did you experience reactance prior to and immediately after the decision? How much dissonance did you feel after making the decision? How did you resolve the dissonance? Explain your answers.

7. According to reactance theory, a consumer's preference between two closely evaluated alternatives tends to converge as decision time nears. What are some actions that a salesperson might take to keep this convergence of preferences from occurring?

8. Ingratiation is a device frequently used to influence others. Describe the various ingratiation tactics an automo-bile salesperson could use and discuss their possible impact on customers.

9. You are working in the marketing department of a firm that does market surveys. Your boss wants to use the foot-in-the-door technique to increase the response rate to telephone interviewers. She asks you to develop the message telephone surveyors will use to implement the foot-in-the-door technique. The research in question involves a ten-minute survey on the use of dishwashing detergent. Write out the specific words that the interviewers should use.

10. You receive the same assignment as in Question 9, except that your boss now favors the door-in-the-face technique. Write the specific words the interviewers should use to implement the door-in-the-face technique.

ENDNOTES

1. Peter Katel and Mary Hager, "Rockers, Models and the New Allure of Heroin," *Newsweek*, August 26, 1996, pp. 50–56.

2. Cecelia Reed, "Partners for Life," *Advertising Age*, November 9, 1988, pp. 122, 126.

3. Michael Ross, "Does Annual Survey of U.S. Drug Use Give Straight Dope?" *The Wall Street Journal*, September 18, 1996, pp. A1, A12.

4. Katel and Hager, "Rockers, Models and the New Allure of Heroin," p. 53.

5. Richard Petty, John Cacioppo, and David Schumann, "Central and Peripheral Routes to Advertising Effectiveness: The Moderating Role of Involvement," *Journal of Consumer Research*, Vol. 10 (September 1983), pp. 135–146. For an article reporting on the relationship between motivation and the route to persuasion, see Scott B. Mackenzie and Richard A. Spreng, "How Does Motivation Moderate the Impact of Central and Peripheral Processing on Brand Attitudes and Intentions?" *Journal of Consumer Research*, Vol. 19 (March 1992), pp. 519–529.

6. Petty et al., "Central and Peripheral Routes to Advertising Effectiveness."

7. Richard Petty and John Cacioppo, "The Elaboration Likelihood Model of Persuasion," in *Advances in Experiential Social Psychology*, Vol. 19, Leonard Berkowitz, ed. (New York: Academic Press, 1986), pp. 123–205.

8. Robert B. Cialdini, Richard Petty, and John Cacioppo, "Attitude and Attitude Change," *Annual Review of Psychology*, Vol. 32 (1981), pp. 357–404.

9. Recent research has supported key elements of the ELM model. See Jong-Won Park and Manoj Hastak, "Effects of Involvement on On-Line Brand Evaluations: A Stronger Test of the ELM," *Advances in Consumer Research*, Vol. 22, Frank R. Kardes and Mita Sujan, eds. (Provo, UT: Association for Consumer Research, 1995), pp. 435–439.

10. John Cacioppo, Stephen Harkins, and Richard Petty, "The Nature of Attitudes and Cognitive Responses and Their Relations to Behavior," in *Cognitive Responses in Persuasion*, Richard Petty, Thomas Ostrom, and Timothy C. Brock, eds. (Hillsdale, NJ: Lawrence Erlbaum, 1981), pp. 31–54. Also see Petty, Cacioppo, and Schumann, "Central and Peripheral Routes to Advertising Effectiveness." A number of studies have found evidence supportive of predictions made by the elaboration likelihood model. The work on the elaboration likelihood model is still relatively new, however, and several authors have noted that it has weaknesses. See, e.g., Charles Areni and Richard Lutz, "The Role of Argument Quality in the Elaboration Likelihood Model," in *Advances in Consumer Research*, Vol. 15, Michael Houston, ed. (Provo, UT: Association for Consumer Research, 1988), pp. 197–203. Also see Paul Miniard, Peter Dickson, and Kenneth Lord, "Some Central and Peripheral Thoughts on the Routes to Persuasion," in *Advances in Consumer Research*, Vol. 15, Michael Houston, ed. (Provo, UT: Association for Consumer Research, 1988), pp. 204–208. Another recent article is Paul W. Miniard, Deepak Sirdeshmukh, and Daniel E. Innis, "Peripheral Persuasion

and Brand Choice, *Journal of Consumer Research*, Vol. 19 (September 1992), pp. 226–239.

11. Scott A. Hawkins and Stephen J. Hoch, "Low-Involvement Learning: Memory Without Evaluation," *Journal of Consumer Research*, Vol. 19 (September 1992), pp. 212–224.

12. Curtis P. Haugtvedt, Richard E. Petty, and John T. Cacioppo, "Need for Cognition and Advertising: Understanding the Role of Personality Variables in Consumer Research," *Journal of Consumer Psychology*, Vol. 1, no. 3, pp. 239–260.

13. Curt Haugtvedt, Richard Petty, John Cacioppo, and Theresa Steidley, "Personality and Ad Effectiveness: Exploring the Utility of Need for Cognition," in *Advances in Consumer Research*, Vol. 15, Michael Houston, ed. (Provo, UT: Association for Consumer Research, 1988), pp. 209–212.

14. S. Ratneshwar and Shelley Chaiken, "Comprehension's Role in Persuasion: The Case of Its Moderating Effect on the Persuasive Impact of Source Cues," *Journal of Consumer Research*, Vol. 18 (June 1991), pp. 52–62. It should be noted that the authors of the study interpreted their results from the perspective of another theoretical model, the heuristic-systematic model. Although their model does make predictions that diverge from the elaboration likelihood model, the results of their study can be interpreted from within that perspective as well.

15. Gita Venkataramani Johar, "Consumer Involvement and Deception from Implied Advertising Claims," *Journal of Marketing Research*, Vol. 32 (August 1995), pp. 267–279.

16. William O. Bearden and Randall L. Rose, "Attention to Social Comparison Information: An Individual Difference Factor Affecting Consumer Conformity," *Journal of Consumer Research*, Vol. 16 (March 1990), pp. 461–471.

17. Fritz Heider, *The Psychology of Interpersonal Relations* (New York: John Wiley, 1958).

18. M. J. Rosenberg, "An Analysis of Affective-Cognitive Consistency," in *Attitude Organization and Change*, M. J. Rosenberg, C. I. Hovland, W. J. McGuire, R. P. Abelson, and J. W. Brehm, eds. (New Haven, CT: Yale University Press, 1960), pp. 15–64.

19. Marvin Shaw and Philip Costanzo, *Theories of Social Psychology* (New York: McGraw-Hill, 1970).

20. For example, see M. Sherif and C. Hovland, "Judgmental Phenomena and Scales of Attitude Measurement," *Journal of Abnormal Psychology*, Vol. 48 (1953), pp. 135–141; and M. Sherif and C. Hovland, *Social Judgment: Assimilation and Contrast Effects in Communication and Attitude Change* (New Haven, CT: Yale University Press, 1961).

21. Gurumurthy Kalyanaram and John D. C. Little, "An Empirical Analysis of Latitude of Price Acceptance in Consumer Package Goods," *Journal of Consumer Research*, Vol. 21 (December 1994), pp. 408–418.

22. E. Walster, "The Temporal Sequence of Post-Decisional Processes," in *Conflict, Choice, and Dissonance*, L. Festinger, ed. (Stanford, CA: Stanford University Press, 1964), pp. 112–127.

23. L. Festinger, *A Theory of Cognitive Dissonance* (Stanford, CA: Stanford University Press, 1957), p. 13.

24. E. Aronson, "Dissonance Theory: Progress and Problems," in *Theories of Cognitive Consistency: A Source Book*, R. Abelson, E. Aronson, W. McGuire, M. Rosenburg, and P. Tannenbaum, eds. (Chicago: Rand McNally, 1968), pp. 5–27.

25. L. LoSciuto and R. Perloff, "Influence of Product Performance on Dissonance Reduction," *Journal of Marketing Research*, Vol. 6 (August 1967), pp. 186–190.

26. For an excellent discussion of the factors required to experience dissonance, see C. A. Insko and J. Schopler, *Experimental Social Psychology* (New York: Academic Press, 1972).

27. David Mazursky, Priscilla LaParbera, and Al Aiello, "When Consumers Switch Brands," *Psychology and Marketing*, Vol. 4 (Spring 1987), pp. 17–30.

28. R. Lowe and I. Steiner, "Some Effects of the Reversibility and Consequences of Decisions on Post-Decision Information Preferences," *Journal of Personality and Social Psychology*, Vol. 8 (April 1968), pp. 172–179.

29. Andrew A. Mitchell and Jerry Olson, "Are Product Attribute Beliefs the Only Mediator of Advertising Effects of Brand Attitude?" *Journal of Marketing Research*, Vol. 18 (1981), pp. 318–332.

30. Richard Lutz, "Affective and Cognitive Antecedents of Attitude Toward the Ad: A Conceptual Framework," in *Psychological Processes and Advertising Effects: Theory, Research and Application*, L. F. Alwitt and A. A. Mitchell, eds. (Hillsdale, NJ: Lawrence Erlbaum, 1985), pp. 45–63.

31. Kenneth R. Lord, Myung-Soo Lee, and Paul L. Sauer, "Program Context Antecedents of Attitude Toward Radio Commercials," *Journal of Academy of Marketing Science*, Vol. 22 (Winter 1994), pp. 3–15.

32. Joseph Phelps and Esther Thorson, "Brand Familiarity and Product Involvement Effects on

the Attitude Toward an Ad-Brand Attitude Relationship," *Advances in Consumer Research*, Vol. 18, Rebecca H. Holman and Michael R. Solomon, eds. (Provo, UT: Association for Consumer Research, 1991), pp. 202–209.

33. These conclusions are based on research by the following authors: Morris Holbrook and Rajeev Batra, "Assessing the Role of Emotions as Mediators of Consumer Responses to Advertising," *Journal of Consumer Research*, Vol. 14 (December 1987), pp. 404–420; Julie Edell and Marian Burke, "The Power of Feelings in Understanding Advertising Effects," *Journal of Consumer Research*, Vol. 14 (December 1987), pp. 421–433; and Mitchell and Olson, "Are Product Attribute Beliefs the Only Mediator of Advertising Effects of Brand Attitude?"

34. Cynthia B. Hanson and Gabriel J. Biehal, "Accessibility Effects on the Relationship Between Attitude Toward the Ad and Brand Choice," *Advances in Consumer Research*, Frank R. Kardes and Mita Sujan, eds. Vol. 22 (Provo, UT: Association for Consumer Research, 1995), pp. 152–158.

35. Thomas J. Olney, Morris B. Holbrook, and Rajeev Batra, "Consumer Responses to Advertising; The Effects of Ad Content, Emotions, and Attitude Toward the Ad on Viewing Time," *Journal of Consumer Research*, Vol. 17 (March 1991), pp. 440–453.

36. Paula Fitzgerald Bone and Pam Scholder Ellen, "The Generation and Consequences of Communication-Evoked Imagery," *Journal of Consumer Research*, Vol. 19 (June 1992), pp. 93–104. For more information on the effects of pictures on information processing and brand preferences, see Carolyn L. Costley and Merrie Brucks, "Selective Recall and Information Use in Consumer Preferences," *Journal of Consumer Research*, Vol. 18, (March 1992), pp. 464–484.

37. Steven P. Brown and Douglas M. Stayman, "Antecedents and Consequences of Attitude Toward the Ad: A Meta-analysis," *Journal of Consumer Research*, Vol. 19 (June 1992), pp. 34–51.

38. Amitava Chattopadhyay and Prakash Nedungadi, "Does Attitude Toward the Ad Endure? The Moderating Effects of Attention and Delay," *Journal of Consumer Research*, Vol. 19 (June 1992), pp. 26–33.

39. James Boles and Scot Burton, "An Examination of Free Elicitation and Response Scale Measures of Feelings and Judgments Evoked by Television Advertisements," *Journal of Academy of Marketing Science*, Vol. 20 (Summer 1992), pp. 225–233.

40. Arthur J. Kover, "Copywriters' Implicit Theories of Communication: An Exploration," *Journal of Consumer Research*, Vol. 21 (March 1995), pp. 596–611.

41. Edward E. Jones, *Ingratiation: A Social Psychological Analysis* (New York: Appleton-Century-Crofts, 1964).

42. Michael J. Dorsch and Scott W. Kelley, "An Investigation into the Intentions of Purchasing Executives to Reciprocate Vendor Gifts," *Journal of Academy of Marketing Science*, Vol. 22 (Fall 1994), pp. 315–327.

43. Daniel J. Howard, Charles Gengler, and Ambuj Jain, "What's in a Name? Complimentary Means of Persuasion," *Journal of Consumer Research*, Vol. 22 (September 1995), pp. 200–211.

44. Edward E. Jones and Harold B. Gerard, *Foundations of Social Psychology* (New York: John Wiley, 1967).

45. Peter H. Reingen and J. B. Kernan, "Compliance with an Interview Request: A Foot-in-the-Door, Self-Perception Interpretation," *Journal of Marketing Research*, Vol. 14 (August 1977), pp. 365–369.

46. Robert A. Hansen and Larry M. Robinson, "Testing the Effectiveness of Alternative Foot-in-the-Door Manipulations," *Journal of Marketing Research*, Vol. 17 (August 1980), pp. 359–364.

47. John C. Mowen and Robert Cialdini, "On Implementing the Door-in-the-Face Compliance Strategy in a Marketing Context," *Journal of Marketing Research*, Vol. 17 (May 1980), pp. 253–258.

48. Robert Cialdini and David Schroeder, "Increasing Compliance by Legitimizing Paltry Contributions: When Even a Penny Helps," *Journal of Personality and Social Psychology*, Vol. 34 (October 1976), pp. 599–604.

49. For a single theoretical explanation of the four compliance techniques based on the availability-valence hypothesis, see Alice Tybout, Brian Sternthal, and Bobby Calder, "Information Availability as a Determinant of Multiple Request Effectiveness," *Journal of Marketing Research*, Vol. 20 (August 1983), pp. 279–290. Also see Edward Fern, Kent Monroe, and Ramon Avila, "Effectiveness of Multiple Request Strategies: A Synthesis of Research Results," *Journal of Marketing Research*, Vol. 23 (May 1986), pp. 144–152.

THE NBA'S GREAT TURNAROUND

In 1981 the National Basketball Association (NBA) was in trouble. During the 1980–1981 season 16 of the league's 23 teams lost money. Attendance at games was declining, and that season CBS television refused to show the sixth game of the NBA Championship series live. Advertisers had begun to shun the league. To sell advertising, representatives had to first persuade companies that NBA players weren't all on drugs. The nadir in that perception was reached in 1982, when the *Los Angeles Times* reported that 75 percent of the league's players were on drugs.[1]

By 1995, a metamorphosis had occurred: the NBA was the hottest sports enterprise going. The turnaround had started long before—in the 1983–1984 season, when the league broke attendance records. It continued to do so for ten straight years. Fans filled stadiums to 89 percent capacity, and the average value of an NBA franchise tripled. Several teams, such as the Chicago Bulls, the New York Knicks, and the LA Lakers, were worth over $100 million. While the television ratings of every other sport fell, the NBA's increased by 21 percent. From 1983 to 1991 revenues increased from $44 million to over $1 billion. In 1995 two new Canadian teams were added to the league's roster—the Toronto Raptors and the Vancouver Grizzlies. Games were televised to over 170 countries.[2]

What produced this dramatic change in the fortunes of the NBA? According to analysts, it began with the hiring of a new NBA commissioner named David Stern in early 1984. A lawyer with a flair for marketing, Stern brought an entirely new approach to the league. The president of the Players Association, Isiah Thomas (then a star guard for the Detroit Pistons), described it this way: "David came in and looked at the NBA and saw it as something more than just sports. It's really entertainment. It's a Michael Jackson tour, a Rolling Stones tour. He saw it as an NBA tour." David Stern himself compared the NBA to Disney Corporation: "They have theme parks, and we have theme parks. Only we call them arenas. They have characters: Mickey Mouse, Goofy. Our characters are named Magic [Johnson] and Michael [Jordan]. Disney sells apparel; we have apparel. They make home videos; we make home videos." Ad-

vertisers are now beating down the league's doors. As one Madison Avenue executive said, "The NBA is clearly ahead of all the other leagues in terms of the warm and fuzzy feeling that fans and advertisers get as a result of association with the sport."[3]

Thus the NBA was transformed from a narrowly defined sports enterprise to a broadly conceived entertainment organization. By selling videos, clothing, basketballs, and even cologne in Europe, the NBA has become an international money machine. In 1996 the NBA fitted a 67-foot tractor-trailer with hoops and interactive videos and began traveling across the United States to reach kids with contests, promotions, and entertainment. But the biggest growth potential is in Europe, Japan, and China, where the NBA is already selling the rights to broadcast its games. Basketball is now played in 176 countries, and the NBA wants to become a part of the culture of all of them.[4]

Perhaps the best example of the marketing emphasis that Stern brought to the league were the changes in the NBA All-Star game. Prior to his arrival, the game was a nonevent. Under Stern's guidance, it was transformed into an extravaganza—an All-Star Weekend with media parties and a series of competitions (e.g., the slam-dunk, the three-point shot, and the legends' contests) to go along with the All-Star game itself.

None of these marketing actions would have been possible without a basic change in the product itself. Just before Stern was installed as commissioner, new rules were put into effect to control the drug problem. The Players Association created a highly effective drug-screening program, along with a rookie orientation program that coached new players on how to deal with the press and how to adjust to the pressures of playing pro ball. The draft was changed so that first pick of college players was determined by lottery—the idea being to discourage bad teams from losing intentionally at the end of the season to enhance their draft choices. (Last place in the league meant first choice in the draft.) Coaches were sweet-talked—and bullied, if necessary—into cleaning up their act. For example, when the coach of the Utah Jazz continued to complain publicly about the referees, Stern went ballistic because he believed the coach's bad-mouthing was hurting the league's image. He called the coach and was reported to have said, "If you can't control your players and coaches to get them to understand how we do business in this league, I'm going to fine you more money than you make selling tickets."

As a marketing executive at Spalding Sports Worldwide said, "A good marketing guy knows that he has to get the product right before marketing it. That's what Stern did with basketball. He cleaned up the product first. Only then did he start marketing."[5]

2. Discuss the consumer behavior concepts from the chapter that relate to this problem.

3. Identify the managerial applications of those consumer behavior concepts. Discuss the actions taken by Commissioner Stern and show how they illustrate the relationship between the consumer concepts and managerial strategy.

4. In 1997, the NBA was again beginning to have problems. Do a brief literature search to identify these problems, and propose a solution or solutions.

Questions

1. Define the problem faced by the NBA in the early 1980s.

References

1. E. M. Swift and John Steinbreder, "From Corned Beef to Caviar," *Sports Illustrated*, June 3, 1991, pp. 74–90.
2. Jeff Jensen, "NBA Tries Going for 2 in Canada for '95–96,'" *Advertis-*

ing Age, November 13, 1995, p. 12.
3. Swift and Steinbreder, "From Corned Beef to Caviar."

4. Kate Fitzgerald, "Hitting the Road," *Advertising Age*, February 5, 1996, p. 16.
5. Swift and Steinbreder, "From Corned Beef to Caviar."

10

PERSUASIVE COMMUNICATIONS

INTRODUCTORY CASE

Can Bill Cosby Hustle Stocks?

In 1986 E. F. Hutton, the large brokerage firm, pleaded guilty to federal fraud charges. Partly in response to this public relations nightmare, the firm hired Bill Cosby to act as its spokesperson. Some advertising professionals praised the choice, one saying that "they need to do something to repair the damage. It certainly won't rub off on Mr. Cosby, but he just might rub off on the company and it could be a stroke of genius." Another commented, "A lot of Bill Cosby's appeal for consumers is his easy and natural association with an important part of our lives: the goods and services we consume." The president of a West Coast ad agency described Cosby as "so nice and warm that it will have to rub off on the company in a positive way. His friendly, offhanded humor will make the company seem human, which is important in that type of business."[1]

Many advertising professionals, however, had severe misgivings about the choice of Cosby as spokesperson. One critic said, "Everybody loves Bill Cosby. To put it suc-cinctly, I don't buy stocks from my grocer and I don't buy Jell-O from my stockbroker. The audience buying stocks is more sophisticated than the audience buying Jell-O, and if they feel they're being talked down to, it could have a backlash effect." Another observer noted, "Unless Cosby is recognized as a shrewd investor, I don't know what the fit is. The connection between an investment house and a Jell-O huckster and a Coke huckster is not immediately evident." Cosby's potential overexposure was also mentioned by some. "My problem with the whole thing is that I think he is borderline overexposed already. If I were Jell-O and Coke, I would be concerned that his appeal would be diluted."

Another perspective on the issue concerned what Cosby would say. One analyst noted, "It all depends on how he will be used—will he stand up and stare . . . , or will he be in the slice-of-life vignettes, or will they use him as an investor?" A New York City adman believed that the whole thing "depends on the idea, and what he says."

INTRODUCTION

Communications are omnipresent in our lives. Radio and television commercials, print advertisements, billboards, packaging, and sales personnel all seek to communicate with us and ultimately to influence us. Researchers have estimated that American consumers receive from 200 to 500 commercial messages a day. Yet they are aware of only 15 percent of these messages, and actively process a mere 4 to 5 percent.[2] In addition, in our encounters with friends and acquaintances, persuasive communications are commonplace. A friend who says "Hey, there's a great new movie—do you want to go?" is engaging in a persuasion attempt.

Moreover, with the exploding interest in the Internet and E-mail, a telecommunications revolution is under way. For example, in late 1996 Lexus kicked off a $60 million ad campaign for its ES 300 with E-mail messages to drivers of rival car makers.[3] Even greeting card companies are working with firms like Microsoft to give consumers the capability to create their own cards on-line. The cards are then either printed and mailed from the card company's headquarters or transmitted electronically to the recipient via the Internet. The U.S. Post Office estimates that 25 percent of future mail volume is "at risk" because of advances in telecommunications.[4] (Actually, this may be a very low estimate!)

Communication is the use of a sign to convey meaning. A **sign** may be a verbalization, an utterance, a body movement, a written word, a picture, an odor, a touch, or even stones set out on the ground to denote a property boundary. When people use the word communication, they may be referring to the specific words spoken, a subtle change in the speaker's voice quality, written words, a pictorial representation, or a gesture. We receive communications through all our senses. Some extremely unambiguous messages are communicated through smell and touch. Perfumes, for instance, are worn to communicate sensual thoughts and feelings, while a touch can communicate feelings of tenderness, sadness, or anger. Even silence can have meaning, and may enhance listeners' retention of ad information.[5]

The meanings conveyed by signs are strongly influenced by culture. For example, the gesture for indicating "A–O.K." in the United States consists of joining the thumb and index finger to form a circle. However, in many Latin American countries this gesture is an insult having scatological (i.e., obscene references to excrement) connotations. Check out the nearby consumer factoid for various meanings of the "hook-em-horns" sign.[6]

In this chapter on persuasive communications we analyze in detail the two key factors that influence the effectiveness of the communication process: the characteristics of the information source and the characteristics of the message that is communicated. In addition to the source and the message, three other factors are important to the communications process: (1) the context within which the message is delivered, (2) the nature of the channel/vehicle through which the message is communicated, and (3) the receiver of the communication (i.e., an individual). We already explored individual differences in consumer behavior in Chapter 7, (on personality and psychographics). Unfortunately, space limitations preclude us from furthur discussing receiver effects, or saying more than a brief word about channels here.

Channels are the media through which messages flow: for example, face-to-face interactions (e.g., a sales call), television, radio, billboards, newspapers, and magazines. The Internet is the newest channel of communication. Its rapid expansion in the last few years has prompted an explosion in cyberspace advertising. In 1996 ad spending in this channel increased by 83 percent between the first and second quarter of the year![7]

To return to the major topics of this chapter—the influence of the information source and the message on the effectiveness of communications—the introductory case illustrates aspects of both source and message effects. When E. F. Hutton hired Bill Cosby, the brokerage firm was getting a trustworthy and likable person to communicate its message.

There was a problem, however: Exactly what kind of message would Cosby convey? More generally, the company was worried about the trend for celebrities to quickly become liabilities to the firms that hire them as pitchmen. The CEO of the ad agency that handles the Anheuser-Busch account put this concern bluntly: "It is better for a pitchman to die than to be caught alive in a scandal. When the person personifying your brand gets in trouble, the brand indirectly gets into trouble."[8]

One way to avoid being embarrassed by a celebrity endorser is to employ cartoon characters instead: for example, the Peanuts characters that work for Metropolitan Life Insurance Company. Not only do animated characters have the advantage of being scandal-proof, they also add humor to messages.

Humor is just one message characteristic advertisers use. Creating fear is another—notice how deodorant and dandruff shampoo ads deftly exploit the social fears of the target audience. Fear of bodily harm is also used as a message tactic. Look at the advertisement in Figure 10-1, created by the Citizens AgaiNst Drug Impaired Drivers. Its message is that drug-induced drowsiness contributes to over 100,000 auto collisions a year.

We start this chapter by introducing you to a model of the communication process. Next we talk about how source and message characteristics affect consumers. Then, as usual, we conclude the chapter with a managerial applications analysis of the introductory case.

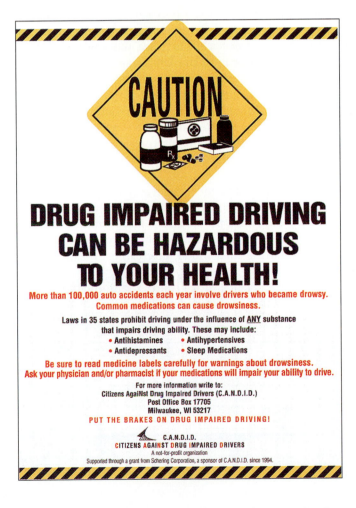

Figure 10-1

This ad from Citizens AgaiNst Drug Impaired Drivers uses a fear appeal to persuade. Also, note the use of symbolism in the "Caution" sign.

Question: What is the "Hook-em-horns" sign? What meaning does it communicate in the United States, Brazil, and parts of Africa and Italy?

Answer: The sign is indicated by holding up the index and pinky fingers with the two middle fingers folded down. For the fans of the University of Texas "longhorn" football team, it is rallying gesture accompanied by a battlecry. In Brazil it is a good luck gesture. In parts of Africa it is a curse. In Italy it is a taunt indicating that your spouse has been unfaithful.

Source: John Kifner, *The New York Times*, August 18, 1996, p. E7.

A MODEL OF THE COMMUNICATIONS PROCESS

Researchers have developed a **communications model** that depicts the relationships among the various factors that influence the effectiveness of persuasive communications.[9] Figure 10-2 presents one version of this model. The model proposes that five separate categories of factors control the effectiveness of communications: source characteristics, message content, medium characteristics, contextual factors, and audience characteristics.

As shown in Figure 10-2, persuasive communications begin with a *source* of information who encodes and delivers a *message*. There are numerous possible strategies for encoding messages: a communicator must think through such issues as whether a fear appeal should be used, whether a conclusion should be drawn at the end of the communication, and whether the message should be one-sided or two-sided.

The message is delivered through some *medium* of transmission. The medium may be face-to-face, print, radio, telephone, billboards, television, or the World Wide Web. The characteristics of the medium influence the interpretation of the message as well as how its information is processed. The message is then *received* by members of an audience, who decode and interpret it.

Various characteristics of the audience—such as personality, sex, intelligence, and involvement in the issue—moderate how receivers decode the information and react to the communication. Finally, the entire process takes place within a general environmental context where different kinds of stimuli may inhibit the communications process by distracting consumers, influencing their mood, or creating "noise" in the transmission of the message.

Because a communication begins with a source of information, this is the element of the communications model that we discuss first.

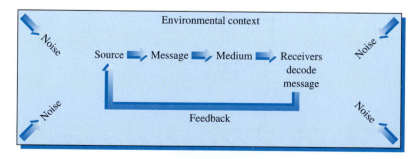

Figure 10-2

A communications model.

SOURCE CHARACTERISTICS

Understanding the factors that influence the effectiveness of sources of information is extremely important to marketing managers and public policy makers. For example, in personal-selling situations the salesperson acts as a source of information, and the salesperson's effectiveness depends in part on how he or she "comes across" to the client. In many advertisements the endorser is a source of information. According to one study that investigated 243 commercials, over 38 percent of them used some type of endorser to advocate a product or service.[10] The importance that advertisers attach to having the "right" source is demonstrated by the huge sums they are willing to pay celebrity endorsers. For example, in 1996, when the young golfer Tiger Woods turned professional, Nike and Titleist paid the 20-year-old a combined total of $40 million to endorse their products over a three-year period.[11]

Just what is a source of information? Many researchers view the term very broadly: a **source** is an individual or character who is delivering a message. Over the past 30 years researchers have identified a number of characteristics that affect the ability of one person to influence another. The principal **source characteristics,** or features of the source that impact the effectiveness of a message delivery, are: credibility, physical attractiveness, likability, and meaningfulness.

Source Credibility

This characteristic has long been recognized as an important element in determining the effectiveness of a source. The term **source credibility** refers to the extent that a source is perceived to have expertise and trustworthiness. The greater the expertise and trustworthiness of a source of information, the more likely an observer will perceive that source as credible.

Source expertise refers to the extent of knowledge the source is perceived to have about the subject on which he or she is communicating. In a recent review of over 150 articles investigating source effects,[12] the researchers found that of all the source variables, expertise had the greatest impact on respondents' reactions to communications. In fact, it had about a *16 percent* impact on respondents' ratings—meaning that 16 percent of the variance in respondents' ratings of communications was accounted for by changes in the level of expertise of the source.

Is a 16 percent change in the impact of a communication large enough to have managerial implications? The answer is "yes"! For consumer goods firms even a 1- or 2-percentage-point change in market share can mean tens or hundreds of millions of dollars in sales. Because consumer responses to marketing communications directly impact sales, maximizing the positive impact of a marketing communication takes on extreme importance.

Source trustworthiness refers to the extent that the source is perceived to provide information in an unbiased, honest manner.[13] Researchers have found that expertise and trustworthiness make independent contributions to source effectiveness. The implication is that a source that is perceived to be trustworthy can influence an audience, even if that source is perceived to have relatively little expertise. It also works the other way around: a source perceived to be untrustworthy, if also perceived to be an expert, has at least some persuasive ability.[14]

One very important factor that influences trust is the attribution the audience makes for the cause of the endorsement. As we explained in Chapter 6, if an endorser is perceived as presenting a message purely out of self-interest, trust in that endorser will be substantially lower. This effect is magnified with multiple endorsers. If multiple untrustworthy endorsers are used in an advertising campaign, trust is dramatically decreased. Conversely, if multiple trustworthy endorsers are employed to convey a message, trust dramatically increases. So companies run a risk if the endorsers of their products all seem to be motivated primarily by money rather than belief in the product.[15]

Advertising campaigns for products such as basketball shoes, beer, and milk have used multiple endorsers. Figure 10-3 presents one of the ads from the award-winning "Milk Mustache" campaign. Some of the endorsers used in this humorous campaign were Spike Lee, Florence Griffith Joyner, Matthew Fox, and Steve Young.

To sum up, highly credible sources are more effective than less credible sources.[16] Highly credible sources have been found to influence consumers in the following ways:

1. They produce more positive attitude change toward the position they are advocating.

Figure 10-3

The "Milk Mustache" campaign illustrates the effective use of a likeable source and of humor in advertisements.

2. They induce more behavioral change than less credible sources do.
3. They enhance the advertiser's ability to use fear appeals, which involve physical or social threats.
4. They inhibit the formation of counterarguments to the message.

This last effect is of great benefit to the advertiser. Advertisers know that consumers often develop their own thoughts in response to a message. These thoughts, called **cognitive responses,** may be positive toward the message (support arguments), negative toward the message (counterarguments), or they may concern the characteristics of the source (source derogations).[17] When an endorser is used, who is perceived as both highly trustworthy and expert, people tend to lower their defenses and not think up so many cognitive responses. Since highly credible sources inhibit the development of counterarguments, they are more persuasive than less credible sources.

Interestingly, some sources of information are trustworthy because of their blunt outspokenness. The nearby Factoid quizzes you on one such person.

Trust and Doing Market Research   The issue of trustworthiness also has an impact on market research. Market researchers are both sources and receivers of information. When gathering information from consumers, they receive information: data from respondents about their perceptions of products, advertising, and other marketing communications. But when they pass their analyses and conclusions on to their clients, market researchers, of course, are sources of information. If market researchers are distrusted by consumers, the data they receive will be flawed. And if they are distrusted by managers, their recommendations and analyses will be ignored.

A study designed to identify the factors that influence managers' trust in the recommendations and data provided by market researchers concluded that managers' trust increased when they believed that the researcher:

1. Possessed personal integrity, expertise, tactfulness, sincerity, and congeniality.
2. Reduced the uncertainty of the findings.
3. Customized the results.
4. Kept the results confidential.
5. Produced the results in a timely manner.[18]

The Physical Attractiveness of the Source

One has only to watch television or look at magazines to realize the importance of **source physical attractiveness.** Most television and print ads use physically attractive people. Actually, physical attractiveness seems to be a requirement for television personalities on news and entertainment shows as well.

Consumer Behavior Factoid

Question: Which Nike endorser said, "I am not a role model. I'm not paid to be a role model. Parents should be role models. I'm paid to wreak havoc. . . ."?

Answer: The basketball star Charles Barkley—in an unusual ad campaign for Nike basketball shoes that broke new ground in the use of famous sports personalities to endorse athletic equipment. Called "unplugged" ads, their goal was to focus on performance on the court or field and depict athletes as real people with real problems.

Research on the Impact of Physical Attractiveness Studies on the impact of physical attractiveness generally confirm what we intuitively know: physically attractive communicators are generally more successful than unattractive ones in changing beliefs.[19] Most men and women form positive stereotypes about physically attractive people. For example, one study found that college students of both sexes expected physically attractive people to be more sensitive, warm, modest, happy, and so forth. Indeed, the title of the article expressed the study's results perfectly: "What Is Beautiful Is Good."[20]

There has been a good deal of research investigating how the physical attractiveness of product endorsers affects consumers. The findings generally indicate that attractive people are perceived more positively and reflect more favorably on the brand endorsed than average-looking people. In one study, for example, respondents were shown slides of either an attractive or an average-looking model engaging in various activities at the Cincinnati Zoo.[21] Respondents were later requested to give their impressions of both the presentation and the model. In addition, they were asked if they would be willing to volunteer at the zoo. The results revealed that impressions of the slide show were significantly more favorable when an attractive model was used. This effect was particularly strong in males who saw an attractive female. These men, in fact, were significantly more interested in attending a meeting and in passing a levy to finance the zoo than those who had seen the average-looking model.

Physical attractiveness interacts with other variables in interesting ways.[22] In one study highly attractive and less attractive people endorsed either a coffee product or a perfume/cologne. The results showed that the sexy model produced greater intentions to buy the product in respondents when the product had a sexual appeal (i.e., the perfume), but when the product had nothing to do with attracting the opposite sex (i.e., coffee), the unattractive source had more impact. Respondents may have inferred that physically attractive endorsers would know something about perfume but little about coffee. So using physically attractive and sexy models in ads may not be appropriate for some types of products.

The managerial implication of this research is that the characteristics of the endorser should fit those of the product. Thus the **matchup hypothesis** states that the dominant characteristics of the product should match the dominant features of a source. Perfume is used to entice members of the opposite sex, so a physically attractive source "fits" this product. In contrast, coffee's dominant characteristic is that it is hard to brew a good cup. This product is not associated with sex—indeed, it is a "wakeup" product people drink to get going in the morning. Physical attractiveness is associated with the bedroom, coffee with the kitchen.

The physical attractiveness and youthfulness of endorsers in cigarette ads has been much criticized over the past decade. In response to the accusation that they were using very young models in advertisements to hook teenagers on their product, the tobacco companies have voluntarily adopted a rule: "Natural persons depicted as smokers in cigarette advertising shall be at least 25 years of age."

Are the tobacco companies living up to their own rule?[23] Not according to one carefully controlled study. The study's authors asked a broad spectrum of consumers (561 people) to estimate the age of the models in a series of print ads for cigarettes that were placed in magazines. They found that 17 percent of the models were perceived to be significantly younger than 25, and that the ads with younger-looking models were placed predominantly in magazines targeted to younger audiences. Furthermore, respondents, regardless of their age, perceived the younger-looking models as more attractive than the older-looking ones. What are the public policy implications of these findings?

Another potentially negative effect of using extremely attractive models is that it can harm females' self-image. Researchers have found that women, teenagers, and even preadolescent girls compare their own physical attractiveness to that of models—and as a result, come to feel inferior in comparison to the social ideal.[24] Indeed, researchers have found that self-comparison to highly attractive models can lower self-esteem.[25]

The Impact of Sexually Suggestive Ads A recent special issue of *Advertising Age* declared, "If you want to catch people's attention—which after all is the point of advertising—sex is one way to break the message out of the clutter. Associating product with pleasure propels purchases."[26]

Advertisers turned up the steam several notches in the mid-1990s with hot underwear ads. TV ads in the United States now show models in their undergarments—a practice that was taboo until 1987. As one ad researcher said, "Sex is everywhere. Advertisers are going to see what they can get away with on network TV."[27] This trend to sexually suggestive ads is not confined to the United States. Billboards for one brand of bras, placed in Britain, Germany, France, and Italy, displayed an underwear-clad model stretched out sexily on a bed of grass. The caption read: "Who Said A Woman Can't Get Pleasure From Something Soft." Such steamy ads have begun to create a backlash, however. For example, in Mexico a women's group forced Playtex to put a dress on a billboard model advertising Wonderbra.[28]

Academic research has shown that sexy advertisements attract attention, enhance ad recall, and improve consumers' attitudes toward the ad. However, responses to highly explicit ads can be negative. For example, one study found that the presence of physically attractive, partially clad models did positively influence an automobile's image—but if the erotic content of the ad was too high, it actually harmed recall of the ad when recall was measured one week after exposure.

Traditionally, most advertising using a sexual appeal has concentrated on the female body—which is why most of the research in this area has investigated the effects of female nudity or near-nudity in ads. Recently, however, with the increasing prevalence of ads, like those of Calvin Klein, in which the male body is eroticized, researchers have begun to analyze consumers' reactions to male nudity.[30] In one study male and female respondents saw male models in various states of dress (from fully dressed to suggestively clothed to nude) in ads for body oil or a ratchet wrench set. The results paralleled the findings for female nudity: individuals of the same sex as the model are influenced negatively by nude models. Male consumers preferred the ads in which the male models had their clothes on, while female consumers preferred the suggestive ads and nude ads for the body oil product. But when the subject of the ad was the wrench set, full nudity turned off the women because it had no relationship to the product.

The following generalizations can be made about using nudity in advertising. First, it should be appropriate to the product. Second, greater nudity draws attention to ads and raises observers' arousal levels. Third, nude images lower consumers' cognitive processing of the brand and the ad message because they are distracting. Fourth, suggestive/nude models appeal more to the opposite sex.[31]

Likability of the Source

Source likability refers to the positive or negative feelings that consumers have toward a source of information. Defining "likability" is difficult because what is likable can vary immensely from person to person. In general, however, source likability refers to the extent to which the source is viewed as behaving in a way that matches the desires of those who observe him or her. In addition, a source's likability tends to increase when he or she says pleasant things.[32] Thus sources are likable because they act or espouse beliefs that are similar to those of the audience.

Likability is an important source quality—the phenomenal success of Shaquille O'Neal and Bill Cosby as endorsers is based on their extreme likability. Other personalities who are equally famous—such as O.J. Simpson and Mike Tyson—cannot be used as endorsers because of their disagreeableness.

Source Meaningfulness

Sources embody meanings, and by connecting sources with their brands, advertisers can transfer those meanings to their products. Thus by hiring Michael Jordan and connecting him with its salty-sweet beverage in advertisements, Gatorade is trying to transfer to its product Jordan's athletic qualities.

Well-known endorsers can bring to a product an entire show business career—an elaborate set of meanings represented by the famous stage persona of the endorser. In discussing the use of James Garner (a long-time endorser of Mazda autos) as an endorser, one analyst commented:

> Garner does not play himself the person nor does he play a particular fictive character [in advertisements]. Instead, he plays what I would call the generalized James Garner role, the type for which James Garner is always cast—handsome, gentle, bumbling, endearing, a combination of Bret Maverick from "Maverick" and Jim Rockford from "The Rockford Files."[33]

The transfer of meaning from celebrity to product to consumer is diagrammed in Figure 10-4. This flowchart illustrates the point that a true celebrity plays many roles in the course of a career.[34] (Note that although celebrities frequently come from show business, they may also gain their fame in politics, sports, business, or another area that puts them in the public eye.) Meanings based upon these roles become attached to the celebrity, and those meanings are widely shared within a culture.

To sum up, the celebrity is a cultural symbol. When the celebrity endorses a product in an advertisement, the audience forms associations such that the cultural meaning of the celebrity is transferred to the product. Eventually, in the consumption phase, that cultural meaning is transferred from the product to the consumer. Thus in drinking Gatorade, consumers are symbolically attaching some of the qualities of Michael Jordan to themselves.

A study was conducted to identify the meanings transferred from the celebrity Cher to Scandinavian Health Spas—a company she has endorsed.[35] Respondents were asked to describe the associations that they made between Cher and the spas on the basis of her advertisements for the company. Table 10-1 presents the six categories in which responses were obtained. Note that the most frequently mentioned association for both men and

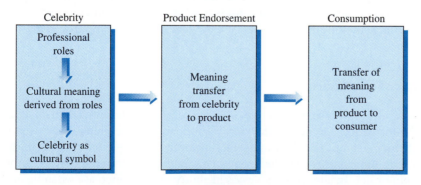

Figure 10-4

The transfer of meaning from celebrity to product to consumer.

Associations Between Cher and Scandinavian Health Spas	Number of Responses Made	
Association	**Males**	**Females**
Attractive/great body like Cher's	15	17
Health/fitness	12	6
Hard work	5	11
Sexy	11	5
Lacks credibility	10	4
Place to meet opposite sex	6	0

Source: Based on Lynn Langmeyer and Mary Walker, "A First Step to Identify Meaning in Celebrity Endorsers," in *Advances in Consumer Research*, Vol. 18, Rebecca Holman and Michael Solomon, eds. (Provo, UT: Association for Consumer Research, 1991), pp. 364–371.

TABLE 10-1

women was becoming attractive and having a "great body like Cher's." Most of the associations were positive, except for the single category of "lacks credibility." For this category, respondents mentioned that Cher obtained her body as much through plastic surgery as hard work. Also note that males and females diverged on some categories. For example, men more frequently viewed a spa as a place to meet the opposite sex, more frequently felt that Cher lacked credibility, and more often associated the word "sexy" with Cher and Scandinavian Health Spas. In contrast, women more frequently associated the words "hard work" with the advertisements.

Managerial Implications of Source Effects

The decision concerning what kind of source to use in an advertising communication is a crucial one for managers because the information source is a vital component of the message. The specific source used can help a company to position a product. For example, consumers would perceive a brand promoted by Bill Cosby quite differently from one promoted by Sylvester Stallone. Marketers should do careful research to determine audience reactions to the source and to track changes in reactions over time.

It is increasingly difficult to find a celebrity willing to make an endorsement who is not already overexposed. In fact, one major advertising firm (Ogilvy & Mather) has stopped using celebrities altogether because research has shown that the audience assumes that a celebrity endorser has been bought off.[36] Because of the likelihood that consumers routinely discount celebrity endorsements, as well as the problem of overexposure, advertisers are willing to pay a premium price for the services of "virgin" endorsers. Most U.S. companies would jump at the opportunity to hire such virgin endorsers as Woody Allen, Robert Redford, Paul Newman, and Sylvester Stallone.

One final managerial issue is whether hiring celebrity endorsers is "worth it." A study that investigated the impact of hiring a celebrity endorser on the stock price of companies revealed that while investors sometimes reacted negatively to the hiring of a celebrity, the action more frequently increased a company's stock price. Overall, the market generally reacts to the hiring of a celebrity as if that action will increase the firm's profits.[37]

Table 10-2 summarizes the major findings on source effects.

MESSAGE CHARACTERISTICS

The effects of message content and construction on receivers has been intensively studied. **Message content** refers to the strategies that are used to communicate an idea to an audience. Examples of such strategies are the decision to use emotional rather than factual advertisements and the decision to develop complex rather than simple messages. **Message construction** refers to the physical makeup of a message. Message construction involves answering such questions as: Where should information be placed in a message to get maximum impact? and How often should information be repeated in a message? Content development and message construction issues are discussed in the next two sections.

Developing Message Content

The logical first step in creating a message is to decide on its content. That is, the sender must choose what signs to use to communicate meaning. Creating an effective message is an art. Some issues that communicators need to consider when developing the content of advertising messages are:

- What rhetorical figures of speech should be employed?
- How simple or complex should the message be?
- Should a conclusion be drawn?
- Should comparisons to competitors be made?
- Should the message be one-sided or two-sided?
- Is it appropriate to use a fear appeal?
- Is it appropriate to use humor?
- To what extent should statistics versus vivid descriptions be used?

Summary of Key Findings on Impact of Source Effects

1. Important source-effect variables include credibility, expertise, trust, physical attractiveness, likability, meaning, and matchup with the product.

2. Source expertise has been found to have a greater impact on consumer responses than other source-effect variables.

3. Sources with high credibility are more effective, enhance the advertiser's ability to use fear appeals, and inhibit the formation of counterarguments.

4. In general, physically attractive people are more effective than less physically attractive people as sources.

5. To maximize source effectiveness, the source and the product should be a good matchup.

6. Meanings derived from the characteristics of the source can be transferred to the product through their close association.

7. The perceived characteristics and personality of the source interact with the nature of the product. Thus in some circumstances highly physically attractive or highly likable people may not be the most effective sources of information.

TABLE 10-2

- Should lectures or dramas be employed to communicate the message?
- What life themes should be used to create meaning?

What Rhetorical Figures of Speech Should Be Employed? As recently described in *The Journal of Consumer Research*, the "central concern of rhetoric . . . is to discover the most effective way to express a thought in a given situation. . . ."[38] Rhetorical figures of speech include rhymes, puns, hyperbole (e.g., exaggerated claims), metaphors, irony, and the construction of arresting phrases. Issues of rhetoric pertain to all marketing messages, from advertisements to packaging, from personal selling to public relations.

Only in the last few years have scholars begun to investigate the impact of rhetorical figures of speech on consumers. Given the recency of the research, definitive statements about the impact of rhetorical devices on consumers would be premature. Still, we can say with certainty that figures of speech make otherwise dull prose more interesting. Suppose that a copywriter is developing an advertisement for a batting glove made by Franklin, Inc. She might say something boring like: "While using our batting glove, Mark McGuire hit 42 home runs last year." Or she could use the principle of paradox and say: "Mark McGuire hit 42 home runs last year. But we held the bat." A *paradox* is a statement that is seemingly contradictory, false, or impossible, and yet is, in some way, true.[39] It can put punch into dull copy.

Another figure of speech often used by copywriters is the metaphor. A *metaphor* substitutes one object for another for the purpose of supplying surplus meaning. In one ad for Johnson and Johnson Band-Aids, the copy read: "Say hello to your child's new bodyguards." Bodyguards are a metaphor for Band-Aids, and the surplus meaning here is strong protection from injury. Interestingly, metaphors can be visual as well as verbal. Figure 10-5 shows an ad for LCI International with a headline that reads, "AT&T, MCI and Sprint Are Making a Killing By Rounding Up to the Next Minute." The photo above the ad shows the yellow tape police use to mark off a crime scene. Rather than depicting the position of a murder victim, however, the white chalk outlines an off-the-hook telephone. The "dead" telephone is a clever metaphor for the "crime" being perpetrated by competing telephone carriers.

Message Complexity From an information-processing perspective, for a message to have impact, the receiver must go through the exposure, attention, and comprehension stages. A factor that strongly influences comprehension is **message complexity.** If the information is too complex—or worse yet, presented in a garbled, confusing manner—receivers are less likely to comprehend and be persuaded by it.[40]

Excessive complexity may also result from attempts to put too much information into a communication. As noted in Chapter 4 on memory processes, consumers have a limited ability to process information. If too much information is given to them, they become overloaded and may react negatively. That is why the general rule for television commercials is that no more than four major copy points can be communicated. And when celebrity endorsers are used, even fewer bits of information can be processed by consumers because part of their cognitive capacity will be allocated to the endorser rather than to the message.

Overly complex marketing messages can have a bad effect on corporate profits. Ever since the deregulation of long-distance telephone service in the early 1980s, consumers have been bombarded with extremely complex pricing schemes, along with constant appeals to change carriers. In the midst of this confusing situation Sprint came out with its "Dime Lady" campaign, in which company spokeswoman Candice Bergen is forced into seclusion because everyone she encounters wants to talk about the "dime-a-minute" price for Sprint calls. In 1995 Sprint's long-distance volume increase was four times greater than AT&T's. This phenomenal growth was fueled, at least in part, by the extremely simple

Figure 10-5
LCI uses a visual metaphor to position itself as the low-cost provider of long distance services.

and appealing message. As said by one Sprint executive, "We recognize that in such a complex category as telecommunications today, that simplicity of product and message is extremely important. . . . That's exactly what Sprint offers."[41]

Drawing Conclusions Another question pertaining to the development of message content is whether the communicator should draw a conclusion for the audience. In many messages the communicator gives a number of arguments that support the advertiser's position. These arguments may logically build on one another and lead to the inference that the audience should buy the product. Thus an advertiser might state: "Our brand is built better, will last longer, and is priced lower than other brands." The conclusion consumers are supposed to draw is that they should go out and buy that brand. The question is: Should the communication *expressly* draw the conclusion for the audience, or should it *imply* a conclusion but let the audience draw it finally for itself?

Research on the effects of **drawing conclusions** indicates that the answer to that question depends on the complexity of the message and the involvement of the audience.[42] If the message is relatively complex or if the audience is not involved in the topic, it is better to expressly draw a conclusion in the message. On the other hand, if the audience is highly involved and the message is strong, without being overly complex, it is better to let the audience make the inference.[43]

Comparative Messages A **comparative message** is one in which the communicator compares the positive and negative aspects of his or her position to the positive and negative aspects of a competitor's position. This approach is frequently used by advertisers who explicitly identify one or more competitors for the purpose of claiming superiority over them.[44]

Since the early 1970s, the Federal Trade Commission has encouraged the use of comparative advertising out of the belief that naming a competitor would assist consumers in evaluating a claim of superiority.[45] Comparative advertising is useful for small companies that are trying to enter a market, particularly if their claims are based on research done by independent third parties.[46] A Coca-Cola executive summed up the opinion of many marketing managers when he said, "Comparative ads are good when you're new, but when you're the standard, it just gives a lot of free publicity to your competitors."[47]

In European countries, however, comparative ads are viewed quite negatively. They are even banned in Germany, Italy, and Belgium. In France one cigarette ad campaign compared smoking to eating cookies. The headline of one of the ads read, "Life is Full of Risks, But They're Not All Equal." Below the headline were three cookies. The ad suggested that because of their high fat content, cookies were more dangerous to health than cigarettes.[48] The claim horrified French regulators and they banned the ads.

Comparative ads can also be used to position and differentiate a brand. By directly comparing a brand with low market share to the dominant brand, managers can anchor their brand close to the position of the dominant brand in the consumer's mind.[49] In studying the product category of toothpaste, researchers found that comparative advertisements seemed to be superior to noncomparative ads for anchoring a new brand closer to a dominant brand and for creating a clear brand image. Direct comparisons between an unfamiliar brand and a market leader apparently reposition the unfamiliar brand so that consumers perceive it to be more similar to the market leader.[50]

Recently, two different types of comparative advertisements were identified. In **direct comparative advertisements** one brand is compared specifically with another brand. In **indirect comparative advertisements** the comparison brand is not specifically mentioned. Rather, the ad compares the brand indirectly to "competitors." Which type of comparison is better? That depends on the market share of the brand. One study concluded that low-market-share brands should directly compare themselves to the market leader, moderate-market-share brands should use indirect comparative ads that do not mention the name of the competitor in order to avoid confusing consumers, and market leaders should generally avoid comparative ads altogether.[51]

Several conclusions can be drawn from the research on comparative advertising:

1. Comparative ads can be effective for low-market-share or new brands in reducing perceived differences with the leading brands.[52]
2. Moderate-market-share brands should use only indirect comparative advertising when comparisons are made to other moderate-share brands.
3. To differentiate its brand from another, a company should compare it to the competitor on important attributes.
4. As a general rule, market leaders should avoid comparative advertising.[53]

One- versus Two-Sided Messages Somewhat related to the use of comparative messages is the question whether a message should give both sides of an issue. Figure 10-6 shows an advertisement that uses a **two-sided message.** The communication is from R. J. Reynolds Tobacco Company, and it addresses the difficult issue of smokers' rights. In one column is information from the nonsmokers' side, and in the other column is information

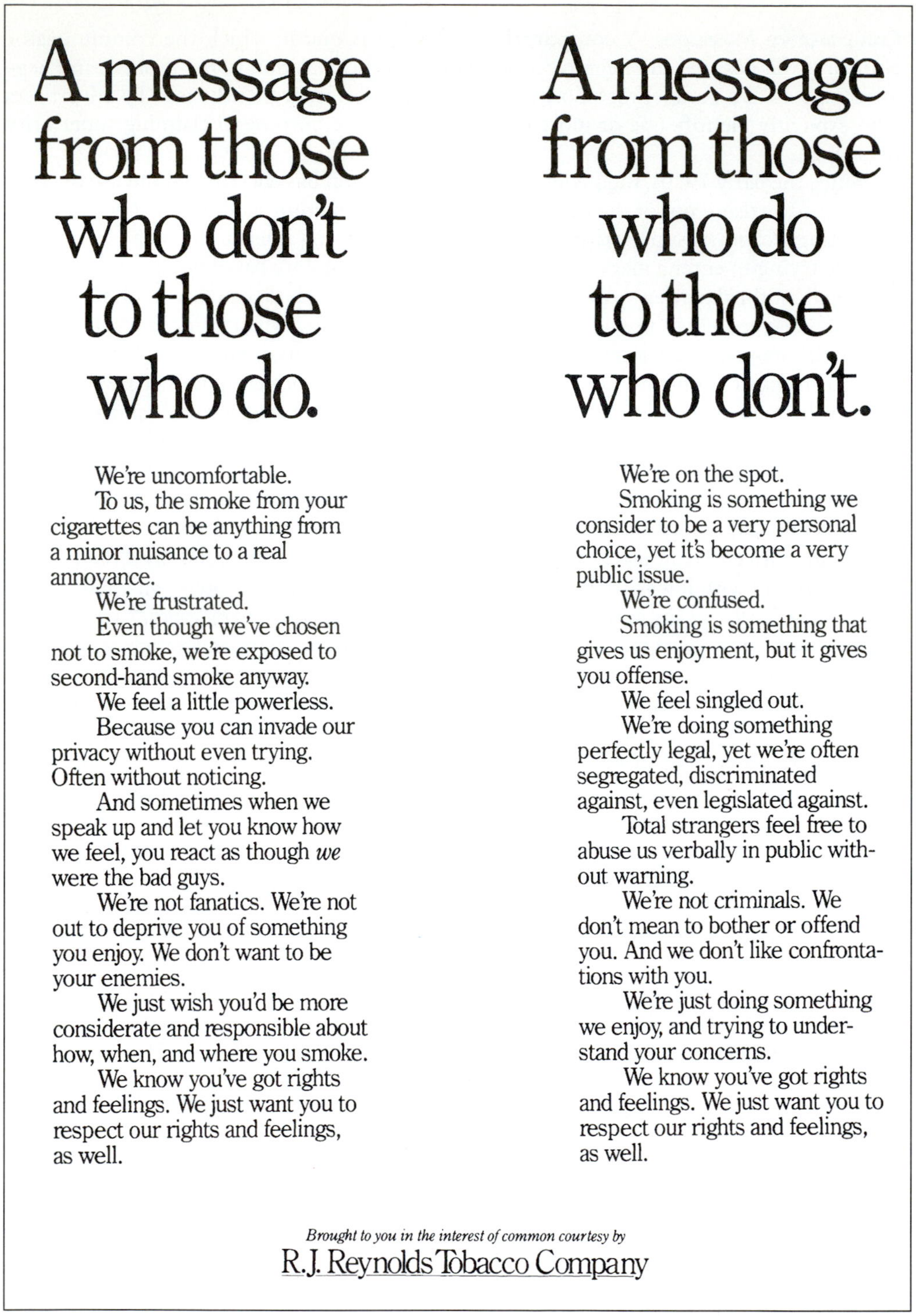

A message from those who don't to those who do.

We're uncomfortable.

To us, the smoke from your cigarettes can be anything from a minor nuisance to a real annoyance.

We're frustrated.

Even though we've chosen not to smoke, we're exposed to second-hand smoke anyway.

We feel a little powerless.

Because you can invade our privacy without even trying. Often without noticing.

And sometimes when we speak up and let you know how we feel, you react as though *we* were the bad guys.

We're not fanatics. We're not out to deprive you of something you enjoy. We don't want to be your enemies.

We just wish you'd be more considerate and responsible about how, when, and where you smoke.

We know you've got rights and feelings. We just want you to respect our rights and feelings, as well.

A message from those who do to those who don't.

We're on the spot.

Smoking is something we consider to be a very personal choice, yet it's become a very public issue.

We're confused.

Smoking is something that gives us enjoyment, but it gives you offense.

We feel singled out.

We're doing something perfectly legal, yet we're often segregated, discriminated against, even legislated against.

Total strangers feel free to abuse us verbally in public without warning.

We're not criminals. We don't mean to bother or offend you. And we don't like confrontations with you.

We're just doing something we enjoy, and trying to understand your concerns.

We know you've got rights and feelings. We just want you to respect our rights and feelings, as well.

Brought to you in the interest of common courtesy by

R.J. Reynolds Tobacco Company

Figure 10-6
This ad uses a two-sided message.

from the smokers' side of the issue. The result is a two-sided message that communicates the idea that there are alternative viewpoints on the topic.

Research on two-sided messages has shown that this can be an effective persuasion technique. Presenting both sides of an argument gives the appearance of fairness and may lower the tendency of consumers to argue against the message and its source. Two-sided communications are particularly effective when the audience is unfriendly, when it knows that opposition arguments exist, or when it is likely to hear arguments from the opposition.[54]

In some instances, however, giving only one side of an issue may result in greater attitude change. **One-sided messages** may be more effective when the audience is friendly, when it is not likely to hear the other side's arguments, when it is not involved in the issue, or when it is not highly educated. In these instances presenting the other side of an issue in a communication may simply confuse the audience and weaken the effects of the arguments *for* the issue.[55] Because so many of the purchases that consumers make occur in low-involvement circumstances, marketers should probably have good evidence from marketing research that a two-sided message will be effective before they use one.[56]

Fear Appeals A **fear appeal** is a message indicating that consumers are in for unfortunate circumstances if they fail to use a particular product or change a certain behavior. Fear appeals activate people's risk perceptions. The risk of bodily harm has been used to generate fear by companies selling burglar alarms and by auto manufacturers advertising the crash protections built into their cars. Fear of financial risk is used by insurance companies. Social risk is used effectively to generate fears by a variety of companies—especially those selling deodorants, dandruff shampoos, and laundry detergents. By buying their products, consumers can avoid such "awful" maladies as "ring around the collar," they can "raise their hand if they're Sure," and they can scratch their heads without people snickering over their dandruff.

Marketers' opinions about the effectiveness of fear-arousing communications have changed considerably over the past 30 years. The first reported study on the use of fear appeals attempted to persuade consumers to brush their teeth more often. In this study one group of high school students was shown gory slides of diseased gums and given messages that tooth infections can lead to heart damage, kidney damage, and other disorders. Other groups received less gruesome messages. The results revealed that the more fear the messages created, the less the behavior change. These early results convinced many researchers that fear appeals were not effective persuaders.[57]

Later studies, however, showed that fear appeals can produce attitude change when used under certain conditions. Indeed, by 1970 there were over 20 studies confirming the effectiveness of fear-producing messages. Advertisers certainly believe in fear appeals, especially in such industries as life insurance, health insurance, burglar alarms, smoke alarms, automobiles, and even computers. Figure 10-7 shows an advertisement from Volvo extolling the virtues of its cars in protecting people in the event of a crash.

For fear appeals to be effective, researchers have found that the message should:

1. Give specific instructions on how to cope with and solve the problem.
2. Provide an indication that following the instructions will solve the problem.
3. Avoid directing high-fear messages at audiences that already feel highly threatened and vulnerable to the threat in question.
4. Avoid directing high-fear messages at audiences with low self-esteem.

As noted by one set of authors, if these precautions are satisfied, "very frightening messages are almost always more persuasive than more factual appeals to reason."[58] One reason fear appeals are sometimes so successful is that they create emotional responses that focus a person's attention on how to cope with a problem. This focus on coping responses

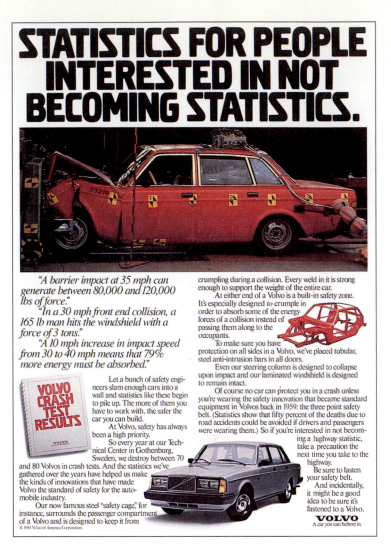

Figure 10-7

Volvo uses an effective fear appeal in this ad.

makes it more likely that the person will learn how to respond to the threat.[59] As long as the emotional response does not interfere with the processing of information about how to solve the problem, the fear appeal is likely to be effective.[60]

Humor in Messages   Like the use of fear appeals, the effectiveness of inserting **humor in messages** has long been debated among marketing researchers. Humor clearly is a frequent element in advertisements: one study found that 24.4 percent of prime-time television commercials run in the United States used humor.[61] A good example is the clever Nike ad campaign that teamed Michael Jordan with Spike Lee. Figure 10-8 presents a print ad from this campaign.

What makes something funny? According to one theory, humor results from incongruity or deviations from expectations.[62] Thus the Nike campaign playfully creates incongruity by pairing the huge basketball player Michael Jordan with the tiny film director Spike Lee in ads for basketball shoes. In addition, a humorous pun is created in the lines "The Best on Earth" and "The Best on Mars."

THE BEST ON EARTH.
Air Jordan from Nike.

THE BEST ON MARS.
Ditto.

Figure 10-8
Nike employs humor to communicate a message in this ad featuring Michael Jordan and Spike Lee.

Humor in ads can produce negative effects as well as positive ones. Managers should be especially mindful of three potential negative outcomes of using humor. First, it can reduce message comprehension. For example, one study that compared the recall of ad content in humorous ads to that in serious ads found that recall was significantly better for the serious version of the ad.[63] Humor often distracts the audience from the message,[64] which is hardly what the advertiser wants. Second, humor generally shortens the life span of an ad. Particularly if it is of the "gag" type, humor tends to fade quickly and lose its positive effects. Third, humorous ads can have unanticipated negative effects on various audiences. For example, ads for Budweiser beer shown in Britain in 1996 used American Indians, who are extremely popular in England. In one ad a truck driver for Chieftain Cement walks into a bar crowded with American Indians. The driver has a ghostly pale face, and is quite out of place in the bar. Just as the scene is about to turn ugly, the driver dunks his head into a pail of water. It turns out that he, too, is Indian, and only looked like a "paleface" because he was covered with cement dust. The scene ends with the Indian gulping down a bottle of beer. While the English loved the ad, Native Americans hated it because it seemed to pander to the stereotype of alcoholism in their group.[65] The British ad executives were quite oblivious to the problem and astonished at the furor it caused.

Perhaps the riskiest thing about using humor in ads is that different audiences react in diverse ways to the same humorous message. One study concluded that females respond more negatively to the injection of humor in ads than males do.[66] Another found that a number of audience characteristics besides sex mediate the effects of humor, including race, national origin, personality, and social attitudes.[67]

That being said, humor can have a very positive impact on persuasive communications. For instance, one field study found that when humorous flyers were handed out to announce social gatherings, such as a neighborhood picnic, over 20 percent more people attended than when informational flyers were used.[68] Another study concluded that a humorous ad improved consumers' attitudes toward the brand and enhanced their recall of information in the advertisement.[69]

Three factors account for the positive effects of humorous messages. One is that humor puts people in a good mood, which makes them less likely to think up counterarguments to the message.[70] Second, humor often attracts people's attention and increases their recall and comprehension of an ad. Finally—and this is the strongest effect—humor enhances consumers' liking for an ad.[71] As described in the previous chapter, attitude toward an ad directly impacts attitude toward the product.

Two additional points about the effects of humor on consumers: first, the humor should be related to the product or service in some way; and second, the effects of humor are moderated by consumers' prior evaluations of the brand.[72] The second point was strongly confirmed in a study that created humorous and nonhumorous ads for a pen and showed them to respondents after the respondents read fictitious *Consumer Reports* ratings of the pens. Thus some respondents saw a very positive rating and others a negative rating. After being shown the ads, respondents were asked to state their attitudes toward the ad and the brand, as well as their purchase intentions. When the ad was humorous and prior evaluations were positive, respondents' attitudes and purchase intentions increased substantially. However, when the ad was humorous and the prior evaluation was negative, their attitudes and purchase intentions plummeted. The opposite pattern occurred with the serious ads. When prior evaluations were negative, attitudes and purchase intentions increased when a serious ad was used and decreased when a humorous ad was used. Figure 10-9 diagrams the effect of humorous ads on purchase intentions when consumers have previously evaluated a brand. From a managerial perspective, then, humorous ads are best employed to reinforce positive attitudes.

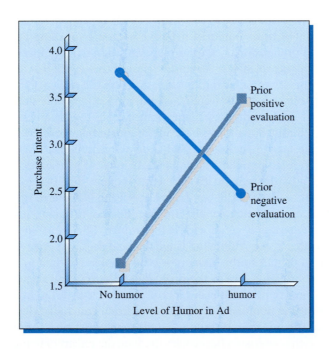

Figure 10-9

The moderating effect of prior brand evaluations of consumer responses to humorous ads. (*Source:* Based on Amitava Chattopadhyay and Kunal Basu, "Humor in Advertising: The Moderating Role of Prior Brand Evaluation," *Journal of Marketing Research*, Vol. 27 [November 1990], pp. 466–476.)

Vivid versus Abstract Information A well-established finding in psychological studies is that messages using vivid, concrete words have a greater impact on receivers than messages containing more abstract information.[73] **Vivid messages** not only attract and hold attention, they also prompt receivers to use their imagination. Therefore vivid messages are more likely to be stored in long-term memory and later recalled than more pallid communications.

What makes a message vivid? Three factors increase the vividness of messages. First, a message that has personal relevance raises the involvement level of receivers, and as involvement increases, so does the impact of the message. The second factor is concreteness. A concrete message gives detailed, specific information about people, actions, and situations. For example, in the early 1900s Upton Sinclair's book *The Jungle* (R. Bentley, 1946) had a major impact on the public and was partly responsible for the passage of legislation creating the Food and Drug Administration to protect Americans from adulterated products. Sinclair's graphic descriptions of working conditions inside meatpacking plants created an uproar that compelled congressional action. Here is his description of the "lard men" whose job it was to render the animal fat into lard used in cooking oils and soap:

> [The men] worked in tank-rooms full of steam, and in some which there were open vats near the level of the floor, their peculiar trouble was that they fell into the vats; and when they were fished out, there was never enough of them left to be worth exhibiting—sometimes they would be overlooked for days till all but the bones of them had gone out to the world as Durham's Pure Leaf Lard. (p. 117)

That is a vivid message.

The third factor that increases the vividness of a message is proximity to the receiver. That is, the information should be as close as possible to receivers in time, space, and sensory experience. *Time proximity* requires using information that is as fresh and new as possible. For example, when they have a product breakthrough, managers should announce the news as quickly as possible. Spatial proximity requires placing the information in a context that is linked as closely as possible to the audience's situation. Thus if a product is targeted to one region of the country, television ads should be filmed in recognizable parts of that region. Sensory proximity requires having the ideas in the message experienced firsthand by the audience or by someone else, such as an endorser, who can tell the audience what he or she experienced. One reason automobile salespeople are so eager to get you to agree to a test drive is to have you obtain firsthand the sensory experience of driving the car they are selling.

Lectures versus Dramas An important distinction has been made between lectures and dramas in communications.[74] When a source speaks directly to the audience in an attempt to inform and persuade, that is a lecture. A lecture resembles a classical oration in which evidence is presented and arguments made. Television commercials frequently use lectures in which a source talks to the audience directly and gives them information about the product. In contrast to a lecture, a **drama** uses indirect address: characters in the commercial speak to each other rather than to the audience. This type of commercial resembles a movie or play. Television commercials often use comic sketches, cartoons, or mini–soap operas in which two or more characters interact with each other about a product. The viewer is an eavesdropper who observes an imaginary setting that concerns a product or service.

When an advertisement uses a lecture, facts are given, and the consumer recognizes that a persuasion attempt is unfolding. In these types of ads the characteristics of the source are extremely important, and the advertiser must be concerned about the audience's cognitive responses. An example of a lecture in print is the advertisement reproduced in Figure 10-1, which presents arguments for believing "Drug Impaired Driving Can Be Hazardous To Your Health!"

Dramas work through an entirely different mechanism. They are stories about the world, and the advertiser's goal is observational learning. That is, viewers are supposed to learn from the lessons revealed by the interplay between the characters (models) in the communication. When a commercial drama rings true, consumers are drawn into it and develop conclusions they can apply to everyday life. As a result, they have less opportunity to develop counterarguments.

Lectures have the advantage of presenting information in a highly condensed form. However, they are frequently dry and boring and spur counterargumentation. Dramas, in contrast, can excite audience interest by creating emotional stories and by transforming the meaning of using a product.

Transformational advertising is advertising that attempts to get consumers to associate the experience of using a product with a set of psychological characteristics not typically associated with the product.[75] Take an advertisement in which a woman is swept off her feet by an impassioned lover after she has gotten the dishes "squeaky clean." Normally, one does not associate sex with dishwashing. This commercial is attempting to transform the experience of washing dishes by giving it a new psychological meaning.

Successful transformational ads are highly experiential. They involve the audience emotionally, and they change how people think and feel about the product or service being advertised. The marketing of perfume and colognes is based largely on attempts to transform the dabbing of a scent on one's skin into a romantic, sensual experience. In fact, the goal of most of these ads is to transform a woman (man) into a gorgeous (handsome) creature having tremendous allure for the opposite sex.[76]

In the last decade or so researchers have been investigating the effects of dramas and lectures on consumer responses. In one study respondents were shown ads for an automobile that employed either a lecture or a drama format. Respondents who saw the ad in lecture format generated more counterarguments and had much less empathy with the ad than did respondents who saw the ad in drama format. In addition, they provided fewer support arguments for the events depicted in the ad.[77]

Overall, dramas evoke greater feeling and less counterargumentation in respondents. Moreover, they increase respondents' perception of the authenticity of a commercial as well as their empathy toward it. Still, researchers have found no overall difference in the effectiveness of drama and lecture ads because lectures are processed evaluatively, whereas dramas are processed empathically. Thus effective lecture ads require high-quality arguments capable of overcoming consumers' counterargumentation. In contrast, effective drama ads involve consumers emotionally, seem authentic, and create empathy.[78]

One critical point is that drama ads require more time. One study found that people's attitudes toward the ad were more favorable and their purchase intentions higher when a 30-second, rather than a 15-second, version of a transformational ad was employed. Results were just the opposite for informational ads: attitudes and purchase intentions actually became less favorable when respondents viewed the longer versions of the ad.[79]

Table 10-3 summarizes the thoughts of one researcher/practitioner on what makes lecture and drama ads effective.

Life Themes and Message Construction

Researchers who study consumer behavior from an experiential perspective and who employ naturalistic methodologies stress the need to understand the meanings receivers derive from communications. They ask such questions as: What meanings do the Pillsbury Doughboy and "Old Joe" the Camel cigarette animal communicate to consumers? One conclusion of this kind of research is that consumers interpret communications from the perspective of their own lives.[80] Consider the copy for this advertisement for Georgia-Pacific that appeared in *Newsweek* magazine:

I. Effective Lectures

A. Lecturer must have *credibility*.

B. Lecture should attract attention via relevant means.

C. Lecturer must appreciate the audience and not talk down to it.

D. Lecturer should use illustrations relevant to the lecture.

E. Lecturer should use illustrations that do not overwhelm the message.

II. Effective Dramas

A. Dramas must pass the *realism test*. (They must live up to the viewer's standards of what seems realistic.)

B. Dramas can use fantasy. (However, characters must follow the rules of the fantasy.)

C. In dramas the characters do *not* lecture each other. (This is not realistic.)

D. The drama must be about the brand.

E. The drama must be rich enough to engage the viewer.

Source: William Wells, "Lectures and Dramas," in *Cognitive and Affective Responses to Advertising*, P. Cafferata and A. Tybout, eds. (Boston: D. C. Heath, 1987).

TABLE 10-3

> You've remade yourself a hundred times, searching for what would fit, and last. College kid, philosopher, James Dean wannabe. Now you're looking at an ad for vinyl siding and it is stirring you to imagine ways of remaking your living space. Would you say your interests have evolved?

The ad goes on to identify one of vinyl siding's key attributes—it is low-hassle because it does not need to be repainted. Targeted to long-time homeowners (middle-class people at least 50 years old), the ad connects vinyl siding to their current life theme (wanting to minimize hassle) and their anticipated life theme (wanting to minimize future costs when they are living on a fixed retirement income). While these themes of avoiding hassle and minimizing future costs appeal to older consumers, they would be completely inappropriate for younger people.

It is essential for marketing managers to identify the life themes that influence the thinking of important market segments. One of the quickest ways to raise consumers' levels of attention and involvement is to link an advertisement to their life themes (e.g., freedom, achievement, the avoidance of hassle). This kind of linkage also creates more positive attitudes toward the ad. Much more research is needed, however, to clarify the types of life themes that appeal most to consumers.

Message Structure

Communicators must be concerned with the structure of messages as well as their content. **Message structure** refers to how the content of the message is organized. One major issue in this area is the placement of important information. Another is how many times key pieces of information should be repeated in a message (e.g., how many times should the brand name be mentioned?).

Primacy and Recency Effects Primacy and recency effects refer to the relative impact of information placed at the beginning or at the end of a message. A **primacy effect** occurs when material early in the message has the most influence, a **recency effect** when material at the end of the message is the most influential. This is a far from trivial question.

Whether in a television commercial or in a formal presentation by a salesperson, the communicator wants to ensure that each piece of information will have the maximum impact on the receiver.

Primacy and recency effects pertain to series of messages as well as to single communications. For example, when a number of commercials run in succession on television, do those at the beginning, middle, or end of the sequence have the most impact?

Some consistent findings are beginning to emerge on primacy-recency effects. First, over time, primacy effects have more impact. Second, when conditions foster high levels of message elaboration (e.g., high involvement processing), primacy effects tend to occur.[81] Finally, researchers report that the primacy effect is stronger for verbal material, such as a radio advertisement, than for visual material, such as a print ad.[82]

One research finding can be stated unequivocally: material presented in the middle of a message is relatively poorly remembered and has the least impact. You will recall from the section on serial learning in Chapter 4 that numerous studies have demonstrated that people have greater difficulty retaining information placed in the middle of lists of material to be learned than information that comes at the beginning or the end. So communicators should avoid placing the important parts of a message in the middle of a communication.

Repetition Effects In Chapter 5 on Behavioral Learning, we discussed the importance of repetition for learning. Whether in classical conditioning, operant conditioning, or cognitive learning, information tends not to be learned unless it is repeated. In organizing an advertising strategy, therefore, marketers must consider **repetition effects.** The major question is: How often should information be repeated? Herbert Krugman has suggested that as few as three exposures to an advertisement may be sufficient.[83] Indeed, evidence suggests that too much repetition may make consumers increasingly negative toward the message—an effect known as **advertising wearout.**

Advertising wearout was reported in one study, where members of church groups received either one, three, or five exposures to an advertisement for a fictitious toothpaste during a one-hour television show. As the number of exposures increased, so did the number of counterarguments to the commercials.[84] Other researchers have likewise found that too much repetition can cause consumers' attitudes toward an ad to turn negative.[85]

For this reason, sophisticated advertisers rarely present the same commercial over and over again. Instead, they create a series of different ads that carry the same basic message. In one study researchers tested such an approach by varying the content of each ad in a series slightly. The finding was encouraging: the number of positive cognitive responses increased and the number of negative cognitive responses decreased as the message was repeated through the varied ads.[86]

To explain the effects of message repetition, **two-factor theory** proposes that two different psychological processes are operating as people receive repetitive messages. In one of those processes the repetition of a message reduces receivers' uncertainty and increases their learning about the stimulus, which results in a positive response.[87] However, in the other process receivers' boredom increases with each repetition. At some point the boredom overtakes the positive effects, and the receiver begins to react negatively to the ad. Two-factor theory suggests that to avoid boring consumers, the communicator should vary the ad a bit with each repetition. Figure 10-10 diagrams the relationships proposed by two-factor theory.[88]

While advertising wearout is a potential danger for corporations, the repetition of a message is critical for learning to occur. One approach to this dilemma, as we have seen, is to use the same basic message, but vary parts of it in order to maintain interest. Researchers have found that such variations in ad execution can substantially improve recall of ads without causing wearout.[89] Another benefit of varying the basic message is that it

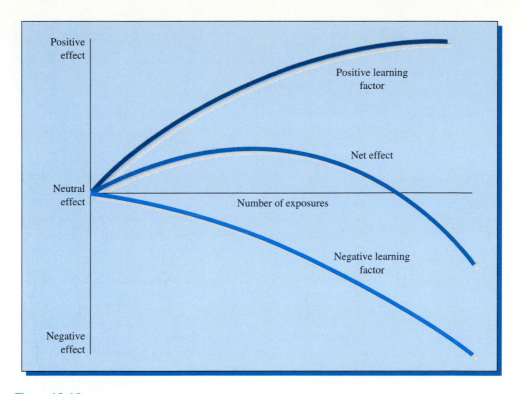

Figure 10-10

Two-factor theory and advertising wearout. (*Source:* Arno Rethans, John Swasy, and Lawrence Marks, "Effects of Television Commercial Repetition, Receiver Knowledge, and Commercial Length: A Test of the Two-Factor Model," *Journal of Marketing Research*, Vol. 23 [February 1986], pp. 59–61, published by the American Marketing Association.)

makes consumers more resistant to attack ads by competitors.[90] Finally, if exposures to repetitive ads are voluntary, distributed over time, experienced in the presence of ads by competitors, and occur in the cluttered environment known as the "real world," repetitive ads actually improve consumers' "top-of-the-mind-awareness" and brand choice.[91]

A MANAGERIAL APPLICATIONS ANALYSIS OF THE BILL COSBY CASE

Problem Identification

E.F. Hutton had to determine how to effectively communicate to consumers the assurance that the firm's legal and ethical problems had been corrected. The question was: How effective would Bill Cosby be as a spokesperson in minimizing the public relations disaster?

The Consumer Behavior Analysis and Its Managerial Implications

Table 10-4 presents the four consumer behavior concepts discussed in this chapter that have specific managerial implications in this case: source effects, message effects, matchup effects, and receiver effects.

Managerial Implications of Consumer Behavior Concepts in the E. F. Hutton Case

Consumer Behavior Concept	Managerial Implications
1. Source effects	*Market research.* Analyze consumer reactions to the endorsement.
	Promotional strategy. Decide if you will employ the endorser permanently.
	Positioning strategy. Determine the effects that using the endorser will have on the positioning of the company. Will the endorser cause the company to be viewed as less serious than it wishes to appear?
2. Message effects	*Market research.* Conduct focus groups in which consumers are exposed to different versions of the message and obtain reactions.
	Promotional strategy. Suggest the type of message that would be most effective for the endorser to use. (In this case a lecture format was chosen.)
3. Matchup effects	*Market research.* Perform analyses to determine the extent to which the target market perceives that the endorser matches the firm and its products.
	Promotional strategy. Carefully consider the meanings that the endorser embodies. Analyze how the message can be constructed to link the positive meanings embodied by the endorser to the firm.
4. Receiver effects	*Market research.* Do analyses to determine if there are different groups of consumers that will respond divergently to the spokesperson.
	Segmentation. Consider developing different messages for different target groups or reaching these divergent groups via different media.

TABLE 10-4

Source Effects A careful reading of the comments by the advertising professionals in the introductory case reveals that these pros were particularly concerned about Cosby's effectiveness as a source of information for a brokerage firm. They recognized his strong personal appeal and likability, but several questioned whether consumers would accept him as an expert on the brokerage business. If the target market failed to perceive Cosby as having expertise in investing, his credibility would be lowered. Another problem with Cosby, according to analysts, was overexposure: he has appeared throughout the years in numerous advertisements. If customers attributed his endorsement of E. F. Hutton to his desire to make more money rather than to his belief in the company, their trust would be lowered. A combination of the perceptions of low trust and low expertise would lead to an ineffective endorsement.

The investigation of source effects applies to the areas of market research, promotional strategy, and company positioning. Clearly, E. F. Hutton needed to do market research to analyze potential consumer reactions to Cosby's endorsement. On the negative side: Would consumers perceive this entertainer as too "lightweight" to endorse an investment firm? Would his many other endorsements cause consumers to distrust him? On the positive side: Would a likable personality be more effective than a "stuffed shirt" type of endorser in helping E. F. Hutton overcome the public relations disaster it had recently suffered? Only market research could obtain for Hutton's managers the information they needed to answer these questions. Hutton's managers also needed to recognize that choosing Bill Cosby as a spokesperson would affect the firm's entire promotional strategy.

Would he become a permanent spokesperson, or would he merely be used until the firm erased consumers' memory of the fraud charges? If management decided to use Cosby for any length of time, he would have a strong impact on how the firm was positioned in consumers' minds. Hutton would need to recognize that a long-term association with this spokesman would probably position the company as less serious—but more human—than other brokerage firms. In short, management would have to carefully analyze Hutton's positioning strategy when they employed Cosby.

Message Effects The importance of the firm's message in the Cosby ads was also emphasized by several analysts who commented on Hutton's move. A critical issue was what Cosby would say. Since he is widely known for his humor, would a humorous appeal be appropriate? Perhaps a lecture format would be most effective in the circumstances.

Management knew that the type of message that Cosby delivered would be crucial to the success of the campaign. As it turned out, they chose a lecture format in which he spoke directly to the audience in a warm and reassuring manner. In such circumstances it is important for firms to do market research to ascertain the target market's reactions to both the endorser and the message he is communicating.

Matchup Effects A critical issue was whether the dominant characteristics of Bill Cosby would fit with the financial services products offered by E.F. Hutton. Does a celebrity comedian fit with a serious product? Would a humorous appeal seem especially inappropriate for a firm trying to recover from the disgrace of having criminal charges filed against it? Once again, market research would be necessary to gauge how the target market viewed Cosby giving different messages. The goal would be to find the message that linked Cosby to the company in a believable manner.

Receiver Effects Advertising professionals noted that the receivers in this case—investors—are sophisticated people who might not respond favorably to a likable celebrity known for a comedy show and for having previously endorsed such products as a gelatin dessert, a soft drink, a car, and a computer. Receiver effects apply to the managerial areas of market research and segmentation. Hutton would need, then, to identify the preferences of the particular segment to which the ads are targeted.

As it turns out, E. F. Hutton employed Bill Cosby for only a short time. No information was made available on the success or failure of the campaign, but it is doubtful that employing Bill Cosby was beneficial to E. F. Hutton. Indeed, a consumer behavior analysis could have predicted that his endorsement would not help the brokerage firm, for he had no credibility in the financial area, he was overexposed as an endorser, and his personal qualities did not match up with those of an investment company.

Managerial Recommendations

Recommendation 1 Work to find a source who has the expertise, trustworthiness, and meaningfulness to make an impact on the targeted group of consumers.

Recommendation 2 Develop a message that employs a lecture format, avoids the use of humor, and presents factual information in a vivid manner.

Recommendation 3 Work hard to ensure that the source and the message match up with the product.

Recommendation 4 Do appropriate market research to test the source and message on targeted consumers.

Summary

The general model of communications consists of several components: source, message, medium, receiver, feedback, noise, and environmental context. In this chapter we identified three major source characteristics. The first, source credibility, refers to the extent to which the audience perceives the sender to have expertise and trustworthiness. Highly credible sources produce greater attitude and behavioral change in response to a communication. They may also enhance the effectiveness of fear appeals and lower the counterarguments of audiences. However, for audiences already favorable to a topic/product, sources of only moderate credibility may actually be more effective.

The second source characteristic is physical attractiveness. Physically attractive communicators are generally more successful than unattractive sources, with this caveat: "physically attractive" should not be equated with "sexually suggestive." In some instances the use of sexually suggestive ads can be counterproductive.

Likability, the third major source characteristic, refers to the extent to which the source creates positive or negative feelings in the audience. Since research findings on the persuasive impact of likable versus unlikable sources are mixed, no firm conclusions can be drawn on the impact of this characteristic at this time.

Message characteristics are another important dimension of the communications process. Messages have differential impacts depending on their content and their structure. One content factor that strongly influences comprehension is the complexity of the message. Other content factors are: whether conclusions are drawn, whether comparative messages are provided, whether the messages are one-sided or two-sided, whether fear appeals or humorous appeals are used, whether concrete or abstract information is included in the message, and whether a drama or lecture format is used. When considering message structure, managers should focus on whether consumers are more likely to be influenced by primacy or recency effects and on the amount of repetition required to influence the consumer.

advertising wearout
channels
cognitive responses
communication
communications model
comparative message
direct comparative
   advertisements
drama
drawing conclusions

fear appeal
humor in messages
indirect comparative
   advertisements
lecture
matchup hypothesis
message complexity
message construction
message content
message structure

one-sided message
primacy effect
recency effect
repetition effects
sign
source
source characteristics
source credibility
source expertise
source likability

source physical
   attractiveness
source trustworthiness
transformational advertising
two-factor theory
two-sided message
vivid messages

REVIEW QUESTIONS

1. Draw the communications model presented in the text. Briefly discuss each of the model's components.

2. Identify six of the different methods for varying message content presented in the text.

3. What are the reasons for and against using comparative advertisements?

4. When should a communicator consider using a two-sided message? A one-sided message?

5. What are the elements a message needs to have to be an effective fear appeal?

6. Identify the advantages and disadvantages of using humor in messages.

7. What are three factors that tend to make messages more vivid?

8. Identify a theoretical explanation for the occurrence of advertising wearout.

9. What are the basic source characteristics identified in the text?

10. What are the components of source credibility?

11. What are the benefits of using a highly credible source?

12. What are the benefits and liabilities of using sexually explicit ads?

13. What are the differential communications effects of lectures and dramas?

14. What is transformational advertising?

DISCUSSION QUESTIONS

1. Briefly describe a television, a print, and a billboard advertisement and, using the communications model, discuss the source characteristics and message techniques used in each ad.

2. Identify one excellent and one poor example of television ads that use celebrity endorsers. Discuss the factors that influence the effectiveness of the ads.

3. Write a television ad for your university. Create two versions—a lecture format and a drama format.

4. You are the account executive for an advertising firm working on a comparative advertising campaign for the Ford Mustang. The Mustang's major competitors are other so-called pony cars, such as the Camaro, Firebird, Eclipse, and Prelude. Sketch out a print advertisement that uses a comparative ad format. What things should you consider in developing the ad?

5. Identify three brands or types of products or services that you believe should use one-sided messages and three brands or types of products or services that you believe should use two-sided messages in their advertising. Explain your answers.

6. Go through magazines and find a print ad that uses a fear appeal. Criticize the ad based upon the criteria identified in this chapter as necessary for the creation of good fear appeals.

7. While you are watching television, identify a commercial that uses humor. Discuss the effectiveness of the advertisement. What do you think were the goals of the ad's sponsors?

8. Write copy that uses highly concrete words and imagery for a print ad for a product of your choice.

9. In the mid-1990s tobacco company ads tended to portray individuals who looked very young. Find a number of print ads for cigarettes and assess how old the models appear to be today. What are the public policy implications of your findings?

1. Information for the introductory case was found in "E.F. Hutton's Spokesman Idea a 'Cos' Celebre," *Advertising Age*, April 21, 1986, pp. 1, 124.

2. Scott A. Hawkins and Stephen J. Hoch, "Low Involvement Learning: Memory Without Evaluation," *Journal of Consumer Research*, (September 1992), pp. 212–226.

3. Bradley Johnson, "Lexus Tries E-Mail for Auto Intro," *Advertising Age*, October 7, 1996, p. 4.

4. Wendy Bounds and Matt Murray, "Card Makers Try New Ways to Greet a Paperless World," *The Wall Street Journal*, March 19, 1996, p. B1.

5. G. Douglas Olsen, "Creating the Contrast: The Influence of Silence and Background Music on Recall and Attribute Importance," *Journal of Advertising*, Vol. 24 (Winter 1995), pp. 29–44.

6. John Kifner, "What's A-O.K. in the U.S.A. Is Lewd and Worthless Beyond," *The New York Times*, August 18, 1996, p. E7.

7. Debra Aho Williamson, "Web Ad Spending at $66.7 Mil in 1st Half," *Advertising Age*, September 2, 1996, pp. 1, 35.

8. Alix Freedman, "Marriages Between Celebrity Spokesmen and Their Firms Can Be Risky Ventures," *The Wall Street Journal*, January 22, 1988, p. 17.

9. C. I. Hovland and I. L. Janis, *Personality and Persuasibility* (New Haven, CT: Yale University Press, 1959).

10. Terence Shimp, "Methods of Commercial Presentation Employed by National Television Advertisers," *Journal of Advertising*, Vol. 5 (Fall 1976), pp. 30–36.

11. Jeff Jensen, "Woods Hits Golf Jackpot," *Advertising Age*, September 2, 1996, p. 6.

12. Elizabeth J. Wilson and Daniel L. Sherrell, "Source Effects in Communication and Persuasion Research: A Meta-Analysis of Effect Size," *Journal of the Academy of Marketing Science*, Vol. 21, no. 2 (Spring 1993), pp. 101–112.

13. Not all researchers define trust in the manner described here. Some define trust as including within its bounds expertise. That is, they define trust in the same manner as we have defined credibility in this chapter. For an example, see Christine Moorman, Rohit Deshpande, and Gerald Zaltman, "Factors Affecting Trust in Market Research Relationships," *Journal of Marketing*, Vol. 57 (January 1993), pp. 81–101.

14. Josh Wiener and John C. Mowen, "The Impact of Product Recalls on Consumer Perceptions," *Mobius: The Journal of the Society of Consumer Affairs Professionals in Business*, Spring 1985, pp. 18–21.

15. David J. Moore, John C. Mowen, and Richard Reardon, "Multiple Sources in Advertising Appeals: When Product Endorsers Are Paid by the Advertising Sponsor," *Journal of the Academy of Marketing Science*, Vol. 22 (1994), pp. 234–243.

16. For an excellent review of the material on source credibility, see Brian Sternthal, Lynn Phillips, and Ruby Dholakia, "The Persuasive Effect of Source Credibility: A Situational Analysis," *Public Opinion Quarterly*, Vol. 42 (Fall 1978), pp. 285–314.

17. Peter Wright, "Cognitive Processes Mediating Acceptance of Advertising," *Journal of Marketing Research*, Vol. 10 (February 1973), pp. 53–62.

18. Christine Moorman, Rohit Deshpande, and Gerald Zalt-man, "Factors Affecting Trust in Market Research Relationships," *Journal of Marketing*, Vol. 57 (January 1993), pp. 81–101.

19. Shelley Chaiken, "Communicator Physical Attractiveness and Persuasion," *Journal of Personality and Social Psychology*, Vol. 37 (August 1979), pp. 1387–97.

20. Karen Dion, E. Berscheid, and E. Walster, "What Is Beautiful Is Good," *Journal of Personality and Social Psychology*, Vol. 24 (December 1972), pp. 285–290.

21. Kathleen Debevec and Jerome Kernan, "More Evidence on the Effects of Presenter's Physical Attractiveness: Some Cognitive, Affective, and Behavioral Consequences," in *Advances in Consumer Research*, Vol. 11, Thomas Kinnear, ed. (Provo, UT: Association for Consumer Research, 1984), pp. 127–132. For additional information on the impact of attractiveness, see Paul Speck, David Schumann, and Craig Thompson, "Celebrity Endorsements—Scripts, Schema and Roles: Theoretical Framework and Preliminary Tests," in *Advances in Consumer Research*, Vol. 15, Michael Houston, ed. (Provo, UT: Association for Consumer Research, 1988), pp. 69–76.

22. Michael Baker and Gilbert Churchill, "The Impact of Physically Attractive Models on Advertising Evaluations," *Journal of Marketing Research*, Vol. 14 (November 1977), pp. 538–555.

23. Michael B. Mazis, Debra Jones Ringold, Elgin S. Perry, and Daniel W. Denman, "Perceived Age and Attractiveness of Models in Cigarette Advertisements," *Journal of Marketing*, January 1992, pp. 22–37.

24. Mary C. Martin and Patricia F. Kennedy, "Advertising and Social Comparison: Consequences for Female Preadolescents and

Adolescents," *Psychology and Marketing*, Vol. 10 (November/December 1993), pp. 513–530.

25. Marshal Richins, "Social Comparison and the Idealized Images of Advertising," *Journal of Consumer Research*, Vol. 18 (June 1991), pp. 71–83.

26. Judy Kuriansky, "Sex Simmers, Still Sells," *Advertising Age*, Spring 1995, p. 49.

27. Pat Sloan, "Underwear Ads Caught in Bind Over Sex Appeal," *Advertising Age*, July 8, 1996, p. 27.

28. Juliana Koranteng and Richard Bruner, "Sexy Bras Drawing Protests," *Advertising Age International*, July 1996, p. 16.

29. M. Steadman, "How Sexy Illustrations Affect Brand Recall," *Journal of Advertising Research*, Vol. 9 (March 1969), pp. 15–19. Also see Robert Chestnut, Charles LaChance, and Amy Lubitz, "The Decorative Female Model: Sexual Stimuli and the Recognition of Advertisements," *Journal of Advertising*, Vol. 6 (Fall 1977), pp. 11–14.

30. Penny M. Simpson, Steve Horton, and Gene Brown, "Male Nudity in Advertisements: A Modified Replication and Extension of Gender and Product Effects," *Journal of Academy of Marketing Science*, Vol. 24 (Summer 1996), pp. 257–262.

31. Stephen M. Smith, Curtis P. Haugtvedt, John M. Jadrich, and Mark R. Anton, "Understanding Responses to Sex Appeals in Advertising: An Individual Difference Approach," *Advances in Consumer Research*, Vol. 22, Frank R. Kardes and Mita Sujan, eds. (Provo, UT: Association for Consumer Research, 1995), pp. 735–739.

32. Jean-Charles Chebat, Michael Laroche, Daisy Baddoura, and Pierre Filiatrault, "Effects of Source Likability on Attitude Change Through Message Repetition," in *Advances in Consumer Research*, Vol. 20, Leigh McAlister and Michael L. Rothschild, eds. (Provo, UT: Association for Consumer Research, 1993), pp. 353–358.

33. Michael Schudson, *Advertising, the Uneasy Persuasion* (New York: Basic Books, 1984), p. 212.

34. Grant McCracken, "Who Is the Celebrity Endorser? Cultural Foundations of the Endorsement Process," *Journal of Consumer Research*, Vol. 16 (December 1989), pp. 310–321.

35. Lynn Langmeyer and Mary Walker, "A First Step to Identify the Meaning in Celebrity Endorsers," in *Advances in Consumer Research*, Vol. 18, Rebecca Holman and Michael Solomon, eds. (Provo, UT: Association for Consumer Research, 1991), pp. 364–371.

36. David Ogilvy, *Ogilvy on Advertising* (New York: Vintage Books, 1983).

37. Jagdish Agrawal and Wagner A. Kamakura, "The Economic Worth of Celebrity Endorsers: An Event Study Analysis," *Journal of Marketing*, Vol. 59 (July 1995), pp. 56–62.

38. Edward F. McQuarrie and David Glen Mick, "Figures of Rhetoric in Advertising Language," *The Journal of Consumer Research*, Vol. 22 (March 1996), pp. 424–438.

39. Ibid.

40. Alice Eagly, "The Comprehensibility of Persuasive Arguments as a Determinant of Opinion Change," *Journal of Personality and Social Psychology*, Vol. 29 (1974), pp. 758–773.

41. Kim Cleland, "Spring Sense Wins Credit for Carrier's Growth Spurt," *Advertising Age*, September 9, 1996, pp. 3, 64.

42. Bertram Raven and Jeffrey Rubin, *Social Psychology* (New York: John Wiley, 1983).

43. Alan G. Sawyer and Daniel J. Howard, "Effects of Omitting Conclusions in Advertisements to Involved and Uninvolved Audiences," *Journal of Marketing Research*, Vol. 28 (November 1991), pp. 467–474.

44. V. Kanti Prasad, "Communications Effectiveness of Comparative Advertising: A Laboratory Analysis," *Journal of Marketing Research*, Vol. 13 (May 1976), pp. 128–137.

45. Gerald Gorn and Charles Weinberg, "The Impact of Comparative Advertising on Perception and Attitude: Some Positive Findings," *Journal of Consumer Research*, Vol. 11 (September 1984), pp. 719–727.

46. William Wilkie and Paul Farris, "Comparison Advertising: Problems and Potential," *Journal of Marketing*, Vol. 39 (November 1975), pp. 7–15.

47. "Creating a Mass Market for Wine," *Business Week*, March 15, 1982, pp. 108–118.

48. Martin Du Bois and Tara Parker-Pope, "Philip Morris Campaign Stirs Uproar in Europe," *The Wall Street Journal*, July 1, 1996, pp. B1, B6.

49. Cornelia Droge and Rene Darmon, "Associative Positioning Strategies Through Comparative Advertising: Attribute versus Overall Similarity Approaches," *Journal of Marketing Research*, Vol. 24 (November 1987), pp. 377–388.

50. For a more detailed look at comparative ads, see Cornelia Pechmann and S. Ratneshwar, "The Use of Comparative Advertising for Brand Positioning: Association versus Differentiation," *Journal of Consumer Research*, Vol. 18 (September 1991), pp. 145–160.

51. Cornelia Pechmann and David W. Stewart, "The Effects of Comparative Advertising on Attention, Memory, and Purchase

Intentions," *Journal of Consumer Research*, Vol. 17 (September 1990), pp. 180–191.

52. Gorn and Weinberg, "The Impact of Comparative Advertising."

53. This last conclusion was recently challenged in the following research: Paul W. Miniard, Michael J. Barone, Randall L. Rose, and Kenneth C. Manning, "A Re-examination of the Relative Persuasiveness of Comparative and Noncomparative Advertising," *Advances in Consumer Research*, Chris T. Allen and Deborah Roedder John, eds. (Provo, UT: Association for Consumer Research, 1994), pp. 299–303.

54. See, for example, studies by Russell Jones and Jack Brehm, "Persuasiveness of One- and Two-Sided Communications as a Function of Awareness: There Are Two Sides," *Journal of Experimental Social Psychology*, Vol. 6 (1970), pp. 47–56; Alan G. Sawyer, "The Effects of Repetition of Refutational and Supportive Advertising Appeals," *Journal of Marketing Research*, Vol. 10 (February 1973), pp. 23–33; and Michael Kamins and Henry Assael, "Two-Sided versus One-Sided Appeals: A Cognitive Perspective on Argumentation, Source Derogation on Argumentation and the Effect of Disconfirming Trial on Belief Change," *Journal of Marketing Research*, Vol. 24 (February 1987), pp. 29–39.

55. G. C. Chu, "Prior Familiarity, Perceived Bias, and One-Sided versus Two-Sided Communications," *Journal of Experimental Social Psychology*, Vol. 3 (1967), pp. 243–254. Also see Cornelia Pechmann, "How Do Consumer Inferences Moderate the Effectiveness of Two-Sided Messages?" *Advances in Consumer Research*, Vol. 17, Marvin E. Goldberg, Gerald Gorn, and Richard Pollay, eds. (Provo, UT: Association for Consumer Research, 1990), pp. 337–341.

56. Raven and Rubin, *Social Psychology*.

57. Manoj Hastak and Jong-Won Park, "Mediators of Message Sidedness Effects on Cognitive Structure for Involved and Uninvolved Audiences," in *Advances in Consumer Research*, Vol. 17, Marvin E. Goldberg, Gerald Gorn, and Richard Pollay, eds. (Provo, UT: Association for Consumer Research, 1990), pp. 337–341.

58. John F. Tanner, Jr., James B. Hunt, and David R. Eppright, "The Protection Motivation Model: A Normative Model of Fear Appeals," *Journal of Marketing*, July 1991, pp. 329–336.

59. Ibid.

60. Punam Anand Keller and Lauren Goldberg Block, "Increasing the Persuasiveness of Fear Appeals: The Effect of Arousal and Elaboration," *The Journal of Consumer Research*, Vol. 22 (March 1996), pp. 448–459.

61. Different studies have obtained divergent estimates of the percentage of commercials using humor. The 24.9 percent estimate came from Marc G. Weinberger and Harlan E. Spotts, "Humor in U.S. versus U.K. TV Advertising," *Journal of Advertising*, Vol. 18 (1989), pp. 39–44. Slightly lower estimates (i.e., 16 percent) were obtained by Dana L. Alden, Wayne D. Hoyer, and Chol Lee, "Identifying Global and Culture-Specific Dimensions of Humor in Advertising: A Multinational Analysis," *Journal of Marketing*, Vol. 57 (April 1993), pp. 64–75. Also see Brian Sternthal and C. Samuel Craig, "Humor in Advertising," *Journal of Marketing*, Vol. 37 (October 1973), pp. 12–18.

One critical issue is: What makes something humorous?

This question is beyond the scope of this textbook, but for a related discussion, see the Alden, Hoyer, and Lee article cited in this reference. Also see Edward F. McQuarrie and David Glen Mick, "On Resonance: A Critical Pluralistic Inquiry into Advertising Rhetoric," *Journal of Consumer Research*, Vol. 19 (September 1992), pp. 180–197.

62. Alden, Hoyer, and Lee, "Identifying Global and Culture-Specific Dimensions of Humor."

63. Joan Cantor and Pat Venus, "The Effects of Humor on the Recall of a Radio Advertisement," *Journal of Broadcasting*, Winter 1980, p. 14.

64. John H. Murphy, Isabella Cunningham, and Gary Wilcox, "The Impact of Program Environment on Recall of Humorous Television Commercials," *Journal of Advertising*, Vol. 8 (Spring 1979), pp. 17–21.

65. Tara Parker-Pope, "British Budweiser Ads Rankle American Indians," *The Wall Street Journal*, July 16, 1996, pp. B1, B5.

66. H. Bruce Lammers, "Humor and Cognitive Responses to Advertising Stimuli: A Trade Consolidation Approach," *Journal of Business Research*, Vol. 11 (June 1983), p. 182.

67. Sternthal and Craig, "Humor in Advertising." Also see Thomas J. Madden and Marc Weinberger, "The Effects of Humor on Attention in Magazine Advertising," *Journal of Advertising*, Vol. 11 (March 1982), p. 1.

68. Cliff Scott, David M. Klein, and Jennings Bryant, "Consumer Responses to Humor in Advertising: A Series of Field Studies Using Behavioral Observation," *Journal of Consumer Research*, Vol. 16 (March 1990), pp. 498–501.

69. Young Zhang and George M. Zinkhan, "Humor in Advertising: The Effects of Repetition

and Social Setting," in *Advances in Consumer Research*, Vol. 18, Rebecca Holman and Michael Solomon, eds. (Provo, UT: Association for Consumer Research, 1991), pp. 813–818.

70. P. Kelly and Paul J. Solomon, "Humor in Television Advertising," *Journal of Advertising*, Vol. 4 (Summer 1975), pp. 33–35.

71. Marc G. Weinberger and Charles S. Gulas, "The Impact of Humor in Advertising: A Review," *Journal of Advertising*, Vol. 21 (December 1992), pp. 35–59.

72. Amitava Chattopadhyay and Kunal Basu, "Humor in Advertising: The Moderating Role of Prior Brand Evaluation," *Journal of Marketing Research*, Vol. 27 (November 1990), pp. 466–476. For another recent study on humor in advertising, see Stephen M. Smith, "Does Humor in Advertising Enhance Systematic Processing?" in *Advances in Consumer Research*, Vol. 20, Leigh McAlister and Michael L. Rothschild, eds. (Provo, UT: Association for Consumer Research, 1993), pp. 155–158. This author found evidence that humor in an ad tends to lead to more peripheral processing, so that the strength of ad claims are not evaluated as closely as they are for more serious ads. Thus a more humorous ad positively impacted ratings only when weak claims were employed.

73. This section relies heavily on material found in Richard Nisbett and Lee Ross, *Human Inference: Strategies and Shortcomings of Social Judgment* (Englewood Cliffs, NJ: Prentice Hall, 1980).

74. William Wells, "Lectures and Dramas," presentation at Association of Consumer Research, Fall 1987.

75. Christopher Puto and William Wells, "Informational and Transformational Advertising: The Differential Effects of

Time," in *Advances in Consumer Research*, Vol. 11, Thomas Kinnear, ed. (Provo, UT: Association for Consumer Research, 1984), pp. 638–643.

76. For a model of transformational advertising, see Vanitha Swaminathan, George M. Zinkhan, and Srinivas K. Reddy, "The Evolution and Antecedents of Transformational Advertising: A Conceptual Model," *Advances in Consumer Research*, Vol. 23, Kim P. Corfman and John G. Lynch, Jr., eds. (Provo, UT: Association for Consumer Research, 1996), pp. 49–55.

77. Gregory W. Boller, "The Vicissitudes of Product Experience: 'Songs of Our Consuming Selves' in Drama Ads," in *Advances in Consumer Research*, Vol. 17, Marvin E. Goldberg, Gerald Gorn, and Richard Pollay, eds. (Provo, UT: Association for Consumer Research, 1990), pp. 321–326.

78. John Deighton, Daniel Romer, and Josh McQueen, "Using Drama to Persuade," *Journal of Consumer Research*, Vol. 16 (December 1989), pp. 335–343.

79. Surendra N. Singh and Catherine A. Cole, "The Effects of Length, Content, and Repetition on Television Commercial Effectiveness," *Journal of Marketing Research*, Vol. 30 (February 1993), pp. 91–104.

80. David Glen Mick and Claus Buhl, "A Meaning-Based Model of Advertising Experiences," *Journal of Consumer Research*, Vol. 19 (December 1992), pp. 317–338.

81. Curtis P. Haugtvedt and Duane T. Wegener, "Message Order Effects in Persuasion: An Attitude Strength Perspective," *Journal of Consumer Research*, Vol. 21 (June 1994), pp. 205–218.

82. H. Rao Unnava, Robert E. Burnkrant, and Sunil Erevelles,

"Effects of Presentation Order and Communication Modality on Recall and Attitude," *Journal of Consumer Research*, Vol. 21 (December 1994), pp. 481–490.

83. Herbert Krugman, "Why Three Exposures May Be Enough," *Journal of Advertising Research*, Vol. 12 (December 1972), pp. 11–14.

84. George E. Belch, "The Effects of Television Commercial Repetition on Cognitive Response and Message Acceptance," *The Journal of Consumer Research*, Vol. 9 (June 1982), pp. 56–65.

85. Marian Burke and Julie Edell, "Ad Reactions over Time: Capturing Changes in the Real World," *Journal of Consumer Research*, Vol. 13 (June 1986), pp. 114–118.

86. See the following study for research that supports this conclusion: Dena Cox and Anthony Cox, "What Does Familiarity Breed? Complexity as a Moderator of Repetition Effects in Advertising Evaluation," *Journal of Consumer Research*, Vol. 15 (June 1988), pp. 111–116. Also see Arno Rethans, John Swasy, and Lawrence Marks, "Effects of Television Commercial Repetition, Receiver Knowledge, and Commercial Length: A Test of the Two-Factor Model," *Journal of Marketing Research*, Vol. 23 (February 1986), pp. 50–61.

87. L. McCullough and Thomas Ostrom, "Repetition of Highly Similar Messages and Attitude Change," *Journal of Applied Psychology*, Vol. 59 (June 1974), pp. 395–397.

88. D. E. Berlyne, "Novelty, Complexity, and Hedonic Value," *Perception and Psychophysics*, Vol. 8 (November 1970), pp. 279–286.

89. The encoding variability hypothesis also applies to the effects of repetition. See H. Rao Unnava and Robert E.

Burnkrant, "Effects of Repeating Varied Ad Executions on Brand Name Memory," *Journal of Marketing Research*, Vol. 28 (November 1991), pp. 406–416. Also see Robert Burnkrant and Hanumantha Unnava, "Effect of Variation in Message Execution on the Learning of Repeated Brand Information," in *Advances in Consumer Research*, Vol. 14, Melanie Wallendorf and Paul Anderson, eds. (Provo, UT: Association for Consumer Research, 1987), pp. 173–176.

90. Curtis P. Haugtvedt, David W. Schumann, Wendy L. Schneier, and Wendy L. Warren, "Advertising Repetition and Variation Strategies: Implications for Understanding Attitude Strength," *Journal of Consumer Research*, Vol. 21 (June 1994), pp. 176–189.

91. Giles D'Souza and Ram C. Rao, "Can Repeating an Advertisement More Frequently Affect Brand Preference in a Mature Market?," *Journal of Marketing*, Vol. 59 (April 1995), pp. 32–42.

HIV STRIKES "MAGIC"

The unexpected announcement shocked the world: "Magic" Johnson revealed he was HIV positive. Earlier in 1991 *The Wall Street Journal* had called him the "perfect advertising spokesman." In fact, Johnson ranked behind only Bo Jackson, Michael Jordan, and Tommy Lasorda as a persuasive sports figure. He had endorsed products for such firms as Nestlé, Converse, Nintendo, Pepsi-Cola, Spalding Sports, and Kentucky Fried Chicken. How would these companies, who paid Magic about $12 million a year for his endorsements, react to his condition?

Initially, the companies, like the world at large, were stunned. A spokesperson for Pepsi said, "There's no road map to tell us where to go. This is all very new and happened very suddenly. No decisions have been made, nor should they be." A manager at Spalding said that although the company was shocked and dismayed, "Magic Johnson has been a member of the Spalding team since he came into the NBA. He's a very important part of our family, and we will support him and his commitment to HIV research."[1]

Although the companies with whom he had contracts cautiously supported Johnson, industry analysts were less sanguine about the effects of his revelation. One suggested that he could be used in public relations capacities to make both him and the companies he was associated with look good. Most observers, however, thought there was a serious danger in associating a brand with AIDS. One analyst commented, "Magic deserved every bit of the tribute he's getting, but the initial coverage is going to be upbeat and positive, and then the reality is going to set in. This is not the kind of thing people want to see in advertising. Advertising is not about grim realities. Advertising is fantasy, and AIDS is not fantasy."[2]

One advertising executive said of the situation, "It's not so cut-and-dried with him. It's not like when Bruce Willis announced he would be going in for alcohol rehab, and they pulled all of the [Seagram's] ads immediately." Another analyst sized up the situation this way: "There is a potential risk, and with anyone else they might not be sure, but Johnson has a unique status. If suddenly Converse or KFC yanked his contract, there would be backlash against the brand. But companies will have to use 'soft sell' on the brand side because the public is going to be sensitive to a brand exploiting this."[3]

When attention shifted from Magic Johnson's endorsement of products to his efforts to educate the public about AIDS, the view of his effectiveness took a 180-degree turn. One leader in the movement to fight AIDS among African-Americans said, "Even though this is a personal tragedy, there is an opportunity to turn this into something positive. I think it will change the way people not only perceive the disease and AIDS, but how they relate to people with HIV because they view him as everyman. They think that if he can get it, maybe I can too. Things will definitely change now that Magic Johnson has spoken out."[4]

Between 1991 and 1997 Magic's endorsement contracts moved in tandem with his on-again-off-again returns to basketball. Things picked up when he was on the U.S. Basketball team in the 1992 Olympics. Then, when he rejoined the Lakers in the 1992–1993 season, endorsements came his way once again. Unfortunately, player complaints forced Magic to retire again in 1993. However, he returned to basketball yet again in February 1996, only to retire once more at the completion of the season. During this time period he signed new endorsement contracts.[5]

It should be noted that payments for endorsements are a small part of Magic Johnson's earnings. Most recently, in partnership with Sony Theatres, he has been opening large multiscreen movie theaters in major cities across the United States.

Questions

1. Define the problem faced by firms that had endorsement contracts with Magic Johnson. Define the problem faced by AIDS activists.
2. What consumer behavior concepts from the chapter apply to this case?
3. What are the managerial implications of those consumer behavior concepts in this case?

References

1. Gary Levin, "Johnson Plans for Future Ads," *Advertising Age*, November 18, 1991, p. 47.
2. "HIV Revelation Tests Magic's Ad Appeal," *Advertising Age*, November 11, 1991, p. 2.
3. Ibid.
4. Cyndee Miller, "Advertisers Forced to Rethink 'Magic' As Their Spokesman," *Marketing News*, December 9, 1991, pp. 1, 2.
5. Denise Gellene, "Will Magic Make a Comeback to Product Pitchman?" *Los Angeles Times*, February 2, 1996, p. D1.

11

CONSUMER DECISION PROCESSES I: PROBLEM RECOGNITION AND SEARCH

INTRODUCTORY CASE

The Rise and Fall of Beer Sales

Between 1982 and 1989 the sales of draft beer in kegs and on tap declined steadily. As one marketing expert explained, "Americans had forgotten to drink draft." Then, in 1990, sales of draft beer suddenly turned around. They grew by 2.7 percent that year, and the following year they were holding their own while sales of canned and bottled beers dropped by over 4 percent. What caused this sudden turnaround in draft beer sales at a time when the consumption of alcoholic beverages in general was falling?[1]

A number of explanations were offered by marketing pundits. One is that draft beer simply tastes better than canned or bottled beer. It is fresher, and because it is not pasteurized, it lacks that slightly cooked taste you get from canned and bottled beers. As one expert said, "Keg beer is in every instance better than bottled beer." The difference in taste may have been accentuated by the advertising campaign for Miller Genuine Draft beer. By heavily advertising its draft bottled beer, Miller alerted consumers to the virtues of draft beer in general.

Pricing issues may also have played a role. Keg beer usually costs less per serving

for taverns and bars, so they frequently give customers discounts on draft. The recession of the early 1990s made consumers more price conscious and willing to shift their buying patterns. In addition, there was a revulsion against the conspicuous consumption of the 1980s. Showing off by buying products for their expensive labels became less socially acceptable in the early 1990s. Sipping draft beer from a glass became the appropriate behavior.

The surge in sales of draft beer, however, proved to be short-lived. In 1994 gallons of draft beer sold decreased by 10.2 percent.[2] One major cause was the 10.8 percent decline in sales of Miller Genuine Draft. Some ad execs speculated that Genuine Draft faltered in the market because Miller dramatically reduced its advertising for the brand as it rolled out a line of specialty beers. A second cause of the decline in draft beer sales was a surge in interest in "specialty" beers produced by microbrewerys. This market segment increased sales by almost 50 percent in 1994.

Could marketing pundits identify a cause for the surge in sales of specialty beers served in brew pubs (i.e., restaurants that make their own beer)? As said by the president of Rock Bottom Brewery in Denver, Colorado, "If people are going to drink less, they want better quality. You can look at corollaries in wine and coffee."[3] A similar view was expressed by a restaurant owner in Atlanta. He suggested that Americans were becoming more selective in their tastes. "You know," he said, "wine carries so much snobbery. We're not really a nation of wine drinkers. . . . Americans are already beer drinkers, so it's easy to have people step up to a higher level."[4]

By 1996 over 500 brew pubs had sprouted up across the United States. Oregon alone had 66 microbreweries within its borders.[5] The Atlanta restaurant owner was bullish on brew pubs, claiming that they "are the restaurants of the future."

Now here is the managerial question: If you were an investor, would you place a significant portion of your investment dollars in microbreweries or specialty beers?

INTRODUCTION

What makes a consumer decide to purchase a specialty beer as opposed to a draft beer or a mainline brand such as Bud? What factors in the decision process cause someone to purchase one brand of car rather than another? These are the kinds of questions pursued by the traditional consumer behavior area of study known as *consumer decision making*. Consumer decision making encompasses all the processes consumers go through in recognizing problems, searching for solutions, evaluating alternatives, and choosing among purchase options.

In this and the next two chapters we discuss the decision-making processes that consumers go through as they acquire, consume, and use products, services, and ideas. Five decision-making stages have been identified: problem recognition, search, alternative evaluation, choice, and postacquisition evaluation. The introductory case can serve to illustrate how consumers move through these stages. For example, what is it that causes a customer to recognize a problem that having a beer will solve? How do customers search through all the brands of beer to decide which one to consume? How do they evaluate and compare brands and ultimately choose which beer to buy? This chapter will answer these questions. (By the way, the nearby consumer behavior factoid will tell you how many brands of beer can be found in the United States.)

We have three major purposes in this chapter. First, we develop a generic flowchart of the consumer decision process and briefly describe each of the decision-making stages. Second, we discuss decision making from the three research perspectives on consumer behavior—the decision-making, the experiential, and the behavioral influence perspectives. Our goal in this section is to give you traditional views as well as more recent views of decision making. Finally, we explore in detail the first two components of the decision-making process—problem recognition and search for information.

A GENERIC FLOWCHART OF THE CONSUMER DECISION PROCESS

At its most complex, **consumer decision making** consists of a series of five stages: problem recognition, search, alternative evaluation, choice, and postacquisition evaluation. (The stages are diagrammed in Figure 11-1.) In the problem recognition stage, consumers recognize that they have a need for something. One goal of advertising, of course, is to cause consumers to recognize a problem. For example, the ad shown in Figure 11-2 on page 350 seeks to activate recognition of a water pollution problem.

If it is sufficiently strong, the need may motivate the person to enter the second stage of the consumer decision-making process: the search for information. The search for information can be either extensive or limited, depending on the involvement level of the consumer. In the third stage consumers evaluate the alternatives they have identified for solving their problem. *Alternative evaluation* is synonymous with the *formation of attitudes regarding the alternatives*, so material from Chapter 8 on consumer beliefs, attitudes, and behaviors is applicable to the evaluation stage.

Choice is the fourth stage of the process. Here consumers decide which alternative action to select (e.g., which brand to choose, whether to spend or save, or from which store to purchase the product). Finally, in the postacquisition stage consumers consume and use the product or service they have acquired. They also evaluate the outcomes of the consequences of their behavior and engage in the ultimate disposal of the waste resulting from the purchase.[6]

This generic decision-making process applies to businesses and other organizations as well as to individual consumers. For example, one researcher sent out questionnaires to over 2,000 purchasing managers at firms of varying sizes.[7] She asked the managers to describe their last purchase for their firm on a series of dimensions, including: search for information, use of analysis techniques, relation to the firm's long-run strategy, and degree

Figure 11-1

A generic flowchart of the consumer decision process.

Figure 11-2
This ad seeks to activate recognition of a water pollution problem.

the purchase was subject to written control procedures. These dimensions closely correspond to the generic decision process. The search-for-information stage is common to both processes. The use of analysis techniques and the relation to the firm's long-run strategy correspond to the alternative-evaluation stage of the generic decision process, while the degree the purchase is subject to written control procedures is similar to the choice stage.

The survey results revealed that purchasing managers employ six general buying approaches: casual; routine, low priority; simple modified rebuy; judgmental new task; complex modified rebuy; and strategic new task. Table 11-1 defines each of these approaches. Note that the buying approaches are arranged in order of importance to the firm. Thus as one moves from a "casual" purchase to a "strategic new task" purchase, the involvement level of the decision maker increases. As we will discuss later, the involvement level of the decision maker has a major impact on which type of decision process is used.

ALTERNATIVE PERSPECTIVES ON CONSUMER DECISION MAKING

From the late eighteenth century through much of the 1970s, researchers viewed people as moving linearly through a decision-making process like that outlined in Figure 11-1. In the late 1970s, however, authors began to question the concept that all consumer purchases result from a careful analytical process. Some suggested that in many instances consumers do not engage in any decision making at all prior to making a purchase. As stated in one article, "We conclude that for many purchases a decision process never occurs, not even on the first purchase."[8] In addition, researchers recognized that many consumer behaviors do not involve the purchase of goods, such as automobiles and toothpaste. People also buy experiences in the form of such services as vacations, rock concerts, theater tickets, parachuting, movies, art, novels, opera, casinos, and houses of ill repute.[9] Moreover, the purchase of some products, like specialty beers, is strongly influenced by the experience and the feelings the product is expected to provide.

Given the limitations of the traditional consumer decision process, researchers have proposed alternative decision-making models that place different emphases on each of the stages identified in the generic flowchart. We will explore three of these models: the traditional decision-making perspective, the experiential perspective, and the behavioral influence perspective. Table 11-2 outlines the differences in these three approaches.

The Decision-Making Perspective

The **decision-making perspective** emphasizes the rational, information-processing approach to consumer purchase behavior. It is closely related to the high-involvement hierarchy-of-effects approach to attitude formation we discussed in Chapter 8. According to this approach, consumers move through the stages of the decision process in a linear fashion, with high levels of information processing occurring at each stage.

In the 1970s, however, researchers realized that consumers do not always go through an extended decision process before they buy. Herbert Krugman was perhaps the first author to suggest that the decision process differs for high- and low-involvement purchases.[10]

Three Perspectives on Decision Making

I. Traditional Decision-Making Perspective

A. *High-Involvement Decisions*

| Problem recognition | →Extensive search | →Extended alternative evaluation | →Complex choice | →Acquisition evaluation |

B. *Low-Involvement Decisions*

| Problem recognition | →Limited search | →Minimal alternative evaluation | →Simple choice processes | →Acquisition evaluation |

II. Experiential Perspective

| Problem recognition (affect driven) | →Search for affect-based solutions | →Alternative evaluation (comparison of affect) | →Choice (affect-based) | →Acquisition evaluation |

III. Behavioral Influence Perspective

| Problem recognition (results from discriminative stimulus) | →Search (learned response) | →Choice (behavior results from reinforcers) | →Acquisition evaluation (self-perception process) |

TABLE 11-2

He suggested that extended decision making occurs in high-involvement conditions, but limited decision making, and less search behavior, are the rule in low-involvement conditions. Further, because the low-involvement hierarchy of effects is operative when consumers are doing limited decision making, the alternative evaluation stage is largely absent from their decision process. Thus in limited decision making the choice among alternative brands is made in a relatively simple manner, with consumers using simplified decision rules.[11]

In summary, the traditional decision-making perspective evolved into a consideration of two routes to making decisions: the high-involvement and the low-involvement routes. Table 11-2 summarizes the stages in each of these routes.

When assessing a managerial problem from the traditional decision-making perspective, then, researchers ask whether consumers move through a high- or low-involvement decision process. The answer to this question affects advertising, sales-management, and pricing strategies. When consumers engage in high-involvement decision making, it is generally because they perceive the purchase as one with significant risk. One way marketers can reduce this perceived risk is to employ skilled sales personnel. Another way is to create more complex, detailed advertising messages that will satisfy consumers in a high-involvement state.

The promotional strategy used to sell products purchased after limited decision making is quite different. Products bought under low-involvement conditions have less risk attached to them. They are frequently low-cost goods that are distributed extensively, and therefore require mass advertising to support them.

Whether target customers engage in limited or extended decision making also influences pricing strategy. For products and services purchased via a limited decision-making process, price may be the single most important consideration. One study found that among consumers who indicated that a purchase was unimportant, 52 percent said price was the determining factor.[12] Often the competition among brands purchased via limited decision processes is fierce, and becoming the low-cost producer may be the key to success in the marketplace.

Table 11-3 summarizes how a firm's marketing-mix strategy is affected by whether its product or service is purchased via a high-involvement or low-involvement decision process.

The Experiential Perspective

In contrast to the decision-making perspective, the **experiential perspective** recognizes consumers as "feelers" as well as thinkers—that is, it assumes people consume many types of products for the sensations, feelings, images, and emotions that these products generate.[13] Of course, the selection of a brand of beer is based predominantly on the feelings and emotions that it produces.

When marketing problems are examined from the experiential perspective, the focus is likely to be on entertainment, the arts, and leisure products rather than on more functional consumer goods. The experiential perspective recognizes that many products carry symbolic meanings for consumers.[14] Flowers, jewelry, perfume, and after-shave lotion, for example, are bought largely for the symbolic meanings they provide. However, products can be purchased for experiential purposes as well. You may buy a certain automobile for the thrill of having your head snapped back as you attack the road. The Pontiac Grand Am GT advertisement shown in Figure 11-3 attempts to influence consumer beliefs about

GRAND AM

THE FUN CHOICE. THE SMART CHOICE.

■ Nothing could be smarter than the safety of its standard airbag. ■ Or the control of its standard anti-lock braking system. ■ Or more thrilling than the kick of its new, available V6. ■ Precisely matched to an agile sport suspension. ■ All for a price thousands less than Accord or Camry.* ■ And all backed by Pontiac Cares' 3-year/36,000-mile no-deductible bumper-to-bumper warranty,† free 24-hour Roadside Assistance and Courtesy Transportation. ■ So visit your Pontiac dealer for a test drive or call 1-800-762-4900 for more information. ■ And discover why Grand Am® is more than the fun choice, it's the smart one, too.

PONTIAC.
WE ARE DRIVING EXCITEMENT

Figure 11-3
Pontiac hopes to influence feeling, as well as beliefs, about driving a Grand Am GT.

performance and price, as well as to depict the exciting experience to be obtained from driving the car.

From an experiential perspective, problem recognition is rooted in the realization that there is a difference between one's actual and one's desired affective state. The search process involves seeking information about the likely affective impact of various alternatives, while the alternative evaluation stage consists of evaluating the various options on the basis of their affective quality. Choice is also based on affective criteria ("Which product will make me feel better?"). Finally, postacquisition evaluation depends upon whether the outcome has met the consumer's emotional expectations.

Besides affect-laden purchases, such as rock concerts and parachuting, three types of purchases can be examined from the experiential perspective: purchases that result from variety seeking, purchases made on impulse, and purchases made out of brand loyalty. Brand loyalty is defined as the degree to which a customer holds a positive attitude toward a brand, has a commitment to it, and intends to continue purchasing it in the future. Because brand loyalty results from postacquisition processes, it will be discussed in Chapter 13. Here we will discuss purchases that result from variety seeking and purchases made on impulse.

Impulse Purchases

An **impulse purchase** is defined as a "buying action undertaken without a problem previously having been consciously recognized or a buying intention formed prior to entering the store."[15] In plain English, impulse buying is a sudden, powerful, persistent, and unplanned urge to buy something immediately, without much regard for the consequences.[16]

Little research has been done on the mechanism responsible for impulse purchases, but it seems likely that such purchases happen when the consumer encounters a product, processes the information about it holistically, and reacts with an extremely strong positive affect.[17] These positive feelings lead to a desire to experience the product or service, which results in a purchase. Impulse purchases are common: various studies have shown that as many as 39 percent of department store purchases and 67 percent of grocery store purchases are unplanned.[18]

Closely related to impulse purchases is **compulsive consumption,** which is defined as "a response to an uncontrollable drive or desire to obtain, use, or experience a feeling, substance, or activity that leads an individual to repetitively engage in a behavior that will ultimately cause harm to the individual and/or others."[19] Researchers have found that consumers who have the compulsive consumption trait more frequently identify with the dysfunctional purchase behavior of others and more often condone the use of a credit card for purchases.[20]

Drug addiction is compulsive consumption. Anorexia and bulimia are also compulsive behaviors. In our view neither the traditional decision-making perspective nor the behavioral influence approach provides a satisfactory explanation of compulsive behavior. Only the experiential perspective is useful for explaining the actions of consumers with compulsive disorders. Here is what one consumer researcher, who had experienced a compulsive disorder herself, had to say on the relationship between compulsions and consumer affect and emotions:

> Addicted consumers appear to have in common an emotional vacancy that they are compelled to fill with *something*. If one substance or behavior is denied to them, they will simply seek out another. What addicts seek most is to escape themselves, their own minds, and their consciousness. They find it very painful to inhibit their own consciousness. Thus virtually any substance or activity that will alter, numb, or erase that consciousness becomes acceptable, if their preferred drug of choice is unavailable. Viewed in this way, it becomes apparent that all possible drugs cannot be removed from the addicted consumer. What must be done, instead, is to repair the emotional hole in the addict's psyche.[21]

Variety-Seeking Purchases

Variety-seeking purchases also fall into the experiential domain. Variety seeking refers to the tendency of consumers to spontaneously buy a new brand of product even though they continue to express satisfaction with their old brand. One explanation of variety seeking is that consumers are trying to reduce their boredom by purchasing a new brand.[22] Recall from Chapter 6 that the theory of optimum stimulation proposes that people need to maintain their appropriate level of stimulation.[23] If that level falls too low or moves too high for them, they will take steps to adjust it. Brand switching is some consumers' method of increasing stimulation by bringing something new into their lives.

Variety-seeking purchases are classified as experiential because they are made to influence feelings. That is, when consumers are bored, they are feeling suboptimal. By purchasing a new brand, they attempt to make themselves feel better.

Approaching Managerial Problems from the Experiential Perspective The traditional methods of marketing research are of little use in the experiential realm. Consider the sport of skydiving. Traditional research methods using questionnaires and/or experiments are inadequate for investigating the decision-making processes that lead to the bizarre behavior of jumping out of a functioning airplane.

In investigating experiential behaviors like skydiving, researchers have borrowed some ethnographic methods from anthropologists. One study of skydivers, for example, used a participant-observer approach.[24] The principal author, Richard Celsi, became an active member of a skydiving club and made over 650 jumps. The second and third authors of the study attended club meetings and observed the jumps from both inside the plane and on the ground. During a 30-month period of investigation, the researchers took copious field notes, conducted 135-plus formal interviews, snapped over 500 photographs, videotaped 50 skydives, and mourned the death of one club member who died parachuting. The team used a triangulation procedure, in which each researcher compared and contrasted his interpretations of the experiences being analyzed with the other researchers' interpretations.

From their ethnographic analysis, the authors concluded people had three motives for skydiving. Foremost was the "normative motive." People take their first plunge in skydiving to become part of a group and to fulfill that group's social expectations. The second motive was hedonic. The authors suggested that the hedonic motive evolves from pure thrill seeking, into pleasure seeking, and ultimately into experiencing "the flow."

The experience of self-efficacy was identified as the third motive for skydiving. As their concerns for safety and survival die down, skydivers begin to focus on the self-confidence and achievement they feel as they learn how to manage risk and exert self-control at the edge. From the perspective of the generic model of decision making, each of these motives—group acceptance, thrill seeking, and self-acceptance—can lead directly to problem recognition, the search for solutions, the evaluation of alternatives, and the eventual choice of skydiving.

The nearby consumer behavior factoid asks a chilling question about this dangerous sport.

The Behavioral Influence Perspective

When approaching problems from the **behavioral influence perspective,** researchers focus on consumers' behaviors and the environmental contingencies that influence those behaviors. Behavioral learning theorists generally avoid discussions of internal states—in fact, many would argue that even a discussion of decision making is inappropriate. Thus

Question: How many people in the United States die parachuting each year?

Answer: About 49—which is 1 out of every 700 participants in the sport.

Source: Richard L. Celsi, Randall L. Rose, and Thomas W. Leigh, "An Exploration of High-Risk Leisure Consumption Through Skydiving," *Journal of Consumer Research*, Vol. 20 (June 1993), pp. 1–23.

Consumer Behavior Factoid

in the introductory case, the focus would be on identifying the reinforcers in the environment that influence beer-drinking behavior. Those reinforcers could be social (the comments of friends), physiological (the taste of the beer), or monetary (sales promotions run to influence consumer demand).

When managers approach a problem from the behavioral influence perspective, they focus on identifying the environmental forces that influence consumers. For example, the physical environment can be used to induce behaviors. As we noted earlier in this text, arranging aisles in a retail store to funnel consumers by products the retailer desires most to sell illustrates how the physical environment can impact consumers' behavior without changing either their beliefs or their feelings.

The use of textures, smells, and lighting can also create an atmosphere that elicits desired responses among consumers. In one field study investigating the effects of lighting on where people sat in a restaurant, the researchers found that patrons tended to sit in the darker areas facing the light. Other researchers have found that as the level of lighting in a room is lowered, people sit closer to each other and talk in lower voices. So if a restaurateur's goal is to create an intimate, quiet atmosphere, low lighting levels should be used.[25]

The mere arrangement of the containers of food products on shelves in a grocery store can affect consumers' buying decisions independently of their beliefs and attitudes about the product alternatives.[26] In most grocery stores managers arrange the containers by brand. In one study the researcher placed respondents in a simulated buying situation in which yogurt containers were arranged either by brands or by flavors. When the containers were arranged by brands, each section would contain one brand (e.g., Dannon) and each of the flavors that brand came in. When the containers were arranged by flavor, there would be a section for vanilla yogurt, another for strawberry, and so on. Within each flavor section different brands would be available. The results revealed that when respondents were asked to buy enough yogurt to last them for six weeks, the shelf arrangement strongly affected their purchase intentions. When the yogurt was arranged by brand, the subjects bought more different flavors of yogurt, but almost exclusively from one brand. When the yogurt was arranged by flavor, the subjects bought more different brands, but fewer different flavors. Thus the mere arrangement of the cartons of yogurt could change the behavior of consumers without altering their beliefs and feelings about flavors and brands.

The Three Perspectives in Summary

The experiential and behavioral influence perspectives are still controversial to some researchers. Indeed, the argument can be made that decision making takes place whenever consumers engage in a behavior. Be that as it may, we have discussed the experiential and behavioral influence perspectives to emphasize the role of affect/feelings and environmental factors in causing certain types of consumer actions. A single-minded focus on belief formation and rational information processing fails to capture the richness of consumer behavior.

The benefits of analyzing managerial problems from each perspective is illustrated by the problems faced by the owner of a restaurant named "Playmakers." He commissioned a consumer behavior analysis of his business because profits were much lower than he had anticipated. The consultant first approached the problem from the decision-making perspective. She examined such factors as the quality of the food, the pricing structure, and the hours of operation. Next she analyzed the restaurant from an experiential perspective. She examined how the decor of the restaurant influenced the feelings and emotions of customers. Finally, she employed the behavioral influence perspective and analyzed the reinforcers and punishers that consumers encountered in the restaurant. In particular, she surveyed patrons on the service and friendliness of employees, two factors that can be strong positive reinforcers or punishers. Based upon the consultant's analysis, the owner made a series of changes. He improved the quality of the food, dramatically improved the atmospherics of his restaurant, and upgraded the training of his waiters and waitresses. Only by analyzing the restaurant from each of the three perspectives on consumer decision making could such a well-rounded set of recommendations have been developed.

As discussed earlier in the chapter, consumers move through a five-stage decision making process. The next two sections discuss the first two of those stages—problem recognition and search.

PROBLEM RECOGNITION

Problem recognition is the discovery of a discrepancy between an actual and a desired state of being. Note that our definition of problem recognition is identical to our definition of a need state in Chapter 6. Thus problem recognition occurs when a need state is felt. Typically, researchers seek to identify consumer problems by analyzing the factors that act to widen the gap between the actual and the desired state. If the consumer's satisfaction with her **actual state** decreases, or if the level of her **desired state** increases, she may recognize a problem that propels her to act. Figure 11-4 diagrams how such a process may work.[27]

Factors Influencing the Actual State and/or the Desired State

A variety of factors may cause the consumer's actual state to slip below acceptable levels. The consumer could run out of a product, such as gasoline or toothpaste. A product could wear out or simply go out of style. Or the consumer could use the product and find that it fails to meet expectations. Another set of factors that influences consumers' actual state are internal, such as perceptions of hunger or thirst or the need for stimulation. Outside stimulation can also cause a negative affective state: the person could receive bad news or be in a situation that makes him uncomfortable (e.g., a new social situation).

The desired state of consumers is influenced by their aspirations and circumstances. Culture, subculture, reference groups, and lifestyle trends can cause people to change their desired state. For example, if you join a fraternity or a sorority, the pressures of that social group may change your perception of the appropriateness of wearing certain types of clothing. When you graduate from college, a whole new set of dress requirements may be imposed upon you. Your desired state will change, and you will develop a need for sober suits, briefcases, and shoes that would have been inappropriate in a college environment.

Figure 11-5 presents a public service announcement developed by the Ad Council. One goal of the ad is to influence the desired state of a young man.

Because consumers have a capacity to think, plan, and dream, they can create new consumption visions. Consumption visions are "self-constructed mental simulations of future

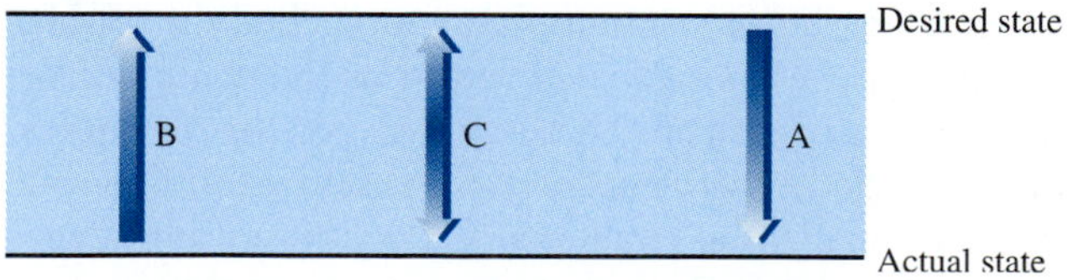

Figure 11-4

The problem-recognition process.

Figure 11-5
This ad seeks to influence the desired state of a young man.

consumption situations."[28] By imagining themselves in new situations or owning new possessions, consumers influence their own desired state. Of course, advertisers encourage such "autistic thinking" by showing off their products and services in highly inviting ways.

In reality, it is often very difficult to state whether problem recognition results from a change in the consumer's desired or actual state. A change in the desired state does tend to create dissatisfaction with the actual state. For example, an increase in salary can make a person dissatisfied with his current house while simultaneously increasing his desire for a larger home in a neighborhood with a higher social status. One of the major purposes of promotional campaigns is to influence the desired and actual states of consumers to create problem recognition. The storyboard shown in Figure 11-6 is for an AT&T ad. It depicts a woman having a nostalgic long-distance conversation with her mother in France. This ad influences the consumer's desired state by showing the wonderful feelings that can

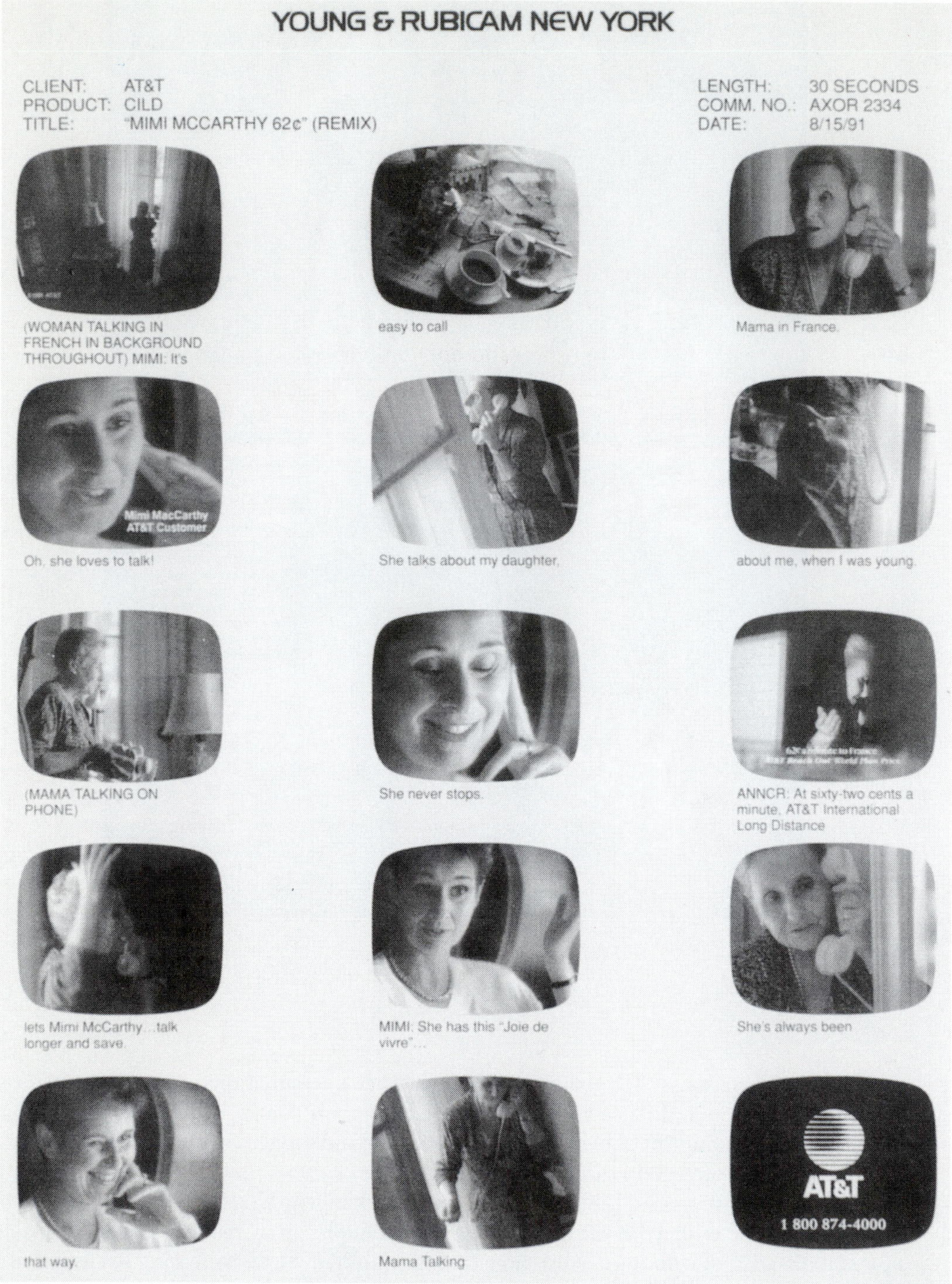
YOUNG & RUBICAM NEW YORK
CLIENT: AT&T
PRODUCT: CILD
TITLE: "MIMI MCCARTHY 62¢" (REMIX)
LENGTH: 30 SECONDS
COMM. NO.: AXOR 2334
DATE: 8/15/91
(WOMAN TALKING IN FRENCH IN BACKGROUND THROUGHOUT) MIMI: It's
easy to call
Mama in France.
Mimi MacCarthy
AT&T Customer
Oh, she loves to talk!
She talks about my daughter,
about me, when I was young.
(MAMA TALKING ON PHONE)
She never stops.
ANNCR: At sixty-two cents a minute, AT&T International Long Distance
lets Mimi McCarthy...talk longer and save.
MIMI: She has this "Joie de vivre"...
She's always been
that way.
Mama Talking
AT&T
1 800 874-4000

Figure 11-6

AT&T attempts to create problem recognition.

result from calling loved ones overseas. It influences the consumer's actual state by focusing attention on how little it costs to make such a call.

One final issue concerning problem recognition must be raised. Because consumers can anticipate future needs, they may purchase products and services before they actually need them. In fact, an entire range of products have been identified as **preneed goods.** Growth areas in preneed marketing include liability insurance, self-diagnostic health kits, prepaid legal services, and prepaid college tuition plans. Perhaps the ultimate preneed purchase is of funeral services and a burial plot long before the consumer's demise.[29]

CONSUMER SEARCH BEHAVIOR

After identifying a problem, the consumer begins a search process to acquire information about products that may eliminate the problem. **Consumer search behavior** refers to all the actions consumers take to identify and obtain information on the means of solving a problem.

Researchers have found that there are two types of consumer **search processes:** the internal search and the external search.[30] The **internal search** is the consumer's attempt to retrieve from long-term memory information on products or services that might solve the problem. The **external search** involves the acquisition of information from outside sources, such as friends, advertisements, packaging, *Consumer Reports*, and sales personnel.

Researchers have also distinguished between the prepurchase search and the ongoing search. The **prepurchase search** involves those information-seeking activities that consumers engage in to facilitate decision making about a specific purchase after they have gone through the problem recognition stage. In contrast, the **ongoing search** involves search activities that are independent of specific purchase needs or decisions.[31] An ongoing search is common among people who have built a hobby around a particular consumer product or activity. Thus car, gardening, computer, and photography enthusiasts are constantly reading up on their topic.

People do an ongoing search because they are heavily involved in the product class, because they are seeking to build a bank of information for future use, or simply because they derive great pleasure from engaging in such activities. One recent study investigated ongoing searches in two product classes—clothing and personal computers. The authors distinguished between heavy and light ongoing searchers. Heavy searchers had greater amounts of product knowledge and engaged in the ongoing search because it was fun. Important to marketers was the finding that they also were heavy spenders within the product class.[32]

The Internal Search

After they recognize a problem exists, consumers engage in an internal search for information. As we said earlier, this internal search is a search through memory for information about products or services that might solve the problem. The degree of internal search depends on the type of problem that needs to be solved. If it is an extensive, high-involvement problem, the consumer may actively search long-term memory for information on brand alternatives. If it is a simple, low-involvement problem, the internal search will probably be quite limited. When the identified problem requires an experiential purchase, consumers will refer to their feelings during this internal search process. (If a behavioral influence process is operating, it is inappropriate to describe a search process as taking place.)

When consumers embark on an internal search for information, they are attempting to retrieve from long-term memory the brands that may solve their problem. Figure 11-7 identifies the five different categories into which a brand may fall.[33] In this figure the internal search is viewed as a two-stage process. First, the consumer retrieves from long-term memory all those products and brands of which he or she is aware. This **awareness set** is a subset of the total universe of potential brand and products available. At a minimum, a company wants its brand to be a part of every consumer's awareness set, for if consumers are unaware of a brand, they will not consider it. About 90 percent of new products are pulled within three years of their introduction. According to one expert, "In most cases, [the] failures were the result of a lack of product recognition."[34]

After retrieving the awareness set from long-term memory, the consumer separates the products and brands into three categories: the **consideration set** (also called the *evoked set*), or those brands and products that are acceptable for further consideration;[35] the **inert set,** or those brands and products to which the consumer is essentially indifferent; and the **inept set,** or those brands and products the consumer considers unacceptable. Of course, a company wants its brand to be part of the consumer's consideration set rather than the inert or, worse still, the inept set.

Research has yielded a number of interesting findings about the size of the average consumer's consideration set. First, it changes over time. From an information-processing perspective, the consideration set equals the contents of working memory elicited when a person is asked to think of acceptable brands within a product class. In this perspective, the consideration set is dynamic and expands as the consumer acquires more information through the external search.[36] As the consumer's consideration set increases, there is a tendency to expand the retailer search, which translates into a greater willingness to switch

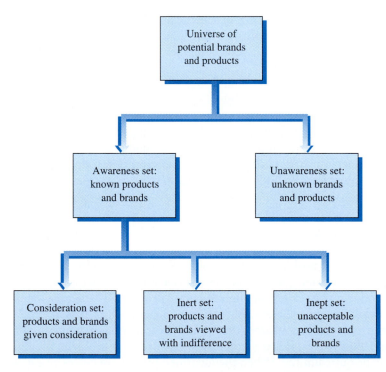

Figure 11-7
Categories of brands that consumers may retrieve from memory during internal search.

from one brand to another.[37] Factors associated with an increase in the size of the consideration set are greater education, bigger family size, a larger awareness set, and the recognition that different brands can be used in different situations.[38] Other evidence suggests that the size of the consideration set decreases as consumers' brand loyalty increases.

How large are the average awareness and consideration sets? One review of the research found that the awareness set ranged from a low of 3.5 brands for mouthwash to a high of 19.3 brands for laundry detergent. The consideration set was 1.3 brands for mouthwash and 5.0 brands for laundry detergent.[39] In general, the larger the awareness set, the larger the consideration set.[40]

The External Search

Consumers engage in an external search for the purpose of obtaining sufficient information to identify and compare alternatives. Formally, external search is defined as the "degree of attention, perception, and effort directed toward obtaining environmental data or information related to the specific purchase under consideration."[41] Table 11-4 identifies the basic types of information consumers look for in the external search. These include alternative brand availability, the evaluative criteria on which to compare brands, the importance of those criteria, and the attribute and benefit performance of the various brands.[42] Note that the amount and types of information consumers seek during the external search can be derived directly from the concepts involved in attitude formation and change we discussed in Chapters 8 and 9.

Measuring External Search Behavior Traditionally, researchers have employed a number of indicators to assess the degree of external search engaged in by consumers. Some of these indicators are:

1. The number of stores the consumer visits.
2. The number of friends with whom the consumer discusses the product.
3. The number of buying guides the consumer consults.
4. The number of store employees with whom the consumer talks.
5. The number of advertisements that the consumer sees, hears, or reads.

Some authors have questioned whether such measures can reliably gauge the extent of the external information search. They propose instead to assess the external search process by measuring the extent to which a consumer relies on the various sources of information.[43] This approach is called the **instrumentality of search.**

The Types of Information Sought via External Search

1. Alternative brands available.
2. Evaluative criteria on which to compare brands.
3. Importance of various evaluative criteria.
4. Information on which to form beliefs:
   Attributes that brands possess.
   Benefits that various attributes provide.

TABLE 11-4

One study that investigated consumers' search behavior for major durable products (such as VCRs, stereo equipment, and televisions) included a measure of instrumentality.[44] The researchers considered the following search categories: stores visited, contacts with acquaintances, contacts with salespersons, neutral sources consulted (e.g., reading *Consumer Reports*), and exposures to advertising. The results revealed that the greatest amount of search occurred within the "stores visited" category. This category was also rated as having the highest degree of instrumentality for making the purchase. This finding does make sense—a rational shopper would search mostly within the category that is the best place to get information (stores).

Factors Influencing the Degree of External Search

There are two divergent approaches to determining the factors that influence external search. The first is known as the economic perspective, and the second is called the decision-making perspective.[45]

The Economic Perspective on Search

Economists argue that consumers search as long as the marginal gains from the search exceed the marginal costs.[46] From this viewpoint, consumers will continue searching for information only for as long as each incremental gain in knowledge exceeds the cost incurred to acquire that extra bit of knowledge.[47] At some point the costs of additional search exceed the benefits gained from it, and the search process stops.[48] In general, the more costly it is for consumers to engage in external search, the less they are to do so. Among the factors that can influence the cost of search are the physical proximity of stores, the cost of gasoline, and the value of the consumer's time.

What factors make it likely that the consumer will benefit from doing an extensive external search? If there are a number of different types of products available in the marketplace and if they are highly differentiated, the consumer can expect to gain large benefits from doing a thorough external search.

The economic perspective on search has some clear managerial applications. Firms that are not brand leaders should lower the costs and increase the benefits of the consumer search process. In contrast, firms that are marketing leading brands should try to convince consumers that an extensive search is a waste of time and money.

The Decision-Making Approach to the Search Process

In general, consumers engage in heavy amounts of external search only when they are in a high-involvement state and doing extensive problem solving. Three primary factors influence the extent of problem solving and external search: factors associated with the risk of the product, factors associated with the characteristics of the consumer, and factors associated with the buying situation.[49] These are outlined in Table 11-5 and discussed in the subsequent paragraphs.

Product Risk Factors. The greater the perceived risk associated with a product, the more likely consumers are to engage in extensive problem solving and search.[50] The risk may be financial, performance, psychological, time, social, or physical. Researchers have found that consumers tend to engage in a more extensive search for services than for goods because they generally perceive services as involving higher levels of risk than goods.[51] Presumably, this is because services are more intangible and less standardized than goods. Also, the greater the choice uncertainty of the consumer about the purchase, the greater the perceived risk—and hence the more extensive the search process.[52]

Consumer Factors. The personality, demographic, and knowledge characteristics of the consumer also influence the extent of problem-solving and external search behavior. For example, consumers who perceive themselves as information seekers engage in a more ex-

Factors Associated with Consumers Engaging in Extensive Problem Solving

A. Factors Associated with Product Risk
1. Financial risk
2. Performance risk
3. Psychological risk
4. Time risk
5. Social risk
6. Physical risk

B. Factors Associated with Consumer Characteristics
1. Consumer knowledge and experience
2. Personality characteristics
3. Demographic characteristics

C. Factors Associated with the Situation
1. Amount of time available for purchase
2. Number of product alternatives available
3. Store locations
4. Information availability
5. Antecedent states of the consumer
6. Social risk of the situation
7. Task definition

TABLE 11-5

tensive external search than other people.[53] Such personality characteristics as open-mindedness and self-confidence have also been associated with greater amounts of external search.[54]

Some researchers have found that the less experience consumers have had with a product category, the greater is their information search behavior.[55] Other studies confirm that as consumers gain experience with a product category, their information search behavior decreases. This relationship between experience and external search, however, holds only for consumers who have some minimal experience. There is evidence that consumers who have had little or no experience with a product class sometimes feel so ignorant and threatened by the search experience that they abandon it quickly.[56] Another factor that shortens the external search process is a tendency to ask advice from other people or to consult expert neutral sources like *Consumer Reports* or hobbyist magazines for information about stores and brands.[57]

One study investigating the search process reported the following findings:

1. As product class knowledge increased, total search effort decreased.
2. As time availability increased, search effort increased.
3. As purchase involvement increased, total search effort increased.
4. As attitudes toward shopping increased, total search effort increased.[58]

The demographic characteristics associated with increased search are greater education, higher income, and higher socioeconomic status.[59] Some researchers have found that search behavior tends to decrease as people grow older.[60]

Situational Factors. The consumer's situation may also influence the amount of external search. Time constraints and such antecedent states as fatigue, boredom, and sickness may affect the ability of consumers to engage in external search. If consumers perceive a high social risk to the purchase, they are more likely to do an extensive search. How the person defines the purchase task is also a factor. If the purchase is to be made for an important occasion, such as the wedding of a close friend or an important party for business clients, consumers will generally do a longer search.

The state of the marketplace is another situational factor. Generally, the greater the number of product alternatives, the longer the external search.[61] Similarly, when stores that carry the product are numerous and in close physical proximity, consumers tend to prolong the external search.[62] Large malls where a number of stores are in close proximity make it convenient for consumers to shop and compare. Remember, when search costs are reduced, search time increases.

How Much Actual Searching Is Done by Consumers?

Now that we have rehearsed all the factors that influence search behavior, it may surprise you to learn that many consumers engage in very little external search, even when they are in an extended problem-solving situation. One study investigating the external search behavior for refrigerators found that 42 percent of the respondents visited only one store and 41 percent considered only one brand.[63] Another study found that 77 percent of consumers out to purchase a small appliance visited only one store.[64] Other researchers who investigated the external search behavior of consumers in the market for major appliances and automobiles concluded that "the amount of information sought by many buyers is small, even though information is accessible."[65]

Do consumers go through a greater external search when options are easily compared, as in a grocery store? Here, where all the product choices are arrayed on the shelves directly in front of customers, how much time do consumers spend before selecting a particular brand? And how much do they remember about the price of the brand they chose?

One study investigating these questions found that shoppers spent, on average, only 12 seconds selecting each good they purchased.[66] Immediately after they made a selection, they were asked to give the price of the brand they had selected. Only 59 percent of the shoppers claimed to have even checked the price, and less than half were actually able to state it correctly. A full 32 percent gave a price that was off by 15 percent. In fact, when a product was selling for a reduced price, fewer than half of the shoppers were even aware of it. The authors of this study noted that their results surprised and dismayed executives of leading packaged-goods firms. If consumers do so little searching, it is difficult to communicate with them via a promotional strategy.

Why do consumers give such short shrift to the external search? One reason is that they may have engaged in an extensive prepurchase search. Research indicates that a majority of consumers do exhibit high levels of presearch activities.[67] These presearch activities range from the passive, low-involvement reception of information from marketing communications to active, high-involvement activities on the part of consumers who have an enduring fascination with a product class.[68]

Another reason consumers fail to devote much time to the information search is that they believe the return in monetary benefits is so low it is not worthwhile. Recall that according to Weber's Law (discussed in Chapter 3), the psychological benefit derived from saving a fixed amount of money (say, $15) decreases as the price of the good increases. Thus while consumers may visit a number of stores to save $15 for a good priced in the $50 to $60 range, they are less likely to visit multiple stores to try to save $15 when the good is in the $500 to $550 range.[69]

Given that consumers search very little, does that mean they make uninformed choices? Probably not, for two reasons. First, the consumer self-report surveys used to gather such information may understate the actual amount of search by consumers—that is, when asked to describe their search process, many consumers forget all the steps they took in the search process.[70] Second, consumers are frequently quite experienced at purchasing the product and therefore do not need to engage in large amounts of external search.

Managerial Implications of the Search Stage

The investigation of the consumer search process is highly important to marketers. In particular, it influences a company's marketing research, promotion, and distribution strategies. First, a company should use marketing research to identify the type of decision process employed by its target market. Suppose the research indicates that consumers use a low-involvement decision process when buying the product in question. This means that they probably engage in very little external search before they make a purchase. In these circumstances it is crucial that consumers immediately think of the company's brand when they recognize a problem. To create such brand awareness, the company needs to do mass advertising so that its brand is quickly recalled from consumers' long-term memory. You can see why the distribution and promotional requirements for low-involvement products like fast-food, soft drinks, and beer are extensive. Recall from the introductory case what happened to sales of Miller Genuine Draft in 1994, when the company reduced its advertising in order to focus on its specialty brands—sales declined dramatically.

A MANAGERIAL APPLICATIONS ANALYSIS OF THE BEER CASE

Problem Identification

The introductory case ended with a practical question. Suppose you are thinking of making a substantial investment in a firm that is seeking to market a specialty beer and you want to analyze the consumer behavior factors that influence the purchase of specialty beers and the marketing strategy implications for the firm. What factors should you be interested in?

The Consumer Behavior Analysis and Its Managerial Implications

Just as with any other good or service, consumers go through a decision process when purchasing beer. Problem recognition occurs, followed by a search process, an evaluation of alternatives, a choice, and a postacquisition evaluation. Four concepts discussed in this chapter apply to the question of whether an investor should consider entering the specialty beer business: the decision-making perspective, the experiential perspective, problem recognition, and external search. Table 11-6 presents the managerial implications of each of these concepts for the beer case.

The Decision-Making Perspective The analyst taking the decision-making perspective would seek to determine whether consumers of the product use extended or limited decision making. Beer consumers use a limited, as opposed to an extended, decision process. Therefore their search process is quite brief and they use only a few attributes to evaluate the alternatives.

Managerial Implications of Consumer Behavior Concepts in the Beer Case

Consumer Behavior Concept	Managerial Implications
1. Decision-making perspective	*Market research.* Track changes in beer preferences over time. Identify key attributes employed by consumers to select beers.
	Advertising. Low-involvement decision making for beer will result in need for high levels of advertising.
	Distribution. Extensive distribution system required within the market area. It will be critical to determine how large the market area is. If financial resources are low, the market area will have to be quite small.
	Product. Identify the attributes possessed by this brand.
2. Experiential perspective	*Market research.* Identify symbolic characteristics of brand that must be communicated to target market. Identify how target market perceives the taste of the beer.
	Positioning. Develop positioning strategy that differentiates brand from competitors and creates the desired product image.
	Advertising. Employ advertising that places brand in consideration set, encourages impulse purchases, and creates the desired image.
3. Problem recognition	*Market research.* Perform research that identifies the factors influencing problem recognition in beer purchases.
	Positioning. Use findings of the research as part of the input to developing a positioning strategy for the brand.
	Advertising. Employ advertising that activates problem recognition and positions the brand as desired.
4. Search stage	*Distribution.* Develop relationships with tavern/bar owners and use persuasive communications and incentives to encourage them to prominently display the brand.
	Advertising. Use high levels of advertising in order to move brand to consideration set. Develop point-of-purchase materials that remind consumers of the brand when in restaurant or bar.

TABLE 11-6

The low-involvement decision-making process used to purchase beer has implications for marketing research, promotional strategy, and distribution. Marketing research should be conducted to track consumer preferences for beer over time and to identify the key attributes patrons use to select their beers. For instance, to what extent do price, a concern for image, and superior taste influence consumers' choices?

The swift rise and fall of draft beer sales in the early 1990s indicates the high impact that advertising has on beer purchases. Because beer is a low-involvement product, there is no way to sustain growth in this highly competitive industry without making significant investments in advertising on a continual basis. This is an extremely expensive proposition for a company.

The low-involvement nature of the beer purchase also means the company must have an extensive distribution system. Here again, large investments are required to distribute a specialty beer widely.

The Experiential Perspective The researcher taking the experiential perspective would seek to identify the feelings and emotions that influence the purchase process. In the case of the purchase of beer, consumers are looking for a brand that will give them the taste sensations they desire and communicate to others a preferred image of themselves. Marketing research is required to identify the taste characteristics of the specialty beer under consideration as an investment. There should be strong evidence that consumers "really like" the taste of the beer. In addition, the research should identify the image of the brand and define the segments of consumers who are attracted to that image. Marketing research should also be conducted to determine to what extent beer purchases involve impulse decisions.

The experiential perspective has implications for positioning, segmentation, and the development of advertising strategy. It is crucial that a specialty beer be uniquely positioned, and the positioning must be supported by strong advertising to communicate the beer's image to customers. In addition, the beer must be targeted to narrowly defined segments of consumers who resonate to the positioning strategy of the brand.

Problem Recognition The analyst working from the perspective of the problem recognition stage would seek to identify the desired and actual states that influence beer consumption. Do consumers drink beer because they are thirsty (i.e., they are seeking to restore an actual state that has declined) or because they want to obtain a "buzz," interact socially with others, and communicate an image (i.e., to obtain a desired state)?

Problem recognition applies to market research, positioning, and advertising. The manager should conduct market research to identify the problems that customers seek to solve when they purchase a specialty beer or go to a microbrewery for a meal. Are they entering the tavern to drink heavily, to interact in a romantic, quiet atmosphere, or to have a great time with a crowd?

Once the problem that drives the consumption process is found, it could be used to position the beer (e.g., as a drink for sharing a great noisy time with others). Advertising would then be used to communicate the desired image to consumers. In addition, the beer would be packaged in a container with a label that communicates these ideas.

The Search Stage The search stage of the decision-making process also has implications for the consumer behavior analysis. Consumers make beer purchases in a low-involvement state. That means they first do a cursory search through internal memory, and in many cases ask for the first brand that comes to mind. If they are in a restaurant or bar, they will be strongly influenced by the choices on the menu or displayed on point-of-purchase reminders. These ideas have application to distribution strategy and promotional strategy.

For the distribution of the brand, it will be important to develop ongoing relationships with owners of restaurants and bars and to use persuasive communications and incentives to prominently display the brand. For the promotional strategy, it will be critical to employ high levels of advertising to get the brand into consumers' consideration sets. Finally, it will be critical to develop and distribute point-of-purchase materials to remind consumers of the brand when they are in the purchase act.

Managerial Recommendations

Our analysis yields several managerial recommendations that have implications for deciding whether to invest in a firm that produces a specialty beer.

Recommendation 1 Carefully analyze the firm's marketing strategy to determine whether its managers recognize the low-involvement, but high-experiential, nature of the beer purchase. Consider whether the firm's promotion and distribution strategies are consistent with the low-involvement, high-experiential nature of the beer purchase.

Recommendation 2 Consider whether the firm's financial resources are sufficient to distribute and promote the brand appropriately. If the firm has only meager financial resources, the brand will be restricted to a narrow local market.

Recommendation 3 Examine the firm's positioning and segmentation strategies to ensure that they maximize the product's appeal to a segment of the population that has the size, willingness, and income to purchase the brand.

Recommendation 4 Determine whether the firm recognizes the impulse nature of the beer purchase and whether its managers have in place a promotional strategy that includes high levels of advertising and point-of-sale reminders.

Recommendation 5 Examine the product itself to ensure that it has the taste and image to make it a long-term player in the highly competitive beer industry.

SUMMARY

The analysis of consumer decision making involves determining how people choose between two or more alternative acquisitions and studying the processes that take place before and after the choice. The generic consumer decision process consists of five stages: problem recognition, search, alternative evaluation, choice, and postacquisition evaluation.

Three divergent perspectives can be used to examine the consumer decision process. The dominant approach in consumer behavior has been the decision-making perspective, in which consumers are viewed as decision makers who make rational decisions regarding the products and services they buy. Researchers have identified two different buying processes within this perspective: high-involvement purchases in which consumers engage in an extended decision-making process, moving through each of the five stages of the action process in a sequential manner; and low-involvement purchases in which they perceive little personal importance in the purchase and move through a limited decision process, minimizing the search stage and perhaps even skipping the alternative evaluation stage.

The second approach to consumer buying, the experiential perspective, views consumers as searching for products and services that elicit sensations, feelings, images, emotions, and fun. Some industries, such as the leisure industry, are based on creating experiences for people. The phenomena of impulse buying, variety seeking, and brand-loyal purchases also result largely from consumers' attempts to gain new and different experiences.

The third approach to consumer buying, the behavioral influence perspective, views certain types of consumer behaviors as resulting from environmental forces rather than from the beliefs or feelings of consumers. In effect, behavior is induced directly. Many of the phenomena of cultures, small groups, other people, and situations can be viewed as resulting from behavioral influence.

This chapter explored the first two stages of the consumer decision process—problem recognition and search. Problem recognition occurs when consumers discover a sufficiently large discrepancy between their actual and their desired state of being. A variety of factors can raise or lower the level of both the desired and actual states.

The search process consists of those steps consumers take to acquire information about the products and services that may eliminate the problem they identified in the first stage of the decision process. Two types of search have been identified: the internal search, which consists of searching through long-term memory for information on brands that may eliminate the problem; and the external search, which consists of seeking outside sources of information on what products may eliminate a problem.

actual state
awareness set
behavioral influence
    perspective
compulsive consumption
consideration set

consumer decision making
consumer search behavior
decision-making perspective
desired state
experiential perspective
external search

impulse purchase
inept set
inert set
instrumentality of search
internal search
ongoing search

preneed goods
prepurchase search
problem recognition
search process
variety-seeking purchases

REVIEW QUESTIONS

1. Explain what is meant by the term *consumer decision making*.

2. Identify the stages of the generic consumer decision process.

3. Identify the three alternative perspectives on consumer acquisitions. How do these perspectives differ from one another in explaining the factors that influence the consumer decision process?

4. How does the movement of consumers through the stages of the decision process differ in high- and low-involvement conditions?

5. Contrast the experiential perspective with the decision-making view of consumer buying behavior.

6. Contrast the behavioral influence perspective with the decision-making view of consumer buying behavior.

7. Discuss the concept of consumer problem recognition. What are the factors that tend to influence the

consumer's actual state and the consumer's desired state?

8. Discuss the factors that cause consumers to engage in extensive problem solving and high amounts of external search.

9. From the perspective of an economist, what are the factors that influence the amount of external search in which a consumer will engage?

10. Give three examples of how marketing-mix strategies should differ under extended versus limited decision making.

11. Identify three implications each for the experiential and behavioral influence perspectives on managerial strategy.

12. Identify the categories of brands that consumers may retrieve from memory during internal search.

DISCUSSION QUESTIONS

1. Identify a consumer purchase you made after engaging in an extensive decision process. What were the steps you went through in selecting the brand you purchased? To what extent did this series of steps match the high-involvement decision process described in this chapter?

2. Identify a consumer purchase you made that was based largely on an experiential buying process. What were the steps you went through in selecting the product or service in this case? What were the types of feelings and experiences you were seeking from the purchase?

3. Identify a recent purchase or activity that resulted largely from behavioral influence. Did you have any feelings about the purchase or activity? Did you engage in an extensive search? What environmental factor was most responsible for the purchase or activity?

4. Try to identify a consumer purchase or action in which more than one of the purchase processes was involved.

Which of the processes were operating simultaneously? Which of the processes tended to dominate your decision?

5. List as many as you can of the purchases of over $5 that you have made during the past several weeks. Categorize these purchases according to whether they fit into the high-involvement decision perspective, the low-involvement decision perspective, the experiential perspective, or the behavioral influence perspective. From which category did most of your purchases come?

6. To what extent do consumers characteristically use one of the purchase approaches more than others? To what extent do consumers show individual differences in their tendency to use one of the perspectives? For example, do some consumers tend to use a decision-making approach, whereas others tend to use an experiential approach in making their purchases?

7. How might advertising for products that are typically purchased under high-involvement conditions differ from that for products bought under low-involvement conditions?

8. Consider the product category of toothpaste. Classify the various brands of toothpaste that you recall as being part of your awareness set, evoked set, or inert set. What could a company do to move its toothpaste from your inert set to your evoked set?

9. Why would a company that markets razor blades be interested in encouraging consumers to engage in problem recognition? How might this company encourage consumers to do so?

10. Under what circumstances would a company want consumers to engage in large amounts of search behavior? Under what circumstances would a company want consumers to minimize their search behavior?

ENDNOTES

1. Marj Charlier, "Bars Cheer as More Patrons Order Drafts," *The Wall Street Journal*, September 27, 1991, pp. B1, B4.

2. "Beer," *Beverage World*, May 1995, p. 52.

3. Carolyn Walkup, "Brewpub Popularity Hops Across the U.S.," *Nation's Restaurant News*, August 28, 1995, pp. 3, 79.

4. Eunice Fried, "Has Beer Gone Upscale?" *Black Enterprise*, June 1996, p. 328.

5. Ibid.

6. For a discussion of cross-cultural issues in consumer decision making, see Kathleen Brewer Doran, "Exploring Cultural Differences in Consumer Decision Making: Chinese Consumers in Montreal," *Advances in Consumer Research*, Vol. 21, Chris T. Allen and Deborah Roedder John, eds. (Provo, UT: Association for Consumer Research, 1994), pp. 318–322.

7. Michele D. Bunn, "Taxonomy of Buying Decision Approaches," *Journal of Marketing*, Vol. 57 (January 1993), pp. 38–56.

8. Richard Olshavsky and Donald Granbois, "Consumer Decision Making—Fact or Fiction?" *Journal of Consumer Research*, Vol. 6 (September 1979), p. 98.

9. Morris Holbrook and Elizabeth Hirschman, "The Experiential Aspects of Consumption: Consumer Fantasies, Feelings, and Fun," *Journal of Consumer Research*, Vol. 9 (September 1982), pp. 132–140.

10. Herbert Krugman, "The Impact of Television in Advertising: Learning Without Involvement," *Public Opinion Quarterly*, Vol. 30 (Fall 1965), pp. 349–356.

11. For an excellent discussion of low-involvement decision making, see Stewart De Bruicker, "An Appraisal of Low-Involvement Consumer Information Processing," in *Attitude Research Plays for High Stakes*, John Maloney and Bernard Silverman, eds. (Chicago: American Marketing Association, 1979), pp. 112–130.

12. John L. Lastovicka, "The Low Involvement Point-of-Purchase: A Case Study of Margarine Buyers," Paper presented at the First Consumer Involvement Conference, New York University, New York City, June 1982.

13. Meera P. Venkatraman and Deborah J. MacInnis, "The Epistemic and Sensory Exploratory Behaviors of Hedonic and Cognitive Consumers," in *Advances in Consumer Research*, Vol. 12, Elizabeth Hirschman and Morris Holbrook, eds. (Provo, UT: Association for Consumer Research, 1985), pp. 102–107.

14. Sidney J. Levy, "Symbols for Sales," *Harvard Business Review*, Vol. 37 (July–August 1959), pp. 117–124.

15. Dennis Rook, "The Buying Impulse," *Journal of Consumer Research*, Vol. 14 (September 1987), pp. 189–199.

16. For a recent review and analysis of impulse purchasing, see James E. Burroughs, "Product Symbolism, Self-Meaning, and Holistic Matching: The Role of Information Processing in Impulsive Buying," *Advances in Consumer Research*, Vol. 23, Kim P. Corfman and John G. Lynch, Jr., eds. (Provo, UT: Association for Consumer Research, 1994), pp. 463–469.

17. Burroughs, "Product Symbolism, Self-Meaning, and Holistic Matching."

18. "Industrial Retail Selling Strategies Designed to Induce Impulse Sales," *Beverage Industry*, June 3, 1977, pp. 6ff.

19. Thomas C. O'Guinn and Ronald J. Faber, "Compulsive Buying: A Phenomenological Exploration," *Journal of Consumer Research*, Vol. 16 (September, 1989), pp. 147–157.

20. Allison Magee, "Compulsive Buying Tendency as a Predictor of Attitudes and Perceptions," *Advances in Consumer Research*, Vol. 21, Chris T. Allen and Deborah Roedder John, eds. (Provo, UT: Association for Consumer Research, 1994), pp. 590–594.

21. Elizabeth C. Hirschman, "The Consciousness of Addiction: Toward a General Theory of Compulsive Consumption," *Journal of Consumer Research*, Vol. 19 (September 1992), pp. 155–179.

22. M. Venkatesan, "Cognitive Consistency and Novelty Seeking," in *Consumer Behavior: Theoretical Sources*, Scott Ward and Thomas Robertson, eds. (Upper Saddle River, NJ: Prentice Hall, 1973), pp. 354–384.

23. P. S. Raju, "Optimum Stimulation Level: Its Relationship to Personality, Demographics, and Exploratory Behavior," *Journal of Consumer Research*, Vol. 7 (December 1980), pp. 272–282. For a review of variety seeking, see Leigh McAlister and Edgar Pessemier, "Variety Seeking Behavior: An Interdisciplinary Review," *Journal of Consumer Research*, Vol. 9 (December 1982), pp. 311–322.

24. Richard L. Celsi, Randall L. Rose, and Thomas W. Leigh, "An Exploration of High-Risk Leisure Consumption Through Skydiving," *Journal of Consumer Research*, Vol. 20 (June 1993), pp. 1–23.

25. Jeff Meer, "The Light Touch," *Psychology Today*, September 1985, pp. 60–67.

26. Itamar Simonson and Russell S. Winer, "The Influence of Purchase Quantity and Display Format on Consumer Preference for Variety," *The Journal of Consumer Research*, Vol. 19 (June 1992), pp. 133–138.

27. Gordon C. Bruner and Richard J. Pomazal, "Problem Recognition: The Crucial First Stage of the Consumer Decision Process," *Journal of Consumer Marketing*, Winter 1988, pp. 53–63.

28. Diane M. Phillips, "Anticipating the Future: The Role of Consumption Visions in Consumer Behavior," *Advances in Consumer Research*, Vol. 23, Kim P. Corfman and John G. Lynch, Jr., eds. (Provo, UT: Association for Consumer Research, 1996), pp. 70–75.

29. C. Jayachandran and Nyroslaw Kyj, "Pre-Need Purchasing Behavior: An Overlooked Dimension in Consumer Marketing," *Journal of Consumer Marketing*, Summer 1987, pp. 59–66.

30. James R. Bettman, *An Information Processing Theory of Consumer Choice* (Reading, MA: Addison-Wesley, 1979).

31. Peter Bloch, Daniel Sherrell, and Nancy Ridgway, "Consumer Search: An Extended Framework," *Journal of Consumer Research*, Vol. 13 (June 1986), pp. 119–126.

32. Ibid.

33. For information on the categories of brands that consumers may retrieve from long-term memory, see F. May and R. Homans, "Evoked Set Size and the Level of Information Processing in Product Comprehension and Choice Criteria," in *Advances in Consumer Research*, Vol. 4, W. D. Perreault, ed. (Chicago: Association for Consumer Research, 1977), pp. 172–175. ALso see Naeim Abougomaah, John Schlacter, and William Gaidis, "Elimination and Choice Phases in Evoked Set Formation," *Journal of Consumer Marketing*, Fall 1987, pp. 67–73.

34. Joseph Pereira, "Name of the Game: Brand Awareness," *The Wall Street Journal*, February 14, 1991, p. B1.

35. For an excellent discussion of the consideration set, see Allan D. Shocker, Moshe Ben-Akiva, Bruno Boccara, and Prakash Nedungadi, "Consideration Set Influences on Customer Decision Making and Choice: Issues, Models, and Suggestions," *Marketing Letters*, August 1991, pp. 181–198.

36. John Howard and Jagdish Sheth, *The Theory of Buyer Behavior* (New York: John Wiley, 1969).

37. Rajan Sambandam and Kenneth R. Lord, "Switching Behavior in Automobile Markets: A Consideration-Set Model," *Journal of Academy of Marketing Science*, Vol. 23 (Winter 1995), pp. 57–65.

38. Ibid.

39. Ayn E. Crowley and John H. Williams, "An Information Theoretic Approach to Understanding the Consideration Set/Awareness Set Proportion," in *Advances in Consumer Research*, Vol. 18, Rebecca Holman and Michael Solomon, eds. (Provo, UT: Association for Consumer Research, 1991), pp. 780–787.

40. For more technical discussions of the factors that influence whether a brand enters the consideration set, see J. Wesley Hutchinson, Kalyan Raman, and Murali K. Mantrala, *Journal of Marketing Research*, Vol. 31 (November 1994), pp. 441–461. Also see Andreas G. Lazari and Donald A. Anderson, "Designs of Discrete Choice Set Experiments for Estimating Both Attribute and Availability Cross Effects," *Journal of Marketing Research*, Vol. 31 (August 1994), pp. 375–383.

41. Sharon Beatty and Scott Smith, "External Search Effort: An Investigation Across Several Product Categories," *Journal of Consumer Research*, Vol. 14 (June 1987), p. 84.

42. See ibid. for an excellent current review of the factors associated with the extent of external search.

43. Jeff Blodgett and Donna Hill, "An Exploratory Study Comparing Amount-of-Search Measures

to Consumers' Reliance on Each Source of Information," in *Advances in Consumer Research*, Vol. 18, Rebecca Holman and Michael Solomon, eds. (Provo, UT: Association for Consumer Research, 1991), pp. 773–779.

44. Ibid.

45. For a review of work on search behavior, see Carol A. Fiske, Lisa A. Luebbehusen, Anthony D. Miyazaki, and Joel E. Urbany, "The Relationship Between Knowledge and Search: It Depends," *Advances in Consumer Research*, Vol. 21, Chris T. Allen and Deborah Roeder John, eds. (Provo, UT: Association for Consumer Research, 1994), pp. 43–50.

46. Arieh Goldman and J. K. Johansson, "Determinants of Search for Lower Prices: An Empirical Assessment of the Economics of Information Theory," *Journal of Consumer Research*, Vol. 5 (December 1978), pp. 176–186.

47. For a discussion of how children respond to the costs and benefits of search, see Jennifer Gregan-Paxton and Deborah Roedder John, "Are Young Children Adaptive Decision Makers? A Study of Age Differences in Information Search Behavior," *Journal of Consumer Research*, Vol. 21 (March 1995), pp. 567–580.

48. For a technical discussion of the economic factors that influence the extent of external search, see William P. Putsis, Jr., and Narasimhan Srinivasan, "Buying or Just Browsing? The Duration of Purchase Deliberation," *Journal of Marketing Research*, Vol. 31 (August 1994), pp. 393–402.

49. For a conceptual discussion of the factors that influence retail search processes, see Philip A. Titus and Peter B. Everett, "The Consumer Retail Search Process: A Conceptual Model

and Research Agenda," *Journal of Academy of Marketing Science*, Vol. 23 (Spring 1995), pp. 106–119.

50. Konrad Dedler, I. Gottschalk, and K. G. Grunert, "Perceived Risk as a Hint for Better Information and Better Products," in *Advances in Consumer Research*, Vol. 8, Kent Monroe, ed. (Ann Arbor, MI: Association for Consumer Research, 1981), pp. 391–397.

51. Keith B. Murray, "A Test of Services Marketing Theory: Consumer Information Acquisition Activities," *Journal of Marketing*, Vol. 55 (January 1991), pp. 10–25.

52. Joel E. Urbany, Peter R. Dickson, and William L. Wilkie, "Buyer Uncertainty and Information Search," *The Journal of Consumer Research*, Vol. 16 (September 1989), pp. 208–215.

53. R. Kelly, "The Search Component of the Consumer Decision-Making Process—A Theoretic Examination," in *Marketing and the New Sciences of Planning*, C. King, ed. (Chicago: American Marketing Association, 1968), p. 273.

54. W. B. Locander and P. W. Hermann, "The Effect of Self-Confidence and Anxiety on Information Seeking in Consumer Risk Reduction," *Journal of Marketing Research*, Vol. 16 (May 1979), pp. 268–274.

55. See, for example, John Swan, "Experimental Analysis of Predecision Information Seeking," *Journal of Marketing Research*, May 1969, pp. 192–197.

56. J. R. Bettman and C. W. Park, "Effects of Prior Knowledge and Experience and Phase of the Choice Process on Consumer Decision Processes: A Protocol Analysis," *Journal of Consumer Research*, Vol. 7 (December 1980), pp. 234–247.

57. Jeffrey G. Blodgett, Donna J. Hill, and George Stone, "A Model of the Determinants of Retail Search," *Advances in Consumer Research*, Vol. 22, Frank R. Kardes and Mita Sujan, eds. (Provo, UT: Association for Consumer Research, 1995), pp. 518–525.

58. Beatty and Smith, "External Search Effort."

59. N. Capon and M. Burke, "Individual, Product Class, and Task-Related Factors in Consumer Information Processing," *Journal of Consumer Research*, Vol. 7 (August 1972), pp. 249–257.

60. J. Newman and R. Staelin, "Prepurchase Information Seeking for New Cars and Major Household Appliances," *Journal of Marketing Research*, Vol. 9 (August 1972), pp. 249–257.

61. D. R. Lehmann and W. L. Moore, "Validity of Information Display Boards: An Assessment Using Longitudinal Data," *Journal of Marketing Research*, Vol. 17 (November 1980), pp. 450–459.

62. G. S. Cort and L. V. Dominquez, "Cross Shopping and Retail Growth," *Journal of Marketing*, Vol. 14 (May 1977), pp. 187–192.

63. W. Dommermuth, "The Shopping Matrix and Marketing Strategy," *Journal of Marketing Research*, Vol. 2 (May 1965), pp. 128–132.

64. J. Udell, "Prepurchase Behavior of Buyers of Small Appliances," *Journal of Marketing*, Vol. 30 (October 1966), pp. 50–52.

65. Newman and Staelin, "Prepurchase Information Seeking."

66. Peter R. Dickson and Alan G. Sawyer, "The Price Knowledge and Search of Supermarket Shoppers," *Journal of Marketing*, Vol. 54 (July 1990), pp. 42–53.

67. Girish Punj, "Presearch Decision Making in Consumer

Durable Purchases," *Journal of Consumer Marketing*, Vol. 4 (Winter 1987), pp. 71–82.

68. Peter Bloch and Marsha Richins, "Shopping Without Purchase: An Investigation of Consumer Browsing Behavior," in *Advances in Consumer Research*, Vol. 10, Richard Bagozzi and Alice Tybout, eds. (Ann Arbor, MI: Association for Consumer Research, 1983), pp. 389–393.

69. Dhruv Grewal and Howard Marmorstein, "Market Price Variation, Perceived Price Variation, and Consumers' Price Search Decisions for Durable Goods," *Journal of Consumer Re-*
search, Vol. 21 (December 1994), pp. 453–460.

70. J. Newman and B. Lockeman, "Measuring Prepurchase Information Seeking," *Journal of Consumer Research*, Vol. 2 (December 1975), pp. 216–222.

KFC FLOUNDERS WITH FRIED FOWL

By the early 1990s, Kentucky Fried Chicken sales per store had begun to fall. Through the first half of the decade, KFC management tried strategy after strategy to halt the deteriorating sales. Here is a description of the process.

Because of disappointing earnings, Kentucky Fried Chicken Corporation changed its strategy in 1991. First, it changed the name of its restaurants from "Kentucky Fried Chicken" to "KFC" in an attempt to downplay the word *fried*. Next, it streamlined its corporate logo, brightened the decor of its restaurants, and added skinless chicken to its menu to appeal to more health-conscious consumers.

This change in strategic direction did little to halt the earnings decline. Still on a corrective path, the company introduced a marinated chicken roast, sold either whole or in quarters, in 1993. The Rotisserie Gold chicken had $750 million in sales the first year, but in later years sales began to falter. By 1996 sales were down by one-third, and KFC began selling the roast chicken only in pieces to differentiate the brand from competitors.[1]

The strategy of going nonfried appeared to make sense, for consumer tastes and preferences were changing and Americans were switching from hamburgers to chicken for health reasons. Through the early 1990s the amount of chicken consumed in fast-food restaurants increased by over 10 percent. At KFC, however, store sales were flat, and executives at KFC's corporate parent, PepsiCo, Inc., were growing impatient.[2]

Meanwhile, other fast-food restaurants launched a host of new nonfried chicken products. Wendy's developed a grilled chicken sandwich, Burger King created the BK Broiler, and McDonald's offered nonfried chicken fajitas. Still, about 90 percent of all fast-food chicken sales are of the fried variety. As one consultant said, "People talk much healthier than they buy." He argued that the jury is still out on whether consumers really want healthy dishes at fast-food restaurants. Indeed, in 1995 KFC decided to resume using the term *fried* in some of its advertising. Fried chicken is simply juicier and tastier than baked chicken.[3]

Some analysts suggested that KFC's sales decline stemmed from a wider range of problems than having the word *fried* in its name. Its stores are generally located in middle- or lower-income neighborhoods, where consumers tend to be less health conscious. In addition, its franchises are independently minded individuals, many of whom have resisted its new product offerings. Finally, the chain is so associated with chicken that a strategy to branch out to other types of entrees (e.g., hamburgers) would be extremely difficult. As one analyst said, "The marketing challenge is a matter of attracting new users without losing their current loyal following."[4]

Then there is the problem of "cannibalization." When the company brought out its Lite 'n' Crispy skinless chicken, consumers in some stores jumped at it. Although it is fried, the chicken does not have any skin, which is the fattiest part of chicken. The problem was that, instead of attracting new customers, the skinless offering merely took sales away from other, higher-margin chicken entrees served at KFC. Another problem KFC faced was that in the mid-1990s hamburger chains (e.g., McDonald's and Burger King) began heavily price discounting their burgers and increasing the number of their chicken offerings. Thus they were competing against KFC on both price and product.

The company tried several other innovations. It introduced baked and broiled chicken entrees. Both efforts failed. It brought out a series of "snack type" chicken dishes, such as bite-sized popcorn chicken and Hot Wings. As said by one spokesperson, the goal of these efforts was to pique consumers' interest and then repique it, and repique it again.[5] Each effort, however, met with only a marginal amount of success. Another corporate insider said, "It's not a no-brainer. We've learned a product has got to be unbelievably indulgent, special and unique and not eminently substitutable at home. Just another roast chicken is not what they're clamoring for."

Questions

1. Identify the problems faced by KFC.
2. What consumer behavior concepts discussed in this chapter apply to the problems?
3. Develop a managerial applications analysis of KFC's problems. Discuss the managerial implications of each of the consumer concepts identified.

References

1. David Goetz, "KFC Chopping Up Its Roasted Chicken," *Courier-Journal Louisville*, March 29, 1996, p. B12.
2. Laurie M. Grossman, " 'Healthful' Approach Is Failing to Bring Sizzle to Kentucky Fried Chicken Sales," *The Wall Street Journal*, September 13, 1991, pp. B1, B8.
3. Karen Benezra, "KFC Set to Win Families' Hearts," *Brandweek*, March 13, 1995, p. 4.
4. Grossman, " 'Healthful' Approach Is Failing."
5. Kyle Craig, "At Long Last, KFC Is Doing Chicken Right," *Brandweek*, January 11, 1993, p. 1.

CHAPTER TWELVE

CONSUMER DECISION PROCESSES II: EVALUATION AND CHOICE

INTRODUCTORY CASE

Evaluating and Choosing Personal Computers

The number of computerized households in the United States broke 40 percent in 1996. In the 20 years since it was introduced, the personal computer has become a mass-market product. With dozens of brands on the market, the process of deciding which computer to purchase has become extremely difficult for consumers. *BusinessWeek* magazine now issues an annual buying guide on computers.[1] The November 1996 guide discussed desktops, laptops, printers, multimedia PCs, and even digital photography. It rated 13 brands of desktop computers. Here is the information provided for five of them:

Overall Rating	Manufacturer Model/Price	Configuration Memory	Comments
16.1	HP Pavilion $2,999	200 MHZ 32 MB/3.1 GB	A very fast Pentium and loads of memory.
13.1	Gateway P5 $2,399	166 MHZ 16MB/2.5 GB	Full-size tower case makes it top choice for expansion.
10.8	IBM APTIVA $3,358	200 MHZ 16 MB/1.6 GB	Slow for a 200 but laden with multimedia features.
9.0	Acer Aspire $2,198	133 MHZ 16MB/2.0 GB	Available with green cases and built-in telephone.
**	Apple Peforma $2,660	200 MHZ 16 MB/2.4 GB	A speedy multimedia workhorse; add a $500 board for video editing.

BusinessWeek developed this table to assist consumers, but it would be confusing to many people, especially those who are not very familiar with PCs. For example, would consumers believe that Apple's position at the bottom means that its model was rated the lowest, even though the double asterisks indicate that the Apple system is not directly comparable to the other models?

Another problem with the table is that it fails to take account of reliability issues, the ease of getting a PC serviced, and the brand's future. For example, in 1996 many observers seriously doubted that Apple and Hewlett Packard would remain in the personal computer business. How would this information affect consumer decision making? *BusinessWeek*'s rating system also ignores aesthetics, although computer makers are beginning to pay attention to the aesthetics of their products. For example, the IBM computer's case is black so that it will match the color of other consumer electronics components.

The key issue in analyzing the *BusinessWeek* report is whether it gives consumers adequate information on which to make a satisfactory purchase decision.

INTRODUCTION

In the last chapter we discussed the first two stages of the consumer decision process: problem recognition and search. This chapter focuses on the next two stages in that process: evaluation and choice. During **alternative evaluation** consumers form beliefs and attitudes regarding the decision alternatives. As you will remember, we covered the topics of consumer beliefs and attitudes in Chapter 8. (That chapter is directly relevant to our present discussion of alternative evaluation, so you might want to review it before continuing on with this chapter.) The introductory case illustrates one issue in the alternative evaluation process: what attributes consumers use to compare the many brands of computers available for purchase.

Choice involves the selection of one option from a set of two or more alternatives. We will discuss a number of approaches for describing how consumers make such choices. Thinking back to the introductory case, one question concerns whether consumers will use the overall rating of the desktop computers developed by *BusinessWeek* when making their choices. A second question concerns whether this rating system captures the factors that consumers employ in evaluating personal computers.

The inkjet printer is another computer industry product racking up huge sales today. These inexpensive devices produce beautiful color documents quickly and easily. The nearby consumer behavior factoid asks what these convenient machines have in common with razors.

ALTERNATIVE EVALUATION

In the alternative evaluation stage of the acquisition process, the consumer compares the options identified as potentially capable of solving the problem that initiated the decision process. As they compare options, consumers form beliefs, attitudes, and intentions about the alternatives under consideration. Thus alternative evaluation and the development of beliefs, attitudes, and intentions are closely related processes.

Question: What do inkjet printers have in common with razors?

Answer: Companies sell razors extremely inexpensively in order to maximize the sale of razor blades, which are their major source of profit. Similarly, firms sell inkjet printers at very low prices in order to maximize sales of ink cartridges, which quickly run out of ink and provide the major source of profit for the firms.

Consumer Behavior Factoid

Alternative evaluation can be analyzed from the viewpoint of the three perspectives on consumer behavior—the decision-making perspective, the experiential perspective, and the behavioral influence perspective. As suggested by the material on attitude formation, the nature of the alternative evaluation process is influenced by the type of hierarchy of effects that is operating. From a high-involvement decision-making perspective, alternative evaluation follows the standard learning model in which the hierarchy of effects flows from belief formation to affect formation to behavioral intentions. In such instances the multi-attribute models of attitude describe the evaluation process. Thus the result of alternative evaluation under high-involvement conditions is likely to be the development of global attitudes toward each of the acquisition options.

In low-involvement situations, on the other hand, alternative evaluation consists of the formation of a few rudimentary beliefs about the options under consideration. Strong affective reactions (i.e., attitudes) develop only after the behavior occurs.

From the experiential perspective, the evaluation process is affect-driven. The focus is not on belief formation, but rather on affect creation. Thus the researcher investigates what feelings and emotions are elicited by an advertisement or by the acquisition that is about to be made. Figure 12-1 shows an ad designed to elicit emotions. Finally, from the behavioral influence perspective, consumers are conceptualized as never consciously comparing alternatives. Table 12-1 summarizes the alternative evaluation process from the decision-making, experiential, and behavioral influence perspectives.

Consumer Judgments and Alternative Evaluation

As noted, alternative evaluation occurs when consumers make overall assessments to compare and contrast options. When evaluating alternatives, consumers make two types of judgments. A **judgment** consists of: (1) estimating the likelihood that something will occur and/or (2) valuing the goodness or badness of something. Judging probabilities and judging value are central to the alternative evaluation process. For example, suppose that a high school senior living in the southern part of Florida is comparing three schools—the University of South Florida, the University of Central Florida, and the University of Miami. In looking at these options, the student will make two types of judgments. First, she will estimate the likelihood that each school will perform as expected on each of the attributes on which it is being evaluated. Second, she will value the goodness or badness of each of the attributes.

You have probably noticed that the judgment of probabilities and values closely resembles the processes described in the Fishbein attitude-toward-the-object model, which we discussed in Chapter 8. First, consumers judge the likelihood that an object possesses an attribute. The scale on which this judgment is made is a probability scale—the process is equivalent to judging the likelihood that something will occur. Second, consumers make a judgment of the value of an attribute in terms of its goodness or badness. In sum, the Fishbein model proposes that consumers make judgments about both probabilities and values.

Consumers also assess risk during the alternative evaluation stage. As noted in Chapter 6, **risk perception** is based upon consumers' judgments of the likelihood that negative outcomes will occur and of the degree of negativity of those outcomes. Thus, besides influencing consumer attitudes, judgments of likelihood and goodness/badness influence risk perception.

Since judging probability and value is central to the alternative evaluation process, the key question is: How do consumers make these judgments of probability and value? There is good evidence that people use judgmental heuristics to make such estimates. **Judgmental heuristics** are the simple rules of thumb people use to make estimates of probabilities and

Figure 12-1
This ad was developed to elicit sufficient emotion to cause someone to act.

values. In the next two sections we discuss some of the factors that influence judgments of probabilities and values.

Judging Likelihood

An entire area of research has developed around the topic of how people judge likelihood. When people say "I think that," or "Chances are that," or "I believe that," they are implicitly making a judgment of the likelihood that something will occur. Probability judgments are made quite frequently in the consumer setting. For example, when people es-

Alternative Evaluation and the Hierarchies of Effects

Hierarchy of Effect	How Alternatives Compared
High-involvement hierarchy	Beliefs about attributes are compared. Affective reactions are compared.
Low-involvement hierarchy	Limited number of beliefs about attributes are compared.
Experiential hierarchy	Affective reactions are compared.
Behavioral influence hierarchy	No internal comparison processes are recognized as occurring prior to behavior.

TABLE 12-1

timate the quality of a product, they are attempting to determine the likelihood that the product contains the attribute of quality. Similarly, when people estimate the preferences of another person, they are evaluating the likelihood that the other has certain likes and dislikes.

Researchers have identified a number of judgmental heuristics that consumers use to estimate probabilities. Three of these heuristics have particular relevance to consumer decision making. They are anchoring and adjustment, availability, and representativeness.

The Anchoring and Adjustment Heuristic When judging probability, people frequently start from an initial value and then adjust upward or downward to obtain the final answer. This process is called **anchoring and adjustment.** The problem with this heuristic is that different starting points often result in different answers because the upward and downward adjustments are often insufficient. Thus the starting point acts to distort the estimate.

One study found that anchoring influenced probability estimates in predicting the preferences of spouses.[2] Husbands and wives must frequently estimate each other's preferences when making purchases. In this study the husbands and wives were asked to predict their spouses' preferences for 20 new-product concepts. The results revealed that both husbands and wives anchored heavily on their own preferences. That is, they tended to ask themselves what *they* would like, and then use that as the starting point, or anchor, for their prediction of their spouse's preference.

The interesting—and somewhat surprising—finding was that using one's own preference was the best strategy for estimating one's spouse's preference. When respondents attempted to adjust from their own preference, they tended to use criteria that were poor predictors of their spouse's preference. Thus in many instances using one's own reactions may be the best strategy for judging the likes and dislikes of others similar to you.

Another study also found that anchoring on one's own reactions improves judgment accuracy.[3] In this study MBA students, marketing managers, researchers, and everyday consumers made predictions about the activities, interests, and opinions of the typical American consumer. The actual preferences of American consumers were obtained through appropriate survey research techniques that used a national sample. All groups in the study made rather poor predictions. The experts (i.e., line managers and market researchers) were no better able to predict the preferences of American consumers than everyday consumers were, and the MBA students were significantly worse. The results also revealed that because the "typical American consumer" was so similar to the everyday consumer group in the study, this group had only to anchor on their own opinions to set a major advantage over MBA students and line managers. The specialized knowledge of the line managers enabled them to make more accurate adjustments than the typical consumer or

The Average American Consumer Quiz*

The following is a series of statements that have been used in attitude surveys of American consumers. Only *married* U.S. men and women participated in these surveys. The people were selected because they were representative of a broad cross-section of all American consumers. The survey respondents were selected through a quota sample, balanced on age, income, geographical area, and population density.

Consumers were asked whether they agreed or disagreed with each statement. For each statement, please estimate what percent of *married* American men and women agreed with each statement in 1986. Write a number between 0% to 100% in the columns to the right to indicate the percentage agreement.

	Percentage of Consumers Agreeing	
	Men	**Women**
1. A nationally advertised brand is usually a better buy than a generic brand.	____	____
2. I went fishing at least once in the past year.	____	____
3. I am a homebody.	____	____
4. Communism is the greatest peril in the world today.	____	____
5. The government should exercise more control over what is shown on television.	____	____
6. Information from advertising helps me make better buying decisions.	____	____
7. I like to pay cash for everything I buy.	____	____
8. The working world is no place for a woman.	____	____
9. I am interested in spices and seasonings.	____	____
10. The father should be the boss in the house.	____	____
11. You have to use disinfectants to get things really clean.	____	____

*Answers to the quiz are found in endnote 3.

Source: Stephen Hoch, "Who Do We Know: Predicting the Interests and Opinions of the American Consumer," *Journal of Consumer Research*, Vol. 15 (December 1988), pp. 315–324. Reproduced with permission.

TABLE 12-2

MBA student could. Finally, because the MBA students were so different from the average consumer and had little specialized knowledge, they were least accurate in their judgments. Table 12-2 presents the quiz used in the study. (Answers to the quiz are found in Endnote 3.)

That prior beliefs form anchors was found by other authors who investigated how marketing research studies influence the beliefs of simulated market researchers.[4] In the study MBA students assumed the role of assistant product managers at Campbell Soup Company. They were given information about consumer reactions to two commercials. This information was either consistent or inconsistent with their prior beliefs about which of the two commercials was superior. The results revealed that when the market research confirmed the students' prior beliefs, it tended to be rated higher and used in the decision making. However, when it was inconsistent with the students' prior beliefs, it was evaluated as poorly done and was less likely to be used.

Research on anchoring and adjustment in consumer behavior literature reveals that many consumers routinely use this heuristic device and that in some instances it actually improves judgment accuracy. This is the case when the evaluators making the judgment are highly similar to those whom they are assessing. However, if the evaluator is dissimilar to the target person, anchoring can lead to poor estimates.

The Availability Heuristic The **availability heuristic** states that people assess the probability of an event by the ease with which the event can be brought to mind. Thus the easier it is for people to recall an outcome, the more likely they are to think that it will occur. In one classic demonstration of this effect, respondents were given lists that contained the names of men and women. In half the lists the men were more famous (hence more available in memory and easily recalled), and in the other half the women were more famous. The respondents were asked to judge which of the lists contained more names of men and which more names of women. In reality, both lists contained the same number of male and female names. The only factor that differed was how famous the males or females on the list were. The results showed that when the list contained names of famous males, respondents would estimate that it contained more names of males, and conversely, when the list contained names of famous females, respondents would estimate that it contained more names of females. Because the names of the famous were easily recalled to mind, subjects' estimates were influenced by the availability heuristic.[5]

One of the major goals of advertising is to make information about a product highly available to memory. Thus if one company is more successful than its competitors in associating its brand with a positive attribute, it will have a strong competitive advantage. Even though competing brands may rate just as highly on the attribute, if consumers cannot bring to mind the association, they will rate the likelihood of the competing brands' possessing the attribute as low.[6]

Researchers have found that one method of making an action or outcome available in memory is to induce consumers to imagine its occurrence. In one study homeowners in a middle-class suburb were approached by a person selling cable television services.[7] In the information condition, the respondents were simply given factual details on the benefits of subscribing to the service, such as the costs and the programming available. In the imagination condition, respondents were given the same information, but additional words were inserted into the sales message that encouraged respondents to imagine the various benefits. For instance, the homeowners were asked to imagine how it would feel to be able to watch movies on the system. The results revealed that respondents in the imagination condition rated the service as more likely to provide the benefits suggested. Furthermore, homeowners in the imagination condition were more likely to subscribe to the cable TV service than were homeowners in the information condition.

Closely related to the availability heuristic is the hindsight bias. The **hindsight bias** states that people consistently exaggerate what could have been anticipated through foresight. So pervasive is this tendency that people often misremember their own predictions, exaggerating in hindsight what they knew in foresight. Because information on what happened in the past is so available to memory, people assume that these events must have been highly likely to occur.

The hindsight bias is responsible for the Monday morning quarterback phenomenon, in which armchair coaches second-guess the decisions made in the "heat of battle" during Sunday afternoon's game. In the consumer arena this heuristic leads people to be highly critical of management for blunders they believe should have been anticipated.

The Representativeness Heuristic The **representativeness heuristic** is a rule of thumb by which people determine the probability that "object A" belongs to "class B" by assessing the degree that object A is similar to or stereotypical of class B.[8] Marketers frequently attempt to take advantage of this heuristic. For example, companies will bring out "knock-off" brands that have names and packaging similar to those of leading brands. The goal is to convince consumers that the knockoff brand also performs like the national brand. To the extent that consumers use the representativeness heuristic, the ploy will be successful. An interesting question is: Are such practices ethical?

An offshoot of the representativeness heuristic known as the **law of small numbers** says that people have a strong tendency to believe that a sample is a true representation of a population even when the sample is extremely small. This heuristic is frequently found among marketing managers who observe focus groups. Because the opinions expressed in focus groups are so vivid and salient, managers often assume that they must represent the views of the entire target market. However, everyone familiar with survey research knows that one simply cannot use a small sample of people to make predictions about a large population. The problem is that the people in the focus group *appear* to represent the target group, and therefore to depict all relevant aspects of the target group. Of course, this is an erroneous perception. Some companies have recognized this problem and do not allow their managers to observe focus groups directly.[9]

The law of small numbers may help explain the great influence of word-of-mouth communications. The reported experiences of others have a strong impact on consumers, even though the experience of one or two people is an extremely poor predictor of the experiences of millions of consumers. But from the perspective of a multiattribute model, the representativeness heuristic—of which the law of small numbers is an offshoot—influences estimates of the probability that an object has a particular attribute. Suppose that a friend describes to you an occasion at a restaurant in which he found a long piece of hair in the lasagna he ordered. If his description is believable and you consider it representative of what can happen at a restaurant, it is likely to influence you strongly—that is, you will probably form the belief that this restaurant has a major problem with the attribute of cleanliness. Of course your friend's experience represents only one observation; it could have been a unique event in an otherwise spotless kitchen. However, because of the representativeness bias, your evaluation of the restaurant will be highly negative.

The representativeness heuristic may explain why consumers sometimes behave atrociously. For instance, customers sometimes treat the people who dress up like cartoon characters and roam the grounds of Disney Land/World and Universal Studios as though they were indestructible "Toons." They punch them, taunt them, and even try to set them on fire. Consider Betina Becker. One day, dressed as Daffy Duck, she was walking around Six Flags Magic Mountain theme park, which lies just north of Los Angeles. Suddenly a large man decided to show off for his wife and grandchildren by slugging Daffy in the ribs. However, unlike Daffy, who can come back from anything, Betina's ribs were broken.[10]

Why do some consumers carry the "representative heuristic" to such ridiculous extremes? It seems these disturbed people see the cartoon character, place it in the "Toon" category, and then treat the person inside the hot, sweaty suit as though he or she were an indestructible cartoon character. (See the nearby consumer behavior factoid.)

Question: What is a "walkaround"?

Answer: A walkaround is a person who strolls through Disney World (or some other theme park) dressed as a cartoon character.

Source: Christine Gonzalez, "This Daffy Duck Has Ribs, and They Can Really Be Broken," *The Wall Street Journal*, August 3, 1993, pp. 1, 4.

Consumer Behavior Factoid

Judging Goodness or Badness

In addition to judging the probability that something will occur, consumers evaluate the goodness or badness of the potential outcomes of their decisions. As noted earlier, the perception of the goodness/badness of the attributes of an object will influence a consumer's attitude toward that object. Two general classes of factors influence people's judgment of the goodness/badness of potential outcomes. The first concerns how consumers value the alternatives, and the second concerns how they relate the outcomes to the goodness/badness of the associations they have made between the outcome and their memories. Each of these classes of factors is discussed in the paragraphs that follow.

Valuing Gains and Losses The **valuation of gains and losses** refers to an individual's psychological assessment of the goodness/badness of an outcome based on the level of the outcome in relation to some reference point or adaptation level. One approach to understanding how people value the goodness or badness of an object is prospect theory.[11]

According to **prospect theory,** how people psychologically interpret the goodness or badness of an option (i.e., a prospect) does not necessarily match any "objective" or "actual" measure of its value. This difference between "actual" and "psychological" valuations is captured in a graph called the *hypothetical valuation function*, which is displayed in Figure 12-2. The **hypothetical value function** is defined as the relationship between the psychological valuation of gains and losses that may result from a course of action and the actual valuation of those losses and gains.[12]

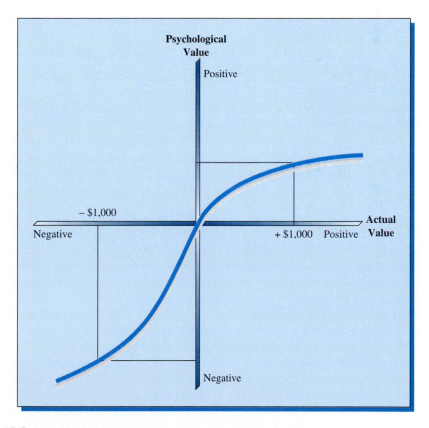

Figure 12-2
Prospect theory's hypothetical value function.

In Figure 12-2 the horizontal axis represents the actual value of a bet. Thus $1,000 is represented at the +$1,000 point on the horizontal axis. The vertical axis represents the psychological value of the bet. The basic idea behind the hypothetical value function is that psychological values do not necessarily match actual values. The curve shows how the psychological values are predicted to deviate from the actual values. (*Note*: If the psychological values precisely coincided with the actual values, there would be a straight line running diagonally through the origin of the curve.) In the figure the curve in the gain quadrant (i.e., the upper-right-hand part of the diagram) starts out steep and then flattens as it moves away from the origin. This shows that increasing gains have decreasing psychological value. It is consistent with the economic concept of decreasing marginal utility, which states that each additional unit of something obtained brings proportionally less utility or satisfaction.

The hypothetical valuation function curve is steeper in the domain of losses (i.e., the bottom left quadrant) than in the domain of gains. Thus all else being equal, losses are weighted more heavily than gains. The curve also flattens out in the domain of losses so that each additional loss means less to the person.

Four managerial implications about how consumers value gains and losses can be deduced from the shape of the hypothetical value function:

Implication 1. Losses are given more weight than gains. Because the curve is steeper in the loss domain than in the gain domain, a loss of $1,000 will have a greater psychological impact than a gain of $1,000.

Implication 2. If people perceive that they are in the gain domain, they will tend to act conservatively.

Implication 3. If people perceive that they are in the loss domain, they will tend to take more risks.

Implication 4. The same decision can be framed from either a gain or a loss position.

Implications 1, 2, and 3 are directly related to consumers' risk-taking tendencies. In general, people like to avoid risk. However, if a person perceives that he is already behind and in the loss domain, he will be much more prone to take risks. Consider the behavior of people who bet at horse races. As the end of the day approaches, gamblers increasingly bet on long shots. Why is this? Because they are in the loss domain (i.e., most gamblers have lost money by the end of the day). Since each additional loss has *less* psychological value, people are willing to take bigger risks to get even. For someone who has lost $100, the psychological value of gaining $100 and pulling even is much greater than the psychological value of losing another $100.

Framing and Prospect Theory As noted in Implication 4, one of the key points of prospect theory is that the same decision problem can be framed in different ways. **Framing** refers to whether a person perceives a decision as being made from a position of gain or a position of loss. That is, depending upon the decision maker's reference point, the same decision dilemma may be framed as involving either a gain or a loss.[13] This phenomenon is analogous to describing a glass as either "half empty" or "half full" of water. If a decision problem is framed as involving a gain, risk aversion can be expected. Conversely, if a decision is framed as involving a loss, greater risk taking can be expected.[14]

One team of researchers demonstrated a framing effect in the risk-handling strategies of those selecting industrial vendors.[15] In this experimental study subjects were asked to respond to a written scenario describing a modified rebuy-purchase situation. They had to decide whether to award a contract to a vendor offering a certain guaranteed profit or to a vendor offering a 50-50 chance of either beating or falling below the guaranteed offer. The subjects were given a series of descriptions of various frames of reference they could use to make the decision. The results revealed that subjects who framed the decision in terms of the worst-case outcome (focusing on losses) or who calculated expected values tended to choose the risky option, while those who framed the decision in terms of factors that caused them to focus on gains (e.g., historical performance and guaranteed performance) tended to choose the conservative option.[16]

Another study found strong evidence that framing influences consumer preferences. In this experiment respondents were asked to give their impressions of ground beef, which was described to them as being either 75 percent lean or 25 percent fat. Notice that, even though identical information was given to the consumers, the product was framed either positively or negatively. Ratings were taken on four scales: (1) good-tasting/bad-tasting, (2) greasy/greaseless, (3) high-quality/low-quality, and (4) fat/lean. In each instance ratings differed significantly as a result of the framing manipulation. Thus when the ground beef was framed as 75 percent lean, subjects rated it as significantly leaner, better-tasting, less greasy, and higher in quality than when it was framed as 25 percent fat.[17] This study shows that how information is framed in promotional messages can have a strong impact on how consumers value the goodness or badness of the information.[18]

The research on framing and prospect theory also has application to how consumers respond to changes in the price of a product. If a price change is framed as a change from the base price of the product, its impact will not be as great as it would if it were framed as a change from the zero point on the prospect theory curve. To see what this means, suppose that the price of a $1,000 product is reduced by $90. If framed as a change in the base price of the product, the impact of this price reduction on the typical consumer will be small because of the shape of the value function curve. That is, in relation to $1,000, a $90 rebate is small change. However, if the price change is framed as a gain of $90—which makes it independent of the base price of the product—it will have a much larger psychological impact because the curve is much steeper as it passes through the origin of the hypothetical value function. In the second framing, the $90 feels like "found money" that can be used to buy something else.

How can companies induce consumers to perceive a price reduction as a *gain* of *x* amount rather than as a *change* in the base price of the product? Many of the sales-promotion devices used by corporations are designed to do just that. Rebates are particularly good for framing the price change to the company's advantage. By mailing a consumer a $500 check after the purchase of a $15,000 car, the car company gets the consumer to think of the money as a gain of $500. If the price were merely reduced by $500 at the time of purchase, the consumer would interpret it quite differently. Psychologically, a $14,500 price is not very different from $15,000. In contrast, a $500 rebate seems like a large sum of money because the comparison is to getting nothing back.

Other sales-promotion devices, such as gifts, operate like rebates. For example, if a customer buys an expensive suit from a clothing store and the owner throws in one or two silk ties for nothing, the gifts will be valued independently of the cost of the suit. The customer will perceive the ties' $50 to $60 value as a gain rather than as a reduction in the price of the $600 suit, and as a result, it will have much greater psychological value. In general, sales-promotion devices such as rebates, gifts, and sweepstakes are more effective than a mere reduction in price because of the effects of framing.

Time Framing and Valuing Gains and Losses Time plays an important role in consumer and managerial decision making. For example, the headline in the advertisement shown in Figure 12-3 for CFO Vision emphasizes the critical nature of time in making tough decisions.

One way that time impacts decisions is through the discounting of gains and losses the further into the future that they occur. That is, the distance in time between when a decision is made and when the gains or losses from that decision are realized also influences their valuation. Researchers have found that consumers psychologically discount gains and

Figure 12-3

CFO Vision emphasizes the importance of time in the decision-making process.

losses differently. Thus people would rather receive $1,000 today than wait a year to receive it, but they would rather pay $1,000 a year from now than pay it today.[19]

In other words, consumers prefer to take their gains in the present and postpone their losses.

Marketers can develop sales-promotion devices to take advantage of this preference. "Buy now—pay later" promotions are based on consumers' tendency to want to delay payments. When customers are encouraged to receive a good or service in the present and to pay for it at a later date, there is said to be a **delay-payment effect.** Because people tend to discount the psychological value of a future loss and because having the good *now* is so important to them, many consumers are willing to pay a much higher price in the future to have what they want in the present. Credit cards, "buy now—pay later plans," and loans of all types are highly appealing to consumers because of this delay-payment effect.[20] The consumer behavior factoid on the purchase of inkjet printers also illustrates the delay-payment effect. At least, part of the popularity of these inexpensive printers is that they allow consumers to save money in the present and put off to a later date payments for the expensive cartridges that quickly run out of ink.

The temporal distance between when something actually happens and when it could have happened also influences consumers' judgments of the goodness and badness of things.[21] Consider how you would feel if the transmission on your car burned out the very day after its warranty expired as opposed to six months after the warranty expired. When a positive outcome is "just missed," people have a much stronger affective reaction. This idea has been used by advertisers. For example, ads soliciting organ donations (e.g., hearts and kidneys) have told stories of children dying because a liver became available one week too late.[22]

Consumer self-control may also be explained by this phenomenon of discounting heavy losses that occur in the future. **Consumer self-control** refers to the ability of people to avoid making purchases that provide pleasure in the present but pain in the future. Why is it that some consumers have great difficulty controlling their impulses? For example, people with food or drug addictions cannot resist the impulse to consume if a cookie or cocaine is available. For these unfortunate individuals, the pleasure of obtaining the cookie or drug in the present is overwhelming and the potential loss that could occur from ingesting the substance is remote in time. As a result, the addict consumes now and regrets later. For some people, the pleasure of the moment is so positive and the discounting of losses in the future is so great that self-control is out of the question.[23]

Finally, the discounting process also explains why coupon expiration dates strongly impact redemption patterns. That is, right before the expiration date of the coupon, coupon redemptions increase.[24] One explanation for this finding is that when the expiration date is in the future, consumers discount the costs of *not* using the coupon. However, as the deadline approaches, the costs of failing to redeem the coupon take on increased salience (i.e., are given more weight), and coupon use increases.

Memories, Meanings, and Judging Goodness/Badness In the course of considering the possible outcomes of a decision, consumers recall semantic memories of similar events in the past. These semantic memories provide meanings that strongly affect how they interpret and value the goodness/badness of the various alternatives before them. Two types of meanings have been identified.[25] *Public meanings* are those assigned by outside observers and social convention—for example, a shirt that has a red-white-and-blue design with stars and stripes has an unmistakable patriotic meaning in the United States. *Private meanings*, in contrast, are personal memories and associations held by the individual. One type of private meanings is the nostalgic association.

Nostalgia "refers to a longing for the past, a yearning for yesterday, or a fondness for possessions and activities associated with days of yore."[26] Research evidence suggests that the targets of nostalgia are generally those things experienced in one's late teens and early 20s. For example, nostalgia for music appears to center on songs that were popular when the person was about 23 years old.[27] In the late 1990s we are seeing a resurgence of advertisements employing symbols and images from the 1960s. Thus a midwestern chain of fast-food restaurants called "Sonic" is rapidly growing partly because of its use of television commercials featuring Frankie Avalon, known for his "Beach Blanket" movies of the 1960s. Why are symbols from the 1960s so "hot" in the 1990s? It was during the 1960s that the older members of the baby-boom generation were in their late teens and early 20s. Advertisers hope to reach this huge group of now-middle-aged consumers with nostalgic appeals employing the icons of their youth.

Recent research on nostalgia suggests that it is an individual difference variable.[28] This study assessed preferences for Academy Award–winning movies, which were released at varying points in time. The results revealed that women showed more nostalgic tendencies than men did. Moreover, people who were more nostalgic tended to like musicals

A Nostalgia Scale

1. They don't make 'em like they used to.
2. Things used to be better in the good old days.
3. Products are getting shoddier and shoddier.
4. Technological change will ensure a brighter future. (reversed)
5. History involves a steady improvement in human welfare. (reversed)
6. We are experiencing a decline in the quality of life.
7. Steady growth in GNP has brought increased human happiness. (reversed)
8. Modern business constantly builds a better tomorrow. (reversed)

Note: Nine-point, agree—disagree scales were used.

Source: Morris B. Holbrook, "Nostalgia and Consumption Preferences: Some Emerging Patterns of Consumer Tastes," *Journal of Consumer Research*, Vol. 20 (September 1993), pp. 245–256.

TABLE 12-3

rather than violent films. Finally, as one might expect from differences in cultural tastes, men preferred more violent movies than women did. Table 12-3 presents the items on a scale designed to measure "nostalgia proneness."

How does nostalgia influence people's determination of the goodness or badness of an option? Since nostalgia is remembrance of a past experience as more pleasurable than it actually was, if a brand can link itself to these types of positive memories, the positive affect from the memories will be transferred to the brand. In this manner consumers' evaluation of the brand can be positively influenced.[29]

Forecasting How Consumer Evaluations Will Change Over Time. An important issue for market researchers is how consumers' feelings toward something new will change over time. In one interesting study the researchers had art experts rate 20 artworks of widely varying quality.[30] They also asked a sample of undergraduate students to rate the same artworks once a week for four weeks. The results revealed that the experts' ratings were highly correlated with the *changes* in the ratings of the novices over the four rating periods. That is, the novices ratings of the high-quality prints tended to improve with each repetition, while their ratings of the poor-quality prints tended to get worse with each rating. In sum, the research suggests that experts can be highly useful in predicting how consumers will respond over time to marketing offerings having a strong aesthetic-hedonic component.[31]

THE CONSUMER CHOICE PROCESS

After evaluating all the alternatives, the consumer's next step in the decision process is to make a choice. Consumers choose among alternative brands or services, and they also make choices among stores. In addition, they choose between **noncomparable alternatives.** For example, people may choose between going on an expensive vacation, purchasing a car, and building a swimming pool in their backyard. This section discusses each of these types of choices—choices between brands, between stores, and between noncomparable alternatives.

How people go about making choices is strongly influenced by the type of decision process in which they are engaged. The choice process differs when consumers use a high-involvement approach as opposed to a low-involvement approach. Similarly, when consumers are using an experiential orientation, the choice process is altered. (Of course, according to the behavioral influence perspective, consumers do not make any type of conscious, mentalistic choice.) In the next three sections we discuss the choice process from the high-involvement, low-involvement, and experiential perspectives. Table 12-4 summarizes these approaches to the choice process.

Choice Under High- and Low-Involvement Conditions

Researchers studying consumer choice under high- and low-involvement conditions have focused identifying the types of rules that people use to decide which alternative to purchase and how they restructure the information they receive so that they can make choices.[32] These investigations have identified two broad categories of models—compensatory and noncompensatory—that explain and predict how consumers make choices. The terms *compensatory* and *noncompensatory* refer to whether high ratings on one attribute can compensate for low ratings on another attribute. In high-involvement conditions consumers use compensatory models, while in low-involvement conditions they tend to use noncompensatory models of choice.[33]

Table 12-5 illustrates the differences between the various models of choice. The example we are using concerns a decision faced by one of the authors of this text: Which brand of power lawn mower should he buy? His consideration set consisted of four brands of self-propelled, gasoline-powered, 21-inch lawn mowers: a Toro recycler, a Toro bagger, a Lawnboy bagger, and a John Deere bagger. The Toro recycler was specially designed so that it would grind grass clippings into a fine mulch and deposit them back on the lawn so that they would be undetectable. The other models were standard rear-bagging lawn mowers with mulching attachments. The table identifies the attributes on which the lawn mowers were evaluated, the evaluations of the goodness/badness of the ratings, the estimates of the likelihood that the models possessed the attributes (both of the latter two concepts were derived from the Fishbein attitude-toward-the-object model), and the importance ratings for each of the attributes.

Alternative Approaches to Predicting Choice

I. **High-Involvement Choice**
   A. Compensatory models (e.g., Fishbein model)
   B. Phased models
II. **Low-Involvement Models**
   A. Conjunctive rule
   B. Disjunctive rule
   C. Elimination by aspects
   D. Lexicographic rule
   E. Frequency heuristic
III. **Experiential Choice Processes**
   A. Brand-loyal purchases
   B. Affect-referral heuristic
   C. Impulse purchases
IV. **Noncomparable Choice Processes**
V. **Store Choice**

TABLE 12-4

TABLE 12-5

Which Lawn Mower to Choose? An Example of the Use of Alternative Choice Models

Attribute	Evaluation Rating	Importance Rating	Belief Rating and Consideration Set*†			
			Toro Recycler	Toro Bagger	Lawnboy Bagger	John Deere Bagger
Low cost	+1	4	7(7)	2(2)	2(2)	6(6)
Blade brake clutch‡	+2	8	1(2)	9(18)	10(20)	8(16)
Ease of operation	+2	7	9(18)	5(10)	4(8)	5(10)
Mulching§	+3	9	9(27)	5(15)	6(18)	5(15)
Consumer Reports rating	+2	5	8(16)	7(14)	6(12)	5(10)
			$\Sigma b_i e_i = 70$	$\Sigma b_i e_i = 59$	$\Sigma b_i e_i = 60$	$\Sigma b_i e_i = 57$

*Assume that a 5 or better on the belief ratings is required to surpass cutoff points on conjunctive and elimination by aspects models. Assume that 10 is required as a cutoff for the disjunctive model.

†$\Sigma b_i e_i$ is the formula for the Fishbein attitude model discussed in Chapter 8. Numbers in parentheses represent the multiplication of the evaluations times the belief ratings.

‡The blade brake clutch allows the engine to run without the blade turning. This is important when bagging grass.

§The mower cuts grass into fine bits, which then are deposited back on the lawn. If this works well, no grass clippings are detectable after mowing.

High-Involvement Choice Under conditions of high involvement, consumers act as though they are using a compensatory model. According to **compensatory models of choice,** people analyze each alternative in a broad evaluative fashion so that high ratings on one attribute may compensate for low ratings on other attributes.[34] In this kind of evaluative process, all the information on the attributes of a brand are combined into an overall judgment of the brand. The process is repeated for each of the brand alternatives, and the brand that has the highest overall preference is chosen. The Fishbein attitude-toward-the-object model discussed in Chapter 8 is a compensatory model of choice.

One aspect of compensatory models should be noted: an alternative is not necessarily rejected because it has low ratings on any particular attribute. Thus a consumer may rate a particular brand of automobile as poor in acceleration, but, because she has rated the car highly on other attributes and because her choice is based on a global evaluation, she may choose the brand anyway. The fact that high ratings on some attributes can compensate for low ratings on other attributes is the basis for calling these models *compensatory*.

To return to our lawn mower choice, if it can be assumed that the author employed a high-involvement decision process, a Fishbein attitude-toward-the-object model should predict the purchase selection. Table 12-5 shows that the lawn mower with the highest rating was the Toro recycler, with an overall attitude score of 70. The closest competitor was the Lawnboy, with a rating of 60. The major reasons for selecting the Toro recycler would be its mulching feature and its ease of operation. High scores on these attributes were able to compensate for the very low rating on the blade brake clutch attribute, which this model lacked entirely.

Low-Involvement Choice In low-involvement circumstances consumers generally act as though they are using **noncompensatory models of choice.** According to these models, high ratings on some attributes do not necessarily compensate for low ratings on other attributes. Noncompensatory models are also called **hierarchical models of choice** because the consumer is viewed as comparing alternatives on attributes one at a time. One attribute is chosen, and all the alternatives are compared on it. The person then moves to the next attribute and compares all alternatives on it. The process continues in a hierarchical manner until all attributes have been covered. One advantage of noncompensatory choice models for the decision maker is that they are fairly simple to implement. When consumers are in a low-involvement situation, they are not willing to engage in the large amounts of information processing required by a compensatory model.

Noncompensatory models are used as shortcuts to reach satisfactory decisions rather than optimal ones—a process known as **satisficing**.[35] Noncompensatory models have also been called *heuristic models of choice*. As noted earlier in the chapter, heuristics are simple rules of thumb that people use to make satisfactory decisions rather than perfect ones. The use of heuristic choice models in low-involvement circumstances makes sense. In such cases consumers are unconcerned with reaching optimal decisions; they merely want to make a decision that is "good enough."

Several noncompensatory choice models have been identified. We discuss four of them here: the conjunctive rule, the disjunctive rule, the elimination-by-aspects heuristic, and the lexicographic heuristic.[36]

The Conjunctive Rule. Consumers are often compelled to decide among a large number of brand alternatives. Clearly, it would be impossible to investigate each brand in detail, so people need a shortcut to simplify the process. One such shortcut involves the use of the **conjunctive rule,** in which the consumer sets minimum cutoffs on each attribute that he or she wishes to investigate. If a brand fails to surpass the minimum cutoff level, it is summarily rejected. If the cutoff levels are set very stringently, it is possible that only one alternative will be standing at the end of the process. In most cases, though, consumers set the cutoff points low enough so that a number of brands survive the cut. The conjunctive rule serves, then, as an initial screening device to eliminate enough brands so that the consumer can apply a more complex decision approach, such as a compensatory model, to select from the remaining alternatives.

In the lawn mower example, belief ratings had to equal or surpass a cutoff of 5 or more to be considered. Using this rule, only the John Deere bagger had belief ratings that reached the cutoff on each attribute. Each of the remaining alternatives had at least one belief rating below the cutoff point. Therefore, based upon the conjunctive model, the John Deere would be selected.

Disjunctive Rule. The **disjunctive rule** resembles the conjunctive rule in that minimum standards are set for each attribute under consideration and alternatives are evaluated on the attributes. It differs from the conjunctive rule in that any alternative that surpasses the minimum cutoff on any attribute is accepted. Usually the cutoff points are set very stringently, so the alternative chosen according to the disjunctive rule is the one that is rated extremely high on some attribute. It is as though the consumer were saying that he or she wants an alternative that is "great" on some attribute.

In the lawn mower example, belief ratings would have to reach the extremely high cutoff score of 10 for the alternative to be considered under a disjunctive model. The only brand to have a 10 on any attribute was the Lawnboy bagger, which had a 10 on the blade brake clutch feature. Thus if a disjunctive model were employed, the analysis would predict that the author would select the Lawnboy.

Let us reiterate the key difference between the conjunctive and disjunctive models. Both set minimum standards for each attribute. However, in the conjunctive model, if a rating falls below the standard on any attribute, it is rejected. In the disjunctive model, if a rating is above the cutoff level on any attribute, that alternative is accepted. Therefore cutoffs for the disjunctive model are typically set higher than for the conjunctive model.

Elimination by Aspects. According to the **elimination-by-aspects heuristic,** each alternative is a collection of aspects or attributes. Choice is arrived at via a hierarchical process in which the alternatives are compared on the attribute that is most important to the decision maker. Any alternatives that do not surpass the cutoff on that attribute are eliminated. The decision maker then moves on to the next most important attribute, and again eliminates alternatives that fail to surpass the cutoff point. The process continues until only one alternative remains.

Applying the elimination-by-aspects heuristic to the lawn mower example, one would predict that the John Deere bagger would be chosen. On the most important attribute of mulching, all brands surpassed the cutoff point of 5. On the second most important attribute, "blade brake clutch," the Toro recycler was eliminated. On the third most important attribute, "ease of operation," the Lawnboy bagger was eliminated. This left the Toro bagger and the John Deere bagger as the two remaining options. Both surpassed the cutoff on the *Consumer Reports* ratings, but because the Toro bagger was below the cutoff on the final attribute of price, the model would predict that the John Deere bagger would be chosen if an elimination-by-aspects heuristic were used. Note that the conjunctive and the elimination-by-aspects models yield the same choice prediction if the same cutoff level is used. In this case both heuristics used a cutoff of 5. If a cutoff of 6 had been employed, however, the results would have been different. On the first attribute of mulching, both the Toro bagger and the John Deere bagger would have been eliminated. On the second most important attribute of blade brake clutch, the Toro recycler would have been eliminated, leaving the Lawnboy bagger as the predicted choice.

The Lexicographic Heuristic. The **lexicographic heuristic** has strong similarities to the elimination-by-aspects approach. Both start with the consumer ranking the attributes in order of importance and then rating all alternatives on the most important attribute. At this point, the two approaches diverge. If a lexicographic model is used, the consumer next selects the alternative that is best on the most important attribute. If there is a tie, the consumer moves to the next attribute and selects the alternative rated best on that attribute, and so forth. Thus the lexicographic model uses a harsher standard of choice than the elimination-by-aspects model, which eliminates alternatives only if they fail to surpass the cutoff point on an attribute. The lexicographic model eliminates an alternative if it does not have the highest rating on the most important attribute. Only in the case of a tie does the decision maker consider the next most important attribute.

Looking again at the lawn mower example, if the lexicographic heuristic were used, the analysis would predict the choice of the Toro recycler, for on the most important attribute of mulching it received the highest rating.

You can readily see why the lexicographic model is noncompensatory. Under this model, an alternative is eliminated automatically if it does not at least achieve a tie in the rating of the most important attribute.

Figure 12-4 presents an ad for Sprint that would be effective for consumers employing a lexicographic model. For consumers who place extremely high importance on getting something free, the ad's announcement that "Fridays are Free" would strongly influence choice.

Additional Choice Models Two additional choice models have been identified: the frequency heuristic and phased strategies.

The Frequency Heuristic. The **frequency heuristic** states that when consumers are in a low-involvement state, choice may be influenced by the "mere number of positive and negative attributes associated with a brand or by the mere number of dimensions on which one brand outperforms another."[37] When a frequency heuristic is used, consumers act as though they simply count the number of features on which one brand surpasses another, allocating little or no attention to the relative importance of the features.[38]

Figure 12-4

The ad for Sprint effectively influences choice for consumers using a lexicographic choice model in which "free service" is the most important attribute.

When advertisers air commercials that use a **piecemeal report strategy,** they are employing the frequency heuristic. For example, auto companies run comparative advertising in which they selectively compare their brand to a series of competitors on a number of different attributes. The ad might state that the vehicle has a trunk larger than a Mercedes, goes from 0 to 60 miles per hour faster than an Audi, and has more leg room than a BMW. In fact, the car might be a very poor brand and be exceeded by its competitors on every other dimension. But by systematically selecting attributes on which it surpasses the competition, the advertiser is able to create the illusion that the car has a great many positive attributes.

Phased Strategies. In a **phased strategy** consumers sequentially use two noncompensatory models, or first use a noncompensatory model and then a compensatory approach. For example, a consumer may use a conjunctive model to reduce the alternatives to be considered to three or four, and then use a lexicographic approach or even a Fishbein model to make the final choice. Phased models are most likely to be employed under high-involvement conditions.

By the way, which lawn mower was chosen by the author? The answer—the Toro Recycler, using a high involvement, compensatory choice model.

Which Choice Models Do Consumers Actually Use? One study asked respondents to make choices among various automobile alternatives after being given seven attributes on which to rate the cars.[39] Table 12-6 presents the results. The study found that almost 61 percent of the respondents used a lexicographic model. Next most frequently used was a compensatory model (32.1 percent). A phased strategy of using a conjunctive model to screen alternatives, followed by a compensatory approach, was used 5.4 percent of the time. These three strategies accounted for 98.2 percent of the choices. Although this was only a simulated buying situation and the respondents were students, the study does give a fair indication that consumers frequently use noncompensatory models in their decision making. It should be noted, however, that this study did not analyze the extent to which respondents used all the types of choice models. For example, it did not analyze whether respondents used an elimination-by-aspects model or the frequency heuristic. More research is needed on this important issue.

Experiential Choice Processes

From the experiential perspective, consumers make a choice after considering their feelings about alternatives; this perspective places little emphasis on the development of beliefs about attributes.[40] Several types of consumer choice can be categorized as experiential processes: choices based upon affect-referral, choices influenced by the effects of brand awareness, choices based upon impulse, and choices influenced by mood.

Frequency of Use of Choice Models in Brand Choice

Model/Choice	Verbal Description	Percentage Using Approach
Conjunctive (noncompensatory)	I chose the car that had a really good rating on at least one characteristic.	0.6
Lexicographic (noncompensatory)	I looked at the characteristic that was most important to me and chose the car that was best in that feature. If two or more cars were equal on that feature, I then looked at my second most important feature to break the tie.	60.7
Multiattribute (compensatory)	I chose the car that had a really good rating when you balance the good ratings with the bad ratings.	32.1
Phased (conjunctive-compensatory)	I first eliminated the cars with a really bad rating on any feature and then chose from the rest the one that seemed the best overall when you balance the good ratings with the bad ratings.	5.4
Other	(Category composed of several other types of heuristic models.)	1.8

Source: Adapted from M. Reilly and R. Holman, "Does Task Complexity or Cue Intercorrelation Affect Choice of an Information Processing Strategy? An Empirical Investigation," in *Advances in Consumer Research*, Vol. 4, W. D. Perreault, Jr., ed. (Atlanta, GA: Association for Consumer Research, 1977), p. 189.

TABLE 12-6

The Affect-Referral Heuristic When consumers employ the **affect-referral heuristic**, they base their choice on their overall emotional response to an alternative. Thus rather than examining attributes or their beliefs about attributes, they use a holistic approach in which they choose the alternative toward which they have the most positive feelings.

The affect-referral heuristic explains why consumers make brand-loyal purchases. Purchases made out of brand loyalty have a strong affective component—indeed, consumers who express strong brand loyalty almost invariably reveal highly positive attitudes toward the brand. When making a purchase, they do not go through an extended or even a limited decision process. Rather, they simply refer to their feelings. For example, suppose that after many years a consumer's Maytag washing machine finally breaks down. She would be revealing brand loyalty if she merely called the local Maytag dealer and asked him to deliver the newest model available. When explaining her choice, she would say something like: "I love my Maytag. It works great. I would never dream of changing."

The effects of brand loyalty on choice were illustrated in one study, which found that consumers shopping for laundry detergent spent a median time of only 8.5 seconds making their selection.[41] Clearly, very little information processing occurred during that brief period. The study found that over 90 percent of the respondents had something positive to say about the brand they purchased. Many of these consumers based their choice on brand loyalty.

The Effects of Brand Awareness Brand awareness may also influence consumer choice through an affect-referral process. New brands often have an extremely difficult time capturing market share because consumers have so much positive affect for national brands. One explanation for this is the mere-exposure phenomenon discussed in Chapter 8. Because national advertising of a brand results in frequent exposure to it, consumers become familiar with it. This familiarity breeds positive feelings, so consumers are likely to choose the familiar brand over newer entrants into the market.[42]

The effects of brand awareness were demonstrated in a study in which respondents were asked to choose among three alternative brands of peanut butter. In the *awareness condition*, one of the brands was a well-known national brand. In the *unawareness condition*, all three brands were unknown regional brands. As might be expected, 93.5 percent of subjects in the awareness condition chose the national brand.[43] Interestingly, the effects of brand awareness were more important than the actual taste of the peanut butter, for the researchers had varied the quality of the peanut butter independently of the brand name. When the good-tasting peanut butter was placed in the unknown brand's jar, only 20 percent selected it—even after they had tasted the inferior alternatives. In contrast, when the good-tasting peanut butter was placed in the national brand's jar, 77 percent chose it.[44]

Impulse Purchases When consumers utilize an experiential choice process, the purchase is made with little cognitive control and seems to happen in a largely automatic manner.[45] This description applies to impulse purchases as well as to brand-loyal purchases. An **impulse purchase** has been defined as a "buying action undertaken without a problem having been previously recognized or a buying intention formed prior to entering the store."[46] An impulse purchase may be described as a choice made on the spur of the moment because of a strong positive feeling regarding an object.

How frequent are impulse purchases? Various studies have found that as many as 39 percent of department store purchases and 67 percent of grocery store purchases are unplanned.[47] Impulse purchases have been described as "mindless reactive behavior."[48] Other researchers have noted that these purchases involve strong affective states in which consumers behave somewhat automatically, exercising little intellectual control over their actions. Impulse buying is the antithesis of the rational consumption process that characterizes most high-involvement purchases and even many low-involvement ones.[49]

In one study researchers conducted depth interviews asking respondents to report on their feelings when they made impulse purchases.[50] One subject stated:

> I was in Beverly Hills just walking around, not intending to buy, when I saw some shoes on sale. So I went inside and tried them on and they fit fine. At that time I thought about buying one pair, then I got the feeling I had to try everything. They were just calling to me. You suddenly feel compelled to buy something. It feels like getting an idea. It's a fast feeling, and if I don't get it right away, I'll think of reasons why I don't need it.

Other respondents also reported having a strong feeling that a product should be purchased, and then going ahead and buying it. The affective state led directly to purchase behavior, without the person forming beliefs or thinking very hard about the purchase. It seems that in impulse buying consumers repress thinking because it might dampen their feelings and inhibit their actions.[51]

Researchers have developed a scale to test for buying impulsiveness.[52] Individuals who score high on this scale are prone to make impulse purchases. The scale is reproduced in Table 12-7 so you can take the test yourself and discover your impulsiveness rating.

Effects of Mood States on Choice Mood states influence whether consumers will use a decision-making or an experiential approach to choice. One research team found that people in a positive mood respond more favorably to emotional appeals than to informational appeals. In contrast, people in negative mood states respond more favorably to informational appeals. These findings were extended by the researchers to the choice process. They found that when people were in a negative mood, they tended to rely on an informational approach to product selection. When they were in a positive mood, they were more likely to focus on their feelings and fantasies about using particular brands.[53]

The Buying Impulsiveness Scale

1. I often buy things spontaneously.
2. "Just do it" describes the way I buy things.
3. I often buy things without thinking.
4. "I see it, I buy it" describes me.
5. "Buy now, think about it later" describes me.
6. Sometimes I feel like buying things on the spur-of-the-moment.
7. I buy things according to how I feel at the moment.
8. I rarely plan most of my purchases.*
9. Sometimes I am a bit reckless about what I buy.

Scoring Instructions: To assess your impulsiveness, first rate your level of agreement with each item using a scale on which 1 = strongly disagree and 5 = strongly agree. Second, add up your score. If you score above 25, you are in the upper half of the population on impulsiveness. If you score above 39, you have extremely strong impulsiveness tendencies.

Note: Item 8 is changed from the original scale. The original item read: "I carefully plan most of purchases." The item was changed in order to avoid having to reverse score it, which would have made calculating your impulsiveness score more difficult.

Source: Dennis W. Rook and Robert J. Fisher, "Normative Influences on Impulsive Buying Behavior," *Journal of Consumer Research*, Vol. 22 (December 1995), pp. 305–313.

TABLE 12-7

Choices Among Noncomparable Alternatives

As we noted earlier in the chapter, choices are not always made among comparable alternatives. Rather than merely deciding which brand of 35mm camera to purchase, a consumer must sometimes decide how to allocate resources among several general alternatives. So the question might be: Should I spend $600 on a high-quality camera, new stereo speakers, or a business suit? The traditional noncompensatory models are of no use here because they require the decision maker to form beliefs about alternatives on common attributes. What do consumers do when the purchase alternatives have no attributes in common other than price?

In a study where subjects had to choose among noncomparable alternatives, researchers noticed two trends.[54] First, subjects tended to use more abstract attributes for their comparison of alternatives. Thus when comparing cameras to speakers to business suits, they would concentrate on such attributes as necessity, stylishness, cost, and innovativeness. Second, the respondents shifted to a more holistic strategy in which they compared overall attitudes toward the alternatives. Besides comparing each alternative on abstract attributes, then, the respondents tended to evaluate each alternative separately to form and compare overall impressions of the various products.[55]

The study of noncomparable alternatives is important to marketing managers because some of the most important decisions consumers make involve noncomparable alternatives. For example, consumers often have to choose between purchasing an auto or building a new kitchen, between going to college or taking a job, between starting a family or concentrating on a career or trying to do both. The nearby consumer behavior factoid addresses one startling change in consumer choices among noncomparable alternatives that took place between the mid-1980s and the mid-1990s.

Choices Among Stores

A critical issue for retailers is the factors that consumers use in selecting a store from which to purchase a product. The approaches to choice identified in the preceding sections are directly relevant to this issue. Using a decision-making perspective, retailers can identify the attributes that people use to evaluate alternative stores, determine whether consumers are in high- or low-involvement states, and identify the appropriate choice model. Researchers have found that consumers consider such attributes as the store's distance from their home, the overall prices of brands carried, and service.[56]

Another factor that influences store choice is the **decision context,** or those situational or extrinsic factors that dictate the options available to the decision maker.[57] Thus the types of stores available, the number of stores available, and the presence or absence of mail-order alternatives influence the choice process.

Consumer Behavior Factoid

Question: What were the top three items on consumers' wish lists for big-ticket items in 1995? Where was buying a new car on the list?

Answer: (1) Remodeling the kitchen, (2) saving to start a business, and (3) buying a home computer. Buying a new car was number 11 on the list. In 1984 buying a new car was number 3 on the consumer wish list. Factors causing the decline of interest in cars include: better used cars, sticker shock, the increasing number of women buyers (they are less status conscious), and changes in attitudes about what types of products show status.

Source: Oscar Suris and Gabriella Stern, "Six Reasons People Are Buying Fewer New Cars," *The Wall Street Journal*, May 3, 1995, p. B1.

Other research on store choice has focused on the type of choice set consumers employ for this decision.[58] Consumers use the same types of sets discussed in the last chapter (i.e., awareness, unawareness, inert, inept, and consideration sets) to evaluate retailers. In addition, researchers found two new types of sets: the interaction and the quiet set. The **interaction set** consists of those stores where the consumer allows himself or herself to be exposed to personal selling. These stores have an opportunity to sell that is not shared by stores in the **quiet set.** Consumers may enter stores belonging to the quiet set, but they tend not to interact with any sales personnel while inside them.

Managerial Implications of Choice Processes

Knowledge of consumer choice processes is useful for designing the marketing mix, segmentation, environmental analysis, and marketing research. Carefully developed market research studies are needed to identify the type of choice process consumers use to purchase a product or service. Researchers need to determine whether the target market engages in high- or low-involvement purchasing and to assess the extent to which the target market uses an experiential approach to purchasing.

The choice process consumers use to purchase a product or service will directly affect the marketing mix. If the research reveals, for example, that the target market regards the marketer's product as a low-involvement purchase and uses a lexicographic approach to choice, the marketer knows that consumers are going to identify the most important attribute and select the brand that rates highest on this attribute, and that if two or more alternatives tie on the first attribute, they will move to the second attribute, and so on. The implication for product development strategy is that the product must be designed so that it performs well on the dominant attributes. Similarly, promotional strategy should emphasize product competence on the dominant attribute. Finally, if price happens to be a dominant attribute—as it so often is—then knowledge of the consumer choice process will influence pricing strategy as well.

Knowledge of the choice process used by consumers also has implications for segmentation and positioning strategies. At times it may be necessary to segment the market based on the choice process used, so that the type of information given in advertisements to high-involvement, low-involvement, and experiential purchasers will be very different. Also, if market researchers identify segments of consumers who desire different attributes, a strategy should be developed to create and position the product to fulfill these diverse desires.

A MANAGERIAL APPLICATIONS ANALYSIS OF THE PERSONAL COMPUTER CASE

Problem Identification

The introductory case discussed a 1996 *BusinessWeek* article on personal computers. The problem can be stated as follows: How do consumers evaluate and make choices among computers, and what information should be provided in the article to assist consumers in the decision process?

You will note that the problem addressed in the case is different from those previously tackled in this textbook. The other cases focused on the development of marketing strategy by firms. In this case the problem concerns how to provide information to consumers so that they can make the best decision.

Managerial Implications of Consumer Behavior Concepts in the Personal Computer Case

Consumer Behavior Concept	Managerial Implications
1. Alternative evaluation	*Market research.* Perform studies to identify attributes employed by consumers to evaluate PCs. Research how each of the brands rate on each of the attributes.
	Article content. Give consumers information on how each of the brands rate on each of the attributes.
2. Attribute importance	*Market research.* Develop an understanding of the uses of PCs by consumers. Identify for each of the uses dominant attributes employed by consumers to evaluate alternatives.
	Article content. Recognize that consumers can be segmented based on how they plan to use their computers. Specifically identify these segments and provide appropriate information.
3. Choice processes	*Market research.* Develop an understanding of the choice process employed by consumers. Consumers will likely employ a high-involvement phased strategy in which they first use a conjunctive model to eliminate options, and then a compensatory model to make the final choice. Identify minimum standards for key attributes to assist the conjunctive model analysis.
	Article content. Specify the minimum standards required for a modern PC. Provide information on the relative importance of the attributes for various uses. Provide a clear explanation of how the overall rating developed by *Business Week* was obtained. Treat Apple computer fairly by developing an overall rating for its model.

TABLE 12-8

The Consumer Behavior Analysis and Its Managerial Implications

Table 12-8 summarizes the consumer behavior concepts that apply to a consumer's decision to purchase a personal computer and lists their managerial implications.

Alternative Evaluation and High-Involvement Decision Making Buying a PC is normally a high-involvement purchase that calls for extended decision making. Thus in the *evaluation of alternatives* stage buyers will develop beliefs about what attributes a PC should possess and will make judgments about the probability that competing brands possess those attributes and about the goodness/badness of the attributes.

The managerial implication for *BusinessWeek* is that a careful study must be made of the attributes consumers use to make computer-buying decisions. The magazine should also identify factors that are not necessarily employed by consumers but are important. For example, consumers may not be aware that video cards can dramatically improve a personal computer's ability to play back information from compact disks. The *Business-Week* guide failed to provide this information and also ignored such important attributes as reliability, service quality, aesthetics, and the possibility that certain brands of PCs may not be available in the future.

Judgments of Attribute Importance When evaluating alternatives, consumers judge the importance of the attributes that form the basis for the comparison. (This process is closely related to that of judging the goodness/badness of attributes.) To assist consumers in this process, it is necessary to identify the various uses of a PC, for different attributes are more or less important depending upon how the PC is to be used. Clear statements should be made of what attributes are important for various uses. For example, if the buyer thinks she will want to expand her computer in the future, it is critical that she purchase a PC with expansion slots. Unfortunately, the *BusinessWeek* chart and writeup failed to compare the computers on this important attribute. Overall, no systematic attempt was made to provide consumers with information that would allow them to develop importance ratings for many attributes.

Consumer Choice Processes Because buying a computer is a high-involvement purchase, and because there are so many brands available, consumers are likely to employ a phased choice process. That is, they may first employ a conjunctive model to narrow down the choice options, and then use a compensatory model to decide among the remaining options.

When consumers use a conjunctive model, they set cutoffs for each attribute, and eliminate all alternatives that fail to rate at or above the cutoff point on that attribute. For the *BusinessWeek* guide, then, it would be important to specify minimum standards for what features a PC should possess, and then eliminate all brands that do not meet those standards.

In order to implement a compensatory choice process, consumers must have information on each of the salient attributes so that they can develop belief and importance ratings. *BusinessWeek* provided an overall rating of each of the computers (except Apple), but failed to provide the criteria on which the ratings were based. Since consumers would have no inkling of what attributes were employed and what the belief and importance ratings were, they could be severely mislead by the overall numbers *BusinessWeek* provided.

Finally, Apple's desktop computer was treated unfairly by not being given an overall rating. Apple's product is not a noncomparable alternative, so an attempt should have been made to employ criteria that would allow a comparison.

Managerial Recommendations

To ensure that consumers receive enough information to make an informed decision, the following recommendations are made:

Recommendation 1 Do the necessary research to identify the salient attributes used by consumers to evaluate brands.

Recommendation 2 Provide meaningful information on the extent that each brand possesses each of the attributes.

Recommendation 3 Provide information on the factors that influence the importance of each of the attributes.

Recommendation 4 Assist consumers in narrowing their choice by identifying the minimum acceptable level of each of the attributes and eliminating alternatives that do not meet the criteria.

Recommendation 5 Provide explicit information on how the overall rating was obtained.

Recommendation 6 Develop appropriate criteria so that an overall rating of Apple's desktop computer could be developed.

SUMMARY

In the consumer decision process, the alternative evaluation and choice stages follow the problem recognition and search stages. Alternative evaluation, which concerns how consumers form overall evaluations regarding each of the alternatives under consideration, can be analyzed from the decision-making perspective. Here the researcher focuses on whether a high-involvement or a low-involvement process is taking place. Alternative evaluation can also be analyzed from the experiential perspective. Here the consumer researcher analyzes the extent to which evaluations are based on feelings and emotions.

When approaching alternative evaluation from the decision-making perspective, the researcher must be concerned with the judgment process. A judgment consists of estimating the likelihood that an event will occur or the goodness or badness of something. When judging the likelihood of an event occurring, people may use judgmental heuristics—or rules of thumb—such as anchoring and adjustment, availability, and representativeness.

When evaluating the goodness or badness of something, people's judgments may follow the predictions of prospect theory. Prospect theory suggests that the psychological value of a stimulus is different from its actual value, and this makes people respond differently to losses and gains. Prospect theory has important implications for understanding how consumers respond to various types of sales-promotion devices as well as to changes in the prices of products. In addition, it has relevance to the risk-taking tendencies of consumers.

Consumers must frequently choose among alternative courses of action. Such choices could involve deciding how much search to engage in, which product or service to purchase, and from which store to make a purchase. When analyzing the choice process, researchers should investigate whether choice is made under high- or low-involvement circumstances. Evidence indicates that for high-involvement purchases, consumers tend to use compensatory choice models. Alternatively, they may use a phased model, in which first they employ a noncompensatory model, such as the conjunctive rule, and then follow that with a compensatory approach. In contrast, for low-involvement purchases, consumers generally use a noncompensatory model. Examples of noncompensatory models are the conjunctive, disjunctive, lexicographic, and elimination-by-aspect rules.

Another perspective on choice is to view it as an experiential process. Here consumers are thought of as using affect and feelings as the basis for making their choices. Purchases and choices based on affect-referral, brand loyalty, brand awareness, and impulses come under the experiential perspective.

Finally, it is important to recognize that consumers also make choices among noncomparable alternatives. In fact, many of the most important purchase decisions involve choosing among options that represent different product categories, such as selecting between a new car and a European vacation.

affect-referral heuristic
alternative evaluation
anchoring and adjustment
availability heuristic
choice
compensatory models of
    choice
conjunctive rule
consumer self-control
decision context

delay-payment effect
disjunctive rule
elimination-by-aspects
    heuristic
framing
frequency heuristic
hierarchical models of
    choice
hindsight bias
hypothetical value function

impulse purchase
interaction set
judgment
judgmental heuristics
law of small numbers
lexicographic heuristic
noncomparable alternatives
noncompensatory models of
    choice
nostalgia

phased strategy
piecemeal report strategy
prospect theory
quiet set
representativeness heuristic
risk perception
satisficing
valuation of gains and losses

REVIEW QUESTIONS

1. What occurs during the alternative evaluation process? How does involvement influence the alternative evaluation process?

2. Define consumer judgment. How do consumer judgments relate to the attitude-toward-the-object model?

3. What is a judgmental heuristic? State briefly the three types of judgmental heuristics used for estimating probabilities.

4. Draw a diagram of prospect theory's hypothetical value function. What does prospect theory say about how people judge the value of something?

5. What is meant by the term *framing*? How can framing influence the risk-taking tendency of a consumer?

6. What is meant by noncomparable alternatives of choice?

7. How does the choice process differ under high- and low-involvement conditions?

8. How do the heuristic models of choice lead to satisfying behavior?

9. What is a conjunctive model of choice?

10. What is a disjunctive model of choice?

11. What is an elimination-by-aspects model?

12. How does a lexicographic choice model work?

13. How does a phased choice model work?

14. What would the attitude-toward-the-object model suggest about choice?

15. From the experiential perspective, how does choice occur?

16. What is the impact of mood on choice behavior?

17. How are choices among noncomparable alternatives likely to be made?

18. What are the factors that influence store choice?

DISCUSSION QUESTIONS

1. Describe how you evaluated alternatives when choosing which college to attend. Did your evaluative process conform more closely to what would be expected from a high-involvement, low-involvement, experiential, or behavioral influence perspective?

2. Now recall exactly how you made your final choice. Describe the choice process you used and state which type of choice model discussed in this chapter most closely matches what you did.

3. Go to a large mall and identify the various means the retailers there use to influence your feelings. Describe as precisely as you can what is being done to manipulate consumers' emotions and moods.

4. Consider how you go about choosing gifts for other people. As part of the process, you probably try to make a probability judgment on the likelihood that the receivers will like the various gifts you are considering. How do you estimate the probability that they will like the gifts? Provide an example of an instance in which judgmental heuristics would impact the decision.

5. In 1996 a TWA flight out of New York City crashed into the ocean as a result of an explosion. Analyze how the news media and consumers of airline services reacted to the tragedy. What judgmental heuristics would impact how consumers responded to the tragedy?

6. Conduct an experiment on ten of your friends. Ask five of them to imagine that it is ten years in the future and that things have gone extremely well financially for them. In fact, they have managed to build up savings of over $50,000. Tell them that they have a chance to get

involved in a business deal. There is a two-in-three chance that the deal will be successful, and if it is, they stand to make $50,000. However, there is a one-in-three chance that the deal will fail, and if it does, they will lose $50,000. Ask them if they would invest in the deal. Now tell your other five friends that it is ten years into the future and things have not gone well for them. In fact, they are $50,000 in debt. Present them with the same opportunity on the deal. Ask both groups to explain their decision. What does prospect theory predict that people in the two groups will do? Do your results support prospect theory?

7. Conduct an interview with five of your friends. Ask them to list their last two impulsive purchases. Ask them to analyze why they engaged in this impulsive buying. Which of the models of choice described in the text seems to best describe what happened?

8. Consider how you allocate your budget among different activities and purchases. What kind of trade-offs do you make in your purchases? How do you decide whether to spend your money on clothing, trips, school supplies (e.g., computers), or CDs? To what extent do your actions follow the process of making choices among noncomparable alternatives?

9. Describe the factors that most markedly influence which grocery store and department store you patronize. Do these correspond to the factors discussed in the text as influencing store choice?

10. Consider the various types of purchases that you or your friends have made. Describe a purchase that was made through each of the following choice processes: compensatory, conjunctive, and lexicographic.

ENDNOTES

1. Stephen H. Wildstrom, "Annual Guide to Computers: Desktop Systems," *BusinessWeek*, November 4, 1996, pp. 118–124.

2. Harry Davis, Stephen Hoch, and E.K. Ragsdale, "An Anchoring and Adjustment Model of Spousal Predictions," *Journal of Consumer Research*, Vol. 13 (June 1986), pp. 25–37.

3. Stephen Hoch, "Who Do We Know: Predicting the Interests and Opinions of the American Consumer," *Journal of Consumer Research*, Vol. 15 (December 1988), pp. 315–324. Answers to the consumer attitude quiz are:

   1. Men = 36; Women = 35
   2. Men = 52; Women = 34
   3. Men = 75; Women = 71
   4. Men = 63; Women = 61
   5. Men = 29; Women = 33
   6. Men = 66; Women = 74
   7. Men = 72; Women = 70
   8. Men = 17; Women = 11
   9. Men = 57; Women = 79
   10. Men = 68; Women = 50
   11. Men = 48; Women = 54

4. Hanjoon Lee, Acito Acito, and Ralph Day, "Evaluation and Use of Marketing Research by Decision Makers: A Behavioral Simulation," *Journal of Marketing Research*, Vol. 24 (May 1987), pp. 187–196.

5. Amos Tversky and Daniel Kahneman, "Availability: A Heuristic for Judging Frequency and Probability," *Cognitive Psychology*, Vol. 5 (1973), pp. 107–232.

6. For more work on estimations based on information in memory, see Geeta Menon, Priya Raghubir, and Norbert Schwarz, "Behavioral Frequency Judgments: An Accessibility-Diagnosticity Framework," *Journal of Consumer Research*, Vol. 22 (September 1995), pp. 212–228.

7. W. Larry Gregory, Robert Cialdini, and Kathleen Carpenter, "Self-Relevant Scenarios as Mediators of Likelihood Estimates and Compliance: Does Imagining Make It So?" *Journal of Personality and Social Psychology*, Vol. 43 (1982), pp. 89–99.

8. Daniel Kahneman and Amos Tversky, "Subjective Probability: A Judgment of Representativeness," *Cognitive Psychology*, Vol. 3, pp. 430–454.

9. Daniel Kahneman and Amos Tversky, "Choices, Values, and Frames," *American Psychologist*, Vol. 39 (1984), pp. 341–350.

10. Christine Gonzalez, "This Daffy Duck Has Ribs, and They Can Really Be Broken," *The Wall Street Journal*, August 3, 1993, pp. 1, 4.

11. Daniel Kahneman and Amos Tversky, "Prospect Theory: An Analysis of Decisions Under Risk," *Econometrica*, Vol. 47 (March 1979), pp. 263–291.

12. For recent review articles on prospect theory and framing, see Alice A. Wright and Richard J. Lutz, "Effects of Advertising and Experience on Brand Judgments: A Rose by Any Other Frame," in *Advances in Consumer Research*, Vol. 20, Leigh McAlister and Michael L. Rothschild, eds. (Provo, UT: Association for Consumer Research, 1992), pp. 165–169. Also see Donald J. Hempel and Harold Z. Daniel, "Framing Dynamics: Measurement Issues and Perspectives," in *Advances in Consumer Research*, Vol. 20, Leigh McAlister and Michael L. Rothschild, eds. (Provo, UT: Association for Consumer Research, 1992), pp. 273–279.

13. Kahneman and Tversky, "Choices, Values, and Frames."

14. For a recent discussion of the impact of framing on direct-mail solicitations, see Gerald E. Smith and Paul D. Perger, "The Impact of Framing, Anchorpoints, and Frames of Reference on Direct Mail Charitable Contributions," *Advances in Consumer Research*, Vol. 22, Frank R. Kardes and Mita Sujan, eds. (Provo, UT: Association for Consumer Research, 1995), pp. 705–712. For a discussion of the impact of presentation format on framing, see James E. Stoddard and Edward F. Fern, "The Effect of Information Presentation Format and Decision Frame on Choice in an Organizational Buying Context," *Advances in Consumer Research*, Vol. 23, Kim Corfman and John G. Lynch, Jr., eds. (Provo, UT: Association for Consumer Research, 1996), pp. 211–217. Also see William D. Diamond and Abhijit Sanyal, "The Effects of Framing on the Choice of Supermarket Coupons," in *Advances in Consumer Research*, Vol. 17, Marvin E. Goldberg and Gerald Gorn, eds. (Provo, UT: Association for Consumer Research, 1990), pp. 488–493. In addition, see John Mowen, Alan Gordon, and Clifford Young, "The Impact of Sales Taxes on Store Choice: Public Policy and Theoretical Implications," *Proceedings of Summer Educators' Conference* (Chicago: American Marketing Association, 1988).

15. Christopher Puto, Wesley Patton, and Ronald King, "Risk Handling Strategies in Industrial Vendor Selection Decisions," *Journal of Marketing*, Vol. 49 (Winter 1985), pp. 89–98.

16. In other research the investigators found that the framing of information about television sets influenced perceptions of risk. See Dhruv Grewal, Jerry Gotlieb, and Howard Marmorstein, "The Moderating Effects of Message Framing and Source Credibility on the Price-Perceived Risk Relationship," *Journal of Consumer Research*, Vol. 21 (June 1994), pp. 145–151.

17. Irwin Levin, "Associative Effects of Information Framing," *Bulletin of the Psychonomic Society*, Vol. 25 (1987), pp. 85–86.

18. For additional research on the effects of framing, see Lauren G. Block and Punam Anand Keller, "When to Accentuate the Negative: The Effects of Perceived Efficacy and Message Framing on Intentions to Perform a Health-Related Behavior," *Journal of Marketing Research*, Vol. 32 (May 1995), pp. 192–203.

19. John C. Mowen and Maryanne M. Mowen, "Time and Outcome Valuation: Implications for Marketing Decision Making," *Journal of Marketing* (October 1991), pp. 54–62.

20. Stephen J. Hoch and George F. Lowenstein, "Time-Inconsistent Preferences and Consumer Self-Control," *Journal of Consumer Research*, Vol. 17 (March 1991), pp. 492–507.

21. Joan Meyers-Levy and Durairaj Maheswaran, "When Timing Matters: The Influence of Temporal Distance on Consumers' Affective and Persuasive Responses," *Journal of Consumer Research*, Vol. 19 (December 1992), pp. 424–433.

22. Ibid.

23. For another view of how problems of consumer self-control occur, see Stephen J. Hock and George F. Lowenstein, "Time-Inconsistent Preferences and Consumer Self-Control," *Journal of Consumer Research*, Vol. 17 (March 1991), pp. 492–507.

24. J. Jeffrey Inman and Leigh McAlister, "Do Coupon Expiration Dates Affect Consumer Behavior?" *Journal of Marketing Research*, Vol. 31 (August 1994), pp. 423–428.

25. Marsha Richins, "Valuing Things: The Public and Private Meanings of Possessions," *Journal of Consumer Research*, Vol. 21 (December 1994), pp. 504–521.

26. Morris B. Holbrook, "Nostalgia and Consumption Preferences: Some Emerging Patterns of Consumer Tastes," *Journal of Consumer Research*, Vol. 20 (September 1993), pp. 245–256. For other research on nostalgia, see William Havlena and Susan Holak, "The Good Old Days: Observations on Nostalgia and Its Role in Consumer Behavior," in *Advances in Consumer Research*, Vol. 18, Rebecca Holman and Michael Solomon, eds. (Provo, UT: Association for Consumer Research), pp. 323–329.

27. Morris B. Holbrook and Robert M. Schindler, "Some Exploratory Findings on the Development of Musical Tastes," *Journal of Consumer Research*, Vol. 16 (June 1989), pp. 119–124.

28. Holbrook, "Nostalgia and Consumption Preferences."

29. For more recent research on nostalgia's impact on aesthetic tastes, see Morris B. Holbrook and Robert Schindler, "Age, Sex, and Attitude Toward the Past as Predictors of Consumers' Aesthetic Tastes for Cultural Products," *Journal of Marketing Research*, Vol. 31 (August 1994), pp. 412–422.

30. Robert M. Schindler, Morris B. Holbrook, and Eric A. Greenleaf, "Using Connoisseurs to Predict Mass Tastes," *Marketing Letters*, Vol. 1 (1989), pp. 47–54.

31. For another view of the effects of time on consumer behavior, see Patricia Ann Walsh, "The Impact of Temporal Orientation on Higher Order Choices: A Phenomenological Investigation," *Advances in Consumer Re-

search, Vol. 22, Frank R. Kardes and Mita Sujan, eds. (Provo, UT: Association for Consumer Research, 1995), pp. 311–317.

32. Eloise Coupey, "Restructuring: Constructive Processing of Information Displays in Consumer Choice," *Journal of Consumer Research*, Vol. 21 (June 1994), pp. 83–99.

33. For recent discussions of choice models, see Pratibha A. Dabholkar, "Incorporating Choice into an Attitudinal Framework: Analyzing Models of Mental Comparison Processes," *Journal of Consumer Research*, Vol. 21 (June 1994), pp. 100–118; and Maryon F. King and Siva K. Balasubramanian, "The Effects of Expertise, End Goal, and Product Type on Adoption of Preference Formation Strategy," *Journal of the Academy of Marketing Science*, Vol. 22 (Spring 1994), pp. 146–159.

34. This section on noncompensatory models relies heavily on work by Peter Wright, "Consumer Choice Strategies: Simplifying versus Optimizing," *Journal of Marketing Research*, Vol. 11 (February 1976), pp. 60–67. Also see Dennis Gensch and Rajshekhar Javalgi, "The Influence of Involvement on Disaggregate Attribute Choice Models," *Journal of Consumer Research*, Vol. 14 (June 1987), pp. 71–82.

35. Alan Newell and Herbert Simon, *Human Problem Solving* (Englewood Cliffs, NJ: Prentice Hall, 1972).

36. Wright, "Consumer Choice Strategies."

37. Joseph W. Alba and Howard Marmorstein, "The Effects of Frequency Knowledge on Consumer Decision Making," *Journal of Consumer Research*, Vol. 14 (June 1987), pp. 14–25.

38. Ibid.

39. M. Reilly and R. Holman, "Does Task Complexity or Cue Intercorrelation Affect Choice of an Information-Processing Strategy? An Empirical Investigation," in *Advances in Consumer Research*, Vol. 4, W. D. Perreault, Jr., ed. (Atlanta, GA: Association for Consumer Research, 1977), pp. 185–190.

40. Banwari Mittal, "A Study of Affective Choice for Consumer Decisions," *Advances in Consumer Research*, Vol. 21, Chris T. Allen and Deborah Roedder John, eds. (Provo, UT: Association for Consumer Research, 1994), pp. 256–263.

41. Wayne Hoyer, "An Examination of Consumer Decision Making for a Common Repeat Purchase Product," *Journal of Consumer Research*, Vol. 11 (December 1984), pp. 822–829.

42. Marc Vanhuele, "Why Familiar Stimuli Are Liked. A Study on the Cognitive Dynamics Linking Recognition and the Mere Exposure Effect," *Advances in Consumer Research*, Vol. 22, Frank R. Kardes and Mita Sujan, eds. (Provo, UT: Association for Consumer Research, 1995), pp. 171–175.

43. Wayne D. Hoyer and Steven P. Brown, "Effects of Brand Awareness on Choice for a Common, Repeat-Purchase Product," *Journal of Consumer Research*, Vol. 17 (September 1990), pp. 141–148.

44. Not all research is supportive of mere exposure effects. For example, see John W. Pracejus, "Is More Exposure Always Better? Effects of Incidental Exposure to a Brand Name on Subsequent Processing of Advertising," *Advances in Consumer Research*, Vol. 22, Frank R. Kardes and Mita Sujan, eds. (Provo, UT: Association for Consumer Research, 1995), pp. 319–327.

45. P. Weinberg and W. Gottwald, "Impulsive Consumer Buying as a Result of Emotions," *Journal of Business Research*, Vol. 10 (March 1982), pp. 43–87.

46. Dennis Rook and Stephen Hoch, "Consuming Impulses," in *Advances in Consumer Research*, Vol. 12, E. Hirschman and M. Holbrook, eds. (Ann Arbor, MI: Association for Consumer Research, 1985), pp. 23–27.

47. "Industrial Retail Selling Strategies Designed to Induce Sales," *Beverage Industry*, June 3, 1977, p. 6.

48. Weinberg and Gottwald, "Impulsive Consumer Buying as a Result of Emotions," pp. 43–57.

49. Rook and Hoch, "Consuming Impulses."

50. Rook and Hoch, "Consuming Impulses."

51. Recently, researchers have suggested that normative evaluations of whether a purchase is "correct" in a particular situation moderate behavior. See Dennis W. Rook and Robert J. Fisher, "Normative Influences on Impulsive Buying Behavior," *Journal of Consumer Research*, Vol. 22 (December 1995), pp. 305–313.

52. Ibid.

53. Meryl Gardner and Ronald Hill, "Consumers' Mood States: Antecedents and Consequences of Experiential vs. Information Strategies for Brand Choice," *Psychology and Marketing*, in press.

54. Michael Johnson, "Consumer Choice Strategies for Comparing Noncomparable Alternatives," *Journal of Consumer Research*, Vol. 11 (December 1984), pp. 741–753. Also see Barbara Kahn, William Moore, and Rashi Glazer, "Experiments in Constrained Choice," *Journal of Consumer Research*, Vol. 14 (June 1987), pp. 96–113.

55. A topic related to choice comparability is decision difficulty.

For a discussion, see Eloise Coupey and Carol W. DeMoranville, "Information Processability and Restructuring: Consumer Strategies for Managing Difficult Decisions," *Advances in Consumer Research*, Vol. 23, Kim Corfman and John G. Lynch, Jr., eds. (Provo, UT: Association for Consumer Research, 1996), pp. 225–230.

56. James Bruner and John Mason, "The Influence of Driving Time upon Shopping Center Preference," *Journal of Marketing*, Vol. 32 (April 1968), pp. 57–61.

57. Susan Spiggle and Murphy Sewall, "A Choice Sets Model of Retail Selection," *Journal of Marketing*, Vol. 51 (April 1987), pp. 97–111.

58. Susan Spiggle and Murphy Sewall, "A Choice Sets Model of Retail Selection," *Journal of Marketing*, Vol. 51 (April 1987), pp. 97–111.

BUICK RECLAIMS CUSTOMERS

During the 1980s consumer perceptions of American automobiles reached an all-time low. Despite incentives such as rebates, below-market interest rates, and creative advertising, market shares for U.S. autos plummeted. Very many consumers shifted to Japanese brands. This trend continued into the early 1990s. For example, in 1991 General Motors lost another one-half-point market share—falling to 35.6 percent. The huge automaker had begun the 1980s with a roughly 55 percent share of the U.S. auto market. By the mid-1990s, however, the trend had been halted. U.S. automakers had finally gotten their collective act together. In 1996 they achieved record profits. GM, for example, reported profits of $6.9 billion that year.[1]

As other U.S. brands lost market share in the early 1990s, the Buick Division of General Motors was bucking the trend. In 1990 Buick's sales increased by 6.6 percent, and in 1991 the division gained a full 1 percent increase in share, to claim over 6 percent of the market. Perhaps most important, the company made these gains without resorting to profit-eroding rebates and sales incentives. What happened to cause this turnaround in Buick's fortunes?

Buick's recent success represents a "bounce-back" from its problems of the early 1980s. Then management made a decision to reposition the division to appeal to younger customers. Sporty Skyhawks, cheapie Skylarks, turbocharged Gran Sports, and boring Rivieras were produced. The promising two-seat Reatta was created in a configuration that was underpowered and uncompetitive with the import challengers against which it was targeted. Quality was sacrificed as cars came off the production line with bad paint jobs, poorly fitting body panels, and windows that wouldn't stay up. Consumer satisfaction surveys ranked Buick near the bottom of the list. As a result of this confluence of problems, Buick's traditional buyers (white-collar professionals aged 45 and older) abandoned the venerable brand and the younger buyers never materialized.

Buick's turnaround began in 1986, when a new general manager, Edward Mertz, was hired. He quickly recognized that the company was selling a supermarket of brands with greatly varying images, so that people didn't know exactly what to expect from a Buick. Mertz decided to take the company back to its roots of building substantial vehicles for professionals. He saw Buick as the "Premium American Motorcar"—distinctive, substantial, powerful, and mature. Perhaps most important, he reoriented the division to focus on quality. By 1989, the J. D. Powers market research firm was rating the Buick LeSabre second in quality only to the Nissan Maxima. During 1990 and 1991 Buick was ranked first among American cars in quality.

Inspired by the favorable reviews, Buick initiated a series of changes. Mertz discontinued the smallest cars and the smallest engines and focused on building compact to full-size luxury models with V-6 and V-8 engines. Although still conservative, Buick styling became distinctive. Priced between $15,000 and $26,000, its vehicles were targeted to traditional Buick buyers—60-year-olds with a median income of $42,700, and 35 percent of whom had a college education. Roomy, easy to drive, with good power and good gas mileage, the "new" Buick's qualities matched those desired by the target market. (A full-size, top-of-the-line Park Avenue gets better highway mileage than a similarly equipped Toyota Camry that is 560 pounds lighter.)

Mertz's attention to providing the car desired by Buick's target market can be seen in the last-minute design changes made in the new Regal only a year prior to its introduction in 1990. A dull gray vinyl dashboard was covered with wood-grain "appliqués." Chrome accents were added to the exterior, and a choppy ride was smoothed by fine-tuning the suspension. As a result, the Regal went on to outsell its major competitor, the Ford Thunderbird, and became the most popular car in its class.

Buick continued to be a profit center for GM through much of the 1990s. Sales held up as the company continued to appeal to professionals. In 1996 the division went a step further and announced that it was consolidating Buick dealerships in major metropolitan areas in order to make showrooms fit the brand message. The goal was to have dealerships that looked and felt like country clubs.[2]

This case was prepared by Carol Hisey.

Questions

1. Define the problem faced by Buick in the 1980s.
2. Discuss the consumer concepts from the chapter that apply to the case.
3. Do a managerial applications analysis of the case. Discuss the managerial strategies that Buick developed and how they relate to the consumer concepts identified.

References

1. James Flanigan, "With Little Room, GM Turns Itself Around," *Los Angeles Times*, February 4, 1996, p. D1.

2. Steve Gelsi, "GM Looks to Consolidate Buick Retail," *Brandweek*, March 11, 1996, p. 8.

13

POSTACQUISITION PROCESSES, CONSUMER SATISFACTION, AND BRAND LOYALTY

INTRODUCTORY CASE

Delta Flight 149 and Consumer Satisfaction

After spending nine hours in cramped coach seats on their flight from Rome to New York, the couple was anxious to catch their connecting flight to Dallas–Ft. Worth. Once in Dallas, they would fly to Oklahoma City. If all went well, they would get home that night to see their children. They were flying Delta Airlines—a company to which they felt brand loyalty.[1]

The flight touched down in New York with an hour to spare before their 4:30 P.M. connecting flight. The ticket agents gave them boarding passes. At 3:45 P.M. an announcement was made that Flight 149 to Dallas–Ft. Worth had changed gates. After hustling to the new gate, they waited as the clock ticked to 4:00 P.M., then to 4:15, and then to 4:30, when the departure time was changed to 5:00 P.M. A number of passengers asked the reason for the delay. The attendant said that the servicing of the plane was taking longer than expected. Over the PA system passengers could hear change after change being made in the departure times of Delta flights. Another half hour passed, and the passengers began to worry about catching their various connecting flights out of Dallas.

Finally, at 5:45 P.M. boarding began, and the announcer asked that all passengers, except first class and business travelers, pick up a Delta Airlines deli-pack. The dinner planned for the flight could not be served to coach passengers. At 6:15 Flight 145 left the gate—1 hour and 45 minutes late.

Once in the air, the pilot announced that the plane was late because no one had been there to clean it and stock it with food and refreshments. He asked the passengers not to take out their frustrations on the flight attendants. Meanwhile, the attendants offered free alcoholic beverages and earphones for an inflight movie.

The flight landed, and the couple dashed to the lineup to see a Delta ticket agent. They hoped that Delta had held up their plane to Oklahoma City. However, the representative said that the plane had taken off on time, there were no other Delta flights to Oklahoma City that day, and that all American Airline flights were full. She gave the couple a ticket for a night's stay at the airport hotel and booked them on the first Delta flight to Oklahoma City the next morning. They received $40 to spend on dinner and breakfast the next morning.

The next morning the plane took off on time, but the couple arrived home 14 hours later than they had expected. In addition to the inconvenience of the delay, they had out-of-pocket expenses for an extra day of airport parking, an extra day's pay for the children's companion, and a half day of lost work for two professionals.

In looking back on the situation, the couple believed that the company hired to service Delta's planes did not have enough personnel to handle all Delta flights leaving New York City. They also believed that Delta had made a calculated financial decision to delay their flight out of New York City because it was only half full. The couple wrote a letter to Delta complaining that the company's financial decision had cost them substantial out-of-pocket expenses and that they should be compensated for their loss with frequent flyer miles. After a long delay, the couple received a letter from Delta. It stated that the flight had been delayed for mechanical reasons and that the company would not compensate them in any way.

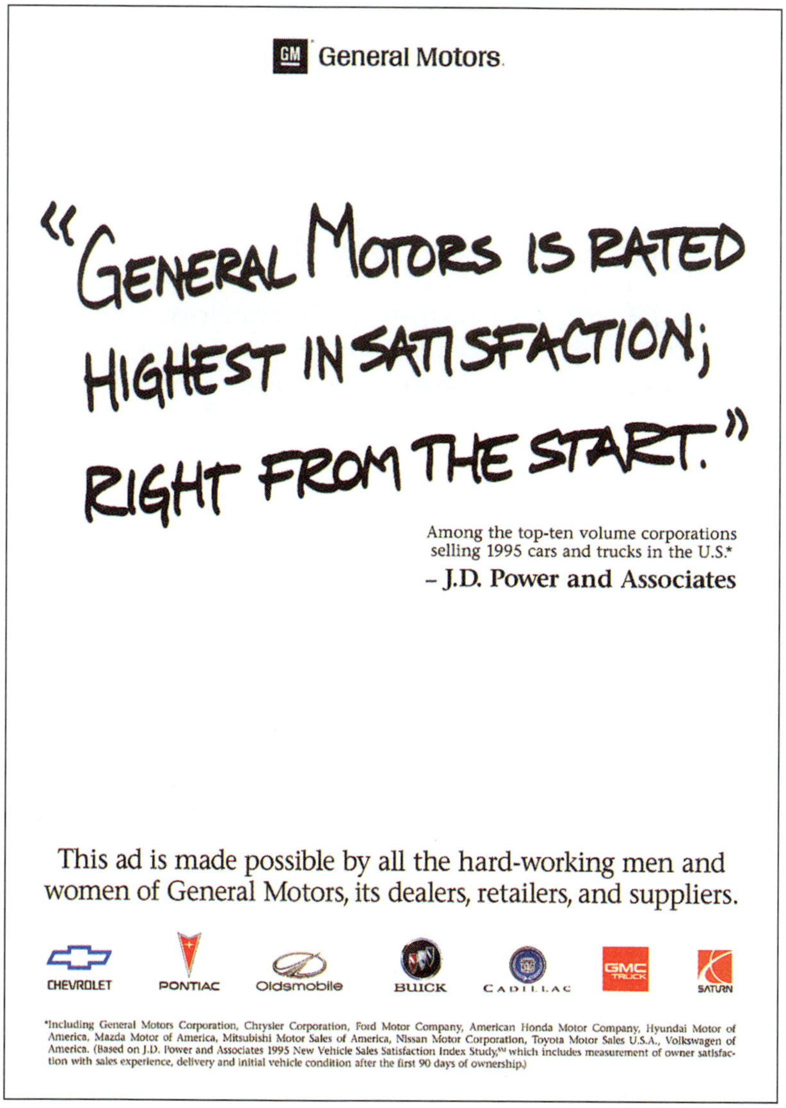

Figure 13-1

Corporations recognize the importance of satisfying their customers. In this ad General Motors touts the results of the J.D. Power's survey.

INTRODUCTION

In the last two chapters we explored the first four stages of the consumer decision process: problem recognition, information search, alternative evaluation, and choice. In this chapter we focus on the last stage of consumer decision making: postacquisition processes. **Postacquisition processes** refer to the consumption, postchoice evaluation, and disposition of goods, services, experiences, and ideas. During the postchoice evaluation stage consumers generally express satisfaction or dissatisfaction with their purchase. Providing high levels of postpurchase satisfaction is a major goal of most companies, from the local restaurant to Delta Airlines to General Motors, because they know that repeat purchase behavior depends on it. Figure 13-1 presents an ad from General Motors that touts the satisfaction of its customers.

Figure 13-2 presents a model of the consumer postacquisition process, which encompasses five major phases: (1) product usage/consumption, (2) consumer satisfaction/dissatisfaction, (3) consumer complaint behavior, (4) the disposition of goods, and (5) the formation of brand loyalty. During the consumption phase consumers use and experience the product. This phase is followed by the development of satisfaction or dissatisfaction with the product. If consumers are dissatisfied with the product's performance, they may complain about it to the retailer or to the manufacturer. The final two phases of the postacquisition stage involve how consumers ultimately dispose of the goods they purchased and whether they form brand loyalty and future buying intentions.

The introductory case illustrates a number of the concepts that we will be discussing in this chapter. Before we get into the chapter proper, we ask you to consider three questions concerning the case. First, what specific aspects of the Flight 149 would influence the satisfaction level of the couple? Second, did Delta respond appropriately to the situation? Third, would the couple's brand loyalty be influenced by Delta's actions?

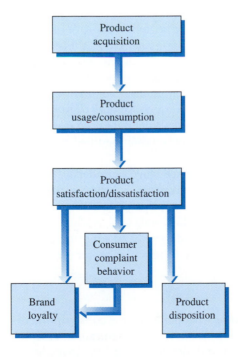

Figure 13-2
A model of the consumer postacquisition process.

THE CONSUMPTION EXPERIENCE

A **consumption experience** may be defined as the cognitions and feelings the consumer experiences during the use of a product or service. In this section of the chapter we consider the three elements of the consumption experience: product use, the consumption of performance, and the impact of moods and feelings on the overall consumption experience.

Product Use

Product use involves the actions and experiences that take place in the time period in which a consumer is directly experiencing a good or service. The observation of how consumers use goods often leads managers to develop new market offerings. For example, a general manager at Kodak once observed a tourist in Japan attempting to pry open a Kodak film container while holding his camera. The feat was impossible with one hand—the man had to use his teeth to tear off the lid. The manager returned to headquarters and reported the problem, and now Kodak film container lids can be pulled off with one hand.[2]

Information on product usage is also important for avoiding product liability problems. Of course, companies must design products so that they are safe for the uses for which they were intended. But that is not enough. They also need to anticipate *unintended* uses of their products, and either design them so that they will be safe for those uses too or warn consumers that they are dangerous in certain applications.[3] For example, manufacturers of aluminum stepladders warn consumers not to stand on the top of the ladder and also to avoid using the ladder near an electrical line.

Marketers have identified three factors that are particularly important when assessing product usage.[4] The first is **consumption frequency.** Some products are used continuously (e.g., refrigerators and hot-water heaters); most, however, are used discontinuously (e.g., dishwashers, medical services, toothpaste, autos). Generally speaking, companies want consumers to use products or services as frequently as possible. (There are exceptions to this, such as when an organization is attempting to get consumers to reduce or eliminate the use of drugs.)

Consumption amount is the second factor that needs to be analyzed. Firms often create strategies to increase the average usage of a product. This is what General Foods Corporation did with its breakfast cereal Grape-Nuts.[5] Market research had discovered that 18 percent of Denver families had purchased Grape-Nuts during a six-month period. This was the fourth best performance among all cereals, but still, purchase volume was significantly less than average. General Foods devised new ways for consumers to use Grape-Nuts and publicized them. Some ads suggested heating Grape-Nuts and eating it as a warm cereal, others proposed that consumers sprinkle Grape-Nuts on their oatmeal, which was then becoming popular as a healthy breakfast food.

Consumption purpose is the third factor to be assessed when considering product usage. A classic example of a company that has successfully expanded the purposes of a product is Arm & Hammer. Through a long-running ad campaign, Arm & Hammer has made consumers aware of many alternative uses for its baking soda: as a tooth powder, as a carpet freshener, as an antacid, and as a refrigerator deodorizer. Consumption purpose is closely related to what is called *usage occasion*, a topic we discuss in Chapter 14.

The Consumption of Performance

Marketing researchers suggest that in Western society people frame the consumption experience as though they were participating in a performance. Using naturalistic research methods borrowed from the fields of anthropology and sociology, they have investigated especially dramatic consumer performances such as skydiving[6] and white-water river rafting.[7]

What does it mean to say that consumers are participating in a performance? From a dramaturgical perspective, consumers and marketers often act as though they are participating in a theatrical performance.[8] For example, when white-water rafting down the Colorado River, the participants and their guide are actors. The boat, life vests, food, mosquito repellants, and all the other trappings are the props for the play. The Colorado River and the canyon form the stage. Within this backdrop, a story is told. In the first stage of the story, conflicting forces are introduced. That is, the participants ask themselves if they really want to put life and limb at risk in order to have a white-water experience. During the second stage tensions and emotions build as they experience fear, hunger, and cold. At the conclusion the conflict is resolved and emotions are released.

Consumers and marketers can be viewed as actors in an "exchange play" in which each performs to a greater or lesser degree. In the introductory case a dramatistic performance was taking place with the couple and Delta Airlines employees as the actors. For the purposes of this text, a **consumer performance** is an event in which a consumer and marketer act as performers and/or audience in a situation in which obligations and standards exist.[9] It is important to distinguish a performance from an occurrence. An occurrence is the result of an accident or an "act of nature." It is unplanned, and does not arise from any obligation.

Table 13-1 gives a succinct description of the three types of consumer performance possible in a marketing exchange. In a **contracted performance** the consumer and marketer play only minimal roles. Contracted performances most frequently involve the purchase and use of low-involvement products like detergents, toothpastes, motor oil, and checking accounts. In an **enacted performance** the consumer and/or the marketer have a clear stake in the success of the exchange. The exchange occurs in a manner in which the consumer or marketer has latitude to blame or to give credit to the other for the outcome of the transaction. Enacted performance occurs most frequently in service exchanges or with high-involvement goods. For example, being a passenger on an airline is to involve oneself in an enacted performance. Similarly, the purchase of a car involves both the consumer and the salesperson in a complex exchange in which blame or credit can be assessed by either party.

The third type of performance, **dramatistic performance,** occurs when both the consumer and marketer know that a show is occurring, and each is alert to the other's role. Dramatistic performance is characteristic of situations in which the stakes are large and the consumer's and marketer's involvement level is quite high. Each actor is an audience to the other, and each becomes alert to the motives of the other in the performance, recognizing that the other's actions could be contrived. An example is a situation where a consumer believes that she has been wronged by a company and begins to complain. Other

Types of Consumer Performances

1. *Contracted performance*. Both the consumer and the marketer have minimal interactions. Occurs with low-involvement goods.

2. *Enacted performance*. Both the consumer and the marketer have sufficient latitude to place blame for the outcome of the transaction. Occurs most frequently with high-involvement products.

3. *Dramatistic performance*. Both the consumer and the marketer know that a show is occurring. Each party becomes concerned with the motives of the other. Occurs most frequently in the highest-involvement situations, such as skydiving or buying an automobile.

TABLE 13-1

examples of dramatistic performances are white-water rafting expeditions and skydiving. It is during dramatistic performances that stories unfold, consumer emotions run their highest, and the flow is most likely to be experienced.

The drama metaphor is particularly appropriate when consumers are purchasing services. For example, in the introductory case, Delta Airlines and its passengers at the New York airport were involved in a drama centered around whether passengers would make their connecting flights and get to their destinations that night. The drama continued when the passengers made complaints.

The drama metaphor may hold for the purchase and use of goods as well as services. Indeed, a good can be described as having a "frozen potential for performance,"[10] so that consumers do not just choose a good, but also consume performances when they use the good. Figure 13-3 shows a photo of the world's greatest salesman, who works for a trading post just outside of Mexico City. In his dramatistic performance, he first entertains a busload of tourists by showing them how a cactus can provide food, clothing, and drink. He then takes the group through the ritual of downing a shot of tequila, licking salt off of one's hand, and then biting a lime. After plying the group with another shot of a strange, but delicious, liquor, he takes the tourists into the store and shows them handmade rugs, sculptures, and jewelry. By the end of his carefully orchestrated dramatistic performance, the consumers practically buy everything in the store.

Figure 13-3

This Mexican salesperson uses dramatistic performance to seduce consumers to purchase rugs and sculptures from the Los Artes Internacionales Piramides outside of Mexico City.

Mood States and the Consumption Experience

Moods are temporary positive or negative affective states. What impact do they have on the consumption experience? As you will recall from in the chapters on information processing (Chapter 4) and choice (Chapter 12), moods often have a strong impact on what consumers remember and on which brand they choose. Mood states may be influenced by what happens during the consumption of a product, and the mood state that is created during the consumption process may, in turn, affect the consumer's overall evaluation of the product. Thinking back to the introductory case, after having flown for over nine hours from Rome to New York, the couple was extremely tired and cranky. Their mood state was definitely negative, and it was from within the confines of this mood state that they interpreted all the events of the drama.

One study investigated the impact of music on consumers' mood states and on their subsequent product evaluations.[11] Respondents either heard music that they rated very positively or music that they rated very negatively. While listening to the music, they rated the taste of peanut butter. Pretesting indicated that the positively rated music put the respondents who heard it in a more positive mood than the respondents who were exposed to the negatively rated music. Different groups of subjects rated one of three different types of peanut butter, which in pretests were determined to taste very good, neutral, or very bad. The results revealed that the type of music did *not* impact evaluations for the good or the bad-tasting peanut butter. However, for the neutral-tasting peanut butter, brand evaluations were significantly higher when the music was liked than when it was disliked.

In sum, consumers' feelings about the consumption experience will affect their evaluations of the product independently of the actual quality of the product. Postpurchase evaluations of products is closely related to the development of feelings of satisfaction or dissatisfaction with the exchange process, which is the topic of our next section.

THE DEVELOPMENT OF POSTACQUISITION SATISFACTION/DISSATISFACTION

During and after the consumption and use of a product or service, consumers develop feelings of satisfaction or dissatisfaction. **Consumer satisfaction** is defined as the overall attitude consumers have toward a good or service after they have acquired and used it. It is a postchoice evaluative judgment resulting from a specific purchase selection and the experience of using/consuming it.[12]

From a managerial perspective, maintaining and/or enhancing customer satisfaction is critical. One recent study that examined the satisfaction level of customers with Swedish firms found that over a five-year period an annual 1 percent increase in customer satisfaction resulted in an 11.4 percent increase in the firms' return on investment. These results revealed that satisfied customers positively influence a company's future cash flows. Managers should therefore view programs to increase customer satisfaction as investments.[13]

What are the factors that contribute to consumer satisfaction or dissatisfaction (CS/D)? Figure 13-4 presents a model of CS/D that shows consumers consuming/using a good or service and, based on this experience, evaluating its overall performance. This assessment of performance has been found to be closely related to the ratings of the quality of the product.[14] Consumers compare their perceptions of product quality after using the product to their expectations of the product's performance before they purchased it. Depending on how actual performance stacks up to expected performance, they will experience positive, negative, or neutral emotions. These emotional responses act as inputs into their overall satisfaction/dissatisfaction perception.

The level of satisfaction/dissatisfaction will also be affected by consumers' evaluation of the equity of the exchange, as well as by their attributions of the cause of the product's performance. The following sections discuss each of these ideas.

The Evaluation of Product Performance and Quality

Over the past 15 years companies throughout the world have embraced the concept of total quality management. **Total quality management (TQM)** is a management philosophy based on the ideas that successful companies continuously improve the quality of their products and that quality is defined by the customer.[15] Producing high-quality products

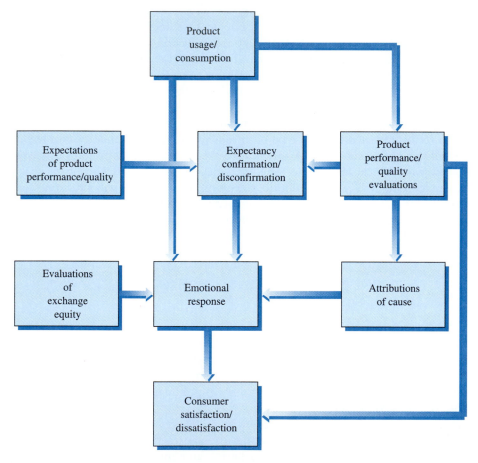

Figure 13-4

A model of consumer satisfaction/dissatisfaction.

is critical to success in international marketing today and in business-to-business marketing as well. An essential element in the implementation of TQM programs is the concept that quality is *consumer driven* and that companies must therefore assess consumer perceptions of quality.

Product quality, then, is defined as customers' overall evaluation of the excellence of the performance of a good or service.[16] A key issue in assessing perceived product performance is what dimensions consumers use to make their evaluations. Researchers in the services area have identified five dimensions on which consumers evaluate service quality. They are given in Part A of Table 13-2.[17]

These five dimensions of service quality can be viewed as attributes on which consumers evaluate the overall performance of *services*. As applied to *goods*, however, they present a major problem because, except for the "tangibles" category, they focus exclusively on the interaction between employees and customers. What is needed is a set of dimensions that includes the concrete attributes consumers associate with goods.

Such a set of eight dimensions has been proposed to assess product quality. These eight categories are listed in Part B of Table 13-2. In addition, other researchers have presented a set of quality dimensions used by customers to evaluate retail stores.[19] We believe that it is possible to combine the three approaches to identify seven basic dimensions of quality. They are:

1. *Performance*. The absolute level of performance of the good or service on the key attributes identified by customers. The extent that the product or service is

---

The Dimensions of Quality

A. Dimensions of Service Quality

1. *Tangibles*. Include physical facilities, equipment, and appearance of personnel.
2. *Reliability*. The ability of personnel to perform dependably and accurately.
3. *Responsiveness*. Providing customers with prompt service.
4. *Assurance*. The knowledge and courtesy of employees, as well as their ability to inspire trust and confidence.
5. *Empathy*. The ability of employees to care and to provide individualized attention.

Source: A. Parasuraman, Valarie A. Zeithaml, and Leonard L. Berry, "SERVQUAL: A Multiple-Item Scale for Measuring Consumer Perceptions of Service Quality," *Journal of Retailing*, Vol. 64 (Spring 1988), pp. 12–36.

B. Dimensions of Product Quality

1. *Performance*. Performance on primary operating characteristics.
2. *Features*. The number of bells and whistles that supplement primary characteristics.
3. *Reliability*. Probability of failing or malfunctioning.
4. *Durability*. The life of the product.
5. *Serviceability*. Ease of repair, and the speed, courtesy, and timeliness of personnel.
6. *Aesthetics*. How the product looks, feels, and sounds.
7. *Conformance to specifications*. Degree to which the product meets production benchmarks.
8. *Perceived quality*. A catchall category that includes the effects of brand image and other intangible factors that influence customers' perceptions of quality.

Source: David A. Garvin, *Managing Quality: The Strategic and Competitive Edge* (New York: The Free Press, 1988).

TABLE 13-2

"done right." The number of attributes offered. The ability of employees to handle problems well. The quality of the information provided to the customer.

2. *Employee interactions*. The courtesy, friendliness, and empathy shown by people delivering the service or good. The overall credibility of the employees, including consumers' trust in employees and their perceptions of employee expertise.

3. *Reliability*. The consistency of the performance of the good, service, or store.

4. *Durability*. The product's life span and general sturdiness.

5. *Timeliness and convenience*. How quickly the product is delivered or repaired. How quickly information or service is provided. The convenience of the purchase and service process, including acceptance of credit cards, store operating hours, and parking.

6. *Aesthetics*. The physical appearance of the good or store. The attractiveness of the presentation of the service. The pleasantness of the atmosphere in which the service or product is received. How the design of the product looks to people.

7. *Brand equity*. The additional positive or negative impact on perceived quality that knowing the brand or store name has on consumers' evaluations.[20]

Research is necessary to establish whether these seven categories fully represent the dimensions on which consumers evaluate quality. In particular, the category of aesthetics requires additional research. One exploratory study on product design did find that consumers evaluated design in a gestalt (i.e., wholistic) manner and did so largely unconsciously. Two factors seemed to be related to aesthetic preferences: proportion (the ratio of the length to the height of an object) and unity (the extent that design elements appeared "to go together").[21]

Table 13-3 provides examples of how each of the seven categories we have proposed can be applied to a good (an automobile) or a service (an elegant restaurant).

A key question concerns how each of the dimensions of product quality are combined to form an overall impression of quality. We view the formation of overall product quality as a type of overall consumer belief. That is, we think that consumers form beliefs about each of the product's quality dimensions, and then sum up these beliefs to form an overall belief regarding the quality of the product. In effect, people act as though their perception of the overall performance quality of a product is formed via a type of multiattribute model.

The Development of Satisfaction/Dissatisfaction

A model critical for understanding and influencing consumer satisfaction/dissatisfaction (CS/D) is the expectancy disconfirmation model. The expectancy disconfirmation model defines CS/D as the "evaluation rendered that the experience was at least as good as it was supposed to be."[22] Three additional approaches have been taken to explain the formation of CS/D: equity theory, attribution theory, and experientially based affective feelings. In addition, the actual performance of a product has been found to impact CS/D.[23] We discuss all of these approaches in this section.

Question: How do you minimize dissatisfaction in consumers who are waiting for a service?

Answer: Set clear expectations for how long customers must wait, and fill their time with something to do.

Source: Shirley Taylor, "The Effect of Filled Waiting Time and Service Provider Control Over the Delay on Evaluations of Services," *Journal of the Academy of Marketing Science*, Vol. 23 (Winter 1995), pp. 28–38.

Consumer Behavior Factoid

A Revised Set of Categories of Product Quality Applied to a Good and a Service	
Product Quality Dimension	**Automobile Quality**
1. Performance	Level of horsepower, handling, fit and finish, resale value, the number of features, such as air bags, ABS breaking system, premium sound system, cup holders.
2. Employee interactions	Friendliness, helpfulness, empathy, and credibility of service personnel.
3. Reliability	Freedom from breakdown of vehicle, consistency of personnel in providing expected levels of service.
4. Durability	How long the car lasts before it wears out from use or before it becomes technologically out-of-date.
5. Timeliness/convenience	The ability of the company to provide the vehicle and its service in a timely way. The convenience of providing service.
6. Aesthetics	The attractiveness and functionality of the layout and style of the car.
7. Brand equity	The extent that the vehicle's brand name results in customers believing that it has high or low quality.
Product Quality Dimension	**Restaurant Meal Quality**
1. Performance	The degree to which the food is prepared according to standards of taste and temperature. The degree to which staff know their jobs. The number of extra features provided with the meal, such as fresh flowers on the table, special breads provided as appetizers, free desserts.
2. Employee interactions	The friendliness and helpfulness of the staff.
3. Reliability	The consistency with which the restaurant provides a high-quality dining experience.
4. Durability	The number of years that the restaurant successfully pleases its customers.
5. Timeliness	The ability of the staff to provide service in a timely way.
6. Aesthetics	The atmosphere of the restaurant, the degree to which the food is pleasing to the eye, the physical attractiveness of the staff.
7. Brand equity	The extent that the restaurant's brand name results in customers believing that it has high or low quality.

TABLE 13-3

The Expectancy Disconfirmation Model The expectancy disconfirmation model of consumer satisfaction/dissatisfaction is shown in Figure 13-5. Note that the process through which CS/D is formed begins with the use of other brands in the product class as well as with the use of the brand in question. Through this usage behavior, and through communications from firms and other people, consumers develop expectations of how the brand *should* perform.

In the next stage consumers compare their performance expectations to **actual product performance** (i.e., the perception of the product's quality). If quality falls below their expectations, they experience **emotional dissatisfaction.** If it is above their expectations, they feel **emotional satisfaction.**[24] If performance is perceived as equal to expectations, consumers experience **expectancy confirmation.**[25] Actually, when expectations and actual

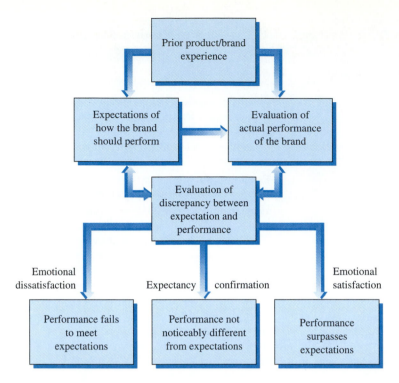

Figure 13-5

The expectancy disconfirmation model of consumer satisfaction/dissatisfaction. (*Source*: Adapted from a discussion in R. B. Woodruff, E. R. Cadotte, and R. L. Jenkins, "Modeling Consumer Satisfaction Processes Using Experience-Based Norms," *Journal of Marketing Research*, Vol. 20 [August 1983], pp. 296–304, published by the American Marketing Assocation.)

performance coincide, evidence indicates that consumers may not consciously consider their level of satisfaction with the product. So although expectancy confirmation is a positive state, it often does not result in strong feelings of satisfaction. Strong satisfaction is apparently experienced only when actual performance is markedly superior to expected performance.

Product expectations are the standard against which the actual performance of the product is assessed.[26] The level of performance expected of a product is influenced by the nature of the product itself, by promotional factors, by the effects of other products, and by the characteristics of the consumer. Concerning the nature of the product, consumers' prior experiences with the product, its price, and its physical characteristics all influence how they will expect it to perform. Thus if the product has a high price or if it has performed extremely well in the past, consumers will expect it to meet high performance standards.

How the company promotes the product both through its advertising and through the communications of its sales personnel also influences performance expectations. A consultant with a market research firm noted that advertising hype can create expectations that are impossible to satisfy.[27] The advertisement shown in Figure 13-6 illustrates how a company can create great expectations. This American Express ad provokes the expectation that if billing problems occur, someone will use "judgment and initiative" to solve the problem.

Consumers' expectations of performance are also influenced by their experience with other, similar products. For example, one key factor influencing consumer perceptions of the quality of medical services is the timeliness with which medical care is delivered.

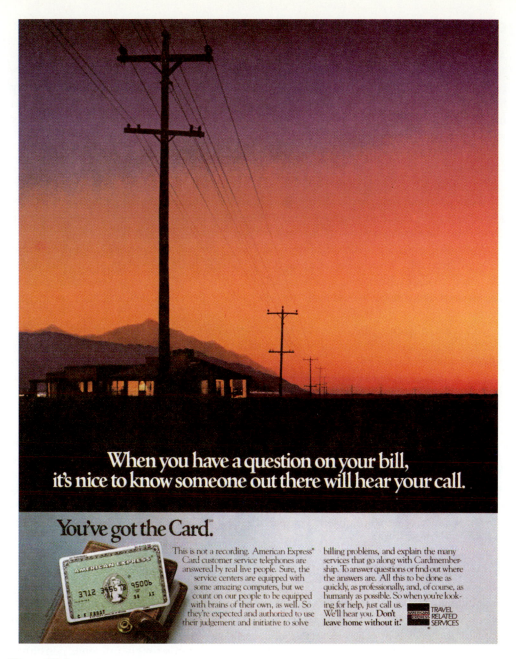

Figure 13-6

American Express attempts to create service expectations.

Physicians and hospitals have been slow to recognize that consumers form their expectations of timeliness as much from their experiences with banks and restaurants as from their experiences with other medical facilities.

Finally, expectations of performance are influenced by the individual characteristics of the consumer.[28] Some consumers simply expect more of products than others do. Likewise, some consumers have wider latitudes of acceptance than others do. Consumers with very narrow latitudes of acceptance are, of course, more easily dissatisfied than those with broad regions of acceptance.

Equity Theory and Consumer Satisfaction

Another approach to understanding consumer satisfaction is through equity theory. Researchers have found that people analyze exchanges between themselves and other parties to determine the extent to which those exchanges are equitable or fair.[29] **Equity theory** holds that people will analyze the ratio of their **outcomes** and **inputs** to the outcomes and inputs of their partner in an exchange, and if they perceive that their ratio is higher, they will experience feelings of inequity. The following equation shows these ratios:[30]

$$\frac{\text{Outcomes A}}{\text{Inputs A}} \approx \frac{\text{Outcomes B}}{\text{Inputs B}}$$

The outcomes that person A receives from an exchange divided by the inputs of person A to the exchange should approximate the outcomes of person B from the exchange divided by the inputs of person B to the exchange.

According to equity theory, the norm is that each party to an exchange should be treated fairly or equitably. Thus satisfaction occurs when the ratios of outcomes and inputs for each party to the exchange are approximately equal. When the buyer believes that his ratio of inputs to outcomes is worse than the seller's, he experiences inequity, and this feeling of inequity leads to dissatisfaction.

Just what are inputs and outcomes to a consumer exchange? From the consumer's perspective, inputs are the information, effort, money, or time exerted to make an exchange possible. Outcomes for the consumer are the benefits and liabilities received from the exchange. Outcomes could consist of the good or service received from the marketer, the performance of the product, and the feelings obtained from the exchange.

A number of authors have investigated how equity theory may be applied to consumer behavior. One study looked at the exchange process between consumers and an airline.[31] For consumers, the inputs to the exchange consisted primarily of the money they paid for the ticket, and the outcomes consisted of the quality of the service they received on the flight and the speed with which the airline got them to their destination. The results of the study revealed that if consumers perceived their inputs to be large because they paid higher-than-average fares, they tended to be dissatisfied with the service. Also, if they perceived that outcomes were poor because flights had been delayed for two hours, they revealed more dissatisfaction.[32]

Other researchers have found that people consider the outcomes of other consumers in determining their own satisfaction with a transaction.[33] In this study respondents pretended to be automobile buyers. After their purchase they found out that another buyer had obtained either a better or a worse deal on the same car. When the other consumer got a better deal on the same car, the respondents were less satisfied with their own transaction and with the auto dealer than when the other consumer got a worse deal. This study shows that factors other than the performance of the product can strongly influence consumer satisfaction—specifically, the evaluation of the overall equity of the purchase transaction.

Note that the process equity theory proposes to explain CS/D is different from the process proposed by the expectancy disconfirmation model presented in Figure 13-4. In the expectancy disconfirmation model CS/D results from the comparison of actual performance to expected performance. In contrast, equity theory holds that satisfaction *also* results from comparing one's inputs and outcomes with those of others.[34] What are the relative impacts of equity and expectancy disconfirmation on consumer satisfaction? In a study of over 400 new car buyers, researchers obtained measures of satisfaction with the salesperson, of the degree of equity or fairness in the transaction, and of the inputs and outcomes of the salesperson and the buyer.[35] The finding was that fairness or equity was highly self-centered for most buyers. That is, they perceived they got a fair deal when their outcome was high and the seller's input was high. A further finding was that perceptions of fairness/equity had a greater impact on consumers' overall satisfaction than perceptions that expectations were disconfirmed.

The managerial implications of equity theory are as follows. First, marketers should ensure that customers recognize all of the inputs the company has added to the transaction. Second, marketers should realize that, as the authors of the new car buyer study stated, "equitable exchange from the point of view of the buyer may be seen as inequitable exchange by the salesperson."[36] Third, consumers do form judgments of equity, and these judgments may have a greater impact on their satisfaction than expectancy disconfirmation. This combination of findings makes the salesperson's job extremely difficult, for it forces the salesperson to manage impressions so that buyers believe they are getting a great buy and the salesperson is giving up a great deal to make the sale. Unfortunately, the need to give such an impression encourages salespeople to use hype and false statements to make sales.

On the Relation Between Attribution Theory, Product Failure, and Consumer Satisfaction

When we discussed **attribution theory** in Chapter 6, we said it was concerned with how people identify the causes for action. The attributions consumers make can strongly influence their postpurchase satisfaction with a product or service. If a product fails (i.e., performance is below expectations), consumers will attempt to determine the cause of the failure. If they attribute the failure to the product or service itself, they are likely to feel dissatisfied, but if they attribute the failure to chance factors or to their own actions, they are not as likely to be dissatisfied.[37]

One study investigating CS/D with airlines that were experiencing a lot of delayed flights found that satisfaction depended on the types of attributions consumers made.[38] When they attributed delays to uncontrollable situational factors, such as fog or ice, they did *not* tend to get angry. However, when they attributed delays to stable factors, such as the actions of airline personnel over whom the airline had control, they were likely to feel angry and dissatisfied. In general, attributional processes are most likely to impact CS/D when consumer involvement in and experience with (i.e., knowledge of) the good or service is high.[39]

Actual Product Performance

Researchers have found strong evidence that actual product performance influences consumer satisfaction independently of expectations, equity, and attributions. Thus even when consumers fully expect a product to perform poorly, they still feel dissatisfied when it does. A study investigating the effects of performance as well as the impact of attribution, expectations, and equity on consumer satisfaction with a stock market selection found that performance influenced satisfaction independently of expectations.[40] It has also been found that perceived product performance/quality directly influences CS/D, particularly when the product is unambiguous and easy to evaluate.[41]

Affect and CS/D

CS/D may also be analyzed from an experiential perspective. The term **affect and CS/D** refers to the concept that the level of consumer satisfaction is influenced by the positive and negative feelings that consumers associate with the product or service after purchase and during use. One researcher investigating the level of satisfaction with automobiles and cable television services after their purchase found that there were two dimensions of affective responses: a set of positive feelings and a set of negative feelings.[42] Interestingly, these feelings were independent of each other. That is, consumers could simultaneously feel both positively and negatively toward a purchase. Of course, it is possible to experience joy, interest, and excitement while also feeling anger, disgust, and contempt in this as in other areas of life. Thus after purchasing an auto a consumer may feel excited and proud about the car itself, while feeling simultaneously irritated and unhappy with the salesperson.[43]

The study also found that measures of CS/D were directly influenced by consumers' affective feelings.[44] Researchers discovered a relationship in which a purchase led to affective reactions, which, in turn, led to feelings of CS/D. Thus in addition to the cognitive knowledge that expectancies were confirmed or disconfirmed, the feelings that surrounded the postacquisition process also appeared to affect consumers' satisfaction with a product. A similar pattern of results has been found in CS/D with restaurants and with automobiles. Affective responses predicted satisfaction independently of customers' cognitive thoughts (i.e., beliefs about the server's attentiveness, friendliness, etc.). Particularly in high-involvement situations, such as the purchase of an automobile, consumer satisfaction tends to have a strong emotional component.[45]

Table 13-4 summarizes the factors that influence CS/D with a purchase. These factors were diagramed in Figure 13-4. If you look back at that figure, you will see that after purchasing and using/consuming a product, consumers go through a series of cognitive and emotional reactions, including expectancy confirmation/disconfirmation, evaluations of the equity of the exchange, evaluations of actual product performance/quality, and attributions of the cause of the outcomes.

Also note that Figure 13-4 depicts emotions and attributions as interacting to influence consumer satisfaction/dissatisfaction. For example, if a product important to the consumer fails, the consumer is likely to have the immediate emotional response of anger. However, that anger will be influenced by the attribution of cause made by the customer. If the cause of the failure is attributed to factors beyond the control of the company, the dissatisfaction and anger are likely to be mild. The intensity of satisfaction/dissatisfaction, then, results from the interaction of cause attribution with product performance evaluation.[46]

Another recent finding is that as consumers' involvement level in the purchase situation increases, their satisfaction or dissatisfaction with the purchase tends to be magnified.[47] So if outcomes exceed expectations, consumers will have higher levels of satisfaction when they are highly involved in the purchase. Of course, if outcomes fall below

---

Summary of Factors Influencing Consumer Satisfaction/Dissatisfaction

I. **Expectancy Disconfirmation**
   A. Factors influencing expectations
      1. Characteristics of the product
      2. Promotional factors
      3. Other factors
      4. Characteristics of the consumer
   B. Factors influencing perception of actual performance

II. **Equity Perceptions**

III. **Attributions of Causality**

IV. **Actual Product Performance**

V. **Consumer's Affective State**

TABLE 13-4

expectations, they will also have higher levels of dissatisfaction when they are highly involved in the purchase.

Measuring Consumer Satisfaction

Traditional measures of consumer satisfaction have assessed people's overall evaluation of the product, as well as their evaluations of specific attributes. Likert scales are frequently used for this purpose: a statement is made and consumers are asked to indicate their level of agreement with it. For example, to assess overall satisfaction with an airline, a questionnaire might present this item: "Overall, I was highly satisfied with the service provided by Delta Airlines." A 5-point scale could be used: *Agree 1 2 3 4 5 Disagree*.

A newer approach to satisfaction measurement is to use rating scales on which respondents evaluate the performance of a service or good on various dimensions. Thus one question might be: "Rate the timeliness of how the airline service was provided." A 5-point scale could be used: *Very Bad 1 2 3 4 5 Very Good*. Other questions would probe consumers' opinions about other characteristics of airline service, such as customer-employee interactions, the aesthetics of the airplane (e.g., was it clean), and the reliability of the service. Frequently, regression equations are developed in which the attribute questions are used to predict overall satisfaction rating. This general approach can be used to evaluate satisfaction with virtually any good or service.

Researchers who use Likert and other rating scales to assess satisfaction treat consumer satisfaction as though it were an attitude, and indeed, recent studies of airline services have confirmed the validity of viewing satisfaction as an attitude.[48] That being so, we would expect customers to place different importance weights on the various attributes of a good or service. That is, some dimensions of the good or service will have a greater impact on overall satisfaction than others. For example, the research study on airlines found that punctuality and the quality of the meals served were extremely important in consumers' eyes. If the flight was delayed, not only did the importance of punctuality in predicting satisfaction increase, but satisfaction ratings on other dimensions of the flight were lower than they were when there was no delay in the flight. This finding illustrates the halo effect, which says that extreme ratings on one dimension of performance will influence ratings on other dimensions of performance.

Recently, researchers have identified a strong positivity bias in traditional approaches to measuring satisfaction.[49] That is, in self-reports of customer satisfaction, most respondents said they were satisfied. The authors of this study found that across hundreds of different studies, on average, 65 percent of customers reported "high levels of satisfaction." These findings should be noted by managers. They need to recognize that a report that states "the majority of customers revealed high levels of satisfaction" is virtually meaningless because almost always this result is obtained regardless of the quality of the service.

One way to correct this problem is to ask about dissatisfaction rather than satisfaction. Asking respondents to agree or disagree with the statement "I was highly dissatisfied with the product" counteracts the positivity bias and allows managers to focus on areas of dissatisfaction.

Consumer Behavior Factoid

Question: What are the two factors that predict alumni satisfaction with universities?

Answer: The perceived quality of the intellectual environment and the employment opportunities of graduates.

Source: Diane Halstead, David Hartman, and Sandra L. Schmidt, "Multi-source Effects on the Satisfaction Formation Process," *Journal of the Academy of Marketing Sciences*, Vol. 22 (Spring 1994), pp. 114–129.

CONSUMER COMPLAINT BEHAVIOR

When consumers perceive that they are dissatisfied with a product or service, what do they do about it? **Consumer complaint behavior** is a term that covers all the different actions consumers take when they are dissatisfied with a purchase.[50] Researchers have identified the following five common complaint behaviors:

1. Deal with the retailer in some manner.
2. Avoid using the retailer again and persuade friends and family to do the same.
3. Take overt action involving third parties (e.g., launch legal action to obtain redress).[51]
4. Boycott the firm or organization.
5. Create an alternative organization to provide the good or service.[52]

See Table 13-5 for a list of specific actions associated with the first three behaviors.

The first three behaviors—dealing with the retailer, not patronizing the brand or store and asking friends to also shun it, and complaining through third parties—are straightforward responses to product or service problems in which consumers seek redress either by personally punishing the retailer through a withdrawal of business or by seeking some type of refund. The refund could be in the form of money or a replacement product. The last two behaviors are more far-reaching. Instead of merely withdrawing their own business (and perhaps that of friends and family), consumers who launch public boycotts are out to change marketing practices and/or to promote social change. Perhaps the most drastic behavior is the last: creating an entirely new organization to provide the good or service. Examples of such organizations are: Consumers Union, food-buying co-ops (e.g., IGA grocery stores), credit unions, and the American Association of Retired Persons.

Studies of consumer complaint behavior have shown that only a minority of dissatisfied customers take overt action against the company. For example, one study found that in a sample of 2,400 households about one in five purchases resulted in some degree of dissatisfaction, but the buyer took action in less than 50 percent of these instances. The

---

Types of Complaint Actions

1. Do nothing or deal with the retailer.
   a. Forget about the incident and do nothing.
   b. Definitely complain to the store manager.
   c. Go back or call retailer immediately and ask manager to take care of the problem.
2. Avoid using the retailer again and persuade friends to do the same.
   d. Decide not to use the retailer again.
   e. Speak to friends and relatives about your bad experience.
   f. Convince friends and relatives not to use the retailer.
3. Take overt action with third parties.
   g. Complain to a consumer agency.
   h. Write a letter to a local newspaper.
   i. Take some legal action against the retailer.
4. Boycott the organization.
5. Create an alternative organization to provide the good or service.

TABLE 13-5

type of action consumers took depended partly on the type of product or service. For low-cost, frequently purchased products, fewer than 15 percent of consumers took any action when they were dissatisfied. But, for household durables and automobiles, over 50 percent of dissatisfied consumers took some sort of action. Actually, though, the product that consumers are most likely to take action on when they are dissatisfied is clothing. As many as 75 percent of those experiencing dissatisfaction with clothing took some form of complaint action.[53]

The models of consumer complaint behavior have identified two major purposes for complaining.[54] First, consumers complain in order to recover an economic loss. They may seek to exchange the problem product for another product, or they may seek to get their money back, either directly from the company or store or indirectly through legal means. The second reason consumers engage in complaint behavior is to rebuild their self-image. In many instances a product purchase is tied to the buyer's self-image, so that if the product performs poorly, the person's self-image is lowered. To restore self-image, the consumer may use negative word-of-mouth communications, stop buying the brand, complain to the company or Better Business Bureau, or take legal action. The self-image maintenance aspects of consumer complaint behavior have been insufficiently studied by researchers and companies.

Factors Influencing Complaint Behavior

A number of factors have been found to influence whether or not consumers complain. As noted above, one of them is the type of product or service involved. Another factor is the cost and social importance of the product. Some authors have suggested that the likelihood of complaint behavior increases when:

1. The level of the dissatisfaction increases.
2. The attitude of the consumer toward complaining increases.[55]
3. The amount of benefit to be gained from complaining increases.
4. The firm is blamed for the problem.
5. The product is important to the consumer.
6. The resources available to the consumer for complaining increase.[56]

Previous experience with complaining is also associated with increased complaint behavior. People who have complained in the past know how to go about contacting appropriate authorities and therefore are less bothered by the task than neophytes are.[57]

Attributions made by consumers relate to complaint behavior. Researchers have found that when consumers attribute product problems to the company rather than to themselves, complaints increase. Furthermore, if the problem is viewed as under the control of the company, complaining increases.[58] For example, if consumers attribute a problem with airline service to decisions purposely made by the company, they are much more likely to complain than if they believe the problem is beyond the company's control. Recall from the introductory case that the couple attributed the cause of the delay in their flight to deliberate decisions made by Delta to maximize its revenue. Had they attributed the cause of the delay to external causes like the weather or mechanical problems, they would have been far less likely to complain.

Researchers have been only partially successful in relating demographic factors to complaint behavior.[59] Actually, experience with complaining was a far better predictor of complaint behavior than any demographic factors.[60] Still, a modest correlation has been found between age and income and complaining behavior.[61] Consumers who engage in complaining behavior tend to be younger and to have higher incomes and more education.[62]

Investigations of the relationship between complaining and personality variables have found that people who are more dogmatic (close-minded) and self-confident are somewhat more likely to complain.[63] Consumers who value their individuality and a sense of independence also tend to complain more often than others. Perhaps by complaining these people make themselves feel important and different from others.[64]

Corporate Reactions to Consumer Complaints

Somewhat surprising is the finding that many companies make no systematic effort to investigate the extent of CS/D with their products or services. For example, one survey of food marketers found that 60 percent had little or no idea of how satisfied consumers were with their products.[65] However, many consumer-oriented firms do make special efforts to track CS/D with their products and services. In fact, the use of consumer hotline numbers for this purpose is becoming increasingly popular. Procter & Gamble, Whirlpool, and 3M are companies that have used such toll-free numbers effectively.

Public policy makers take a great interest in consumer complaints. If they believe that consumer complaints are too frequent in an industry, they are likely to develop regulations to ameliorate the problem. Managers, of course, prefer to avoid the encroachment of government—the mere possibility of government intervention is often a strong impetus to establish industry standards. The Council of the Better Business Bureaus has compiled information on the types of industries that receive the most complaints.

Managers should have mechanisms in place to handle consumer complaints. Toll-free numbers is one highly effective means of handling complaints. In addition, firms should establish a means of redress for legitimate consumer complaints.

When not at fault, companies should try hard to break the connection between themselves and a negative event. Several approaches are possible in these situations. First, the company can deny involvement (i.e., we didn't do it). Second, the company can deflect blame by pinning it on someone else (i.e., a maniac is poisoning Tylenol pills). Third, the company can give explanations for the event and identify extenuating circumstances. Note that in the third case the company is not denying all responsibility. Rather, it is encouraging consumers to make a stronger external attribution for the event instead of blaming it altogether on the company.

One interesting research study analyzed company reactions to corporate complaints and, in addition, had consumers evaluate the types of excuses offered by the companies. Most companies attempted to avoid responsibility, and this type of approach was viewed negatively by consumers. Consumers gave the highest ratings to companies that sought to minimize the unpleasantness of an outcome for the consumer and gave a reason for the action.[66]

The authors of this research suggested that companies use excuses strategically so that they accurately describe the causes and outcomes of the negative events that caused the complaints. The excuses provided by companies are an important source of information for consumers when they are deciding what course of action to pursue to correct a perceived wrong. Of course, consumers are not always right and companies are not always wrong, so sometimes a courteous explanation can clear up a misunderstanding.

Complaints and Exit Behavior

Exit behavior refers to the consumer choice to either leave a relationship or to lower consumption levels of the good or service. Researchers investigating complaint behavior in the cellular telephone industry have found that consumers who complain are (1) more likely to leave a relationship and (2) more likely to decrease their consumption levels of the good or service. In addition, it was found that as the level of dissatisfaction increased, the likelihood of complaining increased. The researchers recommended a "get it right the first time" attitude on the part of companies because in many cases it is simply not possible to appease a complaining customer. This recommendation is particularly important in businesses where the costs of obtaining new customers are high. In the cellular telephone industry, for example, it costs $600 to obtain a new customer, but only $20 to retain an existing one.[67]

PRODUCT DISPOSITION

Although how consumers dispose of acquisitions is a fundamental part of the consumer decision process, little research has been done in this area. Figure 13-7 presents a taxonomy of **product disposition**.[68] Basically, a consumer has three dispositional strategies to choose from after using a product for some period of time: keep it, get rid of it permanently, or get rid of it temporarily. Each of these alternatives has suboptions. For example, if the decision is to keep the product, the consumer may continue to use it, convert it to a new use (e.g., use an old toothbrush to clean the grout around shower tiles), or store it. Similarly, if the decision is to get rid of the product permanently, the consumer has a number of options: throw it away, give it away, trade it, or sell it.

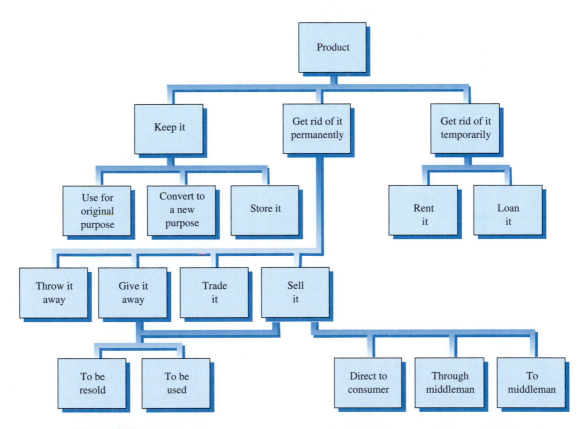

Figure 13-7

A taxonomy of product disposition. (*Source*: Adapted by permission from J. Jacoby, C. Berning, and T. Dietvorst, "What About Disposition?" *Journal of Marketing*, Vol. 41 [April 1997], p. 23, published by the American Marketing Association.)

Disposition Decisions of Six Test Products

	All Products	Stereo Amplifier	Wrist-watch	Tooth-brush	Phono Record	Bicycle	Refrigerator
Converted	7.9%	1.6%	1.8%	17.2%	9.6%	1.5%	7.5%
Stored	12.7	—	28.7	—	32.8	3.1	—
Thrown away	39.7	11.5	30.6	79.7	43.2	17.3	22.6
Given away	17.1	31.1	23.1	—	9.6	40.2	19.3
Sold	11.5	42.6	5.6	—	—	17.3	25.8
Rented	0.7	—	0.9	—	—	—	3.2
Loaned	0.3	—	—	—	—	1.5	1.0
Traded	5.3	4.9	5.6	—	0.8	3.2	20.4
Other	4.8	8.3	3.7	3.1	4.0	15.9	—

Source: J. Jacoby, C. Berning, and T. Dietvorst, "What About Disposition?" *Journal of Marketing*, Vol. 4 (April 1977), p. 26, published by the American Marketing Association. Used by permission.

TABLE 13-6

Table 13-6 presents the results of a study that investigated consumers' disposition decisions regarding six different products.[69] One clear pattern was that the higher the value of the product, the more likely consumers were to dispose of it in ways that maximized return. Thus refrigerators and stereo amplifiers were frequently sold, while toothbrushes were usually just thrown away.

Product disposition can be extremely profitable. For some types of products, there is a thriving aftermarket that seriously cuts into sales of new products. For example, sales of used textbooks can severely lower the sales of new textbooks. Although students benefit in the short term by having to pay less for their textbooks, in the long run the cost of new textbooks is increased because fewer new books are sold and that raises the unit cost of production. Another enterprise based on product disposition is the used-car market. Hundreds of thousands of people make their living buying and selling used cars. And with publications such as *Consumer Reports* rating used cars, new-car buyers are beginning to make the resale value of a car one of the attributes they consider in their initial purchase decision. Companies have even been formed to sell used sports equipment. Figure 13-8 presents an ad for a retail store that specializes in the sale of used golf equipment.

Another product disposition issue is the handling of the garbage resulting from consumer purchases. Indeed, dealing with the environmental hazards posed by the mountains of waste we create each year in using products is now a major public concern. Consumers have generally positive attitudes toward programs designed to reduce waste, such as recycling, garbage reduction, and composting,[70] but despite these positive attitudes, participation in waste-reduction programs varies widely.[71] Researchers investigating the factors that spur people to participate in such programs have found that the individual's attitudes predicted participation to a greater extent than the opinions of other people do (i.e., the subjective norm component of the theory of reasoned action discussed in Chapter 10). Moreover, the greater the individual's perception that a recycling action would have societal benefits, the stronger was that individual's intention to take the action.[72]

The nearby consumer behavior factoid deals with one type of consumer waste product—the bolus.

Figure 13-8
This ad illustrates one means of disposing of used golf equipment—selling it.

BRAND LOYALTY

Closely related to consumer satisfaction and consumer complaining behavior is the concept of brand loyalty.[73] We define **brand loyalty** as the degree to which a customer holds a positive attitude toward a brand, has a commitment to it, and intends to continue purchasing it in the future. Brand loyalty is directly influenced by satisfaction/dissatisfaction with the brand that has accumulated over time as well as perceptions of the product's quality.[74] Because it is from four to six times less costly to retain old customers than to obtain new ones, managers should give top priority to creating strategies that build and maintain brand loyalty.[75]

Air France has a program to nurture brand loyalty among the "jet setters" who ride its supersonic Concorde on a once-a-month basis. These frequent fliers are given unusual gifts, like a videocassette of Jean Cocteau's *Beauty and the Beast*, rather than a coupon for $50 off their next $6,000 round trip. As one well-known marketing consultant said, the point is to "bond a customer to a marketer."[76]

We have defined brand loyalty as the degree to which a customer holds a positive attitude towards a brand, has a commitment to it, and intends to continue purchasing it in the future. This definition is based on two general approaches to understanding the concept: behavioral measures and attitudinal measures of brand loyalty.

Behavioral Approaches to Brand Loyalty

The behavioral approaches measure consumers' actual purchase behavior. The **proportion-of-purchases method** is the most frequently used measure of brand loyalty in empirical research. In this approach all of the brands purchased within a particular product category are determined for each consumer and the proportion of purchases going to each brand is identified. Brand loyalty is then measured in terms of some arbitrary proportion of purchases going to a particular brand. For example, if more than 50 percent of a consumer's purchases were of a particular brand during some time period, that consumer would be said to be loyal to the brand.

The behavioral approaches make it clear that brand loyalty is not an all-or-nothing phenomenon. Instead, the behavior is viewed as taking place across a continuum from complete loyalty to complete brand indifference. There are several types of brand loyalty besides undivided loyalty. In some cases consumers have a divided loyalty between two brands. In other cases they are largely loyal to one brand, but occasionally switch to other brands, perhaps to break the monotony and raise their levels of arousal. In still other instances consumers are completely indifferent to distinctions among brands.[77] These different buying patterns, in which A, B, C, and D are different brands, may be portrayed as follows:

1. *Undivided loyalty*: A A A A A A A.
2. *Occasional switch*: A A B A A A C A A D A.
3. *Switch loyalty*: A A A A B B B B.
4. *Divided loyalty*: A A A B B A A B B B.
5. *Brand indifference*: A B D C B A C D.

From the marketer's perspective, the problem with these behavioral measures of brand loyalty is that they do not identify the reasons consumers purchase a brand. A particular brand could be purchased because of convenience, availability, or price. If any of these factors changed, consumers might rapidly switch to another brand. In such instances consumers cannot be said to exhibit brand loyalty, because implicit in the idea of loyalty is that the consumer has more than a passing infatuation with the brand.

Another behavioral measure of brand loyalty is based on the number of customers who stop using a product. See the nearby consumer behavior factoid for a brief example of this measure.

Attitudinal Measures of Brand Loyalty

The problems encountered in the behavioral measures of brand loyalty illustrate why it is important to distinguish between brand loyalty and repeat purchase behavior. **Repeat purchase behavior** means that the consumer is merely buying a product repeatedly, without any particular feeling for it. In contrast, the concept of brand loyalty implies that a consumer has some real preference for the brand. In light of this distinction, another approach to assessing brand loyalty was developed, one based on the consumers' attitude toward the product as well as on their purchase behavior. According to this approach, consumers exhibit brand loyalty only when they actively prefer the product.[78]

With brand loyalty comes commitment. **Brand commitment** has been defined as an emotional/psychological attachment to a brand within a product class.[79] Whereas brand loyalty has both a behavioral and an attitudinal component, brand commitment tends to focus more on the emotional/feeling component. In one study of the brand commitment of consumers to soft drinks, the researchers found that commitment results from purchase involvement, which, in turn, results from ego involvement with the brand category.[80] According to the authors, such ego involvement happens when a product is closely related to the consumer's important values, needs, and self-concept.

In sum, brand commitment occurs most frequently with high-involvement products that symbolize consumers' self-concepts, values, and needs. These products tend to be higher-priced consumer durables that possess greater perceived risk,[81] though they may be such everyday emotion-laden products as soft drinks. Some evidence indicates that brand preferences are formed during childhood and adolescence,[82] which would suggest that managers should begin targeting customers early in their life cycles.

Identifying Brand-Loyal Customers

One intriguing question for market researchers is whether there is a type of consumer who is brand loyal across various kinds of products. Research evidence so far indicates that brand loyalty is a product-specific phenomenon. Consumers who are loyal in one product category may or may not be loyal in any other product category. Efforts to identify demographic, socioeconomic, or psychological characteristics predictive of brand-loyal behavior have generally been unsuccessful.[83] There is, however, one variable that does predict brand loyalty, and that is store loyalty. Consumers who are loyal to particular stores also tend to be loyal to certain brands.[84] The connection here may be that by repeatedly shopping at the same stores, consumers are forced to buy certain brands because they are the only ones available in those stores.

The monitoring of brand loyalty should be a constant, ongoing process by managers. As one research article noted, "Things are happening in the marketplace on a week-to-week basis that have long-run implications for profitability and long-term survival."[85]

We noted this earlier in the text, but it bears repeating: marketing strategies involving sales-promotion devices may work to inhibit brand loyalty. If consumers purchase brands because of sales promotions rather than because of the products' intrinsic positive qualities, they may get into the habit of buying only when there are sales promotions. One study found that sales-promotion devices can cause even brand-loyal customers to switch brands. However, these researchers also found that the likelihood that consumers would repurchase the new brand was low.[86] All the evidence points to the conclusion that the quality of the product and the advertising of the brand are the key factors in creating long-term brand loyalty.

A MANAGERIAL APPLICATIONS ANALYSIS OF THE DELTA CASE

Problem Identification

Two problems can be identified in the Delta case. First, what consumer behavior factors impacted the reaction of the couple on Flight 149, given the sequence of events and Delta's handling of them? Second, what could Delta have done to improve its management of the situation?

The Consumer Behavior Analysis and Its Managerial Implications

Seven consumer behavior concepts described in the chapter have direct bearing on the two problems identified: (1) the consumption experience, (2) the service quality provided by the airline, (3) the attributions made by the couple, (4) the impact of equity, (5) the satisfaction level of the consumers, (6) complaint behavior, and (7) the brand loyalty of the consumers. Table 13-7 summarizes these concepts and their managerial implications.

The Consumption Experience The couple and other Delta passengers encountered a negative consumption experience—both the performance dimension and the mood dimension of their experience were negative. First, it quickly became apparent to all the passengers that a dramatistic performance was occurring in which a story was unfolding. The story centered on the conflict of whether they would reach their destinations that day. Because of the importance to the passengers of the resolution of this conflict, they began to examine carefully every move made by Delta's employees. Second, the passengers' mood had a strong impact on their reactions to the situation. The nine-hour flight from Rome to New York had left the couple extremely tired, and the poor quality of the food provided on the connecting flight once it took off contributed to their negative mood state. On top of that, they had been forced to sit in an uncomfortable airport waiting room for an extended period of time, which did nothing to improve their negative mood state.

The actions of the pilot and flight attendants on the flight to Texas were exemplary. Providing free alcoholic beverages and movie service temporarily improved the mood of the passengers.

From a managerial perspective, consumption experience issues impact decisions regarding the product, promotion, and segmentation. First, concerning the product, Delta should have taken appropriate steps to ensure that food service was available as promised. Second, in the promotion arena, the company should have trained its employees at the terminal to show sympathy for passengers and their discomfort. Third, the company clearly revealed an awareness of segmentation issues by giving special treatment to first-class and business travelers, but this decision alienated another important segment—frequent flyers— and made the regular passengers unhappy as well. Finally, in the market research arena, the company should perform a series of experiments to determine the most effective means of handling similar situations in the future.

Service Quality A number of the quality dimensions identified in the chapter apply to the case. Foremost is the airline's failure on the critical attribute of "getting the passengers to their destination at the time promised." Second, Delta's performance on food quality was low. Third, it performed badly on the issue of delivering timely information to passengers

Managerial Implications of Consumer Behavior Concepts in the Delta Case

Consumer Behavior Concept	Managerial Implications
1. Consumption experience	*Product.* Take appropriate steps to ensure that food service is available when promised.
	Promotion. Train employees in terminal to show sympathy for passengers and their discomfort.
	Segmentation. Seek to improve service provided to frequent flyers, as well as first-class and business travelers.
	Market research. Perform experiments to determine most effective means of handling delays and missed connections.
2. Service quality	*Product.* Take appropriate steps to ensure that firms hired to provide plane servicing and meals perform at high-quality levels.
	Promotion. Take care in setting expectations of customers regarding when flights will leave. Seek to ensure that the information provided by employees is accurate. Develop better procedures for informing passengers of flight status in waiting area.
3. Passenger attributions	*Promotion.* Communicate to passengers in an accurate, believable manner. Provide truthful reasons for the cause of the flight delay.
4. Equity issues	*Promotion.* Communicate to passengers information that would influence their belief that Delta maximized its revenues at their expense.
	Pricing. Take steps to compensate passengers for their losses so as to reduce their costs in the equity equation.
5. Consumer satisfaction	*Product.* Follow steps identified above.
	Promotion. Follow steps identified above, and in general communicate apologetically and with empathy with passengers.
6. Complaint behavior	*Promotion.* Communicate more quickly with passengers after they have complained. Answer their complaints fully rather than relying on the all-purpose "mechanical difficulty" answer.
	Pricing. Show more willingness to provide redress to consumers for legitimate losses.
7. Brand loyalty	*Promotion.* Through the actions Delta risked losing the brand loyalty of the couple and other passengers. Communications and sales-promotion incentives to recapture the passengers are in order.

TABLE 13-7

on the status of their flights. Fourth, on reliability, Delta gave a dismal performance because it posted and changed times several times. Finally, the credibility of airline employees quickly sank in passengers' eyes since they appeared not to have valid information.

These issues have application to both product and promotion. From a product perspective, Delta should take appropriate steps to ensure that the firms it hires to service its planes live up to the highest quality standards. From a promotion perspective, the airline should empower its ticket agents to provide timely and accurate information to passengers and train them to take care in setting passenger expectations.

Passenger Attributions The passengers made an internal attribution for the cause of the flight delay. That is, they perceived that the airline deliberately delayed their flight in order to fill up the plane and maximize its revenue at the expense of the passengers. This attribution had a negative effect on the passengers' feelings regarding Delta Airlines. Compounding that effect was the belief of some passengers that the airline had deliberately avoided telling them how late the plane would be in order to prevent them from finding seats on other airlines that might have gotten them to their destination on time.

Attribution issues have application to the promotional communications of the airline. Delta's employees should have communicated accurate, believable information. They should have sought to provide credible reasons for the cause of the delay. This information should have been provided not only while the problem was taking place but also in any communications the company had with passengers after they filed complaints.

Equity Issues When the couple evaluated the ratio of their outcomes to inputs in comparison to the outcomes and inputs experienced by the airline, they found that their inputs were large (the cost of the ticket) and their outcome was poor (the waiting, the extra day spent traveling, the poor quality of the on-flight food, and the extra out-of-pocket expenses). In contrast, they perceived that the outcome for Delta was positive because the airline maximized its revenue. In addition, Delta's inputs were relatively modest: the cost of the extra night's lodging and the small amount of money passengers received for meals. In sum, the passengers perceived the exchange as inequitable.

Equity issues have application to promotion and pricing. First, the airline should have communicated to passengers information that would have changed their belief that the company maximized its revenues at their expense (assuming, of course, that the belief was erroneous). Second, Delta should have compensated the passengers for their losses and thereby reduced the inequity of the exchange.

Consumer Satisfaction Consumer satisfaction is influenced by perceived equity, the attributions consumers make, and the actual performance of the service. Each of these factors, as we have seen, was extremely negative for Delta. Satisfaction is influenced by consumers' comparison of the quality of the service provided to their expectations for that service. On this dimension Delta also came out badly. A number of the couple's expectations were violated, including the departure time of their connecting flight, the ability to make the connection in Dallas–Ft. Worth and arrive at their final destination on the day promised, and the promised hot meal in flight. When these violations of their expectancies were combined with the negative attributions the couple made, their negative mood state, their feelings of inequity, and the general poor quality of Delta's service, it could safely be predicted that the couple was extremely dissatisfied with Delta Airlines.

Satisfaction issues influence the product and promotion elements of the marketing mix. From a product perspective, Delta must eliminate the plane servicing problems that caused the problems. From a promotion perspective, the company must train its employees to communicate in ways that appropriately set expectations and positively influence passengers' attributions and perceptions of equity.

Complaint Behavior On a number of dimensions, the couple described in the case were prime candidates to launch complaints against Delta. Both individuals were highly educated and had experience with complaining. They had the necessary resources to complain, including the time and money. Finally, they possessed the self-confidence required to make complaints.

The company should have responded much more quickly to the complaint than it did. It should also have answered the complaint fully instead of relying on the "mechanical difficulty" standby—which was not credible without some sort of explanation for why the pilot's in-flight explanation was different. In addition, the company should have provided redress to the couple in the form of a partial rebate of the price of their tickets.

Brand Loyalty Brand loyalty has both a behavioral and an attitudinal component. The couple already had a divided loyalty between Delta and other airlines. For example, each of them had frequent flyer accounts with other airlines, and their level of commitment to Delta was relatively low. The strong level of dissatisfaction and the negative feelings the couple experienced significantly lowered the brand loyalty they originally felt.

Managerially, Delta needed to take steps to retain the brand loyalty of the passengers after this incident. Communications and sales-promotion incentives to recapture their loyalty would have been appropriate.

Managerial Recommendations

How should Delta have handled the situation? There are several specific recommendations we would make.

Recommendation 1 Train ticket agents at the gate to handle this type of situation more effectively. Make more frequent announcements over the public address system to keep passengers informed on the status of their flight. In addition, train agents to show more empathy and to set expectations more appropriately.

Recommendation 2 Reward the pilot for his good work in this case. In general, train pilots and flight attendants to apologize for poor service whenever it occurs. Continue the policy of providing free drinks and movies in such situations.

Recommendation 3 Offer frequent flyer passengers who missed their connecting flights 20,000 additional frequent flyer miles.

Recommendation 4 Offer nonfrequent flyer passengers who missed their connecting flights coupons for lower fares on future Delta flights.

Recommendation 5 Take appropriate managerial steps to ensure that the company hired to service the planes provides a high-quality product.

Recommendation 6 Write or telephone passengers who missed their connections within one week to express regrets and provide appropriate incentives to retain their brand loyalty.

By following these actions, Delta would maximize the possibility of retaining and/or even increasing the brand loyalty of its customers. Moreover, these actions would minimize the likelihood of passengers lodging formal complaints against the airline and seeking redress through the legal system.

SUMMARY

This chapter focused on the postacquisition stage of the decision process and brand loyalty. The postacquisition stage of the consumer buying process consists of four phases: acquisition consumption/usage, the formation of postacquisition purchase satisfaction or dissatisfaction, consumer complaint behavior, and product disposition. The postacquisition stage plays a major role in consumers' decisions to repurchase a product or service. Expectations of treatment in the postacquisition phase can also influence consumers' brand loyalty.

Despite its importance, the consumption/usage phase of the postacquisition stage has received little attention from consumer researchers. Four areas of importance to managers in this phase are the frequency, amount, interval, and purpose of product or service consumption. One problem for managers is that consumers do not always use products in the ways expected by manufacturers—in fact, product misuse is a major cause of consumer injuries. However, the study of product usage can also be an opportunity for managers to make positive changes in current products or develop new products.

The satisfaction or dissatisfaction that consumers feel during and after product use influences their postacquisition attitudes. Feelings of satisfaction result from any one of several processes. One such process is expectancy disconfirmation. When the product's performance fails to meet expectations, consumers often experience emotional dissatisfaction. When performance merely meets expectations, consumers experience expectancy confirmation, but probably do not think much about their satisfaction with the product. It is when performance surpasses expectations that emotional satisfaction is likely to result. Performance expectations are influenced by the nature of the product, by promotional factors, by the effects of other products, and by the characteristics of the consumer.

Satisfaction with a purchase is also influenced by the actual performance of the product, by feelings of inequity, and by attributions. Consumers will experience feelings of inequity when they perceive that the ratio of their outcomes to inputs is inferior to another's ratio of outcomes to inputs. That other could be a retailer, a manufacturer, a service agent of some type (e.g., a real estate agent or stockbroker), or even another consumer. Consumers make attributions when they identify the cause of a negative outcome. If they make an internal attribution to the firm, they are likely to be dissatisfied.

Consumers who are dissatisfied with a purchase may engage in complaint behavior. Complaints take several different forms, from simply not buying the product or service again, to telling friends about the problem, to making verbal or written complaints, to seeking redress from the business or from the legal system. Consumers complain for two reasons: (1) to recover an economic loss or (2) to restore their self-concept, which may have been injured as a result of a product or service problem. Research reveals that most consumers are satisfied with their purchases. Of those who are dissatisfied, the percentage who take some action to resolve their problem depends upon the type of product purchased. For low-cost household items, as few as 15 percent of consumers take action. However, for socially visible products, such as clothing, the figure rises to about 75 percent. Corporations need to monitor consumer complaint behavior and institute programs to deal equitably with complaints. Some ways of dealing with complaints are using warranties, service contracts, consumer hotlines, and regional service representatives who are empowered to redress a complaint.

The final phase of the postacquisition process is product disposition. Consumers can dispose of a product in three general ways. They can store it for later use, they can get rid of it permanently, or they can get rid of it temporarily by renting it or lending it out. Managers should be aware of these various means of disposition. For certain consumer durables, such as automobiles, how much a product can be sold for after the consumer is finished using it is an important factor in brand selection. Some auto manufacturers, such as BMW, stress the high resale value of their cars in their advertising. Regulations determine how some products can be disposed of—particularly industrial products like hazardous chemicals, which must be disposed of in highly specific and often expensive ways.

Another important issue concerning postacquisition processes is brand loyalty. Brand loyalty is a nonrandom behavioral response that occurs over time and involves a strong positive attitudinal component. It is similar to the concept of brand commitment, which focuses largely on the extent to which consumers have positive feelings toward a specific brand. Brand loyalty is differentiated from repeat purchase behavior, in which a consumer merely buys a brand over and over again because no others are available. Brand loyalty can result from store loyalty—consumers forced to select from the limited choices at their favorite store are ipso facto brand loyal.

actual product performance
affect and CS/D
attribution theory
brand commitment
brand loyalty
consumer complaint
   behavior
consumer performance

consumer satisfaction
consumption amount
consumption experience
consumption frequency
consumption purpose
contracted performance
dramatistic performance
emotional dissatisfaction

emotional satisfaction
enacted performance
equity theory
exit behavior
expectancy confirmation
outcomes
postacquisition process
product disposition

product expectations
product quality
product use
proportion-of-purchases
   method
repeat purchase behavior
total quality management
   (TQM)

REVIEW QUESTIONS

1. What factors influence the formation of postacquisition satisfaction and dissatisfaction?

2. Identify the factors that influence the formation of brand expectations.

3. How do feelings of equity influence satisfaction/dissatisfaction with an exchange?

4. How does the equity approach to understanding postacquisition satisfaction differ from the expectation confirmation approach?

5. What actions may consumers take when they are dissatisfied with a product or service?

6. What are the two major reasons consumers complain about a good or service?

7. To what extent do consumers take overt action to complain when they are dissatisfied?

8. Eight factors were identified that influence consumer complaining. Identify six of them.

9. Discuss the various ways in which consumers may dispose of a product.

10. Identify four actions companies can take to help ensure postacquisition satisfaction.

11. What is the definition of brand loyalty?

DISCUSSION QUESTIONS

1. Think back on your own behavior and identify instances in which you have misused products. (For example, did you ever stick a knife into a toaster without unplugging it first?) Did your consumer misbehavior result in any problems? Could the manufacturer have done anything to prevent you from acting as you did?

2. Go through a magazine looking at the advertisements. What kinds of expectations do these ads create—for example, regarding product performance, postacquisition satisfaction, and the social benefits of owning the product? To what extent do you believe that the products will fulfill these expectations?

3. What are some actions the real estate industry might take to convince consumers that the relationship between the sellers of homes and real estate agents is an equitable one?

4. Equity theory proposes that consumers analyze their purchases in relation to similar purchases made by other consumers. Identify one or two instances in which you compared the outcomes of a purchase you made to the outcomes of a similar purchase made by another consumer. What bases for comparison did you use? Did

you experience any feelings of inequity/dissatisfaction as a result of the comparison?

5. List several occasions when you expressed some type of consumer dissatisfaction. On the occasions when the retailers could do something about the problem, was the outcome satisfactory for you? What could the retailers have done to improve your outcome?

6. To what extent would you consider the resale value of a car prior to purchasing it? Go to a store and find a magazine that lists resale values of automobiles. Based upon the resale value, which of the following sports cars would you purchase: a Nissan 300ZX, a Porsche 911, or a Chevrolet Corvette?

7. Consider the sports car that you found to have the highest resale value in Question 6. How might its manufacturer emphasize this point in promoting the car? Describe any advertising you have seen that does mention the resale value of an automobile or other product.

8. Identify a good or service toward which you feel brand loyalty. Identify the reasons for your loyalty. Next identify a good or service you repeatedly purchase, but without feeling any brand loyalty. What

could the firm that offers that good or service do to move you from simple repeat purchase behavior to brand loyalty?

9. Consider the occasion on which you were most angry with a firm as a result of a purchase of a good or service. What did the firm do to cause your anger? What role did your own attributions play in increasing or decreasing your anger? What specific actions could the firm have taken that would have helped to resolve your complaint?

ENDNOTES

1. The introductory case is based on an experience had by the first author of this textbook and his wife in the spring of 1996.

2. Leslie Helm, "Why Kodak is Starting to Click Again," *Business Week*, February 23, 1987, pp. 134–138.

3. For a review of many of these problems, see John C. Mowen and Hal Ellis, "The Product Defect: Managerial Implications and Consumer Implications," in *The Annual Review of Marketing*, Ben Enis and Kenneth Roering, eds. (Chicago: American Marketing Association, 1981), pp. 158–172.

4. Philip Hendrix, "Product/Service Consumption: Key Dimensions and Implications for Marketing," Working Paper, Emory University, Atlanta, GA, August 1984. Hendrix identified consumption interval as a fourth factor. However, we believe interval and frequency of usage are essentially identical.

5. Joanne Lipman, "Learning About Grape-Nuts in Denver," *The Wall Street Journal*, February 16, 1988, p. 33.

6. Richard L. Celsi, Randall L. Rose, and Thomas W. Leigh, "An Exploration of High-Risk Leisure Consumption Through Skydiving," *Journal of Consumer Research*, Vol. 20 (June 1993), p. 8.

7. Eric J. Arnould and Linda L. Price, "River Magic: Extraordinary Experience and the Extended Service Encounter," *Journal of Consumer Research*, Vol. 20 (June 1993), pp. 24–45.

8. Erving Goffman, *The Presentation of Self in Everyday Life* (New York: Basic Books, 1959).

9. This definition of performance was developed for the textbook and specifically designed to incorporate the notion that an exchange process is taking place. It borrows ideas from the work of John Deighton, "The Consumption of Performance," *Journal of Consumer Research*, Vol. 19 (December 1992), pp. 362–372.

10. Ibid., p. 362.

11. Paul W. Miniard, Sunil Bhatla, and Deepak Sirdeshmukh, "Mood as a Determinant of Postconsumption Product Evaluations: Mood Effects and Their Dependency on the Affective Intensity of the Consumption Experience," *Journal of Consumer Psychology*, Vol. 1 (1992), pp. 173–195.

12. Richard Oliver has distinguished satisfaction from attitude-toward-the-object in his work. He argues that attitude toward the product or brand represents a more generalized evaluation of a class of purchase objects. The approach taken in this text is that attitudes occur at different levels of specificity. They can be highly abstract, such as one's attitude toward one's country, or highly specific, such as one's satisfaction with a specific purchase. All are affective reactions that range on a hedonic continuum from unfavorable to favorable. For a recent article on Richard Oliver's approach, see Robert A. Westbrook and Richard L. Oliver, "The Dimensionality of Consumption Emotion Patterns and Consumer Satisfaction," *The Journal of Consumer Research*, Vol. 18 (June 1991), pp. 84–91.

13. Eugene W. Anderson, Claes Fornell, and Donald R. Lehmann, "Customer Satisfaction, Market Share, and Profitability: Findings from Sweden," *Journal of Marketing*, Vol. 58 (July 1994), pp. 53–66.

14. J. Joseph Cronin and Steven A. Taylor, "Measuring Service Quality: A Reexamination and Extension," *Journal of Marketing*, Vol. 56 (July 1992), pp. 55–68. Also see R. Kenneth Teas, "Expectations, Performance Evaluation, and Consumers' Perceptions of Quality," *Journal of Marketing*, Vol. 57 (October 1993), pp. 18–34.

15. For example, see W. Edwards Deming, *Quality, Productivity, and Competitive Position* (Cambridge, MA: M.I.T. Center for Advanced Engineering Study, 1982). Also see Joseph M. Juran, *Juran on Planning for Quality* (New York: The Free Press, 1988).

16. This definition extends the definition of service quality to goods. See Valerie A. Zeithaml, "Consumer Perceptions of Price, Quality and Value: A Means-End Model and Synthesis of Evidence," *Journal of Marketing*, Vol. 52 (July 1988), pp. 2–22.

17. A. Parasuraman, Valerie A. Zeithaml, and Leonard L. Berry, "SERVQUAL: A Multiple-Item Scale for Measuring Consumer Perceptions of Service Quality," *Journal of Retailing*, Vol. 64 (Spring 1988), pp. 12–36.

18. David A. Garvin, *Managing Quality: The Strategic and Competitive Edge* (New York: The Free Press, 1988).

19. Pratibha A. Dabholkar, Dayle I. Thorpe, and Joseph O. Rentz, "A Measure of Service Quality for Retail Stores: Scale Development and Validation," *Journal of the Academy of Marketing Science*, Vol. 24 (Winter 1996), pp. 3–16.

20. Kevin Lane Keller, "Conceptualizing, Measuring, and Managing Customer-Based Brand Equity," *Journal of Marketing*, Vol. 57 (January 1993), pp. 1–22.

21. Robert W. Veryzer, "Aesthetic Response and the Influence of Design Principles on Product Preferences," *Advances in Consumer Research*, Vol. 20, Leigh McAlister and Michael L. Rothschild, eds. (Provo, UT: Association for Consumer Research, 1992), pp. 224–228.

22. H. Keith Hunt, "CS/D: Overview and Future Research Directions," in *Conceptualization and Measurement of Consumer Satisfaction and Dissatisfaction*, H. Keith Hunt, ed. (Cambridge, MA: Marketing Science Institute, 1977), pp. 455–488.

23. Richard Oliver and Wayne DeSarbo, "Response Determinants in Satisfaction Judgments," *Journal of Consumer Research*, Vol. 15 (March 1988), pp. 495–507.

24. R. B. Woodruff, E. R. Cadotte, and R. L. Jenkins, "Modeling Consumer Satisfaction Processes Using Experience-Based Norms," *Journal of Marketing Research*, Vol. 20 (August 1983), pp. 296–304.

25. R. L. Oliver, "A Cognitive Model of the Antecedents and Consequences of Satisfaction Decisions," *Journal of Marketing Research*, Vol. 17 (November 1980), pp. 460–469.

26. Woodruff et al., "Modeling Consumer Satisfaction."

27. Patricia Sellers, "How to Handle Customers' Gripes," *Fortune*, October 24, 1988, pp. 87–100.

28. Ernest Cadotte, Robert Woodruff, and Roger Jenkins, "Expectations and Norms in Models of Consumer Satisfaction," *Journal of Marketing Research*, Vol. 24 (August 1987), pp. 305–314.

29. J. S. Adams, "Toward an Understanding of Inequity," *Journal of Abnormal and Social Psychology*, Vol. 67 (1963) pp. 422–436.

30. The equity ratio shown has been criticized and is given primarily for pedagogical purposes. See John C. Alessio, "Another Folly for Equity Theory," *Social Psychological Quarterly*, Vol. 43 (September 1980), pp. 336–340.

31. R. P. Fisk and C. E. Young, "Disconfirmation of Equity Expectation: Effects on Consumer Satisfaction with Services," in *Advances in Consumer Research*, Vol. 12, E. C. Hirschman and M. B. Holbrook, eds. (Ann Arbor, MI: Association for Consumer Research, 1985), pp. 340–345.

32. For other studies of equity in consumer behavior, see J. W. Huppertz, S. J. Arenson, and R. H. Evans, "An Application of Equity Theory to Buyer-Seller Exchange Situations," *Journal of Marketing Research*, Vol. 15 (May 1978), pp. 250–260.

33. John C. Mowen and Stephen L. Grove, "Search Behavior, Price Paid, and the Comparison Other: An Equity Theory Analysis of Post-Purchase Satisfaction," in *International Fare in Consumer Satisfaction and Complaint Behavior*, Ralph Day and H. Keith Hunt, eds. (Bloomington, IN: Indiana University School of Business, 1983), pp. 57–63.

34. J. E. Swan and Alice Mercer, "Consumer Satisfaction as a Function of Equity and Disconfirmation," in *Conceptual and Empirical Contributions to Consumer Satisfaction and Complaining Behavior*, Sixth Annual Conference, H. Hunt and R. Day, eds. (Bloomington, IN: Indiana University Press, 1982), pp. 2–8.

35. Richard L. Oliver and John E. Swan, "Consumer Perceptions of Interpersonal Equity and Satisfaction in Transactions: A Field Survey Approach," *Journal of Marketing*, Vol. 53 (April 1989), pp. 21–35.

36. Ibid., p. 33.

37. Valerie Folkes, "Consumer Reactions to Product Failure: An Attributional Approach," *Journal of Consumer Research*, Vol. 10 (March 1984), pp. 398–409.

38. Valerie Folkes, Susan Koletsky, and John Graham, "A Field Study of Causal Inferences and Consumer Reaction: The View from the Airport," *Journal of Consumer Research*, Vol. 13 (March 1987), pp. 534–539.

39. T. N. Somasundaram, "Consumers' Reaction to Product Failure: Impact of Product Involvement and Knowledge," *Advances in Consumer Research*, Vol. 20, Leigh McAlister and Michael L. Rothschild, eds. (Provo, UT: Association for Consumer Research, 1992), pp. 215–218.

40. Oliver and DeSarbo, "Response Determinants in Satisfaction Judgments." Also see David Tse and Peter Wilton, "Models of Consumer Satisfaction Formation: An Extension," *Journal of Marketing Research*, Vol. 25 (May 1988), pp. 204–212.

41. Youjae Yi, "The Determinants of Consumer Satisfaction: The Moderating Role of Ambiguity," *Advances in Consumer Research*, Vol. 20, Leigh McAlister and Michael L. Rothschild, eds. (Provo, UT: Association for Consumer Research, 1992), pp. 502–506.

42. Robert Westbrook, "Product/-Consumption-Based Affective Responses and Postpurchase Processes," *Journal of Marketing Research*, Vol. 24 (August 1987), pp. 258–270.

43. That positive and negative dimensions of affect exist was also found by Haim Mano and Richard L. Oliver, "Assessing the Dimensionality and Structure of the Consumption Experience: Evaluation, Feeling, and Satisfaction," *Journal of Consumer Research*, Vol. 20 (December 1993), pp. 451–466.

44. Laurette Dube-Rioux, "The Power of Affective Reports in Predicting Satisfaction Judgments," in *Advances in Consumer Research*, Vol. 17, Marvin E. Goldberg, Gerald Gorn, and Richard W. Pollay, eds. (Provo, UT: Association for Consumer Research, 1990), pp. 571–576.

45. Robert Westbrook and Richard L. Oliver, "Dimensionality of Consumption Emotion Patterns and Consumer Satisfaction," *The Journal of Consumer Research*, Vol. 18 (June 1991), pp. 84–91.

46. This model is based in part on Lalita A. Manrai and Meryl P. Gardner, "The Influence of Affect on Attributions for Product Failure," in *Advances in Consumer Research*, Vol. 18, Rebecca Holman and Michael Solomon, eds. (Provo, UT: Association for Consumer Research, 1991), pp. 249–254.

47. Barry J. Babin, Mitch Griffin, and Laurie Babin, "The Effect of Motivation to Process on Consumers' Satisfaction Reactions," *Advances in Consumer Research*, Vol. 21, Chris T. Allen and Deborah Roedder John, eds. (Provo, UT: Association for Consumer Research, 1994), pp. 406–411.

48. Shirley Taylor and John D. Claxton, "Delays and the Dynamics of Service Evaluations," *Journal of the Academy of Marketing Science*, Vol. 22 (Summer 1994), pp. 254–264.

49. Robert A. Peterson and William R. Wilson, "Measuring Customer Satisfaction: Fact and Artifact," *Journal of Academy of*

Marketing Science, Vol. 20 (Winter 1992), pp. 61–72.

50. This definition is highly similar to one developed by Jagdip Singh, "Consumer Complaint Intentions and Behavior: Definitional and Taxonomical Issues," *Journal of Marketing*, Vol. 52 (January 1988), pp. 93–107.

51. The first three complaint actions were identified by William Bearden and Jesse Teel, "Selected Determinants of Consumer Satisfaction and Complaint Reports," *Journal of Marketing Research*, Vol. 20 (February 1983), pp. 21–28.

52. The last two complaint behaviors were identified by Robert O. Herrmann, "The Tactics of Consumer Resistance: Group Action and Marketplace Exit," *Advances in Consumer Research*, Vol. 20, Leigh McAlister and Michael L. Rothschild, eds. (Provo, UT: Association for Consumer Research, 1992), pp. 130–134.

53. A. Andreason and A. Best, "Consumers Complain—Does Business Respond?" *Harvard Business Review*, Vol. 55 (July–August 1977), pp. 93–101.

54. R. E. Krapfel, "A Consumer Complaint Strategy Model: Antecedents and Outcomes," in *Advances in Consumer Research*, Vol. 12, E. Hirschman and M. Holbrook, eds. (Ann Arbor, MI: Association for Consumer Research, 1985), pp. 346–350.

55. Diane Halstead and Cornelia Droge, "Consumer Attitudes Toward Complaining and the Prediction of Multiple Complaint Responses," in *Advances in Consumer Research*, Vol. 18, Rebecca Holman and Michael Solomon, eds. (Provo, UT: Association for Consumer Research, 1991), pp. 210–216.

56. E. L. Landon, "A Model of Consumer Complaint Behavior," in *Consumer Satisfaction, Dissatisfaction, and Complaining Behavior*,

Ralph Day, ed. (Bloomington, IN: Symposium Proceedings, School of Business, University of Indiana, 1977), pp. 20–22.

57. See K. Gronhaug and G. Zaltman, "Complainers and Noncomplainers Revisited: Another Look at the Data," in *Advances in Consumer Research*, Vol. 8, K. Monroe, ed. (Ann Arbor, MI: Association for Consumer Research, 1981), pp. 83–87.

58. Folkes et al., "A Field Study of Causal Inferences and Consumer Reaction."

59. Gronhaug and Zaltman, "Complainers and Non-Complainers Revisited."

60. Ibid.

61. W. O. Bearden and J. B. Mason, "An Investigation of Influences on Consumer Complaint Reports," in *Advances in Consumer Research*, Vol. 11, Thomas Kinnear, ed. (Ann Arbor, MI: Association for Consumer Research, 1987), pp. 223–226.

62. Michelle Morganosky and Hilda Buckley, "Complaint Behavior: Analysis by Demographics, Lifestyle, and Consumer Values," in *Advances in Consumer Research*, Vol. 14, Melanie Wallendorf and Paul Anderson, eds. (Provo, UT: Association for Consumer Research, 1987), pp. 223–226.

63. See J. Faricy and M. Maxio, "Personality and Consumer dissatisfaction: A Multi-Dimensional Approach," in *Marketing in Turbulent Times*, E. M. Mazze, ed. (Chicago: American Marketing Association, 1975), pp. 202–208; and W. O. Bearden and J. E. Teel, "An Investigation of Personal Influences on Consumer Complaining," *Journal of Retailing*, Vol. 57 (Fall 1981), pp. 3–20.

64. Morganosky and Buckley, "Complaint Behavior."

65. R. C. Stokes, "Consumer Complaints and Dissatisfaction," speech before Food Update

Conference, The Food and Drug Law Institute, Phoenix, AZ, April 1974.

66. Donna J. Hill and Robert Baer, "Customers Complain—Businesses Make Excuses: The Effects of Linkage and Valence," *Advances in Consumer Research*, Vol. 21, Chris T. Allen and Deborah Roedder John, eds. (Provo, UT: Association for Consumer Research, 1994), pp. 399–405.

67. Ruth N. Bolton and Tim M. Bronkhorst, "The Relationship Between Customer Complaints to the Firm and Subsequent Exit Behavior," *Advances in Consumer Research*, Vol. 22, Frank Kardes and Mita Sujan, eds. (Provo, UT: Association for Consumer Research, 1995), pp. 94–100.

68. J. Jacoby, C. K. Berning, and T. F. Dietvorst, "What About Disposition?" *Journal of Marketing*, Vol. 41 (April 1977), p. 23.

69. Ibid.

70. R. De Young, A. Duncan, J. Frank, N. Gill, S. Rothman, J. Shenot, A. Shotkin, and M. Zweizig, "Promoting Source Reduction Behavior: The Role of Motivational Information," *Environment and Behavior*, Vol. 25 (1993), pp. 70–75.

71. J. A. McCarty and L. J. Shrum, "Recycling of Solid Wastes: Personal Values, Value Orientations, and Attitudes about Recycling as Antecedents of Recycling Behavior," *Journal of Business Research*, Vol. 30 (May 1994), pp. 53–62.

72. Shirley Taylor and Peter Todd, "Understanding Household Garbage Reduction Behaviors: A Test of an Integrated Model," *Journal of Public Policy and Marketing*, Vol. 14 (Fall 1995), pp. 192–204.

73. For a recent review of work on brand loyalty, see Alan S. Dick and Kunai Basu, "Customer Loyalty: Toward an Integrated Conceptual Framework," *Journal of Academy of Marketing Science*, Vol. 22 (Spring 1994), pp. 99–113.

74. William Boulding, Ajay Kalra, Richard Staelin, and Valarie A. Zeithaml, "A Dynamic Process Model of Service Quality: From Expectations to Behavioral Intentions," *Journal of Marketing Research*, Vol. 30 (February 1993), pp. 7–27.

75. Melanie Wells, "Brand Ads Should Target Existing Customers," *Advertising Age*, April 26, 1993, p. 47.

76. Cyndee Miller, "Rewards for the Best Customers," Vol. 27 (July 5, 1993), pp. 1, 6.

77. A similar point was made by J. Paul Peter and Jerry C. Olson, *Consumer Behavior and Marketing Strategy* (Homewood, IL: Richard D. Irwin, 1990), p. 435.

78. Jacob Jacoby and Robert Chestnut, *Brand Loyalty, Measurement, and Management* (New York: John Wiley & Sons, 1978).

79. Sharon E. Beatty, Lynn R. Kahle, and Pamela Homer, "The Involvement-Commitment Model: Theory and Implications," *Journal of Business Research*, Vol. 16, no. 2, pp. 149–167.

80. Ibid.

81. Charles L. Martin and Phillips W. Goodell, "Historical, Descriptive, and Strategic Perspectives on the Construct of Product Commitment," *European Journal of Marketing*, Vol. 25 (1991), pp. 53–60.

82. Lester Guest, "Brand Loyalty Revisited: A Twenty Year Report," *Journal of Applied Psychology*, Vol. 48 (April 1964), pp. 93–97.

83. See, for instance, Ronald Frank, William Massy, and Thomas Lodahl, "Purchasing Behavior and Personal Attributes," *Journal of Advertising Research*, Vol. 9 (December 1969), pp. 15–24.

84. James Carmen, "Correlates of Brand Loyalty: Some Positive Results," *Journal of Marketing Research*, Vol. 7 (February 1970), pp. 67–76.

85. Richard E. DuWors, Jr., and George H. Haines, Jr., "Event History Analysis Measures of Brand Loyalty," *Journal of Marketing Research*, Vol. 17 (November 1990), p. 492.

86. Michael Rothschild, "A Behavioral View of Promotions Effects on Brand Loyalty," in *Advances in Consumer Research*, Vol. 14, Melanie Wallendorf and Paul Anderson, eds. (Provo, UT: Association for Consumer Research, 1987), pp. 119–120.

THE MEDICAL EXAMINATION

Cal is a highly educated, upper-middle-income male over 40 who is conscious of the need for a healthy lifestyle. Because he has a family history of heart disease, he has regular checkups to make sure all is well. In September 1991 he went in for his standard physical. Cal's expectations were that he would have a normal checkup and that he would be told to watch his cholesterol intake more closely, lose a little weight, continue his healthy lifestyle, and come back in a year.

One component of the physical is an exercise stress test. A bundle of electrodes are attached to the patient's chest, and the patient then begins walking briskly on a treadmill. As Cal was in the midst of this test, his physician and the nurse suddenly looked worried as they scrutinized the computer screen. Cal was quickly taken off the treadmill and placed on the examining table. The physician then explained that his EKG indicated a blockage in the heart. On the spot, the physician ordered more tests for Cal, which were to take place in five days. Cal was told to go home and not exert himself.

Five days passed and Cal arrived at the hospital for the tests. A busy professional, he had rearranged his schedule to fit in this examination. He had been told not to eat for four hours prior to the tests and to show up promptly at 10 A.M. in jogging clothes. He had also been told that the test would last about one and a half hours and that he would have to come back again two hours later to have a second picture taken of his heart, which would take 30 minutes or so.

Understandably, Cal's anxiety level was elevated by the time he showed up for his appointment. He arrived on time, but had to wait 20 minutes to be seen by a nurse. Another 15 minutes went by as the staff hooked him up to the electrodes. An IV was inserted into his arm so that radioactive thallium could be injected into his vein during the exercise. (The amount of radioactivity in his heart would later be measured to determine if an adequate blood supply was reaching it.) After the hookup was completed, he was told to sit on the examining table and wait for the doctor.

Cal sat and waited—alone. Clad only in running shorts, jogging shoes, and the wires, he quickly noticed that it was cold in the room—particularly since a circulating fan was blowing air across his bare torso every seven seconds. His only diversion during this wait was watching his heart rhythms on the monitoring machine to which he was attached. After he had been sitting on the table for 45 minutes, the cardiologist finally arrived and commenced to work on Cal with six attendants. After a huge Geiger counter read the level of radioactivity in his heart, he was told to return in two hours for a second measurement. The cardiologist added that Cal could get the results the next morning from his own physician. So an exam that Cal had expected to take about two hours in total actually took about four hours.

The next morning Cal called his physician to inquire about the results of his tests. The nurse told him the doctor was not available at the moment, but that he would return the phone call later. Not having heard from his physician by early afternoon, Cal decided to call again. Now he was told that his primary care physician had gone on vacation, that the physician's key nurse was off, and that no one in the office knew of him or the tests he had taken the day before. He then asked if someone in the office could call the cardiologist to find out if the results of his tests were ready. A substitute attendant called the cardiologist and got back to Cal. She told him that the results were not ready, but perhaps they would be the next day.

The next day Cal waited impatiently through the morning for a phone call. When no call came by 11:30 A.M., he contacted the head nurse at the clinic. She said that nothing had arrived from the cardiologist, but perhaps they would hear something by the following Monday. Cal asked for the cardiologist's phone number so he could call him directly, but the head nurse said she could not give out that information.

At this point Cal's anxiety and frustration levels were so greatly elevated that he decided to call a friend at the hospital who knew the cardiologist in question. The friend quickly gave Cal the cardiologist's number. Cal then called the cardiologist directly and received the results of his tests. Fortunately, they revealed that the original diagnosis had been a false alarm. There was no blockage, his heart was perfectly normal. In all, the false alarm cost Cal a week of anxiety, $2,000 in medical bills, and intense unhappiness with the way he was treated.

This case was prepared by Jane Licata.

Questions

1. Define the problem faced by the health-care workers who treated Cal.

2. What consumer concepts from this chapter explain Cal's feelings about his experience?

3. For which managerial strategy elements do these consumer concepts have implications?

4. Develop a managerial applications analysis of the case and discuss the managerial strategies that should be employed to improve the quality of the service offered by medical staff.

III

The Consumer Environment

14

The Consumer Environment and the Impact of Situational Influences

INTRODUCTORY CASE

Gasoline Retailing Comes of Age

After being neglected for many years, the gasoline station is receiving increased attention from major oil companies. Several factors account for this renewed focus on marketing. First, gasoline consumption has changed little in the last two decades. Between 1978 and 1996 the number of gallons sold in the United States rose by only 10 percent, and in several of those years there were actual decreases. So gasoline retailers find themselves competing for shares in a market that is growing very slowly. Meanwhile, high real estate costs and stricter environmental regulations have caused a price squeeze (after adjusting for inflation, gasoline prices are near an all-time low).

The new stress on marketing has resulted in a number of changes. First, gasoline stations now sell a diversified array of products. More and more frequently, they are convenience stores where people can purchase food and basic household supplies as well as gasoline. For example, Ashland Oil Company focuses on selling high-margin products like soda, cigarettes, and diapers. At the same time, store layouts have been redesigned to entice customers into purchasing more high-margin impulse items. One Ashland executive says that

the company no longer thinks of itself as an operator of gasoline stations, but rather as a retailing firm. Another oil company, Amoco, has even placed Dunkin' Donuts, Burger King, and Dairy Queen stores in some of its stations.

A study conducted by Phillips Petroleum Company found that speed of service has replaced price as the most important attribute in purchasing gasoline. The company now builds its stations with side lanes so that cars can easily pass by each other to get to empty pumps. Mobil has installed pumps that fill up tanks in half the time. Companies also have developed ways to allow customers to pay at the pump—a system that consumer studies show is favored by motorists.

Research has also shown that the lighting around a filling station strongly influences patronage at night. Female customers are much more likely to purchase gasoline from a brightly lighted station. Shell Oil Company claims that its lights, which are recessed in yellow canopies, provide a competitive edge because of their warm yellow glow.

Another trend in gasoline sales is toward providing a wider range of octane levels for customers. Higher margins on expensive high-octane gasoline mean increased profits. Interestingly, the vast majority of cars need only regular unleaded to run properly. One Mobil executive said, "People buy a premium gasoline because they perceive a need."

INTRODUCTION

This chapter on the impact of situational influences on consumer behavior begins Part III of the text, "The Consumer Environment." The **consumer environment** is composed of those factors existing independently of individual consumers and firms that influence the exchange process. Figure 14-1 diagrams the consumer environment and its effect on the exchange process.

In the figure the components of the consumer environment are placed within the box of dotted lines. At the most macro level of analysis are the economic and cultural/cross-cultural environments. They influence both the subcultural and the regulatory environ-

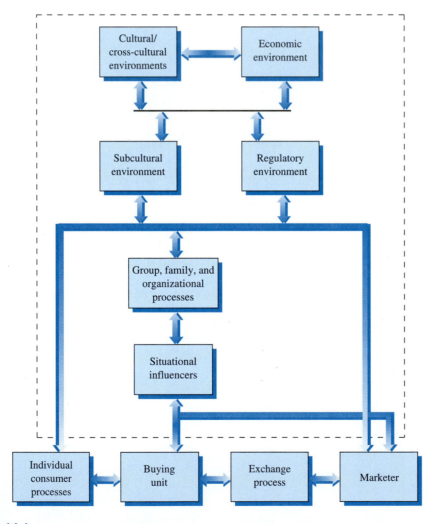

Figure 14-1

The consumer environment and the exchange process.

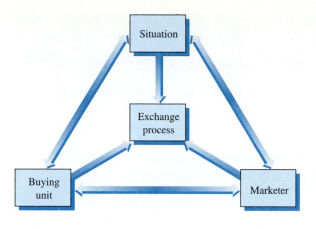

Figure 14-2
The marketing triad: situation, buying unit, marketer.

ments, each of which influences group and family processes. In turn, group and family processes affect the situational influencers, as well as individual consumer processes and the marketer.

At the most micro level of analysis within the consumer environment, one finds situational influencers—the topic of this chapter. Situational influencers affect the buying unit, the marketer, and the exchange process itself. Indeed, a marketing exchange can be conceptualized as resulting from the interaction of the buying unit, the marketer, and the situation at a particular time and place. This important interaction, called the **marketing triad**, is diagrammed in Figure 14-2. All of the other factors identified in the text, from individual consumer processes to environmental influences, come together to influence the situation, the buying unit, and the marketer.

Part III of this text is generally organized from the micro to the macro analysis of the consumer environment. It begins with the analysis of the situational influencers—the environmental factors that operate at the most micro level. In Parts I and II we discussed the individual consumer processes that influence the buying unit. The natural next step is to investigate the situational factors that form the element of the exchange triad that ties directly into the rest of the factors that compose the consumer environment.

INTRODUCTION TO SITUATIONAL INFLUENCERS

Consumer situations consist of those temporary environmental factors that form the context within which a consumer activity occurs at a particular place and time. Thus a consumer situation is composed of those factors that: (1) involve the time and place in which a consumer activity takes place, (2) explain why the action takes place, and (3) influence consumer behavior. Consumer situations are relatively short-term events and should be distinguished from more long-term environmental factors, such as the effects of culture, as well as personal factors that have a more lasting quality, such as an individual's personality. Examples of situations are the physical surroundings, social surroundings, time, the task definition, and antecedent states—all of which are defined in Table 14-1.[1]

The introductory case illustrated a number of aspects of consumer situations. Physical surroundings can have a major impact on the experiences obtained by consumers. Designers of gas stations attempt to create an atmosphere that will make the experience of buying gasoline as painless as possible—for example, by providing good lighting to enhance safety. If the *physical surroundings* are unpleasant, there is always another station down the road. Similarly, *social surroundings* are important. In this case, perhaps the avoidance of unwanted social encounters is critical.

Another situational element is *time*. Purchasing gasoline is not a preferred pastime for consumers. The extent to which the time needed to complete this transaction can be shortened may influence their willingness to use a certain gasoline station.

A fourth situational element is *task definition*, which is the reason or occasion for engaging in a consumer action. A gasoline gauge nearing "empty" defines a task; this is an occasion on which certain activities are expected. By linking gasoline purchases to other activities (grocery shopping, fast-food purchases), companies can enlarge the series of activities that consumers engage in at the "gas station."

The study of situations has important implications for managers; after all, each managerial application area is influenced by situational factors. Products may be defined by the situations in which they are used. For example, wristwatches are positioned, and consumers of watches are segmented, on the basis of usage situations. There are formal watches, sports watches, everyday watches, and specialty watches (e.g., diving watches). Also, groups of people (i.e., segments) may be identified with an unfulfilled situational need, such as a desire to have a watch with a timing function for jogging. A product would then be developed to fit the needs of that situation—in this case a durable timepiece with a stopwatch capacity. Similarly, promotional materials may be created that clearly position the product in reference to its situational use and to its competitors.

In addition to product design, segmentation, and positioning, the study of situations has a variety of other managerial uses. People may obtain information on products in specific situations (e.g., via the car radio while commuting). Thus the promotional method may be influenced by situational variations in information reception. Similarly, certain products may be bought only in certain situations (e.g., as a gift). Such information has an impact on pricing, promoting, and distributing the product.

In this chapter we discuss each of the situational factors that may influence consumers, paying special attention to the effects of the physical environment on consumers. In addition, we extensively treat the effects of time and the task definition. We pay less attention to the impact of the social surroundings, which are fully discussed in Chapter 15. Similarly, we cover antecedent states only briefly because of their close relationship to mood, which we addressed in several earlier chapters. After analyzing the various types of situations, we present the important topic of "situation" by "buying unit" by "market offering" interactions. In the last section we analyze the gasoline station case.

THE PHYSICAL SURROUNDINGS: A FOCUS ON THE STORE ENVIRONMENT

Physical surroundings are the concrete physical and spatial aspects of the environment that encompass a consumer activity. Such stimuli as color, noise, lighting, weather, and the spatial arrangement of people or objects can influence consumer behavior.

Physical surroundings influence consumer perceptions through the sensory mechanisms of vision, hearing, smell, and even touch. Surroundings have particular importance to retailers; perhaps their most important task is to manage the physical environment so as to influence consumers' behaviors, attitudes, and beliefs in a desired direction. For example, physical surroundings have important implications for building a store image. If a retailer wants to present an upscale image, it is crucial that the surroundings match this image.

The perception of safety is another factor controlled in part by the physical surroundings. Ample nearby parking, adequate outdoor lighting, and open spaces enhance shoppers' feelings of security. The presence of such physical attributes could increase nighttime shopping, particularly among the elderly, who are highly conscious of their vulnerability to crime.

Researchers have investigated the impact of the physical environment on consumer perceptions and behavior in several retailing areas. These studies, discussed in this section, have analyzed how music, crowding, store location, store layout, and store atmosphere affect buyers.

The Effects of Music on Shoppers

One component of the physical environment in retail stores that has been shown to influence consumers is background music. Two studies examined the effect of music on consumers. In the first study supermarket shoppers experienced no music, slow-tempo music, and fast-tempo music over a nine-week period. The shoppers walked faster or slower depending on the music, and bought 38 percent more on a daily basis when slower music was played. No differences between the groups were found when customers were asked about their awareness of the music, suggesting that it operated below their consciousness.[2]

The second study obtained similar results. Fast- or slow-paced background music was randomly played on Friday and Saturday nights over eight consecutive weekends in a medium-sized restaurant in the Dallas–Ft. Worth area.[3] The pace of the music influenced the amount of time consumers spent in the restaurant. In the slow-tempo condition patrons took, on average, 56 minutes to complete their dinner. In contrast, it took them only 45 minutes to complete dinner in the fast-tempo condition. The longer time spent in the restaurant had no statistically significant impact on food sales, though liquor sales went up significantly. Overall, the average gross margin per group was $55.82 in the slow-tempo and $48.62 in the fast-tempo condition.

These supermarket and restaurant studies demonstrate that the physical environment can influence buyer behavior. However, one should not immediately generalize and say that all retail stores should play slow-paced music. There may be consumption situations in which fast music would be more appropriate. For example, restaurants that have low margins and depend on high volume must have a high turnover rate. In this case playing fast-paced music may speed up meal consumption, thereby making seats available for other customers more quickly.[4]

Music is a pervasive presence in the consumer environment. For example, when placing a customer on hold on the telephone, many firms play music to fill the silence and help make the wait seem less negative. Surprisingly, however, recent research has found that music rated as more pleasant does *not* make time seem to pass more quickly. Thus "time does not necessarily fly" when people are having fun.[5] These results suggest that playing appealing, peppy music while people are on "musical hold" or in waiting lines may prove counterproductive. A further study suggests that louder music increases people's perception that "the pace of events" is speeding up, but it also raises their estimates of time durations. So keep the volume down.[6]

Research also indicates that music is more effective if it matches the general situational context of the purchase. Thus just as the source should match the message (as discussed in the chapter on communications processes), the type of music should match the purchase context. For example, one study found that when classical music, as opposed to Top Forty selections, was played in a wine store, shoppers selected more expensive wines. As a result, they spent more money.[7] Clearly, the type of music should "fit" the situation.

The Effects of Crowding on Consumers

Crowding occurs when a person perceives that his or her movements are restricted because of limited space. The experience can result from an overabundance of people, from a limited physical area, or from a combination of the two.[8] This concept has particular relevance to retailers who must decide how to arrange floor space. When consumers experience crowding, a number of different outcomes may occur.[9] They may react by reducing their shopping time, by altering their use of in-store information, or by decreasing their communication with store employees. Potentially, crowding increases shopper anxiety, lowers shopping satisfaction, and negatively affects store image.

Researchers have distinguished between the terms density and crowding. **Density** refers to how closely packed people are, while **crowding** refers to the unpleasant feelings that people experience when they perceive that densities are too high and that their control of the situation has been reduced below acceptable levels.

One study investigated the relationship between density, crowding, and perceived control in a service encounter setting. A **service encounter** is one in which interactions occur between a consumer and the representatives of an organization.[10] In this study slides were taken of patrons in a bank and in a bar in high-, moderate-, and low-density situations. Respondents then read descriptions of the banking and bar situations, viewed the photos, and were asked to estimate the reactions of a hypothetical customer to the situation faced. Half of the respondents learned that the customer had little choice about being in the situation, and the other half learned that the customer did have a choice about being in the situation (e.g., in the bank case, the person had to make a deposit immediately or could make it at another time).

The pattern of results supported the model of behavior shown in Figure 14-3. That is, the level of choice and the density of customers influenced the level of perceived control. In turn, perceived control and density influenced the experience of crowding. These factors then affected the feelings of the consumer and his or her tendency to stay or leave the situation. When the hypothetical consumer had no choice, the raters actually perceived levels of density to be higher than when the consumer had a choice. Also, when little control was felt, crowding was perceived as higher, feelings were more negative, and the hypothetical consumer was seen as wanting to leave the situation.

There are, however, instances in which high-density levels are perceived as beneficial. In the bar/bank study higher density levels were associated with more perceived control in the bar setting but lower perceived control in the bank setting. Thus when consumers are seeking a fun social experience, such as drinking in a bar or attending a sporting event, high levels of density may enhance pleasure. In any context there is prob-

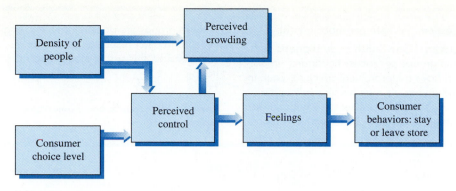

Figure 14-3

The effects of density and crowding on consumer behavior in a retail setting. (*Source*: Figure based on Michael K. Hui and John E. G. Bateson, "Perceived Control and the Effects of Crowding and Consumer Choice on the Service Experience," *Journal of Consumer Research*, Vol. 18 [September 1991], pp. 174–184.)

ably some optimum level of density. For example, dining out is uncomfortable if the restaurant is nearly empty, but if the restaurant is so full that service is poor, the experience is equally negative. The optimum level of density is somewhere between the two extremes.

Finally, it isn't clear that people who perceive that they could avoid congestion by changing shopping times actually do so. Researchers in England found that only 6 percent of a large sample of supermarket shoppers shifted from busy to quiet periods to avoid congestion. Other elements, such as time of shopping in relation to work and weekends, are probably more important to consumers.[11]

Consumer Crowd Behavior In some circumstances consumers behave like hysterical crowds. They do things as part of a crowd that they would never do alone. During the Christmas season of 1983 Cabbage Patch dolls were *the* present for children and stores ran short of them. When news spread that a store had the dolls, mobs formed outside and behavior became so unruly that police were called in to control the situation.

In European and South American countries spectators at important soccer events have been known to turn into mobs. In October 1996, 82 people were killed at a World Cup soccer match in Guatemala City, Guatemala. Too many tickets had been sold, and fans who weren't allowed in tried to squeeze through a small causeway, where people inside were suffocated or trampled. Earlier in 1996 French farmers giving away fruit in Paris to protest low food prices had to stop because unruly crowds overwhelmed them.

The factors that cause normal consumers to evolve into crowds are still not understood completely. In 1896 Gustav Le Bon suggested that people go into hypnotic trances when they are part of a mob, so that the aggregate forms a collective mind. A more likely explanation is that being part of a very large group causes a high degree of physiological arousal, and this high arousal causes each member of the crowd to act on his or her dominant idea. Because it was a similar idea that brought the group together to begin with, the individuals within the crowd are likely to share a common tendency to action. In many instances the dominant tendency is aggressiveness. Since each person in a crowd is inconspicuous, individual responsibility is lost, so the usual norms that control behavior do not apply. The result is an unruly, highly aroused group of people who are not acting as individuals and are not subject to the standard norms that control behavior. The results can be riots, runs on banks, or panic buying of a product in short supply.

The Effects of Store Location

Real estate agents have a rule of thumb stating that the primary factors influencing the value of a piece of property are *location*, *location*, and *location*. Those who study retailing echo this point, so location's contribution to store choice has been extensively researched.

Store location influences consumers from several perspectives. The size of a trading area surrounding a store affects the overall number of people who are likely to be drawn to it. The **gravitational model** uses the analogy of a planet's gravitational effects to predict how many people will go outside of their town's boundaries to shop in other cities.[12]

In addition to actual distance, perceived distance may also influence store selection. Research has shown that consumers have "cognitive maps" of the geography of a city. Interestingly, consumer "maps" of the locations of retail stores may not match reality. Such factors as parking availability, merchandise quality, and the ease of driving to the shopping center can make distances seem shorter or longer than they actually are.[13]

Finally, there is the phenomenon of "image transference": the image of larger "anchor" stores in a shopping center affects the image of smaller stores in the center.[14] Small stores are better off located in a center with a department store as the anchor tenant rather than a discount store, unless the discount store is congruent with the smaller stores' image.

Store Layout

Stores are designed to facilitate customer movement, to assist retailers in the presentation of merchandise, and to help create a particular atmosphere. The retailer's overall goal is to maximize profits by increasing sales through a cost-effective store design. **Store layout** can influence consumer reactions and buying behavior. For example, the placement of aisles influences traffic flow. The location of items and departments relative to traffic flow can dramatically influence sales. One recent suggestion is that all convenience foods—salad bar, deli, bakery, frozen entrees, frozen pizza, rotisserie chicken, and prepared meals—should be brought together for the upscale-but-harried consumer.[15] Figure 14-4 shows the typical layout of a supermarket.

Seating arrangements can dramatically influence communication patterns. It has been argued that airport terminals are designed to discourage people from talking comfortably to each other. Chairs are bolted down and placed so that people cannot face each other and converse from a comfortable distance. The presumed reason for this antisocial arrangement of furniture is to drive people into airport bars and food courts, where space is arranged more comfortably—and where customers spend money. This concept is being taken to great lengths, with casinos and department stores making an appearance in airports. One designer has even described the Pittsburgh Airport as "a mall with planes parked around it."[16]

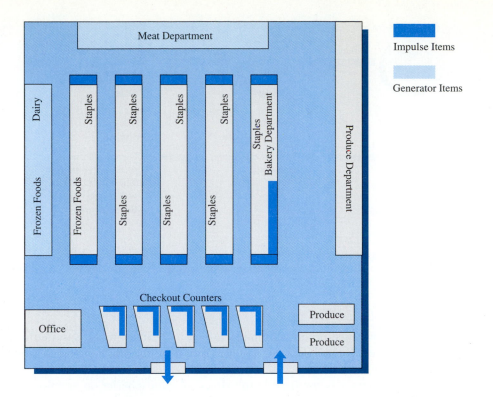

Impulse Items

Generator Items

Figure 14-4

The layout of a conventional supermarket with perishables located around the perimeter. Traffic generators and staples are located to cause shoppers to shop the entire store and to maximize exposure to impulse items. (Courtesy of William W. Thompson.)

The Effects of Atmospherics

A store's atmosphere delivers a message to consumers, such as "this store has high-quality merchandise." **Atmospherics** is a more general term than store layout; it deals with how managers can manipulate the design of the building, the interior space, the layout of the aisles, the texture of the carpets and walls, the scents, colors, shapes, and sounds experienced by customers—all to achieve a certain effect. Even the arrangement of merchandise, the types of displays, and the poses of mannequins can influence consumers' perceptions of store atmosphere. These elements are pulled together well in the definition developed by Philip Kotler, which describes atmospherics as "the effort to design buying environments to produce specific emotional effects in the buyer that enhance his probability of purchase."[17]

Researchers have argued that atmosphere influences the extent to which consumers spend beyond their planned levels in a store.[18] The store's atmosphere influences a shopper's emotional state, which then leads to increased or decreased shopping. Emotional state is made up of two dominant feelings—pleasure and arousal.[19] The combination of these elements influences the consumer to spend either more or less time in the store.

Figure 14-5 diagrams these relationships. When the atmosphere arouses the consumer positively, the buyer tends to spend more time in the store and has an increased tendency to affiliate with people.[20] This situation is likely to result in increased buying. In contrast, if the environment is not pleasurable and arrouses the consumer negatively, the buyer will probably spend less time in the store and make fewer purchases. Research by

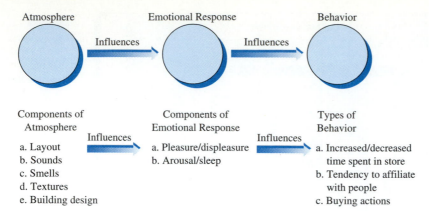

Figure 14-5

Atmospherics and shopping behavior. (*Source*: Adapted from a discussion in Robert Donovan and John Rossiter, "Store Atmosphere: An Environmental Psychology Approach," *Journal of Retailing*, Vol. 58 [Spring 1982], pp. 34–57.)

psychologists has shown that dominant tendencies are more likely to be activated when people become aroused. If the dominant tendency is to leave the store, increased arousal increases the desire to leave.

Kotler, among others, has emphasized the effects of atmospherics on emotions. His approach links the study of atmospherics directly to the experiential perspective on consumer behavior. However, atmospherics can also be understood from the behavioral influence perspective. The layouts of buildings and the design of traffic corridors in cities, malls, and stores directly influence the movements of consumers in many instances without their behavior first being influenced by either beliefs or feelings. As Winston Churchill was quoted as saying, "First we shape our buildings and then they shape us."[21]

A variety of other studies have confirmed that a building's atmosphere influences its inhabitants.[22] Some researchers have suggested that increasing the number of windows and admitting more sunlight improves people's mood states. Wal-Mart opened a prototype store in Lawrence, Kansas, where half of the departments are illuminated by skylights and the other half by artificial light. Sales are higher in the skylit area, and employees in the artificial-light areas of the store have tried to have their departments moved to the skylit part of the store.[23]

One area of atmospherics that has recently attracted attention is olfactory cues. A recent study found that shoppers return more often to scented stores and perceive the goods sold in these stores to be of better quality than the goods sold in unscented stores. The intensity and nature of the scent seem to matter little, as long as it is inoffensive. However, managers should ensure that the scent is distinctive and congruent with product offerings. They also need to pay attention to costs—both scents and diffusion methods can be expensive.[24]

The spatial arrangements in a retail store have important consumer behavior effects, which can be summarized in four statements:

1. Space modifies and shapes consumer behavior.
2. Retail store space affects consumers through the stimulation of the senses.
3. Retail stores, like other aesthetic surroundings, affect perceptions, attitudes, and images.
4. Stores can be programmed via space utilization to create desired customer reactions.[25]

Researchers have proposed that atmosphere becomes more important as the number of competitors increases, as the differences among competitors in product and price fade, and as the market becomes segmented on lifestyle and social-class differences.[26] A retail store's atmosphere can be used as a tool to differentiate it from competitors and to attract specific groups of consumers who seek the feelings signified by the atmosphere.

In general, the nature of the retail store shapes the buyer's experience of acquiring a product or service. In a service setting, the physical and social surroundings may become part of the service itself. For example, the nature of a concert or a play is shaped in large part by lighting, the characteristics of the set, the way the sound is produced, and the characteristics of the other people who are sharing the experience. As a result, the investigation of the physical surroundings is a key element of market research.

SOCIAL SURROUNDINGS

The concept of **social surroundings** deals with the effects of other people on a consumer in a consumption situation. For example, the presence of a group can result in conformity pressures on a consumer. A college student who belongs to a fraternity may feel pressured to purchase particular brands of beverages, clothing, and even automobiles. Similarly, knowledge that a consumption situation involves the presence of other people can dramatically influence a consumer's actions. The type of snack foods that someone buys may be affected by the knowledge that others will be present when the snacks are consumed. Light or salty snacks, for instance, tend to be bought in part as something to have around the house should friends drop by.[27]

Other people also influence the impact of a communication on the consumer. For example, the presence of others in a room causes most television viewers to pay less attention to the advertisements crossing the screen. In a personal-selling situation the presence of a friend can lower the impact of the sales presentation. Research on conformity has found that subjects will conform to the views of a group even when they knew objectively that the group is wrong. However, if at least one other member of the group concurs with the subject, the group conformity effect will be lost.[28] Thus in a sales encounter it is likely that if you bring along a friend, that person will lessen the impact of the sales presentation by buttressing your views.

Social motives explain a certain amount of shopping.[29] Shopping can be an important social experience for consumers, one where they can meet new people and possibly make friends. In one study researchers recorded the social interactions of 100 randomly selected individuals who entered a large mall alone.[30] Fifty-one percent of the interactions between these subjects and others were informational, such as asking someone where to find an item. Twenty-three percent of the interactions were perfunctory,

Question: Can downtowns be rejuvenated by slowing down traffic?

Answer: Traffic engineer Walter Kulash recommends narrowing urban boulevards and making them two-way streets with street parking. For customers to want to stop, he says, traffic needs to be at 20 mph—a horse-and-buggy pace. New York's Greenwich Village, Miami's South Beach, and downtown Santa Fe are examples of congested but vibrant urban communities.

Source: Mitchell Pacelle, " 'Traffic Calming': Some Urban Planners Say Downtowns Need a Lot More Congestion," *The Wall Street Journal*, August 7, 1996, pp. A1, A4.

---

such as acknowledging another person's presence. A full 26 percent of the interactions, however, were social—that is, a real conversation took place between the person and someone else. The authors of this study interpreted these results as indicative of the importance of social interaction in the shopping experience. They even suggested that the rebirth of central business districts and older malls depends on the rejuvenation of their social significance.[31]

For retailers, it is usually beneficial to encourage the social aspects of shopping. The shopper who is with others tends to visit more stores and make more unplanned purchases.[32] In fact, many products would not exist unless people gathered into social groupings. A small industry exists just to supply party needs—noise makers, party napkins, specialized mixers, and so on. Even a basic beverage like beer is frequently consumed in contexts that are social in nature. In an inventory of beer-drinking situations, half of the contexts dealt with social situations, such as: entertaining close friends at home; attending a social event for which you bring your own beverages; going to a tavern after work; going to a restaurant or lounge on Friday or Saturday night; taking a camping trip, a beach trip, or an extended picnic.[33]

THE TASK DEFINITION

The reasons people buy and consume a product or service are varied. These buying purposes form what is called the consumer's **task definition**, or the situational reasons for buying or consuming a product or service at a particular time and place. Examples of such buying purposes are plentiful. A purchase could be occasioned by some type of gift situation, such as Christmas, a birthday, a graduation, or a wedding. The reason for buying a beverage could be to satisfy thirst, to get "high," or to stay awake. In fact, the number of ways consumers define the task situation is probably infinite. It is up to the skilled marketing manager to identify those buying reasons t hat are not adequately met by existing products.

Closely related to the task definition is the usage situation. **Usage situations** form the context in which a product is used and influence the product characteristics sought by a consumer. For example, the usage situation of camping presents unique requirements for eating utensils, food packaging, bedding, and shelter. These requirements center around the needs for light weight, portability, and durability. The task definition of "going camping," therefore, is a situational factor that influences the design of products. Those who choose the situation of living outdoors for short periods of time are a heavy-spending market segment, as Coleman Company, Inc., has discovered. Figure 14-6 illustrates a usage

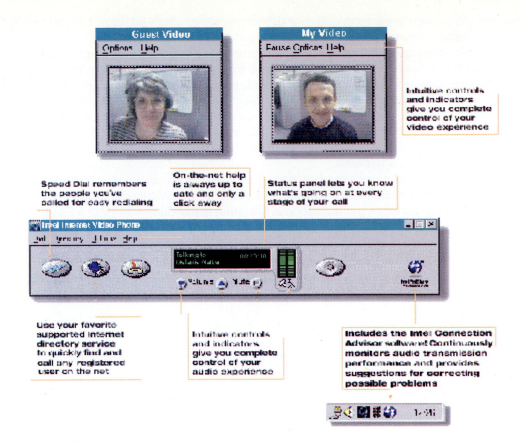

Figure 14-6

This Internet ad for Intel Corporation's Video Phone illustrates a usage situation (calling relatives) for which their product offers a significant improvement over the existing offering, the audio-only telephone.

situation—conversing with grandchildren—for which Intel Corporation's Video Phone is ideally suited.

Occasion-Based Marketing Opportunities

Sometimes a product becomes locked into one usage situation, limiting its market potential. Consumers may come to use the product habitually in a particular situation, and consider it inappropriate for all other situations. Orange juice is a good example. By convention, orange juice is associated with breakfast. Although nutritious and tasty, the beverage has not been adopted by consumers as a thirst-quenching beverage in a way that rivals soft drinks. The orange juice trade association has spent millions trying to redefine the task definition of the beverage. The campaign, based around the theme "Orange juice isn't just for breakfast anymore," has brought national attention to the thirst-quenching aspects of the beverage. A second attempt to redefine the task definition of orange juice concerns health. The trade association has teamed up with the American Cancer Society to explain the fruit's relationship to cancer prevention. It has also teamed up with the March of Dimes. The March of Dimes is concerned with birth defects, and one method of preventing birth defects is to increase the mother's intake of folic acid—which is found in orange juice.

Examples of companies or trade associations attempting to change the usage situations of products are numerous. Turkey manufacturers have attempted to persuade Americans to eat the big birds on occasions other than Thanksgiving and Christmas because the seasonal demand for turkey causes production problems for turkey growers. Another example is beef. While beef held a 3:1 market share advantage over poultry after World War II, by the 1990s the shares were about equal.[34] In an attempt to broaden the situational usage of the product, the beef trade association has sponsored commercials suggesting that beef makes a good breakfast meat.

Companies that recognize new or overlooked usage situations can discover highly profitable new market segments. The forerunner of the Internet (the ARPnet) existed for many years as a tool for scientists and intellectuals, but using it was clumsy. In 1988 a Frenchman decided to write a "front end" to make it easier to get into, and maneuver around, the Internet. Thus was born the prototype for the web browser. Later, as the Internet rose in popularity, companies began developing more and more sophisticated browsers. Companies such as Netscape Communications Corporation have increased Internet usage and have become wealthy in the process.

Gift Giving

An important ritual in most societies is the giving and receiving of gifts. People build reciprocal relations by engaging in a ritual pattern of giving, receiving, and giving back, forming bonds of trust and dependence in the process that assist them in their everyday lives.[35] It has been suggested that gifts reflect status hierarchies, denote rights of passage (e.g., high school graduation), and influence the socialization of children through the formation of gender roles (e.g., little boys receive toy soldiers and little girls receive dolls). Gift giving has strong symbolic qualities. Like advertisers, gift givers manage meanings—about who the giver is, who the receiver is, and the nature of their relationship. For example, the failure to remove a price tag from a gift violates the symbolic notion that gifts are nonmonetary expressions of affection.[36]

Gift giving has important economic consequences. In retail stores some 30 percent of sales occur during the Christmas season. More importantly, Christmas buying accounts for 50 percent of annual retail profits. So powerful is the effect of the Christmas season that consumers will even purchase gifts for people they consider to be "difficult"—those who do not want or need a gift, who are likely to be unappreciative of a gift, or who are very different from the purchaser.[37]

Retailers recognize how important gift giving is to their profits and take full advantage of the many gift occasions that have been prescribed by society. Table 14-2 provides a partial listing of the occasions when gifts are expected by children, spouses, or acquaintances.

The type of gift situation may influence a consumer's involvement in the purchase. For example, we usually engage in greater search efforts and buy more expensive, higher-quality presents for a rite of passage (a low-frequency, large-scale event such as the wedding of a close friend) than a rite of progression (a high-frequency, small-scale event such as a birthday).[38] Researchers report that people are more conservative (i.e., purchase "safe" traditional goods) when buying gifts for their spouses than for themselves.[39] One possible reason is that they perceive much greater risk in buying for a spouse than for themselves.

Why do people give gifts? Gift giving can be analyzed from the perspective of the 2×2 matrix shown in Figure 14-7. On the vertical axis one finds two gift types—voluntary and obligatory gifts.[40] Voluntary gifts are those made with a minimum of outside pressure

Some Gift-Giving Occasions

A. Various Religious Days	**D.** Legislated Days
1. Christmas	**14.** Thanksgiving
2. Easter	**15.** Halloween
3. Hanukkah	**16.** Mother's Day
4. Confirmations	**17.** Father's Day
5. Christenings	**18.** Grandparent's Day
B. Birth-Related Days	**19.** Children's Day
6. Birthday	**20.** Valentine's Day
7. A child's birth	**E.** Leaving and Coming
8. Baby shower	**21.** Going on trip—bon voyage
9. Expectant Mother's Day	**22.** Return from trip
C. Wedding-Related Days	**23.** Retirement
10. Weddings	**24.** Graduation
11. Wedding shower	**F.** Miscellaneous
12. Wedding anniversary	**27.** Sympathy
13. Wedding engagement	**28.** Hostess gifts
	29. Congratulations

TABLE 14-2

forcing the action. In contrast, obligatory gifts are the result of strong social norms pressuring the person into action. On the horizontal axis is the degree to which self-interest influences the gift. In cases of low self-interest, the giver has few ulterior motives for the action. When high self-interest exists, however, ulterior motives play a predominant role in the gift giving.

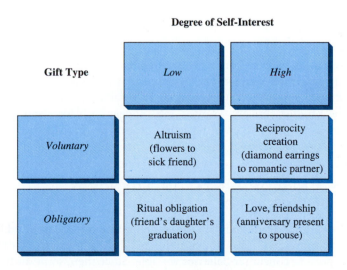

Figure 14-7
Gift-giving motivations result from degree of self-interest and gift type.

Gift-giving motives are found in the four cells of the matrix in Figure 14-7. When the gift is voluntary and self-interest is low, an altruistic motive exists for the action. An example of an altruistic gift is giving a friend a small present completely out of the blue just to cheer her up. In contrast, when the gift is voluntary, but self-interest is high, the motive is frequently one of creating an obligation. Giving a woman an expensive present in the hopes of creating an obligation is an example. On the other hand, low-involvement ritual gifts occur when an obligation exists, but the giver has low self-interest in the exchange. Giving presents to acquaintances at Christmas, birthdays, and graduations fits this category. Finally, when an obligation exists and the person has a high self-interest in the exchange, there is said to be high-involvement reciprocity. In such instances there are strong pressures to give. The exchange relationship may be highly important to the person, and love or friendship may be involved. An example would be purchasing an anniversary present for one's wife because forgetting the event would lead to dire consequences.

A study investigated differences in the gift giving of 299 men and women at Christmas in a large Canadian city. The results revealed that women were much more involved in the task than men were. Women started shopping earlier (October rather than November), spent more hours shopping per gift (2.4 versus 2.1 hours), and fewer of their gifts were exchanged (10 percent versus 16 percent). The only area in which men surpassed women was in the amount spent per gift: $91.25 versus $62.13 (Canadian dollars).[41]

Consumers not only give gifts to others, they also purchase gifts for themselves. Indeed, many of the same situational variables that influence purchasing gifts for others motivate consumers to buy for themselves. **Self-gifts** are premeditated, indulgent, relevant to the self, and context bound.[42] They may be given to reward an accomplishment (e.g., making a high grade on a consumer behavior exam), as therapy for a disappointment (e.g., failing to get a coveted job), or to mark a holiday or life transition (e.g., a birthday, graduation, or divorce).[43] Self-gifts may range from purchasing a donut to reward early-morning exercise to buying a new car to celebrate a promotion. Recent research has found that consumers higher in the personality trait of materialism tend to purchase self-gifts more frequently, particularly as a means to manage their moods. These individuals appear to associate buying with happiness.[44] A quote from one of the respondents in the study illustrates how a self-gift can be purchased in order to buy happiness:

> "I bought a diamond ring for myself. It made me feel worthwhile, loved, secure. My husband doesn't believe in giving diamond rings, so I had to accept the fact that I had to buy one for myself if I wanted to get all those good feelings."

Before leaving the subject of gift giving, we want to emphasize one finding. In a series of four studies a researcher found strong evidence that those who give gifts should take great pains to wrap them nicely.[45] Wrapping a gift results in more positive attitudes toward owning the product. Nicely wrapped gifts appear to place recipients in a better mood state, which causes them to enjoy the entire process more. So, gift givers—*wrap those presents*!

TIME AS AN ENVIRONMENTAL INFLUENCER

In his "Advice to a Young Tradesman" in the eighteenth century, Ben Franklin said, "Remember that time is money." It was not until the mid-1970s, however, that **time** was recognized as an important consumer behavior variable. Since then, some authors have even suggested that time may be the *most important* variable in consumer behavior because it plays a role in so many theoretical areas.[46] As we noted earlier in the text, definitions of brand loyalty should specify the period of time over which the buying behavior is considered. Similarly, studies of the diffusion of innovations need to take into consideration how rapidly a new product or service is adopted. Behavioral learning theory (see Chapter 5) tells us that rewards, to be effective, must be given in close temporal proximity to a behavior. These examples represent only a few of the cases in which time is an important consumer behavior variable.

Time can be analyzed from three different perspectives: (1) individual differences in the conception of time, (2) time as a product, and (3) time as a situational variable.

Individuals and Time

At the individual level, consumers expend their time in four different ways: at work, necessities, housework, and leisure.[47] These uses are arranged on a continuum ranging from obligatory to discretionary. People have little control over when and how long they work. They have somewhat more control over the time they spend on necessities, such as sleeping and eating. The effort spent on housework is much more variable, with dual-earner families spending less time on "household production." Finally, people have the most discretion in how they use their leisure time.

Time can be viewed as a resource, and how people choose to spend that resource says a great deal about them. Activities can be categorized according to whether they are substitutable or complementary.[48] **Substitute activities** are separate activities that satisfy the same need; furthermore, they are mutually exclusive in the sense that they cannot occur together. For example, playing handball and playing racquetball are substitute activities. **Complementary activities** are activities that naturally take place together. Thus a person may jointly engage in gardening and mowing the grass to fulfill the need of having a beautifully landscaped home. Complementary activities do not have to occur simultaneously; they may occur over a period of time, such as a week or a month.[49]

Various constraining factors influence the substitutability and complementarity of activities. For example, the employment status of the wife and the presence or absence of children may strongly influence how couples spend their time. (These issues are discussed in more detail in Chapter 16.) In fact, a husband's and wife's satisfaction with their marriage seems to be influenced by the extent to which they have the same views on the complementarity and substitutability of activities. The evidence indicates that couples who jointly participate in activities have greater marital satisfaction.[50]

How individuals view time is also influenced by their culture.[51] North Americans and Western Europeans tend to run on *linear separable time*: time is divided into the past, the present, and the future; it is allocated to tasks; and there is a future orientation. For those on *circular traditional time*, time doesn't stretch into the future; they tend to do today only what has to be done today. People who live on linear separable time often find it frustrating to deal with those who live on circular time because the latter usually do not see a relationship between time and money. Finally, those who keep *procedural traditional time* are

Consumer Behavior Factoid

Question: Is Franklin's axiom "Time is money" always true?

Answer: No. Researchers have found that we are much more risk-averse with time than money. The reason may be that time is less transferable than money (it can't be as easily stored or recouped). If a taxi ride costs $10 more than expected, we can recoup that loss by cutting con-

sumption elsewhere. But when a trip to the airport takes an hour longer than expected, we can't recoup that hour.

Source: France LeClerc, Bernd H. Schmitt, and Laurette Dube, "Waiting Time and Decision Making: Is Time Like Money?" *Journal of Consumer Research*, Vol. 22 (June 1995), pp. 110–119.

governed by the task rather than the time. For them, a meeting begins when the time is right, and it takes—well, "until it's over." Completing the task is the key; the idea of wasting time is irrelevant. This kind of time is reflected in Native American culture, and is sometimes called "Indian time." Some evidence exists that Asians are also "on procedural time."[52]

Time as a Product

Of course, time can also be a type of product. Many purchases are made to save time. Appliances such as microwave ovens, garbage disposals, and trash compactors exist in part for the purpose of saving time. Fast-food restaurants have flourished because consumers have a need to obtain nourishment while on the go. A name has been given to the individual who engages in such behavior—the time-buying consumer.

Since time acts as a product attribute, advertisers use time-oriented appeals in their promotional materials. One study investigated the changing use of time-oriented appeals between 1890 and 1988 by analyzing ads in *The Ladies' Home Journal* over the period. The authors found that the proportion of ads that used time as the primary appeal increased dramatically. In 1890 less than five percent of the ads did so. By the late 1980s nearly 50 percent of the ads included a time-oriented appeal as a major component. An example can be found in an ad for Hunt's Manwich (from 1986) headlined "When it's dinner time and time is tight."[53]

Time as a Situational Variable

Besides being a product, time is a situational variable. Generally, the situational characteristic of time that influences consumers is its availability. How much time a consumer has available to buy a product will influence the strategy the consumer uses to select and purchase that product. The information search is particularly influenced by the availability of time. Researchers have found that as time pressures increase, consumers spend progressively less time searching for information, use the available information less, and give more weight to unfavorable information in making a purchase decision.[54] The consumers lined up outside Moscow's GUM department store in the photo shown in Figure 14-8 may be influenced by their long wait when they finally enter the store.

An experiment was conducted to directly assess the impact of time pressures on grocery shopping. Actual grocery shoppers were assigned either to the control group, which had no time pressures, or to the experimental group, which was asked to complete their shopping in half the other participants' expected shopping time. The time-pressured group more frequently failed to purchase intended products and made fewer unplanned purchases. They also had a lower total of purchases than the control group. Finally, time pressures caused greater problems when the respondents were shopping in unfamiliar stores.[55] The managerial implication of this study is that retailers should create a shopping environment that makes it easy for time-pressed customers to locate desired products.

Many products and services, from fast-food restaurants to jet aircraft to dental services, have been developed to save consumers time. Figure 14-9 shows a humorous ad for dentures that uses speed of service as an important attribute.

Time may interact with other variables to influence purchase behavior. For example, what shoppers buy at a grocery store is influenced by the length of time that has elapsed since their last meal. Researchers noted that people who shop while hungry may find their

Figure 14-8
Waiting in line outside a GUM department store in Moscow. Time pressure can alter shoppers' behavior.

Figure 14-9
This humorous ad markets the firm's denture services as time-saving.

"imagination readily places potatoes and onions around roasts and transforms pancake mix into a steaming, buttered snack."[56]

Interestingly, a situation-consumer interaction was found in the research on hunger and grocery shopping. The food buying of shoppers classified as overweight was not affected by how long they had gone since their last meal. The effect of buying more when hungry occurred mainly for people of average weight. The authors interpreted the results as indicating that overweight consumers fail to use internal cues to determine their hunger. Rather, they use the presence of food to determine how much to buy and consume.[57] Situation-consumer interactions will be discussed in more detail later in the chapter.

The time of day is an important situational variable that can be used to segment products. For example, food products may be marketed for use in the morning (e.g., breakfast foods) or the evening. Michelob Lite beer created an entire advertising campaign around the theme "The night belongs to Michelob Lite."

The situational element of time can influence distribution strategy as well. Consumers who are short of time want to obtain products quickly and with minimal effort. The drive-through windows at fast-food restaurants exemplify a distribution system that allows customers to get their burgers, fried chicken, and other foods rapidly. Mail-order, telephone-order, and computer-ordering systems (such as found on the Internet) have been developed so that consumers do not have to take the time to go to a retail store to make a purchase.

Finally, taking a long time is not necessarily negative. For example, luxury travel by rail is increasing in the United States. In this case time is a luxury. In Europe the Orient Express between Paris and Istanbul has operated since 1919, despite the availability of faster airline service.[58]

ANTECEDENT STATES

Antecedent states are those temporary physiological and mood states that a consumer brings to a consumption situation. This situational factor is closely related to the individual consumer concepts we discussed in Part II. Examples of antecedent states are hunger, thirst, lack of sleep, and mood. **Mood states** are temporary variations on how people feel, which range from happiness to extremely negative feelings. (The effect of mood on the information processing of consumers was discussed in some detail in Chapter 4.)

An example of how temporary physiological states may influence buying behavior was given in the last section: consumers who shop for groceries while hungry are in danger of making unnecessary impulse purchases. O'Doul's nonalcoholic brew has pursued a strategy of capitalizing on the temporary physiological state of thirst. In a commercial a man dripping with sweat is shown gulping down an O'Doul's while his equally thirsty dog pants unsuccessfully for a drink, then hits his master in the head with his water dish. The goal is to tie the beverage graphically to the physiological state it is designed to remedy.

Temporary physiological states influence buying through two means. First, they can lead to problem recognition. For example, the gnawing pangs in a person's stomach may cause the person to recognize a problem (hunger) that needs to be solved (by purchasing food).

The second way that physiological states influence consumers is by changing the "feeling" component of the hierarchy of effects. (Hierarchy of effects models were discussed in Chapter 8.) For example, when a person is hungry, the presence of food is likely to create highly positive feelings toward consumption. Thus a hungry woman who enjoys red meat will have very positive feelings when she sees a porterhouse steak. These positive feelings may lead to an increased likelihood of her purchasing the steak. Similarly, if a shopper is thirsty while in a store, that physiological state is likely to create positive feelings about thirst-quenching beverages.

The Effects of Temporary Mood States on Consumers

Mood states also influence consumer behavior. In one survey people were asked why they shopped. Two of the reasons given were that they wanted to alleviate either depression or loneliness.[59] Consumers were expressing the idea that they used the shopping and purchasing experience to influence their temporary mood state.

Psychologists have studied the effects of people's mood on gift giving to charities, to others, and to themselves. In some of these studies the researchers actually influenced the mood of subjects. After creating either positive or negative moods in their subjects, the researchers measured how the changes in mood state affected behavior. For example, in one study a group of second- and third-grade children were asked to think of something that made them very happy. Another group was asked to think of something that made them feel very sad. A third group was asked not to think of anything in particular. After their mood was influenced, the children were given a chance to help themselves to candy from a treasure chest. The results revealed that in comparison to the control group, those with either a positive or a negative mood took more candy for themselves. Figure 14-10 shows the results of this study.

This mood study shows that people tend to reward themselves when they feel either good or bad. The mediator of the phenomenon appears to be the affective component of attitudes—the same concept suggested as the explanation for why hungry people buy more in a supermarket. As the authors of the mood study explained, "When one is feeling good, one tends to be more generous to oneself."[60] The phenomenon extends beyond self-generosity: people are also more generous to others when they are in a positive mood state.[61]

But why did the children in sad moods also indulge themselves? The reason seems to be that they took more candy to make themselves feel better. Importantly, the impact of negative moods seems to extend to how much one person will help another. Research evidence suggests that people over the age of 6 will help others more both when they are feeling bad and when they are feeling good, as opposed to when they are in a neutral mood state. Again, the motivation seems to be good feelings. When people feel bad, they may seek to feel better by helping others.

Recent evidence suggests that temporary mood states may influence consumer reactions to advertisements. In one experiment half of the subjects read an uplifting story that put them in a highly positive mood. All the respondents then evaluated a print advertisement. Those in a positive mood state had more favorable brand attitudes and produced

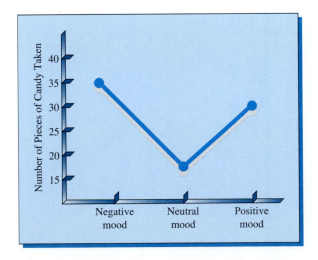

Figure 14-10

Effects of moods on self-reward. (*Source:* Data from D. Rosenham, B. Underwood, and B. Moore, "Affect Moderates Self-gratification and Altruism," *Journal of Personality and Social Psychology*, Vol. 30 [October 1974], pp. 546–552.)

fewer counterarguments to the ad. The author of this study suggested that the respondents who were in a positive mood state engaged in less cognitive processing, which cut down on the development of counterarguments. In addition, a positive mood state tended to cause subjects to process information peripherally. (Recall the elaboration likelihood model in Chapter 10.) Thus the respondents in a good mood were less affected by central cues, such as argument quality, and more influenced by peripheral cues, such as source attractiveness.[62]

Research on the effects of mood on consumer behavior is still in its infancy. We cannot be sure that mood influences the buying of products in the same way that it affects the taking of candy or the distribution of coupons that can be used to obtain a prize.[63] But the evidence indicates that mood states are particularly effective in influencing consumer buying behavior in retail settings—particularly at the point of purchase.

INTERACTIONS AMONG USAGE SITUATION, PERSON, AND PRODUCT

The buying act may be viewed as a two-way interaction in which consumer situations interact with personal factors (a situation-person interaction) or with the type of product or service being offered (a situation-product interaction). Or it can be a three-way interaction between person, product, and situation variables.[64]

An **interaction** occurs when two or more factors combine to cause a consumer to behave in a different manner than the consumer would have behaved had the two factors not been combined. In a situation-product interaction two products are viewed as useful in different situations. For example, Gatorade would be seen by most people as appropriate in situations where one has worked up a great thirst, such as after a competitive tennis match. But drinking Canada Dry ginger ale after a hard workout sounds perfectly awful. In contrast, Gatorade has little appeal as a mixer at a fashionable party, whereas Canada Dry ginger ale would be quite appropriate. Thus the type of product and type of situation interact so that the type of product favored is determined by a situational context. Figure 14-11 diagrams these interactions.

Situation-product interactions form the basis for benefit segmentation. That is, different products are created to offer divergent benefits that appeal in different situations. Consider the various types of watches that are marketed. Diving watches were developed to allow divers to tell time while underwater. The benefit provided is the ability to know

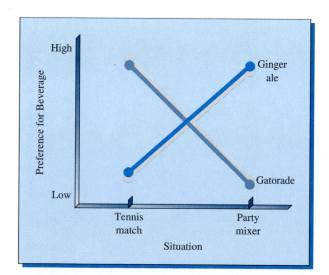

Figure 14-11

Situation-by-product interaction.

when one's air is about to run out. In contrast, formal watches were created as ornaments. Their benefit is that they look pretty.

Situation-product interaction is illustrated by a study developed to probe how purchase agents react to lunches in fancy versus ordinary restaurants. In this study the fanciness of the restaurant represented the type of product, and the reason for the lunch represented the situational factor. (Specifically, the reason for the lunch is a task-definition factor.) The researchers found that the buyers evaluated the suppliers' position more favorably in ordinary restaurant meetings than they did in fancy restaurant meetings. However, if the reason for the lunch had been to celebrate the closing of a contract, the fancy restaurant would have been the more appropriate setting. The authors interpreted the results as indicating that sales representatives should be extremely careful in staging business lunches in fancy restaurants. They argued that the restaurant context should fit the business context.[65]

A MANAGERIAL APPLICATIONS ANALYSIS OF THE GASOLINE RETAILER CASE

Problem Identification

The problem identified in the gasoline retailer case can be stated as follows: How can gas stations remain profitable under conditions of slow market growth and increasing competition?

The Consumer Behavior Analysis and Its Managerial Implications

The changing approach to marketing gasoline illustrates a number of aspects of the situational environment. Table 14-3 summarizes the situational concepts that apply to this case, along with their managerial implications. Three concepts pertaining to the situational environment have particular implications for managerial strategy in this case; the physical environment of the gasoline station, the task definition, and time.

Physical Environment Gasoline marketers are now stressing the physical environment. In deciding where to locate stations, how to arrange the lighting and pump location, and how to design the interior of their retail stores, marketers are attempting to influence consumers' feelings, beliefs, and buying behavior. When considering the physical form of a filling station, managers must seek to understand how the physical environment affects consumers. The design of the store and the arrangement of the gasoline pumps are part of the overall product being offered. Market research should be done to develop an understanding of how consumers react to changes in lighting, the arrangement of pumps, and traffic flow. By creating a physical environment that is safe, clean, and pleasing to the eye, a gasoline marketer will be pursuing a positioning strategy that helps to differentiate his station from competitors.

Task Definition Task definition is related to what consumers purchase at a filling station. The need to fill up one's gas tank is the basic reason for going to a filling station; however, by stocking high-margin impulse items, a retailer may be able to increase the total amount consumers spend at the station. Gasoline stations situated next to interstate highways are particularly appropriate locations for larger retail stores. People traveling long distances frequently have the simultaneous need for gasoline, food, bathroom facilities, and other miscellaneous products, such as games for kids, audiotapes for the cassette player, and medicines to combat motion sickness. As the Ashland executive commented in the introductory case, his company no longer positions its stores as filling stations. Rather, they are

Managerial Implications of Consumer Behavior Concepts in the Gasoline Retailer Case

Consumer Behavior Concept	Managerial Implications
1. Physical environment	*Product.* Design station so that arrangement of gasoline pumps is convenient and they are easy to use.
	Market research. Conduct studies to determine how consumers react to changes in lighting, arrangement of pumps, and traffic flow.
2. Task definition	*Market research.* Identify a task definition of what customers do when they gas up their car.
	Positioning. Based on the market research, design a positioning strategy that fulfills customer needs.
	Product. Design station so as to provide services that match the positioning description.
3. Time	*Market research.* Determine to what extent consumers are pressed for time when using a service station.
	Segmentation. Identify different target groups of customers that may have divergent time pressures.
	Product. Design service stations to meet the time needs of diverse segments of customers.
	Promotional strategy. Promote service stations in a manner that communicates the overall positioning strategy of management.

TABLE 14-3

positioned as retail stores. Understanding the task definition has implications for market research, positioning, and the marketing mix. Managers should perform marketing research to determine what leads consumers to stop at a gasoline station. Based upon this information, they should develop a product and service assortment that fulfills these needs. In turn, the store can be positioned through its promotional activities in a manner that highlights its ability to fulfill these needs.

Time The importance of time to consumers also affects managerial strategy. Efforts are being made to increase the speed with which a customer can fill up a car and pay for the gas. In addition, the smaller scale of a filling station store makes locating items faster, and less time is typically required to pay for the items.

Again, marketing research should be conducted to determine the extent to which consumers are time pressed when they patronize a service station. It may be that there are different segments of customers—for example, a time-pressed group and a more leisurely paced group. Product and service assortments can be developed for each of these groups. In addition, promotional strategy can be employed to position the service station appropriately.

Managerial Recommendations

Three specific recommendations emerge from our analysis of the gasoline station case.

Recommendation 1 As gasoline stations have proliferated, one issue for consideration is positioning and differentiation. Either the physical environment or the time element might be used to differentiate one station from another.

Recommendation 2 As the discussion of the task definition implied, these stores are positioned as retail stores that sell gasoline rather than as gas stations that sell a few other items. Market research might indicate that the typical assortment of grocery and impulse items can be improved upon.

Recommendation 3 Market research may or may not indicate that consumers are pressed for time when they fill up their tanks. For example, there may be a segment that wants quick-filling pumps, and another, more leisurely paced segment that would appreciate the provision of tables and chairs for eating meals. In another era gas stations provided natural gathering places in rural areas. This is a marketing concept that might be returning.

SUMMARY

Consumer situations are those temporary environmental circumstances that form the context within which a consumer activity occurs. Situational factors that influence consumers include physical surroundings, social surroundings, the occasion for which a product is bought (task definition), time, and the consumer's temporary physiological and mood states (antecedent states). These situations may influence consumers when they receive communications about a product or service, when they make a purchase, and when they use the product or service.

The impact of the physical surroundings on consumers is particularly important for retailers. Store layout, atmospherics, crowding, music, and store location are all factors in the physical environment that can affect consumers. Social motives influence why people shop, their involvement in the purchase, and their conformity to the tastes and preferences of others. The task definition deals with the reasons a product or service is bought. One can think of the task definition in terms of the occasion that spurs a purchase, such as a gift occasion, a party, or even a type of meal (e.g., breakfast and orange juice). Usage occasions can be utilized as a potent segmentation tool.

Time is also an important situational variable. Consumers may be segmented on the basis of their perception and use of time. From this perspective, time is a resource. How consumers choose to spend time reveals much about their lifestyles. Time can also be viewed as a product characteristic. Thousands of products have been created and positioned on the basis of their ability to save time. Time may be conceptualized as a situational variable. In this case the availability of time influences consumer actions. In addition, time of day may influence consumer actions, such as product choice and information processing.

Antecedent states are those temporary physical and mood states that influence consumer buying behavior. Whether people are happy or sad, hungry or thirsty, can affect their attitudes toward a purchase and how much they will buy.

The type of situation can directly influence consumers' buying behavior. Frequently, however, the situation interacts with the product and the individual characteristics of consumers to influence buying behavior. For example, situations interact strongly with type of beverage. The type of beverage bought for a party (choice from task definition) may be quite different from that bought for quenching thirst (choice from antecedent state).

antecedent states
atmospherics
complementary activities
consumer environment
consumer situations

crowding
density
gravitational model
interaction
marketing triad

mood states
physical surroundings
self-gifts
service encounter
social surroundings

store layout
substitute activities
task definition
time
usage situation

REVIEW QUESTIONS

1. Define the concept of consumer situation. What are the five types of situations that were identified in this chapter?

2. Give an example of a situation-person interaction. Give an example of a situation-product interaction.

3. The effect of music on shoppers is one example of how physical surroundings can influence buying. Identify five other means through which the physical surroundings can influence buying.

4. What are the effects of a store's location on consumer store choice?

5. Draw the model of how atmospherics influences shopping behavior presented in Figure 14-5. What are the components of store atmosphere?

6. How can the presence of other people influence the consumption situation, the purchase situation, and the communications situation?

7. Define the term *task definition*. Indicate five categories of gift-giving situations.

8. Identify four of the six reasons given in the chapter for gift giving.

9. Identify and give examples of three ways in which time may influence consumption activities.

10. How might a company use information to lower customer dissatisfaction with delays in service?

11. Different cultures view time divergently. Discuss the three views of time held in various cultures.

12. Define the concept of the antecedent state. What are two types of antecedent states and how might each influence consumption?

DISCUSSION QUESTIONS

1. The shoe industry is segmented to a large extent by the usage situation of the product. Identify as many different usage situations as you can for which manufacturers have created different types of shoes.

2. The situation can interact with the type of person and with the type of product. Give an example of each type of interaction. (*Hint*: Think about your own characteristics and preferences and about those of someone else who is quite different from you. Compare how each of you responds to various types of situations and products.)

3. Draw a diagram of the grocery store with which you are most familiar. Identify the specific physical features of the store that are designed to move customers in specific patterns and to encourage them to purchase specific products.

4. Recall from your own experience two consumer behavior settings where large numbers of people were present. To what extent did the presence of people enhance the overall consumption experience? What are the cir-

cumstances in which large numbers of people detract from the consumption experience?

5. Draw a map of your community. Place on the map the locations of your residence and your college. Now draw in the locations of the retailers you most frequently patronize. Do you find any relationship between the location of the retailers and the location of your residence and college?

6. Considering all the components that help to create a store's atmosphere, describe in one or two paragraphs the atmosphere of two popular eating or drinking establishments in your community. To what extent do you think the atmosphere of these establishments was consciously created?

7. List all the gifts you have given to people over the past year. What was the occasion that prompted the giving of each of these gifts? In which instances did you purchase a product that was designed specifically to be given as a gift?

8. Identify five products or services that differentiate themselves from competitors on the basis of saving or using up time. How do these products communicate this benefit to consumers? Try to identify a new product or service that could be marketed as saving time for college students. How much of a market is there for products and services that help you use up time?

9. Suppose you are an advertising executive charged with developing a campaign for a company that sells exotic coffees. Your task is to design an advertising campaign based on the idea that people drink coffee because of their good or bad moods. Develop a print ad carrying out this task.

10. Examine the ethical implications of oil companies selling high-octane gasoline to consumers who own cars that do not need this more expensive product.

E N D N O T E S

1. Russell Belk, "An Exploratory Assessment of Situational Effects in Buyer Behavior," *Journal of Marketing Research*, Vol. 11 (May 1974), p. 160. For a view of situations from a more cognitive perspective, see Luk Warlop and S. Ratneshwar, "The Role of Usage Context in Consumer Choice: A Problem Solving Perspective," in *Advances in Consumer Research*, Vol. 20, Leigh McAlister and Michael L. Rothschild, eds. (Provo, UT: Association for Consumer Research, 1993), pp. 377–382.

2. Ronald E. Milliman, "Using Background Music to Affect the Behavior of Supermarket Shoppers," *Journal of Marketing*, Vol. 46 (Summer 1982), pp. 86–91.

3. Ronald E. Milliman, "The Influence of Background Music on the Behavior of Restaurant Patrons," *Journal of Consumer Research*, Vol. 13 (September 1986), pp. 286–289.

4. For an excellent summary of the effects of music on consumers, see Gordon C. Bruner II, "Music, Mood, and Marketing," *Journal of Marketing*, Vol. 54 (October 1990), pp. 94–104. Also see Judy I. Alpert and Mark I. Alpert, "Contributions from a Musical Perspective on Advertising in Consumer Behavior," in *Advances in Consumer Research*, Vol. 18, Rebecca H. Holman and Michael R. Solomon, eds. (Provo, UT: Association for Consumer Research, 1991), pp. 232–238. There is a growing literature on the impact of music on consumer responses to advertising. For example, see Deborah J. Macinnis and C. Whan Park, "The Differential Role of Characteristics of Music on High- and Low-Involvement Consumers' Processing of Ads," *Journal of Consumer Research*, Vol. 18 (September 1991), pp. 161–173. Finally, tastes differ in music and music possibly should vary according to the time of day, day of week, and type of surroundings. See J. Duncan Herrington and Louis M. Capella, "Effects of Music in Service Environments: A Field Study," *Journal of Services Marketing*, Vol. 10, no. 2 (1996), pp. 26–41.

5. James J. Kellaris and Robert J. Kent, "The Influence of Music on Consumers' Temporal Perceptions: Does Time Fly When You're Having Fun?" *Journal of Consumer Psychology*, Vol. 1, no. 4 (1992), pp. 365–376.

6. James J. Kellaris, Susan Powell Mantel and Moses B. Altsech, "Decibels, Disposition and Duration: The Impact of Musical Loudness and Internal States on Time Perceptions," in *Advances in Consumer Research*, Vol. 23, Kim P. Corfman and John J. Lynch, Jr., eds. (Provo, UT: Association for Consumer Research, 1996), pp. 498–503.

7. Charles S. Areni and David Kim, "The Influence of Background Music on Shopping Behavior: Classical versus Top-Forty," in *Advances in Consumer Research*, Vol. 20, Leigh McAlister and Michael L. Rothschild, eds. (Provo, UT: Association for Consumer Research, 1993), pp. 336–340.

8. Daniel Stokols, "On the Distinction Between Density and Crowding: Some Implications for Future Research," *Psychological Review*, Vol. 79 (May 1972), pp. 275–277.

9. G. Harrell, M. Hutt, and J. Anderson, "Path Analysis of Buyer Behavior Under Conditions of Crowding," *Journal of Marketing Research*, Vol. 17 (February 1980), pp. 45–51.

10. Michael K. Hui and John E.G. Bateson, "Perceived Control and the Effects of Crowding and Consumer Choice on the Service Experience," *Journal of Consumer Research*, Vol. 18 (September 1991), pp. 174–184. A related issue involves the effect of number of employees on customers. Evidence is provided in Julie Baker, Michael Levy, and Dhruv Grewal, "An Experimental Approach to Making Retail Store Environmental Decisions," *Journal of Retailing*, Vol. 68 (Winter 1992), pp. 445–460.

11. Robert East, Wendy Lomax, Gill Willson, and Patricia Harris, "Decision Making and Habit in Shopping Times," *European Journal of Marketing*, Vol. 28, no. 4 (1994), pp. 56–71.

12. David L. Huff, "Defining and Estimating a Trading Area," *Journal of Marketing*, July 1964, pp. 34–38.

13. R. Mittelstaedt *et al.*, "Psychophysical and Evaluative Dimensions of Cognized Distance in an Urban Shopping Environment," in *Combined Proceedings*, R. C. Curhan, ed. (Chicago: American Marketing Association, 1974), pp. 190–193. Also see Priya Raghubir and Aradhna Krishna, "As the Crow Flies: Bias in Consumers' Map-Based Distance Judgments," *Journal of Consumer Research*, Vol. 23 (June 1996), pp. 26–39.

14. David J. Burns, "Image Transference and Retail Site Selection," *International Journal of Retail and Distribution Management*, Vol. 20 (September–October 1992), pp. 38–43.

15. Paul Kelly, "Reorganizing the Store," *Progressive Grocer*, March 1996, p. 21.

16. Paul Tarricone, "Real Estate: Airports Can Be a Launching Pad for Revenue," *Facilities Design and Management*, February 1996, p. 26.

17. Philip Kotler, "Atmospherics as a Marketing Tool," *Journal of Retailing*, Vol. 49 (Winter 1973–74), pp. 48–64.

18. Robert Donovan and John Rossiter, "Store Atmosphere: An Environmental Psychology Approach," *Journal of Retailing*, Vol. 58 (Spring 1982), pp. 34–57.

19. Albert Mehrabian and J. Russell, *An Approach to Environmental Psychology* (Cambridge, MA: M.I.T. Press, 1974).

20. Donovan and Rossiter, "Store Atmosphere."

21. Cited by Mary Jo Bitner, "Consumer Responses to the Physical Environment in Service Settings," in *Creativity in Services Marketing: What's New, What Works, What's Developing*, M.

Venkatesan, Diane Schmalensee, and Claudia Marshall, eds. (Chicago: American Marketing Association, 1986), pp. 89–93.

22. Abraham Maslow and N. Mintz, "Effects of Aesthetic Surroundings," *Journal of Psychology*, Vol. 41 (1956), pp. 247–254.

23. John Pierson, "If the Sun Shines In, Workers Work Better, Buyers Buy More," *The Wall Street Journal*, November 20, 1995, pp. B1, B7.

24. Eric R. Spangenberg, Ayn E. Crowley, and Pamela W. Henderson, "Improving the Store Environment: Do Olfactory Cues Affect Evaluations and Behaviors?" *Journal of Marketing*, Vol. 60 (April 1996), pp. 67–80. See also Deborah J. Mitchell, Barbara E. Kahn and Susan C. Knasko, "There's Something in the Air: Effects of Congruent or Incongruent Ambient Odor on Consumer Decision Making," *Journal of Consumer Research*, Vol. 22 (September 1995), pp. 229–238.

25. Ron Markin, Charles Lillis, and Chem Narayana, "Social-Psychological Significance of Store Space," *Journal of Retailing*, Vol. 52 (Spring 1976), pp. 43–54.

26. Kotler, "Atmospherics as a Marketing Tool."

27. Russell Belk, "An Exploratory Assessment of Situational Effects in Buyer Behavior," *Journal of Marketing Research*, Vol. 11 (May 1974), p. 160.

28. Solomon E. Asch, *Social Psychology* (Englewood Cliffs, NJ: Prentice Hall, 1952).

29. E. M. Tauber, "Why Do People Shop?" *Journal of Marketing*, Vol. 36 (October 1972), p. 47.

30. Richard Feinberg, Brent Scheffler, and Jennifer Meoli, "Social Ecological Insights into Consumer Behavior in the Retail Mall," *Proceedings of the Division*

of Consumer Psychology, Linda Alwitt, ed. (New York: American Psychological Association, December 23, 1987), pp. 17–19.

31. Ibid.

32. Donald H. Granbois, "Improving the Study of Customer In-Store Behavior," *Journal of Marketing*, Vol. 32 (October 1968), pp. 28–33.

33. William Bearden and Arch Woodside, "Consumption Occasion Influence on Consumer Brand Choice," *Decision Sciences*, Vol. 9 (April 1978), p. 275.

34. Eugene W. Anderson and Steven M. Shugan, "Repositioning for Changing Preferences: The Case of Beef versus Poultry," *Journal of Consumer Research*, Vol. 18 (September 1991), pp. 219–232.

35. C. Lévi-Strauss, *Structure Elémentaire de la Parento* (Paris: Presser Universitaires de France, 1954).

36. Mary Finlay, "Motivations and Symbolism in Gift-Giving Behavior," in *Advances in Consumer Research*, Vol. 17, Marvin E. Goldberg, Gerald Gorn, and Richard W. Pollay, eds. (Provo, UT: Association for Consumer Research, 1990), pp. 699–706.

37. Cele Otnes, Young Chan Kim, and Tina M. Lowrey, "Ho, Ho, Woe: Christmas Shopping for 'Difficult' People," in *Advances in Consumer Research*, Vol. 19, John Sherry, Jr., and Brian Sternthal, eds. (Provo, UT: Association for Consumer Research, 1992), pp. 482–487.

38. This distinction is noted in David Cheal, *The Gift Economy* (New York: Routledge, 1988), cited in Mary Finley Wolfinbarger and Mary C. Gilly, "An Experimental Investigation of Self-Symbolism in Gifts," in *Advances in Consumer Research*, Vol. 23, Kim P. Corfman and John G. Lynch, Jr., eds. (Provo, UT: As-

sociation for Consumer Research, 1996), pp. 458–462.

39. E. W. Hart, "Consumer Risk Taking for Self and Spouse," unpublished doctoral dissertation, Purdue University, 1974.

40. The distinction between voluntary and obligatory gifts was pointed out by Cathy Goodwin, Kelly L. Smith, and Susan Spiggle, "Gift Giving: Consumer Motivation and the Gift Purchase Process," in *Advances in Consumer Research*, Vol. 17, Marvin E. Goldberg, Gerald Gorn, and Richard W. Pollay, eds. (Provo, UT: Association for Consumer Research, 1990), pp. 690–698. For another perspective on why consumers give gifts, see Mary Finley Wolfinbarger and Laura J. Yale, "Three Motivations for Interpersonal Gift Giving: Experiential, Obligated, and Practical Motivations," in *Advances in Consumer Research*, Vol. 20, Leigh McAlister and Michael L. Rothschild, eds. (Provo, UT: Association for Consumer Research, 1993), pp. 520–526.

41. Eileen Fischer and Stephen J. Arnold, "More Than a Labor of Love: Gender Roles and Christmas Gift Shopping," *Journal of Consumer Research*, Vol. 17 (December 1990), pp. 333–343.

42. David Glen Mick and Michelle DeMoss, "Self-Gifts: Phenomenological Insights from Four Contexts," *Journal of Consumer Research*, Vol. 17 (December 1990), pp. 322–332.

43. David Glen Mick and Michele DeMoss, "Further Findings on Self-Gifts: Products, Qualities, and Socioeconomic Correlates," in *Advances in Consumer Research*, Vol. 19, John Sherry, Jr., and Brian Sternthal, eds. (Provo, UT: Association for Consumer Research, 1992), pp. 140–146.

44. Kim K. R. McKeage, Marsha L. Richins, and Kathleen Debevec, "Self-Gifts and the Manifesta-tion of Material Values," in *Advances in Consumer Research*, Vol. 20, Leigh McAlister and Michael L. Rothschild, eds. (Provo, UT: Association for Consumer Research, 1993), pp. 359–364.

45. Daniel J. Howard, "Gift-Wrapping Effects on Product Attitudes: A Mood-Biasing Explanation," *Journal of Consumer Psychology*, Vol. 1, no. 3 (1992), pp. 197–223.

46. F. M. Nicosia and R. Mayer, "Toward a Sociology of Consumption," *Journal of Consumer Research*, Vol. 3 (September 1976), pp. 65–76.

47. Laurence Feldman and Jacob Hornik, "The Use of Time: An Integrated Conceptual Model," *Journal of Consumer Research*, Vol. 7 (March 1981), pp. 407–419.

48. Morris Holbrook and Donald Lehmann, "Allocating Discretionary Time: Complementarity Among Activities," *Journal of Consumer Research*, Vol. 7 (March 1981), pp. 395–406.

49. U. N. Umesh, William Weeks, and Linda Golden, "Individual and Dyadic Consumption of Time: Propositions on the Perception of Complementarily and Substitutability of Activities," in *Advances in Consumer Research*, Vol. 14 (Provo, UT: Association for Consumer Research, 1987), pp. 548–552.

50. Ibid.

51. Robert Graham, "The Role of Perception of Time in Consumer Research," *Journal of Consumer Research*, Vol. 7 (March 1981), pp. 335–342.

52. Jay D. Lundquist, Sara Tacoma, and Paul M. Lane, "What Is Time? An Explanatory Extension Toward the Far East," in *Developments in Marketing Science*, Vol. 16, Michael Levy and Dhruv Grewel, eds. (Coral Gables, FL: Academy of Marketing Science, 1993), pp. 186–190.

53. Barbara L. Gross and Jagdish N. Sheth, "Time-Oriented Advertising: A Content Analysis of United States Magazine Advertising, 1890–1988," *Journal of Marketing*, Vol. 53 (October 1989), pp. 76–83.

54. Anthony D. Miyazaki, "How Many Shopping Days Until Christmas? A Preliminary Investigation of Time Pressures, Deadlines, and Planning Levels on Holiday Gift Purchases," in *Advances in Consumer Research*, Vol. 20, Leigh McAlister and Michael L. Rothschild, eds. (Provo, UT: Association for Consumer Research, 1993), pp. 331–335. Also see Peter Wright, "The Harassed Decision Maker: Time Pressures, Distractions, and the Use of Evidence," *Journal of Applied Psychology*, Vol. 59 (October 1974), pp. 555–561; and Frank Denton, "The Dynamism of Personal Lifestyle: How We Do More in Less Time," *Advances in Consumer Research*, Vol. 23, Chris T. Allen and Deborah Roedder John, eds. (Provo, UT: Association for Consumer Research, 1994), pp. 132–136.

55. C. Whan Park, Easwar S. Iyer, and Daniel C. Smith, "The Effects of Situational Factors on In-Store Grocery Shopping Behavior: The Role of Store Environment and Time Available for Shopping," *Journal of Consumer Research*, Vol. 15 (March 1989), pp. 422–433.

56. R. E. Nisbet and D. E. Kanouse, "Obesity, Food Deprivation and Supermarket Shopping Behavior," *Journal of Personality and Social Psychology*, Vol. 12 (August 1969), pp. 289–294.

57. Ibid.

58. John Bigness, "Elegance Does an Encore on U.S. Rails," *The Wall Street Journal*, January 26, 1996, p. B4.

59. Tauber, "Why Do People Shop?", p. 47.

60. D. L. Rosenhan, B. Underwood, and B. Moore, "Affect Moderates Self-gratification and Altruism," *Journal of Personality and Social Psychology*, Vol. 30 (October 1974), pp. 546–552.

61. B. Moore, B. Underwood, and D. L. Rosenhan, "Affect and Altruism," *Developmental Psychology*, Vol. 8 (January 1973), pp. 99–104.

62. Rajeev Batra, "The Role of Mood in Advertising Effectiveness," *Journal of Consumer Research*, Vol. 17 (September 1990), pp. 203–214.

63. D. Kenrick, D. Baumann, and R. Cialdini, "A Step in the Socialization of Altruism as Hedonism," *Journal of Personality and Social Psychology*, Vol. 37 (May 1979), pp. 747–755.

64. S. Ratneshwar and Alan G. Sawyer, "The Use of Multiple Methods to Explore Three-Way Person, Brand, and Usage Context Interactions," in *Advances in Consumer Research*, Vol. 19, John Sherry, Jr., and Brian Sternthal, eds. (Provo, UT: Association for Consumer Research, 1992), pp. 116–122.

65. Paul Schurr and Bobby Calder, "Psychological Effects of Restaurant Meetings on Industrial Buyers," *Journal of Marketing*, Vol. 50 (January 1986), pp. 87–97.

ESKIMO JOE'S: STILLWATER'S JUMPIN' LITTLE JUKE JOINT

Stan Clark graduated from Oklahoma State University in 1975. He put himself through college by selling pizzas, flowers, and hats. After graduation, he took his earnings from selling OSU "Cowboys" hats and leased an old stone building with a partner. Their goal was to open a bar. They tore down an unwanted barn and decorated the building with aged timbers. Clark and his partner did all the carpentry themselves and created a rustic, homey interior.

The next question concerned what to name the joint. The partner suggested "Eskimo Joe's" because they would sell the coldest beer in town. Clark was aghast—whoever heard of Eskimos in Oklahoma? But the partner wouldn't let go of the name. So they commissioned a freshman graphic arts major to design a logo. The student's first draft was a design featuring an Eskimo staring out at customers with a big, toothy grin, accompanied by a huge dog with a long, drooling tongue hanging out. The partners loved it, and made this logo the symbol of Eskimo Joe's. When the bar opened in July 1975, Stan and his partner greeted patrons and sold T-shirts bearing the bar's logo. Their first employee was hired from that first-night crowd. From this unglamorous opening, the bar grew in popularity over the years.

After buying out his partner in 1978, Clark accelerated the marketing of Eskimo Joe's. He understood the importance of creating events to attract customers. The characters in the logo (Eskimo Joe and his dog Buffy) were used to advertise the joint. "T-shirt nights" were created, when patrons who wore Eskimo Joe T-shirts received 10-cent drafts of beer. Each summer the bar celebrated its anniversary with "Joe's Weekend." Alumni of the university would return for a party at Joe's. Slowly the weekend grew in importance until, in the mid-1980s, the mayor of the city condemned the weekend, charging that the crowds it attracted were urinating on her flowers. The media attention only served to attract more people. Clark used the occasion to ask local merchants and service clubs to sponsor booths. By the summer of 1991 Joe's Weekend had become a huge event. Streets were closed and dozens of portable potties were brought in to handle the 48,000 people who arrived for the party.

One of the turning points for Eskimo Joe's came in 1984 when the state of Oklahoma raised the drinking age for liquor to 21. In order to survive, the bar had to generate 50 percent of its sales in food. Clark persuaded a reluctant bank to lend him the money to put in a kitchen and build an atrium for extra room. What looked like a major risk turned out to be a bonanza. The target market suddenly expanded dramatically. As Stan Clark said, "I learned that a lot more people eat every day than drink every day."

By 1991 Eskimo Joe's had become a phenomenon. Eskimo Joe's T-shirts became the second best-selling T-shirt in the world—after Hard Rock Cafe shirts. (As of February 1992 more than 3 million had been sold. Indeed, you can purchase an Eskimo Joe sweatshirt by calling Joe's Clothes Worldwide at 1-800-256-JOES.) The banker who originally lent Stan Clark and his partner the money to start the business says that now Mr. Clark can buy and sell his bank.

When asked what factors are responsible for the remarkable success of Eskimo Joe's Stan Clark says, "Our goal is to exceed customer expectations. You must treat customers right so that they have a great time." Clark believes that you do this by creating an environment where the employees love their job—their enthusiasm will then be transferred to the customers. As Clark said, "Every time an employee interacts with a guest, that's a moment of truth. Guests must be made to feel welcome and wanted." Clark believes that how management treats its employees dictates how they will treat customers. In turn, the interactions of the staff with the customers influences how the customers mingle with one another. Management shares little trade secrets with the staff (e.g., the hamburger is ground fresh every day) and the staff passes this information on to customers, who in turn tell their friends.

The second reason for the success of Eskimo Joe's is its image and atmosphere. The old stone building makes people feel comfortable. The logo creates an offbeat, fun-loving image that carries over to the staff and the customers. The building is filled with music played over an outstanding stereo system. The only guidelines

Figure C-1
Nearly 50,000 people crowd the streets of Stillwater to be part of Joe's Weekend.

for the music played are "no pop" and "no hard rock." When these factors are combined with a menu that features excellent food at low prices, it is understandable that people come to Eskimo Joe's to be seen by others and to meet others (see Figure C-1). As my own students tell me, "Eskimo Joe's is HOT."

Questions

1. Define the problem faced by Stan Clark and his partner when they opened the bar.

2. Discuss the consumer concepts from the chapter that are illustrated by this case.

3. Develop the managerial applications table for this case. Discuss the managerial strategies that emerge from the consumer concepts identified in Question 2.

This case was prepared by John Mowen.

CHAPTER FIFTEEN

GROUP PROCESSES I:
GROUP, DYADIC,
AND DIFFUSION PROCESSES

Bringing Kevlar® to Market

After 25 years of intensive work and over $700 million in capital expenditures, Du Pont Company chemists finally succeeded in producing Kevlar®. When product development began in the early 1960s, the goal was to create a fiber that would duplicate the phenomenal success of nylon and Dacron. Kevlar® was lighter than steel, yet five times stronger. There was a problem, however: In what products could Kevlar® be used?[1]

DuPont managers believed that Kevlar® would replace steel as the material of choice for automobile tires. In comparison to steel it was lighter, stronger, more heat resistant, and more easily woven into rubber compounds for making tires. Only after building a $500 million plant to produce the fiber did the company learn that tire makers had decided to use steel anyway. Steel was cheaper, and consumers liked the phrase "steel-belted radials." By the early 1980s the only commercial demand for Kevlar® was in the manufacture of racing tires. As the marketing manager for the fiber said, "Kevlar® was the answer, but we didn't know for what."

To its credit, DuPont faced the problem squarely in the early 1980s and overhauled its entire product-marketing effort. It put together a team that eventually swelled to over 1,000 people, most of them focused on marketing research and new-applications development. One manager described the turnaround in attitude: "We used to sell what we made. Now we make what we can sell." The company learned the hard way that a technological breakthrough does not necessarily mean financial success. As one consultant said, "If you have a new material, you have to beat the world's door down before it's accepted. You need a strong stomach to be able to withstand the valleys. But when the peak comes, you make obnoxious amounts of money."

By the late 1980s DuPont's tenacity and patience were beginning to pay off as new uses for the fiber were discovered. The breakthrough came when the U.S. Army adopted Kevlar® for use in helmets and flak jackets. Police departments also began to purchase bulletproof vests made of Kevlar. Newer uses include trawling nets, golf clubs, racing sails, protective gloves, oceanic cables, and protective curtains for embassies. Kevlar® is one of the materials in the exotic composites out of which jet aircraft like the Stealth bomber are made, and it is appearing in racecars and motorcycles, and even in stereo speakers. It looks as though the product is finally a success.

On the horizon, however, are new materials that may eclipse Kevlar®. Scientists have identified the genes responsible for producing "drag line," the silk spiders use to frame the spokes of a web. Spider silk is five times stronger than steel, more flexible than nylon, and can absorb three times more impact force without breaking than Kevlar® can.[2]

INTRODUCTION

The Kevlar® case introduces group, word-of-mouth, and diffusion processes as important elements of the consumer environment. A major reason for studying groups is that when people join a group, they frequently act differently than they do when they are alone. As a result, groups are more than the sum of their parts. Why is it that restaurants usually add a 15 percent tip to the bill when more than four or five people eat together? Because each member of the dining party would otherwise give a lower percentage tip than if he or she were eating alone. Being a part of a group apparently causes people to feel less responsible for providing their fair share of the tip.[3]

The impact of groups also shows up in shopping behavior. One study examined people's purchases based on the size of the shopping group they were in. The results showed that when the consumers shopped alone, they tended to make only planned purchases. However, when they shopped in groups, they tended to deviate from their plans. The larger the group, the more pronounced this tendency was. In groups of three or more the number of shoppers who exceeded their planned purchases nearly doubled—and the number who purchased *less* than they had planned more than doubled. Table 15-1 shows these percentages.

This chapter is divided into four major sections. In the first we discuss how groups influence consumption. In the second we explore dyadic exchanges—the information that passes from one individual to another within groups. Such exchanges often have an important impact on consumer decisions as to which product to purchase and which store or service provider to use (e.g., which doctor, dentist, or hair stylist to patronize). In the third section we analyze the processes through which information and innovations diffuse through the environment. Finally, in the last section we present a managerial applications analysis of group processes using the Kevlar® case.

Effects of Group Size on Shopping Purchases

Purchases	Person Alone	Three or More
No items planned or purchased	3.7%	0.0%
Fewer purchases than planned	15.1	31.3
Purchases as planned	58.9	26.6
More purchases than planned	22.8	42.1

Source: Data from Donald H. Granbois, "Improving the Study of Consumer In-Store Behavior," *Journal of Marketing*, Vol. 32 (October 1968), pp. 28–32, published by the American Marketing Association.

TABLE 15-1

GROUP PROCESSES

A **group** is a set of individuals who interact with one another over some period of time and who share a common need or goal. Groups are characterized by the exchange processes that take place among their members. Indeed, people will choose to remain in a group only if they "profit" from it—that is, if the rewards they receive from membership equal or exceed the costs of membership. Consumers belong to numerous groups, each of which has some impact on their buying behavior. For example, college students are likely to be members of families, sororities or fraternities, dorms, student organizations, and clubs. The family group, which is discussed in detail in Chapter 16, is particularly important because it is an important buying unit within the economy.

Groups influence buying in two general ways. First, they affect the purchases made by individual consumers. For example, a member of a fraternity may purchase a fraternity jacket. Second, group members sometimes make decisions as a group. For example, a student club may decide where to hold a party and what refreshments to purchase for it.[4]

The study of group processes is also relevant to decision making within firms. The buying center within a firm is usually composed of several individuals who jointly make purchase decisions. Also, firm employees often form groups to decide where to have parties, which restaurant to go to for a celebration, and which radio station to listen to for background music.

Types of Groups

Sociologists have developed a variety of terms to describe the various types of groups a person may belong to, aspire to join, or avoid,[5] and Table 15-2 provides a brief definition of them. They are: reference groups, primary and secondary groups, and formal and informal groups. The most important is the reference group.

Reference group is a broad term that encompasses a number of more specific types of groups. The common factor among all types of reference groups is that they are used by members as a point of reference to evaluate the correctness of their actions, beliefs, and attitudes.

Types of Groups
Reference group. A group whose values, norms, attitudes, or beliefs are used as a guide for behavior by an individual.
Aspiration group. A group to which an individual would like to belong. If membership in it proves impossible, it becomes a symbolic group for the person.
Dissociative group. A group with which the person does not wish to be associated.
Primary group. A group of which a person is a member and with which that person interacts on a face-to-face basis. Primary groups are marked by intimacy among their members and by a lack of boundaries for the discussion of various topics.
Formal group. A group whose organization and structure are defined in writing. Examples are labor unions, universities, and classroom groups.
Informal group. A group that has no written organizational structure. Informal groups are often socially based, such as a group of friends who meet frequently to play golf, play bridge, or party together.

TABLE 15-2

One important reference group is the aspiration group. An **aspiration group** is a set of people with whom an individual identifies. One can see the effects of aspiration groups on college students in the spring of their senior year, when they are interviewing for jobs. Their aspiration group has suddenly changed, and along with it their clothing—from jeans and cutoffs to business suits.

Another type of reference group is the **dissociative group**. The dissociative group also is a point of reference for the individual—however, it is with which the consumer wants to *avoid* being associated. For example, when individuals are striving to move into higher social classes, they may avoid buying the products and services used by their dissociative reference group. Figure 15-1 shows a dissociative group for some people—smokers forced outside to puff.

How Do Groups Influence Consumers?

Groups affect consumers through five basic means: (1) group influence processes, (2) the creation of roles within the group, (3) the development of conformity pressures, (4) social-comparison processes, and (5) the development of group polarization. These are discussed in the following paragraphs.

Normative, Value-Expressive, and Informational Influence
The type of group that has the most impact on consumers is the reference group. Reference groups affect people through norms, through information, and through the value-expressive needs of consumers. A **norm** is a behavioral rule of conduct agreed upon by over half of the group in order to establish behavioral consistency within the group. Though they are rarely written down, norms are nonetheless generally recognized as standards for behavior by group members. They represent shared value judgments about how things should be done by members of the group.[6] **Normative influence** occurs when norms act to influence individuals' behavior. For example, the effects of unwritten corporate dress codes illustrate the impact of normative influence on the clothing purchased by employees. Similarly, norms

Figure 15-1

An example of a dissociative group for some consumers—smokers forced to move outside to puff.

can influence what and how much a person eats or drinks at a party and even the type of car a consumer purchases.

Groups can also influence consumers by providing them with information and encouraging them to express certain types of values. **Informational influence** operates when the group provides highly credible information that influences the consumer's purchase decisions. **Value-expressive influence** affects consumers when they sense that a reference group has certain values and attitudes pertaining to the consumption process. Because the person wishes to be a member of the group in good standing and to be liked by the other members, he or she may act in ways that express these values and attitudes.

There is one additional important point about reference-group influence that should be made. Reference-group influence varies according to the type of product purchased. There is evidence that reference-group influence is higher for "public" products, such as wristwatches and automobiles, than for "private" products, such as refrigerators and mattresses.[7]

Roles A **role** consists of the specific behaviors expected of a person in a certain position. When one takes on a role, normative pressures exert influence on one to act in a particular way.[8] An important role in consumer behavior is that of the *decider*. This person makes the final decision concerning which brand to choose. In organizational buying settings, identifying the decider is crucial. Often an individual outside of the purchasing department is actually responsible for the buying decision. Reaching this individual with the promotional message can mean the difference between making the sale and failing to make it.

The term **role-related product cluster** has been given to the set of products necessary to play a particular role. For marketing managers, identifying those products that match the roles of consumers can be highly useful. For example, the role-related product cluster in a successful executive's office might include a personal computer, a window on an upper floor, and an exercise device in the corner. An advertising campaign for the exercise equipment could symbolically tie it to the rest of the product cluster as a necessity for the upwardly mobile businessperson.

A classic study relevant to the role-related product cluster was performed in the 1950s. Two groups of housewives were given shopping lists that a "homemaker" had prepared. The shopping lists were identical except that one contained the entry of drip-grind coffee and the other an instant coffee. The homemaker who bought the ground coffee was described by the respondents as "practical and frugal." In contrast, the woman who had bought the instant coffee was seen as lazy, shortsighted, as an "office girl who is living from one day to the next in a haphazard sort of life."[9] The study indicates that in 1950 instant coffee was not a part of the role-related product cluster of a good homemaker. Interestingly, the 1950 study was repeated in the 1970s, and the results were dramatically different. The user of instant coffee was then described favorably, whereas the user of ground coffee was viewed as "old-fashioned."[10]

In a recent study a mostly male sample of professional and skilled workers created sets of living room furniture. The researchers found that the sets created were similar for occupational groups—that is, physicians picked similar furniture, as did firemen and professors—and dissimilar across the groups. For example, professors were more likely to include pianos in the set than either physicians or firemen were.[11] Each group's members had similar ideas of the appropriate product cluster.

Conformity Pressures **Conformity** may be defined as a "change in behavior or belief toward a group as a result of real or imagined group pressure."[12] Two types of conformity can be identified. The first is simple **compliance**, in which the person merely conforms to the wishes of the group without really accepting the group's dictates. The second is **private acceptance**, in which the person actually changes his or her beliefs in the direction

Factors Influencing the Conformity Pressures of a Group
I. Properties of the Group
A. Cohesiveness
B. Size
C. Expertise
D. Group's view of product's salience
II. Properties of the Person
A. Information available to person
B. Attractiveness of the group to person
C. Person's need to be liked
D. Type of decision the person faces

TABLE 15-3

of the group. A number of factors may increase the conformity pressures of a group; these are summarized in Table 15-3.

Factors Within the Group Leading to Conformity. Three aspects of groups act to increase the conformity pressures felt by members. One is *cohesiveness*, which refers to how closely knit a group is. A group whose members feel a high degree of loyalty and identification can exert greater influence on its members. The *expertise* of the group also affects conformity pressures. Because consumers are members of many groups, several different groups may have input into a particular purchase decision. The group whose members have more expertise relevant to the decision will have the greatest influence on the purchase.

The *size* of the group has also been found to influence decisions, particularly when the group is a transient one. In a classic series of experiments the psychologist Solomon Asch had people view a series of lines and judge which of the lines on one card matched the length of a line on another card. The task was quite simple, and when taking the test alone, the subjects made almost no errors. However, in the experimental condition Asch had confederates in a group estimate the relative length of the lines before the subject did. These confederates systematically gave a wrong answer. To the experimenter's surprise, the subjects agreed with the confederates' judgments in 37 percent of the cases. The impact of the group was found to vary with the number of confederates. The likelihood that subjects would agree with the confederates increased until the size of the group reached about four people. After the group size got to four people, the impact of adding more individuals to the group was minimal.[13]

Factors Within the Person Leading to Conformity. The ability of a group to make a person conform depends on the nature and needs of the person as well as on the properties of the group. One such personal factor is the amount of information that the person has available for a decision. When little information is available or when the information is ambiguous, the group has a greater impact on the consumer's decision.

The attractiveness of the group and the person's need to be liked by it often work together to create conformity pressures. Usually, the more the person wants to be part of the group, the more he or she also wishes to be liked by its members. In such circumstances the individual tends to conform to group norms and pressures in order to fit in as well as possible.

Type of Decision. The type of decision is the final factor that influences the amount of conformity pressure felt by the individual. Several studies have suggested that when a product is highly salient and conspicuous to others, conformity pressures increase.[14]

Perhaps the buying situation that best illustrates the impact of group conformity pressures is home shopping parties. One set of researchers who analyzed a number of such parties through participant observation reported, "Generally, the parties had much of the flavor of a bridal shower, a sorority meeting, or even an adolescent girl's pajama party: the sense of being in a private ritual being performed away from men was marked."[15] They noted that nearly everyone who attended purchased something. A norm of purchasing existed to which the women felt pressured to conform. In effect, strong bonds of friendship ties created a type of "moral economy" in which buying was expected.

The term **market embeddedness** has been used to describe situations in which the social ties between buyer and seller supplement product value to enhance overall exchange utility. For example, at a Tupperware party the guests make purchases partly for the worth of the plastic containers themselves and partly for the social benefits gained from going to the party. Those who attend home parties form a group, which for many is a reference group. Because of the close personal ties of the women in the group, conformity pressures are created to make purchases. For many of the women, these pressures actually enhance the overall experience and add utility to the purchase. In other words, they attend the parties as much for the experience of friendship as for the products that they can buy. A study investigating market embeddedness in home buying parties found that conformity pressures to make purchases were strong to the extent that social relations within the group were strong—particularly the tie between the hostess and the guest.[16]

Social-Comparison Processes Another way in which groups influence consumers has to do with people's need to assess their opinions and abilities by comparing themselves to others. The process through which people evaluate the "correctness" of their opinions, the extent of their abilities, and the appropriateness of their possessions has been called **social comparison**.[17] Thus in addition to using groups to obtain factual information, consumers use groups to determine where they stand in terms of their opinions, abilities, and possessions.

Two approaches are used by consumers to obtain ability and opinion information. The first is **reflected appraisal**. In this process the consumer examines the manner in which others in a reference group interact with him. Thus if others respond fondly to the person, compliment him, and generally treat him well, he will conclude that he is acting correctly. In contrast, if the others respond negatively, he will conclude that he is doing something wrong.

The second method of obtaining social-comparison information is **comparative appraisal**. Whereas a person must interact with others in order to do reflected appraisal, interaction is unnecessary in comparative appraisal. The consumer evaluates his own relative standing with respect to an attitude, belief, ability, or emotion by observing the behavior of appropriate reference others.[18]

An important point regarding social-comparison processes is that people typically compare themselves to others who are at about the same level as they are on the given attributes rather than to someone who shows great differences.[19] Social comparison, however, is not limited to contrasting oneself with peers. The idealized images of how one should look that are obtained from advertising can also influence self-image. One study reported a series of experiments on this topic. In one of the experiments college women saw magazine ads that used either highly attractive models or no models. Then they rated photographs of female college students for attractiveness, as well as their satisfaction with their own physical attractiveness. After being exposed to the highly attractive models in the ads, the women were less satisfied with their own physical appearance and also rated the photos of the other college women lower. The authors argued that advertising does cause people to do social comparisons and that these comparisons can negatively affect their feelings about themselves.[20]

Group Polarization Over 20 years ago psychologists began studying a highly perplexing phenomenon called the **group shift**. In early studies researchers presented groups and individuals with decision dilemmas and compared their choices. They found that groups tended to select the riskier alternative. For example, in one situation a man of moderate means was described as receiving a small inheritance. Groups and individuals had to decide how he should invest the money. The groups recommended more often than individuals that he invest in risky securities, which might produce large gains, than in conservative blue-chip stocks.

Later research found that conservative as well as risky shifts could occur in groups. For example, one study investigating racetrack betting found that groups were more cautious in placing bets than individuals were.[21] Such findings caused researchers to change their views on group shifts. As a result, the name of the tendency of groups to cause people to shift their decisions, either in a more cautious or a more risky direction, was changed to the **group polarization phenomenon**.

A variety of explanations have been offered for the group polarization phenomenon. One factor accounting for group shifts is the information transmitted during group discussion of the problem. During the course of discussion, arguments are made for various decisions and, typically, the decision alternative receiving the greatest number of arguments is the one chosen.[22]

Another explanation for the group polarization phenomenon is called the *cultural value hypothesis*. Researchers have found that the shifts are almost always in the direction to which the individuals in the group are already leaning. Thus group interaction tends to emphasize the initial predisposition of individual members. As the social interaction reinforces such predispositions, the group moves to a more extreme position than the average position of the individual members.[23]

The study of group shifts is particularly relevant to organizational sales. If an industrial product or service purchase is a group decision, the salesperson needs to recognize that risky or conservative shifts are likely to occur. Because the dominant culture of most companies is one of financial conservatism, industrial sellers should tailor the marketing mix to this dominant value. The mix of pricing, quality control, performance, and delivery guarantees should emphasize the values likely to be predominant in the buying center. Performing marketing research to identify the dominant values of the buyers' corporate culture would be appropriate in such cases.[24]

Managerial Implications of Group Influence

Group influence applies to several managerial areas. Managers can segment the market based on group membership. Naturally existing groups of consumers make outstanding target markets for firms because they are readily identifiable and reachable. For example, numerous companies target military veterans, public school teachers, government workers, church groups, the National Rifle Association, and so on.[25] Product and service offerings can be developed specifically for the members of such groups, and promotional strategy can be built around the concept that the product or service is being offered specifically to the members of the group. Environmental analysis should be performed to determine the extent to which new groups are establishing themselves. Finally, marketing research should be performed to assess the attitudes and psychographic characteristics of the individuals who make up these groups.

Market researchers should also be aware that group processes may have a large impact on the results of focus groups.[26] In **focus groups** small numbers of consumers (usually six to ten) interact in an open-ended fashion with the assistance of a moderator to provide information on their beliefs and attitudes about specific topics. Because group polarization and social-comparison phenomena operate in focus groups, managers should be highly cautious in interpreting the results that come out of these groups. Since group interaction may change group members' attitudes and beliefs, the results may not represent the beliefs and attitudes of the individuals prior to their arrival for the focus group session.

DYADIC EXCHANGES

Dyadic exchange takes place when two individuals transfer resources between each other. We focus here on two types of dyadic exchange significant in marketing: word-of-mouth communications and the service encounter.

Word-of-Mouth Communications

Word-of-mouth communication refers to an exchange of comments, thoughts, or ideas between two or more consumers, none of whom is a marketing source.[27] Word-of-mouth communications have an extremely strong impact on consumer purchase behavior. When one survey asked consumers what factors influenced their purchases of 60 different products, it turned out that referrals from others accounted for three times as many purchases as did advertising.[28] Another study found that word-of-mouth influence was twice as effective as radio advertising, four times as effective as personal selling, and seven times as effective as newspapers and magazines.[29] Recent research in the United Kingdom shows that although six of seven software users utilize pirated copies, these pirates are responsible for generating over 80 percent of new *legal* software buyers, through word-of-mouth communications with other potential users.[30]

One general finding is that word-of-mouth communications have a **negativity bias**. That is, negative information is given more weight than positive information by consumers. One piece of negative information about a product or service influences a consumer more than two or even three items of positive information. For example, a study of a new coffee product found that after receiving positive information 54 percent tried the product, but after receiving negative information only 18 percent would consent to try it.[31]

A number of reasons have been offered for the disproportionate influence of negative information on purchase decisions. A likely explanation is that because most products are pretty good, negative information is a rather rare occurrence, so when a consumer does receive such information, it then takes on greater importance because of its high saliency.

You will remember from our discussion in Chapter 10 that vivid information has a greater impact than more pallid information. Because word-of-mouth information comes directly from another person who is describing personally his or her own experiences, it is much more vivid to consumers than the information contained in an advertisement. The net result is that word-of-mouth information is more accessible to memory and has a relatively greater effect on consumers.[32]

Why Does Word-of-Mouth Communication Occur? The omnipresence of word-of-mouth communication results from the needs of both the sender and the receiver of the information. Receivers may desire word-of-mouth information because they do not believe advertisements and sales messages. Or they may be seeking additional information to decrease their anxiety about making a risky purchase. When receivers are highly involved in a purchase decision, they tend to go through a longer search process. This search process may include asking friends and "experts" about various alternatives. In these high-involvement situations personal influence is common.

There are three other purchase situations in which consumers are often motivated to seek the input of others:[33] (1) when the product is highly visible to others; (2) when the product is highly complex; and (3) when the product cannot be easily tested against some objective criterion. In each case the consumer is in a high-involvement buying situation.

Word-of-mouth communication also fulfills certain needs of senders of information. The ability to provide information and to sway others in their decisions gives people a sense of power and prestige. Influencing others also helps the influencer erase doubts about his or her own purchase. In addition, by providing information to others, a sender can increase his or her involvement with a group and enhance the social interaction and general cohesion of the group.[34] Finally, a person can obtain a tangible benefit from providing information to others: the norm of reciprocity says that those others should at some point return the favor. Table 15-4 summarizes the factors that promote word-of-mouth communications.

Word-of-Mouth Network Models How do certain service providers, such as doctors and attorneys, build up thriving businesses without engaging in any formal promotional activities? One explanation is the word-of-mouth networks that form among consumers of these services.[35]

Factors That Promote Word-of-Mouth Communications

I. **The Needs of the Sender of Information**
   A. To gain feelings of power and prestige.
   B. To erase doubts about his or her own purchase.
   C. To increase involvement with a desirable person or group.
   D. To obtain a tangible benefit.

II. **The Needs of the Receiver of Information**
   A. To seek information from sources more trustworthy than those who endorse products.
   B. To lower anxiety about a possibly risky purchase.
   1. Risk can result from the product because of its complexity or cost.
   2. Risk can result from the buyer's concern about what others will think.
   3. Risk can result from the lack of an objective criterion on which to evaluate the product.
   C. To spend less time in search of information.

TABLE 15-4

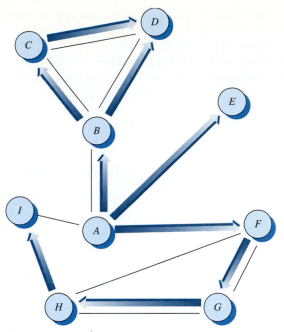

Lines with arrows represent referrals.
Lines without arrows represent strong ties.

Figure 15-2
A word-of-mouth network.

Figure 15-2 diagrams a simple word-of-mouth network that exists among students at a university. The information being passed among the students concerns the work of a certain hair stylist. In the diagram two types of connections can be identified. The lines with arrows represent referral relations—the "who-told-whom-about-the-service" paths. Referral relations depict the word-of-mouth connections along which information on the service was spread. The lines without arrows represent social relations—ties between two individuals, which may be strong or weak. An example of a strong tie would be two friends who frequently visit each other. A weak tie might be two acquaintances who happen to encounter each other and talk about the service during that encounter.[36]

In Figure 15-2 one can see how information about the hair stylist is passed. The information begins with person *A*, who is an opinion leader. She has strong ties with persons *B* and *I*. However, she passes information about the hair stylist to persons *B* and *F*. *B* then passes the information on to persons *C* and *D*. Person *I* actually receives information about the salon from an acquaintance *H*, who obtained it from friend *G*. Person *G* obtained the information from friend *F*, who obtained it from acquaintance *A*. Person *E* is connected only to acquaintance *A* via a referral linkage.

A number of learning points are exemplified in Figure 15-2. First, the fact that two people have strong ties (i.e., are friends) does not necessarily mean that information will be transmitted between them. Even though person *A* had a strong tie with person *I*, she did not communicate information about the stylist to *I*. Second, one can identify small interconnected groups of consumers that share strong ties. Thus individuals *B*, *C*, and *D* form one group, and individuals *F*, *G*, and *H* form a second group. One can also identify the network length by counting the number of referral lines that connect continuously. The longest network length in the figure is composed of four referrals: *A* to *F*, *F* to *G*, *G* to *H*, and *H* to *I*.

One study investigating the information flow about three piano teachers in a southwestern city revealed a complex set of referral and social relations among the individuals.[37] Several interesting findings emerged from this study. One was that weak ties are particularly important for passing information across groups. Indeed, weak ties had a disproportionately greater tendency to act as bridges that allowed information to pass from one distinct group to another. Similarly, in Figure 15-2 one finds that person *A* is connected to group *F-H-G* only via the weak tie of the referral relation.

A second major finding of the research was that, *within groups*, strong ties were more likely than weak ties to activate flows of information because social contact occurred with much greater frequency among friends. A third finding was that persuasion was greater when information came from strongly tied individuals. Weak ties seem to act as bridges *across groups*. Within groups, however, strong ties are crucial to the flow of influence.

Opinion Leadership In studying word-of-mouth communication one finds that some people more frequently provide information than others. Such individuals are **opinion leaders**—consumers who influence the purchase decisions of others.

Opinion leadership does *not* appear to be a general trait held by certain individuals who influence others across a broad range of categories. Rather, opinion leadership is specific to the product category and situation. Within a single product category, such as appliances or household furnishings, an opinion leader may influence others across a number of different products. For example, one study found that people who were opinion leaders for small appliances were also opinion leaders for large appliances.[38] However, opinion leadership does not seem to occur across product categories. Another study found no overlap of opinion leadership across unrelated product categories, such as fashion and public affairs.[39]

Characteristics of Opinion Leaders. Marketers have tried to identify the characteristics of opinion leaders, but their efforts have so far achieved only limited success. Attempts to find demographic and personality characteristics that pinpoint opinion leaders have generally been unsuccessful.[40] The most clear-cut finding is that opinion leaders are involved with the product category. They are interested in it, read special-interest magazines about it, and are knowledgeable about it. Also, there is some evidence that opinion leaders are more self-confident and socially active than followers. They also seem to have a somewhat greater social status than followers, though they do belong to the same peer group. Finally, they tend to be more innovative in their purchases than followers are, but that is not to say that they are "product innovators."[41]

Comparing Opinion Leaders and Product Innovators. Product innovators are that small set of people who are the first to buy new products. In a variety of respects they are like opinion leaders. In a study of physicians, for example, innovators and opinion leaders were found to be similar in a number of ways.[42] As compared to followers or noninnovators, they were more highly socially integrated into the medical community, were more oriented to their professional goals than to their patients, shared offices with other physicians, and attended more medical conferences. Both innovators and opinion leaders showed a pattern of being highly active in their profession, of communicating with other doctors frequently, and of keeping up with new happenings in the medical literature.

Despite all these similarities, however, innovators and opinion leaders differ on some key characteristics. The innovator may be described as an adventurer who strikes off on his or her own to buy new products. In contrast, the opinion leader is like an editor who influences others—but only by never being *too* far away from the goals, values, and attitudes of followers. Innovators are less integrated into social groups and feel freer to break group norms by adopting new products very early in their life cycle. In contrast, opinion leaders are more socially integrated and exert their influence partly because they do not espouse beliefs that are widely divergent from those of the group.[43]

Mavens and Surrogates as Sources of Personal Influence. In addition to opinion leaders and product innovators, market researchers have identified two other sources of personal influence: the market maven and the surrogate consumer. **Market mavens** are "individuals who have information about many kinds of products, places to shop, and other facets of markets, and initiate discussions with consumers and respond to requests from consumers for market information."[44] As this definition suggests, these individuals play a broader personal influence role than opinion leaders do. The expertise of market mavens is not product specific; rather, it is based on general market expertise. Market mavens may seek to obtain marketplace information in order to be useful to others in social exchanges and to provide a basis for conversations. In a sense, they are consumers who adopt the "market maven" role.[45]

The second new type of influencer is the surrogate consumer. A **surrogate consumer** is a person who acts "as an agent retained by a consumer to guide, direct, and/or transact marketplace activities."[46] Surrogate consumers can play a wide variety of roles, such as tax consultant, wine steward, interior decorator, stockbroker, or car buyer. Basically, surrogate consumers act as an additional layer in the channel of distribution between the manufacturer and consumers. They tend to be used in very high involvement purchases in which the consumer desires to surrender some control to a capable external agent. That is, the consumer abdicates to the surrogate many of the information search, evaluation, and choice activities that are part of the consumer decision process. The surrogate consumer plays an important role in the consumer purchase process for certain types of complex products and services, such as expensive furniture and investment securities. Table 15-5 summarizes the characteristics of the four types of influencers in the marketplace: opinion leaders, product innovators, market mavens, and surrogate consumers.

Service Encounters

The **service encounter** is a personal interaction that occurs between a consumer and a marketer. A service encounter can take place in "pure service contexts," such as in a physician's examination, cashing a check, or ordering a meal at a restaurant. In addition, service encounters take place in "mixed service contexts." Consider your involvement with your car. Certainly, the auto is a good (or a bad, depending upon your satisfaction with it). However, a number of service encounters occurred during and after your purchase of the car. When you bought it, you interacted with the salesperson. When having it serviced or repaired, you encountered additional firm representatives. During every service encounter a consumption experience is occurring, and, as we showed in Chapter 13, that consumption experience will have a strong impact on your satisfaction or dissatisfaction with the product.

During a service encounter the consumer and the marketer take on discrete roles,[47] which can be understood through the dramaturgical metaphor used in Chapter 13. This

Characteristics of Four Types of Consumer Influencers		
Influencer Type	**Basis for Expertise**	**Characteristics**
1. Opinion leader	Enduring involvement in product category.	Enduring involvement, higher status, integrated into social group.
2. Product innovator	Purchase of innovative product.	Less integrated into social groups than opinion leaders.
3. Market maven	General market knowledge.	Demographic characteristics unknown; enjoys having general knowledge about the marketplace.
4. Surrogate consumer	Knowledge specific to product category.	Frequently a paid professional.

TABLE 15-5

Question: Are all surrogate consumers human?

Answer: Perhaps not. One new surrogate consumer is the computer "agent." The Bargain Finder, an experiment of Andersen Consulting, burrows through the Internet, querying online stores and finding the lowest price for music CD-ROMS. This computer agent is like a surrogate consumer—both guide a consumer through marketplace activities.

Source: Sam Vincent Meddis, "Welcome to the Future of Online Shopping," *USA Today*, June 13, 1996, p. 7B.

metaphor provides a vocabulary for comprehending the exchange process. The employee and the consumer act as though they are on a stage reading from a common "service script." This script creates expectations on both actors' parts. To the extent that either violates the script in a negative manner, dissatisfaction may result. Thus if the service provider violates expectations (perhaps by being too pushy), the consumer will be dissatisfied with the encounter. Conversely, if the consumer violates expectations (perhaps by ridiculing the employee), the employee will be dissatisfied.[48]

Figure 15-3 is a diagram depicting the service encounter as theater.[49] As in any production, there is a stage where the play takes place. In addition, there are front and back

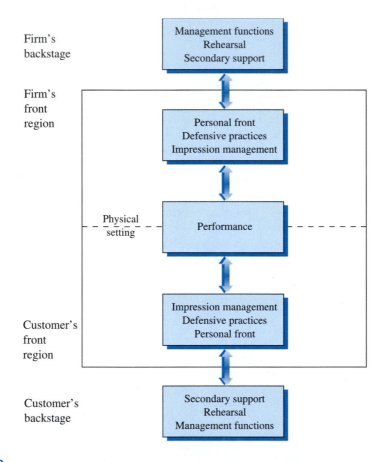

Figure 15-3

The service encounter as theatrical performance. (*Source:* Adapted from Stephen Grove and Raymond Fisk, "The Service Encounter as Theater," in *Advances in Consumer Research*, Vol. 19, John F. Sherry, Jr., and Brian Sternthal, eds. [Provo, UT: Association for Consumer Research, 1992], pp. 455–461.)

regions for both consumer and firm. In the front region both parties reveal impression management and protective practices. In the backstage area both parties undergo rehearsal/practice and seek secondary support (e.g., other people help the production). Here also is where management functions reside.

As we noted earlier, both the consumer and the employee follow scripted roles during the service encounter. Three themes pertain to each party in the encounter.[50] The three themes identified for consumers are autonomy, mutuality, and dependence; these describe the nature of the relationship that the consumer desires to form with the service provider. Consumers desire *autonomy* when they believe they have the information that they need and seek to engage in self-service. Purchasers of low-involvement goods from retail stores frequently desire autonomy. In addition, consumers who have a high degree of expertise often seek autonomy. The sophisticated investor who buys stocks from a discount brokerage house exemplifies this type of consumer.

As product involvement increases and as consumer expertise decreases, consumers may seek either mutual cooperation or dependence in the relationship with the employee. In *mutual cooperation* a feeling of synergy develops between employee and consumer. An example is a purchase of original art by a consumer who has some knowledge of the risks and benefits involved. In contrast, if the consumer has limited knowledge or expertise, *total dependence* may be placed on the employee. In such instances the consumer wants the employee to take an active role and participate fully in the service encounter. At the extreme, the employee becomes a surrogate consumer. The roles aren't static here, however. For example, in an extended service encounter (such as between a guide and a client on a rafting expedition) the customer is in a more dependent state at the beginning, but as the encounter progresses, mutuality often takes over. By the end of the trip, the two are usually—at least temporarily—friends.[51] A similar process may go on between a physician or an attorney and a client over the course of a major illness or an involved case.

Employee themes are symmetrical with the consumer themes. The three employee themes are indifference, cooperation, and dominance. It is critical that employees act as desired by consumers. If the customer wants mutual cooperation, the employee should provide it without attempting to become dominant. The indifference theme, however, is a tricky one. Generally, consumers who want autonomy do *not* want indifferent service providers. Rather they desire providers who leave them alone until they need attention to complete the transaction.

Managerial Implications of Dyadic Exchange Processes

A number of researchers have proposed theories that attempt to identify the underlying factors at work in an exchange. One influential model, developed by George Homans, views the exchange process from the dual perspectives of operant conditioning and economics. From the operant conditioning perspective, Homans argued that if an exchange results in satisfying (i.e., reinforcing) outcomes, it will be repeated. Conversely, if it yields dissatisfying outcomes, it will be discontinued.[52] From the operant conditioning perspective, exchanges involve a complex set of reinforcers and punishers to shape the behavior of the other.

From the economic perspective, Homans proposed that people use a kind of cost-benefit analysis to determine if they will stay in an exchange. To the extent that the rewards from the exchange are greater than the costs, it will be profitable for the participants to continue the exchange. However, if the costs exceed the rewards, the participants will discontinue the exchange or seek to change its nature. The **basic exchange equation** developed by Homans is as follows:

$$Profit = Rewards - Costs$$

Question: Over which area of the service encounter do retailers have the least control?

Answer: Probably over the effect of one customer on another. For example, fervent antismokers may not go back to a business that enforces an antismoking policy laxly. Other behaviors, such as putting one's feet on the table, are less within the realm of control. Employee conduct may help communicate appropriate behaviors to consumers.

Source: Charles L. Martin, "Consumer-to-Consumer Relationships: Satisfaction with Other Consumers' Public Behavior," *Journal of Consumer Affairs*, Vol. 30 (Summer 1996), pp. 146–169.

From the exchange perspective, both consumers and firms attempt to profit from the interaction. The firm calculates its profits by subtracting its monetary costs from its monetary benefits. Consumers calculate their profit by subtracting their monetary and psychological costs from the rewards they derive from the product or service purchased. If either party perceives that he or she is not profiting from the exchange, dissatisfaction will result.

In addition to keeping these underlying factors of all exchanges in mind, a company should have a clear understanding of the types of dyadic exchanges that occur in relation to their product. In particular, they must train their employees to take on the appropriate role when dealing with customers in service exchanges. That is, employees must strive to match their role to the expectations of each customer. Thus if a customer desires to make a purchase decision autonomously, the service provider should respect that wish because a failure to match the customer's service desire is likely to leave the customer dissatisfied.

In addition, the firm should identify the extent to which purchases of its products or services are influenced by word-of-mouth communication and by opinion leadership. It is a function of market research to find and identify opinion leaders, market mavens, and surrogate consumers. If such people exist for the product or service, they should become a segment to which the company targets its promotional messages. In effect, the study of opinion leadership is important to the managerial areas of market research, segmentation, and promotional strategy.

DIFFUSION PROCESSES

The term *diffusion* refers to the idea that substances, or even ideas, gradually spread through a medium until they reach a state of equilibrium. In a consumer behavior setting, **diffusion** refers to the process by which innovative ideas, products, and services spread through the consumer population.

We discuss in this section the three different types of diffusion processes that are of concern to marketers: the diffusion of information and alternative models of information transmission; the diffusion of innovations, including those factors that influence how innovative products become adopted by consumers; and the spread of rumors.

Transmission Processes

How do communications flow within groups and the larger consumer environment? Several models propose to explain how information is transmitted from the mass media to the general population. The **trickle-down theory** holds that trends—particularly fashion trends—begin with the wealthy. The wealthy adopt styles of clothing and attitudes to distinguish themselves from the lower classes, and the lower classes then attempt to emulate the wealthy by copying their fashions. In this way the fashions and behaviors of the wealthy "trickle down" to the general population. One problem with the trickle-down theory is that there is relatively little communication between the classes. Most communications take place between people in the same social class. Another is that in a mass-communication culture information on fashion is transmitted almost instantaneously. Actually, information transmission is much more like a flood than a trickle.

A second approach to explaining the transmission of personal influence is the **two-step flow model**, which posits that mass communications first influence opinion leaders, who then influence followers. Rather than viewing influence as occurring *between* the social classes, this approach regards influence as horizontal *within* a class. The two-step flow model hypothesizes that there are opinion leaders in each class who influence a large group of passive followers. Unfortunately, this model is overly simplistic. No passive group of followers has been identified, and opinion leaders seem to be different for different products.

The approach that appears to best represent the flow of personal influence is the **multistep flow model**. Figure 15-4 diagrams this model. Note that information is transmitted by the mass media to three distinct sets of people: opinion leaders, gatekeepers, and followers.[53] Each type of person is viewed as having the capability of providing information to the other categories of people. The opinion leader is the person who influences others about the particular piece of information being transmitted by the mass media. The gatekeeper is the individual who has the capability of deciding whether or not others in a group will receive the information, although this person's opinions may or may not influence the others. The followers are those who are influenced by the opinion leader or by the information provided by the gatekeeper.

The multistep flow model recognizes a number of important facts of diffusion:

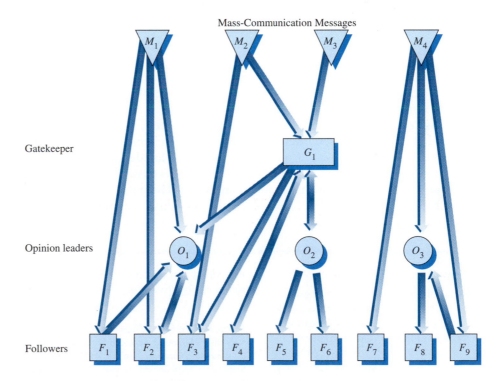

Figure 15-4
The multistep flow model.

1. Mass communications can directly reach nearly everyone in the population.
2. Opinion leaders are able to influence a group of followers. However, for different products, the roles of opinion leader and follower may be reversed.
3. Another group of individuals—the gatekeepers—can choose whether or not to provide information to both opinion leaders and followers.
4. Communications can be transmitted back and forth among the three groups.

The Diffusion of Innovations

The study of the adoption of new products is important for marketers. In order to grow, a company must continually improve its existing products and periodically develop new products for a changing marketplace. The managerial study of product adoption is also important because of the relatively low success rate of new products. The overall cost of introducing a new consumer product has been estimated to be about $6 million, while the chance that a new product will be successful is estimated at a mere 20 percent for consumer goods.[54]

Product innovations come in many varieties, from goods that have a positive impact on society (e.g., antibiotic medicines) to those that harm. Elizabeth Hirschman describes cocaine as a product innovation over the 100 years of its use in the United States. Originally, cocaine was mixed with wine to make a cocktail known as a "Vin Mariani." It was also part of the first Coca-Cola formula. Its use plunged after its addictive properties were recognized. Then it reappeared in the 1970s as a powder to be snorted, and later as a substance to be mixed with ether (freebasing), but these extremely dangerous uses died down, particularly after the comedian Richard Pryor suffered extensive burns while freebasing. The current innovation is known as crack—a more potent but safer form that can be sold in inexpensive packages.[55]

A **product innovation** is a product that has been recently introduced and is perceived by consumers to be new in relation to existing products or services. Several factors help determine whether a product will be perceived as new. Perhaps the most important is the extent to which it changes the consumers' behavior. A product that fails to alter the behavior or lifestyle of consumers cannot be described as new or innovative, while one that causes consumers to engage in entirely new lifestyle patterns is certainly highly innovative.

Figure 15-5 presents a simple model of the diffusion process, identifying six key factors that influence the nature and extent of the diffusion of an innovation.[56] First, diffusion occurs within a social system or market. Second, diffusion depends upon the individual adoption decisions of thousands or even millions of consumers. The individual adoption process is synonymous with individual consumer decision making, which was discussed in Chapters 11 through 13. The decisions of individuals are influenced by three

---

Question: What is "use innovation"?

Answer: Although marketers primarily think in terms of purchase innovation (buying a new product), they should learn to pay more attention to "use innovation" (use of products in a novel way). An example is four-wheel-drive vehicles. Originally designed for rugged rural use, they are now driven on all kinds of roads. Even rental car agencies keep them on hand.

Source: Kyungae Park and Carl L. Dyer, "Consumer Use Innovative Behavior: An Approach Toward Its Causes," in *Advances in Consumer Research*, Vol. 22, Frank R. Kardes and Mita Sujan, eds. (Provo, UT: Association for Consumer Research, 1995), pp. 566–572.

Consumer Behavior Factoid

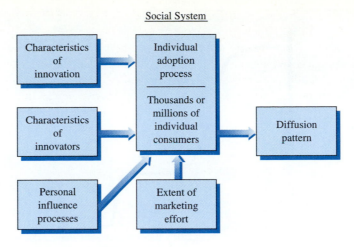

Figure 15-5

A model of the consumer diffusion process. (*Source*: Based, in part, on ideas from Hubert Gatignon and Thomas Robertson, "A Propositional Inventory for New Diffusion Research," *Journal of Consumer Research*, Vol. 11 [March 1985], pp. 849–867.)

factors: the characteristics of the innovation, the characteristics of innovators, and the personal influence process. These three factors make up the third, fourth, and fifth elements of the diffusion process. The final element is the nature of the diffusion process, which is determined by the interaction of the five preceding elements. The following sections discuss in greater detail the elements of the diffusion process.[57]

The Social System The study of the social system in which products are diffused is closely related to the analysis of the impact of cultural and subcultural processes on consumers (which will be discussed in Chapters 17 and 18). Evidence indicates that the speed of diffusion is influenced by several aspects of the social system. First, the greater the compatibility between the innovation and the values of the members of the social system, the quicker the rate of diffusion. Second, the more homogeneous (i.e., nonsegmented) the social system, the faster the diffusion process. The diffusion of innovations across cultures depends on the physical distance between the countries as well as their social similarity.[58]

Characteristics of the Innovation Innovations have been described in terms of the extent to which the new product, service, or idea influences the behavior of consumers. Three categories of innovations have been identified: continuous, dynamic continuous, and discontinuous. What one finds is that the greater the novelty of the innovation, the greater the amount of behavior change required by consumers. In addition, many more continuous innovations enter the marketplace each year than either dynamic continuous or discontinuous inventions. Figure 15-6 diagrams the relationships among the amount of behavior change required, the percentage of new-product innovations in each category, and the type of innovation.

Continuous innovations have the least impact on consumers. These are modifications of existing products to improve performance, taste, reliability, and so forth. An example is the changeover of General Motors from round automobile headlights to rectangular headlights in the 1970s. This innovation had no real impact on the behavior of consumers, but it did work to differentiate GM models from those of other companies.

A **dynamic continuous innovation** influences the lifestyles of consumers to some degree. This type of innovation generally involves some major change in an existing product. An example is the introduction of electrical automobiles. Battery-driven cars present

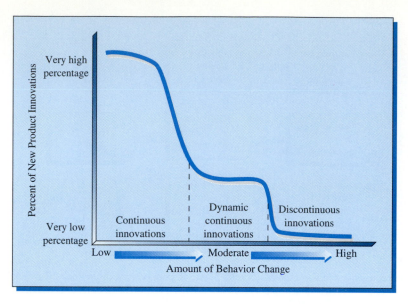

Figure 15-6
A continuum of product innovations and their behavioral impact.

a new set of maintenance requirements and fueling procedures to consumers. Other examples of dynamic continuous innovations are the introduction of the first compact cars and microwave ovens. The introduction of Kevlar® and the potential introduction of synthetic "spider silk" also probably represent dynamic continuous innovations for final users.

Discontinuous innovations produce major changes in the lifestyles of consumers. They come along much less frequently than continuous or dynamic innovations. Examples are computers, televisions, radios, air conditioning, and airplanes. In each of these cases the innovation changed how people lived. For example, radio and television dramatically altered how people spend their leisure hours. Some products from the biotechnology revolution will likely have discontinuous properties, perhaps by dramatically extending the average lifetime.

A number of characteristics have been suggested as necessary for the success of new products:

1. *Relative advantage.* The product must do something better, cheaper, or more reliably than other products on the market.
2. *Compatibility.* The innovation needs to be consistent with the lifestyle, social system, and norms of the target market.
3. *Complexity.* Generally, the less complex a product, the faster it will be adopted and the greater its chances of success will be.
4. *Trialability.* The easier it is for consumers to use the product and experience its benefits firsthand, the greater its chances for success.
5. *Observability.* If consumers can see others successfully using the product, its adoption will be more rapid and its success more likely.[59]

Above all else, of course, a new product must fulfill the needs of a target market.

Figure 15-7 presents an ad for Eagle Creek's Rolling Luggage, which combines rolling capability with convertability into a backpack. This nicely illustrates a continuous innovation. It should succeed in the market because it has the qualities most associated with

Figure 15-7

This combination of a wheeled roller and backpack is a continuous innovation that should find success in the marketplace. Its benefits are clear and require no behavioral changes from the consumer.

the success of innovations: relative advantage, compatibility, simplicity, trialability, and observability.

Another approach to distinguishing innovations is to categorize them as either technological or symbolic.[60] A *symbolic innovation* gives a product a different social meaning than it had previously because of the acquisition of new intangible attributes. An example of a symbolic innovation is the diffusion of a new hair or fashion style. A *technological innovation* results from an alteration in the characteristics of a product or service through the introduction of a technological change. An example of a technological innovation is the compact disc player.

The concept that innovations are either symbolic or technological adds an important dimension to our understanding. Indeed, a key to understanding the diffusion of new political, religious, and lifestyle ideas may be to view them as involving the diffusion of symbols, and the adoption of new symbols may play an important role in fashion trends.

Characteristics of Innovators One of the important challenges faced by marketers of innovative products is to identify the characteristics of people who buy products early in their life cycle. Figure 15-8 depicts the groups who adopt new products at various stages of the product life cycle. Notice that of the five categories of adopters that have been identified, innovators make up a mere 2.5 percent.

Research suggests that innovators tend to have higher incomes, higher levels of education, greater social mobility, higher opinion leadership in the product category, and more favorable attitudes toward risk than other people.[61] One study investigating the characteristics of early adopters of new long-distance services reported that early adopters were

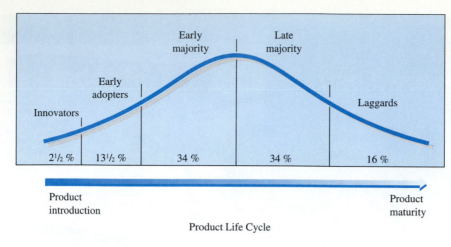

Figure 15-8
Categories of adopters.

younger, better educated, and heavy telephone users. In this study income was not related to early adoption.

Factors Influencing the Diffusion Pattern of Innovations Figure 15-9 identifies the normal pattern of innovative product diffusion through the population. Note that the curve describing the diffusion process is S-shaped. During the introductory phase, the percentage of consumers adopting the product is small and slowly accelerating. As the product moves into the growth stage, the percentage of adopters accelerates, and the curve bends

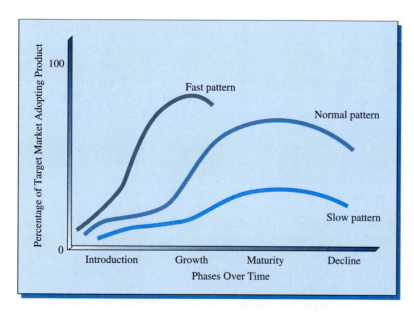

Figure 15-9
The shape of the diffusion process.

upward rapidly. During the maturity phase, growth slows until it turns negative, marking the beginning of decline.

The exact shape of the diffusion curve depends upon a number of factors. Innovations that are adopted very quickly display the fast pattern shown in Figure 15-9. For those whose adoption rate is slow, the pattern is much flatter and more drawn out. Three factors affect the rapidity with which an innovation is adopted and, consequently, the shape of the diffusion curve.

1. *Characteristics of the product.* The same factors that influence the likely success of an innovation also influence the rapidity with which it is adopted. To the extent that it fulfills a need, is compatible, has a relative advantage, has low complexity, has observable positive features, and is easily tried, the product will be adopted more quickly. For example, the Frisbee was widely adopted within six months of introduction.
2. *Characteristics of the target market.* Products targeted to different target groups will exhibit divergent adoption patterns. For example, products that appeal to younger, more highly educated, change-oriented individuals are often quickly adopted, but they also run the risk of rapidly moving into decline.
3. *Extent of the marketing effort.* Companies can influence the growth curve of a product by the quality and extent of their marketing effort.

The diffusion curve is not always S-shaped. In some instances it shows an exponential pattern—the curve starts out slow, and then increases at a rapid rate. Exponential patterns tend to be the rule when the innovation is adopted via low-involvement decision making, when there are low switching costs, and when there is a relative lack of personal influence. In contrast, the S-shaped curve tends to be found when personal influence is operating, when there are high switching costs, and when a high-involvement decision process is taking place.

The Diffusion of Rumors

Since corporations are often plagued by rumors about their products, understanding how rumors are spread is essential for managers. Rumors periodically plague firms both large and small. They are a kind of group contagion that result from fears and anxieties. For example, national hysteria over the AIDS epidemic has, on at least two occasions, spawned the rumor that an employee of a restaurant had AIDS and was infecting patrons' food. As soon as such a rumor begins to spread, business falls dramatically.

In 1978 the rumor spread that the dry toner used by Xerox in its copiers caused cancer. In 1979 Procter & Gamble was plagued by the rumor that the firm embraced Satanism: flyers circulating among conservative Protestant congregations noted that the P&G symbol contained a sorcerer's head and 13 stars—a sign of Satan. McDonald's Corporation has also been hit by rumors alleging Satanism, though even more disturbing was the vicious fiction that the company adds ground worms to its hamburger meat. In 1995 rumors began to spread that subliminal sexual references were included in the Disney movies *Aladdin*, *The Lion King*, and *The Little Mermaid*.[64] The K (for kosher) sign which appears on bottles of Snapple has been interpreted as signaling that the company supports the Ku Klux Klan. A rumor circulated that Liz Claiborne once stated on the Oprah Winfrey show that she didn't want African-Americans wearing her clothes—and has persisted despite Ms. Winfrey's own insistence that she has never interviewed Liz Claiborne.[65] Since the first Tylenol poisoning incident in 1982, the Food and Drug Administration has logged some 500 tampering complaints per year, reaching a peak of over 1,700 complaints in 1986.[66]

Types and Causes of Rumors Sociologists and psychologists have identified a number of different types of rumors. **Pipe dream rumors** represent wishful thinking on the part of the circulators. They are positive hopes—for example, that the Christmas bonus given by a corporation will far exceed last year's bonus.

Another type of rumor, the **bogie**, is fear mongering that spooks the marketplace. This is the type of rumor that plagued Xerox, McDonald's, and Procter & Gamble. A bogie demolished the first king-sized menthol cigarette, Spud, in the 1940s.[67] A rumor spread that a leper worked in the plant where the brand was packaged. In six months the cigarette had disappeared from the market.

Rumors can also be self-fulfilling. In this case the rumor is based on a perception of what could happen in the future if something else were to occur. "Bank runs" are examples of self-fulfilling rumors. It is true that if all of a bank's depositors suddenly withdraw their money, the bank will fail. In bad times this knowledge can "spook" people into the very behavior that is the source of the fear.

In premeditated rumors individuals with something to gain set out to spread false stories that will help them financially or otherwise. Such premeditated rumors can sweep through the stock market and cause short-term shifts in the value of companies, allowing unscrupulous individuals to make a profit. Procter & Gamble believed that the Satanism charge came from the salespeople of a competing firm, who distributed flyers describing P & G's supposed Satanic activities. P & G has had a particularly hard time with Amway distributors. In fact, the company has sued Amway distributors six times for making statements linking the company to Satanism.[68]

Finally, rumors can be spontaneous when people seek explanations for unusual events. One author suggested that the ground-worm rumors striking McDonald's may have begun when a consumer found "tubular" matter in a hamburger.[69] Such matter could easily be a small blood vessel not ground up well. In order to explain the material, the consumer leapt to the conclusion that the tube was a worm.

Rumors need the right environment to be nourished to the point where they sweep through the population. The two factors that seem to be required are uncertainty and anxiety. Rumors generally arise and spread most rapidly when times are bad and people are uncertain about their future. It is not surprising that the rumors that struck McDonald's and P & G were at their worst during the severe recession between 1980 and 1983.

In addition to uncertainty and anxiety, researchers have found that the importance and the ambiguity of a rumor influences its spread. A formula has been created to express this relationship:[70]

$$\text{Rumor} = \text{Ambiguity} \times \text{Importance}$$

Urban legends, a phenomenon related to rumors, are realistic stories about incidents that are reputed to have occurred. They diffuse through the population like rumors, and often appear to have a local connection. One legend has a groom mounting a chair at his wedding party to announce that the marriage will be annulled, and that the reason is underneath everyone's dinner plate. When the stunned guests flip their plate, they find a picture of the bride *in flagrante delicto* with the best man. This story has been set in New York City; New Hampshire; Medford, Massachusetts; and Schenectady, New York. Another version, set in St. Paul, Minnesota, has the groom consorting with the maid of honor. A University of Utah folklorist has found over 400 of these legends. For instance, nearly everyone "knows" that alligators prowl New York City's sewers. Many have heard about the Good Samaritan who approaches a woman slumped in her car. She moans that she's been shot in the head and shows gray matter oozing from the wound. She's actually been hit in the head by the tin at the end of a tube of Pillsbury biscuits, which exploded in the heat, and the "brains" are biscuit dough.[71]

The Managerial Implications of Diffusion Processes

Knowledge of diffusion processes is important to managers, particularly those involved in marketing new products and services. Product managers need to identify whether their innovation is continuous, dynamic continuous, or discontinuous. They need to investigate the extent to which it has a relative advantage over competitors and is compatible with the values and lifestyle of the target market. Furthermore, managers need to assess the product's complexity, trialability, and observability. Only through such analysis will they get a feel for the likely growth curve of the product. Will the product be a slow starter that must be nurtured for a substantial length of time, or will a strong marketing effort allow it to start fast?

New products that are of a dynamically continuous or discontinuous nature may or may not be successful. The digital camera, for example, merges two technologies—photography and computers. A bit like Kevlar® in an earlier era, the digital camera is a solution without a clearly identified problem. Figure 15-10 shows an Apple QuickTake 100

Figure 15-10
Apple Computer has been a market pioneer with innovative digital cameras such as their Apple QuickTake 100.

digital camera. It isn't clear whether these devices will be used primarily for business purposes or recreational use.

Marketing managers also need to monitor information-transmission processes. Marketing research should be employed to identify exactly what a company's customers are communicating to others about its products or services. It is crucially important for firms to track customer satisfaction, and then take quick steps to remedy any problems they become aware of.

Managers should also monitor the environment for the spread of rumors. One expert has suggested that companies go through the following series of actions if a rumor strikes them:[72]

Step 1: Ride out the rumor.
Step 2: Trace its origins.
Step 3: Treat it locally.
Step 4: Rebut it with facts, but don't deny the rumor *before* the public hears about it.

Sad to say, rumors are rarely completely eradicated. The Satan rumor about Procter & Gamble resurfaced in the mid-1990s, some 16 years after P&G thought it had quashed it. Rumors, in fact, can move from company to company. The worms-in-hamburger rumor struck Wendy's prior to jumping to McDonald's.

It should be noted that there is a potential problem with the use of refutational strategies to eliminate rumors. A study investigating the worm rumor attached to McDonald's hamburgers found that when the rumor was refuted with facts (e.g., red worms cost $5 per pound, which is much more expensive than beef, so it would make no sense to use them in hamburgers), the negative impression of McDonald's remained.[73] Because a refutational strategy mentions the rumor, the consumer is reminded of the negative information. One way around the problem may be to give the facts without mentioning the rumor. McDonald's did this with a major promotional campaign advertising the fact that its hamburgers are made with 100 percent pure beef. There was no mention of worms in the advertising campaign.

A MANAGERIAL APPLICATIONS ANALYSIS OF THE KEVLAR® CASE

Several points directly related to group processes are exemplified in the Kevlar® case. The product was an innovation that needed adopters.

Problem Identification

The problem Kevlar® presented to DuPont was succinctly put by the fiber's marketing manager: "Kevlar® was the answer, but we didn't know for what."

The Consumer Behavior Analysis and Its Managerial Implications

The challenges of marketing Kevlar® are readily analyzed by utilizing knowledge of diffusion of innovations, group conformity and polarization, and word-of-mouth processes, or rumors. Table 15-6 summarizes these concepts and their managerial implications.

Diffusion of Innovations Kevlar® is an industrial product. Companies or government agencies would be the first to adopt this product to fashion, say, flak jackets or auto tires. For these buyers, Kevlar® was probably a dynamic continuous innovation. Its properties were quite different from the materials it was meant to replace, such as steel. Thus whole new production processes would have to be developed in order to use it. In such circumstances encouraging adoptions of a product can be quite difficult.

Marketers at DuPont had to go to extraordinary lengths to show the relative advantage of Kevlar®. Further, they had to demonstrate its compatibility with existing procedures and with the materials with which it would be used. DuPont was forced to use some extraordinary but readily observable demonstrations. For example, in order to obtain an order from the U.S. Army for Kevlar® flak jackets, DuPont arranged a demonstration in which the jackets were hung over 100 goats and .38-caliber pistol bullets were fired into the animals. The goats escaped with only minor bruises.

Given these difficulties, it is easy to see why the growth curve of Kevlar® was so slow. Indeed, it was only because DuPont put together a major marketing and new-product development effort that the fiber ever became profitable. It was this marketing team that identified products Kevlar® could be made into, how those products could be positioned, the market segments to which they could be targeted, and how they could be promoted profitably.

From the perspective of both the product developers and the marketing managers, Kevlar® must be continually refined and new uses for it identified, if the material is to retain viability in the marketplace.

The work being done on synthesizing spider silk suggests the dynamic nature of many markets. Like Kevlar®, this new material will have to be accepted through the diffusion process.

Group Polarization Because of the risk involved in adopting a drastically new material like Kevlar®, it could have been anticipated that where purchase decisions had to be made by groups, conservative shifts were a strong possibility. DuPont's best bet would be to develop sales presentations designed to lower the perceived risk of purchasing Kevlar® and the kind of group polarization that would work against the sale.

Group Conformity What we know about the workings of group influence suggests that conformity pressures might very well make it difficult for purchasing agents to specify the purchase of Kevlar®. DuPont's sales personnel should therefore make special efforts to identify the "real" decision makers to whom purchasing agents generally conform and pitch the sales presentation to them.

Rumors DuPont management should be aware that because of the artificial nature of Kevlar®, cancer rumors about the material might surface—especially once it begins to be used in products destined for the general population, such as gloves. An environmental analysis is essential to quickly identify any such rumors. By closely monitoring newspaper, radio, and television communications, the company would be prepared to adopt appropriate public relations strategies to combat damaging rumors.

Managerial Recommendations

Three specific recommendations emerge from our managerial applications analysis of the Kevlar® case.

Recommendation 1 Information on the diffusion of innovations applies to market research, segmentation, product development, and positioning. Market research would be required to identify potential uses for the product, as well as purchasers with needs matching the properties of the product. Using an analysis of needs, new products made from Kevlar® could be developed and promotional strategies designed to increase the rapidity with which the product would diffuse through the environment. Positioning strategies could also be identified that would take advantage of the product's unique capabilities.

Managerial Implications of Consumer Behavior Concepts in the Kevlar® Case

Consumer Behavior Concept	Managerial Implications
1. Diffusion of innovations	*Market research*. Identify potential uses of product and characteristics of potential adopters.
	Segmentation. Based on the market research, identify segments of adopters who have specific needs that could be filled by Kevlar® products.
	Product development. Develop new products that fulfill the needs of these segments.
	Positioning. Develop positioning strategies that employ Kevlar®'s unique characteristics.
	Environmental analysis. Scan the environment for potential new competitors, such as synthetic spider silk.
2. Group polarization	*Market research*. Identify cultural norms within targeted companies/industries that may influence purchase decisions.
	Promotional strategy. Inform sales personnel of the potential effects of group polarization.
3. Conformity	*Market research*. Employ research to identify potential conformity pressures within companies that would impact the buying processes.
	Promotional strategy. Inform sales personnel of the potential effects of conformity pressures. Develop strategies to overcome such pressures.
4. Rumors	*Environmental analysis*. Perform research to analyze the environment for potential rumors that could surface regarding the use of Kevlar®.
	Promotional strategy. Employ appropriate public relations efforts to minimize the chances of rumor transmission.

TABLE 15-6

Recommendation 2 Group polarization and conformity effects have implications for DuPont's market research and promotional strategy. Market research should identify cultural norms within the targeted companies that might influence the decision process.

Recommendation 3 DuPont managers should perform environmental analyses and be alert to the possible development of rumors. Because Kevlar® is a synthetic material, there is always the possibility that damaging rumors concerning its possible health effects will emerge.

SUMMARY

A group is a set of individuals who interact with one another over some period of time and who share some common need or goal. Groups have their own dynamics; they are more than simply the sum of their parts. A variety of different types of groups exist that may have an impact on consumption. These include reference groups, aspiration groups, dissociative groups, formal and informal groups, and primary groups. Such groups influence the behavior of consumers directly through informational influence, normative influence, and value-expressive influence. In addition, groups develop roles that may be adopted by consumers, which may, in turn, influence buying behavior. Finally, groups exert conformity pressures on their members, and when decisions are being made, group discussion may polarize the choice process so that more extreme decisions result.

Within groups, consumers frequently engage in dyadic exchanges. There are two types of dyadic exchanges: the service encounter, in which the customer interacts with the product provider; and word-of-mouth network communications, in which one consumer communicates directly with another to pass on information about a product, a service, or an idea. Word-of-mouth communications can have much greater persuasive impact than impersonal communications. Word-of-mouth network models seek to identify the patterns of information flows among people.

Of the several models developed to explain how personal influence is transmitted, the multistep flow model seems to be the most accurate. According to this model, information moves from the mass media to gatekeepers, opinion leaders, and followers. Communications can pass back and forth among these three groups, and in different situations the members of the groups may be interchangeable.

It is often possible to identify opinion leaders in word-of-mouth communication. These individuals are important to companies because they determine whether the information that others receive will be positive or negative. Although different people tend to be opinion leaders for different product categories, some common factors do characterize opinion leaders. In general, they are heavily involved in and knowledgeable about the product category. Like opinion leaders, market mavens are consumers who have information about many kinds of products and services and who pass that information on to others. Market mavens are generalists who assist other consumers in the marketplace. Surrogate consumers act as agents retained by consumers to guide, direct, and transact marketplace activities. Examples of surrogates are wine stewards, tax consultants, and interior decorators.

Diffusion processes illustrate cases in which ideas, products, or emotions spread through a large population. Consumer researchers are particularly interested in the factors that influence how innovations are adopted by consumers. The rate of adoption is affected by the type of innovation, the characteristics of the target market, and the extent of the marketing effort. Rumors represent another type of diffusion phenomenon. Rumors can be major threats to companies—they have sometimes even resulted in the demise of products.

aspiration group	dynamic continuous innovation	negativity bias	service encounter
basic exchange equation		norms	social comparison
bogie	focus group	normative influence	surrogate consumer
comparative appraisal	group	opinion leaders	trickle-down theory
compliance	group polarization phenomenon	pipe dream rumors	two-step flow model
conformity		private acceptance	urban legend
continuous innovation	group shift	product innovation	value-expressive influence
diffusion	informational influence	reference group	word-of-mouth communications
discontinuous innovation	market embeddedness	reflected appraisal	
dissociative group	market mavens	role	
dyadic exchange	multistep flow model	role-related product cluster	

R E V I E W   Q U E S T I O N S

1. Define the concept of the group and identify the various types of groups.

2. Why is it that "groups are more than the sum of their parts"? Cite a specific example of how people's buying patterns differ when they shop with a group rather than by themselves.

3. Indicate how groups affect people through normative, value-expressive, and informational influence.

4. Define the concept of role. What are some examples of "role-related product clusters"?

5. Identify the various characteristics of the product and the properties of the person that can bring about conformity to group pressures.

6. How do social-comparison processes influence consumers?

7. What is a group shift? What is a likely explanation for why group shifts occur? What types of consumer decisions might be influenced by group shifts?

8. Why is it that groups often give very poor tips in restaurants?

9. What is meant by the term *diffusion*? In a consumer behavior context what is it that is diffused?

10. What are the various types of product innovations that were identified in this chapter?

11. What are the factors that can influence new-product success by affecting the rate of diffusion?

12. What is meant by the term *diffusion pattern*? What are the factors that influence the type of diffusion pattern displayed by a product?

13. Identify the five categories of adopters and state the relative size of each category.

14. What are the various approaches to dealing with corporate rumors? Identify four different types of rumors.

15. What is the negativity bias in word-of-mouth communications?

16. Identify the three models that describe how personal influence is transmitted through the population. Which of the models appears to be the most accurate?

17. What is the difference between an opinion leader and a product innovator?

18. Define market mavens and surrogate consumers.

D I S C U S S I O N   Q U E S T I O N S

1. List the various reference groups that have an influence on you and categorize them into aspiration, dissociative, primary, and informal groups. Rank them in importance in influencing your consumption behavior. On what types of products, if any, do these groups influence your consumption?

2. Groups develop norms to help them function more smoothly. Consider the classroom situation at your university or college. What norms guide the behavior of instructors as well as students in the classroom?

3. Groups can affect consumption through both value-expressive and informational influence. Give some examples of value-expressive and informational influence that could affect fraternity or sorority members in their purchase of an automobile and of a stereo.

4. What products would be considered part of a role-related product cluster for a college student and for a young couple with a new baby?

5. Consider the various groups of which you are a member. In which of these groups are conformity pressures the greatest? Why is this the case?

6. Suppose that you are a member of a buying center for a large, highly conservative corporation. Most major purchase decisions are reached through a consensus process among five members of the group. In the current instance your group must decide whether to purchase a complex and expensive computer system from an established firm that charges high prices or from a smaller but competently run firm that charges lower prices. What would the group polarization phenomenon tell you about the likely decision?

7. Consider the following three products: compact disc players, pump toothpaste dispensers, and computers. Classify each as to its type of innovation. What type of diffusion pattern would you describe each as having? Justify your answers.

8. Identify a recent rumor that involves a corporation or one of its products. What should the company be doing to squash the rumor?

9. Diagram a word-of-mouth network for a service that you have recently obtained, such as a haircut or dental work. Actually go out and conduct brief interviews and attempt to track down the people who formed the linkages in the network.

10. Among your acquaintances identify people who act as opinion leaders, product innovators, market mavens, and surrogate consumers. Describe what each person does.

11. Think about the goods and services that you purchase. To what extent do word-of-mouth communications influence your purchases?

12. Suppose that you are a marketing manager for a regional brewery. How successful do you think a strategy would be of attempting to reach opinion leaders with communications so that they will pass these messages on to followers and thereby influence their behavior?

ENDNOTES

1. Laurie Hays, "Du Pont's Difficulties in Selling Kevlar® Show Hurdles of Innovation," *The Wall Street Journal*, September 29, 1987, pp. 1, 20. One can imagine that the developer of what became Post-it Notes went through a similar circumstance: What does one do with a glue that isn't very sticky?

2. David Graham, "Synthetic Spider Silk," *Technology Review*, October 1994, pp. 16–17.

3. Michael Lynn and Bib Latane, "The Psychology of Restaurant Tipping," *Journal of Applied Social Psychology*, Vol. 14 (November–December 1984), pp. 549–561. For more information on tipping, see Michael Lynn, George M. Zinkhan and Judy Harris, "Consumer Tipping: A Cross-Cultural Study," *Journal of Consumer Research*, Vol. 20 (December 1993), pp. 478–488.

4. James C. Ward and Peter H. Reingen, "Sociocognitive Analysis of Group Decision Making Among Consumers," *Journal of Consumer Research*, Vol. 17 (December 1990), pp. 245–262.

5. Michael S. Olmstead, *The Small Group* (New York: Holt, Rinehart & Winston, 1962). For a fascinating discussion of group influence on decision making, see Irving L. Janis, *Victims of Groupthink* (Boston: Houghton Mifflin, 1972).

6. Marvin E. Shaw, *Group Dynamics* (New York: McGraw-Hill, 1971).

7. Francis Bourne, "Group Influence in Marketing and Public Relations," in *Some Applications of Behavioral Research*, R. Likert and S. P. Hayes, eds. (Basil, Switzerland: UNESCO, 1957). For a study that tested these ideas, see William Bearden and Michael Etzel, "Reference Group Influence on Product and Brand Purchase Decisions," *Journal of Consumer Research*, Vol. 9 (September 1982), pp. 183–194.

8. Shaw, *Group Dynamics*.

9. H. Haire, "Projective Techniques in Marketing Research," *Journal of Marketing*, Vol. 14 (April 1950), pp. 649–656.

10. F. E. Webster and F. von Pechman, "A Replication of the Shopping List Study," *Journal of Marketing*, Vol. 34 (April 1970), pp. 61–63.

11. Kathleen M. Rassuli and Gilbert D. Harrell, "Group Differences in the Construction of Consumption Sets," in *Advances in Consumer Research*, Vol. 23, Kim P. Corfman and John G. Lynch, Jr., eds. (Provo, UT: Association for Consumer Research, 1996), pp. 446–453.

12. Charles A. Kiesler and Sara B. Kiesler, *Conformity* (Reading, MA: Addison-Wesley, 1969), p. 7.

13. Solomon E. Asch, *Social Psychology* (Englewood Cliffs, NJ: Prentice Hall, 1952).

14. V. Parker Lessig and C. Whan Park, "Promotional Perspectives

of Reference Group Influence, Advertising Implications," *Journal of Advertising*, Vol. 7 (Spring 1978), pp. 41–47. Also see J. S. Johar and M. Joseph Sirgy, "Value-Expressive versus Utilitarian Advertising Appeals: When and Why to Use Which Appeal," *Journal of Advertising*, Vol. 20 (September 1991), pp. 23–33.

15. Brenda Gainer and Eileen Fischer, "To Buy or Not to Buy? That is Not the Question: Female Ritual in Home Shopping Parties," in *Advances in Consumer Research*, Vol. 18, Rebecca Holman and Michael Solomon, eds. (Provo, UT: Association for Consumer Research, 1991), pp. 597–602.

16. Jonathan K. Frenzen and Harry L. Davis, "Purchasing Behavior in Embedded Markets," *Journal of Consumer Research*, Vol. 17 (June 1990), pp. 1–12.

17. Leon Festinger, "A Theory of Social Comparison Processes," *Human Relations*, Vol. 7 (May 1954), pp. 117–140.

18. Edward Jones and Harold Gerard, *Social Psychology* (New York: John Wiley & Sons, 1967).

19. Festinger, "A Theory of Social Comparison Processes." For a consumer study that supports these findings, see George P. Moschis, "Social Comparison and Information Group Influence," *Journal of Marketing Research*, Vol. 13 (August 1976), pp. 237–244.

20. Marsha L. Richins, "Social Comparison and the Idealized Images of Advertising," *Journal of Consumer Research*, Vol. 18 (June 1991), pp. 71–83.

21. R. E. Knox and R. K. Safford, "Group Caution at the Race Track," *Journal of Experimental Social Psychology*, Vol. 12 (May 1976), pp. 317–324.

22. Helmet Lamm and David G. Myers, "Group-Induced Polar-ization of Attitudes and Behavior," in *Advances in Experimental Social Psychology*, Vol. 11, Leonard Berkowitz, ed. (New York: Academic Press, 1978), pp. 145–195.

23. Lamm and Myers, "Group-Induced Polarization."

24. One study found evidence that group polarization could also occur when groups were asked to make a choice among restaurants. The article also tested three different mathematical models of group polarization. See Vithala R. Rao and Joel H. Steckel, "A Polarization Model for Describing Group Preferences," *Journal of Consumer Research*, Vol. 18 (June 1991), pp. 108–118.

25. For an interesting examination of an unusual group (Harley Davidson motorcycle enthusiasts), see John W. Schouten and James H. McAlexander, "Subcultures of Consumption: An Ethnography of the New Bikers," *Journal of Consumer Research*, Vol. 22 (June 1995), pp. 43–61.

26. Terry Bristol and Edward F. Fern, "Using Qualitative Techniques to Explore Consumer Attitudes: Insights from Group Process Theories," *Advances in Consumer Research*, Vol. 20, Leigh McAlister and Michael L. Rothschild, eds. (Provo, UT: Association for Consumer Research, 1993), pp. 444–448.

27. This definition is based in part on one developed by Paula Fitzgerald Bone, "Determinants of Word-of-Mouth Communications During Product Consumption," *Advances in Consumer Research*, Vol. 19, John F. Sherry and Brian Sternthal, eds. (Provo, UT: Association for Consumer Research, 1992), pp. 579–583.

28. Stephen P. Morin, "Influentials Advising Their Friends to Sell Lots of High-Tech Gadgetry," *The Wall Street Journal*, February 28, 1983, p. 30.

29. Elihu Katz and Paul Lazarsfeld, *Personal Influence* (Glencoe, IL: The Free Press, 1955).

30. Moshe Givon, Vijay Mahajan, and Eitan Muller, "Software Piracy: Estimation of Lost Sales and the Impact on Software Diffusion," *Journal of Marketing*, Vol. 59 (January 1995), pp. 29–37.

31. Johan Arndt, "Role of Product-Related Conversations in the Diffusion of a New Product," *Journal of Marketing Research*, Vol. 4 (August 1967), p. 292. Similarly, Ford Motor Company found that satisfied customers told 8 people about their cars, but dissatisfied customers told 22 about their complaints. See Damon Darlin, "Although U.S. Cars Are Improved, Imports Still Win Quality Survey," *The Wall Street Journal*, December 16, 1985, p. 27.

32. Paul M. Herr, Frank R. Kardes, and John Kim, "Effects of Word-of-Mouth and Product-Attribute Information on Persuasion: An Accessibility-Diagnosticity Perspective," *Journal of Consumer Research*, Vol. 17 (March 1991), pp. 454–462.

33. Thomas Robertson, Joan Zielinski, and Scott Ward, *Consumer Behavior* (Glenview, IL: Scott, Foresman, 1984).

34. Ernst Dichter, "How Word-of-Mouth Advertising Works," *Harvard Business Review*, Vol. 44 (November–December 1966), p. 148.

35. Peter Reingen and Jerome Kernan, "Analysis of Referral Networks in Marketing: Methods and Illustration," *Journal of Marketing Research*, Vol. 23 (November 1986), pp. 370–378. Also see Karen Maru File, Diane S. P. Cermak, and Russ Alan Prince, "Word-of-Mouth Effects in

Professional Services Buyer Behavior," *Service Industries Journal*, Vol. 14 (July 1994), pp. 301–314.

36. Definitions are taken from Jacqueline Johnson Brown, "Social Ties and Word-of-Mouth Referral Behavior," *Journal of Consumer Research*, Vol. 14 (December 1987), pp. 350–362.

37. Ibid.

38. Charles W. King and John O. Summers, "Overlap of Opinion Leadership Across Product Categories," *Journal of Marketing Research*, Vol. 7 (February 1970), pp. 43–50.

39. Katz and Lazarsfeld, *Personal Influence*, pp. 332–334.

40. Thomas Robertson and James Myers, "Personality Correlates of Opinion Leadership and Innovative Buying Behavior," *Journal of Marketing Research*, Vol. 6 (May 1969), p. 168. For a recent attempt to deal with measurement issues, see Leisa Reinecke Flynn, Ronald E. Goldsmith, and Jacqueline K. Eastman, "Opinion Leaders and Opinion Seekers: Two New Measurement Scales," *Journal of the Academy of Marketing Science*, Vol. 24 (Spring 1996), pp. 137–147.

41. Everett M. Rogers, *Diffusion of Innovations*, 3rd ed. (New York: The Free Press, 1983), pp. 281–284. Note that some of Rogers' views may have changed in the 4th edition (New York: The Free Press, 1995). Also see William H. Redmond, "Contemporary Social Theory and the Bass Diffusion Model," in *Enhancing Knowledge Development in Marketing*, Vol. 7, Cornelia Dröge and Roger Calantone, eds. (Chicago: American Marketing Association, 1996), pp. 176–181.

42. James Coleman, Elihu Katz, and Herbert Menzel, *Medical Innovation: A Diffusion Study* (Indi-

anapolis, IN: Bobbs-Merrill, 1966).

43. Ibid.

44. Lawrence Feick and Linda Price, "The Market Maven: A Diffuser of Marketplace Information," *Journal of Marketing*, Vol. 51 (January 1987), pp. 83–87. Also see Linda Price, Lawrence F. Feick, and Audrey Guskey, "Everyday Market Helping Behavior," *Journal of Public Policy and Marketing*, Vol. 12 (Fall 1995), pp. 255–266.

45. Todd A. Mooradian, "The Five Factor Model and Market Mavenism," in *Advances in Consumer Research*, Vol. 23, Kim P. Corfman and John G. Lynch, Jr., eds. (Provo, UT: Association for Consumer Research, 1996), pp. 260–263. Also see Michael T. Elliott and Anne E. Warfield, "Do Market Mavens Categorize Brands Differently?" *Advances in Consumer Research*, Vol. 20, Leigh McAlister and Michael Rothschild, eds. (Provo, UT: Association for Consumer Research, 1993), pp. 202–208; and Terrell E. Williams and Mark E. Slama, "Market Mavens' Purchase Decision Evaluative Criteria: Implications for Brand and Store Promotion Efforts," *Journal of Consumer Marketing*, Vol. 12, no. 3 (1995), pp. 4–21.

46. Michael Solomon, "The Missing Link: Surrogate Consumers in the Marketing Chain," *Journal of Marketing*, Vol. 50 (October 1986), pp. 208–218.

47. Michael R. Solomon, Carol Surprenant, John A. Czepiel, and Evelyn G. Gutman, "A Role Theory Perspective on Dyadic Interactions: The Service Encounter," *Journal of Marketing*, Vol. 49 (Winter 1985), pp. 99–111.

48. The "employee" viewpoint is well explored in Mary Jo Bitner, Bernard H. Booms, and Lois A.

Mohr, "Critical Service Encounters: The Employee's Viewpoint," *Journal of Marketing*, Vol. 58 (October 1994), pp. 95–106.

49. Stephen J. Grove and Raymond P. Fisk, "The Service Experience as Theater," *Advances in Consumer Research*, Vol. 19, John F. Sherry, Jr., and Brian Sternthal eds. (Provo, UT: Association for Consumer Research, 1992), pp. 455–461.

50. Michael Guiry, "Consumer and Employee Roles in Service Encounters," *Advances in Consumer Research*, Vol. 19, John F. Sherry, Jr., and Brian Sternthal, eds. (Provo, UT: Association for Consumer Research, 1992), pp. 666–672.

51. Linda L. Price, Eric J. Arnould, and Patrick Tierney, "Going to Extremes: Managing Service Encounters and Assessing Provider Performance," *Journal of Marketing*, Vol. 59 (April 1995), pp. 83–97.

52. George Homans, *Social Behavior: Its Elementary Forms* (New York: Harcourt, Brace & World, 1961), p. 235. Also see Marvin Shaw and Philip Costanzo, *Theories of Social Psychology* (New York: McGraw-Hill, 1970). Note that exchange theory has been criticized as focusing too much on the selfish, hedonic aspects of human interactions. See Bergt Abrahamson, "Homans on Exchange: Hedonism Revisited," *American Journal of Sociology*, Vol. 76 (1970), pp. 273–285.

53. Henry Assael, *Consumer Behavior and Marketing Action* (Boston, MA: Kent, 1983).

54. Derived from Glen L. Urban and John Hauser, *Design and Marketing of New Products* (Englewood Cliffs, NJ: Prentice Hall, 1980).

55. Elizabeth C. Hirschman, "Cocaine as Innovation," in *Advances in Consumer Research*, Vol. 19,

John F. Sherry, Jr., and Brian Sternthal, eds. (Provo, UT: Association for Consumer Research, 1992), pp. 129–139.

56. Hubert Gatignon and Thomas Robertson, "A Propositional Inventory for New Diffusion Research," *Journal of Consumer Research*, Vol. 11 (March 1985), pp. 849–867. This article provides an excellent review of the diffusion literature and develops a comprehensive set of propositions concerning the factors influencing the diffusion process.

57. Other diffusion models also exist. A model based on naturalistic observation of diffusion processes in developing countries was developed by Eric J. Arnould, "Toward a Broadened Theory of Preference Formation and the Diffusion of Innovations: Cases from Zinder Province, Niger Republic," *Journal of Consumer Research*, Vol. 16 (September 1989), pp. 239–267.

58. Gatignon and Robertson, "A Propositional Inventory for New Diffusion Research." Also see Kristiaan Helsen, Kamel Jedidi, and Wayne S. DeSarbo, "A New Approach to Country Segmentation Utilizing Multinational Diffusion Patterns," *Journal of Marketing*, Vol. 57 (October 1993), pp. 60–71. Perceived consumption visibility and superordinate group influence might also impact new-product adoption. See Robert Fisher and Linda Price, "An Investigation into the Social Context of Early Adopter Behavior," *Journal of Consumer Research*, Vol. 19 (December 1992), pp. 477–486.

59. Rogers, *Diffusion of Innovations*.

60. Elizabeth Hirschman, "Symbolism and Technology as Sources of the Generation of Innovations," in *Advances in Consumer Research*, Vol. 9, Andrew Mitchell, ed. (Provo, UT: Association for Consumer Research, 1981), pp. 537–541.

61. Gatignon and Robertson, "A Propositional Inventory for New Diffusion Research." A recent study employed cluster analysis techniques to identify a typology of product innovators. Three categories were identified—innovative communicators, less involved, and status maintainers. See David Midgley and Grahame Dowling, "A Longitudinal Study of Product Form Innovation: The Interaction Between Predispositions and Social Messages," *Journal of Consumer Research*, Vol. 19 (March 1993), pp. 611–625. A critique of time-based measures of consumer innovativeness can be found in Ronald E. Goldsmith and Charles F. Hofacker, "Measuring Consumer Innovativeness," *Journal of the Academy of Marketing Science*, Vol. 19 (Summer 1991), pp. 209–221.

62. E. M. Rogers and F. F. Shoemaker, *Communication of Innovations: A Cross-Cultural Approach*, (New York: Holt, Rinehard & Winston, 1971).

63. Gatignon and Robertson, "A Propositional Inventory for New Diffusion Research." For more information on discussion processes, see Frank M. Bass, "A New Product Growth Model of Consumer Durables," *Management Science*, Vol. 15 (January 1969), pp. 215–227; and Vijay Mahajan, Eitan Muller, and Frank M. Bass, "New Product Diffusion Models in Marketing: A Review and Directions for Research," *Journal of Marketing*, Vol. 54 (January 1990), pp. 1–26.

64. Lisa Bannon, "Bazaar Gossip: How a Rumor Spread About Subliminal Sex in Disney's 'Aladdin,' " *The Wall Street Journal*, October 24, 1995, pp. A1, A6.

65. Dorothy Rabinowitz, "Race and Rumor," *The Wall Street Journal*, April 29, 1996, p. A20.

66. John Stockmeyer, "Brands in Crisis: Consumer Help for Deserving Victims," in *Advances in Consumer Research*, Vol. 23, Kim P. Corfman and John G. Lynch, Jr., eds. (Provo, UT: Association for Consumer Research, 1996), pp. 429–435.

67. Robert Levy, "Tilting at the Rumor Mill," *Dun's Review*, July 1981, pp. 52–54.

68. Zachary Schiller, "P&G is Still Having a Devil of a Time," *Business Week*, September 11, 1995, p. 46.

69. James Esposito and Ralph Rosnow, "Corporate Rumors: How They Start and How to Stop Them," *Management Review*, April 1983, pp. 44–49.

70. G. W. Allport and L. Postman, *The Psychology of Rumor* (New York: Holt, Rinehart & Winston, 1947).

71. Neal Gabler, "The Lure of Urban Myths," *Playboy*, August 1996, pp. 70–153.

72. Levy, "Tilting at the Rumor Mill." Problems with aggressive approaches to crisis management are discussed in Stockmeyer, "Brands in Crisis."

73. Alice Tybout, Bobby Calder, and Brian Sternthal, "Using Information Processing Theory to Design Marketing Strategies," *Journal of Marketing Research*, Vol. 18 (February 1981), pp. 73–79.

SHRINERS COME UNDER FIRE

Prospective Shriner Michael Vaughn was quite ready to participate in secret initiation rituals undergone by such notables as John Wayne, Clark Gable, and Gerald Ford before him, but he began to question his decision to join the organization when the festivities turned kinky. Mischievous initiation ceremonies had to be expected from an organization known for its fun-loving public antics, such as riding around in parades on miniature bicycles and elaborate go-carts. But when they included branding irons, electrical shocks, and strawberry sundaes in his underwear, Vaughn found the experience anything but humorous. So much so, in fact, that he filed a lawsuit for damages against the fraternity's Olekia Temple in Lexington, Kentucky, over what he says happened to him during bizarre initiation rites.

The first Shrine temple, known as Mecca, was founded in New York in 1872. Shriners' elaborate rituals and costumes, including the distinctive fez hat, exhibit Arabian themes inspired by actor William J. Florence, a founding father of the organization who was fascinated by Middle Eastern culture. The Ancient Arabic Order of the Nobles of the Mystic Shrine is a hierarchical organization, headquartered in Tampa, Florida. An Imperial Potentate reigns over the fraternity's 725,000 members, who make up 190 temples internationally. Shriners are well known for their philanthropic deeds. They support 22 Children's Hospitals, which provide free care for the needy.

In June 1989 Michael Vaughn was among nearly three dozen initiates at the Olekia temple in Lexington. Several doctors who were present at the initiation excused men with bad backs and heart problems, but they told Vaughn he could "take it," despite the fact that he had recently been treated by a chiropractor. As the initiation ensued, the men were told to strip to their undershorts, blindfolded, and led into a room where a red hot branding iron was waved in their faces. Initiates were then instructed to lie face-down on a table. One by one, they had their undershorts pulled down and, as described by Mr. Vaughn "an unbelievable, painful electric shock was applied to the buttocks." Red dye was then painted on the area. Next the men were made to

sit on a bench which had been electrified, causing a jolt which sent the men "at least two feet in the air."

The delight of the onlooking Shriners continued as they watched the initiates perform their ritual marching, hand in hand, around an electrified floor mat, which supposedly signified the blazing sands of the Sahara desert. This final jolt caused a cramp in Mr. Vaughn's back, at which point he was allowed to rest briefly.

For the final ordeal, a Shriner taped Vaughn's boxer shorts to his legs. Vaughn said afterwards, "I figured they were going to put something down my shorts that they did not want to fall through." He assumed the "something" was in a nearby sink, where he spied strawberries, whipped cream, and ice cream. When Vaughn sat on a table, as the Shriners instructed him to do, the table collapsed. Crashing to the floor, he struck his head on the floor and was knocked unconscious. When he regained consciousness, Mr. Vaughn was administered an icepack and an apology. The table was not supposed to collapse, the Shriners said, and they regretted the accident. Vaughn left within a few minutes.

A few days later he consulted a neurologist who recommended a CAT scan and some physical therapy. Almost a year later Michael Vaughn filed his suit in Fayette County Circuit Court, including charges of fraud, negligence, assault, and a "loss of hedonic pleasure." He also contends that he "wakes up at night with numbness in his arms and feels that he will never fully recover" from the odd rites, an event he describes as "shameful."

Viewpoints differ on the Shriners' rites. In an effort to ensure an impartial jury, Judge George Barker ordered court records sealed and both parties in the case silenced. Parker said he feared that, given the allegations, "some people would laugh the plaintiff out of court," whereas "others would sock it to the Shrine for being a bunch of idiots." Although the Shriners obeyed the judge's orders not to comment on the case, they have acknowledged in court documents that taping boxer shorts and administering electrical shocks can be included in initiation rituals. The Shriners' filing reads, "The defendant cannot confirm that anyone did such an activity" to Mr. Vaughn and "there is no duct tape used in such a procedure, but rather, two-inch masking tape."

The Shriners also admit that a table tipped over on Vaughn but insist that he sustained no injuries as a result of the mishap. John Grant, a Florida state senator and 20-year Shriner says, "Maybe somebody got into some whipped cream or electrical shocks. What's wrong with having a little bit of fun?" According to Cincinnati attorney Robert E. Manley, who specializes in fraternity law, "The event sounds like hazing, and that's generally looked upon as unlawful."

While the Shriners have so far stood their ground defending their traditional rites of initiation, this controversy must be dealt with, as the organization is now being scrutinized in a contemporary light. The Shriners are facing declining membership (off 32 percent since 1979) because fewer young men these days feel the organization has anything to offer them. The Shriners'

hospitals for children are viewed as appealing, but don't provide sufficient grounds to join the organization.

Questions

1. Define the problems faced by the Shriners.
2. What consumer concepts from the chapter help to explain these problems?
3. Construct a managerial applications matrix. Discuss the managerial implications of the consumer behavior concepts for the Shriners.

This case is based on Alecia Swasy, "In the Hot Seat: Joining the Shriners Can Be Electrifying," *The Wall Street Journal*, November 4, 1991, pp. A1, A6; and Dan Fost, "Farewell to the Lodge," *American Demographics*, January 1996, pp. 40–45.

16

GROUP PROCESSES II:
HOUSEHOLD
AND ORGANIZATIONAL PROCESSES

Child Care and the Dual-Career Household

Conrad Lung was having trouble at work after his daughter was born. His wife also worked, and his 1-year-old daughter spent 11 hours per day in child care. "I had this image of my girl crying, and it wouldn't leave me," he said. As his performance at work lagged, he became depressed and considered quitting his job as a vice president of a sporting goods firm. His mind went back to his work only after his parents moved next door and assumed child-care responsibilities for his daughter.[1] Mr. Lung's feelings are shared by millions of working parents. The author of a survey on working couples for *Fortune* magazine said, "Our major finding is that problems with child care are the most significant predictors of absenteeism and unproductive time at work." Indeed, finding satisfactory, much less outstanding, child care is *the* major problem for two-income families. As noted by one researcher, "A parking lot attendant is paid the same as a child-care worker. If we assign the same importance to someone who parks our cars as to those who take care of our children, we have a serious social problem."[2]

In response to this problem some companies are beginning to actively assist their employees with child care. A few firms actually provide facilities themselves, others give financial assistance to working parents, and many more have child-care referral services. Over the last two decades private day-care employment has increased by over 250 percent, representing nearly 400,000 new jobs.[3] Some analysts believe child care may be the fringe benefit of the 1990s. *Fortune* sees the problem of adequate child care as not just the parents'; it is also the employers' problem and, ultimately, society's. As the author of the *Fortune* survey said, "Couples seem to feel that child care is their problem alone. It's not. It's an institutional problem. Families have changed much faster than the institutions that the family relies on."[4]

INTRODUCTION

In the last chapter we analyzed the factors that influence group processes, such as the impact of roles, normative influence, conformity pressures, and word-of-mouth communications. In this chapter we discuss the two most important fundamental groups: families and organizational groups. For many people, the family is the most essential primary group. It not only shapes the individual's personality and general view of others, but also influences the individual's values and attitudes about consumption. In addition, the family is an important consumption unit in and of itself. Most high-involvement consumer decisions involve input from more than one family member. Often the entire family gets involved in such decisions as which car to buy, where to go on vacation, and whether or not to purchase a house. Family members may even express preferences in low-involvement decisions, such as the brand of toothpaste or the kind of toilet tissue to buy. Some researchers have therefore argued that the family, not the individual, should be the primary focus of the study of consumer behavior.[5]

The second important purchase group that we discuss in this chapter is the buying center within an organization. Buying centers purchase the goods and services necessary for organizations to function. Businesses, government agencies, and nonprofit organizations all have a buying center. While they vary in their degree of formalization, these buying centers share the common characteristic of being composed of two or more people who make procurement decisions for the group.

Families and buying centers have a number of similarities as well as several differences. Table 16-1 compares the family with buying centers. One very important difference is that

Similarities and Differences Between Families and Buying Centers

A. Similarities

1. *Role structure*. Each type of group has certain roles, such as deciders and buyers, that someone will have to fill.
2. *Conformity pressures*. Members of each type of group experience pressures to conform to the norms developed within the group.
3. *Group polarization*. When making decisions, each type of group may experience either risky or conservative shifts.
4. *Group conflict*. Within families and buying centers, conflict will inevitably arise as members disagree on the appropriate purchase option to select.

B. Differences

1. Families are formed by marriage or birth, whereas other groups are formed by job or task.
2. Families have permanent relations, whereas other groups have relationships based on contracts.
3. Families are oriented toward interpersonal relationships, whereas other groups are more goal oriented.
4. Families have more emotional ties, whereas other groups have more rational ties.
5. Families are more oriented toward intrinsic values, whereas other groups seek more extrinsic (i.e., material) rewards.
6. Families seek cooperative relationships, whereas other groups are more competitive and self-oriented.

Source: These differences between families and other organizations are based on work done by Jong Hee Park, Patriya S. Tansuhaj, and Richard H. Kolbe, "The Role of Love, Affection, and Intimacy in Family Decision Research," in *Advances in Consumer Research*, Vol. 18, Rebecca Holman and Michael R. Solomon, eds. (Provo, UT: Association for Consumer Research, 1991), pp. 651–656.

TABLE 16-1

family members share a high degree of intimacy and affection that does not exist in buying centers. This results in more permanent relationships, closer personal ties, and more cooperation within the family group.[6] Perhaps the most important similarity is that families and buying centers both have a corresponding set of roles.

Table 16-2 defines the six roles that exist in most groups. In addition, as we showed in the last chapter, conformity pressures, group polarization, and group conflict exist in all types of groups. For example, both families and companies can have conflicts with suppliers.

Within the American family, an important source of conflict in dual-career families involves the nanny. Called the "domestic battle of the 1990s," this clash pits the working mother against the woman hired to care for her children (i.e., the nanny). The nanny's side of the story is summed up in this quote: "I know mothers resent me because their kids take to me." After quitting a child-care job in which the mother would call her at 4:00 A.M. because her baby was crying, she began to clean houses instead. She said, "I can deal with the kids. It's the mothers."

But there is another side to the story. Some nannies fall into the trap of thinking that *they* are the mommies. The president of the National Association of Nannies noted, "A mother senses those kinds of feelings. There's a very fine line between loving a child and caring about a child and stepping over the line and invading a parent's territory." Thus the natural conflict between the maternal instincts of mother and nanny can create difficulties. Clashes can also result from the inevitable differences in the cultural background and socioeconomic status of the nanny and the career woman (or, increasingly, the dad). Disagreements can occur over what television shows to let the children watch and what food

Types of Roles Found in Families and Buying Centers	
Role	**Description**
Users	The persons who use the product that has been purchased. Users may or may not be consulted in the purchase process. They may initiate the decision process, and then have no decision-making authority. Or they may also develop product specifications.
Gatekeepers	The persons who control the information employed by other members of the buying center. They may have influence over who talks to whom in the organization. They may also have influence over what kind of information is obtained within the organization. They screen the types of information that deciders and influencers obtain.
Influencers	The persons who help in the evaluation of alternatives process. In business firms they are frequently engineers and other technicians. Consultants from outside the organization frequently become influencers.
Deciders	The persons who actually make the purchase decision, whether or not they have formal authority to do so. Frequently, deciders are hard to identify. They could be the company CEO or somebody behind the scenes who wields power.
Buyers	The persons who have the formal authority to make the purchase. In a business the buyer may be the purchasing agent. In a family it is frequently the person entrusted with the task of negotiating prices.
Maintainers	The persons who are responsible for the maintenance and upkeep of the product that has been purchased.

Source: Based on Frederick E. Webster, Jr., and Yoram Wind, *Organizational Buying Behavior* (Englewood Cliffs, NJ.: Prentice Hall, 1972), pp. 77–80.

TABLE 16-2

they should eat. The net result is a precarious relationship in which either the nanny or the mommy may fire the other.[7]

Clashes also occur in the business world. Major department chains, in the interest of efficiency, are demanding that small suppliers conform to specifications, including where shipping labels appear on boxes, what direction clothes on hangers face, and when deliveries are made. These efficiencies have become a source of contention, since penalties for ignoring them (called "chargebacks") can cut into suppliers' profits. Some smaller suppliers have stopped marketing to the major chains because of these demands. As a result, chain store departments that once carried 10 or 12 major lines now carry half that many, and many stores now look alike. But as a spokesperson for Federated Department Stores says, "It's not our responsibility to keep vendors afloat. We have a separate philanthropy program."[8]

In this chapter we explore the processes that impact both families and organizational buying centers in the purchase process. We have it divided into three major sections, beginning with an analysis of the family and its relationship to household formation. Within this section we also discuss the important topic of childhood socialization. Then we move on to discuss the organizational buying center, and conclude, as usual, with the managerial applications analysis.

FAMILIES AND HOUSEHOLDS

The term *family* is actually a subset of a more general classification—the household. **Households** are composed of all those people who occupy a living unit. Some examples of households are roommates living in an apartment; unmarried couples living together; a husband and wife living with their children; a husband, wife, children, and grandparents living under one roof; and two couples sharing the same house. The key similarity among all these examples is that the group lives in the same residence. So, based on that definition, a husband, wife, and children who live together are a household as well as a family.

A number of different types of families exist. The **nuclear family** consists of a husband, a wife, and their offspring. The **extended family** consists of the nuclear family plus other relatives, such as the parents of the husband or wife. The high divorce rate in the United States has produced a growing number of single-parent families, which also constitute households.

In many other societies a newly married couple is expected to reside with one or the other set of parents. In the United States and Canada, however, children from middle-class families usually strike out on their own to form families in households separate from their parents'. This arrangement has been called the **detached nuclear family**. The detached nuclear family is associated with the following characteristics:

1. Free choice of mates.
2. Higher levels of divorce.
3. Higher residential mobility.
4. Entry of large numbers of women into the labor force.
5. Lower responsibility of children to care for their parents in their old age.[9]

Over the past two decades major changes have occurred in the nature of households and families in the United States and Canada. New living arrangements have been established that profoundly affect the number and size of households and families. We discuss many of these changes in the next section on the demographics of households.

The Demographics of Households

Two general types of households can be identified: families and nonfamilies. As shown in Table 16-3, each of these categories can be further subdivided so that, in total, nine different household types can be identified, each of which may become a separate segment for marketers. The table shows both the relative size of each of these household segments and projections for how those absolute sizes will change between 1990 and 2000.

Notice in the table that for every six families, there are about three nonfamilies. Among families, married couples outnumber nonmarried couples (nonmarried couples include single fathers, single mothers, and a catchall category of "other families" that includes such families as children living with aunts and uncles). The nonfamily segment includes men and women living alone, as well as "other nonfamilies," composed mostly of cohabitating adults. The household segment that is projected to grow fastest between 1990 and 2000, is "married couples with no children at home." This demographic trend will result from the aging of the baby-boom generation born between 1946 and 1964. Of course, the data in Table 16-3 for the year 2000 are merely estimates. They were derived by editors at *American Demographics* magazine; and as the editors noted, "small differences in assumptions can make a big difference in the final numbers."[10]

Household Changes, 1990–2000

	1990		2000		1990–2000
	Households	% of Total	Households	% of Total	Percentage Change
All Households	93,347	100.0	110,140	100.0	18.0
Families	66,091	70.8	77,705	70.6	17.6
1. Married couples	52,317	56.0	60,969	55.4	16.5
2. With children at home	24,537	26.3	24,286	22.1	−1.0
3. With no children at home	21,522	23.1	31,365	28.5	45.7
4. Single fathers	1,153	1.2	1,523	1.4	9.0
5. Single mothers	6,599	7.1	7,473	6.8	4.1
6. Other families	6,022	6.5	7,741	7.0	28.5
Nonfamilies	27,257	29.2	32,434	29.4	15.6
7. Men living alone	9,049	9.7	10,898	9.9	20.4
8. Women living alone	13,950	14.9	16,278	14.8	14.1
9. Other nonfamilies	4,258	4.6	5,258	4.8	23.5

Source: Based on "The Big Picture," *American Demographics*, December 1993, p. 29.

TABLE 16-3

When targeting market segments, managers must be concerned with their buying power. The household segment with the greatest buying power is childless couples aged 45 to 64. These individuals are in their peak earning years and have no children to support. The households with the least buying power are childless singles aged 45 and older and single parents.[11]

Data from the U.S. Census indicate that household growth has outpaced population growth in recent decades. Since 1970 the average household size has fallen from 3.14 to 2.67 persons, and the average family size has declined from 3.58 to 3.20 persons. This trend toward smaller households can be laid to our rising divorce rate, the decisions of young people to leave home prior to marriage, and the tendency of older people to maintain their own homes after other family members are gone.[12]

A trend toward later marriage is another factor linked to the decreasing size of households. In 1966 the average male was 22.8 years old and the average female 20.5 years old at the time of first marriage. By the late 1980s these ages had risen to 25.8 years for men and 23.6 years for women. The number of women aged 25 to 29 who have never been married has doubled since 1970.[13] In fact, by the mid-1990s, 66 percent of women aged 20 to 24 had never married[14]—more than double the number in 1980.

The trend toward later marriage has a number of implications. First, it suggests that more people will remain single throughout their lives. Second, it implies that fertility rates will decrease because older couples generally have more trouble conceiving than younger couples. Later marriages also increase the chances for premarital pregnancies because women are sexually mature for a longer time before they marry. Finally, by remaining single longer, young people have more time to "invest in themselves" by pursuing educational and work goals.

Divorce is a growing fact of life for contemporary couples. In the late 1970s it was estimated that 35 percent of new marriages would end in divorce. That estimate is now 50 percent. One result of the higher divorce rate is a large increase in the number of single men and women caring for children under 18 years of age. Between 1980 and 1994 this number increased by over 225 percent for men and 142 percent for women.[15] On a more positive note, since the mid-1980s, U.S. divorce rates have declined slightly.[16]

Another major trend in family composition over the past 15 years is the higher incidence of two-career families. By 1993 the wives worked in 64.7 percent of all married couples.[17] A study comparing the overall expenditure patterns of one-earner and dual-earner households revealed a high level of consistency of expenditures between the two groups.[18] Even on such factors as amounts spent on food eaten at home and away from home, the expenditures were virtually identical. Interestingly, the area where the largest differences were found was "apparel and services." Here families with nonworking wives had higher expenditures. The solid finding was that overall family income had by far the largest impact on expenditure patterns.

Changes in family demographics can influence the design of the marketing mix in a variety of ways. For example, the rapid increase in the number of working women has dramatically changed the way marketers attempt to reach this group. The time demands on working women mean that the distribution system has had to be adjusted so that retail stores are open longer hours on weekends and at night. Mail-order purchasing has increased in popularity partly because of the reluctance of working couples to leave home for extended shopping trips after a day at the office. Companies in the clothing industry have introduced more classic suits and blouses for working women that do not go out of style every year. Women are also buying more homes: single women own 13.8 million homes, more than double the number 25 years ago. In a sign of the times, one California builder has hosted Great Expectations, a dating service, and Parents Without Partners to locate "nontraditional" home buyers.[19]

The Family Life Cycle

The **family life cycle** refers to the idea that families usually move through a series of stages in a developmental fashion. Thus a family may begin as a married couple and then move through phases in which children are born, the children grow older and eventually move out, and, finally, the couple grows old. The concept of the family life cycle has been criticized because some people do not go through this cycle at all and others go through other cycles in addition to the family life cycle. Some people never marry and therefore move through a different set of stages. Others get divorced, and move through the family cycle a second time or move through another type of cycle as a single person. Most consumer researchers, however, have retained the term *family life cycle* or *household life cycle* because they think it best represents the idea that people go through identifiable stages in their lives and that this cycle recurs as grown children later marry and procreate.

Table 16-4 presents an 11-stage model of the family life cycle. This model, developed by Mary Gilly and Ben Enis, is widely used in family life cycle research.[20] The Gilly-Enis model has the advantage of focusing on the lifestyle of the stage and the ages of the members of the household. The ages 35 and 65 are employed as cutoffs to distinguish stages of the life cycle. For example, there are three bachelor stages, based on whether the person is under 35, between 35 and 65, or over 65. In the Gilly-Enis model bachelor lifestyle is based on age rather than on whether the person has ever been married. Similarly, the "married" categories include cohabiting adults of any sexual orientation.

A number of studies have investigated the changing consumption patterns of specific products or services throughout the family life cycle. Spending on such items as restaurant

The Gilly-Enis Family Life-Cycle Model

Life-Cycle Stage	Percentage of Total	Description
Bachelor I	7.9%	Unmarried, under age 35
Bachelor II	13.3	Unmarried, under age 65
Newlywed	17.4	Married without children, under age 35
Single parent	5.9	Single parents, under age 65
Full nest I, children <6	9.9	Couple with female under age 35, with children under age 6
Delayed full nest, children <6	3.8	Couple with female over age 35, with children under age 6
Full nest II and III, with children >6 at home	22.2	Couple with children under or over age 6 at home
Childless couple	16.0	Couple under age 65, with no children at home
Older couple	5.9	Couple age 65 or over, with no children at home
Bachelor III	7.4	Unmarried, over age 65
Other	0.5	Miscellaneous other groupings, such as children staying with other kin

Note: The original scale had 14 categories, which were reduced to 11 in this depiction.

Source: Based on Mary C. Gilly and Ben M. Enis, "Recycling the Family Life Cycle: A Proposal for Redefinition," in *Advances in Consumer Research*, Vol. 9, Andrew A. Mitchell, ed. (Ann Arbor, MI: Association for Consumer Research, 1982), pp. 271–276.

TABLE 16-4

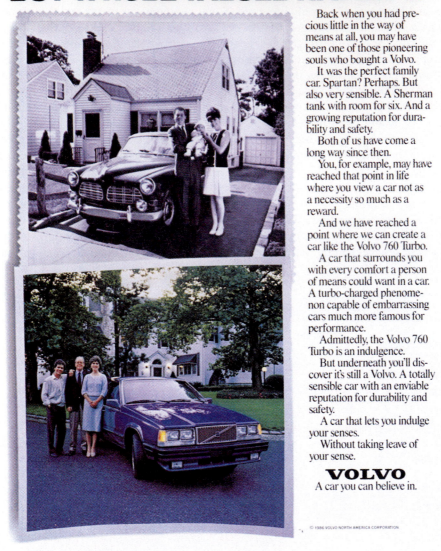

Figure 16-1
In this ad Volvo suggests that it still has a car appropriate for a more mature new life-cycle stage.

meals, telephone service, and energy for home and car diverge dramatically across family life cycle stages. For example, the three most frequently purchased supermarket items by families with children under 6 are disposable diapers, baby bottles and nipples, and baby food, while for families with children from 6 to 17, crayons, bubble gum, and acne remedies top the list.[21] Corporations have recognized that the family life cycle influences purchase patterns. Figure 16-1 shows an ad by Volvo that points out how preferences in autos change as people move through the family life cycle.

A controversial issue is whether life cycle stage or income better accounts for spending differences among households. In one study the authors investigated the clothing expenditures of families.[22] In addition to gathering information on the stage of the family life-cycle, they collected a variety of socioeconomic and demographic data. Their results revealed that income was the best predictor of clothing expenditures. Although the data on life-cycle stage did increase predictive ability, their contribution was extremely small. On the other hand, a recent large-scale study confirms that life-cycle changes are meaningfully related to consumption behavior across 19 of 21 different categories of purchases, from furniture and eating out to apparel.[23] From a managerial perspective, these results suggest that marketers should collect information on the income level of family life segments before targeting them to ensure that they have the required buying power to be a viable market segment.

Family Role Structure

A group's role structure will influence its buying patterns. Figure 16-2 presents an ad for Aunt Jemima pancake syrup targeted to mothers. Although the syrup is consumed by kids, the target of the ad is the mother, who is the decision maker and purchaser of the product.

Figure 16-2
Aunt Jemima targets mothers in this ad, recognizing that moms are the buyers of these products.

Cases where buyers and users of products differ illustrate the point that, within any small group, individuals often take on different roles in order to help the group function more smoothly. One of the results of the increasing tendency of women to work is that men are assuming more purchasing responsibility. Between 1987 and 1994 the number of men shopping from home via catalog increased by 54 percent, compared with only a 39 percent increase in women catalog shoppers.[24]

Role Overload

With the increase in dual-career couples, one or both spouses often are compelled to take on a variety of different roles within the household. **Role overload** has been defined as a conflict "that occurs when the sheer volume of behavior demanded by the positions in the position set exceeds available time and energy."[25] Table 16-5 presents a scale developed to assess the extent of role overload perceived by an individual. The experience of role overload has been found to be related to the wife's work involvement. Of interest to marketers, there is a positive correlation between role overload and the purchase of convenience goods and timesaving durable appliances.

Evidence indicates that both husbands and wives can experience role overload.[26] Figure 16-3 diagrams four possible combinations: (1) wife overloaded/husband underloaded; (2) husband overloaded/wife underloaded; (3) both overloaded; and (4) both underloaded. These particular combinations of role overload were proposed by the researchers to explain information acquisition and decision making within the household. They have argued that when one spouse is underloaded and the other overloaded, information-acquisition activities are carried out by the underloaded spouse. In contrast, when both spouses experience role overload, information-acquisition activities are short-

---

A Scale to Measure Role Overload*

1. I have to do things I don't really have the time and energy for.
2. There are too many demands on my time.
3. I need more hours in the day to do all the things that are expected of me.
4. I can't ever seem to get caught up.
5. I don't ever seem to have time for myself.
6. There are times when I cannot meet everyone's expectations.
7. Sometimes I feel as if there are not enough hours in the day.
8. Many times I have to cancel appointments.
9. I seem to have to overextend myself in order to be able to finish everything I have to do.
10. I seem to have more commitments than some of the other wives (husbands) I know.
11. I find myself having to prepare priority lists (lists that tell me which things I should do first) to get done all the things I have to do. Otherwise I forget because I have so much to do.
12. I feel I have to do things hastily and maybe less carefully in order to get everything done.
13. I just can't find the energy in me to do all the things expected of me.

---

*Items assessed questions on 5-point Likert scales anchored by "strongly agree–strongly disagree."

Source: Michael Reilly, "Working Wives and Convenience Consumption," *Journal of Consumer Research*, Vol. 8 (March 1982), pp. 407–418.

TABLE 16-5

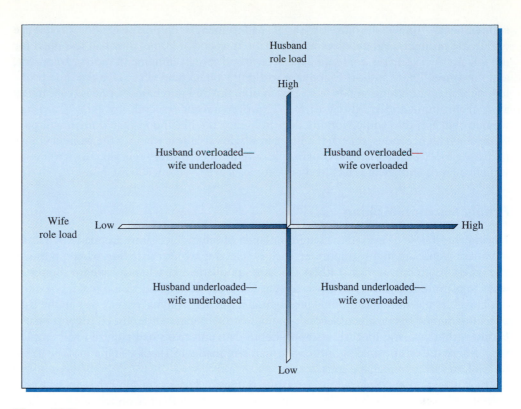

Figure 16-3

Comparison of husband and wife roles loads. (*Source:* Ellen Burns, "Role Load in the Household," in *Advances in Consumer Research*, Vol. 14, Melanie Wallendorf and Paul Anderson, eds. [Provo, UT: Association for Consumer Research, 1987], pp. 458–462.)

ened and joint decision making is minimal. The couple also tends to use convenience items extensively.

Role overload is especially likely when a family consists of two working spouses. There is insufficient time to perform many household tasks, such as cleaning, cooking, paying bills, bathing children, and transporting children to doctors, dance lessons, and baseball practice. Traditionally, these household tasks have fallen upon the wife as the keeper of the household. However, when the wife works eight or more hours per day, performing all of these household tasks is nearly impossible. Researchers have investigated how families with working wives adjust to the time crunch. In one study the authors found that working wives did not substitute capital equipment for their efforts any more than did nonworking wives. They did not use more outside cleaning services than nonworking wives nor did they spend less time at volunteer activities. Neither did employed women substitute the efforts of other family members for their own work. Finally, the employed wives did not sleep less than the wives who didn't work outside the home.[27]

How, then, did the working wives handle their time crunch? The main means was by cutting down on leisure activities. Families with working wives also tended to purchase more meals away from home, to use more disposable diapers, to engage in less housework, and to spend less time caring for family members. The one laborsaving device that has been associated with working wives is the microwave oven.[28]

With the exception of greater use of microwave ovens, researchers have found that durables are *not* substituted for the time wives spend in household activities as they become more involved in outside jobs. Rather, they found that durables and wives' time were complements—that is, the more time a wife had to spend at home, the greater was her use of durable products. When wives had less time to spend at home, they had less need for durable products, such as home appliances, lawn and garden equipment, sports equipment, and furniture. These authors found that working women tended to solve the time problem by utilizing one-use goods (e.g., frozen dinners) and purchased services (e.g., meals away from home and child day care).[29] However, recent research involving Canadian women suggests that while working does influence the likelihood that women will purchase convenience foods, the most important single variable is whether the woman enjoys preparing food. Those who find cooking pleasurable or even stress-relieving use fewer convenience foods and are also less likely to eat meals prepared outside the home.[30]

Family Decision Making

During the course of everyday living thousands of buying decisions are made by family members. Some are highly important, such as selecting which car to buy, where to move, and where to go on vacation. Others are more mundane, like what to have for dinner or what to plant in the garden. For two reasons the study of family decision making is quite difficult. First, as in organizational buying units, the decision maker may not be the user or maintainer of the product. Second, families come in many different configurations. A family with a working mother, a stay-at-home-dad, and two small children will employ very different decision-making processes than one that consists of a single mother living on welfare with two teenage sons.[31]

In this section we explore four key issues in family decision making that are of interest to marketers: (1) which family members have the most influence on various household decisions; (2) the stages in the decision process through which a family moves when making purchases; (3) the role of children in family decision making; and (4) power and conflict in the family.

Relative Influence of Decision Makers A key question for marketers studying family decision making is: Who in the family has the most influence on various types of decisions? An early study of the relative influence of family members on household decisions was conducted in Belgium.[32] This classic research identified four role-specialization dimensions in the buying of products:

1. *Wife-dominated decisions.* The wife is largely independent in deciding what to buy.
2. *Husband-dominated decisions.* The husband is largely independent in deciding what to buy.
3. *Autonomic decisions.* Decisions of lesser importance that either the husband or wife may make independently of the other.
4. *Syncratic decisions.* Decisions in which the husband and wife participate jointly.

Research conducted in the United States has found similar patterns. One study investigated the decision patterns of financially secure middle-aged couples.[33] In this study husband-dominated decisions tended to focus on the details of automobile purchases (e.g., where to purchase the car), while wife-dominated decisions tended to involve the detailed aspects of kitchen and laundry purchases, (e.g., what brand of new washer and dryer to buy). Syncratic decisions appeared to predominate in most other areas, including vacations, home electronic appliances, home selection, when to purchase the next auto, and when to purchase new furniture.

One recurrent problem in researching husband/wife decision influence concerns the reliability and validity of the information obtained. There is a general tendency in some couples for either the husband or wife to systematically overestimate his (her) influence, participation, and authority in household decisions.[34] Researchers have found that 10 percent to 50 percent of couples significantly disagree on their relative influence in buying decisions.[35]

A study investigating investment decision making among couples found that couples sought equitable outcomes when bargaining over the type of investments to make. They tried to avoid conflict and showed empathy for each other's position in order to avoid "making themselves or their negotiating partner unhappy."[36] While couples generally do seek fair outcomes in their decision making, disagreements are inevitable. Five methods have been identified for resolving such conflicts: (1) making a concession now in the expectation that the spouse will reciprocate at a later date; (2) bargaining; (3) withdrawing; (4) overtly capitulating; and (5) compromising.[37]

Family Decision Stages Just as there are different purchase roles in families, so are there different **family decision stages** in a purchase decision. The amount of influence exerted by the husband, wife, and children varies according to the stage of the decision process. In the Belgian study previously mentioned, three family decision stages were identified: problem recognition, search for information, and final choice.[38] According to this study, as the family decision stage moved closer to the final choice, role specialization generally became more syncratic.

Another study undertook to discover which family member had the most influence in buying automobiles and furniture.[39] The decision process for automobiles was divided into six steps:

1. When to buy.
2. How much money to spend.
3. What make to buy.
4. What model to buy.
5. What color to buy.
6. Where to buy.

The decision process for buying furniture was also divided into six steps, which were quite similar.

For the automobile purchase, most of the decision stages were dominated by the husband. The wife consistently shared in or dominated only the decision of what color car to

Consumer Behavior Factoid	
Question: What is causing families to split up?	Express between the mid-1980s and mid-1990s.
Answer: Families are beginning to split up for vacations. Married parents vacationing with kids but without a spouse increased from 2 percent to 5–8 percent of the family vacation business of American	**Source:** Jacqueline Simmons, "Family-Vacation Snaps: Mom and Junior in Barbados, Dad and Daughter in Brazil," *The Wall Street Journal*, November 3, 1995, pp. B1, B6.

buy. For the furniture purchase, the facts were quite different. Here the wife tended to dominate all phases of the decision except for the issue of how much money to spend. An interesting aspect of this study was that each spouse was asked to state an impression of how much influence he or she wielded in the purchase decisions. In most cases there was close agreement in the perceptions of the spouses. The only exception was a tendency for wives to underestimate their dominance in furniture purchase decisions.

Influence in the Family In looking at the ability of family members to influence purchase decisions, researchers have identified three factors that strongly predict influence: the financial resources of the family member, the importance of the decision to the family member, and the gender-role orientations of the spouses.[40] As a member's financial contribution to the family unit increases, so does that member's influence. Similarly, the more important a decision to a family member, the greater that person's influence on the decision. It seems that in the exchange process that takes place within a family trades are made so that a member gives up a degree of influence in one area in order to have greater influence in other areas.

The third predictor of influence, the sex role orientation of the spouses, refers to the extent that a husband and wife follow the traditional normative conceptions of how males and females should behave. One popular approach to studying gender roles is the **Bem Sex-Role Inventory**,[41] which identifies three possible roles. The *masculine role* consists of displaying the characteristics typically ascribed to males, such as strength, forcefulness, aggression, and decision making. The *feminine role* consists of displaying the traditionally female characteristics, such as passivity, nurturance, kindness, and expressiveness. The *psychologically androgynous role* consists of taking on the characteristics appropriate to the circumstances. The androgynous person can be either nurturing or aggressive, depending upon the demands of the situation. Research suggests that families that are less traditional in their gender-role orientation tend to use a joint decision-making style. In general, gender-role orientation is instrumental in defining the decision responsibilities of husbands and wives.[42]

Cross-cultural studies indirectly support these views. One study compared the perceptions of Mexican-American and Anglo wives on the extent to which husbands dominated purchase decisions. The authors found that Mexican-American families tended to be more husband-dominant in the purchase of durables.[43] Since Mexican-American families have more traditional gender-role orientations, these results are compatible with previous research using middle-class Anglo families. As gender roles in a family become less traditional, the influence of female members on purchase decisions generally increases.[44]

One final factor is the change that occurs over the life of the family. Across a wide range of decisions (automobiles, vacations, electronic devices, furniture, and appliances), the wife's influence tends to increase over time, until it peaks in the couple's retirement years. The startling exception is groceries, where the wife's influence actually decreases as the couple ages.[45]

The Role of Children in Family Decision Making All the studies we have discussed to this point ignored the role of children as influencers, decision makers, and users of products and services. Clearly, though, children do make a difference in family decisions.[46] For example, one study found that when children are present in the home, couples more frequently create budgets for their households.[47] Another study investigated the vacation decision process for couples with and without children.[48] The results revealed that in families with children there was less consensus on where to vacation and decisions were likely to be husband-dominated. Although the children did not dominate the decision process, they had the potential to form alliances with either the husband or wife to produce a "majority" decision.

The influence of children on the purchase of breakfast cereals has been extensively investigated. The finding is that children make requests for breakfast cereals more frequently than for other product categories.[49] Almost half of the mothers interviewed at grocery checkout counters mentioned that their child had asked for a particular breakfast cereal. Saturday morning television viewing by children and cereal requests are strongly related: the greater the television viewing, the greater the child's tendency to make requests for specific cereals.[50] In other research it was found that mothers exert little influence over cereal brand preferences among children under 10 years of age. As the researcher noted, "Children appear to develop their own criteria for preferring brands of cereals and beverages that do not correspond with their mother's criteria."[51]

Figure 16-4 outlines the flow of parent-child interaction in breakfast cereal selection based on the findings of a large-scale study in 20 supermarkets.[52] The results are quite interesting and, in some cases, surprising. For example, parents tended to yield more often when the child demanded a cereal than when the child merely requested a particular cereal.

However, when the parent invited the child to make a cereal selection, he or she agreed with the child's selection much more frequently (about 90 percent of the time as compared to 71 percent when the child demanded the cereal). This study also showed that the parent tended to initiate the choice of cereal more often for older children. Furthermore, the percentage of occasions when conflict occurred tended to be at a maximum when the children were between the ages of 6 and 8. Although the sex of the child had little effect in this study, the social class of the family did. Unhappiness with parents' decisions on breakfast cereal purchases tended to occur more frequently among children in working-class families.

Children's influence on household purchase decisions increases as they grow older. One study of 161 adolescents and their parents found that as the adolescents aged, their influence on the various decision stages went up. Another major finding was that peer communication was related to mentioning and discussing purchases with parents. These results demonstrate the large impact that peer groups have on adolescents' product preferences. The study also found that as adolescents earned increasing amounts of money outside the

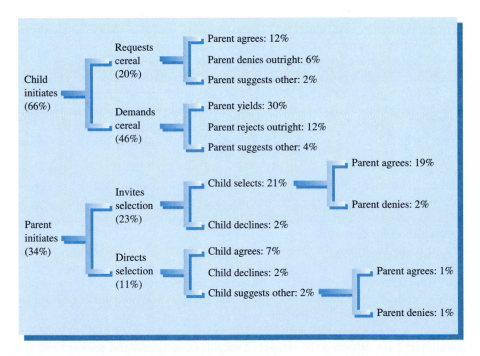

Figure 16-4

Flow of parent-child interaction in breakfast cereal selection. (*Source:* Adapted by permission from Charles P. Atkin, "Observation of Parent-Child Interaction in Supermarket Decision Making," *Journal of Marketing,* Vol. 42 [October 1978], p. 43, published by the American Marketing Association.)

home, they had more input into purchase decisions.[53] This finding is consistent with the concept that financial resources are related to power and influence within the family.

Research comparing adolescents' perceptions of their influence on family purchase decisions with their mothers' perceptions found, unsurprisingly, that teenagers rated their influence as greater than their mothers did. Similarly, the mothers rated their own influence as greater than the adolescents believed it was. This study did show that adolescents are active participants in family purchase decisions, even for products they do not use. For example, in buying a family car, both adolescents and mothers indicated that the young person had some impact on the decision.[54] In another study of adolescent influence on family decisions, the researchers found that the perception of influence was more consistent between husbands and wives than between adolescents and parents[55]—a finding that shouldn't surprise either adolescents or their parents.

Childhood Consumer Socialization

As noted earlier in the chapter, one reason for the family's importance to society is its role as a **socialization agent**.[56] Socialization may be defined as the process by which individuals acquire the knowledge, skills, and dispositions that enable them to participate as members of society.[57] For our purposes, the general concept of socialization can be narrowed to that of childhood consumer socialization.

Childhood consumer socialization refers to the "processes by which young people acquire skills, knowledge, and attitudes relevant to their functioning as consumers in the marketplace."[58] Understanding how children are socialized into consumers is important to marketing managers for several reasons. First, knowledge of the factors influencing consumer socialization can provide information that may be useful in designing marketing communications. In American society children are potent consumers. It is estimated that *children under 12 directly spend nearly $17 billion a year*.[59] Second, public policy decisions concerning the regulation of the marketing of products to children should be based on an understanding of the consumer socialization process. For example, even very young children—just over half of 3- to 6-year-olds—recognize Joe Camel and associate the character with cigarettes.[60]

Unfortunately, public policy officials can't always tell what will appeal to children. For instance, British regulations forbid the use of attractive people in cigarette advertising, so the Embassy Regal brand began using a bald-headed man in ads. He became a hit with British kids. As a spokesman for the Advertising Standards Authority noted wryly, "It was something we could never have foreseen. He was bald and ugly. He became a cult figure in his own right."[61]

A Model of Consumer Socialization
Figure 16-5 presents a simple model of consumer socialization,[62] showing that consumer socialization is based on three components: background factors, socialization agents, and learning mechanisms such as cognitive learning, operant conditioning, and modeling.

Socialization background factors include such variables as the consumer's socioeconomic status, sex, age, social class, and religious background. Socialization agents are those individuals directly involved with the consumer who have influence because of their frequency of contact, importance, or control over rewards and punishments given to the consumer. Examples of socialization agents are parents, brothers and sisters, peers, teachers, the media, and media personalities such as athletes, movie stars, and rock stars.

Researchers have explored the impact of socialization agents and background factors on consumer socialization. In an important early study that analyzed the factors of family, mass media, newspaper readership, school, peers, age, social class, and sex,[63] it was found that the family was crucial for teaching the individual the "rational" aspects of consumption. The amount of communication in the family about consumption was related to how

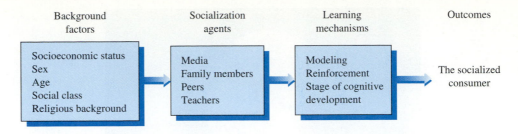

Background factors

| Socioeconomic status |
| Sex |
| Age |
| Social class |
| Religious background |

Socialization agents

| Media |
| Family members |
| Peers |
| Teachers |

Learning mechanisms

| Modeling |
| Reinforcement |
| Stage of cognitive development |

Outcomes

The socialized consumer

Figure 16-5
A model of consumer socialization.

often adolescent children performed socially desirable acts, such as giving to charities. This study also found that the amount of television viewing had a major impact on socialization. Greater television viewing was associated with learning the "expressive" aspects of consumption. Thus high television viewing seemed to encourage consumption for emotional reasons rather than for more rational reasons.

Peers were also found to be important socialization agents. They contributed particularly to the expressive motive, in which one buys for materialistic or social reasons (e.g., buying to "keep up with the neighbors"). For teenagers, buying to impress or be like others was clearly important. However, interaction among peers also was related to an increased awareness of goods and services in the marketplace. The school, on the other hand, had very little influence on the socialization process. For whatever reasons, formal consumer education in school was unrelated to measures of consumer socialization.

A current problem influencing childhood socialization in the United States is teenage pregnancy, which accounted for 12 percent of all births in 1995. "Baby Think It Over," shown in Figure 16-6, is the product of a rocket scientist intended to convince teenagers that having a baby isn't all fun.

Social scientists have long argued that what is learned early in life has an important and lasting effect on people. Particularly in the areas of criminology and psychiatry, theorists have noted that behaviors shown early in life tend to persist into adulthood. There is some evidence that consumption behaviors learned early in life also persist. For instance, brand loyalty may be transmitted from parents to offspring, and brands may be favored for 12 years or longer.[64]

Both parents and peers have a significant impact on product preferences. One study found that the influence of the nuclear family varies according to whether products are publically or privately consumed.[65] Publicly consumed products are those that are visible in use, such as clothing, jewelry, and automobiles, while privately consumed products are those that others do not see one using, such as a refrigerator, mattress, and toothpaste. The results showed that peers strongly influenced teenagers' preferences for public goods, but the nuclear family more strongly influenced their preferences for private goods. Evidence was found for the intergenerational transfer of brand loyalty from parents to children for privately consumed products.

Consumer Behavior Factoid

Question: What new methods are being tried to deal with teenage pregnancy?

Answer: Gem County, Idaho, may be taking the most direct approach. Unwed teenage mothers there have been charged with fornication, and the fathers with lewd and lascivious conduct, a felony.

Source: Quentin Hardy, "Idaho County Tests a New Way to Curb Teen Sex: Prosecute," *The Wall Street Journal*, July 8, 1996, pp. A1, A6.

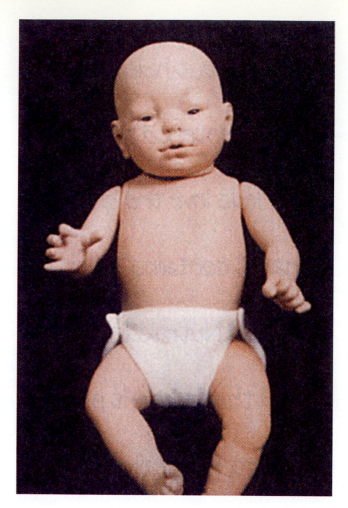

Figure 16-6

Baby Think It Over shrieks at random intervals day and night and has to be held for up to 30 minutes. An internal computer records how long the baby cried before being picked up and fed, and whether it was handled roughly.

In one summary of the findings on childhood socialization, the author noted that parents play an important role in childhood socialization, especially in providing information on the rational aspects of consumption.[66] However, the influence of parents is situation specific. Their impact varies across the stages of the decision process, across various types of products, and across various personal characteristics, such as age, socioeconomic class, and sex of the child. Finally, researchers have recently suggested that children's perceptions of their parents' life satisfaction and financial skills contribute strongly to their willingness to accept parents as consumption "role models." Where parents were perceived as unsuccessful or unskilled, children turned elsewhere for role models.[67]

A critical area of study concerns the impact of divorce and single parenthood on childhood consumer socialization.[68] Some authors have suggested that when there are major life changes, such as when parents divorce, a "teachable moment" occurs for consumers. At these moments perceptions, attitudes, and behaviors can undergo dramatic change,[69] and the impact may be positive or negative for the long-term ability of children to be effective consumers.

Socializing Parents Researchers have recognized that cognitive and social development continues throughout a person's life and that socialization is a reciprocal process within the family. Just as parents socialize children, children also socialize their parents. The information received by parents from their children about the marketplace does, to some degree, influence the adults' beliefs and feelings.[70]

Researchers have been interested in discovering the factors that affect children's influence on their parents.[71] One seems to be the type of family communication pattern. In socio-oriented homes, where controversies are not allowed to surface and children are forbidden to argue with their parents, there is, as might be expected, little parental socialization. In contrast, in concept-driven homes, where children are encouraged to develop their own ideas and communicate them to their parents, there is quite a bit of socialization of parents by children. Other factors that seem to influence parental socialization by children include family structure (more occurs in single-parent homes), socioeconomic status (more occurs in families of higher status), and the extent of the children's resources (more occurs when children earn income outside the home).

ORGANIZATIONAL BUYING BEHAVIOR

Just as individual consumers and families make purchases, so do organizations. Businesses, government agencies, and nonprofit organizations all buy things in order to produce goods and/or services. At the heart of the purchase process in organizations is the buying center. An **organizational buying center** is made up of those people in the organization who participate in the buying decision and who share the risks and goals of that decision.[72] Individuals within a business firm who frequently participate in a buying decision are managers, engineers, marketing personnel, accountants, and purchasing agents. Buying centers are not part of the firm's organizational structure, and their composition varies depending on the purchase situation. For example, physicians aren't involved in determining which floor cleaners to use in a hospital, but are very likely to be active when an expensive piece of diagnostic equipment is being considered.

Because buying centers are composed of people, the same behavioral factors (psychological, sociological, and anthropological) that impact consumers also affect the individuals who make up an organizational buying center. Just as different members of a family exert greater influence over certain purchases, so do members of a buying center use various strategies, such as promises or threats, to influence the final result.[73] However, since organizations differ from families in terms of mission and situational environment, there are major differences between the buying processes of the two types of groups. Table 16-6 compares and contrasts organizational and consumer buying across six dimensions. Notice that on the dimension of price, competitive bidding is used much more frequently in organizational buying than in consumer buying. If a family needs to purchase cooking oil, a member will simply go to a local grocery store and buy a brand at list price. When McDonald's buys cooking oil, the company takes competitive bids, provides detailed specifications for the good, develops long-term relationships with the suppliers, and involves management, R&D, and nutritionists in the decision. Exceptions do exist, however. For example, when purchasing automobiles, homes, and stereo components, consumers also frequently require competitive bids in the bargaining process.

Another difference is that organizational purchases are made in response to derived demand, while consumer purchases are thought to be the result of primary demand. But even here there are exceptions, since some consumer purchases are the result of derived demand. For example, consumers purchase flour, sugar, lumber, and many other products to make something else. And although consumers are often considered to be less "rational" in their

Organizational vs. Consumer Buying

Dimension	Business Purchasing	Consumer Purchasing
Product	More technical; greater quantities purchased; focus on services offered with product.	Less technical and more standardized; smaller quantities purchased.
Price	Frequent competitive bidding; list prices on standard items.	Generally buy on basis of list prices.
Promotion	Rely on information from sales personnel and trade magazines.	Relatively greater reliance on advertising.
Distribution	Short distribution channels; often purchased directly from manufacturers.	Longer distribution channels; most frequently purchase from retail stores or mail-order companies.
Customer relations	More enduring; complex focus on establishing relationships.	Often transaction-specific and quite simple; frequently no long-term relationship formed.
Buying decision process	Involvement of more people in organization with diverse sets of needs; use more structured decision-making process.	Fewer people involved in process; buying process frequently unstructured.

TABLE 16-6

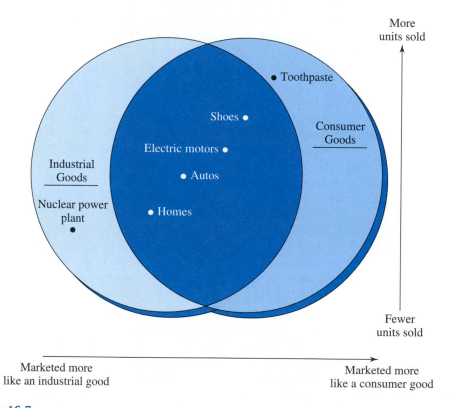

Figure 16-7

Industrial versus consumer goods marketing. (*Source:* Based on a discussion in Jagdish Sheth, "The Specificity of Industrial Marketing," *P.U. Management Review*, Vol. 2 [January–December 1979], pp. 53–56.)

purchases than organizations, they are actually quite systematic and "rational" at times, while organizations can be "irrational" and unsystematic. So the differences are mainly a matter of degree rather than dichotomous.

The relationship between organizational purchases and consumer buying behavior is depicted in Figure 16-7. The number of products bought by organizational buyers and consumers is shown on the vertical axis, and the types of products are shown on the horizontal axis. The intersecting circles suggest that the marketing mix is similar for many products, such as houses and autos sold to consumers and electrical motors sold to a corporation. Differences are found only at the extremes. The marketing mix for a consumer product such as toothpaste does not have a precise industrial counterpart, and purchasing a nuclear power plant certainly has no consumer equivalent. All in all, however, there are more similarities than differences between consumer and organizational purchasing.

Like consumers, organizational buyers move through a decision process that closely resembles the generic decision process we described in Chapter 11. Thus organizational buyers recognize problems, search for information, evaluate alternatives, make a choice, and finally engage in postacquisition processes. Also, as with consumers, the involvement level of organizational buyers differs depending upon the risk level of the purchase. Because of the great complexity of many organizational buying decisions, however, researchers have proposed a more elaborate set of decision stages for organizations. These buying stages are found in Table 16-7. Note that in comparison to consumer decision making, organizational decision making places a greater emphasis on (1) anticipating problems, (2) determining and describing the characteristics of the product needed, (3) qualifying potential suppliers, (4) obtaining and analyzing proposals, and (5) deciding how to make the order (i.e., how many items and over what time period).

When evaluating alternatives, organizational buyers compare the options on the basis of product attributes. Such factors as price, quality, service, continuity of service, and the relationship with the seller have been identified as key attributes on which buying centers evaluate alternatives.[74]

Organizational Buying Situations

Researchers have identified three fundamental task definitions for **organizational buying situations**.[75] In a "new-task" situation the organization is faced with making a purchase that it has not made before. Frequently, new-task situations involve a major high-risk purchase

---

Buying Stages of Organizations

Stage 1. Anticipation of a problem and/or recognition of a problem.

Stage 2. Identification of the characteristics and quantity of the needed product.

Stage 3. Development of a description of the characteristics and quantity of the product.

Stage 4. Search for and qualification of possible suppliers.

Stage 5. Acquisition of and the evaluation of alternate proposals.

Stage 6. Selection of suppliers based upon careful use of choice rules.

Stage 7. Selection and negotiation of how the order will be made.

Stage 8. Evaluation of the performance of the supplier.

Source: Based on Michael D. Hutt and Thomas W. Speh, *Business Marketing Management* (Fort Worth, TX: The Dryden Press, 1995), p. 68.

TABLE 16-7

that compels the organization to engage in extensive problem solving. An example would be a window shutter manufacturer that has decided to purchase large machines to sand the louvers in order to replace workers who have been doing the sanding by hand.

The "straight rebuy" occurs when a company has had long experience with a particular product and thus needs little or no new information to buy it. Frequently, companies develop extensive procedures for making such routinized purchases, and purchasing agents simply follow these procedures.

The "modified rebuy" falls in between the new task and the straight rebuy situations. In this instance the organizational buyer recognizes that benefits could be derived from reevaluating alternatives. In a modified rebuy suppliers will engage in extensive personal selling efforts to influence purchasing agents.[76]

Another important situational variable that heavily impacts organizational buying is time. Increasingly, companies throughout the world are employing just-in-time purchasing practices. In **just-in-time**, or **JIT**, **purchasing**, the organization attempts to have parts and materials delivered to the production process just at the moment they are needed. Developed by Toyota Motor Company, the JIT system has a number of advantages, including reducing waste, lowering the costs of maintaining inventory, improving product quality, and responding very quickly to changes in consumers' needs.[77] The JIT approach to purchasing is closely related to the *total quality management* programs discussed in Chapter 13. The three goals of reducing inventory to the minimal amount possible, of getting close to customers, and of continually improving the quality of products requires that companies develop extremely good relationships with their suppliers.

Building Relationships in Organizational Buying

Perhaps the most discussed concept in the field of marketing in the 1990s is relationship marketing. **Relationship marketing** refers to the overt attempt of exchange partners to build a long-term association characterized by purposeful cooperation and mutual dependence and the development of social, as well as structural, bonds. In sum, when relationships are formed, the parties join together (either formally or informally) so that they share to some degree the gains and/or losses that occur in their business operations.[78] Marketing relationships exist along a continuum from simple, one-time transactions to fully integrated hierarchical firms. Table 16-8 diagrams and defines the seven types of marketing relationships.

The move to relationship marketing by companies in the United States and Canada was spurred by Japanese competition. The success of Japanese corporations with just-in-time systems and their dramatic improvements in product quality necessitated dramatic changes in North American business practices. Without strong mutual cooperation with suppliers, American firms could not hope to implement JIT systems or to achieve the quality levels required to compete against the Japanese in the domestic and world markets. The quality management systems earlier adopted by manufacturers have been applied in recent years to service organizations, such as hospitals, banks, and even universities.

The newest form of relationship marketing in American corporation is the network structure.[79] Similar to the Japanese *keiretsu*, these complex groupings of firms have interlinked ownership and exchange relations. While they possess no formal organization, they are characterized by mutual interdependence and long-term stability. Such networks of firms create a situation in which high levels of mutual trust can be formed.

Given this important trend to form relationships in marketing, organizational buying centers have had to learn to respond appropriately. In many respects the resulting relationships resemble marriages. Like marriages, organizational relationships move through a series of stages: (1) awareness of the other, (2) exploration, (3) expansion, (4) commitment, and (5) dissolution.[80] Like partners in a marriage, managers and suppliers must rec-

The Continuum of Marketing Relationships

Pure Transaction End of Continuum

Relationship Continuum

1.	Transaction	One-time exchange.
2.	Repeated transactions	Frequently a contractual arrangement; transactions that are characterized as being quite formal and done at "arm's length."
3.	Long-term relationship	Engaging in repetitive transactions over time, though adversarial relationships still dominate. However, goals of firms are interrelated and interdependence is recognized. Competitive bidding is used on prices.
4.	Buyer-seller partnership	The recognition of mutual dependence. Each partner approaches total dependence upon the other. Mutual trust is strong. Prices are determined by negotiation rather than competitive bidding.
5.	Strategic alliance	A relationship that emerges when one or more functions between organizations are combined (such as R&D or manufacturing) so that both firms commit resources to reach a joint goal. A joint venture to produce a new product illustrates the strategic alliance.
6.	Network organizations	An organization that has developed multiple relationships (including partnerships, strategic alliances, and long-term relationships) with several other firms.
7.	Vertical integration	A number of organizations formally combined to create a new, larger company.

Fully Integrated Hierarchical Organization End of Continuum

Source: Based on Frederick E. Webster, Jr., "The Changing Role of Marketing in the Corporation," *Journal of Marketing*, Vol. 56 (October 1992), pp. 1–17.

TABLE 16-8

ognize the need for give-and-take. Similarly, the sales force must be willing to adjust rapidly to the changing needs of its customers. Again as in marriages, the dissolution phase is much more difficult than in traditional contractual exchanges.[81] Finally, managers should be aware that the development of buyer-seller partnerships and strategic alliances can create antitrust and ethical problems. This is an area in which the law is still evolving, and managers must try to keep up with it to avert legal difficulties.[82]

The two critical elements for building a long-term marketing relationship are trust and commitment. **Relationship trust** is "a willingness to rely on an exchange partner in whom one has confidence."[83] In order to develop trust in a relationship, the members must reveal vulnerability to each other. They must also learn to entrust control of important resources to the other member of the exchange. Crucially, the exchange members must rely on each other to fulfill their obligations in the exchange. Where there are high levels of trust, the exchange process is flexible, and bureaucratic and legal entanglements are minimized. The other critical element of a long-term marketing relationship, **commitment**, is the belief by an exchange partner that the relationship with the other "is so important as to warrant maximum efforts at maintaining it."[84]

The purchase of market research information is one arena in which trust between organizational buyers and sellers is critical. Because market research information is used to develop new products and evaluate market strategies, there must be a high level of relationship trust between the market research firm and the buying firm. Investigators have identified the factors that predict high levels of trust in market research relationships.[85]

Research integrity is the single most important factor in predicting the level of the purchasing firm's trust. Here integrity refers to setting high standards and to maintaining objectivity throughout the research process. Other important predictors of trust were: (1) willingness to explain the results, (2) maintaining the confidentiality of the results, (3) expertise, (4) tactfulness, (5) sincerity, (6) congeniality, and (7) timeliness.

The Role of Organizational Culture

Organizational culture refers to the shared values and beliefs that enable members to understand their roles and the norms of the organization.[86] An organization's culture influences interorganizational communications, relationships, and decision-making patterns.

A recent review of the literature identified six dimensions on which organizational cultures can be distinguished.[87] Listed and defined in Table 16-9, the six dimensions are: (1) market-driven (external) versus customer-driven (internal); (2) task versus social focus; (3) conformity versus individuality; (4) safety versus risk focus; (5) intuitive versus planning focus; and (6) adaptable versus rigid. When two firms develop a relational buying exchange like that found in a network structure, it is important that there be some degree of match across these six dimensions. Numerous examples exist of partnerships and alliances collapsing because of culture clashes between the two firms. When Imagination Pilots, Inc.,

Six Dimensions of Organizational Cultures

1. *External vs. internal emphasis.* Focus on satisfying customers/clients (market driven) in contrast to an accent on internal organization activities and product-driven orientation.

2. *Task vs. social focus.* Focus on efficiency in reaching organizational activities as compared to fulfilling social needs of members of groups.

3. *Conformity vs. individuality.* Focus on maintaining similarity in work habits, dress, and personal life versus tolerance for individual differences and idiosyncrasies.

4. *Safety vs. risk.* Focus on conservative decision making and slow adoption of new practices versus desire to pioneer new products and give executives autonomy.

5. *Intuitive vs. planning.* Tendency to employ ad hoc solutions and intuition and to place low reliance on numbers and forecasts versus use of mathematical modeling, economic analysis, and elaborate planning.

6. *Adaptable vs. rigid.* Focus on innovation, change, and cultural flexibility versus maintaining the status quo.

Source: Based on John W. Barnes and Edwin R. Stafford, "Strategic Alliance Partner Selection: When Organizational Cultures Clash," in *Enhancing Knowledge Development in Marketing*, Vol. 4, David W. Cravens and Peter R. Dickson, eds. (Chicago: American Marketing Association, 1993), pp. 424–433.

TABLE 16-9

a small developer of interactive CD-ROM games, formed alliances with three larger firms to fund development, distribution, and marketing, the alliances began to founder within a year. The last partnership, with Time Warner, ran into trouble because Time Warner's own multimedia operations were split between the music group in New York and the studio operations in California. Both groups were pursuing their own multimedia activities, and the venture with Imagination Pilots fell thorough the cracks.[88]

Although our discussion of relationships has concentrated on organizational buying, the concepts we have described are also relevant to consumer behavior. For example, the establishment of a relationship with a supplier allows both the individual consumer and the organizational buyer to reduce the costs of search. That is why consumers often purchase the same goods repeatedly from the same store. Brand loyalty likewise can be considered a form of relationship behavior. The idea that many consumers prefer to reduce their choices by engaging in an ongoing loyalty relationship with marketers has been called the "fundamental axiom of relationship marketing."[89] It should be noted that this view is controversial,[90] since when consumers enter a relationship (e.g., by signing up for American Airlines' Frequent Flyer program), they often actually *increase* their choices—first, by developing relationships with several competing airlines; and second, by increasing the information flow from each airline so that they are aware of more, rather than fewer, choices.

A Managerial Applications Analysis of the Child-Care Case

The introductory case discussed the difficulties working parents have in juggling successful careers with their parental responsibilities. Analyzing the problems of parental stress among dual-career couples requires the use of many of the concepts identified in the chapter.

Problem Identification

A key issue for dual-income families is how to arrange for child care. From the child-care provider's standpoint, there are a number of associated opportunities and difficulties.

The Consumer Behavior Analysis and Its Managerial Implications

Three concepts introduced in the chapter have particular relevance to the case of the dual-career couple: household demographics, family role structure, and family decision making. Table 16-10 summarizes these concepts and their managerial implications.

Household Demographics The demographics of households suggest that the problem of parental stress is potentially quite large. Women are increasingly pursuing careers, and men will inevitably have to perform more household duties. An *American Demographics* article noted that in 1985 women spent 7.5 fewer hours per week doing housework than in 1965. In contrast, during the same time period, men spent 5.2 more hours per week doing housework.[91] These trends will have a major impact on how companies promote services and products. In addition, the trend for mothers of young children to work outside the home has created an acute demand for child-care services.

Obtaining high-quality child care is probably the greatest single problem for two-career families. Corporations such as KinderCare Learning Center have recognized the importance to parents of providing their offspring with an excellent child-care environment where the children are happy and learning something. The ad shown in Figure 16-8 effectively communicates to parents the idea that their child will be in a rich environment for learning while at a KinderCare facility.

As a part of their environmental analysis, managers should be on the alert for changes in the number of consumers with children, the number of working mothers, and the number of men who have increased child-care responsibilities. These trends have strong implications for identifying segments of consumers with child-care needs. If the segments are large enough and have sufficient buying power, and if they can be reached, they can

Figure 16-8

KinderCare emphasizes the learning opportunities provided in their child care environment.

be targeted via the development of new products. In addition, promotional strategy can be geared to reaching these segments.

Family Role Structure As women have moved into the full-time work force, they have taken on more and more external roles. In these circumstances role overload is becoming a severe problem for both spouses, but particularly for mothers. In fact, there are increasing time pressures on the entire family. These trends suggest that companies should position products and services for the family experiencing role overload. Of course, environmental analysis would be used to monitor societal changes that influence the extent to which family role structures are changing.

Family Decision Making Contempory families are characterized by more shared decision making. This opens up new opportunities for companies willing to target their marketing strategies to women who have assumed decision-making responsibilities within the family. For example, insurance companies are now targeting working wives with their products. Marketing managers should do research to determine the family decision-making process for their firm's goods or services. Because of changes in role structure and demographic patterns, women are making more decisions for their families—or at least increasingly participating in syncratic decisions. These women represent a market segment to which existing products can be positioned. Likewise, new products might be developed and promoted specifically for such women.

Managerial Recommendations

Three recommendations emerge from our analysis of this case.

Recommendation 1 Do frequent demographic analysis to keep track of changing household patterns. The rise in the number of dual-career families and single-parent households means there are increased opportunities for firms offering child-care services.

Recommendation 2 Position products and services to accommodate the needs of the family groaning under role overload. Continual environmental analysis will be required to assess whether these needs are changing over time.

Recommendation 3 Frame promotions to appeal to the actual decision makers and the actual decision process. Because of the increasing role of the husband in running the household, it will be necessary for marketers to reassess the man's influence in various household decisions.

SUMMARY

Households and organizations are the two basic consumption units. A household consists of all those people living together under one roof. They may or may not be related. Two important types of families are the nuclear family, consisting of husband and wife and their offspring, and the extended family, consisting of the nuclear family plus grandparents or other kinfolk. Tracking the demographics of families and households is important for marketers. Such factors as family size, age at marriage, the divorce rate, and the number of employed women and men all affect family purchase patterns.

Within organizations, buying centers make purchase decisions. A buying center is composed of two or more people who make the procurement decisions for a group. One of the most important similarities between household buying and organizational buying is that both groups have a similar set of roles such as influencers, gatekeepers, deciders, buyers, and users. Family buying differs from organizational buying along several dimensions, however. Families are characterized by more permanent relationships, closer personal ties, and greater cooperation.

The family life cycle is an important idea in marketing. Families are often viewed as moving through a series of stages. As the parents grow older and the children grow up and leave, the family's purchase patterns change. Marketers need to track the number of households in various stages of the family life cycle and project how the distribution may change in the future. For example, as the number of young, single individuals declines, manufacturers of motorcycles may experience problems. Not only will total demand for cycles decrease, but the features desired on a bike will also change. It should be noted that income differences change along with the family life cycle, so many of the changes in consumption patterns may be explained by income differences that occur between the life cycle stages.

Decisions within the family can be classified into four different categories: wife-dominated, husband-dominated, autonomic, and syncratic. These categories refer to the extent to which the husband and wife act independently in making purchases. Research has shown that decision making tends to be increasingly shared as the decision stage moves from problem recognition to search to purchase. Marketers should not forget children. For purchase decisions on certain types of products and services, children have high input.

Another factor that influences family decision making is how power is shared within a family and how conflicts are resolved. Power depends on various factors, including economic means, cultural definitions, and degree of interpersonal dependence. Different people use different techniques to resolve conflicts and achieve desired outcomes. Some employ emotional appeals; others, rewards or bargaining. One important function of the family that should not be overlooked by marketers is its role in the consumer socialization of children. This learning takes place within the context of background factors like social class, religious affiliation, and socioeconomic status. In addition, the process is influenced by socialization agents such as the media, family members, peers, and teachers.

An understanding of the functioning of the family can assist managers in several ways. Tracking demographic and life cycle changes can pay off through finding marketing opportunities and avoiding marketing mistakes. Understanding the family decision process is important for designing the marketing mix. Markets may be segmented and products differentiated on the basis of the family life cycle. Consumer-goods companies need to do continual marketing research to gather information that can be used for segmentation, positioning/differentiation, and promotional strategy. Finally, knowledge of consumer socialization may help managers anticipate changes in the consumer regulatory environment.

Organizations make purchase decisions through organizational buying centers, which are composed of those people in the organization who participate in the buying decision and who share the risks and goals of that decision. Organizational and consumer decision making share many similarities, though organizations put greater emphasis on anticipating problems, qualifying suppliers, and analyzing proposals. Three basic organizational buying situations were identified: the new task, the modified rebuy, and the straight rebuy.

A focus on total quality management has led organizations to stress just-in-time purchasing, in which supplies are obtained just prior to when they are needed in production. In order to implement JIT systems, it is crucial to build close relationships with suppliers. Relationship marketing was defined as the overt attempt of exchange partners to build long-term associations characterized by purposeful cooperation, mutual dependence, and close structural bonds. Particularly important is the building of mutual trust, or a willingness to rely on an exchange partner. Organizational culture refers to the shared values and beliefs that enable members to understand the norms of the organization and their own roles in it. When the cultures of organizations clash, it is difficult for firms to develop the trust and commitment essential to a lasting relationship.

Bem sex-role inventory
childhood consumer
    socialization
commitment
detached nuclear family
extended family

family decision stage
family life cycle
household
just-in-time purchasing
nuclear family
organizational buying center

organizational buying
    situations
organizational culture
relationship marketing
relationship trust
role overload

socialization agent
socialization background
    factors

REVIEW QUESTIONS

1. How do families differ from other types of groups?

2. What types of purchase roles are found in most groups?

3. Differentiate the terms *household* and *family*. Identify three different types of families.

4. Identify three key demographic changes in households expected to occur between 1990 and 2000.

5. Identify three major trends in household demographics that have taken place over the past 20 years.

6. Identify the 11 stages of the family life cycle presented in this chapter.

7. How do people's consumption patterns change as they move through the stages of the family life cycle?

8. Identify and briefly discuss four types of purchase roles that exist within families.

9. Four role-specialization dimensions regarding family decision making were described in this chapter. Identify these dimensions and indicate possible purchases that would fall within each dimension.

10. Researchers have investigated the steps families take in purchasing both furniture and automobiles. What decision steps are common to both types of purchases?

11. What factors affect the extent of influence a family member wields?

12. Children have an important influence on family decision making. What are the major types of decisions on which children influence their parents?

13. Draw the diagram of consumer socialization presented in the text.

14. What factors influence the socialization of parents by their children?

15. Define an organizational buying center.

16. What are the dimensions on which organizational buying differs from consumer buying?

17. What are the three types of organizational buying situations?

18. Identify the seven stages of the continuum of marketing relationships.

DISCUSSION QUESTIONS

1. Consider the changes in U.S. household size over the past 25 years. How have these changes influenced the automobile industry and the housing industry?

2. Ask two female friends and two male friends what they think is the proper age for marriage. How do these ages match the average age at which couples got married in the 1960s and in the 1990s? What do you think will be the trend in age at first marriage over the next ten years?

3. How are the sizes of the various life-cycle stages discussed in the chapter likely to change over the next ten years? What industries are likely to reap positive effects from these changes? What industries are likely to experience problems?

4. Think about your own family. Which individuals in your family have the roles of gatekeeper, influencer, decider, buyer, and user? To what extent do these roles change

across different product categories? Now think about a nonhousehold organization to which you belong (e.g., a fraternity, sorority, or dorm group). Which individuals have these same buying roles in this organization?

5. Identify what you see as husband-dominated, wife-dominated, autonomic, and syncratic purchases for middle-class Americans today.

6. It is interesting to study how mothers and fathers react to the requests of their children in a grocery store. Go to a grocery store and eavesdrop on two parent-child interactions. What type of requests does the child make? How do the parents handle the requests? To what extent do these requests seem to result from the influence of advertising?

7. Consider who influences whom for buying decisions in your own family. Who tends to hold the most influence?

To what extent does the influence change across situations? Why are the influence relationships arranged as they are?

8. In several criminal court cases the defense has argued that the defendant should be found innocent of a crime because he was influenced to commit the crime by television. To what extent do you think that television is a socialization agent of children? To what extent do you believe that television can cause people to commit antisocial acts without recognizing the gravity of their behavior?

9. Compare the brands of products that you prefer to those your parents prefer. To what extent do your preferences coincide? To what extent do you attribute these similar preferences to the socialization process?

10. The decision of how many children to have is an important one. What are the factors that you think you will consider, or that you are now considering, relevant to having children? To what extent do you personally believe that consumer researchers should view children as a "consumption item"?

11. The view of trust developed within the context of organizational buying can be compared with that in the communications literature. In Chapter 10 on persuasive communications we discussed source credibility. From the perspective of communications researchers, source credibility is composed of two factors—expertise and trust. In contrast, those studying organizational buying view trust as composed of integrity and expertise (as well as other variables). Future research is required to untangle this inconsistent use of terminology. Is it possible that the organizational buying researchers have simply replaced the word *credibility* with the word *trust*, and in like manner they are using the word *integrity* in the same manner as the communication researchers use the word *trust*?

12. Consider the relationships that you have formed with various exchange partners, whether in "buying" or in other types of relationships (e.g., friendships, dating). Provide examples of relationships you have that match each of the seven types of marketing relationships depicted in Table 16-8.

E N D N O T E S

1. The example is based on Fern Schumer Chapman, "Executive Guilt: Who's Taking Care of the Children?" *Fortune*, February 16, 1987, pp. 30–37.

2. Ibid.

3. William Goodman, "Boom in Day Care the Result of Many Changes," *Monthly Labor Review*, Vol. 188 (August 1995), pp. 3–12.

4. Chapman, "Executive Guilt."

5. Harry L. Davis, "Decision Making Within the Household," in *Selected Aspects of Consumer Behavior: A Summary from the Perspective of Different Disciplines* (Washington, DC: National Science Foundation, 1977), pp. 73–97.

6. Jong Hee Park, Patriya S. Tansuhaj, and Richard H. Kolbe, "The Role of Love, Affection, and Intimacy in Family Decision Research," in *Advances in Consumer Research*, Rebecca H. Holman and Michael R. Solomon, eds. (Provo, UT: Association for Consumer Research, 1991), pp. 651–656.

7. Clare Ansberry, "Nannies and Mothers Struggle Over Roles in Raising Children," *The Wall Street Journal*, May 21, 1993, pp. 1, 6.

8. Christina Duff, "Big Stores' Outlandish Demands Alienate Small Suppliers," *The Wall Street Journal*, October 27, 1995, pp. B1, B5.

9. Gerald Zaltman and Melanie Wallendorf, *Consumer Behavior: Basic Findings and Managerial Implications*, (New York: John Wiley & Sons, 1983), p. 168.

10. The Editors, "The Future of Households," *American Demographics*, December 1993, pp. 27–40.

11. U.S. Bureau of the Census, *Statistical Abstract*, various years.

12. U.S. Bureau of the Census, *Current Population Surveys*, 1991.

13. James Wetzel, "American Families: 75 Years of Change," *Monthly Labor Review*, March 1990, pp. 4–13.

14. *Statistical Abstract of the United States, 1995*, Item 59, p. 55.

15. Ibid., Item 71, p. 61.

16. Ibid., Item 149, p. 105.

17. Ibid., Item 737, p. 477.

18. Rose M. Rubin, Bobye J. Riney, and David J. Molina, "Expenditure Pattern Differentials Between One-Earner and Dual-Earner Households: 1972–1973 and 1984," *Journal of Consumer Research*, Vol. 17, June 1990, pp. 43–52.

19. June Fletcher, "When Buying a House, Who Needs a Man?" *The Wall Street Journal*, February 9, 1996, p. B10.

20. Robert E. Wilkes, "Household Life-Cycle Stages, Transitions, and Product Expenditures," *Journal of Consumer Research*, Vol. 22 (June 1995), pp. 27–42; and Charles M. Schaninger and William D. Danko, "A Conceptual and Empirical Comparison of Alternative Household Life Cycle Models," *Journal of Con-*

sumer Research, Vol. 19 (March 1993), pp. 580–594.

21. Douglas P. Handler, "Get Ready for More of the Same," *Supermarket Business*, March 1995, pp. 24–29.

22. Janet Wagner and Sherman Hanna, "The Effectiveness of Family Life Cycle Variables in Consumer Expenditure Research," *Journal of Consumer Research*, Vol. 10, December 1983, pp. 281–291.

23. Wilkes, "Household Life-Cycle Stages, Transitions, and Product Expenditures."

24. Callmetta Y. Coleman, "Mail Order Is Turning into Male Order," *The Wall Street Journal*, March 26, 1996, p. A6.

25. Michael Reilly, "Working Wives and Convenience Consumption," *Journal of Consumer Research*, Vol. 8 (March 1982), pp. 407–418.

26. Ellen Foxman and Alvin Burns, "Role Load in the Household," in *Advances in Consumer Research*, Vol. 14, Melanie Wallendorf and Paul Anderson, eds. (Provo, UT: Association for Consumer Research, 1987), pp. 458–462.

27. Sharon Nickols and Karen Fox, "Buying Time and Saving Time: Strategies for Managing Household Production," *Journal of Consumer Research*, Vol. 10 (September 1983), pp. 197–208.

28. R. S. Oropesa, "Female Labor Force Participation and Time-Saving Household Technology: A Case Study of the Microwave Oven from 1978 to 1989," *Journal of Consumer Research*, Vol. 19 (March 1993), pp. 567–579.

29. W. Keith Bryant, "Durables and Wives' Employment Yet Again," *Journal of Consumer Research*, Vol. 15 (June 1988), pp. 37–47.

30. Judith J. Madill-Marshall, Louise Heslop, and Linda Duxbury, "Coping with Household Stress in the 1990s: Who

Uses 'Convenience Foods' and Do They Help?" in *Advances in Consumer Research*, Vol. 22, Frank R. Kardes and Mita Sujan, eds. (Provo, UT: Association for Consumer Research, 1995), pp. 729–734.

31. Robert Boutilier, "Pulling the Family's Strings," *American Demographics*, August 1993, pp. 44–48.

32. Harry L. Davis and Benny P. Rigaux, "Perception of Marital Roles in Decision Processes," *Journal of Consumer Research*, Vol. 1 (June 1974), pp. 51–62.

33. Alvin Burns, "Husband and Wife Purchase Decision-Making Roles: Agreed, Presumed, Conceded, and Disputed," in *Advances in Consumer Research*, Vol. 4, William Perreault, ed. (Atlanta, GA: Association for Consumer Research, 1977), pp. 50–55.

34. Ibid.

35. Elizabeth Moore-Shay and William Wilkie, "Recent Developments in Research on Family Decisions," in *Advances in Consumer Research*, Vol. 15, Michael Houston, ed. (Provo, UT: Association for Consumer Research, 1988), pp. 454–460. Also see Alvin Burns and Jo Anne Hopper, "An Analysis of the Presence, Stability, and Antecedents of Husband and Wife Purchase Decision Making Influence Assessment Agreement and Disagreement," in *Advances in Consumer Research*, Vol. 13, Richard Lutz, ed. (Provo, UT: Association for Consumer Research, 1986), pp. 175–180.

36. Michael B. Menasco and David J. Curry, "Utility and Choice: An Empirical Study of Wife/Husband Decision Making," *Journal of Consumer Research*, Vol. 16 (June 1989), pp. 87–97.

37. William J. Qualls and Francoise Jaffe, "Measuring Conflict in Household Decision Behavior:

Read My Lips and Read My Mind," *Advances in Consumer Research*, John F. Sherry Jr. and Brian J. Sternthal, eds. (Provo, UT: Association for Consumer Research, 1993), pp. 522–531.

38. Davis and Rigaux, "Perception of Marital Roles."

39. A. Shuptrine and G. Samuelson, "Dimensions of Marital Roles in Consumer Decision Making: Revisited," *Journal of Marketing Research*, Vol. 13 (February 1976), pp. 87–91.

40. William Qualls, "Household Decision Behavior: The Impact of Husbands' and Wives' Sex Role Orientation," *Journal of Consumer Research*, Vol. 14 (September 1987), pp. 264–279.

41. Sandra Bem, "The Measurement of Psychological Androgyny," *Journal of Consulting and Clinical Psychology*, Vol. 42 (1974), pp. 155–162.

42. Qualls, "Household Decision Behavior."

43. Giovanna Imperia, Thomas O'Guinn, and Elizabeth MacAdams, "Family Decision Making Role Perceptions Among Mexican-American and Anglo Wives: A Cross Cultural Comparison," in *Advances in Consumer Research*, Vol. 12, Elizabeth Hirschman and Morris Holbrook, eds. (Provo, UT: Association for Consumer Research, 1985), pp. 71–74. A second study shows that as Mexican-American families assimilate and identification with the parent Hispanic culture declines, the role of the husband becomes less dominant. See Cynthia Webster, "Effects of Hispanic Ethnic Identification on Marital Roles in the Purchase Decision Process," *Journal of Consumer Research*, Vol. 21 (September 1994), pp. 319–331.

44. For information on conflict in the family, see William Qualls,

"Toward Understanding the Dynamics of Household Decision Conflict Behavior," in *Advances in Consumer Research*, Vol. 15, Michael Houston, ed. (Provo, UT: Association for Consumer Research, 1988), pp. 442–448; Margaret Nelson, "The Resolution of Conflict in Joint Purchase Decisions by Husbands and Wives: A Review and Empirical Test," in *Advances in Consumer Research*, Vol. 15, Michael Houston, ed. (Provo, UT: Association for Consumer Research, 1988), pp. 436–444; and Rosann L. Spiro, "Persuasion in Family Decision Making," *Journal of Consumer Research*, Vol. 9 (March 1983), pp. 393–402.

45. Cynthia Webster and Samantha Rice, "Equity Theory and the Power Structure in a Marital Relationship," in *Advances in Consumer Research*, Vol. 23, Kim P. Corfman and John G. Lynch, Jr., eds. (Provo, UT: Association for Consumer Research, 1996), pp. 491–497.

46. For a general review and critique of the literature on children's influence on purchase decisions, see Tamara F. Mangleburg, "Children's Influence in Purchase Decisions: A Review and Critique," *Advances in Consumer Research*, Vol. 17, Marvin E. Goldberg, Gerald Gorn, and Richard W. Pollay, eds. (Provo, UT: Association for Consumer Research, 1990), pp. 813–825.

47. Amardeep Assar and George S. Bobinski, Jr., "Financial Decision Making of Babyboomer Couples," *Advances in Consumer Research*, Vol. 17, Rebecca H. Holman and Michael R. Solomon, eds. (Provo, UT: Association for Consumer Research, 1991), pp. 657–665.

48. Pierre Filiatrault and J. R. Brent Richie, "Joint Purchasing Decisions: A Comparison of Influence Structure in Family and Couple Decision-Making Units," *Journal of Consumer Research*, Vol. 7 (September 1980), pp. 131–140.

49. Scott Ward and Daniel Wackman, "Children's Purchase Influence Attempts and Parental Yielding," *Journal of Marketing Research*, Vol. 9 (August 1972), pp. 316–319.

50. For a review of this literature, see Charles K. Atkin, "Observations of Parent-Child Interaction in Supermarket Decision Making," *Journal of Marketing*, Vol. 42 (October 1978), pp. 42–45.

51. Kenneth Bahn, "Do Mothers and Children Share Cereal and Beverage Preferences and Evaluative Criteria?" in *Advances in Consumer Research*, Vol. 14, Melanie Wallendorf and Paul Anderson, eds. (Provo, UT: Association for Consumer Research, 1987), p. 281.

52. Atkin, "Observations of Parent-Child Interaction."

53. George Moschis and Linda Mitchell, "Television Advertising and Interpersonal Participation in Family Consumer Decisions," in *Advances in Consumer Research*, Vol. 13, Richard Lutz, ed. (Provo, UT: Association for Consumer Research, 1986), pp. 181–185.

54. Ellen Foxman and Patriya S. Tansuhaj, "Adolescents' and Mothers' Perceptions of Relative Influence in Family Purchase Decisions: Patterns of Agreement and Disagreement," in *Advances in Consumer Research*, Vol. 15, Michael Houston, ed. (Provo, UT: Association for Consumer Research, 1988), pp. 449–453.

55. Ellen R. Foxman, Patriya S. Tansuhaj, and Karin M. Ekstrom, "Family Members' Perceptions of Adolescents' Influence in Family Decision Making," *Journal of Consumer Research*, Vol. 15 (March 1989), pp. 482–491.

56. For an overview of current research on consumer socialization, see Scott Ward, Donna M. Klees, and Daniel B. Wackman, "Consumer Socialization Research: Content Analysis of Post–1980 Studies, and Some Implications for Future Work," in *Advances in Consumer Research*, Vol. 17, Rebecca H. Holman and Michael R. Solomon, eds. (Provo, UT: Association for Consumer Research, 1991), pp. 798–803.

57. David A. Goslin, "The Nature of Socialization," in *Handbook of Socialization Theory and Research*, D. A. Goslin, ed. (Chicago: Rand-McNally, 1969).

58. Scott Ward, "Consumer Socialization," *Journal of Consumer Research*, Vol. 1 (September 1974), pp. 1–14.

59. Omar L. Gallaga, "Singing About School and Grades, Sextet Wows the Kool-Aid Crowd," *The Wall Street Journal*, June 11, 1996, p. B1.

60. Richard Mizerski, "The Relationship Between Cartoon Trade Character Recognition and Attitude Toward Product Category in Young Children," *Journal of Marketing*, Vol. 59 (October 1995), pp. 58–70.

61. Tara Parker-Pope, "Tough Tobacco-Ad Rules Light Creative Fires," *The Wall Street Journal*, October 9, 1996, pp. B1, B6.

62. Various authors have developed models of the socialization process; see Gilbert A. Churchill and George Moschis, "Television and Interpersonal Influences on Adolescent Consumer Learning," *Journal of Consumer Research*, Vol. 6 (June 1979), pp. 23–35.

63. George Moschis and Roy Moore, "Decision Making Among the Young: A Socialization Perspective," *Journal of Consumer Research*, Vol. 6 (September 1979), pp. 101–112.

64. L. Guest, "Brand Loyalty—Twelve Years Later," *Journal of Applied Psychology*, Vol. 39 (December 1955), pp. 405–408.

65. Terry Childers and Akshay R. Rao, "The Influence of Familial and Peer-Based Reference Groups on Consumer Decisions," *Journal of Consumer Research*, Vol. 19 (September 1992), pp. 198–211.

66. George P. Moschis, "The Role of Family Communication in Consumer Socialization of Children and Adolescents," *Journal of Consumer Research*, Vol. 11 (March 1985), pp. 898–913.

67. Elizabeth S. Moore-Shay and Britto M. Berchmans, "The Role of the Family Environment in the Development of Shared Consumption Values: An Intergenerational Study," *Advances in Consumer Research*, Vol. 23, Kim P. Corfman and John G. Lynch, Jr., eds. (Provo, UT: Association for Consumer Research, 1996), pp. 484–490.

68. Ritha Fellerman and Kathleen Debevec, "Till Death Do We Part: Family Dissolution, Transition, and Consumer Behavior," *Advances in Consumer Research*, John F. Sherry, Jr. and Brian Sternthal, eds. (Provo, UT: Association for Consumer Research, 1992), pp. 514–521; and Aric Rindfleisch, James E. Burroughs, and Frank Denton, "Family Disruption and Consumer Attitudes and Behavior: An Exploratory Investigation," *Advances in Consumer Research*, Vol. 23, Kim P. Corfman and John G. Lynch, Jr., eds. (Provo, UT: Association for Consumer Research, 1996), pp. 83–90.

69. Alan R. Andreasen, "Life Status Changes and Changes in Consumer Preferences and Satisfaction," *Journal of Consumer Research*, Vol. 11 (December 1984), pp. 784–794.

70. Orville Brim, "Adult Socialization," in *Socialization and Society*, J. Clausen, ed. (Boston: Little, Brown, 1968).

71. Karin Ekstrom, Patriya S. Tansuhaj, and Ellen Foxman, "Children's Influence in Family Decisions and Consumer Socialization: A Reciprocal View," in *Advances in Consumer Research*, Vol. 14, Melanie Wallendorf and Paul Anderson, eds. (Provo, UT: Association for Consumer Research, 1987), pp. 283–287.

72. Michael D. Hutt and Thomas W. Speh, *Business Marketing Management* (Fort Worth, TX: The Dryden Press, 1992), p. 66.

73. R. Venkatesh, Ajay K. Kohli, and Gerald Zaltman, "Influence Strategies in Buying Centers," *Journal of Marketing*, Vol. 59 (October 1995), pp. 71–82.

74. Hutt and Speh, *Business Marketing Management*.

75. Erin Anderson, Wujin Chu, and Barton Weitz, "Industrial Purchasing: An Empirical Exploration of the Buyclass Framework," *Journal of Marketing*, Vol. 51 (July 1987), pp. 71–86.

76. For a more complex view of organizational buying situations, see Michele D. Bunn, "Taxonomy of Buying Decision Approaches," *Journal of Marketing*, Vol. 57 (January 1993), pp. 38–56.

77. Ernest Raia, "JIT in Purchasing: A Progress Report," *Purchasing*, Vol. 104 (February 23, 1989), p. 18. Also see Min Chen, *Asian Management Systems* (London: Routledge, 1995), pp. 201–202.

78. This definition of relationship marketing was developed by the first author of this text. Ideas for the definition were derived from Gregory T. Gundlach and Patrick E. Murphy, "Ethical and Legal Foundations of Relational Marketing Exchanges," *Journal of Marketing*, Vol. 57 (October 1993), pp. 35–46.

79. Frederick E. Webster, Jr., "The Changing Role of Marketing in the Corporation," *Journal of Marketing*, Vol. 58 (October 1992), pp. 1–17.

80. F. Robert Dwyer, Paul H. Schurr, and Sejo Oh, "Developing Buyer-Seller Relationships," *Journal of Marketing*, Vol. 51 (April 1987), pp. 11–27.

81. Jeffrey J. Stoltman, James W. Gentry, and Fred Morgan, "Marketing Relationships: Further Consideration of the Marriage Metaphor with Implications for Maintenance and Recovery," *Enhancing Knowledge Development in Marketing*, David Cravens and Peter Dickson, eds, AMA Educators' Proceedings (Chicago: American Marketing Association, 1993), pp. 28–35.

82. Gundlach and Murphy, "Ethical and Legal Foundations of Relationship Marketing Exchanges."

83. Christine Moorman, Gerald Zaltman, and Rohit Deshpande, "Relationships Between Providers and Users of Market Research: The Dynamics of Trust Within and Between Organizations," *Journal of Marketing Research*, Vol. 29 (August 1992), pp. 314–329.

84. Robert M. Morgan and Shelby D. Hunt, "The Commitment-Trust Theory of Relationship Marketing," *Journal of Marketing*, Vol. 58 (July 1994), pp. 2–38.

85. Christine Moorman, Rohit Deshpande, and Gerald Zaltman, "Factors Affecting Trust in Market Research Relationships," *Journal of Marketing*, Vol. 53 (January 1993), pp. 81–101.

86. Rohit Deshpande, John U. Farley, and Frederick E. Webster, Jr., "Corporate Culture, Customer Orientation, and Innovativeness in Japanese Firms: A Quadrad Analysis," *Journal of Marketing*, Vol. 53 (January 1993), pp. 23–37.

87. John W. Barnes and Edwin R. Stafford, "Strategic Alliance Partner Selection: When Organizational Cultures Clash," *Enhancing*

Knowledge Development in Marketing, Vol. 4, David W. Cravens and Peter R. Dickson, eds. (Chicago: American Marketing Association, 1993), pp. 424–433.

88. Michael Selz, "United We Fall," *The Wall Street Journal*, Small Business Supplement, May 23, 1996, pp. R8–R10.

89. Jagdish N. Sheth and Atul Parvatiyar, "Relationship Marketing in Consumer Markets: Antecedents and Consequences," *Journal of the Academy of Marketing Science*, Vol. 23 (Fall 1995), pp. 255–271.

90. Robert A. Peterson, "Relationship Marketing and the Consumer," *Journal of the Academy of Marketing Science*, Vol. 23 (Fall 1995), pp. 278–281.

91. John Robinson, "Who's Doing the Housework?" *American Demographics*, December 1988, pp. 24–28, 63.

Targeting the Family in the 1990s

Companies are recognizing that in marketing their goods and services they must appeal to children as well as to adults—in large part because in the United States children influence the spending of so much money. For example, H. J. Heinz discovered that children under 18 consume one-third more ketchup than adults do, and that they frequently choose the family brand. In response, the company created an ad in which a dark-haired self-confident high-school male impresses a pretty girl by performing the following feat. First, he places a Heinz ketchup bottle on its side on the edge of a roof. He then hurtles down several flights of stairs and buys a hot dog. Next he casually holds it out to catch the first drop of ketchup that has finally oozed from the bottle. A Heinz product manager said, "Our research shows that kids like the commercials because they aspire to be teenagers, and adults like them because they bring back memories of their youth." Heinz believes the ads added 2 percent to their sales volume.[1]

Similarly, executives at movie companies ask themselves how they can create a product that will attract adults as well as children to their films. If a movie company can attract mom and dad *and* the kids, the number of paid patrons will, on average, have doubled. A master at this dual marketing strategy is Disney Studios.

Disney's first direct attempt to target adults as well as children occurred in 1989 with the release of the animated movie *The Little Mermaid*. Disdaining the syrupy-sweet, air-headed heroines of old (e.g., Snow White and Cinderella), animators turned Ariel into a feisty, independent, impetuous young woman. In addition to having a body that would make Mattel's Barbie envious, Ariel possessed a talent (i.e., singing) that many modern parents attempt to instill in their children through endless lessons. In other words, Ariel appealed to fathers and mothers almost as much as she enthralled 6-year-old girls (or boys, for that matter).

Next Disney brought out *Beauty and the Beast*—another animated masterpiece. Promoting this movie even more directly to parents, Disney played up the idea that

some people viewed it as worthy of an Academy Award. Indeed, it initially opened at Cinema I on New York's East Side rather than at local neighborhood theaters, and at the evening shows adults outnumbered children by a ratio of 10 to 1. The company even created different poster art for adults and children. For the kids, there were cheery, vibrantly colorful posters that displayed the various animated characters in the movie. In the newspaper ads Disney appealed to adults with romantic artwork showing muted images of Beauty and the Beast dancing. Belle was the first Disney heroine to be extremely well read—which appealed to parents' desires to have literate kids.[2]

An advertisement run in the Sunday edition of *The New York Times* for the movie transparently depicts Disney's strategy. Quoting liberally from a review by Gene Siskel and Roger Ebert, the ad copy stated:

> One of the very finest films of all time. Two enthusiastic thumbs up, way up. It's a legitimate candidate for Oscar consideration for Best Picture. It's breathtaking. I liked it more than *The Little Mermaid*. Sophisticated and funny, romantic and scary, Disney's *Beauty and the Beast* is an instant classic. It's thrilling, and you don't have to bring a kid along to have fun.

Other recent Disney creations, like *The Lion King*, have employed the same types of dual appeals. Disney has also moved directly into adult-oriented services. The Disney Institute, a "Disneyland for grownups" near Orlando, offers Mom, Dad, and the kids opportunities to learn how to animate movies, attend golf and tai chi clinics, take culinary classes—even compose music with Billy Joel.[3] Another venture is Celebration, an urban development for 20,000 residents that features an 18-hole golf course, its own public school, and a hospital and wellness center.[4]

Questions

1. Define the problem identified in this case. Why is the problem important to marketers?
2. Discuss the consumer concepts from the chapter that apply to this case.

3. Develop a managerial applications matrix for the marketing of *The Lion King*. Discuss the marketing strategies employed by Disney that illustrate the managerial use of the consumer concepts.

4. Can Disney successfully market products such as the Disney Institute and Celebration to the family as a unit? Why or why not?

Thanks to Carol Hisey for her assistance in developing an earlier version of this case.

References

1. Janet Maslin, "Target: Boomers and Their Babies," *The New York Times*, November 24, 1991, Section 2, pp. 1, 39.

2. Patricia Sellers, "The ABC's of Marketing to Kids," *Fortune*, May 8, 1989, pp. 114–120.

3. Patricia Sellers, "Mickey Mouse Aims Higher," *Fortune*, October 3, 1994, pp. 18–20; and Melinda Jensen, "Flying Solo," *Successful Meetings*, July 1996, pp. 39–41.

4. Ruth Eckdish Knack, "Once Upon a Town," *Planning*, March 1996, pp. 10–13.

17

CULTURAL PROCESSES I: CULTURE AND POPULAR CULTURE

INTRODUCTORY CASE

Doc Martens Outruns Athletic Shoes

After soaring for years, sales of athletic shoes leveled off in the mid-1990s, and the earnings of companies like Reebok and Nike fell well below analysts' estimates. Market researchers were perplexed and sought to discover the cause of this sudden and unexpected change in consumer demand.

One culprit they identified was a new fashion trend called the "grunge look." A shoe developed by a German doctor just after World War II to help cure his foot problems fit this trend perfectly. Made of stiff leather and "modernized" with an air-cushion sole, the product was seen on more and more American feet. The shoes are large, ungainly, and ugly! They have successively appealed to workers, soccer fans, neo-Nazis, and punkers, and now are a woman's fashion statement. They are the antithesis of the nimble, fleet athletic shoes that they seem to be replacing.[1]

The original shoe is called Dr. Martens or "Docs." The company, now owned by R. Griggs Group Ltd., saw sales in the United States double in 1993 to about $67 million. By 1995 the U.S. market accounted for 20 percent of the company's revenues, with sales of 125,000 pairs a month. Figure 17-1 shows

a pair of Martens on the feet of a 13-year-old girl.

Meanwhile, dozens of knock-off brands have been hastily introduced into the marketplace. For example, Converse has put out versions called the Lug Boot and the Lug Clog. In a commercial for the shoe entitled "Ugly," a young male says, "There are a lot more, what you call, 'ugly' people in my world than beautiful people."

Why did these shoes so suddenly catch on? According to *The Wall Street Journal*, the key turning point occurred when rhythm and blues performer Bobby Brown and rap star Hammer began performing in Doc Martens in 1992. The shoes nicely matched the grunge look in clothing that began with the Seattle musicians Nirvana, Alice in Chains, and Pearl Jam. As one Kmart executive said, "Kids are stepping out of sneakers and into these shoes for a night out on the town." Meanwhile, a stock analyst noted, "Not everyone these days is a Michael Jordan wannabe."

Moving aggressively to keep their foothold in the market, Griggs now makes 150 styles of Martens in 3,000 versions. But they may be eclipsed by *Hush Puppies*! Clearly fuddy-duddy

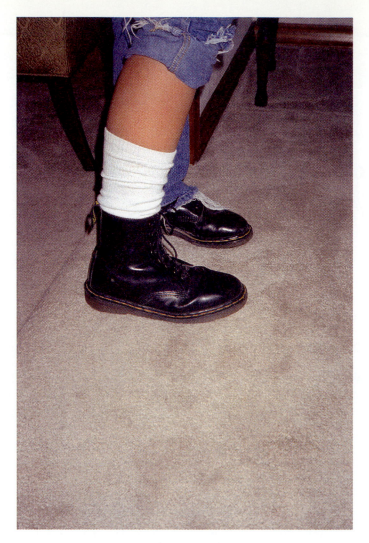

Figure 17-1
These Doc Martens feature the distinctive yellow stitching which sets them apart from other boots.

and long unfashionable, they're now in—in pastel colors. They sell at Macy's and Blooming-dale's. In this case the product was helped by appearing on Tom Hanks' feet in *Forrest Gump*. Even if day-glo Hush Puppies are a casualty of another change in fashion, company executives expect the trend toward more casual work clothing to fuel sales in the long term.[2]

INTRODUCTION

Culture has been defined in a variety of ways. One classic definition states that **culture** is a set of socially acquired behavior patterns transmitted symbolically through language and other means to the members of a particular society.[3] Another definition states that culture is "the interactive aggregate of common characteristics that influence a group's response to its environment."[4] Cultures may be distinguished by their regulation of behavior; by the attitudes, values, and lifestyle of people in the culture; and by their degree of tolerance of other cultures.[5] Another perspective comes from the symbolic interactionists, who view culture as composed of a set of competing images transmitted through media via important signs and symbols.[6]

Broadly speaking, culture is a way of life. It includes the material objects of a society, such as guns, footballs, autos, religious texts, forks, and chopsticks. But it also encompasses ideas and values; for example, most Americans endorse the belief that people have a right to choose among different brands of products. Culture embraces a mix of institutions that include legal, political, religious, and business organizations. Some of these institutions may even symbolically represent a society—for example, McDonald's or French champagne. The ways we dress, think, eat, and spend our leisure time are all components of our culture.

A number of additional ideas are necessary to gain an overall understanding of culture. A culture is *learned*—it is not present in our genes. It is socially transmitted from generation to generation, influencing future members of the society. The process of learning one's own culture is called **enculturation**, while the difficult task of learning a new culture is called **acculturation**. Recently, researchers have distinguished acculturation from cultural identification. **Cultural identification** refers to the society in which a person prefers to live. As such, it is *attitudinal* in nature. In contrast, acculturation refers to the extent that the actions of an immigrant conform to the norms and mores of a new culture.[7] It is *behavioral* in nature.

A culture is also *adaptive*, meaning it changes as a society confronts new problems and opportunities. Just as organisms evolve, so do cultures. They take on new traits and discard old ones to form a new cultural base. The "sexual revolution" that occurred during the 1960s in the United States exemplifies such cultural adaptation. The development of the birth-control pill helped create an environment conducive to changes in the way society viewed women and sexual relations. More recently the AIDS epidemic has influenced sexually active people, whether American, Ghanaian, or Bulgarian, to return to more conservative sexual values.

Finally, culture satisfies needs. By providing **norms**, or rules of behavior, a culture gives an orderliness to society. By providing **values**, it delineates what is right, good, and important. People need to know what is expected of them, what is right and wrong, and what they should do in various situations. Culture fulfills such societal requirements.

Culture is so pervasive and automatically accepted that it is difficult for people to identify the elements of their own culture. In fact, it has been claimed that people do not really understand their own culture unless they know something of another culture—which allows them to realize that other people do things differently.[8] For example, by international standards Americans are fanatics about personal hygiene. Refrigerators only became accepted in this country when their wooden exteriors were replaced by "sanitary" white enamel.[9] In most other parts of the world, deodorants are rarely used, baths are much less frequently taken, and teeth are rarely brushed. Indeed, toilet paper is unheard of in some areas of the globe. However, cultural discomfort is bidirectional. Visitors from mainland China are somewhat revolted when they learn that Americans actually sell food for animals in the same place where food is sold for people.

Components of Culture

Scholars use a number of key concepts to describe cultures. As we noted earlier, every culture has a set of values denoting what end states people should strive to attain. When one compares and contrasts cultures, one sees how the relative importance of various values differs.

All societies have a distinctive set of norms. Norms are more specific than values; they dictate acceptable and unacceptable behaviors. There are two general types of norms. **Enacted norms** are explicitly expressed, sometimes in the form of laws. An example is on which side of the road you drive a car. In the United States people drive on the right side, but in England and in much of the former British Empire (Australia, Hong Kong, Kenya, etc.) as well as in Japan, people drive on the left. When one of us first traveled to Britain, he was almost run over by a car. He was crossing a busy traffic intersection, and a car was turning left in front of him. The person in the right-hand seat was smiling at him—an action he took to indicate that he should cross the street. As he stepped off the curb, the car nearly knocked him over. He had been looking at the passenger rather than at the driver.

The second type of norm, called a **cresive norm**, is embedded in the culture and only learned through extensive interaction with the people of the culture. There are three types of cresive norms:[10]

Customs. Handed down from generation to generation, customs apply to basic actions such as what ceremonies are held and what roles are played by the sexes.

Mores. Mores are customs that emphasize the moral aspects of behavior. Frequently, mores apply to forbidden behaviors, such as the exhibition of skin by women in fundamentalist Moslem countries.

Conventions. Conventions describe how to act in everyday life, and they frequently apply to consumer behavior. For example, the landscaping of yards varies widely from society to society. In the United States yards are frequently very large and covered with grass. In Germany yards often feature neat flower gardens. In Japan yards are small, elaborately planted with bushes, and frequently feature the sound of bubbling water.

Another element of a culture is the myths its people hold. **Myths** are stories that express the key values and ideals of a society. For example, in the United States a popular mythological character is "Superman." Superman displays important values within the American culture, such as great strength hidden behind a mild-mannered exterior. He fights crime and injustice. As noted by one authority on the topic, myths (1) help to explain the origins of existence, (2) reveal a set of values for the society, and (3) provide models for personal conduct.[11]

The creation of myths is extremely important to marketers. The Superman myth was created through a comic book. Other ficitional characters have become consumer myths, such as Santa Claus, the Phantom, E.T., the Playboy Bunny, and the Easter Bunny. (It is ironic that the bunny represents two such different sets of values and behavioral standards.) Other cultural myths are based on real people, such as George Washington cutting down the cherry tree and refusing to lie about it. A more recent cultural myth is based on Sam Walton, who built Wal-Mart and became the richest man in the United States while maintaining a frugal lifestyle.

Every culture also has its own set of symbols, rituals, and values to which marketers can tie their products and services. For example, in the United States the eagle is a symbol of strength, courage, and patriotism. Companies wanting to create such an image for themselves may use the eagle in their advertising or packaging: commercials for Miller Beer, for example, feature an eagle. In Australia the koala is an important symbol that is used by companies to link themselves symbolically to the country. Various rituals are also important to culture. In late January of each year millions of people in the United States gather together in small groups, sit in front of a television set, and eat fattening food while watching behemoths clash on a playing field in an elaborate ritual known as the Super Bowl. In 1996 corporations responded to this mass party atmosphere by spending nearly $1 million for 30 seconds of time to advertise their products. Americans have successfully marketed some of their sports rituals abroad. In the 1990s the U.S. National Basketball Association decided to target Asia, and today NBA games can be seen in most countries in the region. In countries like China where the sport isn't well known, the NBA and sporting goods suppliers are sponsoring competitions and clinics.[12] Similarly, National Football League exhibition games are played in Japan, Europe, and Mexico.

Values also vary widely across cultures. In the United States the freedom to own guns is deeply ingrained. Figure 17-2 shows a photo of a young woman considering the purchase of a pistol for herself: In the early 1990s gun ownership by women increased by 20 percent (although only about 13 percent of American women own guns).[13]

Simultaneously with the consumer rush to purchase guns, a countertrend was occurring. Reebok, Toys 'R' Us, and other retailers were offering to exchange "toys for guns." For example, Reebok and Dial-A-Mattress gave gun owners a $100 gift certificate when they turned in a weapon. The idea originated with a carpet store owner named Fernando Mateo. After his teenage son said that he would give up his Christmas toys to get guns off the streets, Mr. Mateo put up $5,000 of his own money to offer the $100 gift certificates from Toys 'R' Us. The money quickly ran out, and Toys 'R' Us chipped in $20,000. Later Foot Locker pledged $25,000 for its own program. By 1994 over $70,000 in corporate and private donations had gone into these programs.[14]

Thus the surge to purchase guns occurred at the same time as the movement to provide incentives for people to turn in their weapons. This countermovement was rooted in

Figure 17-2
This college-age woman is considering the purchase of a handgun. How does this act illustrate U.S. culture?

another American value—the importance of maintaining social order. Shorter-term changes in the values on which people focus form the popular culture of a society.

The Cultural Matrix

The cultural matrix shown in Figure 17-3 depicts the three sets of factors that compose a culture. It is the interaction of these sets of values—the institutional-social environment, the material environment, and cultural values—that creates the overall cultural fabric of a society. As shown in the figure, the material environment consists of such factors as the technical-scientific level of the society, the extent and type of natural resources that are present, the geographical features of the society, and its degree of economic development. The institutional-social environment includes the legal, political, business, religious, and subcultural institutions and groups that characterize the society. Subcultures, which are discussed at length in Chapter 18, are those subdivisions of a national culture that are centered on some unifying characteristic, such as social class or ethnicity.

A culture is also influenced by the dominant values of the overall society. These cultural values will be discussed in a separate section in the chapter. In the American culture key values are individualism, freedom, and achievement.

It should also be noted that culture can be affected by additional factors, such as natural disasters and wars. For example, when Europeans discovered the Americas, entire civilizations of native people were eliminated by the diseases carried by the invaders. During the recent war in Bosnia and Herzegovina, people laughed off warnings about the long-term effects of smoking. When each day brings the possibility of being killed by snipers or bombs, you don't worry about developing cancer in 30 years. The extremities of war illustrate how the types of consumer goods that are valued in a culture depend a great deal on circumstances.[15]

As time passes, changes occur in the external environment, the social institutions, and the values that make up the cultural matrix. In addition, there is a constant interplay of

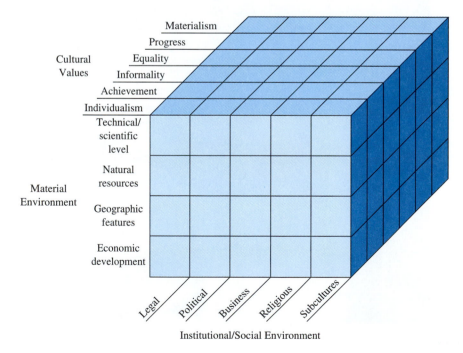

Figure 17-3

The cultural matrix.

movements and countermovements within the matrix. As a result new ideas and trends are constantly bubbling to the surface. These ideas and trends form what is called *popular culture*.

Popular culture is constantly changing, bringing variations in fashion and lifestyles. These changes may lead to corporate catastrophes or to marketing opportunities. For example, in the 1980s popular culture in the United States emphasized fitness and slimness. Marketers of running shoes, weight-lifting machines, and related athletic equipment experienced explosive growth. During this period the sales of a small Tulsa, Oklahoma–based company named Stair Master Corporation exploded as part-time athletes purchased its expensive devices to simulate the exercise of climbing stairs. However, popular culture changed. Between 1985 and 1990 participation in fitness declined by 10 percent.[16] The decline in physical activity occurred for all age groups—not just the aging baby boomers. Such changes created massive problems for companies selling fitness devices. Meanwhile, there was a shift from hard physical exercise to walking, and manufacturers of walking shoes experienced rapid growth. Then in the mid-1990s gyms reported a roughly three-fold gain in participation in boxing, while parents began enrolling their children in private gym programs.[17] The challenge to marketers in the exercise industry is to anticipate these trends.

Chapter Overview

In this chapter we take up culture and its impact on consumer behavior. We begin by analyzing the role of consumer goods within a culture. Next we relate core American values to the cultural meanings that consumers hope to attach to themselves. Then, in the following two sections, we present information on cultural rituals and symbols. The final topic we cover is popular culture, which represents the shorter trends that occur within the overall fabric. We conclude the chapter with a managerial applications analysis of the Doc Martens case.

THE ROLE OF CONSUMER GOODS IN A CULTURE

Consumer behavior researchers have long been interested in the role consumer goods play in a culture. Figure 17-4 diagrams the relationship among consumer goods, individual consumers, and the culturally constituted world. The significance of goods lies in their ability to carry and communicate cultural meaning.[18] **Cultural meanings** refer to those values, norms, and shared beliefs that are symbolically communicated. They are transferred from the culturally constituted world to consumer goods, and from these goods to individuals.

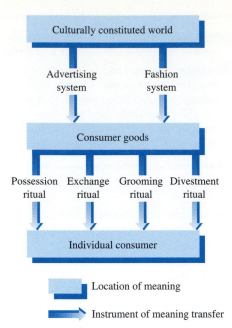

Figure 17-4

Communicating cultural meaning. (*Source*: Reproduced with permission from Grant McCracken, "Culture and Consumption: A Theoretical Account of the Structure and Movement of the Cultural Meaning of Consumer Goods," *Journal of Consumer Research*, Vol. 13 [June 1986], pp. 71–84.)

The culturally constituted world is the lens through which individuals interpret the world around them. It is made up of the values, mores, and norms that define a particular society, and thus it forms a kind of blueprint designating how people should behave. As shown in Figure 17-4, the transfer of meaning from culture to object may occur through advertising and fashion systems, while the transfer of meaning from consumer goods to individuals may take place through various rituals, including possession, exchange, grooming, and divestment.

Advertising is a conduit through which meaning pours from the culturally constituted world to consumer goods. By positioning a product, the advertiser imbues it with meaning. For example, Pontiac has used the theme "We build excitement" extensively. The company's goal is to position Pontiac as an exciting and youthful brand. Through this positioning process, meanings are drawn from the culturally constituted world and transferred to the automobile through the advertisements.

The fashion system is a broader, more diffuse set of agents of transfer. It includes magazines, newspapers, opinion leaders, and, at the margins of society, hippies, punks, and gays. The characters in television shows often give meaning to various products and services. Television programs such as *Dynasty* and *Dallas* acted in the 1980s to transfer meaning to clothing and accessories representing the *nouveau riche* in American society. More recently, *Roseanne* and *The Jeff Foxworthy Show* have done the same for products and services representative of the blue-collar working class.

In Figure 17-4 consumer goods and services are depicted as transferring cultural meanings to individuals. In essence, people use goods to link cultural meanings to themselves. If the meaning that we attach to our material objects is understood by others, we are successfully portraying who and what we are to other people. As one authority has stated, "What can be said of clothing can be said of virtually all other high-involvement product categories and several low-involvement ones. Clothing, transportation, food, housing exteriors and interiors, and adornment all serve as media for the expression of the cultural meaning that constitutes the world."[19]

It has been argued that people use rituals to transfer meanings of objects to themselves and others. A ritual is a symbolic series of actions that link the person to the material good.

The exchange of gifts at birthdays and Christmas is a ritual. Gifts possess symbolic properties that act to transfer cultural meanings, such as love, from one person to another. Rituals will be discussed in more detail later in the chapter.

CULTURAL VALUES IN THE UNITED STATES

Values are enduring beliefs about ideal end states and modes of conduct. Few in number, they are more abstract than attitudes, and they serve as standards to guide actions, attitudes, and judgments. Specific attitudes about objects tend to reflect and support a person's values. Within a society **cultural values** represent the shared meanings of ideal end states and modes of conduct. Thus cultural values depict the shared meaning of what is important and of what end states of existence people in a society should seek.[20]

The values that make up the culturally constituted world in the United States have a variety of sources. One important source of our culture, of course, is the European heritage of the early settlers of the United States and Canada. Their flight from religious persecution and authoritarian monarchies indelibly etched into the American culture the values of individualism and freedom. Some have argued that the frontier created the values of rugged individualism, informality, equality, and diligence.[21] Certainly, the Judeo-Christian heritage of early Americans also influenced what were to become core American values.[22]

A number of authors have developed lists of core American values. Frequently mentioned values include beliefs in the importance of:

1. Individualism
2. Youthfulness
3. Progress
4. Materialism
5. Activity
6. Achievement
7. Efficiency
8. Informality
9. Equality
10. Distrust of government

Other values sometimes mentioned are: freedom, external conformity, humanitarianism, authority, respect for institutions, mastery of the environment, and religion. The "Protestant ethic" is also woven through the social fabric of the United States. Thus values relating to hard work and frugality are important to many Americans. Such themes are sometimes used by advertisers. For example, the Oldsmobile ad pictured in Figure 17-5 positions the Aurora as a reward for hard work. It has been proposed that one advantage of "pioneer brands" is that to Americans being a pioneer signifies innovation and progress.[23]

At the same time, there are in every society countercurrents to the reigning cultural values. For example, in the United States respect for institutions has been steadily falling since the mid-1970s. Similarly, the ecology movement, with its emphasis on living in harmony with nature, is a clear counterforce to the traditional American value of mastering the environment. As we noted earlier, culture is adaptive, so one should expect to occasionally see movements that are inconsistent with the traditional values of a culture.

A psychologist who has investigated values extensively, Milton Rokeach, has identified what he has called terminal values and instrumental values.[24] *Terminal values* are desired

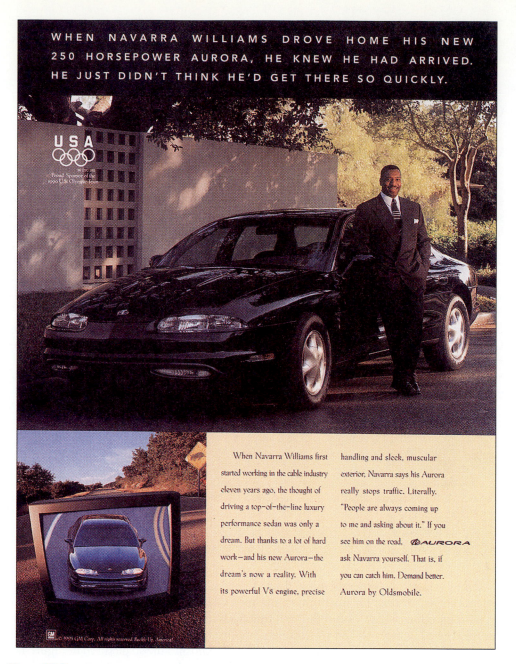

Figure 17-5

This ad for the Oldsmobile Aurora employs the notion that a good car is a suitable reward for those willing to work hard.

end states—how people would like to eventually experience their lives. *Instrumental values* are the behaviors and actions required to achieve the terminal states. Table 17-1 presents a set of 24 terminal and instrumental values identified by consumer researchers as important to consumption.[25] This 24-item list is shorter than the original **Rokeach value scale**, because a number of Rokeach's items, such as "world at peace" and "courageous," have limited applicability to consumer behavior. The Rokeach scale appears to capture values held cross-culturally. For example, it is consistent with the Chinese Value Survey.[26]

Consumer Research on Cultural Values

One important research issue concerns how cultural values influence specific consumption decisions. Figure 17-6 shows how the organization of the individual's belief system moves from global values to domain-specific values to evaluations of product attributes.[27] **Global values**, which correspond closely to Rokeach's terminal values, consist of enduring beliefs about desired states of existence. **Domain-specific values** are beliefs pertaining to more concrete consumption activities—for example, that manufacturers should give prompt service, guarantee their products, help eliminate environmental pollution, and be truthful. Evaluations of product attributes are highly specific beliefs about individual products—for example: How well does a Corvette handle? Is it easy to repair? (Product beliefs were discussed in Chapter 8.)

Researchers have found that people with different global values also exhibited divergent domain-specific values and product evaluations. Indeed, individual differences in global values translate to markedly different product preferences. For example, people

Shortened Rokeach Value Scale

Terminal	Instrumental
1. A comfortable life	14. Ambitious
2. An exciting life	15. Broadminded
3. A sense of accomplishment	16. Capable
4. A world of beauty	17. Cheerful
5. Equality	18. Clean
6. Family security	19. Imaginative
7. Freedom	20. Independent
8. Happiness	21. Intellectual
9. Inner harmony	22. Logical
10. Pleasure	23. Responsible
11. Self-respect	24. Self-control
12. Social recognition	
13. Wisdom	

Source: J. Michael Munson and Edward McQuarrie, "Shortening the Rokeach Value Survey for Use in Consumer Research," in *Advances in Consumer Research*, Vol. 15, Michael Houston, ed. (Provo, UT: Association for Consumer Research, 1988), pp. 381–386.

TABLE 17-1

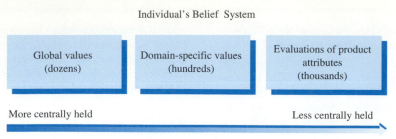

Individual's Belief System

| Global values (dozens) | Domain-specific values (hundreds) | Evaluations of product attributes (thousands) |

More centrally held   Less centrally held

Central-Peripheral Continuum

Figure 17-6

Organization of the value-attitude system. (*Source*: Adapted by permission from Donald E. Vinson, Jerome Scott, and Lawrence Lamont, "The Role of Personal Values in Marketing and Consumer Behavior," *Journal of Marketing*, Vol. 41 [April 1977], p. 46, published by the American Marketing Association.)

whose global values emphasize logic, an exciting life, and self-respect tend to prefer compact cars and outdoor recreation, while those whose global values emphasize national security and salvation are more attracted to standard-sized cars and television.

Figure 17-6 exemplifies what are called **means-end chain models**. Means-end chain models identify the linkages between consumer desires for specific product features with increasingly abstract concepts, such as benefits desired and values that are important to an individual. Suppose a person desires to purchase a car with a small fuel-efficient engine. Three major benefits result from this feature: good gas mileage, lower purchase and operating costs, and protection of the environment. In turn, these benefits lead to a frugal lifestyle. Finally, a frugal lifestyle leads to the terminal value of a clean environment. In sum, the purchase of a car with the attribute of a small engine acts as a means to reach the consumer's desired end-state of a cleaner environment. The process of probing to identify the linkages between means (i.e., attributes) and terminal values (i.e., end states) is called **laddering**.[28]

As we will show later in the chapter, values are also closely connected to social change. As the culture of a society changes, so do the values of the individuals who make up the society. Changes in values can directly influence managerial strategy. For example, Stouffer's recognized that the values of many female grocery shoppers were changing—they were shifting away from emphasizing their role as "servant for the family" toward stressing the value of self-fulfillment. Capitalizing on this recognition, the company successfully introduced a line of frozen entrees that were positioned as fulfillment oriented. In fact, the positioning phrase used in advertisements was "Set yourself free."

Cultural Value Orientations   Researchers have sought to identify the dimensions on which the values of various cultures differ. In a summary of this research scholars identified six basic dimensions of cultural values.[29]

1. *Individual/collective*: the extent to which a culture values the individual more than the group or vice versa.
2. *Masculinity/femininity*: the extent to which the characteristics of one sex are valued over those of the other sex.
3. *Time orientation*: whether members of the society are oriented to the past, present, or future.
4. *Uncertainty avoidance*: the extent to which members of the society are willing to tolerate ambiguity and unusual behavior.
5. *Activity orientation*: the extent to which the society values action over reflection.

6. *Relationship to nature*: the extent to which the society lives in harmony with nature or attempts to dominate nature.

If we compare the United States and Japan on these various dimensions, we will conclude that the Japanese culture is more collective, more masculine, more past and future oriented, more uncertainty avoidant, lower in activity orientation, and more in harmony with nature.

Research on the List-of-Values Scale An index developed to aid consumer research on values is the LOV scale. (LOV stands for List of Values; this subject was discussed in Chapter 7.) The LOV scale is based on Rokeach's Value Survey. One study using the scale investigated how values in the United States changed between 1976 and 1986.[30] The researchers conducted a national survey of consumers in 1976, and again in 1986, asking which values the respondents considered most important. Table 17-2 presents the results. Overall values remained quite stable over the time span: the correlation ratio between the 1976 and 1986 figures was .91 for males and .77 for females. Note that the correlation for females was lower than that for males, indicating a greater change in women's values over the decade. An analysis by age showed that the most change occurred among people under 30.

Research on the LOV scale has found that people's values influence their attitudes, which, in turn, influence their behavior. One study researching the characteristics of people who shop for natural foods revealed that those who emphasize internal values (i.e., self-fulfillment, excitement, sense of accomplishment, and self-respect) like and purchase natural foods more than do people who emphasize external values (i.e., sense of belonging, being well-respected, and having security).[31] A more recent study has suggested the appearance of the "role-relaxed" American in the 1990s. This person is less concerned with seeming "normal" and is more driven by internal values. Consistent with this notion, "role-relaxed" baby boomers score "being well-respected" lower on their scale of values today than did the sample polled in 1986. In other words, the importance of being well-respected seems to be dropping in the 1990s.[32]

Value Changes in the United States						
	Total		**Male**		**Female**	
	1976	**1986**	**1976**	**1986**	**1976**	**1986**
Self-respect	21.1	23.0	21.7	22.4	20.6	23.5
Security	20.6	16.5	20.5	17.1	20.7	15.9
Warm relationships	16.2	19.9	13.1	13.6	18.5	25.7
Sense of accomplishment	11.4	15.9	14.3	20.1	9.2	12.2
Self-fulfillment	9.6	6.5	9.5	7.2	9.6	5.8
Being well-respected	8.8	5.9	8.5	5.7	9.0	6.1
Sense of belonging	7.9	5.1	5.6	3.8	9.6	6.3
Fun/enjoyment/excitement	4.5	7.2	6.9	10.0	2.7	4.6

Source: Lynn Kahle, Basil Poulos, and Ajay Sukhdial, "Changes in Social Values in the United States During the Past Decade," *Journal of Advertising Research*, Vol. 28 (February–March 1988), pp. 35–41. Reprinted with permission of the Advertising Research Foundation.

TABLE 17-2

Environmental analysis and marketing research can help managers understand how cultural values change in a society. For example, an increased desire for pleasure, excitement, and fun among consumers might suggest how products should be named, what their colors should be, and how they should be designed. In advertising, such values would influence the underlying tone of the message and the choice of models. Such a trend can be seen in advertising for Coca-Cola, whose many themes have included "The Pause that Refreshes," "Things Go Better with Coke," "Have a Coke and a Smile," "I'd Like to Give the World a Coke," "It's the Real Thing," "Coke Is It," and "Always Coca-Cola." The theme of "giving the world a Coke" was created in the 1960s, when international tensions were high and Americans were worried about world peace. The advertisement showed people of different countries in a long line, holding hands and passing a Coke. It had a dramatic impact and even spawned a popular song. Similarly, the theme "Coke Is It," which began in late 1982, captured the cultural spirit of the time with its emphasis on self to appeal to the "Me Generation." These themes echoed the changes in cultural values that moved through the United States during the 1960s, 1970s, and 1980s. Figure 17-7 presents several of the print ads from these campaigns.

Research on the Value of Materialism Perhaps the value having the greatest impact on consumer behavior is that of materialism. We discussed materialism as an individual difference variable in Chapter 7. A number of researchers have tried to determine whether the emphasis on the cultural value of materialism has changed in the United States through recent decades. They have approached this question by analyzing the content of popular literature, especially comic books and popular novels. (Content analysis involves coding the themes of written material into various categories.) One study investigated the frequency with which materialistic themes appeared in several comic books, such as *Archie*, *Uncle Scrooge McDuck*, and *Richie Rich*. An example of a materialistic theme is found in a 1965 edition of *Archie*:

> Veronica tells Archie that having everything she wants bore her, and Betty convinces Archie to go out with her instead so that Veronica feels challenged. It works, but Veronica wins, thanks to her new outfits that catch Archie's eye.[33]

After examining the time period from the 1940s to the mid-1980s, the author of this study reported finding little change in materialistic themes. Interestingly, he argued that the comic books may have had a positive socializing influence on children over this 40-year period because the values they have portrayed have been generally positive. The stories indicated that wealth can be either good or bad. When the role models acted poorly, they incurred bad fortune. The wealthy people in the stories were encouraged not to flaunt their riches, and the deserving poor were portrayed as honest, intelligent, and clean people who only lacked the opportunity or circumstances to be wealthy.[34]

Considering sources other than comic books, however, one does find evidence of changes in materialism as a value. For example, one study investigated the frequency with which brand names were mentioned in popular novels.[35] It found a more than fivefold increase in the usage of brand names between 1946 and 1975. Some critics charge that the manner in which companies name products is rendering the "sacred profane." For example, "True" cigarettes and "First Romance" towels can be viewed as profaning sacred words and symbols by connecting them with products. Indeed, these charges seem to have some merit. The word *truth* could be considered tainted by an association with a cigarette brand—especially since tobacco companies have avoided telling consumers the truth about the harmful effects of smoking.

When one looks at the themes in advertisements, one gains another perspective on materialism in American society. Some authors have distinguished two types of materialism—

Figure 17-7

Reading clockwise, these advertisements for Coca-Cola come from the 1930s, 1960s, 1970s, and 1980s. They portray subtle changes in U.S. culture over the time period.

instrumental and terminal. **Instrumental materialism** involves obtaining a material good in order to perform some activity. It is viewed as benign because the good is an instrument for the accomplishment of something else. In contrast, **terminal materialism** involves the possession of a good as an end in itself. Terminal materialism is viewed as potentially destructive because it leads to such unbecoming traits as envy, possessiveness, selfishness, and greed.[36]

One study investigated 2,000 magazine advertisements having to do with the interior or the exterior of houses. The ads, spanning the years 1901 through 1979, were content analyzed to determine the frequency with which material goods were cast in terms of their

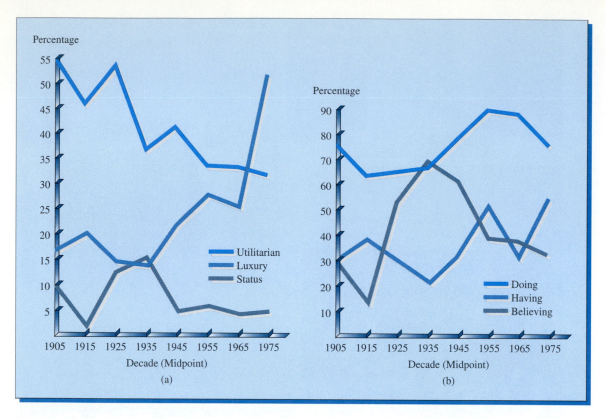

Figure 17-8

Materialistic themes in print advertising. (*Source:* Russell Belk and Richard Pollay, "Materialism and Magazine Advertising During the Twentieth Century," in *Advances in Consumer Research*, Vol. 13, Elizabeth Hirschman and Morris Holbrook, eds. [Provo, UT: Association for Consumer Research, 1985], pp. 394–398.)

appeal or theme. Figure 17-8 diagrams the major findings. Utilitarian themes, in which the product's benefits were described in terms of their practicality and efficiency, decreased in frequency over the time span. In contrast, luxury themes increased dramatically, which superficially indicates an increase in materialistic values. However, while appeals to luxury have risen substantially over time, the underlying themes of such ads have more frequently been of an instrumental nature. As the authors explained:

> It is also evident that this materialistic emphasis has been more involved with instrumental themes of using the advertised items than with terminally materialistic themes of having the product for its own sake. If we have become a culture of consumption, it does not yet appear that this consumption is an end rather than a means to other ends.[37]

Do men or women reveal greater amounts of materialism? In the sixth century B.C. the Greek philosopher Pythagoras suggested that women are more sharing and less materialistic than men. A recent study investigating the materialism and sharing behavior of men and women in Germany and Canada confirms the philosopher's opinion. Women in both countries were found to be more sharing, generous, nurturant, and caring than men. One explanation suggested by the authors was that material goods mean different things to men and women. For men, material goods help establish power and competitive relations, while for women, they are a part of social relations.[38]

We usually think of the United States as a quite materialistic society, but how does it compare in this respect to other industrialized nations? One study undertook to compare materialism in the United States and the Netherlands—a country whose prosperity equals that of the United States.[39] Questionnaires were completed by middle-class households in both countries. The results indicated that the level of materialism was highly similar in each nation across the various scales. The only difference was that the Dutch sample revealed slightly higher levels of "possessiveness" toward material goods than did the American sample.

Another study compared materialistic values among consumers in Europe, the United States, and Turkey.[40] These results revealed that Turkish consumers were simultaneously more materialistic and more generous than American and European consumers. The authors suggested that factors unique to the Turkish culture may account for these surprising findings. That is, Turkey has an ancient history of prosperity, and this cultural legacy may have accustomed the Turks to the idea that they can afford to be generous.

Cross-cultural comparisons of materialistic values suggest that simple statements about *why* people are materialistic must be avoided. Clearly, a variety of factors influence materialistic values—including the overall prosperity and industrialization of a nation, as well as its particular cultural history. The research on materialism as a value in the United States has yielded mixed findings. Some studies find little evidence of any increase in materialism in recent decades, whereas others find ample evidence of a rise in materialism. As the study of interior and exterior housing ads suggested, the difference may be attributable to the type of materialism studied. Americans do seem to have a mistrust of owning things for their own sake. An emphasis on terminal materialism is inconsistent with the American values of practicality and efficiency. Nonetheless, there is overwhelming evidence that the United States is a materialistic society. As one author said, "The findings indicate the pervasiveness of a consumer culture in the mid-twentieth century and suggest that the baby boom generation, reared in material abundance, may be unabashedly materialistic."[41]

When developing the marketing mix, firms should analyze the core values of every culture to which the product is being marketed. This strategy is essential for both American firms marketing in foreign countries and foreign firms marketing in the United States. For example, Anheuser-Busch used Native Americans in television commercials for Budweiser in Britain. This was Budweiser's most popular campaign ever in Britain—viewers even requested photos of the primary actor in the commercial. Brand awareness rose to an all-time high, and Budweiser sales increased by 20 percent. To Britons, Native Americans express "genuine American values," said Lewis Blackwell, editor of the U.K. advertising publication *Creative Review*. However, when Native Americans in the United States got wind of the ad, they asked that it be withdrawn because it was such a painful reminder that the alcoholism rate among American Indians is about five times that of the general population.[42]

Cultural Rituals

Cultural rituals are socially standardized sequences of actions that are periodically repeated, provide meaning, and involve the use of cultural symbols. Rituals can be public or private. They vary from large-scale civic rituals, such as the Super Bowl, to private rituals involving prayer. Ritual behaviors are "scripted," so that they are formal and prescribed by convention, and in many cases they involve the consumption and use of products.

The characteristics of rituals we just identified are embodied in the following formal definition: The term *ritual* refers to an expressive, symbolic activity constructed of culturally sanctioned behaviors that occur in a fixed, episodic sequence, and tend to be repeated over time. Ritual behavior is dramatically scripted and acted out, and is performed with formality, seriousness, and inner intensity.[43]

Rituals should be distinguished from habits. *Habits* are repetitive, engaged in over time, and can have inner intensity. For example, most of us have a sequence of actions we follow in going from home to school or work and back home again. Such sequences of actions are considered habits rather than rituals. Rituals differ from habits on three criteria. First, rituals are prescribed by society rather than by the individual. Second, people are more consciously aware of what takes place in a ritual than they are of what is going on in a habit. Third, rituals have greater symbolic meaning than habits and have more affect attached to them.[44]

Table 17-3 presents a typology of ritual experience. As evident from the table, rituals exist at various levels of abstraction. At their most abstract —as in religious, magic, and aesthetic rituals—they have cosmological value. At their most concrete—as in the grooming and mating rituals of animals—rituals are biologically determined. The types of rituals listed in the table also point out the functional value of rituals. For example, the cultural rituals of graduation and marriage are rites of passage that symbolically denote a change in a person's status. Similarly, rituals can serve to pass on knowledge and create bonds within groups. Thus holiday celebrations, the exchange of birthday gifts, and office luncheons are enacted in order to fulfill specific goals within groups.[45]

Rituals commonly have four elements: artifacts, scripts, performance roles, and an audience. Consider the various aspects of a college basketball game. One can identify in this ritual the artifacts (i.e., basketballs, pompons, beer), the script (i.e., the rules of the game), performance roles (i.e., players, referees, coaches), and the audience. Of course, rituals vary in formality and in the extent to which each of these four elements is present.

At the cultural level, researchers have identified four specific types of rituals.[46] **Exchange rituals** involve the exchange of gifts, information, goods, or money. **Possession rituals** involve acts in which a person lays claim to, displays, or protects possessions. For

A Typology of Ritual Experience

Primary Behavior Source	Ritual Type	Examples
Cosmology	Religious	Baptism, meditation, mass
	Magic	"Healing," gambling
	Aesthetic	Performing arts
Cultural values	Rites of passage	Graduation, marriage
	Cultural	Festivals, Valentine's Day, Groundhog Day, Super Bowl
Group learning	Civic	Memorial Day parade, elections, trials
	Small group	Pancake Day, fraternity initiation, business negotiations, office luncheons
	Family	Mealtime, bedtime, birthday and holiday celebrations
Individual aims and emotions	Personal	Grooming, household rituals
Biology	Animal	Greeting, mating

Source: Dennis Rook, "The Ritual Dimension of Consumer Behavior," *Journal of Consumer Research*, Vol. 12 (December 1985), pp. 251–264. Reprinted with permission.

TABLE 17-3

example, housewarming parties and overzealous car waxing can be viewed as possession rituals. **Grooming rituals** act to ensure that the special perishable properties resident in clothing, hairstyles, and looks are preserved. In some cases the grooming ritual is not performed on the consumer but on a product. An example is the constant grooming of lawns by middle-class homeowners. A fourth type of ritual is the **divestment ritual**, which may be performed to erase the meaning associated with the previous owner of the good. For example, after buying an older house, consumers will frequently engage in cleaning and redecorating behaviors in order to lay claim to their possession. Similarly, a divestment ritual may occur when a person disposes of a personalized item, such as a special coat, car, or house. When one of the authors of this book sold a prized Camaro and asked the new owner for a ride to work, the new owner asked if he wouldn't like to drive the car one last time. She provided him with an additional opportunity for a divestment ritual.

The list of consumption-related rituals is long. They include rites of passage (e.g., weddings, baby showers, and funerals), religious ceremonies, holiday festivities (e.g., Christmas, Thanksgiving), family activities (e.g., television viewing at prescribed times, the summer vacation, and Sunday dinner), and large-scale public rituals, (e.g., singing the national anthem, watching parades and sports events).[47] Some of these rituals have both a religious element and a commercial element. For example, Easter has both religious and secular significance (see Figure 17-9). The television ritual has become extremely important to our society. In fact, the three-hour "prime-time" entertainment block predates television. In the nineteenth century popular theater performances lasted three hours. The three-hour block continued in vaudeville early in the twentieth century, and later was used for double-bill movies.

For manufacturers and retailers, success often lies in recognizing the importance of culturally prescribed consumer rituals and tying the company's products into these rituals. By identifying ritualistic patterns of behavior, marketers can design and promote products that might serve as artifacts in these activities. For example, the beauty ritual involves a long series of steps for many women. Some adroit marketers (e.g., Clinique) have attempted to lengthen the ritual by adding new steps and products, such as using an astringent to close facial pores after washing. Donna Karen, Clinique, and others have assembled similar multistep skin-care systems for men, thus far with only modest success. The idea is to change grooming habits into rituals prescribed by the firm, which promises to provide the important consumer benefit of more attractive skin.

A final point of interest to retailers and service providers is the notion of rituals as catalysts for consumers to construct "small worlds"—that is, to develop and maintain social relationships. Although the rituals may differ ("male bonding" occurs at sports events, while women might socialize at an arts performance), the end result is similar. If facilities and events facilitate the development of "small worlds" of interconnected consumers, perhaps including a sense of belonging, the value provided may be enhanced. For example, some participants have noted that they attend certain events more for social purposes than for the value of the actual performance or event.[48]

Figure 17-9
Easter is a widespread ritual. These shoppers are examining Easter eggs for sale in Warsaw, Poland.

CULTURAL SYMBOLS

In addition to values and rituals, cultures have symbols. **Symbols** are entities that represent ideas and concepts.[49] In Chapter 3 we discussed semiotics, a field of study that investigates the meaning of symbols. As we noted there, symbols are important because they communicate complex ideas rapidly with a minimum of effort. For example, if a company wants to communicate the concept of patriotism, a useful symbol is the American flag. By adroitly using symbols, companies and advertisers can tie cultural values to their products or services, enhancing their products' attractiveness to consumers.

It can be argued that people "consume" symbols.[50] That is, they evaluate, purchase, and use products partly because of their symbolic value. For a product to have symbolic value, it must have a shared reality among consumers, meaning large numbers of consumers must have a common conception of the product's symbolic meaning. For example, in order for an automobile to have "prestige" value, others in the relevant social group must view it in the same manner as the buyer.[51]

Companies frequently symbolize the characteristics of their products through the names they choose for them: one expert insists that names must express the "soul" of the product, as well as strike an emotional chord with consumers.[52] For example, auto manufacturers have been fond of naming their products after the big cats, suggesting swiftness, agility, and aggressiveness. Examples are the Jaguar, Cougar, Lynx, Wildcat, Bobcat, and Puma.

American culture is rife with symbols. The symbol of money—and occasionally power or greed—is the dollar sign ($). The most common symbol for Christian spiritual meanings is the cross. A smoking pipe is often used to symbolize contemplation. Similarly, wearing glasses suggests intelligence and possibly physical weakness—á la Clark Kent, Superman's alter ego. Planting a tree suggests permanence. Figure 17-10 is an advertisement for a store that specializes in symbolic merchandise—memorabilia of famous people.

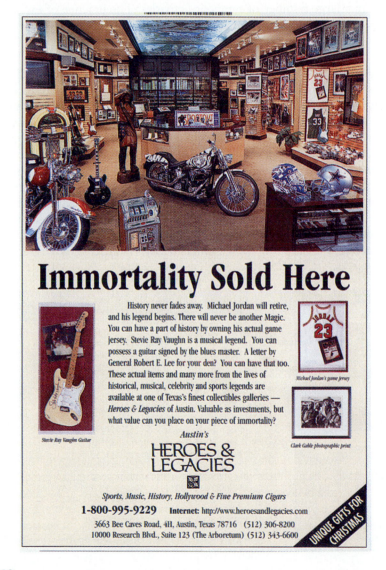

Figure 17-10
This store specializes in symbols, specifically objects belonging to historical or popular culture figures.

Colors can have a variety of symbolic meanings, depending on the context. When worn at funerals, black indicates mourning. In contrast, black bras, garter belts, and panties suggest blatant sex appeal. Blue indicates coolness—for example, "Ice Blue Aqua-Velva." White signifies purity, as in wedding dresses and milk products. Pink is feminine, and for babies, blue is masculine.

Clothing also has important symbolic meaning for consumers. Table 17-4 identifies a variety of functions that clothing can serve, as well as the potential symbolic value of these functions. One function of clothing is to act as an emblem of group membership. The popularity of T-shirts and hats with logos illustrates the symbolic nature of clothing. Designer logos faded after great popularity in the 1980s, but these logos are now back in big, oversized versions.[53]

Although all cultures use symbols, they seem to be more important in some cultures than in others. For example, Japan has been called the empire of signs. Indeed, this statement is true both literally and figuratively. Japan's urban landscape is cluttered with signs, some flashing incessantly and others meticulously lettered. Figuratively, the Japanese culture engages in a large number of symbolic activities. The practice of exchanging business cards (meishi) has a symbolic function. The great care taken in wrapping and packaging plays a role in the spiritual and cultural life of the country. Figure 17-11 shows a portable tearoom, chosen as a symbol of Japan for visiting foreigners.

The Japanese are also fond of using foreign words in promotional materials, which may have several symbolic meanings. The foreign words may connote something new or modern; they may indicate a Western influence; or they may symbolize prestige. One researcher attempted to count the number of English loanwords in a Japanese dictionary, but gave up after recording 7,000. Fully 80 percent of all loanwords in Japanese are taken from English. Examples are *botsu* (boots), *tobako* (cigarette), and *kitchin* (kitchen).

Two researchers spent a summer in Japan investigating the use of English loanwords by Japanese companies.[54] They observed that Japanese beverage companies frequently include English prose in their advertising. For example, one ad for Kirin beer was entirely written in English: "The legendary KIRIN is a symbol of good luck. Open up KIRIN today, and you'll see what it is all about." Japanese promotional messages frequently use similes and metaphors that sound very strange to Americans. One beverage, called Pokka

Clothing: Its Functional Uses and Symbolic Meanings

Function of Apparel	Use of Apparel	Symbolic Meaning	Example of Apparel
Camouflage	Hide the body	Sexually conservative	Robes
	Cover blemishes or injuries		Cosmetics, patches
Display	Reveal body parts	Sexually explicit	Tight or skimpy clothing
Utilitarian	Protect the body	"Down-to-earth," practical	Some jeans, raincoats
Aesthetic	Beautify or enhance the body	Love of beauty	Jewelry
Souvenir	Reminder of the past	Love of family or experience	Charm bracelet
Emblematic	Group membership	Show membership in a group	Fraternity jacket
	Connotative	Reveal social class or wealth	Expensive jewelry

Source: Adapted in part from a table in Rebecca Holman, "Apparel as Communication," in *Symbolic Consumer Behavior*, Elizabeth Hirschman and Morris Holbrook, eds., Proceedings of the Conference on Consumer Aesthetics and Symbolic Consumption (Ann Arbor, MI: Association for Consumer Research, May 1980), p. 8.

TABLE 17-4

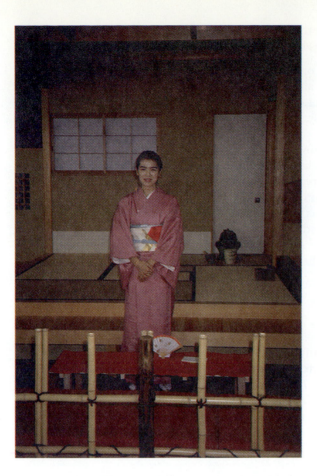

Figure 17-11
This Japanese tearoom is not permanent. It has been brought in and assembled so that foreigners can view the Japanese tea ceremony. The hostess is there to show us how to drink tea correctly.

White Sour, featured a promotional message in English: "Pokka White Sour is refreshing and white like Alpine snow. Its sour taste of yogurt will extend on your tongue softly and be a sweetheart." This usage is merely odd: contrast it with the far less appetizing Pocari Sweat—a brand name for a soft drink.

POPULAR CULTURE

What are the two largest exports by United States firms in the 1990s? Aircraft and related equipment were ranked number one, and popular culture was ranked number two. Just one component of the popular culture scene (popular culture software, which includes movies, music, television programming, and home video) racked up $8 billion on the plus side in our balance of trade. In fact, recordings, films, and books together account for almost as much export revenue as civil aircraft, the only area in which the United States is still considered to have the world's best manufacturers.[55]

So what is popular culture? Many definitions have been proposed. For the purposes of understanding its impact on consumer behavior, the following definition is most appropriate: **Popular culture** is the culture of mass appeal. Popular culture has the following characteristics:

1. It taps into the experiences and values of a significant portion of the population.
2. It does not require any special knowledge to understand it.

3. It is produced in such a way that large numbers of people have easy access to it.
4. It most frequently influences behavior that does not involve work or sleep.[56]

To understand popular culture, one must distinguish it from "high" culture. **High culture** is exclusive in style, content, and appeal. It frequently harks back to the "old masters" of art, theater, music, and literature. To the advocates of high culture, popular culture frequently appears loud, brassy, even immoral. The cult of the pop star Madonna is frequently used as an illustration.

As many scholars have noted, however, the distinction between "high" and "popular" culture is often hazy. For example, when Walt Disney produced *Fantasia*, he borrowed from "high culture" the music of such great classical composers as Beethoven. A huge success, *Fantasia* has become part of popular culture even though it employs elements of high culture. Or consider Leonardo da Vinci's painting, the *Mona Lisa*. She is a high-culture icon, but her image has been used to advertise 9-Lives Cat Food, Lindsay Olives, Prince Spaghetti Sauce, and Minolta copiers. Indeed, Shakespeare's works originated as popular culture—they appealed to mass audiences who sought entertainment in the working-class theaters of his day.

Examples of Popular Culture

Because popular culture involves anything that has mass appeal and is used in nonwork activities, the range of subject matter encompassed by the term is extremely large. For example, in the 1989 edition of the *Handbook of American Popular Culture*, there were 46 articles on distinct subjects. Many of the topics were obvious—advertising, fashion, music, and television, for example. But other topics were unexpected—death, pornography, propaganda, and even science.[57] We briefly discuss several areas of popular culture in this section.

Advertising Advertising becomes popular culture when its images, themes, and icons are embraced by the mass public. Some figures from advertising that have achieved popular culture status are Ronald McDonald, Tony the Tiger, the Energizer Bunny, and the Pillsbury Doughboy.

Television Television does more to create popular culture than any other medium. Indeed, one scholar proclaimed that television "has become preeminently *the* popular culture and a primary purveyor of values and ideas."[58] In the mid-1990s television shows such as *Beavis and Butt-Head* were heavily criticized for promoting mindless gutter humor. Meanwhile, emerging from the throats of countless teenage boys was their familiar laugh, "Huh-huh. Huh-huh."

Researchers have found that heavy television viewing impacts consumers' views of the world. For example, heavy television viewers have been found to overestimate both the amount of violence and the degree of affluence in the United States.[59] Legislation mandating a "V(iolence) chip" in TV sets to allow parents to block their children's access to violent programs has been passed, and a rating system for television is in use.

Music Music also shapes popular culture. The phenomenon of rap music illustrates the enormous impact of music on the consumer behavior of an entire generation. The beginnings of rap music can be traced back to 1968, when it was invented in the Bronx section of New York City. The first rap label was established in 1979. Then, in 1981, Blondie's hit song "Rapture" rose to number one on the charts. In 1985 MTV began a rap program. The first rap-based movie was produced in 1990. By 1993 rap had moved into mainstream popular culture: Coca-Cola employed rap music in its advertising with performers dressed in the baggy, hip-hop fashions associated with the music phenomenon.[60]

Fashion The concept of fashion can be defined either narrowly or broadly. According to the narrow interpretation, fashion is identified with clothing, costumes, and bodily adornment. For example, the practice of body piercing for the purpose of adornment exemplifies fashion in popular culture.

The broader definition of fashion extends the concept to include any use of products to express one's self-image or role position. **Fashion**, then, is the set of behaviors temporarily adopted by a people because they are perceived to be socially appropriate for the time and situation.[61] From this perspective, fashion involves the adoption of symbols to provide an identity. The symbols may be clothing, jewelry, automobiles, housing, artwork, or any other socially visible object that communicates meaning within the popular culture.

Even the books that people read (or whether they read books at all) are symbols that communicate information to others. A consumer researcher analyzed the consumption ideology found in a best-selling author's detective stories—Robert B. Parker, who writes the "Spenser for Hire" series. Noting that detective stories have displaced the cowboy novel in popular culture, the researcher stated that such novels express certain American values. In these novels the detective is a type of mythical hero who possesses special powers and who overcomes personal weaknesses often involving alcohol and women. In the Spenser series an important theme is knowing how and what to consume. As the consumer researcher Cathy Goodwin has said, "Knowing how and what to consume, but sometimes consciously choosing to be inappropriate, is evidence of superiority, strength or originality."[62]

Fashion is inherently dynamic because it constantly changes over time. One cannot overemphasize the importance of the symbolic value of fashion. Indeed, symbolic value frequently overwhelms any "utilitarian" value. One merely has to look at the pain endured by women who wear corsets and high-heeled shoes to understand the relative weights people give to symbolic and utilitarian values. Of course, men have their own fashions and, like women, are ready to endure physical discomfort to look good—witness hair transplants and tattoos.[63]

Fashion trends have a number of characteristics. These are briefly discussed below.[64]

1. Type of trend. Two basic types of fashion trends have been identified. In the **cyclical fashion trend** members of a society adopt styles that are progressively more extreme in one direction or another. Examples are skirt lengths and tie widths. In the **classic fashion trend** particular looks become a "classic," such as the blue pin-striped suit.

2. Speed of trend. The trend may be very fast or slow. Some trends are simple fads that come and go very quickly. An example of such a fad is dyeing one's hair with Kool-Aid. A long-lasting trend is the shaving of facial hair by most men and of underarm hair by most women in the United States.

3. Fashion turning points. Within cyclical fashion trends, at some point in the cycle a turning point occurs because a technological or cultural barrier has been reached. For example, in the late eighteenth century the hoopskirt became progressively wider until women could no longer move through doorways. Similarly, in the early 1970s miniskirts headed upward until a cultural barrier was reached in the form of preserving some modesty. Perhaps the same thing will happen with body piercing, as convenient locations of the body are increasingly "occupied."

4. The degree of individual-level adherence to the trend. While in the overall society fashion trends are clearly discernible, at the individual level each person appears to behave in an almost random manner regarding the trend. Indeed, some people take delight in dressing or behaving in a manner that is exactly the opposite of what is prescribed by the current trend. At times these countertrends become the basis for new fads. The craze for Dr. Martens shoes illustrates a trend away from the pervasiveness of athletic shoes.

How Does Popular Culture Develop?

As we said earlier in the chapter, there are numerous trends and countertrends within the overall cultural matrix of a society. These arise from the interplay of changes in the material environment, the institutional-social environment, and cultural values. The shorter-term trends that bubble up from the cultural matrix come and (in most cases) go. Given the name *popular culture*, such mass trends, while they last, can influence tens of millions of people in their everyday life. In some cases a popular culture trend becomes so ingrained in the overall cultural matrix over time that it becomes a part of "high" culture—witness the works of Shakespeare, jazz music, and certain ethnic cuisines, such as northern Italian food.

As popular culture trends bubble up from the cultural matrix, media and opinion leaders begin to communicate the symbols that carry the meanings of the trend. The media that perform this function include television, radio, print, movies, and the theater. The most important mass opinion leaders are performers, songwriters, journalists, advertisers, sports celebrities, and various editors, though people in other walks of life can act as opinion leaders as well. For example, in 1961 John F. Kennedy broke with custom by walking down Pennsylvania Avenue for his inauguration without a hat. The sight of the youthful bare-headed president resulted in a shift in men's fashion that devastated the hat industry.

In sum, the diffusion of popular culture occurs through a process that mimics the spread of innovations. Thus the material covered in Chapter 15 on diffusion processes directly applies to popular culture. The spread of popular culture can be fast or slow. It diffuses through a process that closely approximates the multistep diffusion model. It has a life cycle that can be short (a fad) or very long (e.g., the Beatles continue to be popular to this day). But its impact cannot be underestimated. Marketers who want to link their products to the fads and fashions that push the hot buttons of masses of people should develop an advanced understanding of popular culture.

A MANAGERIAL APPLICATIONS ANALYSIS OF THE DOC MARTENS CASE

Problem Identification

If the Doc Martens case is approached from the perspective of Nike and Reebok, the problem can be phrased in the following manner: Should these companies begin marketing their own versions of grunge shoes, and if so, what marketing strategy should they use?

The Consumer Behavior Analysis and Its Managerial Implications

Three key consumer behavior concepts from the chapter apply to the case: cultural values, cultural symbols, and popular culture. Table 17-5 summarizes these concepts and their managerial implications.

Cultural Values A number of cultural values prevalent in U.S. society apply to the case. These include individualism, practicality, and informality. Doc Martens and their equivalents tap into these basic beliefs about what is good and proper. Marketing research should be conducted to test the hypothesis that the shoes are linked to the cultural values of in-

Managerial Implications of Consumer Behavior Concepts in the Doc Martens Case	
Consumer Behavior Concept	**Managerial Implications**
1. Cultural values	*Market research.* Perform research to test the hypothesis that grunge shoes are linked to the cultural values of individualism, practicality, and informality.
	Positioning strategies. Position shoes as being worn by individuals who are nonconformist, practical, and informal.
	Segmentation. Identify segments of consumers who respond well to the product and positioning strategy (e.g., teenage females).
	Promotional strategy. Develop advertising and point-of-purchase materials that communicate the positioning strategy.
2. Cultural symbols	*Market research.* Determine what cultural symbols should be associated with the product, such as color. Also determine whether the influence of athletes is waning in the popular culture.
	Promotional strategy. Develop advertising messages, packaging, and point-of-purchase materials that employ the symbols identified.
3. Popular culture	*Market research.* Employ focus groups and depth interviews to probe the target market's perception of athletic shoes. Are there signs that the fashion trend is on the decline? Similarly, probe to determine consumer reactions to the "grunge look" fashion trend.
	Product strategy. Based on the market research, estimate demand for the types of shoes and manufacture appropriate numbers of shoes to meet the demand.
	Promotional strategy. Based on the market research, employ advertising as appropriate to lengthen the product life cycle of athletic shoes and/or speed up the adoption process of "grunge-style" shoes/boots.
	Market research. Employ market research to identify the values associated with current popular culture trends and whether these match the product.

TABLE 17-5

dividualism, practicality, and informality. If the answer is found to be "yes," then companies can develop positioning strategies based upon these ideas. In addition, market segments can be identified for whom these values are particularly important, such as teenagers. Finally, advertising strategies can be created to communicate these values to the target markets.

Cultural Symbols Just as Henry Ford's first cars all came in black, most of the grunge-style boots sold today are black. Unless linked expressly to highly formal occasions, black is associated with a lack of pretentiousness and practicality—hallmarks of the Doc Martens look. Cultural symbols should also be linked directly to the product. In the promotional strategy for the shoes decisions should be made concerning what symbols to link to the product. For example, should the color be emphasized in advertisements and point-of-sale materials? What has happened to this symbolism as Martens have appeared in other colors? Since the fashion trend originated with musicians, should the product be linked symbolically to these individuals in promotional efforts? Does this mean that the importance of athletes for endorsements is diminishing and that of performers increasing? Such questions must be answered by conducting carefully developed market research studies.

Popular Culture Finally, Docs are part of popular culture. Once worn by opinion leaders, the shoes became a fashion statement. One critical question for Nike and Reebok is whether the fashion cycle is changing so that wearing athletic shoes for everyday and formal wear is on the decline. To answer this question, managers should perform market research studies, with emphasis on depth interviews and focus groups. A similar question concerns the length of the trend toward wearing Martens-style boots. Again, carefully designed market research studies are required because the answer will directly influence product strategy (i.e., how much to invest in production of the shoes) as well as how the product is promoted. For example, if managers conclude that Martens are in the mature phase of the product life cycle, they may create advertising designed to lengthen their life.

In sum, given the notoriously short life cycle of fashions among teenagers, Nike and Reebok must look carefully at the movement toward "Marten-style" shoes. They should develop strategies to lengthen the life cycle of athletic shoes for nonathletic wear. In addition, they will have to hedge their bets by developing their own line of grunge shoes.

Managerial Recommendations

Three specific recommendations emerge from our managerial applications analysis.

Recommendation 1 Examine whether athletic shoes no longer represent important cultural values. If they don't, athletic shoe manufacturers must either join the Martens-style trend with their own offerings or reposition athletic shoes to represent current cultural values.

Recommendation 2 Investigate the extent to which musicians may be replacing athletes as cultural symbols. If they are, a new group of product endorsers is a reasonable possibility.

Recommendation 3 Determine the extent to which Martens-style shoes are likely to be a long-term trend and utilize this information in deciding whether to start a competitive line of Martens-style shoes.

SUMMARY

A culture is composed of the socially acquired behavior patterns transmitted symbolically through language and other means to the members of a particular society. Culture is a way of life. It consists of the learned values, norms, rituals, and symbols of a society, which are transmitted through both the language and the symbolic features of the society. Cultural values consist of the shared views of a society concerning the desired states of existence and the appropriate economic, social, religious, and other behaviors in which its members engage. Cultural norms are the rules of behavior that people are expected to follow. The three types of cultural norms are customs, mores, and conventions.

Cultural symbols are concrete objects that represent abstract concepts. Symbols can be utilized by managers in naming their products and in designing promotional materials. Cultural rituals are periodically repeated patterns of behavior. Tying products to the rituals can be a successful marketing strategy. Cultural myths are stories that express the key values and ideals of a society.

One's own culture is learned through the process of enculturation. A new, foreign culture is learned through acculturation. Cultures are adaptive, and their customs, values, and norms fulfill needs in the society. Three important sets of factors compose culture and make up the cultural matrix. These factors are the institutional/social environment, the material environment, and cultural values.

Consumer goods act to transfer meaning from the culturally constituted world to consumers. Goods are "way stations" of meaning. The culturally constituted world acts as a lens through which individuals interpret the world around them. Meaning is transferred from the culturally constituted world to goods through the advertising and fashion systems. Meaning is transferred from goods to people through various types of rituals.

A number of values compose the culturally constituted world in the United States. These include: individualism, youthfulness, progress, materialism, activity, achievement, efficiency, informality, and equality. Research has shown that the values a person holds can influence consumption decisions. Specifically, global values may influence domain-specific values, which, in turn, may influence the purchase decision. Values contained in the List of Values scale have been found to be predictive of the purchase of natural foods. Recent research on the value of materialism has indicated that the United States is a highly materialistic society. However, the focus seems to be on instrumental materialism rather than on the more negative terminal materialism.

Cultural rituals are standardized sequences of actions that are periodically repeated. Rituals are dramatically scripted and acted out with formality, seriousness, and intensity. From a consumer behavior perspective, they serve to symbolically link the meaning of a product to an individual. Rituals are composed of four elements: artifacts, scripts, performance roles, and audience. Four types of consumer rituals have been identified: exchange, possession, grooming, and divestment rituals. Examples of rituals having a strong impact on consumer behavior are Christmas, graduations, and weddings.

All cultures have symbols, which are entities that represent ideas and concepts. People can be said to consume symbols—that is, they purchase products and services partly for their symbolic properties. An important point is that the same symbol may be used to represent divergent ideas in different cultures.

Popular culture is the culture of mass appeal. It taps into the experiences and values of the masses, does not require special knowledge to understand it, and involves nonwork activities. In contrast, high culture is exclusive in content, style, and appeal. Examples of popular culture are advertising, television, music, and fashion. Popular culture develops from the overall cultural matrix of a society.

acculturation	culture	fashion	myths
classic fashion trend	customs	global values	norms
conventions	cyclical fashion trend	grooming ritual	popular culture
cresive norm	divestment ritual	high culture	possession ritual
cultural identification	domain-specific values	instrumental materialism	Rokeach value scale
cultural meaning	enacted norm	laddering	symbols
cultural ritual	enculturation	means-end chain models	terminal materialism
cultural values	exchange ritual	mores	values

REVIEW QUESTIONS

1. Define the concept of culture. What are its basic characteristics?

2. What is the role of consumer goods in a culture? What translates the meaning of culture to consumers?

3. What are the seven core American values that have been identified?

4. Identify four examples each of the terminal values and instrumental values defined by Milton Rokeach. How do instrumental and terminal values differ?

5. Consumers may be regarded as having belief systems that include global values, domain-specific values, and evaluations of product attributes. Define these terms and indicate how they are related.

6. Define the concept of a cultural symbol. Give some examples of clothing that are symbols to consumers.

7. What is popular culture? What are its characteristics?

8. Identify four examples of popular culture.

9. How is popular culture formed?

DISCUSSION QUESTIONS

1. Some editorialists have argued that movies and television shows produced in the United States are teaching children to be violent. Instances of 9- to 12-year-olds actually murdering other children have been cited to prove the point. To what extent do you think that the media influence cultural values?

2. Two popular television shows in 1997 were *Home Improvement* and *Silk Stalkings*. Compare and contrast the cultural values that these two shows portray.

3. Global values, domain-specific values, and evaluations of product attributes are often related. Consider the attributes that you prefer in automobiles. How do these preferred attributes reflect your domain-specific values and global values?

4. Describe a ritual that you go through consistently in your everyday life. It could be a religious ritual, some

type of grooming ritual, or even one involving the preparation of food, among other things. To what extent is this ritual shared by others?

5. Go through a magazine and look at the advertisements. Identify as many cultural symbols shown in the print ads as you can. In each case state what you think the advertiser is attempting to do by using the symbol.

6. Consider the popular singer Madonna. What is the symbolic function of the clothing she wears?

7. Identify a current cultural trend that is influencing the behavior of students at your college campus. From where did this trend emerge? What values are transmitted by this trend? How long do you think its life cycle will be?

ENDNOTES

1. The Doc Martens case is based on Joseph Pereira, "Footwear Fad Makes Nike, Reebok Run for Their Money," *The Wall Street Journal*, June 24, 1993, pp. B1, B5; Colin Brown, "Defining Consumerism," *Consumer Policy Review*, Vol. 6 (March–April 1966), pp. 77–78; and Richard C. Morais, "What's Up, Doc?" *Forbes*, January 16, 1995, pp. 42–43.

2. Keith Naughton, "Don't Step on My Blue Suede Hush Puppies," *Business Week*, September 11, 1995, pp. 84–86.

3. Melanie Wallendorf and M. Reilly, "Distinguishing Culture of Origin from Culture of Residence," in *Advances in Consumer Research*, Vol. 10, Richard Bagozzi and Alice Tybout, eds. (Ann Arbor, MI: Association for Consumer Research, 1983), pp. 699–701.

4. Geert Hofstede, *Culture's Consequences* (Beverly Hills, CA: Sage Publications, 1980).

5. David Tse, Kam-hon Lee, Ilan Vertinsky, and Donald Wehrung, "Does Culture Matter? A Cross-Cultural Study of Executives' Choice, Decisiveness, and Risk Adjustment in International Marketing," *Journal of Marketing*, Vol. 52 (October 1988), pp. 81–95.

6. This comment was made by the sociologist (and friend) Chuck Edgley, who made numerous other helpful comments on this chapter.

7. Sunkyu Jun, A. Dwayne Ball, and James W. Gentry, "Modes of Consumer Acculturation," in *Advances in Consumer Research*, Vol. 20, Leigh McAlister and Michael L. Rothschild, eds. (Provo, UT: Association for Consumer Research, 1993), pp. 76–82. See also James W. Gentry, Sunkyu Jun, and Patriya S. Tansuhaj, "Consumer Acculturation Processes and Cultural Conflict: How Generalizable Is a North American Model for Marketing Globally?" *Journal of Business Research*, Vol. 32 (February 1995), pp. 129–139.

8. Henry Fairchild, *Dictionary of Sociology* (Totawa, NJ: Littlefield, Adams, 1970).

9. Peter H. Bloch, "Seeking the Ideal Form: Product Design and Consumer Response," *Journal of Marketing*, Vol. 59 (July 1995), pp. 16–29.

10. George J. McCall and J. L. Simmons, *Social Psychology: A Sociological Approach* (New York: The Free Press, 1982).

11. Joseph Campbell, *Myths, Dreams, and Religion* (New York: E. P. Dutton, 1970).

12. Fara Wagner, "Basketball Thrills Koreans, as NBA Dribbles into Asia," *The Wall Street Journal*, May 17, 1996, p. B9.

13. Kelly Shermach, "Gun Advocates Decry Study on Firearms Sales to Women," *Marketing News*, January 16, 1995, p. 14.

14. Riccardo A. Davis, "Gun Exchange Strikes Nerve," *Advertising Age*, January 3, 1994, pp. 1, 3.

15. Chuck Sudetic, "Cigarettes a Thriving Industry in Bleak Sarajevo," *The New York Times*, September 5, 1993, p. 5.

16. John P. Robinson and Geoffrey Godbey, "Has Fitness Peaked?" *American Demographics*, September 1993, pp. 36–42.

17. Randall Lane, "A Boxing Boom," *Forbes*, December 18, 1995, p. 207; and Gianna Jacobson, "Booming Baby Market," *Success*, October 1995, p. 30.

18. Much of our discussion of the cultural meaning of goods is based on Grant McCracken, "Culture and Consumption: A Theoretical Account of the Structure and Movement of the Cultural Meaning of Consumer Goods," *Journal of Consumer Research*, Vol. 13 (June 1986), pp. 71–84.

19. Ibid., p. 78.

20. For an interesting discussion of the definition of values, see L. J. Shrum, John McCarty, and Tamara Loeffler, "Individual Differences in Value Stability: Are We Really Tapping True Values?" in *Advances in Consumer Research*, Vol. 17, Marvin Goldberg and Gerald Gorn, eds. (Provo, UT: Association for Consumer Research, 1990), pp. 609–615.

21. Theodore Wallin, "The International Executives' Baggage: Cultural Values of the American Frontier," *MSU Business Topics*, Vol. 24 (Spring 1976), pp. 49–58.

22. Cora DuBois, "The Dominant Value Profile in American Culture," *American Anthropologist*, Vol. 57 (December 1955), pp. 1232–1239. Also see Janet T. Spence, "Achievement American Style," *American Psychologist*, December 1985, pp. 1285–95.

23. Frank H. Alpert and Michael A. Kamins, "An Empirical Investigation of Consumer Memory, Attitude and Perceptions Toward Pioneer and Follower Brands," *Journal of Marketing*, Vol. 50 (October 1995), pp. 34–45.

24. Milton Rokeach, *Understanding Human Values* (New York: The Free Press, 1979).

25. J. Michael Munson and Edward McQuarrie, "Shortening the Rokeach Value Survey for Use in Consumer Research," in *Advances in Consumer Research*, Michael J. Houston, ed. (Provo, UT: Association for Consumer Research, 1988), pp. 381–386.

26. Zhengyuan Wang and C. P. Rao, "Personal Values and Shopping Behavior: A Structural Equation Test of the RVS in China," in *Advances in Consumer Research*, Vol. 22, Frank R. Kardes and Mita Sujan, eds. (Provo, UT: Association for Consumer Research, 1995), pp. 373–380.

27. D. E. Vinson, J. Scott, and L. Lamont, "The Role of Personal Values in Marketing and Consumer Behavior," *Journal of Marketing*, Vol. 41 (April 1977), pp. 44–50.

28. Thomas J. Reynolds and David B. Whitlack, "Applying Laddering Data to Communications Strategy and Advertising Practice," pp. 9–17; Charles E. Gengler and Thomas J. Reynolds, "Consumer Understanding and Advertising Strategy: Analysis

and Strategic Translation of Laddering Data"; Gerald Zaltman and Robin Higie Coulter, "Seeing the Voice of the Consumer: Metaphor-Based Advertising Research," pp. 35–51, all in *Journal of Advertising Research*, Vol. 35 (July–August 1995).

29. John A. McCarty and Patricia M. Hattwick, "Cultural Value Orientations: A Comparison of Magazine Advertisements from the United States and Mexico," *Advances in Consumer Research*, Vol. 19, John F. Sherry, Jr., and Brian Sternthal, eds. (Provo, UT: Association for Consumer Research, 1992), pp. 34–38.

30. Lynn Kahle, Basil Poulos, and Ajay Sukhdial, "Changes in Social Values in the United States During the Past Decade," *Journal of Advertising Research*, Vol. 28 (February–March 1988), pp. 35–41.

31. Pamela Homer and Lynn Kahle, "A Structural Equation Test of the Value-Attitude-Behavior Hierarchy," *Journal of Personality and Social Psychology*, Vol. 54 (April 1988), pp. 638–646.

32. Lynn Kahle, "Role-Relaxed Consumers—A Trend of the Nineties," *Journal of Advertising Research*, Vol. 35 (March–April 1995), pp. 66–71.

33. Russell W. Belk, "Material Values in the Comics: A Content Analysis of Comic Books Featuring Themes of Wealth," *Journal of Consumer Research*, Vol. 14 (June 1987), pp. 26–42.

34. Ibid. The somewhat surprising conclusion that there is little evidence that material values have grown in importance has been found previously. One study compared values in the late 1950s to values in the late 1970s. The values of wealth and accumulation of property and luxury goods actually decreased in frequency during that period, while the values of comfort and relaxed living increased in frequency slightly dur-ing the time span. See Harold Kassarjian, "Males and Females in the Funnies: A Content Analysis," in *Personal Values and Consumer Psychology*, Robert Pitts and Arch Woodside, eds. (Lexington, MA: Lexington Books, 1984), pp. 87–109. Another researcher compared the values portrayed in comic books to those found in underground comix between 1971 and 1972 and 1981 and 1982. Comix books arose on college campuses as a means to provide artistic and journalistic freedom for young writers and authors who opposed the Vietnam War. In general, their messages were antiwar, prodrugs, and pro–sexual freedom. Surprisingly, the results of this study revealed that materialistic themes were more prevalent in the underground comix books than in comic books. Materialistic themes decreased in frequency in the ten-year period in comic books, while increasing substantially in frequency in the underground comix. See Susan Spiggle, "Measuring Social Values: A Content Analysis of Sunday Comics and Underground Comix," *Journal of Consumer Research*, Vol. 13 (June 1986), pp. 100–113.

35. Monroe Friedman, "The Changing Language of a Consumer Society: Brand Name Usage in Popular American Novels in the Postwar Era," *Journal of Consumer Research*, Vol. 11 (March 1985), pp. 927–938.

36. Russell Belk and Richard Pollay, "Materialism and Magazine Advertising During the Twentieth Century," in *Advances in Consumer Research*, Vol. 12, Elizabeth Hirschman and Morris Holbrook, eds. (Provo, UT: Association for Consumer Research, 1985), pp. 394–398.

37. Ibid., p. 397.

38. Floyd W. Rudmin, "German and Canadian Data on Motivations for Ownership: Was Pythagoras Right?" in *Advances in Consumer Research*, Vol. 17, Marvin Goldberg and Gerald Gorn, eds. (Provo, UT: Association for Consumer Research, 1990), pp. 176–181.

39. Scott Dawson and Gary Bamossy, "Isolating the Effect of Non-Economic Factors on the Development of a Consumer Culture: A Comparison of Materialism in the Netherlands and the United States," in *Advances in Consumer Research*, Vol. 17, Marvin Goldberg and Gerald Gorn, eds. (Provo, UT: Association for Consumer Research, 1990), pp. 182–185. Other research has suggested that the level of materialism in Europe has not changed much in recent years. See Caolan Mannion and Teresa Brannick, "Materialism and Its Measurement," *Ibar*, Vol. 16 (1995), pp. 1–16.

40. Guliz Ger and Russell W. Belk, "Measuring and Comparing Materialism Cross-Culturally," in *Advances in Consumer Research*, Vol. 17, Marvin Goldberg and Gerald Gorn, eds. (Provo, UT: Association for Consumer Research, 1990), pp. 186–192.

41. Spiggle, "Measuring Social Values," p. 100.

42. Tara Parker-Pope, "British Budweiser Ads Rankle American Indians," *The Wall Street Journal*, July 16, 1996, p. B1.

43. This definition was taken almost entirely from Dennis Rook, "The Ritual Dimension of Consumer Behavior," *Journal of Consumer Research*, Vol. 12 (December 1985), pp. 251–264. A small change was made to add the idea that rituals are culturally mandated in order to help distinguish the idea of a ritual from that of a habit.

44. These ideas were developed by Mary A. Stanfield Tetreault and Robert E. Kleine III, "Ritual, Ritualized Behavior, and Habit:

Refinements and Extensions of the Consumption Ritual Construct," in *Advances in Consumer Research*, Vol. 17, Marvin Goldberg and Gerald Gorn, eds. (Provo, UT: Association for Consumer Research, 1990), pp. 31–38.

45. Rook, "The Cultural Dimension of Consumer Behavior."

46. McCracken, "Culture and Consumption."

47. Ray Brown, *Rituals and Ceremonies in Popular Culture* (Bowling Green, OH: Popular Press, 1980). For a discussion of funerals and other aspects of death, see James W. Gentry and Cathy Goodwin, "Social Support for Decision Making During Grief Due to Death," in *Marketing and Consumer Research in the Public Interest*, Ronald P. Hill, ed. (Thousand Oaks, CA: Sage, 1996), pp. 55–68; and Terrance G. Gabel, Phylis Mansfield, and Kevin Westbrook, "The Disposal of Consumers: An Exploratory Analysis of Death-Related Consumption," in *Advances in Consumer Research*, Vol. 23, Kim P. Corfman and John G. Lynch, Jr., eds. (Provo, UT: Association for Consumer Research, 1996), pp. 361–367.

48. Brenda Gainer, "Ritual and Relationships: Interpersonal Influences on Shared Consumption," *Journal of Business Research*, Vol. 32 (March 1995), pp. 253–260.

49. Charles Morris, *Signs, Language, and Behavior* (New York: George Braziller, 1946).

50. Elizabeth Hirschman, "Comprehending Symbolic Consumption: Three Theoretical Issues," in *Symbolic Consumption Behavior*, Elizabeth Hirschman and Morris Holbrook, eds., *Proceedings of the Conference on Consumer Aesthetics and Symbolic Consumption*, May 1980, pp. 4–6, 15. See also Morris Holbrook, *Consumer Research: Introspective Essays on the Study of Consumption* (Thousand Oaks, CA: Sage, 1995).

51. However, an object can possess symbolic value for its possessor independent of its value to others. We are unlikely to swap wedding rings even when the alternative offered is of better quality. See Marsha L. Richins, "Valuing Things: The Public and Private Meanings of Possessions," *Journal of Consumer Research*, Vol. 21 (December 1994), pp. 504–521.

52. Cacilie Rohwedder, "Name-Finders Save New Products from Fiascos in Global Market," *The Wall Street Journal*, April 11, 1996, p. B5.

53. Teri Agins, "Signs of the Times: Logos on Clothing are Back and They're Bigger Than Ever," *The Wall Street Journal*, February 22, 1996, pp. B1, B9.

54. This section is based on an article by John F. Sherry Jr. and Eduardo Camargo, "May Your Life Be Marvelous: English Language Labelling and the Semiotics of Japanese Promotion," *Journal of Consumer Research*, Vol. 14 (September 1987), pp. 174–188.

55. Hamish McRae, *The World in 2020: Power, Culture and Prosperity* (Boston: Harvard Business School Press, 1995).

56. This definition, as well as the characteristics of popular culture, was taken from Michael J. Bell, "The Study of Popular Culture," in *Concise Histories of American Popular Culture*, M. Thomas Inge, ed. (Westport, CT: Greenwood Press, 1982), p. 443.

57. M. Thomas Inge, *Handbook of American Popular Culture*, 2nd ed. (New York: Greenwood Press, 1989).

58. Robert S. Alley, "Television," in *Handbook of American Popular Culture*, p. 1368.

59. W. James Potter, "Three Strategies for Elaborating the Cultivation Hypothesis," *Journalism Quarterly*, Vol. 65, (Winter 1988), pp. 930–939.

60. For a discussion of rap music and its impact on children's advertising, see M. Elizabeth Blair and Mark N. Hatala, "The Use of Rap Music in Children's Advertising," *Advances in Consumer Research*, Vol. 19, John F. Sherry and Brian Sternthal, eds. (Provo, UT: Association for Consumer Research, 1992), pp. 719–724.

61. George B. Sproles, *Fashion: Consumer Behavior Toward Dress* (Minneapolis, MN: Burgess, 1979).

62. Cathy Goodwin, "Good Guys Don't Wear Polyester: Consumption Ideology in a Detective Series," *Advances in Consumer Research*, Vol. 19, John F. Sherry and Brian Sternthal, eds. (Provo, UT: Association for Consumer Research, 1992), pp. 739–745.

63. For an excellent discussion of male vanity, see Alan Furnham, "You're So Vain," *Fortune*, September 9, 1996, pp. 66–82.

64. These characteristics were originally developed by Christopher M. Miller, Shelby H. McIntyre, and Murali K. Mantrala, "Toward Formalizing Fashion Theory," *Journal of Marketing Research*, Vol. 30 (May 1993), pp. 142–147.

WILL FUR REVIVE?

In 1987 sales of fur peaked in the United States at $1.8 billion. From that point, things fell apart and sales plunged to just $1 billion in 1991. The impact on manufacturers and retailers was devastating. Bloated inventories and rampant discounting of prices led to losses and bankruptcies.

What caused this dramatic change of fortune in the fur industry? Two factors clearly had an impact. The more publicized one was the efforts of animal rights groups to discourage affluent consumers from purchasing furs. Going so far as to threaten to throw red paint on people wearing fur, animal rights activists received widespread publicity in the late 1980s and early 1990s. However, spokespersons for the fur industry claim that the impact of the antifur crusaders has been vastly overblown. Indeed, as reported in *The Wall Street Journal*, the "Fur Council says its research shows that fur sales reflect the state of the economy and that animal rights activities are not a significant factor."

The second, and possibly more important, factor responsible for the plunge in fur sales, then, was the state of the economy. As the United States slipped into a recession in the early 1990s, sales declined. A tax on expensive luxury goods implemented in 1991 severely hurt sales. When that tax was lifted, sales jumped. Then, in late 1993, when details of the Clinton administration's 1994 budget became public, sales turned down again because of taxes being raised on the wealthy—the main target market for furriers.

Despite these problems, however, sales of furs did increase in 1992 by 10 percent. As a result, prices firmed, and the remaining furriers began to make money. A colder-than-usual winter in 1992–1993 helped fur sales as well.

Some analysts argue that the improving economy and changes in consumer sentiment regarding wearing fur bode well for the industry. Others counter that antifur groups remain a potent force. Antifur parades were held over the Thanksgiving holiday in 1993. In addition, there were "speakouts" in which people wearing fur were confronted on the street by hostile individuals carrying signs saying "There is no excuse for wearing fur."

Still, the fur industry continues to discount the impact of animal rights groups. The industry viewpoint is that furriers need to pay more attention to current fashion trends. As one industry spokesperson said, "Fur needs to look like fashion, instead of just looking like fur." Another industry spokesperson took an even stronger position: "Fur has become a fashion industry, which is better for the future of fur." This attitude appears to be prevailing. In 1994 designer Karl Lagerfeld's collection featured mixed real and fake fur, but in 1995 his line featured rare pale sable coats bearing $150,000 price tags. Lagerfeld told reporters at a Milan fashion show, "I'm tired of being politically correct." Also boosting the industry was the revelation that the group whose members had earlier threatened to throw red paint on fur wearers, People for the Ethical Treatment of Animals, had falsified a story accusing alligator farmers of slowly bludgening alligators to death with baseball bats.

Based on Patrick M. Reilly, "Furriers Hustle to Keep Sales Warm," *The Wall Street Journal*, September 21, 1993, pp. B1, B8; and Nina Munk, "The Beauty in the Beast," *Forbes*, October 23, 1995, pp. 76–80.

Questions

1. Define in your own words the problems faced by the fur industry.

2. What consumer behavior concepts from the chapter apply to the case?

3. What are the managerial implications of these consumer behavior concepts?

4. Consider the cultural matrix identified in the chapter. Which of the consumer concepts identified in the matrix have application to this case?

18

CULTURAL PROCESSES II
THE SUBCULTURAL ENVIRONMENT
AND DEMOGRAPHICS

INTRODUCTORY CASE

Toys for All of Us

An excellent example of an industry heavily influenced by demographic and subcultural trends over the past 30 years is the toy industry. During the late 1950s and 1960s the toy business flourished. Members of the huge baby-boom generation were in their childhood, so the total market for toys grew rapidly. Although the growth of the industry slowed somewhat in the 1970s as the U.S. birthrate declined, sales were surprisingly strong. The reason was that with a rising divorce rate and smaller households, each adult felt obligated to supply toys to the few children being born during the baby-bust years. When births rose again in the early 1980s, as the baby boomers started families of their own, toy manufacturers again got on the fast track. In a given year seven out of ten households buy toys or games, purchasing an average of two at a time on five separate visits to toy stores. One in five parents buys more toys for nieces or nephews, and one in five adults over 60 buys a toy for a grandchild.[1]

The toy business, however, goes far beyond inexpensive presents for young children. Consider Cara, a precocious 8-year-old, who begins and ends each day thinking about

horses. She collects Bryer model horses—which currently number more than 30 in her stable. She attends Bryer model horse shows and subscribes to a newsletter on model horses. At the model horse shows collectors (mostly women in their 30s and 40s and young girls from 6 to 12) buy and sell Man-of-War, Secretariat, and other famous models. In this female market that is the equivalent of baseball card collecting, exceptionally rare models can cost hundreds of dollars. In addition to horses, equine equipment (saddles, etc.) is also available.

Men also collect toys. Indeed, if one subscribes to a magazine called the *Toy Shop*, one finds hundreds of ads for old toys that are now collectibles. The serious collectors tend to be 35 to 54 years old. The readers of *Toy Shop* average over $50,000 in household income and 70 percent have attended college. They spend on average over $2,000 a year on toy collections. What do they collect? The most valuable items tend to come from the 1950s and 1960s. One store owner who specializes in selling collectible toys uses the following rule-of-thumb to decide what collectors want: "If it screwed you up when you were growing up, I deal it."[2]

INTRODUCTION

The United States and Canada are composed largely of immigrants from throughout the world and their descendants. Although U.S. and Canadian "cultures" do exist, the melting pot in either country has not created an entirely homogeneous people out of the hodge-podge of settlers. North America is "a mixture of subcultures reflecting the national heritage, language, religious, racial, and geographic diversity of a vast continent populated primarily by waves of immigrants from many diverse cultures and subcultures."[3]

Within the overall culture of North America, subgroups retain some of the values, beliefs, and symbols of their culture of origin. These groups form subcultures that can be important target markets for marketers. For example, the need of Orthodox Jews for kosher food makes them a tempting target for marketers willing to adequately control the preparation of their food products. Meanwhile, mainstream marketers, such as ConAgra, have begun to market kosher foods because consumers are attracted to the wholesome image of these food products. For example, 60 percent of the sales of Hebrew National's pure beef frankfurters go to non-Jewish customers.[4]

In addition to originating from immigration, subcultures can develop from naturally occurring subdivisions within a society. All societies contain such subgroups, which are usually based on age, social class, and regional differences. In each case there are sufficient differences in values and lifestyles to create a subculture. For example, the commonalities of retirement, the physical ailments of age, and similar housing needs have created an elderly subculture.

A **subculture** may be defined as a subdivision of a national culture that is based on some unifying characteristic, such as social status or nationality, and whose members share similar patterns of behavior that are distinct from those of the national culture.[5] Numerous demographic characteristics have been used to identify subcultures, including:

Nationality (e.g., Hispanic, Italian, Polish)
Race (e.g., African-American, Native-American, Asian-American)
Region (e.g., New England, Southwest)
Age (e.g., elderly, teenager)
Religion (e.g., Catholic, Jewish)
Gender
Social class (e.g., upper class, lower class)

Subcultures versus Demographics

The concepts of subcultures and demographics are closely related. **Demographic variables** describe the characteristics of populations. Examples of demographic variables are:

Nationality	Marital status
Age	Income
Religion	Region
Gender	Ethnicity
Occupation	Education

Of course, many of these demographic variables also describe subcultures. Thus within the demographic category of religion one can identify a number of distinct subcultural groups in the United States, including Jews, Christians, and Moslems. However, when one speaks of cultures or subcultures, the focus is on the group's values, customs, symbols, and behavior. Demographic features merely describe the characteristics of a population of people. The reason a marketer might speak of an African-American subculture is that this demographic characteristic conveniently describes a group of people who have similar behavior patterns.

Changes in age and ethnic distribution and attitudes toward gays and lesbians have had a major impact on marketing strategy. For example, the changing nature of the social classes in recent years has forced retailers to go either upscale or to the lower end of the market. Companies like Sears, which traditionally focused on the middle class, lost market share to specialty stores at the upper end and discount department stores at the lower end. During the 1980s and early 1990s the sales of specialty stores like The Limited and The Gap grew by over 20 percent per year. Sears and J. C. Penney have had to make major adjustments to meet this new competition.

We should also note that large groups of people may form subcultures based on a shared interest in a particular type of product. Professional musicians and artists, for instance, form distinct subcultures that many companies attempt to reach with a unique marketing mix. In the 1960s a psychedelic subculture formed around a shared interest in hallucinogens.

We discuss in this chapter certain key subcultural groups that are more "mainstream" than the subculture of users of hallucinogens. We begin with the important topic of age subcultures.

AGE SUBCULTURES

As consumers move through their life cycle, they undergo predictable changes in values, lifestyles, and consumption patterns. A 5-year-old has a completely different set of needs from a 20-year-old, who, in turn, has different needs from a 65-year-old. Because various age "cohorts" of consumers have similar values, needs, and behavioral patterns, they form subcultures that may constitute important market segments. Furthermore, changes in the numbers of people in age categories because of variations in birthrates create new marketing opportunities.

Marketers are practically obsessed with analyzing age trends because it is much easier to make highly accurate projections of the future age composition of the population than to project other demographic factors, such as income or occupation. These projections allow marketers to recognize potential marketing opportunities years in advance, which greatly simplifies the planning process.

Perhaps as profound as the changing ethnic population of the United States is its changing age composition and income distribution. During the 1980s the number of children under 17 years of age living below the poverty line increased from under 15 percent to over 20 percent (20.8 percent in 1995). At the same time, the poverty rate among people over 65 decreased to 10.5 percent in 1995—which was lower than among either children or the working-age population (11.4 percent).

Consumer Behavior Factoid

Question: What is the oldest business in America?

Answer: Avedis Zildjian Company has been making musical cymbals since 1623—from Mozart to Metallica. Certified as the oldest business in America (but started in Constantinople), Avedis Zildjian has held on to its niche by working closely with its "subculture"—percussionists. Artists often imagine a certain result, and Zildjian makes a cymbal to produce the desired sound. The CEO himself has learned to play the drums.

Source: Thomas Petzinger, Jr., "Craigie Zildjian Aims for Higher Life Forms in Drummers' Cymbals," *The Wall Street Journal*, May 31, 1996, p. B1.

One factor that strongly influences the age distribution of the population is **immigration**. Immigrants, whether legal or illegal, tend to be younger than the native-born population. Immigrant women also tend to have high birthrates. Because of the youth of the immigrants and their higher fertility rates, immigration is the single most important factor retarding the aging trend of the U.S. population.

Four age groups of critical importance to marketers are discussed in this section: the baby-boom generation, Generation X, Generation Y, and the elderly.

The Baby Boomers

Although it is debatable whether the **baby-boom generation** actually forms a subculture, there are sufficient lifestyle similarities in the huge generation of Americans born between 1946 and 1964 for us to say that this group has a large impact on marketers and the economy as a whole. The United States is currently experiencing a fundamental change in the age characteristics of its population, principally because of dramatic changes in birthrates over the last half century. During the Great Depression of the 1930s there was a **baby bust**, as the number of children born to the average woman during her lifetime (i.e., the **fertility rate**) dropped to the replacement level of 2.1 births. Total births declined by 25 percent.[6]

The Depression "birth dearth" was followed by the post–World War II baby boom. The fertility rate shot up past 3.8, and the total number of births increased by one-third over Depression levels. The baby boom lasted through 1964, to be followed by another baby bust. Induced by improvements in the technology of birth prevention (e.g., the "Pill") and the emergence of the working woman, this baby bust sent fertility rates plunging to as low as 1.8 in 1976—a rate far below the replacement level.[7] Lasting from 1965 to 1980, the latest baby bust produced what is known to marketers as Generation X.

This series of changes in the U.S. birthrate created a huge bulge of 77 million baby boomers (over half again as large as the previous generation). As time passes and the boomers grow older, the bulge moves through the population like a melon being digested by a boa constrictor.[8] For example, in 1980 there were fewer than 25 million Americans in their 40s; however, by the year 2000, the number in their 40s will almost double. As the years pass, the bulge moves on, growing older and changing the nature of the marketplace. In 1970 the majority of baby boomers were between 6 and 24 years of age. Marketers of soft drinks and fast foods were ecstatic at the hordes of teenyboppers clamoring for their products. By 1996, though, the earliest baby boomers had reached 50 and the others were in their 30s and 40s. These consumers tend to be affluent and have a new set of product needs and wants. For example, demand for home furnishings is increasing as baby boomers purchase expensive furniture, draperies, and carpets (one indication is that there are now about 100 magazines on home design).

Table 18-1 gives an overview of projected changes in the U.S. population between 1995 and 2005. As you can see, two age groups will shrink considerably during this period: those 25 to 34 years old will decrease by 11.7 percent, and those under 5 years old will decrease by 4.2 percent. A huge increase will occur among those between 45 and 64 years old. These are the baby boomers. The second-greatest increase will occur among those 75 years and older.

Implications for Marketing Strategy One of the prime marketing requirements for consumer-goods firms is to track the baby-boom generation. Indeed, there is a marketing law that might be phrased: "Those who live by the baby boom shall die by the baby boom." As this generation's tastes and preferences change with the passing years, the fortunes of manufacturers are dramatically affected. For example, with their traditional target market of 5- to 17-year-olds declining by more than one-half million during the 1980s,

Projections of the U.S. Population, 1995–2005

Age Group	Population (1,000)		Percentage Distribution		Percentage Change	
	1995	2005	1995	2005	1985–1995	1995–2005
Under 5	20,181	19,333	7.7	6.7	+13.1%	−4.2%
5–17	48,853	53,790	18.4	18.7	+9.1	10.1
18–24	25,465	28,238	10.1	9.8	−11.9	10.9
25–34	41,670	36,792	16.6	12.8	−.1	−11.7
35–44	42,150	43,075	15.7	14.9	33	2.2
45–54	30,224	41,219	10.8	14.3	34.6	36.4
55–64	21,241	28,870	8.2	10.0	−4.0	35.9
65–74	18,963	18,623	7.2	6.5	10.9	−1.8
75 +	14,685	18,347	5.4	6.4	27.1	25.1
Total	263,434	288,286				

Source: U.S. Department of Commerce, *Statistical Abstract of the United States*, 1995 (Washington, DC: U.S. Government Printing Office, 1995).

TABLE 18-1

McDonald's Corporation was threatened with both a decline in revenues and the loss of its primary work force—teenagers. To navigate the treacherous shoals of age demographics, the company hired retired people to work behind its counters.

Other companies also had to make major adjustments. In 1981 Levi Strauss was the world's largest clothing manufacturer, with jeans production peaking at 560 million pairs. However, by the mid-1980s the company's profits began to drop dramatically, and were down 20 percent by 1988. One of Levi's strategic responses was to move into roomier khaki and chino pants, which fit the middle-aged spread of the baby boomers better than jeans did. Levi's now sells about $1 billion worth of Dockers slacks per year. Levi's Dockers sales were also helped by the fact that younger males, who might prefer jeans for everyday wear, need at least one pair of dressier pants, and Dockers fit the bill. Such upscale designers as Geoffrey Beene and Tommy Hilfiger have used elastic waistbands to cope with the expanding middles of baby boomers.[9]

Not all has been positive for the baby-boom generation. Because of their large numbers, the baby boomers have had major problems finding jobs. In fact, many are chronically underemployed. One result is the dependence of some boomers on their parents for financial support even into their 40s.[10] These boomers have been called RYAs (returning young adults who move back in with relatives) and ILYAs (incompletely launched young adults who are not financially independent).

Consumer Behavior Factoid

Question: For what are baby boomers nostalgic?

Answer: Beatlemania. Matchbox cars. Grown women get weepy over Easy Bake ovens. Bullwinkle (one of the authors has a Boris and Natasha tie). Mr. Potato Head. Etch-a-Sketch. These are products that remind baby boomers of their youth, and they're all selling well. Volkswagen may even bring back the Beetle.

Source: Evelyn Neeves, "It's the Era of Nostalgia with Legs," *The New York Times*, December 31, 1995, pp. 4.

Generation X

Born between 1965 and 1980, **Generation X** (the "baby busters") is small, but possesses $125 billion of discretionary income. Given a variety of names, such as "afterboomers" and "flyers" (i.e., fun-loving youth en route to success), the group is noted for valuing religion, formal rituals (e.g., proms), and materialism, and has more negative attitudes toward work and getting ahead than the boomers had at their age.[11] Because of the group's small size, employers must compete for them in the job market. For example, the U.S. Army began its Army College Fund, allowing enlistees to save up to $25,200 during their term of service for college. One research group calls Xers in the United States and Northern Europe the "new realists" because they have resigned themselves to the possibility that they will never achieve the affluence of their parents' generation.[12]

Until recently Generation X was ignored by marketers. But, as one executive pointed out, "as baby boomers enter middle age, marketers are being forced to confront Generation X. These people will fuel the growth for product categories from fast food to liquor to apparel to soft-drinks." In the television arena Fox Broadcasting (e.g., *The Simpsons*) and MTV have specifically targeted Xers. Advertising managers are particularly concerned with how to reach them. A slew of Gen X magazines has been launched, and they are remarkably similar, focusing on music, celebrities and lifestyle. Among those that fell shortly after launch were *Real*, *Forehead*, *The Nose*, and *Hypno*.[13]

Because of its spending power, Generation X is being taken seriously by marketers. This group is moving into the time of life when its members are interested in purchasing autos, houses, and other "big-ticket" items. The VP-general manager of Nissan USA said that Generation X now accounts for 25–30 percent of its auto sales. He added, "As they age and move up in income, they'll grow in importance. We want to make a good first impression."[14]

Xers are also part of a new infatuation called "global teens." For years international marketers have noticed that people in different countries with similar educational and income backgrounds act in much the same way. The Xers may be the first generation to have a great many commonalities: many watch the same TV shows, drink Coke and eat Big Macs, see the same movies, "surf" the Internet, and wear the "global teen uniform": baggy Levi's or Diesel jeans, T-shirt, and Nikes or Doc Martens. This tying together via a worldwide media net may mean that teenagers everywhere are leading "parallel lives," and therefore cross-national marketing opportunities are much greater.[15]

Generation Y

The next cohort to appear on the horizon are the 72 million children of the baby boomers, the first of whom will reach adulthood in the year 2000. Now aged 18 or younger, they represent 28 percent of the current population, rivaling the baby boomers' 30 percent.

Like Xers, **Generation Y** is more heterogeneous in racial and socioeconomic terms than the boomers. For example, the original boomers were 75 percent non-Hispanic

---

Question: What form of gambling have Generation Xers adopted?

Answer: Bingo. Like Tony Bennett and polyester, bingo became a craze of Xers in the mid-1990s. All are retro, and therefore hip.

Source: Andrea Peterson, "Generation Xers Pick Up a New Line At Bars: 'BINGO!'" *The Wall Street Journal*, April 10, 1996, pp. A1, A8.

Consumer Behavior Factoid

white, while the Yers are only 67 percent non-Hispanic white. Generation Y is the first generation to have significant numbers (about 1 in 35) of mixed race, so the traditional racial categories are somewhat obsolete for marketers interested in this group. Another difference is that the older half of the boomers were born in the era of segregation, ancient history to the Yers. The boomers learned that "Father Knows Best," but for the Yers, "Dad isn't home": in 1970 only 12 percent of children lived in a one-parent household, while in 1993 a full 27 percent did.[16] One group of Yers is particularly in demand. There are only 7.4 million 12- to 15-year-old girls, the prime babysitter pool—and 35 million families with children ranging from infancy to 11 years old who need sitters.[17]

The Elderly

A fourth major age trend in the United States is the "graying of America." The aging of the population, in fact, will be one of the most dominant demographic factors for the foreseeable future. Barring global war or other disasters, the U.S. population under 30 will never again be as large as it was in 1983. By the year 2020 Americans over 65 will outnumber teenagers two to one.

A number of factors—birthrates, mortality rates, and immigration rates—will determine the characteristics of the U.S. population in the years ahead. Unfortunately for marketers, each of these factors is difficult to predict accurately. Birthrates are influenced by available contraceptive technology as well as by cultural values and lifestyle patterns. **Mortality rates** have been falling noticeably since the 1970s: life expectancy increased by three years during that decade, and it is estimated that it increased another two to three years in the 1980s. Men born in 1990 will live, on average, 72 years; women, 79 years. Because of the striking difference in the life expectancies of men and women, an aging population means a lot more women. Of Americans over 85 years old today, women outnumber men by almost two and a half to one. Elderly women will increasingly form an important segment for marketers to target.

The Mature Consumer Just who is the **mature consumer**? No specific age is associated with becoming "mature" or reaching one's "golden years." However, a series of events occur between the ages of 55 and 65 that set the aging consumer apart from younger people. During this time retirement has either occurred or is anticipated. In all likelihood income is reduced, and will become relatively fixed after retirement, making inflation a threat. Health concerns become more prominent at about this age, and close friends begin to die.

Mature consumers are generally well off financially. While only 23 percent of American consumers are 55 or older, they control 75 percent of the nation's wealth and about half of its discretionary income.[18] Mature consumers also have a great deal of free time. In 1900, 60 percent of all men over 65 were still working. In 1940 the figure was 40 percent, and by the 1990s only 17 percent of men over 65 were working.[19] This early-retirement trend was largely made possibly by the stronger financial position of mature consumers in the 1980s.

Mature consumers—here defined as age 55 or older—differ from younger people on two major dimensions. First, they process information differently. In particular, their visual, hearing, and taste senses are less acute. One study found that information-processing differences limit the extent to which the elderly are able to utilize nutritional information about cereals. Compared to younger consumers, the elderly were less able to search intensively for nutritional information on packages and to select an appropriate cereal.[20] From a public policy perspective, these results suggest that while nutritional information is more readily available today on packages, the elderly may not be able to make appropriate use of it. The reported changes in older people's information-processing abilities indicate that marketers should be concerned with how much time the elderly are given to make a decision. Providing additional time for information processing—for instance, by lengthening an advertisement or having salespersons make more leisurely presentations—may assist older consumers and make brand- or store-loyal purchasers out of them.

A second way in which mature consumers differ from younger consumers is that their motor skills decline. As people age, their ability to walk, to write, to talk clearly, and to drive a car gradually deteriorates. In many cities companies are now providing a variety of services to the elderly to help them overcome these age-related handicaps. Examples of such services are in-home food delivery, yard and house cleaning, fix-up services, and nursing care. Table 18-2 lists several ways in which the consumption and buying habits of the elderly differ from those of younger consumers.

One major finding concerning the elderly is that they are cautious consumers: they do not tend to risk being wrong for the sake of acting quickly.[21] In fact, the higher the perceived risk, the less likely the elderly are to try a product.[22]

Another difference between the elderly and younger consumers is that as people grow older, they spend more time watching television. While all Americans spend more time in front of a TV than at any other activity except sleep and work, the elderly use TV both for entertainment and for obtaining information. Television is so important as a source of information partly because as people age, they have fewer social contacts.[23]

For all these similarities among the elderly, marketers still find that attitude, more than age, defines the mature marketplace. The U.S. elderly generally feel younger than they actually are.[24] One implication for managers is that promotional materials should portray the elderly at the age they feel rather than at their chronological age.

Consumption and Buying Habits of Mature Consumers Compared to Younger Consumers

1. Shopping Behaviors
   a. Shop more frequently.
   b. Spend less per shopping trip.
   c. Shop less often at night.
   d. Use coupons.
   e. Pay with cash—not credit cards.
   f. Shop less at discount stores.
2. Media Habits
   a. Watch 60% more TV, particularly in the daytime.
   b. Read more newspapers.
   c. Listen to less radio, particularly FM.
3. What They Want from Retailers
   a. Courteous treatment.
   b. Personal assistance.
   c. Delivery service.
   d. Rest facilities (e.g., benches).

Sources: Adapted from K. L. Bernhardt and T. C. Kinnear, *Advances in Consumer Research*, Vol. 3 (Ann Arbor, MI: Association for Consumer Research, 1976), pp. 449–452; and Zarrel Lambert, "An Investigation of Older Consumers' Unmet Needs and Wants at the Retail Level," *Journal of Retailing*, Vol. 55 (Winter 1979), p. 43.

TABLE 18-2

ETHNIC SUBCULTURES

Another demographic variable frequently employed to describe subcultures is ethnicity. Although used in a variety of ways, **ethnicity** generally refers to a group bound together by ties of cultural homogeneity. That is, the group is linked by similar values, customs, dress, religion, and language. Ethnicity is frequently closely related to nationality or region of origin. One may speak of Mexican-Americans and Chinese-Americans as ethnic groups because each shares a common national or geographic ancestry along with a similar culture. Table 18-3 provides population projections for several ethnic groups from 1995 to 2020. In this section of the chapter we discuss three ethnic subcultures of importance to marketers: the African-American, Hispanic, and Asian-American subcultures.

The African-American Subculture

A number of factors shape the **African-American subculture**, which represents almost 13 percent of the U.S. population. One major contributor is income deprivation. In the 1990s, 37 percent of African-American households had incomes of under $15,000. In contrast, 30 percent of Hispanic and 14 percent of white households had incomes this low.[25] Other factors influencing the subculture are (1) educational disparities, (2) a young, highly mobile family structure often headed by a female, and (3) concentration in central cities.

Despite these disadvantages, the black subculture is growing in importance as a market segment. As shown in Table 18-4, it has impressive buying power, it is increasing in size faster than the general population, and it is rising in socioeconomic status.

The African-American subculture is also marked by the importance of religious and social organizations. African-Americans disproportionately belong to fundamentalist Protestant groups and to the Democratic party. There is also a recognized speech pattern, known as AAVE—African American Vernacular English—that is used to some extent by

U.S. Population Projections for White, Black, Asian, and Hispanic Groups, 1995–2020			
	White	Black	Asian	Hispanic*
% Distribution				
1995	82.9%	12.5%	3.7%	10.2%
2000	81.9	12.8	4.4	11.3
2010	80	13.4	5.7	13.5
2020	78.2	13.9	6.9	15.7
% Change				
1995–2000	3.6	7.1	24.3	16.3
2000–2010	6.2	13.4	41.8	30.0
2010–2020	6.0	12.9	31.8	26.4

*Persons of Hispanic origin may be of any race.

Source: U.S. Department of Commerce, *Statistical Abstract of the United States, 1995* (Washington, DC: Government Printing Office, 1995).

TABLE 18-3

1. *Spending power*: Over $213 billion in annual expenditures.

2. *Average annual household income*: $22,393.

3. *Increasing size*: During the 1990s, will increase in size by 12.2% to represent 12.8% of the U.S. population.

4. *Youth*: Median age is 28 years as compared to 34 for whites.

5. *Geographic concentration*: 65% of African-Americans live in the top 15 U.S. markets.

6. *Unique tastes and preferences*: Spend far more than whites on boys' clothing, rental goods, radios, and cognac. Adults are more than twice as likely as whites to own a pager.

Sources: *Statistical Abstract of the United States, 1993, 1995;* Eugene Morris, "The Difference in Black and White," *American Demographics,* January 1993, pp. 44–49; Lisa L. Brownlee, "Motorola Gets Signal on Blacks' Pager Use," *The Wall Street Journal,* June 24, 1994, p. B6; Bureau of the Census press release, September 26, 1996.

TABLE 18-4

80 percent of the African-American population. This dialect form appears frequently in TV programs, but its use in written or spoken advertising is quite limited.[26]

We should note that the African-American subculture is not homogeneous. For example, different groups of African-American consumers have divergent views of rap music. While the sound is popular with lower-class youths, researchers have found that older people in the middle class frequently respond to it negatively. So national advertisers who employ rap music to reach black audiences may, in fact, be offending the very people they are trying to appeal to. The researchers noted that perhaps national advertisers should follow the lead of the Atlanta radio station that plays "songs you grew up on, and no rap."[27]

A critical issue marketers face in promoting products to black consumers involves liquor and cigarette advertising. Blacks spend relatively more of their income on liquor and cigarettes than whites do, and advertising that specifically targets blacks for these products has drawn fire from public interest groups. In 1991, when Heileman Brewing Company attempted to launch PowerMaster, a new brand with a high alcohol content that was targeted to urban blacks, it backed off the brand after a public outcry. The next year the company was again criticized when it sought to bring out Crazy Horse malt liquor—another high-octane brand targeted to blacks. In 1993 Heileman began a repositioning effort for its Colt 45 malt liquor with an ad in which a young black college graduate gives advice to a younger friend. One official with the Institute on Black Chemical Abuse said, "[I]t's in poor taste. It's inaccurate to portray someone like the gentleman, with this sense of mission, yet acting as a proponent of malt liquor right there on the street."[28]

The Hispanic Subculture

Hispanics are the second-fastest-growing ethnic subcultural group in the United States (Asian-Americans are in first place). Hispanics will, in fact, become the largest ethnic minority in the United States by the year 2010 (see Table 18-3). It has been estimated that Mexican admissions alone made up 23 percent of all legal immigration into the United States between 1971 and 1990.[29] A combination of high fertility rates, high immigration rates, and continued illegal immigration from Latin America have led to a rapidly expanding Hispanic population.

The **Hispanic subculture** is based on a number of factors. A common language unites most Hispanics: the primary language of 82 percent of U.S. Hispanic households is Spanish.[30] A common religion, Catholicism, is another binding factor: over 85 percent of Hispanics are Catholic. Hispanics also tend to live in metropolitan areas: 63 percent, compared to 75 percent of the African-American population.[31] Because Hispanics share a language and religion and are geographically concentrated, they may make an outstanding target market for certain products and services.

The Hispanic subculture is marked by a constant influx of new members through legal and illegal immigration. A circular pattern exists in which Hispanics enter the United States, stay for a length of time, and then return to their country of origin. It has been estimated that 30 percent of Mexican immigrants eventually go back to Mexico—but not before they have acquired some American tastes, which may be why American products sell so well in our southern neighbor nation.[32]

Hispanics reveal a highly conservative value structure. They are actually more likely than Anglos to support traditional American values concerning the importance of hard work; they are optimistic regarding their future standard of living; and they are materialistic in that they aspire to the "good life."[33] Hispanics tend to be more family oriented than Anglos, to live more for the present, and to be somewhat less competitive. Table 18-5 presents a number of important facts about the Hispanic market.

Hispanic Segmentation Any marketer studying Hispanics will recognize that they are not one homogeneous group. Therefore it is probably inappropriate to speak of a *single* Hispanic market segment.[34] There are at least four distinct groups, or segments: Mexicans (60 percent of U.S. Hispanics), Cubans (7 percent), Puerto Ricans (14 percent), and Central Americans (18 percent). Among these four groups, Spanish is spoken differently, food preferences differ (Mexicans eat refried beans, Cubans eat black beans, and Puerto Ricans eat red beans), and political attitudes are divergent.

Each of the Hispanic groups is also geographically concentrated. Los Angeles, where 2.1 million Hispanics live, is considered to be the prime target area for reaching Mexican-Americans. Similarly, Miami, which is 62 percent Hispanic, contains the largest concentration of Cubans, and New York City has the largest number of Puerto Ricans.[35]

One other point of differentiation is the degree of acculturation. Hispanics range from "just off the boat" arrivals to tenth-generation descendents of immigrants. In addition to length of stay, facility with the English language and general contact with the majority culture influence the degree of preference for U.S. products. Some products, such as clothing, are easily adopted. Others (long-distance phone call procedures, obtaining and using credit cards) require more learning and adjustment. One study found that Mexican-Americans consumed more white bread, highly sugared cereals, and other unhealthy foods

---

Some Key Characteristics of the Hispanic Subculture

1. Mexican-Americans make up two-thirds of U.S. Hispanic households.
2. The average annual household income is $22,860.
3. 14% of Hispanic households have incomes of over $50,000.
4. Hispanics are heavy users of both long-distance and local phone services.
5. On average, Hispanics spend more on in-home food preparation than non-Hispanics. Large meals are at the center of Hispanic home entertainment.
6. Over 80% of Hispanics watch Spanish-language TV and listen to Spanish-language radio—a percentage that has been rising in recent years.

Sources: Patricia Braus, "What Does Hispanic Mean?" *American Demographics*, June 1993, pp. 46–49; *Statistical Abstract of the United States, 1995*; and U.S. Bureau of the Census press release, September 26, 1996.

TABLE 18-5

than either Anglos or Mexicans. It was suggested that a time-lag effect was involved: Mexican immigrants had assimilated an outdated version of the Anglo-American lifestyle that didn't reflect contemporary health concerns.[36]

Problems in Marketing to Hispanics Marketing managers encounter certain problems in trying to market to the Hispanic subculture. As we mentioned earlier, marketing to Puerto Ricans is not the same as marketing to Cuban-Americans or to Mexican-Americans. Also, there are cultural differences *within* each segment that make marketing to these groups even trickier. An advertising executive once noted that if the United States and Mexico went to war, Hispanics in California would likely fight for Mexico, while those in Texas would fight for the United States.[37]

A second problem in marketing to Hispanics is the differences in the type of Spanish spoken. The word for "earring," *pantella*, can mean "television screen" or even "lampshade" to some Hispanics. In some areas of the United States *bodega* means a small Hispanic-owned grocery, but in South Texas *bodegas* are warehouses.[38]

The Asian-American Subculture

What is the fastest-growing ethnic subculture in the United States? The answer is not African-Americans or Hispanics, but the **Asian-American subculture**. In the 1980s over 40 percent of all immigrants to the United States came from Asia. Some estimate that by the year 2050 the number of Asian-Americans will nearly equal the number of Hispanics, who by then will be the largest minority in the United States. Asian-Americans are already becoming a potent economic and intellectual force. The percentage of Asian-Americans who graduate from college is nearly twice that of white Americans. In addition, family incomes of Asian-Americans are significantly higher than Anglo-Americans (by $4,848), Hispanics (by $17,754), and African-Americans (by $18,221).[39]

To an even greater degree than Hispanics, Asian-Americans differ widely in language and culture of origin. Chinese, Vietnamese, Japanese, and Korean are the most common languages spoken by Asian-Americans, and they are mutually incomprehensible. Tastes also differ. At the 1996 Olympic Games in Atlanta, a Chinese athlete complained that appropriate food wasn't available. Told that there was plenty of kimchee (fermented spicy cabbage), he replied that this was food for Koreans.

Comparing Anglo, African-American, and Hispanic Consumption

One study surveyed Anglo, African-American, and Hispanic consumers in order to compare the groups on a variety of consumption characteristics.[40] The results were inconsistent with a number of stereotypes concerning these groups. First, no evidence was found for differences in brand loyalty among the groups (Hispanics are often assumed to be very brand-loyal), although there was an age difference on this score (respondents over 55 reported being more brand loyal). Second, both African-Americans and Hispanics viewed trading stamps more positively than did Anglo consumers. No differences were found among the groups on coupon proneness, impulse buying, shopping for generic products, and the tendency to shop for specials. Both African-Americans and Hispanics showed a greater tendency to shop for bargains. Overall, though, the results did not reveal large differences among the groups on any of the variables.

Marketers must therefore avoid assuming that stereotypes of ethnic subcultures are accurate. Marketing strategy should be based on sound marketing research and environmental analysis.

Portraying Minorities in Advertisements

An issue of concern has been the degree to which ethnic groups appear in print advertisements and television commercials. Given their proportion in the U.S. population, African-Americans are slightly underrepresented in magazine advertisements, but Hispanics are even more underrepresented, while Asian-Americans are slightly overrepresented. Hispanics and Asian-Americans are also more likely to be depicted in a major role in advertisements than African-Americans are. On the other hand, the Screen Actors Guild reported that in 1995 nonwhites got 21 percent of jobs in television advertisements, which actually exceeds their proportion of the population.[41]

REGIONAL SUBCULTURES

Another major subcultural variable of interest to marketers is the distribution of populations in the various regions of the United States. Measuring and predicting the demographic patterns of **regional subcultures** is important to marketers for two reasons. First, different regions have distinct lifestyles resulting from variations in climate, culture, and the ethnic mix of the people. Consequently, different product preferences exist. For example, there are regional preferences for foods and beverages. Some coffee manufacturers blend their coffee differently for the various regions—heavier for the East, lighter for the West, and with chicory for Louisiana.

A second reason for studying regional subcultures is that their growth rates and size vary dramatically. For many types of goods, it is important to shorten the distribution channel as much as possible, so new production facilities should be built in areas experiencing the greatest population growth. In addition, companies looking for new growth opportunities should probably focus on regions expected to experience population increases.

Dramatic population changes are occurring in regions of the United States. Historically, the Northeast and North Central regions were the most heavily populated, but by the late 1980s three of the five most populated states (California, New York, Texas, Pennsylvania, and Florida) were in the lower half of the United States. In 1990 California and Texas became the two largest states in terms of population. Because of these shifting demographics, corporations are changing their marketing emphasis—and in many cases their corporate headquarters—to take advantage of emerging regional markets.[42]

Table 18-6 shows regional population winners and losers in the 1980s and early 1990s. Note that while California, Florida, and Alaska had large percentage increases during the 1980s, they were replaced by Idaho, Colorado, and Utah as fast-growth states in the early 1990s. The likely explanation for this change is that the economic recession of the early 1990s hit the first three states particularly hard, and as a result, their population growth slowed dramatically.

Regional population shifts occur for several reasons. One is the search for jobs. During the severe recession of 1980–1982, many workers moved from the North Central states to the West and Southwest in search of employment. People also move for lifestyle reasons. Florida has grown rapidly in the last two decades because of the huge influx of retirees seeking the sun. Consequently, Florida is the nation's "oldest" state, with 18.4 percent of the population 65 or over.[43]

A third reason for regional population shifts is a difference in birthrates. These differences take longer to manifest themselves, but over a 10- to 20-year period the variations become meaningful. In general, the West is younger than the Northeast and North Central region. The median age in the Northeast is over 30 years, whereas in the western states it is often well under 30. For example, Alaska's median age is 28.3. Utah is the "youngest" state in the Union, with a median age of 25.5 years. The Mormon population

Percentage Shifts in Population by State			
1990–1994		**1980–1990**	
Fastest Percentage Growth			
Nevada	21.2%	Nevada	50.1%
Idaho	12.5	Alaska	36.9
Arizona	11.2	Arizona	34.9
Colorado	11.0	Florida	32.7
Utah	10.7	California	25.7
Slowest Percentage Growth			
Rhode Island	−0.7%	West Virginia	−8%
Connecticut	−0.4	Iowa	−4.7
North Dakota	−0.1	North Dakota	−2.1
Massachusetts	0.4	Pennsylvania	0.1
Maine	1.0	Louisiana	0.3

Source: *Statistical Abstract of the United States, 1995.*

TABLE 18-6

and influence in the state are large, and a central focus of the Mormon religion is the importance of the family and of childbearing.

The combination of a net inflow of migration and a youthful population portend above-average growth in the Western states. The youthful population there will have higher birthrates than the older populations resident in the Northeast and North Central states.

Figure 18-1 shows the Census Bureau's regional division of the United States. One study found that differences in values on the LOV (List of Values) scale occurred across these divisions.[44] One possible reason for this effect is that the Census Bureau's divisions have a political basis, and political boundaries can take on significance for values as well. For example, a certain pride in one's region exists that resembles rooting for the home team. Thus all of Indiana feels pride when the Hoosiers win a national basketball championship or when Notre Dame is ranked number one in football. Table 18-7 presents the distribution of values across the census regions of the United States.

Geodemographics

One area of study that is having a major impact on marketing research today is geodemographics. **Geodemographics** takes as its unit of analysis the neighborhood (i.e., census blocks) and obtains demographic information on consumers within the neighborhood. Census blocks found to contain people with similar demographic characteristics are then clustered together to form potential target markets for firms. This process of identifying groups of neighborhoods with households that are demographically similar is called **cluster analysis**. One basic concept of geodemographics is that individuals within a neighborhood have similar demographic characteristics, buying patterns, and values. Another is that neighborhoods may be placed into similar categories, even when they are widely separated.[45]

Geodemographic analysis can be a vital managerial tool, particularly in direct marketing. By directly contacting consumers with similar geodemographic profiles through

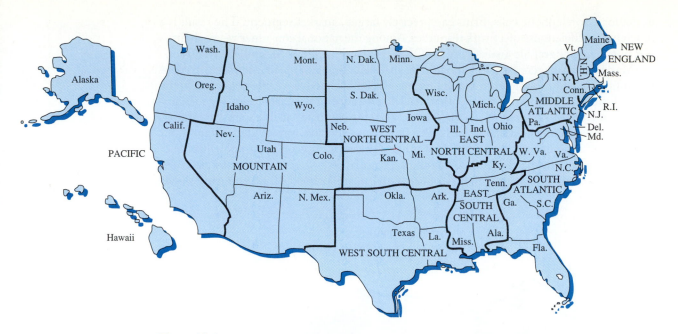

Figure 18-1

Nine Census Bureau regions. (*Source*: Adapted by permission from *Marketing News*, May 13, 1983, Section 2, p. 8, published by the American Marketing Association.)

Distribution of Values Across Census Regions of the United States

Values	New England	Middle Atlantic	South Atlantic	East South Central	East North Central	West North Central	West South Central	Moun-tain	Pacific	N*
Self-respect	22.6%	18.6%	23.1%	23.4%	20.2%	16.7%	23.8%	29.2%	19.8%	471
Security	21.2	18.0	18.3	26.9	22.1	20.6	23.8	18.1	18.5	461
Warm relationships with others	13.9	16.8	15.7	11.4	16.0	21.6	14.9	15.3	17.6	362
Sense of accomplishment	13.9	13.0	10.7	9.6	11.4	14.7	6.8	8.3	12.1	254
Self-fulfillment	8.0	10.0	10.1	7.8	9.3	8.3	6.5	6.9	15.0	214
Being well respected	8.8	7.7	9.8	12.0	10.0	7.4	14.0	4.2	3.5	196
Sense of belonging	7.3	8.8	9.2	7.8	7.4	6.9	6.4	13.9	7.0	177
Fun/enjoyment/excitement	4.4	7.1	3.3	1.2	3.5	3.9	4.7	4.2	6.4	100
Total	100.0	100.0	100.0	100.0	100.0	100.0	100.0	100.0	100.0	2235
N*	137	339	338	167	430	204	235	72	313	

*N = the number of people in the column or row. Thus, for the "self-respect" value, 471 listed it as most important. Of the 137 New Englanders who answered the survey, 22.6 percent listed the self-respect value as most important.

Source: Lynn Kahle, "The Nine Nations of North America and the Value Basis of Geographic Segmentation," *Journal of Marketing*, Vol. 50 (April 1986), pp. 37–47. Published by the American Marketing Association. Reprinted with permission.

TABLE 18-7

direct mail or telephone calls, firms can precisely target a market segment. The result is a much more efficient use of a firm's resources. Among the national consumer research firms offering geodemographic analysis are ACORN, ClusterPlus, PRIZM, and Micro-Vision.

Marketing managers use geodemographic analysis to segment the marketplace, to reposition brands, and to design the marketing mix. Neighborhoods identified as being in the same cluster become market segments. L. L. Bean was one of the early users of geodemographic analysis to segment the marketplace. Since the company mails expensive catalogs to potential customers, its managers had to find a cost-effective way of identifying "L. L. Bean types." A company called PRIZM was hired to develop a geodemographic profile of the market segment that L. L. Bean should target. Catalogs were then sent to zip codes possessing a high percentage of "L. L. Bean–type" neighborhoods. The company slowly

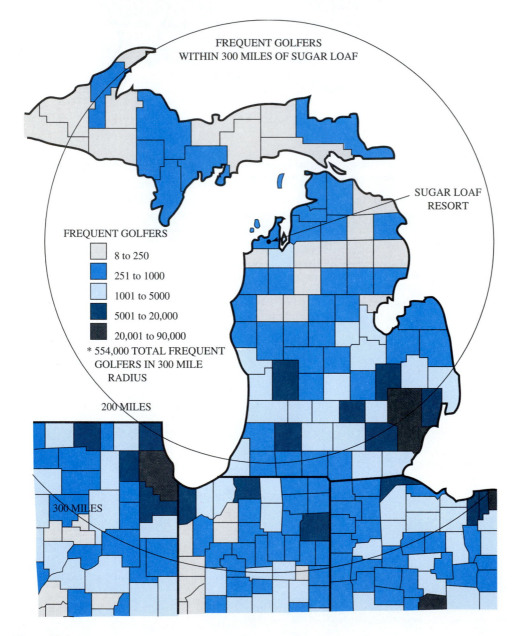

Figure 18-2
A geodemographic map showing the concentration of golfers in Michigan near a new resort—Sugar Loaf.

built a database that not only identified where its clients lived but also what magazines they read, what television shows they watched, and even what products they owned.[46]

So geodemographic analysis helps managers design the marketing mix by providing a detailed profile of where customers live, what they buy, and what their demographic characteristics are. In particular, the location of stores and the selection of merchandise for stores can be guided by geodemographics. Recently, market researchers have used this technique to identify good locations for new golf courses. By determining where golf courses are currently located and by creating a demographic profile of golfers and where they live, researchers can pinpoint areas of the United States that have a surplus of golfers in relation to the number of courses available. Figure 18-2 presents a map that depicts the concentrations of golfers in the Michigan area, with darkly shaded areas representing high concentrations of golfers. The map was drawn to help managers decide whether to build a new golf course near a resort called Sugar Loaf. Based on the map, do you think the golf course would be successful?

Should Companies Segment by Geography?

This question is very similar to the question about global marketing strategy we take up in Chapter 19. Little doubt exists that a national marketing effort is less expensive than a regionally based strategy. As one consultant succinctly said, "Breadth of choice equals complexity; complexity equals increasing costs."[47] For example, when Campbell's Soup Company divided the country into 22 regions, it had to promote 88 employees to brand sales managers, retrain its entire sales force, and make major changes in production—all costly moves. Moreover, targeting a specific region frequently brings retaliation from local companies. Thus when Campbell's introduced Spicy Ranchero Beans into the Southwest, the area's dominant marketer of beans, Ranch Style Beans, fought back with heavy advertising and sales promotions.

Despite these problems with regional marketing strategies, many companies prefer to use regional segmentation. For example, the 30 teams of the National Football League present a dilemma for store chains selling NFL merchandise. While a few teams like the Dallas Cowboys have a national following, in many cases regional teams draw the largest interest. So a national chain such as Footlocker must carefully calibrate the appropriate mix of "national" versus "regional" teams to feature in its stores.[48]

SOCIAL-CLASS SUBCULTURES

Social classes are those relatively permanent strata in a society that differ in status, wealth, education, possessions, and values. All societies possess a hierarchical structure that stratifies residents into "classes" of people. Both actual and perceptual factors distinguish the groups. In concrete terms, classes differ by occupations, lifestyles, values, friendships, manner of speaking, and possessions. In perceptual terms, individuals perceive that different classes have varying amounts of prestige, power, and privilege. Finally, members of a class tend to socialize with one another rather than with members of other classes. As observed by one theorist, social classes are multidimensional. Three primary factors differentiate the social classes: economic status (e.g., occupation, wealth, house type and location), educational credentials, and behavioral standards (community participation, aspirations, and recreational habits).[49]

In the egalitarian culture of the United States, discussions of social class make many people uncomfortable. When answering an interviewer's question about social class, one woman said, "It's the dirtiest thing I've ever heard of."[50] Despite its unpleasant connotations, social class has important managerial implications for marketers.

In comparison to how the term is used by sociologists, marketing managers define social class narrowly. They are, after all, concerned with how the buying patterns of social classes differ, rather than with the political, institutional, and cultural reasons for their existence. To marketers, the social classes are subcultures with distinct lifestyles, buying patterns, and motivations.[51] In other words, they are potential market segments possessing divergent needs, wants, and desires for products and services.

What Are the Social Classes in the United States?

A number of classification schemes have been devised to rank the social classes. One that is frequently used is Warner's Index of Status Characteristics (ISC).[52] Warner's index uses four variables as indicators of social class: occupation, source of income, house type, and dwelling area. The indicators are weighted, with occupation most heavily emphasized and dwelling area least heavily weighted in the composite index. Based on the total ISC score, an individual is classified into one of six categories:

1. Upper-upper class
2. Lower-upper class
3. Upper-middle class
4. Lower-middle class
5. Upper-lower class
6. Lower-lower class

The most valid approach for measuring social class is through the use of multiitem indices. Table 18-8 lists four social-class scales and the variables each uses to rank the social classes.

Measuring Social Class

| Variable | Social-Class Index | | | |
	Hollingshead	Warner	Census Bureau	Coleman
Occupation	*	*	*	*
Source of income		*		
House type		*		*
Dwelling area		*		
Family income			*	
Education	*		*	*
Neighborhood housing				*
Wife's occupation				*
Wife's education				*
Religious affiliation				*
Associations				*

Names of indices:
 Hollingshead: Index of Social Position (ISP).
 Warner: Index of Status Characteristics (ISC).
 Census: Census Bureau Index of Socioeconometric Status (SES).
 Coleman: Index of Urban Status (IUS).
Note: The indices have various "weighting" schemes for the variables—that is, some variables are more important than others in calculating social status in the four indices.

TABLE 18-8

Table 18-9 provides a **social-class hierarchy** scheme and summarizes some of the characteristics of the social classes. The descriptions given in the table have proved quite accurate for at least the last 50 years in the United States. However, recent trends are creating some subtle changes. For one thing, a new group of people who might be placed in the lower-upper class has appeared. These are professionals who marry and form two-career families. Because of their high incomes and their need to juggle two careers, these families have become a separate target market. For example, when one spouse must move because of job relocation, the other spouse may need help finding a job comparable to the one currently held, and businesses have sprung up to cater to this need.[53]

Differences between social classes are manifested in their communication patterns. One study found that people can identify an individual's social class simply by hearing him or her read something.[54] Social classes differ in speech cadence, voice modulation, and fluency of speech. Vocabulary also varies among the social classes.[55] The lower classes describe the world in more concrete terms than do the middle and upper classes. If asked

---

The Social-Class Hierarchy

A. Upper Americans

Upper-upper (0.3%): The world of inherited wealth and old family names. Working is a matter of choice, and members often serve on the boards of directors of major corporations. Serves as a reference for lower classes. Not a major market segment because of its small size.

Lower-upper (1.2%): The newer social elite, drawn from current professionals, corporate leadership. May be extremely wealthy, but the money is relatively new. Is an achieving group and will spend money to show its wealth. Will guard its social-class position because of insecurity. Is a major market for specialized luxury goods, such as Mercedes automobiles.

Upper-middle (12.5%): The rest of college-graduate managers, intellectual elite, and professionals. Lifestyle centers on private clubs, causes, and the arts. Collegiate credentials expected. Housing is extremely important to this group—particularly where the house is located. The quality and appearance of products are also important.

B. Middle Americans

Middle class (32%): White-collar workers and their blue-collar friends. Live on "the better side of town," try to "do the proper things." Have white-collar friends and acquaintances. Respectability is a key idea for this group. Home ownership, high moral standards, and focus on the family are important ideals. They tend to have high school educations or some college but do not reach high levels in their organizations.

Working class (38%): Blue-collar workers; lead "working-class lifestyle" whatever their income, school background, and job. Jobs tend to be monotonous, although affluence is possible if they have a union job. Tend to stay close to their parents and relatives and live in older parts of town. Do have money for consumer products and, with the middle class, represent the market for mass consumer goods.

C. Lower Americans

Upper-lower (9%): Working, not on welfare. Living standard is just above the poverty level. Behavior judged "crude," "trashy." Tend to be unskilled workers.

Lower-lower (7%): On welfare, visibly poverty stricken, usually out of work (or have the "dirtiest jobs"). Some are bums, common criminals. Has become separated from the upper-lower group because it exists mainly on government transfer payments. With the upper-lower class, accounts for only 6–7% of disposable income.

Source: Data adapted from Richard P. Coleman, "The Continuing Significance of Social Class in Marketing," *Journal of Consumer Research,* Vol. 10 (December 1983), pp. 265–280.

TABLE 18-9

where he or she obtained bubble gum, a lower-class child would likely state a person's name. An upper-class child would simply say "from the grocery store."

Although most marketers agree that social class is an important consumer concept, published examples of its use in marketing are sparse because there are so many problems in using this concept as a segmentation variable. Some of these problems are identified in Table 18-10.

One problem in measuring social class is that the measures assume that an individual's social class is an average of his or her position on several dimensions of status. The consistency with which an individual reveals a particular social class across a number of dimensions is called **status crystallization**. Some have argued that people who have low crystallization are more prone to express liberal ideas and advocate changes in the social order.[56] An individual with low status crystallization might be an Hispanic attorney whose parents were laborers.

Social Class and Buying Behavior

Because of the problems of the social-class concept, one must use caution in interpreting the findings of studies investigating its impact on buying behavior. One finding of importance to marketers is that the reasons for shopping differ among the social classes. The upper classes tend to shop not simply out of necessity but also for pleasure.[57] Higher-class women tend to favor stores with a high-fashion image, such as the Neiman Marcus chain, while lower-class women prefer mass merchandisers and stores with price appeal. The importance of maintaining a certain social image is revealed in the shopping patterns of the upper classes. Products that reflect differences in class, like furniture, are viewed as "socially risky." Upper-class consumers tend to purchase such products from specialty shops and department stores geared to providing personal service in an upscale atmosphere. For low-risk products, such as toasters, the upper-class shopper is perfectly willing to buy a brand-name product from a discounter. The relationship between income and willingness to buy store-brand rather than national-brand merchandise may be curvilinear: low-income and higher-income shoppers are less likely to buy store brands than those in between.[58]

Problems in the Use of Social Class by Marketers

1. *What is its definition?* Little agreement has been reached on how to measure the concept.

2. *The choice-behavior fallacy.* Social class by itself is a poor predictor of buying behavior. However, such a result should be expected when only a single indicator such as social class is used. Many factors influence product choice in addition to social class.

3. *The husband-only fallacy.* The social class of the husband cannot be used as the sole criterion for determining a family's status. Because of the prevalence of working wives and because many pairings of husbands and wives are inconsistent regarding social class, this sexist practice is misleading.

4. *The present social-class fallacy.* One cannot assume that a family's current social class is governing their lifestyle and buying behavior. A family's lifestyle, beliefs, and values are based not only on both partners' current status but also on the status of their parents. The socialization process creates a tendency to maintain a certain lifestyle, even if one's social status has moved up or down.

5. *The effect of aspirations.* People differ in their desire to get ahead and move up in social class. In addition, a person's reference group may be of a different social class. Such an individual would tend not to share the consumption behaviors of members of his or her objectively measured social class.

TABLE 18-10

The social classes also differ in information-search behavior prior to and during shopping. Middle- and upper-class consumers tend to engage in more information search before they make a purchase. Before buying appliances, for example, they may read newspaper ads, brochures, and test reports. In contrast, lower-class consumers are apt to rely on in-store displays and the advice of salespeople.[59] In general, lower-class consumers have less product information, are less informed about product prices, and are no more likely to buy products "on sale" than upper-class consumers are. Upper-class consumers are also less likely to use price as an indicator of quality. Instead, they tend to judge the quality of products on their merits.

Social Class and Income

What is the relationship between social class and household income? Some have argued that income is really a better predictor of buying behavior than social class, but research suggests that that depends on the type of product or service being investigated.[60] Social class was found to be a better predictor of purchases that were not expensive but that symbolically represented lifestyles and values. For example, usage of certain food items like sweet beverages and wines could be predicted by social class. On the other hand, income was a superior predictor of purchases of major appliances as well as the frequency of usage of soft drinks, mixers, and distilled alcohol. A combination of social class and income was a good predictor of expensive status products like autos and clothing.

Related to the income–social class debate is the **relative-income hypothesis**. Research conducted in the early 1960s revealed that people within the same social class often have different consumption patterns based on their relative incomes.[61] The people who had high incomes for their social class were labeled **overprivileged**, while those in the same class who had low incomes were labeled **underprivileged**. The relative-income hypothesis insists that income cannot be ignored when investigating consumers. At the same time, income and social class are related. Those with higher incomes tend to have higher educations, more upscale occupations, nicer homes, better furniture, and so forth.

Just what is the relationship between income and social class? One noted researcher estimated the correlation to be relatively low (around $r = .40$) in the 1980s.[62] Three reasons were cited for this rather low correlation. First, social class has historically been based more on occupational differences than on income. Even in the 1990s many blue-collar workers earn more than many white-collar workers, yet their social status is lower. Second, differences in age can lower the correlation. Young workers traditionally earn less than older workers. However, a young stockbroker making $50,000 is in the middle class, whereas a 50-year-old cabinet maker earning $50,000 is in the working class. Finally, family variation in the number of earners has affected the income–social-class correlation. With our rising divorce rates in recent decades, it has become increasingly common for women to head a family. Unfortunately, women still earn less than men, so the incomes of families headed by a female tend to be lower. In contrast, families where both spouses hold jobs have relatively higher incomes. Still, in most cases neither divorce nor two incomes influences social-class status—rather, the relative amounts of income available do.

Psychological Differences Among the Classes

Many of the differences noted in the consumption behaviors of the social classes can be accounted for by differences in the way they view the world. The middle classes tend to focus on the future. They are generally self-confident, are willing to take risks, believe that they

Figure 18-3

In transitional economies such as that of Russia, a larger percentage of the population may be in the lower classes than in richer countries.

can control their fate, and see their horizons as broad. In contrast, the lower classes focus on the present and past. They are concerned with security and with their family and themselves.

Psychological differences in the social classes were demonstrated in a study that investigated how groups of consumers differed in their perception of the symbolism of products.[63] Lower-class people tended to believe that owners of big houses and nice cars had obtained them because of "good luck." In contrast, consumers with higher social status attributed the ability to purchase status symbols to the self-motivation of the owner. Such results indicate a more fatalistic view of life among the lower classes. These psychological and lifestyle differences are summed up by the following quotation:

> For twenty years researchers have found that working-class life styles have been almost impervious to change in their basic characteristics—i.e., the limited horizons, the centrality of family and clan. The chauvinistic devotion to nation and neighborhood have been little altered by the automobile, telephone, or television. The modernity—and change—that these people seek is in possessions, not in human relationships or "new ideas." For them, "keeping up with the times" focuses on the mechanical and recreational, and thus ease of labor and leisure is what they continue to pursue.[64]

Social Class and Lifestyles

As a macroenvironmental force, social class strongly influences consumers' lifestyles. Four generalizations can be made concerning the impact of social class on consumer lifestyles: (1) it strongly influences lifestyle; (2) it is a predictor of resources; (3) people buy products and services to demonstrate their membership in a particular social class; and (4) people also purchase goods and services to help advance their social standing.

Social Class Influences Consumer Lifestyles Perhaps the most important contribution of social class to the understanding of consumer behavior is that it strongly influences lifestyle. Weber was perhaps the earliest researcher to link social class and lifestyle, although he viewed lifestyle as more closely linked to status than to class. Some consumer researchers have even argued that lifestyle is the "essence of social class."[65] The style of consumption (i.e., lifestyle) may be viewed as an expression of a particular social class. How consumers live is directly influenced by their education, household income, occupation, and type of house. Level of education tends to influence a person's activities, interests, opinions, values, and beliefs. Household income determines the capacity to purchase consumer goods and to express other interests. Occupation influences the type of people with whom a person associates, as well as the types of products and services that are purchased to play the occupational role. As noted in Chapter 15, the products and services that a person must have in order to engage effectively in a particular role is called a *role-related product cluster*.[66] A stereotypical view of the role-related product cluster of an successful young attorney or stockbroker might include an Armani suit, a luxury car, a vacation home—and perhaps the watch shown in Figure 18-4.

Social Class Is Predictive of Resources Owned Four resource dimensions have been identified as influenced by social class: financial, social, cultural, and time. First, those in higher social classes tend to have greater financial resources because of their occupations or inherited wealth. Second, as one moves higher in social-class level, opportunities for social participation increase, and associations are made with those of higher social standing. One's level of social participation generally rises as one's social status increases. Furthermore, social skill and social standing appear to be closely linked.[67] Third, those in higher social classes tend to be familiar with cultural matters. In addition, higher-education credentials provide "cultural capital" for individuals. Finally, those in higher social classes tend to have a broader time horizon than those in lower social classes. Membership in the higher social classes requires people to have both longer time horizons and to delay gratification while building personal skills through education. Those in higher social classes frequently have less "free time" than people in lower social classes, but they have more flexibility in choosing the activities on which to spend their time.

Figure 18-4
This advertisement for an expensive watch stresses opulence rather than functionality.

GUCCI
timepieces
AVAILABLE AT GUCCI SHOPS AND FINE STORES WORLDWIDE

Goods May Be Purchased as Status Symbols Products and services are often bought to show one's membership in a particular social class. Goods and services may represent social-class standing because of restrictions that make it difficult for individuals not in the social class to own them—that is, those in lower social classes lack the resources to purchase or effectively use these status symbols. For example, in the United States owning a Mercedes-Benz has come to represent membership in the lower-upper-class for many people. Similarly, a high level of education is required to read and enjoy magazines, such as *The New Yorker*, that are addressed to people of upper-middle-class standing.

It has long been recognized that in order to depict their social status people must display appropriate material items. When we encounter strangers, frequently the only way we have to ascertain their status is through visual cues. Still, there is a problem in portraying social class through material goods. If the ownership of a material symbol is diffused across levels of the class hierarchy, it becomes a **fraudulent symbol**.[68] That is, if members of different social classes display the same symbol of status, it will not accurately depict the meaning desired.

For a material item to adequately symbolize social-class standing, accuracy is required in both the encoding and decoding stages.[69] Accurate encoding is only possible if ownership of the material item is homogeneous within a single social class. Thus people within the class should consistently possess the good, and there must be wide agreement that possession of the item symbolizes a particular social-class standing. Accuracy in decoding demands that a shared status meaning be attached to the material good by society at large. The types of material symbols that people generally decode in a consistent manner are clothing, health care, automobiles, and housing.[70] Another material symbol that is accurately encoded and decoded is the possession of hired household help. The presence of chauffeurs, cooks, and gardeners is indicative of membership in the upper classes.

A review of the literature on status recognition in the 1980s noted that during the 1960s and 1970s there was a decline in the use of material goods as status symbols.[71] This trend may have resulted from a shift in the interests of Americans away from materialism to a simpler lifestyle coupled with the fact that rising affluence during this period made many material goods fraudulent. Indeed, the "radical chic" movement of the era involved people of higher social class adopting the fashion styles of lower classes. Researchers who content-analyzed advertisements confirmed the trend toward disparaging status-oriented themes, particularly during the 1960s.[72]

Consumption of Status Symbols Is a Skill The adroit purchase of goods and services can be used to solidify or help advance an individual's social-class standing. People who fail to represent their social class via the "correct" visible symbols risk scorn and the disrespectful title "nouveau riche." Knowing how to make the correct purchases is a skill. The problems associated with moving rapidly from one class to another have been grist for Holly-

---

Question: What status symbol is long, round, and could cost you $20 or more?

Answer: A cigar. The success of *Cigar Aficianado*, a magazine started in 1992, illustrates the increasing popularity of cigar smoking. Despite championing a politically incorrect activity and celebrating affluence when conspicuous consumption is supposed to be dead, the magazine had 40 percent more ad pages in 1995 than in the previous year. Its success reflects a 30 percent increase in cigar smoking from 1994 to 1996. Formerly known as a pastime of older men, the cigar habit has been taken up by women and young males in droves.

Source: Scott Donaton, "Where There's Smoke, There's Shankan's Star," *Advertising Age*, March 11, 1996, p. 52.

Consumer Behavior Factoid

wood movie makers: In *King Ralph* John Goodman is a Las Vegas lounge singer one day, King of England the next. In *Coming to America* Eddie Murphy goes the other way, from a prince in Africa to working at a fast-food restaurant in the United States.

The argument can be made that there is currently a great deal of status anxiety in the United States. The proliferation of consumption guides, fashion experts, interior decorators, and real estate professionals implies great concern about purchasing the "correct" goods and services to support or help one's advance status. People would not hire these surrogate consumers if the accurate display of symbolic material goods were unimportant to them.

OTHER SUBCULTURES

Space limitations prohibit a discussion of all the various subcultures available for target marketing. One interesting example of a geographically based subculture is the growing rural population. From 1990 to 1995 three-quarters of the rural counties in the United States grew, reversing the pattern of the 1980s. This movement has been spearheaded by those looking for pleasant retirement living or a second, recreational home. The rise in telecommuting and long-distance driving has also spurred the movement of workers into rural areas.[73] Another subculture marketers are becoming interested in is the 49 million U.S. citizens who are disabled in some way.

An Internet Community?

The phenomenal growth of the Internet in the last few years may be spawning a new subculture—that of Web users.[74] In demographic terms, this community is largely male and well educated. Among Web users, "Internet friends" are eclipsing family members, co-workers, and regular friends as sources of information and product recommendations.

A MANAGERIAL APPLICATIONS ANALYSIS OF THE TOY INDUSTRY CASE

Problem Identification

The challenge for the toy industry is to precisely define and market to specific subcultures of the population. Of course, not all of these subcultures are defined in terms of age.

The Consumer Behavior Analysis and Its Managerial Implications

Three concepts from the chapter shed light on the challenges facing the toy industry: the baby-boom generation, ethnic groups, and social class. Skillful appeals to these subcultures can help the industry successfully address the needs of current and potential customers.

Baby-Boom Generation One serious concern for the toy industry is the future of the baby boomers as a market. Currently, this group is in the late middle years of child rearing. Because of the enormous number of parents in this age group, the demand for children's toys is flourishing. However, in the late 1990s the number of new births has begun to decline, which is a potential problem for the industry. As suggested by Table 18-11, marketers' study of the baby-boom group should focus on the development of the marketing mix, segmentation, and environmental analysis. An environmental analysis should be conducted to track changes in the size of the children's toy market so that segments of appropriate size and buying power can be identified and specific products developed and promoted for these target groups.

Managerial Implications of Consumer Behavior Concepts in the Toy Industry Case

Consumer Behavior Concept	Managerial Implications
1. Baby-boom generation	*Segmentation.* Target baby-boom parents and their children as customers.
	Environmental analysis. Track changes in the size, age, and buying power of the baby-boom generation.
	Marketing mix. Develop promotional strategy that is consistent with the values of baby-boom parents. Develop toy products that reflect the values, needs, and wants of the baby-boom generation.
2. Ethnic groups	*Environmental analysis.* Track changes in the size of key ethnic groups.
	Segmentation. Target ethnic groups growing rapidly in size, such as Hispanics and Asians.
3. Social class	*Segmentation.* Identify key market segments based on social class that may have divergent needs and wants for toys. Combine with other subcultural variables, such as age and sex, to pinpoint specific target groups. For example, preteen middle-class girls are a target for model horses. Similarly, middle-class males may be a target for adult toys.
	Product. Develop toy products and promote them in a manner that meets the needs of the social-class subcultures identified.

TABLE 18-11

Ethnic Groups The second consumer concept of importance to toy manufacturers is ethnic groups. In addition to carefully analyzing age trends, toy manufacturers should conduct broader-scale demographic analyses. Environmental analyses should be carried out to identify changes in the ethnic composition of the population, which may reveal new consumer segments to be targeted. For example, the high growth rate of the Hispanic population may make Hispanic children a lucrative target market. Market research can identify the unmet toy needs of Hispanic children so that manufacturers can develop products specifically for them.

Social Class The specific needs and interests of various social classes should also be considered by toy manufacturers. In the introductory case we discussed adult toy collectors. From the perspective of social-class standing, it is apparent that, on the basis of education, income, and occupation, this segment is largely middle class. This information can be used by toy makers to segment the marketplace and to develop elements of the marketing mix. For example, the knowledge that most toy collectors are middle class tells marketers what pricing structure (i.e., moderate prices will work best) and promotional strategy (buyers are too sophisticated for hype tactics) to use.

Managerial Recommendations

Three specific recommendations emerge from our managerial applications analysis.

Recommendation 1 Target baby boomers and their children, but stay attuned to fluctuations in the composition of the toy market as boomers and their children age.

Recommendation 2 Consider the implications of the increasing size of the Hispanic, African-American, and Asian-American subcultures for toy offerings. Can changes be made that would more effectively position toys to appeal to these subcultures?

Recommendation 3 Bear in mind that social class also plays a role in determining key market segments, especially in conjunction with other subcultural variables such as age and gender.

SUMMARY

A subculture is a group of people that makes up a subdivision of a national culture. One or more unifying features distinguish a subculture, whose members share patterns of behavior distinct from those found in the national culture. Demographic characteristics such as age, nationality, and religion are often used to identify subcultures.

Age groupings of particular importance for marketers in the 1990s are the baby-boom generation and the elderly. Although not a subculture in the strict sense of the word, the baby-boom generation does have extreme importance to marketers because of its size and buying power. Now in their 30s to early 50s, the baby boomers are becoming even more influential as they enter their peak earning years. The elderly also represent a legitimate subculture because of their distinct lifestyles and buying patterns.

Relatively little has been written about the consumer behavior of the African-American subculture over the past ten years. Marketers have somewhat downplayed the importance of this large market segment, so astute marketing managers have a wide open field here. A high birthrate and massive inflows of immigrants have contributed to the rapid increase in the number of Hispanics in the U.S. population in recent decades. There are four important Hispanic groups: Cubans, Puerto Ricans, Mexicans, and Central Americans. Asian-Americans are the fastest-growing ethnic subculture.

Another basis for the classification of subcultures is the region of a country. A region may develop a distinct subculture for several reasons. Differences in the religion, ethnicity, and nationality of the people who settle in an area can make for the development of a distinct set of values and behavior patterns. For example, Utah has a distinct subculture largely because of the influence of the Mormon Church.

The social classes also represent distinct subcultures. Social classes are relatively permanent and homogeneous strata in a society. A variety of factors distinguish the social classes, including occupation, wealth, education, possessions, values, housing, and associations. The study of social class has implications for each of the major marketing management areas. In particular, a market may be segmented along lines of social class. Products can be developed, promoted, and positioned in order to appeal to members of a particular class. Managers should use environmental analysis and market research to identify potential changes in the composition of the social classes because such changes can constitute major environmental threats or opportunities for the firm.

A number of social-class scales have been developed. The most common variables used to measure social class are occupation, education, and house type. Family income is another important variable to consider when investigating social class.

Perhaps the most important social-class factor for understanding consumer behavior is that social status strongly influences lifestyles. Social-class membership is often predictive of resources. In addition, many products and services are purchased for their symbolic value in representing a particular social class. The "correct" consumption of status symbols is a skill. Consumers who are uncomfortable with their skill level often hire surrogate consumers to assist them in making the "correct" purchases.

African-American subculture
Asian-American subculture
baby-boom generation
baby bust
cluster analysis
demographic variables

ethnicity
fertility rate
fraudulent symbol
Generation X
Generation Y
geodemographics

Hispanic subculture
immigration
mature consumer
mortality rate
overprivileged
regional subcultures

relative-income hypothesis
social class
social-class hierarchy
status crystallization
subculture
underprivileged

REVIEW QUESTIONS

1. Identify six different types of subcultures in the United States.

2. What is the definition of the term *subculture*? How are subcultures different from demographic variables?

3. Describe the age distribution of the baby-boom group of consumers. Describe the impact of this group on two industries.

4. Table 18-1 presents projected U.S. population trends between 1995 and 2005. Based on this table, identify the age groups that will increase and decrease by the end of the century.

5. What are the factors that influence the accuracy of age projections of the population?

6. Identify three ways in which the elderly process information differently from the rest of the adult population.

7. Identify four factors that make the African-American subculture an important target market. What factors should companies consider when deciding whether to market directly to blacks?

8. What factors make the Hispanic subculture the second-fastest-growing group in the United States?

9. Four segments of Hispanics have been identified, based upon ancestry. Identify these four segments and give their relative sizes.

10. What are the reasons for regional shifts in population?

11. Define the concept of social class. How do marketers tend to use this concept in comparison to sociologists?

12. Identify the social classes as defined by Coleman and found in Table 18-9. What is the relative size of each of the social classes?

13. Indicate the four variables most frequently used to assess social class.

14. Delineate four of the five problems identified in the chapter affecting the use of the social-class concept by marketers.

15. Provide two examples of how upper and lower social classes differ in their shopping patterns and leisure activities.

16. What is the correlation between social class and income? For what types of products may social class be a better predictor of buying patterns than income?

17. Discuss the concept of the relative-income hypothesis.

18. Identify the ways that social class may influence consumer lifestyles.

DISCUSSION QUESTIONS

1. Subcultures can be found in most large collections of people. Identify as many subcultures as you can within the university or college you are now attending. Describe the norms, values, and behaviors of these subcultures that set them apart.

2. Because of the long lead times required for planning and bringing new products to market, managers must often look five to ten years into the future. What marketing opportunities and problems might the baby boomers present to managers between the years 1995 and 2005?

3. You are the marketing director for an investment group that has decided to develop a shopping center specifically targeted to the elderly market. What types of services, stores, and amenities would you attempt to provide in the shopping center? What problems might you encounter in targeting a shopping center specifically for the elderly?

4. Compare and contrast how a company might attempt to market a product, such as blue jeans, to blacks, Hispanics, and Anglos. Specifically consider the selection of media and the development of advertising themes.

5. You are the marketing director for a company that plans to open a chain of new department stores targeted to consumers with incomes above $80,000. What considerations would influence your decisions as to where to locate the stores geographically?

6. Identify a product for which the marketing mix must be varied across the geographic regions of the United States. State the reasons why the marketing mix should be varied for each product.

7. Consider what subcultural variables you would use to divide the United States geographically. Draw a map of the United States that shows the boundaries of the regions you have identified and justify your analysis.

8. Consider the types of department stores in your region of the country. Identify the social classes that each of these stores appears to target.

9. Just as we assign people to social classes, we also rank institutions of higher education by prestige. Identify two universities or colleges that can be placed into each of the following prestige classifications: highest prestige, moderately high prestige, middle prestige, moderately low prestige, and low prestige. What criteria determine how the universities are classified?

10. Why is it that people in the United States (including professors, students, and the authors of this text) tend to be uncomfortable discussing the topic of social class?

11. Given the knowledge you have of your friends and acquaintances, do you think that social-class mobility is increasing or decreasing in the United States? What are the primary means of upward mobility in the United States today?

12. Conduct a quick survey among ten of your acquaintances designed to identify the types of goods and services that they purchase as status symbols.

ENDNOTES

1. Marcia Mogelonsky, "Butterfly Barbie Effect," *American Demographics*, May 1996, p. 8.

2. S. K. List, "More Than Fun and Games," *American Demographics*, August 1991, pp. 44–47.

3. Robert E. Pitts, "Guest Editorial: The Hispanic Subculture: Subcultural Complexity and Marketing Opportunity," *Psychology and Marketing*, Vol. 3 (1986), pp. 243–246.

4. Suein L. Hwang, "Kosher-Food Firms Dive into the Mainstream," *The Wall Street Journal*, April 1, 1993, pp. B1, B6.

5. D. O. Arnold, *The Sociology of Subcultures* (Berkeley, CA: Glendasary Press, 1970).

6. R. T. Reynolds, B. Robey, and C. Russell, "Demographics of the 1980s," *American Demographics*, January 1980, pp. 11–19.

7. "Americans Change," *Business Week*, February 20, 1978, pp. 64–80.

8. Campbell Gibson, "The Four Baby Booms," *American Demographics*, November 1993, pp. 37–40.

9. Teri Agins, "The Status of Denim: Designer Jeans Make a Comeback," *The Wall Street Journal*, July 2, 1996, pp. B1, B3; and Teri Agins, "Like Boomers' Middles, Elastic Waistbands S-p-r-e-a-d," *The Wall Street Journal*, September 19, 1996, pp. B1, B10.

10. Christina Buff, "Passing the Bucks: Aging Boomers Cut the Cord But Can't Let Go of the Wallet," *The Wall Street Journal*, July 8, 1996, pp. A1, A5.

11. Ronald Alsop, "Busters May Replace Boomers as the Darlings of Advertisers," *The Wall Street Journal*, November 12, 1987, p. 35; and Chris Manolis, Aron Levin, and Robert Dahlstrom, "A Generation X Scale: Conceptualization, Measurement and Nomological Validity," *Marketing Theory and Applications*, Vol. 7, Edward Blair and Wagner A. Kamakura, eds. (Chicago: American Marketing Association, 1996), pp. 435–436.

12. Diane Summers, "A View of the X-Files," *The Financial Times*, January 20, 1996, p. 11.

13. Jennifer DeCoursey, "Growing Pains Plague Generation X Magazines," *Advertising Age*, November 5, 1995, p. S-24.

14. Raymond Serafin and Cleveland Horton, "X Marks the Spot for Car Marketing," *Advertising Age*, August 9, 1993, p. 8.

15. Cyndee Miller, "Teens Seen as the First Truly Global Customers," *Marketing News*, March 27, 1995, p. 9. But see Chapter 19 for a discussion of the possible problems of assuming that markets are the same across the world.

16. Susan Mitchell, "The Next Baby Boom," *American Demographics*, October 1995, pp. 22–31: and Melinda Beck, "Next Population Bulge Shows Its Might," *The Wall Street Journal*, February 3, 1997, pp. B1, B6.

17. Emily Nelson, "Why Teenage Sitters Have So Much Power," *The Wall Street Journal*, September 26, 1996, pp. B1, B7.

18. Rick Christie, "Marketers Err by Treating Elderly as Uniform Group," *The Wall Street Journal*, October 31, 1988, pp. B1, B3.

19. Fabian Linden and Paul Ryscavage, "How We Live," The Conference Board and the U.S. Bureau of the Census, 1986; and

Statistical Abstract of the United States, 1995, Item 627, p. 399.

20. Catherine A. Cole and Siva K. Balasubramanian, "Age Differences in Consumers' Search for Information: Public Policy Implications," *Journal of Consumer Research*, Vol. 20 (June 1993), pp. 157–169.

21. Jack Botwinick, *Aging and Behavior: A Comprehensive Integration of Research Findings*, 2nd ed. (New York: Springer, 1978).

22. L. G. Schiffman, "Perceived Risk in New Product Trial by Elderly Consumers," *Journal of Marketing Research*, Vol. 9 (February 1972), pp. 106–108.

23. Rose L. Johnson, "Age and Social Activity as Correlates of Television Orientation: A Replication and Extension," *Advances in Consumer Research*, Vol. 20, Leigh McAlister and Michael L. Rothschild, eds. (Provo, UT: Association for Consumer Research, 1993), pp. 257–261.

24. Gabrielle Sandor, "Attitude (Not Age) Defines the Mature Market," *American Demographics*, January 1994, pp. 18–21; Benny Barak and Leon Schiffman, "Cognitive Age: A Nonchronological Age Variable," in *Advances in Consumer Research*, Vol. 8, Kent B. Monroe, ed. (Ann Arbor, MI: Association for Consumer Research, 1981), pp. 602–606; and Robert E. Wilkes, "A Structural Modelling Approach to the Measurement and Meaning of Cognitive Age," *Journal of Consumer Research*, Vol. 19 (September 1992), pp. 292–301.

25. *Statistical Abstract of the United States, 1995*, Item 736, p. 476.

26. Jennifer Edson Escalas, "African American Vernacular English in Advertising: A Sociolinguistic Study," in *Advances in Consumer Research*, Vol. 21, Chris T. Allen and Deborah Roedder John, eds. (Provo, UT: Association for

Consumer Research, 1994), pp. 304–309.

27. Lydia A. McKinley-Floyd, J. R. Smith, and Hudson Nwakanma, "The Impact of Social Class on African American Consumer Behavior: An Interdisciplinary Perspective," in *Marketing Theory and Applications*, Vol. 5, C. Whan Park and Daniel C. Smith, eds. (Chicago: American Marketing Association, 1994), pp. 384–389.

28. Laura Bird, "Critics Shoot at New Colt 45 Campaign," *The Wall Street Journal*, February 17, 1993, p. B1.

29. Lisa Peñaloza, "*Atravesando Fronteras*/Border Crossing: A Critical Ethnographic Exploration of the Consumer Acculturation of Mexican Immigrants," *Journal of Consumer Research*, Vol. 21 (June 1994), pp. 32–54.

30. Lisa A. Yorgey, "Cultured Creative," *Target Marketing*, November 1995, pp. 22–28.

31. Daniel McQuillen, "Cities of Gold," *Incentive*, February 1996, pp. 38–40. Other estimates place the number of Hispanics living in urban areas at up to 88 percent: See Peñaloza, "*Atravesando Fronteras*/Border Crossings."

32. B. G. Yovovich, "Cultural Pride Galvanizes Heritages," *Advertising Age*, February 15, 1982, pp. M-9, M-44.

33. B. A. Brusco, "Hispanic Marketing: New Application of Old Methodologies," *Theme*, May–June 1981, pp. 8–9.

34. Joel Saegert, Francis Piron, and Rosemary Jimenez, "Do Hispanics Constitute a Market Segment?" *Advances in Consumer Research*, Vol. 19, John Sherry and Brian Sternthal, eds. (Provo, UT: Association for Consumer Research, 1992), pp. 28–33.

35. Marilyn Lavin, "Acculturating the Hispanic Consumer: The Grocery Shopping Experience," *Marketing Theory and Applica-*

tions, Vol. 6, David W. Stewart and Naufel J. Vilcassim, eds. (Chicago: American Marketing Association, 1995), pp. 359–364.

36. Melanie Wallendorf and Michael R. Reilly, "Ethnic Migration, Assimilation, and Consumption," *Journal of Consumer Research*, Vol. 10 (December 1983), pp. 292–302, cited in Peñaloza, "*Atravesando Fronteras*/Border Crossings".

37. John Sugg, "Miami's Latino Market Spans Two Continents," *Advertising Age*, February 15, 1982, pp. M-9, M-44.

38. Additional problems occur when companies are "politically incorrect" in a foreign language. Microsoft Corporation accidentally released a Spanish-language thesaurus suggesting that Indians can be equated with man-eating savages and offering "bastard" as a synonym for those of mixed race. Don Clark, "Hey, #@*% Amigo, Can You Translate the Word 'Gaffe'?" *The Wall Street Journal*, July 8, 1996, p. B6.

39. U.S. Bureau of the Census, press release, "Income and Poverty Status of Americans Improve, Health Insurance Coverage Stable, Census Bureau Reports," September 26, 1996.

40. Robert E. Wilkes and Humberto Valencia, "Shopping-Related Characteristics of Mexican Americans and Blacks," *Psychology and Marketing*, Vol. 3 (1986), pp. 247–259. See also Francis J. Mulhern and Jerome B. Williams, "A Comparative Analysis of Shopping Behavior in Hispanic and Non-Hispanic Shopping Areas," *Journal of Retailing*, Vol. 70 (Fall 1994), pp. 231–252.

41. Charles R. Taylor, Ju Yung Lee, and Barbara B. Stern, "Portrayals of African, Hispanics and Asian Americans in Magazine Advertising," in *Marketing and Consumer Research in the Public Interest*, Ronald P. Hill, ed.

(Thousand Oaks, CA: Sage, 1996), pp. 133–150; and Leon E. Wynter, "Business and Race," *The Wall Street Journal*, November 6, 1996, p. B1.

42. Joe Schwartz, "Fourth to Florida," *American Demographics*, October 1987, p. 14.

43. *Statistical Abstract of the United States, 1995*, Item 34, p. 33.

44. Lynn Kahle, "The Nine Nations of North America and the Value Basis of Geographic Segmentation," *Journal of Marketing*, Vol. 50 (April 1986), pp. 37–47.

45. David J. Curry, *The New Marketing Research Systems: How to Use Strategic Database Information for Better Marketing Decisions* (New York: John Wiley and Sons, 1993).

46. Ibid.

47. Alix M. Freedman, "National Firms Find That Selling Local Tastes Is Costly, Complex," *The Wall Street Journal*, February 9, 1987, p. 17.

48. Andrew Gaffney and Andy Bernstein, "Jim Connelly," *Sporting Goods Business*, February 1996, pp. 62–65.

49. Richard Coleman, "The Continuing Significance of Social Class in Marketing," *Journal of Consumer Research*, Vol. 10 (December 1983), pp. 265–280.

50. R. H. Tawney, *Equality* (London: Union Books, 1981).

51. James Carmen, *The Application of Social Class in Market Segmentation* (Berkeley, CA: Institute of Business and Economic Research, 1965).

52. W. J. Warner, M. Meeker, and K. Eels, *Social Class in America: Manual of Procedure for the Measurement of Social Status* (Chicago: Science Research Associates, 1949).

53. Bill Leonard and Roger D. Sommer, "Relocating the Two-Income Family," *HR Magazine*, August 1995, pp. 55–58.

54. Dean Ellis, "Speech and Social Status in America," *Social Forces*, Vol. 45 (March 1967), pp. 431–437.

55. Leonard Schatzman and A. Strauss, "Social Class and Modes of Communication," *American Journal of Sociology*, Vol. 60 (January 1955), pp. 329–338.

56. Gerhard Lenski, "Status Crystallization: A Non-Vertical Dimension of Social Status," *American Sociological Review*, Vol. 21 (August 1956), pp. 458–464.

57. Stuart Rich and Subhash Jain, "Social Class and Life Cycle as Predictors of Shopping Behavior," *Journal of Marketing Research*, Vol. 5 (February 1968), pp. 43–44.

58. Alan Dick, Arun Jain, and Paul Richardson, "Correlates of Store Brand Proneness: Some Empirical Observations," *Journal of Product and Brand Management*, Vol. 4 (4), 1995, pp. 15–22.

59. V. Kanti Prasad, "Socioeconomic Product Risk and Patronage Preferences of Retail Shoppers," *Journal of Marketing*, Vol. 39 (July 1975), pp. 42–47.

60. Charles M. Schaninger, "Social Class versus Income Revisited: An Empirical Investigation," *Journal of Marketing Research*, Vol. 18 (May 1981), pp. 192–208.

61. Richard P. Coleman, "The Significance of Social Stratification in Selling," in *Marketing: A Mature Discipline*, Martin L. Bell, ed. (Chicago: American Marketing Association, 1960), pp. 171–184.

62. Coleman, "Continuing Significance of Social Class."

63. Russell Belk, Robert Mayer, and Kenneth Bahn, "The Eye of the Beholder: Individual Differences in Perceptions of Consumption Symbolism," in *Advances in Consumer Research*, Vol. 9, Andrew Mitchell, ed. (Ann Arbor, MI:

Association for Consumer Research, 1981), pp. 523–529.

64. Cited in Coleman, "Continuing Significance of Social Class."

65. J. H. Myers and Jonathan Guttman, "Life Style: The Essence of Social Class," in *Lifestyle and Psychographics*, William Wells, ed. (Chicago: American Marketing Association, 1974), pp. 235–256.

66. Another group of authors has called this the "standard package" for both different occupational groups and different cultural groups—e.g., Asian-Americans. See Cecilila Wittmayer, Steve Schulz, and Robert Mittelstaedt, "A Cross-Cultural Look at the 'Supposed to Have It' Phenomenon: The Existence of a Standard Package Based on Occupation," in *Advances in Consumer Research*, Vol. 21, Chris T. Allen and Deborah Roedder John, eds. (Provo, UT: Association for Consumer Research, 1994), pp. 427–434.

67. Much of this section is based on ideas suggested by James Fisher, "Social Class and Consumer Behavior: The Relevance of Class and Status," in *Advances in Consumer Research*, Vol. 14, Melanie Wallendorf and Paul Anderson, eds. (Provo, UT: Association for Consumer Research, 1987), pp. 492–496.

68. Erving Goffman, "Symbols of Class Status," *British Journal of Sociology*, Vol. 2 (December 1951), pp. 294–304.

69. Russell Belk, "Developmental Recognition of Consumption Symbolism," *Journal of Consumer Research*, Vol. 9 (June 1982), pp. 887–897.

70. Scott Dawson and Jill Cavell, "Status Recognition in the 1980s: Invidious Distinction Revisited," in *Advances in Consumer Research*, Vol. 14, Melanie Wallendorf and Paul Anderson, eds. (Provo, UT: Association for Consumer Research, 1987), pp. 487–491.

71. Ibid.

72. Russell Belk and Richard Pollay, "Images of Ourselves: The Good Life in Twentieth Century Advertising," *Journal of Consumer Research*, Vol. 11 (March 1985), pp. 887–897.

73. Scott Kilman and Robert L. Rose, "Population of Rural America is Swelling," *The Wall Street Journal*, June 21, 1996, pp. B1, B4.

74. Neil A. Granitz and James C. Ward, "Virtual Community: A Sociocognitive Analysis," in *Advances in Consumer Research*, Vol. 23, Kim P. Corfman and John G. Lynch, Jr., eds. (Provo, UT: Association for Consumer Research, 1996), pp. 161–166.

MARKETING IN THE GHETTO

Retail is heading to Harlem. In 1995 and 1996 Rite-Aid and Blockbuster Video opened stores on Harlem's famed 125th Street. Walt Disney Company agreed to anchor Harlem USA, a retail and entertainment complex set to open in 1998, and The Gap will open a large store in the complex. Magic Johnson and his partner Sony are looking for a location for a movie theater. In East Harlem developers are trying to lure the suburban fixture Home Depot and discount chain Caldor.

This isn't as risky a proposition as it sounds, since "it's been done before." In May 1991 the Concourse Plaza Shopping Center opened in one of the worst sections of the Bronx. Its first day it sold over $250,000 of merchandise to 10,000 customers. The developer of the shopping center said, "Until recently, most retailers have been too scared to go into inner-city areas. The developers chased easy deals in the suburbs. But now that the suburbs are saturated, the greatest opportunities are in the inner cities." Indeed, a sort of retailing vacuum exists in the inner cities. But savvy marketers are discovering the profit potential of these areas. For example, Woolworth's has developed a corporate strategy of entering "ghetto areas" under appropriate circumstances. An executive said, "If we see a need in the community, we're willing to take a risk and go in there."

As Woolworth's is discovering, marketing in the inner city is different from marketing in the suburbs. For example, different assortments in the sizes of shoes are required, and customers prefer different colors to those favored by customers in the suburbs. Although security costs are higher, the price of land and buildings is lower. As a result, Woolworth's inner-city stores enjoy profit margins a full percentage point higher than those in the suburbs.

Some people argue that the opportunities for grocery stores are even higher than those for department stores. In the inner city most food stores are bodegas—small convenience stores that must charge high prices. Consumers are starved for bargains, so larger grocery stores (e.g., Tops in the Bronx) usually do very well if they take the plunge into the inner city. One executive said, "Quality retailers will always do well here because their competition is shoddy, overpriced merchandisers."

Those with experience in managing retail stores in the ghetto say that inner cities should be viewed as developing countries. Just as Americans tell the Poles, the Peruvians, and the Bangladeshis to free their markets from government control and encourage private enterprise, the same advice holds for the inner city. Analysts argue that ghettos have become pockets of socialism in the United States because federal, state, and local governments are the dominant economic force in these areas. For example, in one area of East Harlem called "El Barrio," the city government owns 62 percent of the land and two-thirds of the residents live in public housing.

One of the biggest problems for potential entrepreneurs in the ghetto is access to capital. Community banks have begun to help in some cities, such as Chicago. In some cases informal credit cooperatives are created. For example, Korean grocers obtain credit from revolving credit associations, and many West Indian businesspeople belong to *sousou* groups. Members of these groups make periodic payments into a pot, and each can take a turn at receiving the whole pot. In another instance small businesses form themselves into groups of five or so. Each receives credit, but if any fail, the entire group loses its credit. The resulting peer pressure forces the members to work extra hard.

Overall, great opportunities exist in the inner cities. For example, one analysis conducted in Harlem concluded that its residents spend $205 million a year on apparel and $33.6 million on books—mostly outside their neighborhood.

Further, inner-city neighborhoods influence fashion nationwide—fashion designer Tommy Hilfiger owes his success largely to his clothings's popularity with blacks and Hispanics. In 1997 advertising firm DDB Needham announced a joint venture with black film director Spike Lee. "Kids from these neighborhoods often set the tone for trends around the country, and we want to be in touch with them," said Keith Reinhard, DDB's chairman.

Already there is competition in the inner city. For example, in Chicago, The Lark stores sell upscale apparel at suburban prices, but manage to prosper thanks to service that is so good it actually attracts shoppers from suburbia. Local marketing helps (The Lark pays employees to drop by local dance clubs to talk about the store), as do attentive salespeople, whom The Lark retains by paying high wages and promoting quickly. As the owner of The Lark chain, Daniel Rothschild, says, "A national chain is like a battleship and turns in a wide arc. We can turn in a tight radius."

Questions

1. Define the problem faced by a retailer considering entering an inner-city area.

2. What consumer behavior concepts from the chapter apply to this case?

3. Take the perspective of a retailer considering entering an inner city market. Develop a managerial applications matrix for the retailer and then discuss the managerial issues the retailer faces, as determined by the consumer analysis.

Based on Mark Alpert, "The Ghetto's Hidden Wealth," *Fortune*, July 29, 1991, pp. 167–173; Laura Bird, "Shunned No More, New York's Harlem Entices Big Chains Seeking Fresh Turf," *The Wall Street Journal*, July 25, 1996, pp. B1, B10; and Robert Burner, "Urban Rarity: Stores Offering Spiffy Service," *The Wall Street Journal*, July 25, 1996, pp. B1, B10: and Victoria Griffith, "Hip-Hop Harlem Trades Up," *The Financial Times*, February 17, 1997, p. 13.

19

INTERNATIONAL ISSUES IN CONSUMER BEHAVIOR

INTRODUCTORY CASE

Amway's Successful Japan Venture

When products do well abroad, it is often because their manufacturers have taken local customs into account. Amway Corporation's sales of $1.9 billion in 1996 made it the third-largest direct-selling organization in Japan, where the size of the direct-sales market is two and a half times that of the United States. Why is the company so successful in Japan, a market where so many other American companies have faltered?[1]

One factor is that an American image remains popular in Japan. The jars and bottles that contain Amway's household products have the "Amway" name and logo written in English on the label. Even the product description is written in English, beside a Japanese translation.

A second factor is that many Japanese in their 20s and 30s are choosing to work in direct distribution in order to avoid the hierarchical arrangements of Japanese corporations that often mean waiting for advancement until one is well into middle age. While most American Amway distributors are retirees, in Japan they are much younger. As one Amway distributor explained, "People are starting to wonder what they could do as a single gear

in a company. They want to have fun, they want to do something. When they join Amway, there's something that clicks."

Although the Amway distributors may be fleeing the rigid Japanese corporate life to go out on their own, they still make full use of the group mentality of the Japanese. In Japanese culture the importance of friendship and group participation leads people to highly value the building of *jinmyaku*, or a network of human contacts. Because Amway distributors sell mostly to friends, the *jinmyaku* are indispensable. The Amway culture emphasizes group meetings and pep rallies, which fit in well with the Japanese value system. Like Japanese corporate workers who go out drinking together at the end of the workday, the distributors gather together for "after-Amway" dinners.

Japanese Amway distributors are well aware of opportunities to enhance their lifestyles. Amway products can be sold part-time, and with commissions of 30 percent, distributors can increase their incomes substantially. Many have been able to buy American-style apartments—a real luxury in Japan. Indeed, the Japanese propensity toward hard work is readily seen in the distributors. Back from an American tour, one Japanese distributor commented, "People in America separate their work from the days they take off. But in Japan, you'd never refuse someone who needs a hand on a particular day."

Finally, the success of Amway can also be ascribed to its distribution system. Because it moves its goods directly to its distributors, the company avoids the import-resistant Japanese middlemen.

As a result of all these factors, Amway is a smashing success in Japan. The company enjoys incredible group loyalty from its Japanese distributors. One employee noted that if polo shirts could be purchased with the Amway logo on them, "we'd line up to buy them."

INTRODUCTION

Understanding culture is never more important than when selling products abroad. By recognizing the differences between their own culture and that of the targeted society, managers can avoid multimillion-dollar mistakes. At the same time, diverse cultures often share certain interests. For example, enthusiasm for basketball is exploding around the world.[2] Many basic needs are similar from nation to nation. The ad for the Gillette Sensor razor for women shown in Figure 19-1, which appeared in the German magazine *Brigitte*, addresses personal grooming needs that are the same for German and American women.

Consumer behavior concepts apply across diverse cultures. The importance of food in France illustrates the role of *cultural rituals* in consumer behavior. Attempting to sell U.S. cheese to the French would probably be an exercise in futility. French *hypermarches* may carry 130 brands of cheese, bottled in oils, rolled in ashes, covered with mold, filled with seasonings, surrounded by rinds or waxes, even in decay. In France cheese consumption, like food consumption in general, is considered extremely important. Cheese is served on a plate, eaten with a knife and fork, and usually accompanied by bread and wine.[3] Fearing that younger French citizens are losing some of their elders' knowledge about how to eat and serve cheese and other traditional French foods, the French government brought top chefs into the nation's primary schools in the 1990s to educate young French palates on food preparation and consumption rituals.

It is important to remember that "cultures" and "nations" are not the same. A nation can be precisely identified, but a "culture" cannot.[4] For example, "Ethiopia" is a country with definite borders, but Ethiopians carry their culture with them when they emigrate to another country or visit as tourists.

Cross-Cultural Use of Symbols

Differences in cultures are readily seen in the use of symbols. For example, Yokohama Rubber Company had to pull hundreds of off-road tires from the market in Brunei after complaints from the Muslim community because the tread left a design that resembles a verse in the Koran.[5]

One class of American products that frequently succeeds abroad is motion pictures. Because of the high profit potential, a U.S. movie is usually distributed overseas within six months of its release in the United States. Despite the strong general appeal of American-made movies overseas, it can be difficult to predict which films will be popular abroad. For example, Al Pacino is a well-known actor here, but he is a bigger star abroad. U.S. posters for *Scent of a Woman* featured Pacino less prominently than did the posters used overseas.[6] The difference between Al Pacino's popularity here and abroad illustrates how symbols may have different meanings to people of different cultures.

The Japanese have a great fondness for borrowing words from other cultures and using them in their promotional materials. Foreign words have several symbolic meanings for

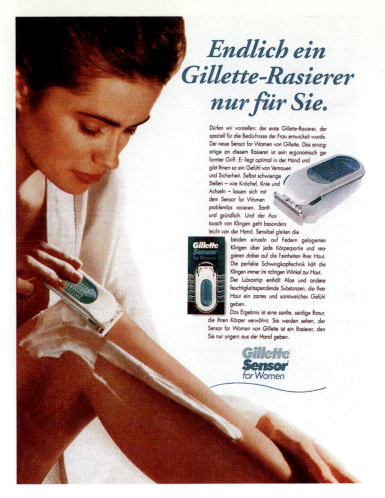

Figure 19-1

This ad from the German women's magazine *Brigitte* suggests the commonality of certain needs, wants, and desires across cultures.

the Japanese. They may connote something new or modern; they may indicate a Western influence; or they may symbolize prestige. Figure 19-2 illustrates the custom of using English loanwords in Japanese advertising. The infiltration of Japanese loanwords into English has been much less prevalent, but some common examples are *sushi*, *samurai*, *keiretsu*, and *kamikaze*.

The symbolic meaning of various holidays also varies across cultures. In Japan, of course, Christmas has little to do with celebrating the birth of Jesus. Rather, Christmas Eve, which is more important than Christmas Day, is to young people a night for romance, so hotels are booked up to a year in advance. For everyone, it's a good day to eat fried chicken and strawberry shortcake. On Christmas Eve KFC's Japan unit sells about five times more food than it does on an average day.[7]

The symbolic meanings of nonverbal communication can create problems for marketers in the international arena. In 1993 AT&T launched its "i Plan" around the world. In print advertisements in the United States, the dot above the "i" in "i Plan" was replaced by a thumbs-up sign. When the symbol was considered for the Russian and Polish markets, there was a problem because in those countries it makes a big difference whether the viewer sees the palm of the hand or the back of the hand. It seems that a "thumbs-up" sign

Figure 19-2

This ad from a Japanese company, Kyocera, appeared in the German magazine *Focus*. Note the mixture of German and English words.

in which the palm is seen conveys an offensive message to Poles and Russians. AT&T decided, of course, to portray the "thumbs-up" sign from a back-of-the-hand perspective.[8]

Knowledge of the implicit meaning of symbols is particularly important when a company begins to market its products or services internationally. The next section discusses this important issue.

INTERNATIONAL MARKETING AND CONSUMER BEHAVIOR

For an international marketing campaign to succeed, managers must have an excellent understanding of culture in the target markets. **Cross-cultural analysis** involves the study of the values, attitudes, language, and customs of other societies.

Table 19-1 identifies seven categories of differences in foreign cultures that affect international business. Of these, perhaps the most important are differences in languages and values. Differences in language can severely impede the communication process. Value differences have a more subtle, but equally important, impact on marketing. For ex-

International Business Cultural Factors

1. *Language*: Spoken, written, mass media, linguistic pluralism.
2. *Values*: As related to time, achievement, work, wealth, change, risk taking, science.
3. *Politics*: Nationalism, sovereignty, power, imperialism, ideologies.
4. *Technology and material culture*: Transportation, energy system, communications, urbanization, science.
5. *Social organization*: Social mobility, status systems, authority structures, kinship.
6. *Education*: Literacy, human resource planning, higher education.
7. *Religion*: Philosophical systems, sacred objects, rituals.

Source: Adapted from Vern Terpstra and Kenneth David, *The Cultural Environment of International Business* (Cincinnati, OH: Southwestern Publishing, 1991).

TABLE 19-1

ample, values related to the acceptability of body hair on women severely limit the ability of companies to market razors successfully in some countries. The Austrian marketing director for Gillette once remarked, "We don't have to advertise women's razors here. I can personally give razors to all four Austrian women who want them."[9] Still, the fact that Gillette is now advertising the Sensor for women in neighboring Germany shows that cultural values can change over time.

Cultural Differences Between East Asia and the U.S.A.

Over the past couple of decades America's trade ties with Europe have decreased in importance as export efforts have been focused more and more on developing countries and the nations around the Pacific Rim. The **Pacific Rim** includes North America, South America, Australia, Indonesia, East Asia, and Siberia. This region holds 50 percent of the world's population, and will contain six of the world's ten "supercities" by the year 2000 (none of the ten will be in Europe).[10]

East Asia in particular is becoming increasingly important to the United States. Composed of Japan, Korea, China, and Southeast Asia, this region has over one-fourth of the world's population and is the dominant exporter of automobiles, electronics, and computer chips. It also has a culture that is markedly dissimilar to our own. East Asian countries are characterized by the Confucian ethic, a philosophy that does not subscribe to a supreme being and that emphasizes the virtues of work, frugality, and education.

Within East Asia Japan is a major trading partner and economic competitor of the United States. Table 19-2 compares and contrasts a number of the values found in the two societies. One of the major cultural differences is how the two societies view the individual. In the United States the individual is seen as more important than the state, whereas in Japan the group, family, and state are more important than the individual.

The cultural differences are also apparent in how companies view their employees and customers. Japanese companies tend to assume that their customers are correct and honest in all instances. The attitude of American companies tends to go in the other direction. Similarly, Japanese firms motivate their employees with job security, although this general statement can be taken too far: part-time workers and women typically have no job security, and many Japanese workers are forced to retire between the ages of 55 and 60 and then need to seek employment elsewhere because their pensions are inadequate or nonexistent.[11]

While cultural values are deeply ingrained and therefore rather difficult to change, the Japanese are beginning to adopt some Western values. After years of working far longer

Comparison of Values in United States and Japan	
United States	**Japan**
Judeo-Christian theism	Confucianism
Individualism	Affiliation
Protestant ethic	Virtues of frugality, work, education
Democracy	Democracy
Liberty	Government over individual
Private property	Close-knit social structure
Merit differentiation	Mutuality of obligations
Equality	Vertical relationships
Self-fulfillment	Family/group orientation
Rationality	Emotion/intuition
Youthfulness	Maturity

Source: Adapted from Robert Bartels, "National Culture—Business Relations: United States and Japan Contrasted," in *International Marketing Management*, Erdener Kaynak, ed. (New York: Praeger, 1984).

TABLE 19-2

hours than their counterparts in other rich countries, for example, the Japanese are now learning to value their leisure time. The government has asked businesses to reduce the traditional five-and-a-half-day workweek, and gave its own employees a five-day work-week in 1992.[12] Millions of middle-class Japanese are now taking foreign vacations, and exposure to consumer goods in other countries has led them to increase their demand for imports when they arrive back home.

One consumption pattern that the Japanese share with us—but that they have taken to greater heights—is the use of automated vending machines. In Japan such machines are grouped into "stores," as shown in Figure 19-3. A larger variety of goods are sold via vending machines, which appear in residential as well as business areas. While the Japanese may buy an entire meal from vending machines, they don't like to eat in public—so the machines must be close enough to either home or work for them to be able to dine in privacy.

Taiwan, South Korea, Singapore, and Hong Kong are also top markets for U.S. products. Many U.S. companies are even more intrigued by the 1.2 billion consumers in the

Figure 19-3

This is an automated "store" in Japan—nothing but vending machines. Illustrating the Japanese penchant for using English words, sometimes without making much sense, the cigarette machine says "speak Lark."

People's Republic of China (PRC). China has the world's fastest-growing economy today, and the preferences of Chinese consumers are changing. A couple of decades ago the "three bigs"—the most longed-for consumer items—were a watch, a bicycle, and a sewing machine. In the 1980s they were a color TV, a washing machine, and a tape recorder, while in the 1990s a VCR, an air conditioner, and a stereo topped the list.[13] Wal-Mart and Sam's Club stores have opened in China, and are planning to have 35 Chinese locations by the end of the century.

Another of the most rapidly expanding markets in the world is Vietnam, where PepsiCo's KFC unit was the first of many U.S. fast-food brands to open stores. North Korea is also finally opening its doors to foreign companies. The cases of Vietnam and North Korea are illustrative of a growing tendency on the part of Western businesspeople to think of developing countries not only as sites for low-cost production but also as markets whose consumers have (or will shortly have) the incomes to purchase significant amounts of Western products.[14]

Researchers have looked at the differences in decision making among people in the United States and East Asia. In one study the researchers investigated differences in the exchange process among executives from the PRC, Japan, Korea, and the United States by asking a sample of executives in each country to engage in a simulated negotiation exercise in which they had to reach an agreement on the price of three products.[15] In all cases the negotiations occurred within the same culture—that is, Americans negotiated with Americans, Japanese with Japanese, and so on. A number of interesting differences were found. First, in both Japan and Korea the buyers had greater status than the sellers and received greater profits than the sellers did. Second, for Americans, the key to successful negotiations was the use of problem-solving strategies involving cooperation and information exchange. Third, competitive strategies yielded higher economic rewards for the Chinese. Fourth, the Koreans' negotiation style incorporated some aspects of the American negotiation model and some aspects of the Japanese model. Finally, the authors concluded that the only universal principle to emerge from this research was that interpersonal attractiveness strongly influences negotiation outcomes for all four cultural groups. The more interpersonally attractive the partners were to each other, the better the outcomes.

Cultural Differences Between Latin America and the U.S.A.

With the ratification of the North American Free Trade Agreement (NAFTA), we can expect that trade with Mexico—already our third-largest trading partner—will leap upward. Nor will trade-expanding agreements stop there. The United States has agreed to negotiate free trade agreements with all other Latin American countries, beginning with Chile. A market scene from Peru, perhaps compatible with our traditional view of Latin America, is shown in Figure 19-4.

American-made products are viewed positively in Latin America. In Mexico about 90 percent of the movie videos rented were made in Hollywood, and most have subtitles rather than Spanish dubbing.[16]

Figure 19-4
This Peruvian market is a high contrast to the automated Japanese "store" shown earlier.

Other U.S. exports are also highly prized. The number of U.S. franchises with outlets in Mexico quadrupled in the early 1990s, to more than 100. *Cristina*, an imported Cuban-American TV talk show, patterns itself after *Oprah* and other American talk shows that dwell on psychological and sexual issues.[17] Not to be outdone, Grupo Televisa, Latin America's biggest media concern, has exported its racy telenovelas to Turkey, China, India, Russia, and elsewhere. The firm is also becoming a force in English-language programming for the U.S. market.[18] Its first English-language soap opera was called *Forever*.

As trade increases with Latin America, however, cultural differences will create difficulties. For example, a nonverbal activity that can discomfit North Americans is the *abrazo*, or embrace—a common mode of greeting in Latin America. It may take some practice for *norteamericanos* to learn how to turn their heads a bit so they don't bump noses!

The Spanish language is a unifying force among most of the peoples of Latin America, but that unity isn't monolithic. Just as the British, Americans, and Australians speak the same language, but with variations—what are "bangers and mash," anyway?—so is

---

Question: Why couldn't moviegoers in Buenos Aires, Argentina, view Oliver Stone's film *Nixon* on one weekend?

Answer: Because the only copy in the city had been borrowed by the president, Carlos Menem.

Source: Observer, "Tricky One," *The Financial Times*, March 19, 1996, p. 15.

Consumer Behavior Factoid

there variability in Spanish throughout Latin America. For example, café (a place for snacks) is *un cabaré* in Colombia, *un cafetín* in Mexico, "*un milonguero*" in Argentina, *un boiti* in Central America—and *una tapesa* in Spain. A variant dialect of Spanish has for years been spoken in Los Angeles, and along the U.S.–Mexican border people speak a Spanish-English mix called "Spanglish"[19] or "Tex-Mex." This "border Spanish," spoken in places like McAllen, Texas, is not viewed with favor by those living in the Mexican interior. Finally, in Brazil Portuguese is spoken rather than Spanish.

As you will recall from our discussion in Chapter 7, cosmetic surgery is a consumption phenomenon related to the self-concept. Perhaps this phenomenon has reached its height in Argentina, where it is estimated 1 out of every 30 people have undergone plastic surgery. One humorist sums up Argentina's philosophy as "I have been operated on, therefore I am." President Carlos Menem has apparently gone under the knife himself. When he appeared in public one day with a swollen face, the official explanation was that he had been stung by wasps. The more accepted version laid the blame on collagen injections in the presidential cheeks, while others said it was a reaction to a hair transplant. Whatever the real story, it prompted the birth of a satirical magazine called *The Wasp*, and a slogan for a hotel that had been refurbished: "We, too, have been bitten by a wasp."[20]

Cultural Differences Between Eastern Europe and the U.S.A.

The Eastern Europe landmass stretches from the eastern border of Germany to the Pacific Ocean, and is composed of people as diverse as the European Czechs and the Mongoloid people of far eastern Siberia. With a population of some 425 million (compared to 357 million in all of Western Europe), this area has enormous potential for marketers.

Incomes in Eastern Europe are much lower than in Western Europe, but productivity is rising after a period of political turmoil and economic readjustment in the early 1990s. The retail setting is still austere: typically, stores have had few toilets, no air conditioning, little in the way of carpeting, and only the most rudimentary displays of goods. In Kazakhstan understanding of capitalism was so weak after generations of communism that a soap opera was put together to demonstrate how market systems work.[21] On the other hand, demand for Western products is high: one Swedish furniture retailer had to drop catalog sales in Hungary and stop advertising in both Hungary and Poland because it couldn't keep up with demand. The combination of high demand and low purchasing power has created new shopping patterns in which consumers accumulate silverware and tableware one spoon or cup at a time.[22]

Not all Eastern European countries are poor, however. The Czechs were the sixth-wealthiest people in the world before World War II, and this background has contributed to the rapid adaptation to market structures and Western tastes in that country.[23] In the Czech Republic U.S. products have a good reputation for quality, although generally the perceived quality of German and Japanese goods is higher. Czech customers are influenced by advertising and price discounting, however, so U.S. suppliers may be able to use both to compete favorably with the Japanese and Germans. Still, at this point Czech customers prefer German, Japanese, and even Czech products.[24]

The disintegration of the Soviet Union and its satellites threw open a huge market hungry for consumer goods, especially for imported goods banned under communism. *Playboy* has licensed overseas editions in Poland, Hungary, and the Czech Republic. It airs selected pay-per-view television offerings in Bulgaria, and sells home videos in Slovenia and Croatia.[25] Not only are the people of Eastern Europe anxious for consumer goods, Western items are status symbols as well. For example, the Twix bar is a favorite for Russian teenage boys hoping to impress their girlfriends with American confections.[26]

Marketing to consumers in Eastern Europe does take an understanding of the different cultures of the people and of their unfamiliarity with "Western-style" business practices. When European and American products first began to arrive in their countries, Eastern Europeans felt that advertising tricked consumers. When Procter & Gamble introduced its shampoo and conditioner Wash and Go, customers had not heard of hair conditioner, nor did they want it. Polish bars began serving a drink derisively called "Wash and Go—a shot of vodka with a water chaser. Wash and go."[27] They greeted free samples with suspicion, reasoning that the product must be of low quality if the company was giving it away.[28]

Gradually, however, these consumers have acquired more experience and are becoming more comfortable with marketing activities. One research study found that 89 percent of a 500-person focus group assembled by Leo Burnett's Prague office believed ads provide useful information, and nearly 60 percent said they use the information in deciding what to buy. According to Marek Janicki, managing director of ITI-McCann-Erickson in Warsaw, "In the past, producers were king. Now the customer is king. People are happy someone is trying to get their attention."[29]

Still, advertising often fails to get the marketer's message across. Hungarian consumers thought the Eveready Energizer bunny was a promotion for a bunny toy, not a battery.[30] Similarly, an ad for a baby bath soap showed a young mother holding a baby, wearing a ring on her left hand. Scandalized Hungarians, who wear wedding rings on their right hand, were aghast that she would tell everybody in Hungary that she wasn't married!

Cultural Differences Between Western Europe and the U.S.A.

By comparison with other areas of the globe, Western Europe seems a very attractive area for U.S. businesses seeking to expand abroad. First, it is large (there are 364 million people in the European Union) and relatively wealthy. Second, Western Europe seems culturally accessible. Even McDonald's is doing well in the land of haute cuisine, with some 500 French locations.[31]

Despite its size and wealth, Western Europe contains remarkable cultural diversity. Cultural differences exist both between the United States and Western Europe, and between the nations and cultures within Western Europe. For example, an important difference between U.S. and German citizens is their attitude toward debt and credit cards. Although we incur debt rather freely, the German word for debt—*schulden*—also means guilt. This may be why Germans make only 1 percent of their purchases with credit cards, compared to 18 percent in the United States.[32]

While the European Union (EU) has a common agricultural policy, a coordinated monetary system, and open borders, there are cultural differences among the member nations

---

Question: Who likes vinegar-flavored potato chips?

Answer: European consumers don't enjoy salty snacks the way we do—we consume eight times the world average of these foods. PepsiCo found that in potato chips Europeans prefer a salt-and-vinegar flavor, Poles and Hungarians like paprika, and Asians like fish flavors. In China the sticky-cheese coating on Cheetos wasn't a hit, so Chinese Cheetos are cheeseless.

Source: Robert Frank, "Potato Chips to Go Global—Or So Pepsi Bets," *The Wall Street Journal*, November 30, 1995, pp. B1, B10.

Consumer Behavior Factoid

of this organization. Also, a small part of Western Europe still does not belong to the EU. Countries within Western Europe have different preferences, even on such mundane matters as the appropriate size of paper napkins.[33] Unilever's food division sells a different tomato soup in Rotterdam than in Brussels, uses another recipe in France, and still another in Germany. Unilever found that Germans want a detergent that is environmentally safe, and will pay a premium for it. Spaniards, however, want a cheaper product that will get shirts white and soft. Greeks want smaller detergent packages to hold down the cost of each store visit.[34] In short, the **Euroconsumer** does not yet exist.

Table 19-3 identifies some of the key dimensions on which cultures in the United States, Mexico, the Czech Republic, France, and Japan can be compared. Each is located in one of the foreign market areas we have examined.

Cross-Cultural Problem Areas

When marketers deal with people from a different culture, a number of difficult problems may arise. We discuss some of these issues in this section.

Translations In addition to coping with the difficulties of everyday speech in foreign countries, marketers must be aware of the problem of accurately translating their product's brand name into new languages. Examples of mistranslations abound.[35] For example, Colgate-Palmolive introduced its Cue toothpaste into France without changing the name. They did not realize that *cue* is a pornographic word in French. A paper manufacturer accidentally had its name translated into Japanese so that it became "He who envelops himself in ten tons of rice paper." When the American film *City Slickers* went to France, its title became *Life, Love and Cows*.[36]

The list of translation *faux pas* is long. One method of avoiding such problems is called **back-translation**, a process that involves successively translating the message back and forth between languages by different translators. In this way, subtle and not-so-subtle differences in meaning can be discovered.

Although back-translation will solve translation issues, there is still the question of context. Is leasing a car meaningful in a culture where leasing isn't prevalent? Even using a

Comparing the United States, Mexico, the Czech Republic, France, and Japan: Key Dimensions					
	United States	**Mexico**	**Czech Republic**	**France**	**Japan**
Attitudes toward uncertainty	Risk acceptant	Risk averse	Risk averse	Risk averse	Risk averse
Individualistic vs. group oriented	Individualistic	Group oriented	Group oriented	Individualistic	Group oriented
Nurturing vs. macho	Macho	Macho	Nurturing	Nurturing	Very macho
Attitudes toward authority*	Low	High	High	High	High

*The degree to which survey respondents felt that authority figures, such as their bosses, were to be deferred to. U.S. respondents were less inclined to defer to their supervisors than were people from the other countries listed.

Source: Adapted from Geert Hofstede, *Culture's Consequences* (Beverly Hills, CA: Sage Publications, 1980).

TABLE 19-3

translator fluent in both languages won't necessarily solve this potential problem. For example, a Nigerian who has spent enough time in the West to speak English with great fluency has also to some degree internalized Western values. To that extent, he no longer reflects the same values as his compatriots in Nigeria.[37]

One new technology with considerable promise is translation software, which offers the alluring possibility of foreign language translation at your fingertips. Earlier attempts at computerized translation in the 1950s led to such howlers as "the spirit is willing but the flesh is weak" rendered as "the vodka is strong but the meat is rotten." More recently, when former prime minister Margaret Thatcher visited a Fujitsu plant near Mt. Fuji, the company's intelligent computer translated her remarks on being honored to visit such a marvelous factory as "This company, having been visited by me today, is honorable." Nonetheless, Fujitsu is confident enough in its product that it has put the English-Japanese translator on the Internet.[38]

National Languages and Dialects Frequently the language question is highly nuanced. In roughly ascending order of the level of confusion, China, India, and Africa present great linguistic challenges to Westerners.

China, a huge country divided by high mountain ranges and peopled by several major ethnic groups, has a number of Chinese "languages" that are mutually unintelligible. One of the authors visited a village in Taiwan where neither the national nor the dominant regional language was spoken, but yet a third "Chinese." He could speak only with children, who had learned the national language in school. But China is slowly being tied together by a common language as children are taught to speak a national language based on the dialect of the capital, Beijing.

Even more languages exist in India than in China: one official census of India gave a figure of 826 different languages and dialects. Although, in fact, there are only four major language families with more than one million speakers each (fewer than in Europe), still there is great diversity.[39] As a practical matter, though, marketers' coverage of India is less complicated. Each of the 26 states has three official languages: English, Hindi, and the predominant state language. To ensure complete coverage, many advertisers place the same ad in an English paper, a Hindi newspaper, and a local-language newspaper.

Language can also affect the location of foreign businesses in India. Hindi is a northern Indian language, and Indians in the south see little reason to speak it instead of English. Their English is therefore generally better than Northerners', and foreign businesspeople may find that southern India therefore provides a better environment in which to work.

Although English, French, and, to a lesser extent, Portuguese are spoken in Africa as a legacy of the colonial past, there are over 1,000 mutually unintelligible languages used on that continent. Some languages (such as Swahili, Hausa, and Mandingo) had become *lingua franca* (universal languages) in certain areas of Africa before the arrival of Europeans. Nonetheless, the problem of linguistic appropriateness is a major challenge to marketers in Africa.[40]

Some linguistic impediments are political in nature. When the Soviet Union disintegrated, the former states declared linguistic as well as political independence from Moscow. Kyrgyzstan, Kazakhstan, and Turkmenistan not only use their own languages in preference to Russian—they have also decided to use the Latin alphabet instead of Cyrillic letters.[41]

Time Perception Time (which is also discussed in Chapter 14) is an important situational factor influencing consumers. In international settings, it can cause problems because different cultures often view time differently. Time is a commodity in the United States. For example, Americans speak of "spending" and "wasting" time. As a consequence, Americans hate to be kept waiting. In many other cultures, time is much less important. A foreign executive may keep an American client waiting for 45 minutes or longer and think nothing of it. To some foreign businesspersons 45 minutes is an insignificant length of time to wait.[42]

A U.S. professor described his experience of teaching classes in Brazil as traumatic at first, because students arrived late to class and then hung around after class for no apparent reason. Partway through the semester, he asked the students how many minutes before and after the agreed time would have to elapse before someone was considered early or late. For Brazilian students, the average was 54 and 34 minutes, respectively. For students in a comparable California university, the times were 24 and 19 minutes. The Brazilian students were simply more casual in their approach to time.[43]

Some argue that an emphasis on time denotes a culture that maintains a very fast paced lifestyle. A study was performed that investigated the accuracy of bank clocks, the average walking speed of pedestrians on a city street, and how long it took postal clerks to sell a stamp in several cultures. On all three measures Japan had the most accurate/fastest times. The United States or England was either second or third on each. Finally, Indonesia tended to have the most relaxed pace.[44]

Symbols As already explained, divergent cultures may have different symbols to communicate meaning. Thus what something means in one culture may not be the same in other cultures. For example, the number seven is unlucky in Ghana and Kenya, but lucky in India and the Czech Republic. The number four is unlucky in Japan because the words for "four" and "death" are pronounced identically; Mandarin and Cantonese speakers have the same attitude, for the same reason. In Hong Kong eight, three, and two sound good since they sound like "good fortune," "alive," and "easy," respectively. The triangle is negative in

Hong Kong and positive in Columbia. Purple is associated with death in many Latin American countries. In Mexico yellow flowers are a sign of death, whereas in France they denote infidelity. The expression "wearing a green hat" means that a man's wife is cheating on him in China. Similarly, gifts may represent different feelings in different cultures.

Never surprise your Japanese host with a gift. By accepting it (and refusal is impossible), he incurs an obligation to reciprocate immediately with a gift of the exact same value. If your gift was not made in Japan, the price may be unknown, and your host will agonize over what to do.

Friendship Americans tend to make friends easily, but they also drop them rapidly. In some countries friendship replaces the legal or contractual system.[45] Therefore friends are made slowly and retained for great lengths of time. As a consequence, the Chinese, Japanese, and others view with skepticism Americans who come on strong; they tend to see such people as insincere and superficial.

Etiquette Matters of etiquette can also create discomfort and misunderstandings. For example, Americans may not understand the Japanese exchange of business cards, or *meishi*, which is a necessary social ritual. These exchanges allow the Japanese individuals to gauge their respective levels of status. There is a precise ritual to exchanging name cards in Japan: they must be given with both hands rather than one (this is also true for China and Korea). In China the exchange of name cards is both a matter of etiquette and practicality. Many people have the same names, and many characters sound alike in spoken Chinese (4,800 people are identically named Liang Shuzhen in Shenyang City alone). Name cards are used to build personal "phone books," since calling "information" might be an exercise in futility!

The exchange of hugs and a kiss on the cheek between males in Eastern Europe strikes many Americans as strange and inappropriate. However, the ritual is a basic part of the manner in which people are greeted in that part of the world. Another matter of etiquette that differs is how food is eaten. For example, many Europeans consider eating food with your fingers (e.g., sandwiches or french fries) quite crude. The Japanese find the Western practice of blowing one's nose in a handkerchief and putting this effluvia in a pocket or purse, rather than disposing of it, disgusting. Instead of getting formal when embarrassed, Thais giggle. Westerners sometimes assume they have missed a joke when actually they have embarrassed their Thai counterpart.[46]

Nonverbal Behavior Nonverbal behaviors are those actions, movements, and utterances that people use to communicate in addition to language. These include movements of the hands, arms, head, and legs, as well as body orientation and the space maintained between people. Different cultures have divergent norms concerning such nonverbal behavior. Take interpersonal spatial relations. Americans have four zones surrounding them: intimate, personal, social, and public.[47] The intimate zone is from zero to 18 inches away. Public zones are from 12 feet or further away. Business tends to be conducted in the social zone of four to seven feet.

People in other cultures, however, do not space themselves in the same way as Americans. In Middle Eastern and Latin American cultures, for instance, people tend to interact at a much closer distance. Consequently, an American may become uncomfortable as a foreign businessman closes in on him. The result of such interaction has been described as a sort of waltz, with the American backtracking and the foreign client pursuing. The problem is that the foreigner sees the American as standoffish, whereas the American sees the foreigner as pushy.[48]

Another aspect of nonverbal behavior is the influence of context—that is, how one says something is as important as what one says.[49] The United States is a low-context country. Most of the information in a message is contained in explicit code—that is, language. In Japan, a high-context country, people look for meaning in what is *not* being said—silences, gestures, and so on. For example, in the United States the precise wording of agreements is very important, and in business transactions this means that contracts are critical. Since attorneys are specialists in writing contracts, legal input is important. In Japan, however, precise wording is less important than the intentions of the parties. Divining intention requires an atmosphere of trust, so agreeing to do business takes a bit longer in Japan. Once someone has agreed to do something, the words written on paper mean proportionately less. So in Japan "a person's word is his bond," but in the United States written contracts tend to be relied upon. For Americans, a disconcerting result is that the Japanese often ask for contracts to be renegotiated based on the intention of the parties. That intention is interpreted from the context of the discussion and not from the precise words used in the contract.

Ethnocentricity **Ethnocentrism** refers to the common tendency for people to view their own group as the center of the universe, to interpret other social units from the perspective of their own group, and to reject persons who are culturally dissimilar. This natural proclivity leads people to blindly accept those who are culturally similar to them. Thus the symbols and values of a person's ethnic or national group become objects of pride, whereas symbols of other groups may become objects of contempt.[50]

When marketing across cultures, business executives must strenuously avoid the tendency to look down on others because they do things differently. They must inhibit the urge to try to change the behavior of their hosts because what they do is not as "good" as the American way.

Similarly, attitudes toward consumption activities differ markedly across cultures. When given the statement "A house should be dusted and polished three times a week," 86 percent of Italians agreed, whereas only 25 percent of Americans did; 89 percent of Americans felt that "Everyone should use a deodorant," but only 53 percent of Australians agreed.[51]

The tendency to exhibit ethnocentrism can be used as a segmentation variable. In fact, a consumer ethnocentrism scale has been developed. As shown in Table 19-4, the scale measures American consumers' tendency to prefer to purchase U.S.-made products. Research conducted on the scale indicates that those who are high in consumer ethnocentrism are more prone to accentuate the positive aspects of domestic products and to discount the virtues of foreign-made ones. They reacted more positively to advertisements that used an "American-made" theme. In addition, a product's American origin and construction were rated higher as purchase considerations by those with higher levels of ethnocentrism.[52] The consumer ethnocentrism scale has been shown to apply cross-nationally to French, Japanese, and German people as well.[53]

Several studies have been conducted to investigate the extent to which "made in America" themes have a positive impact on U.S. consumers' attitudes and buying intentions. It was thought that the use of such themes could evoke feelings of patriotism and prove beneficial for companies. The overall results of the research, however, were quite mixed. For example, one study assessed consumer decision making before and after the introduction of the "Made in the USA" television campaign.[54] The $40 million campaign was financed by a coalition of 245 U.S. textile and apparel companies. It used nationally known celebrities to tout American-made apparel as superior in quality and style. The researchers found that although respondents had positive attitudes toward domestically produced goods, the campaign had little effect on actual purchase preferences compared to other product attributes, such as style, quality, and fiber content.

Early research on the "country of origin" issue found evidence that U.S. consumers *did* consider this factor when making a purchase. For example, a 1985 Wall Street Journal/NBC nationwide telephone poll found that 53 percent of respondents claimed to look at product labels for country of origin. Of those who did, 76 percent said they generally chose domestically produced apparel.[55] Follow-up research in the United States and Canada, however, revealed that when 1,458 consumers were asked why they purchased an

Consumer Ethnocentrism Scale

Item

1. American people should always buy American-made products instead of imports.
2. Only those products that are unavailable in the United States should be imported.
3. Buy American-made products. Keep America working.
4. American products, first, last, and foremost.
5. Purchasing foreign-made products is un-American.
6. It is not right to purchase foreign products, because it puts Americans out of jobs.
7. A real American should always buy American-made products.
8. We should purchase products manufactured in America instead of letting other countries get rich off of us.
9. It is always best to purchase American products.
10. There should be very little trading or purchasing of goods from other countries unless out of necessity.
11. Americans should not buy foreign products, because this hurts American businesses and causes unemployment.
12. Curbs should be put on all imports.
13. It may cost me in the long run, but I prefer to support American products.
14. Foreigners should not be allowed to put their products on our markets.
15. Foreign products should be taxed heavily to reduce their entry into the United States.
16. We should buy from foreign countries only those products that we cannot obtain within our own country.
17. American consumers who purchase products made in other countries are responsible for putting their fellow Americans out of work.

Note: Response format is a 7-point Likert-type scale: strongly agree = 7; strongly disagree = 1. Range of scores is from 17 to 119.

Source: Reprinted with permission from Terence Shimp and Subhash Sharma, "Consumer Ethnocentrism: Construction and Validation of CETSCALE," *Journal of Marketing Research*, Vol. 24 (August 1987), pp. 280–289, published by the American Marketing Association.

TABLE 19-4

article of clothing, only one person gave "country of origin" as the reason. The authors stated that "the percentage of those who searched for domestically produced goods because they cared about protection of the home industry was much lower than the percentage of those who expressed a concern for buying Canadian or U.S.-made clothing."[56]

It seems, then, that while a "Made in the USA" campaign will enhance a company's corporate image, better-made products and price are more important. Still, when quality and price are competitive, American-made goods have a strong appeal, which may be growing.

One factor that may have some influence on ethnocentric buying behavior is the specific area in which consumers live. One study polled consumers in North Carolina about their views on textile imports and the "Made in the USA" campaign.[57] In Greenville, a city whose economy is significantly affected by foreign imports, 92 percent of those polled stated that they would pay more in order to limit imports of both cars and clothing. In the more urbanized Winston-Salem, less economically threatened by foreign imports, only 32 percent of those polled stated that they were willing to pay more to limit clothing imports and only 23 percent said they would pay more to limit auto imports. The likely explanation for these dramatic differences is that consumers' ethnocentrism increases when foreign competition directly affects their own jobs and economic viability.

Binational products The issue of consumer ethnocentrism is made more complicated by the current manufacturing trend to make product components in one country and have the product assembled in another country, or to design a product in one country and manufacture it in another. How are these **binational products** received by consumers? Generally speaking, consumers are influenced by their view of *both* countries. This means that manufacturers need to carefully consider the locations of all of the steps in the production process. For example, having a product designed in Japan can mitigate the effects of having it made in a country that has a poor reputation for quality.[58]

Other Ethnocentrism Effects Ethnocentrism may also be displayed in the tendency for consumers in richer societies to assume that products from poorer countries are less preferable than those from developed countries. This effect may even extend to consumers from poorer countries themselves—who may prefer richer-country products to their native products.[59] This does not necessarily mean that consumers in richer countries do not want to buy any products from poorer countries, only that they display preferences for goods that match their notion of the country of origin. For example, while athletic footwear from China would probably not be attractive to U.S. consumers, sandals might be a good match.[60]

ADAPTING OR STANDARDIZING PRODUCTS AND SERVICES

A major issue in international marketing is whether to standardize the marketing plan across national boundaries. This debate has been led by two well-known marketing thinkers. Philip Kotler argues against standardization across markets, while Theodore Levitt takes the opposite position. Levitt argues that a rapid homogenization of the world's

Figure 19-5
An open-air restaurant in Beijing, China. In another case of adaptation, restaurants string Christmas lights across their awnings so they can be identified at night.

wants and wishes is occurring for "advanced" goods and services. He cites as one example the image, which many retain, of the 1979 Iranian hostage crisis. During the period when the Iranians held the U.S. embassy hostage, one could see on television "inflamed young men in fashionable French-cut trousers and silky body shirts open to the waist, with raised modern weapons, thirsting for blood in the name of Islamic fundamentalism."[61]

There is no simple answer to the question of whether the marketing mix can be standardized. In some countries, like Japan and Russia, distribution systems are quite different from those found in the United States. Likewise, products must often be adapted to the tastes and preferences of different cultures. For example, U.S. companies typically find that the scent of their personal hygiene products must be made stronger to do well in Thailand.

The issue of standardization is most striking in the advertising area. Impulse, a spray deodorant/perfume, followed a global advertising strategy by using a "boy meets girl" love story theme across the 31 countries in which it was marketed. To accommodate cultural differences, however, the company permitted each of the local agencies to shoot its own version of the basic storyboard. Each of the commercials used the same copyline: "If a complete stranger suddenly gives you flowers—that's impulse. Men just can't resist acting on Impulse." The romantic fantasy commercials involved a young man acting irrationally when a woman wearing the perfume walks by. Upon smelling the perfume, he searches for a flower seller, grabs a bunch of flowers, and chases after the woman. The successful brand was first developed in 1972 in South Africa, from where it moved to Brazil. Within two years of its debut in West Germany, it had garnered 36 percent of the country's total deodorant market.[62]

Although standardized marketing efforts across countries are cheaper to develop and put into practice, with many products there are serious problems with this approach. The goal of a **global marketer** is to have what Coca-Cola called "One sight, one sound, one sell."[63] In most cases, however, too many obstacles get in the way of this goal for it to be implemented. Differences in such variables as government regulations, electrical outlets and voltages for electrical products, and customs make standardized marketing impractical in many instances. For example, government authorities in Britain did not allow Philip Morris to use advertisements showing the Marlboro cowboy, on the grounds that children worship cowboys and would therefore be seduced into smoking. So one ad showed a map of the United States, standing for "Marlboro country," above a mandated health warning against tobacco.[64] In other cases the issue is "what works." Pepsi ads in Israel have featured a young man in army boots doing pushups. In Israel the military is held in high esteem by almost everyone, and teenagers idolize soldiers in elite combat units rather than rock stars or sports celebrities.[65] This campaign, while appropriate for Israel, might stimulate controversy elsewhere.

Even in the product category of athletic shoes companies must exercise caution in employing a standardized marketing effort. For example, athletic shoe makers Nike and Reebok now have 50 percent of the $4.5 billion market for athletic shoes in Europe, up from 5 percent just a decade ago. In this case European buyers want the shoes because they are American and are identified with such American icons as Michael Jordan. The popularity of the 1992 Olympic basketball dream team in Europe enhanced the image of these American brands at the expense of their European rivals, Adidas and Puma. "America's image may be the last remaining export by U.S. firms," according to Michael Atmere, publisher of *Footwear Plus*.

European buyers of Nike and Reebok shoes are interested in having an "American experience," so the physical product isn't altered. In both print advertising and on TV, taglines in Italy, Germany, the Netherlands, and France all read the same way, in English: "Just do it" or "Planet Reebok." But subtle changes are necessary. Reebok deleted weightlifting and boxing from commercials in France because of the French aversion to violence.

Europeans don't play sports as much as Americans do, and don't visit sporting goods stores nearly so often. So Reebok also sells its shoes in about 800 traditional shoe shops in France.[66]

A curious case of adaptation has occurred in the case of beer. In 1531 King Ferdinand of Germany liked a South Bohemian beer so much that he adopted it as the beer of his royal court—the "Beer of Kings." The Germans called the beer "Budweiser" after the German name of the town where it was made, Budweis. In 1876 Adolphus Busch of St. Louis, Missouri, created a new beer, trademarked the name Budweiser, and added a new slogan, "The King of Beers." At the turn of the century the two Buds clashed over rights to the name. In 1911 they agreed on a settlement. Budweiser (Europe) remained a robust beer brewed in small batches, while Budweiser (U.S.) was adapted to blander American preferences.[67]

In a way, the Chinese have adapted a Western product to their own uses. Since they don't use strings of lights on a Christmas tree, these light strings have been put into service as outdoor advertising for restaurants.

Examples of the problems of global marketing abound. While forms of clothing in North America and Western Europe are virtually identical, storage isn't. In Europe walk-in or built-in closets barely exist, so freestanding wardrobes, almost a curiosity here, are big European sellers.[68] Kool-Aid sells well in Venezuela but cannot pass muster in Europe. Nestlé, the huge Swiss company, sells coffee in every country in the free world. However, the advertising and the taste of the coffee vary from country to country. Philip Kotler argues that "there are only a very few products, if any, that you can safely standardize."[69] *The Wall Street Journal* reached a similar conclusion in an article entitled "Marketers Turn Sour on Global Sales Pitch Harvard Guru Makes."[70] The article stated:

> Not only are cultural differences very much still with us, but marketing a single product one way everywhere can scare off customers, alienate employees, and blind a company to its customers' needs.

The idea that companies can completely standardize their marketing plans around the world actually contradicts the marketing concept, which insists that the *consumer* be at the center of the marketing plan. Because consumers differ around the world, so, too, should marketing plans. Besides violating the marketing concept, standardization is difficult to pull off. A recent study of "Eurobrands" found that in order to become pan-European, every single brand had to make some alteration in an element of its marketing mix: 75 percent had to make changes in distribution and pricing, 79 percent in promotion, some in every element.[71]

Nonetheless, Dr. Levitt stands adamantly behind his notion that global advertising can succeed with a "homogenized audience all over the world." He tells advertisers to "achieve what MTV achieves. They communicate powerful fashion, design and music messages around the world without using different music videos of the same songs for different countries."[72]

A number of companies have adopted a compromise strategy that consists of developing a base product and customizing the accompanying elements of the offering (i.e., price, promotion, and distribution channels) for a region, such as Latin America, Europe, or Asia. While an overall promotional theme may be developed to be employed worldwide, the implementation of this theme (for example, deciding whether to translate a slogan directly or to paraphrase it) is done locally. Called **pattern advertising**, this approach is an example of what the Japanese call *dochakuka*: "think globally, act locally."[73]

Pattern advertising can even apply to packaging and brandmarks. When Coca-Cola expanded into the former Soviet Union, the company found there was already a high level of awareness of its famous script logo. However, the word "Enjoy," which is part of the logo, connoted sensuality when translated into Russian, which is not appropriate for a soft drink. So "Enjoy" was changed to "Drink."[74] The pattern of the brandmark was retained, but slightly changed for the specific environment. The Impulse perfume promotional campaign mentioned earlier in the chapter is another example of a successful pattern advertising campaign.

Tangible Products versus Services

The degree to which standardization is possible also depends on the nature of the product. As Figure 19-6 illustrates, different types of products are more or less likely to be successful in a standardized format. Generally, services and industrial products are less likely than consumer products to need adaptation to local markets. Management consultants, lawyers, and accounting firms are able to practice in much the same ways in different countries, although specifics (such as laws and accounting practices) differ. Similarly, industrial products are seldom country-specific, since there are few cultural differences in how a screw works! On the other hand, food products are highly likely to be country-specific. The Chinese may like hamburgers as a break in their usual routine, but they have a saying that if they go three days without eating rice, they're still hungry no matter what else they eat.

A Conclusion to the Standardization Debate?

In the long term Professor Levitt may be correct. As their incomes increase, people do seem to want many of the same products. And the younger the customer, the more true this is. London yuppies are probably more like rich young Parisians than like their older countrymen. However, cultural influence remains strong, and it will be quite some time before Professor Kotler's advice can be ignored.

THE ROLE OF MARKETING RESEARCH IN INTERNATIONAL MARKETING

To identify similarities and differences in taste preferences and in the meaning of symbols across cultures, a firm must engage in marketing research. Major problems exist, however, in performing marketing research across cultures. One issue involves how to standardize measures of consumption values. Recently, it was suggested that researchers might be better off focusing on perceived attribute importance as a means of standardizing measures across cultures. Thus a large pool of attributes can be developed that are likely to be important to people in diverse cultures. Studies can be done in each culture to identify those attributes most important to individuals in that culture. A pilot study conducted with individuals in Japan, Singapore, Hong Kong, South Korea, and Taiwan supported this general approach.[75]

Other issues in cross-cultural marketing research involve technical problems. For example, Saudi Arabia officially bans most meetings of four or more people except for family or religious meetings, so a focus group would be difficult to arrange in that country.

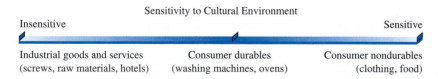

Sensitivity to Cultural Environment

Insensitive ———————————————————————————— Sensitive

| Industrial goods and services | Consumer durables | Consumer nondurables |
| (screws, raw materials, hotels) | (washing machines, ovens) | (clothing, food) |

Figure 19-6
Different types of products tend to be more or less sensitive to foreign environment. The more sensitive a product is, the greater the need to adapt the product to the local environment.

With no published electoral rolls or phone books, telephone surveys would also be difficult. And it's technically illegal to stop strangers on the street or knock on the door of someone's house, so street and door-to-door surveys are out of the question.[76]

Country versus Segment Targets

When a company does business in several countries, managers can choose between two broad segmentation approaches: by country or by market. In the first approach "Turkey" would be viewed as a target market segment. Under the second approach, while Turkey is the physical location of a large group of consumers, the important variables for segmentation would be commonalities in needs and wants among consumers. These consumers reside in different countries and speak different languages, but they have similar needs for a product or service. From this perspective, age, income, or psychographics would be the essential means of identifying market segments. The relevant marketing question is not where consumers reside, but whether they share similar wants and needs. The targeted consumers could be global teens, middle-class executives, or young families with small children: each of these segments shares wants and needs across borders.

A MANAGERIAL APPLICATIONS ANALYSIS OF THE AMWAY CASE

The introductory case described the success of Amway in Japan, which is based, not on adapting the product, but rather on adapting aspects of distribution to the local environment. In particular, while in the United States much of door-to-door selling is done through "cold calls," this would be impossible in Japan, where wide networks of friendship (*jinmyaku*) are critical.

Problem Identification

A key issue for managers in the international environment is to identify the factors that will enhance the suitability of their product for a particular foreign market.

The Consumer Behavior Analysis and Its Managerial Implications

Four consumer concepts from the chapter have particular relevance to the case: cultural values, cultural rituals, cultural symbols, and cross-cultural analysis. Table 19-5 summarizes these concepts and their managerial implications.

Cultural Values One of the reasons for Amway's success in Japan is the company's compatibility with the set of values that dominate that society. The Japanese stress affiliation, and that fits in well with Amway's corporate culture. It has enhanced the ability of the company to create a well-trained, highly motivated sales force. Similarly, the importance the Japanese attach to mutual obligations and group membership helps the distributors find a ready-made set of individuals who might buy Amway products. However, although many of the traditional values of Japan remain strong, some are changing. For example, materialistic values appear to be increasing, so appeals to materialism should certainly play a role in the recruitment of distributors.

Cultural Rituals An example of cultural ritual is the habit of Japanese businesspersons of going out together after work for dinner and drinks. Again, this ritual fits perfectly with Amway's business culture. The distributors maintain important contacts by going to dinner with each other at the end of the business day.

Cultural Symbols Cultural symbols are employed extensively by Amway in Japan. The use of English words and the Amway logo on the labels of products are attractive to Japanese consumers. The Japanese continue to look positively on the American culture overall, even though the relationship between the two nations has occasionally been strained in recent years.

Cross-Cultural Analysis A cross-cultural analysis should be performed by any U.S. company seeking to do business in Japan. For example, a critical issue for firms wishing to enter the Japanese market is how to deal with the Japanese distribution system, which differs dramatically from that found in the United States. Fortunately, Amway was able to circumvent this problem by selling directly to its distributors. In addition, the company created a Japanese subsidiary to make some Amway products in Japan.

Managerial Recommendations

Several recommendations emerge from our managerial applications analysis.

Recommendation 1 Cultural values have particular application to the distribution and promotion of Amway products. For example, the group plays a critical role in tapping potential buyers. Other companies attempting to succeed in Japan will need to consider Amway's brilliant utilization of these cultural values.

Recommendation 2 An understanding of Japanese cultural rituals has helped Amway motivate its sales force. The company uses cultural symbols to link its products to America. Indeed, the name *Amway* literally refers to the "American Way." Symbols of the United States placed on Amway product labels act as promotional tools in positioning the company.

Managerial Implications of Consumer Behavior Concepts in the Amway Case	
Consumer Behavior Concept	**Managerial Implications**
1. Cultural values	*Distribution*. Employ a distribution system that is consistent with values, emphasizing the importance of affiliation, the group, and the extended family.
	Promotion. Train sales personnel so that they understand how to work with the strong social ties among Japanese.
2. Cultural rituals	*Promotion*. Make sales contacts by engaging in Japanese cultural rituals, such as going out for drinks after work with potential clients.
3. Cultural symbols	*Promotion*. Employ symbols that are positively evaluated by the Japanese.
	Positioning. Use appropriate symbols of the United States to position the company.
4. Cross-cultural analysis	*Environmental analysis*. Monitor cultural trends in the United States and Japan for their possible impact on the Japanese. In particular, the potential impact of economic friction between the countries should be carefully monitored.

TABLE 19-5

Recommendation 3 Cross-cultural analysis should be performed to monitor changes in both the Japanese and American cultures. In particular, Amway needs to monitor the environment so that it can react if the economic friction between the two countries develops into deeper cultural resentment.

SUMMARY

Cross-cultural analysis involves the study of the values, attitudes, language, and customs of another society. Factors to consider in international marketing are differences in language, values, laws, politics, technology, education, and religion. Two specific problem areas are translating product names and campaign themes and accounting for cultural differences in time perception, symbols, etiquette, and nonverbal behavior. One tendency successful international marketers have learned to avoid is cultural ethnocentricity—the belief that the values, beliefs, and ways of doing things in one's own culture are right and correct.

Of particular importance to marketers in the United States are the East Asian countries on the Pacific Rim. The cultures of these societies differ in a number of important ways from the culture of the United States, especially in the areas of decision making, face saving, and the role of the individual versus that of the group. However, given their growing economic importance, it is crucial for U.S. firms to engage them in trade. Other important trade areas are Latin America and Eastern and Western Europe.

A major debate in international marketing concerns the extent to which marketing plans can be standardized across cultures. Standardization yields great economies of scale, but the approach is difficult to implement successfully. Although all consumers have similar emotions, such as love, hate, greed, and envy, expression and symbolism can be dramatically different as one moves from culture to culture. Therefore, in most cases, the marketing plan should be tailored to match the consumer preferences of the targeted culture.

KEY TERMS

back-translation	East Asia	Euroconsumer	Pacific Rim
binational products	ethnocentrism	global marketer	pattern advertising
cross-cultural analysis			

REVIEW QUESTIONS

1. Identify five of the seven categories of differences in foreign cultures that may affect international consumer behavior.

2. Compare and contrast the cultural values of Japan and the United States.

3. Eight cross-cultural problem areas were identified in the text. Identify four of these pitfalls and discuss how they could influence the reactions of consumers to marketing offerings.

4. What is meant by cross-cultural ethnocentricity?

5. What problem is back-translation meant to solve?

6. Argue for and against the merits of using a standardized global marketing strategy.

7. Which strategy may be a good compromise between global and adaptive marketing strategies, and why?

DISCUSSION QUESTIONS

1. A U.S. firm in Spain gave a picnic at which U.S. executives donned chef's hats and served food to the workers. The workers felt uneasy and wouldn't socialize with the bosses. Why?

2. The Japanese have a consensus-bonded, group-oriented culture, while Americans are individually motivated and independently oriented. To what extent do you agree with this statement? What are its advertising implications?

3. Compare how easy it would be to standardize the advertising of a perfume versus the advertising of a soft drink around the world.

4. You are the marketing director for the firm that produces California Coolers, the citrus-based alcoholic product that is sold similarly to beer. You wish to sell the product internationally. What types of problems might you have in selling California Coolers in such countries as Mexico, India, Japan, Saudi Arabia, France, and Britain?

5. Increasing numbers of immigrants are buying homes in California. Realtors are finding that they have greater success selling houses that don't have the number "4" in their street address. Why is this true?

ENDNOTES

1. The introductory case is based on Amway Japan Limited (September 18, 1996), "Welcome to Amway Japan," [WWW document], http://www.amway.com/amway/global/japan.htm; Yumiko Ono, "Amway Translates with Ease into Japanese," *The Wall Street Journal*, September 21, 1990, pp. B1, B4; and "CEO Interview: Richard Johnson of Amway Japan," *Institutional Investor*, May 1994, pp. 23–24.

2. Even in Korea! See Fara Warner, "Basketball Thrills Koreans, as NBA Dribbles into Asia," *The Wall Street Journal*, May 17, 1996, p. B9.

3. Scott D. Roberts and Kathleen S. Micken, "*Le Fromage* as Life: French Attitudes and Behaviors Toward Cheese," paper presented at the Annual Conference of the Association for Consumer Research, Minneapolis, MN, October 19–22, 1995.

4. Terry Clark, "International Marketing and National Character: A Review and Proposal for an Integrative Theory," *Journal of Marketing*, Vol. 54 (October 1990), pp. 66–79.

5. "Where the Koran Meets the Road," *Playboy*, March 1993, p. 15.

6. Thomas R. King, "Local Lures: For International Movie Marketers, Posters Are the Center of Attention," *The Wall Street Journal Global Entertainment Supplement*, March 26, 1993, p. R13.

7. Yumiko Ono, "Love and Chicken Fill Christmas Eve in Very Merry Japan," *The Wall Street Journal*, December 17, 1991, pp. A1, A9.

8. Riccardo A. Davis, "Many Languages—1 Ad Message," *Advertising Age*, September 20, 1993, p. 50.

9. Anne B. Fisher, "The Ad Biz Gloms onto Global," *Fortune*, November 12, 1984, p. 80.

10. Donald A. Ball and Wendell H. McCulloch, Jr., *International Business: Introduction and Essentials* (Homewood, IL: Irwin, 1996).

11. Min Chen, *Asian Management Systems: Chinese, Japanese and Korean Styles of Business* (London: Routledge, 1995).

12. "Changes in Japan's Workweek," *The Wall Street Journal*, May 4, 1992, p. A17.

13. Valarie Reitman, "Enticed by Visions of Enormous Numbers, More Western Marketers Move into China," *The Wall Street Journal*, July 12, 1993, pp. B1, B6.

14. G. Pascal Zachary, "Strategic Shift: Major U.S. Companies Expand Efforts to Sell to Consumers Abroad," *The Wall Street Journal*, June 13, 1996, pp. A1, A6; and Joseph Kahn, "Cleaning Up: P&G Viewed China as a National Market and Is Conquering It," *The Wall Street Journal*, September 15, 1995, pp. A1, A6.

15. John Graham, Dong Kim, Chi-Yuan Lin, and Michael Robinson, "Buyer-Seller Negotiations Around the Pacific Rim: Differences in Fundamental Exchange Processes," *Journal of Consumer Research*, Vol. 15 (June 1988), pp. 48–54. For a discussion of differences between Taiwanese and U.S. negotiators, see Ben S. Liu and Wai-kwan Li, "A Friend Is a Friend Even When Money Is the Issue: Differences Between Taiwanese and Americans in Negotiations," unpublished manuscript, 1996.

16. Matt Moffett, "Mexico: JFK, Si! Madonna, No!" *The Wall Street Journal Global Entertainment Supplement*, March 26, 1993, p. R15.

17. Matt Moffett, "Amigos for Now: Mexicans Anticipate Passage of Trade Pact Will Lift Economy," *The Wall Street Journal*, April 20, 1993, pp. A1, A13.

18. Craig Torres and Joel Millman, "Televisa Seeks to Get Big Part in Global Play," *The Wall Street Journal*, May 30, 1996, p. A14.

19. Frances de Talavera Berber, *¡Mierda!: The Real Spanish You Were Never Taught in School* (New York: Plume, 1990).

20. David Pilling, "Rich Argentines Live on a Knife Edge," *The Financial Times*, June 3, 1996, p. 9.

21. Paul Levy, "Showing Kazakhs the Way the World Turns," *The Wall Street Journal*, October 3, 1995, p. A16.

22. Stephen D. Moore, "Sweden's Ikea Forges into Eastern Europe," *The Wall Street Journal*, June 29, 1993, p. A6.

23. Frederick Kempe and Cacilie Rohwedder, "Top Executives Name Czech Republic Most Attractive for Future Investments," *The Wall Street Journal*, July 9, 1993, p. A6.

24. David B. Klenosky, Suzeanne B. Benet, and Petr Chadraba, "Assessing Czech Consumers' Reactions to Western Marketing Practices: A Conjoint Approach," *Journal of Business Research*, Vol. 36 (June 1996), pp. 189–198.

25. Susan Carey, "Playboy Looks Overseas as U.S. Climate Grows Hostile," *The Wall Street Journal*, September 29, 1993, p. B4.

26. Neela Banerjee, "Russia Snickers After Mars Invades," *The Wall Street Journal*, July 13, 1993, p. B1.

27. Dan Michaels and Shailagh Murray, "Advertising: Eastern Europe's Window of Opportunity Is Still Open," *The Wall Street Journal Europe*, July 7, 1993.

28. William P. Putsis, Jr., "Marketing in Eastern Europe: Lessons from Early Entrants," *Yale Management*, 1993, pp. 14–21.

29. Michaels and Murray, "Advertising: Eastern Europe's Window."

30. Tara Parker-Pope, "Ad Agencies Are Stumbling in East Europe," *The Wall Street Journal*, May 10, 1996, pp. B1, B14.

31. Andrew Jack, "McDonald's Makes Fast-Food Inroads on the French Palate," *The Financial Times*, February 21, 1996, p. 14.

32. Greg Steinmetz, "Germans Finally Open Their Wallets to Credit Cards But Aren't Hooked Yet," *The Wall Street Journal*, April 6, 1996, p. A14.

33. Janet Guyon, "A Joint-Venture Papermaker Casts Net Across Europe," *The Wall Street Journal*, December 7, 1992, p. B6.

34. E. S. Browning, "In Pursuit of the Elusive Euroconsumer," *The Wall Street Journal*, April 23, 1992, p. B1.

35. For an excellent discussion of the problems of translation, see David A. Ricks, *Blunders in International Business* (Cambridge, MA: Blackwell, Grid, 1993).

36. "Did We Say That?" *Playboy*, September 1993, p. 15.

37. Eric J. Arnould and Melanie Wallendorf, "On Identical Methods in Cross-Cultural Research, or The Non-Comparability of Data Obtained with Seemingly-Comparable Measures," paper presented at the 1993 American Marketing Association Educators' Meeting, February 20–23, 1993, Newport Beach, CA.

38. Emiko Terazono, "Fujitsu Puts First Japanese Translation Package Online," *The Financial Times*, April 29, 1996, p. 9.

39. *Encyclopedia Americana*, 1991, Vol. 14, pp. 881–882.

40. Ibid., Vol. 1, pp. 269–270.

41. Martha Brill Olcott, "Central Asia's Catapult to Independence," *Foreign Affairs*, Vol. 71 (Summer 1992), pp. 108–130.

42. Edward T. Hall, *The Hidden Dimension* (New York: Doubleday, 1966).

43. Robert Levine and Ellen Wolff, "Social Time: The Heartbeat of Culture," *Psychology Today*, March 1985, pp. 28–35.

44. Ibid.

45. Hall, *The Hidden Dimension*.

46. Karen Swenson, "Roaches and Redheads: Touring a Small Thai Town," *The Wall Street Journal*, July 1, 1993, p. A12.

47. Edward T. Hall, *The Silent Language* (New York: Doubleday, 1959).

48. H. W. Smith, "Territorial Spacing on a Beach Revisited, A Cross-National Explanation," *Social Psychology Quarterly*, Vol. 44 (June 1981), pp. 132–137.

49. Edward T. Hall, *Beyond Culture* (Garden City, NY: Anchor Press, Doubleday, 1976).

50. Terence Shimp and Subhash Sharma, "Consumer Ethnocentrism: Construction and Validation of the CETSCALE," *Journal of Marketing Research*, Vol. 24 (August 1987), pp. 280–289. Also see Subhash Sharma, Terence Shimp, and Jeongshin Shin, "Consumer Ethnocentrism: A Test of Antecedents and Moderators," *Journal of the Academy of Marketing Science*, Vol. 23 (Winter 1995), pp. 26–37.

51. J. T. Plummer, "Consumer Focus in Cross-National Research," *Journal of Advertising*, Vol. 6 (Spring 1977), pp. 10–11.

52. Shimp and Sharma, "Consumer Ethnocentrism." See also Joel Herche, "A Note on the Predictive Validity of the CETSCALE," *Journal of the Academy of Marketing Science*, Vol. 20 (Summer 1992), pp. 261–264.

53. Richard G. Netemeyer, Srinivas Durvasula, and Donald R. Lichenstein, "A Cross-National Assessment of the Reliability and Validity of the CETSCALE," *Journal of Marketing Research*, Vol. 28 (August 1991), pp. 320–327.

54. Richard Ettenson, Janet Wagner, and Gary Gaeth, "Evaluating the Effect of Country of Origin and the 'Made in the USA' Campaign: A Conjoint Approach," *Journal of Retailing*, Vol. 64 (Spring 1988), pp. 85–100.

55. H. Gilman, "Clothing Shoppers Talk Domestic But Look First for Style, Savings," *The Wall Street Journal*, October 15, 1985, p. 31.

56. Susan Hester and Mary Yuen, "The Influence of Country of Origin on Consumer Attitude and Buying Behavior in the United States and Canada," in *Advances in Consumer Research*, Vol. 14, Melanie Wallendorf and Paul Anderson, eds. (Provo, UT: Association for Consumer Research, 1987), pp. 538–542.

57. Sayeste Daser and Havva Meric, "Does Patriotism Have Any Marketing Value?—Exploratory Findings for the 'Crafted with Pride in U.S.A.' Campaign," in *Advances in Consumer Research*, Vol. 14, Melanie Wallendorf and Paul Anderson, eds. (Provo, UT: Association for Consumer Research, 1987), pp. 536–537.

58. Paul Chao, "Partitioning Country of Origin Effects: Consumer Evaluations of a Hybrid Product," *Journal of International Business Studies*, Vol. 24 (Second Quarter 1993), pp. 291–306; and Richard Ettenson and Gary Gaeth, "Consumer Perceptions of Hybrid (Bi-National) Products," *Journal of Consumer Marketing*, Vol. 8 (Fall 1991), pp. 13–18.

59. David K. Tse and Gerald J. Gorn, "An Experiment on the Salience of Country-of-Origin in the Era of Global Brands," *Journal of International Marketing*, Vol. 1, no. 2 (1993), pp. 57–76.

60. Myung-Kyoo Choi, John C. Mowen, and Michael S. Minor, "The Effect of Country of Origin on Product Evaluations: A Test of the Matchup Hypothesis," unpublished manuscript, 1996; and Martin S. Roth and Jean B. Romeo, "Matching Product Category and Country Image Perceptions: A Framework for Managing Country-of-Origin Effects," *Journal of International Business Studies*, Vol. 23 (Third Quarter 1992), pp. 477–497.

61. Theodore Levitt, "The Globalization of Markets," in *The Marketing Imagination* (New York: The Free Press, 1983), pp. 20–49.

62. Brian Oliver, "A Little Romance Puts Impulse on Global Path," *Advertising Age*, June 24, 1985, pp. 39, 40.

63. Fisher, "The Ad Biz Gloms onto Global."

64. Tara Parker-Pope, "Tough Tobacco-Ad Rules Light Creative Fires," *The Wall Street Journal*, October 9, 1996, pp. B1, B6.

65. Amy Dockser Marcus, "Out of Step: The Poor Grow Poorer in Israel as the Army Rejects More Youths," *The Wall Street Journal*, August 13, 1993, pp. A1, A6.

66. Joseph Pereira, "Off and Running: Pushing U.S. Style, Nike and Reebok Sell Sneakers in Europe," *The Wall Street Journal*, July 22, 1993, pp. A1, A8.

67. Shailagh Murray, "Privatization: Emotion Joins Economics as Factor in Czech Sell-offs," *The Wall Street Journal Europe*, June 21, 1993; Roger Thurow, "The King of Beers and the Beer of Kings Are at Lagerheads," *The Wall Street Journal*, April 2, 1992, pp. A1, A8; and "Czech Government Closer to Brewery State Auction," *The Wall Street Journal*, July 28, 1993, p. A10.

68. Allyson L. Stewart, "U.S. Puts Pier Pressure on Europe's Retailers," *Marketing News*, August 2, 1993, pp. 6, 7.

69. Fisher, "The Ad Biz Gloms onto Global."

70. Joanne Lipman, "Marketers Turn Sour on Global Sales Pitch Harvard Guru Makes,"

The Wall Street Journal, May 12, 1988, pp. 1, 8.

71. Jeryl Whitelock, Carole Roberts, and Jonathan Blakeley, "The Reality of the Eurobrand: An Empirical Analysis," *Journal of International Marketing*, Vol. 3, no. 3 (1995), pp. 77–95.

72. Kevin Goldman, "Prof. Levitt Stands by Global-Ad Theory," *The Wall Street Journal*, October 13, 1992, p. B7.

73. An excellent discussion of "going local" can be found in Alan S. Parter, *Going Local: How Global Companies Become Market Insiders* (London: The Economist Intelligence Unit, 1993).

74. Murray I. Tubliner, "Brand Name Selection Is Critical Challenge for Global Marketers," *Marketing News*, August 2, 1993, pp. 7, 11.

75. David Tse, John Wong, and Chin Tiong Tan, "Towards Some Standardized Cross-Cultural Consumption Values," in *Advances in Consumer Research*, Vol. 15, Michael Houston, ed. (Provo, UT: Association for Consumer Research, 1988), pp. 387–395. Other problems exist in doing market research across cultures. For a discussion of problems in measurement, see Jagdip Singh, "Measurement Issues in Cross-National Research," *Journal of International Business Studies*, Vol. 36 (Third Quarter 1995), pp. 597–620.

76. Tara Parker-Pope, "Nonalcoholic Beer Hits the Spot in Mideast," *The Wall Street Journal*, December 6, 1995, pp. B1, B2.

FLORIST'S TRANSWORLD DELIVERY CORPORATION

FTD Corporation, the leader in the $5 billion-a-year flower delivery business since its foundation in 1910, is in an uncharacteristic struggle to maintain its dominance in the world market.

For the last five years FTD's lead has been eroded by companies using innovative marketing strategies like flowers by phone (1-800-FLOWERS) and flowers on the Internet. FTD's once-dominant 80 percent share of the market (in 1989) plummeted to about 50 percent in 1995, as orders decreased from 22 million to 16 million. FTD has recently taken a number of steps in an effort to fight back.

In April 1995 FTD launched a $40 million "Language of the Heart" promotional campaign. Part of this campaign is FTD's new World Wide Web page on the Internet. This Web site allows customers and member florists to place orders to many countries of the world from any computer linked to the Internet. A customer can chose either a North American shop or an International shop, where he or she can view a "virtual" catalog of the products available in specific countries. Once a choice has been made, the customer types in an accompanying message and delivery information, and pays for the arrangement by credit card. If desired, an automated system will remind the customer the next time flowers must be sent to the same person in the coming year. This innovative reminder service includes not only typical holidays and special days but also a customized list of personal occasions. The customer receives an E-mail message 10 to 12 days before the date of the special occasion.

Another step FTD has taken is to upgrade its proprietary Mercury Network, which links 16,400 of its 22,300 florists in 146 countries. A project called Mercury 5000 FTD Floral Expression System aims to replace the outdated personal computer system linking individual florists with more modern and sophisticated client-server technology. In addition to providing faster communication and access to the Internet, these systems will enable more efficient and closer ties among member florists, which is expected to slash product-development time from 24 months to as little as 24 hours. Customers will not only be able to view pictures of the arrangements they will be sending across the globe; they will also be able to browse through libraries of information on flowers and plants.

Among other steps FTD has taken is one forging associations with Gerber, M&M Mars, and Campbell's Soup to establish a line of "branded" products. These products are a unique combination of a "sentiment" bouquet coupled with some tangible item as part of a theme. For example, the "get well" theme includes a can of Campbell's Chicken Soup, while the "bundle of joy" theme includes a number of baby products. In yet another partnership FTD began offering frequent flier miles that are good on American Airlines flights. For a minimum order of $29.95, the customer will receive 300 AAdvantage miles; 100 more miles are added for every $10 over $29.95. The company has also acquired Renaissance Greeting Cards of Sanford, Maine, which puts it in direct contention with one of the biggest players in the "sentiment expression" industry, Hallmark Cards.

FTD hopes that its long experience, coupled with its updated Mercury network and entry on the Internet, will allow it to regain its dominance in both the U.S. and foreign markets.

Questions

1. Define the problems facing FTD.
2. Identify the international marketing customer concepts that are applicable to this case.
3. Develop a managerial applications analysis for the FTD case based on the applicable consumer concepts. Has FTD been responding appropriately to its new competition?

José Castillo developed this case, which is based on Bristol Voss, "Selling With Sentiment," *Sales & Marketing Management*, March 1993, pp. 61–65; Kevin Goldman, "FTD Hopes to Put Bloom Back on Its Image with New Campaign," *The Wall Street Journal*, October 6, 1995, p. B8; Greg Steinmetz, "FTD to Look at Bids to Make It Bloom Again," *The Wall Street Journal*, November 2, 1994, pp. B1–B2; Jennifer Lawrence, "Yet Another Way to Petal Frequent Flyer Miles," *Advertising Age*, March 7, 1994, p. 8; "How Kmart's Former CIO Had Bloomed Anew at FTD," *Chain Store Age*, February 1996, pp. 156–158; and "The Language of the Heart," August 6, 1996 [WWW Document], http://www.ftd.com/.

CHAPTER TWENTY

THE DARK SIDE OF CONSUMER BEHAVIOR

INTRODUCTORY CASE

Sears and Social Responsibility

In 1988 a long battle between Sears, Roebuck & Company and New York City spilled over into the public arena, as the city pressured Sears to stop engaging in various forms of advertising. For one thing, the city wanted the company to stop its practice of promoting a discount price without also explaining whether the markdown was based on the regular price of the merchandise (i.e., the merchandise could be marked *up* prior to announcing the sale). For another, it insisted that Sears stop advertising that a bargain was about to end when in fact the sale would go on indefinitely.

Executives at Sears believed that their advertising was not deceptive and that the company was being unfairly singled out by the New York City Department of Consumer Affairs. In fact, the company issued a press release warning that if it lost its fight, it would "virtually discontinue advertising in New York City, including national publications and network broadcasts in that market." When a Sears attorney was asked if the company's intransigence might harm its image, he was quoted as saying, "I don't care what the public thinks." Sears executives did not seem particularly concerned either. One manager

stated, "Our reputation for dealing with the American public is 100 years old. Our policies haven't changed. The phrase 'Satisfaction Guaranteed or Your Money Back' is still over the door at every store."[1]

Four years later Sears was once again charged with deception—this time on the West Coast. The California Consumer Affairs Department claimed that 33 Sears auto centers in that state had overcharged customers by an average of $223 in nearly 90 percent of the cases investigated. The deception and overcharges were instigated by a quota system established by corporate headquarters that set minimum sales volumes for parts, services, and repairs for every eight-hour shift. Service advisors were instructed to sell a certain number of shock absorbers or struts per hour worked. Those who failed to meet the quotas were transferred.

In an open letter appearing as a full-page advertisement on June 18, Sears' chairman and CEO acknowledged that "mistakes may have occurred" but maintained that the company would "never knowingly violate" customers' trust. A week later New Jersey officials also charged the company with similar violations.

On June 23 Sears' chairman appeared at a press conference and accepted personal blame for the problem. Two days later a second full-page advertisement appeared in which the chairman acknowledged that "our incentive compensation and goal-setting program inadvertently created an environment in which mistakes have occurred." He stated that the Sears' incentive and quota programs that were at fault had been replaced by an incentive system that awarded service advisors for high levels of customer satisfaction. In addition, an outside firm had been retained to conduct unannounced "shopping audits" to ensure that these mistakes would not be repeated.[2]

INTRODUCTION

As the introductory case reveals, companies can prey on consumers through unscrupulous behavior. But, as we will see in this chapter, consumers also engage in negligent behavior—for example, they consume harmful drugs like steroids and cocaine. To decrease the likelihood of harmful activities by companies and consumers, the government regulates the buying and selling of goods and services.

The **regulatory environment** consists of all the laws and regulations established by federal, state, and local governments to exert control over business practices. One goal of these laws and regulations is to protect consumers from the actions of unscrupulous firms. For example, the Federal Trade Commission (FTC) prohibits "unfair or deceptive acts or practices" by merchants and monitors the consumer environment for evidence of such practices.

Regulatory agencies not only seek to protect consumers against outright scams, they also attempt to control less obvious harmful activities of firms, such as the sale of slightly used products as new items. In 1996 the state of California charged Chrysler with reselling 116 cars that had been returned to dealers because of major problems. The new owners had not been informed of the returns, a violation of California law.[3]

In addition to protecting consumers against unscrupulous companies, regulatory agencies try to protect consumers from themselves. Consumers sometimes engage in negligent behavior that poses risks to themselves and to others. The Food and Drug Administration (FDA) is charged with enforcing laws that forbid the misuse of various types of drugs. The use of steroids to build up muscles is one misuse of drugs. Some forms of sexual conduct also pose risks. In fact, advertising campaigns have been initiated to inform consumers of practices that put them at risk of contracting AIDS. Figure 20-1 shows one ad from this campaign.

In this chapter we give you an overview of the development of consumerism, a movement that has heightened both government and corporate sensitivity to consumers' needs in the marketplace. We next present and analyze three major public policy issues: deceptive advertising practices, marketing aimed at children, and environmentalism. This is followed by a discussion of negligent consumer behavior, examples of which are seat-belt use, product misuse, and drinking and driving. We then examine smoking, compulsive drinking, gambling, and other examples of compulsive consumer behavior. Our last topic is the importance of corporate social responsibility. We conclude the chapter, as usual, with a managerial applications analysis of the introductory case.

CONSUMERISM

Consumerism has traditionally been viewed as the "set of activities of government, business, independent organizations, and concerned consumers that are designed to protect the rights of consumers."[4] The development of the consumer movement spans approximately 90 years and can be roughly categorized into four eras.[5]

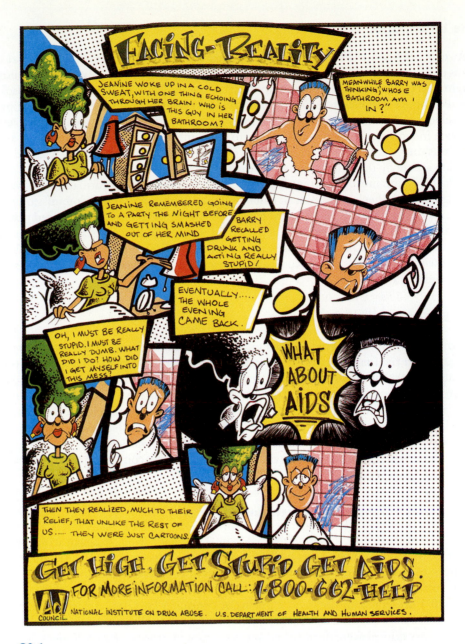

Figure 20-1

Government and advertising organizations sometimes join forces to create messages to warn consumers about AIDS.

The Muckraking Era

The first consumerism era was the muckraking era (1905–1920). In 1905 Upton Sinclair wrote *The Jungle*, which depicted the atrocious conditions then existing in the Chicago meatpacking industry. The public furor that arose over the book's revelations sparked national awareness of the need for consumer protection. Subsequently, Congress passed the Pure Food and Drug Act (1906), the Federal Meat Inspection Act (1907), the Federal Trade Commission Act (1914), and other consumer-oriented legislation.

The Information Era

Between 1927 and 1939 the revelations of Stuart Chase and F. J. Schlink in several editions of the book *Your Money's Worth* again stimulated public concern about the consumer's plight in the marketplace. The primary focus of the book was on advertising and packaging techniques designed to enhance product sales rather than aid the consumer in product selection. *Your Money's Worth* called for objective product-testing agencies that would provide independent product evaluations to consumers. One such agency to arise at this time was the Consumers Union, publisher of the mighty *Consumer Reports*. A single unfavorable article by this nonprofit agency can doom a product.

Probably the most important legal development during the information era was the passage of the Wheeler-Lea Act, an amendment to the Federal Trade Commission Act of 1914. The Wheeler-Lea amendment gave the FTC a more consumer-oriented perspective, along with additional responsibility to investigate deceptive acts and practices. The FTC was granted the power to issue cease-and-desist orders, fine companies for not complying with such orders, and investigate companies even before a formal complaint was made against them.[6]

The Era of Continuing Concern

During World War II and the postwar era (1945–1960), the focus shifted away from consumerism. In the immediate postwar years, U.S. consumers experienced a new prosperity and a hunger for products that had been denied them during the war. As a consequence, fewer major consumer-protection laws were enacted during this era. Among those passed were the Fur Product Labeling Act (which provided mandatory specifications related to the labeling and advertising of fur products), the Flammable Products Act (prohibiting the making of garments from flammable material), and the Hazardous Substances Labeling Act (which required warning labels on household products containing toxic, flammable, or irritating substances).

The Modern Consumer Movement

The modern consumer movement lasted from 1962 until 1980. It began with the enumeration of four consumer rights by President John F. Kennedy in 1962: the right to safety, the right to be informed, the right to gain redress or to be heard, and the right to choice. Many subsequent congressional acts were designed to aid in the protection of these rights. Table 20-1 presents a chronology of the major consumer laws passed during the modern consumer era.

One very critical event during this time was the publication of Ralph Nader's book *Unsafe at Any Speed*. Nader criticized General Motors' attitude toward automobile safety, with particular emphasis on the Chevrolet Corvair. The attention his book drew incited interest in other consumer areas.

Several important acts were passed between 1962 and 1980. For example, the Cigarette Labeling and Advertising Act (1966) required that tobacco companies print the surgeon general's warning regarding the health hazards of smoking on all cigarette packages. The Child Protection Act (1966) banned the sale of hazardous toys and goods intended for children, while the Consumer Credit Protection Act (1968) required that consumers be informed of the full terms of finance charges for loans and installment purchases. In addition, the Consumer Product Safety Act of 1972 established the Consumer Product Safety Commission.

One former government official described the consumer movement as going "from Nader to nadir after President Reagan took office"[7] in 1980. A combination of factors

Developments in the Modern Consumer Movement and the Current Era

Modern Consumer Movement

1962	Kennedy's Enumeration of Consumer Rights
1965	Ralph Nader's *Unsafe at Any Speed*
1966	Cigarette Labeling and Advertising Act
1966	Fair Packaging and Labeling Act
1966	Child Protection Act
1966	National Traffic and Motor Vehicle Safety Act
1968	Consumer Credit Protection Act
1972	Consumer Product Safety Act
1975	Magnuson-Moss Warranty–Federal Trade Commission Improvement Act

The Current Era

1984	Toy Safety Act
1990	Nutrition Labeling and Education Act
1990	Children's Television Act
1994	Dietary Supplement Health and Education Act

Source: Data adapted from Rogene Buchholz, *Business Environment and Public Policy* (Englewood Cliffs, NJ: Prentice Hall, 1982), with additions by the authors of this text.

TABLE 20-1

appeared to be responsible for the movement's decline. Perhaps foremost was the severe reduction in the funding of government agencies.[8] Another important factor was the Reagan administration's preference for market regulation in the form of incentives (e.g., marketable air pollution permits) and disincentives (e.g., advance disposal fees on nonrecyclable products and packaging) over "command-and-control" forms of nonmarket regulation.[9]

Future Directions in Consumerism

What future orientation might consumerism take? For the consumer, health and safety issues will increase in importance even as industrialized societies become healthier and safer. From the regulator's perspective, one major area of concern will be the commercial use of the Internet: as use has increased (consumer purchases through the Internet may reach $200 billion by the year 2000),[10] the dissemination of pornography, the sale of unsuitable products to the underaged,[11] and the security of financial transactions have become major issues.

The internationalization of the U.S. economy will increase Americans' exposure to consumer-related practices in other countries. One concern during the negotiation of NAFTA (the North American Free Trade Agreement) was possible health hazards to U.S. citizens living near the Mexican border because Mexico's environmental enforcement policies are less stringent than those of the United States.

Actually, several countries have gone further than the United States in protecting consumers. Norway, for instance, has banned several forms of sales promotion—trading stamps, contests, premiums—on the grounds that they are "unfair" instruments for promoting products. Thailand requires food processors selling national brands to market low-price brands as well so that low-income consumers can also find affordable goods on the grocery shelves. In India the 15th of the month is "Customer's Day" at all nationalized banks: bank management fields routine complaints from customers.[12] In China nationwide television has been used to encourage viewers to call special hotlines to expose substandard products.[13] These and other consumer-related developments have not surfaced in the United States, but they suggest some directions regulation could take here to constrain marketing practices.

Some Current Public Policy Issues in the Consumer Domain

During the 1960–1980 period three major consumer issues emerged: deceptive advertising, advertising aimed at children, and environmental protection. Each of these issues remains very much "on the public policy agenda."

Deceptive Advertising

Deceptive advertising is either literally false or potentially misleading. Some ads are easy to evaluate: for example, "guaranteed to last ten years" is a statement that is either true or false. Potentially misleading ads are more difficult to assess, since their effect depends on consumers' interpretations. When ads are interpreted incorrectly, we have a case of *miscomprehension*.

Miscomprehension is actually quite common. One study showed that, on average, consumers had a miscomprehension rate of 30 percent for television advertisements. Another study by the same authors of print advertisements indicated that 21.4 percent of the meanings in magazine advertisements were misunderstood, and in a further 15.5 percent of cases consumers did not comprehend the message at all.[14] Although the precise rate of miscomprehension and noncomprehension is somewhat controversial, the potential for miscomprehension of advertisements is clearly significant. The managerial implication is that a certain proportion of the audience is likely to miscomprehend, or fail to comprehend, the advertising message.[15]

The Federal Trade Commission is charged with regulating deceptive advertising, rather than with monitoring consumer miscomprehension of ads. Table 20-2 lists and describes a number of categories of deceptive safety claims that come under the scrutiny of the FTC.

In 1991 the FTC acted against deceptive advertising for Kraft Singles (individually wrapped cheese slices). After losing market share to imitation-cheese products, Kraft launched a campaign positioning its Singles as containing as much calcium as 5 ounces of milk. Since about 30 percent of the calcium was lost in processing, however, the real calcium content of the cheese was equivalent to that in 3.5 ounces of milk. The FTC determined that Kraft had made a deceptive claim and ordered the company to desist from making it. One of the controversies in the Kraft case was whether the difference between the calcium in 5 and 3.5 ounces of milk was material—that is, did Kraft want consumers to make their purchase decision based on the fact that Singles had more calcium than its artificial competitors, or was it the *actual* amount of calcium that consumers were supposed to consider? The FTC and consumer researcher David Stewart argued for the latter position, while analyst Jacob Jacoby argued for the former.[16] As you can see, what constitutes deceptive advertising is not always clear-cut.

The agency has issued a series of advertising guidelines and enforcement policy statements on advertising claims that range from the product-specific (for example, metallic

Misleading Safety Claims	
Misleading affirmative safety claims	Untrue claims that the product is safe. For example, the manufacturer of Jazz nontobacco cigarettes was enjoined from making claims about the safety of the product and its ability to help people stop smoking.
Deceptive denials of product risks	No assertions that the products are safe are made, but it is asserted that its lack of safety hasn't been scientifically proven. R. J. Reynolds asserted for years that a causal relationship between smoking and heart disease had not been scientifically proven.
Deceptive information omissions	Claims that are partially true but contain significant omissions. For example, liquid diets requiring very low food intake were deceptively called "risk-free" because advertisements did not disclose that monitoring by a physician is required to minimize health risks.
Unfair information omissions	A plastic surgery center did not disclose the fact that breast implants interfere with mammography. This is an unfair omission because while implants may otherwise have an acceptable risk level, this risk is significant.

Source: Based on Ross D. Petty, "Regulating Product Safety: The Informational Role of the U.S. Federal Trade Commission," *Journal of Consumer Policy*, Vol. 18 (1995), pp. 387–415.

TABLE 20-2

watch bands and hosiery) to the general (e.g. use of the word *free* in advertising, and environmental marketing claims).[17] Many of the early FTC cases involved offers by small companies to repair consumers' credit records.[18] The FTC has brought the first regulatory cases involving deceptive advertising on the Internet.

Unfair Advertising In 1976 the FTC attempted to rule that *all* advertising aimed at children was unfair. Here the issue wasn't deception, but whether advertising directed at young children was inherently unfair because children might not be able to understand the messages. This led to a 14-year battle between Congress and the advertising industry over the legal definition of what was "unfair." During this legal limbo the FTC could cite "unfairness" in individual cases, but couldn't issue industry-wide rules on "unfairness." As a result, "unfairness" played only a minor role in FTC actions in the 1980s and early 1990s. Agreement on a definition was finally reached in 1994, but it is still unclear whether this will prompt major new rulings from the FTC.[19]

Corrective Advertising In response to the increased concern about deceptive advertising tactics in the '60s and early '70s, the FTC began to order corrective measures from some of the guilty parties. The incident that sparked **corrective advertising** involved Campbell's soup advertisements in which clear marbles were placed in the bottom of a soup bowl to force the vegetables to the surface. Consumers were obviously meant to believe that the soup contained more vegetable pieces than it actually did. The FTC issued a cease-and-desist order that banned this practice.[20]

Perhaps the most famous of all corrective advertising cases involved Warner-Lambert's false claim that Listerine mouthwash could prevent or lessen the severity of colds and sore throats. The company, which began manufacturing Listerine in 1879, had been advertising this claim since 1921—that is, for over half a century. In 1975 the FTC ordered Warner-Lambert to correct the misimpression that the advertisements had created. So in 1978–1980 Warner-Lambert spent more than $10 million on corrective advertising. Nearly 95 percent of this money was devoted to television commercials.[21]

Future Directions Despite the government's attempts to monitor deceptive advertising, studies show that consumers continue to express concern over potentially misleading ads. One study investigated consumers' perceptions of the proportion of misleading advertising across the various media. The respondents viewed telephone advertising as the form with the greatest proportion of misleading information, and direct mail as a close second.[22] These results suggest the need for consumer education material that addresses the issues of mail fraud and telephone misuse.

Children's Advertising

Both marketing managers and public policy makers have reacted to criticisms of advertising directed at children. Children are a significant target market. They represent $8.6 billion in direct purchasing power, and influence some $35 billion of grocery purchases, $22 billion of fast-food items, and $11 billion of children's clothing. Advertisers spend $100 million on Saturday morning child-focused advertising.[23]

Children prefer national brands—which are usually more profitable than private-label brands. While 70 percent of adults have become major buyers of private-label store brands, only 7 percent of children would even consider the stuff: they want brand-name gifts and designer clothes. Brands offer children a common commercial language, something that identifies them as part of a group.[24]

Marketing managers and public policy makers have benefited from consumer behavior research and theory that examines children's responses to advertising. Here are some of the key issues that researchers have investigated:

- Can children tell the difference between commercials and programming?
- Do children understand the selling intent of commercials?
- Do commercials make children want products that are not good for them?

The concern about children's exposure to television is justifiable considering the strong influence this medium has on children. According to some researchers, the commercial influence of TV has slipped in recent years as such countermeasures as children's membership clubs and catalog-marketing programs have flourished.[25] One other reason the commercial influence of TV may have declined is that children are seeing fewer commercials. In 1990 the Children's Television Act limited the advertising on children's television programs to no more than 10.5 minutes per hour on weekends and no more than 12 minutes per hour during the week. A more recent agreement commits television stations to carry at least three hours of educational children's shows a week.[26] Turner Broadcasting's Cartoon Network broke new ground by "bookending" its show *Big Bag* (created

---

Question: Why did Ford Motor Company (U.K.) formally apologize and pay compensation to four black, Indian, and Pakistani assembly workers in 1996?

Answer: The workers had been part of a group photograph but their faces and arms had been lightened. (In one case a white head had been superimposed on a worker wearing a turban.) Ford said that the retouched photo was originally intended for use in an advertising campaign in Poland, and the dark faces "did not portray the ethnic mix in Poland." In fact, Polish advertisers agreed that it didn't make sense to use such an ethnically diverse group there.

Source: Andrew Bolger, "Ford Apologises to Black Workers over Advertising," *The Financial Times*, February 21, 1996, p. 9; and Tara Parker-Pope, "Ford Puts Blacks in Whiteface, Turns Red," *The Wall Street Journal*, February 22, 1996, p. B8.

Consumer Behavior Factoid

by the Children's Television Workshop, the producers of *Sesame Street*) with only 4.5 minutes of ads per hour. This policy of running no commercials during the program is a startling new concession.[27]

Environmental Protection

The United States produces over 200 million tons of household and commercial refuse annually. In all of the Organization for Economic Cooperation and Development members except Germany, municipal waste output has increased since 1980. The Japanese are building islands of waste in Tokyo Bay to cope with over 22,000 tons of trash generated by the city daily.[28]

Environmental "consciousness" has certainly increased in the last two decades. According to studies, 78 percent of consumers would switch to an environmentally friendly product container even it were priced as much as 5 percent higher than a less friendly package. An *Adweek* poll reported that 96 percent of consumers say environmental concerns influence their purchase decisions. Public compliance with recycling campaigns and regulations led to a glut of recycled newsprint and cans in 1996.[29] In surveys of international executives over 90 percent of respondents report that their companies are making changes to existing products and new-product offerings to conform to environmentalists' demands.[30] The number of new "green" product introductions soared from 0.5 percent of all new-product introductions in 1985 to 13.4 percent in 1991.[31] One business response, which is more formalized in Europe than here, is the idea of "product stewardship"—manufacturer responsibility for a product from "cradle to grave," including disposal without harming the environment.[32]

In actuality, however, most consumers seem to be willing to make only minor concessions in convenience to environmentalism. Few are willing to make major behavioral changes. For example, 70 percent of Canadians indicated that they would participate in household recycling programs, but only 50 percent would use returnable containers, and only 33 percent would pay more for environmentally safe products.[33]

One major obstacle hindering the transition from environmental consciousness to effective conservation programs is the notion of personal responsibility. Consumer researcher Russell Belk and his associates have stressed that the attribution of causality is critical in determining whether or not an individual will conserve. When people attribute the cause of an energy shortage to a nonpersonal source (such as the government, foreign powers, or major oil companies), they feel that a nonpersonal solution (such as government intervention) is the answer. Only when they perceive that the general public is to blame for the problem are they likely to engage in conservation behavior.[34] Along similar lines, researchers stress that people who feel that their actions make a difference are more likely to recycle than those who don't think their behavior truly matters. A recent study found that perceived individual effectiveness was the most important variable explaining environmentally conscious consumer behavior.[35]

Conservation behavior can be divided into three basic categories: curtailment behavior, maintenance behavior, and efficiency behavior.[36] *Curtailment behavior* involves reducing consumption by modifying current behavior. Examples of this form of conservation are adjusting the thermostat downward whenever possible, washing clothes in cold water, and driving less. *Maintenance behavior* involves making sure that energy-consuming equipment and appliances are in good working order. Tuning up the car and getting the furnace cleaned are two examples of maintenance behavior. *Efficiency behavior* focuses on reducing energy consumption via structural changes in the home or travel environment. Purchasing a more fuel-efficient car, installing solar panels, and insulating the attic are examples of efficiency behavior. The degree of information seeking, financial risk, and lifestyle modification varies with the type of conservation behavior. Therefore policy makers need to design their conservation programs to complement the form of conservation behavior they are trying to encourage.

NEGLIGENT CONSUMER BEHAVIOR

Most of us would agree with the statements "Smoking is hazardous to your health," and "Drinking and driving don't mix." Both are negligent behaviors. Yet many consumers exhibit negligent behavior in some form or another. **Negligent consumer behavior** consists of actions and inactions that may negatively affect the long-term quality of life of individuals and society. This type of behavior comes in two forms. The first form of negligent behavior consists of consuming a product that in and of itself presents a hazard of some sort. The consumption of cigarettes and heroin are two examples that fall into this category. The second type of negligent behavior consists of using a product in an unsafe manner or failing to use the safety features of the product or to follow the safety instructions. Neglecting to buckle up seat belts and failing to follow the dosage instructions for over-the-counter drugs are examples of the second form of negligent behavior.[37]

There are two possible approaches to inducing people to act in a safer manner. One is passing laws—forcing consumers to wear seat belts, banning the advertising and sale of cigarettes, and imposing stiffer penalties for drunk driving, for example. The other is employing marketing techniques to encourage more appropriate consumer actions. Consumer behavior research and theory provide insight into how marketers and public policy makers can influence consumers to behave in a safer manner.

Getting People to Buckle Up

Automobile accidents claim the lives of more than 30,000 Americans a year and result in 500,000 less-than-fatal injuries. Seat belts could prevent more than half of these deaths and injuries, yet only about 15 percent of American drivers and passengers wear their seat belts.[38] The beliefs that *they* will never be in an accident, that seat belts do not really provide much protection, and that they are uncomfortable besides are just a few excuses offered by consumers for this negligence.

Early attempts to persuade consumers to wear their seat belts were characterized by fear appeals depicting the grisly results of nonuse. A National Safety Council campaign in 1969 involved more than $50 million worth of public service media space and airtime, but had no discernible effect on consumers' use of seat belts. A subsequent campaign in Michigan used the more emotionally charged theme of "Somebody needs you." At a cost of some $2.1 million, this campaign raised the observed usage of seat belts by 4.4 percent (about 270,000 persons). Despite the expense of this and similar projects, however, the change in behavior has proved short-lived. If the reminder to buckle up is absent, many people do not make the effort because it is not ingrained in their routine or because they are not really concerned about the issue. Still, the campaign to get people to buckle up continues.

The theory of operant conditioning can give us an additional perspective on this problem. As noted in Chapter 5, the positive reinforcement of a behavior increases the likelihood that that behavior will be repeated. The application is clear. Increasing the probability that people will wear seat belts requires rewarding them when they buckle up. Some studies have found that rewarding people for wearing seat belts can more than double the practice.[39] The rewards need not be elaborate—perhaps discount coupons or bingo chips—and they can easily be administered at drive-through locations.

An interesting adjunct to the discussion over seat belt use is the question of compensatory behavior.[40] As early as 1970 an argument was made that seat-belt use should not be mandatory because wearing a seat belt gives the driver a sense of security that might translate into more reckless driving. According to a recent study, however, this compensatory behavior is likely to occur only among drivers who are "risk lovers."[41]

Product Misuse

Most of us would never think of using a blow dryer in the shower or a lawn mower to trim the hedges. Nor would we think that using a cellular phone while driving a car may lead to a serious accident. Consumers' misuse of products in the latter fashion has prompted public policy makers to urge, and marketers to exert, special precautions in the design and testing of products. In fact, the majority of product-related injuries result not from a flaw in the product itself but from misuse of an otherwise safe product.[42] As one person put it, "The most dangerous component is the consumer, and there's no way to recall him."[43] Another pointed out that "the actual hazard arises in the kitchen or in the hedgerow, not in the store."[44] Table 20-3 shows various possible explanations for consumer misuse of "safe" products.

As we mentioned earlier, one method of preventing product misuse is legislation. In addition to regulating consumer behavior, this might involve setting government safety standards for almost every type of industry. If a company's products fail to meet such standards, they would be subject to recall. However, it has been estimated that "no more than 20 percent of all consumer product related injuries can be addressed by feasible regulation of the production and distribution of consumer products."[45]

We also said earlier that a second method of preventing product misuse is to increase consumer information. However, this alternative, too, has been called into question. There is a practical limit to the amount of information that can be presented on a label, and inserts and manuals are usually discarded early in the life of such products as power tools. Even experience may not be helpful, since novices are often more careful and vigilant than the experienced user.

Consumer Misuse of "Safe" Products: Some Potential Explanations

1. *Action slip*. A performance error resulting from faulty cognitive processing. This is particularly likely when the consumer is focusing on desired end results rather than the more mundane actions necessary to arrive at the desired state.

2. *Error proneness*. The tendency not to be vigilant, especially during routinely performed activities.

3. *Reinforcement*. The consumer takes a risk, but doesn't suffer any consequences. Each successive trial that doesn't result in harm reinforces the proneness to risky behavior.

4. *Hedonic goals*. Consumers focused on fantasy, fun, and feelings are less likely to calculate the risks involved in their behavior.

5. *Ritual/socially sanctioned misuse*. Campus beer bashes, for example.

6. *Individual irrationality*. The actions of obsessive, compulsive, or addictive personalities.

7. *Advertising*. Advertising representations may be partially responsible for unsafe behavior because they encourage extreme forms of product use.

Source: Adapted from Jeffrey Stoltman and Fred Morgan, "Psychological Dimensions of Unsafe Product Usage," in *Marketing Theory and Applications*, Vol. 4, Rajan Varadarajan and Bernard Jaworski, eds. (Chicago: American Marketing Association, 1993), pp. 143–150.

TABLE 20-3

What about product design? The argument has been made that this third alternative is the best insurance against product misuse. Before we put too much reliance on design, we need to do a lot more research on how products are actually used. For example, the oval-shaped Ford Taurus instrument panel, which is a departure from previous designs, partly came about because of customer complaints that previous panels had too many small buttons that were too close together to manage easily while driving.[46]

Drinking and Driving

Although alcohol-related traffic fatalities have declined by 20 percent in the 1990s, some 17,700 still occur every year in the United States.[47] In the 1980s drinking and driving became an urgent political issue because of the efforts of groups like Mothers Against Drunk Driving (MADD). Public policy makers could make greater use of consumer behavior research in this area. In this section we describe some of the methods currently used, along with their strengths and weaknesses.[48]

Informing and Educating This approach assumes that individuals will act rationally to further their self-interest—if they know what their self-interest is. Thus the public should be presented with objective information about the hazards of drunk driving.[49] Creators of such information campaigns have frequently used a fear-inducing message appeal. An ad that was part of the Department of Transportation and the Ad Council's campaign against drinking and driving is shown in Figure 20-2. The strong fear appeal of this message is difficult to misperceive.

Social Controls Most liquor ads portray the beverage as a drink consumed in the presence of others to heighten one's social acceptability. This strategy plays on the understanding that people are influenced by the actions and attitudes of those around them. The same social-controls strategy has been used in campaigns against drunk driving. Examples of this strategy are campus meetings of SADD (Students Against Drunk Driving) and commercials showing relatives or friends taking car keys away from a person who has overindulged.

Economic Incentives Concepts from behavior-modification theory suggest that a successful approach might be to reward people for demonstrating the desired behavior. Insurance companies currently make use of this approach by giving reduced rates to people who agree not to drink and drive. Some restaurants give a free meal to the designated nondrinker in the group, who will drive his or her indulging friends home. The limitation of this approach is that many people will refrain from drinking and driving only if they perceive the benefits as outweighing the costs.

Figure 20-2

A strong fear appeal developed to reduce drunk driving.

Economic Disincentives Rather than rewarding people for not drinking and driving, the economic-disincentives approach punishes those who do drink and drive. This punishment could be direct—in the form of fines, car repair costs, or high insurance premiums—or indirect—in the form of an excise tax on alcohol that would raise liquor prices. Again, the problem is that many people will disregard the disincentives if they feel the benefits of their behavior outweigh the costs.

COMPULSIVE CONSUMPTION

Some negligent consumer behaviors involve the use of products that are hazardous in and of themselves. Over time, many of these behaviors become compulsive or addictive. Other behaviors are not harmful in moderation, but become harmful when the behavior gets compulsive. We discuss three **compulsive consumptions** in this section: smoking, compulsive drinking, and compulsive gambling.

Smoking

Until the late 1960s, consumers were exposed to nearly 3,000 cigarette commercials per week by 38 different brands. Concern about the health hazards of cigarette smoking arose in the 1950s, but it was not until the issuance of the surgeon general's report in 1964 that policy makers began to exert considerable efforts to alter the public's smoking behavior. The Department of Health and Human Services (DHHS) used such tactics as bumper stickers that read "Smoke, Choke, Croak" and negative endorsements by athletic stars like Peggy Fleming and Bart Starr claiming, "I don't smoke." In general, the approach was to depict smokers as distraught coughers and nonsmokers as happy and healthy.[50]

These promotional efforts had some limited impact. Between 1967 and 1968 cigarette sales fell by 1.3 billion cigarettes, and the number of U.S. smokers dropped by 1.5 million to 70 million. However, rather than a steady decline in cigarette sales or the number of smokers, the major behavioral trend has been toward the purchase of low-tar and low-nicotine brands.

Despite a ban on television commercials promoting the product, the cigarette industry continues to survive. Some researchers believe that poor communications strategies by antismoking groups are partly to blame, but the root causes are the strong social reward for smoking in some circles (e.g., among teenagers) and certain deeply held cognitive positions. In fact, consumer awareness of the major health effects of smoking is now quite high. Researchers have found that smokers now overestimate, rather than underestimate, the risk of lung cancer from smoking.[51] These results suggest that many smokers simply tune out or develop counterarguments for antismoking messages.

During the mid-1990s the negative publicity concerning smoking and the actions of cigarette manufacturers grew in intensity. In particular, the advertising campaign employing "Joe Camel" was attacked for targeting the youth of America. In 1994 *Advertising Age* and the Roper organization conducted a national poll that found that 68 percent of Americans believe that cigarette ads influence children and teens to smoke. Further, the results revealed that two-thirds of Americans, including half of all smokers, wanted the U.S. government to increase restrictions on cigarette advertising. Over 50 percent of those polled wanted all cigarette advertising banned.[52] In 1996 the federal government instituted new restrictions on cigarette advertising and sales, with the aim of halving tobacco use by children and adolescents. The new guidelines ban cigarette vending machines and self-service displays except where those under 18 aren't allowed, require photo identification for anyone under 27 buying cigarettes, ban cigarette advertising billboards near schools and playgrounds, limit such billboards and advertisements in magazines with a young readership to black-and-white text only, and restrict the distribution of promotional items (such as clothing).[53]

In the mid-1990s a group of 60 attorneys banded together and pledged to spend $100,000 a year pursuing a major class-action lawsuit against the cigarette companies. The suit was later rejected, however, on the grounds that with up to 90 million potential plaintiffs, with varying claims and seeking damages under different tort systems in different states, the matter couldn't be handled on a class-action basis across the United States.[54]

Despite all this antismoking activism, cigarette consumption has stopped declining. Although smoking went down during the 1980s at a rate of 2 to 3 percent a year, 1995 was the third year in a row during which the percentage of high school smokers increased.[55] New cigarette brands designed to appeal to young adults, such as Red Kamels (revived after a 60-year hiatus) and Moonlight Tobacco, have been introduced, and the controversial Joe Camel has been brought back as well. A recent study indicates that adolescents are three times more responsive to cigarette ads than adults are, leading the study's authors to conclude that "cigarette advertising for market share is primarily a battle of brands for consumption by the young."[56] So the battle over this issue is by no means over.

A new group of actors entering the antismoking arena in the late 1990s were the makers of such products as nicotine gums and patches. These alternatives to cigarettes are available as over-the-counter drugs. Since their manufacturers are well versed in consumer advertising, their antismoking message may be more successful than public-interest commercials have been.[57] Figure 20-3 presents an ad positioning NicoDerm CQ as an aid to stop smoking.

Figure 20-3

Nicoderm CQ is one of several over-the-counter products designed to provide a supply of nicotine while consumers try to quit smoking.

Compulsive Drinking

The decline in alcohol-related deaths on the road, mentioned earlier, may be partly a consequence of the overall decline in alcohol consumption in recent years. The National Institute on Alcohol Abuse and Alcoholism reported that in 1991 drinking per capita fell to its lowest mark since 1965, with hard liquor intake declining to near-1949 levels.[58] In 1995 alone consumption of hard liquor dropped 1.6 percent. As further evidence of the downward trend, a decades-old voluntary moratorium on television advertising by makers of hard liquor ended with Seagram's airing of commercials in 1996.[59] Moreover, distillers such as Jack Daniels and Bacardi Ltd. were considering developing beers under their label to make up for the decline in liquor sales.

Despite the decrease in sales of hard liquor, there are at least three disturbing trends in alcohol consumption. First, one of the newer drinking fads involves alcoholic soft drinks ("alcopops") that taste like colas or fruit juices but often contain more alcohol than beer. The British market (where these drinks were developed) was estimated to be $385 million in 1996. Going under such names as Cola Lips, Two Dogs, Mrs. Puckers', Hooper's Hooch, Lemonhead, and Moog in Britain, these products are now being test-marketed in the United States.[60] Second, in the 1990s "binge" drinking increased dramatically: 42 percent of college students have engaged in binge drinking (more than five drinks at a time), and 35 percent of college women now drink to get drunk, over three times the percentage found in 1977.[61] Third, the "gender gap" in use of alcohol by teenagers is disappearing: on average, boys and girls now start to drink at the same age—15.[62]

Compulsive Gambling

Gambling as an addictive consumption affects an estimated 8 to 12 million Americans. While a compulsive gambler is most likely to make less than $25,000 a year, many are high-income professionals. Like drug users, compulsive gamblers often experience a "high" while engaging in the activity, followed by depression when they stop.[63] We often think of gambling in connection with casinos, which have spread from landlocked locations in Las Vegas and New Jersey to numerous riverboat locales. In addition, 36 states now have state-run lotteries that make it easy to gamble with nothing more than a visit to the local convenience store.[64]

Gambling is prevalent in many countries. In Japan 17.8 billion yen a year—equal to one-fourth of the national government's budget and more than the Japanese car industry's production revenues—is spent on *pachinko*, a game that is addictive for some Japanese.

Consumer Behavior Factoid

Question: Do fear appeals work to curb smoking?

Answer: It depends on the level of fear. When the appeal doesn't induce much fear (e.g., consequences such as coughing are referenced), consumers have little incentive to embrace the solution. When the appeal induces too much fear (atherosclerosis, heart attacks, death), consumers tend to reject it and ignore the solution. When low-fear appeals are used, targets need additional stimulation to encourage them to focus on the solution. When high-fear appeals are used, targets need to be given appealing reasons to really think about the consequences—because stern warnings alone generally induce people to ignore both the problem and the solution.

Source: Punam Anand Keller and Lauren Goldberg Block, "Increasing the Persuasiveness of Fear Appeals: The Effect of Arousal and Elaboration," *Journal of Consumer Research*, Vol. 22 (March 1996), pp. 448–459.

Pachinko is played on an upright pinball-like machine, where steel balls drop through formations of nails. It is even easier to play than the state lotteries in the United States, since *pachinko* parlors are found on virtually every busy urban street, with over 14,500 parlors and 3.1 million machines in operation nationwide. *Fortune* magazine estimated that the owner of a *pachinko* machine manufacturing company, Kenkichi Nakajima, is the fourth-wealthiest individual in the world.[65] Figure 20-4 shows a *pachinko* hall.

Gambling is a widespread attraction in other countries. In Taiwan a state-run lottery was reinstated in 1993,[66] and Katmandu, Nepal, is becoming the gambling capital of South Asia.[67] In China lotteries are run under the name of "social welfare projects" to avoid government prohibitions. Chinese gambling on horse racing is called an "intelligence competition"—participants guess which horse is "smart enough" to finish first or—in an "intelligence trifecta"—" first, second, and third![68]

The gambling industry seems to be on a roll. British Airways, Swissair, and Singapore Airlines have plans to add gambling devices on their planes, and U.S. carriers have ordered equipment. The theory is that, particularly on international flights lasting up to 15 hours, a "captive audience" will be delighted to try their luck.[69]

Other Compulsions

Some people "shop till they drop." They turn to shopping compulsively, as other addicts turn to alcohol or drugs. And like other addicts, they seek the experience to boost their self-image, but when it is over, they feel more self-loathing and are subjected to the disapproval of others, which produces guilt. Compulsive buyers attempt to escape the guilt

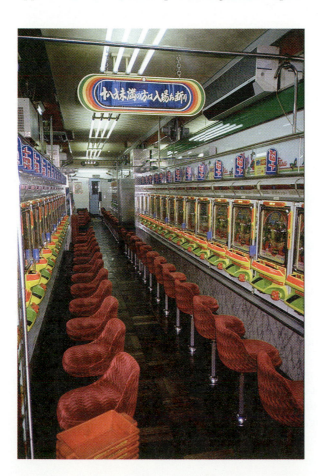

Figure 20-4

An empty *pachinko* parlor, photographed early in the morning before the start of the business day

Compulsive Consumption: Some Examples

Substance abuse	Alcoholism
	Stimulants and sedatives
	Cannabis, opioids, cocaine, hallucinogens
Eating disorders	Anorexia
	Bulimia
	Binge eating disorder
Impulse-control disorders	Compulsive gambling
	Compulsive buying
	Compulsive sexuality
	Kleptomania
	Compulsive working
	Compulsive exercising
	Compulsive television watching

Sources: Based on Elizabeth C. Hirschman, "The Consciousness of Addiction: Toward a General Theory of Compulsive Consumption," *Journal of Consumer Research*, Vol. 19 (September 1992), pp. 155–179; and Ronald J. Faber, Gary A. Christenson, Martina de Zwaan, and James Mitchell, "Two Forms of Compulsive Consumption: Comorbidity of Compulsive Buying and Binge Eating," *Journal of Consumer Research*, Vol. 22 (December 1995), pp. 296–304.

TABLE 20-4

and self-loathing by engaging in the experience again. According to some psychologists, this type of experience isn't pleasurable even while the addict is engaged in it.[70]

Other forms of compulsive consumption are shown in Table 20-4. One of the more interesting compulsions is overwork. In 1996 a Japanese court ordered Dentsu, the world's largest advertising agency, to pay $1.2 million to the survivors of Ichiro Ishima, who during his last 8 months of employment at Dentsu had worked from early in the morning to 2 A.M. on 105 days and beyond 4 A.M. for 49 days. His family said he averaged only 2 to 4 hours of sleep a night.[71]

Until the 1980s, perspectives on compulsive behavior emphasized sociological and psychological influences. However, recent research on compulsive behavior has evolved in two directions. One is based on the possibility that various forms of addiction have physical roots,[72] since certain addictive tendencies seem to be inheritable (e.g., there is evidence that alcoholism "runs" in families).

The other new direction of research suggests that several forms of compulsive behavior may be driven by the same forces—that is, may occur together. For example, a recent study found that compulsive buyers also tended to be binge eaters. In fact, compulsive buyers were more likely than others to suffer from a range of eating disorders, substance abuse or dependence (alcohol, sedatives, cocaine, etc.), and other compulsive consumptions, such as gambling and kleptomania.[73]

These new directions, as well as sociologically and psychologically oriented studies, may give us a better understanding of compulsive consumption behaviors. Compulsive consumption may be more widespread than currently thought. Much research on compulsive behaviors depends on self-reporting, and since these behaviors aren't socially desirable, respondents may be unwilling to admit to them.[74]

CORPORATE SOCIAL RESPONSIBILITY

Until the 1960s most Americans generally accepted the idea that business's primary objective was to make a profit. This thinking began to change, however, as America's social values changed. Today 95 percent of Americans believe that companies have responsibilities toward their employees and communities beyond making profits.[75] Many companies exert much energy, time, and money portraying themselves as good corporate citizens who act in a socially responsible manner. **Corporate social responsibility** refers to the idea that business has an obligation to help society with its problems by offering some of business's resources. Several arguments support the notion that developing a positive image in terms of social responsibility is important for companies.

Succeeding in the Long Run

One argument for being socially responsible depends on a long-term rather than a short-term perspective. It says that a business's self-interest could be advanced when the business embraces a long-run view. This position encourages expenditures in support of socially responsible activities on the grounds that they will yield future benefits in the form of consumer approval and loyalty. A focus on short-run profits, in contrast, discourages expenditures devoted to societal problems. For example, in 1996 the nation's largest waste-management company, WMX Technologies, Inc., secretly sponsored an engineering study for an environmental group, the North Valley Coalition of Concerned Citizens. The Coalition, which was underfunded, needed sophisticated evidence to aid it in its efforts to keep the second-largest waste-management company, Browning-Ferris, Inc., from reopening its Sunshine Canyon Landfill in the Los Angeles area.[76] Although WMX's action might keep its rival from reopening the dump in the near term, in the longer term such behavior will only make the job of securing approval of dump sites more difficult for all waste-management companies, including WMX.

Acquiring a Positive Public Image

Companies can create a positive public image for themselves by acting in socially responsible ways. One study revealed that customers are less likely to blame a manufacturer for accidents with its products if those products have safety standards that exceed—rather than simply meet—those mandated by the government. Also, consumers are less likely to blame the manufacturer when products include safety warnings.[77]

Another way that companies can behave in a socially responsible manner is by making speedy product recalls when defects are discovered. Some researchers have suggested that firms view product recalls as corporate opportunities because they show the company acting in a proconsumer fashion.[78] A series of studies by one of the authors of this book examined the impact that product recalls have on consumers' impressions of a company. These studies found: (1) consumers perceived a familiar company as significantly less responsible for a product defect than an unfamiliar company[79]; (2) consumers viewed companies that reacted to product defects prior to intervention by the Consumer Product Safety Commission as less responsible for the defects[80]; and (3) consumers' impressions of the company were influenced by the speed with which it initiated a product recall.[81] Table 20-5 gives an overview of the implications of these findings.

Avoiding Government Regulation

A final reason to act in a socially responsible manner is to avoid government regulation. Given current societal values, if business does not respond to societal demands on its own, consumer groups will almost certainly pressure the government to intervene.

All business functions are concerned to some degree with social responsibility, but the responsibility burden falls most heavily on the marketer. Indeed, when a company is perceived as acting unethically or in an irresponsible fashion, marketing is the function most likely to be blamed.[82] Marketers can best avoid blame by following the strategies we have suggested—namely, maintaining a positive initial corporate image and responding quickly when difficulties arise. An advertisement for Coors is reproduced in Figure 20-5. An ever-increasing amount of money is shown to represent higher salaries for women who are literate. The ad doesn't address the benefits of Coors products, but is intended to position Coors as a company fulfilling its social responsibilities.

Overview of Product-Recall Implications

- Companies should strive to maintain a highly visible positive corporate image. Such a company is less subject to a negative consumer response when a recall is initiated.

- Companies should establish a recall plan that can be quickly implemented should disaster strike. Consumers have a more favorable impression of companies that react quickly in a product-safety situation.

- When a problem is first discovered, it may be best to overstate the problem to the public. Consumers will subsequently develop more favorable impressions of the company when they hear that the problem is not as severe as first expected. If the company displays the reverse behavior—that is, minimizes the problem, only to later discover that the difficulty is worse than first announced—the result can be negative consumer impressions.

- Companies should endeavor to manufacture the safest products possible. The safer the products, the less likelihood of severe injuries, negative consumer opinions, and product liability awards.

- Companies should not shy away from press coverage of product recalls. Information from independent sources such as the media, especially when the company is described as behaving in a socially responsible manner, can generate favorable consumer impressions.

Source: Adapted from Joshua Wiener and John C. Mowen, "Product Recalls: Avoid Beheading the Messenger of Bad News," *Mobius*, Vol. 4 (1985), pp. 18–21.

TABLE 20-5

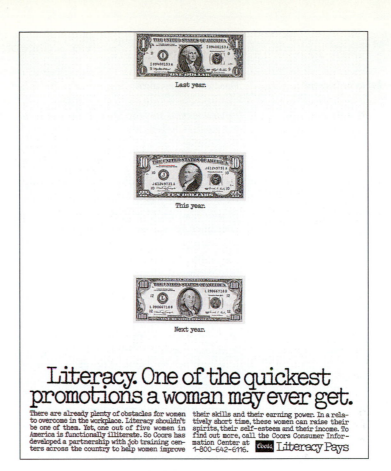

Last year.

This year.

Next year.

Literacy. One of the quickest promotions a woman may ever get.

There are already plenty of obstacles for women to overcome in the workplace. Literacy shouldn't be one of them. Yet, one out of five women in America is functionally illiterate. So Coors has developed a partnership with job training centers across the country to help women improve their skills and their earning power. In a relatively short time, these women can raise their spirits, their self-esteem and their income. To find out more, call the Coors Consumer Information Center at 1-800-642-6116. *Coors* Literacy Pays

Figure 20-5

By showing corporate responsibility, firms can win over the respect of consumers. Coors has long practiced this philosophy as illustrated by their program to improve women's skills and earning power.

A MANAGERIAL APPLICATIONS ANALYSIS OF THE SEARS CASE

The introductory case detailed how Sears Roebuck & Company got into hot water with various regulators because of what were deemed deceptive practices. In this section we discuss what Sears did well and where the company might have improved its response.

Problem Identification

Sears' problem was that it denied wrongdoing. The company not only took an intransigent position but also—in at least one instance—threatened to retaliate economically against a city whose government accused the company of deceptive practices.

The Consumer Behavior Analysis and Its Managerial Implications

What do you think of Sears' strategy in 1988? When concepts from the chapter are used to analyze the problem, four categories of issues emerge: government regulations regarding sales promotions, consumerist groups, sensitive consumer issues, and corporate

Managerial Implications of Consumer Behavior Concepts in the Sears Case

Consumer Behavior Concept	Managerial Implications
1. Regulatory agencies	*Environmental analysis.* Do appropriate legal analysis to ensure that actions are in compliance with laws and regulations.
	Promotional strategy. Develop public relations and advertising strategies for coping with adverse publicity that could result from charges filed by legal or regulatory agencies.
2. Consumerist groups	*Market research.* Use market research to determine how consumer groups view the company.
	Promotional strategy. Employ public relations and advertising to influence how the company is perceived by consumerist groups.
	Positioning. Position the company as being proconsumer in its activities.
	Marketing mix. Develop marketing-mix strategy that implements the proconsumer strategy.
3. Sensitive consumer issues	*Promotional strategy.* Evaluate advertising to ensure that it is not misleading and does not offend minority groups.
	Market research. Analyze marketing-mix strategy to ensure that vulnerable segments (e.g., children and the elderly) in the marketplace are treated fairly.
4. Corporate social responsibility	*Marketing mix.* Analyze the entire marketing-mix strategy to ensure that it follows principles that represent socially responsible behavior.
	Market research. Do research to determine if consumers perceive the firm to be socially responsible.
	Positioning. Develop strategies to position the firm as being socially responsible.

TABLE 20-6

social responsibility. Table 20-6 summarizes these consumer behavior concepts and their managerial implications.

Nature of Regulations The first consumer concept to consider when analyzing the case is the nature of the regulations that pertain to sales promotions and the capabilities of the regulatory agencies to enforce their regulations. In the New York City case Sears was being sued in civil court, so the company stood a chance of "winning." However, if the case had gone to trial, it would certainly have resulted in massive negative publicity against the firm. In addition, the company could have lost and incurred large fines. Meanwhile, the attention being given to the case in New York was beginning to cause other states to look at Sears' practices.

The examination of regulatory agencies and applicable laws has implications for environmental analysis and promotional strategy. Sears should have performed a careful environmental analysis of its situation to precisely identify the reactions of competitors, such as Kmart, as well as the various regulatory agencies. The company needed to ascertain whether it was failing to comply with appropriate regulations. Whenever charges are filed by a regulatory agency, companies must stand ready to change their promotional strategy to respond appropriately.

Consumerist Groups The study of consumer groups is a market research function. Sears' marketing managers should have analyzed the company's problem from the perspective of how consumerist groups might react. Obviously, whenever a charge of deceptive practices is brought, the public reaction can be quite negative. One consumer advocate stated, "Sears has the strange idea that they should abide by the lowest common denominator of consumer protection behavior." An attorney for a consumer interest group stated that he would begin lobbying for tougher consumer advertising laws. Again, based on the reactions of the consumer groups, Sears should have been ready to change its promotional strategy.

Sensitive Consumer Issues Sears should have known from the beginning that it was involved in a sensitive public policy issue. In general, misleading advertising is considered by regulators to be sensitive. In fact, had it been found that certain vulnerable population groups, such as the elderly, were negatively affected, Sears' problem could have become far worse. This possibility underscores the importance of using market research to identify groups of customers who may be particularly vulnerable to certain kinds of promotional strategies and changing those strategies if warranted.

Corporate Social Responsibility When Sears' problem is analyzed from the viewpoint of corporate social responsibility, it must be said that the company's actions were not what one would expect from a socially responsible firm. At a minimum, Sears should have stopped the promotions in question while fighting New York City in court. One New York City official stated that "Sears is the largest and most consistent consumer law breaker in New York City." Sears' tactics were even criticized by securities analysts—a group known for its focus on profits rather than social responsibility. As one analyst said, "This is bureaucratic management rigidity, not good business sense. You'd think Sears would say, 'You're right. Let's get on the consumer side of this thing.' Instead, they seem to want to get dragged kicking and screaming into losing market share."

Managerial Recommendations

Sears' response to the 1992 California charges was more in line with the analysis presented here. In this instance the company quickly complied with the law and made a large public effort to convince consumers that their interests were high on Sears' agenda. As a result, the problem disappeared.

Three recommendations emerge from our analysis of this case.

Recommendation 1 The concept of corporate social responsibility has direct implications for the positioning of the firm. Efforts to create a "good citizen" image help to position a company as one that puts customers first.

Recommendation 2 Accomplish these actions through the marketing mix. Pricing, promotion, product development, and distribution should be undertaken in a manner that is socially responsible. Communicate these actions via public relations.

Recommendation 3 Managers must understand the regulatory environment, know the positions of consumer groups vis-à-vis their firm's products or services, and be aware of the sensitivity of issues affecting the firm's products or services.

Summary

The regulatory environment consists of the laws and regulations that governments develop to exert control over businesses and consumers. Such laws and regulations may be enforced by organizations at the federal, state, or local level.

Consumerism consists of the activities of government, business, independent organizations, and concerned consumers that are intended to protect the rights of consumers. The movement in the United States is over 90 years old. Four major eras of the consumer movement have been identified: the muckraking era (1905–1920), the information era (1927–1939), the era of continuing consumer concern (1951–1960), and the modern consumer movement (1962–1980).

Certain issues and groups are of particular importance in our society and, as a result, receive a good deal of regulatory attention. One such issue is deceptive advertising. Because of the potentially large impact of the media on consumers, lawmaking bodies have passed laws making it illegal to mislead consumers. One group of consumers that regulatory agencies particularly seek to protect is children. Whenever companies market products to children, they must take special care to ensure that they are acting responsibly. A third sensitive area is environmental protection.

Another problem area in public policy is negligent consumer behavior, a term that refers to those actions and inactions that negatively affect the long-term quality of life of individuals or society in general. Failure to wear seat belts, smoking, drunk driving, and product misuse are a few examples of negligent consumer behavior. It is often difficult to draw the line between individual freedom and the public policy interest in restricting the negligent actions of consumers.

Compulsive behavior, whether drug abuse, kleptomania, gambling, or other compulsions, may actually be increasing. Gambling, for example, is becoming more accessible as the number of venues increases. The introduction of gambling on the Internet may result in an increase in this activity. Current research on compulsive behavior is investigating possible physical, as well as psychological and social factors.

Corporate social responsibility is clearly an important concept. In general, the more socially responsible corporations are, the less need there is for consumer-oriented laws and regulations. Acting in a socially responsible manner can help a company survive in the long run, improve its public image, and decrease the likelihood of government intervention in corporate affairs.

KEY TERMS

compulsive consumption

conservation behavior

consumerism

corporate social
responsibility

corrective advertising

deceptive advertising

negligent consumer behavior

regulatory environment

REVIEW QUESTIONS

1. Identify the four phases of the consumer movement presented in the text.

2. What is the current status of the consumer movement?

3. In 1982 one of the three most important consumer concerns was high prices. What do you think is the primary consumer concern today?

4. What are the categories of deceptive advertising that the FTC has considered in the past?

5. To what extent can children tell the difference between commercials and programming?

6. To what extent do commercials tend to make children desire products that are not good for them?

7. What are the three basic types of conservation behaviors?

8. What is the definition of negligent consumer behavior?

9. Identify four examples of negligent consumer behavior.

10. What are the primary methods now being used to attack the problem of drunk driving?

11. What is meant by the idea of corporate social responsibility? Give four examples of how companies can act in a socially responsible manner.

12. Identify the reasons for and against businesses actively attempting to portray themselves as socially responsible.

13. According to the text, what are the factors that influence consumer reactions to companies that issue product recalls?

14. What are three ways that companies might be able to make children's advertising more acceptable to parents?

DISCUSSION QUESTIONS

1. Which consumer issues do you think are most important—deceptive advertising, waste disposal, drunk driving, or some other problem area? Do you believe that corporate treatment of consumers has improved or worsened over the past five years?

2. Some have argued that the modern consumer movement ended with the beginning of the Reagan presidency in 1980. To what extent do you agree or disagree with this statement?

3. In 1986 the Federal Trade Commission began to consider whether it should take action to force the large car rental corporations (e.g., Hertz and Avis) to comply more quickly with manufacturers' recall requests to bring cars in to get mechanical problems fixed. To what extent do you think government agencies should intervene to force such companies (or, for that matter, individuals) to comply with manufacturers' requests to bring cars in when there is a product recall? What kinds of actions could or should a government agency take?

4. What do you think of the notion of "product stewardship"? Should a manufacturer's responsibility for a product extend through product disposal?

5. From an attributional perspective, what may have been the effect of Listerine's corrective ad, which read,

"While Listerine will not help prevent colds or sore throats or lessen their severity, breath tests prove Listerine fights onion breath better than Scope." (*Note*: Attribution theory was discussed in Chapter 6, "Consumer Motivation and Affect.")

6. Political commercials have been called the most deceptive advertisements of all. Discuss the types of deception that you have seen or heard in political advertisements. Give specific examples of each type of deception.

7. Discuss the distinction between deceptive ads, miscomprehension of ads, and noncomprehension of ads. What can management do to reduce the incidence of each of these three problems?

8. Watch Saturday morning cartoons and observe the advertising directed at children. What types of advertising appeals are being used? To what extent are cartoon characters being featured in the advertising? What sort of guidelines do you think companies that advertise to children should follow?

9. By the mid-1980s conservation efforts had waned from levels found in the 1970s. What are some of the reasons for this falling off in conserving resources? What types of programs do you feel are most effective in promoting the conservation of various natural resources?

10. A variety of approaches may be taken to control negligent consumer behavior. Discuss the alternative means through which public policy makers can attempt to reduce drunk driving. Which approaches do you consider to be most effective?

11. Two different viewpoints exist concerning the social responsibility of corporations. One is that the only responsibility of a company is to make a profit for its stockholders, and the other holds that businesses have a responsibility to help improve society. Defend your viewpoint on this issue.

12. Compare the behavior of Sears management in 1988 and 1992. Which response to the regulatory environment is likely to serve the company best in the long run?

ENDNOTES

1. Robert Johnson and John Koten, "Sears Has Everything, Including Messy Fight over Ads in New York," *The Wall Street Journal*, June 28, 1988, pp. 1, 14.

2. Tung Yin, "Sears Is Accused of Billing Fraud at Auto Centers," *The Wall Street Journal*, June 12, 1992, pp. B1, B5; Gregory A. Patterson, "Sears' Brennan Accepts Blame for Auto Flap," *The Wall Street Journal*, June 23, 1992, pp. B1, B4; and "Open Letter to Sears Customers," advertisements, *The Wall Street Journal*, June 15, 1992, p. C15, and June 25, 1992, p. C11.

3. John Howard, "Chrysler Faced with 'Lemon Law' Sanctions," *The McAllen Monitor*, June 1, 1996, p. 7A.

4. Louis Harris et al., *Consumerism in the Eighties*, Study No. 822047 (Louis Harris and Associates, 1983), p. 12. Referenced in D. S. Smith and P. N. Bloom, "Is Consumerism Dead or Alive? Some New Evidence," in *Advances in Consumer Research*, Vol. 11, Thomas C. Kinnear, ed. (Ann Arbor, MI: Association for Consumer Research, 1984), pp. 369–373.

5. David A. Aaker and George S. Day, *Consumerism: Search for the Consumer Interest* (New York: The Free Press, 1974).

6. Rogene A. Buchholz, *Business Environment and Public Policy* (Englewood Cliffs, NJ: Prentice Hall, 1982).

7. Joe L. Welch, *Marketing Law* (Tulsa, OK: Petroleum Publishing Co., 1980).

8. *The New York Times*, January 21, 1983, p. A16.

9. Thomas A. Hemphill, "Self-Regulating Industry Behavior: Antitrust Limitations and Trade Association Codes of Conduct," *Journal of Business Ethics*, Vol. 11 (December 1992), pp. 915–920.

10. John Kavanaugh, "Purchases on the Internet 'Could Potentially Exceed $200 Billion by Year 2000,'" *The Financial Times*, November 1, 1995, p. 12. See also Donna L. Hoffman, William D. Kalsbeek, and Thomas P. Novak, "Internet Use in the United States: 1995 Baseline Estimates and Preliminary Market Segments," Vanderbilt University Working Paper, Nashville, TN; April 12, 1996.

11. Victoria Griffith, "Sex, Lies and the Internet," *The Financial Times*, February 12, 1996, p. 15.

12. Gurjeet Singh, "Business Self-Regulation and Consumer Protection in India," *Journal of Consumer Policy*, Vol. 16 (1993), pp. 1–33.

13. Youngho Lee and Ann C. Brown, "Consumerism in China," in Salah S. Hassan and Roger D. Blackwell, eds., *Global Marketing: Perspectives and Cases* (Ft. Worth, TX: Dryden Press, 1994).

14. Jacob Jacoby and Wayne D. Hoyer, "Viewer Miscomprehension of Televised Communication: Selected Findings," *Journal of Consumer Research*, Vol. 15 (March 1989), pp. 434–443. Also see Jacoby and Hoyer, "The Miscomprehension of Mass-Media Advertising Claims: A Re-Analysis of Benchmark Data," *Journal of Advertising Research*, Vol. 30 (June–July 1990), pp. 9–16.

15. See Gita Venkataramani Johar, "Consumer Involvement and Deception from Implied Advertising Claims," *Journal of Consumer Research*, Vol. 32 (August 1995), pp. 267–279.

16. Jacob Jacoby and George J. Szybillo, "Consumer Research in FTC vs. Kraft (1991): A Case of Heads We Win, Tails You Lose?" *Journal of Public Policy and Marketing*, Vol. 14 (Spring 1995), pp. 1–14; David M. Stewart, "Deception, Materiality and Survey Research: Some Lessons From Kraft," *Journal of Public Policy and Marketing*, Vol. 14 (Spring 1995), pp. 15–28; and Seymour Sudman, "When Experts Disagree: Comments on the Articles by Jacoby and Szybillo and Stewart," *Journal of Public Policy and Marketing*, Vol. 14 (Spring 1995), pp. 29–34.

17. Arent Fox, "FTC Advertising Guidelines," www.webcom.com/lewrose/guides.html, October 22, 1995, pp. 1–2.

18. "Sellers Beware On-Line," *Sales and Marketing Management*, December 1994, p. 16; and Arent Fox, "FTC Tackles Fraud on the Information Superhighway, Charges Nine On-Line Scam-

mers," www.webcom.com/lewrose/article/ftcnet.html, April 28, 1996, pp. 1–4.

19. Ivan L. Preston, "Unfairness Developments in FTC Advertising Cases," *Journal of Public Policy and Marketing*, Vol. 14 (Fall 1995), pp. 318–320.

20. For an account by an advertising executive involved in the controversy, see Dick Mercer, "Tempest in a Soup Can," *Advertising Age*, October 17, 1994, pp. 25–29.

21. William L. Wilkie, Dennis L. McNeill, and Michael B. Mazis, "Marketing's 'Scarlet Letter': The Theory and Practice of Corrective Advertising," *Journal of Marketing*, Vol. 48 (Spring 1984), pp. 11–31.

22. Howard G. Schultz and Marianne Casey, "Consumer Perceptions of Advertising as Misleading," *Journal of Consumer Affairs*, Vol. 15 (1981), pp. 340–357.

23. Jennifer Gregan-Paxton and Deborah Roedder John, "Are Young Children Adaptive Decision Makers? A Study of Age Differences in Information Search Behavior," *Journal of Consumer Research*, Vol. 21 (March 1995), pp. 567–580. Also see M. Suzanne Clinton and Ronald D. Taylor, "Advertising to Children: A Synthesis of the Literature," *Advances in Marketing*, Daryl O. McKee, Daniel L. Sherrell, and Faye W. Gilbert, eds. (New Orleans, LA: Southwestern Marketing Association, 1993).

24. Kyle Pope, "Better to Receive: How Children Decide on Gifts They Want, and Plot to Get Them," *The Wall Street Journal*, December 24, 1993, pp. A1, A5.

25. Ibid.

26. Elizabeth Jensen and Albert R. Karr, "White House, TV Industry Compromise on Educational Programs for Children," *The Wall Street Journal*, July 30, 1996, p. B14.

27. Elizabeth Jensen, "Turner Will Offer Preschoolers a Show with Ads as 'Bookends,' " *The Wall Street Journal*, May 31, 1996, p. B5.

28. Faye Rice, "Where Will We Put All That Garbage?" *Fortune*, April 11, 1988, pp. 96–100; and Leyla Boulton, "Making a Golf Course from a Trash Mountain," *The Financial Times*, June 3, 1996, p. 4.

29. Lee Berton, "Highflying Recycler Lands in the Dumps," *The Wall Street Journal*, August 12, 1996, pp. B1, B2.

30. Lisa Collins Troy, "Consumer Environmental Consciousness: A Conceptual Framework and Exploratory Investigation," in *Enhancing Knowledge Development in Marketing*, Vol. 4, David W. Cravens and Peter R. Dickson, eds. (Chicago: American Marketing Association, 1993).

31. Jacquelyn Ottman, *Green Marketing* (Chicago: NTC Business Books, 1994).

32. Peter Knight, "The Empty Promise: The Idea of 'Product Stewardship' Is Unlikely Ever to Work," *The Financial Times*, June 5, 1996, p. 12.

33. Ida E. Berger, "A Framework for Understanding the Relationship Between Environmental Attitudes and Consumer Behaviors," in *Marketing Theory and Applications*, Vol. 4, Rajan Varadarajan and Bernard Jaworski, eds. (Chicago: American Marketing Association, 1993).

34. Russell Belk, John Painter, and Richard Semenik, "Preferred Solutions to the Energy Crisis as a Function of Causal Attributions," *Journal of Consumer Research*, Vol. 8 (December 1981), pp. 306–312.

35. James A. Roberts, "Green Consumers in the 1990s: Profile and Implications for Advertising," *Journal of Business Research*, Vol. 36 (July 1996), pp. 217–231. Also see L. J. Schrum, Tina M. Lowrey, and John A. McCarty, "Using Marketing and Advertising Principles to Encourage Pro-Environmental Behaviors," in Ronald P. Hill, ed. *Marketing and Consumer Research in the Public Interest* (Thousand Oaks, CA: Sage Publications, 1996), pp. 197–216

36. J. R. Brent Ritchie and Gordon H. G. McDougall, "Designing and Marketing Consumer Energy Conservation Policies and Programs: Implications from a Decade of Research," *Journal of Public Policy and Marketing*, Vol. 4 (1985), pp. 14–32.

37. Thomas C. Kinnear and Cynthia J. Frey, "Demarketing of Potentially Hazardous Products: General Framework and Case Studies," *Journal of Contemporary Business*, Vol. 7 (1978), pp. 57–68.

38. E. Scott Geller, "Seat Belt Psychology," *Psychology Today*, May 1985, pp. 12–13.

39. Ibid.

40. Michael Minor, "Accident Risks and Automotive Safety: Safety Belt Use in the U.S.", *Proceedings of the First U.S.–Japan Conference on Risk Management*, Saburo Ikeda and Kazuhiko Kawamura, eds. (Nashville, TN: Vanderbilt University, 1984).

41. Harinder Singh and Mark Thayer, "Impact of Seat Belt Use on Driving Behavior," *Economic Inquiry*, Vol. 30 (October 1992), pp. 649–658. Similar results are found in the case of airbags. See Steven P. Peterson and George E. Hoffer, "The Impact of Airbag Adoption on Relative Personal Injury and Absolute Collision Insurance Claims," *Journal of Consumer Research*, Vol. 20 (March 1994), pp. 657–662.

42. Richard Staelin, "The Effects of Consumer Education on Consumer Product Safety Behavior," *Journal of Consumer Research*, Vol. 5 (June 1978), pp. 30–40. For a philosophical view of why

safety devices lead to complacency and similar paradoxes, see Edward Tenner, *Why Things Bite Back: Technology and the Revenge Effect* (New York: Alfred A. Knopf, 1996).

43. Walter Guzzardi, "The Mindless Pursuit of Safety," *Fortune*, April 9, 1979, pp. 54–64.

44. Jeffrey J. Stoltman and Fred W. Morgan, "Expanding the Perspective on Consumer Product Safety," in Ronald P. Hill, ed., *Marketing and Consumer Research in the Public Interest* (Thousand Oaks, California, Sage Publications, 1996), pp. 177–195.

45. Staelin, "The Effects of Consumer Education."

46. John Pierson, "Ford Labors over Tiny Buttons and Dials in Quest for a Driver-Friendly Dashboard," *The Wall Street Journal*, May 20, 1996, pp. B1, B7.

47. J. Craig Andrews and Richard G. Netemeyer, "Alcohol Warning Label Effects: Socialization, Addiction and Public Policy Issues," in Ronald P. Hill, ed., *Marketing and Consumer Research in the Public Interest* (Thousand Oaks, CA: Sage Publications, 1996), pp. 153–175.

48. Laurel Hudson and Paul N. Bloom, "Potential Consumer Research Contributions to Combating Drinking and Driving Problems," in *Advances in Consumer Research*, Vol. 11, Thomas C. Kinnear, ed. (Provo, UT: Association for Consumer Research, 1984), pp. 676–681.

49. Janet R. Hankin, Ira J. Firestone, James J. Sloan, and Joel W. Ager, "The Impact of the Alcohol Warning Label on Drinking During Pregnancy," *Journal of Public Policy and Marketing*, Vol. 12 (Spring 1993), pp. 10–18.

50. Kinnear and Frey, "Demarketing of Potentially Hazardous Products."

51. John E. Calfee and Debra Jones Ringold, "The Cigarette Advertising Controversy: Assumptions About Consumers, Regulations, and Scientific Debate," in *Advances in Consumer Research*, Vol. 19, John F. Sherry, Jr., and Brian Sternthal, eds. (Provo, UT: Association for Consumer Research, 1992), pp. 557–562.

52. Steven W. Colford and Ira Teinowitz, "Teen Smoking and Ads Linked," *Advertising Age*, February 21, 1994, pp. 1, 36.

53. Richard Tomkins, "Advertising Curb May Lift Tobacco Industry Profits," *The Financial Times*, August 26, 1996, p. 4. Also see Tara Parker-Pope, "Tough Tobacco-Ad Rules Light Creative Fires," *The Wall Street Journal*, October 9, 1996, pp. B1, B6.

54. Richard Tomkins, "Big Tobacco Takes a Break," *The Financial Times*, May 25–26, 1996, p. 3.

55. Gene Koretz, "Economic Trends: More Teens Are Lighting Up," *BusinessWeek*, February 26, 1996, p. 27; and Suein L. Hwang, "Cigarette Sales Steady as Young Find Habit Hip," *The Wall Street Journal*, January 30, 1997, p. B12.

56. Richard W. Pollay, S. Siddarth, Michael Siegel, Anne Haddix, Robert K. Merritt, Gary A. Giovino, and Michael P. Eriksen, "The Last Straw? Cigarette Advertising and Realized Market Shares Among Youths and Adults, 1979–1993," *Journal of Marketing*, Vol. 60 (April 1996), pp. 1–16.

57. Suein L. Hwang, "Slick New Ads by Drug Firms Decry Smoking," *The Wall Street Journal*, May 21, 1996, pp. B1, B7.

58. Tim W. Ferguson, "Calm Down: Risk Is Not All Around," *The Wall Street Journal*, December 14, 1993, p. A17; and Judith Valente, "Scotch Makers Tell Youth It's Hip to Be Old-Fashioned," *The Wall Street Journal*, December 29, 1993, pp. B1, B5.

59. Yumiko Ono, "Some Liquor Makers Are Happy if You Switch to Beer—As Long as It's Theirs," *The Wall Street Journal*, May 23, 1996, pp. B1, B5; and Sally Goll Beatty, "Seagram Flouts Ban on TV Ads Pitching Liquor," *The Wall Street Journal*, June 11, 1996, pp. B1, B6.

60. Tara Parker-Pope, "Spiked Sodas, an Illicit Hit with Kids in U.K., Head for U.S." *The Wall Street Journal*, February 12, 1996, p. B1; and Roderick Oram, "Sweet Taste of Success," *The Financial Times*, December 24, 1995, p. 9.

61. J. Craig Andrews and Richard G. Netemeyer, "Alcohol Warning Label Effects: Socialization, Addiction, and Public Policy Issues."

62. "Women and Drugs," *The Wall Street Journal*, June 6, 1996, p. A14.

63. Bob Smith, "Compulsive Gamblers: In Over Their Heads," *HR Focus*, February 1992, p. 3.

64. R. S. Salomon, Jr., "Hooked," *Forbes*, May 10, 1993, p. 197.

65. "Lots of Lovely Silver Balls," *The Financial Times*, May 22, 1996, p. 13; and Masayasu Goto, "Letters: Pleasures of Pachinko," *Japan Update*, December 1993, p. 1.

66. Lisa Gates, "Place Your Bets: Taiwan Plans to Reintroduce State Lotteries," *Far Eastern Economic Review*, March 1993, p. 51.

67. Thomas Wagner, "The Las Vegas of South Asia," *The McAllen Monitor*, January 23, 1994, p. 7F.

68. "Gambling on the Rise in China," *China News Daily*, June 27, 1996.

69. Michael J. McCarthy, "In-Flight Gambling Is Ready to Take Off," *The Wall Street Journal*, May 24, 1996, pp. B1, B7.

70. Gerhard Scherhorn, "The Addictive Trait in Buying Behav-

ior," *Journal of Consumer Policy*, Vol. 13 (1990), pp. 33–51; Elizabeth C. Hirschman, "The Consciousness of Addiction: Toward a General Theory of Compulsive Consumption," *Journal of Consumer Research*, Vol. 19 (September 1992), pp. 155–179; and Elizabeth C. Hirschman, "Cocaine as Innovation: A Social-Symbolic Account," in *Advances in Consumer Research*, Vol 19, John F. Sherry, Jr., and Brian Sternthal, eds. (Provo, UT: Association for Consumer Research, 1992), pp. 129–139.

71. Emiko Terazono, "Suicide of Employee Who Worked Excessive Hours Costs Japanese Company $1.2 Million," *The Financial Times*, March 30–31, 1996, p. 3.

72. Elizabeth C. Hirschman, "Professional, Personal, and Popular Culture Perspectives on Addiction," in Ronald P. Hill, ed., *Marketing and Consumer Research in the Public Interest* (Thousand Oaks, CA: Sage Publications, 1996), pp. 33–53; and James A. Roberts, "The Antecedents and Incidence of Compulsive Buying in the Baby Bust Generation," paper presented at the 1996 Texas Marketing Faculty Consortium, Waco, TX, April 12, 1996.

73. Ronald J. Faber, Gary A. Christenson, Martina de Zwaan, and James Mitchell, "Two Forms of Compulsive Consumption: Comorbidity of Compulsive Buying and Binge Eating," *Journal of Consumer Research*, Vol. 22 (December 1995), pp. 296–304.

74. David Glen Mick, "Are Studies of Dark Side Variables Confounded by Socially Desirable Responding? The Case of Materialism," *Journal of Consumer Research*, Vol. 23 (September 1996), pp. 106–119.

75. Nancy Dunne, "Portrait of an American Dilemma," *The Financial Times*, June 17, 1996, p. 10.

76. Jeff Bailey, "The Dump's Foe Is Indignant and Has Money for a Fight," *The Wall Street Journal*, June 7, 1996, pp. A1, A4.

77. Mitch Griffin, Barry J. Babin, and William R. Darden, "Consumer Assessments of Responsibility for Product-Related Injuries: The Impact of Regulations, Warnings, and Promotional Policies," in *Advances in Consumer Research*, Vol 19, John F. Sherry, Jr., and Brian Sternthal, eds. (Provo, UT: Association for Consumer Research, 1992), pp. 870–878.

78. G. Fisk and R. Chandran, "How to Trace and Recall Products," *Harvard Business Review*, November–December 1975, pp. 90–96.

79. John C. Mowen, "Further Information on Consumer Perceptions of Product Recalls," in *Advances in Consumer Research*, Vol. 7, Jerry Olson, ed. (Ann Arbor, MI: Association for Consumer Research, 1980), pp. 519–523.

80. Ibid.

81. John C. Mowen, David Jolly, and G. S. Nickell, "Factors Influencing Consumer Responses to Product Recalls: A Regression Analysis Approach," in *Advances in Consumer Research*, Vol. 8, Kent Monroe, ed. (Ann Arbor, MI: Association for Consumer Research, 1981), pp. 405–407.

82. Patrick Murphy and Gene Laczniak, "Marketing Ethics: A Review with Implications for Managers, Educators, and Researchers," in *Review of Marketing*, Ben M. Enis and Kenneth J. Roering, eds. (Chicago: American Marketing Association, 1981), pp. 251–266.

McDonald's in the Internet McSpotlight

The degree of business concern with social responsibility issues has ebbed and flowed during the past 30 years. Corporate concerns have mirrored fluctuations in the society, from the politically active 1960s, through the consumer movement of the 1970s, into decline in the acquisition-dominated 1980s, and reemergence in the rapid communication environment of the 1990s. Today new communication tools are making social responsibility a major planning challenge for businesses.

When activists first challenged the societal role of business, the tools available to them were limited and in most cases permitted only local efforts to pressure corporations to adopt a desired stance toward specific social responsibility issues. Unless an issue was perceived to affect the country as a whole, the mass media were not ready partners of activists in their battles against corporations. The outcry against the nuclear power industry following the Three Mile Island incident in the 1970s and the boycotts and condemnations of Exxon Corporation that followed the *Exxon Valdez* oil spill in the 1980s were perhaps the last successful national advocacy campaigns directed against American business. Since then, most of the social responsibility battles have been local skirmishes, such as the efforts to save an old-growth forest in the Northwest and the blind cave pup fish in Texas. These efforts have failed to attract national exposure.

New communication tools may be ending the isolation of social responsibility clashes. With the expansion of the Internet and its connection to a large percentage of the international population, activists can now mount a social responsibility attack anywhere in the world and of whatever magnitude they want to spend the time and effort to create.

The Internet now reaches into 130 countries, with millions of "surfers" in virtually every industrialized and emerging nation in the world. For example, the number of host computers grew in China by 1,003 percent from 1995 to 1996, and Russia, Singapore, and Brazil expanded by over 300 percent in the same time period. Setting up an Internet site for distribution of cause information is relatively inexpensive. A World

Wide Web server can be purchased and loaded with all necessary software for about $2,000. A dedicated connection to the Internet through an Internet service provider (ISP) can cost as little as $100 per month. Some environmental groups have even established Web servers to host pages produced by activists who cannot afford their own dedicated connections to the Internet (http://www.envirolink.org/).

In 1986 two activists in England objected to the arrival of McDonald's in their country. They printed a six-page fact sheet to inform anyone they could get to listen about their perceptions of McDonald's social irresponsibility.

This incident would likely have remained a local skirmish had not McDonald's England sued the pair for libel in 1990. At this point the trial is the longest-running civil court case in English history. The activists created a Web site to apprise the Internet community of the case, which has been dubbed "McLibel" (http://www.McSpotlight.org/). The McSpotlight site asked others who have had problems with McDonald's to contribute information about their concerns, and it even includes discussion bulletin boards for real-time discussions of issues. The very slickly done Web site now houses more than 1,600 files on McDonald's alleged social irresponsibility.

On its side, McDonald's corporate headquarters established its own Web site (http://www.McDonalds.com/). Although the site contains typical corporate files, including investor and franchising information, it also features a kids' section outfitted with animated pictures (at the time it was prepared, this was not an easy process to build into Web pages), coloring books, and other information targeted at younger Web surfers. And, the site contains a section devoted to McDonald's community social responsibility. In fact, the link to these pages is plainly labeled "social responsibility."

Since no one polices content on the World Wide Web, information put on a Web site is not reviewed for accuracy by anyone but the site's Web master or reviewers asked to examine the material as a part of organizational policy. This means that views on social issues are no longer being scrutinized by professional editors for appropriateness, accuracy, and legality before being presented to a mass-media audience. Diligent promoters who place their site's address in directories and make it accessible to search engines can garner 100,000 hits or more per month after only a few days of promotional activity.

Questions

1. Define the problems faced by businesses that suffer an Internet attack on their social responsibility.

2. Discuss the consumer behavior concepts from the chapter that apply to this case.

3. Construct a managerial application matrix for an Internet retail business. Discuss the managerial implications of the consumer concepts you identify.

David L. Sturges developed this case, based on "The Other Half of Web Users," (1995/1996) SRI International [WWW document] (URL http://www.sri.com); Rabikar Chatterjee, Sunil Gupta, and Jim Pitkow (1995/1996), *The Hermes Study*, University of Michigan [WWW document] (URL http://www.umich.edu/~sgupta/hermes); Jim Pitkow, "Surveys 1, 2, 3, and 4," Graphics, Visualization, and Usability Center, Georgia Institute of Technology, 1994–96 [WWW document] (URL http://www.gatech.edu/pitkow/survey/); McDonalds (n.d./1996), "McDonalds Corporation" [WWW document] (URL http://www.mc-donalds.com/); McSpotlight (n.d./1996); "McInformation Network" [WWW document] (URL http://www.McSpotlight.org/); and Robin Frost, "Web's Heavy U.S. Accent Grates on Overseas Ears," *The Wall Street Journal*, September 26, 1996, pp. B6, B8.

NAME INDEX

SUBJECT INDEX

PHOTO/AD CREDITS

American Express, Inc. 435 Courtesy of Play It Again Sports.

Chapter 14

463 Courtesy of Intel Corporation. 469 Photo by Douglas L. Bartley 469 Courtesy of Drs Dental Lab 482 Courtesy of Stan Clark Worldwide.

Chapter 15

486 Photo by John Mowen 503 Courtesy of Eagle Creek Travel Gear 507 Courtesy of Apple Computer, Inc.

Chapter 16

526 Courtesy of Volvo Cars of North America Corporation. 527 Courtesy of The Quaker Oats Company 536 Courtesy of Baby Think It Over, Inc. 544 Courtesy of KinderCare Learning Centers, Inc.

Chapter 17

556 Photo by Michael Minor 559 Photo by John Mowen 564 Courtesy of Oldsmobile Div., General Motors Corp. 569 Coca-Cola and Coke are trademarks of the Coca-Cola Company and are used with permission. 574 Photo by Douglas L. Bartley 575 Courtesy of Heroes & Legacies 577 Photo by Michael Minor

Chapter 18

610 Photo by Douglas L. Bartley 611 Courtesy of Gucci Timepieces

Chapter 19

625 Courtesy of The Gillette Company 626 Courtesy of Kyocera Europe GmbH, Germany; ZEFA, Germany; Daimler Benz AG, Germany 628 Photo by Michael Minor 630 Photo by John Mowen 639 Photo by Michael Minor

Chapter 20

653 Courtesy of the Advertising Council. 663 Courtesy of the Advertising Council 665 Courtesy of SmithKline Beecham Consumer Healthcare 667 Photo by Michael Minor 671 Courtesy of Coors Brewing Company